the concise ne
of modern culture

A *Who's Who* of Western and world culture, from Woody Allen to Émile Zola ...

Containing over four hundred essay-style entries, and covering the period from 1850 to the present, *The Concise New Makers of Modern Culture* includes artists, writers, dramatists, architects, philosophers, anthropologists, scientists, sociologists, major political figures, composers, film-makers and many other culturally significant individuals and is thoroughly international in its purview.

Next to Karl Marx is Bob Marley, with John Ruskin is Salman Rushdie, alongside Darwin is Luigi Dallapiccola, Deng Xiaoping rubs shoulders with Jacques Derrida as does Julia Kristeva with Kropotkin.

With its global reach, *The Concise New Makers of Modern Culture* provides a multi-voiced witness of the contemporary thinking world. The entries carry short bibliographies and there is thorough cross-referencing as well as an index of key subjects.

Justin Wintle is an author, editor and journalist who has contributed to a wide variety of media outlets. He is editor of the original *Makers of Culture*, *Makers of Modern Culture* and *Makers of Nineteenth Century Culture* and the updated *New Makers of Modern Culture*.

the concise new makers
of modern culture

edited by
justin wintle

Routledge
Taylor & Francis Group

LONDON AND NEW YORK

First published 2009
by Routledge
2 Park Square, Milton Park, Abingdon, Oxon OX14 4RN

Simultaneously published in the USA and Canada
by Routledge
270 Madison Avenue, New York, NY 10016

Routledge is an imprint of the Taylor and Francis Group, an informa business

Editorial Selection and Material © 2009 Justin Wintle
Individual Entries © the Contributors

Typeset in Bembo by
Taylor & Francis Books
Printed and bound in Great Britain by
CPI Antony Rowe, Chippenham, Wiltshire

British Library Cataloguing in Publication Data
A catalogue record for this book is available from the British Library

Library of Congress Cataloging in Publication Data
   The concise new makers of modern culture / edited by Justin Wintle.
      p. cm.
   "Simultaneously published in the USA and Canada"–T.p. verso.
   "An abridgement of the two-volume reference set New makers of
modern culture (2006), which in turn was a re-compilation of two
earlier volumes, Makers of modern culture (1981) and Makers of
nineteenth century culture (1982)"–Intro.
   Biography–19th century–Dictionaries. 2. Biography–20th century–
Dictionaries. 3. Civilization, Western–Dictionaries. 4. Intellectual
life–History–19th century–Dictionaries. 5. Intellectual life–History–
20th century–Dictionaries. I. Wintle, Justin.
   CT103.C59 2008
   920.009'04–dc22
                                                      2008028378

ISBN10: 0-415-47782-4 (hbk)
ISBN10: 0-415-47783-2 (pbk)
ISBN10: 0-203-88428-0 (ebk)

ISBN13: 978-0-415-47782-6 (hbk)
ISBN13: 978-0-415-47783-3 (pbk)
ISBN13: 978-0-203-88428-7 (ebk)

contents

introduction   vi

acknowledgements   ix

list of entries with contributors   x

entries   1

index   847

introduction

The Concise New Makers of Modern Culture is an abridgement of the two-volume reference set New Makers of Modern Culture (2006), which in turn was a re-compilation of two earlier volumes, Makers of Modern Culture (1981) and Makers of Nineteenth Century Culture (1982).

The two-volume edition of New Makers of Modern Culture, published as a library edition by Routledge, contains 957 entries and a full index arranged in double columns over 1,759 pages. Approximately sixty-five per cent of the material included derived from the earlier volumes. This was updated wherever appropriate. A key decision in producing the new work was to incorporate many of the entries from Makers of Nineteenth Century Culture in order to accommodate such figures as Charles Darwin and Karl Marx, integral to any understanding of 'modern culture'. The boundaries of modern culture were therefore pushed back from the beginning of the twentieth century to circa 1850.

The same strategy has been broadly followed in the present volume, although there is a slightly greater emphasis on the twentieth century in its selection of entries. Some notable mid-nineteenth century figures – for instance, Alexis de Tocqueville, Victor Hugo, Ivan Turgenev, Hector Berlioz and Ralph Waldo Emerson – have been omitted, mainly for reasons of space.

Any division of history, cultural or otherwise, is arbitrary, since the seeds of one period or era are invariably contained in its predecessor or predecessors. Can Wagner, for instance, be understood without reference to Beethoven, or the Impressionist painters without reference to Turner? Set against this is the simple fact that 'modern' as a term applied to the present, the recent and not-quite-so-recent past enjoys a distinctive near-global usage quite separate from (say) 'contemporary'; and there is also the simple need to present a body of information, ideas and interpretation in more or less digestible and portable parcels.

Our sense of what is 'modern' is in constant flux. Even during the quarter-century or so since I devised the Makers project, profound changes have occurred. Outside of the People's Republic of China, Marxist communism – the greatest single challenge to traditional political and social values that the world has perhaps experienced – appears to have run its course. Similarly, in the West, Sigmund Freud is no longer regarded as the touchstone of our understanding of the human psyche. Rather his reputation and authority have been badly dented. This in turn has limited the remit of the 'post-modernist' movement, a largely French intellectual foment that owed at least some of its inspiration to both Marxist and Freudian concepts. Indeed one may now begin to speak of the demise of post-modernism.

But culture, like nature, abhors a vacuum. Since the beginning of the 1980s computers and the Internet have come to dominate much of our daily lives – an astonishingly rapid technological revolution that, even more than Marxism in the hundred years that preceded it, has spread worldwide. In the same quarter-century we have adopted a model of the human being based on genetics, and become more urgently concerned with the health of the planet itself. Whereas in 1980 we were worried that oil and other fossil fuels must eventually run out, now we worry that the same finite resources will destroy Earth's eco-fabric.

The intervening years have also witnessed an upsurge in religious fundamentalism, most notably within Islam, and most forcibly brought home by the events of 9/11. While the attack on the World Trade Center in New York has been variously characterized, ranging from the pursuit of a justified holy war provoked by prolonged Western incursions into Middle Eastern territories to a civilian slaughter of the most barbarous kind, it signalled yet another aspect of 'globalization' – of all the buzzwords that have surfaced during the last two or three decades arguably the most compellingly apposite. As two world wars should have taught us, conflictual violence is no longer to be contained *in situ*.

In compiling *New Makers of Modern Culture* I sought to take account of these developments whilst remaining faithful to my original definition of 'culture', namely 'how we see ourselves', whether through literature, the other arts, architecture, a variety of academic disciplines (sociology and anthropology for instance), the work of some scientists and the visionary politics of some statesmen and revolutionaries (of whatever hue). Above all, I sought to preserve the notion of an inter-disciplinary inter-connectedness in a format that encourages readers and users to think and explore outside their immediate preserves.

That said, there have been constraints and restrictions all along. Most obviously, there is the old saw, that the more one learns the more there is to learn. However one may define it, modern culture is its own library, virtually limitless in size. Then there is the bald fact that *New Makers* is an English-language compilation, and is therefore necessarily slanted toward British and American perspectives.

This shows in my selection of subjects – those figures of whatever profession or calling

accorded an entry. Globalization is not yet so far advanced that the averagely educated citizen of London or Los Angeles knows who's reading what in Paris or Milan, let alone Moscow or Beijing. While *New Makers* is significantly more 'open' to the achievements of the non-Anglophone world than its parent volumes, satisfying the curiosity and immediate needs of the 'native' constituency has remained a priority. Conveniently, the Anglophone world still, just about, rules the global roost, though for how much longer that will pertain is, or has become, a main issue.

Within these parameters there have been more particular constraints. It will be noticed that, where I have fished in 'foreign waters', novelists, for instance, predominate over poets. This is not at all to disparage what poets do; rather it is to acknowledge that the relationship between a poet and the language he or she works in has an intimacy that rarely survives translation. While the same is true of some novelists, fiction is the more exportable commodity. Ditto cinema, and ditto the other visual arts. Paradoxically, though, the same seems to apply less to music. Both China and India, for example, have their own hugely rich musical traditions, yet to the untutored Western ear the music of those civilizations is seldom more than something exotic. That's our failing of course, reinforced by the extraordinary narrative of the mainstream Western musical tradition, which does transgress national boundaries. For a long time now Western concert halls have been graced by Japanese, Korean, Chinese and even Thai performers of the Western repertoire.

The most internationalized languages perhaps are those of the sciences and mathematics, where 'translation' becomes an almost mechanical, minimalist operation. A scientific paper either is or isn't translated accurately. In so far as 'modern' culture at the 'material' level, in the sense adumbrated by (mainly Western) anthropologists and archaeologists, is often stridently secularist, technology and science are the mainsprings; but just because they tend not to consciously articulate 'how we see ourselves', I have resisted including very many scientists, technologists and mathematicians in *The Concise New Makers of Modern Culture.*

The downside of that is that, based on the present volume, my take on culture must, in the eyes of some, too readily approximate to a somewhat conventional notion of 'high culture' – as opposed to what, for perhaps a majority of the planet's denizens, goes on nightly on their television screens. It will be noticed, for example, that I have given the performing arts (actors, singers, comedians etc.) a wide berth, except where performers give renditions of their own exceptional material. But for all that I make no apology. My aim has been to provide a resource stimulus for the Anglophone learning and teaching community and its visitors, again within the limited space available.

Even so, I have made room where room is at a premium for the likes of the Beatles and the Rolling Stones, for Elvis Presley and Bob Marley and Monty Python. To deny the genius of, say, Bob Dylan would be a travesty by any standard; and giving at least an intimation of the scope and variety of our articulated culture has also been a goal.

All of which made drawing up the original and subsequent lists of entries – whether for *Makers of Modern Culture, Makers of Nineteenth Century Culture* or *New Makers of Modern Culture* – a formidable challenge. Throughout, however, I have found myself indebted to many of the several hundred distinguished contributors, for their enthusiasm, encouragement and sometimes contrary views. But if, far more than most reference works, the Makers project has been a collaborative venture, then that is altogether fitting. Quite deliberately I invited my writers to furnish interpretations of their chosen subjects, rather than more matter-of-fact dictionary-type appraisals, so that overall the *Makers of Culture* volumes are in themselves a multi-voiced cultural expression.

Some critics quickly cottoned on to this, none more so than Peter Conrad. 'For Arnold and Eliot,' Conrad wrote in a review of *Makers of Modern Culture* for the *Observer* in 1981, 'the purpose of culture was conservation. Wintle and his cohorts treat their field more radically and progressively. They're not dealing with an inheritance entrusted to the present from the past, but with ideas which provoke the future into being . . . '

These were words I greatly warmed to, even though I sensed an element of regret – Conrad I think would have preferred it had I followed the Arnold-Eliot path more closely. How much of the frisson he describes carries through into this, *The Concise New Makers of Modern Culture*, is, however, another matter. In order to create a portable edition of *New Makers of Modern Culture* I have had to wield the axe as never before. If devising the lists of entries for the original volumes was fraught with anxieties, making this further selection has been little short of tortuous.

Mainly I have opted to retain those figures and those entries I imagine a majority of users would expect to find contained between its covers, at the expense of abandoning many other entries of equal intrinsic interest. Some fields and disciplines have suffered more than others. I have kept only a handful of sociologists, anthropologists and their ilk, on the grounds that few of these are 'household names', even within academic households; and I have dispensed entirely with a tranche of theologians whose Bible scholarship unwittingly contributed to our culture's progressive secularization from the early nineteenth century onwards.

And so on and so forth – an invidious pruning for which I expect to take some flak. Yet even so, and rather like the British Chancellor who invariably winds up his annual House of Commons address by 'commending this budget to this House', I am pleased to offer this concise edition in the hope that it may assist its users in that process of intellectual exploration and self-enrichment which happily is still a part of our civilization.

Justin Wintle, May 2008

acknowledgements

It will be noticed that some entries have been 'updated and revised by the Editor' or by another hand. Inevitably, and sadly, some of those who contributed to the original volumes are now deceased. Twenty-five years on, it also proved impossible to trace a handful of others. But to these as to every other contributor my sense of vast gratitude remains intact. While it is perhaps invidious to single out individual contributors for particular thanks in helping guide *New Makers of Modern Culture* home – so many have had an input beyond the call of duty, sparing the need to work through a cumbersome 'editorial board' – I wish to acknowledge the special generosity of the following in giving freely of their time and thoughts: Professor Roger Cardinal; Professor John Cottingham; Sir Bernard Crick; Professor Antony Flew; Professor John Hamilton Frazer; Professor Andrew Gibson; Professor Charles Gregory; Professor Paul Jorion; Professor A. Robert Lee; Professor Sebastian Lucas; Nick Reyland; the late Professor James Richmond; Professor Stephen Serafin; Charles Warren; Gary Watson; and my brother Christopher Wintle. Alan Bold, His Excellency José Guilherme Merquior, Professor Eric Mottram and Professor Anthony Storr have not survived to witness the present work, but their helpful encouragement of the original two volumes are keenly remembered. Outside the magic circle of contributors, I must thank Andrew Lockett and Joe Staines for their help and advice, as also young Angela Mardle. Various members of the staff at Routledge, among them Gerard Greenway, Natalie Foster, Dominic Shryane, Charlotte Wood and Anna Callander in London, and Kate Aker, Beth Renner and Ruth Gilbert in New York, provided invaluable support. The index was prepared by Frances Mather. Last, but perennially first, I thank my wife, Kimiko Tezuka-Wintle, for her altogether disproportionate, and therefore mystifying, patience. *Pace* Jacques Derrida *et al.*, altruism – if one must call it that – is alive and kicking.

entries and contributors

AALTO, Hugo Alvar Henrik
Ranulph Glanville

ADAMS, John Coolidge
Peter Dickinson

AFGHANI, Jamal Uddeen Al
Dilip Hiro

ALBEE, Edward Franklin
C.W.E. Bigsby (revised and updated by the Editor)

ALLEN, Woody
Ahron Bregman

ALTMAN, Robert
Charles Warren

AMIS, Martin Louis
Boyd Tonkin

ANDRÉ, Carl
David Raskin

ARMSTRONG, Daniel Louis (Satchmo)
Christopher Wagstaff

ARNOLD, Eve
Caryn E. Neumann

ARNOLD, Matthew
Simon Rae

ASHBERY, John Lawrence
Jodi Cressman

ASHBY, William Ross
Ranulph Glanville

ASIMOV, Isaac
Charles Gregory

ATTENBOROUGH, (Sir) David Frederick
Alexandra Freeman

AUDEN, Wystan Hugh
Janet Montefiore

AUSTIN, John Langshaw
Antony Flew

AYER, (Sir) Alfred Jules
John Cottingham

BABBAGE, Charles
Christopher Ormell

BACON, Francis
Patrick Conner

BAIRD, John Logie
Justin Wintle

BAKST, Léon Samölivich
Richard Humphreys

BALLARD, James Graham
Roger Luckhurst

BARBER, Samuel
Peter Dickinson

BARNUM, Phineas Taylor
Charles Gregory

BARTH, John
A. Robert Lee

BARTHES, Roland
Andy Stafford

BARTÓK, Béla
Ronald Lumsden

BAUDELAIRE, Charles Pierre
Roger McLure

BEARDSLEY, Aubrey Vincent
Richard Humphreys

BEATLES, The
Duncan Fallowell

BECKETT, Samuel
Derval Tubridy

BELL, Alexander Graham
Justin Wintle

BELLOW, Saul
David Corker (revised and updated by the Editor)

BERG, Alban
Douglas Jarman

BERGMAN, Ernest Ingmar
Roy Armes (revised and updated by the Editor)

BERLIN, Irving
Stephen Banfield

BERLIN, (Sir) Isaiah
Sir Bernard Crick

BERNERS-LEE, (Sir) Timothy
Ranulph Glanville

BERNSTEIN, Leonard
Stephen Banfield

BEUYS, Joseph
Stuart Morgan

BIN LADEN, Osama
Dilip Hiro

BIZET, Georges
David Cox

BOAS, Franz
Marianne Boelscher

BORGES, Jorge Luis
D.L. Shaw

BOULEZ, Pierre
Paul Griffiths

BRADBURY, Raymond Douglas
Viv Horwitz

BRAHMS, Johannes
Malcolm MacDonald

BRANCUSI, Constantin
Slavka Sverakova

BRAQUE, Georges
John Milner

BRECHT, Bertolt
Martin Esslin

BRETON, André
Roger Cardinal

BRITTEN, Benjamin (Lord)
Arnold Whittall

BROWNING, Robert
Joseph Bain

BRUCKNER, Anton
Basil Lam

BRUNEL, Isambard Kingdom
Frederick Scott

BUÑUEL, Luis
Paul Sidey

BURGESS, John Anthony
Philip Gooden

BURROUGHS, William Seward
Duncan Fallowell

CAGE, John
Michael Alexander

CALDER, Alexander
Slavka Sverakova

CAMUS, Albert
Ted Freeman

CANTOR, Georg Ferdinand Ludwig Philipp
W.H. Newton-Smith

CAPA, Robert
Caryn E. Neumann

CAPOTE, Truman
John Daniel

CARROLL, Lewis (Charles Lutwidge DODGSON)
Duncan Fallowell

CARSON, Rachel
Sasha Norris

CARTER, Elliott Cook
Stephen Pruslin

CARTIER-BRESSON, Henri
Roger Cardinal

CÉZANNE, Paul
Simon Watney

CHAGALL, Marc
John Milner

CHANDLER, Raymond Thornton
Philip Gooden

CHAPLIN, Charles Spencer
Charles Gregory

CHEEVER, John
A. Robert Lee

CHEKHOV, Anton Pavlovich
Paul Nicholls

CHIRICO, Giorgio de
Roger Cardinal

CHOMSKY, Avram Noam
Hilary Wise (revised and updated by the Editor)

CHRISTIE, Agatha
Philippa Morgan

CHURCHILL, (Sir) Winston Leonard Spencer
Justin Wintle

COETZEE, John Maxwell
Derek Attridge

COLLINS, William Wilkie
Christopher Heywood

CONRAD, Joseph
Jonathan Keates

COPLAND, Aaron
Paul Griffiths

COPPOLA, Francis Ford
Gino Moliterno

CORBUSIER, Le *see*: LE CORBUSIER

CRICK, Francis Harry Compton
Robert Olby

CUKOR, George
Nigel Algar

CUMMINGS, Edward Estlin
Alan Bold

CUNNINGHAM, Merce
Anne K. Swartz

DALAI LAMA *see*: GYATSO, TENZIN, 14TH DALAI LAMA

DALÍ y Domenech, Salvador Felipe Jacinto
Conroy Maddox

DARWIN, Charles Robert
Justin Wintle

DAVIES, (Sir) Peter Maxwell
Christopher Dromey

DAVIS, Miles Dewey, Jr
Christopher Wagstaff

DAWKINS, Clinton Richard
Michael Ruse

DE KOONING, William
James Faure Walker

DEBUSSY, (Achille-) Claude
David Cox

DEGAS, Edgar
Richard Humphreys

DeLILLO, Don
Charles Gregory

DeMILLE, Cecil Blount
Steve Jenkins

DENG XIAOPING (TENG HSIAO-PING)
Justin Wintle

DERRIDA, Jacques (Jackie)
Justin Wintle

DIAGHILEV, Serge (Sergei Pavlovich)
John Milner

DICKENS, Charles John Huffam
Philip Collins

DICKINSON, Emily
Helen McNeil

DISNEY, Walt
Clare Kitson

DOSTOEVSKY, Fyodor Mikhailovich
Richard Freeborn

DOYLE, (Sir) Arthur Conan
Philip Gooden

DUBUFFET, Jean-Philippe-Arthur
Roger Cardinal

DURKHEIM, Émile
Bobbie Lederman

DVOŘÁK, Antonin
Paul Griffiths

DYLAN, Bob (Robert Allen ZIMMERMAN)
John Porter (revised and updated by the Editor)

EDISON, Thomas Alva
Eric Mottram

EIFFEL, Gustave
John Furse

EINSTEIN, Albert
Michael Redhead

EISENSTEIN, Sergei Mikhailovich
Philip Drummond

ELGAR, (Sir) Edward William
Ian Parrott

ELIOT, George (Mary Anne or Marian EVANS)
Neil Roberts

ELIOT, Thomas Stearns
Valentine Cunningham

ELLINGTON, Duke
Philip Larkin

EPSTEIN, (Sir) Jacob
Simon Wilson

ERNST, Max
Gray Watson

FASSBINDER, Rainer Werner
Gray Watson

FAULKNER, William
Andrew Gibson

FAURÉ, Gabriel Urbain
J. Barrie Jones

FELLINI, Federico
Christopher Wagstaff

FITZGERALD, Francis Scott Key
Geoffrey Moore

FLAHERTY, Robert Joseph
Pat Cook

FLAUBERT, Gustave
David Meakin

FLEMING, Ian Lancaster
Philip Gooden

FORD, Henry
Duncan MacLeod

FORD, John
Steve Jenkins

FORSTER, Edward Morgan
Jonathan Keates

FOSTER, Norman Robert (Lord)
Robert Maxwell

FOUCAULT, Paul Michel
Paul Jorion

FREUD, Lucian Michael
T.G. Rosenthal

FREUD, Sigmund
Todd Dufresne

FRIEDAN, Betty
Gayle Graham Yates

FRIEDMAN, Milton
Roger Opie (revised and updated by the Editor)

FROST, Robert
Geoffrey Moore

FULLER, Richard Buckminster
John Hamilton Frazer

GABO, Naum
John Milner

GALBRAITH, John Kenneth
Roger Opie

GALLUP, George Horace
Tom Williams

GANCE, Abel
Philip Drummond

GANDHI, Mahatma (Mohandas Karamchand)
Dilip Hiro

GARCÍA MÁRQUEZ, Gabriel
D.L. Shaw

GATES, Bill (William Henry)
Ranulph Glanville

GAUDÍ, Antoni (Antonio)
Mark Burry

GAUGUIN, Paul
Pat Turner

GEHRY, Frank Owen (Ephraim GOLDBERG)
John Hamilton Frazer

GENET, Jean
David Bradby

GERSHWIN, George
Wilfrid Mellers

GIACOMETTI, Alberto
Slavka Sverakova

GIDE, André-Paul-Guillaume
Christopher Bettinson

GILBERT & GEORGE
Duncan Fallowell

GINSBERG, Allen
Jodi Cressman

GLASS, Philip
Peter Dickinson

GODARD, Jean-Luc
Roy Armes (revised and updated by the Editor)

GOLDING, (Sir) William Gerald
Jonathan Keates

GORBACHEV, Mikhail Sergeevich
Richard Sakwa

GORKY, Maxim (Aleksey Maximovich PESHKOV)
Richard Freeborn

GOULD, Stephen Jay
Mark Ridley

GRAHAM, Martha
Franc Chamberlain

GRASS, Günter Wilhelm
Frank Steele (revised and updated by the Editor)

GREENE, Graham
Philip Gooden

GREER, Germaine
Monica Petzal (revised and updated by the Editor)

GRIFFITH, David Wark
Steve Jenkins

GROPIUS, Walter
Penny Sparke

GUEVARA, Che (Ernesto GUEVARA DE LA SERNA)
Mike Gonzalez

GYATSO TENZIN, 14th Dalai Lama
Charles Allen

HARDY, Thomas
C.H. Sisson

HAVEL, Václav
April Carter

HAWKING, Stephen William
Justin Wintle

HAWKS, Howard Winchester
Chris Auty

HEANEY, Seamus
Stephen Regan

HEIDEGGER, Martin
David J. Levy

HEISENBERG, Werner
D.R. Murdoch

HELLER, Joseph
Dennis Paoli

HEMINGWAY, Ernest
A. Robert Lee

HENDRIX, Jimi
Kevin Greene

HENZE, Hans Werner
Paul Griffiths (revised and updated by Stephen Downes)

HEPWORTH, (Dame) Jocelyn Barbara
Richard Calvocoressi

HERZL, Theodor
David Dinour

HERZOG, Werner
Gray Watson

HESSE, Hermann
A.V. Subiotto

HIRST, Damien
Judith Bumpus

HITCHCOCK, (Sir) Alfred Joseph
Geoff Brown

HITLER, Adolf
Anthony Glees

HOCKNEY, David
Gray Watson

HOLABIRD, William and ROCHE, Martin
Pat Turner

HOMER, Winslow
Stuart Morgan

HOPKINS, Gerard Manley
Alan Bold

HOPPER, Edward
Samantha Goat

HUGHES, Ted (Edward James)
Neil Roberts

HUXLEY, Aldous Leonard
Ronald G. Walker

HUXLEY, Thomas Henry
Vincent Brome

IBSEN, Henrik
David Thomas

IVES, Charles Edward
Michael Alexander

JAMES, Henry
Jonathan Keates

JAMES, William
Robert Olby

JANÁČEK, Leoš Eugen
Paul Griffiths

JOBS, Steven
Ranulph Glanville

JOHNS, Jasper
Stuart Morgan (revised and updated by the Editor)

JOYCE, James Augustine
Andrew Gibson

JUDD, Donald
Adrian Kohn

JUNG, Carl Gustav
Anthony Storr

KAFKA, Franz
Corbet Stewart

KANDINSKY, Wassily (Vasilii Vasilievich)
John Milner

KAWABATA YASUNARI
Edward Seidensticker

KEATON, 'Buster' (Joseph Francis)
Charles Gregory

KENNEDY, John Fitzgerald
Anthony Glees

KEROUAC, Jack
Eric Mottram

KESEY, Ken
Eric Mottram (revised and updated by A. Robert Lee)

KEYNES, John Maynard
Roger Opie

KHOMEINI, Ruhollah Musavi
Dilip Hiro

KING, Martin Luther, Jr
Lester C. Lamon

KIPLING, Joseph Rudyard
Janet Montefiore

KITAJ, Ronald Brooks
Judith Bumpus

KLEE, Paul
Roger Cardinal

KLEIN, Yves
Gray Watson

KLIMT, Gustav
John Milner

KOONING, Willem de see: DE KOONING, WILLEM

KOONS, Jeff
David J. Getsy

KROPOTKIN, Petr Alekseyevich
R.M. Davison

KUBRICK, Stanley
Roger Hillman

KUHN, Thomas Samuel
Christopher Ormell

KUROSAWA, AKIRA
Isolde Standish

LACAN, Jacques
Lorenzo Chiesa

LANG, Fritz
Philip Drummond

LARKIN, Philip Arthur
Valentine Cunningham

LAWRENCE, David Herbert
G.M. Hyde

LE CARRÉ, John (David John Moore CORNWELL)
Philip Gooden

LE CORBUSIER (Charles-Édouard JEANERET)
Ranulph Glanville and Sam Stevens

LEAN, (Sir) David
James Chapman

LEARY, Timothy
Eric Mottram (revised and updated by A. Robert Lee)

LENIN (Vladimir Ilyich ULYANOV)
Athar Hussain

LEVI, Primo
Jonathan Keates

LÉVI-STRAUSS, Claude
Paul Jorion

LICHTENSTEIN, Roy
Gray Watson

LINCOLN, Abraham
Duncan MacLeod

LISZT, Franz
Michael Alexander

LONDON, Jack (John Griffith)
David Corker

LORENZ, Konrad Zacharias
Mark Ridley

LORCA, Federico García
Jason Wilson

LOSEY, Joseph Walton
Tom Milne

LOVELOCK, James Ephraim
Sasha Norris

LOWELL, Robert
John Haffenden

LUTOSŁAWSKI, Witold
Nick Reyland

MACHADO DE ASSIS, Joaquim Maria
J.G. Merquior

MACKINTOSH, Charles Rennie
Penny Sparke

MAGRITTE, René-François-Ghislain
Roger Cardinal

MAHLER, Gustav
Douglas Jarman

MAILER, Norman
David Corker (revised and updated by the Editor)

MALEVICH, Kazimir
Robin Milner-Gulland

MALINOWSKI, Bronislaw Kaspar
Peter Gathercole

MALLARMÉ, Stéphane
Roger McLure

MANDELA, Nelson
J.D.F. Jones

MANET, Edouard
Michael Wilson

MANN, Thomas
Corbet Stewart

MAO ZEDONG (MAO TSE-TUNG)
Justin Wintle

MARC, Franz
Brian Petrie

MARCONI, Guglielmo
Christopher Ormell

MARINETTI, Filippo Tommaso
Christopher Wagstaff

MARLEY, Bob (Robert Nesta)
Joan Bird

MÁRQUEZ, Gabriel García,
see: GARCÍA MÁRQUEZ, GABRIEL

MARX, Karl Heinrich
G.H.R. Parkinson

MATISSE, Henri
Pat Turner

McLUHAN, Herbert Marshall
Eric Mottram

MEAD, Margaret
Adam Kuper

MELVILLE, Herman
A. Robert Lee

MENDEL, Gregor
Robert Olby

MESSIAEN, Olivier Eugene Prosper Charles
Christopher Wintle

MIES VAN DER ROHE, Ludwig
Frederick Scott

MILL, John Stuart
Bernard Crick

MILLER, Arthur
Ann Massa

MILLETT, Kate (Katherine Murray)
Gayle Graham Yates

MIRÓ, Jóan
David Sweet

MISHIMA YUKIO (HIRAOKA KIMITAKE)
William Horsley

MIZOGUCHI KENJI
Sterling Van Wagenen

MODIGLIANI, Amedeo
Richard Humphreys

MONDRIAN, Piet
Pat Turner

MONET, Claude
Pat Turner

MONTY PYTHON
Robert Cushman

MOORE, (Sir) Henry
Patrick Conner

MOORE, Marianne Craig
Helen McNeil

MORRIS, William
David Meakin

MORRISON, Toni
Susanna Roxman

MUNCH, Edvard
Gray Watson

MUSSORGSKY, Modest Petrovich
Stuart Campbell

NABOKOV, Vladimir Vladimirovich
G.M. Hyde

NEEDHAM, Jospeh
Justin Wintle

NERUDA, Pablo (Neftalí REYES)
Jason Wilson

NICHOLSON, Ben
Patrick Conner

NIEMEYER, Oscar
John Furse

NIETZSCHE, Friedrich
John Carroll

NOBEL, Alfred Bernhard
Derek Gjertsen

NUSSBAUM, Martha Craven
John Cottingham

OATES, Joyce Carol
A. Robert Lee

ŌE KENZABURŌ
Mark Williams

OLDENBURG, Claes
Gray Watson

O'NEILL, Eugene Gladstone
C.W.E. Bigsby

ONO, Yoko
Anne K. Swartz

OPPENHEIMER, J. Robert
Justin Wintle

ORWELL, George
Bernard Crick

OWEN, Wilfred
Jon Stallworthy

PALMER, Samuel
Gray Watson

PAOLOZZI, (Sir) Eduardo
Robin Spencer

PARKER, Charles Christopher, Jr (Bird)
Christopher Wagstaff

PASOLINI, Pier Paolo
Geoffrey Nowell-Smith

PASTERNAK, Boris Leonidovich
Peter France

PAVLOV, Ivan Petrovich
Robert Olby

PENDERECKI, Krzysztof
Nick Reyland

PICASSO, Pablo (Ruiz y)
Pat Turner

PINTER, Harold
Ronald Knowles (revised and updated by the Editor)

PIRANDELLO, Luigi
Brian Moloney

PLATH, Sylvia
Helen McNeil

POLANSKI, Roman
Chris Petit (revised and updated by the Editor)

POLLOCK, Jackson
Gray Watson

POPPER, (Sir) Karl Raimund
John Cottingham

PORTER, Cole
Stephen Banfield

POULENC, Francis
Paul Griffiths

POUND, Ezra Loomis
Stephen Fender

PRESLEY, Elvis Aaron
Duncan Fallowell

PRICE, Cedric John
John Hamilton Frazer

PROKOFIEV, Sergei Sergeievich
Rita McAlister

PROUST, Marcel
Alison Finch

PUCCINI, Giacomo
Roger Parker

PYNCHON, Thomas
David Corker (revised and updated by the Editor)

QUTB, Sayyid Muhammad
Dilip Hiro

RACHMANINOV, Sergei
Michael Alexander

RAUSCHENBERG, Robert
Gray Watson

RAVEL, Joseph Maurice
Paul Griffiths

RAWLS, John Bordley
Rex Martin

RAY, Man
Gray Watson

RAY, Satyajit
Roy Armes (revised and updated by the Editor)

RENOIR, Jean
Roy Armes

RENOIR, Pierre-Auguste
Michael Wilson

RESNAIS, Alain
Roy Armes (revised and updated by the Editor)

RICHARDSON, Henry Hobson
Frederick Scott

RIEFENSTAHL, Leni (Helene Bertha Amalie)
Michael Pick

RILKE, Rainer Maria
Corbet Stewart

RIMBAUD, Arthur
Margaret Davies

RIMSKY-KORSAKOV, Nikolay Andreyevich
Stuart Campbell

ROBBE-GRILLET, Alain
Ann Jefferson

ROCHE, Martin *see*: HOLABIRD, WILLIAM AND
ROCHE, MARTIN

RODIN, François-Auguste-René
Stuart Morgan

**ROGERS (of Riverside),
Richard George (Lord)**
Robert Maxwell

ROLLING STONES, The
John Porter

ROOSEVELT, Franklin Delano
Samuel H. Beer

**ROSSETTI, Dante Gabriel (Gabriel Charles
Dante ROSSETTI)**
Duncan Fallowell

ROTH, Philip Milton
A. Robert Lee

ROTHKO, Mark
Gray Watson

ROUAULT, Georges
Richard Humphreys

ROUSSEAU, Henri ('Le Douanier')
Roger Cardinal

RUSHDIE, Salman
Phil Baker

RUSKIN, John
Patrick Conner

RUSSELL, Bertrand Arthur William (Earl)
J.E. Tiles

SAID, Edward Wadie
Ahron Bregman

SALINGER, Jerome David
E.A. Abramson

SARGENT, John Singer
Malcolm Warner

SARTRE, Jean-Paul
Keith Gore

SAUSSURE, Mongin-Ferdinand de
Geoffrey Sampson

SCHOENBERG, Arnold Franz Walter
Malcolm MacDonald

SCORSESE, Martin
Gino Moliterno

SCOTT, Ridley
Philip Gooden

SEBALD, Winfried Georg
Duncan Fallowell

SEN, Amartya
Polly Vizard

SEURAT, Georges Pierre
Richard Humphreys

SHAW, George Bernard
Michael Holroyd

SHOSTAKOVICH, Dmitri Dmitrievich
Malcolm Barry

SIBELIUS, Jean
Robert Layton

SINGER, Isaac Bashevis
Susanna Roxman

SIRK, Douglas
Linda Miles

SKINNER, Burrhus Frederic
John Cottingham

SOLZHENITSYN, Aleksandr Isayevich
Richard Freeborn

SONDHEIM, Stephen
Stephen Banfield

SPENCER, (Sir) Stanley
T.G. Rosenthal

SPIELBERG, Steven
Dennis Paoli

STALIN, Joseph
Michael Cox

STANISLAVSKY, Konstantin (Konstantin Sergeyevich ALEXEYEV)
Paul Nicholls

STEINBECK, John Ernst
Geoffrey Moore

STEVENS, Wallace
Geoffrey Moore

STOCKHAUSEN, Karlheinz
Richard Toop

STOPPARD, (Sir) Tom
Robert Cushman

STRAUSS, Johann
Andrew Lamb

STRAUSS, Richard George
Alan Jefferson

STRAVINSKY, Igor Fedorovich
Francis Routh

STRINDBERG, Johan August
Mary Sandbach

SULLIVAN, Louis Henry
Frederick Scott

SULSTON, (Sir) John Edward
Rachel A. Ankeny

SUZUKI DAISETSU TEITARO
Hisao Inagaki

TAGORE, Rabindranath
Dilip Hiro

TÀPIES, Antoni
Ming Tiampo

TCHAIKOVSKY, Peter Ilich
Michael Alexander

TENNYSON, Alfred (Lord)
Michael Schmidt

THOMAS, Dylan Marlais
Alan Bold

THOMAS, Ronald Stuart
M. Wynn Thomas

THOREAU, Henry David
A. Robert Lee

TIPPETT, (Sir) Michael
Arnold Whittall

TOLKIEN, John Ronald Reuel
Janet Montefiore

TOLSTOY, (Count) Lev Nikolaevich
Richard Freeborn

TOULOUSE-LAUTREC, Henri de
Pat Turner

TROLLOPE, Anthony
Jonathan Keates

TROTSKY, Leon
Norman Geras

TURING, Alan
Christopher Ormell

TWAIN, Mark (Samuel Langhorne CLEMENS)
Eric Mottram

TZARA, Tristan (Samuel ROSENSTOCK)
Roger Cardinal

UPDIKE, John Hoyer
David Corker (revised and updated by the Editor)

VALÉRY, Paul
Margaret Davies

VAN GOGH, Vincent
Pat Turner

VARGAS LLOSA, Mario
Jason Wilson

VAUGHAN WILLIAMS, (Sir) Ralph
Paul Griffiths

VERDI, Giuseppe
Pierluigi Petrobelli

VERLAINE, Paul
Clive Scott

VERNE, Jules
David Meakin

VIDAL, Gore
Philip Gooden

VISCONTI, Luchino
Geoffrey Nowell-Smith

VON STERNBERG, Josef
Philip Drummond

VONNEGUT, Kurt, Jr
Gary Thompson (revised and updated by the Editor)

WAGNER, Richard
Christopher Wintle

WALCOTT, Derek
Stephen Regan

WARHOL, Andy (Andrew WARHOLA)
Peter Gidal

WATSON, James Dewey
Robert Olby

WAUGH, Evelyn Arthur St John
Ian Littlewood

WEBER, Max
John Rex

WEBERN, Anton von
Christopher Wintle

WELLES, George Orson
Nigel Algar

WELLS, Herbert George
Vincent Brome

WHISTLER, James Abbot McNeill
Simon Watney

WHITMAN, Walt
Eric Mottram

WILDE, Oscar Fingal O'Flahertie Wills
Duncan Fallowell

WILLIAMS, Tennessee (Thomas Lanier)
Ann Massa

WITTGENSTEIN, Ludwig Josef Johann
John Cottingham

WODEHOUSE, (Sir) Pelham Grenville
R.B.D. French

WOLF, Hugo
Derrick Puffett

WOLFE, Tom
Duncan Fallowell

WOOLF, Adeline Virginia
Michael Rosenthal

WRIGHT, Frank Lloyd
John Furse

WYETH, Andrew Newell
Samantha Goat

YEANG, Ken
John Hamilton Frazer

YEATS, William Butler
Joseph Bain

ZAMYATIN, Yevgeniy Ivanovich
Neil Cornwell

ZOLA, Émile
David Lee

A

AALTO, Hugo Alvar Henrik

1898–1976

Finnish architect and designer

Some eleven years younger than **Le Corbusier**, Alvar Aalto belonged to the second generation of architects in the International Modern movement, the architecture dominant in the twentieth century in much the same way that baroque was dominant in the seventeenth. To it Aalto brought an informality and sensitivity, deriving ultimately from the crudely charming but usable vernacular of his country, that most commentators would agree had previously been lacking. Partly because he eschewed theorizing and polemics, and partly because of the enormous variety of his invention over a period of more than fifty years, he qualifies more than any other as the architect's architect, among both his contemporaries and his successors.

Aalto was born into a family with strong rural traditions. While his mother's father was a Swedish-speaking forester, his own was a land surveyor concerned chiefly with the construction of railroads through forests. For most of his childhood he lived in Jyväskylä, in a house shared by a Russian countess and an alcoholic confectioner. Admonished 'always to remain a gentleman' by his father, he left home at eighteen to study architecture at what is now the Helsinki Technical University, but returned to Jyväskylä after he had qualified five years later. There he set up his first office (1923–7) and began the career that was to make him famous. Broadly this can be divided into three periods (although elements characteristic to each tended to reappear in the others): an early white period of the International style; a red, or brick period; and a marble period, beginning *c.* 1960. His earliest works, however, were in a neo-classical idiom. These include the Jyväskylä Workers' Club (1923–5) and the rather delicate church at Muurame (1926–9). It was not until he moved his office to the old Finnish capital, Turku, in 1927, that his originality began to assert itself. Probably the decisive inspiration came from his first wife, the architect Aino Marsio, a designer of considerable imagination whom he married in 1925, and with whom he worked in closest collaboration until her death in 1949. The changes in his style can be most clearly observed in the development of his designs for the town library at Viipuri (now Vyborg in the USSR). This project began in 1928 along neo-classical lines, but by the time of its completion in 1935 it had been transformed into an obviously modernist building. With its sunken reading-well, its cylindrical skylights, and the wavy form of its lecture-hall ceiling, it also served as a test-bed for many of Aalto's prototypes. Concurrently he worked on a number of other projects in the same idiom, of which the most important are the newspaper offices of Turun Sanomat in Turku (1927–9), and the remarkable Tuberculosis Sanatorium at Paimo (1927–33), one of the outstanding buildings of the International style.

In 1933 he again moved offices, this time to Helsinki. This coincided with the creation of Artek, a firm he set up to produce the furnishing, light-fittings and vases which he had also begun to design for his interiors. Aalto's furniture, made inexpensively from bent-wooden laminates that gave him the fluidity of form he so liked while straightforwardly satisfying the obvious functional requirements, has had considerable impact and, unlike the furniture designed by most other eminent architects, is still in production. To finance this operation he sought the patronage of Harry and Maire Gullischen, for whom he later built the Villa Mairea (1938–9), one of the great modern houses, referred to by Siegfried Giedeion as 'architectural chamber music'.

It was towards the end of the 1930s that Aalto evolved his second, 'red' phase – although such a soubriquet does little justice to the variety of either materials or designs employed. The most important constructions here were the expressionistic Cellulose Sulphate Factory at Sunila (1936–9); the Baker House Dormitory for MIT in Chicago (where he was Professor of Architecture 1945–9), his first foreign commission; the Iron Federation Building in Helsinki (1951–5); the complicatedly sited National Pensions Institute (1952–6); the Jyväskylä Pedagogical University (1950–7); the Communist Party Headquarters and Culture House (1955–8), with its curvy walls built out of a specially designed reinforced brick; and Louis Carré's private villa at Bazoches in France. But of all his buildings in this style the Town Hall and Civic Centre for the small community at Säynätsalo (1950–2) in the centre of Finland was the masterpiece, where he achieved a dignified harmony between his materials (brick, wood and copper) and the surrounding forest.

Aalto's last period was altogether more mannerist in its approach, and is characterized by the use of white marble and blue ceramic tiles. Although even his earliest buildings showed an unusual interest in fragmented forms, curves and non-right-angles, these themes now became particularly prominent, perhaps encouraged by the nature of the commissions he received, often for churches and auditoria, buildings that demand unusual forms and precise foci. Among these he seems to have considered Finlandia Hall, with its added Conference Centre (1967–75), his testament, realizing the main generative element of his partially executed and slightly Italianate Central Helsinki plan (1959–64). The Cultural Centre at Wolfsburg, West Germany (1953–63), the suite of public buildings at Seinäjoki (1959–65) and the lonely Scandinavian House in Reykjavik, Iceland, (1965–8) are also outstanding. These projects were carried out in partnership with his second wife, Elissa Mäkiniemi, whom he married in 1952.

As is the case with most architects, Aalto's reputation rests on his larger, public buildings, and yet he was also involved with work of a humbler kind. After the Second World War, when Finland was in need of massive reconstruction, Aalto played a major role in the re-planning of Lapland, an area particularly devastated by the German withdrawal. As a part of this responsibility he designed a series of self-help, minimal space, expansible timber houses of remarkable ingenuity.

Further reading

Aalto's relatively scant literary output has been collected in *Alvar Aalto*, ed. Karl Fleig (3 vols, Zurich 1963). See also: George Baird, *Alvar Aalto* (1971); Paul David Pearson, *Alvar Aalto and the International Style* (1978); Malcolm Quantrill, *Alvar Aalto: A Critical Study* (1990); Richard Weston, *Alvar Aalto* (1995); Michael Tencher, *The Alvar Aalto Guide* (1996).

RANULPH GLANVILLE

ADAMS, John Coolidge

1947–

American composer and conductor

At the turn of the century, with the premiere of his Nativity Oratorio *El Niño* (2000) at Le Théâtre du Châtelet in Paris, John Adams was being acclaimed as the most prominent American serious composer on the international scene. He grew up under the influence of minimalist composers Steve Reich and **Philip Glass** but, a decade younger, he inherited American music of all kinds which he has fused in a uniquely individual way. His operas on contemporary subjects such as *Nixon in China* (1987) and *The Death of Klinghoffer* (1991) brought him to a wide public and courted controversy, but by the time of his musical response to the attack on the World Trade Center – *On the Transmigration of Souls* (2002) – he had become a kind of laureate among American composers.

Adams was born in Worcester, Massachusetts, in 1947 and grew up in East Concord, New Hampshire; he soon became a proficient clarinetist and later played professionally; by the age of ten he was having composition lessons and four years later heard his first orchestral piece. He took his MA at Harvard where his teachers included Leon Kirschner, who found him 'not quite in the twentieth century' because he failed to respond to serial music and preferred to listen to Jefferson Airplane and the Grateful Dead. He then moved to San Francisco in 1971, in what he has called 'the typical romantic gesture of a twenty-two-year-old', where he taught at the Conservatory for a decade. It was during this period that he wrote his minimalist piano piece *Phrygian Gates* (1977), inspired by the repetitive patterns in architecture in Florence, and the orchestral *Shaker Loops* (1983), based on American traditional practices. These were followed by *Harmonium* (1981), settings of poems by John Donne and **Emily Dickinson**, and *Harmonielehre* (1985), both written for the San Francisco Symphony where Adams worked closely with Edo de Waart. By this time the lavish expansion of minimalist procedures, which Adams regarded as 'the essential fulcrum of my personal language', showed him breaking away and establishing his own territory, although he has always recognized his starting point.

A major landmark was the opera *Nixon in China*, suggested by director Peter Sellars, based on President Nixon's 1972 visit to Beijing to meet **Mao Zedong**. Alice Goodman's libretto allows for a mixture of documentation and commentary in music that is both lyrical and heroic. Adams said: 'The Nixon/Mao encounter, puffed-up and media-driven as it was, lent itself perfectly to a parody in the **Verdian** *verismo* tradition', and he had to learn to write melody. The opera's success was immediate, following its premiere at Houston Grand Opera in 1987, and the *New York Times* said that Adams had done for the arpeggio what McDonald's did for the hamburger. Adams made an even wider impact when the same operatic team embarked on *The Death of Klinghoffer*, about the American Jew confined to a wheelchair who was murdered by Palestinian terrorists on the cruise ship *Achille Lauro* in the Mediterranean in 1985. The premiere was in Brussels in 1991 during the first Gulf War, but the even-handed, non-partisan treatment of the subject was too controversial for a revival in the US after the performances by San Francisco Opera. It has since made a searing impact as a film.

Adams' next theatre piece, *I Was Looking at the Ceiling and Then I Saw the Sky* (1995), is based on a story by June Jordan about seven youths in a tough part of Los Angeles. The score boldly plunges into the vernacular with pop songs and a rock band. But by the early 1990s Adams was being increasingly represented in the concert hall and conducting himself. His *Chamber Symphony* of 1992 came to terms with the two examples by **Schoenberg**, and his Violin Concerto for Gidon Kraemer appeared in the following year.

Less than a year after the Paris premiere of *El Niño* came 9/11, and six months after that Adams was commissioned by the New York Philharmonic to commemorate the event. *On the Transmigration of Souls* was not a requiem but, like the operas, was partly documentary, including voices speaking about their bereavement. The final words are 'I love you', and Adams said: 'The meditative ending, I hope, demonstrates that life can – and does – go on.'

Now Adams' career is still in full swing, but at his fiftieth birthday Sir Simon Rattle said that he was 'a ten times better composer than all the minimalists put together'. In terms of the impact of his music and the relevance of his concerns to large numbers of people, that looks like a judgement that may stand.

PETER DICKINSON

AFGHANI, Jamal Uddeen Al

1838–94

Islamic teacher and writer

An Islamic scholar, philosopher, teacher, orator, linguist, journalist and politician, Jamal Uddeen Al Afghani played a leading role in arousing anti-imperialist consciousness in the Muslim world, then dominated by European powers, and encouraging reformist and constitutional movements within Muslim countries. This brought him into conflict with not only Britain, the foremost imperialist nation of the time, but also the rulers of Egypt, Iran and Turkey.

He was a controversial figure, spartan in habits, and a life-long bachelor. His death was kept a secret for many years; and his national origin and birthplace are still a subject of debate. He claimed to have been born of Sunni parents at Asadabad near Konar, in the district of Kabul, Afghanistan, in 1838. But his critics insisted that his birthplace was Asadabad near Hamadan in western Iran, that his parents were Shia, a minority sect, and that he lied about his Shia origin so as not to alienate the Sunni majority.

There is, however, no doubt that he spent his childhood and adolescence in Kabul where he studied Islam as well as philosophy and exact sciences. He left Afghanistan when he was eighteen, and was abroad for five years. He stayed in India for over a year; and after his pilgrimage to Mecca went to Karbala and Najaf in Iraq. On his return to Afghanistan he helped the ruler, Dost Mohammed Khan, to mount a successful attack on Herat. After

Khan's death in 1863, he became involved in the civil war which broke out. His patron lost; and he was expelled from Afghanistan in September 1868. He went to India and Egypt and then Istanbul, where he was well received.

Afghani lectured at such prestigious places in Istanbul as Sultan Ahmed's mosque and Aya Sofia. In one of his lectures he described imparting prophetic teachings as a human craft or skill. This offended the religious establishment, headed by the Shaikh al Islam (Wise Man of Islam), Hasan Fahmi, who was jealous of his scholarship and popularity. Under the circumstances Afghani considered it prudent to leave Istanbul.

He arrived in Cairo in March 1871, and was given an annual allowance of 12,000 Egyptian piastres by the ruler, Khedive Ismail. Besides teaching his disciples theology and philosophy, he urged them to take up journalism, since he regarded the written word as the most effective method of influencing the minds of contemporaries. Among his students were Mohammed Abdu and Said Zaghlul Pasha: the former was to become the grand mufti of Egypt, and the latter a founder of the nationalist Wafd Party. He helped establish a daily newspaper and a monthly journal. He encouraged patriotic resistance to growing British and French interference into Egypt's affairs, attacked Khedive Ismail for his spendthriftness, and proposed a parliamentary system of government.

When, in early 1879, Tawfiq succeeded his father, Khedive Ismail, the British advised him to expel Afghani. He did so. In September, Afghani was deported to Hyderabad, India, and then to Calcutta, and kept under British surveillance. This continued until the simmering nationalist movement in Egypt had burst out as an armed uprising in 1881–2, and had then been crushed by British troops.

In January 1883, Afghani turned up in Paris. Four months later he published an article in the Journal des Débats in which he refuted Joseph-Ernest Renan's arguments, delivered in an earlier lecture, that Islam and science were incompatible. With the help of Indian Muslims living in Paris, he and Mohammed Abdu started a journal, *Al Urwat al Wuthqa* ('The Indissoluble Link'), in March 1884. Because of its opposition to the British policies in such countries as Egypt and India, the journal was banned by the British in their colonies. It ceased publication seven months later.

Following an invitation in 1886 by Nasir Uddeen Shah, the ruler of Iran, Afghani went to live in Tehran. But his popularity there soon disconcerted the shah. The next year he left for Uzbekistan province of tsarist Russia. There he engaged in propaganda against the British in India; and this pleased the tsar. At his urging, the tsar allowed the publication of the Koran and other Islamic literature in Russia for the first time.

In 1889, on the way to the Paris World Exhibition, he met the shah of Iran in Munich. Accepting the shah's invitation, he returned to Tehran. But his stay there was short and unhappy. His plan for reforming the judiciary aroused the shah's suspicion; and he retired to a religious sanctuary near the capital. In early 1891, the shah sent a large force of cavalry to arrest him and banish him to Khaniqin on the Iranian–Turkish border.

After Afghani had reached Basra and recovered his health, he attacked the shah for giving tobacco concessions to a British company. His disciple, Mirza Hassan Shirazi, the first clergy of Samarra, decreed that the faithful should stop smoking until the shah had withdrawn his tobacco concession. The shah yielded.

Afghani then travelled to London and carried out a sustained campaign against the dictatorial rule of the shah, chiefly through *Diyal al Khafikayn* (Radiance of the Two Hemispheres), a monthly journal published in Farsi and English. He thus helped to build a reformist movement in Iran, under the leadership of the clergy, which was dedicated to the shah's overthrow.

When the sultan of Turkey invited Afghani to Istanbul, he went. There the sultan gave him a generous monthly allowance and tried to persuade him to cease his propaganda against the shah. He refused and sought, in vain, to leave. On 11 March 1896 the shah of Iran was murdered by Mirza Mohammed Reza, a disciple of Afghani. This led to the accusation that Afghani had guided the assassin's hand, a charge he denied in an interview with the Paris-based *Le Temps*. About a year later he died of cancer of the chin, and was buried in Nishantash. In December 1944 his body was removed from there and sent to Ali Abad, a suburb of Kabul, where it has rested since then.

Afghani made four major contributions to Islamic and secular thought and action. He argued that each believer had the right and responsibility to interpret the Koran and the Sunna ('custom') for himself. He wanted the people to help themselves, and often quoted the Koranic verse which states: 'Verily, Allah does not change the state of a people until they change themselves inwardly.' He urged Muslims to master science as a means of liberating themselves from the domination of Western nations. While he stressed the pan-Islamic concept throughout his life, in his writings and lectures on India he underlined the need for unity between Muslims and Hindus in their struggle against British rule.

As the anti-imperialist movement sharpened in Islamic and non-Islamic colonies in the wake of the Second World War, interest in Afghani's teachings rose dramatically. The success of the Islamic revolution in Iran in 1979 reiterated the significance of Afghani and his views.

Further reading

See: E.G. Browne, *The Persian Revolution of 1905–1909* (1910); Elie Kedourie, *Afghani and Abduh: An Essay on Religious Unbelief and Political Action in Modern Islam* (1966); Nikki R. Keddie, *An Islamic Response to Imperialism: Political and Religious Writings of Sayyid Jamal ad-Din 'al-Afghani'* (1968) and *Sayyid Jamal ad-Din 'al-Afghani': A Political Biography* (1972); A. Albert Kudsi-Zadea, *Sayyid Jamal ad-Din Al Afghani: An Annotated Bibliography* (1970). See also: Dilip Hiro, *War Without End: The Rise of Islamist Terrorism and the Global Response* (2001).

DILIP HIRO

ALBEE, Edward Franklin

1928–

US dramatist

The adopted son of a millionaire, Albee was quickly promoted as a natural successor to **Arthur Miller** and **Tennessee Williams**, both of whose careers seemed in decline in the late 1950s. But when he refused to capitalize on his early success by obligingly abandoning what many critics regarded as a wilful experimentalism, his reputation suffered an ill-deserved decline.

His first one-act play, which received its premiere in Berlin in 1959, was *The Zoo Story*. Not the absurdist play which it was taken to be, it was in fact a powerful plea for the centrality of human relationships and a rejection of what is presented as a destructive materialism. Much the same could be said of his first Broadway production, *Who's Afraid of Virginia Woolf?* (1962). Ostensibly a **Strindbergian** drama of sexual conflict, it was also a Catonian warning against the erosion of human values and the consequence of a failure to engage the real. Set in the ironically named New Carthage, it combines a brilliantly witty drama of personal relations with an articulate assault on the collapse of private and public values. In his early works, indeed, he is something of a social critic, insisting that, while 'we are no longer looking for panaceas against all evils or solutions manufactured abroad', his concern was 'to prevent our political system from being denatured by too much facile conformism', asserting that this 'is already a programme in itself'. But if *Who's Afraid of Virginia Woolf?* advocated a confrontation with social and sexual realities, it evaded the question of definition. Reality was taken to be substantial and immediate. In subsequent plays he pressed his enquiry further. *Tiny Alice* (1965), for example, examines the nature of religious conviction in a play whose symbols many found baffling and whose characters have begun a slide towards abstraction which now intensified in his work. In *A Delicate Balance* (1966),

awarded the Pulitzer Prize denied to his earlier and more worthy *Who's Afraid of Virginia Woolf?*, he dramatized his sense of an absurdity which could no longer be neutralized by a quixotic gesture or even a determined effort to re-establish communal values.

And so the confidence of his early plays slowly erodes until, in *Quotations from Chairman Mao Tse-tung* (1968), words become found-objects and character little more than social role, a series of contingent acts. The play combines literal quotations from **Mao's** work with a poem by the nineteenth-century American sentimental poet Will Carleton. Only one character speaks lines actually written by Albee and each narrative is broken into fragments, these being juxtaposed to one another. The effect is to create occasional moments of consonance, as passages seem to comment on one another. But for the most part any coherent meaning must be the product of individual members of the audience as they struggle to create totality out of fragments – a process which is offered as an accurate account of the process whereby experience is reduced to meaning.

Albee's experiments continued in this direction. The world, which in his early plays he still believed could be saved with compassion and a liberal respect for reality and a language which, if wilfully deceptive, could still offer hints for the restoration of harmony, collapses. In *Counting the Ways* and *Listening*, rather as in **Pinter's** and **Beckett's** later work, the word 'reality' lost all meaning. We are left with a present which is no more than the recalling of a past which may never have happened. Even the substance of the physical surroundings has shrivelled into a space which offers no clue as to meaning or time.

For a time Albee tended to alternate original plays with adaptations. But the latter were almost invariably disappointing. Either he set himself to dramatize the undramatizable – in the form of Carson McCullers's southern grotesques in *The Ballad of the Sad Café* (1963), or James Purdy's surreal characters in *Malcolm* (1966) – or he simply adapted a work, like Giles Cooper's *Everything in the*

Garden (1968) which benefited little from transposition from an English to an American environment. His real talent lay in the consummate skill with which he dissected private and public deceptions and articulated first his liberal convictions, and subsequently his deepening scepticism about life and art. Only with *Three Tall Women* (1991), which won another Pulitzer drama prize, did Albee begin to re-emerge, both critically and commercially.

Of the recent work, it is *The Goat, or Who is Sylvia?* (2002) that has attracted most attention, though not all of it positive. An architect and those around him are thrown into emotional and intellectual disarray when he becomes physically enamoured of the animal of the play's title. An allegory about how individuals deal, or fail to deal, with being gay, it draws upon the dramatist's considerable linguistic and intellectual resources to the full. For some Broadway audiences this was disconcerting: but in London, where *The Goat* was first staged in 2004, acclaim was instant and almost unconditional.

In 2005 – the same year as his longstanding partner Jonathan Thomas died of cancer – Albee was given a Tony Award for Lifetime Achievement. At its best his work is characterized by a coruscating wit, an articulacy that can become his subject as well as his method, a fascination with language, and a sensitive control over rhythm and tone, which at times gives it a musical structure. No other American dramatist has been as dedicated to examining the essence of theatricality, or dissecting the nature of his own language and art.

Further reading

Albee's many other works include: the one-act plays *The American Dream* (1962), *The Sandbox* (1960), and *The Death of Bessie Smith* (1960); *All Over* (1971); *Seascape* (1974); *The Lady from Dubuque* (1980); *Lolita* (stage adaptation of the novel by **Vladimir Nabokov**, 1980); *The Man Who Had Three Arms* (1981); *The Lorca Play* (1992); *Peter & Jerry* (2004). See: C.W.E. Bigsby, *Albee* (1969) and *Edward Albee* (1975); Michael Rutenberg, *Edward Albee: Playwright in Protest* (1969); Anne Paolucci, *From Tension to Panic: The Plays of Edward Albee* (1972); G. McCarthy, *Edward Albee* (1987); Mel Gussow, *Edward Albee: A Singular Journey* (2000).

C.W.E. BIGSBY
(REVISED AND UPDATED BY THE EDITOR)

ALLEN, Woody

1935–

US comedian and filmmaker

Woody Allen was born Allen Stewart Konigsberg in New York into a Jewish family and was educated at Midwood High School in Brooklyn. He was a talented writer from a young age and at fifteen started selling one-liners to gossip columns. In 1952 he adopted his stage name and a year later, in 1953, enrolled in New York University's film programme. But failing the course 'Motion Picture Production', he dropped out of university after one semester and started writing material for television comedians.

In 1961, Allen began performing as a stand-up comedian with a comic persona of an insecure, doubt-ridden character who exaggerates his own anxieties. His career as a filmmaker began in 1965 when he wrote and starred in *What's New, Pussycat?* in which the subjects that have always obsessed him and which would become his trademarks in future films – relationships, sex, death and the meaning of life – could already be detected. In it Michael James desperately wants to be faithful to his fiancée, Carole Werner, but finds it difficult as women he meets all seem to fall in love with him. His therapist Dr Fritz Fassbinder (played by Peter Sellers) cannot help him either, since he is busy courting one of his patients who in turn longs for Michael. A climax is reached as all the characters check into the same hotel for the weekend, not knowing of each other's presence.

Allen's directorial debut – *What's Up, Tiger Lily?* (1966) – was an interesting experimental exercise, but not properly original.

Instead, Allen took a Japanese film called *Kagi No Kagi* (1964) – 'Key of Keys' – and dubbed it in his own unique style and with completely new comic dialogue.

The films that followed – *Take the Money and Run* (1969), a farcical comedy about an incompetent would-be criminal called Virgil Starkwell in which Allen starred, co-wrote and directed; *Bananas* (1971); *Everything You Always Wanted to Know about Sex but Were Afraid to Ask* (1972); and the futuristic comedy *Sleeper* (1973) – all employed a highly inventive, joke-oriented style. Allen's 1975 *Love and Death* signalled his desire for respect as a serious filmmaker; a satire of the Napoleonic wars, it included references to history, Russian culture (with an obvious nod to **Tolstoy**) and showed that beneath Allen's comic surface there was seriousness.

Annie Hall (1977), a funny but also serious and often moving observation of urban romance, was a breakthrough, turning Allen into one of America's most prominent directors. In it, a stand-up comedian, Alvy Singer, a clumsy, anxiety-ridden, neurotic New York Jew – much like Allen himself – meets aspiring singer Annie Hall. They fall in love and a romance develops, but the cultural gap between the two is insurmountable, so beautifully shown in the way Alvy's boisterous Jewish family's dinner table (Allen derived much of his comic material from his Jewish background) shares a split screen with the Hall's tight-lipped dinner table. The complicated relationships disintegrate and Alvy and Annie eventually separate. *Annie Hall*, which won four Academy Awards, embraced Allen's central themes, namely how impossible relationships are and his fear of death.

Allen's subsequent films contained comedy, philosophy and a unique combination of trivialities with major concerns. The commercial failure of the theatre-style drama *Interiors* (1978), inspired by the films of his hero **Ingmar Bergman**, was followed by *Manhattan* (1979), an autobiographical ode to Allen's beloved New York City, shot in black and white and underscored with **Gershwin's** music; hailed as a masterpiece,

Manhattan remains perhaps Allen's definitive work.

In later films such as *Stardust Memories* (1980); the documentary *Zelig* (1983); *The Purple Rose of Cairo* (1985); *Hannah and Her Sisters* (1986), which won favourable comparisons to **Chekhov**; *Crimes and Misdemeanors* (1989); *Side Effects* (1989); and *Alice* (1990), Allen attempted with varying success to blend his vein of absurd humour with a wider range of character portrayals and light but basically serious themes.

Further reading

See: *Woody Allen on Woody Allen: In Conversation with Stig Bjorkman* (1995); Foster Hirsch, *Love, Sex, Death, and the Meaning of Life: The Films of Woody Allen* (1981); Richard A. Schwartz, *Woody, From Antz to Zelig: A Reference Guide to Woody Allen's Creative Work, 1964–1998* (2000).

AHRON BREGMAN

ALTMAN, Robert
1925–2006
American film director

A native of Kansas City, Missouri, of German Catholic ethnic background, Altman moved to Los Angeles and worked extensively in television before making a Hollywood breakthrough with *M.A.S.H.* (1970), a dark comedy set among the American medical corps in the Korean War but widely taken as a depiction of the then current Vietnam War. Altman took the film as a directing assignment and made it into something highly original. The sense of life's absurdity, the irreverence towards authority, the frankness about sex, mutilation and death, look back to **Joseph Heller's** World War II novel *Catch-22*. But the behavioural world of the film is entirely of the 1960s, scruffy, uninhibited, mad, embodied in a range of vivid new film actors: Elliott Gould, Donald Sutherland, Sally Kellerman and others. And nothing had been seen and heard like Altman's film images crowded with inventive detail and activity, lacking a centre, pulling the attention in different directions, the camera constantly in motion, simultaneous separate conversations and other sounds woven in and out of each other. The world comes to life here in a new way, and the vast energy of it all seems a protest of life against death. (Altman had nothing to do with the much softer long-running television series *M.A.S.H.*)

The commercial success of *M.A.S.H.* gave Altman an authority in the film industry that helped to keep him going for decades as he worked on the border between Hollywood and the independent realm, conceiving his own projects, finding material and working closely with writers, drawing on Hollywood personnel and money. Altman brought out a film every year or two from the late 1960s until his death, in the process devising a singular portrait and critique of America, and giving unprecedented space to human oddity and to not usually acknowledged regions of motivation.

In the 1970s Altman took an interest in recasting American film genres. *McCabe and Mrs Miller* (1971) is a Western without heroism starring Warren Beatty and Julie Christie as brothel entrepreneurs in a frontier community struggling to realize itself in face of big business tyranny and common human pettiness. Shot on location in the Pacific Northwest, the film has great beauty of a bleak sort and an intense lyrical elegiac mood. Death is felt as inevitable and ever present. Life is full of desire and passion, but ultimately pitiable. *The Long Goodbye* (1973) is *film noir* set in 1970s Los Angeles rendered with an inquiring documentary quality in all its squalor, eccentricity, opulence and violence. Elliott Gould, in the role of Raymond Chandler's Philip Marlowe, is an odd, isolated figure of ambiguous sexual identity, given to talking to himself (like McCabe and many other Altman characters), who is more buffeted and used by the world around him than able to control it.

With the musical *Nashville* (1975) Altman made his most acclaimed film, a picture of America in the microcosm of the country music business, with a presidential political campaign in progress involving the singers. Altman fields a large array of characters and perfects his characteristic narrative style of moving around among separate stories seemingly at random, showing human pursuits and frustrations in great variety, drawing comparisons, giving scope to odd players such as Shelley Duvall, Keith Carradine, Lily Tomlin and Karen Black. Some of the songs are parody, pointing up American bad taste and smugness. Others are genuine, especially those of the star, Ronee Blakley, expressing great longing, ecstasy and despair. There is considerable interest taken here in abused, passionate, even mad women as setting a standard for judging the world, knowing more than the world knows. This interest carries on into one of Altman's most powerful and interesting films, *Three Women* (1977), with Shelley Duvall and Sissy Spacek, set in consumerist southern California.

The decidedly non-generic *Three Women* along with other challenging experiments such as *Buffalo Bill and the Indians* (1976), set in William Cody's Wild West Show, and the futurist apocalyptic *Quintet* (1979) gave Altman the reputation of an art film director and made large budget productions not viable for a time. In the 1980s he turned to films of stage plays, sometimes made for television, and made an art form of this kind of film. Altman's moving, probing camera and pointed editing transfigure the plays into dreamlike experiences with powerful, haunting outbreaks of physical or emotional violence. Film takes us where only film can go. *Streamers* (1983), *Secret Honor* (1984), about President Nixon, *Fool for Love* (1985), *The Dumb Waiter* (1987) and others follow from *Come Back to the Five and Dime, Jimmy Dean, Jimmy Dean* (1982), one of Altman's best, and bleakest, films. A group of women meet in a dying Texas town for a reunion of their 1950s James Dean fan club and talk themselves into painful confessions. Karen Black in the role of a transsexual leads everyone to acknowledge violent change, mutilation, death and self-delusion as the most persistent of realities. Altman's camera moves inventively between two stage areas, one seen through a mirror, bringing together past and present, reality and fantasy.

The commercial success of *The Player* (1992), Altman's satire of Hollywood, starring Tim Robbins, made possible a late phase of large-production filmmaking. The most important work here is *Short Cuts* (1993), a three-hours-plus study of lives lived in and around Los Angeles, loosely based on Raymond Carver stories, moving, like *Nashville*, constantly in and out of people's separate stories, featuring a vivid cast of a newer generation of actors: Frances McDormand, Julianne Moore, Jennifer Jason Leigh, Matthew Modine, Robert Downey Jr and others. As so often in Altman, a seeming randomness and spontaneity in narrative and in the camera's observing eye becomes a means to revelation, virtually on the level of metaphysics. The rhythms and outbursts of one life seem actually to affect another as we cut from story to story, and all lives are cast under a pall of environmental poisoning and coming apocalypse.

Nevertheless, there is considerable inventive humour, coming from Altman and from the characters, which suggests hopefulness about carrying on with life. *Kansas City* (1996) is a compelling dark film about jazz and political corruption in the 1920s. But *Cookie's Fortune* (1999), after a half hour of mystical confrontation with death, turns into gentle comedy of community life in the South, with a focus on the young. *Dr T and the Women* (2000) has a large element of satire (set in Dallas, Texas), but is more than anything a manic celebration of femininity. The English country house film *Gosford Park* (2001) moves from social realism and tragedy to a saving farce. And *The Company* (2003), largely a documentary about the Joffrey Ballet, celebrates creativity. Altman was a disappointed idealist who forged new cinematic forms to critique his culture, project his sense of doom, and look for signs of life in odd places. In the end he seems to have found more of the positive than he could have anticipated.

Further reading

Other films include: *That Cold Day in the Park* (1969); *Brewster McCloud* (1970); *Images* (1972); *Thieves Like Us* (1974); *California Split* (1974); *A Wedding* (1978); *Popeye* (1980); *Tanner '88* (1988); *Vincent and Theo* (1990), about **Van Gogh**. See: Robert Phillip Kolker, *A Cinema of Loneliness* (1980); Patrick McGilligan, *Robert Altman: Jumping Off the Cliff* (1989); Helene Keyssar, *Robert Altman's America* (1991); David Sterritt (ed.) *Robert Altman Interviews* (2000); Robert Self, *Robert Altman's Subliminal Reality* (2002).

CHARLES WARREN

AMIS, Martin Louis

1949–

English writer

Money (1984), the supercharged satire of ambition, greed and vanity in London and New York that remains the author's most accomplished work of fiction, features an anti-hero narrator named 'John Self' and a minor character named 'Martin Amis'. From early novels such as *Success* (1978) through to the mid-career manifesto of *The Information* (1995), the world of Martin Amis abounds in doublings, distortions and twisted reflections of identity. In his novels, stories and in numerous essays and articles, the mirror of the self, and of the society it inhabits, shatters into glittering but disconnected fragments and facets. From the late 1990s, however, the mood changes. This postmodern game of doubles, pairs and repetitions yields to a more single-minded quest for unity and authenticity, in his fiction and non-fiction.

Ever since his precocious debut, the British novelist, journalist and memoirist has enjoyed (and endured) a career seen by many of his peers as exemplary. From the early 1980s, he became a semi-reluctant model, for good or ill, of 'success' in the style-obsessed, fashion-driven upper reaches of Anglo-American literary life. That the millennium, and his own middle age, should see Amis pull decisively away from the forms of the culture that celebrated him may give us valuable information about the times as well as the man.

The author Martin Amis has always had to struggle against the ghostly double 'Martin Amis', an object of envy, admiration, resentment and derision – sometimes all at once. He was born in Oxford in 1949, younger son of the epoch-defining post-war comic novelist Kingsley Amis. This relationship shadows and shapes much of Martin's work. After feckless and disrupted teenage years, his seemingly effortless early brilliance as a student at Oxford University, as a wickedly stylish journalist and reviewer, and as a coruscating satirical novelist, became the stuff of legend. The *New Statesman* magazine, where he worked as deputy literary editor and made his name as a slash-and-burn critic, once ran a competition that asked for inappropriate pairings of authors and works. *My Struggle* by Martin Amis was among the winners.

This heartless swagger, delivered in a style steeped in the modern literary canon yet enthralled by the rip-roaring energies of pop culture, belonged to the period as well as the personality. In snappily cadenced, button-bright prose, the honed ironies of **Saul Bellow** (mentor and model for a novelist who always looked to the US rather than Europe) merged with the hip sloganeering of the style magazine and the advertising billboard. With Amis, the British – and transatlantic – 1980s found their voice: smart, sharp and often savage. His themes, from the bitterly farcical male rivalry of *Success* to the demented consumerism of *Money*, matched the age as much as did his style. Profoundly cool (in every sense), this cruel divinity looked down on absurd, struggling humanity with a pitiless extraterrestrial's eye. 'Martian Amis' became another favourite critics' soubriquet. Meanwhile, scores of younger novelists and journalists made life mimic art as they played their own games of imitation and emulation with the Amis manner and career.

Yet, in true Amis fashion, another self partnered and sometimes punctured this glacially clever *persona*. This second Amis, anxiously and passionately immersed in the mysteries of identity and mortality, had announced itself with the otherworldy enigmas of *Other People* (1981). Amis followed his father not merely in an uproarious comic gift but in his fascinated respect for science fiction, with its non-naturalistic narratives that pose the most challenging questions about selfhood and society. This was the writer – a genre-bending moralist as much as a satirist – who told the story of the holocaust backwards in *Time's Arrow* (1991), and explored the anguish of the nuclear age in the fables of *Einstein's Monsters* (1987). In this light, *London Fields* (1989) reads like a pivotal work: not only an exuberant tragi-comic carnival of metropolitan low (and high) life, but a futuristic eco-fantasy darkened by the ageing of the planet and the dying of the sun.

Entropy, the 'measure of disorder' within any system and the seed of its extinction, has long acted as a master-metaphor behind Amis's work. That entropy governs persons as well as planets became laboriously plain in *The Information*. This digressive novel, in patches both banal and brilliant, met a mixed reception that hastened the twilight of 'Martin Amis' as a cultural idol. It functioned both as a return to his archetypal motifs – with a doppelgänger feud between a failed novelist and his glib superstar friend – and a middle-aged meditation on death, the 'information' that comes to all of us, and its bone-aching messengers.

Death, in its genre-fiction guise, also informed his take on the American hard-boiled thriller in *Night Train* (1997). Closer to home, death brooded over his extraordinary memoir, *Experience* (2000). From the passing of his father, his own mid-life perplexities, and his first cousin's hideous death at the hands of the serial killer Fred West, Amis spun a life-story of grief, loss and love which at last blended all his talent for narrative pyrotechnics with a whole-hearted drive towards wonder and wisdom. Inspired in part by **Nabokov** (another literary touchstone), *Experience* in large measure achieved Amis's longed-for marriage of ingenuity and insight; of self and soul.

Since the millennium, Amis's life and his books have simplified. After a divorce and re-marriage, he now has five children and – although still based in London – has for long periods opted out of the capital's literary scene. *Koba the Dread* (2002) was a short book of anger and lament about the horrors of **Stalinism** and the left's refusal to treat them with due solemnity. It can be seen as another act of homage to his famously anti-Communist father, as well as a public quarrel with his old and close friend, the journalist and polemicist Christopher Hitchens. The novel *Yellow Dog* (2003) showed Amis marking time. Further whispers of mortality combined with a reversion to heavy-duty satire, here directed at the parasitic media which for so long flattered, and then flayed, the postmodern icon known as 'Martin Amis'.

That figure died, unmourned, a decade ago. The writer who remains clearly wishes to put his sensitive social antennae and vast stylistic resourcefulness at the service of work that marks, but in some way mitigates, the terrible vulnerability of human life, love and culture. In fiction, he has yet to find the most effective vehicle for his aims. His progress so far suggests that he will.

Further reading

Other works include: *The Rachel Papers* (1973) and *Dead Babies* (1974), and two collections of essays, press pieces and interviews: *Visiting Mrs Nabokov and Other Excursions* (1993), and *The Moronic Inferno: And Other Visits to America* (1986). See: A. Mars-Jones, *Venus Envy* (1990); J. Diedrick, *Understanding Martin Amis* (1995).

BOYD TONKIN

ANDRÉ, Carl

1935–

US sculptor and poet

Carl André has repeatedly insisted that sculptures are about the physical properties of their materials (mainly wood or metal), taking an anti-allusive position that puts him at odds with what most people expect from visual art. Born in Quincy, Massachusetts, and educated at the prestigious Phillips Academy in Andover, his position is best understood in the context of the American artistic empiricism of the 1960s, the decade in which André made his most important contributions. Many then thought art's viability as an expressive medium demanded formalist self-criticism, a conviction that was in part somewhat para-doxically committed to the literal, seemingly objective use of materials to secure metaphysical knowledge. Unlike the influential critics Clement Greenberg and his disciple Michael Fried, who believed that this type of material fidelity afforded viewers an intuitive sense of absolute moral values, André and the other Minimalists – especially Frank Stella (with whom he once shared a studio), **Donald Judd**, Robert Morris, Dan Flavin and Sol LeWitt – thought that literalism washed art clean of such lofty pretensions. Without this transcendent register, the knowledge that André claimed his art provided was one restricted to scientific fact in that it was observable, verifiable and, most importantly, limited in reach. It was in this sense that he told one interviewer in 1968, 'I am the exact opposite of an idealist. I am a materialist exactly. Matter is my subject-matter.'

A work like the Tate Modern's *Equivalent VIII* (1966, 1969), notorious for the scandal it caused in Britain (i.e. the 'Tate Bricks'), gives a sense of what André means by this statement. Seizing the floor, this work of art is a six-brick-wide by ten-long grouping of 120 white firebricks stacked two high on the floor. It presents the classic serial construction and anaxial symmetry of most Minimal works, a strategy designed to void art of the solipsism these artists thought inherent in traditional European artistic practices. As a grouping of eight 'equivalent' 120-brick rectangular works, André showed how each retains the same weight while *appearing* (falsely) to have different masses and volumes, which places factual knowledge at odds with visual perception. Other pieces like *Copper-Lead Plain* (1969), a chequerboard patterned floor piece on which gallery-goers are permitted to walk, shows how visual knowledge comes up short against the countervailing tactile sensations in revealing the nature of the art. This conflict, again, between visual experience and knowledge acquired by touch remains one of André's recurring themes.

Early works include the stacked wood *Pyramid (Square Plan)* (wooden beams, 1959) and display André's interest in the Romanian Constructivist artist **Constantin Brancusi** (1876–1956), while in more recent pieces including *Pb Cu* (lead and copper cubes, 1995) the visually sensuous properties of his materials come to the fore. Of late, his art has been somewhat overshadowed by the premature death of his wife, the artist Ana Mendieta, for whose murder he has twice been tried and twice acquitted. Also a poet until the mid 1970s, André has used words in a manner akin to the modular components of his sculptures, relating them more through juxtaposition than by connotation. Though loosely narrative, the poems function mainly as drawings or images, and are likewise displayed.

André's materialist thinking was not restricted to aesthetic pursuits alone; it formed the basis of his political writing and leftist activism with the Art Workers Coalition during the 1960s and 1970s. In one notorious statement from 1965 quoted in an art magazine, he offered a Swiftian solution to the Vietnam War: 'Let them eat what they kill.' (He was himself a soldier in the US Army from 1955 to 1956.) And in a rather more developed **Marxist** analysis from 1976 of art's relationship to other commodities, André and his co-author disputed the self-satisfied radicalism of conceptual artists:

> the most farcical claim of the conceptualizing inkpissers is that their works are somehow antibourgeois because they do away with objects. In fact, doing away with objects and replacing them with such reifications of abstract relations to production as stockshares, contracts, liens, options, and paper money itself . . . is exactly the final triumphant form of the bourgeois revolution.

What unites André's art, poetry and politics is his desire to strip culture of allusion and metaphor in favour of the blunt physical facts of social reality, unwelcome though they be.

Further reading

See: Jeanne Siegel, 'Interview with Carl André: Artworker', *Studio International* (November 1970); Carl André and Jeremy Gilbert-Rolfe, 'Commodity and Contradiction, or, Contraction as Commodity', *October*, No. 2 (Summer 1976); Pieter de Jonge (ed.) *Carl André* (1987); Ian Cole (ed.) *Carl André and the Sculptural Imagination* (1996).

DAVID RASKIN

ARMSTRONG, Daniel Louis (Satchmo)
1900–71
US jazz cornetist, trumpeter, singer, actor

Louis rose from a poor New Orleans background to become one of the greatest of all jazz musicians. At the age of twenty-two he was in Chicago, second cornetist in King Oliver's Creole Jazz Band, and even at this stage the younger man's advanced conception of improvisation in comparison with the sober, classic New Orleans style of Oliver is apparent. He moved on to New York in 1924, to small group recordings with Clarence Williams and Sidney Bechet, to backing blues singers like Bessie Smith, and to big band work with Fletcher Henderson in 1924–5.

Back in Chicago in 1925, he formed a small pick-up group and called it the Hot Five. This group revolutionized jazz. It contained New Orleans musicians with the standard instrumentation. The New Orleans style had the three front-line wind players improvising a collective polyphony, interspersed with solos. Louis broke with tradition, increased the domination of the cornet lead and the proportion of soloing to ensemble playing, and organized the three minutes permitted by the 10-inch, 78-rpm disc into a slowly developing climax of intensity and virtuosity. The pianist Earl Hines then joined the fluid personnel of the Hot Fives and Hot Sevens, and from 1927 to 1929 Louis produced, one after another, about fifty of the greatest jazz recordings ever made.

Typical of Louis's soloing during these years are the use of the 'break', when the rhythm section stops playing for a few bars and the soloist continues alone, and the solo against stop-chords in the accompaniment (the other players sound only the first beat in each, or in every other, bar). Both these devices are used by Louis to enable him to rise away from the implied beat and superimpose on it complex rhythmical patterns of his own, full of syncopation and of triplets. In a stop-chord solo he tends to build his lines in two-bar phrases, leaping and winding through the chords, each phrase expanded by the next, with the solo fitting together as a whole both on the rhetorical level, as a gradual crescendo of emotional tension, and on the melodic level, as a developing variation on the melody of the song. A fine example of his style is 'Basin Street Blues' of 1928, in which can be found twelve-bar blues soloing where he gradually increases the density of notes and rhythmical complexity after the fourth bar, a scat-sung (i.e. wordless) chorus, four solo choruses where he builds to a climax and then winds down, and an example of his restraint where three choruses are played quietly around one low-register note.

In 1929 he was featured in a Broadway show, *Hot Chocolates*. By now he was on the one hand the model for every jazz trumpeter, and on the other the happy entertainer and singer for mainly white audiences. If Louis distinguished between the two, it was to give precedence to the art of communicating with the greatest number of people through his music. From 1930 onwards he led a succession of big bands, with which he recorded a large number of popular songs of the day in a fairly constant format: he would play the melody once with the band, sing it, and then take one or more solo choruses, leading the band out at the end – often soaring into the upper register. In nearly all of these performances he transcended the material, and in many of them he played magnificent solos. He toured widely in Europe, and acted in Hollywood films – throughout his life he appeared in about fifty in all. His singing gradually began to dominate his performances, and it may be for this that his influence has been widest. His gravelly, laughing voice had immense charm, but more importantly, he was able to dismantle a song into short, rhythmically strong phrases which he sang slightly behind the beat, mingled with scat-sung interjections and 'fills'. In this way he took the art of the crooner and gave it swing and vitality by tempering his melodies with the speech–rhythms characteristic of Southern black folk song.

In the 1940s he formed a small group (the All-Stars) of first-rate musicians (including the trombonist Jack Teagarden), and rode the crest of the New Orleans revivalist wave. But he was always reaching towards the biggest audiences as well. There is no reason to believe that Louis saw his record 'Hello Dolly', which pushed the **Beatles** from the top of the lists of best-selling records in 1964, as being a lesser achievement than his magnificent 1927 'Potato Head Blues'. Not only was he indisputably superior to any other jazz musician of his time between 1924 and 1932, but the magnitude of his achievement during that period, in establishing standards of musicianship and a vocabulary of improvisation, is unsurpassed.

Further reading

Most of Louis's original 78-rpm records have been reissued on long-playing discs, notably on World Records – EMI, CBS, RCA, MCA. Books by Armstrong: *Swing That Music* (1936); *Satchmo: My Life in New Orleans* (1955). Books about him and his music: Max Jones and John Chilton, *Louis* (1971); Albert McCarthy, *Louis Armstrong* (1961); Richard Meryman, *Louis Armstrong – A Self-Portrait* (1971); Hugues Panassié, *Louis Armstrong* (1971); Laurence Bergreen, *Louis Armstrong: An Extravagant Life* (1997). Studies of his solos are to be found in: André Hodier, *Jazz: Its Evolution and Essence* (1956); Richard Hadlock, *Jazz Masters of the Twenties* (1965); Gunther Schuller, *Early Jazz:*

Its Roots and Musical Development (1968). Louis' solos transcribed can be found in: *44 Trumpet Solos & 125 Jazz Breaks* (published by Charles Hansen, New York); and *Louis Armstrong, A Jazz Master* (twenty solos, published by MCA, New York).

CHRISTOPHER WAGSTAFF

ARNOLD, Eve

1913–

American/British photographer

Born in Philadelphia, Pennsylvania in 1913 to immigrant Russian-Jewish parents, Arnold began photographing in 1946 while working at a photo-finishing plant in New York City. She decided to take a six-week course in photography offered by Alexei Brodovitch at New York City's New School for Social Research in 1948. Impressed by her pictures of a Harlem fashion show, Brodovitch encouraged Arnold to keep shooting. Her first professional photograph was a 1949 Bowery bum sleeping off his excesses on the New York waterfront.

Throughout the 1950s, Arnold continued with portraiture usually as an assignment for a magazine or a film production. A 1952 picture story of Marlene Dietrich recording songs she had sung to Allied troops during the war acted as a launch pad for Arnold to personality and star photography. Her unglamorized and unretouched photographs revealed the changes taking place in portraiture. Arnold first became associated with Magnum Photos in 1951, becoming a full member in 1955.

To move around easily and elicit more from her subjects, Arnold streamlined her equipment early in her career, never using motor drives, lights or tripods, and carrying the minimum amount of gear in a single bag. She took a low-key approach based on establishing contact with the subject and using whatever light was available. To choose her photographs, she always asked if the subject was visual and if words would enhance the picture. Rather than selecting the sensational, Arnold let the subject dictate the treatment, angle of approach and point of view. Describing her vision, she stated that if a topic interested her then she believed that she could make it interesting to others. She often liked to use colour as an accent or as part of the design and believed that muted colour often proved more effective than stark tones.

Arnold focused on Hollywood stars, political figures and religious leaders as well as ordinary people. The photographs for which she is best known are those of Marilyn Monroe. She had a total of six sessions with Monroe, ranging from press conferences to her last film, *The Misfits*. With Monroe, Arnold saw what many male photographers did not, specifically that Monroe could switch her sexual aura on and off.

In 1961, Arnold began work with the London *Sunday Times* and stayed under contract with them for the next ten years. She moved permanently to England in 1962. Despite her desire to cover a war, *The Times* refused to send her to Vietnam because of the dangers involved. Managing to receive an assignment in 1979 to produce the book *In China*, Arnold sought to reflect the happiness that most Chinese felt about the approach of industrialization. The pictures brought Arnold her first major solo exhibition, a display of the China photographs at the Brooklyn Museum in 1980. Arnold delved into filmmaking and made *Beyond the Veil* (1971) for the BBC about life in a harem. Put off by the expense and the numbers of people involved with a film, Arnold never attempted a second project.

Further reading

The best source on Eve Arnold is her autobiography, *In Retrospect* (1996). The chief critical appraisal of her photographs is Sarah Brown's 'Eve Arnold', *British Journal of Photography*, 5 January 2000. Her other works include: *The Unretouched Woman* (1976); *Flashback: The 50s* (1978); *In China* (1980); *In America* (1983); *Portrait of a Film: The Making of White Nights* (1985); *Marilyn for Ever* (1987); *Marilyn Monroe: An Appreciation* (1987); *Private View: Inside Baryshnikov's American Ballet Theatre* (1988); *All in a Day's Work* (1989); *The Great British* (1991); *Magna Brava: Magnum's*

Women Photographers (1999); and *Film Journal* (2002).

CARYN E. NEUMANN

ARNOLD, Matthew

1822–88

British poet and critic

Matthew Arnold, the eldest son of Thomas Arnold, was born at Laleham in 1822. He was educated at Winchester and, from 1837, at Rugby. In 1841 he went to Balliol College, Oxford, on an open scholarship, but neglected his work and, like his close friend Arthur Hugh Clough, failed to take a first-class degree. However, in 1845 he joined Clough as a fellow at Oriel, though he had no intention of teaching. In 1847 he became private secretary to the Marquis of Lansdowne, who later appointed him an Inspector of Schools (1851). This post enabled Arnold to marry Frances Lucy Wightman. Before his marriage Arnold had frequently visited the Continent, and in 1848 and 1849 had met at Thun the mysterious 'Marguerite' about whom he wrote the love poems collectively entitled 'Switzerland'. Arnold remained a school inspector for thirty-five years. As a break from his normal duties he was occasionally sent abroad to investigate continental education. These assignments resulted in such books as *The Popular Education of France* (1861), *A French Eton* (1864) and *Schools and Universities on the Continent* (1868). He also wrote a number of official reports, selections of which were published in 1889 and 1908. Although Arnold's work was with elementary schools for the working class, his personal preoccupation was with middle-class education, improvement of which he regarded as a most pressing national priority.

In 1849 Arnold published *The Strayed Reveller, and Other Poems*, which surprised those who knew him as something of a dandy by its vein of stoical melancholy. 'The something that infects the world' ('Resignation') is a theme present in most of the poems, despite their exotic settings in myth or the classical past. *Empedocles on Etna, and Other Poems* (1852) gives further expression to a personal and general malaise, the nineteenth century being characterized as 'this iron time/Of doubts, disputes, distractions, fears' in 'Memorial Verses' (1850) commemorating Wordsworth. Arnold's feeling that the modern intellect was inimical to man's spiritual and creative needs is most powerfully embodied in 'Empedocles' which follows the Greek philosopher and poet through a crisis of world-weariness culminating in his suicide in the crater of Etna. The volume also includes the 'Marguerite' poems which extrapolate from the lovers' predicament a pessimistic view of the individual's isolation – 'We mortal millions live *alone*' ('To Marguerite – Continued'). In 1853 Arnold brought out *Poems: A New Edition*, notable for the Preface which justified the omission of 'Empedocles' on the grounds that it was morbid. Arnold quoted Schiller – 'All art is dedicated to Joy' – and insisted that poems should be based on 'great actions, calculated powerfully and delightfully to affect what is permanent in the human soul'. In a letter to Clough of 1853 he emphasized that poetry should '*animate* and *ennoble*'. The preface also inveighed against Romantic subjectivity and what Arnold saw as the contemporary fixation with details of imagery and sensuousness of expression at the expense of overall structure or *Architectonicé*, arising, he thought, from the deleterious influence of the Elizabethans. He wanted poets to revert to classical models and he wrote to Clough 'modern poetry can only subsist by its *contents*: by becoming a complete magister vitae as the poetry of the ancients did'. Arnold tried to live up to his own standards, producing the long poems 'Sohrab and Rustum' (1853) and 'Balder Dead' (1855) in 'the grand style' of the classical epic, and a Greek tragedy, *Merope* (1858), but the strength of his poetry remained in the personal and elegiacal mode of 'The Scholar-Gipsy' (1853), 'Thyrsis' (1866) and 'Dover Beach' (1867). Although Arnold published further collections of poetry in 1855 and 1867, his inspiration was waning and these contained little new apart from occasional poems and memorial verse such as 'Rugby Chapel' (1867) on his father, 'Heine's Grave' (1867) and 'Haworth Churchyard' (1867) on Charlotte Brontë. 'Obermann Once More' (1867), Arnold's last major poem, shows the earlier melancholy giving way to the more hopeful meliorism of his prose.

In 1857 Arnold was elected Professor of Poetry at Oxford and he held the chair for ten years. His first published lectures were *On Translating Homer* (1861) in which he characterized Homer's distinctive qualities and laid down guidelines for translators, taking exception to Francis Newman's recent version of the *Iliad* because it failed to render Homer's 'nobility'. Another series of lectures resulted in *On the Study of Celtic Literature* (1867). In 1865 *Essays in Criticism* (First Series) appeared. In 'The Function of Criticism at the Present Time' Arnold says that the task of criticism is to 'make the best ideas prevail' in order to create a proper climate for a literature 'adequate' to the needs of a complex modern society, and to help the individual to an awareness of 'the best that is known and thought in the world'. In 'The Literary Influence of Academies' he castigates the English for their 'intellectual eccentricity' and lack of the critical spirit, while in 'Heinrich Heine' he hails 'a brilliant soldier in the Liberation War of humanity', and also acknowledges Goethe as the outstanding critical intelligence of Europe whose 'imperturbable naturalism' was responsible for eroding the last vestiges of medieval Europe. 'Dissolvents of the old European system ... we must all be,' Arnold declared.

Although criticism was 'disinterested' and above party, class or sectarian interests, Arnold was drawn to comment on social and political affairs. His underlying conviction was that the 'ideas' of the French Revolution were bound to prevail, that the *Zeitgeist* or 'time-spirit' was on the side of democracy as against the old aristocratic order. There was, however, a conservative element in Arnold's politics, and in *Culture and Anarchy* (1867) he

warned that personal liberty must be contained by 'a principal of Authority' if anarchy were to be avoided: 'Without order there can be no society, and without society there can be no human perfection.' The state was 'sacred'. The book is most celebrated for Arnold's conception of culture as 'a study of perfection', and for his attack on the Philistinism of the English middle class, which lacked 'sweetness and light'. In contrast to their 'Hebraism', dourly concerned with work and morality, 'money and salvation', Arnold proposed 'Hellenism', the spirit of the Greek Humanism with its ideal of the wholly developed man. His onslaught on Philistinism was also carried out in a series of satirical letters to the *Pall Mall Gazette* (1866–70) which he published as *Friendship's Garland* in 1871.

In the 1870s Arnold turned his attention to religion, producing *St Paul and Protestantism* (1870), *Literature and Dogma* (1873) and *God and the Bible* (1875). Arnold wanted to preserve Christianity, but saw that its traditional defenders were in fact imperilling its chances of survival. 'Christianity is true; but in general the whole plan for grounding and buttressing it chosen by our theological instructors is false, and, since it is false, it must fail us sooner or later.' Arnold wished to dispense with the miraculous and supernatural elements of religion which science was discrediting, clear away the accretions of dogma and *Aberglaube* ('extra-beliefs'), and return to the essentials of Christianity, the person and example of Jesus. The anthropomorphic deity of popular theology, characterized by Arnold as a 'magnified non-natural man', was to be replaced by 'the eternal not ourselves which makes for righteousness'. Religion for Arnold was 'morality touched by emotion', and he was writing in the tradition of Coleridge and his father by placing the emphasis on the moral validity and 'natural truth' of Christianity. Like his father, he believed in a national church which would embrace Christians of all doctrinal persuasions.

After *Last Essays on Church and Religion* (1877) Arnold returned to social and political commentary and literary criticism in *Mixed Essays* (1879), *Irish Essays* (1882) and *Discourses in America* (1885). His concern in these last years was with 'the humanization of man in society', and while he saw dangers in American democracy (he visited America to lecture in 1883 and 1886), he remained convinced of the need for greater equality in England. Arnold's later literary criticism, contained in *Essays in Criticism* (Second Series, 1888), attaches great importance to poetry in a scientific world. In 'The Study of Poetry' Arnold wrote, 'More and more mankind will discover that we have to turn to poetry to interpret life for us, to console us, to sustain us.' In the same essay he promulgated his system of judging poetry by 'touchstones' from the classics. Other essays give final assessments of the Romantic poets, of whom Wordsworth and Byron were 'first and pre-eminent, a glorious pair'.

In 1883 Arnold accepted a Civil List pension of £250 and in 1886 he retired from the inspectorate. He died suddenly of heart failure at Liverpool in 1888.

Throughout his adult life Arnold read widely and his *Note-books* (ed. H.F. Lowry, K. Young and W.H. Dunn, 1952) are filled with quotations from classical, European and English writers. As a young man Arnold had delighted in the novels of George Sand, and while at Oxford read Carlyle and Emerson. Goethe and Sainte-Beuve helped form his regard for criticism while his political thought was influenced by Burke. Spinoza was an important influence on his religious writing, and he was well read in contemporary European theologians such as Renan and Strauss. Writing in 1872, he acknowledged Wordsworth and Cardinal Newman as formative influences, and another was undoubtedly his father from whom he took both a strong sense of personal morality and his interests in education, religion and society. The contemporary who affected him most was Clough, to whom he wrote in 1853, 'I am for ever linked with you by intellectual bonds – the strongest of all.'

As a critic, Arnold's importance lies in his championing of the critical spirit and his insistence, against English insularity, on the concept of a European culture. Though his critical methods have not survived the various revolutions in literary criticism of this century, his essays express that critical tact and sensitivity towards literature that he sought to inculcate, and even if his evaluations have not necessarily stood the test of time, his criticism will always remain worth reading. His other prose writings shed light on major issues of the nineteenth century and are saved from the polemical excesses of some Victorian 'sages' by Arnold's urbanity and wit. Several of his phrases have passed into the language, and *Culture and Anarchy* is indisputably a prose classic.

As a poet, Arnold ranks below **Tennyson** and **Browning**. His output was uneven and he was handicapped by his own wilfully imposed poetics and the pressure of his work. He was right, however, when he wrote in 1869, 'my poems represent ... the main movement of mind of the last quarter of a century', and as well as this representative quality the canon includes a number of individual poems of the highest standard.

Further reading

Other works include: *The Poems of Matthew Arnold* (2nd edn), ed. Miriam Allott (1979); *The Complete Prose Works of Matthew Arnold*, ed. R.H. Super (1960–77); *Reports on Elementary Schools 1852–1882*, ed. F.S. Marvin (1908); *Letters of Matthew Arnold, 1848–1888*, ed. G.W.E. Russell (1895); *The Letters of Matthew Arnold to Arthur Hugh Clough*, ed. H.F. Lowry (1932); *Unpublished Letters of Matthew Arnold*, ed. Arnold Whitridge (1923). See: Lionel Trilling, *Matthew Arnold* (1939); Park Honan, *Matthew Arnold: A Life* (1981); on the poetry: C.B. Tinker and H.F. Lowry, *The Poetry of Matthew Arnold: A Commentary* (1940); A.D. Culler, *Imaginative Reason: The Poetry of Matthew Arnold* (1966); W.A. Madden, *Matthew Arnold: A Study of the Aesthetic Temperament in Victorian England* (1967); see also: E.D.H. Johnson, *The Alien Vision of Victorian Poetry* (1952); on the prose: S. Coulling, *Matthew Arnold and His Critics* (1974); D.J. DeLaura, *Hebrew and Hellene in Victorian England*

(1969); John Holloway, *The Victorian Sage* (1953); P. Honan, *Matthew Arnold* (1983).

SIMON RAE

ASHBERY, John Lawrence

1927–

US poet

One way or another, every great poet writing in the twentieth century grappled with chaos. Poets writing in the grain of high modernism responded to the experience of chaos sorrowfully: their poetry voices a lament for lost order. The postmodern poets who followed on their heels often found relief and artistic material in whatever semblance of order is offered by autobiographical experience.

John Ashbery – New York-born and Harvard-educated – instead attempts to capture the experience of disorder – what he sees as the experience of experience – itself. 'My poetry is disjunct, but then so is life,' he once remarked. Like Gertrude Stein, whom he openly admires, Ashbery develops a poetics of dissociation: in his work, experience always eludes intellection and, so, meaning always outreaches his poetry's grasp. His poems are like kaleidoscopic compositions built from the shards of meaning; they fail to form a familiar image, but are beautiful and radiant in their own right.

Indeed, in addition to Stein, **Stevens**, **Auden** and **Whitman**, and fellow New York School poets Frank O'Hara, Kenneth Koch and James Schuyler, Ashbery was deeply influenced by the abstract expressionist painters. In his early career he was an art critic, writing for the Paris edition of the *New York Herald* during the 1950s. 'I attempt to use words abstractly, as an artist uses paint,' he has said. This means that no overarching narrative form emerges to bind various images: pronouns may have no clearly discernible antecedents, lines may not appear to follow one another logically, and poems may consist of mere fragments. 'When the squall hit', for example, is a poem in its entirety, as it lies beneath the (much lengthier) title 'We Were on the Terrace Drinking Gin and Tonics' (from *As We Know*, 1979). Rather than develop an underlying connection that binds poem to title, Ashbery instead draws our attention to their adjoining surfaces. Here and elsewhere in Ashbery's work, the poetic elements adhere on a spatial plane instead of through a narrative arc that unfolds over time. In this way, the verbal art of poetry approaches the visual art of painting. This is poetry as daring as **Pollock's** splattered canvases, but as Ashbery has argued, 'most reckless things are beautiful in some way, and recklessness is what makes experimental art beautiful'. Even so, if Ashbery's reckless poetry is experimental, it is also deeply anchored to reality, as the experience of experience is marked by fragmentation, redirection and false starts. Clichés, perseverated phrases and disjoined memories all float in the stream of consciousness.

While his first published volume, *Some Trees*, would win the Yale Series of Younger Poets Prize, coming out in 1956 with a preface by Auden, Ashbery's poetry did not receive widespread attention until 1975 with the publication of *Self-Portrait in a Convex Mirror*. Ashbery would later say that he 'never cared' for *Self-Portrait*, but the critics clearly did: it won the Pulitzer Prize, the National Book Award and the National Book Critics Circle Award. The title poem, an extended reflection on Francesco Parmigianino's painting of the same name, explores the inevitable imprisonment and distortion inherent in artistic representation. 'Everything is surface,' the poet declares: 'The soul is a captive' in its portrait. Neither Parmigianino's painting nor Ashbery's poem offers a transcendence; instead, these instruments of discovery merely turn us back on ourselves. Like its subject's hand, the meaning of the painting 'swerv[es] easily away, as though to protect/What it advertises.' And, as for Ashbery's poem, 'the words are only speculation/(From the Latin *speculum*, mirror).'

Another major work is *Flow Chart* (1991), a book-length work that is at once a serious meditation on the difficulties (or impossibilities) of charting experience and an extended, oftentimes playful engagement with his critics. 'I see you are uncertain where to locate me:/here I am,' the poet wryly states before, of course, moving on. His words remind his readers that he and his poems will always, necessarily, elude their grasp. But Ashbery is not being coy, he is being true to the dissociated nature of consciousness that prevents us from locating – and thereby fixing – 'some point of concentrating around which a person can collect itself'. Ashbery's ambitions in *Flow Chart* actually resemble those of his critics. He wishes to see his imagination – his mind – at work, but in order to capture consciousness, one has to arrest and step outside it. Instead, Ashbery offers us what he can – partial angles, refracted light. His words, though 'distant now, and mitred, glint'.

Further reading

Other works include: *The Tennis Court Oath* (1962); *Rivers and Mountains* (1966); *Houseboat Days* (1977); and *Shadow Train* (1982). *A Nest of Ninnies* (1969) is a novel written in collaboration with James Shuyler. See: D. Shapiro, *John Ashbery: An Introduction to the Poetry* (1979); Harold Bloom (ed.) *John Ashbery* (1985); and John Shoptaw, *On the Outside Looking In* (1994).

JODI CRESSMAN

ASHBY, William Ross

1903–72

English neurologist, psychiatrist and cybernetician

W. Ross Ashby was born in London and educated at the Edinburgh Academy, Sidney Sussex College, Cambridge, where he took a degree in natural sciences, and at St Bartholomew's Hospital, London, qualifying as a psychiatrist. Following this he worked as a research pathologist at St Andrew's Hospital, Northampton, concentrating on neurology, until the beginning of the Second World War, when he became an officer in the Royal Medical Corps. When hostilities

ended he became director of research at Barnwood House, a psychological institute in Gloucestershire. The publication of *Cybernetics* by Norbert Wiener in 1948 provided Ashby with a discipline which could unite his interests in neurology and psychiatry, and the field in which his most important work was subsequently accomplished.

Cybernetics, in Wiener's words, purports to study 'communication and control in man and machine', and as such grew out of a series of discussions between Wiener and the physiologist Arturo Rosenbleuth at MIT concerning the workings of feedback and servomechanisms. While it is not clear to what extent Ashby worked independently of Wiener, his *Design for a Brain* (1952) immediately established him as a leading exponent of the new science. In it Ashby reaffirmed the simulative and descriptive nature of scientific knowledge in a manner that has been of general use in, for instance, computer modelling studies. His purpose, he insisted, was not to imitate the detailed action of the (human) brain, but rather to build descriptions which, while as a theoretical computer producing the same behavioural patterns as (a part of) the brain, would not necessarily function in the same manner.

This simulative approach was made even more explicit in Ashby's following book, *An Introduction to Cybernetics* (1956). Here he states that the reality of our knowledge of reality is made up of a collection of 'black boxes', which provide simulations of the performance of an entity, and through which we make descriptions that allow us to predict behaviours. Such description-building corresponds to what Wiener referred to as 'making a black-box white', and which he, in turn, had derived from the Scottish physicist J.C. Maxwell. The particular value of *An Introduction,* however, is the bringing together of three separate phenomena within a common theoretical structure. First the cybernetic concept of 'state' is refined and elaborated as a precise and powerful tool. Then state and state change are used as a basis for the modelling of behaviours. Not surprisingly, in view of his background in neurology, the demonstrations Ashby provides are applied to organisms as they function *in vivo* (and not *in vitrio,* as a dead brain does not of course 'behave'). One of the most significant characteristics of living systems is their stability in different circumstances and environments, known as homeostasis, of which, using his concept of state, Ashby produced a working description and then an electro-mechanical device with a similar performance. This allowed the concept to be understood much better than it had been previously. The third phenomenon was the invention of the measure 'variety'. Variety is a measure of the states – and their interconnectedness – that a system may have. A generalization of Claude Shannon's measure 'information', it also relates to the concept of entropy as used in Information Theory, which was developed contemporaneously with cybernetics. The particular power of variety is embodied in the Law of Requisite Variety, which requires that a control system has as much variety as the system it is to control if it is to be effective.

Although the generality and profundity of the Law of Requisite Variety is still being discovered, it may be said to represent Ashby's special contribution to cybernetics. After the publication of his two books, first as Director of the Burden Neurological Institute, then as Professor of Electrical Engineering at the University of Illinois, Ashby continued his theoretical work, applying his conclusions and techniques in a way that has increased our understanding of theoretical computers.

Further reading

A list of publications and a representative selection of Ashby's papers may be found in Heinz von Foerster, *Cybernetics of Cybernetics* (1974). See: John Bryant, *Systems Theory and Scientific Philosophy: An Application of the Cybernetics of W. Ross Ashby to Personal and Social Philosophy, the Philosophy of Mind, and the Problems of Artificial Intelligence* (1991).

RANULPH GLANVILLE

ASIMOV, Isaac

1920–92

US writer

Isaac Asimov wrote, taught, preached and played with science and ideas his entire life, producing around 500 books in his lifetime. He wrote science fiction, mysteries, general science works, science columns, and hosted the TV show *Nova*. By 1979, he could claim in his autobiography to have published thus far more than fifteen million words.

Asimov's most important work began as a science fiction writer barely in his twenties when he wrote the pulp stories that would become the basis for his most influential work which he continued revising and refining in the last decade of his life.

Born in Russia, he came to America in 1923, becoming a citizen at the age of eight. His Brooklyn upbringing was hardly typical since his accelerated education enabled him to graduate from Columbia University at the age of nineteen. His father's corner store, however, was filled with the gaudy lure of pulp magazines. The year he graduated he published his first story in *Amazing Stories,* 'Marooned Off Vesta'. Graduate degrees came swiftly when you consider he was publishing so many stories; he earned an MA in 1941 and a PhD in biochemistry in 1948. After taking his doctorate, Asimov joined the faculty of the Boston University School of Medicine, eventually becoming a full professor at that institution.

Asimov's major contribution to science fiction was first felt in the 1940s in *Astounding Science Fiction* under the guidance of the legendary editor John W. Campbell Jr where he published most of his early stories about robots (formulating his still monumental 'Three Laws of Robotics') and the stories that would eventually provide the basis for his *Foundation* trilogy. Before Asimov, robots were mostly mechanical monsters, higher-tech versions of Frankenstein, with the same theme of Man challenging God by creating 'life'. Asimov explained that while 'Knowledge has its dangers, yes, but is the response to be a retreat from Knowledge? I began in 1940, to write robot stories of my own … my robots were machines designed by engineers, not pseudo-men created by blasphemers.' The special 'positronic' brains of these robots allowed them to think logically guided rigidly by the Three Laws.

Asimov's robots were thinkers and doers and – because of the Three Laws – they often faced ethical dilemmas.

The Three Laws are: (1) a robot may not injure a human being or, through inaction, allow a human being to come to harm; (2) a robot must obey the orders given it by human beings except where such orders would conflict with the First Law; (3) a robot must protect its own existence, as long as such protection does not conflict with the First or Second Laws.

Whether these robots were really human became the question faced often by Asimov's human protagonists. The stories collected under the title *I Robot* (1950) were the first stories, but the most important, *Caves of Steel* (1954), introduced the robot detective R. Daneel Olivaw who would grow to dominate the 'robot series'.

Asimov's *Foundation* trilogy was originally published in the 1940s in *Astounding Science Fiction* and then in novel form in the early 1950s: *Foundation* (1951), *Foundation and Empire* (1952) and *Second Foundation* (1953). Asimov's concept of 'Psychohistory' in the trilogy seems firmly based on **Karl Marx's** beliefs in the patterns of history and **Freud's** insights into basic psychological motivations. Thus 'psychohistorians' with the use of certain mysterious mathematical formulae could predict future patterns for the Galactic Empire: its fall, the aftermath and the establishment of new empires. Knowing these patterns meant that such historians could interfere at the correct moment to assure the continuation of the 'right' patterns. Such a concept was plotted over thousands of years and hundreds of solar systems; yet Asimov's stories usually found the right combination of concrete human conflict in specific situations to match his grander pattern. While the 'foundation' guided the empire, a mysterious 'second foundation' was rumoured to aid humankind when all else failed. Scientific gods always have a backup.

Most critics credit Asimov with establishing not only patterns by which robots must behave but civilizations as well. Indeed, some historians of the science fiction field insist that Asimov provides a symbolic 'Before Asimov/After Asimov' dividing line. Modern science fiction begins with the stories collected in *I, Robot* and the *Foundation* trilogy. The dramatic movement of Asimov's robots towards individualism while human history could be predicted mathematically because humans fall so often into inevitable patterns became Asimov's great paradoxical theme, which he slowly realizes and works to consolidate in his entire fiction.

In the last decade of his life Asimov deliberately set out to link his robot and foundation and empire series together with a group of novels: *The Robots of Dawn* (1983), *Robots of Empire* (1985) and *Prelude to Foundation* (1988). Here we discover that detective R. Daneel Olivaw has been helping behind the scenes for thousands of years nudging humankind in the right direction at key moments, a one-man Second Foundation. The books provide a special pleasure to those familiar with the series as things fall into place with what you might call positronic precision.

Asimov became a publishing industry unto himself, letting his curiosity take him into many areas where fans accumulated from the science writings and fiction followed him in his studies of the Bible, Shakespeare, humour and history among other topics. His influence thus extends far beyond that of even the finest current science fiction writers (inheritors of the tradition he helped establish) due to his endless speculations and his facility with words and concepts. Asimov, after all, always insisted that, 'If knowledge can create problems, it is not through ignorance that we can solve them.'

Further reading

See: *The Autobiography of Isaac Asimov 1920–1954* (1979); and *I Asimov* (1994).

CHARLES GREGORY

ATTENBOROUGH, (Sir) David Frederick

1926–

British broadcaster and naturalist

Known to millions around the world for his role as a presenter of natural history programmes, David Attenborough's influential career at the BBC had an unpromising start. Turned down for a job in radio, he was offered instead a traineeship in the fledgling medium of television – despite only knowing one person with a set at the time.

After his first foray on screen as an interviewer, the producer wrote, 'David Attenborough is intelligent and promising and may well be producer material, but he is not to be used again as an interviewer. His teeth are too big.'

He was indeed 'producer material', and used his natural sciences background and interest in anthropology to bring many early programmes such as *Animal, Vegetable, Mineral* to our screens in the 1950s. The most famous of his programmes, however, was *Zoo Quest* in 1954. This successful format featured a presenter wrestling to catch animals in the wild, and then bringing them back to a studio to talk about them. Attenborough was able to fulfil his longing for travel to far-flung places, and after the tragic death of the original presenter, London Zoo's Jack Lester, he found himself back on screen as an intrepid explorer and animal-catcher in *Zoo Quest for a Dragon* (1957).

The enthusiasm, intelligence and imagination that led to his success as a presenter also led to Attenborough rising up the ranks of BBC producers. At the same time as presenting *Zoo Quest*, he became the founder of the Travel and Exploration Unit within the BBC in London, as a complement to the new Natural History Unit in Bristol which had just been set up by Desmond Hawkins to bring British natural history to the television audience. As the Head of the Travel and Exploration Unit, Attenborough produced studio-based series such as *Travellers' Tales* and *Adventure* in between his own expeditions for *Zoo Quest*. By 1962, though, his enthusiasm for anthropology, and the invention of a method of recording sound alongside and synchronized with film, led to the series *Quest Under Capricorn* where Attenborough travelled to northern Australia and revealed the world of the Australian Aboriginal people.

This latest journey inspired Attenborough to take a break from the BBC and return to academia to study for a postgraduate degree in anthropology at the London School of Economics, and a brief period as a freelance television producer. Both these new enterprises were ended in March 1965, though, when Attenborough was appointed Controller of a brand new channel, BBC2. In this role he shaped the channel as the antithesis of BBC1 and ITV, providing provocative alternative programmes. Here he initiated 'landmark' BBC series as well as the first 'live events' such as a live broadcast of a BBC-financed excavation of Silbury Hill – formats that continue to be the backbone of the BBC's factual programming output today.

In 1967, television underwent a revolution with the introduction of colour, and it came first to Attenborough's channel, BBC2. It was a chance for him to reshow many of the Travel and Exploration and Natural History Units' programmes, originally shot on colour film, in their full glory. This he did under the strand title *The World About Us*, a format so successful that it remained a staple Sunday evening show for thirty years. The first programme he commissioned to be filmed especially to celebrate the dawn of the age of colour, however, was the first BBC 'landmark' series: *Civilisation*, a celebration of the achievements of two thousand years of European civilization narrated by Sir Kenneth Clark, which was closely followed by *The Ascent of Man* presented by Jacob Bronowski. These series were enormously popular with viewers and critics alike, and many followed on a range of subjects.

Attenborough was soon promoted to Director of Programmes, an appointment which he admits filled him with misgivings. During his role as Controller of BBC2 he had found time to take short breaks in order to quench his thirst for travel by producing and presenting occasional programmes for the Bristol-based Natural History Unit. His four years as Director of Programmes found him wrestling with the BBC's finances rather than the problems of filming animals in their natural habitat, and in December 1972 he resigned in order to return to his great passion by producing and presenting for the BBC Natural History Unit, as a freelancer.

Now free from the shackles of managerial responsibility, Attenborough was able to fulfil an ambition that he had harboured since the success of *Civilisation* – to present his own landmark series on natural history. So *Life on Earth* was born: a thirteen-part series starting with the beginnings of life and explaining the evolution of all living things today. Three years in the making, *Life on Earth* was revealed to the public in 1979 and had a dramatic impact. Attenborough's technique of starting a paragraph in one continent and finishing it in another as he moved from one example to another, and featuring animals of which most people had never heard, made for compelling viewing.

A sequel was called for, and Attenborough and the Natural History Unit were more than willing to supply one. *The Living Planet* (1984) took ecology, rather than evolution, as its theme, and Attenborough took his viewers on a journey around the world's habitats, introducing them to the plants and animals that had adapted to live in each. His reputation as an inspirational and imaginative presenter was established around the world as foreign broadcasters bought the BBC's series, and he has remained the most influential presenter in the genre as he continues to produce series on natural history and anthropology.

Further reading

Books by David Attenborough based on his television work include: *Zoo Quest to Guiana* (1956); *Zoo Quest for a Dragon* (1957); *Zoo Quest to Paraguay* (1959); *Zoo Quest to Madagascar* (1961); *Quest Under Capricorn* (1963); *The Tribal Eye* (1976); *The First Eden* (1987); *Life on Earth* (1979); *The Living Planet* (1984); *The Trials of Life* (1990); *The Private Life of Plants* (1995); *The Life of Birds* (1998); *The Life of Mammals* (2002); *Life in the Undergrowth* (2005).

ALEXANDRA FREEMAN

AUDEN, Wystan Hugh

1907–73

English/US poet, dramatist, librettist and essayist

W.H. Auden was born in York, the youngest son of a doctor (all his life, Auden was to take an interest in sickness and healing, though defining neither in orthodox medical terms). His childhood, spent in Solihull, then a village just outside Birmingham, was a happy one, apart from the crucial absence of his father during the war years 1914–19. The atmosphere of the Auden home combined affectionate family life with high Anglican Christianity, lively interest in the arts, especially music, and a penchant for intellectual pursuits. Auden's interests as a child included Icelandic sagas and the construction of an imaginary world whose main features were a northern limestone landscape and a lead-mining industry.

Auden was educated at St Edmund's Preparatory School, where he first met his future collaborator and life-long friend, Christopher Isherwood, and at Gresham's School, Holt, where **Benjamin Britten** was a much younger pupil. Auden's interests as a schoolboy were mainly scientific (he intended to become a mining engineer), though he also profited greatly from the music teaching. By his own account, he did not then think of himself as a writer, and only when a friend asked him if he wrote poetry did he suddenly realize his vocation. By the time Auden went up to Oxford, he was already a technically highly accomplished poet in the Georgian mode, **Hardy** being his first poetic master. In 1925, he entered Christ Church College, Oxford, as a scholar in Natural Sciences. He soon, however, changed his course, first to Philosophy, Politics and Economics and then to English Language and Literature, in which he was tutored by Nevill Coghill, later the translator of Chaucer, and attended **J.R.R. Tolkien's** lectures on *Beowulf* and other Old English poetry. Auden was particularly fascinated by Old English poetry, echoes, phrases and rhythms from which haunt both his early and later work.

Auden, as an undergraduate who had read **Freud** and **Jung** during his schooldays, was far more intellectually sophisticated than most of his Oxford contemporaries. He became something of a legendary figure, dispensing psychological and aesthetic wisdom (he had by now been converted to 'modernist' writing) in his artificially darkened college rooms. He was a central figure in a group of talented young men, including Stephen Spender. During this time Auden was also reintroduced to Isherwood and their friendship reopened. Via Isherwood, he met the writer Edward Upward and was initiated into 'Mortmere', the surreal imaginary world whose grotesqueness parodies English conventionality, which Upward and Isherwood had invented during their Cambridge undergraduate days. Although the direct influence of 'Mortmere' on Auden's work seems comparatively slight except in *The Orators* (1932), it certainly contributed to the making of the imaginary worlds that both stand apart from and explain or criticize 'reality', which are such a marked feature of Auden's work both during the 1930s and after.

In 1928 Auden spent a year in Berlin, where he enjoyed the homosexual night life, was fascinated by the cultural and political milieu of Weimar Germany, and began writing some of his finest poems. In Berlin he also met and was much influenced by John Layard, a disciple of the recently dead Homer Lane, a psychologist who taught that all disease was psychosomatic, the result of psychic conflicts or repressions. This doctrine provided the framework of many poems, although it is not quite certain how literally Auden took it. All his life he had a love of totalizing intellectual models in which to systematize human experience and make it intelligible and coherent. The systems might be psychoanalytic, philosophical or theological; Auden used all but retained a permanent allegiance to none. He would employ such models in poetry (or conversation) with a dogmatism which contained a discernible element of high camp.

In 1930 Auden made his public début with the appearance of the charade *Paid on Both Sides* in the *Criterion* and then of *Poems*, his first full-scale collection, which includes the justly famous 'Consider this and in our time', '1929', and 'Sir, no man's enemy'. The date of this collection's publication is appropriate, for Auden was to be regarded as the 'poet of the 1930s' *par excellence*. This is not just because Auden was generally acknowledged then and now as the central figure of the 'thirties group' of young writers (usually identified as Auden, MacNeice, Day Lewis, Spender and Upward) who were left-wing in their politics and 'modified modernist' in their technique, but because Auden's poems set the tone of the public poetry that was to dominate the decade. The intellectual structure of these poems owes much to **Marx** and Freud (the latter definitely predominating in *Poems*, 1930); their tone is characteristically one of didactic diagnosis, and their technique combines the sophisticated exploitation of, usually, traditional verse-forms with casually witty language and with vivid images or vignettes which are frequently small allegories in themselves. Also immensely influential (and often copied) were the landscapes of Auden's early poetry: desolate frontier regions marked by a derelict industrialism, whose compelling power not only had an obvious contemporary relevance to the economic Depression, but also in a more subterranean way evoked folk memories of the devastated no-man's land of the trenches in the First World War.

Poems was succeeded by *The Orators*, a parodic mélange of discourses both public (the joke Litany, the Odes) and private (the 'Journal of an Airman'). All the speakers in the book insist that England is 'a country where nobody is well'; the difficulty for the reader is that all the speakers appear to be at least as sick as their subjects.

Auden supported himself during the early and mid-1930s by various schoolmastering jobs. In 1935 he spent six months working with Grierson's GPO film unit, for which he wrote the words for the documentaries *Coal Face*, *Night Mail* and *The Road to the Sea*. In this work he met Britten, who was in charge of composing the music and sound effects. The two became friends, and Britten set many of Auden's lyric poems to music, as well as composing the music for the Group Theatre productions of the Auden and Isherwood plays. Many of the poems Britten set to music (including the song cycle *On This Island*, 1938) were published in *Look, Stranger!* (1936), which contains, as well as many beautiful lyric poems, the famous public poems 'A Bride in the Thirties', 'A Summer Night', 'The Malverns' and 'To a Writer on his Birthday'.

In the summer of 1936 Auden went to Iceland with Louis MacNeice for a long holiday, which produced the collaborative *Letters from Iceland* (1937), a delightfully unsystematic travel book which contains the splendid autobiographical 'Letter to Lord Byron'. While Auden was in Iceland, the Spanish Civil War broke out. Auden went to Spain, intending first to fight on the Republican side and then to work as an ambulance-driver. In the event, he took no active part in the war but wrote his finest political poem 'Spain 1937' (collected in *Another Time*, 1940). In this poem, the political/military conflict is presented as a point of momentous choice between a past stretching back to prehistory and forward to a possible future of human justice. The choice, it is insisted, is urgent: 'the time is short, and/

History to the defeated/May say alas but cannot help or pardon.' (This conclusion the poet was later to repudiate as immoral because 'it equates goodness with success'.)

Auden returned from Spain in 1937. The following year he and Isherwood set off for China to write a book about the Sino-Japanese war. *Journey to a War* (1939) offers the reader an odd contrast between a mainly comic travel diary ascribed to Isherwood and Auden's very serious and ambitious sonnet sequence 'In Time of War'.

The 1930s was also the period of Auden's plays. His first publicly performed play, *The Dance of Death* (1933), an allegory of the decline of the bourgeoisie, has some fine songs but was too frivolous and unstructured to be successful. This was succeeded by *The Dog beneath the Skin* (with Isherwood, 1935), in which a Candide-like public school hero wanders around two imaginary European countries, reactionary royalist (Ostnia) and fascist (Westland), in search of the missing heir of Pressan Ambo, a parodic imaginary English village like 'Mortmere'. The play, owing much to **Brecht**, is episodic and non-naturalistic in form, cut up by superb poetic choruses and songs. *The Ascent of F6* (1936), Auden and Isherwood's most ambitious play, followed; it is the tragedy of Michael Ransom, a hero recalling T.E. Lawrence, who dies attempting to climb the inaccessible mountain F6. Ransom's action is determined partly by the manipulation of reactionary capitalist politicians, and partly by his own neurotic Oedipal compulsions, for he represents the Truly Weak Man, a mythical/parabolic figure invented by Isherwood, whose 'heroic' deeds are really attempts to escape his own inner weakness (as opposed to the Truly Strong Man, a less interesting character who has no private fears and consequently doesn't do heroic things because he doesn't need to prove himself). The last play that the two friends collaborated on was *On the Frontier* (1938), a much more directly political play than its predecessors, in which Ostnia and Westland slide towards a disastrous war that neither side really wants.

Another Time (1940), the last of what Auden's executor-bibliographer has styled the 'English Auden' collections, contains 'September 1939', 'Spain' and the elegies on **Yeats** and Freud as well as the famous lyric 'Lullaby'. But by the time it appeared, Auden together with Isherwood had left for America, an act for which both writers were heavily criticized and for which some of Auden's English readers never forgave him. He had been celebrated for years as the admired poet of the Left (a position which in fact had increasingly irked him), and his departure from England just before the war against the fascism he had been condemning for years seemed to his admirers a betrayal of what he had been thought to stand for. It is certainly clear that 1939–40 was a turning point in Auden's life and works. Several important events in his life occurred then; he met Chester Kallman, his lover and life-long companion; he returned to the church, becoming an existentialist Kierkegaardian Anglican; and his mother died in 1941. A marked change came over Auden's poetry at this point, both in style and content. Auden had always been much concerned as a poet with what art was *for*. In the 1930s, he tended to state or imply that art has a social or humane value, as in his much-quoted formulation of the two kinds of art: 'escape-art, for man needs escape as he needs food or deep sleep, and parable-art, that art which shall teach man to unlearn hatred and learn love' (*Psychology and Art*, 1932). This stance ('We must love one another or die') changed, partly under the pressure of political events, since poetry had demonstrably failed to stop **Hitler**, and partly through personal Christian conviction. Already in his elegy on *Yeats* (1939) Auden had asserted that 'Poetry makes nothing happen'; to this was added the conviction that poetry is a purely aesthetic, not an ethical or religious practice. His own art, in its exploitation of pastiche and parody, had always partially depended on raising a game of nuances between poem and reader; this game now became the basis of his aesthetic. From this time on, Auden insisted that poetry

was 'only' a game (which did not prevent him from writing religious didactic poems). He was thus in the paradoxical role of being a magician who did not approve of magic.

The first fruit of Auden's conversion to Christianity and America was a series of long poems. *New Year Letter* (1941, entitled *The Double Man* in America) is a discursive philosophical poem in octosyllabic couplets accompanied by a long commentary and a sonnet sequence, 'The Quest'. It attempts, first through 'conversational' argumentative verse, and then through the metaphor of the 'Quest', to question what the human condition in 1940 is, and to give a Christian answer. It was followed by *For the Time Being* (1944), a 'Christmas oratorio' which dramatizes states of mind and dilemmas both Christian and humanist. It was published together with *The Sea and the Mirror*, a verse commentary on *The Tempest* which is the most brilliant of Auden's longer poems. The Shakespearean reference point gives the poem a strong and flexible structure both dramatically and intellectually, while the overcoming of technical difficulties (it is an expertly fertile *tour de force* of verse forms) is accompanied by extraordinary verbal richness and vitality, not least in Caliban's baroquely **Jamesian** 'Speech to the Audience'. The last of these long poems is *The Age of Anxiety* (1947), a 'baroque eclogue' of four persons written in alliterative accentual metre (the metre of *Beowulf*), which although it is not easy to read contains some of the richest of the 'middle Auden' poetry.

By the end of the war, Auden had made New York his permanent home, although until the end of his life he usually summered in Europe: from 1948 to 1957 on the island of Ischia in the Bay of Naples, and thenceforward in Austria, after winning the Feltrinelli Prize for Literature in 1957 enabled him to buy a farmhouse in the village of Kirchstetten, 40 km from Vienna. Partly under the influence of Kallman, Auden became an opera-lover. His interest in combining words and music was longstanding; his creative collaborations with

Britten in the late 1930s and early 1940s had produced two song cycles, the much-loved 'Hymn to St Cecilia' (1940) and the Auden/Britten opera *Paul Bunyan* (composed and performed in 1941, first published 1976), though the Auden/Britten collaboration ended in 1942 when Britten broke off communications after a tactless letter from Auden. Now Auden had come to value opera as 'the last refuge of High Style among the arts that use words', his collaboration with Chester Kallman on their libretti occupied a key focus for his creative energies. He and Kallman first collaborated on the libretto for **Stravinsky's** score of *The Rake's Progress* (1951), and many other librettos followed, including a translation of *The Magic Flute* (1955) and *The Bassarids* (1963). He was also a reviewer and lecturer of distinction. From 1955 to 1958 he was Professor of Poetry at the University of Oxford. His lectures were collected in the acclaimed book of criticism *The Dyer's Hand* (1962), and he gave a generous amount of time and help to students interested in poetry. His poetic output also remained prolific and impressive. *Nones* (1950) was his first post-war collection, whose lyric poems are especially fine; it also contains the beautiful 'In Praise of Limestone'. It is followed by *The Shield of Achilles* (1955), Auden's most impressive post-war collection. The title poem is one of his finest; the book also contains the brilliant allegorical landscape poems 'Bucolics' and 'Horae Canonicae'. *Homage to Clio* (1960) has some fine pieces, particularly the title poem, and is the first collection in which Auden included a large proportion of his light verse 'shorts'. *About the House* (1965) is mainly a sequence of discursive syllabic poems, each of which starts off from some aspect of his Kirchstetten farmhouse. *City Without Walls* (1969) is darker in tone and more nostalgic. It contains more translations and occasional verse than previous collections, including the short but very telling political epigram 'August 1968', alluding to the USSR invasion of Czechoslovakia. *Epistle to a Godson* (1972) has poems of great skill, wit, learning and

technical accomplishment; but Auden's final collection, *Thankyou, Fog* (published posthumously in 1974), seems the work of a poet still in command of his powers but increasingly weary of the world. The apparent cosiness and actual cold detachment of its last poem 'Lullaby' (a title shared by his famous 1930s love-lyric) make it one of the most haunting poems Auden ever wrote.

All of Auden's later poems have a discernibly similar tone. Technically, they are often virtuoso performances; they are humane and conversational in style, and they carry with ease and grace a load of quirky learning and outlandish words which send the reader to the dictionary more often than to Freud or Kierkegaard. While most English readers found it less exciting than the shifting rhythms and obscure challenge of Auden's early poems, this later writing certainly adds up to much more of a whole man's life, embracing work, love, play, learning, religion and pleasure. 'Late Audenesque' is a style in reading and appreciating as much as writing; it ranges from theology to cookery books, from biology to opera. Auden certainly regarded his work from 1940 on as his most important. He repudiated most of his best-known political poems of the 1930s, omitting many of them from *Collected Shorter Poems 1927–1957* (1966), and others were radically revised. With or without the political poems, Auden's poetic achievement remains the richest, most wide-ranging, ambitious, impressive and influential of any English poet of the twentieth century.

Further reading

Professor Edward Mendelson, Auden's literary executor, is editing a multi-volume scholarly edition of *The Complete Works of W.H. Auden*, published by Princeton University Press. The following have appeared to date: *Libretti (with Chester Kallman)* (1993); *Plays (with Christopher Isherwood)* (1995); *Prose Vol. 1 Prose and Travel Books* (1997), *Prose Vol. 2 1939–1948* (2002). See: W.H. Auden *Collected Poems* (1976), ed. Edward Mendelson; *The English Auden: Poems, Essays and Dramatic Writings 1927–1939* (1977); *Forewords and Afterwords* (1970). See also: B.C. Bloomfield and

Edward Mendelson (eds) *W.H. Auden: A Bibliography* (1970) and for studies of Auden: Richard Hoggart, *Auden: An Introductory Essay* (1951); John Bayley, *The Romantic Survival* (1957); Monroe Spears, *The Poetry of W.H. Auden* (1963); John Fuller, *A Reader's Guide to W.H. Auden* (1970, revised edition 2000); Samuel Hynes, *The Auden Generation* (1976); Edward Mendelson, *Early Auden* (1981), *Later Auden* (1999); Katharine Bucknell and Nicholas Jenkins (eds) *'The Map of All My Youth'* (1990); Lucy MacDiarmuid, *Auden's Apologies* (1990); Anthony Hecht, *The Hidden Law* (1993); Stan Smith, *W.H. Auden* (1997). For biographical studies, see Charles Osborne, *W.H. Auden: The Life of a Poet* (1980); Humphrey Carpenter, *W.H. Auden: A Biography* (1981); Thekla Clark, *Wystan and Chester* (1997).

JANET MONTEFIORE

AUSTIN, John Langshaw

1911–60

British philosopher

The father of this 'implacable professor' was an architect who, after service in the First World War, became secretary of St Leonard's School in the ancient Fifeshire university town of St Andrew's. The son went to Shrewsbury School (where **Charles Darwin** had been a pupil), proceeding from there on an open scholarship to Balliol College, Oxford. Except for a wartime interlude of outstandingly valuable service in the Intelligence Corps, and two short visiting appointments at Harvard and the University of California, Austin's entire working life was spent at Oxford, where he became successively Fellow of All Souls, Fellow of Magdalen, and White's Professor of Moral Philosophy.

Austin's influence on and through his colleagues and pupils was far greater than the small extent of his publications would suggest. His main mission – pursued with a formidable combination of intensity, intellectual force and wit – was to apply the methods and standards of a scholar of the Greco-Roman classical texts to various, usually non-technical areas of contemporary English discourse. For how else are concepts to be elucidated if not by meticulous attention to the usage of the words through which these concepts are expressed?

The nature of this mission, and the philosophical profit to be won from it, is perhaps best seen in the articles 'Other Minds' (1946) and 'A Plea for Excuses' (1956), reprinted in the posthumous *Philosophical Papers* (1961). The former contains Austin's first account of performatory utterances: speech-acts which are in themselves the performance of an action. Thus to say 'I promise' in the appropriate conditions is in itself the making of a promise, not a mere statement about a promise. The latter article brings out the great richness and some of the detailed characteristics of our everyday vocabulary of extenuation and excuse. It also contains, on one and the same page, Austin's most incisive repudiations of two views often but falsely attributed to him by those hostile to his philosophical methods: first, that any such map-work is the be-all and end-all of philosophy (as opposed to the begin-all); and second, that our untechnical vocabulary never needs to be revised or supplemented. His true thesis was that the resources of any vernacular, as the naturally selected product of generations of practical experience, are likely to be greater than those of some hastily and uncritically contrived professional jargon: here as everywhere, the reform which is to be improvement must wait on an understanding of the status quo.

In his again posthumously published lectures on *Sense and Sensibilia* (1962) Austin dissected, and some would say demolished, the entire tradition, dating back through Descartes to the Greek Sceptics, which denied that we can be immediately aware of anything but our own most private sense data.

In his last years – represented by the 1955 William James Lectures, published as *How to do Things with Words* (1962) – Austin sophisticated upon the notion of performative utterances. He distinguished, for instance, the illocutionary force of a speech-act (what is done *in* saying something) from its locutionary force (what it is the act *of* saying), and its perlocutionary force (what is effected in others by the saying). Because Austin always somehow 'failed to leave enough time in which to say why what I have said is interesting' his later work has often been thought to be philosophically irrelevant linguistics.

Further reading

See: K.T. Fann (ed.) *Symposium on J.L. Austin* (1969); Isaiah Berlin (ed.) *Essays on J.L. Austin* (1973); G.J. Warnock, *J.L. Austin* (1991).

ANTONY FLEW

AYER, (Sir) Alfred Jules

1910–89

British philosopher

A.J. Ayer's career was a paradigm of academic success. A King's scholar at Eton, he went on to become a classical scholar and later lecturer in philosophy at Christ Church, Oxford. From 1946 to 1959 he was Professor of Philosophy at University College, London, and from 1959 to 1979 he held the Wykam Professorship of Logic at Oxford. He was knighted in 1970.

From the philosophical point of view the most important event of Ayer's life was his visit to Vienna as a young graduate in 1933. Armed with a letter of introduction from Gilbert Ryle, Ayer was able to attend the discussions of the celebrated Vienna Circle (Wiener Kreis) of philosophers, containing brilliant figures such as Moritz Schlick and Rudolf Carnap. Ayer was deeply impressed by the philosophical approach of the circle, which came to be known as Logical Positivism. Soon after his return to England he published his first and easily best-known book, *Language, Truth and Logic* (1936). This rapidly became, for the English-speaking world, the manifesto of the Logical Positivist movement, and it remains in many ways the definitive exposition of positivist philosophy.

The central demand of Ayer's treatise was for the 'elimination of metaphysics' (the title of Chapter 1):

No statement which refers to a reality transcending the limits of all possible sense experience can possibly have any literal significance; from which it must follow that the labours of those who have striven to describe such a reality have all been devoted to the production of nonsense.

The tool for the removal of metaphysics was the famous Principle of Verification: 'A sentence is factually significant to a given person if, and only if, he knows how to verify the proposition it purports to express.' The results of applying this criterion were devastating: apart from the tautologies of logic and mathematics, no statement was to be accepted as meaningful which could not be checked by empirical observation. Thus the whole of substantive ethics, and the entire body of religious claims are discarded as a collection of meaningless pseudo-propositions. The only statements to survive the holocaust turn out to be those of science: 'Philosophy is virtually empty without science'; there is no future for philosophy except as the Logic of Science.

The details of Ayer's argument are of an extraordinary rigour and clarity, and the catch-words of *Language, Truth and Logic* – 'empirical', 'criterion', 'factual significance', 'observation-statement' – were to dominate the philosophical scene for the next quarter-century. What led to the eventual decline of Positivism was that it slowly became clear that its own darling, natural science, could not pass the test of strict verifiability. The highly generalized statements of scientific theory just cannot be reduced to observation statements; and if the verification test is made less rigorous so as to accommodate scientific theory, then religion and metaphysics will be able to creep back in as well. This is a problem with which Ayer wrestles in the long Introduction to the second edition of *Language, Truth and Logic* (1946); but he was later forced to admit that it could not be solved.

It would be wrong to say that Ayer's reputation rests on *Language, Truth and Logic* alone. But his prolific subsequent writings have never achieved the pivotal importance of the first book. It is often asserted that its central ideas are now dead and buried, but this is seriously misleading. Although it is true that most philosophers (including Ayer himself) had, by the late 1960s, abandoned strict verificationism, much subsequent philosophy has developed as a response to Ayer's radical empiricist challenge. As for 'metaphysics', this is once again a respectable term; but the kind of metaphysics practised in academic departments is of a highly analytical kind, and is very largely conducted within the strictly logical and linguistic philosophical framework which Ayer helped create.

Further reading

Other work includes: *Philosophical Essays* (1954); *The Problem of Knowledge* (1956); *The Concept of a Person* (1964); *Metaphysics and Common Sense* (1967); *The Central Questions of Philosophy* (1973); *The Origins of Pragmatism* (1968); *Russell and Moore, the Analytic Heritage* (1971). He is also the editor of *Logical Positivism* (1959), a collection of expository and critical materials. See: A. Phillips Griffiths, *A.J. Ayer: Memorial Essays* (1992); Ben Rogers, *A.J. Ayer: A Life* (2000).

JOHN COTTINGHAM

B

BABBAGE, Charles

1792–1871

English mathematician

It is possible that at some future date a film will be made of the life of Charles Babbage, polymath, tabulator and premature inventor of the computer. If such a film is made, it will dwell, no doubt, on Babbage's early, confident years – years in which our rich and handsome hero introduced continental methods of mathematics to Cambridge, helped to found the Astronomical Society, received its gold medal, became a fellow of the Royal Society (at twenty-three), was elected Lucasian Professor of Mathematics, was received by the Chancellor of the Exchequer, and was awarded an annual grant of £1,500 for work on his remarkable invention, the 'Difference Engine'. Babbage involved himself in a hundred and one practical and taxing problems, from pin manufacture to crypt-analysis, from light-houses to statistical linguistics. He actually lived the kind of colourful, multi-sided life sometimes depicted for fictional academics on the silver screen.

The promise of Babbage's early years was not merely bright, it was astonishing. He set himself a series of large and ambitious tasks. He appeared, both to himself (no doubt) and to his contemporaries, to have the capacity to pull them off. Yet the early promise gradually turned to dust. The Difference Engine was never completed. Babbage shamelessly neglected his Lucasian chair. In his later years

he became a crotchety, tiresome, disappointed and greatly impoverished man. During the 1860s Babbage must often have ruefully reflected that had he attempted less, he must have achieved more.

Babbage was born on 26 December 1792 in Teignmouth, Devon. His family was not poor, and he was educated at private schools in Alphington and Enfield. He taught himself algebra and calculus, with the aid of books, prior to entering Trinity College, Cambridge, in 1811. But after a personal mathematical preparation of this kind, Cambridge was rather a disappointment. The notation and methods of calculus used were those of Newton, and the superior flexibility and explicitness of the continental, Leibnitzian notation was totally ignored. Babbage, typically, wasted no time in trying to put this right. In 1812 he helped to form – with fellow undergraduates Herschel and Peacock – the Analytical Society, a body whose aim was to introduce Leibnitzian notation into the university. Whereas Newton represented the derivative of a function $\dot{y}$, Leibnitz denoted it dy/dx, or sometimes Dy. Babbage described the object of the new society, facetiously, as that of promoting 'the principles of pure D-ism in opposition to the Dot-age of the university'! The incident shows many sides of Babbage's unique personality: his impatience, his underestimation of the inertia opposing change, his courage in going for a bold solution, his capacity to reduce an issue to a slogan with the object of marshalling support, his scorn for the established wisdom.

Babbage graduated from Peterhouse in 1814, wrote three articles on the calculus of functions, and was elected Fellow of the Royal Society in 1816. In 1820 he was one of the chief architects of the foundation of the Astronomical Society. And he began to turn his attention to the problem of producing accurate tables for astronomical, navigational and mathematical purposes. The tables in use at the time had been compiled laboriously item by item and contained innumerable errors. It is true that the computation had been done on simple calculating machines, but these machines had to be set up by hand, repetitively, and it was this intervention of the human operator which was responsible for the errors. Babbage realized that it would be possible to use the method of differences to devise a machine which, once set in motion, would compute item after item, basing each new result on the preceding one. This would effectively eliminate human error and should result in tables of superb accuracy and consistency.

Babbage's case was very powerful: such tables were evidently needed; there seemed no impediment in principle to the construction of a machine of the kind envisaged. British power was at its zenith; this, it was felt, was the kind of lead Britain *should* set – a project which would benefit her people, and also anyone who needed tables of proven accuracy, proven authority.

Babbage's methodology is hard to fault. He had a model of his Difference Engine constructed in 1820–2 and it worked admirably. He issued a volume of logarithms of natural numbers from 1 to 108,000. He drew up impressive plans of the full-size Difference Engine, and even invented a notation for recording the mode of operation of the moving parts. He travelled abroad to learn something of the clockwork and gear-wheel technology of the continent. He invented new tools for the manufacture of components. He was continually thinking of ways to streamline the design and improve its operation.

Not surprisingly, Babbage's ambitions imposed strain on those around him, and Clement, the engineer in charge of the work on the Difference Engine, rebelled openly in 1828: he even removed the special tools Babbage had designed, so that there was no way in which work could proceed. For fifteen months work on the Difference Engine was at a standstill.

It was during this period of hiatus that Babbage began to wonder whether there was not a still more dazzling goal to be achieved, only slightly beyond the Difference Engine. Instead of building a machine which would automate a *single* table-making task, why not make a machine which would work automatically on *any* arithmetic task? What was needed was a method to instruct the machine, and such a method already existed, in the cards used on the Jacquard loom. There would be two sets of cards: 'variable' cards, containing the numbers on which computation would proceed, and 'operation' cards embodying the sequence of operations required. The machine would print its own answers. Babbage called his new machine the 'Analytical Engine' and for eight years actively worked on it. Finally, in 1842, the government said no to the request for further funds.

Unfortunately the rising sun of the Analytical Engine had distracted Babbage's attention from the Difference Engine, still hopelessly incomplete. A portion of the Difference Engine was put together in 1833, was later shown at the International Exhibition of 1862, and finally moved to the Science Museum, South Kensington, where it may be seen today. The Swedish engineer Georg Scheutz, after reading an article in the *Edinburgh Review*, built himself a less ambitious version of the Difference Engine, which worked well and was in use in an observatory for many years.

But Babbage's heart was now in the Analytical Engine. His friend Lady Lovelace wrote programs for it. It was, in effect, a mechanical computer of ambitious power, though Babbage did not take the final step – that of arranging for the machine to modify its own program. Had Babbage done this, he would have realized that a more modest machine of this kind, being recursive, can do many things as effectively as a large machine, albeit more slowly. Altogether Babbage spent thirty-seven years on the Analytical Engine, and by his death it was still far from being a reality.

Babbage's life was a warning to any lesser mortal who might have been tempted to move towards automated calculation. If Babbage failed, with his incomparable gifts, there was only one conclusion to be drawn – the task was beyond nineteenth-century man. It may be noted that a century later, in the 1930s, it proved impossible to construct a really effective electromagnetic computer, in spite of all the advances of the preceding years and the considerable advantages of electrical operation with binary codes. The valve computers of the 1940s and 1950s were perpetually breaking down, and it was only the invention of the transistor, with its negligible current consumption, which created the near-miraculous standards of reliability needed to get a programmable computer to work in a satisfactory way.

Babbage's life was not entirely a failure. He was responsible for the logarithmic tables mentioned above; he made various minor inventions, including signalling 'by occulting solar lights' which was used by the Russians at the Battle of Sevastopol. Lord Rose commented that Babbage's engineering improvements 'more than repaid the sum expended' by the government. He wrote a number of books and numerous articles, none of which, however, became a classic. These are, of course, mere fragments of achievement resulting from a talent of impressive boldness, intelligence and verve, which broke, finally, on a task beyond its strength.

Further reading

Babbage's works include: *The Ninth Bridgewater Treatise* (1837); *The Exposition of 1851* (1851); *Passages from the Life of a Philosopher* (1864). See: *The Dictionary of National Biography*, Vol. 2 (1885); Anthony Hyman, *Charles Babbage: Pioneer of the Computer* (1982); Bruce Collier and James MacLachlan, *Charles Babbage and the Engines of Perfection* (1999); J.M. Dubbey, *The Mathematical Work of Charles Babbage* (2004).

CHRISTOPHER ORMELL

BACON, Francis

1909–92

Anglo-Irish artist

Francis Bacon was born in Dublin, the son of a successful English horse-trainer, and spent an unsettled childhood in Ireland and England. At the age of twenty he achieved some celebrity as a designer of fabrics and steel-framed furniture. At about this time he began to paint in oils, exhibiting occasionally, but very few of his works of the years 1930–44 survive – partly the result of Bacon's life-long habit of destroying much of his own work. His artistic endeavour began in earnest just before the end of the war, when *Three Studies for Figures at the Base of a Crucifixion* was shown in April 1945 at the Lefèvre Gallery in London. This triptych of contorted monsters, grimacing against a strident orange background, was unacceptable to many who sought distraction from the genocide and unprecedented destruction which that year revealed.

Dictatorial, enthroned figures and dismembered carcasses were themes which dominated Bacon's paintings of the following years. In 1951 he executed the first series of 'Popes', shown staring intently or screaming with rage, within a rectangular framework reminiscent of his earlier furniture designs. In particular he adapted Velázquez's *Pope Innocent X* to achieve a formidable expression of savagery and naked power. He made use of **Van Gogh's** paintings, the cinematic stills of Eadweard Muybridge and photographs discovered in newspapers, to produce an effect quite different from that of the initial inspiration. Many of Bacon's images gain force from the ambiguity of their reference: the associations of butcher's meat with the Crucifixion, of a hypodermic syringe with the nailing of Christ, and of wrestlers with lovers are repeatedly exploited. Bacon has often emphasized the role of chance in his work; fortuitous juxtapositions are developed and semi-accidental blobs and smears of paint are allowed to remain on the canvas.

After a period in the 1950s in which his work was characterized by dark tones and blurred forms, Bacon returned to sharper contours and more vivid colours, not only in his backgrounds but in limbs, nose and lips, accentuating the powerful effect of his brushstrokes. In 1962 he painted his second triptych, a format which he was to employ many times subsequently. In the same year a retrospective exhibition of his work was held at the Tate Gallery, before being circulated in Europe, where his reputation was consolidated. Neither the product nor the initiator of an artistic 'movement', he has won international respect through the unabated ferocity of his personal vision.

Some of Bacon's most arresting works are portraits, and in the traditionally respectful genre of portraiture he has overthrown convention. In the 1960s his portraits became increasingly violent, with facial features obscured or blurred in parabolic swathes of pigment. His figures sit or lie in a space defined only by a grid of intersecting lines, or in a stark room supplied with one or two characteristic items – an unshaded light bulb, a swivel chair or bar stool, cigarette butts, a window blind, a washbasin or lavatory. The tendency of Bacon's work is to expose his subjects, alone and often naked, without the support of the setting in which they are customarily seen; all that is homely or comforting is stripped away in his relentless pursuit of the individual in isolation.

Further reading

The illustrated catalogue of Bacon's work exhibited at the Grand Palais, Paris, in 1971–2 contains a full bibliography and an introduction by Michael Leiris. The outstanding critical study is John Russell, *Francis Bacon* (1979). See David Sylvester, *Interviews with Francis Bacon* (1975).

PATRICK CONNER

BAIRD, John Logie

1888–1946

Scottish inventor

So globally ubiquitous has television become there is scarcely any need to comment on its primacy as a disseminator of entertainment, live sport, news, documentaries, advertising and political propaganda, though inevitably the mix varies, depending on local circumstances, local broadcasting laws and the whims of particular governments and regimes. Its origins, however, are more obscure. Like any complex technological entity, the television was the end-product of any number of contributory discoveries and inventions. Certainly it did not come about by chance. In the early twentieth century the presence of photography, film, radio broadcasting and the telephone wire had put the notion of television – the direct transmission of moving pictures to a receiver distant from the transmitter – into the minds of many scientists, engineers and inventors. But who really got there first? The answer, it would appear, was a Scotsman, John Logie Baird, largely working on his own, sometimes with only scratch materials, and without the back-up of any large corporation or university department.

Baird was the archetypal independent inventor. The son of a Presbyterian minister born in Helensburgh, he built a telephone system in the family house as a child, and duly progressed to read engineering at the University of Glasgow after passing through the Royal Technical College (later Strathclyde University). But the outbreak of the Great War cut short his studies. Because of ill-health (which persisted throughout his life) he could not enlist as a soldier, but instead worked as a superintendent at the Clyde Electrical Power Company. Early on he put down a marker by designing, manufacturing and making some money from a medicated sock (the Baird Undersock) intended to prevent 'damp foot' and its associated problems. Then in 1920 he tried his hand at manufacturing jam in Trinidad, only to be thwarted by Caribbean insects.

Returning to Britain in 1922, Baird joined the race to produce a functional television. Already, as early as 1908, Alan Campbell Swinton had adumbrated in an academic paper how a television might work, by employing the cathode ray tube, invented by Karl Ferdinand Braun in 1897. But while Baird saw the possibilities latent in the cathode tube, he preferred instead to go down a non-electronic 'mechanical' path, favouring a system of more conventional projection, using mirrors, spinning discs and penny lenses.

By 1924 Baird had worked out how to transmit a still image (of the Maltese Cross) from one room to another. The following year he progressed to transmitting a moving picture, and on 26 January 1926 he demonstrated the result before forty scientists drawn from the Royal Institute in a Soho attic: the world's first authenticated television broadcast. Then, in 1930, came the first public television service, with the BBC (British Broadcasting Corporation) adopting Baird's system under licence. In 1931 Baird was also responsible for the first 'live' television transmission, of the Epsom Derby horse race.

Baird continued to make seminal advances. He pioneered colour television, the flying spot scanner, the optic fibre cable, facsimile transmission and (arguably) radar. Others, however were hot on his heels, and were mastering the use of the cathode ray tube. In the United States, although the television images he produced in 1928 were unequal to Baird's, Philo T. Farnsworth, following Campbell-Swinton's lead, developed a system ultimately superior to the Scotsman's, and it was this that became the industry standard. Although Baird himself shifted his energies into electronic transmission, in 1937 his 240-line system was rejected by the BBC in favour of a 405-line system developed for Marconi.

While, curiously, public television broadcasting did not begin in America until 1939 – Baird in fact was refused a broadcasting licence by the Federal Communications Commission in 1931 – thereafter it was the United States that provided technological leadership. Baird was down, but not, as is often supposed, out. Nor did he die impoverished. During World War II he worked on more or less secret government projects, and in 1946 built a 1,000-line colour television (the 'Telechrome') that was a marked improvement on anything he or anyone else had thus far come up with. Simultaneously he was experimenting with 'stereoscopic' or 3-D television. But within two months of the Telechrome's successful demonstration Baird was dead, and his masterpiece became quickly forgotten.

Further reading

See: Geoff Hutchinson, *Baird: The Story of John Logie Baird 1888–1946* (1985).

JUSTIN WINTLE

BAKST, Léon Samölivich

1866?–1924

Russian painter and theatre designer

Bakst was born in Grodno, near St Petersburg. (There is, in fact, no certainty that this was in 1866.) He studied at the academies in Moscow and St Petersburg but always found academic standards reactionary and deadening. He was expelled from the St Petersburg Academy for painting the Virgin Mary and Joseph as contemporary Jewish peasants. The artist he admired most as a student was the religious 'Wanderer' painter Neskerov. In the early 1890s he travelled to Paris where he studied under the Finnish painter Edelfelt. Upon his return to Russia he met Benois, Filosofov, Roerich, Serov and other radical artists and became a portrait painter and theatre designer. In 1899 he joined **Diaghilev's** newly founded Mir Iskusstva (World of Art) group in St Petersburg and from then on until its demise in 1904 contributed to the group's magazine. The group's main aim, under the influence of the diplomat Charles Birlé, was to rejuvenate Russian art and literature by importing the most recent ideas from the rest of Europe, such as the Art Nouveau style practised by **Beardsley** and **Mackintosh**, the Post-

Impressionism of **Cézanne** and **Gauguin** and the Symbolism of Moreau, **Rimbaud** and others. The predominant aesthetic of Mir Iskusstva was Symbolist and Bakst's paintings, like *Terror Antiquus* (1906), reflect the impact of the poetry of Blok and Balmont as well as of painters like Puvis de Chavannes, and the designer Victor Vasnetsov. Bakst believed, along with Benois and Diaghilev, that the arts should become reintegrated and saw an opportunity for this on the stage. He was particularly impressed by similar attempts in England by Edward Gordon Craig. In 1902 he designed his first sets and costumes for the St Petersburg Theatre. In 1905, having travelled with Serov in Greece, the archaic art of which was a persistent influence on his mature style, he decorated the vestibule of the show of Russian art at the Tauride Palace with sculptures and a trellised water-garden. This exhibition was organized by Diaghilev who was also responsible, in 1906, for the twelve rooms dedicated to Russian art at the Salon d'Automne in Paris. Once again Bakst designed the setting. In 1908 he designed sets and costumes for Fokine. In 1909 he travelled to Paris with Diaghilev's Ballets Russes and designed the costumes for many of the series of ballets performed from then on. This year also saw his first major one-man show of watercolours at the Bernheim Gallery in Paris. Although he often quarrelled with Diaghilev he became the Russian impresario's chief and most celebrated designer. All his work was conducted in full collaboration with the musicians, choreographers and producers and this helps to explain the quite extraordinary overall visual unity which each ballet seems to have. His main designs were for *L'Aprés-midi d'un faune*, *Schéhérazade*, *Narcisse*, *L'Oiseau de feu*, *Héléne de Sparte* and *Salomé*. Bakst's work was not confined to the stage alone and he also produced fashion and textile designs for famous houses like Worth and continued to paint portraits and to produce illustrations. His influence upon fashion design and the development of textile design during the 1920s and 1930s was considerable. He died near Paris.

Bakst was largely responsible during his career for the revival of costume design and theatre sets in Europe. The sources of his art are many and varied and include Indian, Persian and Hellenic period styles as well as the Sezession art of **Klimt** and Schiele and Art Nouveau. The key to his work's power lies less in the technical innovation, for which he is rightly revered, than in his acute feeling for the emotional values of colour, texture and movement. He wrote, 'From each setting I discard the entire range of nuances which do not amplify or intensify the hidden sense of the fable.' His figures are never static but seem charged with a concentrated dynamism dictated by their own rhythmic logic. In talking of his use of colour he explained,

> in each colour of the prism there exists a gradation which sometimes expresses frankness and chastity, sometimes sensuality and even bestiality ... This can be felt and given over to the public by the effect one makes of the various shadings. That is what I tried to do in *Schéhérazade*. Against a lugubrious green I put a blue full of despair, paradoxical as it may seem.

Such notions of colour show the close proximity of Bakst's ideas to those of his compatriot **Kandinsky**, one of the fathers of abstract painting.

Further reading

See: A. Alexandre and Jean Cocteau, *Decorative Art of Léon Bakst* (1913, trans. 1972); Raymond Lister, *The Muscovite Peacock* (1954); Charles Spencer, *Bakst* (1977); Alexander Schouvaloff, *Leon Bakst: The Theatre Art* (1991); Skira Edotore (ed.) *The Art of Alexandre Benois & Leon Bakst: Theatre of Reason Theatre of Desire* (1999).

RICHARD HUMPHREYS

BALLARD, James Graham

1930–

English novelist

J.G. Ballard was born in Shanghai into a wealthy expatriate family. He was interned in a prisoner-of-war camp during the Second World War by the Japanese, and travelled to England for the first time in 1946. These early experiences of extremity and displacement, the basis of his fictionalized autobiography *Empire of the Sun* (1984), no doubt contributed to Ballard's total detachment from conceptions of cultural respectability and the tradition of the English novel. Precisely because of his subversion of the indigenous novel, many critics now regard Ballard as one of the most important post-war writers. This recognition has been slow, largely because he was identified as a writer of science fiction for the first half of his career. One of his major achievements has been to help transform perceptions of this despised pulp genre, which he did by fusing the low cultural energies of science fiction with the avant-garde in the 1960s, using it to produce an extraordinary vision of alienated, science-fictionalized existence in the advanced capitalist West.

He began publishing short stories in English and American science fiction magazines in 1956. The monthly pulp magazines were often stuffed with poorly executed and utterly conventionalized writing; from the start, Ballard wrote in a highly stylized way about vividly realized landscapes. Early stories were collected as *Vermilion Sands* (1971), in which a desert resort is the backdrop for the psychological games of profoundly traumatized people. *Vermilion Sands* showed Ballard's interest in exteriorizing psychic states in extreme physical settings. The clearest and most sustained influence on his work in this regard has been Surrealist painting, particularly the work of Paul Delvaux and **Salvador Dali**. The stories also introduced Ballard's interest in repetition and modulation: he tells the same story over and over, obsessively teasing out different resonances from the same scenario. His work comes in clusters as he pursues a particular idea until all of its potential is exhausted. This was evident in his first four novels, known as the 'Disaster Quartet' (1962–6). Each explores a global disaster and the perverse reactions of the dwindling

survivors. Unlike the heroic tradition where a band of scientists or engineers reverse the disaster and save humankind, Ballard's enervated figures seek ways of actively embracing the post-disaster world, often finally choosing physical death. *The Drowned World* (1962), in which London is submerged by floods, openly carried debts to Surrealism and the holistic psychology of **Carl Jung**. It secured the attention of mainstream literary commentators while the passivity appalled many in the American science fiction world.

Ballard's main association in England was with the science fiction journal *New Worlds*. In 1962, the editorship of *New Worlds* passed to Michael Moorcock. With Ballard and others, Moorcock planned to revolutionize the journal in the hope of making science fiction an aesthetic and political avant-garde. Moorcock proved to be in complete synchronicity with the times: between 1962 and 1970, *New Worlds* became a leading London avant-garde journal and the home of so-called New Wave science fiction. Ballard wrote a manifesto in 1962, 'Which Way to Inner Space?', in which he demanded a science fiction that abandoned outer space for the kinds of psychological climates and emotional territories his own work had been exploring. Ballard then embarked on a series of extreme experiments in 'condensed novels' that attempted to find a new form to address violent times. Eventually published as *The Atrocity Exhibition* in 1970, these difficult and confrontational works explore the assassination of **John F. Kennedy** and the psychic impacts of televised wars like Vietnam and Biafra, and detail the cultural obsession with celebrity and violent death. They are his most important but also most uncomfortable works.

After 1970, Ballard wrote fewer short stories and has concentrated on the novel. He wrote a trilogy of books about the transformation of the London landscape (*Crash*, 1973, *Concrete Island*, 1974, and *High-Rise*, 1975), which explored the sexual psycho-pathology of new technologies and their environments. This has become Ballard's abiding theme. Indeed, for anyone who reads these works, the epithet

'Ballardian' becomes an unavoidable term to describe those strange modern spaces that we increasingly inhabit: shopping malls, airport terminals, highway interchanges. Later work has included two volumes of fictionalized autobiography and a further trilogy on the boredom and psychosis induced by the globalized world of transnational business parks and gated communities.

Further reading

Other works include: *The Wind from Nowhere* (1962); *The Burning World* (1964); *The Terminal Beach* (stories, 1964); *The Drought* (1965); *The Crystal World* (1966); *The Atrocity Exhibition* (1970); *The Unlimited Dream Company* (1979); *Running Wild* (1988); *The Kindness of Women* (1991); *The Complete Short Stories* (2001); and the trilogy *Cocaine Nights* (1996), *Super-Cannes* (1999) and *Millennium People* (2003). See also: Peter Brigg, *J.G. Ballard* (1985); and Roger Luckhurst, *The Angle between Two Walls: The Fiction of J.G. Ballard* (1997).

ROGER LUCKHURST

BARBER, Samuel

1910–81

American composer

Barber was one of the most successful American classical composers of the twentieth century. His romantic music, confidently conservative in idiom, has survived changes of fashion and now seems as enduring as that of **Copland** or **Gershwin**, although it lacks their obviously American profile.

Samuel Barber was born in 1910 in comfortable circumstances at West Chester, Pennsylvania, where his father was a respected doctor. His mother played the piano and his aunt was the international opera singer Louise Homer, whose husband Sydney was a composer known especially for his songs. Barber started composing at the age of seven and two years later wrote in a letter to his mother: 'I was not meant to become an athlete. I was meant to be a composer, and will I'm sure.' The Curtis Institute had recently been founded in Philadelphia and he enrolled in 1924 to study singing, piano, conducting and composition. It was here four years later that he met Gian Carlo Menotti, fresh from Italy and able to speak very little English. Their professional and personal partnership lasted almost a lifetime. In a late interview Barber said: 'There's no reason music should be difficult for an audience to understand, is there?' He and Menotti shared an ability to communicate directly, a quality which came under suspicion with the professional musical establishment of the 1960s.

After graduating, Barber spent some time in Europe, especially Italy, but he also studied in Vienna and began a brief career as a singer. Rosario Scalero, an admirer of **Brahms**, had given him a strong traditional grounding at Curtis and his polished student scores gained him awards for further study. After he attracted the attention of conductors as prominent as Rodzinski and Toscanini he never looked back – the latter gave the premiere of what became Barber's best-known work, the *Adagio for Strings*, in 1938. In a remarkable way this elegiac score, arranged from an earlier string quartet, has summed up the emotions of the American people on momentous occasions such as national funerals.

Barber's literary connections included a setting of the **Matthew Arnold** poem 'Dover Beach' for baritone and string quartet (1931), which he sang and recorded himself; an overture *The School for Scandal* (1931); and *Music for a Scene from Shelley* (1933). He provided a score for **Martha Graham's** ballet *Medea* (1946) and wrote two concertos before turning to opera. The first of his two grand operas, *Vanessa* (1958), was to a libretto by Menotti, based on a story by Isak Dinesen. Eleanor Steber, for whom Barber had written *Knoxville: Summer of 1915* (1947), took the title role at the Met in New York. Menotti directed, sets and costumes were by Cecil Beaton, and the opera was a success. The gloomy foreboding of the story, with echoes of **Ibsen**, suited Barber's melancholic nostalgia and he found his own approach to traditional arias, duets and ensembles.

Before Barber returned to opera he had composed another concerto. The Piano Concerto (1962), written for John Browning, may not be as popular as the vernal Violin Concerto (1939) but it is just as characteristic, with a total command of its resources, including a magical slow movement.

His second grand opera, *Anthony and Cleopatra*, was commissioned for the opening of the new opera house at New York's Lincoln Center in 1966 and seems to have been torpedoed by the occasion itself, the difficulties of setting word-for-word Shakespeare and Zefirelli's over-elaborate production. This failure, compared with *Vanessa*, had a disastrous effect on Barber even though future revivals have questioned this verdict, and he subsequently composed less. Another blow came in 1973 with the sale of the house he had shared with Menotti for thirty years.

Barber wrote songs throughout his career. With great sensitivity he set a variety of poets from different centuries, often mixing poets in cycles. The texts represent personal responses and show an understanding of the medium from the inside – his own singing and the family connections with his aunt and uncle. His songs may lack the magisterial quality of Copland's *Twelve Poems of Emily Dickinson* or the cycles of **Britten** but they have attracted some of the finest international singers as well as amateurs.

Barber's legacy demonstrates that great imaginations are conservative. He took the mainstream idiom of the early twentieth-century inheritance, positioning himself somewhere between Brahms and **Stravinsky** but never varying in his determination to be true to himself. Audiences have been grateful that they would not be challenged beyond their capacity and there is every reason to expect that Barber will retain his position in the pantheon of American composers.

Further reading

See: Barbara Heyman, *Samuel Barber: The Composer and His Music* (1992); D.A. Hennessee, *Samuel Barber: A Bio-Bibliography* (1985).

PETER DICKINSON

BARNUM, Phineas Taylor

1810–91

US showman, publicist and author

To call P.T. Barnum the first great 'showman' is to neglect an essential part of his greatness, for Barnum was among the first to understand the nature of advertising his product not only by posters but also by manipulating the existing media and word of mouth. In many ways he was the Founding Father of Madison Avenue. The small village of Bethel, Connecticut, where he was born, would hardly seem a fertile place for such talents. And yet biographers and critics have stressed the atmosphere of practical jokes and exaggerated rhetoric in which Barnum grew up. Although Barnum attended grammar school for at least six years, his first major 'lesson' for his future came from his grandfather Phineas Taylor, who gave him a property called Ivy Island when the child was four, telling him that this fabulous property would make him wealthy when he came of age. At ten he visited this 'property' and discovered it to be 'an almost inaccessible, worthless bit of barren land, and while I stood deploring my sudden downfall, a huge black snake (one of my tenants) approached me with upraised head.' Memories of this hoax combined with experiences working in a country store where he learned 'that sharp trades, tricks, dishonesty, and deception are by no means confined to the city' were the most important schooling Barnum had in his formative years.

Barnum's first adult venture was a newspaper, the *Herald of Freedom*, first published on 19 October 1831, whose critics labelled it 'Masonic and anti-priestcraft'. More formidable opponents brought three suits of libel against him, the third landing him in jail for accusing a local deacon of 'usury'. The anti-clerical stance of this tabloid would continue to be one of the major forces directing Barnum throughout his life in the rather grimly puritan days of the first half of the nineteenth century. More than any other individual, Barnum made public entertainments popular and respectable in an age that frowned on the masses enjoying anything other than religion. In his own defence Barnum once said, 'This is a trading world and men, women and children need something to satisfy their gayer, lighter moods and hours, and he who ministers to this want is in a business established by the Author of our nature.'

In 1835 Barnum began his show business career in New York City with the exhibition of an old Negro woman whom he claimed to be George Washington's 161-year-old former nurse, thus shrewdly cloaking his entertainment in the acceptable colours of science and patriotism, somewhat tarnished by later revelations that she was a fake.

Barnum continued to tour and exhibit until 1841 when he bought the American Museum in Manhattan and turned this curious old warehouse with its waxworks, freaks, animals and a lecturing 'professor' into one of the most famous entertainment places in the country. He doubled the museum space and added transient attractions such as educated dogs, 'industrious fleas, automatons, ventriloquists, living statuary ... the first English Punch & Judy in this country, Italian Fantoccini, mechanical figures ... dissolving views, American Indians who enacted their warlike and religious ceremonies on the stage'. In doing all this Barnum began to change the very nature of entertainment in America and in the process accumulated his first fortune, grossing over $300,000 in the first three years.

This fortune and reputation were greatly enhanced by the tours Barnum made in the early 1840s with Charles S. Stratton, the 25-inch midget known professionally as General Tom Thumb. The General did monologues and historical and mythic roles, playing everything from Cupid to Napoleon. With Tom Thumb as his vehicle Barnum fulfilled a longtime ambition to tour England and Europe, exhibiting the advertising shrewdness that made him both rich and notorious. He let Tom perform for three nights in London and then stalled until he received the coveted invitation to Buckingham Palace for an audience with Queen Victoria, which was quickly followed by a second to see the three-year-old Prince of Wales. Barnum exploited all this quickly and broadly and soon the midget was known in the press as the 'Pet of the Palace'. Barnum snowballed this first royal audience into others on the continent and returned to the United States with an even more valuable human property, one that is estimated at selling about twenty million of the eighty-two million admission tickets sold by Barnum in his career.

Despite his success with the museum, General Tom Thumb, the famous 'Siamese twins', Chang and Eng, and other attractions, Barnum still sought to 'place himself before the world in a new light' by elevating public taste. And so, without ever having heard her sing, he booked Jenny Lind, 'The Swedish Nightingale', for an American tour of 150 concerts which would earn the then astounding figure of over $700,000. No foreign artist had been so fully accepted, praised and paid for by the American public, thus climaxing the exhibition phase of Barnum's career.

After two publicized 'retirements' in 1855 and 1868, Barnum returned to show business in 1871 to demonstrate once more his place as the premier promoter of the century. He became partners with William Cameron Coup and Dan Castello to build a travelling circus with innovations such as travel by rail, Ben Lusbie who could sell 6,000 tickets in one hour, a half-ton seal, and the permanent base of P.T. Barnum's Great Roman Hippodrome in New York City. Eventually, Barnum bought out his partners and travelled as 'Barnum's own Greatest Show on Earth', slowly increasing the size until the overheads were $3,000 a day. In 1881 he merged with Allied Shows Circus owned by James E. Cooper, James L. Hutchinson and James Anthony Bailey. Thus was the *three-ring* circus born on 18 March 1881, establishing new definitions of extravagance for an age-old form. In 1882 the new partners bought 'Jumbo', a 12-foot tall, six and a half ton elephant, from the London Zoological Gardens. Jumbo quickly became one of Barnum's biggest successes and was often presented in tandem with General Tom

Thumb. Barnum is often credited with 'inventing' the circus, an institution that has existed for perhaps thousands of years. What he really did – with the help of shrewd partners like Coup and Bailey – was truly American: through money, size and advertising he simply created 'the greatest show on earth'.

During his various retirements Barnum wrote two books which reveal both his character and his interests. His frequently revised autobiography first came out in 1855, and in 1865 he published *Humbugs of the World*. The latter attacks spiritualists, quacks, swindlers, ghosts and certain religious cultists, while the former outlines 'Forty Busy Years' of providing 'Healthful entertainment to the American people'.

P.T. Barnum was that typical nineteenth-century American success, the sincere charlatan: a man who believed that all his tricks, deceptions, braggadocio and sheer size were in the best interests of the public. He brought entertainment on a vast public scale to a nation that in its youth had shunned it. He made public spectacle and pleasure not only acceptable, but necessary and profitable.

Further reading

See: *How I Made Millions: Or the Secret of Success* (1884, the last rewrite of his autobiography); *Why I Am a Universalist* (1895); Phineas T. Barnum and James W. Cook (eds) *The Colossal P.T. Barnum Reader: Nothing Else Like It in the Universe* (2006); M.R. Werner, *Barnum* (1927); Constance Rourke, *Trumpets of Jubilee* (1927); Irving Wallace, *The Fabulous Showman* (1959); Neil Harris, *Humbug: The Art of P.T. Barnum* (1973); Joel Benton, *Life of Honorable Phineas T. Barnum* (1891); Alice Curtis Desmond, *Barnum Presents: General Tom Thumb* (1954); A.H. Saxon, *P.T. Barnum: The Legend and the Man* (1989); Philip B. Kunhardt Jr, Philip B. Kunhardt III and Peter W. Kunhardt, *P.T. Barnum: America's Greatest Showman* (1995).

CHARLES GREGORY

BARTH, John

1930–
US novelist

Postmodern might almost have been a designation expressly invented for John Barth. Along with similarly inclined contemporary US literary authorship like that of **Thomas Pynchon**, William Gaddis, Donald Barthelme, Ron Sukenick, Robert Coover, **Kurt Vonnegut** and Raymond Federman, or at a more distant reach **Vladimir Nabokov**, **Jorge Luis Borges** and **Samuel Beckett**, his novels have been nothing if not determinedly, even lavishly, full of inventive consciousness as to their own fashioning. 'Process as content' continues to win favour from among his hallmark phrases.

Two seminal essays written for the magazine *Atlantic*, 'The Literature of Exhaustion' (1967) and 'The Literature of Replenishment: Postmodernist Fiction' (1980), usefully set out his literary credo. Drawing on narrative sources from *The Thousand and One Nights* – especially its use of Scheherazade as a framing device – through to **James Joyce's** *Ulysses*, as well as language philosophy and phenomenology, he argues that fiction as mimesis has long run itself into the ground. The old stories, form and content, increasingly risk imaginative fatigue, even stasis. Fiction's best new turn, he goes on to suggest, is to be arrived at not only through the author's acknowledgement of his or her artifice but its uninhibited exploitation: storytelling, thereby, as its own self-referential making of reality. True to postmodern as against modernist writ, no one grand narrative presides for either the world or its telling, rather, and co-existingly, *les petits récits*.

Born in Cambridge, Maryland, briefly a music student at New York's Juilliard School for the Performing Arts, Barth studied at Johns Hopkins University in Baltimore before embarking on a career as writer and professor which took him to Pennsylvania State University, the State University of New York, Buffalo, Boston University, and a long stint back at Johns Hopkins from 1973 through to retirement in 1995. From the outset his fiction gave evidence of a rare, parodic-philosophical talent. *The Floating Opera* (1956) thus offers a pastiche of **Camus** on suicide pitched as the pleasure boat might-be death day of Todd Andrews. Ribald narrator, lawyer and anti-hero, Todd lives with a sense of utter contingency. His back and forth ruminations, even his role in a rakish sex-triangle, act as commentary. *The End of the Road* (1958) continues the theme in the life of Jacob Horner, Instructor in Prescriptive Grammar at Wicomico State Teachers' College, whose academic specialism is mocked both by his own life and by those of his husband-and-wife friends Joe Morgan, a would-be relativist in values, and Rennie Morgan, who having had an abortion absurdistly chokes to death after eating. Debate was early to join. Was Barth the instinctive master of life-as-carnival or comic nihilist?

The former, certainly, seemed the more likely with his launch into mock-epic. In *The Sot-Weed Factor* (1960) Ebenezer Cooke, tobacco vendor and would-be poet laureate of eighteenth-century colonial Maryland, serves as protagonist in a rollicking Menippean comic satire. The parody turns not just upon Barth's inveterate wordplay and bawdy, or the reeling impostures and reversals, but upon history as always the one or another competing fiction of fact. With *Giles Goat-Boy* (1966, revised 1967) he envisions the Cold War world as a university run by the WESAC computer, its glitches to be put to rights by an Orpheus updated from Greek myth or the anthropologist Joseph Campbell's greatly influential *The Hero with a Thousand Faces* (1949).

Barth offers few more emphatic examples of postmodern theory-into-practice than *Lost in the Funhouse* (1968), especially its title-story. Told first by a narrator suffering writer's block, then by his alter ego, Ambrose Mensch, whose life is disclosed not a little fantastically from sperm to adulthood, it works as though one continuous narrative loop. The World War II literal seaside funhouse into which Ambrose first enters does duty for the world as ancient maze, a hall of mirrors, and yet always impatient for new, and so authorially self-renewing, narrative. A shared ambition, not to say at times startling exuberance and virtuosity, marks out the subsequent fiction.

Chimera (1972) yields a three-novella irreverent reworking of ancient myth in the

figures of Dunyazade as Scheherazade's sister, Perseus and Bellerophon. *LETTERS: A Novel* (1979) uses its intertextual reference-back into the epistolary hey-day of the eighteenth century and its seven personae to rewrite the 1960s. *Sabbatical* (1982), another cruise format, deploys the lives of Fenwick and Susan Turner to rebuke all binary versions of the human condition. *The Tidewater Tales: A Novel* (1987), also set aboard ship in Barth's domain of the Chesapeake Bay, gives a mythic reworking of four literary classics. *The Last Voyage of Somebody the Sailor* (1991), *Once Upon a Time: A Floating Opera* (1994), *On with the Story: Stories* (1996) and *Coming Soon!!!* (2001), each panoramic in canvas and the further refusal to settle for closure of life or word, confirm no drop of inventive daring on Barth's part.

Both in his postmodern tapestries, as they have been called, and in the discursive work of *The Friday Book: Essays and Other Nonfiction* (1984) and *Further Fridays: Essays, Lectures, and Other Non-Fiction 1984–94* (1995), the insistence on storytelling's autonomous dynamic, its metafictive or ludic circling, has not always earned him approval. There has been talk of mere virtuosic spiral. For admirers, however, the challenge of Barth's visionary fabulation bespeaks a quite indispensable American literary figure.

Further reading

See: Robert Scholes, *The Fabulators* (1967); David Morrell, *John Barth: An Introduction* (1976); Joseph J. Waldmeir (ed.) *Critical Essays on John Barth* (1980), Charles B. Harris, *Passionate Virtuosity: The Fiction of John Barth* (1983); E.P. Walkiewicz, *John Barth* (1986); Heide Ziegler, *John Barth* (1987); Patricia D. Tobin, *John Barth and the Anxiety of Continuance* (1992).

A. ROBERT LEE

BARTHES, Roland

1915–80

French writer-critic and teacher

The writing of Roland Barthes embraces literature and the arts, as well as a much wider range of cultural phenomena: he wrote, for example, on women's fashion, on advertising, food and the Citroën DS. His interest was in cultural phenomena as sign/language systems, and to this extent he may be thought of as a Structuralist. Broadly speaking, his work belongs within an anti-positivist, anti-empiricist tradition whose basic references are **Marx**, **Nietzsche**, **Saussure** and **Freud**. Barthes published some fifteen books and a sizeable body of articles and prefaces. Chronologically two major shifts of emphasis, and therefore three phases, may be distinguished.

In the first phase the emphasis is twofold: (1) on demystifying the stereotypes of bourgeois culture; and (2) on studying culture as form. Barthes is concerned with literature, literary form and the history of French literature in *Writing Degree Zero* (*Le Degré zéro de l'écriture*, 1953, trans. 1967), with the link between writing and biography in *Michelet par lui-même* (1954) and with so-called mass culture as a sub-product of bourgeois culture in *Mythologies* (1957, trans. 1972) and *The Eiffel Tower and Other Mythologies* (1979–80). His early work is much influenced by **Sartre** and **Brecht**.

The second phase may be labelled the semiotic phase. It begins with Barthes's reading of Saussure in 1956, and the methodological appendix to *Mythologies*. In this phase Barthes takes over Saussure's concept of the sign and analysis of language as a sign system. 'Elements of Semiology' ('Éléments de sémiologie', *Communications 4*, 1964, trans. 1967) is a theoretical work in which Barthes considers the adaptation of Saussure's model to the study of cultural phenomena other than language. *Système de la mode* (1967, 'The Fashion System', trans. in Susan Sontag (ed.) *A Barthes Reader*, 1982) applies the methods of semiology to a corpus of fashion articles from *Elle* and *Jardin des Modes*.

It is during this second phase that Barthes acquired the label of a Structuralist. Vladimir Propp's theories on folk tales are applied to a James Bond novel (*Communications 8*, 1965, trans. 1981), in which Barthes shows painstakingly how the levels of the story can be assigned functions in the narrative, suggesting that the seemingly endless production of stories in advanced Western societies in fact involves a much smaller number of variants that rely on a surprisingly limited stock of certain themes. Such an approach – 'structural' in the sense that it looks at the *form* a story takes, in relation to its 'content' – was updating the (Russian) formalist debates of the 1920s. Using Saussure's 'differential' view of language and applying this differential approach to everyday stories has inevitably proved rich in all forms of media studies, especially televisual and cinematic research. Following **Lévi-Strauss's** idea of 'bricolage' (amateur DIY), Barthes 'borrowed' also from linguistics, this time in his analysis of fashion. Having given up the study of historical clothing forms as futile, he decided on a more synchronic study of clothing: how women's magazines present fashion styles verbally. In other words, Barthes was suggesting, once again, that verbalizing (here, *speaking* clothes, using language on fashion items) could be part of the 'hidden persuasion' that the fashion system operates. This approach was the key meeting point of Lévi-Strauss's structural anthropology with Saussurean linguistics.

The third phase is established with the publication of *S/Z* (1970, trans. 1974), alongside a seminal article called 'The Death of the Author' (1968, trans. in *The Rustle of Language*, 1986). At this point Barthes moves away from Saussurean semiology towards a theory of 'the text', defined as the field of play of the signifier and of the symbolic (*vide* **Lacan**). 'The Death of the Author' is a stark but playful reminder, at the height of the May 1968 uprising in France, that 'author' and 'authority' may have more in common than mere shared etymology. A key Barthesian suggestion is that it no longer matters what an author *thinks* (or thought) his/her novel is about: it is up to the reader, liberated from the tyranny of imposed meaning, to read the novel how he or she may wish. But rather than an 'anything-goes' view of literary criticism, Barthes insisted in good Sartrean fashion that this freedom carried responsibilities. *S/Z* puts this ethos into practice. It is a reading of Balzac's *Sarrasine* which plots the migrations of five 'codes', understood as open groupings of signifieds and as the points of crossing with other texts (or 'intertext'). The distinction between '*le scriptible*' (the writeable) and '*le lisible*' (the readable), between what can be written/rewritten today, i.e. actively produced by the reader, and what can no longer be written but only read, i.e. passively consumed, provides a new basis for evaluation, and is extended in *The Pleasure of the Text* (*Le Plaisir du texte* 1973, trans. 1975) via the metaphor of the body as text and language as an object of desire.

S/Z, The Pleasure of the Text, as well as other books published by Barthes in the 1970s, have in common that they are written in the form of fragments. This represents for Barthes a conscious retreat from what he sees as the discourse of domination and power, caught in the subject/object relationship and the habits of rhetoric. He distinguishes now between 'the ideological' and 'the aesthetic', between the language of science, which deals in stable meanings and is identified with the sign, and (following **Derrida**) the language of writing and criticism, which aims at displacement, denaturalization, dispersion. Barthes offered 'textual' readings of Japan in *L'Empire des signes* (*The Empire of Signs*, 1970, trans. 1983), of the founders of new languages in *Sade-Fourier-Loyola* (1971, trans. 1976), of himself in *Roland Barthes by Roland Barthes* (*Roland Barthes par Roland Barthes*, 1975, trans. 1977) and of the outdated, discredited discourse of love in *A Lover's Discourse* (*Fragments d'un discours amoureux*, 1977, trans. 1978). Barthes's lectures at the Collège de France from 1976 until his death in 1980, published posthumously (see below) show a dedicated but sceptical academic fascinated by the essayistic and provisional nature of 'learned' public discourse. Barthes's final text – an emotional and rich journey through photographs that have moved him during his quest for a satisfying photographic representation of his recently deceased mother – has had significant impact on photographic theory: *Camera Lucida. A Note on Photography* (*La Chambre claire. note sur la photographie*, 1980, trans. 1984) no longer claimed to be using semiology, but a whole panoply of post-semiotic (even anti-semiological) terms such as *pathos*, self, emotion, subjectivity, to account for the (seemingly) most 'scientific' of media. Here Barthes was crowning his unpredictable career with a return, in 'spiral' (a favoured metaphor), to his earlier concerns with truth and access to the past, clearly influenced by the maverick nineteenth-century French historian Jules Michelet.

More generally, Barthes's mode of progress is itself characterized by displacement. Apart from the major shifts of emphasis already described, shifts and turns can occur from one work to the next, and even from one sentence to the next and within single words. 'Semiology', for instance, is used quite differently in the 1970s, in association with art, aesthetics and theories of the subject.

Barthes was from 1960 to 1962 Chef de travaux and from 1962 to 1976 Directeur d'études at the École Pratique des Hautes Études, Paris. In 1976 he became professor of literary semiology at the Collège de France. His life ended when he was struck down by a van in a Parisian street. Teaching was for him an important activity, closely related to writing. He was interested especially in the forms through which knowledge and culture are conveyed, speaking latterly of the digression, the equivalent of the fragment in writing, as a means whereby teaching might be freed from didacticism. His later work is undoubtedly problematical in its insistence that the essential struggle is against the sign. On the other hand, there can be no return to the positions which, indirectly, he did so much to help us criticize; and he leaves for us the very considerable pleasure of his own texts.

Further reading

Other works include: *On Racine* (*Sur Racine*, 1963, trans. 1964); *Critical Essays* (*Essais critiques*, 1964, trans. 1972); *Critique et vérité* (*Criticism and Truth*, 1966); 'L'ancienne rhétorique (Aide-mémoire)' (Classical rhetoric, working notes), *Communications 16* (1970); and the lecture *Leçon* (1978, trans. 1979). *Image-Music-Text* (1977) contains essays selected and translated by Stephen Heath. Other work that has appeared posthumously in translation includes: *The Responsibility of Forms* (1986); *The Semiotic Challenge* (1987); *Sollers Writer* (1987); *New Critical Essays* (1990); *Incidents* (1992); *The Language of Fashion* (2006); interviews are translated in *The Grain of the Voice* (1985). Barthes's complete works have appeared, in French only, in two editions (1993–5 and 2002). Lecture notes from the 1976–80 period are published as *Comment vivre ensemble* ('How to Live Together', 2002), *The Neutral* (trans. 2005) and *La Préparation du roman* ('Preparing to Write a Novel', 2003), as yet available only in French. See: L.-J. Calvet, *Roland Barthes. Un regard politique sur le signe* (1973) and a biography (1994); S. Heath, *Vertige du déplacement* (1974); P. Thody, *Roland Barthes: A Conservative Estimate* (1977); A. Lavers, *Structuralism and After* (1982); J. Culler, *Barthes* (1983); P. Roger, *Roland Barthes, roman* (1986); M. Moriarty, *Roland Barthes* (1991); A. Brown, *Roland Barthes: The Figures of Writing* (1992); C. Coste, *Roland Barthes moraliste* (1998); D. Knight, *Barthes and Utopia* and *Critical Essays* (1997 and 2000); A. Stafford, *Roland Barthes, Phenomenon and Myth* (1998); G. Allen, *Roland Barthes* (2003). M.-A. Burnier and P. Rambaud, *Le Roland-Barthes sans peine* (1978) is a work of parody.

ANDY STAFFORD

BARTÓK, Béla

1881–1945

Hungarian composer

A fervent nationalist, Bartók relinquished the opportunity of studying in Vienna in favour of the Budapest Royal Academy of Music where he became known less as a composer than as a brilliant pianist. From 1907 his own teaching there was influential and, with concert tours, provided the means by which he sustained his folk-music research until becoming a member of the Hungarian Academy of Science in 1934. By then, too, the radical individuality of his music was established abroad. With the increasing Nazification of Hungary he departed for the United States in 1940 and was awarded an honorary doctorate at Columbia University, where he continued his research until 1942. During the remaining three years, despite recurring illness, he composed the *Concerto for Orchestra* (1943), Sonata for solo violin (1944) and the Third Piano Concerto (1945).

With **Schoenberg** and **Stravinsky**, Bartók is one of the great innovators of his epoch. The image of him as 'folklorist', while true, can be deceptively facile. His individuality arises from the rare concurrence in one intelligence of elements both scrupulously scientific enough to seek out, analyse and classify a forgotten language, and powerfully creative enough to evolve a new one.

His output falls broadly into two periods: the first (*c.* 1903–23) is involved with the assimilation of folk music and the development of his style; a second period (from 1924) is dominated by the synthesis of large-scale forms. He subscribed to none of the accepted contemporary musical tendencies but, being eclectic, aimed for a measured balance of these elements. His music, lyrical and dramatic in expression, depends on sonata-type forms for its fulfilment and is characterized by the intensely organic way in which these are evolved and interrelated (thematically, through a process derived from **Franz Liszt**).

The monumental set of six String Quartets (No. 1, Op. 7, 1909; No. 2, Op. 17, 1915–17; No. 3, Op. 1927; No. 4, Op. 1928; No. 5, Op. 1934; No. 6, Op. 1939), long regarded as the core of his work, display such formal preoccupations. Of the First it could be said that its main theme only emerges in the third (last) movement, whereas in the Second everything is contained in the opening. The Third, based on some two or three motives, is reduced to one movement of four sections whose first and third have related material: the nascent arch-form. The Fourth and Fifth show elaborated arch-forms of five movements (schematically ABCBA), while the Sixth forsakes them for an introductory motto-theme which introduces each movement and is developed in the last.

Up to 1905 Bartók's style was compounded of popular Hungarian and teutonic elements (**Brahms**, **Wagner**, **Richard Strauss**), but a basic change took place then because of the ethnomusicology begun with Kodály. Revealed to him was the spirit of a 'new Hungarian art-music' and melodies of 'unsurpassable beauty and perfection'. They were the spontaneous expression of the rural peasantry, completely unknown and distinct from the gypsy music of urban civilization. Unlike Kodály, Bartók extended his interest to Slovak, Romanian, Arabic and Turkish music. The hours spent collecting this music were the happiest of his life, his identification with rural life and art complete. The allegorical *Cantata Profana* (1930) is the quintessence of this spirit.

But the most direct interaction with folk music can be traced in the numerous song-settings and piano transcriptions. Bartók's vitality of rhythm is greatly influenced by improvisatory speech-rhythm (*parlando rubato*), dance-rhythm (*tempo giusto*, mainly duple pulse except for the pliancy of Bulgarian rhythms) and the 'dotted' rhythm derived from the Hungarian language. Moreover, these melodies were based on pentatonic, modal and oriental scales, not the diatonic ones of Western classical music. Harmonies derived from the first led to a more free use of seconds, fourths and sevenths, traditionally considered dissonant. If these were applied (chromatically) to modal tunes the increased possibilities resulted in a mixture of modes, hence bi- and poly-modality. However, Bartók retained, at any given moment, the authority of a fundamental tone, unlike the claims of 'atonality' and 'polytonality'. Although one of various principles, modality identifies some of Bartók's characteristics: the gravitation of his (own) melodies around specific tones, the variation of otherwise strict contrapuntal forms (canon, fugue, inversion) and the rich diversification of his harmonic palette generally. The last of the *Eight Improvisations on Hungarian Peasant Songs*, Op. 20 (1920) was admitted to be the extreme limit reached by him in adding daring accompaniments to simple folk tunes. So complete was his absorption that the creation of original works in imitation of folk music followed naturally, of which the *Piano Suite*, Op. 14 (1916) and orchestral *Dance Suite* (1923) are fine examples.

From the speculative *Fourteen Bagatelles*, Op. 6 (1908) which mark the beginning of his personal style, up to the two Violin and Piano Sonatas (1921/2) there is a swing from the simpler to the more complex, from Romanticism to expressionism, from the opera *Duke Bluebeard's Castle*, Op. 11 (1911), through *The Wooden Prince* ballet (1914–16) and *Songs*, Op. 15 and 16 (1915–16), to *The Wonderful Mandarin* pantomime, Op. 19 (1918–19). The piano music alone affords a varied panorama of this period and sees the beginning of his overtly pedagogical music which, from *Ten Easy Pieces* (1908) to the *153 Mikrokosmos* (1926–39) and *Forty-four Duos* (1931) for two violins, was without equal in the twentieth century. Liberally endowed with folk material and stylistic innovations, their often graphic qualities enhance the musical points made. Instrumental technique was highly developed in Bartók but never exaggerated. His treatment of percussion instruments was actually refined while his exploitation of stringed instruments was little short of miraculous.

Coinciding with editions of baroque keyboard music, the three works of 1926 are marked by economy of line and propulsive rhythm (Piano Sonata, First Piano Concerto, *Out of Doors*). While the Second Piano Concerto (1930–1) might be termed 'neo-classic' in its interlocking patterns and confessed aim to be more pleasing, this music indicates a more raw awareness of the reality in the ethnic experience and its alignment to art-music. Stripped of the inessential except in the pursuit of sonority, an unyielding force flows through it which yet contains the delicacy of 'Musiques Nocturnes' (*Out of Doors*).

The elucidation of golden sections and tonal axes of symmetry confirm what is already felt in the dynamic equilibrium of the succeeding works. All kinds of scale-segments are drawn upon for the compression and expansion of pitch (and rhythm) that transforms one idea over a span of four movements in *Music for Strings, Percussion and Celesta* (1936), whose fugal first movement is itself a unique structuring of musical space. A constant regeneration of invention promotes a form as large as the first movement of the *Sonata for Two Pianos and Percussion* (1937). A vision which can seem to question the very substance of musical material in the Fourth Quartet can later embrace the variational exuberance of the Violin Concerto (No. 2, 1937–8). With these achievements comes a rejuvenation of classical proportions which *Contrasts* (1938) and the *Divertimento* (1939) share with the works of the American period, granting Bartók a wide appeal and understanding which has not diminished. His influence on post-war composers was selective, as witness **Stockhausen's** early dissertation on the rhythmic aspects (alone) of the *1937 Sonata*; or the fascination, particularly for serially minded commentators, of the Fourth Quartet's integration. Others have emulated subtleties of sound and texture or his pedagogical style. The humane integrity of Bartók's utterly musical art remains invincible.

Further reading

An unfinished Viola Concerto (1945) was reconstructed and orchestrated by Tibor Serly. See: Serge Moreux, *Béla Bartók* (trans. 1953); Halsey Stevens, *The Life and Music of Béla Bartók* (1953, revised 1964); Ernö Lendvai, *Béla Bartók* (1971); *Béla Bartók Essays*, ed. Benjamin Suchoff (1976); P. Griffiths, *Bartók* (1984); K. Chalmers, *Béla Bartók* (1985).

RONALD LUMSDEN

BAUDELAIRE, Charles Pierre

1821–67

French poet

Throughout his life Baudelaire maintained an intense and often anguished relation with his mother, a woman of some taste but little understanding. As a child of seven he felt deprived of her affections when in the year following his father's death she took as her second husband Colonel Aupick, a decent if unimaginative man who partly fuelled the adolescent Baudelaire's postures of revolt against conventional morality. Judging from the poet's letters, his stepfather nevertheless seems to have stood as a symbol of his deeper desire to achieve moral worth. The family background goes some way to explaining two fundamental tensions that are expressed in his poetry: his need for woman's love set against scorn for uncomprehending female superficiality; and his deep-rooted need for personal piety and worth, coupled with an uncompromising awareness of the 'worm' at the heart of virtue. His feeling of dispossession was exacerbated when to cure him of his profligate habits as a dandy in the *Bohème*, the management of his inheritance was removed from his control and entrusted to a lawyer friend of the family, Ancelle. Lumbered by debts, kept constantly short of money, unfavoured by the patronage of established men of letters, dogged by sequences of misfortunes that seem so diabolically schemed as to suggest complicity (see **Sartre's** study, below), Baudelaire's life is a story of frustrations, humiliations and procrastinations. In 1841 his parents sent him on a voyage to India, in the hope of weaning him from what they judged to be his depraved Parisian life. He got only as far as Mauritius, returning to Paris in 1842. The journey proved fruitful, however, from the creative point of view, since it stocked his mind with the exotic imagery on which his poetry was to draw. Otherwise Baudelaire barely stirred from Paris during the twenty-eight years (1836–64) that he lived there continuously. He interested himself briefly in Republican politics and played a minor part in the 1848 Revolution. But he was by temperament too aristocratic and too 'metaphysical' in his conception of evil to sustain a commitment to the prevailing liberal doctrines of human perfectibility.

By mid-century Baudelaire had earned himself a reputation as an art critic and as the author of a number of essays including, as one of his most striking pieces, a non-psychological interpretation of laughter in its relation to original sin. He also produced remarkably good French translations of some of the works of Poe, with whose ideas on the creative imagination he had felt an immediate affinity. Despite some success in placing his poems with prestigious journals, Baudelaire's reputation was by 1855 still that of an eccentric vampire of legendary lubricity (mostly his own invention) attempting to shock his way to public recognition. The same lack of understanding greeted the publication, in 1857, of the volume of poetry on which his fame rests, *Les Fleurs de mal*. He was put on trial for obscenity in the same year, fined and forced to publish an expurgated version of his collection. The ban – on six offending poems – was not lifted until 1949, though publishers contrived to incorporate them in most post-1857 editions. A second edition containing fresh poems, but not the banned ones, appeared in 1861. This being the last edition which Baudelaire was able to supervise personally, it is generally considered to be the most trustworthy guide to his intentions with regard to the thematic groupings and sequences which, he believed, would best convey the 'architecture' of the whole collection: a synopsis of human destiny in its progress through the stations of illusory salvation. The first posthumous edition, again substantially enriched, came out in 1868 (*Les Nouvelles Fleurs de mal*).

The originality of Baudelaire's achievement does not lie in any novelty of theme, versification or even supporting theories of art. The focus on everyday life, the satanical, the macabre, the exotic and erotic, the suffering of the artist, his role as intercessor between the human and the divine, the thirst for the absolute were all part of the stock-in-trade of the contemporary Romanticism. In versification he tends to work his own variations within traditional forms of euphony, particularly the alexandrine, which gives even his lesser poems a stately dignity. His special sound effects tend to come from assonances and alliterations within the line rather than from innovations in rhyme or rhythm.

As regards his theories of art, though, if they were 'in the air' at the time they had not before been fixated by an intelligence comparable to Baudelaire's in keenness and imaginative scope. He saw clearly what the contemporary Art For Art's Sake movement failed to understand – that technique is not its own end but the servant of vision. Against the Realist aesthetics he maintained that beauty is a spiritual product of the imagination and not a property of some aspects of the world ('nothing of what is satisfies me'; 'the beautiful is always the effect of art'). Against the Parnassians, who had turned from the ugliness of modern civilization to seek consolation in the emotional and philosophical abstractions of Classicism, he maintained that beauty, although admittedly not of the world, must be wrought from it by a process of imaginative alchemy ('God gave me mud and I made gold of it'). In contrast to the Romantic poets, he believed that if nature can be made to appear beautiful it is as the result of the poet infusing it with his personal vision and not of his having made perfectly manifest God's presence in it. Baudelaire is one of the first poets consciously and philosophically to centre the poetic universe on man. In this he is an early 'modern'.

His preoccupation with evil is best understood in the light of his conviction that poetic vision is personal in its origin and bizarre in its effects: 'The beautiful is always bizarre.' Independently of both his belief in original sin as in the essential evil of the universe, and of the extent and nature of any private perversities, the *aesthetic* value which evil held for Baudelaire lay in the effects of strangeness and surprise that it would yield if it could be subjected to an imaginative transmutation. The presence of goodness, moreover, as what is found strange or surprising given its origin in evil, is indispensable to the dialectic of Baudelaire's alchemy. We find, accordingly, that the 'gold' of the poetry is suffused with a warm radiance. It has a moral or redemptive quality that is inseparable from its beauty and quite distinct from the didacticism against which he often protested.

In his concept of the poet as visionary or seer Baudelaire had been anticipated by Victor Hugo, and there was nothing particularly new about the idea that what the poet was gifted to 'see' and interpret for the rest of humankind was the latently visible system of universe analogy or *correspondances* placed by God in nature. On the subject of correspondences Baudelaire's thinking is at its least cogent. For one thing, his theoretical writings lump together the Fourierist doctrine of terrestrial or 'horizontal' correspondences, such as are perceived in synaesthetic experience, with the 'vertical' or transcendental correspondences linking heaven with earth and deriving from a more ancient Platonic-Augustinian tradition. Furthermore, it is hard to reconcile his aversion to nature with his adherence to either doctrine of analogy: for must nature not compel love and reverence if it is the repository of divinely appointed analogies? Finally, Baudelaire states that the interrelations between symbols (objects as terms of analogic relations), being providentially ordained, are 'mathematically exact'. But if this is the case, poetic vision loses the personal and creative character which he praises elsewhere, becoming a contemplative faculty for the revelation of a pre-ordained world-system. This 'objective' conception of analogy is not, however, carried over into his poetic practice, where we find the same sensory datum playing shifting and variable symbolic roles in response to changing mood, sometimes passing into its opposite. Images of flux and mobility, for example, are consubstantial now with spiritual decay, now with the fluid patternings of creation. Sensations of lulling and swaying render sometimes the hypnotic fascination of evil, sometimes the gentle swell of nascent creativity. The impression of deep tension combined with fluidity which much of the poetry gives depends in part on this deliberate play with polyvalent analogy.

Yet in the sphere of correspondence theory Baudelaire had an original and powerfully influential insight which survives the contradictions mentioned: that the poet's gift for apprehending analogies, a gift assisted in Baudelaire's case by a lifelong addiction to hashish, could and should be embodied in the literary devices of metaphor, simile, allegory, etc., which are thereby promoted from decorative effects to epistemological instruments for perfecting his analogic intuitions and transcribing them into a public medium. Baudelaire believed that the precision and intersubjective value of a metaphor had their explanation in the fact that, being 'drawn from the inexhaustible storehouse of universal analogy', it captures the mathematical exactness of a pre-existent analogic relation. But he could have justified the literary use of metaphor by pointing, less metaphysically, to the reality of synaesthetic experience. This would not, however, have been a perfect solution either, for while synaesthesia allows for subjective variations it leaves obscure the intersubjective value of successful poetic metaphors, the speculative explanation of which constitutes the attractiveness of the 'objective' theory.

From the technical viewpoint Baudelaire's originality undoubtedly rests on his suggestive use of language and of familiar, trivial objects to conjure up subtleties of feeling and thought. He excels in the art of suggesting the infinite through the finite, particularly the ugly. He regarded poetic language as an 'evocative bewitchment', magical in its effects, though as scientific as mathematics or music in the precision of the handling through which these are achieved: 'There is no chance in art ... the imagination is the most scientific of the faculties.' Suggestion differs from description in that what it evokes leaves 'an absence to be completed by the imagination of the listener'. Here again, technique is at the service of a personal vision of beauty, as possessing 'some slightly indeterminate quality ... leaving room for conjecture.' Baudelaire is a master of the aspect of the art of suggestion which calls for a delicate striking of the balance between an over-exact use of terms that would stultify reverie and, at the other extreme, an insufficiency of definition such as would leave the reader's imagination unstimulated and inert.

The 'new shiver' which Hugo credited Baudelaire with having brought to French poetry arises from the distinctive tonality that accrues to beauty when it is extracted from ugliness. The distillations of memory, filtered through imagination, succeed in salvaging from the thwarted aspiration to perfection a value that is limited inasmuch as impregnated with the failure on which it feeds, while yet being absolute in its suggestion of mystery and invitation to renewed spiritual voyages. One lovely species of this 'flower' arises from the granting of absolute value to what is known to be in one sense illusory: it is recognized that the mysteries of a mistress's eyes are unbacked by corresponding qualities of heart and mind; they are empty – but 'emptier and deeper than even you, O Heavens'. The pit of hell is an inverted vision of the vault of heaven.

The influence of Baudelaire cannot be overstated. He is the most important forerunner of Symbolism (**Mallarmé**), which adopted in an even more self-conscious and thoroughgoing style his notions of poetry as verbal sorcery with a strong emphasis on word-music, of the analogic value of objects and their indeterminacy as symbols, of the role of imprecision and of precision, as well as of that of the reader as active participant in the production of the poem.

Further reading

Baudelaire's complete oeuvre is collected in the Bibliothèque de la Pléiade edition (1961). His prose writings include: *La Fanfarlo* (a thinly disguised autobiographical novel); *Paradis artificiels*; *De l'essence du rire et généralement du comique dans les arts plastiques*; *L'Oeuvre et la vie d'Eugène Delacroix*; *Salon de 1846*; *Salon de 1859*; *Journaux intimes*. His *Sur la belgique* is a vituperation against what he sees as Belgian pusillanimity. There is an English edition of most of the poems of *Les Fleurs du Mal* in the original French, but with good plain prose translations and an introduction: F. Scarfe, *Baudelaire* (1962). The standard English biography is by E. Starkie, *Baudelaire* (1957). The best introduction to understanding Baudelaire's poetry is A. Fairlie, *Baudelaire* (1960). Other critical studies in English include: W.F. Leaky, *Baudelaire and Nature* (1969); P. Quennell, *Baudelaire and the Symbolists* (1954).

Among studies in French are: J. Prévost, *Baudelaire* (1953); M.A. Ruff, *L'Esprit du mal et l'esthetique baudelairienne* (1955); J. Pommier, *La Mystique de Baudelaire* (1964); J. Lonke, *Baudelaire et la musique* (1975); Richard D.E. Burton, *Baudelaire and the Second Republic: Writing and Revolution* (1991); J.A. Hiddleston, *Baudelaire and the Art of Memory* (1999); Eugene W. Holland, *Baudelaire and Schizoanalysis: The Socio-poetics of Modernism* (1993); and Rosemary Lloyd (ed.) *The Cambridge Companion to Baudelaire* (2006).

ROGER MCLURE

BEARDSLEY, Aubrey Vincent

1872–98

British illustrator and writer

Aubrey Beardsley was born in Brighton. From an early age he had tubercular tendencies and his work was often interrupted by severe attacks of haemorrhaging. As a child he was a precocious draughtsman and pianist. After attending Brighton Grammar School he took a job with a surveyor and then with the Guardian Life Assurance Company in London. He wrote verse and drama and drew in the evenings. In 1891 he introduced himself to the famous painter Burne-Jones, who was impressed by his work and who helped and encouraged Beardsley in his career as an illustrator. Beardsley began to study in particular the drawings of Mantegna, Dürer and Botticelli. He was also greatly impressed by the 'Peacock Room' **Whistler** had designed for the shipping magnate Frederick Leyland; the American artist had made especially elegant and original use of the Japanese style. Beardsley attended some evening classes at Westminster School of Art in 1892 – the only training he received. During this early period he met and was influenced by Puvis de Chavannes, became interested in Japanese prints and Greek vase decoration, became a 'Wagnerite' and was acquainted with **Oscar Wilde**.

In 1892 he received his first commission from the publisher John Dent to provide a large number of line-block illustrations to an edition of Malory's *Morte d'Arthur*. These showed the strong impact of Walter Crane, **William Morris** and Burne-Jones and yet, in their extraordinary electric and complex effects, reveal Beardsley's own powerful and individual artistic personality. In 1893 he illustrated Wilde's *Salome*, published in 1894 by The Bodley Head, which by its form and contents shocked critics and public. *The Times* reported the edition as:

> fantastic and grotesque, unintelligible for the most part, and, so far as they are intelligible, repulsive. They would seem to represent the manners of Judaea as conceived by a French décadent. The whole thing must be a joke, and it seems to us a very poor joke!

Hostility is often very accurate, at least in its empirical descriptions. In the same year Beardsley founded the *Yellow Book* with Henry Harland, and acted as art editor. In 1895 he was dismissed from the magazine by its publisher John Lane, having been implicated in the Wilde trial, and replied by founding the *Savoy* with Leonard Smithers in 1896. His other major works include illustrations to *The Lysistrata of Aristophanes* (1896), *The Rape of the Lock* (1896) and *Ben Jonson His Volpone* (1898). In 1897 Beardsley became a Catholic convert under the influence of his benefactor André Raffalovich. He died in Menton in the south of France, after chills and haemorrhaging, in 1898 at the age of twenty-five.

During his lifetime Beardsley's drawings, his friends and his habits made him a spectacular and scandalous figure. His art transforms the Romanticism of artists like Morris and Burne-Jones into a bitter and erotic fantasy. He achieved this technically by using a fine steel pen and dense black ink, with which he virtually scraped his designs into the cartridge paper. He rarely sketched preliminary studies but rather drew directly with pencil and then went over this with pen and sable brush. Most of his work was executed for photo-mechanical line-block processes. His style of dramatic black and white contrasts and an extremely fine and sinuous line varied from his early complex arts-and-crafts effects to a classical but personal art nouveau in *Salome* and finally, in *The Rape of the Lock*, to a novel reinterpretation of rococo profusion. This movement shows how far Beardsley naturally veered between extreme minimalism and a profound *horror vacui*. A disturbed but free sexuality informs almost all Beardsley's best work, even when the imagery is not explicitly erotic, and his imagery and style accurately represent the attempt by an avant-garde in English art and letters to wholly undermine Victorian morality and aesthetics. Not until Wyndham Lewis was England again to find such an ideologically subversive artist. Beardsley illustrated his own erotic prose story, *Under the Hill*, published posthumously, and this shows him to have had an original literary talent. The critic Roger Fry prophesied Beardsley's future fame as 'the Fra Angelico of Satanism'. His influence, however, was less in matters of immorality than in the visual arts and, significantly, in literature. Artists like **Léon Bakst**, **Toulouse-Lautrec**, **Paul Klee** and **Picasso** can be counted, along with Englishmen like Laurence Housman, Arthur Rackham and Eric Gill, as those directly influenced by his linear and asymmetric art. His influence has also extended to descriptive passages in the works of writers who include **D.H. Lawrence**, Ronald Firbank and **William Faulkner**. His purely formal powers as an illustrator, or perhaps interpreter, of literary texts seems to have provoked a response in many different spheres of creativity. This is the greatest testimony to his genius.

Further reading

See: Robert Ross, *Aubrey Beardsley* (1909); Brian Reade, *Aubrey Beardsley* (1967); Bridgit Brophy, *Aubrey Beardsley* (1976); Stanley Weintraub, *Aubrey Beardsley, Imp of the Perverse* (1976); Simon Wilson, *Beardsley* (1983); C. Snodgrass, *Aubrey Beardsley: Dandy of the Grotesque* (1995).

RICHARD HUMPHREYS

BEATLES, The

1962–70

British pop group

Teenage culture, which had emerged so suddenly with **Elvis Presley** as its figurehead, was widened and deepened by the Beatles, the biggest phenomenon in the history of pop music. The group, which consisted of John Lennon (1940–80, rhythm guitar), Paul McCartney (1942–, bass guitar), George Harrison (1943–2001, lead guitar) and Ringo Starr (1940–, drums), all came from Liverpool. Their first phase, that of spontaneous and hysterical idolatry, began in 1963 with the release of their second single 'Please Please Me'. Beatlemania, as it was called, gathered momentum throughout that year with the further release of 'From Me to You', 'She Loves You', 'I Wanna Hold Your Hand', each a number one hit, by which time they had passed from obscurity, through commercial success, to the point at which they were generating the most extreme fanaticism ever accorded entertainers. Like Presley, the Beatles focused adolescent energy quite abruptly, and caused a similarly radical alteration in the behaviour and appearance of young people. Unlike Presley, they wrote their own material, which was the main factor in their far greater liberating influence. Presley may have excited a rebellion but the Beatles also suggested a thousand places you might go afterwards.

As individuals too they possessed disarming intelligence. John Lennon in particular was a bravura personality. This coupled with the skill and beauty of the Lennon and McCartney songs, plus the aggressive simplicity with which they were originally performed, gave them a unique status, and they rose to the occasion so well that in the heady mood of the Swinging Sixties, at whose apex they quickly stood, they won over those establishment and parental figures who had been discomfited by the appearance of a generation which seemed to be running wild. That the Beatles were able to navigate this unprecedented adulation and continue to develop

was almost as remarkable as Beatlemania itself. They toured the world; they made two films (*A Hard Day's Night* and *Help!*) with Dick Lester, which epitomize as well as anything else the exuberant weirdness of London at the time; and they were awarded the MBE.

Beatlemania came to an end at the beginning of 1967 with the release of the single 'Penny Lane/Strawberry Fields'. Neither pop music nor avant-garde classical, this record suggested that music might go in a different direction altogether. It failed to reach the number one spot. The group had begun serious experimentation on the album *Revolver* the previous year, introducing chamber music into 'Eleanor Rigby' and electronic distortions into 'Tomorrow Never Knows', a song marking their public association with the Flower Power movement whose prime mover was **Timothy Leary**. With the release of the album *Sergeant Pepper's Lonely Hearts Club Band* in the summer of 1967, the traditional melodiousness of popular songs meshed with surreal poetry, intellectual games and strangely alluring tonal and structural inventions: pop music had boldly announced itself as a modern art form.

It was during the 1967 Summer of Love that the Beatles became involved with the Indian mystic the Maharishi Mahesh Yogi, a symptom of the growing interest in Eastern thought being taken by non-specialists. Unlike many of their contemporaries the Beatles never committed themselves wholeheartedly to the drug culture or (with the exception of George Harrison) to oriental philosophies. After *Sergeant Pepper* their albums plot the disintegration of their collective identity, brilliantly turned to account with *Abbey Road* (1969) and less well on their last *Let It Be* (1970). It was no surprise when they disbanded in 1970.

Their subsequent careers remained newsworthy. John Lennon abandoned the celebrity roundabout to live quietly in New York; he was about to get back on it when he was murdered. George Harrison had a brief explosion of creativity before falling away into good works and reclusiveness. Ringo

Starr moved to Monaco. Paul McCartney, whose subsequent career was more prosperous than that of the others, has been acknowledged in *The Guinness Book of Records* as the world's most commercially successful composer, but the new directions seen in 'Strawberry Fields' turned out to have been essentially John Lennon's and were never pursued on McCartney's own records. He has received a knighthood.

The Beatles are important for their role in providing the 'bonding' soundtracks and, on a global scale, for a decade which saw extraordinary social developments and changing attitudes. They promoted progressive causes. They encouraged people to do things for themselves in defiance of corporate interests. The corporations have since reasserted themselves but pop music has never lost the confidence in its own significance and powers which the Beatles gave to it. This has also operated retroactively so that earlier masters such as **Cole Porter** and even Noël Coward are now accorded greater respect. Indeed, the popular song can now be seen as one of the most fertile art forms of the last hundred years. It is a short cameo medium, incapable of intellectual development, but enormously flexible, particularly adept at dealing with emotion and sex. At the same time it was the Beatles who burst the boundaries of the pop song, turning it into a no-limits musical space. This fostered the instrumentally ambitious genre of 'rock' which opened up the traditional three-minute track into an extended musical ride based on strong rhythms, as well as the adoption of advanced studio electronics as a compositional resource.

Since the Beatles, notable advances in the pop field have been made by David Bowie (especially as a songwriter), the Velvet Underground and, above all, Can who seized on the rock milieu as a way of invigorating the extreme sophistication of the classical German avant-garde from which they had emerged. There has subsequently arisen a whole school of experimental music to which the old division of classical and popular can no longer be applied.

Further reading

See: Hunter Davies, *The Beatles* (1968); Chris Ingham, *The Rough Guide to the Beatles* (2003).

DUNCAN FALLOWELL

BECKETT, Samuel

1906–89

Irish novelist, playwright and poet

Samuel Beckett was born in Dublin, the second son of William Beckett (a quantity surveyor) and May Roe. He was educated at Portora Royal School, Enniskillen, and at Trinity College Dublin where he read French and Italian. He was a keen sportsman, excelling in cricket, tennis and boxing. Graduating with a first-class degree he taught at Campbell College, Belfast, then at the École Normale Supérieure in Paris 1928–30. There he became a close admirer of **James Joyce** who strongly influenced the young writer. Beckett's essay 'Dante … Bruno. Vico … Joyce', written in support of Joyce's *Finnegans Wake,* was published in the journal *Transition* (1929) along with his first prose piece 'Assumption'. In 1930 Beckett's *Whoroscope,* a long poem on time narrated by Descartes, won a competition sponsored by Nancy Cunard's Hours Press. During the summer of that year Beckett wrote a study of **Proust** (1931) in which we find the beginnings of a particular Beckettian aesthetic as well as insights on a key French novelist.

Beckett returned to Dublin to take up a lectureship in French at Trinity College, but resigned abruptly after four terms because he could not bear to teach others what he did not know himself. The year 1932 saw Beckett in Paris working on his first novel *Dream of Fair to Middling Women.* Beckett was deeply affected by his father's death in 1933. The same year his cousin Peggy Sinclair, with whom he had been close, also died. His relationship with his mother during this period was, at times, difficult and fraught. The 1930s saw Beckett in London. Depressed and ill, he undertook a course of **Jungian** psychotherapy under Wilfrid Bion of the Tavistock Clinic. He also travelled around Germany exploring modern art.

Beckett's early writing includes short stories *More Pricks than Kicks* (1934) and poems *Echo's Bones, and Other Precipitates* (1935). In 1937 he left Ireland for Paris, disaffected by the conservatism and nationalism of Irish society at the time. There he finished *Murphy*, a comic novel that plays on Descartes's mind/body dualism. Walking in Paris one December night Beckett was randomly stabbed. Recovering in hospital he renewed an acquaintance with Suzanne Deschevaux-Dumesnil who became his partner and wife. Beckett remained in Paris during the occupation of World War II. Encouraged by his friend Alfred Péron, he joined the Gloria SMH cell of the French Resistance. When the cell was betrayed to the Nazis, Beckett and Suzanne fled Paris for Rousillon where Beckett worked as a farm labourer and continued his resistance activities, for which he was awarded the Croix de Guerre. In Rousillon he finished *Watt* (1953), a novel that explores the relationship between language and reality in a narrative full of repetition and permutations. With the end of the war Beckett went to Ireland to see his mother but had difficulty re-entering France because of his Irish nationality. In order to ensure his return, Beckett volunteered for an Irish Red Cross job in St-Lô, arriving in Paris finally at the end of the year.

With the completion of *Watt* Beckett began writing in French, citing the need to write without style. Beckett's first novel in his adopted language, *Mercier et Camier,* was completed in 1946 yet published much later, in 1970. He subsequently wrote a number of short pieces ('La Fin', 'L'Expulsé', 'Le Calmant' and 'Premier amour') before turning to theatre. Beckett's first play, *Eleutheria,* was written in 1947 but never published or produced in his lifetime. The late 1940s and early 1950s were a period of intense productivity resulting in what many consider to be Beckett's finest work. Most remarkable is the trilogy of novels *Molloy, Malone meurt* and *L'Innommable,* translated as *Molloy, Malone Dies* and *The Unnamable*. The first two novels explore the difficulty of narrative progression and the impossibility of self-knowledge through a text that is acutely conscious of its own fictionality. Beckett's narrative, which begins to fragment at the end of *Malone Dies,* is further destabilized in *The Unnamable.* Written in the first person, the novel raises questions about the subjectivity of the speaking voice and the paradoxical obligation of speaking in order to be silent. *Molloy* was translated into English by Patrick Bowles with Beckett's assistance. Finding it easier to translate alone rather than revise another's work, Beckett translated *Malone Dies* and *The Unnamable* himself, producing versions that are also revisions of the original text. This inaugurated Beckett's practice of translating all subsequent work so that each work exists in the original in both English and French.

In August 1950 Beckett's mother died, followed by his brother Frank in September 1954. During this period Beckett wrote his second play, *En Attendant Godot* (*Waiting for Godot*): on a spare stage two characters debate the passage of time and the futility of action while waiting for an unknown person who never arrives. It was premiered in Paris in 1953 under the direction of Roger Blin. The play brought Beckett success and security at last. Subsequent plays, *Endgame* (1957), *Krapp's Last Tape* (1958) and *Happy Days* (1961), explore the ability to endure under hostile circumstances, and the difficulty of self-knowledge. Beckett involved himself increasingly in the production of his work, often directing the plays. He returned to prose with *How It Is* (1961), a disjointed narrative that explores love, torment and language. These works develop Beckett's distinctively spare style that strips language to its bare essentials, placing it under stress until form and content fuse. A phrase that Beckett used to describe Joyce's work becomes just as relevant to his own: 'form *is* content, content *is* form'.

Beckett married his companion Suzanne in a private ceremony in England on 25 March 1961. In 1969 he was awarded the Nobel

Prize for Literature 'for his writing, in which – in new forms for the novel and drama – the destitution of modern man acquires its elevation'. Uncontactable in Tunisia, Beckett retained a low profile, sending his French publisher Jérôme Lindon to Stockholm to accept the award. The secretary of the Swedish academy, Karl Ragnar Gierow, explained how Beckett's writing 'rises like a miserere from all mankind, its muffled minor key sounding liberation to the oppressed and comfort to those in need'.

Beckett's late plays display a minimalism and visuality that strip theatre to the basics of space, sound, bodies and movement. These include *Play* (1964), *Come and Go* (1966), *Breath* (1969), *Not I* (1973) and *Rockaby* (1981). His theatre is complemented by plays for radio and television such as *All That Fall* (1957), *Embers* (1959) and *Eh Joe* (1966). His late prose is characterized by a spare and rigorous style, including the evocative *The Lost Ones* (1970) and the powerful trilogy of short novels *Company* (1980), *Ill Seen Ill Said* (1981) and *Worstward Ho* (1983). Suffering from emphysema, Beckett spent his last years working on translations. His final work, *What is the Word?* (1988), asks a question that is fundamental to all of Beckett's writing. A year later, on 17 July, Beckett's wife Suzanne died. Beckett did not survive her long, dying on 22 December 1989. He is buried in Paris in Montparnasse Cemetery.

Further reading

There are two excellent biographies on Beckett: James Knowlson, *Damned to Fame* (1997); and Anthony Cronin, *Samuel Beckett: The Last Modernist* (1999). Jennifer Birkett and Kate Ince, *Longman Critical Readers: Samuel Beckett* (1999) contains excellent theoretical responses to Beckett's work, while Lois Oppenheim, *Palgrave Advances in Samuel Beckett Studies* (2004) contains essays that both review and advance critical approaches to Beckett's work. See also: Hugh Kenner, *Samuel Beckett: A Critical Study* (1961); Ludovic Janvier, *Beckett par lui-même* (1969); A. Alvarez, *Beckett* (1973); P.J. Murphy (ed.) *Critique of Beckett Criticism* (1994); R. Begam, *Samuel Beckett and the End of Modernity* (1996).

DERVAL TUBRIDY

BELL, Alexander Graham

1847–1922

Scottish/US inventor and entrepreneur

As with the television (see **John Logie Baird**) there was a certain inevitability about the invention of the telephone. Since the middle of the nineteenth century the telegraph had been transmitting information around the world: famously, *The Times* correspondent W.H. Russell sent dispatches from the Crimean War of 1853–6 by wire to London. A next step was to transmit the human voice itself, not just electronically encrypted words. It was Alexander Graham Bell who won the inventors' race, but only by two hours: the interval between his applying for a patent to the US Patent Office, on 14 February 1876, and his closest rival, Elisha Gray, doing the same. Subsequently it emerged that an Italian, Antonio Meucci, had successfully demonstrated a telephone at the Havana Club in Cuba as early as 1849. Meucci, however, was too impoverished to apply for a patent, and had to wait until 2002 before the US Congress passed a resolution affirming his priority – a posthumous victory resented, and sometimes contested, by Bell's latterday champions.

Bell himself had well-honed business instincts as well as the financial backing of his about-to-be father-in-law, whose deaf daughter Mabel Hubbard he married shortly after his patent was granted (on 7 March 1876). In a bid to improve his own invention he bribed a patents officer to divulge the details of Gray's application, leading to just one of several hundred lawsuits Bell became embroiled in. But in 1893 no less an authority than the US Supreme Court gave judgment in Bell's favour in a patent hearing, and thereafter Bell just was the creator of what became the world's most popular means of communication between individuals separated by distances great and small.

That Bell's wife was deaf fitted his background. His father, Alexander Melville Bell, was an educationalist who developed a sign system called 'Visible Speech' to help deaf-mutes acquire spoken language skills. The younger Bell, born in Edinburgh, taught elocution at the Weston House Academy in Elgin as a sixteen-year-old, before becoming an instructor at Somersetshire College in Bath and spending a year at Edinburgh University. But in 1870 the family, decimated by tuberculosis, moved to Canada, where Bell helped his father set up a Visible Speech centre in Montreal. Then in 1872 Bell transferred to Boston in the United States. A year later he was appointed Professor of Vocal Physiology and Elocution at Boston University. Mabel was one of his students.

Bell worked on telephony at Boston from 1874 onwards. The significant breakthrough came on 10 March 1876, almost a month after he had applied for his patent. Having set up a transmitter and two receivers, Bell heard his assistant, Thomas Watson, shuffling about in an adjoining room when the transmitter was switched off. The magnetic coils inside the receivers turned out to be two-way: not only did they convert electric current into speech, but they converted sound into electric current. At once Bell spoke the celebrated message: 'Mr Watson, come here: I want you.' Watson responded, and telephonic communication as a public utility was launched. In 1877 Bell founded the Bell Telephone Company, which after a series of mergers became AT&T (American Telephone and Telegraph Company), and which in time provided Bell with a personal fortune.

Bell worked on many other projects, though with varying success. In 1880 he patented the photophone, that used light beams to transmit non-visual data. The following year, he urgently devised the first metal detector, known as an 'induction balance', after an assassin's bullet lodged in the body of President James Garfield. Bell reckoned without the metal frame of the

Garfield's bed, however, and the president did not survive. In the same year he designed a metal vacuum jacket, a forerunner of the iron lung, after a son died of respiratory disorders. From 1886, acquiring an estate on Cape Breton Island off Nova Scotia (Canada), he spent several years experimenting with sheep, wrongly believing that a ewe's fertility is proportionate to the number of her teats. In league with **Thomas Edison**, he invented the wax recording cylinder, fundamental to the phonograph. Then, from around 1895, his interest switched to aeronautics. Although it was the Wright brothers who, in 1903, staged the first manned flight, in 1907 Bell established an Aerial Experiment Association. Among his contributions to aviation were a tricycle undercarriage, and the aileron, an adjustable wing section that acts as a stabilizer during flight. Finally, in 1919, with Casey Baldwin, Bell produced a hydrofoil that attained a water-speed of just over 70 mph – a record not broken for many years.

Bell was far more than an inventor who struck lucky. Like other Victorian entrepreneurs he gladly played the part of philanthropist, helping deaf-mutes especially. Simultaneously he exhibited what later generations regarded as a discordant interest in eugenics. In 1921, as honorary president of the Second International Congress of Eugenics, he advocated the compulsory sterilization of 'defective varieties' among the human race, including those born deaf or blind. But there was no malice in this. Rather, he was swept along by the tide of Social **Darwinism**, as were many others, believing that people as well as machines could be perfected and certain types of misery eradicated.

Further reading

See: *The Dispositions of Alexander Graham Bell* (1908); Alvin F. Harlow, *Old Wires and New Waves* (1936); R.U. Bruce, *Alexander Graham Bell and the Conquest of Solitude* (1973); Naomi Pasachoff, *Alexander Graham Bell: Making Connections* (1995); Edwin S. Grosvenor, *Alexander*

Graham Bell (1997); Struan Reid, *Alexander Graham Bell* (2000).

JUSTIN WINTLE

BELLOW, Saul

1915–2005
US novelist

Born in Quebec, Canada, of Jewish immigrant parents who moved to Chicago when he was nine, Saul Bellow attended Chicago, Northwestern and Wisconsin Universities. He has been acclaimed as an exponent of the Jewish comic story tradition and his characters seen as schlemiels; as a liberal-humanist; and as a follower of the Naturalist tradition, exploring the social forces impinging on the individual. Undoubtedly, all these are influences, plus the example of Existentialist writers, such as **Sartre**, especially upon his first novel, *Dangling Man* (1944). In his hands, however, the central theme is not nihilism versus commitment, but the need to recognize one's continuity with others and one's era. His protagonists all believe themselves to be privileged to inhabit a sphere of intellectual and spiritual freedom and regard those who occupy roles or defend boundaries with bewilderment, fascination and contempt. The comedy of Bellow's writing stems from the ironic contrast between their personalities, usually childish, sulky, ingenuous, and their pretensions to the cherished values of the Western intellectual tradition, that is: detachment from self-interest or worldly ambitions, the pursuit of self-knowledge by introspection, and aesthetic contemplation of the products of both nature and culture.

Bellow's novels raise no significant epistemological problems and break no new ground stylistically, being first-person narratives shifting between conversation, narration, journal or letter-writing and inner monologue. It is the juxtaposition of these varying perspectives which reveals the persona of the narrator, his defences and pretences. Usually the protagonists confront not only the conventional but also 'reality-instructors', people whose beliefs or behaviour point to those areas forbidden to common sense and rational scepticism. Thus, Allbee in *The Victim* (1947) confronts Leventhal with the consequences, albeit unintended, of his past actions, by blaming him for his being sacked and made unemployable. This not only challenges Leventhal's sense of superiority and his innocence, but makes him question the boundaries we normally establish between people and between our motives and our actions. Bellow's conclusion seems to be that we draw the lines arbitrarily but must take full responsibility for our choice as to where to draw them.

Henderson of *Henderson the Rain King* (1959), driven by a craving for fulfilment and significance, voyages through a surreal Africa to find a version of himself as saviour, symbol or hero. He wins the title of Rain King with the Wariri, but only slowly realizes what King Dahfu tries to tell him: that, although we choose our roles, we do so totally, for they remake our bodies and our lives. The title carries with it a function and a destiny, to be king and to be slaughtered, and from this fate Henderson flees, but not unchanged by his awareness of the reality of symbols. Similarly, Moses E. Herzog of *Herzog* (1964) blames his wife, her lover, his producer, the whole twentieth century for the dissatisfactions he feels. He wants to put himself in the position of knowing why our situation is as it is, but such a contemplative, detached awareness, brilliant though it may be, cannot solve the problems of how to act, as he finds out when he tries to murder his wife's lover. Again, the gulf to be bridged is that between ideas and their embodiment, for in isolation the mind breeds only the delusions of pride, megalomania and embittered impatience.

While Herzog's answers centred around Romanticism and Existentialism, Sammler of *Mr Sammler's Planet* (1970) has the rational humanism and elitism of **H.G. Wells** and the Bloomsbury Group. Against his experience of Auschwitz or New York in the 1960s such a perspective can only act as a defence until he can be drawn to see the same valuable human reasoning powers operating through the seemingly irrational modes of aggression, display, sexuality and even obsession and impulsiveness. The lesson here is that each intellectual or rational mode of thought must be seen as part of a historical and cultural setting rather than some timeless Platonic realm. Charley Citrine of *Humboldt's Gift* (1975) takes up this train of thought for, as a dramatist, he is offended by Humboldt's fascination with money, politics, power and historical trends, preferring the serene world of Steinerian spirituality. However, it is Humboldt, with all his quirks and failings, who provides the inspiration for Citrine's art, and he is eventually forced to accept the common origins between art and history.

Bellow won the Nobel Prize for Literature in 1976, yet seems not to have been overwhelmed by the honour. His later novels, beginning with *The Dean's December* (1982) – a portrait of a deracinated Chicago academic (Albert Corde) briefly set loose in still communist Romania – are increasingly characterized by authorial misanthropy. As the arteries hardened his defence of traditional Christo-Judaic humanism found expression in attacks on feminism, postmodernism and the 'politically correct'. In 1987 he caused controversy by asking, in a preface to his friend Allan Bloom's account of *The Closing of the American Mind*, 'Where is the Tolstoy of the Zulus?' He also became progressively disillusioned with Chicago itself, the city that forms the backdrop of most of his best work, and where he had pursued his other incarnation as an academic. Eventually, in 1993, he upped sticks and transferred to Boston University, accompanied by his fifth wife and former seminar student, Janis Friedman.

Besides the novels, Bellow wrote short stories and two plays. As one of the greatest mid to late twentieth-century American novelists, his consistent thrust was against the atomic individualism of most Western sociological and psychological thought, and to assert the continuity between mind and body, individuals and their forms of expression, whether social, aesthetic or intellectual, and between people themselves, sharing a common condition.

Further reading

Other works include: *The Victim* (1947); *The Adventures of Augie March* (1953); *Seize the Day* (1956); *The Last Analysis* (1965), a play; *To Jerusalem and Back: A Personal Account* (1976); *More Die of Heartbreak* (1986); *Something to Remember Me By: Three Tales* (1991); *It All Adds Up* (essays, 1994); *The Actual* (1997); *Ravelstein* (2000); *The Collected Stories* (2001). See: Marcus Klein, *After Alienation* (1964); Tony Tanner, *Saul Bellow* (1965); John J. Clayton, *Saul Bellow: In Defense of Man* (1968); Malcolm Bradbury, *Bellow* (1982); J. Braham, *A Sort of Columbus: The American Voyages of Bellow's Fiction* (1984); James Atlas, *Saul Bellow* (2000).

DAVID CORKER
(REVISED AND UPDATED BY THE EDITOR)

BERG, Alban

1885–1935

Austrian composer

Born in Vienna, Berg began to compose while still a teenager. From 1904 to 1910 he studied composition with **Arnold Schoenberg** and his earliest published works date from this period of his life. These early works demonstrate the gradual development of Berg's musical style from the Schumann, **Wolf** and, occasionally, **Debussy**-inspired idiom of the *Seven Early Songs* (1905–8) to the post-**Wagnerian** Piano Sonata Op. 1 (1907–8) and thence to the highly chromatic expressionism of the *Four Songs* Op. 2 (1909–10) and the String Quartet Op. 3 (1910).

By the early 1910s Berg's music, like that of his teacher Schoenberg and of his fellow pupil and life-long friend **Anton von Webern**, had reached a point at which traditional tonal criteria no longer operated. The disappearance of the tonal relationships upon which the formal designs of eighteenth- and nineteenth-century music had depended inevitably created acute structural problems. For a period both Schoenberg and Webern attempted to overcome these problems by devoting themselves, almost exclusively, to the composition of short pieces, and something of the influence of his two colleagues can be seen in the miniature forms of Berg's *Altenberg Lieder* Op. 4 (1912) and the *Four Pieces* for clarinet and piano Op. 5 (1913). Berg, however, was never really attracted to the miniature as a form of expression. His greatest and most individual achievements lie in his organizing of large-scale structure and the *Three Orchestral Pieces* Op. 6 (1914–15), which are **Mahlerian** in both size and emotional atmosphere, are more characteristic of his work.

In May 1914 Berg attended a performance of Büchner's *Woyzeck* and immediately began work on an opera based on the play. First performed under Erich Kleiber in Berlin in December 1925, *Wozzeck* established Berg as one of the foremost composers of his generation. A 'free' atonal work, completed before Schoenberg had evolved his twelve-note system, *Wozzeck* exhibits the intricate, labyrinthine formal design and that fusion of traditional and radical elements that characterize all Berg's mature music. Each of the three acts of *Wozzeck*, and each scene within each act, is designed as a self-contained unit based upon a traditional musical form, usually a form associated with 'absolute' instrumental music. Thus Act I sc. 4 is a Passacaglia, Act II sc. 1 a strict Sonata form movement, Act II sc. 2 a Fantasia and Fugue and so on. Within this structure operate both a complex leitmotiv system and a variety of intricate, predetermined compositional schemes. In *Wozzeck*, as in all Berg's music, the rigorous and highly calculated compositional techniques give rise to a work of overwhelming, and apparently spontaneous, emotional and dramatic effect. With *Wozzeck* and his subsequent works Berg, alone among the three composers of the so-called 'Second Viennese School', achieved critical and popular success, and from 1926 until 1933, when his music was banned in Germany by the Nazi party, he was able to live on his royalties.

In the last song of the *Altenberg Lieder* and in sections of *Wozzeck* Berg had employed a twelve-note theme as the basic structural element. A number of twelve-note themes also appear in the *Chamber Concerto* (1923–5). It was not until 1925, when writing the *Lyric Suite* for string quartet, however, that Berg deliberately employed (albeit in only a few of the work's six movements) Schoenberg's method of composition with twelve notes for the first time.

Berg's handling of the twelve-note technique differs radically from that of his colleagues. In the music of Schoenberg and Webern the twelve-note row is defined by interval succession; in Berg's music the note row is assumed to have other characteristics (such as melodic contour and quasi-tonal connotations) which are regarded as being as important as – and, sometimes, more important than – the interval sequence. Thus, for example, Berg frequently employs within a single work a number of different rows which are related through the common harmonic content of their various segments. Similarly, the interval succession may be modified in order to enhance the melodic or tonal relationship between different row forms.

In 1928 Berg began work on an opera based on Frank Wedekind's two *Lulu* plays, *Erdgeist* (1895) and *Die Büchse der Pandora* (1904). Work on *Lulu* was interrupted by the composition of the concert aria *Der Wein* (1929) and the Violin Concerto (1935), and Berg died having completed the opera in short score but without having finished the orchestration of Act III. The first performance of the work as a three-act opera, with the orchestration of Act III completed by Friedrich Cerha, took place in Paris in February 1979.

More complicated even than *Wozzeck* in its structural design, *Lulu* combines the vocal forms of the traditional 'number opera' with both a large-scale formal plan, in which each of the three acts is dominated by a single self-contained musical form, and an intricate network of musical, dramatic and textual cross-references. The leitmotiv system of the opera affects not only melodic and harmonic elements but is extended in such a way that it embraces twelve-note rows, rhythms, metres, instrumental colours, production details (such as the casting of performers in specific double and triple roles) and almost every other aspect of the work.

At a time when music was undergoing one of the most profound changes in its history Berg seems to have felt the need to assert the relationship between the new musical language that he and his colleagues were evolving and the great eighteenth and nineteenth-century tradition of Austro-German music. His natural lyricism, his traditional conception of thematic structure and development, his feeling for large-scale theatrical and dramatic gesture and the intense emotional atmosphere of his music all look back to the world of the late Romantics and the Mahlerian symphonic tradition. For many years Berg's critical standing rested upon the response to these apparently traditional elements and, consequently, fluctuated wildly as critical fashions changed. Thus, for example, the fact that Berg's twelve-note works employed note rows designed to give rise to melodic and harmonic formations reminiscent of those of tonal music was initially hailed by many commentators as an indication of Berg's 'innate musicality' and his lack of dogma; the same features were subsequently condemned by composers such as **Boulez** as indicating Berg's failure to understand, or at least his refusal to accept, the true structural implications of the twelve-note method.

It is now possible to appreciate that Berg's attitude to the procedures and designs of earlier music was far more ambivalent than is generally recognized and that, alongside its more obviously traditional aspects, Berg's music demonstrates a number of radical, and, indeed, revolutionary, features. While some of these features – such as his almost obsessional interest in palindromic and other complicated symmetrical structures – seem to have had a deeply personal significance, many are peculiarly relevant to more recent musical developments. Thus one can find in Berg's music constructive note rows some ten years before Schoenberg developed the twelve-note system, symmetrical arch-forms which predate those of **Bartók**, systematically applied rhythmic and durational patterns of a kind later associated with **Messiaen**, metric modulations (**Elliott Carter**), schematic metronome marks (**Stockhausen**), superimposed tempi (Stockhausen and Ligeti) and the use of elaborate numerological and other precompositional determinants that look forward to the work of **Peter Maxwell Davies** and many other contemporary composers.

Further reading

Other works include: eighteen works (although over eighty early songs remain, as yet, unpublished), the most important of which are mentioned above. All Berg's music is published by Universal Edition. About Berg: H.F. Redlich, *Alban Berg* (1957); W. Reich, *Alban Berg* (1957); Mosco Carner, *Alban Berg* (1975); and Douglas Jarman, *The Music of Alban Berg* (1979); G. Perle, *The Operas of Alban Berg* (1980–5); A. Pople, *The Cambridge Companion to Berg* (1997). See also: George Perle, *Serial Composition and Atonality* (1962); and *Alban Berg: Letters to His Wife*, edited and translated by Bernard Grün (1971).

DOUGLAS JARMAN

BERGMAN, Ernest Ingmar

1918–2007

Swedish film, theatre and television director

Ingmar Bergman was the son of a Lutheran clergyman and all his work is marked far more by spiritual anguish than by social or political concern. As a child he was fascinated by the mysterious imaginary worlds opened up by his magic lantern and toy theatre, and later he left the University of Stockholm without completing his degree to become a theatre director, first in Halsingborg, then in Gothenburg.

His work in the cinema began with the script *Frenzy* in 1944 and he made his début as a film director with *Crisis*, released in 1946. In these early films the themes of youthful despair and impotent revolt are already apparent. Bergman has always been a prolific director. He had made nine feature films and scripted five others by the time his first major work, *Summer Interlude*, appeared in 1951. From the start he shared many of the metaphysical and existentialist concerns of the new writers and artists who emerged in Sweden during the 1940s.

In the early 1950s, while simultaneously working as a stage director in Malmö, Bergman began to attract a wider audience with films like *Summer with Monica* (1952) and *Sawdust and Tinsel* (1953). The contrast of these two works – the first a simple, directly told story of a short-lived love affair, the second a complex intermixing of a circus troupe's hopes, inadequacies and humiliations shot in a totally expressionist style – points to the breadth and versatility of Bergman's style at this period. His international career began with the award-winning *Smiles of a Summer Night* (1955), an uncharacteristically light work, reminiscent of **Jean Renoir's** *La Règle du jeu*, which remains his most satisfying comedy. This opened the way to an uneven period of intense creativity, marked by a number of striking and ambitious works of which *The Seventh Seal* (1956), with its portentous symbolism, and the complexly structured *Wild Strawberries* (1957) are perhaps the most successful.

In 1961 he embarked on what was to become a major trilogy – *Through a Glass Darkly* (1961), *Winter Light* (1962), *The Silence* (1963) – which gave fresh expression to the themes of solitude, suffering, religious doubt and anxiety which had haunted his work up to this point. Bergman's developing relationships with his players were always crucial to his work and, in both theatre and film, he constantly used the same small group of performers in leading roles. In the 1950s and early 1960s his style continually changed so as to capture the specific qualities of his

actors, Gunnar Bjornstrand and Max von Sydow, and, more especially, his actresses: Harriet Anderson, Eva Dahlbeck, Bibi Andersson and Ingrid Thulin. From 1963 to 1966 he deepened his theatrical involvement by taking on the post of head of the Royal Dramatic Theatre in Stockholm. Then, with *Persona* in 1966, he began a deeply personal exploration of the problems of human communication which, through *Hour of the Wolf* (1966), *The Shame* (1967) and *A Passion* (1969) to *Cries and Whispers* (1972), featured the Norwegian-born actress Liv Ullman.

Subsequently Bergman turned away to some extent from the mainstream of Swedish cinema – a departure hastened by allegations of tax fraud that encouraged him to move to Munich. Although the allegations proved false, he remained in Germany, where much of his energy was channelled into theatre direction, as well as scriptwriting for other directors. *The Magic Flute* (1974) is a film version of his own production of the Mozart opera. Equally, he turned towards television. *Scenes from a Marriage* (1973) and *Face to Face* (1975) both began life as television dramas, before being re-edited for the cinema. Four German-made features – *The Serpent's Egg* (1977), *Autumn Sonata* (1978), *From the Life of the Marionettes* (1980) and *After Practice* (1982) – preceded what Bergman declared would be his last film, the explicitly autobiographical and uncharacteristically tender *Fanny and Alexander* (1982), which won him an Academy Award for the Best Foreign Language Film. This was followed by further television dramas, including *Karen's Face* (1986), *In The Presence of a Clown* (1997) and *Saraband* (2003), which in its film version won widespread critical acclaim.

Bergman's earlier career particularly has been amongst the most significant in modern European cinema. Until the 1970s he resisted the lure of international co-production and rooted his work firmly in the context of Swedish life and culture. In the 1950s and 1960s he established the concept of the film-maker as a self-conscious artist in quite a new way for a whole generation of critics and film directors. Unsurprisingly, he was consistently hailed as one of cinema's premier *auteurs*. His work was always deeply personal – reflecting the joys and contradictions of an emotional life marked by no fewer than six marriages. In the 1960s and early 1970s he pioneered a form of intensely, even painfully, direct expression of these themes in a pared-down, brilliantly controlled yet innovative style which confirmed his status as a filmmaker of the very first rank. That Bergman himself said toward the end of his life that he was no longer able to watch the films that established his international reputation is testament of their rare capacity to disturb their audiences at the deepest psychological level.

Further reading

Bergman's other films are: *It Rains on Our Love* (1946); *A Ship to India* (1947); *Night is My Future* (1948); *Port of Call* (1948); *Prison/The Devil's Wanton* (1949); *Thirst* (1949); *To Joy* (1950); *This Can't Happen Here* (1950); *Waiting Women* (1952); *A Lesson in Love* (1954); *Journey into Autumn* (1955); *So Close to Life* (1958); *The Face/The Magician* (1958); *The Virgin Spring* (1960); *The Devil's Eye* (1960); *Now About These Women* (1964); one episode in *Stimulantia* (1967); *The Rite* (1969); *Faro Document* (1970); *The Touch* (1970). See also: *Bergman on Bergman* (1973); Jörn Donner, *The Personal Vision of Ingmar Bergman* (1964); Robin Wood, *Ingmar Bergman* (1969); John Simon, *Ingmar Bergman Directs* (1972); Stuart M. Kaminsky (ed.) *Ingmar Bergman: Essays in Criticism*; and Ingmar Bergman, *Images: My Life in Film*, trans. Marianne Ruuth (1994).

ROY ARMES
(REVISED AND UPDATED BY THE EDITOR)

BERLIN, Irving

1888–1989

US popular composer

Irving Berlin was a parable of America and seems to span the vast space between pre-modernity and the late twentieth century. Born in the Russian Pale, he began life as a peasant and ended it the multi-millionaire Sutton Place recluse, his last, possibly misanthropic years thereby casting something of a Citizen Kane question mark over the entire enterprise, although much earlier, when asked what was Berlin's place in American music, his fellow-songwriter Jerome Kern supposedly replied, 'Irving Berlin has no place in American music. He *is* American music.' Berlin's family left Russia in 1893 for New York, where the father worked as a cantor and in a kosher abbatoir but died in 1901. Young Israel Baline supported the family by selling newspapers and by leaving it early. He soon by transferring his eye for a headline to his way of selling and later composing a song became, by stages and with little education, street busker, singing waiter, staff lyricist with song publisher Ted Snyder, composer and publisher of his own songs, musical theatre impresario, and theatre and publishing company owner.

Berlin epitomizes Tin Pan Alley, the song-plugging place (a music publishers' section of New York's 28th Street) and system of the early twentieth century. He helped bring popular song to the point at which brash topicality and *chutzpah* would subsume Victorian gentility into an irresistible product that on stage or screen in the American musical proved equal to the full range of bourgeois emotion and topic. 'White Christmas', first heard by millions as sung by Bing Crosby in the film *Holiday Inn* in the second year of America's Second World War, still ranks as the commercially most popular song of all time; *Annie Get Your Gun* (1946) as the Broadway musical with the greatest number of hit tunes (including 'You Can't Get a Man with a Gun', 'There's No Business like Show Business', 'Anything You Can Do'); 'God Bless America' (1938) as an unofficial national anthem; 'Alexander's Ragtime Band', not a ragtime song (though Berlin wrote plenty), as the emblem of America's demotic triumph before, during and after the First World War, its catchiness the perfect embodiment of jazz-age compulsion in rhythm and speech, speech which for Berlin had been solely Yiddish until he was five.

It should not be forgotten that Berlin sang as well as wrote, with a small but unmistakably cantorial voice that helps define the popular address in his songs and represents the shift in emotional sensibility that mass immigration afforded urban entertainment. His army shows, *Yip, Yip, Yaphank* (1918) and *This is the Army* (1942), had him seen and heard in person on the stage, the little man of ordinary America expressing, unlike **Chaplin**, not bewilderment but good-humoured conviction. 'Oh, How I Hate to Get Up in the Morning' penetrated the private's mindset; its performance could be started solo and finished by thousands as Berlin toured the camps. Berlin never learnt to read music, played the piano apparently only in F sharp major, and had no musical style as such; yet his melodies, instantly memorable, command harmonic depth, just as his songs overall embody a perfect relationship between their vernacular words, notes and scenarios. 'Cheek to Cheek', one of his numbers for *Top Hat* (1935), perhaps the best of the Fred Astaire and Ginger Rogers films, is as glorious a match for their dancing as is 'A Couple of Swells' (*Easter Parade*, 1948) for the vaudeville precision of Astaire and Judy Garland. Altogether, Berlin was one of the most extraordinary twentieth-century artists.

Further reading

A six-volume selection of Berlin's songs (1991) is usefully divided into 'Novelty', 'Movie', 'Broadway', 'Patriotic', 'Ballad' and 'Ragtime and Early' volumes. The three volumes of collected early songs (1907–14) in the *Music of the United States of America* series (*MUSA* II, 1994) is as important for the editor Charles Hamm's masterly introduction as for the texts themselves. *Annie Get Your Gun* is available in piano/vocal score. Robert Kimball has edited *The Complete Lyrics of Irving Berlin* (2001). For biographies and critical studies see Laurence Bergreen: *As Thousands Cheer: The Life of Irving Berlin* (1990), Charles Hamm: *Early Berlin: Songs from the Melting Pot* (1997), Mary Ellin Barrett: *Irving Berlin: A Daughter's Memoir* (1994) and Ian Whitcomb: *Irving Berlin and Ragtime America* (1988).

STEPHEN BANFIELD

BERLIN, Sir Isaiah

1909–97

English academic intellectual

Isaiah Berlin was the most famous English academic intellectual of the post-Second World War era, an outstanding lecturer, peerless conversationalist and superlative essayist. His career began in pure philosophy but he became interested in the history of ideas, especially those thinkers who claimed – falsely in his view – to offer a comprehensive view of human purposes. He had a genius for expounding empathetically the plausibility of such thinkers, even those he detested, and for evoking the relationship of character to ideas, but always to expose the danger to freedom and human diversity of all ideologists who claim to have, or to lead towards, a single goal or truth. To Berlin the plurality of human beliefs has to be accepted. Philosophy no more than brute force can resolve conflicts of values. His pluralism was not an uncritical exaltation of variety, still less the postmodern cynicism of 'anything goes'; rather he articulated the recurrent pain, at times the tragedy, of knowing that whatever values we pursue are always at some cost to other values, and often to other people. To be humane and tolerant and to act honourably we must know both our own limitations and appreciate the almost boundless oddity of others.

He was born in Riga, Latvia, the only child of a prosperous timber merchant. His parents were secular but his grandparents were pious Chabad Hasidim. He grew up speaking Russian and German. The family moved in 1915 from Riga to Andreapol, and on to Petrograd in 1917 of which he had vivid memories. In 1921 his parents left for England. He was put to school at St Paul's, studying classics but picked up French as well, achieving a greater linguistic range and proficiency than most of his Oxford contemporaries. In 1932 he won a prize fellowship to All Souls, and became a fellow of New College in 1938.

His promise as a philosopher was clear in that he became one of a small circle, convened by **J.L. Austin** which included **A.J. Ayer** who met to discuss the purest problems of the new analytical philosophy. After the war he hinted with good humour that while this activity was probably important and very exhilarating, it was no longer for him. He had become interested in the history of ideas that either shape historical events or how we perceive them.

Even in his Oxford analytical phase, he had written in 1939 a short, lucid and judicious *Karl Marx: His Life and Environment* (1939). It was the first remotely objective account of what **Marx** had actually said, who he was, why he said it, his Hegelian roots and his Jewish ethos. The book was, with austere provocation, only about Marx, ignoring Marxism and international Communism. Berlin's critique of determinism was already clear and firm, but not laboured. He always had the good manners to enjoy unlikely company and to draw out, not to put down or caricature, interesting people, whether living or dead, whose ideas he thought quite wrong-headed.

He spent the war in New York and then at the British Embassy in Washington sending despatches on American opinion, read and much admired by **Churchill**. And for a few months at the end of 1945 he was in the embassy at Moscow. There he met semi-clandestinely **Boris Pasternak** and the great poet Anna Akhmatova, and later wrote a memorable account of their conversations about Russian literature and the condition of writers under **Stalin**. Akhmatova in her isolation was to attach an exalted, almost a crazed significance, to their meeting: art and intelligence could rise above and annul all political oppression universally. The encounter affected Berlin greatly. To his natural gaiety, literary facility, vanity and pyrotechnic intellectuality was added a deep moral seriousness.

When he returned to Oxford he had re-read **Tolstoy's** *War and Peace* and plunged deeply into the Russian novelists, poets and social thinkers of the mid-nineteenth century. 'Their approach seemed to me essentially moral: they were concerned most deeply with what was responsible for injustice, oppression, falsity in human relations, imprisonment whether by stone walls or conformism – unprotesting submission to manmade yokes – moral blindness, egoism, cruelty, humiliation, servility, poverty, helplessness, despair, on the part of so many.' So he turned his back on analytical philosophy; but with a mind sharpened by those ultra-intelligent mental exercises, he evoked the dilemmas inherent in great or hitherto obscure but interesting figures in the history of ideas.

His inaugural lecture as Chichele Professor of Social and Political Theory was on 'Two Concepts of Liberty'. It has provoked lasting debate on both sides of the Atlantic. Many called it at the time, 'a classic restatement of English liberalism'. But that was only a half-truth. Few recognised the more pessimistic tones of Russian nineteenth-century liberalism, quite different to **J.S. Mill's** optimistic rationalism. Its manner became the hallmark of all his writing. He could be and was read by both academics and general intellectuals – he joked against himself that he was 'a general intellectual, by analogy to "general domestic"; will tackle anything', for he affably ignored the rigid disciplinary boundaries of English academic life. He combined rhetoric with analytical rigor in an unusual but characteristic way.

Essays flowed out and honours flowed in thick and fast. He had twenty-three honorary doctorates and in 1971 came the Order of Merit. He willingly served on numerous time-consuming scholarship, fellowship and award committees in Britain, the USA and Israel, enjoying meeting the rising stars of each generation, asking them searching, interesting questions – and often immediately answering them himself.

His bibliography is confused because he rewrote speeches and essays for different occasions, and published some in different collections with varying titles and some repetition and revision. But basically there are four books: *Karl Marx*; *Four Essays on Liberty* (1969), *Vico and Herder* (1976) and *The Magus of the North: J.G. Harmann and the Origins of*

Modern Irrationalism (1993). However more typical and more important are the seven volumes of his widely ranging essays carefully edited by his friend Henry Hardy – history of ideas, political philosophy, Russian thinkers, studies of contemporaries etcetera.

He loved England as often only émigrés can and he appeared so very English, and it was 'England' almost too specifically, he never spoke or wrote of Great Britain or the United Kingdom, and had no interest in Scottish, Welsh or Irish literature. He was aware that the Scottish enlightenment of David Hume and Adam Smith was part of the history of British empiricism, but on neither did he write, nor ever on Edmund Burke. Almost too English, in this sense, but also so naturally cosmopolitan, always introducing forgotten or misunderstood continental figures, especially those who had thought on a continental scale.

The speed and restlessness of his thinking made the essay his métier, not the book, never the monograph. He was brilliantly evocative and empathetic, but much of his writing is dramatic evocation, not explanation. The twists and turns of 'the crooked timber of humanity', a phrase of Kant he made his own, were not capable of explanation, in any strict sense, only of understanding. He wrote for intellectuals more than for disciplinary scholars. He evoked the plausibility of ideas and the characters of their protagonists, especially those that threaten freedom. He was a humanist who believed that morally the happiness and dignity of individuals counts more than the pride and power of nations or ethnic groups. He was a Zionist, indeed, but not so much because he was Jewish, but because Jews were persecuted and thus needed, contingently not in principle, the protection of a national home. Yet he had a darker view of human nature than liberals who thought that goodwill and the UN could achieve a peaceful coexistence in the Middle East without paying a heavy price. We cannot live without group identities, hence his interest in Herder and the German romantics; but individuals can and sometimes should take on other identities, or challenge dominant beliefs of their group in the name of freedom.

'Two Concepts of Liberty' (first published in *Four Essays on Liberty*, 1969) distinguished between negative and positive liberty, and argued that to seek to go beyond negative liberty – that is freedom from restraint – into positive liberty – that is freedom as achieving some positive good – is politically dangerous, morally dubious and even logically self-contradictory. Positive liberty is when I *feel* more free when I know the truth ('the truth shall set you free') or am serving a just cause. But all such 'freedoms' involve direct restrictions on others, a certainty that their values or views are false – as in Rousseau's 'forcing people to be free'. There are often good reasons for restricting freedom but let us recognize, he said, that to do so is not to increase freedom. Freedom is a basic human value, but not the only value. It may be right and just that I should be taxed so that you do not starve; but do not say that either of us is then positively free, otherwise the price of restraining freedom is not even recognized.

If he was a libertarian, it was in the sense that the protection of negative freedom is a necessary condition of any just social order; but it is never a sufficient condition, as the market liberals tried to argue. Like **Popper**, his views on social policy were pragmatic, though both were misrepresented by socialist critics. 'Where does he stand?', some asked scathingly. He stood as definitive critic of single-truth systems of thought and systematic ideologies; but with their threat diminished, some of his finest writings may loose the bite of relevance they once had.

Perhaps more lasting will be his understanding of pluralism, but it is not a comfortable one. He was not a relativist. Some values are universal, like freedom and science; and some value systems threaten or distort both. Nonetheless we live in a world of diverse values, not all of them equally pleasing for good reason, but which we can, with knowledge and empathy, understand; and are then able to build tolerant compromises.

Further reading

Other works include: an anthology of 'the best of Berlin' see *The Proper Study of Mankind* ed. Herny Hardy & Roger Hausheer (1997). Michael Ignatieff, *Isaiah Berlin: A Life* (1999) is both an intimate and brilliant biography. See also: Alan Ryan ed., *The Idea of Freedom: essays in honour of Isaiah Berlin* (1979); Ramin Jahanbegloo, *Conversations with Isaiah Berlin* (1992); John Gray, *Isaiah Berlin* (1995).

SIR BERNARD CRICK

BERNERS-LEE, (Sir) Timothy

1955–

English computer scientist

Of all the great inventions, intellectual and practical, of the late twentieth century, perhaps none surpass in general application, speed of adoption or influence on how we can think more than the world wide web. The creator of this medium was Tim (now Sir Tim) Berners-Lee. Born in London, he gained his degree in computer science from the University of Oxford in 1976. His parents were pioneers among computer scientists who had worked on the first commercial computer, the Ferranti mark 1, so computing was in his blood.

While working as a computer scientist for CERN (the European Council of Nuclear Research) in 1989, Berners-Lee suggested a simple way of managing and sharing information using computers and the already familiar internet. His proposal was essentially a form of hypertext, not that dissimilar to a proposal of Gordon Licklader ('Main-Computer Symbiosis', 1960), Ted Nelson's project Xanadu and Gordon Pask's *Entailment Meshes for Knowables*. But Berners-Lee's proposal differed in four respects: he saw this as free (in the hacker tradition), something that would exist democratically, without charge and between all possible machines; he understood that rather than copying material from one machine to another, material should remain resident on one machine only but be viewable to any others; he realized that access had to be from the user's end,

rather than by being sent; and he was a computer scientist who could construct the code to make it work.

Joined in 1990 by Robert Cailliou, he set about constructing a general-purpose set of computer protocols (hypertext transfer protocols – http) and commands (hypertext mark-up language – html) that could be interpreted into a local version suitable for particular computers (or, more exactly, their operating systems). The outcome, first demonstrated in the 1991 CERN telephone directory, was a way of communicating between individual machines over the internet such that material stored on machines located anywhere on the internet could be woven into any web of interconnections the user wanted. Hence, the world wide web – www: a map stored in Helsinki could be called into position by a document being written in Melbourne, made visible through a virtual window looking from Melbourne into the Helsinki computer.

This singular achievement finally freed the computer from its role of super-calculator that **Babbage** had envisioned to become the sort of communication enhancer early cyberneticians and later visionaries in the entertainment world (especially **Steve Jobs** at Apple) had begun to imagine. The computer becomes ubiquitous and all-pervasive rather than being a specialist piece of equipment. The (world wide) web became, through accident of timing and excellence of implementation, the standard medium for doing almost everything on the internet. Specialized activities, such as email, remained separate, although they could be handled through the world wide web by web-browser. (The first web-browser, Mosaic, was created by Mark Andreesson in 1993.) With the world wide web, the internet became a public forum, a place in which even under-resourced people could gain access to anything placed there.

Berners–Lee's achievement in creating the web (recognized by a knighthood, and the first Millennium Technology Prize) is remarkable enough. Its effect can be seen not only in its all-pervasiveness and universality, but in how it has entered our consciousness: the web, in the form Berners-Lee made, has enormously expanded the ways we can conceive the world we find ourselves in.

At the most basic level, the web allows access to a vast quantity of knowables (to use Pask's term). The democratic basis that allows anyone to publish anything without censorship raises difficult questions concerning how we understand the status of the knowable and its relationship to any world we may wish to describe, at least given how we currently think about it. It has allowed enormous industries to grow where previously censorship restrained them (e.g. notably pornography), which infuriates many and may create a shift in morality some welcome and others resist. It has provided a new way of selling. It allows us to visit many places without going there vicariously. And it encourages us to think quite differently about place, space and time – and such social activities as the practice of friendship. It permits us to access the previously inaccessible (driving the Mars rover) and to become part of a massive global computer that can tackle inconceivable problems through borrowing processors on computers that are resting, distributing tasks among them.

The world wide web also requires us to rethink what it means to be a human who knows others and who knows the world: it is an epistemological conundrum. It has changed how we can think of ourselves. Perhaps its most important aspect is what Berners-Lee has done – and not done – with it. In agreement with CERN, the code that makes the web possible was released to anyone who wanted it: it is, in the best hacker tradition, free. Whereas other major programmers such as **Bill Gates** have fought to keep possession of their code, Berners-Lee has wanted his to belong to everyone. Nor does he want to determine where the web should go, but to protect its openness and free availability to all. The world wide web consortium (W3C, run out of MIT where Berners-Lee is professor), which he chairs, provides guidelines

that arise from how the web is being used and what people propose. This is a framework that allows. The consortium tries to keep the intentions clear and clean. It is not always possible, but the web remains a good and free place that stubbornly resists those such as moralizing politicians and self-appointed evangelists who wish to own or otherwise control it. The web is not just a technology that creates opportunities and questions: it is also an example of a deeply held ethical belief in the value of being human and in making what we can, well.

Further reading

See: Tim Berners-Lee, with Michael Fischetti, *Weaving the Web* (1999).

RANULPH GLANVILLE

BERNSTEIN, Leonard
1918–90
US conductor and composer

At the time of his death there was reason to call Bernstein the best-known modern musician, for his crossover success between international maestro, mass music educator and composer of perhaps the most iconic musical ever, *West Side Story* (1957), was on a unique scale, altogether making for a larger and more sustainable public reach than Paderewski's popular pianism at one end of the century, a pop idol's media domination at the other, or the liberal obeisance commanded by conductors and composers such as Toscanini, Karajan and **Copland** in the middle. Since then, while Bernstein's name and personality may have faded somewhat – posthumous promotion has been modest – it has been less possible than might have been predicted to say that the achievement was shoddy; if anything, his work begs to be taken more seriously.

Darling of the liberal New York establishment, Bernstein and his conquests make for heady columns of addition. The USA, unlike Britain, has never resented the advantages of the best education that money or talent can procure, and the young man's success as he made his stormy way through Harvard, the Curtis Institute in Philadelphia, and the hair of several senior conductors (Reiner, Koussevitzky, Mitropoulos and Rodzinski) was not to be doubted, in many ways more that of the nineteenth-century Romantic musician than could have been accommodated in twentieth-century Europe. Appointed assistant conductor of the New York Philharmonic Orchestra at the age of twenty-five, he sprang to fame when he deputized for Bruno Walter at short notice in a broadcast concert in November 1943, and as a conductor never once looked back. The NYPO was his for over a decade, and then for life as 'laureate conductor'; he was the first American to conduct at La Scala (*Medea* with Maria Callas), found his spiritual home with the Israel Philharmonic and, most extraordinarily for this unexampled Jewish extrovert, was taken to heart by the Vienna Philharmonic with its anti-Semitic legacy. A brilliant pianist, he could join the ranks of executant virtuosi such as Barenboim and Zukerman, yet this talent remained in service to his role as educator, not just before an international public on television but with academic plausibility when he gave the Charles Eliot Norton lectures at Harvard in 1973, published as *The Unanswered Question*.

As a composer and, indeed, as public figure it would be too easy to write Bernstein off as facile mouthpiece of the *Zeitgeist*, as the spoilt celebrity consorting with the Black Panthers in radical chic solidarity, flaunting a chaotic personal lifestyle (probably only the exercise of conducting kept him living as long as he did), holding on to superannuated youth with the hippy sensibility of *Mass* (1971), and charting a course of existentialist *angst* through his three symphonies, the *Jeremiah* (1942), *The Age of Anxiety* (1949) and the *Kaddish* (1963), this last posthumously dedicated to **John F. Kennedy**, with whom Bernstein's charisma was naturally linked. 'Kennedy was accident-prone,' wrote Colin Wilson of the *Kaddish*, 'but nothing as bad as this happened to him while he was alive.' Bernstein certainly lacked taste, but much of his output may seem more, not less, palatable as the manners of his time are overlaid with others and his ongoing concerns are appreciated for the personal odyssey that they undoubtedly were. His work for the musical theatre bears closer scrutiny: the miniature opera *Trouble in Tahiti* (1951) was much later incorporated into the agonized *A Quiet Place* (1983), that opera's title epitomizing something of the quest sensed also in *West Side Story*, the ballets *Fancy Free* (1944) and *Facsimile* (1946), and the superb film score for *On the Waterfront* (1954). Bernstein's personal style, eclectic though it was, never falters and indeed develops through these works, for all their instability, a challenging monument to a heroic, sometimes tragic muse. Nor should it be forgotten that he knocked the Broadway tradition into a cocked hat with his musicals, never once prey to the conventions of the 32-bar tune throughout *On the Town* (1944), *Wonderful Town* (1952), *West Side Story* and *Candide* (1956), any more than to the English choral tradition in the *Chichester Psalms* (Chichester Cathedral, 1965), yet in both cases satisfying his public with little resistance.

Musicals have never been the same since *West Side Story*. Whether *1600 Pennsylvania Avenue* (1976), a soul-searching history of the USA and its presidency misjudged for the bicentennial, will eventually find its place on the American stage is less easy to predict. It is not currently possible for white Jews to speak for black slaves; Bernstein and his librettist Alan Jay Lerner tried to.

Further reading

Most of Bernstein's musical works are available in score, the theatre pieces not only in the standard piano/vocal format but, unusually, *West Side Story* and *Candide* in full orchestral score (Boosey and Hawkes edition, 1994). The most comprehensive biography is Humphrey Burton, *Leonard Bernstein* (1994); Joan Peyser, *Leonard Bernstein* (1987), is more sensationalist. There is not yet an authoritative study of his music. Bernstein's writings, especially *The Joy of Music* (1954, expanded 1959) and *The Unanswered Question* (1976), are important. Many of his recordings are still available.

STEPHEN BANFIELD

BEUYS, Joseph

1921–86

German sculptor

Like **Warhol**, Beuys constructed his own legend as his career took shape. Before the 1960s, therefore, the facts of his life are hotly debated. As promulgated by the artist himself, they can be summarized as follows. At the age of seven he moved from Kleve to Rindern but ran away to join a travelling circus, performing as an escapologist. In the Second World War he served first as a radio operator, then a combat pilot, was injured five times and nearly died in 1943 when his plane crashed in the Crimea and he was rescued in a snowstorm after German search parties had given up hope. Tartars took him to their tents, covered his body in fat and wrapped him in felt. Three years later he returned to Kleve and throughout the 1950s worked on a farm there, in a state of profound mental disturbance caused by the war. After working on a zoological film with the naturalist Heinz Sielmann, he enrolled at the Düsseldorf Academy under Ewald Mataré, who passed on to him a commission for a church door for Cologne Cathedral.

In 1961 Beuys was appointed Professor of Monumental Sculpture at the Academy, and between 1962 and 1965 was closely involved with Fluxus, a group of international neo-Dadaists dedicated to collective activity. Gradually his work became more overtly political. Teaching and forming groups was important: the German Student Party (1967), the Organization for Direct Democracy (1970), the Organization for Non-Voters and Free Referendum (1970) and the Free University (1977). In 1972, however, he was sacked from his teaching position. A six-year lawsuit followed. At last Beuys won his case for wrongful dismissal against Johannes Rau, Minister for Science and Research for Northern Westphalia. By the end of the 1970s his political aspirations had intensified; in 1979, the year of his great retrospective at the Guggenheim Museum, New York, Beuys stood for election to the European Community Parliament.

Despite the fiasco at Düsseldorf Beuys's title of 'monumental sculptor' describes his achievement well; the balance between 'public' issues and more private 'artistic' concerns, maintained for twenty-five years, served to sketch a theory of sculpture as activity, demonstration and social comment, with no sacrifice of aesthetic power. His art arises naturally from the testing of his world view and the fictionalization of incidents in his life. Operating in every conceivable mode, he employs an unsystematic personal mythology – rooted in the folkloristic and scientific strains of German Romantic thought – to redress failure of intuition and spiritual awareness in an era of disintegrating capitalist values. If topics of world importance are tackled, they are dealt with obliquely. A felt-covered piano is devised for pieces composed by thalidomide children. He suggested that the Berlin Wall be raised five centimetres 'for aesthetic reasons'. Beuys's technique may resemble a more obviously political version of Duchamp's ready-mades; he creates a bone radio or an earth telephone, or constructs his *Fond* series, as batteries which do not work. And, like Duchamp, he rises to levels of precarious, perhaps confused, allegory. Invited to design sets for *Iphigenie* and *Titus Andronicus* at the Frankfurt Theatre Festival in 1969, Beuys offered to perform them simultaneously instead. On a stage with chalk diagrams and scores for the performance, Beuys, dressed at first in a white fur coat, recited *Iphigenie* while behind him a white horse stood on a sheet of iron. Over loudspeakers actors recited a montage of both plays, while Beuys repeated a set of gestures, reading lines and moving away, making flying movements, feeding sugar to the horse, crouching, measuring his head in both hands, making animal noises and spitting margarine into an empty area of the stage. In *I Like America and America Likes Me* Beuys was blindfolded, flown to New York, taken in an ambulance to the gallery and locked in a cage for a week with a wild coyote, armed only with a felt blanket, a stick and a triangle, gloves and, every day, fifty copies of the *Wall Street Journal*. The coyote, revered by the Red Indian as a shape-changer, was despised by the White Man and reduced to the level of a trickster. By making friends with the coyote and adopting his way of life temporarily Beuys attempted to make contact with what he regarded as an American trauma. In both *Aktionen* the physical manifestation meshed with Beuys's own complex theories – explained more directly by the artist in his *Energy Plan for Western Man* lectures – yet the visual impact was undiminished. Remembering *Iphigenie*, wrote the playwright Peter Handke, 'an excited state of stillness comes over me – it activates me; it is so painfully beautiful that it becomes Utopian, and that means political.'

Even without his physical presence Beuys's sculpture speaks eloquently of the social significance of the act of its making. *Tallow*, created for an outdoor site in Münster, resulted from filling a huge useless area in a badly designed concrete underpass. A ply-wood mould was made and twenty tons of mutton fat – plus a little beef fat for firm-ness – was melted and poured in. It took three months to cool and was cut into five great sections, like icebergs. *Honey-Pump* at Documenta 6 in Kassel in 1977 was in action for the hundred days of the Free University. Two ships' engines pumped two tons of honey through plastic pipes connect-ing every room in the building. Honey, fat, felt – however unfamiliar his strategies, Beuys's compulsive repetition of materials, his desire to inject significance into every aspect of the surrounding world – even his clothes – are reminiscent of the story of the airman who returned to life. Beuys became a survival artist, intent on showing others how to go on living.

Further reading

See: G. Adriani, W. Konnertz and K. Thomas, *Joseph Beuys* (1970); Caroline Tisdall, *Joseph Beuys* (Solomon R. Guggenheim Museum, 1979); H. Szeeman (ed.) *Beuys* (exhibition catalogue, 1993).

STUART MORGAN

BIN LADEN, Osama

1957–

Saudi Islamist, leader of Al Qaida

Born in Jiddah, Saudi Arabia, to Muhammad Awad bin Laden – a South Yemeni brick-layer who became Saudi Arabia's leading construction magnate – and Alia Hamida Ghanoum, Osama bin Laden completed his secondary education at an elite high school in 1974, and graduated in civil engineering four years later.

After visiting Peshawar, Pakistan, in 1980, he successfully raised large donations from his relatives and friends for the anti-Soviet struggle in Afghanistan, and returned to Pakistan with several Afghan and Pakistani employees of the Saudi Binladin Group, owned by his family. Working with Pakistan's Inter-Services Intelligence (ISI) and the US Central Intelligence Agency (CIA), which oversaw the conduct of the anti-Soviet campaign, he opened an office to support non-Afghan *mujahedin* (jihadists).

He collaborated with Abdullah Azzam, a Palestinian Islamist ideologue, who in 1984 established the Maktab al Khidmat (Bureau of Service) for the non-Afghan *mujahedin* in Peshawar. Bin Laden vetted non-Afghan volunteers and sent them to one of the con-stituents of the Afghan Mujahedin Alliance for training, supervised the construction of roads and the refurbishing of caves for storing weapons in the Mujahedin-controlled areas, and participated in guerrilla actions and armed encounters.

In 1986 he oversaw the construction of a tunnel complex at Zhwahar Killi near the Pakistani border, to house a training centre, weapons store and medical facility with electricity and piped water.

When the Soviets left Afghanistan in February 1989, he declared it to be a victory for the Islamic *jihad* (holy struggle). Following the assassination of Azzam, his intellectual mentor, in November, he resolved to run Maktab al Khidmat under the new title of Al Qaida ('The Base') with the aim of creating an international network of *jihadis*, those who had participated in the successful anti-Soviet *jihad*.

Frustrated by the internecine violence among the victorious Afghan Mujahedin, centred round ethnic differences, bin Laden returned to Jiddah in the spring of 1990. In Saudi Arabia his taped speeches became best-sellers.

Following Iraq's invasion of Kuwait in August, he offered the authorities a plan to defend the kingdom by mobilizing citizens and his veteran *mujahedin*. They rejected the offer. He disapproved of the stationing of over half a million Western troops – predominantly American – on Saudi soil. When, after the end of the Gulf War in February 1991, many thousands of US soldiers stayed on, he protested vehemently.

Soon after he flew to Pakistan and then to Sudan, ruled by an Islamist military government. In Khartoum he set up several varied businesses. During his five years there, Al Qaida's policy-making Shura Council of twelve was served by four committees: military, business, Islamic studies, and media and public relations. He continued to attack the presence of infidel troops on Saudi Arabia's holy soil and the Saudi regime.

He waged the anti-American *jihad* by financing directly Al Qaida's terrorist actions and sponsoring like-minded groups abroad and training their activists at Al Qaida camps in Sudan. Al Qaida established associate relationships with jihadist groups in Algeria, Chechnya, Egypt, Ethiopia, Lebanon, Libya, Philippines, Syria and Yemen, and maintained guesthouses in different countries.

In 1992–3, bin Laden intervened in the civil war in Somalia, with Al Qaida's military chief Muhammad Atef supervising the training of the Somali tribes opposed to the United Nations intervention in the conflict. In 1994

the Saudi government revoked his citizenship and froze his assets of $20–25 million. There was an unsuccessful attempt on his life. He established the Committee for Advice and Reform with the purported aim of promoting peaceful reform in Saudi Arabia, which opened an office in London.

To see its name removed from Washington's list of states that support international terrorism, Sudan's government agreed in early 1996 to put bin Laden under surveillance, thus following the lead of the CIA, which had established a special Bin Laden Station.

Neither America nor Saudi Arabia wanted him on its soil, the former because it lacked evidence to convict him for killing Americans, and the latter because it feared violent reaction to his trial. So, in May 1996, yielding to Sudan's pressure, he and his entourage left for Jalalabad in Afghanistan, then in the throes of a civil war between a ramshackle government in Kabul and the newly established, Pakistan-backed Taliban. Jalalabad was outside the Taliban's control.

After Jalalabad and Kabul fell to the Taliban in September, he sought its protection. He got it, but only after swearing a loyalty oath to Mullah Muhammad Omar, the Taliban's spiritual leader. Assisted by his 3,000-strong, experienced fighters, Omar's Taliban militia extended its control over seven-eighths of Afghanistan. Omar allowed bin Laden to open training camps.

Inaugurating the World Islamic Front for Jihad against Crusaders and Jews in February 1998, bin Laden and four other Islamist leaders deplored the suffering of Palestinians and Iraqis, and declared it the religious duty of Muslims everywhere to kill the Americans and their allies – civilian and military – to liberate the Al Aqsa Mosque in Jerusalem and the Holy Mosque in Mecca from the control of the Crusaders and Jews.

Following the bombing of the US embassies in Nairobi and Dar as Salaam on 7 August 1998, which killed 227 people, Washington held bin Laden responsible for the deadly blasts, and called on the Taliban to hand him over. Omar refused.

The US Federal Bureau of Investigation included bin Laden in its list of 'Ten Most Wanted Fugitives', with a $5 million reward for information leading to his arrest, a sum later raised to $25 million.

Washington detected Al Qaida's involvement in the bombing of *USS Cole* in Aden in October 2000. Two months later, at America's behest, the UN Security Council demanded the extradition of bin Laden from the Taliban-controlled Afghanistan within a month on pain of imposing of arms embargo on the Taliban regime. Omar ignored the resolution.

The February 2001 trial in New York of four Al Qaida operatives – charged with conspiracy for the bombings in Nairobi and Dar as Salam – gave bin Laden a higher profile in the Muslim world and raised his influence over Omar. When, following the terrorist attacks in New York and Washington on 11 September (9/11), US President George W. Bush held bin Laden responsible, and called on Omar to hand him over to Washington, Omar argued that bin Laden could not have been the culprit.

Later, during his videotaped meeting with Khalid Harbi, a visiting radical cleric from Jiddah, bin Laden named nine of the fifteen Saudi hijackers involved in 9/11, adding that they had been instructed to go to America. The videotape was obtained by the US in the third week of November – soon after the Taliban's flight from Kabul on 12–13 November following a Washington-led bombing campaign against the Taliban regime on 7 October.

By mid-December, bin Laden, accompanied by Ayman Zawahiri, his intellectual mentor, had escaped to the tribal area along the Afghanistan–Pakistan border and found a sanctuary there. He resorted to sending audio-taped statements to Al Jazeera and other Arabic satellite television channels on well-chosen dates such as the first anniversary of 9/11 and the high point of the *hajj* (the pilgrimage to Mecca) in February 2003 during the American military build-up to invade Iraq. In his later statements he attacked the US-led coalition that invaded and occupied Iraq in April.

Further reading

See: Peter L. Bergen, *Holy Wars Inc: Inside the Secret World of Osama bin Laden* (2001); Jason Burke, *Al-Qaeda: Casting a Shadow of Terror,* I.B. Tauris (2003); Dilip Hiro, *War Without End: The Rise of Islamist Terrorism and Global Response* (2002); Gilles Kepel, *Jihad: The Trail of Political Islam* (2002); Jonathan Randal, *Osama: The Making of a Terrorist* (2004).

DILIP HIRO

BIZET, Georges
1838–75
French composer

A great composer of diverse talents, Bizet had the misfortune to be largely misunderstood and underestimated during his short life, and was equally unlucky in the treatment of his works after his death. The beginnings were auspicious: a child prodigy who was admitted to the Paris Conservatoire at the age of ten. There his teachers included Gounod and the composer Jacques Halévy (who later became his father-in-law). His Symphony in C, written when he was seventeen, was unrecognized until 1935, when it was at last published and performed. Its Mozartian freshness, vitality and charm have since won it ever-increasing popularity. His accomplished one-act opera *Le Docteur Miracle* (1857) won a competition sponsored by Offenbach; and his cantata *Clovis et Clothilde*, of the same period, won him the important Prix de Rome in 1857. The three years which Bizet spent in Italy, free from financial concern, were probably the happiest of his life. At this time, also, Bizet was not only blossoming as a composer, with an *opéra bouffe*, *Don Procopio*, and a choral symphony, *Vasco de Gama*, but he was also showing great talent as a pianist. Even **Liszt** was impressed.

The trouble started when, returning to Paris in 1860, he began his uneasy career as a composer for the theatre. Impulsive by nature, he withdrew and destroyed a one-act opera which the Opéra-Comique had accepted. Then his exotic full-scale operas *Les Pêcheurs de perles* and *La Jolie Fille de Perth* (after Walter Scott) were only moderately successful. There followed a spiritual crisis in which Bizet re-examined his whole attitude towards his art. His health, which was never good, deteriorated. Unlike Gounod, he had not been able to accept the teaching of the church; he turned for a time to a study of the history of philosophy. As a result of all this, the change in his style of composing was radical – as can be seen in what remains of his opera *La Coupe du Roi de Thulé*, a work which may well have been of outstanding importance, but was mutilated after his death and only fragments remain. These show, however, a vastly increased range of melodic and dramatic power, and an elaborate use of 'leading motifs', stemming from the powerful influence which **Wagner** then had on him. The culmination was to come later. Disquieting circumstances persisted – an unhappy marriage in 1869 to Halévy's daughter, who was neurotic and emotionally unstable, and participation in the Franco-Prussian War.

During the last four years of his life, however, Bizet produced some of his finest works. The early and largely hampering influences of Meyerbeer and Gounod were now thrown off, and a striking originality is found in the one-act opera *Djamileh* (1872). In this work, despite a poor libretto, Bizet felt he had found his true style – a form of dramatic realism through music which led directly to *Carmen*, his masterpiece. In a lighter vein he also composed at this time the witty and delightful suite for piano duet, *Jeux d'enfants*, five movements of which (with additions) were arranged as the *Petite Suite* for orchestra. A masterpiece also of this period was the incidental music which he wrote for Daudet's *L'Arlésienne*. Certain parts of this are well known through the two concert suites drawn from the total of twenty-seven numbers. At first it was not a success: audiences predominantly interested in the drama were

irritated by the (for them) unwanted intrusion of music. The *mélodrames*, however, demonstrate Bizet's remarkable capacity to underline and sum up, orchestrally, the emotional and dramatic content of the play. Unfortunately, he was not able to witness its highly successful revival at the Paris Odéon in 1885.

The four-act opera *Carmen* (1875) undoubtedly represents the summit of Bizet's achievement. **Tchaikovsky's** prophecy in 1876 that it would become the most popular opera in the world has been vindicated. In this work, based on Mérimée's novel, Bizet transformed the current concept of *opéra-comique*: drama, characterization, music were completely at one, and passion, jealousy, tragedy were all vividly represented with a 'realism' that was never crude, always artistically controlled. It was a style which had an immense influence on subsequent opera-composition. Composers as different as **Puccini**, Busoni and **Stravinsky** have all paid tribute to the Bizet style. But to the first audiences, the originality, the unexpectedness, the 'shocking' subject-matter – all proved disturbing, and the opera was initially a failure. The failure plunged the composer into a deep depression which was undoubtedly a contributing cause of his death a few months later at the age of thirty-seven. He died just when his genius had really begun to blossom: an incalculable loss to the world of music. Bizet was not a great innovator: his importance lay in his gifts as a melodist and as a musical dramatist. His work is full of original harmonic touches, and as a master of orchestration his skill was of the highest order. Another orchestral master, **Richard Strauss**, once advised young composers not to study Wagner's scores if they wanted to learn how to orchestrate, but to study the score of *Carmen*: 'What wonderful economy . . . and how every note and every rest is in its place.'

Further reading

Mina Curtiss's valuable study, *Bizet and His World* (1958), was based on much research into unpublished documents. Other studies include: Martin Cooper, *Georges Bizet* (1951); F. Robert, *Georges Bizet* (1965); Winton Dean, *Georges Bizet: His Life and Work* (1965; rev. 1975); S. McClary, *Carmen* (1992).

DAVID COX

BOAS, Franz

1858–1942

US anthropologist

Although born and educated in Germany, Franz Boas is considered the founding father of American anthropology. His contributions, ranging from vast collections of ethnographic data, statistical studies in physical anthropology and descriptive studies of American Indian languages, to treatises on the aims and methods in the study of the subject, shaped anthropological research into a science and had an immense impact on future generations of anthropologists.

The son of a prosperous businessman, Boas was born in Minden, Westphalia, and was educated at the universities of Heidelberg, Bonn and Kiel. Majoring in physics with geography as a minor, he received his doctorate in 1881 with a thesis called *Beiträge zur Erkenntnis der Farbe des Wassers* ('Contributions Towards the Understanding of the Colour of Water', 1881). His interest, however, soon turned to cultural geography, influenced by his teacher Theobald Fischer and the writings of Friedrich Ratzel and Wilhelm Wundt. His growing interest in the relationship between environment and culture took him on a research expedition to the Arctic in 1883–4 which resulted in a number of geographical and ethnographic articles on the Eskimo as well as his monograph *The Central Eskimo* (1888). It was this trip that also established the basis for the dominant aspect of his anthropological thinking: the awareness of the infinite complexity of human culture and how it came into being.

While he was assistant at the Berlin Völkerkunde Museum under A. Bastian in 1885, a group of Indians from the north-west coast of America were 'exhibited' there, which inspired him to do field research among the Kwakiutl Indians of British Columbia, whose study was to become his lifelong occupation.

Upon his return from the field he decided to emigrate to America and subsequently settled and married in New York. After holding a number of poorly remunerated positions as assistant editor of the journal *Science*, docent in anthropology at Clark University and curator at the Chicago Field Museum, he became curator of the American Museum of Natural History, and then professor in anthropology at Columbia University, where he stayed until his retirement in 1936. In addition, Boas played an instrumental role in the establishment of professional organizations and was the editor of the *American Anthropologist* and the *Journal of American Folklore*, as well as founding and editing the *International Journal of American Linguistics*.

The large bulk of Boas's publications consists of his ethnographic material on the Indians of the Pacific coast. Over a period of almost six decades, he published more than ten thousand pages on the natives of this area. While these writings include such synthesized accounts as *The Social Organization and Secret Societies of the Kwakiutl Indians* (Report of the US National Museum for 1895, 1897) and the posthumously published *Kwakiutl Ethnography* (1966), it is characteristic of his approach that the remainder of the materials are collections of texts recorded in the native language. With the help of a native informant, George Hunt, he transcribed, translated and edited thousands of pages of texts, including myths, family histories, customs, dreams, accounts of religious ceremonies and even recipes. Only texts collected in this manner, he believed, were undistorted and presented the view from within the culture. Moreover, he had little regard for the description of informal behaviour: with the American Indian way of life quickly disappearing under the impact of the white man, his preoccupation was with the symbolic and ceremonial aspects of native mentality.

It is difficult to label Boas's contribution to anthropological theory, since he usually presented his views as critiques of what he took to be others' reductionist assumptions. In a number of essays reprinted in *Race, Language and Culture* (1940), he incessantly points out the immense complexity of cultural growth, employing the concept of historicity: the particular shape individual cultures take is due to multiplex processes of adaptation and borrowing from other cultures. With the time factor introduced, there is a dynamic relationship between single cultures, between culture and environment, between individual and society. He thus argued both against the evolutionists' assumption of universal laws governing the development of civilization and against theories of environmental determination: culture itself emerged as a factor shaping human civilization.

His investigations in physical anthropology ultimately point in the same direction: in *The Mind of Primitive Man* (1911, revised 1938) – a book on the purge list of the Nazi German book-burning in 1933 – he demystified the concept of race, heretofore dominated by Eurocentric notions of superiority; his statistical studies on growth, heredity and modification of bodily form among descendants of immigrants pointed out the impact of cultural environment on physical growth. Interestingly, these studies had some practical significance, being utilized, for example, in the administration of American orphanages. Last, and not least, he used the results of his studies on race in his outspoken opposition against the racism of the German Nazi regime.

In linguistics, Boas was completely self-taught, although he was influenced by the humanistic language theories of W. von Humboldt, J.G. Herder and H. Steinthal. His study of Indian languages taught him that these operate with categories not assumed by Indo-European linguistics. These categories, however, must be analysed and described in their own terms, undistorted by the categories of Indo-European languages. Examples of such linguistic analysis are his short grammars of Chinook, Tsimshian and Kwakiutl in the *Handbook of American Indian Languages* (1911), which he also edited, and his extensive, posthumously published *Kwakiutl Grammar* (1947). Linguistic analysis, however, to him was not an aim in itself, but was part of ethnographic analysis. In fact, as he pointed out in his famous introduction to the *Handbook*, language, as a manifestation of the human mind which is yet empirically observable, helps us to gain a clearer understanding of ethnological phenomena, precisely because of its unconscious nature: the very nature of other languages' lexical and grammatical categories points to different ways of categorizing experience. These notions opened the way to more radical hypotheses on the relationship between language and world view brought forth by his student Edward Sapir and by B.L. Whorf.

Finally, one concept emerges from all of Boas's investigations into race, language and culture: the study of different and strange ways of behaviour enables us to free ourselves from the 'shackles of our own civilization' and to view it more objectively (*The Aims of Ethnology*, 1889). Boas trained a whole generation of American anthropologists and linguists, who in turn spread his legacy. Among them are, to name only a few: A.L. Kroeber, Ruth Benedict, R.H. Lowie, **Margaret Mead**, Sapir, M.J. Herskovits and P. Radin.

Further reading

Other works include: *Tsimshian Mythology* (Bureau of American Ethnology, 31st Annual Report, 1916); *Primitive Art* (1927); *Anthropology and Modern Life* (1928); and editorship and contributions to *General Anthropology* (1938). See also: Melville Herskovits (ed.) *Franz Boas, The Science of Man in the Making* (No. 61 of the Memoir Series of the American Anthropological Association, 1943); Walter Goldschmidt (ed.) *The Anthropology of Franz Boas* (Memoir No. 89, 1959); Leslie A. White, *The Ethnography and Ethnology of Franz Boas* (1963); Vernon J. Williams, *Rethinking Race: Franz Boas and His Contemporaries* (1996); Douglas Cole, *Franz Boas: The Early Years, 1858–1906* (2000).

MARIANNE BOELSCHER

BORGES, Jorge Luis

1899–1986

Argentine short-story writer, essayist and poet

Of mixed British and Argentine stock, he has published both in Spanish and English. After a private education in Geneva, he moved to Spain and came under the influence of the innovatory poetic movement *ultraismo*, whose aim was to break away from formal constraints and express complex and beautiful patterns of rhythms and images in free verse. He introduced the movement to Argentina, with momentarily striking success, in 1921. Between 1921 and 1930 he published numerous essays and three collections of poetry including *Fervor de Buenos Aires* (1923), moving away from experimentalism towards more meditative verse. In his later poetry (for example, *El otro, el mismo*, 1969), after a long gap, increasing blindness – and maturity – led him back to traditional metres and added new themes drawn from his study of old Germanic languages, his obsession with time, his philosophical interests, dominated by Schopenhauer and Berkeley, and his cult of his forebears. His later poetry shows almost classical restraint and depth.

In 1938 he came close to death from septicaemia. On his recovery, fearing that his creative abilities might have been affected, he wrote a spoof learned article to test them. This became one of the stories of *Ficciones* (1944; trans. A. Kerrigan, 1962) which, with *El Aleph* (1949) (trans. Borges and Di Giovanni, 1970) established him as the most influential prose writer in Spanish since Miguel de Unamuno. Later collections include *El informe de Brodie* (1970) and *El libro de arena* (1975). His most characteristic tales can be described as fantastic fables which illustrate the collapse of man's comforting certainties and the bewildering possibilities which thus emerge. Borges holds that belief in the meaningfulness of existence is hard to maintain, that confidence in our ability to understand reality is probably an illusion, and that we ourselves are a mystery.

All combinations of experience are theoretically possible; anything, logical or illogical, can happen; any explanation, credible or incredible, may be true.

Many of his best short stories examine existence and reality as if they formed part of some strange and bewildering puzzle. Among his favourite themes are: the impossible quest (for some ultimate certainty); the ironic fulfilment of man's greatest dreams (of immortality, of changing the past, of total knowledge); the implications of philosophical idealism; the nonexistence of the individual personality; the chaos and futility of existence; the circularity of time; and the defeat of reason. His attitude, however, is not one of spiritual stress but rather one of gentle humour, the expression of a detached, playful awareness of the absurdity of the human condition. For a long time his favourite symbol of this last was that of a circular labyrinth without a centre, since an endless maze perfectly conveys the combination of apparently significant regularity and total bafflement. But occasionally in his work men by acts of courage reach the centre of their own private existential labyrinths and discover their real identities.

Borges wrote extremely slowly and meticulously. Each 'inlaid detail' of the meaning can be seen to fit, each feature of the narrative technique performs a conscious function. This produces a **Kafka**-like density of texture (though Borges prefers to describe the Argentine Macedonio Fernández, along with Hawthorne, R.L. Stevenson and G.K. Chesterton, as major influences). Borges's impact on Latin American literature, where he led an entire generation of younger writers towards a new conception of the ambiguity of reality and the role of the creative imagination, has been immense. It has also been attested by writers in North America and France especially.

Further reading

Other works include: *Obras completas* (2002). See: *Jorge Luis Borges: The Total Library: Non-fiction*

1922–86 ed. Eliot Weinberger, trans. Esther Allen, Suzanne Jill Levine and Eliot Weinberger (2000). For poetry in translation: *Selected Poems 1923–67* (bilingual edition, 1972) and *In Praise of Darkness* (1974). For stories and essays other than those mentioned: *Labyrinths* (1961); *Dreamtigers* (1964); *Other Inquisitions* (1964); *A Personal Anthology* (1967); *The Book of Imaginary Beings* (1969); *A Universal History of Infamy* (1972); and *Doctor Brodie's Report* (1972). See also: A.M. Barrenechea, *Borges, The Labyrinth Maker* (1965); R.J. Christ, *The Narrow Act: Borges' Art of Allusion* (1969); and for beginners M.S. Stabb, *Jorge Luis Borges* (1970); Beatriz Sarlo, *Jorge Luis Borges: A Writer on the Edge* (1993); James Woodall, *The Man in the Mirror of the Book: A Life of Jorge Luis Borges* (1996); Julio Woscoboinik, *The Secret of Borges: A Psychoanalytic Inquiry into His Work*, trans. Dora C. Pozzi (1998); Evelyn Fishburn and Psiche Hughes (eds) *Dictionary of Borges* (1990); Edwin Williamson, *Borges: A Life* (2004).

D.L. SHAW

BOULEZ, Pierre

1925–

French composer

The son of an industrialist, he studied with **Olivier Messiaen** at the Paris Conservatoire in 1944–5 and also had lessons in serial technique from René Leibowitz, a pupil of **Schoenberg** and **Webern**. At once he recognized serialism as the necessary basis for a new musical language, to be joined by the rhythmic procedures he found in **Stravinsky** and Messiaen. His first published works, the *Sonatina for Flute and Piano* and the First Piano Sonata (both 1946), show his Webern-inspired use of serialism to develop small patterns of notes, but the Schoenbergian frenzy of his piano writing, the restless rhythms and the rapidity of the musical thought announce a quite individual style, one of impatient vehemence. The cantata *Le Visage nuptial* (1946–7), originally scored for two female voices and instrumental quartet but later revised for soprano, contralto, women's chorus and large orchestra (1951–2), gives this forceful rhetoric a focus in the response to the highly charged poetry of René Char.

Boulez's early style reached a climax of complexity and violent passion in his Second Piano Sonata (1947–8), where he subjects his small musical cells to elaborate development in dense contrapuntal textures; the work remains one of the most fearsome – and rewarding – tests of a pianist's intellectual stamina. It was followed by the *Livre pour quatuor* for string quartet (1948–9), where the new medium imposes a certain reticence, but where too the development of cells is carried still further in a quest for perpetual variety.

Influenced by Messiaen's *Mode de valeurs et d'intensités* (1949) Boulez appears to have recognized that his music was leading him towards total serialism, i.e. the application of serial methods to the non-pitch parameters of music: duration, loudness and timbre. This he put into practice in *Polyphonie X* for eighteen instruments (1951), in two *Études* composed on tape (1951–2) and in the first book of *Structures* for two pianos (1951–2). *Structures Ia* is the *locus classicus* of total serialism, a piece of rigorous construction whose discipline Boulez felt necessary to liberate him from the burden of the past and to open the way towards a richer serial grammar, towards the more flexible manner of *Structures Ib*.

Even more importantly, it was the experience of *Structures Ia* which made possible *Le Marteau sans maître* (1953–5). This work gained an immediate success, thanks partly to its unusual instrumentation: the nine movements use various combinations from an ensemble of alto flute, viola, guitar, vibraphone, xylorimba and untuned percussion, with a contralto voice singing short poems by Char in four of them. As Boulez has pointed out, the ensemble can allude to the sounds of Balinese (vibraphone) or of black African (xylorimba) music, though in style *Le Marteau* is not at all exotic. Indeed, it shows Boulez's serial proliferations working at high pressure along routes of allusive connection, and it draws together threads from Schoenberg, Webern, Messiaen and **Debussy**.

Boulez's next objective was to find a more general way of balancing free invention with strict technique; his solution was to include a role for chance within the composition itself. His Third Piano Sonata (1956–7) is in five movements, or 'formants' as he prefers to call them, which may be arranged in various possible orders and which contain other opportunities for the performer to exercise choice: passages which may be omitted, alternative routes through given material, variable tempos and so on. In the second book of *Structures* for two pianos (1956–61) he adds further mobility in the relationship between the players, and in *Pli selon pli* (1957–62) he deploys his recent innovations on a grander scale to create a portrait of Mallarmé, the literary source of his aleatory thinking.

Since this period Boulez's works have tended to appear piecemeal. Only two formants of the Third Sonata have been published, and *Pli selon pli* grew gradually from a pair of pieces for soprano and resonant percussion ensemble to an hour-long composition for soprano and orchestra. Similarly, the short *Éclat* for fifteen instruments (1965) has been greatly extended to form *Éclat/multiples* for orchestra (begun 1966), and various other projects – including *Figures–Doubles–Prismes* for orchestra (begun 1957–8), *Domaines* for clarinet and six instrumental groups (begun 1961) and *'explosantefixe'* for eight instruments and electronics (begun 1971) – remain to be completed.

To some degree Boulez's slower pace of creative activity since 1960 may be attributed to his growing activity as a conductor. In 1954 he established a Paris concert series, eventually known as the Domaine Musical, for furthering modern music, and since 1957 he has appeared widely as a conductor, at first specializing in twentieth-century music but later ranging into the standard repertory, particularly while he held appointments with the New York Philharmonic (1971–7) and the BBC Symphony Orchestra (1971–5). But his reluctance to bring works to completion also has less mundane causes. His musical world is one of constant variation, and ideas, as in the case of *Éclat*, will suggest almost limitless extension. Furthermore, his assumption of a duty to establish a general

framework for musical discourse – a duty which he is now fulfilling as director of the Institut de Recherche et de Coordination Acoustique/Musique in Paris – makes his an onerous task in an age of such stylistic diversity.

Further reading

Other works: *Le Soleil des eaux* (1948, revised 1958, further revised 1965), cantata to poems by Char; *Poésie pour pouvoir* (1958, withdrawn) for tape and orchestra, after Michaux; 'Cummings ist der Dichter' (1970) for chamber chorus and small orchestra; *Rituel* (1974–75) for orchestra; *Messagesquisse* (1970) for solo cello and six other cellos. Writings: *Penser la musique aujourd'hui* (1963, trans. Susan Bradshaw and Richard Rodney Bennett, *Boulez on Music Today*, 1971); *Relevés d'apprenti* (1966, translated as *Notes of an Apprenticeship*, 1968); *Werkstatt-Texte* (1972); *Anhaltspunkte* (1975); *Par Volonté et par hasard: entretiens avec Célestin Deliège* (1975, translated as *Conversations with Célestin Deliège*, 1977). About Boulez: Antoine Goléa, *Rencontres avec Pierre Boulez* (1958); Joan Peyser, *Boulez: Composer, Conductor, Enigma* (1976); Paul Griffiths, *Boulez* (1978); G. Born, *Rationalizing Culture: IRCAM, Boulez, and the Institutionalization of the Avant-Garde* (1995); J. Vermeil, *Conversations with Boulez: Thoughts on Conducting* (1996).

PAUL GRIFFITHS

BRADBURY, Raymond Douglas

1920–

US science fiction writer

Ray Bradbury was born in Waukegan, Illinois, and was then moved by his parents to Los Angeles. Although he graduated from high school there, his family could not afford to send him to college. Instead, from an early age, he built up a living contributing stories to newspapers and pulp science fiction magazines, publishing his first book, *Dark Carnival*, in 1947. His writings have as their core a potent nostalgia for the 'paradise lost' of small-town America. As the United States became more and more urbanized, the rural idyll and its values (church, mom, apple pie) became touchstones of a mass culture. Bradbury's genius was his ability to blend a Norman Rockwell-style idealized small town with the paraphernalia of imaginative progress: rockets, robots and spaceships.

In the early 1950s, when he started selling his work seriously, science fiction was still the preserve of the acne-ed adolescent male. Through a series of more or less dystopian books consisting mostly of short stories tenuously linked by some central theme and peopled with characters of the purest cardboard, Bradbury helped bring the idea of 'out there' to the mainstream of American and thereafter European awareness. There were better writers crafting SF stories at the time, and better scientists speculating in science fiction, yet nobody sold more books or had a greater influence on the general public – largely because Bradbury's stories were easily adapted into comic books and then for TV and film. His strength was that his stories had 'hooks': moments which simply replay themselves endlessly in the mind. Like the best pop music they transcend their triviality.

Bradbury is very much an 'outsider artist'. Leaving school at sixteen, in his own words he 'read the library'. Like most autodidacts, the way he organized the knowledge so acquired was eccentric, and this shows in his writing. *Fahrenheit 451* (1951), his undoubted masterpiece, is at once more memorable and a lesser novel than that other great vision of a fascist dystopia, **Orwell's** *Nineteen Eighty-four*. Written within five years of each other, Orwell's bleak communism contrasts wonderfully with Bradbury's post-literate consumer hell. But it is the endings that point up the differences. If Bradbury's 'hobo-professors' with their memorized books are rather silly, he finds in small-town USA a touchstone to save the world. The religiosity, the naivety are almost embarrassing, and yet, perhaps because there is the chance of salvation and there remains some little cause for optimism, the book sticks in the memory like a burr. And even though it is the lesser work, it was and is more grounded in reality, and so in the end, it is still scarier, more 'real'.

It is hard now to regain the mindset of the 1950s, to appreciate how ignorant of the universe we were, how racist the world was, and how little real social criticism ever penetrated to the mass market. It is thus doubly hard to realize the effect some of Bradbury's work had. *Fahrenheit 451* was almost unpublishable – it finally found print in one of the first editions of *Playboy* magazine, itself a revolutionary publication. While not written as a critique of Joe McCarthy and his witch-hunts, it did very well as one anyway. Likewise, 'Way Up in the Middle of the Air' (from *The Martian Chronicles*, 1950), and its sequel 'The Other Foot' (from *The Illustrated Man*, 1951), were probably more subversive of mainstream American racism than (the far greater literature of) James Baldwin. Bradbury brought issues such as race discrimination, poverty in the developing world and threats to the environment to the attention of a huge audience of 'acne-ed adolescent males' who had simply not thought about such matters before. They went on to become the professors, businessmen and politicians of the 1960s, 1970s and 1980s, and the concerns Bradbury had raised in the 1950s were taken up by them in part because of Ray Bradbury.

Bradbury did not make science fiction respectable, but he did expand its appeal, and he most certainly created some of its most abiding clichés. The science may be bunk, the characters may be straight out of central casting, and the writing is either purest poetry or cringe-inducingly florid, but either way, Bradbury was and remains an influential maker: it is unimaginable, for instance, that *Back to the Future* and other of **Steven Spielberg's** films, similarly blending the cosiness of American suburbia with hi-tec fantasy, would have seen the light of day without his example.

Further reading

Other works include: *The Silver Locusts* (1951); *The Golden Apples of the Sun and Other Stories* (1953); *Dandelion Wine* (1957); *A Medicine for Melancholy* (1959); *The Day It Rained Forever* (1959); *The Small*

Assassin (1962); *Twice 22* (1966); *Tomorrow Midnight* (1966); *I Sing the Body Electric* (1969); *The Wonderful Ice Cream Suit and Other Plays* (1972); *When Elephants Last in the Dooryard Bloomed* (1973); *Pillar of Fire and Other Plays* (1975); *Long After Midnight* (1976); *Where Robot Mice and Robot Men Run Round in Robot Towns* (1977); *Death is a Lonely Business* (1985) and *A Graveyard for Lunatics* (1990). See: J.L. Garci, *Ray Bradbury: humanista del futuro* (1971); Jerry Weist, *Bradbury: An Illustrated Life* (2005).

VIV HORWITZ

BRAHMS, Johannes

1833–97

German composer

Brahms was born in a tenement in the poorest quarter of Hamburg, son of a young town musician and a seamstress already in her mid-forties. He was always intended for a musical career, studying first with his father and a local piano teacher; at the age of eleven recognition of his unusual gifts induced the noted teacher Edouard Marxsen to accept him as a pupil for both piano and composition. The family's poverty forced Johannes to play for money in the seaport's taverns and brothels, and his health was undermined for a time, though he gave some public recitals on his own account and began teaching and arranging popular music. In 1853, his life was transformed when he undertook a concert tour with the Hungarian violinist Reményi, which led him first to a meeting at Göttingen with the composer–violinist Joachim (who became a life-long friend and champion); then to Weimar, where he met **Liszt**; and finally to Düsseldorf, where he enormously impressed Robert and Clara Schumann with the playing of his own compositions. Schumann responded with a wildly enthusiastic article in *Neue Zeitschrift für Musik* hailing Brahms as a long-awaited master, 'one who should utter the highest ideal expression of his time, who should claim the Mastership by no gradual development, but burst upon us fully equipped': which instantly made Brahms an object of controversy and

scepticism. This new-found friendship was tragically clouded by Schumann's mental breakdown in 1854, which propelled Brahms into the position of chief confidant and protector of his wife and children. He fell deeply in love with Clara Schumann, fourteen years his senior – it is unclear whether this passion, which was certainly mutual, was ever consummated, but they remained close friends for the rest of their lives.

In the later 1850s Brahms was employed at the princely court of Lippe-Detmold; afterwards he lived in Hamburg before becoming conductor of the Vienna Singakademie in 1863. He resigned the post in the following year, but henceforth resided in Vienna. The première of *Ein Deutsches Requiem* ('A German Requiem', Op. 45, to his own selection of texts from the Lutheran Bible), which he conducted at Bremen in 1868, marked his public acceptance as an artist who had fulfilled Schumann's early prophecies; and the appearance of a First Symphony (Op. 64) in 1876 which Hans von Bülow was moved to call 'the Tenth' – suggesting that at last a worthy successor had appeared to the symphonies of Beethoven – confirmed his position as a 'living classic' in the eyes of all but ultra-Romantics of Wagnerian persuasion.

Brahms's life after he settled in Vienna was unremarkable in its externals: despite several liaisons of varying emotional depth he never married; and though one of the first great composers to earn a considerable fortune in his lifetime (chiefly from his immensely popular *Hungarian Dances* for piano duet) he lived a frugal bachelor's existence in a small flat, devoting much of his money to helping fellow-musicians – he was instrumental, for instance, in furthering **Dvořák's** early career. Concert tours and walking holidays, often in Switzerland or Italy, varied his routine. His last years were shadowed by the deaths of several close friends, and after Clara Schumann's in 1896 he went into a decline; he himself died of cancer of the liver (as had his father) the following year.

In 1860 Brahms had been unwise enough to sponsor, with Joachim, a 'manifesto' criticizing the so-called 'New German School' of high Romantic composition, headed by Liszt. As a piece of propaganda it was a failure, but it was symptomatic of his reverential attitude towards tradition which cast him, in hostile eyes, into a 'reactionary' role; even today the image is of a solid, unadventurous composer, a classicist antipope to **Wagner**. These two great figures seem in retrospect the coeval Alpha and Omega of nineteenth-century German music (though Brahms was the younger man by nearly a generation). Wagner is only too clearly the revolutionary, with his operas' strong appeal to the ungovernable emotions and his vastly enlarged harmonic language; Brahms, with his symphonies, concertos and chamber works that sit so comfortably and immovably in the mainstream repertoire, seems by contrast the embodiment of bourgeois conservatism, even if raised to the highest power of genius. In fact he is one of the most complex, and ultimately ambiguous, figures in the history of music; and it is arguable that if he had been less lavishly endowed with sheer musicality the potent contradictions of his art would be more readily evident. He was probably the subtlest and most comprehensive musical mind since Beethoven, and it is in his music, and not before, that Beethoven's profoundest examples are fully understood and developed upon.

The nineteenth-century debate about 'Music of the Future', which ranged Brahms and Wagner on opposite sides, concerned the proposition that the traditional musical forms were exhausted, and that music must move on to 'freer' forms that would develop with the depiction of intense emotion. The classical hierarchies of tonal relationships and balanced, ordered structures were progressively loosened in Schubert's, Chopin's and Schumann's lyric forms; the programmatic symphonies of Mendelssohn, Berlioz, Raff and Goldmark; Liszt's tone-poems and 'cyclic' forms; and ultimately Wagner's music-dramas with their leitmotivic structures and dramatic periods. The concepts of 'form' and 'content' had become distinct as they had never been

in the Classical era: the idea of 'sonata-form' itself, seen as that era's most characteristic achievement, was a description *post hoc* (actually *c.* 1840) of normative practices in Haydn, Mozart and Beethoven. The early Romantics were much impressed by the vigour and intensity of Beethoven's ideas, but were either unprepared to submit to his structural disciplines (Liszt, Wagner), or attempted to apply those disciplines for the sake of their honoured associations, rather than as an organic outcome of the potential of the basic material (Schumann).

Brahms, too, was a Romantic, of the most passionate kind: his early piano works are as turbulent as Schumann's, and the massive opening movement of the First Piano Concerto (Op. 15, 1854–8) is a *ne plus ultra* of *Sturm und Drang* emotionalism and tragic power. But it also deploys and organizes its explosive material, on the largest scale, with complete understanding of the fundamentally *dramatic* nature of sonata-style: and perhaps its chief model is the first movement – in the same key, D minor – of Beethoven's Ninth Symphony. Meanwhile the First Serenade for orchestra (Op. 11, 1857–8) had already displayed how his melodic thinking, which possesses a very personal breadth and flexibility, could give rise to structures of Haydnesque wit and formal clarity, propelled by a Beethovenian dynamism. Brahms did not revert to the structural norms of the classical style, but built upon the foundation of its more unorthodox inspirations, which until then had exerted little influence.

This makes him a Janus figure in musical history. There is no doubt that his personal historical sense was very highly developed: he himself performed and edited music of the Baroque and Classical eras, was keenly interested in the work of contemporary musicologists, and had an intimate and admiring knowledge of Mozart, Haydn, Beethoven and Schubert. Their example was the basis for his own language, yet he was no epigone: his historical sense included the certainty of the irrecoverability of the past. Charles Rosen has observed that

The depth of his feeling of loss gave an intensity to Brahms's work that no other imitator of the classical tradition ever reached: he may be said to have made music out of his openly expressed regret that he was born too late.

There is a large element of truth here, but it remains a one-sided view. The intensity of Brahms's feelings was not simply for the loss of the classical style. He was a man of his own times, and his imaginative identification with aspects of earlier music was his personal approach to writing music of those times.

Brahms essayed all the traditional musical genres except opera: his major works include four symphonies, four concertos and several choral works with orchestra; a large body of chamber music including three string quartets as well as sextets, quintets, trios and sonatas; a great number of songs and unaccompanied choruses, including nearly a hundred settings of German folk songs; and a substantial output of solo piano music which concentrated, after his early years, on sets of variations and the smaller forms of the ballade, rhapsody and intermezzo. There is an apparent preference for 'abstract' or 'pure' designs: no avowedly programmatic works, though many private, concealed programmes may well lurk in pieces of such tightly controlled emotionality as the C minor Piano Quartet (Op. 60, 1874).

But these time-honoured forms arise now from different premises, to articulate new orders of material. Brahms's harmony could be as chromatically complex as Wagner's, though arrived at from a more diatonic basis; and his treatment of tonality in large-scale forms seldom fulfils traditional expectations, but instead makes new departures which in retrospect prove justified and satisfying. His study of older music led him to create an enriched polyphonic texture in which each contrapuntal voice has an increased independence and life of its own: his success in this was due to the plasticity of his melodic gift and, especially, to his subtle and all-pervasive mastery of rhythm to point up contrasts of line and shifts of pulse.

It is precisely here that he ceases to be a classic and becomes rather the first of the moderns, the initiator of that drive for absolute polyphonic freedom which characterized the early development of **Schoenberg**, who revered Brahms and summed up his importance for later generations in a classic essay with the seemingly paradoxical title 'Brahms the Progressive'. It was, perhaps above all, Brahms's infinite resource in motivic development that Schoenberg admired, and in this connection it is relevant to note Brahms's predilection for variation form, apparently as a means of fully defining the essence, and exploring the infinite latent possibilities, of any given thematic idea. The piano variation-sets on themes by Handel (Op. 24, 1861) and Paganini (Op. 35, 1863), the slow movement of the First String Sextet (Op. 18, 1860), the finale of the Clarinet Quintet (Op. 115, 1891), and the orchestral *St Antoni Variations* (Op. 56, 1873) are all distinguished examples. Perhaps the summit is the astonishing passacaglia on a theme derived from Bach that is the finale of the Fourth Symphony (Op. 98, 1885): a display of 'pure' musical invention of the utmost tragic power. But this finale is itself but a crystallization of processes adumbrated in the three previous movements: the symphony's opening idea of falling thirds is organically developed throughout its whole length with allusive ingenuity – just as, in the Third Symphony (Op. 90, 1883), all movements made use of multifarious developments of a three-note figure F–A flat–F – and the *idea* of passacaglia form is already implied in the character of the counterstatement of the first movement's first subject.

At certain points in the late piano pieces (Op. 116–19, 1891–3) and the *Vier ernste Gesänge* (Op. 121, 1896) motivic elaboration in melodic and harmonic spheres is almost total. It was these aspects of Brahms's practice that were the ultimate sanction for Schoenberg's rigorously motivic twelve-note method. It is probable, too, that Brahms's creative mixing of old and new musical resources made a profound impression on Ferruccio Busoni; and the power of certain of his inspirations continued to haunt the consciousness of twentieth-century composers (the openings of such diverse works as Carl Ruggles's *Sun-Treader* and Bernd Alois Zimmermann's *Die Soldaten*, for instance, are most likely attempts at re-creating, in their own voices, the tremendous timpani-pinned impression of the start of Brahms's First Symphony).

Brahms has generally been acknowledged as one of the supreme craftsmen among composers, and he was highly self-critical, destroying all that he imagined to be substandard work. Even his orchestration, once unfavourably compared to the pyrotechnics of Berlioz or **Tchaikovsky**, is now generally understood as brilliantly suited to the nature of his inspiration, and is one of the secrets of the quality – which he shares with Beethoven – of intimacy on a grand scale. The worst that can be charged against his music is that occasionally he relies on technique alone, and produces a dry discourse – the first two String Quartets (Op. 51, 1873) are especially disappointing in this respect for a composer with Beethoven's examples before him. But the creator of such fullhearted love-music as the Double Concerto (Op. 102, 1887), or merely such a sumptuous tune as the trio-melody in the scherzo of the C major Piano Trio (Op. 87, 1882) can be forgiven anything. 'Such a great man! Such a great soul!' sorrowed Dvořák: 'And he believes in nothing!' But there is nothing nihilistic about Brahms's music: rather, it is the work of a great *humanist* mystic who, aware of the tragedies, paradoxes and imponderables of existence, wrote his works to provide sustenance for the here and now.

Further reading

The collected edition of Brahms's works is published by Breitkopf & Härtel, Leipzig, and a large number of individual pieces are widely available in many other editions. He was a copious correspondent, and revealing collections of his letters include *Letters of Clara Schumann and Johannes Brahms 1853–1896*, ed. Berthold Litzmann (1922) and *Johannes Brahms: The Herzogenberg Correspondence*, ed. Max Kalbeck (1909). See: Karl Geiringer, *Brahms: His Life and Works* (2nd edn, 1947); Hans Gal, *Johannes Brahms: His Work and Personality* (1963); Bernard Jacobson, *The Music of Johannes Brahms* (1977); Julius Harrison, *Brahms and His Four Symphonies* (1939); S. Avins, *Johannes Brahms: Life and Letters* (1997); L. Botstein (ed.) *The Complete Brahms: A Guide to the Musical Works* (1999); M. Musgrave (ed.) *The Cambridge Companion to Brahms* (1990); *A Brahms Reader* (2000).

MALCOLM MACDONALD

BRANCUSI, Constantin

1876–1957

Romanian sculptor

Hailed as the pioneer of modern sculpture by some, and blamed for its degeneration by others, Constantin Brancusi can without doubt be placed at the forefront of those who created an abstract idiom to replace figurative representation for the art in its Western form. Born in Hobitza, a hamlet of Pestisani in southern Romania, he received no formal schooling, but worked first as a shepherd, then at a variety of menial jobs in nearby towns. With the help of a local industrialist, who was impressed by Brancusi's skill at carving domestic artefacts in wood (a traditional peasant craft), he attended the School of Arts in Craiova (1895–8), and then the National School of Fine Arts in Bucharest (1898–1902), where he trained as a sculptor, simultaneously teaching himself to read and write. Drawn to Paris by the reputation of **Auguste Rodin**, he arrived there in 1904, having spent some months in Munich, and making most of his journey on foot. In 1905 he enrolled at the École des Beaux Arts, and in 1907 received his first important commission, a statue for the tomb of Peter Stanescu, in Buzau Cemetery, Romania. This work, *The Prayer*, depicts a young girl kneeling and, although recognizably classical, already suggests the artist's move towards apparent simplicity of form. During the next twelve years he worked on many of his most important themes: *The Kiss*, *Sleeping Muse*, *Torso*, *Narciss*, *The Wisdom of the Earth*, *Prometheus*, *Maiastra*, *Mlle Pogany*, *Penguins*, *The Newborn*, *Princess X*, *Endless Column* and *Bird in Space*. During the 1920s, while continuing to develop most of these, he added *Adam and Eve*, *The Fish*, *Leda*, *The White Negress* and the *Cock*. The high abstraction he attained at this period is attested by an attempt made by the US Customs Department to have Brancusi arraigned for secretly importing industrial parts into America, following their unwillingness to believe that a bronze *Bird in Space* was a sculpture. The main addition to his work in the 1930s was the sculptural programme for the Public Park in Tirgu Jiu (Romania): *The Table of Silence*, two benches, *The Gate of the Kiss*, and the 100-foot-high *Endless Column*, constructed from steel (all 1937–8). At the same time he travelled to India, where the Maharajah of Indore had asked him to create a temple, but the Maharajah's death prevented the project's fruition.

Unlike some other modern artists and sculptors, Brancusi's style did not suddenly emerge, or come into its own as an all-of-a-piece affair, but developed gradually over a period of twenty-five years. His achievement therefore has the advantage of being self-documented; while the full force of it can only be experienced by contrasting 'early' and 'mature' pieces. Thus, while the bronze *Torment* of 1907 presents the notion of mimesis of a natural form, full of details to convey deep emotion, subsequent works (the marble *Prometheus* of 1911, through the bronze *Prometheus* of the same year, the bronze *Newborn* of 1915, to the bronze, egg-like *Beginning of the World* of 1924, also known as the *Sculpture for the Blind*) exhibit a progressive refinement, or as some would say reduction, towards the essence of the sculpted object, achieved by a fusion of the internal substructure and sculptural detail in the plane of a skin-deep surface. Increasingly, as the plane rotates, the unessential details (neck, nose, lips, eyes, hair) decrease. The essential form then enters into a reflective relationship

with its base, be it a plate or a cushion. The abstracting force of this creative process, however, is, in Brancusi, balanced by his deep, often sensual, response to the particular materials used, from the direct rough carving in wood to the highly polished metals. From this he also developed a sophisticated spatio-temporal idea. Traditionally the space of a sculpture was understood to be underneath, or contained within, its surface. But Brancusi activated the space between the surface and the beholder, making that space subjective, to be experienced and lived through in time. His larger works have the power to enclose the viewer at a distance – hence their 'closed' form, and the 'silence' that envelops them. His final images, clear, exact and precise, become mysteries.

Brancusi claimed that 'a well-made sculpture should have the power to heal the beholder', and that 'it must be lovely to touch, friendly to live with'. His work, whose idiom has to a large extent become the *lingua franca* of modern sculpture, was an extraordinary marriage of distinct backgrounds. His attitude towards materials and craftsmanship, his repetitiveness, and the rejection of haste and willingness to work on a piece over a number of years, together with a personal self-effacement, were as Romanian as his themes: the pagan myths of rebirth (egg, cock, bird), the sky – earth axis (endless column) – so important in the lives of Romanian farmers, and the solar motifs (love, birth, growth). While it has been suggested that these aspects may have been further cultivated by Brancusi's reading of a treatise by the eleventh-century Tibetan monk Milarepa, the impact of French culture was the other important determinant. It furnished Brancusi, on the one hand, through the later works of Rodin, with the idea that the meaning of a sculpture was located on its surface; and on the other, with the neo-platonic view advanced by Charles Blanc in 1880, that the role of sculpture 'is to create a life of images analogous to real life'.

Although the full catalogue of Brancusi's oeuvre is relatively small, individual works have found their way into museums throughout Europe and America. This, together with the considerable critical attention he has received, has ensured Brancusi a high place in modern sculpture. If the ambiguous interfusion between the primitive and high art was neither inevitable nor peculiar to Brancusi, its continuation has in turn been abetted by the ambivalence of his reputation.

Further reading

See: D. Lewis, *Brancusi* (1957); C. Giedion Welcker, *Constantin Brancusi* (1959); H. Read, *A Concise History of Modern Sculpture* (1964); S. Geist, *Brancusi* (1968); A.T. Spear, *Brancusi's Birds* (1969); S. Miller, *Constantin Brancusi* (1995).

SLAVKA SVERAKOVA

BRAQUE, Georges

1882–1963

French painter

It was as a decorator that Braque arrived in Paris in 1900 to attend evening courses in painting and design at the Cours Municipal des Batignolles. In later life, even in his severest works, there survived a decorative sense of great beauty. Only after military service in 1901–2 did Braque enrol at the Académie Humbert in Paris, and begin to execute oil paintings of his family.

During 1902 his involvement with painting grew and developed through visits to the Louvre, through an increasing circle of friends amongst practising painters, including Marie Laurencin and Francis Picabia, but also through the experience of Impressionist and Post-Impressionist paintings seen at the commercial galleries of Vollard and Durand-Ruel. By 1903 Braque was committed to painting. He entered the École des Beaux-Arts under Bonnat but subsequently returned to the Académie Humbert. In 1904 he was working independently and the following year was overwhelmed by the ferocity and vitality of the Fauve painters at the Salon

d'Automne. From this moment forward, a moment of insight into possibilities within his reach, Braque never ceased to explore and consolidate his achievements. Never reaching beyond the lucid tracing of his tactile and sensual experience, Braque became a connoisseur of visual sensation, committed at once to freshness of colour and touch, an explorer of visual experience. Within such a development the particular blend of rigid discipline and sensual delight that distinguishes a brilliant decorative painter was never absent.

His links with the Fauve painters flourished through his personal friendships with Othon Friesz and Raoul Dufy. For Braque the bright explosion of Fauve paintings by Derain, **Matisse** and Vlaminck in particular signalled the final and decisive acceptance of brilliant Post-Impressionist colour and the lively articulation of individual brushmarks. Pointillisme in particular had emphasized both of these qualities, and Signac had communicated their principles directly to Matisse. The fresh *tache*, recording the touch of the brush, was given new force and vitality. Into so rhythmic and colourful an effusion of paint Braque saw room for the extension of his own abilities. He painted Fauve paintings throughout 1906 and exhibited the following year at both the Salon des Indépendants and at the Salon d'Automne, making his aesthetic allegiance clear. *The Port at Antwerp* (1906) reveals Braque's debt to the Fauves. The calligraphic qualities of this painting, where balcony ironwork is depicted in a singular curling line and the reflections of boats in the harbour are loose dashes of colour, combine a natural painterliness with the freshness and immediacy of the Fauves. Yet Braque's colour in 1906 is not fully recognizable as Fauve unless it is comparable with that of his friend, Othon Friesz, whose vibrant but dense and slow-moving mauves do find a response in Braque's 1906 sea- and riverscapes. They lack the fiery crackling of wilder Fauve brushwork. Braque retains a strength of compositional structure comparable to that which Matisse had only briefly abandoned.

Fauve painting was, however, for Braque a vital initiation into a new range of painterly techniques and priorities.

In 1908 Guillaume Apollinaire wrote an introduction for Braque's one-man exhibition at Kahnweiler's gallery in Paris. By this time his work had undergone dramatic modification. During the intervening years two major artistic experiences followed upon the impact of Fauvism. First, Braque was overwhelmingly impressed by a memorial retrospective of **Cézanne's** work, and second, Braque became friendly with **Pablo Picasso** whose *Demoiselles d'Avignon*, an unresolved and violently new work, was glimpsed by Braque in Picasso's studio. Both events encouraged a fierce disciplining of the energy let loose by Fauve painters, and until the First World War when Braque was called up for military service, the colour-range of his palette was severely limited to black, earth browns and ochres. Through their creative repartee, through innovations in aim and technique, exchanged and extended continuously, Braque and Picasso during this period evolved the central core of Cubism, perhaps the single most influential development in twentieth-century art in Europe and America. From the monumental and Cézannesque strength of paintings executed at L'Estaque in 1908, Braque, in collaboration with Picasso, evolved a more crystalline and rhythmic style in which forms resembled fragmented geometrical solids; single viewpoint perspective was abandoned and contradictory light sources were employed. This complex faceting of forms locked objects into the context of their immediate surroundings. Their forms were recorded as much in intellectual as in visual terms, reducing a guitar to a few recognizable elements of shape and detail, an approach that was analytical and devoid of accidental effects of light, weather or application. As the subject became more difficult to recognize, except through hints and clues left within the crystalline framework by the painter, this analytical phase of Cubism came more and more to rely upon identifiable signs. In effect analytical Cubism

radically altered the painter's visual language, while remaining firmly committed to depiction: the very means of painting and the nature of representation were brought into consideration by the Cubist works of Braque and Picasso. As the means and techniques employed for such references were extended, Cubism increasingly played off against each other differing forms of representation. The viewer, alerted by recognizable clues, was encouraged to interpret further images within the painting. For example, the crystalline and vigorously modelled planes of Braque's *Violin and Palette* (1910) emphasize an implied depth within the picture space, yet the *trompe l'oeil* nail at top centre of the painting appears to fasten the canvas to a wall, and the viewer is forcefully reminded of the flat surface of the canvas. Such a painting as the equally vigorous *Still Life with Playing Card* (1913) reveals much of the subsequent development of Cubism. Colour remains restrained and certain images are at once recognizable: the drawing of a cluster of grapes and the imagery of playing cards are an example. Beyond this, Braque is more suggestive and less explicit, and in these areas more recent Cubist techniques are clearly evident. Lettering, introduced by Braque to Cubism in 1911 with his painting *Le Portugais*, inhabits the flat canvas surface and recalls printed text, perhaps a newspaper. Elsewhere Braque has imitated decorators' woodgraining techniques to suggest material qualities. Furthermore, the shapes of these woodgrained sections are such as to suggest that they have been cut from a printed woodgrain wall covering and stuck on to the canvas, a technique employed from 1912 by both Picasso and Braque in Cubist collages.

This slowing down of interpretation led to a more intimate examination of the techniques, concerns and methods of representation open to the painter and employed by him. These means, more than any specific style or technique, were to spread throughout the world. Georges Braque's contribution before 1914 was inextricable from that of his close friend and collaborator Pablo Picasso. Indeed, after the war, Braque retained Cubist devices and constructions in his paintings, adding an intellectual delight to the sensually ravishing surfaces of many of his later paintings. The Tate Gallery's *Still Life with Mandolin, Glass, Pot and Fruit* (1927) exemplifies this. Sombre, resonant colour inhabits the most liquid of lines, yet the division of the pot into areas of light and shade is effected decisively with a single zigzag line. Into so severe and intellectual a system of painting Braque has reintroduced a different form of exploration that rivals Matisse as readily as Picasso, for in the manipulation of colours Braque became a great explorer and an epicurean sensualist. The hints he gives of succulence or rigidity, of translucency or weight, all testify to an almost tactile immediacy of sensation. His complexity and his confidence in this achievement made of his later still-lives an orchestration of sensual associations in which perception and articulation appear to flow one from the other completely without hindrance. *The Shower of Rain* (1952) shows no loss of this succinctness: the suddenness and transparency of a shower are caught in a group of descending lines: the perception, astutely edited, is presented by means entirely appropriate to painting.

Braque's contribution to Cubism and to later painting was increasingly recognized. He was invited to present a special exhibition at the Salon d'Automne in 1922, and major exhibitions followed at the Galérie Paul Rosenberg, Paris, from 1924, the Basle Kunsthalle in 1933, the San Francisco Museum of Art in 1940, the Museum of Modern Art in New York in 1948, the Kunsthalle at Berne in 1953, and the Basle Kunsthalle again in 1960.

Further reading

See: Georges Braque, *Le Jour et la nuit* (1952). See also: Guillaume Apollinaire, *Les Peintres cubistes* (1913); P. Heron, *Braque* (1958); John Golding, *Cubism: A History and Analysis 1907–1914* (1959); John Russell, *Georges Braque* (1959); Edwin Mullins, *Braque* (1968); K. Wilkin, *Georges Braque* (1991).

JOHN MILNER

BRECHT, Bertolt

1898–1956

German poet, playwright and director

Brecht, one of the most influential playwrights of the twentieth century, was the son of the manager of a paper mill in the Bavarian city of Augsburg. When he left grammar school (*Gymnasium*) at the age of eighteen, he decided to study medicine, largely in order to avoid combat duty in the First World War, then at its height. He succeeded in being assigned to a military hospital in his native city as a medical orderly and it is said that the suffering of the wounded he saw there instilled in him the passionate hatred of war, and the bourgeois society that had instigated it, which determined his later political development.

During his pre-medical studies at the University of Munich after the war he drifted gradually into theatrical circles, wrote ballads he himself sang to the guitar and published poems, stories and theatre reviews. His first play to be performed, *Drums in the Night* (*Trommeln in der Nacht*, written 1920; first performed Munich 1922), won the coveted Kleist Prize and established him as one of the most promising playwrights of the new post-war generation. From 1922 onwards he spent more and more time in Berlin, where he settled in 1924. From 1926 onwards he became increasingly interested in **Marxism** which he came to regard as a strictly scientific doctrine that alone would be capable of eradicating war and poverty from the earth. Brecht's first major theatrical success was the *Threepenny Opera* (*Dreigroschenoper*, 1928). After **Hitler's** accession to power in Germany Brecht went into exile and settled in Denmark (1933–9) but, after brief interludes in Sweden (1939–40) and Finland (1940–1), decided to go to America. Not only is it significant that he did not want to stay in the Soviet Union, where **Stalin** was conducting a vigorous campaign against avant-garde art, but that, to get to the United States in June 1941, he had to cross the entire Soviet Union to reach Vladivostok, where he embarked on a boat going to California a few days before the Germans invaded Russia. In Hollywood he tried to make a living as a film scriptwriter. Although he sold a few ideas, only one of his scripts ever reached the screen: *Hangmen Also Die* (directed by **Fritz Lang**, 1942). In 1947, having been subpoenaed as a witness by the House Un-American Activities Committee investigating Communist subversion in the film industry, and having skilfully avoided implicating any of his friends, he returned to Europe. After some time spent in Switzerland, devoted to a cautious exploration of the possibilities for creating a theatre of his own, he decided to accept an East German offer to start his own company in East Berlin. This company, the Berliner Ensemble, was formally inaugurated in 1949. But before he returned to East Berlin Brecht had laid the foundations for freedom of movement and independence in publishing his work by applying for Austrian citizenship and by vesting the copyright of his writings in a West German publisher.

Brecht's massive oeuvre can be divided into a number of fairly clearly distinct phases: a wildly anarchic period of exuberantly poetic plays, reflecting an intense sensual enjoyment of life coupled with a deeply pessimistic conviction that all is futile and must end in a senseless death – 1918 to *c.* 1928; among the plays of this period are *Baal* (1918); *Drums in the Night* (1920); *In the Jungle of the Cities* (*Im Dickicht der Staedte*, 1922/3); *Edward II* (a free adaptation of Marlowe's Elizabethan tragedy, first performed in Munich, 1924); and *Man equals Man* (*Mann ist Mann*, 1926). Brecht's greatest success, the *Threepenny Opera* (1928), marks his transition from this exuberantly anarchic phase to the period of his austerely didactic *Lehrstuecke* (didactic plays, teaching plays): 1929 to *c.* 1934. These concise, pared-down, almost diagrammatically schematic works, relying often so heavily on music that they become operas or oratorios rather than plays in the usual sense, were designed not so much for the instruction of an audience as for that of the actors and other participants, to whom they would give an opportunity of

learning, by actually experiencing it, what it was like to be oppressor and oppressed, or an individual sacrificed for the benefit of society and the beneficiary of that sacrifice. As this implies, Brecht insisted that the actors in the didactic plays should play all parts in turn. Outstanding among these didactic plays are the 'school operas', *The Yes-Sayer* (*Der Jasager*, 1930) and *The No-Sayer* (*Der Neinsager*, 1930); the oratorio *The Measures Taken* (*Die Massnahme*, music by Hanns Eisler, 1930); *The Exception and the Rule* (*Die Ausnahme und die Regel*, 1930, first performance, Paris 1947); *The Mother* (*Die Mutter*, after a novel by **Gorky**, 1932). In a less austere style but with equally didactic intentions, Brecht wrote, in the same period, the opera *Mahagonny* (*Aufstieg und Fall der Stadt Mahagonny*, 1930, music by Kurt Weill, who had also largely contributed to the phenomenal success of the *Threepenny Opera*), and the play *St Joan of the Stockyards* (*Die Heilige Johanna der Schlachthoefe*, 1931, first performed in Hamburg, 1959).

In the years of his exile Brecht at first (1934–8) tried to make an active contribution to the overthrow of Hitler by writing what amounted to topical propaganda material of small artistic merit. When it became clear, after Hitler's occupation of Austria in March 1938, that such contributions had become futile, Brecht could return to more ambitious projects. He thus entered on the most fruitful period of his playwriting career: 1938 to 1947, the period of his great parable plays: *The Life of Galileo* (*Leben des Galilei*, 1938, first performance Zürich 1943); *The Good Woman of Setzuan* (*Der Gute Mensch von Setzuan*, 1938–40, first performance Zürich 1943); *Mother Courage* (*Mutter Courage und ihre Kinder*, 1939, first performance Zürich 1941); *Mr Puntila and his Man Matti* (*Herr Puntila und sein Knecht Matti*, 1940–1, first performance Zürich 1948); and *The Caucasian Chalk Circle* (*Der Kaukasische Kreidekreis*, 1944–5, first performance Northfields, Minnesota, 1948).

After his return to East Berlin Brecht devoted himself mainly to the production of these plays and of adaptations of the classics he had made for the Berliner Ensemble.

Much of Brecht's immense worldwide impact on modern drama derives from his attempts, after his conversion to Marxism, to develop what he regarded as the only possible aesthetic theory for a Marxist theatre, his theory of 'epic theatre' and the *Verfremdungseffekt* (strange-making effect, distancing or 'alienation' effect). Brecht was convinced that the traditional theory of drama (which he called 'Aristotelian' but actually derived from the German eighteenth-century classics Goethe and Schiller) is based on the assumption that in the theatre the audience should be made to believe that they are witnessing an event actually taking place before their eyes in an 'eternal present' and that therefore the actors should identify themselves as much as possible with the characters they are portraying, so that the audience in turn can identify with the action of the play and feel what the characters are experiencing. These assumptions, Brecht maintained, imply that throughout the ages human emotions have always been the same, that, in fact, there is such a thing as a permanent, unchangeable 'human nature'. But Marxism, Brecht asserted, is based on the opposite assumption, namely that human nature, human consciousness, human values, are constantly changing, in accordance with changes in the economic and social basis of material conditions. If, therefore, a spectator, as the Aristotelian theory postulates, could really say, 'Yes, I felt exactly what Oedipus or Lear or Macbeth must have felt', that would imply that the Marxist view of human nature was invalid. What was needed, therefore, was a truly Marxist theory of drama, which would not only show that human nature has radically changed throughout the ages, but also that it would still further have to be transformed by changing the organization of society. Hence the devices, usually called 'dramatic', of breathless suspense, high emotional intensity, total identification of actor and character, maximum involvement in an action happening 'here and now', must be rejected and replaced by devices, such as obtain in narrative literature, epic poetry: reflective detachment, critical and relaxed observation of events which are experienced as happening in a distanced past tense, 'there and then'. In other words the theatre must cease to be 'dramatic' in the traditional sense and become 'epic'. The spectator should now see Oedipus or Lear or Macbeth as specimens of humanity determined by different social conditions, as useful examples of changes in human development upon which he could sharpen his critical perception of present social conditions as a preliminary to changing those for the better. In recognizing that Oedipus, for example, was the victim of taboos which have now become senseless, the spectator should realize that similar taboos of his own time might be equally ripe for rejection. Thus, by *historicizing* the dramatic performance, the audience could be induced to think critically about their own society.

The means by which Brecht wanted to bring about this *epic* theatre were what he called his *distancing effects* (*V-Effekte*): chief among these are an avoidance of relentless climaxes in the writing of the play and the avoidance of suspense by announcing the outcome of the action beforehand (so that the audience should direct their attention not on what is going to happen next, but on *how* it is happening); a detached and cooled-down acting style; the avoidance of anything designed to make the audience forget that they are in a theatre, i.e. non-illusionistic scenery; unconcealed lighting apparatus and brilliant, unchanging lighting throughout to inhibit the production of moods and emotions through sentimental lighting effects; the independence of music and design from the words, so that rather than reinforcing them, these elements would act as a contrapuntal critical commentary on the action, i.e. harsh music would expose the false sentimentality of a love song, projections of rotting corpses would comment on a patriotic speech; to show that they are not identifying with their characters, the actors will talk directly to the audience, etc., etc.

Brecht discussed these ideas in voluminous theoretical writings, the most important among which is his *Little Organon for the Theatre* (*Kleines Organon fuer das Theater*, 1948).

Whether the philosophical and psychological basis of these theories is correct or not, their use results in an immensely interesting poetic style of theatre. Brecht's own practice as a director with the Berliner Ensemble in the last years of his life produced performances of an elegance, lightness of touch and grace unusual in the German theatre which had always tended to rely on heavily emotional effects and an intensity which often resulted in screaming and grandiloquent bombast. What is far more questionable is the political impact of the Brechtian theatre. It has been argued that Brecht was too good a dramatist, by instinct, ever to have been able to produce work which would be biased enough to achieve the intended effect of converting audiences to his own political views. Indeed, in his plays, the characters he intended to have a negative impact often arouse more sympathies than the positive heroes, where, in fact, there are any; most of Brecht's later plays heavily rely on irony, in showing what *not* to do rather than trying to influence the public by positive precept. In practice his plays, therefore, often achieve a different effect from the one he intended: Mother Courage, who is supposed to show that being a trader (hence a capitalist) in a war must inevitably lead to the death of her children, is often felt by the public to be a rousing example of selfless devotion and mother love. Brecht was distressed by this, but refused to alter the play to comply with the demands of the Communist authorities who wanted a more direct impact for their cause.

What was even more galling to Brecht was the fact that in his lifetime the aesthetics of drama officially prescribed in the Soviet Union were based on the ideas of **Stanislavsky**, which are in direct contradiction to what Brecht regarded as the truly Marxist aesthetics of drama, the Brechtian epic theatre. Brecht's theories and his plays were long rejected and suppressed in the Soviet sphere of influence as smacking of formalism and avant-garde experimentation. It was only in East Germany that Brecht was tolerated in his lifetime, because the presence of Germany's foremost playwright within its borders shed lustre on a regime struggling for international recognition. But even here Brecht's plays and his productions often met official disapproval and had more than once to be withdrawn. Only after his death was he canonized into a great national classic.

Brecht was, above all, a supreme master of the German language and a very great poet. Even his plays, ultimately, owe their greatness to the sheer brilliance of their language rather than any other, purely dramatic, qualities. Hence it is difficult for non-German audiences to experience their full impact, as all translations must of necessity be imperfect. His theory, although put forward in a highly contemporary Marxist idiom, owes a great deal to his acknowledged models and forerunners, above all the Elizabethan theatre, the classical drama of China and Japan, and the Austro-Bavarian folk-theatre. Seen in its historical context, Brecht's theory emerges as an attempt to reject the bourgeois respectability and academic pretensions of the nineteenth-century theatre and the dominance of the photographic illusionism of the naturalistic stage, and to return to a barnstorming, crudely vital popular proletarian theatre which has its roots in the music hall and the fairground. To achieve this end Brecht forged a splendid idiom of earthy speech, in striking contrast to the highly artificial traditional stage-German. In his poetry Brecht acknowledged the influence of poets as diverse as Villon, **Rimbaud**, **Rudyard Kipling**; of Luther's Bible as well as obscene folk ballads. He also made frequent use of other poets' work through parody; many scenes in his plays are savage parodies of Shakespeare, Schiller and Goethe. In this and in his many adaptations of acknowledged classics Brecht expressed his convictions that the literature of the past was useful only as 'raw material' for quarrying.

Further reading

Collected editions of Brecht's plays in English translation are in the course of publication in Britain (Eyre Methuen) and the United States

(Random House). For Brecht's principal theoretical writings, see John Willett, *Brecht on Theatre* (1964). See also: Klaus Voelker, *Brecht: A Biography* (1976); and an excellent pictorial survey of Brecht's life, *Bertolt Brecht. Sein Leben in Bildern und Texten*, ed. W. Hecht (1978). Critical overviews of Brecht's life and work can be found in John Willett, *The Theatre of Bertolt Brecht* (1959); Martin Esslin, *Brecht – A Choice of Evils* (1959, revised 1980); P. Kleber and C. Visser (eds) *Re-interpreting Brecht: His Influence on Contemporary Drama and Film* (1990); Peter Thomson and Gendyr Sacks (eds) *The Cambridge Companion to Brecht* (1994).

MARTIN ESSLIN

BRETON, André

1896–1966

French writer

During the four decades he spent at the centre of that tumult of debate and agitation which was French Surrealism, André Breton aroused many passions. He was always a man whose temperament required him to define and defend with total intensity certain ideas which mattered to him. If at times this cost him the pain of broken friendships, as witness his quarrels with Antonin Artaud and Louis Aragon, it also gained him the lifelong support of the poet Benjamin Péret and the allegiance of a stream of younger Surrealists eager to further the Surrealist project. As mentor, spokesman and animator of the Surrealist movement – never its bigoted, infallible pope, as his enemies have charged – Breton exerted enormous influence over the French cultural scene from the 1920s onwards. In many ways he was a most self-concerned writer, fascinated by his personal intellectual co-ordinates and his private responses; and yet he became a voice for the modern artistic sensibility at large, a cultural exemplar of a rare kind.

Drawn to poetry at an early age, Breton first published sonnets in the Symbolist style of **Paul Valéry**. But during the First World War he came upon the hallucinatory writings of **Arthur Rimbaud** and this discovery, along with his brief friendship with the sardonic iconoclast Jacques Vaché, led Breton to envisage a purely literary career as narrow and artificial. His work as an orderly in a military hospital had put him in direct contact with the strange utterances of the mentally deranged on whom he had (as one of the first to do so in France) essayed the techniques of Freudian analysis. By 1919 he had produced, in collaboration with Philippe Soupault, the texts of *Les Champs magnétiques* ('Magnetic Fields', 1920), the first sample of Surrealist automatism or trance-writing. After the wild interlude of Paris Dada, the nascent Surrealist group found its charter in Breton's *Manifeste du surréalisme* of 1924, which not only codified automatic practice as a prospection, in the light of **Freud's** researches, of the raw material of the unconscious made available in the form of non-directed language, but defined poetry as a purposeful activity which must lead the poet out of the closed space of literature and into the real world.

The scandalous 'secret society' of Surrealism manifested itself in various acts of revolt against the status quo, with virulent attacks on the Catholic church or establishment writers like Anatole France, and in the publication of a journal, *La Révolution surréaliste* ('The Surrealist Revolution', 1924–9), of which Breton became editor. Following his enthusiastic reading of **Trotsky's** *Lenin*, Breton was converted to dialectical materialism and led the group into protracted negotiations with the French Communists in an effort to conciliate the Surrealist quest with the militant aims of the Party. The latter was, predictably, reluctant to envisage avant-garde experimentation as an integral part of the proletarian struggle. Breton's patchwork book *Les Vases communicants* ('Communicating Vessels', 1932) reflects his efforts to reconcile the idea of the poet as dreamer with that of the poet as revolutionary: but his enquiries into his personal sleeping and waking experiences, in the manner of Freud's auto-analyses, sit ill beside political passages laced with quotations from Engels, **Marx** and other like authorities.

The break with official Communism was sealed with the news of the Moscow Trials in 1936 when Breton showed himself one of the fiercest European critics of the **Stalinist** betrayal of the great idea of the Russian Revolution; his political sympathies now lay with Trotsky, whom he visited in Mexico in 1938. Following the Second World War and his own exile in the USA, Breton shifted his ground somewhat, propounding the central relevance to the Surrealist cause of the writings of the utopian socialist Fourier (*Ode à Charles Fourier*, 1947). The Paris group, reconstituted after Breton's return in 1946, moved eventually towards a libertarian position, collaborating with the *Fédération anarchiste* during the early 1950s. Unfortunately Breton did not live to witness the brief realization of many aspects of the Surrealist poetico-political vision in the May Events of 1968 in Paris.

Breton's writings range from the dreamy suggestiveness of the fantastic worlds evoked in the automatic prose of *Poisson soluble* ('Soluble Fish', 1924) to the persistent argument of programmatic texts like the three Surrealist manifestos (1924, 1930, 1942) or the hard-edged political articles he wrote for the 1930s magazine *Le Surréalisme au service de la révolution*. A genre in which he excels is the personal memoir in which the record of private experiences – dreams, love affairs, visits to such distant places as Tenerife in *L'Amour fou* ('Mad Love', 1937) or the Gaspé peninsula in *Arcane 17* (*Arcanum XVII*, New York 1945) – forms the raw material on which his associative imagination can work, eliciting from particular facts whole chains of analogies and new meanings such that the accidents of an individual life are transcended in a series of propositions about the collective perspectives of Surrealism. In this sense, all Breton's works hover between being confessions and proclamations: his most public statements (such as *Position politique du surréalisme*, 1935) contain passages of intimate reflection, while his most lyrical writings, including a poetry of cascading images (*Poèmes*, 1948), bear the imprint of a mind intent on universal resonances. The mode of Breton's thinking is resolutely analogical: no idea or image emerges in one domain which is not immediately tested for its appropriateness to other, wider domains.

Throughout the history of the political and artistic experiments of Surrealism, Breton pursued knowledge with the passion of one whose final purpose was the delineation of an entirely new mentality, liberated from the orthodoxies of reason and habit. Scornful of the cultural moulds he had inherited, Breton took as his measure the Surrealist commitment to the future and the discipline of spontaneity, of loyalty to the secret self, as evinced in the experiments of automatism and in the wider-ranging adventures of falling in love or, eventually, of taking part in an insurrection.

Reinstating what he saw as a primary faculty shared by children and primitive peoples, Breton sought to define an approach to experience which would reconcile dream-life with actual perceptions and exploit the creative interpenetration of inner and outer reality. Surreality is nothing less than the passionately witnessed coincidence of individual and world, of representation and perception, the imaginary and the tangible, the pleasure principle and the reality principle.

A host of associated values – the marvellous, the enigmatic, the delirious, the convulsive – echo throughout Breton's work. Books such as *Nadja* (1928), in which he relates his affair with an inspired mad girl, point to the emergence of an attitude of delightful susceptibility to the invitations of chance and love: in describing his wanderings through the Paris streets, Breton effectively elaborates a method of intellectual enquiry into the correspondences between mental and material phenomena, and, extrapolating from an essentially Romantic vision of the universe mediated through the imagination, points toward a revolutionary thesis: that the overthrow of repressive political systems is inseparable from poetic revolution within the individual consciousness. Breton's watchword 'the imaginary is that which tends to become real' is the corollary of the premise that allegiance to one's total being – in both its irrational and rational aspects – is the sole guarantee of a fully satisfying implementation of desire at the level of material existence.

As a thinker receptive to many out-of-the-way ideas, Breton followed a zigzag intellectual path, fervently admiring by turns such figures as the Decadent writer Huysmans, the neurologist Babinski, the poets Apollinaire and **Tzara**, the psychoanalyst Freud, the revolutionaries **Lenin** and Trotsky, the erotic novelist Sade, the social theorist Fourier. The intellectual system which he evolved owes its richness and fluency to his capacity for synthesizing such diversely stimulating influences. Breton's synthesis has in turn exercised its own influence. In the political sphere, his ideas find an echo in the writings of Herbert Marcuse and anticipate many theses of the Situationists. Many of his insights into the nature of language have filtered through into the thinking of such post-Freudian theorists as **Jacques Lacan** and **Roland Barthes**. In literary terms, Breton did much to help rewrite nineteenth-century literary history, rescuing neglected figures like Nerval, Lautréamont and Jarry. In the field of the visual arts, he contributed, through such authoritative texts as *Le Surréalisme et la peinture* ('Surrealism and Painting', 1928), to the evolution in perception that has led to the public recognition of **de Chirico**, Duchamp, **Ernst** and **Picasso** as major artists of the age.

Breton was equally alert to a host of other art forms, including naive painting, mediumistic and psychotic art, and tribal art: he owned a considerable personal collection of Polynesian and Red Indian artefacts. In this, as in his other seemingly eccentric enthusiasms – for Gothic novels or rare texts on alchemy, for agate stones or butterflies – Breton displayed the virtues of a sensibility at one with itself and thus able to commit itself unhesitatingly to any and every genuinely felt attraction.

A system of thought which encompasses incredible disparities within an overall unity; a prose style in which explosive images are marshalled by a concern for lucid theoretical formulation; a moral rigour in relationships which nonetheless allowed for a well-attested capacity for loyalty even beyond the limits of the 'reasonable' – these are just a few of the paradoxes which emerge from a consideration of Breton's complex career. They are factors of confusion in an exact portrayal of where he stood and what he was: yet there is no denying that Breton occupied a central position in French cultural life during his lifetime and that his example remains a powerful, if often occulted, force in contemporary France. If for nothing else he will be remembered for his unswerving commitment to the theme of prospecting man's hidden potentialities.

Further reading

Other works: *L'Immaculée Conception* (with Paul Eluard, 1930); *Anthologie de l'humour noir* (1941); *Entretiens* (1952); *L'Art magique* (1957). See also: J. Gracq, *André Breton: quelques aspects de l'écrivain* (1948); M. Carrouges, *André Breton et les données fondamentales du surréalisme* (1950); C. Browder, *André Breton: Arbiter of Surrealism* (1967); S. Alexandrian, *André Breton par lui-même* (1971); M. Bonnet, *André Breton: naissance de l'aventure surréaliste* (1975); G. Legrand, *André Breton en son temps* (1976); Mark Polizzotti, *Revolution of the Mind: The Life of André Breton* (1995).

ROGER CARDINAL

BRITTEN, Benjamin (Lord)

1913–76

English composer

Benjamin Britten was born in Suffolk, an area of England to which he remained devoted, and where he lived for most of his life. Yet he was in certain significant respects an outsider. He was a homosexual, without the bohemian flair which would have enabled him to live in places where conventional morality could be more easily discounted. His contacts with the **Auden** and Isherwood circle in the 1930s encouraged a move to America at the start of the war, but the establishment of a permanent relationship with the singer Peter Pears combined with a longing for Suffolk to bring him home in 1942. He was also a pacifist, but after World War II this naturally affected the character of his work more than that of his everyday life.

As composer, conductor, pianist and director of the Aldeburgh Festival, Britten was for thirty years after 1945 a central figure in British musical life. This period saw substantial changes in taste and style, so it was inevitable that Britten should, at the end, seem old-fashioned alongside Harrison Birtwistle or **Peter Maxwell Davies**. Even after his first major success, the opera *Peter Grimes* (1945), he was still regarded by some as a clever but superficial composer, and this reaction was one result of his earlier rejection (with the encouragement of his principal teacher Frank Bridge) of much that was most insular in the British music of the inter-war years. His early taste was for **Mahler**, **Stravinsky**, some **Berg** and **Schoenberg**, and various popular idioms, and his style soon cast off any trace of British pastoralisms in favour of an expanded tonal harmony relating to **Bartók** and Stravinsky, and a technique of thematic integration comparable to Bartók or even Schoenberg. Britten was always a highly economical composer, a supreme miniaturist, as the song cycles prove. Yet he was also skilled at sustaining tensions over the largest scale available to a composer, opera, where the conflicts of the plot could be mirrored in purely musical tensions and interactions.

With the exception of a rather sprawling *String Quartet* (1931), Britten's early works – for example, the *Sinfonietta* Op. 1, and the choral variations *A Boy Was Born* Op. 3 – are notable for tight formal control, textural inventiveness and a remarkably mature technique of thematic manipulation. Between 1933 and 1939, he spent much time working on various radio, film and theatre projects, but during the late 1930s and early 1940s he composed several fine song cycles, including the *Seven Sonnets of Michelangelo* (1940), and some important orchestral works, including the Violin Concerto (1939) and the *Sinfonia da Requiem* (1940). With the first performance of *Peter Grimes* the foundations were laid for a contribution to opera which embraced works for children (*Let's Make an Opera*, 1949), chamber opera (*Rape of Lucretia*, 1946; *Albert Herring*, 1947; and *The Turn of the Screw*, 1954) and larger-scale works (*Billy Budd*, 1951; *Gloriana*, 1953; *A Midsummer Night's Dream*, 1960; and *Death in Venice*, 1973), as well as three 'parables for church performance' (*Curlew River*, 1964; *The Burning Fiery Furnace*, 1966; and *The Prodigal Son*, 1968) and one opera specifically for television, *Owen Wingrave* (1971). Opera was the genre in which Britten worked most consistently, though he also composed a wide variety of other vocal works, from song cycles to the celebrated *War Requiem* (1961), whose juxtaposition of the Latin liturgy with **Wilfred Owen's** poetry – the work was commissioned for the dedication of the new Coventry Cathedral – has remained a notably powerful embodiment of Britten's ability to express profoundly ambivalent feelings in striking direct and affecting ways. In the field of instrumental music particular artists stimulated the creation of some important compositions: for example, a sonata with piano, three solo suites and a symphony with orchestra were all written for the cellist Mstislav Rostropovich.

It is not in itself remarkable that Britten's preferred texts dealt with various forms of vulnerability, nor that his operatic subject-matter returned obsessively to the outsider, the alienated, the lonely. Serious poetry and drama, especially of the more Romantic variety, deals constantly with these issues. But it is remarkable that, given the recurrences of these ideas and images, Britten's music evolved so distinctively, while remaining essentially concerned with the purely musical techniques for exploring fundamental tonal relationships and the forces capable of undermining them. Britten was never a teacher, and although his style, like any distinctive form of expression, lends itself to mimicry, his influence has been most fruitful on composers who have preserved his concern for communicating through lyric melody in which goal-directed linear processes project the essence of a firm harmonic logic, even when that logic is no longer governed by traditional triadic progressions.

Further reading

Other works include: *Our Hunting Fathers* (1936, text devised by Auden); *Variations on a Theme of Frank Bridge* (1937); *Les Illuminations* (1939); *The Young Person's Guide to the Orchestra* (1945); *Spring Symphony* (1949); *Cantata Misericordium* (1963); *Songs and Proverbs of William Blake* (1965). Britten's principal publishers are Boosey and Hawkes and Faber Music. Britten's writings are in *Letters from a Life* (Vols 1 and 2, 1991: Vol. 3, 2004), and *Britten on Music*, ed. Paul Kildea (2003). For a comprehensive biography, see Humphrey Carpenter, *Benjamin Britten: A Biography* (1992). See also: Peter Evans, *The Music of Benjamin Britten* (revised edn, 1996) and Philip Rupprecht, *Britten's Musical Language* (2001).

ARNOLD WHITTALL

BROWNING, Robert

1812–89

English poet

It has been Browning's fate that he fell a prey in his later years to the sort of snobbish adulation which often attends obscurity of expression. After early comparative neglect, the poet's reputation fell into the hands of readers and critics who saw in him a seer and moral teacher with a tough but reassuringly optimistic message; a thinker who, despite – perhaps even because of – his verbal difficulty, could provide for the initiated a strenuous assurance that God was in his Heaven, that doubt could be conquered by persistent faith and that an intellectually consistent poetic argument could be adduced in defence of anti-intellectualism. Browning's poetry seemed bracing, free of the morbidity of much late-Victorian art, gratifyingly taxing in its expression, but confident and life-enhancing. The tone of much Browning criticism up to the First World War tended to follow such lines, and even if George Santayana and others reacted strongly against this fashion, the very course their criticism took tended still to

attack him on his qualifications as a thinker and teacher, rather than on his artistic qualities.

Since then poets of greater obscurity have carried messages more in keeping with this present age and Browning has been largely ignored, apart from a handful of well-known school anthology pieces. Even here his moral heartiness has tended to make him a poet more popular with teachers than pupils. Not having gone so deeply through the purgatorial period of critical antagonism meted out to such contemporaries of his as **Tennyson**, Browning has not benefited from rediscovery and reassessment. He lacks the dark pessimism of Tennyson, the cultured melancholy of **Arnold** or the metaphysical anguish of **Hopkins**. He seems altogether too normal, too sane, and perhaps too verbose, while the verbal complexities that tantalized his age have become merely irritating in a century accustomed to the conundrums of **Pound**, **Eliot**, **Yeats**, **Wallace Stevens**, Empson and their followers. An enormous proportion of his verse is dismissed – unread – as unreadable. This includes all his plays, most of his poems before 1843 and virtually everything after 1869. Even *The Ring and the Book* (1868–9), considered his masterpiece, is almost certainly far more often praised than read. Not that Browning himself is guiltless in this matter: *Sordello* (1840), despite its fine passages, remains one of the most obscure poems ever written and seems to most readers a puzzle whose solution ill repays the effort, while the plays are of interest merely to students of Victorian drama, and only not inferior to most examples of that luckless genre, while *The Ring and the Book*, despite its acknowledged mastery, is terrifyingly long. The late poetry, though, is another matter altogether and hardly deserves the almost total neglect into which it has fallen. Not that Browning has lacked sympathetic critics and biographers: they have so far failed to carry the public with them.

Yet Browning's poetry was extremely influential in the twentieth century: more so than has sometimes been acknowledged by his debtors. Pound's admiration for Browning is well known and accounts for some of the worst as well as some of the best features of his poetry, but T.S. Eliot's *Journey of the Magi* and *Prufrock* and much besides are inconceivable without Browning's example; and the dramatic monologue has had a significant place in the work of many modern English and American poets, while in 'St Martin's Summer' and other poems in his later volumes there is more than a suggestion of **Hardy**.

Browning was born on 7 May 1812 in Camberwell, then a village. His father was a clerk in the Bank of England and his mother was from Dundee, the daughter of a Scottish mother and a German father. She had a keen interest in natural history and music, which her son was to share, and was a deeply religious nonconformist – an influence which was to prove strong but ambiguous. Between mother and son there was an exceptionally close bond. He remained all his life a man who needed the society and support of women, and to his mother he was entirely devoted. His father was an unworldly erratically scholarly man: 'My father was a scholar and knew Greek,' wrote Browning in 'Development', one of his last poems. From this poem we catch a glimpse of Browning senior's method of teaching, for it was from him rather than from his formal education that Robert learnt most, though he went to school after a fashion and, for a very brief spell, to London University. He shared his father's delight in the odd, the out-of-the-way, and from him too came his love of painting. His father's educational methods, though strangely modern and calculated to interest and stimulate a sensitive and inquiring mind, were probably not very systematic – Browning, like Yeats, had an eccentric area of knowledge – and Santayana was later to pour scorn on, and read a lot into, this unconventional education. Yet the strange by-ways of knowledge, picked up partly from his father, partly from his browsings in his father's library, partly from what he called his 'university' of Italy, give the characteristically wide range of his subject-matter. From his exceptionally sheltered childhood

Browning took away a love of the unusual, a need to be mothered and an easily wounded sensibility.

Though probably too much has been made of Browning's distress over the reception of his first published poem, 'Pauline' (1833), a Shelley-like effusion, uncharacteristic of his later work, he remained conscious of his own fear of self-revelation. He writes to Elizabeth Barrett, 'You speak out, *you*, – I only make men and women speak – give you truth broken into prismatic hues, and fear the pure white light, even if it is in me.'

Yet the paradox of Browning is that he is at his most personal when appearing most objective. He is best known for his dramatic monologues. He did not invent the form, but he and Tennyson independently and almost simultaneously brought it to perfection in their different ways. Browning perhaps developed it more consistently, and it represents some of his finest work. Browning's art in the dramatic monologues has been compared to that of the actor assuming a role, but it is surely more than this. The characters are created from within, and poet and reader and character participate in the same ritual. The monologue is not an argument presented to the reader, but an act in which the reader is made to share. In so far as the individual poem is successful it involves a fusion of the reader's personality with that of the protagonist; we do not judge Andrea del Sarto or Count Guido, we collaborate with them. The drama of the monologue is a quarrel, not between different characters on the stage, but between the reader's desire for freedom and sense of moral order, or what Robert Langbaum (see below) refers to as 'sympathy versus judgement'. Hence Browning's fondness for disreputable characters and extreme dramatic situations. The danger of the method, and one that Browning does not always escape, is wordiness. It is this ability to make the reader identify with characters whom he cannot necessarily admire that reaches its highest point in *The Ring and the Book*. This 'theme and variations' forces one to modify one's response to a central event in such a way that the crude story is made to reveal the greatest range of interpretation – one's instinctive responses are repeatedly shaken.

Two fine and unaccountably neglected poems of his late 'unreadable' period – 'Red Cotton Night-Cap Country' and 'The Inn Album' – are again evidence of his ability to handle extreme and apparently unsuitable material with astonishing virtuosity.

It may seem odd that a writer so well versed in drama of character, so expert at variations of speech, should have made such heavy weather of writing for the stage. Perhaps one is here misled by the term 'dramatic monologue'. The monologue is dramatic in so far as it shows conflict emerging in speech; but drama requires visual action, and interplay between characters. Browning's plays remain wordy and introspective, a series of self-explanatory speeches rather than an interplay of character, speech and action. Perhaps the monologues should be called 'psychological monologues': the drama is entirely interior and entirely self-sufficient. The poet assumes the personality of the speaker and this allows both anonymity and universality.

But it is not only the dramatic monologues that are in this sense 'dramatic': Browning's love poetry, another aspect of verse at which he is a master, is oblique too. Not usually in any conventional sense lyrical, the poems have a deep but muted sensuality and a sense of the physical, and are often concerned with a moment of union between the sexes, all too fleeting and rare: the 'good minute' is a moment of mutual illumination, endlessly sought for and as real, though the poetic means are different, as such moments in Donne's poetry. Yet again the poet avoids too direct a personal reference: the poem keeps its distance: it is 'Any Wife to Any Husband' or 'One Way of Love' and 'Another Way of Love'.

One of the facts that everybody knows about Browning is his elopement in 1846 with the poet Elizabeth Barrett and their life together in Italy until her death in 1861. Italy, and particularly Renaissance Italy, gave to Browning a sense of freedom and colour and an escape from Victorian England. His poetry is a poetry of extremes, that plunges passionately into violent action. Italy provided the electric charge that his work needed:

Open my heart and you will see
Graved inside of it, 'Italy'.

Elizabeth and Italy were the inspiration of some of his happiest and some of his intensest poetry. Italy stimulated too his love of art. No poet writes better about the other arts, particularly music, than Browning.

Browning's mind was quick rather than profound and his philosophy is as superficial and commonplace as the 'philosophy' of most of us. His work is weakest when most concerned with abstractions, and his attempts at systematic teaching have worn badly. His insistence on the efficacy of struggle for its own sake – the 'I was ever a fighter' strain in his work – and his confessional poems such as 'Easter Day' have lost much of their appeal, but the idea of Browning as a mindless optimist is contradicted by much of his poetry: not only such poems as 'Caliban upon Setebos' and 'Childe Roland', but much of his love poetry is aware of the tragic and gloomy side of life and the frailty of relationships.

He wrote too much, too carelessly and too easily, but his own satiric comment, 'That poet's a Browning: he neglects the form', is scarcely accurate. There are few poets with a more adventurous sense of form: indeed, the form of the poems is sometimes their most ingenious characteristic. Nor is he deficient in musicality: the falling cadences of 'A Toccata of Galuppi's' and the rhythmic control of such poems as 'The Last Ride Together' would give that the lie. It is a lack of pruning, an over-emphasis and long-windedness that make even such poems as 'Fifine at the Fair' tedious despite their ingenuity:

Volubility
with him, keeps on the increase

as he says of one of his characters. All the same, with his colloquialisms, his Chaucerian skill as a storyteller, his liberation of poetic speech from the over-sophistication and conscious polish of much Victorian verse, his obsession with the brutal and the prosaic, his acceptance of women as partners rather than idealized mistresses, he would seem to speak very much to us today. It is true that there is a sort of brashness in his work that can repel the more fastidious: he writes too much at the top of his voice.

A young woman meeting him for the first time wrote:

> He talks everybody down with his dreadful voice, and always places his person in such disagreeable proximity to yours and puffs and blows and spits in your face. I tried to think of 'Abt Vogler' but it was no use – he couldn't ever have written it.

Further reading

See: G.K. Chesterton, *Robert Browning* (1903); B. Miller, *Robert Browning. A Portrait* (1952); W.C. DeVane, *A Browning Handbook* (1955); R. Langbaum, *The Poetry of Experience: The Dramatic Monologue in Modern Literary Tradition* (1957); B. Litzinger and D. Smalley, *Browning: The Critical Heritage* (1970); I. Jack, *Browning's Major Poetry* (1973); N. Irvine and P. Honan, *The Book, the Ring and the Poet: A Biography of Robert Browning* (1974); C. de L. Ryals, *Browning's Later Poetry – 1871–1889* (1975); G.R. Hudson, *Robert Browning's Literary Life* (1993); Pamela Neville-Sington, *Robert Browning: A Life After Death* (2004).

JOSEPH BAIN

BRUCKNER, Anton

1824–96

Austrian composer

Bruckner's uniqueness among major composers could be defined in several ways. No one of comparable stature left so few important works; an accomplished organist in his eleventh year, he continued his technical studies until he was thirty-seven; happy to give before large audiences organ recitals consisting mostly of improvisations, in society

Bruckner was totally without self-confidence. Several years after becoming principal organist at the monastery of St Florian he doubted his musical gifts to the extent of studying Latin with a view to becoming a schoolmaster. Having composed his mature symphonies he humbly permitted well-meaning conductors to make cuts during rehearsal. To the end of his days this profoundly inspired artist and consummate craftsman remained obedient to priests and respectful to the upper classes.

Bruckner was born at the village of Ansfelden in Upper Austria in 1824, the descendant of a line of peasants and artisans traceable as far back as the fourteenth century. His father and grandfather were both teachers at the village school. The musically gifted father played for dancing to augment his meagre salary and became the prey of convivial drinking; in 1836 his health broke down so completely that the boy Anton had to return home from Linz where he had been sent to improve his education. After his father's death a year later Anton entered the choir at St Florian, the great Benedictine House that was to be the centre of his personal life. Here he studied organ and violin and, during a year at Linz before qualifying as school assistant, heard for the first time music by Beethoven. With dedicated patience he copied out the whole of Bach's *Kunst der Fuge*. In 1841 Bruckner became assistant in a village school, living the life of the rural poor; besides teaching, his duties included work in the fields with the labourers. He began to compose church music and, later, choruses for men's voices. In 1845 a post as regular school assistant brought the security of ten years at St Florian. Even after composing a Requiem and being confirmed in his position as first organist he continued to doubt his vocation and in 1854 applied for an administrative vacancy in the monastic chancellery. Failures in love (to the end of his life Bruckner was susceptible to the charms of too-young girls) and self-doubt drove him to the brink of collapse, though he soon recovered sufficiently to compose his first significant work, the Mass in B flat minor, performed in 1854. Almost against his will he accepted the post of organist at Linz Cathedral, fearful at the thought of having to emerge from the seclusion of his beloved St Florian.

The time at Linz began with a period of comparative happiness; Bruckner conducted choral concerts, was well received in local society and, with almost fanatical diligence ('I worked seven hours daily for Sechter') perfected his technique, though in his compositions he remained cautiously derivative, modelling his style largely on Schubert or Mendelssohn. Knowledge of the great masters of instrumental music came from studies with Otto Kitzler, ten years Bruckner's junior. Other Linz friends made him aware of **Wagner** and in 1865 he was present at the first performance of *Tristan* in Munich, having heard *Tannhäuser* three years earlier. In 1864 he completed the D minor Mass, the work which showed for the first time more than hints of future greatness. The earliest symphonies, No. 0 *(Die Nullte)* and No. 1, belong to this period; with the success of the D minor Mass, the encouragement of Wagner and a passing acquaintance with **Berlioz**, **Liszt** and Anton Rubinstein, anyone but Bruckner would surely have begun to feel secure in the larger world of music.

On the contrary, having completed the two symphonies and a second Mass (a commission from the Bishop of Linz) he suffered a total collapse from which he recovered completely to apply for a lectureship at Vienna University. Failure here was mitigated by an appointment at the Vienna Conservatorium, to succeed his own mentor, Simon Sechter, but the prospect of moving from the security of Linz precipitated another crisis of indecision. At Linz Bruckner was well paid and, like any worthy servant of the establishment, could look forward to the security of a pension. No disrespect for a visionary artist is intended by the observation that these intense disturbances of mind may have sprung as much from a peasant-like fear of penury as from spiritual malaise. Certainly the acceptance of the Vienna post was made

less painful by an increase in the salary offered and a promise that his position at Linz would be held in suspension should he wish to return.

At first all went well in Vienna: Bruckner proved an excellent teacher and in 1872 the third of his Masses, performed in the Augustinerkirche, was praised by Hanslick, later to be a relentless opponent. Symphonies were another matter. Dessoff, conductor of the Philharmonic concerts, rejected No. 1 in 1869 and No. 2 three years later. It was Dessoff who, beginning to rehearse No. 0, had asked its unfortunate composer to tell him where the first subject began. ('And where are you going to put your brown tree?') Neither of the rejected symphonies betrayed any lack of invention or of technical skill, but the abundance of motifs and the absence, even thus early in Bruckner's maturing style, of the classical impetus preserved by **Brahms**, must have seemed evidence of mere incapacity. No. 3, with its majestic trumpet theme that so impressed Wagner (in its first version the work contained quotations from the *Ring*), was still less acceptable. The doubtless inadequate performance under Bruckner himself in 1877 was a disastrous failure, promoting only the self-distrust that led to the usually regrettable revisions of many works. Isolation and incomprehension were in part the consequence of this naive artist's unforeseen involvement in the musical politics for which he could not have been worse suited. In their feud with the classicists the Wagner party needed a symphonist to set against Brahms, while Hanslick (the model for Beckmesser), though far from being a fool and more appreciative of Wagner's genius than has been pretended, found in Bruckner the unresisting victim of his brilliant and obtuse polemics. (Brahms refrained from attacking a colleague, but in private expressed his doubts as to Bruckner's sense of movement by references to 'symphonic boa-constrictors'.) If Brahms's resolution of the problem facing the composer of symphonies in the later nineteenth century still seems more convincing than Bruckner's, this is because he was able to limit its scope by adhering to the harmonic rhythms of the classical masters and thus retaining the guide-lines of sonata form – the distinction between exposition and development, the structural emphasis on the beginning of the recapitula-tion and its transition to coda. The nature of Bruckner's genius left him no choice but to embody in musical architecture the range, scope and time-scale of Wagner's mature dramas; only a profoundly thoughtful artist could have sustained the dual burden of defining and then creating a new kind of symphony containing valid equivalents for no longer available procedures.

The Fourth Symphony (composed 1874, revised 1878, performed 1881) was, in its first movement at least, the evident product of a major composer. As yet the enlargement of the classical time-scale does not preclude the observance of traditional structures, but in the symphonies that followed processes of transition became increasingly continuous until, in No. 7, the letter of sonata form had virtually disappeared, leaving its spirit all the more enhanced in the first of Bruckner's works to win acceptance. Neither the Fifth nor the Sixth was heard by the composer but the first performance of No. 7, at Leipzig, not Vienna, was immensely successful, as was the second, at Munich. Bruckner rightly feared the worldly Viennese, for when they heard the work, under Richter, in March 1886, the insufferable Hanslick described the symphony, full of exalted vision and wonderful tone-colours (original, not taken from Wagner), as 'unnatürlich, aufgeblasen, krankhaft und verderblich' ('forced, inflated, morbid and pernicious'). However, several eminent conductors were now favourable, notably Hermann Levi (Wagner's tolerated Jew) for whom Bruckner had profound regard. No. 8, even more monumental than No. 7 – it had taken three years to write – was sent to Levi in 1887 for inclusion in his winter season, but having seen the score he rejected it as incompre-hensible. Hard-won confidence was destroyed and the symphony was submitted to drastic revision, to be performed in 1892,

by Richter, not Levi. No omen deterred Bruckner from planning his ninth symphony in D minor but it was never finished. Even with the fragmentary last movement it is clearly the most daringly original of the series, harsh and tormented as though all that remained of the New Testament for this devout artist was Revelation, in its most forbidding aspect. At the last concert he attended, nearly a year before his death in October 1896, Bruckner heard his own *Te Deum*.

No other great composer's fame can have rested on so few works. Of the symphonies, the first three are imperfect, the last unfinished. Three Masses, some motets, the *Te Deum*, of chamber music one quintet.

Such is the sum of a master who, so far from being a Romantic, was perhaps the last repre-sentative in the nineteenth century of the Great Tradition, reaching back to the Middle Ages, of a music that drew life from its own nature and substance, not from the private emotions and fantasies of those who composed it.

Further reading

See: Robert Simpson, *The Essence of Bruckner* (1967); Philip Barford, *Bruckner Symphonies* (1968): Hans Redlich, *Bruckner and Mahler* (1955 rev. 1963); Erwin Doernberg, *The Life and Symphonies of Anton Bruckner* (1960); T. Jackson and P. Hawkshaw (eds), *Bruckner Studies* (1997); S. Johnson, *Bruckner Remembered* (1998); C. Howie, *Anton Bruckner: A Documentary Biography* (2001).

BASIL LAM

BRUNEL, Isambard Kingdom

1806–59

Anglo-French engineer

Of all the great engineers of the first age of the machine, Isambard Kingdom Brunel was undoubtedly the most original, and arguably the greatest. He is remembered equally for his failures as for his successes, for they both share the same qualities of grandeur, of being the produce of creative genius working always to advance the art of engineering.

His father was the celebrated French émigré Marc Isambard Brunel. Isambard Kingdom was born in Portsea, near Portsmouth, on 9 April 1806, during the time that his father was finishing the revolutionary block-making machinery in the naval dockyard. His education was carefully overseen by his father, who encouraged him to draw as a child, and later sent him to Paris to learn mathematics and to undergo an apprenticeship with Louis Breguet, the maker of chronometers and scientific instruments. On his return to England in 1822, he began to work with his father, and also spent time working with the consummate craftsman engineer and associate of his father's, Henry Maudsley. Thus his early experience was with two of the finest exponents of the new machine technology. Consequently, Brunel stands apart from Samuel Smiles's ideal of self-help, of the ultimately shallow and philistine tradition of the self-taught, self-made engineer/entrepreneur.

His father began work in 1824 on the second great project of his career, the Rotherhithe Tunnel beneath the Thames in London. The undertaking was prolonged, difficult and dangerous. In 1828 there was a major flood in the tunnel, in which Brunel, by then engineer-in-charge, was seriously injured. His description of the accident, written shortly afterwards, contains a revealing item: 'When standing there the effect was grand – the roar of the rushing water in a confined passage, and its great velocity rushing past the opening was grand, very grand.' This appreciation of such proximity of the dark power of nature was strangely in tune with the spirit of the art of the time, with the poetry of Blake and the paintings of John Martin. It reveals a sensibility that was to inform much of his finest work.

At the end of a long convalescence, Brunel moved to Bristol, a city whose setting, with the fantastic gorge of the Avon, must have appealed to him. He entered and finally won the competition for the design of a bridge to span the gorge. Because of problems of finance, his design was to remain unbuilt until after his death. Finally it was to be completed by a consortium of those who had been both associates and opponents of his during his lifetime. It stands today with its high suspended single span, a graceful soaring memorial, this bridge which was, in his own words, 'my first child, my darling'. After several years of frustration, he was invited, in 1833, by a group of Bristol merchants, concerned for the future of the city as a port, to survey a possible route for a railway from the city to London. He promised to discover 'not the cheapest, but the best route'. He undertook the survey on horseback. From this beginning, the Great Western Railway was formed, and Brunel was appointed engineer.

Thus began a life of continuous hectic endeavour which was to prove finally fatally exhausting, a life paralleled by many of his contemporaries in this most explosive of ages.

Brunel's essential nature as an engineer was always to innovate, always to find a fitting originality for each new problem, eschewing established solutions, always working from what he took to be basic principles. Thus the railway as it unfolded became a line of constant invention across southern England. He determined from the outset to make what he called 'the finest work in England' perfect in execution. Rejecting all precedents, he decided that the line should consist of a broad gauge of 7ft to facilitate speed and comfort. This was to cause considerable controversy as there already existed an established gauge of 4ft 8½ins pioneered by George Stephenson, and widely adopted. That this gauge had pragmatic origins in the coal mines of the north of England would have been sufficient to condemn it in Brunel's eyes. His indifference to the foreseeable problems of a mixture of gauges on a national scale is an indication of his vision of the Great Western Railway as a singular work, a demonstration of excellence. Consistent with this, he insisted on having total responsibility for all aspects of the work, and, with the exception of the building surrounding his great roof at Paddington Station, his finger was on every detail.

He moved his office to London, which allowed him to exercise his love of society. Through a common interest in music he became friends with the Horsley family of Kensington, and in 1836 he married Mary, one of the daughters.

Throughout his life, until his final great work, he attracted to him devoted colleagues of almost equal brilliance to his own. Such a man was David Gooch, the designer of a series of beautifully proportioned powerful engines for the Great Western Railway. With these locomotives the railway was able to demonstrate journeys at unprecedented speeds, regularly averaging over 50 mph.

The first section from Paddington to Taplow was opened on 31 May 1838. In 1840 Queen Victoria travelled by special train from Windsor to London, with Gooch and Brunel on the footplate. The final joining of the two lines emerging from Bristol and from London required the driving of what was then the longest tunnel in the world, through solid stone at Box Hill, near Bath. On the last day of June 1841, a garlanded train travelled the completed route in four hours.

By 1844, the extended broad-gauge line was running express trains from London to Exeter. The excellence of Brunel's conception was proven, but it was to be finally a Pyrrhic victory. Throughout England more cautious railway engineers had adopted the narrow gauge, and finally the inescapable fact emerged that in order to overcome the inconvenience of changing between the two gauges, it was easier and cheaper to narrow a line rather than broaden it. The Great Western Railway however, rather heroically, maintained the broad gauge until 1892.

West of Exeter, on the line to Plymouth, Brunel undertook what must be considered his strangest and certainly least successful work. Concerned partly by the steep inclines involved in the route between Exeter and Newton Abbott, he decided to construct an atmospheric railway. The driving mechanism he constructed was a buried tube between the lines, which was maintained as a partial vacuum by pumping stations built at intervals. Within the tube, a piston was drawn along by the unequal air pressures. This was connected through a continuous slot in the top of the tube to the carriages on the rails above. The success depended upon the linear valve remaining air tight while allowing the repeated passage of trains. This proved impossible to achieve for any length of time. While it worked it fulfilled its author's specification 'moving trains at up to 54 mph and up to 100 tons in weight at slower speeds', but its final total failure was unavoidable. It proved to be the most costly failure in the history of civil engineering. Within this defeat, however, as his biographer L.T.C. Rolf has pointed out, can be detected a clear indication of his finest qualities.

> He was building through a landscape of great beauty. From his efforts can be read an intention of fitting his own work into the greater work of nature. The trains would be moved by a silent force; the pumping stations were carefully considered and sited. It is as if some deeper vision urged on his vaunting inventiveness, a vision that once developed would have stood as a moral principle of harmony between nature and the machine, a principle capable perhaps of transforming the dark horror of the early industrial landscape.

It is some measure of his esteem that despite the disaster he was retained as engineer for driving the railway further westward. It is some measure, too, of his resilience that in the process he built a series of brilliant stone and wood viaducts and finally, carrying the line across the broad Tamar river at Saltash in 1849, began his last and greatest bridge. With one of the two great spans in place by 1857 he was as ever ready to move on, leaving it to be completed by his associates, who finished it in the year of his death.

As early as 1835 he had suggested to the amazed directors of the Great Western Railway that the western terminus should be New York, rather than Bristol. While intensely involved with the railways, he designed and had built by the Great Western Steamship Company in 1836 the first of his three great ships, the *Great Western*. The purpose of the ship for its designer was to prove the viability of crossings under continuous steam power. He was the first to realize the theoretical relationship between performance and form and the gain by building large ships. His ships were therefore to be big and fast, as were the locomotives that he and Gooch designed for the Great Western Railway. Each of the three ships at its launching was the largest ever built. The first two were intended for the Atlantic crossing, the third for the journey to Australia. All three, the *Great Western,* the *Great Britain* and the *Great Eastern*, were plagued by bad luck. The first two were built in Bristol and the third, the *Great Eastern*, was built at Millwall on the Thames, close to his father's tunnel, the site of his first serious work and the place where the river had nearly taken his life. The misfortunes that danced attendance around the building, launching and maiden voyage of his last gigantic ship were to exhaust him, break his spirit and kill him. Most of the problems stemmed from Brunel's choice of contractor, who turned out to be very different from his devoted associates on previous work. Also the undertaking became a public event, prone to ridicule or praise through the newly powerful popular press. A new age had arrived, populist and disrespectful, quite out of sympathy with the intensity and integrity of his brilliance.

He collapsed aboard the great ship three days before its first sailing and died on 15 September 1859. The last report he had, hours before his death, of the *Great Eastern* out in the English Channel on her maiden voyage, was that there had been an explosion on board, with several fatalities.

From the life and work of Isambard Kingdom Brunel can be discerned an image of an industrialized society free from the compulsion of mass production, producing through the concerted efforts of the people, orchestrated by genius, fine works. His finest remaining memorials, the bridge at Saltash and the route of the Great Western Railway, stand therefore also as mitigating to the first half of the nineteenth century, to the great energy of the working people of the dark enflamed first Machine Age.

Further reading

See: L.T.C. Rolf, *Isambard Kingdom Brunel* (1957); L.T.C. Rolf, *Victorian Engineering* (1970); Adrian Vaughan, *Isambard Kingdom Brunel: Engineering Knight-errant* (1991).

FREDERICK SCOTT

BUÑUEL, Luis
1900–83
Spanish film director

A man (Buñuel himself) stands by a window sharpening a razor. Outside a cloud passes across a full moon. A woman stares in impassive close-up towards the camera. The razor is drawn across her eyeball.

After three-quarters of a century this opening sequence from Buñuel's first 17-minute film has lost none of its power to shock. *Un Chien andalou* (1928), made in collaboration with **Salvador Dali**, was a Surrealist *succès de scandale*.

Buñuel described his second independent feature, *L'Age d'or* (1930s, with Dali), as a 'desperate and passionate appeal to murder'. In Paris, where it was first shown, the police had to be called in to clear the cinema. To convict Buñuel of the charge of anarchy, blasphemy, pornography or even high seriousness would be to reduce his obsessions to the literal banality of moral and aesthetic terrorism. His genius was to combine the unnatural, the incongruous, the outrageous with an unblinking matter-of-factness that not only subverts the narrative preconceptions of his audience, but which also dramatizes an emotional collage of images and associations that haunt the mind.

In Buñuel's words, 'Neo-realist reality is incomplete, official, and altogether reasonable; but the poetry, the mystery, everything which enlarges tangible reality is missing.' However, Buñuel's next venture was an uncompromising documentary, *Land Without Bread* (1932). With cool, almost surgical precision, scenes of appalling poverty, sickness and despair in a small Spanish village are contrasted with the rich and remote trappings of the church. It was too much for the Republican authorities. The film was banned.

For seventeen years Buñuel's career went into eclipse. He did a dubbing stint for Paramount in Paris, produced for Warner in Spain, and was even invited to Hollywood to make anti-Nazi propaganda. But an accusation from his old friend Dali that he was an atheist, communist, or both, forced his resignation. He emigrated to Mexico, and directed a musical box-office flop, then a comedy hit which permitted him to make the award-winning *Los Olvidados* (1950). After Vittorio de Sica's sentimental social indictment of slum life, *Bicycle Thieves* (1948), Buñuel's underworld of beggars, assassins, the blind, the drunken and the innocent strikes with the iconoclastic force of hallucinatory vision.

'I am against all conventional morals, traditional fantasies, sentimentality, and all that moral filth,' he said. 'Bourgeois morality is for me anti-morality, because it is based on three unjust institutions – religion, family and country.'

Shock tactics had scored Buñuel high critical ratings. But for almost the next ten years he was to concentrate on more obviously popular and commercial cinema. It is a prolific and varied interlude – ranging from 'B' feature potboilers, picaresque melodramas, quirky interpretations of classic novels like *Robinson Crusoe* (1952) and *Wuthering Heights* (1953), to the morbid paranoia of *El* (1952), revolutionary thrillers, and the deliriously erotic black comedy of *The Criminal Life of Archibaldo de la Cruz* (1955).

Just in case there was any danger of his audience being lulled into a false sense of security, Buñuel responded first with the stark ferocity of *Nazarin* (1958), and two years later with *Viridiana* (1960). In both films a character who is religiously committed to a concept of goodness and charity is forced into dramatic confrontation with its physical, mental and social antithesis. In both cases the moral code disintegrates. *Viridiana* caused a sensation. It won the Palme d'Or at Cannes, but was immediately banned by the Spanish authorities who had felt safe to make the picture their official entry at the festival. The beggars' banquet which freezes into a 'Last Supper' tableau ensured that once more Buñuel was firmly back on the Catholic Church's blacklist.

But Mexico was not so squeamish. Buñuel returned there to make *The Exterminating Angel* (1962), a *Huis Clos* surreal drama, where a group of bored, wealthy socialites, mysteriously confined in an elegant house, are slowly but surely stripped of their protective, civilized layers.

> Surrealism taught me that life had a moral meaning that man cannot ignore. Through surrealism I discovered that man is not free. I used to believe that man's freedom was unlimited, but in surrealism I saw a discipline to be followed. It was one of the great lessons of my life; a marvellous, poetic step forward.

Buñuel can create images with the emotional resonance of depth-charges. In *Diary of a Chambermaid* (1965), a snail slowly crawls up the exposed thigh of a young girl who has been sexually assaulted and murdered.

Buñuel's world is anything but black and white, but working with colour and Catherine Deneuve, *Belle de Jour* (1968) made bourgeois sado-masochistic fantasy chic for a whole new audience. But Buñuel had not sold out. The limpid elegance of his later films does not reflect a sudden slump towards fashionable cynicism, erotica, and style for style's sake. The shocking and the startling are still viewed with the same unblinking gaze. Perhaps the old anarchic anger had been tempered into a more humorous compassion in films like *The Discreet Charm of the Bourgeoisie* (1972) and *The Phantom of Liberty* (1974). However, at the age of seventy-seven, partially deaf, but claiming, 'I'm still an atheist, thank God!'

Buñuel could still make magic with *That Obscure Object of Desire* (1977), a profound, sensual and ironic study of *l'amour fou*, which teasingly used two different actresses in the same part.

This was to be his last piece of cinema. An autobiography, *My Last Sigh*, was published after his death in 1983 in which he claimed he would be happy to burn the prints of all his films. Like some of the facts in his book, this statement wasn't necessarily true. As Angela Molina observed: 'Bunuel had the art of provocation ... That's what he wanted – to disturb people, make them question things, and have fun at the same time.'

Further reading

See: Ado Kyrou, *Luis Buñuel* (1963); Freddy Buache, *Luis Buñuel* (1964); Raymond Durgnat, *Luis Buñuel* (1967); Isabel Santaolalla and Peter William Evans (eds), *Luis Buñuel: New Readings* (2004); Gwynne Edwards, *A Companion to Luis Buñuel* (2005).

PAUL SIDEY

BURGESS, John Anthony

1917–93

English novelist and critic

Anthony Burgess Wilson was born in Manchester in 1917 and educated at the Xaverian College and Manchester University. After military service during the Second World War he taught in England before working as an education officer in the colonial civil service in Malaya. In 1959 he was invalided home with a suspected brain tumour. Given one year to live, he produced five novels and lived for another thirty-three years. Although he had written fiction earlier, this was the real beginning of Burgess's career as a full-time novelist, critic, scriptwriter, reviewer – and sometime composer. A long-standing love of music (he sometimes claimed to rate his composing more highly than his writing), linguistics and phonetics always informed his work.

Burgess's prolific output, his range, responsiveness and invention marked him out from most other authors. In *Shakespeare* (1970) he commented: 'A snapper-up of unconsidered trifles – that is Autolycus in *The Winter's Tale*; it is also Shakespeare and, indeed, any writer of drama or narrative fiction.' Living by his own dictum, Burgess ransacked any cache of history and information, especially those stored up by other artists. His novel *1985* (1978) is an ingenious variant on *Nineteen Eighty-Four* by **George Orwell**; *Nothing Like the Sun* (1964) is a fictional recreation of Shakespeare's early life; *ABBA ABBA* (1977) describes Keats's dying days in Rome; *Tremor of Intent* (1966) is partly a parody of **Ian Fleming's** spy stories; the structure of *Napoleon Symphony* (1974) is based on the pattern provided by Beethoven's Eroica Symphony; the anthropological jokes and riddles of *MF* (1971) are a nod in the direction of **Lévi-Strauss**, fashionable at the time of the book's appearance.

Linguistically the chief influence on Burgess was **James Joyce**, although he cited Shakespeare and **Gerard Manley Hopkins** almost as often, while the puzzle-playing of some of his novels is reminiscent of **Nabokov**. 'All art springs from delight in raw material,' Burgess claimed in *Language Made Plain* (1964). His preference for exotic locations in his novels came from a well-conveyed sense that countries less temperate than England offered a rawer, more confused material on which to work. The Malayan Trilogy (*Time for a Tiger*, *The Enemy in the Blanket* and *Beds in the East*, 1956, 1958 and 1959 respectively), and *Devil of a State* (1961) describe the uneasy shoulder-rubbing of different cultures in Asia and Africa during the waning of colonialism. Burgess exploited the farcical discomforts of racial and religious collision and dived enthusiastically into a linguistic melange, using to the full his talent for mimicry. The return to England was without illusion: the anaemic tellyland of, for example, *The Right to an Answer* (1960) was projected into the future in the anti-utopian novels *A Clockwork Orange* (1962), *The Wanting Seed* (1962) and

1985, with their visions of a half-hearted totalitarianism and individual protest.

The fiction dealing with famous historical figures, the sequence of novels about the poet Enderby (who composes best in the lavatory), the gloomy prospects of the future showed Burgess's distrust of the state and all its organizations. There was a complementary emphasis on the individual, although the heroism of his central characters is based more on quirkiness and a lack of allegiances rather than any positive acts of defiance. The jaunty hero of *A Clockwork Orange*, a book for which Burgess created a special argot derived from Russian, is a teenage hooligan who robs, rapes and kills for pleasure. Forcibly and chemically rehabilitated by the state, he can choose only to be good; simultaneously he loses his love of classical music, just as the hero of *Inside Mr Enderby* (1963) loses his poetic faculty after psychiatric treatment.

Burgess preferred voluntary damnation to enforced social salvation. His Catholic background coloured his fiction, not just in its pessimistic view of human progress but in its conviction of human evil and corruption. His most substantial fiction is *Earthly Powers* (1980), narrated by a Somerset Maugham–like novelist looking back over a long life which encompassed much of twentieth-century history. An ambitious and encyclopaedic work, it was followed by *The End of the World News* (1982) which combined science fiction with excursions into the lives of **Freud** and **Trotsky**.

Burgess's final novel was a 'biography' of Christopher Marlowe. In no way the work of an ageing novelist, *A Dead Man in Deptford* (1993) is infused with the linguistic energy of the Elizabethans and the sense of the modern world on the verge of discovery. Burgess also produced two volumes of autobiography, *Little Wilson and Big God* (1987) and *You've Had Your Time* (1990).

Further reading

Other works include: *The Doctor is Sick* (1960); *The Piano-players* (1986); *Any Old Iron* (1989). The only biography to date, Roger Lewis's *Anthony Burgess* (2002), is highly idiosyncratic. Lewis is half in love with his subject, but also frequently scornful of him. The book has something of Burgess's mad-cap inclusiveness to it.

PHILIP GOODEN

BURROUGHS, William Seward

1914–97

US novelist

William Burroughs's grandfather invented the adding machine and it is said that the Depression scotched what would have been a considerable family fortune. Burroughs's parents made him an allowance of $200 a month and it was this which enabled him to live modestly in foreign lands and pursue his non-commercial writing. He has written:

> As a young child I wanted to be a writer because writers were rich and famous. They lounged around Singapore and Rangoon smoking opium in a yellow pongee silk suit. They sniffed cocaine in Mayfair and they penetrated forbidden swamps with a faithful native boy and lived in the native quarter of Tangier smoking hashish and languidly caressing a pet gazelle.

Drugs, travel, homosexuality, sardonic humour, the contemplation of unusual wealth and secret worlds – the most striking aspects of his life and work are present in this recollection.

Born in St Louis, he graduated in English from Harvard, then travelled to Vienna where in 1936 he studied medicine at the university for one term. Later, on a GI grant, he investigated pre-Columbian civilizations in Mexico City (where accidentally he killed his wife with a revolver) and lived subsequently in New York, Tangier, Paris and London, ending his days in the small university town of Lawrence, Kansas. He is the father of the Beat movement, though not quite of it, and his disciples – **Kerouac**, **Ginsberg**, Corso – were always slightly awed by him. The Beats were in love with uninhibited, jazz-inspired forms of self-expression, but Burroughs also had epistemological interests about the nature of consciousness and reality which set him apart.

His first major novel *Naked Lunch* (or *The Naked Lunch* – Burroughs himself used both titles), published in 1959 by Maurice Girodias at the Olympia Press in Paris, adumbrates the essential preoccupations which made him for many years one of the most notorious and least accessible of modern novelists. Wilfully encompassing philosophy, poetry, psychology, journalism, cybernetics, sociology, medicine and politics, all stirred together in a wild and phantasmagorical burlesque, and having a number of features associated with speculative physics (namely probability, indeterminacy, synchronicity, acausality), *Naked Lunch* replaces linear narrative and enclosed characterization with a new model which closely resembles montage. Burroughs added a further element of vagary to it by handing the untidy pages to Allen Ginsberg who was responsible for the final sequence. Many of the episodes were based on Burroughs's oral 'routines' when, in the company of friends and intoxicated by various substances, he would conjure hilarious and imaginative sophistries out of the air.

He pursued his experiments in *The Soft Machine* (1961) and *The Ticket that Exploded* (1962), which introduced the 'cut-up/fold-in' method, a technique developed from the ideas of Brion Gysin. 'Cut-up' refers to the practice of randomizing his own or borrowed texts with the help of scissors; while 'fold-in' involves folding a page down its middle and typing out the resulting interpenetration of words. This recourse to chance in the preparation of a final text was a violent attempt to release language from its formulaic tendencies and thereby produce unplanned effects and meanings. It was rewarding when not overused but in several books became another intransigence of style.

Burroughs's use of these external processes was paralleled by his use of drugs. He wasn't the first writer to be a heroin addict – Anna Kavan became addicted in the 1930s and injected it for the rest of her life while crafting superb novels of modernist alienation. But Burroughs was the first to create for narcotics addiction an outlaw mystique by representing it as both dangerous and an elite interest. He claimed to have been cured in London by a treatment based on apomorphine, a drug which acts upon the hypothalamus to reduce anxiety and reschedule the metabolism, but one which provokes severe vomiting. This purgation, described as 'mediaeval' by some other addicts, would appeal to a man with a sado-masochistic temperament such as his. The characters who flicker through his lurid pages are either masters or slaves, hunters or the hunted, eaters and the eaten. One is never far from a cruel symbolism based on control and submission. In his own words 'a paranoiac is a man in possession of all the facts'.

Only love or crime may briefly break this vicious circle. For Burroughs both are valuable as transgressions. Therefore love must be homosexual. Yet unlike, say, **Genet**, whose passions moved outward in a clear intoxication, Burroughs is a man staunched by mid-Western reserve. His lust is erratic and hyper-obsessive, given to endless repetitions produced by cut-up/fold-in, and the vehemence with which he constructs homosexuality into a bio-evolutionary command seems to be a way of unlocking himself. Crime is glamorized as the alternative to imprisonment.

However wanton it may sometimes appear, Burroughs's writing is conventionally redeemed by the quality of its satire and its acute delineations of underworlds and parallel realities. At the time of its publication *Naked Lunch* was admired for being a courageous, unflinching look into the hell of drug addiction and social breakdown, but what really comes across in rereading is the abandoned glee of a man smashing up the furniture and remaking it in alarming, obscene shapes. Burroughs has a tendency to list images rather than develop ideas but in his finest passages the master of high camp collides with the prophet of doom in bursts of outrageous comedy, surreal perversions and extraordinary speculation. Despite their apparently casual arrangement, the books are greatly enhanced if not merely dipped about in but read through from start to finish, when the recurrences and transformations of texts, scenes and phrases produce a unique kind of iridescence.

In the 1970s Burroughs eased up on his use of the cut-up/fold-in method. *The Wild Boys* (1971) is almost agreeably comprehensible as a futuristic fantasy, although its content (gangs of youths terrorizing the world) is hardly pleasant or nowadays so very fantastical. In the 1980s his life altered. He was taken up and organized by a group of young fans who cleverly repackaged him for the mainstream. He became a celebrity associated with the **Warhol**/pop star set in New York and published his fiction trilogy: *Cities of the Red Night* (1981), *The Place of Dead Roads* (1984) and *The Western Lands* (1987). These are certainly the work of 'weird old Bill' but the pressure of risk and adventure is much reduced and it is his earlier, uncompromising

books which increasingly resonate with the way the world is going. The spark of aggressive, disquieting originality transferred in his last years to a new activity – artworks – created by firing shotguns at painted plywood panels. After his death it emerged that he had been projecting a deceit: the famous apomorphine cure hadn't really worked and he had continued to inject heroin or (more usually) one of its substitutes until the end of his life.

Further reading

Other works include: *Junkie* (1953); *Dead Fingers Talk* (1963); *The Yage Letters* (with Allen Ginsberg, 1963); *Nova Express* (1964); *Exterminator!* (1974); *The Third Mind* (with Brian Gysin, 1978); *Ah Pook is Here* (1979). *The Job* (1969) is a book of interviews with Burroughs conducted by Daniel Odier. See: Eric Mottram, *William Burroughs: The Algebra of Need* (1977); Ted Morgan, *Literary Outlaw: The Life and Times of William S. Burroughs* (1988).

DUNCAN FALLOWELL

C

CAGE, John

1912–92

US composer

'I have nothing to say and I am saying it and that is poetry' sums up Cage's own assessment of his contribution to twentieth-century art. Such a dictum is intentionally paradoxical, for most of his musico-philosophical statements over the past thirty years reflect not only his adherence to the tenets of Zen Buddhism but also his unique approach to the world of sound. The son of an inventor, Cage was born in Los Angeles and received instruction from Henry Cowell and **Arnold Schoenberg**, two of the most influential composer-teachers in America during the 1930s. His early chamber works and songs are generally chromatic, dissonant and confined to ranges of twenty-five notes arranged in contrapuntal textures. Study under the guidance of Cowell at the New School for Social Research, New York, enabled him to survey developments in contemporary, oriental and folk musics with the result that he formed a percussion group which specialized in the use of unusual instruments such as tin cans, brake drums, water gongs and flower pots creating wholly new sonorities. Representative works of this period are three pieces entitled *Construction in Metal* and *Amores* which includes a part for Cage's own invention, the 'prepared piano' whose sound is modified with the addition of screws, bolts, pieces of wood and rubber placed between the strings: later pieces using this medium were the *Sonatas and Interludes* (1946–8), a host of works written in collaboration with the **Merce Cunningham** Dance Company, and the *Concerto for Prepared Piano and Chamber Orchestra* (1951). A continuing interest in the musical potential of unusual sounds promoted experiments with electronic sources such as variable speed turntables and radio signals (*Imaginary Landscape*, Nos 1 and 4 of 1939 and 1951); later gramophone cartridges, contact microphones and amplifiers were used.

Soon after the war Cage made a study of the music of Eric Satie and **Webern** at a time when neither composer's work was yet acknowledged as musically significant. He prophesied that their attitudes towards and treatment of musical form via proportional time lengths would point the way to future methods of composition, and as a result silence could only be perceived in terms of time duration and not as an opposition to melody and harmony. Demonstrations of such theories found shape in the *String Quartet in 4 Parts* of 1950 and the silent piece *4ʹ33²* of the following year, a work which depended on audience and environmental response for its effect. It was also at this time that Cage took studies in Zen Buddhism under **D.T. Suzuki** at Columbia University and came under the influence of the *I Ching*. By employing 'chance' in his ensuing compositions he could ensure that they were free of individual taste and memory in their order of events. From now on the concept of Indeterminacy would be used as a guide towards the placing of tempi, durations, sound and dynamics in most of his new compositions. *Music of Changes* for piano solo (1951) was the first work to employ such a system and very soon was followed by similarly inspired compositions from Cage's close associates Earle Brown, Morton Feldman and Christian Wolff.

From an early age John Cage had been interested in a synthesis of the creative arts but the opportunity to hold such a mixed-media event did not arise until the summer schools at Black Mountain College, North Carolina, where between 1948 and 1952 he was encouraged to work with Charles Olson, **Robert Rauschenberg**, Merce Cunningham (dancer) and David Tudor (pianist) to produce the first 'Happening' which incorporated music, dance, painting, poetry reading, actions, recordings, films and slides. Such a collaboration was to herald a host of similar events in the 1950s and 1960s which were put on tour around the country and abroad. Later works in this genre include *Theatre Piece* (1960), *Musicircus* (1967), *HPSCHD* (1969), *Apartment House 1776* and *Renga* (1976). Besides the promotion of intermedia events Cage continued to construct scores for traditional instrumental forces even though at times these were for unusual combinations and often called for additional electronic sound sources. His last preoccupation was with the use of amplified plant materials, a concept appropriately entitled 'Biomusic'.

The example of John Cage, lifelong musical inventor, experimenter and revolutionary, continues. His innovations in the realm of new sound sources, indeterminacy, graphic notation and artistic integration have influenced most of the post-war avant-garde and contemporary experimental composers.

Further reading

Other works include: *Silence* (1968); *A Year from Monday* (1968); *M-Writings '67–'72* (1973); *Notations* (1969); *Empty Words* (1980). See also:

C. Tomkins, *Bride and the Bachelors* (USA) / *Ahead of the Game* (UK) (1965); R. Kostelanetz (ed.), *John Cage* (1971); H. Wiley Hitchcock, *Music in the United States* (2nd edn, 1974); P. Yates, *Twentieth-Century Music* (1967); W. Mellers, *Music in a New Found Land* (1965); D. Revill, *The Roaring Silence: John Cage: A Life* (1992); J. Pritchett, *The Music of John Cage* (1993).

MICHAEL ALEXANDER

CALDER, Alexander
1898–1976
US sculptor

Famous as the man who invented the 'mobile', who introduced motion into sculpture, it was not until his mid-twenties that Alexander Calder purposively turned his attention to art, despite the fact that both his father and grandfather were sculptors. In 1919 he graduated from the Stevens Institute of Technology in Hoboken, New Jersey, with a degree in mechanical engineering. A gifted draughtsman, his initial ambition was to become a successful commercial artist, and with this in mind he signed up as an illustrator for the *National Police Gazette* in 1924. The drawings, which Calder dubbed 'man-made approximations', revealed a rapid observation and abstracting power. His experiments with the use of wire as a means of lifting line off the page resulted in *Josephine Baker 1*, which, with a number of other 'wire portraits', was exhibited in a one-man show at the Weyhe Gallery in New York (1927). At the same time he made his first journey to Paris (in 1926), and devoted much of his time and energy to making the small figures that together composed his *Circus* (1924–31), which he loved to 'perform' for small invited audiences to the sound of the record 'Ramona'. These pieces were constructed from corks, pieces of felt, wood and whatever other scraps of material came to hand. They were anthropomorphic, capable of transformation into 'live' creatures with magic immediacy. In the sense that it tackled the problems of balance and of space, the *Circus* was the prototype mobile.

Calder's childhood memories, recollected in *An Autobiography with Pictures* (1966), dictated to his son-in-law, were full of the observation of mechanical movement, of trains, bicycles and coasters. Also warmly remembered were the toys he made for his sister Peggy. 'I have always been delighted by the way things are hooked together,' he said – a delight which was transmitted later through the delicate spins of his sculptures. As a student he was similarly drawn to the 'discussion of the laws governing the plane motions of rigid bodies, with applications to machines, compound and torsion pendulum, translating and rotating bodies'; and he was inculcated with a picture of the universe as a mechanical structure of moving parts.

Except for a brief flirtation with Abstraction-Creation (1932–4) Calder never attached himself to any artistic school. On the other hand Paris, which he made his second home after his marriage to Louisa James in 1931, brought him in contact with the newest ideas and many of their exponents, including Léger, **Mondrian**, **Miró** and Duchamp. It was in fact Duchamp who provided his moving figures with the label 'Mobiles', and Arp who termed the frozen mobiles 'Stabiles'. According to their construction, the mobiles divide into two types: standing and hanging. Both were collapsible, and could therefore be transported easily. The earlier ones incorporated 'found objects', while the later ones were made from designed metal pieces painted either black or in primary colours. Finally, the mobiles of the 1970s used steel. But while his work can be seen to develop towards increasingly larger structures (*The Four Elements*, 1962, and *Hello Girls*, 1964, both standing mobiles) sometimes serving a directly representational purpose (*The Circle*, 1935, or *Spirale*, 1958), most of Calder's work is underlined by a basic sense of play, which on occasion manifested itself as a pure, abstracted humour (*Performing Seal*, 1950). This was reflected in his choice of titles. Behind their whimsicality there was usually a perfectly matter-of-fact

explanation. Either they referred to the natural phenomena that had prompted the piece in question (*Snow Flurry*, 1948), or to the thickness of the material employed (*.125*, 1958), to the person who had commissioned it (*Gwenfritz*, 1969 = Gwendolyn Cafritz), or simply to the place of installation (*La Défense*, 1975). But such betrayal of sophistication was indicative of Calder's attitude: he would never, for example, refer to himself as an artist.

Calder's output extended to motorized mobiles, tapestries, stage designs, oil paintings, woodcarvings, bronzes, toys, magazine covers, etchings, lithographs, household utensils, jewellery, two fountains, an acoustic ceiling and the decoration of two aeroplanes and a BMW motorcar. In addition he was a gifted illustrator of children's books. But it was his hanging mobiles that captured the public's imagination and accounted for a worldwide reputation that began in the 1950s, after taking the First Prize for sculpture at the Venice Biennale (1952). People simply enjoyed watching them without feeling a need for explanation. As Pierre Restany put it, 'He was Francis of Assisi turned lay engineer.' Some of the later mobiles (e.g. the series *Gongs*) had polished bronze elements, which produced a resonant ring when struck by other parts. If this draws attention to a range of artefacts produced in the Orient from time immemorial, in the context of contemporary Western sculpture Calder has, almost playfully, inserted a new dimension. A mobile 'spins out its tale of achieved volume' (Kraus).

Further reading

Several films portraying Calder's work include: *Works of Calder* (1951); *Mobiles* (1966); *Calder un portrait* (1972). See: J.J. Sweeney, *Alexander Calder* (1951); H.H. Arnason, *Calder* (1966); J. Lipman, *Calder's Universe* (1976). See also R.E. Kraus, *Passages in Modern Sculpture* (1977); J.M. Master, *Alexander Calder* (1991).

SLAVKA SVERAKOVA

CAMUS, Albert

1913–60

French writer

One of the most significant, and redeeming, features of cultural life in France is its willingness to welcome a major intellectual who has emerged from a humble background and whose work remains accessible to a wide reading public. Such a writer is Albert Camus, whose origins as a *pied noir* from the working-class district of Algiers were as obscure as those of any of the eight French winners of the Nobel Prize for Literature who preceded him. He first became known in metropolitan France towards the end of the Second World War through his work on the Resistance newspaper *Combat*. In the years immediately following the war he was rapidly established, together with his contemporary **Jean-Paul Sartre** and the latter's mistress Simone de Beauvoir, as one of the leaders of the new generation of committed French writers, philosophers and critics. Their common concern was the struggle for the freedom, justice and dignity of man in an age of successive and conflicting tyrannies which could be fought only in circumstances of considerable moral ambiguity.

Camus had in fact been active as early as 1935, while a student at Algiers University, in the propaganda warfare against international fascism, and had also taken on the conservative French establishment in defending the rights of the Arab population. From the middle 1930s onwards Camus's career reflects both in his creative works and his journalism a quarter-century of intense debate of the great issues of the times: fascism, genocide, the savage post-war purges of French collaborators, repressive colonialism (e.g. the French in Madagascar and the British in Cyprus), the death penalty, torture, racialism and conscientious objection among others. All of these drew from Camus a clear moral response. So too did **Stalinism** and revolutionary terrorism from the late 1940s onwards. The widening gulf between Camus and the French left as a result of the latter reached unbridgeable dimensions after the outbreak of the Algerian War in 1954, when Camus refused to support the FLN, *grosso modo*, in their struggle for Algerian, i.e. Arab, independence from France. He was killed in a car crash in January 1960. Although only forty-six he was considered by his critics to be a spent force; the Nobel Prize award in 1957 had been regarded as the consecration of his passage to the ranks of the *bien-pensants*.

Like many French intellectuals of his time Camus expressed himself creatively in the two major literary genres, prose fiction and the theatre, as well as in philosophical essays and copious journalism. Camus's reputation was made very quickly while he was still young in the five years immediately following the Second World War (sometimes on the strength of work first published or performed earlier). His four original plays, *Caligula* (1944), *Cross Purposes* (*Le Malentendu*, 1944), *State of Siege* (*L'État de siège*, 1948), *The Just Assassins* (*Les Justes*, 1950, all four trans. 1958); his two major philosophical essays, *The Myth of Sisyphus* (*Le Mythe de Sisyphe*, 1942, trans. 1955), *The Rebel* (*L'Homme révolté*, 1951, trans. 1953); and particularly his novels, *The Outsider* (*L'Étranger*, 1942, trans. 1946, as *The Stranger* in the US) and *The Plague* (*La Peste*, 1947, trans. 1948), brought him a considerable degree of material ease and fame. Camus' early popularity was enhanced by his personal image and lifestyle: the 'Mediterranean' type (of mixed French–Spanish origins), handsome, athletic, a lover of football, swimming, dancing and womanizing. This is particularly the vestigial Camus of the Algerian period, the 'Philosopher of the Absurd' who wrote *The Outsider*, *The Myth of Sisyphus* and short essays such as *Nuptials* (*Noces*, 1939, trans. in *Lyrical and Critical* 1967):

> In Algiers whoever is young and alive finds sanctuary and occasion for triumphs everywhere: in the sun, the bay, the flowers and sports stadiums, the cool-legged girls. But for whoever has lost his youth there is

nothing to cling to and nowhere for melancholy to escape itself.

('Summer in Algiers')

In these early works Camus is stressing certain *essences* such as what we would now recognize as the machismo of the *pied noir* and southern Europeans generally, a continuity of pagan Greek values and, less credibly, a symbiosis of European and Arab cultures. Life is short; the simple, sensual pleasures of Mediterranean man, swimming, sun-bathing, making love, are to be enjoyed while one is young, as they are by Meursault, the enigmatic hero of *The Outsider*. The more keenly man enjoys these pleasures, the more scandalous is the fact of his mortality. For Camus the crime, on discovery of this mortality and of the limitations on man's ability to comprehend and order the universe, is to do one of three things: (1) to commit suicide literally; (2) to commit intellectual suicide by looking to a life after death; or (3) to do what Caligula does in Camus' play, rush headlong into a destructive rebellion against a world which can offer man the most intense physical joys only to mock him and cast him off irrevocably at the cruellest moment: a sort of metaphysical coitus interruptus. The stoic but life-enhancing course to adopt, as expounded in *The Myth of Sisyphus*, is not to attempt to defeat the absurd (or, to be precise, destroy the absurd *relationship* between man and the resistant external world) but to maintain it with courage and lucidity. Man must take up the challenge of the absurd and live in a state of spiritual tension to which Camus gave the name *revolt*.

The great divide in Camus's work occurs in the early 1940s in the face of the harsh realities of the German occupation. The exalted, solipsistic world of *The Myth of Sisyphus* was soon left behind as Camus came to feel increasingly during the 1940s, especially as Nazism was succeeded by Stalinism, that revolt degenerated all too easily into what he considered to be a nihilistic and cynically pursued absolute, *revolution*. The result was that Camus waged an increasingly shrill campaign towards the end of the decade not just against revolutionary violence and the ethic of ideological expediency but specifically against communism and its **Marxist** philosophy of history. *State of Siege* and *The Just Assassins* were skirmishes before the full-scale battle provoked by *The Rebel* in 1951 and the consequent break with Sartre and friends. Many readers, particularly in the United States, prefer (or know only) this Camus, the Cold Warrior of the middle period. But with the passage of time it will surely be recognized that his masterpiece is not *The Plague*, with its botched allegory of the Occupation and its cosy, up-beat conclusion ('what one learns in time of pestilence is that there are more things to admire in man than to despise'), but rather *The Fall* (*La Chute*, 1956, trans. 1957). This last major piece of prose fiction, produced during the relatively barren last decade of Camus' life, is a brilliantly ironic, mock-cynical *tour de force* in confessional form. The confession, in this work rich in puns and sly cultural allusions, is that of Jean-Baptiste Clamence, a man who, like Camus and many of his fellow intellectuals, has spent his life in the liberal conscience industry. The captain of such an industry should go down with his ship; Clamence failed even to attempt to rescue a girl who plunged into the Seine. The ship that Camus declined to go down with was that of justice in Algeria. *The Fall* is Camus's best work: his most deeply personal, his most tragic, and at the same time – an effect he sought unsuccessfully to capture previously – his most comic.

Further reading

Gallimard's 2-volume Pléiade edition of Camus's works is comprehensive and scholarly: *Théâtre, Récits, Nouvelles* (Vol. 1); *Essais* (Vol. 2). See also: *Exile and the Kingdom* (*L'Exil et le Royaume*, stories, 1957, trans. 1958). See: J.-C. Brisville, *Camus* (1960); J. Cruickshank, *Albert Camus and the Literature of Revolt* (1960); C.C. O'Brien, *Camus* (1970); R. Quilliot, *La Mer et les prisons* (1956); Herbert R. Lottman, *Albert Camus* (1979); David Sprintzen, *Camus* (1988); Joseph McBride, *Albert*

Camus: Philosopher and Littérateur (1993); Olivier Todd, *Camus: A Life* (1997).

TED FREEMAN

CANTOR, Georg Ferdinand Ludwig Philipp

1845–1918

German mathematician and logician

Georg Cantor, the creator of set theory, was born in St Petersburg in 1845 and moved with his parents to the south of Germany in 1856. Against his father's wishes he studied mathematics at Berlin University from 1863 to 1869. There he was greatly influenced by Theodor Weierstrasse's seminal lectures on the real numbers. After obtaining a doctorate for work on number theory he settled in Halle where he spent the remainder of his life, becoming Professor Extraordinary of the University of Halle in 1872 and Professor Ordinary in 1879. His most productive decade ended in 1884 when he suffered a breakdown of health. He was subsequently plagued by mental illness and largely ceased mathematical work in 1897.

During his lifetime his highly original work in logic and mathematics received a mixed reception. The severe criticism of Leopold Kronecker and Poincaré, among others, greatly distressed him and may have contributed to his breakdown. Poincaré regarded Cantor's set theory as 'pathological' and confidently predicted that it would come to be regarded as a disease from which mathematics had recovered. However, in time his work gained general acceptance, particularly through the support of David Hilbert, and Cantor is now regarded as one of the greatest logicians and mathematicians of the nineteenth century. Cantor's difficulties in gaining a sympathetic hearing from the mathematical establishment prompted him to become a founder and first president of the Deutsche Mathematiker Vereinigung (German Mathematical Assembly).

Prior to Cantor and Dedekind there was no adequate theory of the real numbers. In particular a satisfactory definition of the notion of an irrational number was lacking. Following a suggestion of Weierstrasse, Cantor defined irrational numbers as certain infinite ordered sets of rational numbers (fractions). On this approach $\sqrt{2}$ can be taken to be the sequence of rational numbers 1.4, 1.41, 1.414, . . . , the squares of which progressively approximate the value 2. This led Cantor to develop a theory of sets within which to study infinite sets which, he maintained, existed actually and not merely potentially. His theory was based on the simple but powerful notion that two sets have the same number of members just in case the members of the two sets can be placed into a one–one correspondence. Cantor defined an infinite set as one which can be put into a one–one correspondence with a proper subset of the set (i.e. to a selection of some members of the set). For instance, the set of natural numbers 1, 2, 3, . . . is infinite for it can be put into a one–one correspondence with the set of even natural numbers 2, 4, 6, . . . , a result which also shows that these two sets have the same number of members. Cantor defined denumerable sets to be those that can be put into a one–one correspondence with the natural numbers and used the symbol a_0 for the number of members in any such set. He established the counterintuitive result that the set of all rational numbers is denumerable and using his famous diagonal method showed that the infinite set of all real numbers is not denumerable. Using the symbol 'c' for this larger infinite number which gives the size of the set of all real numbers Cantor laboured in vain to answer the question as to whether there are any infinite numbers between a_0 and c. The continuum hypothesis which states that there are no such infinite numbers is now known to be consistent with the postulates of set theory but not a consequence of them.

Cantor discovered the existence of an infinite hierarchy of ever larger infinite sets which Hilbert referred to as 'Cantor's Paradise'. The crucial element in this is Cantor's theorem which states that the number of members of the power set of a given set A is greater than the number of members of A. The power set of A is the set of all sub-sets of A. It turns out, as Cantor showed, that the power set of the set of all natural numbers is the same size as the set of all real numbers. By Cantor's theorem the power set of the set of real numbers is an infinite set of even greater size. Taking the power set of that set in turn gives a still larger set. And repeating this operation gives an endless sequence of ever larger infinite sets. Cantor went on to develop the laws of arithmetic for the resulting hierarchy of infinite numbers.

In the course of his work on infinite sets Cantor attempted to prove that the infinite set of points on a line of unit length was smaller than the infinite set of points in a unit square. However, in 1877 he established that in fact these sets are of the same size, a result which he said he saw but did not believe. Indeed, this result holds if one moves to three or more dimensions. This meant that one could no longer understand an increase in dimension in terms of an increase in the number of points. While Cantor was himself unable to produce a satisfactory alternative account of dimension his work prompted others to do so.

In his development of set theory Cantor had defined a set to be 'a collection into a whole of definite distinct objects of our intuition or our thought'. Cantor became aware that on this understanding of a set the resulting theory had problematic aspects, discovering in 1895 what is now known as the Burali–Forti paradox and in 1899 the paradox that bears his name. This latter paradox arises if one posits (as the definition would seem to allow) the existence of a set S consisting of all sets. By Cantor's theorem, the power set of S must be larger in size than S itself. But by the definition of S the power set of S must be a sub-set of S and hence it cannot be larger in size. Mathematicians have had to add restrictions to Cantor's theory of sets to prevent these and other paradoxes. However, these restrictions do not affect Cantor's results concerning infinite sets which remain the basis of our understanding of infinities in mathematics.

Further reading

See: *Gesammelte Abhandlungen*, ed. Ernst Zermelo (1932), contains Cantor's collected works. His most influential papers appear in translation in *Contributions to the Founding of the Theory of Transfinite Numbers* (1955), which contains an introduction to his work by P.E.B. Jourdain. See: Joseph Warren Dauben, *George Cantor: His Mathematics and the Philosophy of the Infinite* (1990).

W.H. NEWTON-SMITH

CAPA, Robert
1913–54
Hungarian/American photographer

The man who would become Robert Capa was born Endre Ernö Friedmann on 22 October 1913 in Budapest, Hungary, as the second of the three sons of Julia and Dezsö Friedmann. Always irrepressible, the teenage Capa ran afoul of the Hungarian government by promoting left-wing politics. He spent a few days in jail before his father managed to get him out. After finishing high school, Capa went to Berlin in 1931, partly for further study but also to get away from the watchful Hungarian authorities.

In Berlin, Capa studied journalism at the University of Berlin. As the Great Depression worsened, his parents could no longer afford to provide Capa with funds. Forced to make a living and already self-taught in photography, Capa decided to pursue work as a photographer. This new profession was as close to journalism as he could get without a strong command of German.

Capa got his first steady job in the darkroom of DEPHOT (Deutscher Photodienst) as a lab technician. Given a Leica camera by his boss, Capa began going out on simple assignments in 1932. He showed a knack for capturing exciting images and received more assignments. Just as his star began to rise, Capa's German photography career was cut short by the rise of the Nazis. As a foreigner, a leftist and a Jew, Capa epitomized everything that the Nazis hated. With a valid Hungarian passport Capa could easily leave Germany, and he did so in 1933.

Moving to Paris, Capa found work with Agency Hug Block. He enjoyed the acclaim that his pictures received but retained a very ambivalent attitude towards photography. Capa seems to have been most annoyed by the fact that he couldn't make a decent living as a photographer. He constantly had to scramble for work, and many assignments paid little. To increase his marketability and his pay, Friedmann changed his name to Capa in 1936. The new name was easy to pronounce, easy to spell, and easy to remember. It could be French or American in origin and also sounded a bit like the name of famous American filmmaker Frank Capra. Pretending to be a rich, successful American photographer, Capa sold photographs for more money than Friedmann could ever receive.

In 1936, Capa began to photograph the Spanish Civil War as a freelance photographer. Among the pictures that he offered for sale, Capa included a photograph of a Loyalist militiaman at the moment when the shock of being hit by an enemy bullet registers on his body and he begins to collapse into death. It became Capa's most famous shot. No one had ever seen such a photograph before. It brought the viewer the sensation of being close to the killing and being killed.

The success of the Loyalist militiaman photograph taught Capa that a photojournalist needed to be right in the centre of the action to produce powerful images. His maxim became, 'If your pictures aren't good enough, you aren't close enough.' Capa snapped both soldiers and civilians, showing that the effects of war could be found not only in the battle but also in the fear, suffering, and loss at the edge of the action. Always primarily a photographer of people, Capa's pictures of war are extraordinarily sympathetic and compassionate studies of people under extreme stress.

In 1938, Capa emigrated to the United States. When World War II began, Capa found it difficult to get to the front lines because Hungary had allied with Germany. In 1943, he was sent to North Africa as a fully accredited photographer/correspondent for Collier's. Chosen to cover the start of the D-Day invasion in Normandy, Capa accompanied the American amphibious troops into France.

Capa became a US citizen in 1946. Despite his fame, he still struggled to make a living. In an effort to make more money while retaining the rights to his own work and the negatives of his pictures, Capa joined with several other prominent photographers in 1947 to form the Magnum photo agency.

On 25 May 1954, Capa went to Southeast Asia to photograph the war between the Vietnamese and the French. As always, he wanted to get as close to the action as possible. Outside the village of Thai-Binh, he stepped on a Vietminh antipersonnel mine and died of blood loss.

Further reading

Capa's autobiography, *Slightly Out of Focus* (1947), sacrifices accuracy for a good story. The best sources on Robert Capa are Richard Whelan's biography *Robert Capa* (1985) and Alex Kershaw's *Blood and Champagne: The Life and Times of Robert Capa* (2002). For Capa's photographs, see *Robert Capa: Photographs from Israel, 1948–1950* (1988); *Robert Capa: Photographs* (1996) and *Robert Capa: The Definitive Collection* (2001).

CARYN E. NEUMANN

CAPOTE, Truman
1924–84
US novelist

Born Truman Streckfus Persons in New Orleans in 1924, Capote has described his early years as 'the most insecure childhood I know of' – a statement which reveals his tendency towards self-dramatization as well as how he felt about his childhood. He had little formal schooling and claimed to be unable to recite the alphabet. His parents divorced when he was four years old and his mother later married a Cuban textile manufacturer named Capote. Until he was ten he lived mainly in Monroeville, Alabama, with three maiden cousins and one man. 'I used up some of my loneliness by writing,' he said later. He was taken to Millbrook, Connecticut, where he spent a year at Greenwich High School, running away repeatedly, once, he reported, with an older girl who later achieved notoriety as the 'Lonely Hearts murderer'. By the age of seventeen he was in New York, employed on the staff of the *New Yorker*. After the publication of a short story, 'Miriam', in *Mademoiselle* he signed a publisher's contract and moved back to New Orleans where he wrote his first novel, *Other Voices, Other Rooms* (1948). He remained in New York but travelled extensively, often as a guest of the wealthy and the internationally famous.

Capote has a reputation as a short-story writer, as the author of *Breakfast at Tiffany's* (1958), and as the inventor of the 'non-fiction novel' exemplified by *In Cold Blood* (1966). In all his work he is known as a meticulous, rather ornate stylist. He is not immediately thought of as a writer from the deep South, perhaps because his two most famous books are set in New York and Kansas, but his chosen themes are connected with the South: Gothic horror, breakdown and a claustrophobic society in which the individual is hopelessly yearning for an elegant past or a glittering future. His literary ancestors include Edgar Allan Poe and **William Faulkner** as well as **Flaubert** and Turgenev; his near contemporaries are Flannery O'Connor, Eudora Welty and **Tennessee Williams**.

Other Voices, Other Rooms is a superb evocation of the Old South, especially in its descriptions of natural scenery where Capote has few equals. Although less well known than his later books and less valued by the author, it has a texture and density which his subsequent work lacks. The self-conscious aestheticism matches the subject-matter

which deals with a small boy, Joel Knox, trapped in a decaying mansion surrounded by distant, eccentric adults. There is a fine, unique portrait of the tomboy Idabel beside whom the more celebrated Holly Golightly in *Breakfast at Tiffany's* now seems rather dated and sentimental, although she made an electric effect when the book was published and in the film (1961), where she was played by Audrey Hepburn. Holly too is a waif from the poor South, longing for brilliance (Tiffany's) but only disappearing into blankness and probable death. In both these works homosexuality appears as a major theme but is presented with a certain evasion and coyness.

Capote spent five years researching *In Cold Blood*, carrying out exhaustive interviews with two murderers, Dick Hickcock and Perry Smith, as with everyone else connected with the murder of the Clutter family in their Kansas farmhouse. He became intensely involved in this case, particularly with Perry Smith who resembles the orphan-like protagonists in his earlier stories. The result is compulsive reading: the riveting attention that every macabre murder story commands, but in spite of the careful arrangement of chapters it lacks the inwardness of a novel. It owes its genesis, as does much of Capote's reporting and interviewing, to the long feature in the *New Yorker*. Like them, Capote's articles are beautifully crafted, precisely observed and somewhat long-winded.

Further reading

Other works include: *A Tree of Night and Other Stories* (1949); *The Grass Harp* (1952); *The Dogs Bark* (1974) and *Answered Prayers* (1986), an unfinished novel. *Music for Chameleons* (1981) is collection of journalism. He has also written plays, *The Grass Harp* and *House of Flowers*, and film scenarios, *Beat the Devil* and *The Innocents*. See: William L. Nance, *The Worlds of Truman Capote* (1973) Gerald Clarke, *Capote: A Biography* (1988) and *Too Brief a Treat: The Letters of Truman Capote* (2006); George Plimpton, *Truman Capote* (1997); Joseph J. Waldmeir and John C. Waldmeir, *The Critical Response to Truman Capote* (1999).

JOHN DANIEL

CARROLL, Lewis (Charles Lutwidge DODGSON)

1832–98

British children's author

The life of the Rev. Charles Lutwidge Dodgson, alias Lewis Carroll, is uneventful: born in Cheshire, the son of a clergyman; Richmond Grammar School; Rugby; Christ Church, Oxford, where he became a tutor in mathematics and logic until his death at his sisters' house in Guildford. He travelled abroad only once, to Russia, preferring Eastbourne or the Isle of Wight. Much photography and writing, including many academic books – *Euclid and His Modern Rivals* (1879) is the best known of these. No love affairs – a sigh in the direction of the young Ellen Terry is usually jumped on by biographers eager for material. As a result his diaries, letters, and the biographies of him are dull. More stimulating are those books which seek to partake of the imaginative world he created as Lewis Carroll, a world of such mythic force that it became self-propagating and beyond conventional critique: *Aspects of Alice* by Robert Phillips (1971), *The Magic of Lewis Carroll* by John Fisher (1973), *The Philosopher's Alice* by Peter Heath (1974), *The Raven and the Writing Desk* by Francis Huxley (1976), *Fragments of a Looking-Glass* by Jean Gattégno (1978). The most successful of these, the least beset by psychological triteness, is *The White Knight: A Study of C.L. Dodgson* by Alexander Taylor (1952).

Dodgson was a shy and fastidious bachelor with a marked stammer, sometimes priggish or melancholy, not especially likeable. Like **Ruskin**, he loved young girls. In their company he was unusually animated. His letters to them are full of brilliant nonsense, unlike his other correspondence. Later in life he liked to photograph them unclad. But as they entered puberty he lost interest, and young boys he actively disliked. Dodgson's most famous companion was Alice Liddell, daughter of the dean of Christ Church. The stories he extemporized for her on boating trips from Oxford were the basis for *Alice's Adventures in Wonderland* (1865) and *Through the Looking-Glass, and What Alice Found There* (Christmas 1871, dated 1872). With the long nonsense poem *The Hunting of the Snark* (1876), they form the essence of his literary output.

This work is the characteristic Victorian attempt to enter the dream world – and it succeeds utterly. Part poet, part logician, Lewis Carroll was better adapted to this task than any comparable writer and the outcome is an autonomous creation free from the folksiness of the Brothers Grimm, the sentimental realism of Hans Andersen, or the tendency towards inconsequential whimsy which one finds in Edward Lear. Carroll is a precursor of Surrealism (Aragon translated him) and Absurdism (their humour is his invention), hence the enormous increase in his status among intellectuals since the Great War. The ages of Freud and Jung transformed the *Alice* books from a children's story into something profoundly mysterious and there is no doubt that the title 'children's author' has always been incorrect, despite Dodgson's own modest intentions ('I meant nothing but nonsense,' he said). Nonetheless, it is true that to notice, for example, that the trial of the Knave of Hearts is father to **Kafka's** *Trial*, or that Humpty Dumpty's 'portmanteau' language is the prototype of the punning technique of *Finnegans Wake* (dubbed 'superjabberwocky' by **Anthony Burgess** enlarging Edmund Wilson's connection), does not really get one very far. It throws some light on Kafka and **Joyce** but none at all on Carroll, whose creations always remain gleefully superior to this kind of exercise.

More than most works of genius, the *Alice* books defy explication, because they travel with us from childhood, changing as we change, comforting, disturbing, each aspect acting as the foil for the other, and in that tension we are spellbound. They are short, very pure works, outside time, concrete, written without discursiveness at a level of inspiration that is effortlessly high. They are always fresh – with every reading a new vista springs up in the landscape. Yet there is virtually no background. They are all character and drama, full of dialogue and action, which the illustrations of Sir John Tenniel (1820–1914) exactly reinforce. Like minor deities these characters move mischievously in a clatter of laughter between our world and their own, and the chief of them is Alice herself, sensitive and robust, one of literature's archetypal figures. She returns us to the uncynical state of wondrous curiosity associated with childhood and, like a genuine goddess, leads us into strange, eternal places without leading us astray.

Further reading

The Lewis Carroll Handbook (1970) is the standard bibliographical reference work. See also: Stuart Dodgson, The Life and Letters of Lewis Carroll (1898); Derek Hudson, Lewis Carroll (revised 1977); M.N. Cohen, Lewis Carroll (1995).

DUNCAN FALLOWELL

CARSON, Rachel

1907–64

US naturalist

Rachel Carson's greatest talent lay in writing luminescent prose on scientific subjects. Her gift to humanity was that she chose environmental subjects, without knowledge of which our world and our health would have suffered even more through the ensuing decades.

Born in Springdale, Pennsylvania, Carson specialized in English at Pennsylvania College; she went on to graduate magna cum laude in 1929 in Biology from Johns Hopkins University. For five years she taught Zoology at the University of Maryland, continuing her studies in the summer at the Marine Biological Laboratory at Woods Hole, Massachusetts. There she was able to explore scientifically her childhood fascination for marine life. From 1936, for fifteen years she worked first as a geneticist and then editor-in-chief for the US Fish and Wildlife Service. She studied offshore life under a Guggenheim fellowship from 1951 to 1952.

Her fascination culminated in her three biographies of the seas: Under the Sea-wind (1941); The Sea Around Us (1951) and The Edge of the Sea (1955). The Sea Around Us was first place on the national best-seller list for thirty-nine weeks, won the John Burroughs Medal, then the National Book Award, and within the year sold more than 200,000 hardback copies. By 1962 it had been published in thirty languages. Through her career, Carson also received the Gold Medal of New York Zoological Society and the Conservationist Award from National Wildlife Federation, and was a Member of the National Institute of Arts and Letters and a Fellow of the Royal Society of Literature. Her success allowed her to retire from the Wildlife Service in 1952 to write full-time.

Although Carson was reluctant to give up her focus on pure natural history and turn to tackling environmental problems, she felt compelled to speak out. DDT was introduced for use in 1942 and by 1945 Carson had become interested in pesticide problems. Insecticides, such as dieldrin and malathion, were killing off wildlife never intended as 'pests'. They were also damaging human health. 'The more I learned about the use of pesticides, the more appalled I became,' Carson recalled: 'everything which meant most to me as a naturalist was being threatened ... nothing I could do would be more important.'

Among many notable events which galvanized her efforts to write her most famous book, Silent Spring (1962), was the fire ant control programme in which 20 million acres in nine states were treated, leaving the land desolate, and the fire ants still going strong. To convey these and other effects of indiscriminate pesticide use, Carson used the metaphor of a town in which 'all life seemed to live in harmony with its surroundings'. Then, 'a strange blight crept over the area and everything began to change'. She describes how animals, domestic and wild, perished and failed to reproduce, people fell ill, no bees pollinated the apples, bird tables were bare, children even died after playing outside. Her vivid prose captured the imagination of the American people. Four and a half years in the writing, and serialized in the *New Yorker*, *Silent Spring*, whose publication date was broken, became a best-seller even before it hit the shelves.

Carson was by all accounts a quiet, intellectual and unassuming woman, and although confident in her facts and ability to convey them, could not be described as a campaigner. However, her view was that the public deserved to understand all the facts on the use of pesticides and that public opinion should inform policy. Despite a massive counter-attack by industry and being decried 'an hysterical woman', Carson's desire came to fruition when her book prompted a government investigation into the dangers of pesticides. In May 1963, after a long study, President **Kennedy's** Science Advisory Committee issued its pesticide report, warning against indiscriminate use of pesticides. It called for more research into potential health hazards, and the committee chairman, Dr Jerome B. Wiesner, said the uncontrolled use of pesticides was 'potentially a much greater hazard' than radioactive fallout. Also in 1963 Carson advised Congress on better ways to protect public health and the environment.

Unlike many for whom the claim is made, Rachel Carson's relevance today truly is as great as ever. Many of the key organizations which criticized her are now at the hub of new environmental controversies, such as genetically modified foods. Carson refers to a 'tide of chemicals born of the Industrial Age'. Today the number of chemicals in daily domestic use exceeds 60,000 and 400 toxic chemicals have been found inside human bodies. As Carson put it in 1962, 'the average purchaser is completely bewildered by the array of available insecticides, fungicides, and weed killers, and has no way of knowing which ones are ... deadly'. This statement is ever more true and it's hard to say where we would be without her. Her brilliance at conveying the wonder of nature is another lasting legacy.

Carson died of breast cancer, in spring 1964, Silver Spring, Maryland.

Further reading

Carson's three marine books were also published as a combined volume, *The Sea* (1968). See: Carol B. Gartner, *Rachel Carson* (1983); L. Lear, *Witness for Nature* (1998).

SASHA NORRIS

CARTER, Elliott Cook
1908–
US composer

Elliott Carter was born in New York on 11 December 1908 and received early encouragement from **Charles Ives**, who recommended him to Harvard University. There, Carter studied literature until his final year, when he began composition study with Walter Piston. He subsequently studied with Nadia Boulanger in Paris.

His early music, in common with that of many of his colleagues, bears the imprints of **Stravinskian** neo-classicism, which he had imbibed during his time in Paris. With the Piano Sonata of 1945–6, however, a powerful individual voice makes itself unmistakably felt. In this and in the succeeding works, the cogent Cello Sonata (1948), the First String Quartet (1951), which brought him to international prominence, and the exquisite *Sonata for flute, oboe, cello and harpsichord* (1952), the neo-classic element is at once paid tribute to, brought to a head and exorcized, as the mature musical personality comes more and more into focus.

Since then Carter has slowly but inexorably amassed an impressive series of masterpieces which collectively have established his position as one of the most significant figures at work in the world today. Although the surface of his music has grown steadily more complex for listeners and performers alike, this is an inseparable part of his own growth process and is accepted as such by his steadily increasing admirers in both groups, who also recognize that Carter's refusal to write down to them is the sign of his taking them seriously.

But even more than an act of faith on the part of his devotees, what has allowed Carter steadily to consolidate his position while maintaining an absolutely single-minded attitude to his own linguistic growth is the presence of certain constant attitudes through the entire oeuvre. He seems to have inherited from his mentor Ives not only a specific interest in the musical representation of simultaneity, but also a general measure of American transcendentalist common sense. With unerring instinct he balances his technical and conceptual flights by keeping several feet firmly on the ground.

When asked after a public lecture why instrumental difficulty seemed an essential ingredient of his music, Carter replied, 'These people spend years practising all of these beautiful instruments, and I feel it's my job to give them something to do on them.' The charming pragmatism of this remark bears fruit time and time again as we sense that here is someone who is literally writing for instruments and not against them – who positively delights in the things instruments can do. And every performer of Carter's music who has gone through all the rigour of learning one of his works for the first time must subsequently have had a feeling of surprise and gratification at how much has remained in the fingers and brain. For all of its difficulty, Carter's music feels right to a performer – the difficulty is justified, exhilarating and intrinsically related to the music's message.

And what helps get the message across is that every work is based on a powerful image that allows Carter to proliferate a density of event and a complexity of form without losing touch with the work's root experience. Very often this image concerns the use of the instruments themselves as the personae of an unstated but unmistakable drama: the unforgettable confrontation of darkness and light represented by the separation of high and low instruments in the slow movement of the First Quartet, the 'personalizing' of each instrument through a cadenza and an individual repertory of intervals in the Second

Quartet (1959), reinforced by a wide spatial positioning on stage, and the synchronous juxtaposition in the Third Quartet (1971) of two duos (violin/viola and violin/cello) who play in a 'strict non-relation' to each other throughout the work – in all these cases, the listener's initial impression of linguistic complexity is immediately tempered by the recognition of a tangible intellectual and physical drama which is the more articulate for not being expressed in any overt programme.

Other works depend not on inbuilt dramas, but on the recognition of fundamental images from other areas of experience: the gritty, demanding surface of the *Duo for Violin and Piano* (1974) eventually yields, to reveal a purely instrumental version of a classical *pas de deux*, with the piano and violin taking on the respective qualities of the male and female dancers to an astonishing degree – while the large-scale wave motions of the *Double Concerto* for harpsichord, piano and two chamber orchestras (1961) suggest cosmic rhythms expressive of the formation, flourishing and destruction of the physical universe. And these are aurally and viscerally palpable even without reference to Carter's literary analogue with Lucretius.

All of the music so far discussed is 'absolute' and without text. No one else in the modern period has so individually reinterpreted known genres (e.g. String Quartet, Piano Concerto, 1965, *Concerto for Orchestra*, 1969, *Symphony of Three Orchestras*, 1976) yet succeeded in restoring so much of their archetypal meaning. To one who has so purposefully achieved this, words come as a well-earned luxury in *A Mirror on which to Dwell* (1975). But Carter would never be content to rest even at this stage of his journey: in *Syringa* (1978) the baritone soloist sings ancient Greek texts about Orpheus while the mezzo-soprano retells the myth in the verse of the American poet **John Ashbery**, the result being one of Carter's most absorbing studies in simultaneity to date. With *Night Fantasies* (1980) he returns to the medium of solo piano, with which his mature music had begun thirty-five years before.

Since then, Carter's work has continued to unfold across a fruitful Indian summer characterized by an increased profusion right across the genres. Having earlier spent long periods of time carving out the language for each successive stage in his compositional journey, these newer works seem to have flowed more quickly and fluently from his pen, while maintaining the same immaculate craftsmanship.

Stylistically there have been new developments. Important among these is the greater prominence of wit and humour as a component of the musical fabric. This comes particularly to the fore in the *Triple Duo* (1983), within whose timbrally mixed sextet the three duos enter into animated musical conversation with each other. Such mercurial exchanges can also be understood as an instrumental preparation for Carter's only opera: the one-acter *What Next?* (1999) is about a car crash on the way to a wedding, inspired by Jacques Tati's film, *Traffic*.

Carter has also revealed a penchant for writing slenderer works, in which he becomes not a minimalist but a translucent miniaturist. These have included occasional pieces conceived as tributes to close musical friends and colleagues, such as *Au quai* (2002) for bassoon and viola, written for the fiftieth birthday of Oliver Knussen, and whose title is a pun on Knussen's initials. A similar sense of play informs *Réflexions* (2004), dedicated to **Pierre Boulez** on his eightieth birthday, in which Carter has imbedded a musical cryptogram of Boulez's surname, while the percussion includes a rolled stone that acts as a sonic symbol of the word 'Pierre'.

This lightness of spirit does not mean that Carter has abandoned his previous *gravitas*. One of the most profound later examples of this is undoubtedly the orchestral triptych *Symphonia: sum fluxae pretium spei* (1993–6). Its constituent movements were premièred individually, though the work achieves its greatest impact as an integral experience. In its own right, however, the final, dazzling

Allegro scorrevole lays claim to being the closest musical equivalent in Carter's output of Dante's *Paradiso*.

In a way utterly characteristic of Carter, the plenitude of his prolonged creative autumn has always been suffused with the pristine freshness of a vernal equinox.

Further reading

Other works include: *The Minotaur* (ballet, 1947); *Wind Quintet* (1950); *Eight Etudes and a Fantasy* (for woodwind quartet, 1950); *Eight Pieces for Four Timpani* (1950, 1966); *Variations for Orchestra* (1955); *Brass Quintet* (1974); *Penthode* (1985); String Quartet No. 4 (1986); Violin Concerto (1990); String Quartet No. 5 (1995); Cello Concerto (2000); *Boston Concerto* (2002). See: Jonathan W. Bernard (ed.), *Elliott Carter: Collected Essays and Lectures 1937–1995* (1997). See also: Charles Rosen, *The Musical Language of Elliott Carter* (1983); William T. Doering, *Elliott Carter: A Bio-Bibliography* (1993); Max Noubel, *Elliott Carter ou Le Temps fertile* (2000).

STEPHEN PRUSLIN

CARTIER-BRESSON, Henri

1908–2004
French photographer

When Henri Cartier-Bresson died in Provence in 2004 at the age of ninety-five, having put away his camera some three decades before, obituaries issued worldwide were unanimous in saluting him as the master of twentieth-century art photography, as well as a pioneer of modern photojournalism. Nonconformist by nature, the young Cartier-Bresson spurned a career in his family's manufacturing business and spent two years studying with the post-Cubist artist André Lhote, from whom he derived an unswerving sense of aesthetic rigour. A dalliance with the Paris surrealist group encouraged his taste for enigmas and coincidences. In 1931, he spent a year hunting in French West Africa before being invalided back to Europe after a severe bout of blackwater fever.

As a child he had tinkered with a Box Brownie, but now he treated himself to the latest camera, a Leica 35 mm rangefinder with a 50 mm lens. Hand-held and unobtrusive − he camouflaged it with black tape − it was ideally suited to his surreptitious style and became his indispensable talisman. Travelling in Italy, Spain and Mexico for the illustrated magazine *Vu*, Cartier-Bresson took his first serious photographs. By 1935, his reputation had led to a joint New York show alongside the emerging talents Walker Evans and Manuel Alvarez Bravo. However, he chose to set photography to one side and, back in France, worked for a while as assistant to the film-director **Jean Renoir**. Later, his political instincts, aroused by the rise of the Popular Front and fuelled by his deep disdain for his class origins, drew him back to photojournalism and a job with the left-wing daily *Ce Soir*. One of his assignments was to cover the coronation of George VI in May 1937, when he focused largely on working-class revels in the London streets.

Drafted into the French army, Cartier-Bresson was captured by the enemy in 1940 and imprisoned in camps in southern Germany; in 1943, at the third attempt, he managed to escape and returned to Paris to join the Resistance. After the Armistice, he busied himself with a documentary film about the homecoming of French prisoners of war. Meanwhile, thinking he was dead, the Museum of Modern Art in New York had begun organizing a posthumous exhibition of his work: happily, the photographer was able to attend the opening in 1947.

In that same year, Cartier-Bresson became a co-founder of the Magnum photo agency, along with **Robert Capa**, George Rodger and David Seymour. He would soon become the outstanding photojournalist of his epoch, visiting dozens of countries, covering events from a gypsy horse-fair to **Gandhi's** funeral, and publishing in such magazines as *Life*, *Harper's Bazaar* and *Paris-Match*. From his fertile archives emerged a succession of themed albums: *Europeans* (1955), *The People of Moscow* (1955), *The Face of Asia* (1972), *Henri Cartier-Bresson in India* (1985) and *America in Passing* (1991). The classic collection is *Images à la sauvette* (literally 'Pictures on the Run') of 1952. The book's English title, *The Decisive Moment*, launched a motto-phrase which would be for ever linked to his name as a shorthand for a principle of photographic practice based, in his words, on 'the simultaneous recognition, in a fraction of a second, of the significance of an event as well as of a precise organization of forms which give that event its proper expression'.

Cartier-Bresson was the virtuoso of the candid camera, deftly indiscreet and aspiring to pass unnoticed as he tracked down the unsuspected surreality of circumstance. He liked to invoke the Zen approach to archery adumbrated in a celebrated treatise by Ernst Herrigel, which recommends the dissolution of the ego and the cultivation of a poised tenseness. The snapshots embrace all sorts of bizarre or poignant conjunctures: kids larking about on a bombed site in Seville, a businessman dozing on Boston Common, a French workman sneaking a glass of wine at a riverside picnic, Kashmiri women outlined against distant mountains, a French customs-officer sweeping slush from a border-crossing, three prostitutes posed balletically in an Alicante brothel, a Serb cyclist with a cello on his back, an intertwined young couple slumbering on a train in Romania. Often the apparently artless image secretes a secondary, discrepant detail that lifts it above anecdote and discloses a poetic or humorous dimension.

Occasionally, he would indulge in landscape studies, producing a small number of brisk, spare masterpieces. Collected in *Tête à tête* (1998) are his memorable portraits of such cultural celebrities as **Jean-Paul Sartre** and **Albert Camus**, along with revealing studies of artists like **Matisse**, **Braque** and **Giacometti**, with whom he felt an affinity. Allergic to bravura techniques, Cartier-Bresson kept things simple: he shunned contrived or manipulated imagery, abhorred cropping and flash, and used colour but rarely. For most of his career he judged it healthy to assign responsibility for darkroom processing to impartial technicians.

In 1973, Cartier-Bresson abandoned the camera and returned to an earlier love, the pencil. His drawings – of such motifs as nudes or the Tuileries Gardens seen from his apartment window – are disappointing when compared with his incisive photography. Nevertheless, the work was exhibited with some success in New York in 1975 and published in book form as *Line by Line* (1989).

Though no longer producing photos, and averse to interviews, the retired image-maker was amused to find his reputation continually expanding. A retrospective comprising 400 prints had toured the United States in 1960; the early work was shown in New York in 1987, *Europeans* in Paris and London in 1998. In 2003, the year before his death, an exhaustive retrospective was held at the Pompidou Centre, supported by the newly established Cartier-Bresson Foundation.

Further reading

See: Lincoln Kirstein and Beaumont Newhall, introductions to *The Photographs of Cartier-Bresson* (1947, reissued 1964); Henri Cartier-Bresson, *The World of Cartier-Bresson* (1968); Yves Bonnefoy, introduction to *Henri Cartier-Bresson, Photographer* (1982, reissued 1992); Peter Galassi, *Henri Cartier-Bresson. The Early Work* (1987); Jean-Pierre Montier, *Henri Cartier-Bresson and the Artless Art* (1995); Claude Cookman, *Henri Cartier-Bresson* (1997); Pierre Assouline, *Cartier-Bresson. L'Oeil du siècle* (1999); Philippe Arbaïzer *et al.*, *Henri Cartier-Bresson. The Man, the Image and the World* (2003).

ROGER CARDINAL

CÉZANNE, Paul

1839–1906

French painter

Paul Cézanne was born in Aix-en-Provence on 19 January 1839, the third of five children. His parents did not marry until 1844. He received a traditional classical French education at a local lycée, where a close friend and contemporary was **Émile Zola**.

His artistic training was also highly traditional. He studied at the Aix Drawing School, but having failed to achieve a credit at his matriculation he succumbed to his father's wishes and registered at the local faculty of law. A **Wagner** enthusiast, he played second cornet in an orchestra for which Zola was flautist. Two years later he finally persuaded his father to let him go to Paris to study painting. His early academic style was quickly called into question as the result of his getting to know the Impressionist painters Armand Guillaumin and Camille Pissarro, and he was duly rejected by the École des Beaux Arts.

After a brief flight back to Provence, where he worked for a time as a clerk for his father's bank, he returned to Paris in 1862, extending his circle of colleagues to include Sisley, **Monet**, **Renoir** and Bazille. The next ten years were divided between Paris and Provence, with a strong gravitational pull southwards. In 1874 he exhibited at the First Exhibition of the Société Anonyme des Artistes, Peintres, Sculpteurs et Graveurs, the first Impressionist exhibition. He thus acknowledged his own position outside the official French art world. With a monthly allowance of 300 francs from his father he was able to work exclusively as a painter, and was largely untroubled by the poverty which affected so many of his acquaintances. Spending most of his time now in and around Provence, he became increasingly reclusive and estranged from the Parisian avant-garde of which he had been a member. A difficult and querulous man, he quarrelled with most of his former friends, including Zola and Monet, retreating increasingly into the life of a semi-recluse, though he assiduously cultivated his growing reputation with younger painters as a solitary genius. In 1906 he died of pneumonia, contracted while out painting *sur le motif*, and was buried in the cemetery of Aix. He was given one-man shows in 1904 and 1905 at the Salon d'Automne and the Indépendants, and in 1907 the first major retrospective of his works was also shown at the Salon d'Automne. He left a wife,

Hortence, whom he had married after the birth of their only child, Paul, who also survived him. In 1894 the French government refused a legacy of three Cézanne paintings. In 1936 *The Card Players* was bought by an American collector for five million francs.

The facts of Cézanne's working life are important in relation to the various received images of his achievements and influence as a painter. Writing in 1917 Roger Fry described him as 'the type of the artist in its purest, most unmitigated form ... in a world where everyone else is being perpetually educated the artist remains ineducable – where others are shaped, he grows' ('Paul Cézanne', in *Vision and Design*, 1920). Fry valued Cézanne's work in so far as it represented to him a way of painting in which 'all is reduced to the purest terms of structural design'. For this reason he described him, together with such other artists as **Gauguin** and **Van Gogh** and **Seurat**, as a 'Post-Impressionist', an appellation which has stuck owing to its immense convenience. Convenience is not, however, necessarily an unmixed blessing. For in combining the work of such very different artists of the same generation Fry was able to create a stick with which to beat the dog of academic naturalism, which he detested in the collective name of Impressionism. It has also ensured that the work of this generation has in general been regarded until recently in primarily formal terms, to the exclusion of any very penetrating consideration of the differences between these artists, or the social context in which and for which they worked. It also, interestingly enough, recycles the traditional Romantic picture of the artist as a particular kind of person, a heroic individual outside society, for twentieth-century consumption. It is around such myths that the legend of Cézanne has been sustained, and it is a myth to which Cézanne himself undoubtedly subscribed. He explained in a letter to Émile Bernard on 12 May 1904 that 'Art addresses itself to an excessively small number of individuals.' And to Joachim Gasquet on 30 April 1896: 'To be sure an artist wishes to raise his standard intellectually ...

but the man must remain in obscurity.' Many critics and artists have employed these beliefs to 'explain' the complex sociology of modern art and its tiny public in terms of a theory of the supposed nature of the artist, and of art itself. This was Cézanne's lasting significance – he preserved intact the person and the ideology of the aesthete drained of all connotations of languor and lilies.

Throughout the paintings of the 1860s Cézanne can be seen to be working his way through the gamut of alternatives available to him to the dominant styles of French official Salon painting. In particular he looked at Courbet, violently exaggerating that artist's break with traditional means for constructing the illusion of space. The violence with which the means of painting are themselves stressed is paralleled by a subject-matter of complex social and especially sexual significance, for example *The Rape* of 1867, in which a naked man carries off a woman into a landscape which makes no pretensions whatsoever to actuality. In the 1870s Cézanne worked in a more recognizably Impressionist manner, particularly in relation to his friend Pissarro, laboriously building up his picture space in related tints, already hatching his brush-strokes in groups which possess an identity of direction which is unrelated to their representational function. He was working very much against current conventions of landscape painting and the sense of the picturesque of his day, rejecting chiaroscuro modelling in favour of a sense of space constructed through the tonality of colour. As he wrote in evident excitement to Pissarro from the south on 2 July 1876: 'The sun is so terrific here that it seems to me as if the objects were silhouetted not only in black and white, but in blue, red, brown and violet. I may be mistaken but this seems to me the opposite of modelling.'

In this way he developed away from a mainstream Impressionist emphasis on the single moment of sensory perception as the cardinal criterion for aesthetic authenticity. For an ideal truth to the moment he exchanged a concern with the flow of observation over an indefinite period of time, a value he came to describe as the sense of 'duration', borrowing a term from the philosopher Henri Bergson. Hence his retention of profiles and contours which are frequently out of alignment with one another, but 'true' in so far as each registered a different and equally valid moment, in the production of the picture which, by definition, could never be finished. In this respect again he embodies the Romantic view of art as an unachievable ideal. Cézanne's stress on the primacy of his 'little sensation' bears witness to his own belief in the uniqueness of the artist as a person, best summarized in his friend Zola's definition of a work as 'a man: I wish to find in this work a temperament, a particular and unique accent.' Such a philosophy fitted very well with the increasing formal daring of his compositions, such as the various late *Baigneuses* pictures of the 1880s and 1890s. And in the criticism of Fry and many of his French contemporaries Cézanne emerges as a model for a new kind of Bohemianism, in which the artist's essential greatness is seen to reside not in living life to the full, but in his (or her) abstemious devotion to aesthetic sensation to the exclusion of life altogether. Hence Cézanne can emerge as heroic in his way as **Rimbaud** – and how much more palatable to a bourgeois audience!

Cézanne's late paintings offer a wealth of suggestions of how we are to think the problem of pictorial space. Gone are all the last vestiges of comfortable reassuring Renaissance perspective, with its endless homogeneous vistas and solid tangible forms. He insisted that pictures are not true to the objects they depict, but to the sensation the painter has of them. In this manner Cézanne wrote off the nineteenth-century Realist tradition and opened up the prospect of a grand Romantic revival, albeit a revival which continues to call upon the tones and values of classicism. Indigestible in his own time for Naturalists and Symbolists alike, he was able to draw on both as theoretical resources with which to bolster his own increased fascination with the conventions of European art themselves. His late pictures, such as *Bathers* of 1900–1906, push the sense of duration to its most extreme and vulnerable point – the exchange of a mark of paint for an object in space in an almost totally arbitrary relation. This was Cézanne's importance to the next generation: he legitimated the practice of painting as an end in itself. He made 'art for art's sake' respectable and, more to the point, modern. At the same time his remark in April 1906 to the German collector Osthaus that he had tried 'to render perspective uniquely through colour' pointed the way to the subsequent achievements of **Matisse** and all his followers. It should, however, be pointed out that this same goal of creating a universal pictorial language, in opposition to speech and writing, of rejecting hierarchies of genre and letting nature 'speak', was nothing new. Rather, Cézanne realized one strand of the Romantic tradition, and carried it across to this century triumphantly draped with legends of innovation and timeless value which remain as misleading as they are ubiquitous.

Further reading

Cézanne's *Letters*, ed. J. Rewald (trans. 1941), were republished in 1976. The standard biography remains that by Ambroise Vollard, *Paul Cézanne* (1914, trans. 1924). The best recent collection of Cézanne criticism is Theodore Reff, Laurence Gowing and others, *Cézanne, The Late Work* (1977). The most influential British study of the artist was Roger Fry, *Cézanne, A Study of His Development* (1927). See also: J. Rewald, *Paul Cézanne: The Watercolours* (1983); R. Shiff, *Cézanne and the Ends of Impressionism* (1984); R. Kendall, *Cézanne by Himself: Drawings, Paintings and Writings* (1998).

SIMON WATNEY

CHAGALL, Marc

1887–1985

Russo-French painter

Born at Vitebsk in western Russia, Chagall inherited the myths and traditions of folk legends, Jewish lore and the imagery of

Russian orthodox churches. To this vital source, Chagall brought the sophisticated practices of Parisian art. Chagall's paintings have evoked emotion and a poetic sense of beauty that they have drawn from direct experience: for Chagall painting was, of necessity, an autobiographic activity, even when his themes as such are not directly observed. He made of narrative paintings so succinct a vehicle for his emotional and spiritual life that their density and brilliance of colour, and even their supernatural or fantastic subjects, appear mischievous, rapturous or even epic. It is, however, for all his originality, a mistake to see Chagall out of context. He was first a student under Jehuda Pen in Vitebsk, and the Jewish community at Vitebsk, with which Chagall was closely associated, provided themes, such as the fiddler on the roof, to which Chagall was to return many times. In 1907 Chagall entered the Imperial School for the Encouragement of the Arts in St Petersburg where the love of decoration and of lavish colour characteristic of his tutor, **Léon Bakst**, served to confirm this tendency in Chagall's work although the elegance of Bakst found no reflection in the fierce individuality of Chagall's early works. Bakst also encouraged a lasting love of the theatre in Chagall, an outlet that has provided a regular activity for Russian painters. In this respect Chagall seems to have approached the World of Art circle whose cosmopolitan outlook did much to make Chagall more aware of French Post-Impressionist painting. On the other hand the ostensibly natural primitivism of Chagall's early work, its roughness and directness of expression, places him closer to the cultivated primitivism of such Russian contemporaries as Larionov, Goncharova and **Malevich**. In this respect Chagall's fantastic themes appear less the products of an extraordinary and isolated imagination and more a lively contribution to a current vogue. The apparently unconventional qualities of his paintings frequently obscure the intellectual as well as emotional effort that has produced them. When Chagall travelled to Paris in 1910, living in the studio complex known as La Ruche, he found himself at the centre of a changing group of Russian artists and writers who had the most intimate links with French literary and artistic pioneers, among them Apollinaire, Delaunay, Cendrars, **Picasso**. Chagall's *Self Portrait with Seven Fingers* painted in Paris sums up his union of dreams of Russia with urban Paris, and of primitive painting with the devices of Cubism.

Upon the outbreak of war in 1914 Chagall returned to Russia, where particularly after the Revolutions of 1917, his achievement was recognized and his talents employed. He designed murals, sets and costumes for Granowsky's Moscow Jewish Theatre and was placed in control of the art-activities, teaching and exhibitions of Vitebsk. His paintings of this Russian period are exquisite evocations of Vitebsk, of rural Russian-Jewish life and of the elation of his relationship with Bella, his wife.

Chagall returned to Paris in 1922, retaining his extraordinary individuality and increasing his vocabulary of themes, potent images, some Jewish, some Christian and all suggestively powerful, that he characteristically isolated as being of importance to his expression. Their autobiographical sources were developed into more broadly applicable human themes. The breadth of Chagall's humanity in this sense is a central feature of his achievement. In 1933 he published the autobiographical *Ma Vie* in French (trans. *My Life*, 1965). He had seen his first retrospective exhibition in Paris in 1924 and his French links became extremely strong, alongside the Russian and Jewish elements of his identity and cultural life. Despite the fantastic features of his painting, Chagall remained unaffected by the Surrealist movement whose founding manifesto was published in Paris in 1924. Yet during the later 1930s his work reflected political developments and in particular the suffering of the Jews. In 1939 he was invited to New York by the Museum of Modern Art there and did not return to France until 1944.

If there are elements of his work that recall the grotesque fantasy of Nikolai Gogol's stories, there are elements also that recall Apollinaire or Cendrars. Chagall became an international public figure whose ability to raise personal experience to a broadly human expression made him brilliant in the execution of public works devoid of the ballast of affectation. His book designed for Vollard, his stained-glass windows, his theatrical design and his colossal ceiling painting for the Paris Opera, unveiled in 1964, testify to his broadening scope and his indefatigable vitality.

Further reading

See: J.J. Sweeney, *Marc Chagall* (1946); F. Meyer, *Marc Chagall* (1961); Jean Cassou, *Chagall* (1965); J. Baal-Teshuva (ed.), *Chagall: A Retrospective* (1995).

JOHN MILNER

CHANDLER, Raymond Thornton

1888–1959

US thriller writer

Raymond Chandler was born in Chicago but educated largely in England, at Dulwich College. After a period in London and service during the First World War in France he returned to America and worked at a variety of jobs (including the vice-presidency of a group of oil companies) before becoming a full-time writer in early middle age. Chandler did not create the detective story format but adapted it from the 'pulp' magazines of the 1930s, in particular the *Black Mask*, to which he contributed. His most notable predecessor is Dashiell Hammett, author of *The Maltese Falcon* (1930). The private eye, the lone and usually lonely individual who battles against a society and solves a mystery which springs from its corruption, can be traced back in some form at least as far as Edgar Allan Poe's amateur detective Auguste Dupin. Chandler found insulting and distasteful the sterile contrivance and lack of realism that characterized the so-called Gold Age of detective fiction, the early twentieth century. In his essay 'The Simple Art of Murder' (*Atlantic Monthly*, 1944) he claims that Hammett 'took murder out of the

Venetian vase and dropped it into the alley'. In preferring the squalid-glamorous to the genteel, Chandler was following an increasingly confident American tradition.

For his locale Chandler used Los Angeles, as far away in spirit as it was possible to get from murder in the English vicarage. Mystification rather than the neat, logical problems set by an **Agatha Christie**; a range of social types rather than the upper middle-class inhabitants of the drawing-room; a laconic and witty style, and a certain disconnectedness in narrative, instead of the pedestrian parade of suspects and motives – these were some of the ways in which Chandler broke from the standard English and American whodunnit. In California he found an atmosphere as much as a setting, one that appealed to the strong elements of romanticism and exoticism in him. Philip Marlowe, his hero, appears in seven novels; having found a satisfactory vehicle for his and his readers' fantasies, Chandler developed Marlowe little. 'Down these mean streets a man must go who is not himself mean, who is neither tarnished nor afraid': the famous rhapsody to the private-eye-as-hero describes a figure who is recognizable from the first novel, *The Big Sleep* (1939), to the last, *Playback* (1958). The format too hardly varies. Marlowe is approached by a client, accepts the case with weary charity, and pursues his quest, usually in search of a missing person, over dead bodies, through the estates and dubious private clinics of the rich, in the interrogation rooms of corrupt police forces, in the bars and boulevards of Los Angeles and its environs. Throughout Marlowe retains his independence, signified by his obstinacy in upholding his client's interests in the face of threats, bribes and sexual temptation.

This quixoticism – it is significant that one of Marlowe's earlier incarnations in the pulp magazine period was named Mallory, recalling the author of *Morte d'Arthur* – reaches its peak in Chandler's most ambitious and substantial novel, *The Long Goodbye* (1953), the plot of which turns on Marlowe's irrational and unrewarded loyalty to a male friend. In the sexually ambiguous nature of their friendship, in the lengthy portrait of another character, an alcoholic writer whose survival and eventual death are in some way dependent on the hero, we see the closest approach between the author and his creation. In the later novels, apart from the atypical *Playback*, Marlowe also becomes more sententious, more invulnerable to temptation and perhaps less plausible.

The direct and laconic style which owes something to **Hemingway**, the wisecracking, the startling similes for which Chandler is noted, are to be found in their most unalloyed forms in the earlier novels. It becomes clear in retrospect that the claims of realism Chandler made for the genre are only partially valid; that the Philip Marlowe novels are as stylized, ordered and remote from everyday experience as the classical detective stories of which Chandler was so disdainful. But his books skilfully embody certain heroic fantasies, being witty, tough and compassionate while remaining always loyal to an inner unstated conception of integrity, being able to move easily in any level of a tainted society.

Further reading

Other works include: *Farewell, My Lovely* (1940); *The High Window* (1942); *The Lady in the Lake* (1943); *The Little Sister* (1949). See also: *The Raymond Chandler Papers: Selected Letters and Non-fiction, 1909–1959* (2000). About Chandler: Frank MacShane, *The Life of Raymond Chandler* (1976); and *The World of Raymond Chandler*, ed. Miriam Gross (1977); J. Kenneth van Dover, *The Critical Response to Raymond Chandler* (1995); Gene D. Phillips, *Creatures of Darkness: Raymond Chandler, Detective Fiction and Film Noir* (2000); Toby Widdicombe, *A Reader's Guide to Raymond Chandler* (2001).

PHILIP GOODEN

CHAPLIN, Charles Spencer

1889–1977

British/US film actor and director

Born into a family of struggling music hall entertainers, Chaplin experienced the ugly, poverty-stricken side of Victorian London in his childhood which undoubtedly contributed greatly to his 'little tramp' and his narrative settings. By the time he was approached by Mack Sennett in 1913, Chaplin had finished a long apprenticeship in the English music halls and was the star of Fred Karno's vaudeville Mumming Birds company. Chaplin made thirty-five shorts for Sennett and as early as the second had evolved the costume for which he is famous: little bowler, tiny coat, baggy pants and cane. 'Tillie's Punctured Romance' made him a star in 1914 and he left Sennett shortly after to work for Essenay, then Mutual, and First National. Chaplin quickly became one of the richest and most popular stars in Hollywood, and perhaps the only one to gain any prestige for the infant art form among intellectuals, earning praise from critics as diverse as **T.S. Eliot** and Gilbert Seldes. In 1920 Chaplin directed his first feature-length film, *The Kid*. In 1923 he joined United Artists which he had helped Douglas Fairbanks, Mary Pickford and **D.W. Griffith** to form in 1919. Although he made his first sound films in 1931 (*City Lights*) and 1936 (*Modern Times*), Chaplin refused to allow any dialogue. Sound seems to discourage Chaplin, perhaps as representative of the modern technology and values that seemed so far away from his Victorian youth. His films became fewer and fewer. In 1940 he made *The Great Dictator*, a satire on **Hitler** that probably earned him that unusual label from the American right of 'premature fascist'. His blackest comedy *Monsieur Verdoux*, a story about a Bluebeard-type murderer with a pacifist sub-theme, was released in 1947. The overly sentimental *Limelight* (1952) was set in the London of his childhood and featured a guest appearance by his great comedic rival **Buster Keaton**. His last two films, *A King in New York* (1957) and *A Countess from Hong Kong* (1967), were kindly ignored by the majority of critics and audiences.

Throughout his career in the United States Chaplin was pursued by controversy and court cases, first in his sensational marriage and divorce to teenage co-star Lita Grey (resulting in an underground best-seller called *Complaints of Lita Grey* based on the divorce proceedings); then his 1944 indictment under the Mann Act for which a jury eventually acquitted him on the fourth vote; and finally a September 1952 order from the Attorney General's office to refuse Chaplin re-admittance to the country under the undesirable aliens clause Section 137, Paragraph (c) of Title 8 of the US Code. Chaplin had been named many times as a 'commie' or left-winger by witnesses in the notorious Hollywood purge by the House Committee on Un-American Activities. *Limelight* was picketed by the American Legion and Chaplin did not return from his 1952 European vacation until the end of the 1970s when Hollywood offered him a belated award. Chaplin's bitterness at this ludicrous political purge deprived Americans of any chance to see his major features for the better part of two decades since he owned the rights to them (except *The Gold Rush*) and refused to allow them to be shown in America. Slowly he relented and the films became more available in the 1970s.

Chaplin's genius can best be compared with that of the great nineteenth-century stage producer/star who knew exactly how best to mount a production to showcase his particular talents. From the very beginning Chaplin somehow understood that the 'Keystone style' was too frenetic, and he played against this prevailing mode with an infinitely more graceful and restrained style that quickly separated him from his cohorts who mugged and jumped their way into history in the homogeneous and anonymous Keystone style. Chaplin's Victorian roots became more and more evident as he moved from shorts into feature films. He offered himself as Everyman, an innocent victim, unconquerable idealist, and sentimental unrequited lover. His scripts were almost always episodic, absurdly sentimental, and outrageously simplistic. Yet his physical grace, his pantomime, his impregnable optimism and irresistible wistfulness always seemed to overcome the dated vehicles in the minds of his audiences.

His career as a director, however, emphasizes his limitation as a filmmaker while continuing to enhance his reputation as a performer. *The Kid* made a star out of child actor Jackie Coogan and wrung tears from every child-loving American and hardly anyone noticed that the situations and characters seemed ludicrous in the beginnings of the Jazz Age and the angst following the slaughter in the just-ended war. *The Gold Rush* (1925) underlined his habit of worshipping young women without reason or realism while demonstrating how little he had noticed the technical and visual advances in cinema since his career began twelve years earlier. One has only to look at Keaton's *The General*, made in the same year, to see how Chaplin was falling behind as a director. Yet no one will ever forget Charlie sitting down to eat his boot with shoestrings as spaghetti or the parody of Robert Service in the saloon scenes. *City Lights* emphasizes his essentially Victorian sentimentalism with its street-ballad plot of the poor blind girl who befriends the little tramp and deserts him in the end. Chaplin's dramatic structure rarely escapes the obvious excesses of nineteenth-century melodrama even thirty or forty years into the twentieth century. *Modern Times* is perhaps his richest attempt to deal with contemporary issues, although he stubbornly refuses to use dialogue. The early sequences of the Chaplin tramp caught up in the super-modern factory machinery and eventually leading – by accident – a radical demonstration were superseded by concentration on the gamine figure that obsesses Chaplin throughout his career. Thus Chaplin's social observations are overwhelmed by the female entanglements that ensnare the tramp far more totally than any technology can do. Even Chaplin's most tightly organized script, *Monsieur Verdoux*, suffers from a few gratuitous episodes and lacklustre camera movement and editing. Verdoux himself, however, is that much more moving as a man out of place in his own time, a gentleman murderer in an age of mass murderers. Verdoux's last moments before execution are a fitting epitaph for

Chaplin's own career. After dismissing the priest with the words, 'I am at peace with God, my conflict is with man,' he decides to accept the offer of a glass of rum because he has never tried rum before. Then he takes the long walk to the prison courtyard, the last road the little tramp will ever walk because the horizon has become a stone wall.

Further reading

See: *Charlie Chaplin's Own Story* (1916); *My Autobiography* (1964). See also: Louis Delluc, *Charlie Chaplin* (1922); Theodore Huff, *Charlie Chaplin* (1951); Robert Payne, *The Great God Pan: A Biography of the Tramp played by Charles Chaplin* (1952); Isabel Quigley, *Charlie Chaplin: Early Comedies* (1968); Donald W. McCaffrey, *Focus on Chaplin 9* (1971); David Robinson, *Chaplin: His Life and Art* (1985).

CHARLES GREGORY

CHEEVER, John

1912–82

US story writer and novelist

The Chekhov of the suburbs. Such, if a touch inflatedly, has become the critic John Leonard's familiar catchphrase for John Cheever. The meticulous, stylish portraiture of well-appointed American East Coast society, with irony to match, has long won high esteem in contemporary literary ranks. It is not that America as suburban life has lacked its chronicles, whether the fiction of James Gould Cozzens or John O'Hara or, subsequently, the Pennsylvania quartet of novels **John Updike** inaugurated with *Rabbit Run* (1960) or the portrait of township Dixie in Allan Gurganus's *White People* (1991). But the dozen story collections and novels under Cheever's name win their own distinctive standing. His New York of residential Westchester or Manhattan's Upper East Side, along with Connecticut, New Hampshire or Massachusetts, serve as moral playground, the interior hinterland of self-loss and foible behind the WASP upper middle-class writ of corporate affluence and office, dinner party and the cocktail hour.

Born into an affluent family in Quincy, Massachusetts, Cheever witnessed his factory-owner father's ruination in the 1929 crash and subsequent desertion, left school early, sold his first story to *The New Republic* at eighteen, wrote MGM script synopses, lived with his brother in Boston, and moved into literary life in New York as a contributor to *Collier's Story*, *The Atlantic* and, from 1935, the *New Yorker*. There followed marriage to Mary Winternitz in 1941 and three children, war service in the signals corps, TV writing, a Guggenheim Fellowship in 1951, teaching stints variously at the University of Iowa, Sing Sing Prison, Barnard College and Boston University, and a stay at New York's Smithers Rehabilitation Center to combat depression and alcoholism. But as the posthumous issue of *The Letters of John Cheever* (1988) and *The Journals of John Cheever* (1991) make clear this success, not least as an output of more than two hundred magazine and other stories, masked complex fissures within, whether self-doubt, betrayals, drinking, or guilt at his long concealed but in later years active bisexuality.

Cheever's stories offer a repertoire of lives caught up in shadow. Miscued desire offers one staple, the anxiety, often the melancholy, at a given life opportunity missed. Business connivance recurs. Loneliness, illness, drink, aging, petty adultery, alienated offspring or the fret and ritual of pool or golf club all become working features within the larger realm of suburban affluence. The upshot has been talk of Cheever Country for which one centre has been the township of Shady Hill. This urbane, closely observed portraiture, whether first published in the *New Yorker* or elsewhere, made for a formidable run of collections beginning from *The Way Some People Live* (1943). In turn followed *The Enormous Radio and Other Stories* (1953), *The Housebreaker of Shady Hill* (1958), *Some People, Places and Things That Will Not Appear in My Next Novel* (1961), *The Brigadier and the Golf Widow* (1964) and *The World of Apples* (1973), with *The Stories of John Cheever* (1978) as omnibus edition and which won him the

Pulitzer Prize. *Thirteen Uncollected Stories* (1994) supplies an epilogue.

Examples of Cheever's craft would deservedly include 'The Swimmer', Ned Merrill's slightly surreal action of swimming home through the neighbourhood pools of suburbia as the refraction of lives past or blighted and to include his own. It gave rise to an underrated 1968 film with Burt Lancaster in the prime role. 'The Worm in the Apple' adds a companion version of this suburbia of tarnished lives as the portrait of the Crutchmans, a family in every respect seemingly above reproach except for the narrator's suspicion of the debilitating cost of routine. 'The Enormous Radio' gives a virtuoso anatomy of the fall from psychological innocence of Jim and Irene Wescott as the radio's imperfect, and sometimes sinister, sound illuminates both the charade of their own Sutton Place apartment lives and those of their close neighbours. 'A Woman Without a Country' beautifully pursues the life of Anne Tomkins, monied expatriate on the grounds of an accidental family scandal, and able neither fully to return to the America she misses nor to accomplish a wholly right Europeanism. 'The Housebreaker of Shady Hill' offers a kind of reverse burglary story, John Hake's furtive return of a neighbour's cash he has stolen to bail out his business after circumstances return him to financial viability. He ends up a kind of moral oddity, the lie he tells a suspicious cop about being out only to walk his dog obliquely at one with his action over the money.

Cheever's novels invite matching recognition. *The Wapshot Chronicle* (1957), spanning a heritage of seven generations in the Massachusetts fishing village of St. Botophs, deals in the knots of dynasty: Leander Wapshot, seafarer and suicide, his wife Sarah, two sons Coverly and Moses, and maverick Cousin Honora. *The Wapshot Scandal* (1984), a savvy, often witheringly comic, sounding board for America's post-war temper, takes the story forward. Coverly gets embroiled in the politics of McCarthyism, Moses in sexual despair, and Honora in taxation woes. *Bullet*

Park (1969) satirizes suburban white-collar mores through the name-linked Eliot Nailles and Paul Hammer. *Falconer* (1977) uses its Hudson River Prison format to explore related other modes of incarcerated self. *Oh What a Paradise It Seems* (1982), magic realist fare, makes the defence of Beasey's Pond by the ageing Lemuel Sears into a swansong for the America Cheever loved but believed, literally as figurally, at risk of polluting its own best promise.

Further reading

See: Lynne Waldeland, *John Cheever* (1979), *Conversations with John Cheever*, ed. Scott Donaldson (1987), Scott Donaldson, *John Cheever: A Biography* (1988), Patrick Meanor, *John Cheever Revisited* (1995), James O'Hara, *John Cheever: A Study of the Short Fiction* (1989), Susan Cheever, *Home Before Dark: A Biographical Memoir of John Cheever* (1984), *Treetops: A Family Memoir* (1999).

A. ROBERT LEE

CHEKHOV, Anton Pavlovich
1860–1904
Russian dramatist and short-story writer

Anton Chekhov was the third of six children born to Pavel and Yevghenia Chekhov in Taganrog in the North Caucasus. His father, a shopkeeper, had a great interest in the arts, which he pursued to the neglect of his business. This resulted in financial difficulties, and physical hardships for his children. Chekhov attended secondary school, but his home was not conducive to study and he had to stay on for two extra years to work up to standard. In 1876 his father went bankrupt, and the family moved to Moscow, leaving Chekhov behind to finish school. Already a prolific writer, he became editor of the school magazine called the *Stutterer*. In 1879 he rejoined his family, entering the Medical Faculty of Moscow University. In his spare time Chekhov continued to write for publication, but he worked hard at his medical studies, and not until 1883 was there any marked increase in his literary output. During this period he was mostly writing humorous short stories, poor in quality, and viewed by Chekhov simply as a means of earning extra money. It was around 1886 that he began to take writing seriously, and from then on it increasingly absorbed his time, at the expense of his medical practice.

Chekhov had written his first play, *The Fatherless* (*Bezzotsovshchina*) in 1877, while still at school. His brother Alexander, whose opinion Chekhov always valued, disliked it, and the play was neither performed nor published during the author's lifetime. The same fate befell *On the High Road* (*Na Golshoydorage*, 1886), adapted by Chekhov from his own short story, 'Autumn'. From 1887 onwards he began to devote more attention to drama, and produced a series of one-act comic sketches known collectively as the 'vaudevilles'. These were well received by the public, and one in particular, *The Bear* (*Medved*), was quite profitable. Chekhov's first full-length play, *Ivanov*, was performed in 1887, but he was by now becoming dissatisfied with the over-theatricality of the contemporary stage, believing that actors should 'show life and men as they are, and not as they would look if you put them on stilts'. However, he found it difficult to convey these ideas to actors, and the first production of *Ivanov* was not to his liking, although a reasonable success with the public. Chekhov drastically rewrote it, and the new version was staged in 1889, to critical acclaim. In his next play, *The Wood Demon* (*Leshy*, 1889), Chekhov eschewed most of the stage conventions of the day in a search for a new 'structure of feeling'; the work failed to repeat the success of *Ivanov*, and he withdrew it. Eight years later a rewritten version was to appear as *Uncle Vanya* (*Dyadya Vanya*). After a tour of Western Europe, Chekhov bought a small estate near Moscow, and wrote his next play, *The Seagull* (*Chayka*), in 1895, a production of which was very badly received in St Petersburg the following year. Chekhov wrote afterwards: 'I left Petersburg full of doubts of all kinds.' His self-confidence, never great, had been

severely shaken. Shortly afterwards he fell ill; tuberculosis was diagnosed, and after a period in a Moscow clinic, Chekhov left for the south of France, returning to Russia in 1898.

That same year the face of Russian theatre was radically altered by the birth of the Moscow Art Theatre, established by **Konstantin Stanislavsky** and Vladimir Nemirovich-Danchenko as a protest against the current artificiality of Russian drama. Like Chekhov, they looked for sincerity in acting rather than flamboyance and trickery. Nemirovich-Danchenko persuaded Chekhov, against both his and Stanislavsky's better judgements, to allow them to include *The Seagull* in their opening season. Stanislavsky co-directed and also took the part of the writer Trigorin. It proved to be the most successful play in their repertoire. The Moscow Art Theatre went on to establish a reputation as the greatest exponent of Chekhov's art, though the writer himself was not always satisfied with Stanislavsky's interpretations. Chekhov did not actually see them perform his work until 1900 when they toured the Crimea, where he had moved for the sake of his health shortly before the first night of *The Seagull*. In 1899 Stanislavsky had staged *Uncle Vanya*. It did not repeat the triumph of *The Seagull*, and indeed, Moscow audiences tended to be slow to appreciate any of the works of Chekhov's maturity.

In 1900 Chekhov began work on *Three Sisters* (*Tri sestry*), but ill-health made writing an exhausting task, and he described the play as 'dreary, long, and awkward'. Nevertheless, he took the manuscript to Moscow himself, and played an active part in rehearsals, although he was again out of the country, this time in Nice, when it was premièred in January 1901. Later that year Chekhov married Olga Knipper, an actress with Stanislavsky's company. It was a happy marriage, though they were apart for much of the time, he in Yalta, she in Moscow. They had no children.

Chekhov found working on his final play, *The Cherry Orchard* (*Vishnyory sad*), extremely difficult: 'I write about four lines a day, and even that costs me an intolerably painful effort.' The play was finally performed on 17 January 1904, Chekhov's birthday. He had again attended rehearsals, where there had been serious disagreements between himself and Stanislavsky. Chekhov insisted that the play was 'a light comedy', while the director saw it as a 'serious drama of Russian life'. However, Chekhov attended the opening night and was fêted by the audience, at considerable cost to his health. He died six months later, and his remains were buried in Moscow.

Chekhov's major plays focus upon the lives of the privileged landowning class of tsarist Russia, and all are set on or around provincial estates. Yet they were written during a period of political ferment. They are therefore frequently held to be 'elegies' for the passing of an age. It is argued that Chekhov presents the cultural values of the Russian upper class in their struggle for survival against the social transformation urged by middle-class intellectuals and businessmen. Hopeless though the struggle may be, it is at least, so the theory goes, the occasion for a heartening idealism, the expression of belief in traditional virtues. But this interpretation wrongly labels Chekhov's drama as reactionary and sentimental. The later plays are certainly concerned with resistance to social change: the three sisters create a myth around their Muscovite past to insulate themselves against the ugly realities of provincial life; an axe fells the trees of the cherry orchard, and a social order approaches its end. But far from mourning its decline, Chekhov's work exhibits a profound understanding of the necessity of its passing. He portrays a class becoming painfully aware of its own impotency and inability to change. Self-delusion is no escape because, as Gayev remarks in *The Cherry Orchard*, 'the greater the number of cures you suggest for a sickness, the more certain you can be it's incurable'. Unlike **Ibsen**, Chekhov placed no faith in personal rebellion, and the last plays have no clearly defined central character. He rejected the possibility of heroic action:

Our life is provincial, the cities are unpaved, the villages poor, the masses abused. In our youth we chirp rapturously, like sparrows on a dung heap, but when we are forty, we are already old and begin to think about death. Fine heroes we are!

The ruling class in Chekhov's plays is presented as morally stagnant, capable only of looking to its own past; that is its tragedy. But the plays themselves are clear-sighted and far removed from sentimentality.

A leading dramatist, Chekhov also ranks alongside **Joyce** as one of the greatest of short-story writers. His best fiction, notably 'Lady with a Lapdog' ('Dama s sobachkoy', 1899) and 'The Darling' ('Dushechka', 1898), display his ability to combine tragedy and comedy in a fine balance. 'Ward 6' ('Palata No. 6' 1892) presents a ward in a mental hospital as a symbol for Russian society. Ragin, a doctor, condones the neglect and cruelty rampant in the hospital, but is tricked into himself becoming a patient, a victim of the logic that, while there are mental wards, patients must be found to fill them. An austere work, 'Ward 6' was much admired by the young **Lenin**.

In all his writing Chekhov was able to convey depths of feeling – the enormity of personal tragedy, the joy of hope, the absurdity of human behaviour – through a word or a gesture. He fought, often against his own inclinations, to remove the melodramatic from his work, relying on atmosphere rather than action; it was his boast, of *The Cherry Orchard*, that there is 'not a single pistol shot in it'. Few dramatists have equalled his understanding of people's fears and weaknesses, while rejecting any indulgence in pessimism or despair.

Further reading

Chekhov has not always been well served by his English translators. The best edition of his work remains Ronald Hingley, *Oxford Chekhov* (1961–75), but there is an adaptation of *The Cherry Orchard* by the playwright Trevor Griffiths which deserves to be read widely. The authoritative biography is E.J. Simmons, *Chekhov: A Biography* (1962), See also R. Williams, *Drama from Ibsen to*

Brecht (1952); R. Hingley, *A New Life of Anton Chekhov* (1976); Donald Rayfield, *Anton Chekhov: A Life* (1997); Victor Emiljanow (ed.), *Anton Chekhov: Collected Critical Heritage* (1997); Vera Gottlieb and Paul Allain (eds), *The Cambridge Companion to Chekhov* (2000); Janet Malcolm, *Reading Chekhov* (2003).

PAUL NICHOLLS

CHIRICO, Giorgio de

1888–1977
Italian artist

Giorgio de Chirico was born in Greece of Italian parents and first studied art in Athens. In 1907 he went to Munich, where he experienced what he called 'severe crises of melancholy', becoming a devotee of the poetic gloom he found in certain writings of Schopenhauer and **Nietzsche**. On moving to Italy in 1909, he began painting in an unnatural, sepulchral manner derived from Arnold Böcklin. *The Enigma of the Oracle* (1910) shows the mysterious rear view of a dark figure gazing out to sea, balanced by a white figure (a statue?) practically hidden by a black drape. Already de Chirico was fascinated by the principle of simultaneously revealing and hiding his subject-matter. When in 1911 he moved to Paris and got to know Apollinaire, he began to produce his so-called metaphysical paintings, commonly seen as the first manifestations of Surrealist art.

De Chirico's metaphysical work combined Mediterranean sunniness with a distinctly Nordic chill, opening on to dream spaces that relate uneasily to the world of straightforward perception. 'One must picture everything in the world as an enigma,' he wrote, 'and live in the world as if in a vast museum of strangeness.' *Mystery and Melancholy of a Street* (1914), in which a girl with a hoop runs past a parked removal van towards an unseen figure whose shadow, cast by the late afternoon sun, creeps menacingly forth from behind a building, introduces us to a city in the grip of invisible forces and conveys a sense of queer foreboding.

De Chirico's city contains gaping piazzas framed by Italianate buildings with sharply angled façades, spectral arcades and narrow towers and chimneys. These look as if they were cut from cardboard with fanatic care and are painted in dry neutral colours that lend an air of feigned innocence. Architectural incident is often cramped into the corners of the canvas, and the multiplication of vanishing points produces an effect of dizziness: 'Who can deny the troubling connection between perspective and metaphysics?' the artist once asked. Almost the only inhabitants of the city are classical statues (*Ariadne*, 1913) or faceless mannequins (*The Fatal Light*, 1915).

Often small objects are portentously arrayed in the foreground of the paintings – artichokes, gloves, biscuits, cotton-reels. 'He could only paint when he was *surprised* by certain dispositions of objects which presented to him a flagrant particularity,' observed **André Breton**. In *The Uncertainty of the Poet* (1913), de Chirico shows an instinctive grasp of the Surrealist principle that visual surprise springs from violently illogical juxtapositions: a nude female torso in stone and a sheaf of bananas meet on an empty piazza, with a locomotive passing at the skyline (this last apparently in homage to the artist's father, a railway engineer).

The effect of such works is to instil a mood which has been variously categorized as nostalgic, fateful or melancholic. In detailing for us what he called 'the signs of the metaphysical alphabet', the artist developed a captivating idiom of cryptic allusion. *Self-Portrait* (1913) depicts a plaster cast of a left foot, a right foot which might be reality or replica, a rolled map, an egg and two chimneys. On a wall is inscribed a large letter X which both 'marks the spot' and masks the identity of the sitter. If this *is* a self-portrait, it seems the artist is either unwilling or unable to reveal who or what he really is. Other works, such as *The Song of Love* (1914) or *The Enigma of Fatality* (1914), use the motif of the glove or gauntlet to stage a gesture of urgent but unspecified pointing. The typical de Chirico effect is one of oracular profundity, the sensation of an impending revelation whose proper articulation is, however, always deferred. The viewer is kept hovering between puzzlement and understanding.

After a wartime association with the Futurist Carlo Carrá (who founded a short-lived *scuola metafisica*), de Chirico returned to Rome in 1918 to study the techniques of the Old Masters. 'It was in the museum of the Villa Borghese one morning, standing before a Titian, that I received the revelation of what great painting is: in the gallery I beheld tongues of flame.' Almost from that moment on, de Chirico's career moved in a resolutely reactionary direction. Through the 1920s he distanced himself from the modern movement in general and Surrealism in particular. Though he produced a few sporadic pictures in a more or less Surrealist vein and even wrote a Surrealist novel, *Hebdomeros* (1929), de Chirico effectively spurned the Surrealists at the very time his influence over them was at its height. Painters like **Ernst**, Tanguy, **Magritte** and **Dalí** ignored the artist and concentrated on adjusting to their individual preoccupations the key formula offered by his work, namely the poetic suggestion of unconscious states in terms of the relations of objects in space.

Over the half-century of his post-metaphysical career, de Chirico produced academic canvases in a neoclassical or baroque manner which are, in the view of most critics, disappointingly derivative if not downright trashy, and certainly bereft of the hallucinatory magic of the metaphysical style. It may be surmised that he had come to see in his early work the symbolic record of feelings which he could not consciously tolerate. One senses an undercurrent of panic. The 'revealing symptom of the *inhabited depth*' which the artist saw as typifying the metaphysical perception of reality may have become for him the revealing symptom of personal insecurity; perhaps he eventually read the 'metaphysical alphabet' as registering an absurd lack of meaning in the world, emptiness rather than plenitude, paralysis rather than vibration. But

whatever the meaning of these works for de Chirico (who repeatedly argued from the late 1920s on that 'nobody has ever understood them, either then or now'), there is no denying that the few brief years (*c.* 1911–*c.* 1919) of his metaphysical inspiration constitute a distinctive landmark on the map of modern art.

Further reading

de Chirico's metaphysical period is fully documented in J.T. Soby, *Giorgio de Chirico* (1966). See also *Catalogo general Giorgio de Chirico*, ed. C. Bruni (3 vols, 1971–3). Other writings by the artist: *The Memoirs of Giorgio de Chirico* (*Memorie della mia vita*, trans. 1971); selected texts in M. Carrá, *Metaphysical Art* (1971). See also: R. Vitrac, *Giorgio de Chirico et son oeuvre* (1927); I. Faldi, *Il Primo de Chirico* (1949); M. Jean, *The History of Surrealist Painting* (1960); R. Martin (ed.), *Late de Chirico* (exhibition catalogue, 1985).

ROGER CARDINAL

CHOMSKY, Avram Noam

1928–

US linguist, philosopher and polemicist

Son of an eminent Ukrainian Hebrew scholar, Noam Chomsky has succeeded in combining a brilliant academic career with an active political life. He studied mathematics and philosophy at the University of Pennsylvania where he was drawn to the study of linguistics by Zellig Harris, whose political thinking had much in common with his own. His early work on Modern Hebrew attracted the interest of philosophers rather than linguists; it was as a research fellow at Harvard and later at the Massachusetts Institute of Technology that he developed the theory of generative grammar which was to earn him an international reputation by the age of forty.

It is common to talk of Chomsky's 'revolution' in linguistic theory, and certainly in the context of American structural linguistics his ideas represent a dramatic break with tradition. The structuralist method consists essentially in segmenting a large corpus of utterances into recurring sequences of sounds, which are then classified into units according to their function and distribution. Impressive results were obtained at the levels of phonology and morphology, but structural techniques were less effective in revealing the syntactic structure of a language.

It is this latter weakness that is the focal point of Chomsky's attack, in *Syntactic Structures* (1957), on the methods, goals and assumptions of the structuralist school. He demonstrates clearly that a taxonomic approach can reveal no more than the most superficial syntactic relationships. Moreover, no body of data, however extensive, will contain all possible syntactic constructions; the resulting description is bound to be incomplete.

Chomsky proposed a radically different model in which the rules underlying the construction of all possible sentences in a language must be specified; structurally ambiguous sentences are assigned descriptions which reflect their different semantic interpretations and formal relationships are established between superficially differing structures. Rather than applying mechanical discovery procedures of segmentation and classification, the linguist must try to formalize the 'competence' or intuitive knowledge which enables the native speaker to relate sequences of sounds to their semantic interpretation. The broader goal of linguistic theory is to 'discover the general properties of any system of rules that may serve as a basis for a human language, that is, to elaborate . . . the general *form of language* that underlies each particular realization, each particular natural language'. Descriptions of natural languages are therefore primarily of interest for the light they throw on the general theory of language, which in turn provides insights into the nature of mental processes, and in particular the mechanisms by which knowledge is acquired and stored. For Chomsky, linguistics is not an autonomous discipline but a major branch of cognitive psychology.

The impact of *Syntactic Structures*, first in the United States and later in Europe, was dramatic. It engendered bitter hostility on the part of scholars committed to the behaviourist-empiricist position, who accused Chomsky of being 'mentalistic' and 'unscientific'. At the same time his ideas aroused considerable interest among psychologists and philosophers, who had hitherto found little stimulus in the work of contemporary linguists. Chomsky rapidly attracted an impressive circle of graduate students to MIT, where he held the Ferrari P. Ward Chair of Modern Languages and Linguistics.

By the late 1960s Chomsky's ideas had engaged the younger generation of linguists in Europe and the United States, although many disagreed on the precise formulation of the theory. The basic distinction between a speaker's 'competence' and his 'performance' (the actual manifestation of his internalized system of rules) is now widely accepted (though many query whether the line between them has been drawn in the right place). Performance is the indirect reflection of competence, which may be affected by a wide range of extra-linguistic factors, such as memory span, the physical and emotional state of the speaker, and so on. Chomsky claims that a model of linguistic performance can only be seriously attempted once the facts of competence have been established. Underlying the competence–performance distinction is the rejection of psychology as a behavioural science; the observable facts of human behaviour are clues to the innate principles of mental organization, but their description is not in itself the ultimate goal.

Although there was little dialogue in the 1940s and 1950s between linguists and psychologists, it had been generally assumed that the facts of language acquisition and use could be accounted for within the then accepted framework of behaviourist psychology. In 1959, in his scathing review (in *Language*, p. 35) of **Skinner's** *Verbal Behaviour*, Chomsky exposed the inadequacies of reinforcement theory when applied to the complexities of linguistic behaviour. He stressed the creative aspect of language – our ability to produce and understand sentences we have never heard before – and the unpredictable nature of linguistic 'responses', which renders the notion of 'stimulus' in this context vague to the point of vacuity. Neither intelligence nor motivation appear to be vital factors in the acquisition of language, as every normal child can acquire her mother tongue on the basis of patchy and often imperfect data, with little direct reward. Chomsky concludes that genetic endowment must play a major role in the acquisition process: a child must be born with a knowledge of the basic principles of linguistic structure. Whether this knowledge takes the form of a specific set of rules governing the possible form of sentences in any human language, or whether the child is endowed with learning strategies which enable her to deduce the rules of the language to which she is exposed is still largely a matter for conjecture; some would claim that no genuine distinction exists between the two views.

Structural linguistics had tended to stress the differences between languages, partly because taxonomic techniques could be most successfully applied at levels where differences are most marked. Chomsky's insistence on the need to explore the more abstract levels of linguistic structure made possible the investigation of the common properties of natural languages. The existence of certain substantive universals, such as the distinction between nouns and verbs, had been recognized, but these had generally been explained in terms of universal features of the external world. Chomsky and his colleagues have suggested that *formal* universals, for which no such explanation can be invoked, closely constrain the structures and processes to be found in every language. The precise formulation and testing of such hypotheses has proved to be one of the most fruitful areas of recent research.

Chomsky has related his view of language to the seventeenth-century Rationalist tradition of the continental Cartesians and the British Neo-Platonists, while rejecting any sharp distinction between body and mind:

the acquisition and use of language must ultimately be explained in terms of neural structures, of which our knowledge remains rudimentary. The idea that universal structures underlie superficially diverse forms is to be found, for example, in the *Port-Royal* grammar of 1660. But in the absence of precise techniques for investigating the structure of language it had not been possible to develop the notion of a 'universal grammar'. In a sense, Chomsky's work can be seen as a synthesis of the insights of the Rationalist tradition and the rigorously objective methodology developed initially by the structuralists.

The essence of Chomsky's mature theory is contained in his *Aspects of a Theory of Syntax* (1965), in which the model proposed in *Syntactic Structures* is extended to account for the relationships between sound, syntactic structure and meaning. The model can be seen as a device capable of generating all (and only) the grammatical sentences of a language. The central component is a set of ordered syntactic rules which expand the basic element 'sentence' until the level of individual lexical and grammatical categories is reached. These 'phrase structure rules' produce tree-like 'deep structures' in which each branch is assigned a label in the course of the derivation. At this point the device has access to a lexical or dictionary component, from which words of the appropriate category are selected to substitute for the terminal elements in the tree. The semantic component operates on the deep structure of a sentence, combining an interpretation of the syntactic configuration with the interpretation of its individual elements.

As Chomsky points out in *Syntactic Structures*, phrase structure rules are implicit in many structuralist models, but are by themselves inadequate to account for all the syntactic structures of a language, and the semantic relations between them. He therefore proposes a second set of syntactic rules which operate on the output of the phrase structure rules, deleting and reordering elements in the underlying tree. An essential feature of these 'transformational rules', as proposed in the *Aspects* model, is that they should not affect the meaning of a sentence, only its 'surface structure'. A structurally ambiguous sentence, like 'flying planes can be dangerous' would therefore be assigned two quite different deep structures; it is the operation of the transformational rules which produces a common surface structure. When a sentence has been processed by the syntactic component the surface structure is converted into a sequence of speech sounds by a series of phonological rules. The syntactic component is central to Chomsky's model, with the semantic and phonological components playing interpretative roles. The precise relationship between the various components has given rise to much controversy, even within the 'generativist' camp. Chomsky himself has conceded that the surface structure of a sentence can partly determine its meaning, while some have argued that surface structures can be assigned semantic interpretations without the need for an intervening level of deep structure. Yet another breakaway group have proposed a theory of 'generative semantics' in which there is no clear boundary between syntax and semantics. Despite the disagreement surrounding the correct formulation of the theory, generative linguistics share the same basic assumptions about language and have succeeded in demonstrating beyond doubt the innateness and complexity of the language faculty.

Chomsky's work in linguistics has profound implications for our understanding of humanity, which Chomsky himself has been assiduous to exploit. In particular his concept of a 'grammar' shared by all underwrites the notion of universal equality, while what people do with their innate linguistic abilities reinforces notions of individual autonomy. Referring to himself variously as a 'liberal anarchist' and as an 'anarchic socialist', across five decades Chomsky has sustained a scathing polemics against aspects of American foreign policy and against the 'corporatist' state, sometimes lampooned by him as all but synonymous with the 'industrial-military complex'.

Chomsky has claimed that at the age of ten he wrote an essay about the threat of fascism, following the fall of Barcelona to Franco's nationalist forces during the Spanish Civil War. In 1967 he achieved celebrity with 'The Responsibility of Intellectuals', a keynote attack on America's involvement in Vietnam published in the *New York Review of Books*. Since then he has regularly challenged received definitions of 'terrorism', claiming that more often than not such violence is the product of particularly American intervention in the affairs of smaller, weaker nations by stronger, mainly Western powers. A persistent critic of both the Israeli and Saudi Arabian states, he has voiced support for the Palestinian cause. In the 1970s he challenged Western media coverage of alleged human rights abuses in **Mao Zedong's** China and in Cambodia under the Khmer Rouge, although he later retracted his views once the 'facts' had become established. Most controversially, in 1979 he defended Robert Faurisson's right to question whether the Jewish Holocaust had really happened, even though Chomsky himself was fiercely critical of Faurisson's arguments. For the radical professor of linguistics, freedom of speech is more important than any version of events sponsored by the establishment, however consonant the latter may appear to be with evidential truth.

Chomsky's assault on American foreign policy and on some American institutions has continued into the new millennium. His *9–11* (2001) – his analysis of al-Qaeda's attack on New York and the Pentagon as something the USA had brought upon itself – angered liberals as well as conservatives, but also became a best-seller, winning him fresh admirers among younger readers, especially those deemed 'anti-capitalist'. Predictably he vociferously opposed George Bush Jr's incursions into Afghanistan and Iraq. But to dismiss Chomsky as an 'anti-American', as many of his critics have attempted, is ill-considered. His own arguments are always more subtle than that, and as his commentaries on other powers make plain, he cherishes those liberties embedded in the American constitution. His polemics can as easily be read as a lament for what might have been as an impassioned critique of how things are.

Further reading

Other important linguistic works by Noam Chomsky are: *Cartesian Linguistics: A Chapter in the History of Rationalist Thought* (1966); *Language and Mind* (1968); *The Minimalist Program* (1995). His many political writings include: *For Reasons of State* (1973); *American Power and the New Mandarins* (1969); *At War with Asia* (1970); *Reflections on Justice and Nationhood* (1974); *Language and Responsibility* (1979); *The Fateful Triangle: The United States, Israel, and the Palestinians* (1983 revised 1999); *Turning the Tide: US Intervention in Central America and the Struggle for Peace* (1985); *Pirates and Emperors: International Terrorism and the Real World* (1986); *Manufacturing Consent: The Political Economy of the Mass Media* (1988, with Edward Herman); *What Uncle Sam Really Wants* (1992); *Rethinking Camelot: JFK, the Vietnam War, and US Political Culture* (1993); *Profit over People* (1999); *Rogue States: The Rule of Force in World Affairs* (2000); *Hegemony or Survival* (2003); *Chomsky on Anarchism* (2005). See: C.F. Hockett, *The State of the Art* (1967); John Lyons, *Chomsky* (1970); Milan Raj, *Chomsky's Politics* (1995); Robert Barsky, *Noam Chomsky: A Life of Dissent* (1997). See also: Peter Collier and David Horowitz (eds), *The Anti-Chomsky Reader* (2004).

HILARY WISE
(REVISED AND UPDATED BY THE EDITOR)

CHRISTIE, Agatha

1890–1976

English crime fiction writer

How to account for the mystery of Christie? How to explain the fact that, when her 'golden age' detective fiction contemporaries such as Dorothy Sayers (1893–1957) or Margery Allingham (1904–66) struggle to hold on to an ageing readership or drop out of print altogether, the Agatha Christie industry is booming? Even the critical hostility of earlier days, most famously summed up in Edmund Wilson's essay 'Who Cares Who

Killed Roger Ackroyd?' (1945, *New Yorker*), has been replaced by an increasing willingness to see her as a significant cultural phenomenon. And, of course, her global audience, whether for the novels or for the many film, stage and television versions of them, is greater than it was even in her lifetime.

Despite this extraordinary success, the charges levelled against Christie are largely true. Her characters have little depth and their dialogue is often banal; the milieu in which they move is almost entirely upper-middle class; the solutions to the mysteries may surprise but they are generally implausible, sometimes absurd. Looked at another way, though, Christie was simply doing her job of providing entertainment – undemanding perhaps but in no way mindless – and paring down her narratives so that they contained only those elements necessary for the setting up of a problem and its solution. Virtually every detail in her stories, however minor or seemingly incidental, has the function either of misdirecting her readers or of pointing them towards the truth which will emerge in the closing pages. Narrative is therefore invested with constant meaning and purpose, something which is certainly part of her consoling appeal.

Agatha Christie had a great hit with her first novel, *The Mysterious Affair at Styles* (1920), but her supremacy in the field only became clear with *The Murder of Roger Ackroyd* (1926), a novel in which the concept of the unreliable narrator – the kind of high critical construct which Christie would have found laughable or irrelevant – reaches an apotheosis. Her readiness to break the rules of detective fiction, or at least to artfully subvert them, is evident also in *Murder on the Orient Express* (1934) and *And Then There Were None* (originally *Ten Little Niggers*, 1940). All of these novels, with the exception of the last named, feature her Belgian detective, Hercule Poirot, whose prowess with his 'little grey cells' is responsible for uncovering the truth. Like G.K. Chesterton's priest-detective Father Brown, Poirot has the observer's knack of going unremarked, so that the people around him are less guarded in their behaviour. Poirot will also travel, as he does in *Death on the Nile* (1937) or *Appointment with Death* (1938), two examples of the author's fondness for well-realized Middle Eastern settings and the product of her tours with her second husband, the archaeologist Max Mallowan.

Christie's other most important detective is a stay-at-home: Jane Marple, the beady-eyed spinster of the archetypal village of St Mary Mead. Either by chance or by invitation, Miss Marple finds herself investigating a sequence of baffling mysteries as in *The Body in the Library* (1942) and *A Murder is Announced* (1950). Frequently she uses her knowledge of village life, with its petty but deeply felt jealousies and hatreds, to illuminate the grand murders, and there is a sense – as there is in Jane Austen's *Emma* (1816), also a village-based mystery – that all (or at least a great deal of) human life can be contained within a small compass. As well as producing spy/conspiracy thrillers, Christie also employed other sleuths, notably Inspector Battle, whose stolid skills are effectively shown in the ingenious and manipulative *Towards Zero* (1944).

As the publication dates of the above novels indicate, Agatha Christie enjoyed her own 'golden period'. She produced entertaining later work, for example in *They Do It With Mirrors* (1952) and *Endless Night* (1967), but nothing matched the clarity, originality and high spirits of the interwar mysteries or those she wrote in the 1940s. At her best she was able to turn her limitations of narrow focus, an often pedestrian style and schematic plotting, into strengths. Above all, she returns us to the pleasures of the tale.

Further reading

For a very readable discussion of Christie's output see Robert Barnard, *A Talent to Deceive* (1980). For autobiographical material, particularly on Christie's mysterious disappearance in 1926, see Jared Cade, *Agatha Christie and the Eleven Missing Days* (1998).

PHILIPPA MORGAN

CHURCHILL, (Sir) Winston Leonard Spencer

1874–1965

English statesman

The most admired European politician of modern times, Winston Churchill was in his mid-sixties when he first became Britain's Prime Minister – in May 1940, at the head of a wartime coalition government. Eighteen months before he was widely considered a has-been, a once-brilliant but disruptive maverick who had blotted his copybook too often. He was, however, the leader of a small group that had from the start taken the threat of **Hitler's** Germany seriously, and alone among senior politicians he seemed to have the wherewithal to co-ordinate an effective response. No come-back from the political wilderness has been more startling.

It was as a militarist that Churchill triumphed, some would say against all odds. Yet the pedigree was there. He was born at Blenheim Palace, the stately home of his ancestor John Churchill, Duke of Marlborough, whose victories during the Europe-wide War of the Spanish Succession (1701–14) accelerated England's Great Power pretensions. His father too – Lord Randolph Churchill – was a man of prominence, having served as Chancellor of the Exchequer, while his American mother, neé Jennie Jerome, was the daughter of a noted New York financier.

Despite such antecedents, Churchill was a slow starter. Neither parent offered him much warmth or attention. A dull pupil at Harrow School, he gained entrance to the Royal Military Academy at Sandhurst only at the third attempt. Although as a subaltern he performed well enough, serving under Lord Kitchener on the Nile as well as in India, his restless energies were too easily distracted to concentrate on soldiering. Partly he wanted to follow his father into politics, partly he wished to become a writer. In 1899 he resigned his commission, having published *The Story of the Malakand Field Force* (1898).

In the same year he stood as Conservative candidate for Oldham at a general election. Failing to win the seat, he became the *Morning Post*'s South Africa correspondent, to cover the Boer War. There he achieved instant celebrity by organizing the rescue of an armoured train ambushed by the 'enemy', and then escaping from a Boer prison. Returning to England, he succeeded in winning Oldham in the 1900 election, and for the next thirty years was seldom out of the public eye.

Churchill's early parliamentary career was both chequered and controversial. Opposed to his party's trade protection policies, in 1904 he 'crossed the floor' to join the Liberals, and was castigated as a 'traitor' by the Conservatives. In 1908 Herbert Asquith made him President of the Board of Trade. Encouraged by David Lloyd George, Churchill introduced several reforms, and in 1911 supported the Parliament Act that limited the powers of the House of Lords. As Home Secretary, however, he acted ruthlessly towards both strikers and anarchists and was swiftly transferred to the Admiralty, where, with Sir John Fisher, he was tasked with refurbishing the Royal Navy in anticipation of a war with Germany.

During the Great War itself Churchill's stock fell rather than rose. Closely associated with, though unfairly blamed for, the catastrophes of the Dardanelles and Gallipoli (1915), he was removed from the Admiralty and made Chancellor of the Duchy of Lancaster: a demotion which soured his relations with the Liberal leadership. In 1916 he resigned from government, only to return as Minister of Munitions in 1917, in which role he keenly advocated the use of poison gas as well as tanks as instruments of war.

In January 1919 Lloyd George made Churchill Secretary of State for War, the war being over, and in 1921 gave him the Colonial Office. But already Churchill's love affair with the Liberal Party was over. In the 1923 general election, wanting to return to the Conservative fold, he stood as an 'independent anti-socialist'. Attaching himself to

the tails of Prime Minister Stanley Baldwin, he became Chancellor of the Exchequer in 1924, but this was the beginning of his eclipse. Still distrusted by many Conservative colleagues, his ill-inspired economic policies, persistently attacked by **John Maynard Keynes**, were largely responsible for the General Strike of 1926.

By 1929 Churchill was consigned to the back benches of the House of Commons, and seemed likely to remain there. An implacable foe of Soviet-style communism, he opposed every attempt to introduce self-rule in India or grant Britain's largest colony dominion status. But in the one, crucial respect he was ahead of his contemporaries. From the outset he recognized that German National Socialism must challenge the values of European civilization at large.

Churchill put himself back on the map in September 1938, when he denounced Neville Chamberlain's Munich Agreement with Hitler as an abhorrent defeat. Thereafter the tide turned inexorably in his favour. When on 3 September 1939 Prime Minister Chamberlain finally and reluctantly declared war on Germany, following the invasion of Poland, Churchill was immediately given his old job as First Lord of the Admiralty. 'Winston's back,' the Navy cheered, in a celebrated signal. Nine months later, Churchill was himself Prime Minister, the only man with a strategy of any kind to contain a rampant Germany that had, by then, seized Norway and the Netherlands, and was closing in on Paris.

The cornerstone of Churchill's war policy was to cement and maintain a grand alliance against the Axis powers, much as Marlborough had done against Bourbon France at the beginning of the eighteenth century – even though this meant doing business with **Joseph Stalin** and the USSR. Well before Japan's attack on Pearl Harbor, in December 1941, Churchill primed relations with US President **F.D. Roosevelt**, and it was American intervention that tipped the scales against Hitler in Europe. But Churchill's non-strategic contribution to an eventual victory was also significant. He gave several Labour politicians, including Clement Attlee and Ernest Bevin, key government posts, so that his coalition really was a government of national unity, while his powerful oratory sustained British morale in the face of severe military setbacks in the eastern Mediterranean, North Africa and the Far East.

The British electorate, however, was equally canny. The war in Europe over, in July 1945 Churchill was voted out of office, and a Labour government under Attlee introduced the most radical reforms of any British administration, establishing the welfare state, instituting a mixed economy in which key industries were taken out of private hands, and relinquishing many of Britain's imperial possessions, including India and Burma.

Churchill returned to power at the end of 1951, at the age of seventy-seven, but his second spell as Prime Minister was unequal to the first. His dreams of maintaining the British empire already shattered, he failed to convince his cabinet of the importance of forming a European union. Instead he emerged as a Cold War warrior, in league with US President Dwight Eisenhower, and overseeing Britain's acquisition of the hydrogen bomb.

Ill-health forced an octogenarian Churchill to resign office in April 1955, though he did not relinquish his Commons seat until the year before his death, and he refused the offer of a dukedom. Among the many honours bestowed on him were the first honorary citizenship of the United States (in 1963, at the instigation of **J.F. Kennedy**) and a state funeral at his death. The most curious honour was the Nobel Prize for Literature, in 1953. Although his many publications, including *Marlborough: His Life and Times* (1933–8), and his monumental *The Second World War* (6 vols, 1948–54), were compellingly written, he set no new historiographic standard, and it is as a conserver of an existing culture, not the instigator of cultural change, that he is remembered.

More recently, Churchill has been attacked by the 'post-colonial' studies lobby. He stands accused of riding roughshod over Palestinians' interests, of allowing a devastating famine in Bengal to run its course unchecked (to hamper any Japanese invasion of eastern India in 1942–3), of authorizing the bombing of civilian Dresden in 1945, of complicity with Stalin in the redrawing of Poland's post-war boundaries, and of meddling in Iranian politics during his second premiership. But such contentions scarcely dent his enduring popular reputation as first among Britain's 'bulldog' breed. To no one's surprise, in a nationwide survey conducted by the BBC in 2002, Churchill was ranked 'greatest Briton ever', comfortably ahead of Nelson, Shakespeare, Newton and **Darwin**.

Further reading

Other works include: *The River War* (1899); *Lord Randolph Churchill* (1906, revised 1953); *The World Crisis* (6 vols, 1923–31); *My Early Life* (1930); *History of the English-Speaking Peoples* (4 vols, 1956–8). See: Lady Violet Bonham-Carter, *Winston Churchill As I Knew Him* (1965); Randolph S. Churchill and Martin Gilbert, *Winston S. Churchill* (6 vols, 1966–88); William Manchester, *The Last Lion: Vision of Glory* (1983) and *The Caged Lion* (1985); Roy Jenkins, *Churchill* (2000).

JUSTIN WINTLE

COETZEE, John Maxwell
1942–
South African novelist

The award of the Nobel Prize for Literature to J.M. Coetzee in 2003 confirmed the global reputation achieved by a novelist who will always be associated with his birthplace, South Africa, but whose fiction is written in, and against, the tradition of the great works of European literature. Another geographical connection is suggested by *Elizabeth Costello* (2003), the hybrid work – part novel, part lecture series – he published in that year: its eponymous hero is an Australian novelist, a fact perhaps not unconnected with Coetzee's own move from South Africa to Australia in 2002.

Two important periods of Coetzee's early life are recorded – with a degree of fictional licence – in his memoirs, *Boyhood* (1997) and *Youth* (2002). Raised in a family in which English was spoken in preference to Afrikaans, he left South Africa after gaining degrees in English and Mathematics to work for four years as a computer programmer in London. The second memoir ends around 1964, a year before he started a PhD on **Samuel Beckett** at the University of Texas in Austin, followed by a position at the University of Buffalo. His American academic career was cut short when his application for permanent residence was refused, and the University of Cape Town became his professional home instead.

While at Buffalo, he had written a short fiction expressive of his opposition to the Vietnam War and on his return to Cape Town he wrote another novella, based on an eighteenth-century ancestor's depredations as a hunter-adventurer in the South African interior. Published together as *Dusklands* in 1974, they attracted little attention outside South Africa. *In the Heart of the Country*, a female monologue whose intense emotional expressiveness is countered by the numbered paragraphs in which it is presented, appeared in 1977; set in the barrenness of the Karoo, it mixes Beckettian self-mockery with postmodern referential instability.

The novel that established an international reputation for Coetzee was *Waiting for the Barbarians* (1980). Its hero is an ineffectual, liberal town governor on the fringes of an unnamed empire who is driven to a recognition of the reality of authoritarian power – the kind of power that was keeping South Africa in the hands of a white minority. The novel has more obscure elements too, including the strange sexual need that draws the central figure to the tortured prisoner in his charge.

Coetzee returned to a recognizable Cape Province for the setting of *Life & Times of Michael K* (1983) in order to tell the story of the hare-lipped, inarticulate Michael K, evading the armed state's regulatory machinery through an inviolable innocence. In *Foe* (1986) we find ourselves in eighteenth-century London, attending to a woman's attempts to have her story – a spell on a desert island with two men called Cruso and Friday – told by a well-known writer, Daniel Foe. The resonances of the novel include the racial situation in South Africa – especially in the ominous presence of Friday, who is unable to speak – but radiate much further as well.

The next novel, *Age of Iron* (1990), was Coetzee's most direct engagement thus far with the South Africa of his time: another female monologue, this time from a retired classics teacher dying of cancer who, confronted by the realities of the war in the townships, develops an intense relationship with a vagrant of uncertain origins. Questions of the artist's responsibilities and struggles come to the fore in *The Master of Petersburg* (1994), in which the central character is a fictionalized **Fyodor Dostoevsky**. Less well known than Coetzee's other novels of the 1990s, it finds a compelling fictional form for some of the author's most individual concerns and fears (given fullest expression in the interviews with David Attwell in *Doubling the Point*, 1992).

Coetzee's second Booker Prize (the first was for *Michael K*) was won by *Disgrace* (1999), a novel that unflinchingly observes, from the inside, the downfall of a white university teacher in conflict with the mores of post-apartheid South Africa. In most of Coetzee's novels, an irresolvable conflict is staged between two principles, the end-determined, calculable imperatives that govern the political domain and a barely articulable commitment to something incalculable – at once transcendent and singular – motivating a resistant character: the state apparatus against the Magistrate in *Waiting for the Barbarians*; the controllers of the camps against Michael K; the township fighters against Mrs Curren in *Age of Iron*; the revolutionaries against Dostoevsky in *The Master of Petersburg*. There is nothing so simple as moral victory for the second of these; in the devastating final pages of *Disgrace* David Lurie's commitment to the dignity of dead dogs is either a remarkable acceptance of an ethics opposed to the demands of incessant productivity or an emblem of the final irrelevance of old standards in a permanently changed world.

Further reading

Coetzee's literary and cultural criticism is collected in *White Writing* (1988), *Doubling the Point* (1992), *Giving Offence* (1996) and *Stranger Shores* (2001). See also David Attwell, *J.M. Coetzee: South Africa and the Politics of Writing* (1993) and Derek Attridge, *J.M. Coetzee and the Ethics of Reading: Literature in the Event* (2004).

DEREK ATTRIDGE

COLLINS, William Wilkie

1824–89

British novelist

The most brilliant of the circle of young writers working with **Charles Dickens** was Wilkie Collins, elder son of William Collins, RA, a successful painter who died young. Wilkie Collins's work combined narrative exuberance with tenacious observation and a rich pictorial imagination. His fiction moves freely among the classes of society and reflects his preoccupation with physical handicaps and disorders of mind and body. The later writings of Dickens bear many traces of the gifted younger writer's impact on his patron, especially in the move of the later 1850s towards an interlocking narrative form and a sombre sensationalism. The success of *All the Year Round* in its early years from 1859 was due mainly to the serialization of *The Woman in White* (1860), Collins's most successful novel and his favourite among his own works.

Collins's achievement as a novelist was buttressed by his work as essayist, critic and writer of melodramatic plays. His essays on literary and other topics were reprinted in *My Miscellanies* (1863). His essay on Balzac in *All the Year Round* (1859), together with Routledge's issue of a good translation of *Eugénie Grandet* in that year, was the culmination of the shift of taste in the 1850s which paved the way for the fiction of **Henry James**, George Moore and **Joseph Conrad**. The play *The Frozen Deep* (1857), Collins's most successful work of collaboration with Dickens, was a melodramatic tale of male rivalry ending in reconciliation and death. Other writings for the stage were failures which attracted ridicule. In the novels and short fiction which form his main work, Collins pioneered the closely woven tale of detection and multiple viewpoint. Though sympathetic to the problem of women's disabilities in society, he was only rarely able to portray female characters with warmth and sympathy.

Collins's major novels span the 1860s and are among the most important writings of the decade. In *The Woman in White*, *No Name* (1862), *Armadale* (1866) and *The Moonstone* (1868) he established himself as a master of narrative but retained the social commitment of his masters, Dickens, Victor Hugo and Balzac. In the critical essay which dominated the critical discussion of fiction for two decades until the advent of **Zola**, Henry Longueville Mansel ('Sensation Novels', *Quarterly Review* 1863) took the negative view of Collins which reappeared in **Ruskin's** essay 'Fiction, Fair and Foul' (*Contemporary Review*, 1880). 'Sensation' writing was, however, an integral part of the move towards realism and was inseparable from the main development of the novel in the century, as **Trollope** argued in an essay which later formed part of his *Autobiography*. The most judicious among early views of Collins was that of Émile Forgues, editor of the *Revue des deux mondes*, whose essay 'Le Roman anglais contemporain' (*Revue des deux mondes*, 1863) recognizes the *balzacien* elements of the genre and tacitly acknowledges its affinity with New England romantic fiction, in which Forgues was adept.

The Woman in White explores the exposure of two women to the machinations of two scheming villains, Sir Percival Glyde and Count Fosco. Like the plays of Webster, with which it has many affinities, it owed its germ to an account of a judicial trial; Collins owned and treasured a copy of Maurice Méjan's *Recueil des causes célèbres*, from which he took his principal motif. In showing the abuses associated with private asylums, Collins gave direction to an important strand in the social literature of his age. In *No Name* he showed how a vengeful quest for the retrieval of property by a disadvantaged woman (another important 'sensation' theme) can be tempered by the effects of romantic love. In *The Moonstone* he inaugurated the modern cult of the detective novel. His novels of the 1870s increasingly shed the paraphernalia of suspense and detection. In *Man and Wife* (1870), *The New Magdalen* (1873), *The Law and the Lady* (1873) and *Fallen Leaves* (1879), Collins developed further the interest which he first explored in *No Name*, in the penalties imposed by society on illegitimate or compromised women.

The close relationship between Collins's fiction and the facts of his life was carefully screened from view until the appearance of recent biographical studies. The dominance in his life of an over-protective mother, herself the victim of early widowhood, undoubtedly contributed to his incapacity to form stable domestic relationships. His meeting with the first of two mistresses is vividly told in the opening of *The Woman in White*. His second mistress bore his three children. Myopic, of slight stature and tenacious manner, Collins never lost the combination of eloquence and tortuousness which undoubtedly owed much to his training as a barrister, a profession he never practised. Though principally associated with the 'sensation' writer's creed as expressed in a phrase attributed to him, 'make 'em cry, make 'em laugh, make 'em wait', his novels made a distinctive contribution to the pictorialism and psychological intensity which dominated the fiction of the second half-century.

Further reading

See: Michael Sadleir, 'Wilkie Collins', in *Excursions in Victorian Bibliography* (1922); T.S. Eliot, 'Wilkie Collins and Dickens', in *Selected Essays* (1945); Kenneth Robinson, *Wilkie Collins: A Biography* (1951); N.P. Davis, *The Life of Wilkie Collins* (1956); C. Peters, *The King of Inventors: A Life of Wilkie Collins* (1991).

CHRISTOPHER HEYWOOD

CONRAD, Joseph
1857–1924
Anglo-Polish writer

Conrad's work is marked by the overriding paradox of a Pole whose second language was French fervently desiring to become an Englishman. Jozef Konrad Korzeniowski was the son of a Polish revolutionary poet, with the bitter experience of having seen his country thoroughly cowed under Russian imperial domination. The boy's reading of English authors during his Cracow schooldays may have encouraged a wish to assume British nationality, but it was not until 1884, after ten years of seafaring and painstaking study of the English language, that he was able to realize his ambition and become a naturalized subject.

He was a capable sailor and had already gained his Board of Trade certificate as a Master. His travels took him all over the world during the last great era of sail as opposed to steam, and he was clearly alive to the romance of a fully rigged ship, just as he was conscious of the essentially prosaic image of the steamer (for his views on this, see *An Outcast of the Islands*, 1896). One area in particular has been associated with him. The 'Conrad world' is that of the East Indian islands around Java, Malaya, Sumatra and the Philippines, and especially the islands of the Molucca archipelago which provide the backgrounds of *Lord Jim* (1900), *Victory* (1915) and *An Outcast of the Islands*. Other exotic settings are an imaginary South American republic in *Nostromo* (1904) and the River Congo in the short story 'Heart of Darkness' (1902).

His first novel, *Almayer's Folly* (1895), was written during his last years at sea. Imperfect as it is, it shows an astonishing stylistic maturity in a first book whose author was writing in, essentially, a foreign language. A year after its appearance Conrad married and settled down quietly in Kent. He was admired and befriended by such disparate figures as **Henry James**, Ford Madox Ford (with whom he also collaborated) and **H.G. Wells**, and came increasingly to be seen, in the company of writers like **Kipling** and R.L. Stevenson, and the eccentric adventurer Cunninghame-Graham, as the visionary analyst of British colonial experience.

Not all his novels, however, encompass a common subject-matter. Two of the finest, *The Secret Agent* (1907) and *Under Western Eyes* (1911), deal with the activities of anarchists and revolutionaries in England and Russia, and are undeniably coloured with recollections drawn from his family's own revolutionary tradition. *The Secret Agent* shows Conrad's astonishing ability to absorb and transmit the atmosphere of his adopted country and is as near perfect in its overall achievement as anything written during the immensely fertile period of English letters between the death of Queen Victoria and the First World War. Its single serious flaw is the outrage which the author chooses to place at the centre of the action. The destruction of Greenwich Observatory by a bomb seems altogether too abstract a process to engage our interest.

Conrad's increasing mastery of English is the first thing which strikes anyone who studies him seriously. Cautious, halting and occasionally inexact in the earlier novels and stories, his style flowers, in *Lord Jim* and 'Heart of Darkness', into something of great richness, sonority and weight, moderated continually by his evident respect for this, his third language. His narrative technique too acquires a corresponding complexity, adding to *Nostromo*, with its contrasted time-shifts and varied character perspectives, a degree of experimental skill hitherto unknown in the European novel, with the possible exception of Sterne's *Tristram Shandy*.

His main concern, however, is not with style, technique, the evocation of atmosphere or the expression of socio-political criticism, so much as with the idea of a single man, or group of men, in a situation which will test human endurance to breaking point. Faced with danger and distress, his characters are summoned to proclaim their moral toughness. We think, for example, of Kurtz in 'Heart of Darkness', who is found 'hollow at the core', or the slow destruction of Willems in *An Outcast of the Islands*. The conclusions of his books are thus bleak, fatalistic, often, by implication, terrifying in their visions of darkness and disorder. The positive occupies a restricted domain and Conrad takes the true traveller's delight in exploiting the simple antithesis between the savage and the civilized.

Beginning with *Chance* (1913), and with the notable exception of *Victory* (1915), his later novels saw a decline into the sort of romantic yarn-spinning his public best liked. He is often verbose and tumid in his narrative, and his 'man is a man' world's view of women as either generally time-wasting or purely destructive (but not so Mrs Gould in *Nostromo*) has sometimes a dire effect on credibility. But his influence on later novelists, especially in America, has been immense, and he has been deservedly rescued from a role as a mere writer of adventure stories by the intensive reappraisal of the post-war decades.

Further reading

Other work includes: *The Nigger of the 'Narcissus'* (1897); *The Inheritors* (with Ford Madox Ford, 1901); *Youth: A Narrative and Two Other Stories* (1902); *Typhoon and Other Stories* (1903); *The Rescue* (1920); *The Rover* (1920). See also: F.M. Ford, *Joseph Conrad: A Personal Remembrance* (1924); F.R. Karl, *A Reader's Guide to Joseph Conrad* (1960); F.R. Leavis, *The Great Tradition* (1948); Leo Gurko, *Joseph Conrad: Giant in Exile* (1962); Jocelyn Baines, *Joseph Conrad: A Critical Biography* (1960); Edward Crankshaw, *Joseph Conrad* (1976); Frederick Karl, *Joseph Conrad: The Three Lives* (1979); Norman Sherry, *Conrad's Western World* (1971); C.D. Bennett, *Joseph Conrad*

(1991); K. Carabine (ed.) *Joseph Conrad: Critical Assessments* (4 vols, 1992).

JONATHAN KEATES

COPLAND, Aaron

1900–90

US composer

The son of Lithuanian-Jewish immigrants, Aaron Copland studied with Rubin Goldmark in New York and then with Nadia Boulanger in Paris (1921–5). Under Boulanger he came to admire the neo-classical **Stravinsky**, whose influence is evident in such spare, driving works as the Symphony for organ and orchestra (1924) and the Dance Symphony (1925), but after his return to New York he decided that his music must be more American in character. He first tried to achieve this by using jazz idioms, most abundantly in his Piano Concerto (1926). The jazz phase, however, was short-lived, and in his next group of works, including the Piano Variations (1930) and the *Short Symphony* (1933), he developed an imposing but austere style in which the thorough motivic working shows some connections with serialism.

Copland's continuing concern for a specifically American music, coupled with his feeling that composers were drawing apart from their audiences, led him next to simplify his manner and look for local colour. The first result was *El salón Mexico* (1936), a vibrant orchestral impression, and this was followed by three American ballets drawing on indigenous hymns, folk songs and popular music: *Billy the Kid* (1938), *Rodeo* (1942) and *Appalachian Spring* (1944). The fresh colours and the clear, widespread harmonies of these scores seemed to conjure the virginal open spaces of America, and provided composers of film scores with the perfect style for Westerns. Yet at the same time Copland was pursuing his more abstract style, notably in his Piano Sonata (1941), and in his ambitious, public Third Symphony (1946) he brought together the two currents in his music of the previous decade.

In 1950, with his Piano Quartet, he began to use serial methods while retaining, like Stravinsky, his own distinctive feeling for chord placement and his own voice. The Piano Variations now gained added importance as the herald of this later style, and in 1957 Copland orchestrated the work. His other major serial compositions include the *Piano Fantasy* (1955–7) and two orchestral scores, *Connotations* (1961–2) and *Inscape* (1967), of which the second became his last undertaking on a large scale.

Throughout his career Copland was active in various fields outside composition. His pride in America, musically expressed not only in the cowboy ballets but also in the *Lincoln Portrait* for narrator and orchestra (1942), inspired him to work tirelessly on behalf of native composers: he founded the American Composers Alliance in 1937 and served on various other boards. Similarly his democratic spirit, which has a musical emblem in his *Fanfare for the Common Man* (1942), also stimulated his work in popular musical education besides affecting the direction of his own music.

Further reading

Other works include: *Music for the Theatre* for orchestra (1925); Symphony No. 1 (1928); *Symphonic Ode* (1928, revised 1955); *Vitebsk* for piano trio (1929); *Statements* for orchestra (1934); Sextet for clarinet, piano and string quartet (1937); *Quiet City* for orchestra (1940); *Danzón cubano* for orchestra (1942–4); Violin Sonata (1943); Clarinet Concerto (1948); *Twelve Poems of Emily Dickinson* for voice and piano (1950); *Old American Songs* for voice and piano (1950–2); *The Tender Land*, opera (1954); *Dance Panels* for orchestra (1959, revised 1962); Nonet for strings (1960); *Emblems* for band (1964); *Music for a Great City* for orchestra (1964); *Duo* for flute and piano (1970–71). Writings: *What to Listen for in Music* (1938); *Our New Music* (1941, revised as *The New Music*, 1968); *Music and Imagination* (1952); *Copland on Music* (1960). *Composer for Brooklyn* (1984) is Copland's autobiography. See also: Arthur Berger, *Aaron Copland* (1953); H. Pollack, *Aaron Copland: The Life and Work of an Uncommon Man* (1999).

PAUL GRIFFITHS

COPPOLA, Francis Ford

1939–

American screenwriter, director and producer

Now that the dust of so many battles has settled and with a seat on the Board of MGM, Coppola indeed seems to have become, in Kent Jones' apt phrase, the 'creative grand old man of Hollywood'. Coppola has not personally directed a film since his competent, if rather unspectacular, adaptation of John Grisham's *The Rainmaker* in 1997 but he has continued to exert a benign influence from afar and, through American Zoetrope, to produce films for others, including feature films directed by his children, Sofia and Roman. Nevertheless, in 2005, Coppola's name is more likely to appear on the Internet in connection with *Zoetrope: All Story*, the high-quality literary magazine he founded in 1997, or in glossy ads for the Rubicon wine which he now produces in abundance on his Napa Valley Estate in California (and which he rates on a par with some of the best Italian wines). For four decades, however, beginning in the early 1960s when Coppola was officially enrolled in the UCLA graduate film programme but in reality much of the time away making Z-grade films with Roger Corman, Coppola's unique gifts as a scriptwriter and producer-director marked him out as the most creative – and most contentious – presence in the so-called New Hollywood.

In those years, as all the official biographies now testify, from as early as the schlock-horror *Dementia 13* (1963) which Coppola made with funds wheedled from Corman, behind every film released under Coppola's name lay the tangled history of an arm-wrestle between Mammon and the creative artist, a struggle between the exigencies of Hollywood studio executives and the money they managed, and Coppola's artistic ambitions, passion and projects. Given the trials and tribulations behind each project and all the inevitable compromises forced on Coppola along the way, the wonder may be

that many made it to the screen at all, much less that, for the most part, they turned out to be such good, indeed often great, films.

Coppola's greatest claim to fame, of course, will always be linked to the Godfather films, especially *The Godfather* (1972) and *The Godfather: Part II* (1974) which between them netted him ten Oscars, including Best Picture and Best Director. The recent release on DVD in box set of all three Godfathers, which has made it possible to watch them all at one sitting, has allowed the tragic denouement operating throughout *Part III* to emerge much more clearly than before, thus prompting a greater appreciation of the overarching unity and the epic dimension of the family saga.

But it will be *Apocalypse Now* (1979) which, with all its political ambivalence and its moral and narrative aporias, will undoubtedly remain as Coppola's greatest testament to not only his subject, the Vietnam War, but also to himself as an entrepreneurial filmmaker with visions to burn. It's telling that the recent release of *Apocalypse Now Redux* (2001), with its extra hour of footage, has done nothing to fill in the gaps, but it has confirmed that Coppola made the right choices when he edited it down to its original theatrical release length. In any case, especially since the appearance of *Hearts of Darkness: A Filmmaker's Apocalypse* (1991), the remarkable documentary on the making of the film, it seems unlikely that the artistic validity of the film will now ever be separable from the accounts of the ordeals that Coppola put himself and others through to achieve it.

Coppola would provide a much rosier, and certainly more ingenuous, self-reflexive portrait of the visionary artist-entrepreneur struggling against the system in the later *Tucker: The Man and His Dream* (1988) although it's significant that the film was produced and supervised by George Lucas, since in the wake of the financial collapse of the Zoetrope Studios and the cost overruns on films like *The Cotton Club* (1984), Coppola's own fortunes had sunk to an all-time low ebb from which he would not recover until the runaway success of *Bram Stocker's Dracula* (1992).

And yet, leaving aside the impressive grandeur of the larger projects – the ones that did make it to the screen and the scores of others, like *Pinocchio* or *Megalopolis* that never did – perhaps Coppola's most memorable and artistically realized film would undoubtedly have to be *The Conversation*, the film which won him the *Palme d'or* at Cannes in the same year as *The Godfather: Part II* triumphed in America (1974). In the story of Harry Caul, an audio-surveillance expert who finds himself under surveillance, Coppola achieved a narrative concision and a moral complexity that he would seldom achieve elsewhere. And if, as Kent Jones has argued, in spite of Coppola's natural gregariousness it is the theme of loneliness that subtly runs through much of Coppola's work, there can be no more effective representation of absolute loneliness than the final image of *The Conversation* with Harry Caul alone in a gutted apartment blowing a plaintive riff on the saxophone.

Nevertheless, it's clearly too early to attempt any final pronouncements on Coppola and his work. After so many twists and turns in such a fruitful and eventful career, Coppola may yet deliver us the ultimate surprise with *the* mega film to top them all.

Further reading

Best comprehensive biography on Coppola, which includes an examination of all the films, is Michael Schumaker, *Francis Ford Coppola: A Filmmaker's Life* (1999). Best short critical overview of Coppola's work is Kent Jones, 'Mythmaker: Francis Ford Coppola, The Great Conductor of American Cinema', *Film Comment*, March/April 2002. The ill-fated Zoetrope adventure is analysed in great detail in Jon Lewis, *Whom God Wishes to Destroy … Francis Coppola and the New Hollywood* (1995).

GINO MOLITERNO

CORBUSIER, Le *see:* LE CORBUSIER

CRICK, Francis Harry Compton

1916–2004

English molecular biologist

Francis Crick was the central figure in the molecular revolution that swept through biology in the 1950s and 1960s. A master of exposition, inveterate conversationalist, highly articulate, a great listener, humorous, often flamboyant, he packed the lecture halls of universities, as he sought to convert reluctant biologists, geneticists and biochemists to the new knowledge of the molecular mechanisms underlying life.

Born in the provincial town of Northampton, he was raised in the traditional manner of a well-to-do family in business, a family supportive of nonconformist religious institutions and beliefs. These he rejected by the time he was twelve years of age. Henceforth he nurtured the ambition to become a research scientist with the aim of making discoveries that he expected would banish mysticism and undermine faith in the supernatural. His enthusiasm for the wonders of astronomy and the mysteries of the atom led him to physics, the science he studied at Mill Hill School and at University College London. Before he had completed his doctoral research, war was declared and he was directed to research for the navy, working chiefly on mine design.

The war over, Crick joined Naval Intelligence at the Admiralty. By this time his six-year military interlude had destroyed his hope of making a successful career in the rapidly moving subject of physics. Research in the borderline between physics and biology – biophysics – however, he found appealing. Supported by the Medical Research Council and aided by his wealthy Uncle Arthur, Crick stepped back into the lowly world of a research student to find his feet in biology. In 1949 he joined Max Perutz's MRC Unit for the Study of the Structure of Biological Systems in the Cavendish Laboratory in Cambridge, directed by Sir Lawrence Bragg. There Crick plunged into the world of protein structure and the technique of X-ray diffraction analysis. His first talk to members of the Unit was given to criticizing the methods being used by Perutz and Bragg. After further clashes with Bragg it became clear that Crick had no future at the Cavendish. Fortunately, the postdoctoral visitor from America, **James Watson**, teamed up with Crick in an effort to discover the structure of the genetic material, DNA. Aided by knowledge of the X-ray crystallographic research of Rosalind Franklin in London, they solved its structure, much to Bragg's delight, and revising Bragg's evaluation of Crick.

Following this discovery Crick spent a year in Brooklyn, New York, studying protein structure. But his sights were set on the implications of the DNA model. Composed of two long polynucleotide chains held together by hydrogen bonds between the 'bases' (purines and pyrimidines), the sequence of these bases must encode the genetic information. What are the rules governing the translation of the sequences in DNA into the proteins synthesized under DNA's instruction – the genetic code?

To the MRC Unit Crick had drawn the South African biologist Sydney Brenner, to work to answer this by genetic methods. In 1961 they succeeded in establishing the general principles of the code, the same year in which the biochemists Nirenberg and Matthaei discovered the code letter for the first amino acid.

Crick's concern with these questions occupied him until 1966, by which time the role of each of the sixty-four groups of three bases in DNA – the codons – had been assigned. That year Crick presided over the symposium at the Cold Spring Harbor Laboratory, New York, given to the genetic code, a triumphal event.

In the intervening years Crick's international reputation and that of the MRC Unit in Cambridge had been growing. In 1962 he shared with James Watson and Maurice Wilkins the Nobel Prize for Physiology or Medicine. Since then Crick turned to the

difficult field of embryological development, and brought the embryologist, Peter Lawrence, into his group. He also made excursions into the structure of the chromosomes, the origin of life, the origin of the genetic code, and the origin of protein synthesis.

Crick spent his sixtieth year on a sabbatical at the Salk Institute in La Jolla where he had for many years been a Visiting Fellow. Approaching retirement under MRC rules and very happy in Southern California, he resigned from the MRC, to become Kieckhefer Distinguished Professor at the Salk. Now, he felt, was the time to turn to the other subject that had so engaged his attention when he first thought about going into biology – consciousness and the brain. Plunging into neuroscience he mastered in amazing detail the extensive literature in this growing field. In typical fashion he found an ideal collaborator in Christof Koch. Together they published extensively on the neural correlates of consciousness. But Crick's main contribution was to make the study of consciousness respectable in scientific circles and to build a community of researchers in the field in the San Diego area.

The molecular revolution of the 1950s and 1960s created the simple picture of the gene and gene expression in molecular terms. Its basic features were first set out by Crick in 1957 embodied in two principles – the Sequence Hypothesis and the Central Dogma – both of which have since been critiqued in the light of revelations about the nature of gene expression. The molecular approach also played its part in undermining further the already battered classical concept of the gene as a bead on a string. Crick commented on these developments with equanimity, seeing in such revisions evidence of the incredible sophistication of the systems that evolution by natural selection has fashioned.

Crick sought to avoid publicity for himself, while at the same time spreading the word about the wonders of molecular biology. To concentrate his life on research he avoided university teaching, sitting on committees and attending public functions. After the award of the Nobel Prize and especially after the appearance of Watson's book *The Double Helix*, privacy became more difficult to preserve. As a public figure he received many requests to support petitions, but he signed only those he felt passionately about, the last being for instituting a **Darwin** Day in the UK calendar. The Queen awarded him the Order of Merit in 1995.

Further reading

Other works include: *What Mad Pursuit* (1989) and *The Astonishing Hypothesis: The Scientific Search for the Soul* (1994). See: James Watson, *The Double Helix. Norton Critical Edition* (1980); David E. Newton, *James Watson and Francis Crick: Discovery of the Double Helix and Beyond* (1992).

ROBERT OLBY

CUKOR, George

1899–1983

US film director

The key to Cukor's work lies in his concept of 'performance' and in the subtle shading that he brings to the delineation of role-playing within the explicit theatricality of the stage as well as the implicit theatricality of everyday life. His own direction of acting performances from Greta Garbo, Ingrid Bergman and, most notably, Katharine Hepburn won deserved acclaim, but it has required the more flexible critical ideology of the 1970s, open to notions of performance and anxious to evaluate representations of women in Hollywood cinema, to exhume Cukor's reputation from the shallow graves dug by earlier critics, prepared only to see him as a 'woman's director' or as a compliant, if high-grade, contract director.

In the 1920s Cukor rose to prominence on the Broadway stage with interpretative productions of such plays as *The Great Gatsby* and *The Constant Wife*. The Depression crash of Broadway theatre and the arrival of

sound pictures hastened him westwards and he was initially engaged by Paramount as a dialogue director, later to direct his first film after working on the hugely successful *All Quiet on the Western Front* (1930). Cukor was one of the first sound-only directors to gain recognition for his skill in directing film adaptations of precisely those witty and literate salon plays that had resisted silent film treatment. His longevity as a director – more than fifty films in fewer years – was tribute to his ability to work within the parameters of Hollywood studio production and contrasts with the fate allotted such self-proclaimed auteurs as **Von Sternberg** and **Welles**.

From *What Price Hollywood?* (1932) to its virtual remake *A Star is Born* (1945) and beyond, via *Dinner at Eight* (1933), *A Double Life* (1948), *The Actress* (1953) and others, Cukor's films have often taken place within the worlds of theatres, movies or show business and equally frequently presented characters, especially women, who are obliged to assume a particular deliberate role. In her swan song, *Two-Faced Woman* (1941), Garbo plays a wife who decides to impersonate an imaginary loose-living twin sister to regain her husband's affections. Hepburn's ambiguous sexual appeal is used to advantage in *Sylvia Scarlett* (1935), in which she masquerades as a boy. Unlike the major genres which traditionally assign a limited range of stereotypes to women, Cukor's work is peopled with emotionally resilient heroines who, while acknowledging patriarchal might, nonetheless challenge the male's authority and frequently outflank him by the use of his own most cherished weapons of wit and intelligence. The bright and innovative series of Garson Kanin and Ruth Gordon scripted films, in particular the Hepburn/Tracy vehicles of *Adam's Rib* (1949) and *Pat and Mike* (1952), lay out the terrain on which the sexes engage, but the hostilities are less than grim and lead less to victories than to shared emotional growth. The presentation of the courtroom drama in *Adam's Rib* as a series of carefully constructed performances conveys Cukor's view of role-playing: he is no moralist, concerned to expose 'artifice' or 'deceit' in the name of Truth, but a benign explorer of all the discourses that make up a multiplicity of truths.

The literary and stage antecedents to much of Cukor's earlier work obscured the view of his discreet but effective style, that none-theless took unobtrusive risks with lengthy takes or hand-held camera, and could assume more highly inflected characteristics when required for melodrama, as in *A Woman's Face* (1941) or *Gaslight* (1944). Rejecting the option of 'opening out' stage plays in a sup-posedly 'cinematic' way, Cukor preferred to concentrate his direction on the management of performances through the cinematic means of pacing, composition and camera place-ment. With *A Star is Born*, however, his first venture in Cinemascope and colour, Cukor discovered a new stylistic richness and chro-matic complexity in a project that yoked together the disparate genres of musical comedy, Hollywood chronicle and domestic drama to provide Judy Garland with a quasi-confessional role and Cukor with a new boost of critical life. The musicals that followed were generally more uneven works, despite the massive popular success of *My Fair Lady* (1964), and his career beached after the wreck of an attempted American–Russian co-production of *The Bluebird* (1976).

Further reading

Other works include: *A Bill of Divorcement* (1932); *David Copperfield* (1934); *Camille* (1936); *Gone with the Wind* (1939) (Cukor worked on pre-produc-tion for a year and shot some material); *The Women* (1939); *The Philadelphia Story* (1940); *Born Yesterday* (1950); *It Should Happen to You* (1954); *Bhowani Junction* (1956); *Les Girls* (1957); *Heller in Pink Tights* (1959); *Let's Make Love* (1960); *The Chapman Report* (1962); *Travels with My Aunt* (1972). See: Carlos Clarens, *Cukor* (1976); Patrick McGilligan, *George Cukor: A Double Life* (1992); James Bernardoni, *GeorgeCukor: A Critical Study and Filmography* (1986).

NIGEL ALGAR

CUMMINGS, Edward Estlin

1894–1962

US poet

E.E. Cummings (or e. e. cummings as 'Mr Lowercase Highbrow' preferred) was born on 14 October 1894 at Cambridge, Massachusetts; his father taught at Harvard and subsequently became minister of Old South Church, a celebrated Unitarian institution in Boston. Cummings's background was thus eminently respectable and he gravitated naturally to the academic life. In 1911 he enrolled at Harvard where he contributed lush Keatsian verse to the college magazine and played a prominent part in establishing the Harvard Poetry Society. In 1915 he received his BA in English and Classics and the next year took his MA. Then, unpredictably, he quit academic life and went to New York to work for a mail order firm. It was an early assertion of his refusal to be typecast in a given social role.

In 1917, before the USA had entered the hostilities of the First World War, Cummings enlisted in the Norton-Harjes Ambulance Corps and was sent to France on active ser-vice. Because of his association with a friend whose letters criticizing the French war effort were discovered by the censor, Cummings was classified as a suspicious person and detained for three months at the French prison camp of La Ferté Macé. There sixty men were kept under surveillance in an oblong room 'about 80 feet by 40, unmis-takably ecclesiastical in feeling' – *The Enormous Room* (1922) of his first book. To Cummings the indignities so stoically endured by the inmates proved emphatically that the gifted individual could always transcend the hostile conditions inflicted by society; his personal credo of individualism was embodied in the Delectable Mountains, four supremely human beings. The shape of the book was suggested by Bunyan's *Pilgrim's Progress* (hence the Delectable Mountains) and the style was visionary: 'In the course of the next ten thou-sand years it may be possible to find Delectable Mountains without going to prison ... it may be possible, I dare say, to encounter Delectable Mountains who are not in prison.'

After the war Cummings remained in Paris to study painting which, as is evident from his pictorial collection *CIOPW* (1931), remained a passion with him. He was impressed by the textural experiments of the French painters who used the anti-illusionistic method of Cubism to restore the subjective element to figurative art: the artist's vision was to transcend the objects that inspired it. Cummings applied this textural approach to poetry and discovered that he could revitalize traditional literary themes by presenting them in a typographically novel format. He had already published poems in the *Dial* magazine and his first collection *Tulips and Chimneys* (1923) brought him to the notice of a puzzled public. In the section 'Chansons Innocentes' Cummings evoked childhood with his visually attractive metrics:

In Just—
Spring
when the world is mud-luscious
the little
lame balloonman
whistles far
and wee.

Cummings also showed, by the inclusion of sixty-one sonnets in his first collection, that he was no destructive enemy of formal poetry; his method was (and remained) a means of shocking readers out of their complacent familiarity with the world.

Cummings had found in France, as he put it in his Charles Eliot Norton lectures *i: six nonlectures* (1953), 'an immediate reconciling of spirit and flesh, forever and now, heaven and earth. Paris was for me precisely and complexly this homogeneous duality: this accepting transcendence; this living and dying more than death or life.' In 1924 he returned to New York where he published *&* (1925) and received the *Dial* prize for poetry. Cummings then made a dramatic theatrical entrance with his play *Him* (1927) which was first performed by the Provincetown Players in 1927.

In a programme note he warned the audience 'DON'T TRY TO UNDERSTAND IT, LET IT TRY TO UNDERSTAND YOU' and confronted them with the conflict between Him (an artist unable to function because of his denial of love) and Me (a pregnant woman frustrated by Him's resistance to domesticity). By rotating the theatrical room in which Him and Me performed Cummings deliberately denied the audience the reassurance of a fixed viewpoint.

In 1931 Cummings spent a month in the USSR; his vivid journal of this visit was published as *Eimi* (1933). With his transcendental belief in the sanctity of the individual, Cummings was appalled at the regimentation he saw in Russia: 'Russia, I felt, was more deadly than war; when nationalists hate, they hate by merely killing and maiming human beings; when internationalists hate, they hate by categorying and pigeonholing human beings.' Some of this political indignation entered his collection *No Thanks* (1935), so called because the manuscript was rejected by fourteen publishers whose names Cummings catalogued on his dedication page. However, the positive aspect of the poet was expressed in typographically extreme poems which juxtaposed images inside and outside parentheses:

swi(
across! gold's
rouNdly
)ftblac
kl(ness)y.

Cummings was now a poetic law unto himself though his roots in the radical individualism of Blake, Emerson and **Thoreau** were obvious enough. He resisted Grand Old Man status by remaining true to his initial insights, and in his fifth Charles Eliot Norton 'nonlecture' defined his abiding transcendental vision:

We should go hugely astray in assuming that art was the only selftranscendence. Art is a mystery; all mysteries have their source in a mystery-of-mysteries who is love; and if lovers may reach eternity through love herself, their mystery remains essentially that of the loving artist whose way must lie through his art, and of the loving worshipper whose aim is oneness with his god.

He continued to make this philosophy startling by his technical vivacity, and his poetry – right up to the posthumous collection *73 Poems* (1963) – revealed, rather than concealed, a touching belief in humanity and a dazzling lyric gift.

Further reading

Cummings's poetry is collected in *Complete Poems* (2 vols, 1968; 1972); useful critical studies include Norman Friedman's *E.E. Cummings: The Growth of a Writer* (1964) and Charles Norman's *The Magic Maker: E.E. Cummings* (1969); Christopher Sawyer-Laucanno, *E.E. Cummings: A Biography* (2004); Harold Bloom (ed.), *E.E. Cummings* (2005).

ALAN BOLD

CUNNINGHAM, Merce

1919–

US dancer and choreographer

Insofar as it makes sense to speak of a revolt against abstract expressionism in dance, then Merce Cunningham has been its leading exponent. In the 1950s and 1960s and beyond he advanced a choreographic revolution that detached dance from its traditional narrative enfoldment, and also redefined its relationship to both musical accompaniment and what Cunningham called 'décor' – the costumes and stage scenery. Instead, Cunningham set out to explore the whole spectrum of human movement, drawing on sources well outside conventional ballet. Walking, marching, prancing and falling down are just some of the elements he introduced into his choreographic repertoire. Typically his pieces are non-linear and non-climactic, the movements of their dancer or dancers independent of the score.

Born in Centralia, Washington State, Cunningham first studied dance at the Cornish School of Fine and Applied in Seattle, then at Mills and Bennington Colleges, and also at George Ballantine's School of American Ballet. While at Bennington he was noticed by **Martha Graham**, the pioneer of modern dance, and invited to join her company in 1939. Soon he was creating roles as a solo dancer, and by 1944 had begun choreographing. On stage, he was noted at this time for his irregular rhythms and his subtly expressive movements.

Cunningham left Martha Graham's company in 1945, her influence being replaced by that of the avant-garde composer **John Cage**, whom Cunningham had first encountered as a faculty member at the Cornish School.

In 1948 both men found themselves teaching at the legendary Black Mountain College in Asheville, North Carolina. The College had been founded in 1933 in order to 'educate the whole student', who was expected to perform manual labour as well as explore a cross-section of intellectual interests. Although Black Mountain closed in 1953 following acrimonious disagreement between some of its senior faculty members, while it lasted it attracted an extraordinary array of creative talents, among them Josef Albers and **Allen Ginsberg**. Its interdisciplinary ethos particularly suited Cunningham and Cage, who formed a close collaborative partnership. Thus, when in 1953 Cunningham formed his own dance company, Cage would frequently accompany it on tour. To Cage's influence may be ascribed two important 'firsts' achieved by Cunningham. His *Suite by Chance* (1952) was the first dance-sequence to be performed to an electronic score, while *Collage* (also 1952) was the first ballet to utilize *musique concrète* (in essence tapedrecorded sounds derived from natural and urban environments).

The Merce Cunningham Dance Company, destined to tour Europe and Japan as well as North America, provided its founder with the perfect vehicle to further his innovative approach to dance, and Cunningham himself was to choreograph in excess of 150 pieces for it. Always eschewing the maudlin and sentimental, he aimed at 'pure movement', in which emotion played little or no ostensible part. Instead he relied on chance and sudden, seemingly inexplicable choreographic shifts, the sequencing of at least one of his pieces being determined literally by the toss of a coin. At the same time he strove to maintain a separation between dance and music, often rehearsing his dancers without benefit of the score, which might only become known to them the day before a performance.

The independence of dance, score and décor correlated with the independence of the senses, functioning in alliance with, but not beholden to, each other. Thus in *Summerspace* (1958) the sets and costumes designed by **Robert Rauschenberg** bore no obvious relation to the choreography. Rather, the dancers moved about on stage like whimsical animals, birds flitting about or insects scurrying within an arbitrary, random environment.

More recently Cunningham has distinguished himself by his willingness to employ animation technology through his use of *Lifeforms* software – responding perhaps to the bald fact that dance is seldom satisfactorily captured by film, television and video, making it the most ephemeral as well as most spontaneous art. Asked once by a bewildered audience member what a work of his had actually meant, Cunningham pointed at a moth darting about in the warmth of an exposed light bulb. His dances, he said, were 'about' that kind of freed motion.

Further reading

See: Richard Kostelanetz (ed.), *Merce Cunningham: Dancing in Space and Time* (essays, 1998); Germano Celant, *Merce Cunningham* (1999); and Roger Copeland, *Merce Cunningham: The Modernizing of Modern Dance* (2004).

ANNE K. SWARTZ

D

DALAI LAMA *see:* GYATSO, TENZIN, 14TH DALAI LAMA

DALÍ y Domenech, Salvador Felipe Jacinto

1904–89

Spanish artist

'With the coming of Dalí,' wrote **André Breton** in his introduction to the first Paris exhibition of 1929, 'it is perhaps the first time that the mental windows have been opened really wide, so that one can feel oneself gliding up towards the wild sky's trap.' For Surrealism it was a year of crisis and redirection. Since the movement's inception in 1924 the emphasis had been on automatism and the advantage of chance discovery as a contribution in artistic and literary creation. The Surrealists were to draw their inspiration not from reality but from a 'purely interior model'. But it was becoming increasingly apparent that the process had inherent weaknesses. The essentially passive role in which the writer and painter became instruments no longer had any validity. That 'state of effervescence' had degenerated into repetition, monotony and disillusionment. It did not mean a lack of faith in the process, but rather a recognition that it no longer constituted for Surrealism an end in itself. Dalí fully shared the Surrealists' commitment to the automatic processes, which he had read about in various reviews and catalogues. In 1927, according to his own *The Secret Life of Salvador Dalí* (1942),

when he was still living in his home town of Figueras, near Barcelona, he 'spent the whole day seated before my easel, my eyes staring fixedly, trying to "see", like a medium, the images that would spring up in my imagination.' Two paintings date from this period, *Apparatus and Hand* and *Blood is Sweeter than Honey*, which not only reveal Surrealist influences but also show that, for the involuntary images inspired by a dream state to achieve their full potential, they had to be developed in a fully conscious manner. By 1929, using his technical dexterity as a 'means of forcing inspiration', he had produced some of the most genuinely Surrealist paintings of the time. For the next four years, according to Breton, Dalí 'incarnated the Surrealist spirit and his genius made it shine as could only have been done by one who had in no way participated in the often ungrateful episodes of its birth'. There is little argument that he became the movement's most spectacular exponent, bringing to Surrealist art a new objectivity, painting like a madman rather than an occasional somnambulist. From the time when he had been a student at the Madrid School of Fine Arts he had expressed a preference for those artists who used a precise technique, and his own convincingly illusionist realism was now put to the use of painting as an illustrative medium and to revive a return to anecdotal art. A group of small works of hallucinatory intensity crystallized Dalí's mature style: *The Lugubrious Game, Illumined Pleasures* and *Accommodations of Desire* (all 1929) combined photographic realism (at this time he even called his paintings 'handmade photography') with bits of collaged colour engravings and photographs to establish an all-over pattern of exactitude. Painted replicas of the collage elements were so carefully executed as to be indistinguishable.

Dalí's intervention was ceaseless and on all levels, including revolutionary critical interpretation of familiar works of art. Millet's *Angelus* he saw as a monument to sexual repression, while in *The Legend of William Tell* he discovered not filial devotion but incestuous mutilation. In his own *The Enigma of William Tell* a kneeling figure with the face of **Lenin** appears trouserless with an extended buttock supported by a crutch. Along with his fascination of all aspects of aberration, the provocative scatology of his subject-matter and his understanding of **Freud's** psychology on which he based much of his early work led to the development of his theory of 'paranoiac-critical activity', which he describes as 'a spontaneous method of irrational knowledge based upon the critical and systematic objectification of delirious associations and interpretations'. It is, in fact, a form of image interpretation, in which the spectator sees in a picture or object a different image depending upon his or her own imaginative ability. Not unrelated to this method is one of his most lyrical paintings, *The Phantom Cart* of 1933, in which a horse-drawn cart is going towards a distant eastern city. The two seated figures, we realize, are also the buildings in the city, suggesting that the cart has already reached its destination. Another influence on Dalí was Art Nouveau architecture and decoration, which he called the 'undulant-convulsive' style. Many of the ectoplasmic forms in his paintings during the years 1930–4 are based on the decorative busts in that style or the wrought-iron vegetation of the Paris Métro.

Dalí always refused to explain the meaning of his paintings, adding that he was as astonished as anyone by the images that appeared on his canvases. Yet we know from his account of his childhood in *The Secret Life*, from his interpretative studies of Millet, the Pre-Raphaelites and William Tell, that there is evidence of a meaning behind many of his fetish symbols. One obsessional image is watches, which first made their appearance in *The Persistence of Memory* (1931). He makes them limp, soft and pliable, hanging over ledges and tree trunks to express eternity and the flexibility of time. Equally dominant is the crutch which he uses to prop up fantastic forms. He sees in the bifurcated shape the whole concept of life and death, but the emphasis he places on them in his autobiography suggests homosexual meaning and the need for masculinity. As a substitute for his father he uses the grasshopper. It is an image of fear, of discipline. Dalí called these objects 'a tangible, objective, and symbolic materialization of desire by sublimation, a wish or a prayer'.

More purely aesthetic influences became noticeable in a number of works between 1934 and 1936, in particular a growing interest in the nineteenth-century Romantic tradition. More serious perhaps were his political tendencies and the interest he began to show in Nazism, which gave rise to heated discussions within the Surrealist group, some of whom saw no reason to sponsor any of his private obsessions. Although an attempt to exclude him was not unanimous, he ceased to attend group meetings. Nevertheless he was still invited to contribute to the exhibitions.

Prior to the outbreak of the Second World War (which he spent in America) Dalí made three visits to Italy. The works of Botticelli, Piero di Cosimo and Caravaggio, as well as Vermeer and Velázquez, began to play an important part in the iconography of his paintings. This return to classicism demanded a more conscious objectivity and a close study of the pictorial science of the Renaissance. For Dalí it meant 'integration, synthesis, cosmogony, faith'. Not surprisingly this shift was accompanied by an increased belief in the Catholic hierarchy.

Further reading

Other works include: *Hidden Faces* (a novel, 1944); *Diary of a Genius* (1966); and *Dalí by Dalí* (1970).

See: David Gascoyne, *A Short Survey of Surrealism* (1936); Fleur Cowles, *The Case of Salvador Dalí* (1959); Marcel Jean, *The History of Surrealist Painting* (1960); Patrick Waldberg, *Surrealism* (1965); Roger Cardinal and Robert Short, *Surrealism – Permanent Revelation* (1970); R. Descharnes, *World of Salvador Dalí* (1972); Conroy Maddox, *Dalí* (1979); Robert Descharnes, *Salvador Dalí* (1986).

CONROY MADDOX

DARWIN, Charles Robert

1809–82

British naturalist

Darwin made the doctrine of the evolution of species, which until the publication of *The Origin of Species* in 1859 had existed only as a sporadic and uncertain hypothesis, overwhelmingly probable by showing that natural selection, as an evolutionary mechanism, is and must be operating. Because his theory convincingly replaced religious doctrines about the special creation of each species, its dissemination and acceptance marked a significant as well as substantial expansion of the role of empirical science within our culture. Just as the terms 'evolution' and 'Darwinism' have tended to become synonymous, so too has an antithesis between science and religion aptly been laid at Darwin's door.

Charles Darwin was born in Shrewsbury, the son of a doctor, Robert Waring Darwin, and grandson of both Erasmus Darwin and of the industrialist Josiah Wedgwood. In 1818 he entered Shrewsbury School, where, according to his mildly disingenuous *Autobiography*, he was a very average pupil who preferred dogs, angling and shooting to the prescribed classical studies. In 1825 he was sent by his father to study medicine at Edinburgh University; but, nauseated by the one surgical operation he attended, young Charles was obviously unsuited to the profession, and in 1827 he was transferred to Cambridge to prepare for holy orders. However, although at this period Darwin entertained a belief in 'the strict and literal truth of every word of the Bible', he was no more minded to take up the cloth than he had been the stethoscope (an invention of 1816), and he continued to cause his family concern by his 'idle, sporting' behaviour. But in reality his time at the two universities was by no means wasted. At Edinburgh he had mixed with several naturalists, among them Robert Edmund Grant, a supporter of the evolutionary views of Lamarck, views which Darwin had already encountered in Erasmus Darwin's *Zoönomia* (1794–96); and at Cambridge he came to be known by some of the dons as 'the man who walks with Henslow'. The Rev. John Stevens Henslow was Professor of Botany, and, although entirely conservative in his adherence to the doctrine (most widely disseminated at the time through William Paley's *Natural Theology* of 1802) that all species were separately created and immutable, a field observer of considerable acumen. Darwin's friendship with him, which he described as the 'circumstance which influenced my career more than any other', was fruitful in three respects: it sharpened Darwin's own powers of observation; it directed his attention towards geology; and it secured him a berth on the *Beagle*.

This last was all-important, for the five years (from December 1831 until October 1836) Darwin spent aboard HMS *Beagle* furnished the material and experience without which *The Origin of Species* could not have been written. He was taken on as ship's naturalist by the ship's master, Captain Robert Fitzroy, after an introduction by Henslow. Fitzroy, later sacked as Governor of New Zealand for defending Maori land claims, was commissioned by the Admiralty to conduct a detailed survey of the coasts of South America and to set up chronometrical stations around the globe. This journey gave Darwin a prolonged exposure to an area of the world radically different in its fauna and flora from his native England, as well as a more general sweep of the entire southern hemisphere. Darwin seems to have endured the hazards of the voyage remarkably well; but within a few months of his return home he became a semi-invalid. His illness, sometimes identified as Chagas' Disease (his symptoms were lassitude, digestive disorders and vomiting), affected the rest of his life. From 1842, three years after his marriage to his cousin Emma Wedgwood (by whom he had ten children, eight surviving infancy), he lived in near-reclusion at Down House in Kent. The success of his father's practice combined with a judicious investment policy enabled him to live independently, and to the end of his days he maintained a firm belief in the social benefits of an intelligensia freed from the burden of employment.

From the notes, observations and collections made during the *Beagle*'s long circumnavigation Darwin worked on a number of publications that gave him a solid position in the British scientific community. These included *The Structure and Distribution of Coral Reefs* (1842). But the first work to reach a wider audience and which is remembered by non-specialists is the *Journal of Researches into the Geology and Natural History of the Various Countries Visited by H.M.S. Beagle* (1839, rev. 1846), better known as *The Voyage of the Beagle*. Quite apart from its virtues as the most informed travel book of its time and the most readable of all Darwin's output, it can be seen as setting the stage for the theory that was to come. Beneath its light and often anecdotal surface, *The Voyage* displays a remarkable familiarity with existing botanical, zoological and geological literature; and behind its scholarship lurk those acute questions which led its author towards an evolutionist explanation of speciation.

William Paley had used an analogy to summarize the orthodox position. Finding a watch in a field, it would be reasonable to infer that the object owed both its gross design and intricate mechanism to the inspiration and labour of a watchmaker. And so it was with the world and its organic contents. All had been made and designed by a God, each species having its place in a grand hierarchy of living beings, in which man, by his rationality, enjoyed special pre-eminence. Each species was suited to its climate and habitation by its special characteristics; or, put

another way, geographic and climatic diversity existed in order to support the broadest possible spectrum of living things, knowledge of which best equipped man to learn of the existence of his creator.

There was nothing original in Paley's teleological formulation. In the main it harked back to such works as John Ray's *Wisdom of God Manifested in the Works of Creation* (1691); and, in its adherence to Usher's biblical chronology that dated the Creation in 4004 BC, it proved vulnerable to two immediate threats: the discovery of extinct species in the fossil record, and the emergence of a geology that described the inorganic world as having changed through periods of time far greater than anything suggested in Genesis. Here the decisive publication was Sir Charles Lyell's *Principles of Geology* (3 vols, 1830–2), the first volume of which Henslow had urged Darwin to take with him on the *Beagle*. In it Lyell argued that, far from being designed, the features of the contemporary earth have emerged from, and are explicable wholly by, the gradual accumulative operation of such forces as earthquakes, volcanic eruptions and the weather.

Lyell's non-catastrophic model of evolution Darwin made his own. In his work on coral reefs he embraced it directly, showing how polyps-built atolls are signposts for submerged islands; and in the *Voyage* he adopted it as his perceptual framework. It was precisely the apprehension of current appearances through a corridor of projected past time that generated his famous observations on the Galapagos Islands. There he found that not only were many species unique to the archipelago, but they were often unique to the individual islands. But what mattered was the degree of relationship between species: for whereas the closest ties existed between species on separate islands, the fauna and flora of the Galapagos resembled that of South America much more than that of any comparable basaltic larval terrain, for instance the Cape de Verd islands. Darwin's comments on the Galapagos finches show clearly the direction of his thoughts: 'Seeing the gradation and diversity of structure in one small, intimately related group of birds, one might really fancy that from the original paucity of birds in this archipelago one species had been taken and modified for different ends.' Why is it, he asks elsewhere, that living marsupials are found only in South America and Australia (which had once been joined)? And why is the closest relation of the South American rhea the South African ostrich?

In fact, when the *Voyage* was first published, Darwin had already come to the main conclusions of his theory of descent with modification. He opened his first notebook on evolution in July 1837, and in 1838 a reading of Malthus's *Essay on the Principle of Population* suggested to him the mechanism of natural selection. In 1842 he wrote a thirty-five-page sketch on the subject, which in 1844 he elaborated into a 230-page essay that he showed to the botanist Joseph Dalton Hooker (both are published in Gavin de Beer, *Evolution by Natural Selection*, 1958). But it was not until 1856, on the advice of Lyell himself, that he began preparing his views for publication. And even this bore only an indirect relation to what finally appeared, for Darwin originally intended writing a work three or four times the length of the *Origin*, which he referred to as an 'abstract' only. The delay, between 1844 and 1856, can be explained by Darwin's keen awareness of the momentousness of the issues at stake, and his recognition that acceptance of his theory would depend on the maturity of its presentation; although during the interim much of his time was devoted to four monographs that set out to classify the different orders of living and fossilized barnacle. What forced his hand was the arrival from the Malay Archipelago of Alfred Wallace's paper, expressing ideas identical to his own. With Wallace's consent, papers by both men were read at a meeting of the Linnaean Society on 1 July 1858. *The Origin of Species* was then written and published on 24 November of the following year. The first edition of 1,250 copies sold out on the same day.

If caution was Darwin's strategy, his instinct was faultless, for *The Origin of Species* is still, in its close argument, an impressive piece of advocacy, the more so as its author took particular pains to forestall his enemies by previewing their likely criticisms. Evolution by natural selection, or descent with modification as Darwin often calls it, is extrapolated from three broad areas of fact: the 'struggle for life', variation and inheritance. Malthus, in his *Essay*, had argued that so long as human populations are permitted to increase geometrically while the food supply increases only arithmetically, famine and death are inevitable. And this, says Darwin, is exactly what happens in the animal and vegetable kingdoms, on the largest possible scale:

> as more individuals are produced than can possibly survive, there must in every case be a struggle for existence, either one individual with another of the same species, or with the individuals of distinct species, or with the physical conditions of life.

Nature 'red in tooth and claw' (the phrase is **Tennyson's**) affords no 'artificial increase of food, and no prudential restraint from marriage'. From this it follows that 'any being, if it vary however slightly in any manner profitable to itself, under the complex and sometimes varying conditions of life, will have a better chance of surviving, and thus be *naturally selected*'. Finally: 'From the strong principle of inheritance, any selected variety will tend to propagate its new and modified form.' Let this process of random adaptation to a dynamic environment continue long enough and new species, new genera, new families and new orders will be co-evolved.

The most difficult term in Darwin's tripartite equation was variation, and to this topic he devoted the opening chapters of his book. Variation is first demonstrated not among feral creatures, but among the domesticated, such as dogs and pigeons; for every trainer knew that by careful selecting new breeds could be developed within fairly short periods of time. Thus, all varieties of tame pigeon are known to derive from a single species of rock-pigeon. In the wild, human control is merely substituted by the struggle for life. A powerful support for this view can be found in the vagaries of classification itself. Ever since Linnaeus had provided naturalists with a system for ordering the different species, arguments had raged about what did and what did not constitute a distinct species. Darwin concluded that if hard and fast lines between species and sub-species are difficult to draw, then that is because hard and fast lines do not naturally occur. Rather, species are separated by degree, not kind. As Linnaeus himself had said, it is the characteristics that make the genus, not the genus that makes the characteristics.

Having thus presented his theory, Darwin moved on to corroborate it with circumstantial evidence from four important areas: the fossil record, the distribution of species, morphology and embryology. For the theory itself, as Darwin himself admitted, could never be proved: the great span of evolutionary time was simply irrecoverable. Indeed, one of the hardest tasks facing him was the reconciliation of his thesis with contemporary palaeontology: for whereas fossils provided ample evidence of the extinction of species, which one would predict from the theory, few if any of them could be identified unequivocally as 'intermediate' varieties – although one fossil discovery, that of the archaeopteryx, unexpectedly linking birds back to reptiles, was hailed as irresistible confirmation of the evolutionary position. Yet, quite apart from the fact that the fossil record was as yet relatively unexplored, Darwin was able to point out that the record never would be 'complete' because geologically it was impossible: sedimentary beds are not laid down continuously, and however long it might take for a species to become modified, the period during which it remains unchanged is incomparably longer. On the other hand, affinities between extinct and living species greatly enhanced the theory, particularly with regard to distribution: for the fossils of one area are generally more closely allied to living species of the same area than those of any other. And fossil resemblances formed only a part of the larger morphological picture: for, throughout nature, diversity of function is consistently located in similarity of structure. The wings and legs of a bat, like the legs of a horse and the arms of a chimpanzee, are not only built up from the same basic bone units, but the bone units always appear in the same sequence. In embryology we can virtually see such implicit adaptation taking place, for the embryos of different species are frequently alike in their early stages. 'Thus, community in embryonic structure, reveals community of descent.' Or, as Darwin's German champion, Haeckel, put it (much too crudely): ontogeny recapitulates phylogeny.

The morphological and embryological arguments applied as much to man as to any other species. Although *The Origin of Species* carefully refrained from making a point of this, it became, in the public's mind, the key issue in the controversy that followed publication. Darwin himself took very little part in the great debate, and willingly allowed **T.H. Huxley** to lead the evolutionist charge. It was Huxley too who first gave an extended account of man the primate in his *Evidence as to Man's Place in Nature* (1863). But Darwin did take up the subject himself in his widely influential *The Descent of Man, and Selection in Relation to Sex* (1871).

In *The Descent of Man* Darwin offered the first comprehensive account of sexual selection, an accomplice of natural selection, operating among many of the more developed species. In such species striking differences between males and females are said to have come about adaptively. Thus, the peacock's tail has evolved by virtue of the advantage it bestows on the peacock's chances of attracting a peahen. Among some species of beetle the two sexes appear so unalike that previously naturalists had been misled into assigning them to different species altogether. Among humans, too, sexual selection is used to explain why women are generally smaller, less hairy, less muscular and, according to Darwin, less well-equipped mentally. Darwin also ascribes racial differences to the same cause, while proposing that the various races (many of which he refers to as 'savages') be regarded as subspecies. He does not, like so many of his contemporaries, argue that the different races represent originally different species; yet the characteristic that separates man from all other species is his moral sense – in a famous passage he describes how man alone possesses the capability to judge his own actions; and this quality, he says, has only been brought to a pitch among Caucasians.

Clearly *The Descent of Man* exhibits some of the white supremacism and the sexism regarded by many commentators as an unfortunate consequence of the application of Darwin's ideas during the last decades of the nineteenth century. But while some of what he says must be put down to the prejudices of his age, and while 'Social Darwinism' derived at least so much from the *laissez-faire* philosophy of Herbert Spencer, his plea for human subspeciation needs to be regarded as an attempt to reinforce his main scientific argument – man's commonality with nature. In the same spirit, and prefiguring the main concerns of ethology, his chapter on 'Mental Powers' describes the incidence of such behaviour as curiosity, fear, imitation, attention, memory, imagination, reason, language, even the sense of beauty, and above all the 'social instinct', among many animals other than man. What sets the latter apart is merely the concentration of all these qualities (acting together to produce moral sense) in one species.

Darwin's vivid account of man as one species among many underpins the social sciences; his picture of man's mind as the product of different and variously developed biological skills serves as an antidote to idealist philosophies; his rejection of orthogenesis constitutes a repudiation of the Judaeo-Christian and Islamic concepts of God; and his theory of evolution provides the framework of the modern understanding of the life process. While together these ideas make up

the core of 'Darwinism', separately they each had clear antecedents in an increasingly materialist and secular European culture. Atheism was a widespread, age-old phenomenon. By the mid-nineteenth century discoveries in prehistoric archaeology had already abetted geology's rejection of biblical chronology (the Frenchman Boucher de Perthes in the late 1830s established the dates of the Stone Age); early ethnologists, like some social theorists (notably Condorcet, and later **Marx**), had embarked on stadial models to explain the route from 'savagery' to 'civilization'; at least two physical anthropologists, W.C. Wells (in a paper given to the Royal Society in 1813), and James Cowles Prichard (in the second edition of *Researches into the Physical History of Mankind*, 1826), had proposed theories of natural selection; and Spencer, who coined the tautological phrase 'survival of the fittest', had espoused Lamarck's theory of the inheritance of acquired characteristics throughout the 1850s. Although Darwin drew relatively little upon sources outside the natural sciences (the major exception being his reading of Malthus), the implications of his work were quickly apprehended, and often assimilated, by a very broad cross-section of the intellectual community at home, in Europe and in America.

The reason why this was so lies as much in the quality of Darwin's thought as in any contemporary disposition towards loosely evolutionist attitudes. In both the *Origin* and the *Descent*, as in the early notebooks, his great strength lies in his ability to discern broad patterns amidst a mass of observation; and it is the compatibility of his theory of adaptive modification with findings from a very wide range of scientific inquiry that has stood surety for its proof, and which explains why it has so often carried the day against creationism. It is, for example, quite remarkable that the major discoveries in experimental biology and chemistry, from **Mendel** to **Watson** and Crick's work on DNA, have squared comfortably with the Darwinian hypothesis. Indeed, modern biology is founded upon the synthesis of Darwinian natural selection and Mendelian genetics effected by the statistical analyses of Sir Ronald Fisher and J.B.S. Haldane in the late 1920s and early 1930s. That is not to say that in some respects Darwin's theory has not itself been modified. It is now thought by some that he placed too much emphasis on the graduality of evolution and on species rather than individuals; and a leniency towards Lamarck exhibited in later editions of the *Origin* was exorcized in the 1890s after advances in cytology offered a convincing refutation of the French biologist. But the principle of evolution by natural selection is still accepted by a vast majority of biologists, and fundamentalist criticisms of Darwin tend also to be a fundamental rejection of scientific logic.

In the years immediately after 1859 attempts were made to reconcile Darwinism with traditional religious dogma, by asserting that natural selection was God's chosen method of creation – what John Dewey dubbed 'design on the instalment plan'; and even today there are those who interpret spontaneous mutation as a form of sublime intervention. In general, however, it remains one of the great ironies that natural history, which flourished in the early nineteenth century as the handmaiden of religion, turned traitor on its cause. Indeed, what distinguished Darwin's theory of evolution from others of the period, and what provoked so much hostility, was precisely its insistence that the growth of complex out of simple forms is a matter of chance rather than design. Even Lamarck had upheld the ordinary teleological view of progress as necessary progress.

Darwin himself worked on indefatigably during the 1870s, publishing works of high scientific value, among them *The Expression of the Emotions in Man and Animals* (1872), *The Effects of Cross and Self Fertilization in the Vegetable Kingdom* (1876), containing an explanation of the adaptive advantages of sexual selection, and *The Formation of Vegetable Mould through the Action of Worms* (1881). He died in 1882, of a heart attack, and upon the intercession of twenty MPs was buried in Westminster Abbey.

Further reading

The full text of Darwin's *Autobiography* first appeared in *The Autobiography of Charles Darwin*, ed. Nora Barlow (1958), although a theologically 'expurgated' version was included in *Life and Letters of Charles Darwin*, ed. Francis Darwin (3 vols, 1887). Darwin's other works include: *Geological Observations on the Volcanic Islands Visited During the Voyage of H.M.S. Beagle* (1844); *Geological Observations on South America* (1864); *A Monograph on the Subclass Cirripedia* (2 vols, 1851 and 1854) and *A Monograph of the Fossil Lepudidae, or Pedunculated Cirripedes of Great Britain* (1851); *A Monograph of the Fossil Balanidae and Verrucidae* (1854); *On the Various Contrivances by which British and Foreign Orchids are Fertilized by Insects* (1862). For Darwin's 'Notebooks' see *Bulletin of the British Museum (Natural History)*, Vol. 2 (1960) and Vol. 3 (1967). See: Julian Huxley, *Evolution: The Modern Synthesis* (1942; 3rd edn, 1974); Gavin de Beer, *Charles Darwin: A Scientific Biography* (1963); John Maynard Smith, *The Theory of Evolution* (2nd edn, 1966); Lynn Barber, *The Heyday of Natural History* (1980); Ronald Good, *The Philosophy of Evolution* (1981); Peter Brent, *Charles Darwin* (1981); Jonathan Howard, *Darwin* (1982); Wilma George, *Darwin* (1982); Peter J. Bowler, *Charles Darwin: The Man and His Influence* (1990); Janet Browne, *Charles Darwin: A Biography* (2 vols, 1995–2002); Harold Orel (ed.), *Charles Darwin: Interviews and Recollections* (2000). Two collections of essays by Stephen Jay Gould are also recommended: *Ever Since Darwin* (1977) and *The Panda's Thumb* (1980).

JUSTIN WINTLE

DAVIES, (Sir) Peter Maxwell

1934–

English composer

Peter Maxwell Davies was born in Salford, Lancashire (now Greater Manchester), and began to compose at an early age. He won a scholarship to study music at Manchester University in 1953. Self-taught until then, Davies was influenced in his youth by many composers. The *Quartet Movement* (1952) exhibits an interest in folkloric writing reminiscent of **Béla Bartók**, and a witty and parodic flair which would characterize Davies's mature style. This synthesis was totally alien to the dominant trends of British music at the time, and Davies's musical curiosity caused him difficulty while at university. Rejecting classes on figures no more contemporary than **Edward Elgar** and Frederick Delius, Davies preferred to attend Richard Hall's composition classes at the Royal Manchester College of Music. He found there a group of performers and composers more sympathetic to advancing new music: other members of the Manchester School, as it became known, included Harrison Birtwistle, Alexander Goehr, Elgar Howarth and John Ogdon. The works Davies wrote during this period, the *Sonata for Trumpet and Piano* (1955) and the *Five Piano Pieces* (1955–6), reveal the influence of continental exponents of modernism such as **Anton Webern** and **Olivier Messiaen**.

Study with Goffredo Petrassi in Rome followed in 1957. Davies never became a typical member of the European avant-garde: his fascination with the medieval and renaissance periods did not allow it. Encouraged by Petrassi, Davies increasingly drew on plainsong to generate material in his works. However, these sources were often distorted beyond recognition by old and new techniques of development: mensural canon and serialism co-exist in *Alma Redemptoris Mater* (1957), yet to all but the analyst its submerged Marian antiphon and eponymous Dunstable motet are undetectable.

Davies was appointed Director of Music at Cirencester Grammar School in 1959, acquiring there a reputation as a music educationalist. He has since inherited the mantle of **Benjamin Britten** by becoming the country's leading composer for children. This has not always led Davies to dilute his idiosyncratic, progressive style. The creative pinnacle of his work in Cirencester, *O Magnum Mysterium* (1960), continued to reconcile the past and present through its constant displacement of sources, and placed considerable demands on the school's musicians. Davies

relinquished his post in 1962 to study at Princeton University, USA, where faculty members included the composers Milton Babbitt, Earl Kim and Roger Sessions.

Returning to Britain, Davies was soon reunited with Birtwistle and Goehr. Dissatisfied with the frequency and standard of performances of their music, they organized two summer schools at Wardour Castle (1964/5). **Michael Tippett** was enlisted as president, and the week-long events assembled Britain's new generation of composers and performers. In 1965 the Melos Ensemble presented at Wardour **Arnold Schoenberg's** *Pierrot Lunaire* (1912). Birtwistle, Davies, the clarinettist Alan Hacker and the pianist Stephen Pruslin decided to form their own ensemble based on the work's instrumentation. Davies's agreement to become composer-in-residence at the University of Adelaide postponed their plans, although he met in Australia the group's first manager, James Murdoch. In Britain, Mary Thomas (voice), Judith Pearce (flute, piccolo), Duncan Druce (violin, viola) and Jennifer Ward Clarke (cello) were also recruited, and in a novel modification of Schoenberg's line-up, the percussionist Tristan Fry completed the membership of this new British 'Pierrot' ensemble. In May 1967, the Pierrot Players staged their first concert. Rigorously rehearsed, their performance of *Pierrot* now had a progeny in the form of Davies's instrumental overture *Antechrist* (1967). The group gave Davies a platform to compose a string of incendiary works. The critical clamour caused especially by *Eight Songs for a Mad King* (1969), reliving George III's mental derangement, catapulted him to the forefront of British musical life.

Co-directing the Pierrot Players, Davies now put parody, sensationalism and melodrama at the heart of his style. His treatment of sources became more overt. In *Fantasia and Two Pavans* (1968) and *St Thomas Wake* (1969), pavans by Bull and Purcell respectively are resurrected as foxtrots; in *Missa super L'Homme Armé* (1968, rev. 1971), a mass undergoes the same transformation, a demonic transposition that attracted the interest of film director Ken Russell, for whom Davies wrote scores for *The Devils* and *The Boy Friend* (both 1971). The themes which had preoccupied Davies up to this point were embodied by his first opera *Taverner* (1962–70), based on a since discredited account of the life of the Tudor composer. Fascinated yet repulsed by religion, Davies was driven by two major anxieties: the hypocrisy of institutionalized belief and the betrayal and persecution of innocence. These have never receded, but events in 1971 led to changes in their musical expression: Davies moved to Orkney in January of that year and has since identified himself and his music with Orcadian culture, history and natural surroundings; a few months later, Birtwistle's fear of his unreasonable comparison with Davies reached its nadir, and he left the Pierrot Players.

Reconstituted as 'The Fires of London', the group continued under Davies's sole direction. He met in Orkney the poet and author George Mackay Brown, on whose work he has frequently drawn. Inspired by the stark sights and sounds of the extreme north, *Stone Litany* (1973) and *Ave Maris Stella* (1975) show Davies's evolution towards a symphonic language which culminated in Symphony No. 1 (1973–6), Symphony No. 2 (1980) and the six other symphonies he has composed since (1984–2000). New possibilities of form intrigued him, from sonata principles to magic squares, and these resources showcased fresh extramusical concerns. Prompted by numerology, mysticism and even alchemy, they reflected legends of Orkney and Scandinavian-influenced lore. The musical and theatrical shock tactics of the previous decade relented, but early works for the Fires – *From Stone to Thorn* (1971) and *Hymn to St Magnus* (1972) – scaled new heights of virtuosity. The group's near-complete change of personnel during the 1976/7 season triggered a renaissance of music theatre. *The Martyrdom of St Magnus* (1976), on the life and death of the Orcadian patron saint, and *Le Jongleur de Notre Dame*

(1977–8) were premiered in Orkney at successive St Magnus Festivals, which Davies founded in 1977 and has since helped every midsummer to direct. *The Lighthouse* (1979) and *The No. 11 Bus* (1983–4) broadened Davies's experimentation with the timbre of his group. Where once a solo dancer (*Vesalii icones*) and tape (the first version of *Missa super L'Homme armé*) were occasional partners to the ensemble, now mime artists, extra instruments (particularly the horn, trumpet and double bass) and groups of singers and dancers became more likely features.

The Fires disbanded in 1987, the same year Davies was knighted. First associate composer-conductor, then composer laureate of the Scottish Chamber Orchestra (from 1985), his direct, regular engagement with performers was uninterrupted. He has so far written nineteen works for them, including ten *Strathclyde Concertos* (1986–96). The erstwhile *enfant terrible* who shocked countless audiences with his dramatization of a senile king succeeded Malcolm Williamson as Master of the Queen's Music in 2004.

Davies's lasting stature is guaranteed by the new canon of music for the 'Pierrot' ensemble he established through his own works and those he commissioned from other composers (including **Elliott Carter**, **Hans Werner Henze** and Judith Weir). His twenty years of domestic and foreign tours also spawned a tradition in which similarly configured groups such as Psappha (UK) and Eighth Blackbird (USA) now tread. Some query whether Davies's prolific urge to compose sustains the quality of his output. This question has recurred as he completes a projected series of ten *Naxos String Quartets* in five years (2002–7). Others observe a composer unafraid to write in a light idiom, yet critical of popular music. Certainly Davies has often used 'commercial' music, especially foxtrots, to represent crudity and moral offence. But the release of extracts in this style, as in *Farewell to Stromness*, currently his best-known work yet derived from *The Yellow Cake Revue* (1980), and *Rock Songs* from the opera *Resurrection* (1987), has attracted a new audience to his music. Because of this, *Resurrection*, especially, may be the work by which his latest period is most appropriately understood. Its allegorical assault on mediocrity and commercial crassness reinvented Davies as a protest figure. *Naxos Quartet No. 3* (2003), denouncing the war in Iraq, shows that despite his royal endorsement he retains that position still.

Further reading

See: Paul Griffiths, *Peter Maxwell Davies* (1982); Richard McGregor (ed.), *Perspectives on Peter Maxwell Davies* (2000). The most recent catalogue of Davies's music is Stewart Craggs (ed.), *Peter Maxwell Davies: A Source Book* (2003). The composer's website (http://www.maxopus.com) offers the latest details on new works, performances and recordings. Most of Davies's music is published either by Schott, Boosey and Hawkes or Chester Music.

CHRISTOPHER DROMEY

DAVIS, Miles Dewey, Jr

1926–91

US jazz trumpeter, composer, bandleader

Miles Davis played a major role in the development of jazz from the mid-1940s to the mid-1970s. His contributions were a personal and influential style of trumpet playing and improvisation, the leadership of innovative bands and recording sessions, and the ability to sense the potential in new forms of music and exploit them.

He was born into a well-to-do Illinois family and was destined for college when he chose music instead. He sought out and attached himself to **Charlie Parker** in New York, becoming the trumpeter in his quintet from 1945 to 1948, and playing on most of Parker's famous Savoy and Dial recordings. His tone was weaker and his articulation less sure than those of other bop trumpeters, but his mastery of the idiom and his improvisation were impressive for a nineteen-year-old.

In 1949 nine musicians gathered for a short engagement at the Royal Roost, and were recorded by Capitol. They made a sound quite unlike swing or bop music hitherto. The arrangements were relaxed, reflective and intimate, and caused the recordings to be titled 'The Birth of the Cool'. Even though he was not perhaps the originator of its ideas, Davis led the band, which was one of the sources of the 'cool jazz' of the 1950s. Most of the players were to be prominent in important bands of their own. Davis himself went on, after a struggle with heroin, to lead a series of quintets through the 1950s, through which passed many major jazz musicians of the period, and whose recordings are considered classics of the post-war era. Davis made a virtue out of necessity where his trumpet playing was concerned, and further refined the small-scale, intimate sound, often playing through a Harmon mute with the stem removed. Whereas bop musicians used flurries of notes, Davis used few, well-chosen, and uttered with emotional intensity, as if to express a restrained passion. Young musicians everywhere began imitating his lack of vibrato, his cracked grace notes, his way of half-valving to make a note droop at the end, his way of giving a new flavour to what seemed unpromising material (e.g. *Bye Bye Blackbird*). In live performances, his personality also added to the aura: he was without consideration for the audience, would play with his back to them, leave the stage when he had finished soloing, and generally maintain that his music was all that he owed the listener. Davis's style was complemented by the very different style of his most important saxophonist, John Coltrane, an improviser of awesome energy.

At the end of the 1950s Davis began playing numbers that, instead of having a sequence of rapidly changing chords, were based on a mode which lasted for a number of bars, and on which the player had more time to improvise melodies (the LP *Kind of Blue*). Meanwhile his trumpet tone developed a broad, rich, burnished quality which was unique in the idiom. In this same period the arranger Gil Evans wrote orchestrations that highlighted Davis's soloing on trumpet or fluegel horn (*Miles Ahead*). The record *Sketches of Spain* (in which Rodrigo's *Concierto de Aranjuez* is played with Evans's arrangement and Davis's trumpet replacing the guitar) belongs in a category of music which has been called 'third stream', attempting to bring classical music and jazz together.

Towards the end of the 1960s, many jazzmen were moving in one of two directions: towards 'free jazz' (in which improvisers were no longer bound to harmonic structures), or towards a 'fusion' with rock music (intenser and more repetitive rhythms, simpler melodies, more use of electronic instruments and effects, less emphasis on solo improvising). Davis experimented with rock, and using a tenor saxophonist, guitarist, rhythm section augmented with assorted percussion, and various players at electronic keyboards, began a series of recordings and live performances which led to his being credited with the innovation of jazz-rock or electro-jazz (*In a Silent Way*, 1968). *Bitches Brew* (1970) established a blend of polyrhythmic free ensemble improvisation which would characterize his music henceforth.

In 1975 Davis retired from performing and recording, partly as a result of poor health. Still not fully fit, he returned in 1981, with rock-based ensembles producing a tighter, more commercially popular retrenchment of his 1970s style (*Star People*, 1983), in which Davis offered himself more affably to the audience than in the past. Overcome by illness, he died in September 1991.

Ever innovating, and refusing to 'repeat', as he put it, the ballad-playing in which he excelled, and which he loved, Davis had transformed bop with his quintets of the 1950s, widening the popularity of modern jazz (*Kind of Blue* is one of the best-known recordings in the history of jazz), and his move towards rock had the same effect, bringing thousands of young people into contact with a jazz music (diluted, perhaps) they would otherwise have ignored.

Further reading

Selected recordings: 1940s on Spotlite and Savoy, Capitol (*Birth of the Cool*); his 1950s recordings

reissued by Prestige, and for CBS: *Milestones* (1958), *Kind of Blue* (1959), *Porgy and Bess* (1958), *Sketches of Spain* (1960), *My Funny Valentine* (1964), *E.S.P.* (1969), *Bitches Brew* (1970), *Live-Evil* (1972), *The Man with Horn* (1981), *Star People* (1983). See: Ian Carr, *Miles Davis: A Biography* (1982); Jack Chambers, *Milestones: The Music and Times of Miles Davis* (2 vols 1983, 1985). See also: Mark Gridley, *Jazz Styles* (1978). Further information at website Miles Ahead: http://www.plosin. com/milesAhead.

CHRISTOPHER WAGSTAFF

DAWKINS, Clinton Richard

1941–

British evolutionist, popular science writer and atheist

Richard Dawkins (he is always known by his second Christian name) was born of an upper-middle-class farming family in Kenya that moved to England when he was eight. He was educated first at Oundle School and then Oxford University, where he studied biology and fell under the influence of the Nobel-Prize winning ethnologist Nikolaas Tinbergen. On receiving his doctorate, Dawkins spent a short time at the University of California at Berkeley, returning then to Oxford where he has been since. He is now the Charles Simonyi Professor of the Public Understanding of Science. He is a Fellow of the Royal Society, and recipient of many awards for his writing as well as numerous honorary degrees.

Dawkins first came to public attention with *The Selfish Gene* (1976), a work of popular science in which he introduced the world to the major moves that had been occurring in recent evolutionary biology, as it turned to look at issues to do with social behaviour. In particular, Dawkins highlighted the way in which evolutionists now adopt a minimalist approach to the mechanism of natural selection, arguing that one should always think of competition as occurring between individuals rather than groups, and preferentially should think of the ultimate processes of evolution as focusing on the units of heredity, the genes, rather than physical organisms. Because evolution pits individual against individual, ultimately gene against gene, the effects are going to be features, adaptations, that benefit the individual rather than the group, one gene rather than another. Hence the title of Dawkins's book, for in the end evolution is producing genes that have or cause features that speak to their own self-interests rather than those of others.

What made Dawkins's book a deserved best-seller was his brilliant use of language, metaphors especially, and the way in which he could so clearly and simply explain the models, especially those drawn from game theory, that are now used extensively by today's evolutionary biologists. At the end of the book, Dawkins suggested that human culture might be driven by units analogous to genes at the biological level. The supposition that there might be such units, that Dawkins labelled 'memes', has attracted some attention in recent years, although many argue that this is a simplistic approach to the complexities of culture.

The years after this first book saw Dawkins extending his scope and interests. His next best-selling book was *The Blind Watchmaker* (1986) where he covered the whole of evolutionary biology, arguing that Darwin's mechanism of natural selection is overwhelmingly the key to ongoing organic change. A particularly attractive feature of this book was the way in which Dawkins drew on a longstanding interest in computers to make points about the possibility of an unguided natural process to produce the complex adaptations that we see in the living world.

An underlying theme of this book, one that has become more and more prominent in Dawkins's writings in the subsequent twenty years, was that natural selection explains the features that in pre-Darwinian times had been explained as the direct intervention of the Christian God. At this point Dawkins was primarily concerned to show that modern biology can do all that traditionally the deity was supposed to do. Hence the subtitle of his book: 'Why the Evidence of Evolution Reveals a Universe without Design'. However, in subsequent writings, Dawkins showed greater and greater antipathy to any and all kinds of religious belief, arguing that it is both false and dangerous.

Since the destruction of the World Trade Center in 2001, Dawkins has been ecumenical in his hatred of all religions, arguing that Islam is if anything an even greater threat to humankind than is Christianity. It is not always obvious why Dawkins thinks that religion is false. Sometimes he appeals to the traditional problem of evil. Sometimes he simply assumes that in an age of science it is obvious that religion must be false. It is even less obvious that Dawkins's deep hatred of religion is always helpful in achieving the ends that he desires. Particularly in America, the biblical literalists welcome all and any writings by Dawkins, justifiably confident that his extremism will upset all theists, even those of moderate persuasion, and that people will naturally link Dawkins's positive passion for evolutionary biology with his negative passion for Christian belief.

Dawkins's most recent work, *The Ancestor's Tale: A Pilgrimage to the Dawn of Life* (2005), is the story of life's evolution, with the twist that Dawkins starts in the present with our own species, and then works back to the first forms of living beings. By using *Homo sapiens* as a starting point, Dawkins makes completely explicit a theme that underlies much of his writings, namely that although he rejects the Christian claim that humans are special because we are made in the image of God, he does agree that humans are in some sense the pinnacle of evolution. He has often written favourably of the notion of biological arms races, where organisms compete against each other and thereby improve, and he argues that the end process of this kind of competition is the human species. Dawkins denies vehemently that this is providing the basis for a secular religion that can replace Christianity, but it is certainly the case that, like many humanists, Dawkins is drawn to a world picture that makes sense precisely because we humans are in some sense different from and above the rest of the living world.

Further reading

Other than the two best-selling popular books noted above, Dawkins most detailed scientific book is *The Extended Phenotype* (1982), a careful discussion of the workings of natural selection. More popular, recent works, where the hostility towards Christianity starts to appear strongly, include *River out of Eden* (1996) and *A Devil's Chaplain* (2003). A good overview of his thinking, comparing him with his fellow evolutionist and popular science writer **Stephen Jay Gould**, is *Dawkins vs Gould* (2001), by the philosopher Kim Sterelny.

MICHAEL RUSE

DE KOONING, Willem

1904–97

US artist

Willem de Kooning was born in Rotterdam, studied at the Academy there, and in 1926 emigrated to the United States as a stowaway. He took a studio in New York where he became friends with Arshile Gorky, and in 1935 worked on the federal WPA (Works Progress Administration) project. He was a leader of what subsequently became known as 'Abstract Expressionism', and it was his vigorously physical approach to painting, the seemingly endless search for the right 'fit', each stage of the process a challenge to ever bolder revisions, that provided the model for Harold Rosenberg's existentialist interpretation 'Action Painting'. De Kooning's influence was at its height in the 1950s (his first one-man show was not until 1948) but his art has developed uninterrupted from the 1930s to the 1980s, when ill-health forced him to stop work.

The early paintings – tense abstractions drawing on **Mondrian** and **Miró**, and solitary figures disintegrating into melancholy but luminous backgrounds – have a hard and repressed quality. Opaque planes alternate with transparent apertures across the surface, and focal points (such as the eyes, the exposed shoulder-joints, the vase in the beautiful portrait, *The Glazier* of 1940) control the eye's travel. Only the sinewy contour, an incisive line that seeks out its own shapes – shapes that become distinctively de Kooning's own and reappear through all his phases – disturbs the stillness. Gradually the paintings gain in fluency, as the implied formal metamorphoses of the image, the restless ambiguity of its space, become fused with the physical momentum – the thrusts and drips of the brush, the energized glare of heightened colour – of the painting process. A series of paintings of women became increasingly urgent or 'pressured', the line thrusting and looping, the colour rising to pinks, reds, yellows, blues, until the figure dissolved in a swirl of disembodied limbs (e.g. *Pink Angels* of 1945). There followed a magnificent group of black paintings with white linear motifs (deriving from the alphabet or landscape details) carrying a continuous rhythm of light and texture across the entire surface (see *Light in August*, 1946, or *Dark Pond*, 1948, for example). It was at this time that **Pollock** and de Kooning were at their closest, both using dripped black enamel paint across all-over undifferentiated fields. But de Kooning's shapes came to re-establish their identity, to separate from the pattern in sharp juxtaposition (they were frequently derived from collaged drawings, a practice that was to remain constant), with white and flesh tints now predominating over black (e.g. *Attic* of 1949) culminating in *Excavation* of 1950, where flashes of eyes, teeth, lips intersperse the seething crush of form.

De Kooning's grimacing goddess/pin-up, *Woman I* of 1950–2, his best-known work, surprised many of his followers who took abstraction to be an irreversible step. Both hilarious and hysterical, the painting marked an extreme of painterly ferocity, the brush gouging, tearing, slapping the surface. The *Women* series evolved into gritty 'urban' abstract paintings (e.g. *Easter Monday* of 1956), with the same high velocity and impacted scaffolding, giving way to much simplified landscape images (e.g. *Suburb in Havana*, 1958) of boldly gestured verticals, diagonals and horizontals. Hereafter his paintings became calmer and more pastoral (he moved to the countryside outside New York in 1963), reaching new extremes of loose watery handling and soft exultantly erotic colouring (e.g. *Clam Diggers*, 1964, or *Untitled II*, 1976). Figures shimmer and dissolve into landscape, and landscape merges into gestural rhythm, so that the figurative/abstract polarity has little meaning. Counteracting the elusive immateriality of these images perhaps, de Kooning became preoccupied with aggressively massed clay sculpture.

If the earlier work synthesized cubist linear discipline and surrealist freedom, this late work can be seen to incorporate the sensuality of Rubens or Boucher, the rich physicality of Courbet, and yet it remained as toughly measured, and free of the rhetoric of Expressionism, as ever. It's arguable that it's the unlikely compass of de Kooning's art, combined with its pressing vitality, each phase a complete renewal, that puts it on a par with **Picasso** and **Matisse**. And like them, his importance is not as an innovator but as an artist who embodied, to a spectacular degree, an irrepressible inventiveness.

Further reading

See: Harold Rosenberg, *The Tradition of the New* (1959) and *William de Kooning* (1974). See also *William de Kooning*, exhibition catalogue of the Museum of Modern Art (New York, 1968); S. Yard, *Willem de Kooning* (1995).

JAMES FAURE WALKER

DEBUSSY, (Achille-) Claude

1862–1918

French composer

The composer who liked to sign himself '*musicien français*' was born of a line of farmers and artisans, and nothing in his heritage appears to have predisposed him to a musical career. In fact, his parents envisaged for him a career as a sailor. What may well have been a decisive influence came when he was eight years old – a meeting with Madame Mauté de Fleurville, a pupil of Chopin and mother-in-law of the poet **Verlaine**; and for three years he studied piano with her prior to entering the Paris Conservatoire. This early link with Chopin and Verlaine is indeed peculiarly significant: Chopin was perhaps the most important single musical influence in the formation of Debussy's highly individual style of composition; while Verlaine and other poets and writers of the time were part of an immensely influential literary ambience into which Debussy entered completely. At the Conservatoire he showed a mixture of brilliance and waywardness which led (not without difficulties) to his being awarded the coveted Prix de Rome. In Rome, however, he disliked intensely his stay at the Villa Medici, and fled from it twice, back to Paris, the second time for good.

His first work of lasting interest from about this time is *La Damoiselle élue* (written in 1887–8), a setting of a French version of Rossetti's 'Blessed Damozel' for solo voices, chorus and orchestra – a work which struck the academic judges as 'vague', with its fluctuating harmonies and rhythms. **Wagner** at the time was the idol of the Paris artistic world. Debussy greatly admired his *Tristan and Isolde*, and had the opportunity to hear Wagner operas at Bayreuth in 1888 and 1889. It was a strong influence against which he was later to react. Meanwhile, a Wagnerian richness pervaded some of his earlier compositions. Then he became acquainted with the score of **Mussorgsky's** opera *Boris Godunov*, and immediately he was an ardent admirer of that composer's original and very personal form of expression. This and other Russian influences, the fascination of the Javanese gamelan (heard at the Paris Exposition Universelle), and contact with the economical style of the composer Erik Satie – all these elements were reflected in Debussy's work; in the String Quartet (1893), and above all in the *Prélude à l'après-midi d'un faune* (1892–4) which was his first fully personal expression. In this work he conveyed the spirit of the poem *L'Après-midi d'un faune*, by his close friend **Mallarmé**, in a style which was closely related to the Symbolist movement in the arts – a style in which ideas and states of mind are *suggested* by symbols, and these symbols become more significant, in the inner world of reflection, than any external reality. Herein lies the essence of Debussy's mature style – and comparisons with Impressionism can be quite misleading. Some of Debussy's most fully characteristic work is found in his songs – his settings of Symbolist poets such as Verlaine, **Baudelaire**, Mallarmé: the *Fêtes galantes* (Verlaine) of 1903 which range from the brilliantly imaginative 'Fantoches' to the quiet intimacy of the 'Colloque sentimental'; the passionate hope and despair of the *Cinq Poèmes de Baudelaire* (1887–9); the mixture of depth of expression and preciosity in his Mallarmé settings. The *Chansons de Bilitis* (1897) captured perfectly the simple, clear, erotic character of the prose-poems (supposed to be the work of a girl of Ancient Greece) by his friend Pierre Louÿs, for whose writings Debussy felt a particular sympathy. And there is a stark dramatic quality in the *Trois Ballades de François Villon*, a striking impression of the past seen through modern eyes. For the set of *Proses lyriques* (1892–3) Debussy wrote his own poems, with mixed results.

His freedom from conventional formulae is clearly shown in his opera *Pelléas et Mélisande* (composed between 1892 and 1902), which reflects the elusive, legendary atmosphere of Maeterlinck's play, all half-lights and suggestion. Revolutionary in its unemphatic recitative-like style, the opera was ridiculed by the critics, but it was nevertheless a success with the public and had a number of performances, later becoming part of the standard operatic repertoire. He tried other operatic ideas, but they were not brought to satisfactory completion. The elaborate incidental music which Debussy wrote for Gabriele D'Annunzio's spectacular mystery play *Le Martyre de Saint-Sébastien* contains much of importance; but performances are rare, and without the dramatic context the music loses much of its point.

In the *Prélude à l'après-midi d'un faune* Debussy was translating sensual and emotional impressions into the symbolic language of music, and was departing from traditional and fixed forms, 'liquidating' tonality and tonal procedures in ways that were as significant and far-reaching as the processes which **Schoenberg** was carrying out at about the same time. Important to Debussy also was tone-colour and rhythmic subtlety as ingredients in his style – a style which profoundly affected the work of practically every twentieth-century composer.

It is mostly through the earlier orchestral works that Debussy's full development as a composer is seen: the *Nocturnes* (1887–9), *La Mer* (1903–5), and *Images* (1906–12). The three *Nocturnes* may well have been suggested directly by the series of paintings with the same title by Whistler, whom Debussy admired – and the composer himself said that the movements were intended to convey 'all the various impressions and special effects of light that the word suggests'. With *La Mer* (a work in three closely linked movements, like a symphony) the first impulse may have been pictorial also – Turner's sea pictures, which made a deep impression on the composer. Form and content are both strong in this work, but we see it against a many-sided background, a fusion of the arts, a fusion of nature and art. It is far more than a purely musical impact. In the scherzo movement ('Jeux de vagues') Debussy showed that he was able to unify, to bind together consistently, extremely diverse textures and timbres on a background of ever-changing tonalities. This technique was further explored in the ballet *Jeux* (1912) – a technique (or style) which has been described by **Pierre Boulez** as follows: 'A component section of a theme is defined as another is suggested; another phrase is added and we have the beginnings of a form. More material is added and we have a structure.' On the face of it, *Jeux* is not sensational (its thunder was stolen by **Stravinsky's** *Rite of Spring*, which appeared at the same time and was more obviously revolutionary); the advance was a logical stage in Debussy's evolution – a greater degree of clarity in the freedom of form and the attitude to thematic material, structure, orchestral textures, timbres, rhythm. It was an outlook and technique which immediately foreshadowed later 'avant-garde' procedures.

The orchestral *Images* are three separate compositions – not a unified structure as *La Mer* was. Each is an extremely personal expression of a composer at the height of his powers. The first section, 'Gigues' (originally 'Gigues tristes'), was probably suggested by a poem of Verlaine, 'Streets', written in London (which city Debussy visited on more than one occasion), and the work incorporates treatments of 'The Keel Row', a dance-song associated with England's Tyneside district. In the second movement, 'Ibéria', the atmosphere and rhythms of Spain are brilliantly conveyed. With the third movement, 'Rondes de Printemps', we are back in France: a complex and subjective evocation of the reawakening of nature, introducing some very unobvious treatments of folk-song material.

The important piano compositions of Debussy belong to the later part of his life: the two series of *Images* (1905 and 1907), and in particular the twenty-four *Préludes* (in two books, 1910 and 1910–13), which sensitively explore an enormous range of mood, character and feeling, within the expressive and technical range of the piano as opened out by Chopin. We know that Debussy was a fine pianist. Those who heard him play have told of his remarkable quality of touch and an entirely personal way of using the sustaining pedal. A further development in his piano style was the remarkable *Douze Études* (1915), in a sense a homage to Chopin, but also a personal technical accomplishment of vital importance.

In the early years of the century, Debussy wrote: 'Every sound you hear around you can be reproduced. Everything that a keen ear perceives in the rhythm of the surrounding world can be represented musically.' The result was a richly imaginative world of elusive harmonies and rhythms; melodies and chords drawn from the whole-tone scale and other unusual scales; chords regarded as colour, often with 'dissonances' unresolved,

and colour many times as an end in itself; the placing of an unusual chord (related to overtones) on every note of a melodic phrase; oriental flavour and design in ornamental passages; abrupt, unprepared modulations, 'false' relations, and tonally rapidly shifting focal points. As Verlaine had suggested that the poetic image should be '*plus vague et plus soluble dans l'air*' – so too with music, more indefinite and more fluid in the air, with nothing to weigh it down.

Although Debussy, through this kind of freedom, loosened classical tonality, he did not destroy it, as Schoenberg had felt obliged to do. Focal points remained, however flexible. A richer, freer and essentially positive attitude towards tonality was the result of Debussy's innovations. His sensual and picturesque imagination created a new, instinctive, dreamlike world of music, lyrical and pantheistic, contemplative and objective.

Further reading

The most important works of Debussy are all mentioned above. They are mostly published by Durand, Paris. About Debussy: Léon Vallas, *Debussy, sa vie et ses oeuvres* (1926, trans. 1933); Edward Lockspeiser, *Debussy, His Life and Mind* (2 vols, 1962 and 1965); Stefan Jarocinski, trans. Rollo Myers, *Debussy – Impressionism and Symbolism* (1976); David Cox, *Debussy's Orchestral Music* (1974); Roger Nichols, *Debussy* (1972); Alfred Cortot, *The Piano Music of Debussy* (1922); M. Cobb, *The Poetic Debussy* (1994); R. Langham Smith, *Debussy Studies* (1997); R. Nichols, *A Life of Debussy* (1998).

DAVID COX

DEGAS, Edgar

1834–1917

French painter and sculptor

Edgar Degas was born in Paris, the eldest child of a banker. His grandfather, whose family bank it was, had fled to Naples during the Revolution. Degas's mother was a Creole from the United States and died when the artist was thirteen. After a sound classical education Degas enrolled as a law student in

1853 but soon abandoned his studies in favour of painting. He copied the drawings of masters like Mantegna and Leonardo in the print-room of the Bibliothèque Nationale and began to frequent the studio of an Ingres disciple, Louis Lamothe. As a boy Degas had met Ingres who greatly impressed him and who advised him to '*Faites des lignes et des lignes.*' For Ingres, as for Degas, drawing was the 'probity of art'. From 1857 until 1860 Degas spent much time in Italy where he continued to study drawing and painting. He became intimate with the group of French artists, writers and musicians who stayed at the Villa Medicis and met great luminaries such as Gustave Moreau, **Bizet** and Edmond About.

Moreau particularly influenced Degas's early preference for history painting. Examples of these early works include *The Young Spartans* (1860) and *The Daughter of Jephthah* (1861–4). In *The Young Spartans* Degas's concern with contemporary reality can be discerned in the deliberately Montmartre-style snub-noses of the children. Degas's return to Paris in 1859 decisively altered the course of his career. He became familiar with the newly fashionable Japanese prints which were available at the print-shop of Mme Desoye in the rue de Rivoli and began to form contacts with the more radical realists and future Impressionists. Men like **Manet** and **Renoir**, the painters, and **Zola** and Duranty, the writers, became his closest intellectual companions. The master-piece of his early career is probably the group portrait *The Belleli Family* (1860–2), in which one can see his various interests perfectly balanced. The drawing is classically cool and precise; the grouping of the figures against the rectangles of the background and the slight tensions between the poses of the figures show an interest in Japanese composition, as does the use of the patterned wallpaper; and the youngest girl's left leg 'replaced' as it were by the legs of the chair she is sitting on reveals Degas's slightly bleak humour and his sense of the artificiality of his work.

During 1860s Degas began to draw and paint race-horses, theatre scenes and ballet dancers. In 1870, during the Franco-Prussian War, he served in the Garde Nationale and may have injured his eyesight while sleeping out in the cold. In 1872–3 he visited his mother's home town of New Orleans in America and was greatly exhilarated by the change of culture. His *Cotton Market* (1873) shows his increasing concern for the canons of naturalism and his great skill with a limited palette. In 1874 his father died and he was forced to sell some of his now large drawings collection to help the family. It was during this year that he played a decisive part in organizing the first Impressionist exhibition, held at the old studio of the photographer Nadar. Degas was not an Impressionist *pur sang* for, although he was friendly with **Monet**, Renoir and others, he believed deeply in the virtues of fine draughtsmanship and in the necessity for deliberated composition. He preferred artificial to natural light and was more interested in the movement of the human figure than in landscape or *plein air* effects. Very late in his life he said, 'If I were the government I would have a company of police watching out for men who paint landscapes from nature,' adding good-humouredly that his friend Renoir could do as he wished. Degas, however, contributed many works to all the remaining Impressionist shows, including decorated fans and sculpture. His later life was spent producing an enormous amount of work. He became interested in photography, which he used as an aid in composition, and was particularly fascinated by the work of Muybridge whose chrono-photography allowed one to catch the progressive changes of movement in a human body performing an action. This was of great use to Degas in his studies of dancers and horses. Degas was also a remarkable technical innovator and may be said to have radically expanded the possibilities of the graphic arts. Like a number of artists often dubbed 'conservative' he believed that a very great part of the artist's power lay in his craft knowledge and dedication to study. He told Vuillard, 'A painting is an artificial work existing outside nature and it requires as much cunning as the perpetration of a crime.' In 1887 he travelled in Spain and Morocco. In the 1890s, although he drew and painted (often using curious techniques like pastel brushed with hot water on to the paper), his eyesight was deteriorating seriously and he executed more sculptures, in wax and plaster, which were easier for him to work. He continued to extend his superb collection of art. He virtually stopped work in 1908 and died in Paris in 1917. He had told a friend to avoid making a long oration at his funeral and that 'You might just say he loved drawing.'

Degas's influence on the visual arts has been very great. He brought to perfection the possibilities of the naturalist aesthetic while retaining those traditional elements of painting he so greatly valued. He sought an art which combined rigorous drawing with realist subject-matter. His style is as greatly informed by a study of Titian and Delacroix as it is by a temperamental preference for Ingres and Mantegna; as much by Leonardo's observation of surface as by the snapshot of photography and Duranty's realist credo. Although he was a political conservative, being an anti-Dreyfusard and holding a dandyish contempt for the masses, he was concerned with men and women in their social aspect. His influence on painters like Sickert, **Gauguin**, **Toulouse-Lautrec**, Bonnard, Vuillard and **Picasso** is perhaps incalculable. His celibacy and utter dedication to his art, his prizing of the intellect and inherited sensibility and taste, were the qualities that drew the poet **Valéry** to him. In his story *An Evening with Monsieur Teste* Valéry tells of an aloof and lonely figure who observes the audience at the opera with a visionary precision and control and whose personal habits are few and astringent. He has Leonardo's intellect and **Mallarmé's** remote imagination. Monsieur Teste was in part Valéry's idealized perception of Degas's mind itself.

Further reading

See: *Lettres de Degas*, ed. M. Guérin (1945, trans. 1947); John Rewald, *Degas' Sculpture: The Complete Works* (1956); J. Adhémar and F. Cachin, *Edgar Degas: Gravures et Monotypes* (Paris, 1973); *Notebooks of Degas*, ed. T. Reff (2 vols, 1976); T. Reff, *Degas: The Artist's Mind* (1976); R. McCullen, *Degas: His Life, Times and Work* (1984); D. Sutton, *Edward Degas: Life and Work* (1986).

RICHARD HUMPHREYS

DeLILLO, Don

1936–

US novelist

Don DeLillo was born in New York City of Italian immigrant parents where he recalls playing football and baseball on the streets of the Bronx. He has always said that he slept through Cardinal Hayes High School and learned everything by rote at Fordham University, thus summing up what he thought of Catholic education. His degree was in a then new discipline invented in the 1950s in several American universities: 'communications art'. The new degree attempted to combine traditional journalism and literature with the new medium of television. It also provided DeLillo with the training for postgraduate employment with a large advertising agency, Ogilvie & Mather.

His first short story was published in *Epoch* in 1960 and he managed to place several stories in the next few years, enough to encourage him to quit the ad agency in 1964. He supported himself with freelance writing of various kinds while working on his first novel *Americana* which was not published until 1971. This was followed by two more novels about 'Americana': *End Zone* (1972) about college football; and *Great Jones Street* (1973) about the rock music world. In each novel the protagonist tries to find and protect his own individual expression, often by abandoning his skills in a group and isolating himself in some small chosen room. His early themes seem concentrated in his examinations of American pop culture and life, but they are also rooted in his undergraduate studies of 'communications' and his first job of media manipulation through advertisements. He clearly fears the mass manipulation of people through the corruption of word and image.

By 1980 reviewers and academic critics were beginning to hail DeLillo as part of the next generation of 'postmodernist' novelists: following in the tradition of **John Barth**, **Thomas Pynchon** and Robert Coover. DeLillo has given a few interviews in which he has brushed aside who his literary influences are; instead he suggests the question should be 'What is there in your life – public or private – that has influenced you?' And he has his own answer, of course: the 1963 **Kennedy** assassination. What has informed his writing since then is the difficulty of perceiving truth. The famous Zapruder film of the seconds of the actual shooting – now a piece of Americana for ever – is engraved in many American minds. So many people have created so many conspiracy/fictions based on the film and other evidence that DeLillo has clearly learned the essential difficulties of reading and recording reality. If it is difficult to know who you are in the bewildering world of American media and communication, then how much more difficult it must be to understand the external world.

In 1985 DeLillo published *White Noise* which won the National Book Award and widespread praise. His hero, a professor of **Hitler** Studies, hides that he hasn't a word of German. Many academics have rejoiced in the satiric comments on university 'communication' and the depiction of middle-class consumerism, family and campus life. The white noise is all the babble of advertisements, radio transmissions, TV programmes and other emissions of cultural noise that interferes with people seeing their world.

Ironically, his biggest commercial success was *Libra* in 1988, a drama around the John F. Kennedy slaying which featured both fictional characters and a detailed imagining of assassin Lee Harvey Oswald's life and character. One can't help thinking that the convoluted plot of the novel and the killing end up being another conspiracy theory instead of the intended explanation of why Americans need conspiracy theories to explain the world. DeLillo, when he fails, fails always on the side of ambition.

His most ambitious novel *Underworld* (1997) sketches a portrait of America over five decades beginning with a dazzling scene at perhaps the most famous baseball game in US history, certainly so for most New Yorkers of DeLillo's generation: a game of last-minute heroics between the New York Giants and Brooklyn Dodgers in which a home run in the final seconds defeated the Dodgers for a league championship in 1951. DeLillo places J. Edgar Hoover in the stands with the then very popular TV star Jackie Gleason, and a frenetic Frank Sinatra. It's a great beginning that becomes lost in the 800 pages that follow. The author wants to document the paranoia of the Cold War in the second half of the century, but loses his readers in too much seemingly unrelated detail. As one exasperated critic remarked, 'it's a very powerful book and heavy too. Just right for smacking noisy children.'

His most recent novel, *Cosmopolis* (2003), examines the world of instant millionaires and stock manipulation with its billionaire 'asset manager', who is spending his time in a new kind of 'small room' (a limo), struggling to cross town to get a haircut in the midst of a presidential visit that has tied up traffic while gambling on the exchange market. Here different characters drop into his limo from a chaotic and valueless world that seems increasingly threatening. Billionaires may also be Americana, especially the youthful bubble millionaires of recent decades.

DeLillo loves the immigrant American dreams of his parents ('the sense of possibility') and longs to see them continue, but he is at his strongest with his brilliant images and situations reflecting the isolation of people in the midst of a deterioration of language. None is stronger than the *Cosmopolis* image of the frustrated hero struggling in the clogged streets jammed with trapped people trying to do a simple task while being besieged by a world he has tried to avoid. DeLillo refuses to accept all the white noise of an increasingly rootless culture. In his own increasingly challenging and technically brilliant novels, he continues to follow his own advice: 'American writers ought to stand and live in the margins and be more dangerous.'

Further reading

See: Douglas Keesey, *Don Delillo* (1993).

CHARLES GREGORY

DeMILLE, Cecil Blount

1881–1959

US film director

Claudette Colbert bathing in ass's milk in *The Sign of the Cross* (1932) is an image which encapsulates a commonly held view of Cecil B. DeMille's work. He is often associated only with vulgar Hollywood versions of biblical and Roman history, Christian moralizing sold with sex and spectacle in films like *The Ten Commandments* (1923, remade in 1959), *King of Kings* (1927), *Cleopatra* (1934) and *Samson and Delilah* (1949). However, such a view hardly does justice to the interest of the director's forty-two-year Hollywood career, and the seventy-six films he made between 1914 and 1956.

From 1900 DeMille was involved with theatre, as actor and playwright, and also opera, as singer and director, until, in 1913, together with Samuel Goldwyn and Jesse Lasky, he established the Lasky Feature Play Company, which would later form part of Paramount. DeMille directed *The Squaw Man* (which he would remake twice) in 1914 – the company's first production and the first-ever feature to be made in Hollywood. It was a huge success, costing $25,450 and grossing $255,000. DeMille's subsequent silent films, fifty-one in all, are extraordinarily diverse in character. They include Westerns,

supernatural and psychological dramas, and range from the historical spectacle of *Joan the Woman* (1916), through powerful, exotic melodramas like *The Cheat* (1915), to social comedies such as *Male and Female* (1919) and *Why Change Your Wife?* (1920). The latter are particularly interesting as worthy forerunners of Ernst Lubitsch's later, similar and more celebrated work within the genre.

DeMille formed his own production company in 1925, which was responsible for five films, including *King of Kings*. Then, after a brief period with MGM, for whom he made *Dynamite* (1929), his first sound movie, he returned to Paramount in 1932. His association with the latter company continued until the end of his career. DeMille's best work from the 1930s and 1940s is his series of big-budget adventure films, dealing with events, and semi-legendary characters, from eighteenth- and nineteenth-century American history. *The Plainsman* (1936) starred Gary Cooper as Wild Bill Hickok, while Fredric March played Jean Lafitte in *The Buccaneer* (1938). *Union Pacific* (1939) dealt, in spectacular fashion, with the building of the famous railroad, and was followed by *North West Mounted Police* (1939), *Reap the Wild Wind* (1942) and *Unconquered* (1947). DeMille's achievement in these films was to combine pleasing spectacle (they are all to a degree 'epics') with a very sure sense of narrative construction and pace. Perhaps the most useful point of comparison, in terms of locating the films within American culture, is Fenimore Cooper's *Leatherstocking Tales*. As a group they clearly contrast strikingly with the 'sophisticated' comedy and musicals with which Paramount is usually associated at this time.

The director's last three films tie in squarely with his 'public image'. *Samson and Delilah* and *The Ten Commandments* featured, respectively, Victor Mature as Samson and Charlton Heston as Moses, while *The Greatest Show on Earth* (1952) was an all-star circus drama. They were all massive financial successes, aided by DeMille's customary vigorous promotion campaigns, but certainly compare unfavourably with his earlier sound work.

DeMille is one of the comparatively few filmmakers who might justifiably be described as a 'household name'. But whereas 'Hitchcock' is associated with an identifiable body of work, 'DeMille', rather like 'Walt Disney', has the strong connotation of Hollywood as institution – its supposed values, its cynicism, excess and success. This is deceptive, as regards both the man and the oeuvre. Many of his early films failed in financial terms. He regarded himself as a thwarted 'serious' artist, whose later success was the result of consciously conceding to Hollywood's commercial demands – he gave them the product they required while believing that he was, to some extent, compromising himself. And his oft-proclaimed belief in the moral worth of his epics ('Who else – except the missionaries of God – has had our opportunity to make the brotherhood of man not a phrase but a reality?') may well have been as sincere as his passionate post-Second World War campaign against communism. In terms of the films themselves, DeMille's considerable achievements in the silent era have been overshadowed by the critical attention paid to **D.W. Griffith**. The former should be recognized as an equally crucial figure in the early history and development of the American cinema. And the solid virtues of the previously mentioned adventure films should not be overlooked – DeMille is too easily and often dismissed as signifying only Bible and box-office.

Further reading

See: *The Autobiography of Cecil B. DeMille*, ed. Donald Hayne (1960); Gene Ringgold and DeWitt Bodeen, *The Films of Cecil B. DeMille* (1969); Paolo Cherchi Usai and Lorenzo Codelli (eds), *The DeMille Legacy* (1991); Sumiko Higashi, *Cecil B. DeMille and American Culture: The Silent Era* (1994); Robert S. Birchard, *Cecil B. DeMille's Hollywood* (2003).

STEVE JENKINS

DENG XIAOPING (TENG HSIAO-PING)

1904–97

Chinese leader

In the twenty-one centuries of China's imperial history it was often the second emperor of a new dynasty who determined whether the dynasty survived and prospered. Thus was the Tang dynasty secured by the Emperor Taizong (r. 626–49), and the Manchu Qing dynasty by the Kangxi Emperor (r. 1661–1722). Similarly, the contemporary People's Republic of China (PRC), inaugurated in 1949 after a protracted civil war between communists and nationalists, may be said to owe its continuance to its 'second emperor', Deng Xiaoping. If **Mao Zedong** was the architect of the communist victory and the establishment of China's one-party state, it was Deng who, following Mao's death in 1976, made the system work, even though supreme power was nominally exercised by the relatively ineffectual Hua Guofeng until 1981.

Deng was born Deng Xiansheng into the 'small landlord' class in a village near Guangan, Sichuan province. 'Xiaoping', meaning 'Little Peace', was only adopted, as a *nom de guerre*, in 1926. He was educated, at his father's expense, locally and at middle school in Chongqing, before embarking for France in 1920. Li Yuying, a wealthy and patriotic philanthropist who subscribed to the 'self-improvement' ideals touted by Kang Youwei and other late nineteenth-century progressives, had some while before set up the Sino-French Education Association to enable Chinese students to study in Europe, and Deng was among many hundreds who benefited from this imaginative but overly-ambitious scheme. Within a year of his departure the Association was bankrupt, and Deng's five years in France were spent scratching a living as an ill-paid factory worker when he was not engaged as a political activist on behalf of a **Marxist** youth party. His editorship of an agitprop newssheet called 'Red Light' led to his being nicknamed the 'Doctor of Mimeography';

and in France Deng struck up an enduring relationship with Zhou Enlai, a fellow student destined to become the PRC's foreign minister, as well as, in many ways, Mao's right-hand man.

In 1926 Deng left Paris for Moscow, a day before a warrant was issued for his arrest as a subversive. There he enrolled first at the University for the Toilers of the East, sponsored by **Stalin** to incubate Asian revolutionaries, and then at the Sun Yat-sen University. At the end of the same year he returned to China as a political officer in the entourage of Feng Yuxiang, the 'Christian' warlord whom the Comintern had decided to offer limited support; and in June 1927 Deng was ordered to Hangzhou, where he was given the sensitive position of secretary to the Communist Party's Central Committee by the CCP's leader, Chen Duxiu.

Deng's star rose rapidly. In 1929, having narrowly escaped a purge of communists in Shanghai, he was made political commissioner for Guangxi province, charged with building up party membership, and then preparing an uprising. The uprising failed, and even more disastrous was Deng's participation in an attempt to capture Wuhan from the nationalists (Guomindang) on the orders of Li Lisan. But although Deng was briefly 'disciplined' in 1931, his obvious organizational abilities meant that he was quickly appointed general-secretary of the Red Army's political department. He also became editor-in-chief of the communist military's principal propaganda vehicle, the *Red Star*.

Over the next two decades Deng excelled as an increasingly senior party member, and as a supporter of Mao. Together with the soldier Liu Bocheng he created an extended communist 'base area' on the borders of Shanxi, Hebei, Shandong and Henan provinces, from which an important element of the war against the occupying Japanese (1937–45) was fought. For his efforts Deng was elevated to the Central Committee in 1945, being listed twenty-eighth in the overall party rankings. During the civil war against the Guomindang he again linked up

with Liu, with whom he directed the communist campaign between the Yellow and Yangtze rivers, culminating in the capture of Nanjing and Shanghai in 1949.

The People's Republic established, Deng became political commissioner and Party Secretary for the south-western provinces of Sichuan, Guizhou, Yunnan and Xikang. There he hunted down remnants of the Guomindang, oversaw the dismantling of the landlord class, and was the man immediately responsible for the military operations that led to the annexation of Tibet as an 'autonomous region' within the PRC. For these endeavours Deng was made a state vice-premier in 1952, and shortly afterwards appointed Minister of Finance.

These promotions gave Deng sixth overall party ranking, but also placed him in hazardous proximity to Mao. His appointment as Secretary-General of the Central Committee in 1954 in particular proved a poisoned chalice, since it later enabled Mao to accuse Deng of running an 'autonomous empire' within the party. Although Deng supported, and implemented, Mao's 'anti-rightist' campaign of 1957, matters began coming to a head in 1958, when to Deng, Liu Shaoqi and others on the politburo it became transparent that Mao's Great Leap Forward, designed to fast-track China's economic development, was backfiring miserably. At the same time, in a prolonged debate about the place of individual leadership within the communist movement, Deng refused to embrace Mao's Stalinist view that the party leader was necessarily beyond reproach, arguing instead that the leader should 'stand above' neither the party nor the masses.

In the short term such differences between Deng and Mao cost Deng little. Indeed, when Liu effectively took over the reins of government in 1961, Deng played a crucial role in the programme of reconstruction needed to reverse the pitfalls of the Great Leap Forward. In the longer term, however, they nearly cost Deng his life. When in 1966 Mao regrouped and launched the 'Great Proletarian Cultural Revolution', Deng was castigated as 'Number Two Capitalist Roadster', second only to Liu. Harassed by the Red Guards, in 1967 he was made to offer 'self-criticism' before being stripped of his offices and banished to Nanchang (Jiangxi province) to work in a tractor-repair factory. That he did not suffer graver punishment, and was allowed to keep his party membership, was almost certainly due to the intervention of Zhou Enlai.

Zhou may also have been responsible for Deng's recall in 1973, when Mao needed old party stalwarts to contain the extreme radicalism of his wife Jiang Qing and her 'Gang of Four'. Zhou's death in January 1976, however, and the temporary resurgence of Jiang, forced Deng to flee Beijing for Guangzhou, and it was not until 1977 that he resumed his positions in Beijing, under Hua Guofeng. By 1981, through astute politicking, Hua had been comprehensively sidelined, and Deng was China's undisputed 'paramount leader'.

Deng had already embarked on the programme of economic reform and liberalization for which the period of his leadership is chiefly celebrated by the Chinese – even though the 'Four Modernizations' (of agriculture, industry, defence, and science and technology) adumbrated by him in 1978 had first been proposed by Zhou twelve years earlier. To make modernization work, Deng restored incentive by reintroducing private ownership – helped by the systematic transfer of state assets into the hands of individuals closely connected to government at both the national and provincial levels. He encouraged the opening of China's first stock markets, and created 'special economic zones' that accelerated capitalist enterprise, at the same time opening China's doors to massive inward investment by American, Japanese, European and other foreign companies.

Through such devices Deng reversed the crippling legacy of ailing state-owned industries that were not only uncompetitive in the international market, but were domestically suffocating. In defiance of much of what Mao and particularly Jiang Qing had stood for, Deng proclaimed that 'to get rich is glorious'.

Other lauded triumphs of his leadership included negotiating the return of Hong Kong, a British colony, to Chinese rule, although it was his own technocrat successor, Jiang Zemin, who reaped the full benefit of this initiative, in July 1997. Deng also cemented Mao's rapprochement in Sino-American relations by paying a state visit to the United States. But, as the world haltingly came to realize, Deng's progressive policies, summarized in his slogan 'socialism with Chinese characteristics', did not extend to the political arena. He was, and always had been, committed to the one-party state. He had no sympathy for Western-style democracy, and under his rule dissidents continued to be persecuted, and freedom of expression discouraged.

Yet economic liberalization inevitably raised hopes of political liberalization, and the tensions such aspirations produced led, almost inexorably, to 'Tiananmen Square' – the squalid butchering of as many as three thousand civilian protestors, mainly students and workers, in the heart of the capital in June 1989. Whereas Western perceptions of what the tens of thousands of protestors who had poured into Tiananmen Square from April onwards actually wanted were severely distorted – although the protestors certainly clamoured for democracy, they also expressed resentment at the 'Westernization' of Chinese society that seemed to be generating both soaring inflation and the creation of a super-rich elite – Deng's decision to use units of the army to clear the square is still seen as a regrettable and unnecessary affront to the Chinese people.

Deng's 'knee-jerk' response to the Tiananmen protests has been explained by the fact that they coincided with a showpiece state visit to Beijing by the Russian leader **Mikhail Gorbachev**. Above all, the Chinese leadership could not run the risk of losing face by allowing the protests to escalate out of control in front of the world's assembled media. But it is unlikely Deng would have reacted otherwise. Outstanding pragmatist though he was, he had grown up with, and been moulded by, the Chinese communist revolution. As his writings show, his political commitments were explicit and consistent. He made no significant or original contribution to communist theory, simply wanted, and worked, to demonstrate the viability of the party he served from the 1920s until 1995, when he slipped into a coma. His dedication was manifest in his unremitting attention to detail over seventy years. Refreshingly, he eschewed the trappings of power. Famously, the only official position he held from 1987 onwards was 'Chairman of the Chinese Bridge Association'. Yet he was also a master of spin. He maintained that whereas Mao was 30 per cent wrong, he was 70 per cent right, as Mao had once said of Stalin – a borrowed formula that enabled Deng to transform China's prospects. With rather more accuracy, the same formula may be applied to Deng himself. In Chinese history his place as a consolidator and constructionist seems already assured.

Further reading

See: *Selected Works of Deng Xiaoping 1977–82* (1984) and Deng Xiaoping, *Fundamental Issues in Present-Day China* (1987) – both available from the Foreign Languages Press, Beijing. See also: David Bonavia, *Deng* (1989); Harrison Salisbury, *The New Emperors: China in the Era of Mao and Deng* (1992); Richard Evans, *Deng Xiaoping and the Making of Modern China* (1993, rev. 1997); and Andrew J. Nathan and Perry Link (eds), *The Tiananmen Papers* (2002). Jasper Becker, *The Chinese* (2000) casts a critical eye on the effects of the one-party state during the latter stages of the twentieth century; Joe Studwell, *The China Dream: The Elusive Quest for the Greatest Untapped Market on Earth* (2002) asks searching questions about the mechanics underpinning Deng's 'economic miracle'.

JUSTIN WINTLE

DERRIDA, Jacques (Jackie)

1930–2004

French/Algerian philosopher

Jacques Derrida was one of the brightest, most controversial stars in the Western philosophical firmament during the last third of the twentieth century. He is frequently, but not always helpfully, associated with both post-structuralism and postmodernism. His principal, and most celebrated, contribution to philosophical activity was 'deconstruction', a critical practice that deliberately sought to undermine traditional European philosophizing, outside as well as inside formal philosophy, by re-examining key texts with a particular eye to exposing what he termed their 'metaphysics of presence' and so accessing their alleged internal contradictions. But Derrida himself never definitively formulated deconstruction as a theory, indeed explicitly said that such a task is impossible; and one of the problems with his oeuvre is the way in which, during a writing career that spanned forty-five years, he employed the same terms with different nuances, sometimes different meanings.

Another problem is Derrida's style of writing: distrusting established modes of discourse, he often depends on the first person to carry his investigations forward, while also progressively indulging in textual and semantic experimentation that left some readers bewildered, particularly within the fraternity of Anglo-Saxon analytical philosophy. In 1992 a furore erupted when twenty philosophers, among them Willard Quine, made an unsuccessful attempt to prevent Cambridge University awarding Derrida an honorary doctorate, on the grounds that his work did not satisfy 'accepted standards of clarity and rigour'. If anything, his stock rose yet further as a result.

A more rounded view would give Derrida prominence in a long line of European sceptics, from Montaigne through **Nietzsche**. In another register he may be seen as one of the great contemplatives, whose spirited and intermittently humorous meditations were inscribed even as they were spun, generating a prodigious output – scores of books, and innumerable essays and articles that have yet to be adequately catalogued. But that Derrida achieved fame during his lifetime had much to do with his performances in academe. Always a brilliant presenter of his own ideas, he packed international conferences and lecture halls as few other of his contemporaries could, making a particular splash in America, and becoming the participatory subject of a commercial film – Amy Ziering-Kofman's *Jacques Derrida* – released in 2002, two years before his death from cancer of the pancreas. He had the looks, and he had the charm.

Derrida was born in el-Biar, outside Algiers. Under the wartime Vichy administration he was removed from school for being a Jew. In 1949 he relocated to Paris to complete his secondary education at the Lycée Louis-le-grand, and entered the École Normale Superieure only at the third attempt, in 1952. His mentors there included **Michel Foucault** and Louis Althusser. Between 1957 (the year he married Marguerite Aucoutourier, a psychoanalyst) and 1959 he was conscripted into the French army, serving as a language teacher in the Algerian War. From 1960 until 1964 he taught philosophy at the Sorbonne, before returning to the ENS as a staff member. There he remained until 1984, when he transferred to the École des Hautes Études en Sciences Sociales, taking formal retirement in 1998. From 1986 he also held a chair at the University of California, Irvine, having previously run seminars at Yale.

Derrida first came to the fore in 1966, when, during a seminar at Johns Hopkins University, Baltimore, he outshone **Jacques Lacan** and other heavyweights. The following year he consolidated his position with the publication of three books: *Speech and Phenomena* (*La Voix et le phénomène*, 1967, trans. 1973), a study of Edmund Husserl, and two collections of essays – *Writing and Difference* (*L'Écriture et la différence*, 1967, trans. 1978) and *Of Grammatology* (*De la Grammatologie*, 1967, trans. 1976). These, together with an earlier publication – a critical translation of Husserl's *The Origin of Geometry* (1962, trans. 1978) – put 'deconstruction' (a term initially adapted from **Martin Heidegger**) firmly on the map, with *Of Grammatology* and its critique of the Swiss linguist **Ferdinand de Saussure** generally being regarded as Derrida's seminal text.

The relationship between language and thought was a principal concern among philosophers throughout the twentieth century. Thus the Logical Positivists, in the interests of good housekeeping, sought to establish new rules of clarity and verification in philosophical discourse; **Ludwig Wittgenstein** made the question 'what is it that can be said?' central to his work; and **J.L. Austin** focused on the mechanics of what he called 'speech acts'. In France, **Claude Lévi-Strauss**, **Roland Barthes** and other Structuralists went rather further, claiming that 'meaning' is the product of closed sign systems and little else. Through deconstruction, Derrida challenged even this view: meaning, if it exists at all, necessarily lies beyond our reach – though this did not prevent Derrida himself assiduously promoting his own understandings, which amounted to a non-systematic, and some would say peripheral, assault on all prior Western philosophy.

Chronologically at least, Derridean deconstruction begins with a specific dismissal of Husserlian phenomenology, as well as a more diffuse recognition of **Freud's** insistence on covert mental processes. For Derrida there is, and can be, no immediate *now*, no true certainty or *presence*. Rather, whether we speak or write, our words (even our thoughts) are refracted representations only, deferrals muddied by hierarchic dualisms that constitute what Derrida adumbrates as an embedded metaphysics. Examining texts by such disparate authors as Plato, Rousseau, Freud, Lévi-Strauss and Emmanuel Lévinas, he identifies a series of core oppositions – for example good/evil, positive/negative, pure/impure, essential/accidental, as well as (less convincingly) speech/writing itself – whose deployment is 'metaphysical' in two ways: first, in the assumption that such dualisms have some or other descriptive relevance to how things are; and second, because in every case one term is preferred, or 'privileged', above the other (leading to an arbitrary hierarchy of values). Simultaneously, Derrida acknowledges that he is unable to dispense with oppositional dualisms altogether without himself adding to their number. Rather, his strategy – which takes as given that philosophy should never stray into the prescriptive, but always stick to the descriptive – is to 'resist' found dualisms, as a means if not of acquiring truth, then of stepping back from error, or metaphysical contamination.

These moves made, deconstruction is developed by Derrida into a formidable apparatus with its own terminology, for all that what he seems to want is a suspension of philosophy. His characteristic method is to treat a text in such a way that it appears to 'deconstruct' itself. Out of his consideration of oppositions, Derrida extracts the concept of 'supplementarity'. For example, masturbation is normally presented as something supplemental or secondary to coitus, but that, says Derrida, is just another metaphysical trap, or bias. Another term he uses is 'undecidability' (or 'indeterminability'): investigate any idea or notion long enough and we will reach a point of impasse (called by Derrida an *aporia*, a term also employed by Theodor Adorno) where 'meaning' becomes, at best, ambiguous. A simple example of this is the word 'ghost': does a ghost 'exist' or not? Where there is a signifier, something or other is signified. But perhaps the best known of all his weapons is 'différance', a neologism made up of the two words 'difference' and 'defer', wielded by Derrida to demonstrate that, try as we may, we can never succeed in finally pinning down a certainty.

Deconstruction so presented is, as Derrida's critics were swift to remark, parasitic. In his early (but highly influential) works, continuing to around 1980, the Parisian bobby-dazzler seems unable or unwilling to proceed without devouring others, and it is noticeable that he gives little or no account of such nonverbal, and arguably primary, experiences as seeing, hearing and smelling. Rather, he provides a series of commentaries, somewhat in the manner of a medieval theologian keen to identify heresies in the canon of his predecessors while allowing that he may himself be transgressing. Post-1980, however, while

never abandoning his quest to disfigure what he conceived to be false transparencies, he moved more into the open, tackling social, political and religious, as well as personal, themes. In *The Gift of Death* (*Donner la morte*, 1992, trans. 1995) and *The Politics of Friendship* (*Politiques de l'amitié*, 1994, trans. 1997), and also in *On Cosmopolitanism and Forgiveness* (*Cosmopolites de tous les pays, encore un effort!* 1997, trans. 2001), Derrida ruminates on such actions as giving, forgiving and offering hospitality, demonstrating linguistically and psychologically as well as logically that the implicit altruism of such behaviours is always compromised – something already long familiar to anthropologists. More urgently, he questions whether, since the future is always occluded, decision-making can ever be even a halfway rational process – quite apart from ethical considerations, which are invariably fraught with their own problematics. Rather, for Derrida, to take a decision is akin to Kierkegaard's 'act of faith', a blind, mad leap into the dark.

Darkness is also apparent in a number of texts Derrida wrote following the deaths of friends and colleagues, notably *Memoires: for Paul de Man* (*Memoires: pour Paul de Man*, 1984, trans. 1989), where he deconstructs 'mourning' – incapable of completion unless the sentiment of fidelity to the lost one is abandoned. In this instance, though, Derrida's attachment to a longstanding colleague is troubled by the knowledge, acquired late on, that de Man, like **Martin Heidegger**, had once been a Nazi collaborator. Politically Derrida swung leftwards, though always with trepidation, since for him all causes involve indeterminability, and dogma of any kind is the enemy. Undecidability led him to oppose the death penalty. He gave vociferous support to **Nelson Mandela** and the struggle against apartheid, but on other public issues he more often than not sat on the fence, as is evident in his most overtly political book, *Spectres of Marx* (*Spectres de Marx* 1993, trans. 1994).

His being so recently deceased, it would be futile to attempt any evaluation of Derrida's lasting contribution to philosophy, though it is likely that future generations will see him as less of a subversive, and more of a revitalizer most skilled in the art of reading whose findings, in their combative attentiveness to textual subtleties, lie well within the mainstream of Western philosophical culture. Perhaps, like Pascal in the seventeenth century, he will be viewed as a man compulsively engaged in some principal intellectual debates of his era whose thought was just too subtle, and sometimes too abstruse, for quick-fix characterization. Like Pascal too, he belongs equally to literature. Significantly, at the time of his death his impact appears to have been most marked in the field of literary criticism. A generation of academic critics on both sides of the Atlantic have been beguiled by Derrida to exhibit a trenchant disrespect for the reputations of the authors they study, though seldom with his commanding (and eclectic) *élan*.

Further reading

Other works include: *Dissemination* (*La Dissémination*) (1972, trans. 1981); *Margins of Philosophy* (*Marges de la philosophie*, 1972, trans, 1982); *Positions* (*Positions*, 1972, trans. 1982); *L'Archéologie du frivole* ('Archaeology of the frivolous', an essay on Condillac, 1973); *Glas* (*Glas*, 1974, trans. 1986); *Spurs* (*Éperons*, an essay on Nietzsche, 1976, trans. 1979); *La Vérité on peinture* ('The Truth in Painting', 1978); *The Post Card* (*La Carte postale*, 1980, trans. 1987); *Aporias* (*Aporias*, 1984, trans. 1993); *Adieu to Emmanuel Levinas* (*Adieu á Emmanuel Levinas*, 1997, trans. 1999); *The Work of Mourning* (*Chaque fois unique, la fin du monde*, 2003, trans. 2003). For a fuller list of Derrida's work go to: http://www.hydra.umn.edu/derrida/jdalf. See: Jonathan Culler, *On Deconstruction: Theory and Criticism after Structuralism* (1982); David Wood and Robert Bernasconi (eds), *Derrida and Difference* (1985); Christopher Norris, *Derrida* (1987); K. Hart, *The Trespass of the Sign: Deconstruction, Theology and Philosophy* (1989); J. Caputo, *The Prayers and Tears of Jacques Derrida* (1997); Geoffrey Bennington, *Jacques Derrida* (1993) and *Interrupting Derrida* (2000); Herman Rapaport, *Later Derrida* (2002); Tom Cohen (ed.), *Jacques Derrida and the Humanities: A Critical Reader* (2002).

JUSTIN WINTLE

DIAGHILEV, Serge (Sergei Pavlovich)

1872–1929
Russian impresario

No more vital figure than Diaghilev was instrumental in introducing an awareness of Russian cultural vigour into the West. His role was catalytic: he provided for Russians a link with the West, and for the West his exhibitions and subsequently his brilliant Ballets Russes came as a revelation of the latest Russian developments in stage design, choreography, dancing and music. The impact of the Ballets Russes was sufficient to ensure for it as much a place in the history of French culture as of Russian culture.

Diaghilev was born of a noble family in the Novgorod region. His interest in music and fine art were early developments and his family had close contact with both **Tchaikovsky** and **Mussorgsky**. Studying in St Petersburg, Diaghilev met the painters Alexandre Benois and **Léon Bakst**, with both of whom he collaborated on his periodical *Mir Iskusstva* (*The World of Art*) from its inception in 1898; subsequently Diaghilev, Benois and Bakst were to collaborate too upon the productions of the Ballets Russes.

Diaghilev's brilliant eye for talent, his thirst for astonishment and the force of his will in the increasingly complex area of his activities made him a significant contributor to the history of the theatre, of music, of art and, above all, of ballet. Directly active in none of these spheres, Diaghilev's indirect achievement was to influence each of them enormously. His ruthless determination to elicit the best from his designers, composers, choreographers and dancers is well documented. As a result his ballets were never apologetic but were emphatically assertive in their modernism. His designers, dancers and choreographers worked so closely together that it is not possible to revive a Ballets Russes production without attempting to revive the union of these three. Diaghilev made maximum use of the designers, employing many remarkable painters. By the time of the Exhibition of Russian Art at the

1906 Salon d'Automne in Paris, Diaghilev's links with painters extended from the florid languor of Bakst to the fierce primitivism of Larionov. Through the Ballets Russes he was to work with very many French as well as Russian artists.

Diaghilev's initial theatrical season in Paris, 1908–9, at once relied heavily upon designers. Chaliapine sang *Boris Godunov* at the Paris Opera in 1908 clad in a densely jewelled costume designed by the painter Golovin and redolent of barbaric splendour. In the production of Borodin's *Prince Igor* which followed, the balletic explosion of the Polovtsian dances was equally un-European, with sets and costumes by Nikolai Roerich as tribal and wild as the frenzied music, a blend of wildness and sophistication, of barbaric vigour with a leap of the imagination, that electrified Parisian audiences and assured Diaghilev of fame, with a measure of infamy, from the very beginning of his musical and theatrical career in Paris.

A second phase of productions followed in which the urbane and cultivated luxury of Bakst alternated with the lightness and eighteenth-century freshness of Benois's *Pavillon d'Armide* (music Tchérépnine, choreography Fokine and design by Benois). *Les Sylphides*, which was orchestrated by **Stravinsky** from Mozart, choreographed by Fokine and danced by Karsavina, Pavlova and Nijinsky, confirmed that during 1909, in one brilliant year, Diaghilev had established a complex, vital and innovatory company that was strong in every part of its creative work. Diaghilev astonished his audiences with the combined talents of Fokine, Stravinsky, Bakst, Nijinsky and Karsavina. Contrast followed contrast as the other-worldly luxury of *Schéhérazade* (1910), *Le Spectre de la rose* (1911) and the infamous *L'Après-midi d'un faune* (1912) gave way to Stravinsky's *Petrouchka* (1911) and *Rite of Spring* (1913), where the vigorous ferocity of folk and peasant themes returned. Increasingly the lavishness of Bakst gave way to the more angular but equally spectacular designs of Larionov, Goncharova, and eventually to French Cubist and Italian futurist

designs. *Parade* (1917), choreography by Massine, music by Satie, theme by Cocteau and design by **Picasso**, was again revolutionary and of an originality that Diaghilev maintained until the end of his life. He continued to employ Russian designers after the Revolution in Russia but remained based in the West. The year 1927 saw **Gabo** and Pevsner design *La Chatte*, Yakulov design *Pas d'acier* and Tchelichev design *Ode*. George Balanchine became the prominent new choreographer of the closing years of Diaghilev's Ballets Russes. The final production *Le Fils prodigue*, opened in Paris in May 1929, bringing sets by **Rouault** to music by **Prokofiev**: Diaghilev's unique ability to unite diverse talents had continued to the end of his career.

Further reading

See: Richard Buckle, *Nijinsky* (1975), W. MacDonald, *Diaghilev Observed* (1976); Serge Lifar, *Serge Diaghilev: His Life, His Work, His Legend* (1977); Lynn Garafola, *Diaghilev's Ballets Russes* (1990); John Drummond, *Speaking of Diaghilev* (1997); Stephen D. Press, *Prokofiev's Ballets for Diaghilev* (2005).

JOHN MILNER

DICKENS, Charles John Huffam
1812–70
English novelist

Dickens's lengthy career as an author, during all of which he manifestly was at the top of the tree, occupied the middle third of the nineteenth century – from 1836–7 when *Pickwick Papers* (his first novel and, as many contemporaries thought, his best) became a best-seller of unprecedented popularity and established him immediately as a literary eminence, to 1870 when he died suddenly while writing *Edwin Drood*. Thus, as Humphry House remarked, 'his writing life coincided almost exactly with the rule of the Ten-Pound Householders', that is, between the Reform Acts of 1832 and 1867 (*The*

Dickens World, 1941), and many contemporaries saw him as the product, and the voice, of this period of reform. Immediately before becoming a full-time novelist, he had been on the staff of the Benthamite *Morning Chronicle*, and though he was never an avowed Utilitarian or Philosophical Radical – 'Isms!' he once exclaimed: 'oh Heaven for a world without an *ism*' – his critique of Victorian society and its institutions owed something to that intellectual tradition. Not, of course, that his significance was only, or even primarily, political. He was a prolific creator of characters, a compelling narrator, the greatest of English humorists, a master of pathos, a highly original stylist, and a wide-ranging depicter of the urban life of his age: and in all these respects he had a large influence. Outside his fiction, he was brilliantly and energetically active in many areas, as a magazine editor and journalist, an amateur actor, a remarkable solo recitalist, an eloquent public speaker, and a philanthropist.

Lower middle class in origins (his father was a Royal Navy pay-clerk), he experienced in his childhood a sudden and painful though impermanent descent into the working class when, in 1824, his father's financial ineptitude landed the family in bankruptcy and himself in jail. Charles, who had ceased attending school, was sent to work in a bottling warehouse. As his intimate friend and official biographer John Forster commented, the 'very poor and unprosperous' in his novels 'were not his clients whose cause he pleaded with such pathos and humour … but in some sort his very self.' The boy hero of his second novel, *Oliver Twist* (1837–9), was the first of a series of lost, bewildered and oppressed children in his fiction, inspired by this experience. He indeed virtually introduced the child, the child's-eye view upon life, and the school into English fiction, and in this, as in much else, was soon followed and imitated. Oliver had been born in a workhouse, Dickens thus creating an opportunity to attack the controversial Poor Law Amendment Act (1834). Such topicality and this concern with social institutions were to be characteristic of his fiction, where characters are often seen in relation to institutions: schools, prisons, the churches, the money market, the law courts, the civil service, and officialdom in general.

Oliver is born in the provinces and comes to and stays in London: so do many Dickens heroes, who thus repeat the pattern of his own life. (Born in Portsmouth and raised mostly in Chatham, he moved finally to London when aged ten.) This immigration from the country to the large town or the metropolis was moreover a conspicuous feature of Britain at this time; as the 1851 Census showed, the majority of people now lived in large towns, for the first time in history. 'Dickens describes London like a special correspondent for posterity,' observed Walter Bagehot in 1858. London was much the most frequent, and successful, setting for his fiction; his presentation of the countryside is perfunctory, but he writes with verve about some overseas environments, the America of *Martin Chuzzlewit* (1843–4) for instance, or the Italy of *Little Dorrit* (1855–7). Eminently he was the novelist of urban experience, to a degree and with a density achieved by no predecessor. London specially suited his genius, being the country's political, commercial, administrative and artistic centre, and presenting conspicuously such extreme contrasts between affluence and destitution, power and powerlessness, and containing both cosy and quaint neighbourhoods and the possibility of urban *anomie*. He was at his most powerful as an explorer of urbanism in certain novels of his maturity: *Bleak House* (1852–3), *Little Dorrit* and *Our Mutual Friend* (1864–5). He is interesting, though less knowledgeable and effective, on the purely industrial town in *Hard Times* (1854) and incidentally elsewhere.

From the start, he offered in every novel a variety of contents. Comedy, including the farcical, was prominent in *Pickwick*, and is never absent thereafter, though later it is less pervasive; and his narrative tone, which is rarely self-effacing, is most characteristically comic or ironic. Pathos, often centring on a child or some other disadvantaged or easily oppressible character, provided an important element in his original popularity, though it was less admired and less conspicuous later. Violence, crime, murder, hidden secrets and skulduggery added excitement and suspense to his narratives, and gave opportunities for him to present human nature in its most extreme forms. (Dickens was much concerned with, and perceptive about, criminal psychology, mental disturbance and madness, as well as with the more common reaches of individual and social behaviour.) Most of his novels refer to, or have as a prominent subject, contemporary political or social issues, generally treated from a reformist standpoint, though on some issues, such as 'the Woman Question' then emerging, he was conservative or retrograde. Very young when he achieved fame, he developed greatly in technique and in intellectual command of the large swathe of society and emotionally varied materials which, ambitiously, he took as his province. Love and marriage are generally less central and less impressive in his novels than in most fiction, but are more prominent in his two first-person (and partly autobiographical) novels *David Copperfield* (1849–50) and *Great Expectations* (1860–1).

The wide diffusion of his novels to a heterogeneous audience was much assisted by their all being serialized. They were thus bought by many who could never have afforded the lump-sum purchase of a hardback book, and they became a regular topic for conversation over a lengthy period. (The impact of radio and television series and serials presents obvious analogies.) 'His current serial was really a topic of the day; it seemed something almost akin to politics and news – as if it belonged not so much to literature as to events' (*Daily Telegraph*, 18 June 1872). The publishers of *Pickwick* created what remained Dickens's favourite serial form: twenty monthly numbers, each with two illustrations – and these illustrations, mostly by 'Phiz' (Hablot Browne), were, and remain, important in providing unforgettable visual images of his people and places. This serial pattern was much imitated, as was Dickens's invention of the Christmas book with *A Christmas Carol* (1843); he was an influential pioneer in the forms, as well as the content, of popular literature, as Robert L. Patten (cited below) most amply demonstrates. Similarly his giving public readings from his works, from 1853, led to a vogue for such author-recitals.

His attachment to Christmas, evident throughout his career, was notable and significant. In Christmas are concentrated many of his fondest tastes and beliefs: the stress upon family and the hearth, and the special care for children's happiness; simple unsophisticated good living and jollity; benevolence and generosity; hope, in a dark world; a stress on what unites rather than distinguishes people (for all classes celebrate Christmas in similar ways). His special feeling for Christmas, as novelist, magazine editor, public reader and paterfamilias, is a prime instance of his being the spokesman for a widespread popular sentiment or conviction. (**Anthony Trollope** nicknamed him, with unkindly intent, 'Mr Popular Sentiment', in *The Warden*, 1855). As indeed his vast – and soon international – popularity suggests, his artistic temperament was far from that of an outsider or a crier in the wilderness. In denouncing social evils, he was articulating the conscience of his times, but rather as a member of a loyal opposition than as a rebel or revolutionary: and the shortcomings of his sympathies corresponded to common English prejudices – against blacks, for instance, or Jews, or the Irish, or Roman Catholicism.

Shortly before his death, he had an audience with Queen Victoria. A courtier briefed her for this meeting with 'the author whose name will hereafter be closely associated with the Victorian era' – a sound forecast, for his novels take in so many of the central preoccupations of the times that 'Dickens's England' remains a meaningful concept. Queen Victoria would like him, this courtier advised: 'He, too, has the most anxious desire to raise what we call "the lower classes"; and would sympathize with Your Majesty in many of The Queen's views and aspirations.' She found it so, and on his death wrote in her diary:

> He is a very great loss. He had a large, loving mind and the strongest sympathy with the poorer classes. He felt sure that a better feeling, and much greater union of classes would take place in time. And I pray earnestly it may.

Dickens was not so 'safe' or conformist as this community of outlook with his queen might suggest, but this anecdote better suggests his standpoint than some more exciting recent views represented by the influential Edmund Wilson's assertion that 'Of all the great Victorian writers, he was probably the most antagonistic to the Victorian Age itself' (*The Wound and the Bow*, 1941) – unless Wilson was implying that no great Victorian authors were much at odds with their age. Without insincerity, Dickens gave his large public much what it wanted, both in entertainment and literary satisfactions, and in eloquent and impatient reformism. His enormous literary skills and his standing as a much-loved as well as admired personality gave wide currency, and weight, to his ideas, which in general were not far in advance of public opinion. Certainly he was credited with great influence: 'Pen in hand, he wielded a power superior to that of a whole House of Commons,' wrote one obituarist, somewhat extravagantly; 'In his own inimitable way,' wrote the radical publicist Charles Knight, 'he has perhaps done more to expose wrong and injustice and to improve society socially and morally than any other worker or writer of the present century.'

To adapt a line of Wordsworth's: 'He gave them eyes, he gave them ears', making the reading public more vividly aware of the world – including its submerged tenth – around them; imposing upon them, indeed, a new way of seeing, hearing and interpreting. But, very sensitive visually and aurally, and widely exploratory in his range of perception, his was a highly imaginative, not merely a recording, mind. Characteristically he spoke of his mind's taking 'a *fanciful* photograph' of a scene; his natural tendency was thus to yoke the imaginative with the literal, for example demanding 'a little standing-room for Queen Mab's Chariot among the Steam Engines', or 'blessing the South-Eastern Railway Company for realising the Arabian Nights in these prose days' (when railway speed had a magic-carpet effect). His art straddled, and at its best uniquely combined, the journalistic and the poetic; his narrative prose was much more intense and more highly metaphoric than any of his predecessors' in the novel. Not only in content and in reformist rhetoric but, more fundamentally, in vision and in imaginative construction, he enlarged the forms of fiction and the sensuous capacities of English prose. His influence was apparent in Russian and French as well as in Anglo-Saxon fiction: see George Ford, *Dickens and His Readers* (1955) and *Dickens and Fame* (centenary issue of *The Dickensian*, 1970). As House concluded his seminal study *The Dickens World*: 'He made out of Victorian England a complete world, with a life and vigour and idiom of its own, quite unlike any other world there has ever been.'

Further reading

Dickens's novels, much reprinted and widely translated, are most conveniently available in trustworthy annotated form in the Penguin English Library (1966–78). Five novels have so far appeared in the textually authoritative Clarendon Press Dickens (1966–). The Clarendon Press also publishes the scholarly editions of his *Speeches*, ed. K.J. Fielding (1960), *Letters*, ed. Madeline House *et al.* (from 1965), and *Public Readings*, ed. Philip Collins (1975). His plays and poems, few in number, are of negligible interest, but his essays are often excellent and very relevant to his fiction: *Reprinted Pieces* (1858), *The Uncommercial Traveller* (1861, 1868, 1875), *Miscellaneous Papers*, ed. B.W. Matz (1908), all reprinted later. See: John Forster, *Life of Dickens* (1872–4), the official biography, often reprinted; G.K. Chesterton, *Charles Dickens* (1906); Edgar Johnson, *Charles Dickens: His Tragedy and Triumph* (1952), the standard biography; John Butt and Kathleen Tillotson, *Dickens at Work* (1957); J. Hillis Miller, *Charles Dickens:*

The World of His Novels (1958); Angus Wilson, *The World of Charles Dickens* (1970); F.R. and Q.D. Leavis, *Dickens the Novelist* (1971); *Dickens: The Critical Heritage*, ed. Philip Collins (1971): Robert L. Pattern, *Charles Dickens and His Publishers* (1978); M. Andrews, *Dickens and the Grown-up Child* (1994); B. Murray, *Charles Dickens* (1994); J. Schad, *Dickens Refigured: Bodies, Desires and Other Histories* (1996).

PHILIP COLLINS

DICKINSON, Emily

1830–86

US poet

Emily Dickinson and **Walt Whitman**, the two greatest nineteenth-century American poets, were contemporaries who appear not to have read each other's work. Both rebelled successfully against the limited subject–matter and traditional form of poetry in their society, but they used almost diametrically opposed methods. Whitman dilated his ego into a national and universal self, embracing a potentially hostile audience with his long, free-verse poems. Dickinson's highly condensed, often ironic first-person lyrics set forth alternately exuberant, tormented and fragmented selves. She deliberately turned her back on a public that encouraged even more insipid 'Dimity Convictions' (poem 401) of its 'refined' 'Brittle' 'Gentlewomen'. 'Civilization – spurns – the Leopard!/Was the Leopard – bold?' she asked sarcastically (492). Knowing that 'Much Madness is Divinest Sense' (435), Dickinson damned the 'majority':

> Assent – and you are Sane –
> Demur – you're straightway dangerous –
> And handled with a Chain –

Of the more than 1,700 lyrics that Dickinson wrote (some 500 or so during 1862–3) she published only seven, anonymously, during her lifetime; many of her poems were hardly 'written' at all – inscribed on scraps of paper or bound into eight-poem packets. In 1890 a much-acclaimed selection of Dickinson's poems appeared, edited and regularized by Mabel Todd and Col. T.W. Higginson, a minister, Civil War hero and the 'Preceptor' who had advised Dickinson in 1862 to 'delay' publishing what he felt to be her 'spasmodic' verse.

Only with T.H. Johnson's *Complete Poems* (1955) were Dickinson's poems printed as they were written, with irregular rhythms, slant rhymes, capitalization and, most valuably, with the dashes which give even her shortest lines a floating, resonant quality. Dickinson's rich, elliptical letters first appeared in 1958. Thus Dickinson's reputation, like **Herman Melville's**, has relied upon twentieth-century assessments; neglect during her lifetime has made her in effect a modern poet. Since Dickinson is the most important American woman poet, her deliberate testing of the range and intensity available to a female poetic have made her work a challenge to the critic and an inspiration and warning to the poet; her influence, unmistakable in the work of Theodore Roethke and **Sylvia Plath**, increases annually as critical studies based on her complete works appear.

Since Dickinson almost never titled or dated her poems, Johnson's chronological numbering, based upon internal evidences and handwriting, is necessarily conjectural. Nevertheless it is possible to distinguish three overlapping phases in Dickinson's work. First was a celebratory phase, influenced by Ralph Waldo Emerson, in which Dickinson's voice is often an Emersonian imperial self, or a joyous child in a nature where 'Apprehensions – are God's introductions – / To be hallowed – accordingly – ' (797). A second, more psychological phase in the early to mid-1860s depicted torment, estrangement and occasional passionate affirmation. In a third phase from the late 1860s to Dickinson's death in 1886, earlier themes were expressed more epigrammatically, with a stable and often scathing irony: 'Far from Love the Heavenly Father/Leads the Chosen Child' (1021).

Emily Dickinson grew up in western Massachusetts as part of the New England professional, political and intellectual elite.

Her lawyer father, treasurer of Amherst College and member of the US House of Representatives, dominated an oppressively closely knit family, with an invalid wife and two daughters, Emily and Lavinia, who never married. Emily Dickinson's beloved brother Austin, also a lawyer, lived next door with his vivacious wife Sue; when Emerson lectured at Amherst in 1858, he stayed with Austin and Sue (but Emily did not attend the lecture). For a woman of her day, Emily Dickinson had an excellent education, first at Amherst Academy, then at the Mount Holyoke Seminary (later College), where she cut short her studies after a year to return to the parental home, living there for the rest of her life. As Dickinson's confident poetic allusions to astronomy, botany and geology show, she was a serious student of the natural sciences, influenced by the Amherst scientist Edward Hitchcock's view of 'natural language' as well as by Emerson's more ecstatic celebration of the legible 'hieroglyphic' of experience and nature. Dickinson once remarked that she did not understand why it should be necessary to read anyone but Shakespeare, but aside from Shakespeare, the pervasive Emerson and the inevitable – and deeply absorbed – Bible, she read and used contemporary writers such as **George Eliot** (her poetry as well as her novels), Robert and Elizabeth Barrett Browning, the Brontë sisters and Henry Wadsworth Longfellow (for his novel *Kavanagh* as much as for his poetry).

Even when Dickinson's poems doubt her personal worthiness, they never question her intellectual powers or fear her ability to express herself. Dickinson's notorious reclusiveness freed her from conformist demands imposed by her class, sex and religion; it was a strategy as well as a fate. 'The Soul selects her own society/Then – shuts the Door – ' (303). In 1862–3 Dickinson appears to have suffered a severe crisis of identity which her poetry both expressed and to some extent probably healed; she often uses writing and speech as metaphors for life, while erasure and silence signify death, loss or destruction of self. 'They shut me up in Prose,' poem 613

recounts, 'As when a little girl/They put me in the closet – /Because they liked me "still" – '. But, the poem continues, she has 'abolished' her captivity. Many poems and the famous 'Master' letters, addressed to an unknown recipient (possibly Rev. Samuel Bowles) set love next to a self-annihilating despair. 'She dealt her pretty word's like Blakes,' Dickinson wrote (479), probably referring to her insensitive sister-in-law.

Yet Dickinson's love poems, like her many poems on the 'flood subject' death, make joy or sorrow secondary to sheer intensity of experience. 'I like a look of Agony,/Because I know it's true – ' (241). But she asserts even more strongly in 'Wild Nights – Wild Nights!' (249) that 'Were I thee/Wild Nights should be/Our luxury!' Dickinson was aware that she used emotion, even victimization, to generate her power. 'Power is only Pain – / Stranded, thro' Discipline' (252). In one remarkable poem she wrote, 'My life had stood a loaded gun' until 'The Owner passed – identified – /And carried, me away –!' Although now 'I speak for him', her lover will die some day. The 'Vesuvian' poet, however, is immortal: 'For I have but the power to kill/Without – the power to die – ' (754). Dickinson's greatest terror is of 'Bandaged Moments' when the Soul is 'too appalled to stir' and submits to the caress of 'Goblin' 'Horrors' (512). Repression, substitution or 'balm' only exacerbate anguish:

> To fill a Gap
> Insert the Thing that caused it –
> Block it up
> With Other – and 'twill yawn the more –
> You cannot solder an Abyss
> With Air.
>
> (546)

Dickinson is sometimes carelessly called a Puritan poet; aside from her loathing of the self-proclaimed Elect or 'meek members of the Resurrection' (216) and her distaste for the 'Eclipse ... whom they call their "Father"' (letter to Higginson, 1862), Dickinson never accepted original sin and was repelled by the concept of Heaven as a 'great schoolroom in the sky' – though of course she did find it necessary to attack these concepts in quatrains parodic of the Bay Psalm Book and sermon citation. Dickinson's Puritan inheritance shows up positively in her concentration on joy in experience of the created world, in her bouts of self-denial, and in her love of dialectic – whose terms she characteristically inverts in mid-poem.

The Dickinsonian speaker witnesses the present moment: noon, sunset, ecstasy, death, recognition. Even Dickinson's shortest poems employ several image systems; she is anti-Platonic; her metaphors function as facets of an action defined by the poem's 'circuit'. Her condensed, often ambiguous syntax, riddling word plays, omissions and shifting emblems all embody the flux of complex processes which were her great subjects. More deeply even perhaps than Whitman (because she dealt with less tractable material), Dickinson was a poet of experience.

Further reading

See: *The Manuscript Books of Emily Dickinson*, ed. R.W. Franklin (2 vols, 1982). See also: Richard B. Sewall, *Emily Dickinson* (2 vols, 1974), which is the definitive biography; Ruth Miller, *The Poetry of Emily Dickinson* (1968); Robert Weisbuch, *Emily Dickinson* (1975); Sharon Cameron, *Lyric Time: Dickinson and the Limits of Genre* (1979); Joel Myerson, *Emily Dickinson: A Descriptive Bibliography* (1984); Jane Donahue Eberwein, *An Emily Dickinson Encyclopedia* (1998); Wendy Martin (ed.), *The Cambridge Companion to Emily Dickinson* (2002).

HELEN MCNEIL

DISNEY, Walt

1901–66

US filmmaker

In 1964 Walt Disney was awarded the President's Medal of Freedom, with the citation 'artist and impresario, in the course of entertaining an age Walt Disney has created on American folklore'. Had the world stopped when he died it would have been found to contain more reproductions – in films,

books, toys, clothes, even wrist-watches – of the most famous of his creations, Mickey Mouse, than any other image, with the possible exceptions of the Crucifix and the Buddha. The first universal icon that expressed a sense of fun, the Mouse symbolized nothing so much as his creator's talent. That talent was somewhat more complex than any of its products. It grasped three things: line, business and technology. More importantly, it grasped the potential of the relations between them.

Though born in Chicago, Disney spent his early childhood on a farm in rural Missouri, which left a small-town mid-American stamp on the boy for life. His father Elias was a carpenter and failed entrepreneur, forever moving house and veering from one money-making project to another, pushing the young Walt (and his brothers) out to work at a very early age. Thus imbued with a recognition of the need to make money from the start, Disney had his first taste of success when he was seventeen: having volunteered for driving service in France in 1918, he earned considerable sums painting fake medals and German helmets to sell to returning soldiers.

An early interest in cartoons (he did not invent animation, but simply became its by-word) led him to work for a number of commercial art firms, including the Kansas City Film Ad Company. Then, with his brother Roy Disney as the business manager, he opened his own company, Laugh-O-Grams, to make freelance advertisements for the Newman Theatre in Kansas. At the age of twenty he had already acquired a team of collaborators – including Ub Iwerks, Hugh Harman and Rudolph Ising – whom he recognized as superior draughtsmen to himself, but who were nonetheless prepared to defer to him. At the same time his skill for adapting technology began to assert itself. A team called the Fleischers had made their animated Koko pop out of an inkwell into the live-action world. Disney made his live-action Alice jump back into Cartoonland. The success of this was modest, but Disney was sufficiently inspired to set up a studio in Hollywood. There it was not until the release of *Steamboat Willie* in 1928 that Disney's pre-eminence in the cartoon world was established, for it was *Steamboat* that introduced Mickey Mouse to the public. But it was not the small-town, resourceful entrepreneurialism of the character that seized the imagination: it was the combination of sound and animation. This was the first sound cartoon, and from that day close synchronization of sound and picture was known as 'Mickey-mousing'. The technique was used to greater effect in *Skeleton Dance* (1928), and reached its first apogee in *The Band Concert* (1935), in which Mickey conducts the *William Tell* Overture while a tornado, in line with the music, wreaks havoc with his orchestra.

Other technological breakthroughs succeeded throughout the 1930s. *Flowers and Trees* (1932) was the first-ever colour cartoon; and Disney in fact negotiated a deal with Technicolor that gave him an exclusive franchise for the three-colour process, so that other studios had to make do with two-colour systems. Then came the multiplane camera, which set artwork at different levels, thereby giving the illusion of a third dimension in a two-dimensional medium, used most effectively in *Pinocchio* (1940). *Pinocchio* was also an example of another frontier that Disney crossed: from shorts to full-length features, beginning in 1937 with *Snow White and the Seven Dwarfs*, and continuing with *Fantasia* (1940), *Dumbo* (1941) and *Bambi* (1942). But if the shorts gradually became the bread-and-butter of his company, it is among them that the essential Disney is to be found. Mickey Mouse was joined by Donald Duck (1931), Goofy (1932) and Pluto (1933), each of them 'created' by Disney himself, as well as the *Silly Symphony* series. *Three Little Pigs* (1933), released at the height of the Depression, became a rallying point for popular audiences, while *Who Killed Cock Robin?* (1935), satirizing the stars of the day (Mae West, Bing Crosby and Harpo Marx among them), marked a change from simple slapstick

towards a form of sit-com related to contemporary live-action comedies.

The 1930s were the golden era of Disney films, and all his productions of that period are immediately recognizable as Disney products. They are characterized by two aspects: a certain narrowness in the range of their plots and emotions (though this impression owes much to the fact that there were just so many Disney cartoons), and superb craftsmanship. They also bore the name of Disney, to the exclusion of those of his collaborators. In 1941 this led to a crisis from which Disney never fully recovered. Having opened a new studio, streamlined and rationalized, his animators went on strike. Disney, they felt, had not only monopolized the credit for their work, but had established an aesthetic dictatorship. They were the most talented draughtsmen in the business, but they were restricted, by and large, to actualizing Disney's conceptions. Harmony was eventually restored, but only after the strike leaders had seceded to set up their own studio, UPA; and it was the new UPA style, angular and determinedly two-dimensional, that dominated the post-war period. More and more Disney himself turned to live-action filming, or a mixture of live-action and animation, as in *Make Mine Music* (1946), *Song of the South* (1946) and *Melody Time* (1948). By the 1950s Disney Productions, while continuing to produce full-length animated features, was becoming less distinguishable from other Hollywood studios. In particular it devoted itself to live-action adventures, many of them specifically for children. With his unflagging instinct for good business, Disney brought to the family entertainment feature high technical standards (viz. *Davy Crockett*, 1955, or *Swiss Family Robinson*, 1960); but increasingly his films became recognizable as assembly-line products. A truer expression of the man was the first Disneyland, opened in 1954, an adventure park that combines all that is 'safe' with high spirits and precise technological organization.

Perhaps the most interesting feature of Disneyland is a series of figures, most notably **Abraham Lincoln**, animated by sound impulses activating pneumatic and hydraulic valves. Looked upon by many as monstrosities of bad taste, they embody perfectly Disney's vision of immediate entertainment supported by technological sophistication. His success was commercial because his products exuded inventiveness in an age that had an appetite for invention, and aestheticians seeking to find in him an aspect of primitivism are misguided.

Further reading

See: Richard Schickel, *The Disney Version* (1968); Ercole Arseni, Leone Bosi and Massimo Marconi, *Walt Disney – Magic Moments* (1973); Bob Thomas, *Walt Disney: An American Original* (1976); Christopher Finch, *The Art of Walt Disney* (1975); Eric Smoodin (ed.), *Disney Discourse: Producing the Magic Kingdom* (1994); Alan Bryman, *Disney and His Worlds* (1995); Janet Wasko, *Understanding Disney: The Manufacture of Fantasy* (2001).

CLARE KITSON

DOSTOEVSKY, Fyodor Mikhailovich

1821–81

Russian writer

Born in Moscow, the second son of a doctor at the hospital for the poor, his early life appears to have been enclosed and solitary. Deliberately segregated from local children, he was educated at home and at local schools, always in the company of his elder brother Mikhail. His father was short-tempered, domineering and fond of drink, but well educated by the standards of the time; his mother was more cultivated and of finer breeding. Apart from the Bible, the Dostoevsky family had reading tastes which embraced Russian literature and some of the most important journals of the day. Probably the most significant of Dostoevsky's childhood recollections concerns a visit to the theatre at the age of ten to see a production of Schiller's *The Robbers*. The dramatic qualities of the work and its romantic plea for freedom were to have enduring and profound meaning for Dostoevsky's development as a writer.

Of equal importance was the fact that his father acquired in 1831 an impoverished estate of two peasant villages in the province of Tula on which the Dostoevsky family used to spend their annual holidays. This was Dostoevsky's only real introduction to the Russian people, or *narod*, about whom he was to write so eloquently. From Schiller and the wretched Tula estate grew themes and incidents stretching the length of Dostoevsky's life and receiving their fullest treatment in the last of his novels, *The Brothers Karamazov* (*Brat'ya Karamazovy*, 1878–80).

The death of his mother in 1837 was followed by the death of his father two years later, supposedly murdered by his peasants. The Dostoevsky family broke up. Dostoevsky himself had already entered the military engineering institute in St Petersburg where, though he received a technical education, he seems to have devoted a great deal of his time to reading the Russian classics and an assortment of European writers from Walter Scott to Hoffmann, De Quincey and Balzac. A predilection for the horrific and supernatural is evident in his tastes at this time. When he had completed his engineering training, he obtained permission to retire from army service and devoted himself to a literary career. A translation of Balzac's *Eugénie Grandet* was quickly followed, in 1846, by Dostoevsky's first original work, *Poor folk* (*Bedniye lyudi*), which received the accolade of high praise from the leading critic V.G. Belinsky, and established the author's place in Russian literature almost overnight. The first success was not repeated with his second work, *The Double* (*Dvoynik*, 1846), and on the whole his career showed signs of dribbling away into various unsatisfactory experiments with such themes as the power of legend (*The Landlady, Khozyaika*, 1847) or the power of dreams (*White Nights, Beliye nochi*, 1848). Towards the end of the 1840s he was drawn into discussions about utopian socialism and revolution at meetings of the Petrashevsky group. He was certainly influenced by such ideas at the time, though there are no grounds for assuming that he was ever sincerely committed to revolutionary views. In the spring of 1849 he was arrested along with other members of the Petrashevsky group, imprisoned, summoned before a military tribunal and sentenced to death. The evidence against him was based principally on his having read aloud at a meeting Belinsky's famous 'Letter to Gogol' in which the critic had attacked Gogol for his religious mania and declared that the Russian people were profoundly atheistic. It was not so much the content of the 'Letter' as its illegality which condemned Dostoevsky. The enactment of the death sentence, a horrific charade devised on Tsar Nicholas I's orders to strike terror into the convicted men, ended with the announcement that the sentences had been commuted to terms of penal servitude and exile.

At the beginning of 1850 Dostoevsky was put in chains and carried away to Siberia to spend four years in the penal settlement at Omsk. The experience was shattering. Whether or not it was a major cause of his epilepsy, which may have manifested itself earlier, remains unclear, but there is no doubt that for the rest of his life Dostoevsky was to suffer terribly from epileptic attacks. His account of his four-year incarceration in the penal settlement is a classic of prison literature (*Notes from the House of the Dead, Zapiski iz myortvogo doma*, 1861–2), telling both of the literal privations, chiefly the sheer absence of privacy, and of the stoic nobility of the convicts. When he was released in 1854, he was still confined in Siberia but able to live a relatively free life, especially after being commissioned as an officer. He married the widow of a colleague and was finally permitted to return to European Russia in 1859.

His marriage was on the whole unhappy. Moreover, he was now faced by the task of rehabilitating his reputation as a writer in a Russia dominated by talk of reform and possible revolutionary changes. His experiences had strongly confirmed in him the religious feelings latent in him during the 1840s and when with his brother's help, he launched a journal, *Vremya* (*Time*), in 1861 his politics were conservative, jingoistic and vaguely 'populist' in the sense that they advocated a belief in the Russian peasantry and urged the intelligentsia to learn from them. It was in *Time* that he published his first novel, *The Insulted and Injured* (*Unizhenniye i oskorblyonniye*, 1861), as well as his account of his first trip to Western Europe, *Winter Notes on Summer Impressions* (*Zimniye zametki o letnykh vpechatleniyakh*, 1863). The metropolitan capitalism of the West, particularly as he encountered it in London, shocked him and aroused in him strong anti-Western, anti-radical attitudes. Infatuated with a young woman, Polina Suslova, he gambled on his European trips and became addicted to it. Indebtedness increased and misfortunes followed. His journal was closed down by the authorities for printing an article on the Polish rebellion of 1863 and the following year, despite receiving permission to launch a second journal, *Epoch* (*Epokha*), disasters befell him in the shape of his wife's death, his brother's death and the death of one of his closest collaborators, Apollon Grigor'yev. Though he published his most outstanding work to date, *Notes from the Underground* (*Zapiski iz podpol'ya*, 1864), in *Epoch*, his journal soon faltered and then failed completely, leaving him with heavy debts which he attempted to recoup by gambling sprees abroad. In desperate straits, in Wiesbaden, in the early autumn of 1865, he conceived a project for a long novel, *Crime and Punishment* (*Prestupleniye i nakazaniye*, 1866), which he wrote the following year. In order to fulfil a contractual obligation for a novel to be completed by a deadline in 1866, he temporarily abandoned his major work to write *The Gambler* (*Igrok*, 1867), a novel which he dictated to a young stenographer. This young lady, Anna Snitkina, became his second wife early the following year, and despite the quarter of a century which divided their respective ages it proved to be an exceedingly happy and successful marriage.

It began inauspiciously with the newly married couple forced into European exile in order to escape Dostoevsky's debtors. Four years were spent abroad, chiefly in Dresden, during which he completed two major novels, *The Idiot* (*Idiot*) (1868) and *The Possessed* or *The Devils* (*Besy*, 1871–72). On returning to Russia in 1871 his wife assumed the role of his publisher and created a stable, tranquil home life. Her careful, devoted management of Dostoevsky's finances gradually brought an end to his indebtedness. Although the early deaths of some of his children and serious epileptic attacks clouded the last decade of his life, his literary reputation prospered both through his publicistic activity (his *Diary of a Writer, Dnevnik pisatelya*, begun in 1873; continued, with intervals, until his death) and through his public readings, his editorial work (of the journal the *Citizen, Grazhdanin*, 1873–74) and his work as a novelist (*The Raw Youth, Podrostok*, 1875), crowned by the appearance of his greatest novel, *The Brothers Karamazov*, in 1879–80. His greatest triumph occurred during the celebrations associated with the unveiling of the Pushkin memorial in Moscow in June 1880 when his speech was greeted by an enormous popular ovation. His funeral on 1 February 1881, after his death on 28 January, was an occasion for large-scale mourning.

Dostoevsky's first work, *Poor Folk*, may have the old-fashioned appearance of an exchange of letters between an impoverished middle-aged clerk, Devushkin, and a much younger girl, but this simple formula is given psychological depth and its particular Dostoevskian character through the way in which Devushkin's letters become intricate confessions not only of his passion for the girl but also of a dawning awareness of his own identity, his social place and the meaning of his poverty. Devushkin's sense of alienation in an urban world is the first instance of a major concern of Dostoevsky: the problem of human identity in urban society. Dostoevsky's second work, *The Double*, demonstrated on a pathological level a confusion over identity already discernible in Devushkin, though in this case the dilemma of Golyadkin senior persecuted by his malicious double, Golyadkin junior, has as many comic as schizophrenic features and is on the whole more noteworthy for its dramatic concentration of events in time and its use of the *skandal* scene than for its psychology. The greatest of Dostoevsky's works all have such a 'dramatic' time-scheme and are built on successive 'scandalous' scenes involving the public humiliation of one or another character. Dostoevsky experimented with many forms and themes in his work of the 1840s, but strictly speaking he became master of none. Nor is there any real evidence of prominence being given to socio-political or religious ideas, and it is hard to discern more than the faint lineaments of the writer's future stature in these beginnings.

On his release from penal servitude in 1854 he confessed to a correspondent his doubts and his faith in one of the most remarkable testaments of the nineteenth century:

> I will tell you about myself that I am a child of the age, a child of disbelief and doubt up to this time and even (I know) to the end of my life … And yet God sometimes sends me moments when I am completely at peace; at those times I love, and I find that I am loved by others, and in such moments I have composed for myself a symbol of faith, in which everything for me is lucid and holy. This symbol is very simple, it is: to believe that there is nothing more beautiful, profound, loving, wise, courageous and perfect than Christ, and not only is there not, but I tell myself with jealous love there cannot be. What is more, if someone proved to me that Christ was outside the truth, and it was really true that the truth was outside Christ, then I would still prefer to remain with Christ than with the truth.
>
> (Letter to N.D. Fon-Vizina,
> February 1854.)

This testament only began to achieve a specific literary relevance in his work some ten years later when, in his *Notes from the Underground*, he proclaimed his doubts about the scientism, materialism and radicalism of the 1860s by opposing the notion of man as an essentially rational creature with his own concept of man as essentially capricious, sceptical and wilful. But his first successful realization of this concept in a literary characterization came with Raskolnikov, the student drop-out of the novel *Crime and Punishment* who commits murder in order to prove his right to be a self-willed Napoleon but eventually discovers his fallibility and the nihilistic futility of his motives. Raskolnikov is confronted by a dilemma of choice which is reflected also in his own divided character. These choices are between the arrogance of man who has usurped the place of God (Svidrigaylov) and the humility of the prostitute Sonya who acknowledges the need for faith and forgiveness. Whether or not Raskolnikov achieves moral regeneration under Sonya's influence must remain in doubt, but the dramatic power of this majestic noveltragedy, the profundity of its ideas and its nightmarish blending of a squalid urban reality with the characters' fevered subconscious has made it the basis of Dostoevsky's reputation as Russia's leading nineteenth-century novelist.

In his second major novel, *The Idiot*, Dostoevsky attempted to embody his concept of a contemporary Christ in the child-like 'idiot' Prince Myshkin, whose gospel is a mixture of salvation through the power of beauty and Russian messianism. Brilliant though the first and final parts of the novel are, as a whole the work is overburdened with talkative, polemicizing characters and sub-plots. If there is hope for Russia through the promise of a Russian Christ in *The Idiot*, in Dostoevsky's third great novel, *The Possessed* (or *The Devils*), the future of Russia is projected as one of turmoil in which an intelligentsia, poisoned by Western ideas and nihilistic influences, cannot discover a faith in itself or in the God-carrying Russian people. Stavrogin, the supposed saviour of the intelligentsia, is apparently torn between a nihilistic vision of freedom (represented by his disciple Kirillov) and the possibility of religious faith (embodied in the faith-seeking Shatov), but is eventually manipulated by the terrorist Pyotr Verkhovensky to serve his own destructive ends. As a diagnosis of the political tyranny awaiting Russia as a result of revolution this novel proved to be the most difficult of Dostoevsky's novels for Soviet critics to interpret.

After this powerful, if black, comedy, Dostoevsky aspired to reappraise the situation of Russia in more positive terms, but his study of an 'accidental family' (*A Raw Youth*) contributed little to this process and it was not until he attended the trial of the terrorist Vera Zasulich in 1878 that he found the formula for his last and greatest novel, *The Brothers Karamazov*. This novel is built around the trial of Dmitry Karamazov for the murder of his father. The result was a miscarriage of justice and the novel is so structured as to reveal, through an analysis of motive, why such a miscarriage should have occurred.

The Karamazov family is treated as a microcosm of the Russian situation. The three legitimate brothers represent, in Dmitry's case, mundane contemporary Russia, in Ivan's, the influence of the West and, in Alyosha's, holy Russia with its spirit of true Christian faith. Though Ivan's critique of the church and denial of God (especially in the famous 'Grand Inquisitor' chapter) appear to make an unanswerable attack on the injustice of the world, it is counterbalanced by the vision of a just world based on mutual responsibility for the world's sinfulness which Alyosha's mentor, Father Zosima, offers in his teaching. The ultimate guilt rests with those, like Ivan, who incite humanity to a total nihilistic freedom in the moral sphere.

The Brothers Karamazov, as the culmination of his achievement, sets in relief Dostoevsky's lifelong concern with the paradoxes of choice which confront humankind. Posed always in highly dramatic confrontations for and against, in fictional worlds that are as resonantly polyphonic as they are teeming with characters, Dostoevsky's heroes live their convictions and commitments at fever pitch; and in this intensity of commitment to life, as if to an act of faith that has passed through all the crucibles of doubt, lies Dostoevsky's greatness.

Further reading

Other works: (in Constance Garnett's translations) *The Eternal Husband, and Other Stories*; *An Honest Thief, and Other Stories*; *The Friend of the Family, and Other Stories*; (in Jessie Coulson's translation) *The Gambler/Bobok, A Nasty Story*; translations of Dostoevsky's notebooks for his major fiction are available in editions by the Chicago University Press and Ardis, Ann Arbor, Michigan. See: Joseph Frank's five-volume of life of Dostoevsky (1976–2002): *The Seeds of Revolt, 1821–49* (1976); *The Years of Ordeal, 1850–59* (1987); *The Stir of Liberation, 1860–65* (1992); *The Miraculous Years, 1865–71* (1995); and *Mantle of the Prophet 1871–81* (2002). Other biographies available in English are by L. Grossman (trans. Mary Mackler, 1974), R. Hingley (1978) and K.V. Mochulsky (trans. M.A. Miniham, 1967). See also: M.M. Bakhtin, *Problems of Dostoevsky's Poetics* (trans. R.W. Rotsel, 1973); D. Fanger, *Dostoevsky and Romantic Realism* (1967); J. Frank, *Dostoevsky, The Seeds of Revolt, 1821–49* (1976); a chapter on *Crime and Punishment* in R. Freeborn, *The Rise of the Russian Novel* (1973); M. Holquist, *Dostoevsky and the Novel* (1977); M. Jones, *Dostoevsky, The Novel of Discord* (1976); R. Peace, *Dostoyevsky: An Examination of the Major Novels* (1971); *Dostoievsky: A Collection of Critical Essays*, ed. R. Wellek (1962); Malcolm V. Jones, *Dostoyevsky after Bakhtin: Readings in Dostoyevsky's Fantastic Realism* (1990); Peter Kaye, *Dostoevsky and English Modernism 1900–1930* (1999); Kenneth Lantz (ed.), *The Dostoevsky Encyclopedia* (2004).

RICHARD FREEBORN

DOYLE, (Sir) Arthur Conan

1859–1930

British novelist

Arthur Conan Doyle was born in Edinburgh in 1859. A member of an Irish Catholic family, he was educated at Stonyhurst in Lancashire and studied medicine at Edinburgh University. For a few years, before the success of his writing gave him a substantial income, he had a medical practice near Portsmouth. An adventurous temperament and an innate curiosity had already prompted him to spend several months as ship's doctor on an Arctic whaler. These qualities, together with his humanitarianism, later took him to South Africa during the Boer War. His work there as a doctor and, more importantly, his polemical writings on behalf of the British cause earned him his knighthood in 1902.

It was the Sherlock Holmes stories that gave Doyle his first public success and it is with Holmes and his narrator, Dr Watson, that their creator is lastingly associated. Doyle was, however, a prolific and tireless worker who wrote historical romances, supernatural tales, a series of short stories featuring the bombastic Brigadier Gerard, and a group of novels and tales about Professor Challenger, the irascible scientific genius whose theories (like Holmes's) are always proved right. Ironically, Doyle expended more creative effort on historical works while the Holmes stories were produced quickly and to order. Doyle put much research into such novels; from his mother and his childhood reading he inherited a love of an age of romantic and chivalrous simplicity which in a novel such as *The White Company* (1891) is qualified by a mild irony. Also evident in this early production is his narrative dexterity. Another side of Doyle's nature is suggested by the words of the storyteller in the short tale of the supernatural, *The Leather Funnel* (1900): 'I have myself, in my complex nature, a hunger after all which is bizarre and fantastic.' This is exemplified by some of the memorably odd concepts to be found in Doyle's work: the survival in South America of a dinosaur-filled plateau in *The Lost World* (1912); the notion that the earth is the shell of a monstrous animal like a sea-urchin (*When the World Screamed*, 1929). Bizarre mysteries and riddles abound in the Holmes canon and elsewhere, for example the complete disappearance of a train in *The Lost Special* (1919) or the reasons behind the existence of a society which promotes the welfare of red-headed men (*The Red-Headed League*, 1891). The riddles are soluble but a trace of the grotesque and of the Victorian macabre still clings to facts which can be rationally explained. Doyle also attempted scientific investigations himself in the miasma of spiritualism, of which he was a fervent proponent in the last years of his life.

This is reflected in the Professor Challenger story, *The Land of Mist* (1926).

The model for Sherlock Holmes, and in part for his deductive methods, was Dr Joseph Bell, a surgeon and lecturer at Edinburgh University. Holmes's principal literary antecedent is Auguste Dupin, the amateur detective created by Edgar Allan Poe. Holmes and Watson first appeared in *A Study in Scarlet* (1888), subsequently in three novels and over fifty short stories. What distinguished Doyle from his predecessors in the genre and from most of those who have come after is narrative pace, directness and simplicity of characterization, the ability to create economically a sense of place. Almost invariably the stories begin with Holmes's being offered a problem by an anguished or baffled client; the detective's importance is suggested by the frequency with which the famous find their way to Baker Street, his chivalry and benevolence by a willingness to help the underdog. Holmes's eccentricities, his powers of observation, his application of logic to situations where whimsy seemed the dominant factor became as familiar to British and American readers as his appearance, 'that pale, clear-cut face and loose-limbed figure'.

The detective's popularity was so great that when Doyle, anxious that his literary energies should not be directed too much into one channel, killed Holmes off in *The Final Problem* (1893), public entreaties and financial inducements caused the author to bring him back to life (the resurrection is made plausible in *The Empty House*, 1903). The problems in the stories, although central to their interest, never overshadow every other element. The best illustration of Doyle's vigorous, often sombre imagination is the Holmes novel *The Hound of the Baskervilles* (1902), in which the author transforms Gothic nightmare into Victorian crime. The Holmes stories perhaps provided for their public a heightening of the details of an everyday life threatened by the bizarre and criminal but ultimately controlled by an heroic intelligence.

Further reading

Conan Doyle's other works include: *Uncle Bernac* (1897); *The Adventures of Gerard* (1903); *The Poison Belt* (1913); *The Maracot Deep* (1929). See: Erik Routley, *The Puritan Pleasures of the Detective Story* (1972); Julian Symons, *Bloody Murder* (1972); Charles Higham, *The Adventures of Conan Doyle* (1976); J.L. Lellenberg, *The Quest for Sir Arthur Conan Doyle* (1987); H. Orel (ed.), *Critical Essays on Sir Arthur Conan Doyle* (1992); M. Booth, *The Doctor, the Detective and Arthur Conan Doyle* (1997).

PHILIP GOODEN

DUBUFFET, Jean-Philippe-Arthur
1901–85
French artist

A former wine merchant, Jean Dubuffet pursued a highly successful artistic career on the premise that originality stems from calculated acts of dissociation from the habits of perception and cultural conditioning. In the lecture 'Anticultural Positions' (1951), he announced that 'our culture is a garment which no longer fits. It is more and more estranged from our true life. I aspire to an art plugged directly in to everyday living.' His early paintings of ordinary people – a man on a bike, a girl milking a cow – combine the awkwardness of child art with the anonymity of graffiti, and reflect the artist's flair for making what seems least 'beautiful' become seductive. The scandalous *Corps de dames* series (1950), in which that touchstone of traditional aesthetics, the female nude, is caricatured as a horrendous hag, jaggedly incised into messy impasto, led to Dubuffet's installation as the *peintre maudit* of post-war international art.

Dubuffet's concern has been systematically to break the rules of orthodox representation and painterly technique; in so doing he has spawned a number of varied styles in a wide range of media, some of them suggesting (perhaps superficially) analogies with artists like Grosz, **Klee**, **Pollock**, Fautrier or **Tapiès**. In the late 1950s he celebrated the amorphous textures of non-human surfaces in resin-based pictures like *Exemplary Life of the Soil* (1958), which offers the spectator the equivalent, hung on the gallery wall, of a section of earth underfoot.

In 1962, Dubuffet arrived at his *ne plus ultra*, the *Hourloupe* style (allegedly inspired by a telephone-pad doodle), an idiom of interlocking irregular shapes grossly hatched in anti-natural colours (bold reds, blues, blacks) which flatten any object depicted and create an eerie continuum of busy segments without depth or differentiation. Over the next twelve years the *Hourloupe* cycle progressed in scale, with three-dimensional objects of painted polystyrene, then larger ones in epoxy such as the monumental *Group of Four Trees* (1969), set outside the Chase Manhattan Bank in New York. The cycle culminates in the *Closerie Falbala* (1969–76), an immense environmental work of white polyester striated in black, covering some 1,600 square metres, inside which the visitor may well experience a final sense of estrangement not only from culture but even from natural sensation. This unearthly edifice has been erected outside Paris as the centrepiece of the Dubuffet Foundation.

Of constant inspiration to the artist was his collection of *Art brut* or 'raw art' – the work of madmen, mediums, hermits and other marginals who, in Dubuffet's view, create inventive art by virtue of their imperviousness to established culture. It is largely thanks to his sponsorship that the psychotic artists Adolf Wölfli and Aloïse Corbaz achieved international recognition.

Further reading

Dubuffet's work is exhaustively detailed in the multi-volumed *Catalogue intégral des travaux de Jean Dubuffet*, ed. M. Loreau (1964–). His writings include *Prospectus et tous écrits suivants* (2 vols, 1967) and *Asphyxiante culture* (1968). See also: P. Selz, *The Work of Jean Dubuffet* (1962); *L'Herne*, No. 22, ed. J. Berne (1973); M. Loreau, *Jean Dubuffet: Stratégie de la création* (1973); *Chambres pour Dubuffet* (exhibition catalogue, 1995).

ROGER CARDINAL

DURKHEIM, Émile
1858–1917
French sociologist

Durkheim is generally regarded as one of the founders of sociology. More than any other single figure he is responsible for the branch of sociology that approaches social phenomena from the scientific standpoint. The notion that society is susceptible to scientific investigation is, however, only derivatively his. It is rather a systematic rationale for this conviction, together with his application of it in practice, which elevated Durkheim to a position of eminence unsurpassed within the discipline.

Of Jewish parentage, Durkheim was born in Épinal, Lorraine. He gained entry to the École Normale Supérieure in 1879 and later took one year's leave of absence (1885–6) to study in Germany. In the course of these formative years he was influenced by figures prominent in the French intellectual tradition, most notably Saint-Simon, Comte, Fustel de Coulanges and Émile Boutroux. Significant also were the neo-Kantian Renouvier and the German psychologist Wilhelm Wundt. He held a combined chair of sociology and education at Bordeaux from 1887 to 1902, and one at the Sorbonne from that time until his death. During this latter period he was instrumental in founding an influential journal for the yearly review of literature pertaining to the social sciences, *L'Année sociologique*. His own authorship in the field was considerable, the major works being *The Division of Labour in Society* (*De la Division du travail social: étude sur l'organisation des sociétés supérieures*, 1893); *The Rules of Sociological Method* (*Les Règles de la méthode sociologique*, 1895); *Suicide* (*Le Suicide: étude de sociologie*, 1897); and *The Elementary Forms of Religious Life* (*Les Formes élémentaires de la vie religieuse*, 1912).

Durkheim was the beneficiary of two streams of thought which gathered force towards the end of the nineteenth century. The first was a fervent optimism in the capacities of science; the second, a new conception of society based on considering it as an entity in its own right rather than a simple conglomerate of individual lives. Applying the first to the second of these ideas, Durkheim sought to establish a science of society. Early in his career he defined the distinctive character of the discipline he envisaged and clarified the ways in which it differed from psychology and biology, sciences which had already embarked upon the task of unravelling the mysteries of human behaviour. Society, he argued in *The Rules*, warrants its own scientific enterprise because the interaction of individuals generates customs, traditions and codes of conduct which themselves constitute an original and irreducible body of data. Although they exist in and through the minds of men, these phenomena are external to the individual in that they await him at birth and continue after his death. They are not products of his own creation but are received by him as part of his cultural heritage. Furthermore, they impose upon his will. Constraining the basic self-seeking impulses of his psyche, they regulate his conduct to conform with community standards. Hence they are not accurately classified as psychological. Yet neither are they biological in character. Social phenomena are not physical but ideational. They are 'ways of acting, thinking and feeling' (*RSM*, 3), which are, nevertheless, 'real' in the sense that they are objects of perception conceived from data drawn from outside the mind. Awareness of them comes from observation; it is through experience that we learn of their existence. To these phenomena Durkheim gave the name 'social facts'. For the sociologist:

> A social fact is recognized by the power of external coercion which it exercises or is capable of exercising over individuals, and the presence of this power may be recognized in its turn either by the existence of some specific sanction or by the resistance offered against every individual effort that tends to violate it.
>
> (*RSM*, 10)

Having thus specified his subject-matter Durkheim set out the method by which it was to be investigated. Since the founding of an empirical science was his aim, the model he advocated was, in all fundamental respects, that of the natural sciences. Causal analysis was the keystone. Sociology was to determine the causal connections operating between human associations (as cause) and states of the 'conscious collective' (as effect). By the former Durkheim understood 'the ways in which the constituent parts of society (individuals) are grouped' (*RSM*, 112); by the latter, the set of beliefs and sentiments, duties and obligations commonly held within a given society (*DLS*, 79), which renders its individual members solidarity. In *The Division of Labour in Society* he identified two such organizational aspects of the social milieu: '(1) the number of social units, or ... the *size of a society*; and (2) the degree of concentration of the group ... the *dynamic density*' (*DLS*, 113). These, he found, were correlated with states of the *conscience collective* as it changed over time. Durkheim endeavoured to show that, due to the division of labour, the *conscience collective* of modern Western society had been transformed. While in the past the form of association had been segmental (all units identical) and communal solidarity based on similarity ('mechanical solidarity'), modern society was evolving a co-operative form (units differentiated) and a solidarity based on interdependence ('organic solidarity'). In the social aggregates of primitive peoples uniformity was undisturbed by factors of diversity. Daily existence was the same for all, each man being himself responsible for all items of sustenance. The division of labour brought diversity of occupation and with it individual variability. But even though social solidarity has thus been lessened, the weakness is only temporary. The emergent individuation of the species carries with it the seed of a new organic form of solidarity wherein each unit exists in a network of interdependent social relations.

There is, for the sociologist, an important lesson to be learned from this work. Here,

Durkheim exemplifies his point (elaborated in *The Rules*) that the sociologist must beware of taking a lay definition of his subject of investigation as his starting-point. Dealing with that most familiar of phenomena, the social world, we must be constantly critical of the unconsidered assumptions upon which we order our daily lives. In Durkheim's time, the division of labour was commonly regarded as an obnoxious development which would corrupt or restrict the natural unfolding of human nature. His analysis exposed the latent prejudice in this assumption, a prejudice carried over from the layman's fear of the novel. Far from being an undesirable feature of the evolution of the species, the division of labour was, in Durkheim's view, destined to produce a tighter and more resilient social bonding than that which had existed previously. Again, the common-sense assumption that crime and deviance are social evils and disruptive of community will be shown false when subjected to dispassionate examination. According to Durkheim, moral sentiments are inculcated in the young and sustained in society at large, mainly through the witnessing of socially expressed disapproval: the application of sanctions. Hence it follows that society must have the opportunity to punish which only crime and deviance provide, and that therefore these elements are a functional necessity of social life.

This introduces another important aspect of Durkheim's sociology, viz. his functionalism. The aim of sociology is, he holds, to determine not only the causes of social phenomena but also their social function. It is through functional analysis that sociology will benefit mankind. Stripped of prejudice the sociologist's analyses would discriminate between 'normal' and 'pathological' developments. For instance, while the division of labour was found to be a normal development, suicide (in particular its increasing incidence in the Western world) is, Durkheim maintained, pathological. In *Suicide* he utilized the 'comparative method', this being his one methodological concession to the difference between the natural and

social sciences. Due to the lack of experimental opportunity and the complexity of the causal networks operating in the social world, the sociologist must compare sets of social facts drawn from different societies, or different segments of the one society, in order to arrive at his generalizations. By comparing statistics of suicide rates, Durkheim was able to pinpoint specifically social causes for what appears to be a psychological or biological phenomenon. Finding the suicide rate to be correlated with religious affiliation, the divorce rate and severe disruptions in the social order – and this to be true of different societies – he exposed the integrative function of religion, marriage and family, and politico-economic stability. The obligations and duties imposed by the institutions of religion and family bind the individual to fellow members of these social groupings. And on a more general level, that individual is bound to his society as a whole by the moral order which establishes an equilibrium between, on the one hand, his situation in society and the purposes, ambitions and desires appropriate to it, and on the other, the social means and natural talents which render the attainment of these a real possibility. In modern society, both the political and economic spheres are in constant fluctuation and hence the individual's position and expectations are abruptly and frequently altered. He no longer knows what society expects of him or thinks proper to apportion to him, with the result that he himself has no notion of what he may reasonably desire or, in justice, be asked to give. He thus falls prey to discontent and uncertainty. In principle, everything is possible, for society fails to perform its delimiting and defining role. In practice, the inequality of human talent and ability determine that it is not. Society has cast him loose in a sea of infinite desires with no directions for selecting those possible of fulfilment.

Implicit in this is a view of human nature and a conception of the essence and role of morality. For all that Durkheim wants to establish sociology as a discipline independent of psychology, his social theory is founded on the assumption that men have a vital psychological need of morality. Far from being a mere social contrivance to oil the wheels of social intercourse, morality is essential to psychological well-being, for it not only constrains but actually defines the purposes and desires of human existence. Unlike those of other animal species, human desires are boundless. Once the conditions necessary for his physical maintenance are supplied, man craves a higher standard of comfort. And once that is attained, he wants still more. Without the external regulating force of the moral order his passions are insatiable. The ungoverned imagination cannot escape 'the futility of an endless pursuit' that ends finally in consummate weariness and disillusionment (*Suicide*). This condition, a pathology of the modern world, Durkheim called 'anomie'. He saw it, however, as a transitory phase. Society being now an organic entity, the dysfunction of one component will, in time, be compensated by adjustment. For example, the decline in religious observance, seen by Durkheim as a concomitant of the progress of science, heralds the emergence of new secular religious forms which will, ultimately, fulfil the same integrative function as the religions of the past. This prediction follows from the main line of his argument in *The Elementary Forms of Religious Life*.

As in all his substantive work, Durkheim begins his study of religion by questioning the validity of the received conception of the phenomenon under investigation. The notion that the defining characteristic of religion is a belief in the supernatural does not, he found, stand up to examination. Some religions (an instance is Buddhism) do not hold this belief. What is common to all is a conceptual division of the world into the two domains of the sacred and the profane. Unlike profane objects which men deal with intellectually and practically, sacred objects elicit the religious feelings of awe and reverence. The true referent of these feelings is not, however, any supernatural being but is society. The gods, according to Durkheim,

are the symbols which represent community. The religious conviction that there exists a transcendent entity is in fact man's awareness of his relation to society. Hence, although science will bring about the demise of particular religions founded in earlier centuries by rendering their particular symbols inappropriate, new forms will inevitably arise as men seek to restore their communion with the social milieu.

For Durkheim, all ideas issue from the collectivity and their emergence and decline reflect the changing character of society as it moves through time. It is this notion that underlies the sociology of knowledge, a field upon which he has had considerable impact. Durkheim holds that it is social organization that generates ideas. Even the most fundamental have this origin. Our ideas of space derive from the spatial organization of primitive community life. Likewise our organization of time into calendar units once corresponded to cyclical community celebrations and ritual observances. The *tabula rasa* is writ upon not by experience *per se* but by social experience. The very categories of thought are produced – not merely influenced – by the social environment.

In this extreme form Durkheim's conception of the societal input to knowledge has not found adherents. It is now regarded as an overstatement of the more modest yet indubitable truth that ideas are in large part shaped by the social context in which they arise. Nevertheless, it was with these arguments that Durkheim, together with **Marx** and Mannheim, initiated the study of correlations between systems of thought and forms of social structure. He has been particularly influential in this and also one other development within the discipline. Both are forms of 'structuralism', but the other, through the Parsonian synthesis, is less concerned with thought systems and places more emphasis on the organizational aspects of the social order and the structural relations among their elements. But Durkheim's greatest contribution to sociology has been the general one of setting the example for rigorous and innovative research guided by a clear conception of subject-matter and a systematic methodology.

Further reading

See: T. Parsons, *The Structure of Social Actions* (1937); R.K. Merton, *Social Theory and Social Structure* (1957); A. Giddens, *Émile Durkheim: Selected Writings*, Introduction (1972); S. Lukes, *Émile Durkheim: His Life and Work* (1973); R.A. Nisbet, *The Sociology of Émile Durkheim* (1975); K. Thompson, *Émile Durkheim* (1989); Stjepan G. Mestrovic, *Émile Durkheim and the Reformation of Sociology* (1993); Anthony Giddens, *Durkheim* (1997).

BOBBIE LEDERMAN

DVOŘÁK, Antonin

1841–1904

Bohemian (Czech) composer

A butcher's son, Dvořák was slow to make his way as a composer, producing nothing significant until he was in his thirties. Once started, however, he wrote copiously in all the standard genres: ten operas, nine symphonies, a host of other orchestral works, several quartets, a variety of large-scale choral works, numerous songs and many sets of piano pieces. Indeed, like Schubert he gives the impression of having composed sponta-neously and with ease. He had a great gift for melody, and he had no problems with orchestration, having in his youth worked as a professional viola player in the Prague opera orchestra under Smetana (1866–73). And it was Smetana's example that was to be so useful to him in giving a distinctively Czech flavour to his music.

However, at first he was most influenced by **Wagner**, as is evident in the early sym-phonies that were never published during his lifetime: No. 1 in C minor (1865), No. 2 in B flat major (1865), No. 3 in E flat major (1873) and No. 4 in D minor (1874). The third won him an Austrian national prize and brought him to the attention of **Brahms**, who was on the jury. Brahms became a per-sonal friend and champion of his music, but it was only when he had taken note of

Smetana, in the *Three Slavonic Rhapsodies* and *Eight Slavonic Dances* for orchestra (all 1878), that his mature style began to form, and indeed the great majority of his most familiar works were composed after the mid-1880s. Of his later symphonies, for example, Nos 5 in F major (1875) and 6 in D major (1880) have never been as popular as Nos 7 in D minor (1885), 8 in G major (1889) and 9 in E minor (1893). No. 7, unusually dramatic and firmly unified, was consciously composed in emulation of Brahms, whereas the other two later symphonies concentrate on what came most naturally to Dvořák: flowing melody and fresh woodwind scoring redolent of the countryside.

His Ninth Symphony bears the subtitle *From the New World* (*Z noveho svéta*) and was one of the works he composed in America as director of the National Conservatory of Music in New York (1892–5). In it he was stimulated by Black American and Indian music, though the feeling is just as much Czech: the case of the 'American' Quartet in F major (also 1893) is precisely similar. For Dvořák's procedure was to use general fea-tures of folk music rather than quote specific melodies, and his American material offered the same kind of modal patterns that he found in the music of his own country. In matters of rhythm, though, he was more inclined to borrow directly from folk music; for example, the scherzos of both his Sixth and his Seventh Symphonies use the crossed metres, triple and duple, of the *furiant*, a Czech dance.

Dvořák's period in America was produc-tive, seeing the composition not only of the 'New World' Symphony and 'American' Quartet but also of his Cello Concerto (1895), his last great essay in standard symphonic form. Moreover, as the first distinguished European composer to spend time in the New World, he had a notable influence on the emergence of American music, encouraging composers to seek stimulus in the music they found around them, as he had done. But he felt a strong need to return to his own terri-tory, and he spent the last decade of his life teaching at the Prague Conservatoire. The major works of this period were a set of symphonic poems based on fairy tales and three operas, *The Devil and Kate* (*Čert a Káča*, 1898–9), *Rusalka* (1900, another fairy-tale piece) and *Armida* (1902–3), all of which show some return of his Wagnerism.

These interests of his late years draw attention to the strain of **Liszt–Wagner** descriptiveness in Dvořák's musical character, for although his orchestral output is dominated by works in the abstract forms – symphonies, concertos (one for piano, 1876, and one for violin, 1879, as well as that for cello) and the Symphonic Variations (1877) – he also wrote a triptych of overtures under the title *Nature, Life and Love*, comprising *Amid Nature* (*Vpírod*, 1891), *Carnival* (*Karneval*, 1891) and *Othello* (1891–2), apart from the final symphonic poems: *The Water Sprite*, (*Vodnik*, 1896), *The Noonday Witch* (*Polednice* 1896), *The Golden Spinning Wheel* (*Zlatý kolovrat* 1896), *The Wood Dove* (*Holoubek*, 1896) and *Heroic Song* (1897). In all but the last of these he derived melodies from lines of Czech verse, a conscious intensification of his normal practice of letting Czech speech patterns influence his melodic thinking.

Inevitably this happened most conspicuously in his operas. The first of them, *Alfred* (1870), was a Wagnerian piece with a German libretto, but in all the others he used his native language, contributing with Smetana and Fibich to the great flowering of Czech opera in the last three decades of the century. These operas include two comedies, *The Pig-Headed Peasants* (*Tvrdé palice*, 1874) and *The Peasant a Rogue* (*Selma sedlàk*, 1877), and two grand operas, the tragedy *Vanda* (1876) and the historical epic *Dimitrij* (1881–2), which continues the story of **Mussorgsky's** *Boris Godunov*. But his operatic masterpiece was *The Jacobin* (*Jakobin*, 1887–8), concerned with life in a Bohemian village and filled with romantic melody, especially associated with the figure of a schoolmaster-musician with whom the composer obviously identified.

Among his other vocal works were two popular sets of songs, the four *Gypsy Songs* (1880, including 'Songs My Mother Taught Me') and the ten *Biblical Songs* (1894, texts from the psalms), as well as three bigger pieces composed for English audiences: the cantata *The Spectre's Bride* (1885), the oratorio *St Ludmila* (1886) and the *Requiem* (1891). Like Mendelssohn before him, Dvořák enjoyed great favour in England, not only on account of the melodiousness of his contributions to the oratorio tradition – including also a *Stabat Mater* (1876–7), a Mass in D (1887) and a *Te Deum* (1892) – but also for his symphonies, among which the Seventh and Eighth were given their first performances by the Philharmonic Society of London.

Unlike his colleague Smetana, therefore, Dvořák was established internationally long before his death and was able to prove the possibility of a Czech voice in all the customary musical forms. And though his own brand of romantic nationalism barely outlasted him, his work as a teacher (of his son-in-law Josef Suk among others) encouraged others to take up the challenge presented by his achievements.

Further reading

Other works include: Serenade for string orchestra, 1875; Serenade in D minor for wind and low strings, 1878; *Legends* for piano duet or orchestra, 1881; Scherzo capriccioso for orchestra, 1883; Piano Quintet in A major, 1887; Piano Trio in E minor 'Dumky', 1890–1; String quartets in A flat major and G major, both 1895. See: John Clapham, *Dvořák: Musician and Craftsman* (1966); Robert Layton, *Dvořák Symphonies and Concertos* (1978); M. Beckerman (ed.), *Dvořák and His World* (1993); B. Beveridge (ed.), *Rethinking Dvořák: Views from Five Countries* (1996); Kurt Honolka, *Dvořák: Life and Times* (2004).

PAUL GRIFFITHS

DYLAN, Bob (Robert Allen ZIMMERMAN)
1941–
US rock 'n' roll musician

Even his disclaimers ('I'm just an entertainer . . . a song and dance man . . . a trapeze artist') are part of the picture of Dylan as the articulate consciousness of his generation in the mid-1960s, the 'Angelic Dylan singing across the nation' of **Allen Ginsberg's** 1966 *Wichita Vortex Sutra*. As a focus first for radical dissent, then for psychic revolution, he altered sensibilities and political attitudes; as a performer in the traditions of blues, rock and country music his influence is huge; as a poet and songwriter he is *the* major artist of rock 'n' roll.

Born in Duluth, Minnesota, and brought up in the nearby iron-ore mining town of Hibbing, he learnt piano, guitar and harmonica as a child, experiencing America's musical richness through radio. In his teens he played in high-school rock bands, and after a brief spell at the University of Minnesota in Minneapolis (1959–60) he left for New York, impassioned by the discovery of Woody Guthrie, the source of his early vocal style and political awareness, which he began to channel through the current vogue for folk-lyricism.

The first record, *Bob Dylan* (1962), presents arrangements of traditional songs and blues, delivered in a harsh nasal voice already showing the control, intensity and immaculate timing of a brilliant talent, suggesting depths of experience and suffering, as well as humour and sincerity. *The Freewheelin' Bob Dylan* (1963) is a variety of his own compositions: castigations of the war machine, dream-framework songs of nuclear insanity, wit and candour in love relationships, all with a chary clear-eyed wisdom. He transcends the folk idiom by refusing its nostalgia and by confronting current issues with imaginative breadth.

The label 'protest singer' was a commercial tag too narrow to define the visionary tone of *The Times They Are A-Changin'* (1964). The disgrace of a supposedly impartial justice when dealing with crimes against the Negro, the divisive tactics of a class society in fostering such crimes, are paired with vignettes of poor-white despair under the neglect and inhuman fluctuation of capitalist economics. An optimistic counterpart is in the album's title track, whose image of revolutionary flood

under a new consciousness is extended in 'When the Ship Comes In', when 'The chains of the sea/Will have busted in the night/And will be buried at the bottom of the ocean.'

While such anthems were making him the spokesman for activism, Dylan was already claiming greater freedom of expression. 'Restless Farewell' is his goodbye to 'The dirt of gossip ... And the dust of rumours', and heralds the change from objective to subjective which is begun in *Another Side of Bob Dylan* (1964), and completed in *Bringing It All Back Home* (1965). Under the influence of **Kennedy's** assassination, drugs, the reading of poets like Ginsberg and **Rimbaud**, confidence in his own artistic power, and the rock revival launched from England, he returned to the native traditions of Chicago, Memphis and the Mississippi Delta.

In 1964 he said, 'I don't want to write *for* people anymore ... I want to write from inside me', and this desire emerges in the Blakean visions and personal venom of *Another Side*, as well as in the generally more emphatic syncopation. The transition to a fuller musical sound is made with Side 1 of *Bringing It All Back Home*, when studio musicians are first used to accompany his guitar and harmonica. Zany, surreal, nihilistic fantasies full of tumbling images and transcendent juxtapositions complete this major statement. His ideas were now couched in an entirely different perceptual mould, the songs capable of simultaneously rewarding and evading intense scrutiny. The American Nightmare is indicted through invitation to enter a nightmare condition in which the promise of any security in known points of contact is withheld. Millions in the West were prepared to follow.

The final break with, or, in his own terms, the re-synthesis of American folk music, was made at the Newport Folk Festival in 1965, when Dylan performed with full electric blues-rock accompaniment. In the same year he worked with The Hawks, later known as The Band. Tuneful organ punctuations, percussive piano and tambourine, whining harmonica and wailing guitars achieve 'that thin, that wild mercury sound … metallic and bright gold' of his stated ideal on the two definitive rock albums of the 1960s, *Highway 61 Revisited* (1965) and *Blonde On Blonde* (1966). Here a painful, violent rage overspills through a weird swirl of imagined characters and situations, unresolved mysteries, the sense of confusion and alienation hurled in bitter accusations of which Dylan himself is the target as much as the disoriented victims of the songs. In this whirlwind period the pressure is towards reliance on imagination, creativity and self, rather than facts, culture and the other.

In August 1966 Dylan broke his neck in a motorcycle crash. The enforced rest was followed by several years of uncertain experiment in his music and attitudes, some of which is reflected in informal sessions with The Band, recorded in 1967 and released in 1975 as *The Basement Tapes*. The tone of his work in the next five years is predominantly low-key, even mellow. The simple melodies of *John Wesley Harding* (1968), using only bass and drum backing, deal in pity, guilt, remorse and loneliness, with a sense of order and morality replacing chaotic vision. *Nashville Skyline* (1969) is a happy country-style collection, and *Self-Portrait* (1970) an accomplished double album, mostly of other people's songs. *New Morning* (1970) begins a revival fully achieved in *Planet Waves* (1973), consisting largely of romantic love songs in which at least some of the productive ambiguity of the 1960s is apparent. The style is fresh, the voice strong, The Band's music a subtly beautiful counterpoint to the dominant themes of security in rural family seclusion and religious fundamentalism.

The year 1971 saw the publication of his book *Tarantula*, 'a series of thoughts as they came to me … not judgments but comments'. His triumphal return to major public performance with The Band is recorded on *Before the Flood* (1974). *Blood on the Tracks* (1974) treats the theme of dissolution through powerful lyrics in which security is again lost in uneasy quest. *Desire* (1975) brings his continued reinvention of himself as artist to a new peak,

treading on the heels of Rimbaud moving like a dancing bullet thru the secret streets of a hot New Jersey night filled with venom and wonder, meeting the Queen Angel in the reeds of Babylon and then to the fountain of sorrow to drift away in the hot mass of the deluge.

(cover notes)

More successful touring with The Rolling Thunder Review (*Hard Rain*, 1976, and *Bob Dylan at Budokan*, 1978) was combined with the production of his film, *Renaldo and Clara* (1978).

To the surprise, frustration and often dismay of many of his followers, in 1979 Dylan became a 'born-again' Christian, reflected in the album *Slow Train Coming* (1979). He began sermonizing between songs on stage, and for a decade his genius seemed in abeyance. Only a handful of tracks – 'When the Night Comes Falling from the Sky' (1985), for instance, or 'Blind Willie McTell' (1988) – evinced critical enthusiasm. Perhaps just because *Down in the Groove* (1988) was so bad, the more polished but still evangelical album that followed, *Oh Mercy* (1989), won a smattering of praise. But then Dylan's career slowly took off again. Embarking on 'The Never Ending Tour', he began playing live gigs twice a week at least, always mixing up his routine, and returning to his folk and blues roots. *Time Out of Mind* (1997) may have been his first collection of original songs for seven years, but tracks like 'To Make You Feel My Love' reconnected Dylan to young audiences.

A special moment for Dylan came in 2001, when he was awarded an Academy Oscar for 'Things Have Changed', written and composed by him for the film *Wonder Boys*. In the same year he released *Love and Theft*, musically as well as commercially his most successful album for a quarter of a century. Since then the still-performing 'found again' Dylan has moved back centre stage, his legendary status affirmed by *No Direction Home: Bob Dylan* (2005), a two-part **Martin Scorsese** bio-pic covering the years 1961–6, with Dylan himself narrating.

Further reading

Since 1991 seven volumes of 'Bootleg Series' recordings have been issued, collecting together takes and songs not previously released. Bob Dylan's books include *Writings and Drawings* (1973), *Lyrics 1962–1985* (1990), *Lyrics 1962–2001* (2004), and *Chronicles: Vol. One* (2004), the first of a projected five volume autobiography. About Dylan: Michael Gray, *Song and Dance Man* (originally 1972, but twice revised); Toby Thompson, *Positively Main Street* (1969); Anthony Scaduto, *Bob Dylan* (1972); *Bob Dylan: A Retrospective*, ed. Craig McGregor (1972); Sam Shepard, *Rolling Thunder Logbook* (1977); Robert Alexander, *Bob Dylan* (1968); Alan Rinzler, *Bob Dylan* (1978); Howard Sounes, *Down the Highway: The Life of Bob Dylan* (2001); Clinton Heylin, *Bob Dylan: Behind the Shades Revisited* (2003); Greil Marcus, *Like a Rolling Stone: Bob Dylan at the Crossroads* (2005). See also: David Hajdu, *Positively 4th Street: The Lives and Times of Joan Baez, Bob Dylan, Mimi Baez Farina, and Richard Farina* (2001).

JOHN PORTER
(REVISED AND UPDATED BY THE EDITOR)

E

EDISON, Thomas Alva

1847–1931

US inventor, engineer and manufacturer

As a boy in Ohio Edison gained a reputation for being odd, asking so many questions which infuriated his teachers that his mother, a teacher herself, decided to educate him at home. He read quickly and memorized easily; at twelve, only Newton's *Principia* seems to have floored him. To afford chemicals for his home laboratory he worked as a newsboy on the railroad between Port Huron and Detroit, and then, graduating to a printing press, issued his own newspaper, the first to be printed and published on a train. After his baggage coach laboratory caught fire, he and his gear were thrown off. In 1862, a station agent, father of a boy he had rescued from train rails, offered to teach Edison to be a telegrapher. He became the fastest in America; with the earnings he reinforced his technological knowledge, buying (amongst others) Faraday's writings. During the Civil War years he wandered the central states, one of those tramp operators – skilled, in demand and intellectually alert – who were transforming American communications and thereby the structure of society. He liked *Othello* and copied plays for a Cincinnati theatre. In 1868 in Boston he patented his first invention – a mechanical vote-recorder, which failed because Congress did not particularly want voting procedures speeded up – lesson number one for the young inventor: only invent what is needed. Waiting to be interviewed in New York City in 1869, he repaired a telegraph machine (basic for speculation) and immediately got a job. During the speculation burst that year, the president of a Wall Street firm paid him $40,000 for a stock ticker. So, at the age of twenty-three, he could found the first firm of consulting technologists, and for six years in Newark, New Jersey, invented continuously – practical quadruplex telegraphy in 1874, the mimeograph, telegraphic improvements, waxed paper, etc., always basing invention on social justification and commerciality. In 1876 he founded Menlo Park, New Jersey, the first industrial research factory – to produce, he planned, an invention every ten days, from a technological and scientific team. This method was a major advance on the tradition of chance individual cleverness. Before his death 'the wizard of Menlo Park' had issued nearly 1,300 inventions including radio aerials (purchased by **Marconi**), the dictaphone and gummed paper. In one four-year period the rate became one invention every five days. He had converted the lonely study, partly resulting from his deafness, into a group industry.

In 1877, he worked on and improved **Bell's** telephone to make it practical. Then he put tin foil on a cylinder and connected the waves from a needle skimming it to a receiver. The sound wave track on the foil was reproduced – the basic phonograph, for which Edison wrote out ten uses, including phonographic books for the blind. (His London company staff at this time included

Bernard Shaw.) In 1878, he improved on Sir Joseph Wilson Swan's incandescent bulb, with carbon filament, by a wire filament which would heat to white light in a vacuum without melting. Patent No. 222,898 thus ruined the gas market: two months after its invention, the electric light bulb illuminated the main street of Menlo Park. Then Edison worked to invent a generating system for the variable power needed – achieved in 1881, the year he encouraged one of his employees, a car enthusiast named **Henry Ford**. Edison's peculiar need for controlled enterprise now moulded his character in battle with his one-time associate Nikola Tesla. The latter backed alternating current against Edison's direct current in electricity transportation. He lost the electric-chair contract to Tesla and George Westinghouse (who obtained the alternating current victory to develop Niagara Falls power). The struggle was bitter and neurotic. In 1899, Edison recorded a series of images on an Eastman film-strip, flashed their projection on a screen in rapid succession, controlled by perforations fitting sprocket wheels turning at regular speed. In 1903 the Edison Company issued the first story film, *The Great Train Robbery* (director, Edwin S. Porter; length, 800 feet; with Marie Murray in the first screen cabaret; Harry Davis opened his Pittsburgh nickelodeon with it in 1905).

The electronic industry in fact begins with Edison's flair for concentrated, resistant absorption of each invention in the field in order to change it – 'genius is one per cent inspiration and ninety-nine per cent perspiration': his most famous maxim summarizes his method. He made technological inventions practical for the mass public as never before and confirmed the American legend of the poor boy becoming the self-made wealthy industrialist. It took him 8,000 experiments to produce a better storage battery than Gaston Planté's 1859 and Charles Francis Brush's 1881 inventions: the steel alkaline battery of 1905. To the public he became, according to *Harper's Weekly* in 1897:

a midnight workman with supernal forces whose mysterious phenomena have taught men their largest elemental power; a modern alchemist, who finds the philosopher's stone to be made of carbon, and with his magnetic wand changes everyday knowledge into the pure gold of new applications and original uses.

The sinister isolated genius, prominent in earlier American fiction, is characteristically offset by the boy Edison, tinkering with gadgets and delivering newspapers, and by the adult engineer technocrat and tycoon. Edison became, like Franklin, a certain kind of American mythic ideal in his own lifetime. In old age he could remember seeing the prairie schooners, or covered wagons, in Milan, Ohio, setting out for the Californian goldfields. At the end of his life he worked for nine years on the magnetic separation of iron ore from rock. But the method did not work for the rich ores in the Missah Range. His vision of controlling the world steel industry failed, his savings of two million dollars were lost. He turned to cement manufacture, hoping to produce prefabricated concrete houses in large numbers at low cost.

Further reading

See: Thomas Alva Edison, *Diary and Sunday Observations*, ed. D.D. Runes (1948). Also: Matthew Josephson, *Edison: A Biography* (1959); Ronald W. Clark, *Edison: The Man who Made the Future* (1974); Paul B. Israel, *Edison: A Life of Invention* (2000).

ERIC MOTTRAM

EIFFEL, Gustave
1832–1923
French engineer

A construction engineer of great ingenuity and versatility, Gustave Eiffel is justly renowned as the builder of the dramatic 300.51-metre Eiffel Tower, which still dominates the city of Paris. Designed for the

Universal Exhibition of 1889 it symbolizes French recovery from humiliating defeat in the Franco-Prussian War and is both a supreme technical achievement and a bizarre structure that aptly reflects the frivolity of the Belle Époque. It was, however, as a builder of railway bridges and train-sheds of a strict functional simplicity that he made his prime contribution to the French Industrial Revolution. The railways were the vehicles of that revolution and a new approach to architectural engineering was essential and vital to it. In 1867 he opened his own metal-working shops in Levallois-Perret, an industrial suburb outside Paris, and Eiffel and Company soon established an international reputation. The high bridge across the Sioule river north of Clermont-Ferrand, completed in 1869, is the direct ancestor of the Tower with its wrought-iron trusswork, its careful attention to wind bracing and the utilization of a system of rollers and rockers to launch the structure pier by pier across the wide chasm. In 1876 the magnificent span across the Douro river at Oporto was completed for the Portuguese National Railway, the challenge of the 525-foot width surmounted by building the two halves of the arch out towards each other supported from above by steel cables attached to piers set on either bank. Its success led to further important undertakings, not all linked to the ever expanding railway system, including a gasworks at Clichy, a covered market in Bordeaux and the enlargement of the Bon Marché department store in Paris in 1879.

The year 1884 saw the completion of the bridge at Garabit 400 feet above the Truyere river, and until the construction of the tallest tower Eiffel considered it 'one of the victories of modern engineering' and thought of it as his masterpiece. The subtle design for the highest arched bridge in the world left nothing to chance, and the same method used at Oporto again proved effective and the daunting project was completed in less than five years. In 1881 Eiffel had played an important part in the making of another dramatic national symbol, 'Liberty Enlightening the People', and his iron skeleton for the hollow Statue of Liberty, designed by Frédéric Auguste Bartholdi, with the supporting beams for the extended right arm running through the body to counterbalance the upward thrust is one of his most inventive solutions. A complete understanding of the capabilities of a given material enabled him to overcome the most complex structural problems, and when he came to build his finest work it was to wrought iron, the material that had revolutionized nineteenth-century industrial construction, that he turned. Above all it is the Tower that we see as the high point of Eiffel's career, and it remains a triumphant reminder of the ties between the engineer who made it possible and the painters who came to see it as a symbol of hope for the new opportunities offered by twentieth-century technology.

Further reading

Joseph Harriss, *The Tallest Tower* (1975); Jean Roman, *Paris 1890s* (1961); David I. Harvie, *Eiffel: The Genius who Reinvented Himself* (2004).

JOHN FURSE

EINSTEIN, Albert
1879–1955
German/Swiss/US physicist

Albert Einstein was born in Ulm of middle-class Jewish parentage. His early academic career was not particularly brilliant. He disliked the rigid discipline of the Luitpold Gymnasium in Munich and later succeeded in entering the prestigious Swiss Federal Polytechnic School at Zürich only at the second attempt. Here he studied mathematics and physics, but on graduating in 1900 failed to obtain an academic appointment. Instead in 1902 he secured the post of Technical Expert (Third Class) in the Swiss Patent Office at Berne. (He had renounced his German nationality in 1896 and become a Swiss citizen in 1900.) It was while working at the Patent Office that Einstein in his spare time wrote his epoch-making papers of 1905 including his announcement of the special theory of relativity. His genius in theoretical physics was soon recognized. In 1908 he was appointed *Privatdozent* in the University of Berne and then in 1909 was made associate professor of theoretical physics in the University of Zürich. In 1911 he was appointed professor at the German University in Prague (temporarily acquiring Austro-Hungarian nationality), but returned to a chair in mathematical physics at the Polytechnic in Zürich in 1912. Then in 1914 he was appointed director of the new Kaiser Wilhelm Institute for Physics in Berlin, was made a member of the Prussian Academy of Sciences and was also given a professorship in the University of Berlin. It was here that Einstein produced the final version of his general theory of relativity. However, Einstein was awarded the 1921 Nobel Prize in Physics for his work on the photoelectric effect rather than the more speculative relativity. In 1933 he left Germany due to the Nazi persecution and became a member of the new Institute for Advanced Study at Princeton in the USA. Here he remained until his death, becoming a naturalized American in 1940.

Apart from his scientific work Einstein was a passionate advocate in the causes of pacifism and Zionism. Indeed, in 1952 he was offered, but declined, the presidency of Israel. His pacifist views were profoundly affected by **Hitler's** rise to power in Germany, and in 1939 he wrote a famous letter to **Roosevelt** warning him of the danger of atomic weapons and recommending a US programme of research in this field.

In the popular imagination Einstein is regarded as a mathematician who invented an impossibly recondite theory, relativity, according to which time is relative, space is curved, light does not travel in straight lines and so on. In fact Einstein's early work, prior to general relativity, used quite simple mathematics and was distinguished rather by an amazingly clear physical insight. In the case of general relativity Einstein did not

himself invent new mathematical tools, but applied ideas on non-Euclidean geometry developed by Riemann, Ricci, Levi-Civita and others. As a mathematician Einstein was not particularly outstanding and in this respect must be regarded as the inferior of Newton. Indeed, his later work on generalizations of relativity, unified theories designed to accommodate both electromagnetism and gravitation, was largely mathematical in character and showed a considerable falling off as compared with the quality of his earlier work.

It should be stressed that much of Einstein's most original work had nothing to do with relativity. His first research interest was in thermodynamics and statistical mechanics. He virtually invented the latter discipline for himself in papers published between 1902 and 1904, independently of the more widely known work of J. Willard Gibbs (1839–1903). Stressing the importance of fluctuations in statistical theories Einstein applied his ideas to the quantitative elucidation of the Brownian motion of suspended particles in a liquid. This was one of his three famous 1905 papers, all published in the Germany monthly journal, *Annalen der Physik*. It had a profound significance in demonstrating the essential correctness of the kinetic-atomic theory of matter.

The next field in which Einstein made a major contribution was the newly discovered Quantum theory in which Planck in 1900 had introduced an element of fundamental discontinuity into the physics of blackbody radiation. In 1905 Einstein boldly applied this idea to the radiation field itself so that light and other forms of electromagnetic radiation were to be regarded as exhibiting a corpuscular aspect in addition to their wave-like properties. He applied the new theory to explain among other things the detailed quantitative laws of the photoelectric effect, which were later to be brilliantly confirmed by the experiments of Robert A. Millikan. During the next twenty years Einstein continued to develop a number of significant aspects of the Quantum theory, in particular the theory of specific heats dating from 1907, and culminating in 1924 with his theory of gas degeneration, a phenomenon wherein he anticipated a wave aspect for material particles, which, together with the independent work of Louis de Broglie, led directly to Schrödinger's development of wave mechanics. But Einstein was not in sympathy with the later interpretations of this theory and the closely associated Quantum mechanics of **Heisenberg**. At this point Einstein fell out of line with the orthodox development of physics as reflected particularly in the views of Niels Bohr and refused to accept a statistical instrumentalism as an ultimate account of happenings in the world of atoms and electrons. Einstein regarded the new Quantum theory as 'incomplete' and alien to the realistic interpretation of physical theories he had espoused since his early work on kinetic theory. It is fair to say that Einstein's sustained critique of the new micro-physics served to sharpen the at times rather unclear formulation of the orthodox Copenhagen school, but in combination with his long and unsuccessful attempts at extending general relativity it left Einstein for the last thirty years of his life almost completely isolated from the mainstream developments in theoretical physics.

It was Einstein's third 1905 paper which introduced the special theory of relativity. This was not unconnected with his light-quantum hypothesis in the theory of radiation. Since Einstein believed that Maxwell's equations of the electromagnetic field could not be an exact description, he wanted to distil from these equations a principle which would survive in any more accurate future theory of light. This led him to his formulation of a new relativity principle. In classical mechanics there was already incorporated the principle of Galilean relativity according to which the laws of mechanics were unchanged in form when referred to any so-called inertial reference frame, any two such frames being in uniform relative motion with respect to each other. As a result no purely mechanical phenomena could distinguish a state of absolute rest or motion, only the relative motion of bodies could be established – hence the term 'relativity'. Although motion was relative according to the Galilean principle, spatial extensions and temporal intervals were considered to be 'absolute' in the sense of being the same when measured with respect to any of the inertial reference frames. However, the equations of electromagnetism, namely Maxwell's equations, failed to satisfy the relativity principle and suggested the possibility of identifying 'absolute' states of motion. Experiments designed to test the predicted failure of the principle in respect of electromagnetic phenomena, such as the propagation of light, showed apparently that the principle did hold here as well. Einstein was not really influenced in his work by these experimental findings (there is some doubt as to whether he even knew of them). Instead, he proposed as a new principle of physics to extend relativity to cover all physical phenomena. In order to comprehend electromagnetism this meant revising the kinematic relationships between moving reference frames embodied in the Galilean principle. Since these in turn were based on the notion of absolute space and time the new Einstein principle resulted in a frame-dependence or 'relativity' of spatial and temporal interval measurements. (The Einstein transformations were formally identical with, although conceptually quite distinct from, earlier results of H.A. Lorentz.) Velocity was still in general 'relativized' with the exception of the unique velocity accorded by the Maxwell equations to the propagation of light in a vacuum. The velocity of light became the new 'absolute' element in the kinematic relationship between moving frames. The new Einstein relativity principle while designed specifically to accommodate electromagnetic phenomena as described by Maxwell's equations now failed in respect of the laws of classical mechanics. So Einstein proceeded to modify Newton's laws of mechanics in such a way as to conform to his new principle. In particular the mass of an object ceased to be an 'absolute' quantity but now varied in a characteristic manner with velocity. One consequence of this was the famous $E = mc^2$ relation between energy and mass where c is the velocity of light. (Incidentally this equation is often erroneously claimed to identify a new source of energy, namely mass, which is then said to be the origin of 'atomic energy' – in fact, it applies to *all* forms of energy.) Einstein's special theory of relativity was a rather complicated blend of conventional or definitional components associated with his analysis of the relativity of simultaneity and a direct physical component which explained, for example, the null results of optical experiments designed to measure absolute motion. The unravelling of these two components was only cleared up satisfactorily in the work of J.A. Winnie (1970). Einstein seems to have been influenced psychologically by the writings of the positivist philosopher of science Ernst Mach, in particular in his approach to the analysis of the time concept in physics, but the resulting theory with its continuing but revised blend of 'relative' and 'absolute' elements is far removed from Mach's crude sensationalism.

Although with special relativity Einstein had abolished the notion of absolute rest, the question of absolute acceleration – as, for example, in rotational motion – remained. Under transformations to arbitrary reference frames the laws of physics would change their form even when they were adjusted to be invariant under transformations to uniformly moving reference frames as required by the special theory. However, Einstein proposed that this change in form could be compensated by a change in the gravitational field experienced by the physical system described by the law in question. In this way the relativity principle could be generalized from uniformly moving reference frames to arbitrarily moving reference frames. In order to implement this programme Einstein first invoked a principle of equivalence according to which the effect of an accelerated reference frame was 'equivalent' to an appropriate gravitational field in the unaccelerated frame.

Extending this idea to the case of 'permanent' gravitational fields which could not be globally but only locally eliminated by a change of reference system, Einstein arrived at his theory of general relativity, which he thought would provide a solution to the absolute acceleration problem and also give a geometrical theory of gravitation in which the metrical properties of a non-Euclidean space–time continuum would be determined by the local distribution of matter and radiation. Considered as a theory of gravitation, general relativity made three immediate predictions: a small correction to the motion of the planet Mercury which was already known to be required for agreement with observation; an effect of a gravitational field on the frequency of spectral lines; and, most striking of all, the bending of light in a gravitational field. This latter effect was strikingly confirmed in 1919 by observation of the shift in apparent direction of stars near the eclipsed sun. It was this successful novel prediction that made Einstein famous overnight to an amazed but almost totally uncomprehending public. In 1917 Einstein applied this new theory to the cosmological problem of the universe as a whole and showed by a slight and later rejected modification of his field equations the possibility of a static, spatially closed, but unbounded universe. This was the starting point of the great explosion of interest in theoretical cosmology of the past eighty years.

Paradoxically it turned out that one of the guiding principles that led Einstein to general relativity, Mach's principle or the elimination of absolute acceleration, was not exemplified in the final theory. Exactly how one should attempt to incorporate Mach's principle into a physical theory has been one of the most debated issues of modern cosmology. Furthermore, a second guiding principle of general covariance, according to which one should eliminate in all respects the frame-dependence of the laws of physics, turned out to be vacuous. Unlike the relativity principle of the special theory, it actually placed no constraint on possible physical theories, as was pointed out by Kretschmann in 1917. Nevertheless, as a theory of gravitation, general relativity has acquired an increasingly secure reputation, although it was in fact only after Einstein's death that it began to rival the special theory in scientific respectability due to a number of sophisticated experimental tests making use, for example, of satellite and radar technology. (The unequivocal detection of predicted gravitational waves remains, however, a major challenge to the experimentalists.) Furthermore, the theoretical implications of the theory in respect of the intense gravitational fields associated with space–time singularities and 'black holes' have only come to be properly understood during the past fifteen years. General relativity has become the working tool of modern astrophysics and cosmology just as surely as special relativity has become second nature to the elementary particle physicist.

It is on the basis of detailed quantitative predictions, i.e. considered as a precise physical theory, that relativity is judged by physicists. Einstein, however, never paid much attention to the experimental tests of his theories. For him they were 'free inventions of the human intellect', discovered quite independently of anomalous observational data, guided by considerations of mathematical elegance and conceptual unity, and their very success has counterpointed the narrow positivistic and operationalist philosophy espoused by many contemporary physicists. Einstein was by far the greatest theoretical physicist of his age, and arguably in this field must rival even Newton, whose work in so many respects he was to overthrow.

Further reading

The best popular exposition of relativity remains Einstein's own book *Relativity: The Special and the General Theory* (1920). Einstein's major papers on relativity are included in the collection translated by W. Perrett and G.B. Jeffrey, *The Principle of Relativity* (1923). Einstein's own autobiography is contained in P.A. Schilpp (ed.), *Albert Einstein: Philosopher-Scientist* (1949). See also: R.W. Clark, *Einstein: The Life and Times* (1973); P. Frank, *Einstein: His Life and Times* (1947); J. Bernstein, *Einstein* (1973); S.W. Hawking and W. Israel (eds), *General Relativity: An Einstein Centenary Survey* (1979); G. Holton and Y. Elkana (eds), *Albert Einstein: Historical and Cultural Perspectives* (1982); Abraham Pais, *Subtle is the Lord: The Science and Life of Albert Einstein* (1982); D. Howard and J. Stachel (eds), *Einstein and the History of General Relativity* (1989); M. White, *Albert Einstein: A Life in Science* (1993); A. Whitaker, *Einstein, Bohr and the Quantum Dilemma* (1996).

MICHAEL REDHEAD

EISENSTEIN, Sergei Mikhailovich
1898–1948
Russian film director

Eisenstein was born into the family of a city architect in Riga, and spent his childhood there and in St Petersburg before studying architecture and engineering at the Petrograd School of Public Works. In 1918 he enlisted in the Red Army, where he produced posters and theatre designs. After the Civil War, he moved to Moscow to study Japanese, but was diverted into the theatre after a chance encounter with a childhood friend, Maxim Strauch. It was in his theatrical work between 1920 and 1924 that Eisenstein was exposed to a range of Modernist experiments in dramaturgy that were to lead him in the direction of the cinema.

In the theatre he worked on a number of productions for the Proletcult between 1920 and 1921, then enrolled in Meyerhold's State School for Stage Direction, where he made the acquaintance of Sergei Yutkevich, with whom he was to produce a number of stage-pieces after leaving Meyerhold. Further encounters with Foregger's Workshop Theatre and the Factory of the Eccentric Actor led back to an assistantship with Meyerhold and then to the directorship of a branch of Proletcult, where Eisenstein's first production (Ostrovsky's *Even a Wise Man Stumbles*) included his first short film, *Glumov's Diary*, and triggered his first theoretical article, linking theatre and film, 'The Montage of Attractions', published by

Mayakovsky in *LEF* in 1923. The period as a whole is marked by Eisenstein's rejection of the psychological realism of the Moscow Art Theatre tradition and his search for new dramatic models in the general field of Constructivist aesthetics.

While with Proletcult, Eisenstein moved fully into film production with his exuberant and dynamic first feature, *Strike* (1925), the story of the bloody suppression of a factory strike in pre-Revolutionary Russian. By the end of the same year he had completed his second film, the stern five-act drama of *Battleship Potemkin* (1925), recounting the mutiny aboard the battleship in June 1905. Work on *October* (1927), a poetic chronicle for the tenth birthday of the Revolution, displaced the preparations for *Old and New* (formerly *The General Line*), a film dealing with the co-operativization of agriculture and the acquisition of new farming technologies, eventually premiered in 1928. These films and the theoretical writing that accompanies them established Eisenstein as the major new talent in Soviet cinema in the 1920s, and quickly led to international acclaim.

With this clutch of silent masterpieces behind him, Eisenstein set out in mid-1929 to tour Europe and to visit the United States. In Hollywood he and his collaborators Tisse and Alexandrov were hired by Paramount but were unable during 1930 to bring any projects to fruition. As a result the next three years were spent in vexed attempts, far from Hollywood, to produce *Que Viva Mexico!* independently for Upton Sinclair, an experience which brought Eisenstein into close proximity with the religious mysticism and eroticism of Mexico, its history and mythology. *Time in the Sun*, compiled by Eisenstein's biographer-to-be Marie Seton in 1939, is the best generally available record of this fraught endeavour.

The experience of surrendering his footage to Sinclair as the project failed was a severe blow to Eisenstein, who returned to the USSR and only gradually made his way back into the mainstream of Soviet film production, in a climate much less sympathetic than

before. Between 1935 and 1937 his new film on agriculture, *Bezhin Meadow*, was halted first by Eisenstein's smallpox and then by state edict; with remaining material being destroyed in the war, it survived only as a half-hour montage of stills and music compiled by Sergei Yutkevitch in 1966. Eisenstein's only finished project of the 1930s is his contribution to the anti-Fascist programme, *Alexander Nevsky* (1938), which dramatizes the defence of Novgorod and Pskov against the Teutonic Knights in 1242, although his theoretical and academic work continued and in 1939 he became the artistic head of Mosfilm.

Eisenstein's final film was *Ivan the Terrible*, an unfinished trilogy about the sixteenth-century Tsar who destroyed the autonomy of the nobles and created a united Russia. Part 1 was released in 1944, Part 2 in 1946, with Eisenstein now using colour for the first time for part of the film. In 1946 Eisenstein suffered a coronary; the second part of the trilogy was denounced by the Central Committee on Cinema and Theatre, sensitive to the unflattering parallels between **Stalin** and Tsar Ivan; in 1947, working on Part 3 of *Ivan*, he was heartbroken by his first sight of the American versions of his early 1930s Mexican material; early in 1948 he died of a further heart attack.

The work of Eisenstein has spheres of influence too numerous to catalogue. The cinema has not ceased to absorb his ideas and his examples, or to acknowledge their importance by contesting them. He is invariably invoked in discussions of the cinema and the politics of socialism, both at the level of ideologies in general and in terms of the ideology of film form. His films, with their constant return to history, form part of those central debates over the cinema and ideas of realism, with particular reference to the question of historical representation. His theories of film editing and film style are central to discussions of film 'language', while his interest and involvement in other media (theatre, literature, music, opera) also gives his work keen purchase on more general questions about artistic media and aesthetics.

Fundamental to these questions was Eisenstein's approach to problems of film form. The task of creating a new Soviet cinema led Eisenstein to dismantle the continuum of realist fiction, and to concentrate attention upon its constituent units, in particular the role of individual frames and shots and the system of connection, editing, that organized their flow. Editing then became a compositional principle, became the activity of 'montage', for which Eisenstein began to elaborate a possible typology of functions: metric, rhythmic, tonal, overtonal and intellectual. For Eisenstein, drawing upon such diverse influences as dialectical materialism, ideogrammatic writing, **Pavlov's** work on motor-reflexes and his experience of theatrical presentation as a 'montage of attractions', montage opened up new ways of modelling film form beyond the linearity of the dominant model. The complexity it suggested was to be embodied in such different examples as the spatial and temporal disjunctions of the massacre on the Odessa Steps in *Battleship Potemkin*, the lyrically fragmented closing of the bridge in *October*, the climactic animation of the cream-separator in *Old and New*.

Montage cinema then broke with traditional film form and involved spectators in new reflexive modes of reading cinema. But for all its multivalence and polyphony, montage in Eisenstein is always contained by larger-scale dramatic principles. It never reaches the degree of riotous profusion that creates the semiotic complexity of Vertov's *Man with a Movie Camera*, for instance, perhaps the supreme example of the anti-realist drive of the Soviet montage aesthetic. For the disruptive and disintegrative powers of montage are contained in Eisenstein by a more classical impulse for organicism and coherence, which becomes more marked in Eisenstein's later work as montage cinema as a whole is overhauled by the return to Classicism, in the 1930s, in the form of Socialist Realism. By the time of Eisenstein's sound films this has become the case in two main ways. First, Eisenstein's concerns with montage at the level of film editing are displaced by an increasing interest in the internal organization or montage of the image and of the shot, marking an increased concern with *mise-en-scène*. This is more than partly because the late historical dramas, *Alexander Nevsky* and *Ivan the Terrible*, now centre individual 'character' as never before in Eisenstein, thus emphasizing the centrality of the film actor, and the space and time in which he moves. Editing in these later works thus sacrifices its disruptive potential in the service of the coherence of the pro-filmic event, preferring to assume instead a heightened function of ensuring complex but classical continuity of dramatic space and time. It is in this period that Eisenstein can look back on *Battleship Potemkin* as a model of organic unity and symmetry. Second, the organicism of Eisenstein's late works is also determined by his acceptance of a classical aesthetic of coherence for the combination of sound and image. Sound, like montage, is used to enrich and reinforce, rather than to disrupt. The call for contrapuntal use of sound embodied in Eisenstein's, Pudovkin's and Alexandrov's 1928 manifesto instead gives way to the sumptuous synchronicity of the late films, particularly in their plangent and emotive use of scores by **Prokofiev**. In his book *The Film Sense*, Eisenstein is even able to claim a note-to-image correspondence between the music-track and picture-track of a segment of *Alexander Nevsky*. It is perhaps the tension between these two modes – the disruptive montage aesthetic of the 1920s compared with the organic classicism of the later period – that focuses the importance of Eisenstein for ideas about the differing possibilities of film form, and of the ideological systems underpinning them.

Further reading

Other works include: Eisenstein, *Izbrannyiye Proizvededea v shesti tomakh*, ('Selected Works', 6 vols, 1964–71); *The Film Sense* (1942); *Film Form* (1949); *Notes of a Film Director* (1959); *Film Essays* (1968); See: Yon Barna, *Eisenstein* (1973); Marie Seton, *Eisenstein* (2nd edn, 1978); Jean Mitry,

Eisenstein (1975); Leon Moussinac, *Sergei Eisenstein* (1970); Peter Wollen, *Signs and Meaning in the Cinema* (3rd edn, 1972); David Bordwell, *The Cinema of Eisenstein* (1993); Anne Nesbet, *Savage Junctures: Sergei Eisenstein and the Shape of Thinking* (2003); Richard Taylor (ed.), *The Eisenstein Reader* (1998); Al LaValley and Barry P. Scherr (eds), *Eisenstein at 100: A Reconsideration* (2001). See: Jay Leyda, *Kino: A History of the Russian and Soviet Film* (2nd edn, 1973); Sylvia Harvey, *May '68 and Film Culture* (1978).

PHILIP DRUMMOND

ELGAR, (Sir) Edward William

1857–1934

English composer

At a period when it was assumed that England was '*Das Land ohne Musik*' and where only foreigners would compose or play, Elgar was born to an obscure piano tuner's wife a few miles from the cathedral city of Worcester. Recognition was slow in coming to this composer, who was almost entirely self-taught. He learnt his craft partly by helping his father at the organ of St George's Roman Catholic Church, by playing violin in the Worcester Festival Choral Society's orchestra, by his careful copying and paraphrasing of the works of the great masters, by his visits to Germany where he listened to **Wagner**, and by his somewhat strange appointment as Band Instructor to the City of Worcester Pauper Lunatic Asylum. He did not receive the normal instruction of a young musician of the time and was always somewhat self-conscious and even bitter on this account. Nevertheless, he not only built up a formidable technique worthy to place alongside the giants in Germany such as his contemporary **Richard Strauss**, but he became a composer with a recognizable style of international standing.

Indeed, Elgar changed from a provincial nobody to a world-famous genius round about the turn of the century when he completed his now famous *Variations on an Original Theme* (Op. 36). It is probable that when he wrote the word 'Enigma' on the first page of the score he was thinking of his attendance at St Joseph's, Malvern, on Quinquagesima Sunday, 1899, when he heard the words of St Paul, ending with '*aenigmate*', in which we are like 'men looking at puzzling reflections in a mirror. The time will come when we shall see reality whole and face to face.' In this composition Elgar wrote character-sketches of his friends 'pictured within' – perhaps a mirror is implied here. The 'break-through' (for the second part of St Paul's lines) came sooner than was expected. The *Variations* were performed with resounding success in June 1899. The conductor was, of course, foreign, an Austrian, Hans Richter (1843–1916). Another man of German blood who helped to put Elgar on the international map was Julius Buths (1851–1920). This time the inadequacies of British choral societies of the time are seen to be painfully obvious. *The Dream of Gerontius* (Op. 38 and based upon a poem by Cardinal Newman) was too 'modern' for the Birmingham Festival performers in 1900 and it was due to Buths that a successful second performance was given in Düsseldorf the following year, which led Strauss later to refer to Elgar as the 'first English progressive musician'.

If Elgar's music was not violently revolutionary it was certainly new and frequently upsetting to many of the conventional members of Edwardian society. Now, however, well into his forties, the composer was accepted both artistically and socially. He continued to live in the world of the Three Choirs Festival (where his music is especially cherished) and from 1904 to 1911 he and his wife and one daughter occupied a house called Plas Gwyn on the outskirts of Hereford, but he was much in demand in London – about which he had written colourfully in *Cockaigne* (Op. 40). Works of this period include the two fine Symphonies (No. 1 in A flat, 1908; No. 2 in E flat, 1911) and the Violin Concerto (Op. 61) which, together with some passages in the two oratorios, *The Apostles* (Op. 49, 1903) and *The Kingdom* (Op. 51, 1906), contain his maturest and most characteristic music.

Elgar was knighted in 1904 and was also given a Festival to himself that year. Gradually his name became associated with the more extrovert side of the buoyant and confident British Empire. The trio tune of the first of a series of five *Pomp and Circumstance* military marches was put into the *Coronation Ode* (Op. 44) in 1902 and later became a song in its own right as 'Land of Hope and Glory'.

Despite Elgar's clear love of outward pageantry, there was another dreamy and introspective side to his nature, never far from the surface, giving a tinge of whimsical melancholy even to his happy children's music. The tunes from the two suites *The Wand of Youth* (Op. 1) date back to his earliest years, but were published in 1907 and 1908. *The Nursery Suite*, a similar work put together as late as 1931, was dedicated to H.R.H. Queen Elizabeth II and Princess Margaret when the sisters were children. The nervous melancholy broke through with the onset of the First World War. The world's values would never be the same, and Elgar knew it. He was wrong to think that future generations would not care for his music, but he was right to suppose that post-war composers would write experimental heartless non-national works instead of music which might stir, exalt or ennoble. Works such as the *Introduction and Allegro* for strings (Op. 47, 1905) and *Falstaff* (Op. 68, 1913) have sad interludes in otherwise jaunty and optimistic settings, the one a nostalgic reminiscence of Welsh voices singing over the hills at Llangranog in Dyfed, the other of a young Falstaff, a 'Dream Interlude'. Whereas the former work ends with a flourish, the latter paves the way for the desperately unhappy ending to the Cello Concerto (Op. 85). Although performed before the death of his wife in 1920, it is full of foreboding; the composer published nothing more of significance and his style became less adventurous. At his death, however, notes existed for a 'Third Symphony', commissioned by the BBC, and these were eventually elaborated into a full orchestral score by Anthony Payne, and first performed in 1998.

Elgar's impact has grown steadily. At one time it was thought that **Debussy** was inevitably more important since he broke the conventions in harmonic progression and in form. Elgar was then being judged by the classical romantic standards which would apply to **Brahms**. Just as *The Dream of Gerontius* represented a break with the recitative and aria tradition of English choral music, so the Symphonies broke with traditional sonata form in many respects, especially with regard to the key scheme in the first. It is now recognized that his use of mosaic-like units in, say, *The Apostles*, is much nearer to the structuring of *La Mer* (1905) than was realized and his reacting against the rules of the textbooks was no less fierce than that of the Frenchman. His musical language was, however, steeped in the Germanic tradition. An English tradition? There was none. The only British composer immediately before him of stature was Arthur Sullivan – who studied, as he did, in Leipzig.

Further reading

Most of Elgar's works are published by Novello or by Boosey. See: P.M. Young, *Elgar O.M.* (1955); Diana M. McVeagh, *Edward Elgar: His Life and Music* (1955); Michael Kennedy, *Portrait of Elgar* (1968); Ian Parrott, *Elgar* (2nd edn, 1977); Jerrold Northrop Moore, *Edward Elgar: A Creative Life* (1984); R. Monk (ed.), *Elgar Studies* (1990); R. Anderson, *Elgar in Manuscript* (1990); Michael Kennedy, *The Life of Elgar* (2004).

IAN PARROTT

ELIOT, George (Mary Anne or Marian EVANS)
1819–80
English novelist

The hero of George Eliot's greatest novel, *Middlemarch*, is a scientist: a medical practitioner and researcher whose attempts to introduce modern medicine are thwarted by his entrapment in the complex social network of an ignorant, conservative provincial town. In the same novel she gives tragic portrayals of the corrupted conscience of an Evangelical zealot and the emotional sterility of a theological scholar, self-induced by wilful blindness to the futility of his labours. These are some of the fruits of a life that encompassed most of the stresses and intellectual dramas of the mid-nineteenth century. The daughter of the steward of a landed estate in Warwickshire, she fervently espoused Evangelical Christianity – the Christianity of William Wilberforce and Hannah More – in her teens, and in her early twenties rejected Christianity in favour of an equally committed quest to reconcile a causal, scientific interpretation of the world with the ethical imperatives of her former religion. In the next fifteen years she translated two of the major German critiques of Christianity: David Strauss's *Life of Jesus* (trans. 1846) and Ludwig Feuerbach's *Essence of Christianity* (trans. 1854). A statement of George Eliot's own, 'The idea of God, so far as it has been a high spiritual influence, is the ideal of a goodness entirely human', is a précis of Feuerbach's thesis.

Despite the serious strain caused by her loss of religious faith, she remained close to her family until her father's death in 1849, after which she moved to London to pursue full-time literary work. This was still, and was to remain for a few years, of a 'secondary' kind: translating and literary journalism. This was, however, of the most serious and demanding kind and her lengthy reviews (the best of which are collected in her *Essays*) helped to prepare her for novel-writing by requiring her to articulate her thoughts on literature, religion and the study of society. Most of this work was done for the *Westminster Review*, the leading organ of secular, moderately radical intellectuals. She was effectively its editor for a few years in the early 1850s.

A major influence that helped her to crystallize her views was the work of Auguste Comte. His combination of scientific materialism, humanized religion, altruism (his coinage) and reverence for the past, and his elevation of feeling over intellect, were ideally suited to a secular intellectual of George Eliot's temperament. His espousal of 'sociology' (another coinage), the scientific study of humanity, was to be particularly influential on the novels. But she was not a slavish follower of Comte. She was never a regular attender at the Positivist Church established by friends of hers in London, refused the request of a friend to write a positivist Utopia and, most importantly, she radically modified one of Comte's major dogmas. He claimed that the individual does not exist, only humanity is real. Eliot, as a novelist whose attachment to theory was subordinate to her imaginative absorption in experience, embodied in her fiction a more subtle, dialectical understanding of the mutual dependence of the individual and the group.

The second great crisis in George Eliot's life came in 1854 when she fell in love with George Henry Lewes. Lewes was legally married but George Eliot acted out her own belief in marriage as a voluntary commitment by eloping with him and living as his wife until his death in 1878. She was ostracized, particularly by women, and her family broke with her. This isolation was undoubtedly painful and possibly damaging, but Lewes crucially helped her to work up the confidence to start writing fiction.

One essay written in this period is a manifesto for the kind of fiction George Eliot was about to start writing. It is a review of a German work of social documentation, and in it she argues that a novelist who adopted the methods of the social scientist, and studied the actual behaviour, motives and circumstances of the various classes, particularly the common people, would succeed in fostering in his readers a fruitful sympathy for men and women as they are, rather than a false and vitiating sympathy for ideal types. 'Realism' is upheld above all for its *moral* value. The essay is significantly titled 'The Natural History of German Life': her model for the practice of fiction is the science of organisms in relation to their environment.

The hallmark of the early creative work that followed is the recovery of the world of her childhood in the analytic light of her subsequent development. At the same time the ideas she had absorbed from Comte, Feuerbach and other sources are dissolved in the dense medium of that recovered world – so that it was possible for enthusiastic early readers of *Adam Bede* to suppose that 'George Eliot' was a country clergyman, rather than the atheistic and adulterous translator of Feuerbach and Strauss.

Most of her fiction is historical, not simply because it is set in the past, but because an apparently stable and entrenched social world is presented with a consciousness of the historical forces that are about to change it. In most of them the action takes place at an historically pregnant moment for the community it studies – the arrival of Evangelicalism in a provincial town in *Janet's Repentance*, the First Reform Bill in *Felix Holt* and *Middlemarch*, the impact of Savonarola on Florence in her most recognizably historical novel, *Romola*. Even *Daniel Deronda*, set in the present, works a similar process projectively, prophesying the State of Israel. Her narratives frequently represent the dilemma of individuals who have risen spiritually and intellectually above the level of their communities, who embody 'development' (like many of her contemporaries George Eliot interpreted evolution as a mechanism of moral progress) but are incapable of changing their world and are moreover tied to it 'by the strongest fibres of their hearts'. Maggie Tulliver in *The Mill on the Floss* is an obvious example.

George Eliot began with a series of three *Scenes of Clerical Life* (echoing Balzac). The first of these, *Amos Barton* (1857), shows her most literal practice of the doctrine stated in 'The Natural History of German Life'. She attempts to win the reader's sympathy for a provincial clergyman who is as plain, unintelligent and ineffective as she can make him. She achieves a limited success but seems quickly to have realized that such a medium was inadequate to her larger themes. In subsequent work she focuses on more exceptional protagonists and in the third of the *Scenes, Janet's Repentance* (1857), she

anticipates most of the characteristics of her mature work.

Adam Bede (1859), the first major novel, which secured George Eliot's reputation while she was still anonymous, is the most nostalgic and overtly moralistic of her novels. Although there is evidence of her powers of social analysis, particularly in the relations between the squire and his tenants, the presentation of the rural world of Hayslope is strongly influenced by pastoral models. It is not, like most of her communities, seen historically; it is, rather, a secular and plausibly imperfect paradise from which the sinners Arthur and Hetty are expelled in punishment. The process of self-deception by which the well-meaning young squire destroys both his own life and Hetty's without ever intending to exemplifies George Eliot's understanding of moral action. The portrayal of Hetty's vanity, fantasies and egocentricity, though harsh, is equally convincing. The relentless causal sequence of pregnancy, infanticide and death-sentence is, however, too evidently selected to favour a moral *parti-pris*.

The world of *The Mill on the Floss* (1860), her second novel, is much more analytically presented and firmly rooted in historical processes. Maggie's mother and maternal aunts are not only great comic creations but subjects of an anthropological study of class customs. In contrast to the morality-fable design of *Adam Bede*, where the virtuous hero Adam is perfectly adapted to his environment and the sinners Arthur and Hetty are expelled from it, Maggie, the most morally developed character, can neither fit into her world nor leave it. The limbo into which the logic of her dilemma drives her anticipates the open endings of many twentieth-century novels (such as **D.H. Lawrence's** *The Rainbow*, which was clearly influenced by *The Mill*) but George Eliot, who had planned a tragedy, resolves all with the *deus ex machina* of the flood. George Eliot's attachment to the Comtean principle of 'continuity' shows here not in overt nostalgia but in the overwhelming power of the past over the moral and emotional lives of the characters. Maggie herself asserts the principle that makes escape impossible for her: 'If the past is not to bind us, where can duty lie? We should have no law but the impulse of the moment.'

Silas Marner (1861) is the last of the novels to draw freely and spontaneously on the impressions of George Eliot's childhood. Its composition interrupted work on her first consciously researched novel, *Romola*. It is her most successful attempt at overtly poetic narrative, strongly indebted to Wordsworth, grounded less on analysis of motive than on apprehensions of spiritual growth that defy analytic presentation. The scene in which the embittered and alienated miser gropes for his lost gold and feels the blonde curls of the little girl who is to redeem him is one of the most moving and pregnant images in English fiction.

With *Romola* (1862–3) George Eliot begins a major development. As *Villette* is to *Jane Eyre* and *Little Dorrit* to *David Copperfield*, so are her last four novels to her first three. She leaves behind the peculiarly English and Victorian type of novel that overlaps with 'children's classics' and begins to develop into a major European writer. *Romola* itself does not put George Eliot in that class, but it signals her refusal to repeat her successes or pander to her audience. It is a detailed and deeply informed study of Renaissance Florence, and is interesting for that reason alone. But despite the mass of circumstantial detail with which George Eliot strives to emulate the density of her earlier fictional worlds, the didactic and emotional drives behind the book stand out too nakedly. On the one hand, in Romola herself she indulges a craving for ideal action that she had analysed in Maggie Tulliver and would once again in Dorothea Brooke. On the other, she hunts down Tito Melema (a more sinister and accomplished Arthur Donnithorne) with a cold and abstract ruthlessness.

The didactic and schematic treatment of Tito contrasts markedly with the portrayals of the varied, variously reprehensible egotists in her last three novels. Mrs Transome in *Felix Holt*, Casaubon, Lydgate and Bulstrode in *Middlemarch*, and Gwendolen Harleth in *Daniel Deronda* are portrayed with a new kind of depth and intimacy. This is achieved mainly by what F.R. Leavis called 'psychological notation', an essentially poetic method of giving the most private and tenuous experience the status of a perceived reality: '[Mr Casaubon's] soul was sensitive without being enthusiastic: it was too languid to thrill out of self-consciousness into passionate delight; it went on fluttering in the swampy ground where it was hatched, thinking of its wings and never flying.' Judgement is not withheld, but the exposure of the inescapable self, the knowledge that in real life is matched only by self-knowledge, constitutes an authentic tragic vision.

In *Felix Holt* and *Daniel Deronda* these achievements belong to the less obviously ambitious parts of the novels. The treatment of industrial unrest in *Felix Holt* (1866) is a failure. Industrialism is the one major aspect of Victorian life that defeated George Eliot's imagination, and on this subject she compares unfavourably with less gifted novelists such as Mrs Gaskell and even Charles Kingsley. The stiffness in the characterization of Felix himself reflects the failure to grasp the larger reality. The sympathetic portrayal of Zionist idealism in *Daniel Deronda* (1876) is more interesting because it is unparalleled, because it springs from a nobler impulse than the industrial part of *Felix Holt*, and because it entails a bolder imaginative experiment. Nevertheless, George Eliot fails with this theme for the same reason that she failed with the heroine of *Romola*: when stripped of her entirely creditable sympathy for the Jews, the story amounts to an indulgence of the desire for ideal action unhampered by the psychological, circumstantial and material complexities that are the very substance of her creative genius.

The other half of *Daniel Deronda* concerns Gwendolen Harleth, a more profoundly analysed Emma whose vitality and intelligence are channelled by narrowness of circumstance into ignorant egocentricity. Her nemesis in the form of the numbingly but tenaciously lifeless Grandcourt is a strikingly original study of evil. Her story, with its account of moral growth, is perhaps Eliot's greatest single achievement, but *Middlemarch* (1871–2) is undoubtedly her greatest novel. Its doomed scientist hero Lydgate is quoted as saying, 'A man's mind must be continually expanding and shrinking between the whole human horizon and the horizon of an object-glass.' This describes the method of the novel. It is conceived between the poles of intimate psychological detail and historical events of national importance (the First Reform Bill, the spread of the railways). The latter are there not so much to influence the action as to remind the reader that the resistant world of *Middlemarch* will suffer change regardless of the fate of people such as Lydgate and Dorothea who have a vision of a better future. George Eliot did not unequivocally think that the world was better in 1870 than in 1830. The question is not whether change will come, but whether it will come through morally responsible vision such as that of her protagonists rather than through the random forces of political and economic expediency. In the novel we see the former happening only to a very small degree. Between the poles are the subtly distinguished circles of the social world, themselves constantly shifting, which shape, confine and resist the inner selves of the characters. If realism can be defined as the creation of a fictional world which seems to be continuous with the real world of history, *Middlemarch* is a model of realistic technique. There not only seems to be but is in the mind of the author an enormous range and depth of knowledge beyond the pages of the book, to which we are directed by the subtlest hints. Behind the stories of Lydgate, Casaubon and Bulstrode, for example, there is far more knowledge of medical history, theological controversy and Evangelical religion than George Eliot directly exploits in the novel.

By the end of her life George Eliot was respected and by some almost worshipped not only as a novelist but as a moral teacher.

This helped her to overcome the isolation caused by her union with Lewes but it contributed to a decline in her reputation after her death, when her work was misrepresented as heavy moralizing in laboured prose. Despite this she was a formative influence on **Hardy**, **Henry James** and Lawrence, and the authority of *Middlemarch* is an important reason for the lure that realism still has for English novelists today.

Further reading

Other works include: 'The Lifted Veil' (1859); 'Brother Jacob' (1864); *The Spanish Gypsy* (1868); *The Legend of Jubal and Other Poems* (1874); *Impressions of Theophrastus Such* (1879); *The George Eliot Letters*, ed. Gordon S. Haight (7 vols, 1954–5); *Essays of George Eliot*, ed. Thomas Pinney (1963). See: Gordon S. Haight, *George Eliot: A Biography* (1968); Jerome Beaty, *Middlemarch from Notebook to Novel* (1960); Barbara Hardy, *The Novels of George Eliot* (1959); *Middlemarch, Critical Approaches to the Novel*, ed. Barbara Hardy (1967); R.T. Jones, *George Eliot* (1970); F.R. Leavis, *The Great Tradition* (1948); Neil Roberts, *George Eliot: Her Beliefs and Her Art* (1975); Rosemary Ashton, *The German Idea* (1980); S. Graver, *George Eliot and Community: A Study in Social Theory and Fictional Form* (1994); J. Rignall (ed.), *The Oxford Reader's Companion to George Eliot* (2000).

NEIL ROBERTS

ELIOT, Thomas Stearns

1888–1965

US/British poet, critic and playwright

T.S. Eliot was arguably the most important English poet and critic of the twentieth century (he was baptized into the Church of England and took out British naturalization papers in 1927). His long poem *The Waste Land* (1922) helped to crystallize the sense of spiritual desolation, social chaos and failure of linguistic nerve that became widespread in the West, especially in the aftermath of the First World War, and thus to define some fundamental aspects of literary modernism's pervasive negativity and pessimism. Certain phrases from his essays – 'dissociation of sensibility' (to define the seventeenth-century break he alleged had occurred in 'the English mind'), 'objective correlative' (coined to help explain *Hamlet*'s failure) – quickly passed (to Eliot's embarrassment) into the common stock of critical terminology. As editor of the *Criterion* (1922–39) he pushed his own poems (*The Waste Land* first appeared in the *Criterion*'s opening number), the European and American authors he admired, his discoveries in the next generation of English poets (notably **Auden** and Stephen Spender) and his own critical and political preferences, into the centre of English intellectual life. As a member (from 1925) of the publishing firm of Faber's he helped to build up what quickly became England's central corpus of published poets (Auden, Barker, MacNeice, **Pound**, Read, Sassoon, Spender). It was to Eliot as editor and publisher, as much as to his work as poet and critic, that the definition of modernist poetry in English is owed: *The Faber Book of Modern Verse*, edited by Michael Roberts (1936), was only one among several of Eliot's central signposting activities.

In an unguarded moment in the Preface to *For Lancelot Andrewes: Essays on Style and Order* (1928) Eliot defined his 'point of view' as 'classicist in literature, royalist in politics, and anglo-catholic in religion'. An Englishing of a description of the policies of Charles Maurras's right-wing French monarchist movement, *Action Française*, the formula (which Eliot occasionally attempted to blur) was an apt summary of the position put by his poems and essays. It remained true for the rest of his life and work. A writer must have a living relation to the tradition, he argued, in 'Tradition and the Individual Talent' (in his first volume of essays, *The Sacred Wood*, 1920), and before long Eliot had settled on the early seventeenth century (roughly Shakespeare and the Metaphysicals) as the centre of an ideal tradition, a time when English literature was continuing Dante's Christianity with the intellectual sprightliness of an un-Victorian amalgamation of thought and feeling such as he admired in some modern European authors (notably Jules Laforgue). The sermons of Jacobean Bishop Lancelot Andrewes epitomized for Eliot the preferred prelapsarian blend of monarchism (they were preached to King James), Anglicanism (Andrewes was Bishop of Winchester) and classicism (his discourses, formidably learned, quote freely from the ancient tongues). Pre-Civil War, they helped undergird Eliot's notion that the great English poetic tradition had been destroyed by the onset of parliamentary democracy, the abolition of the peerage and the episcopate, and by the killing of King Charles. So Eliot's work did not only keep expressing anti-democratic and anti-humanist, anti-Romantic and anti-Semitic sentiments, it continually sought to reconnect his readers to the contrasting Andrewes tradition that would be a salvation from the modern plight. It was an educational task that he sought to effect through two parallel activities: by quoting and remodelling bits of the admired literature in his poems (Andrewe's sermons, for instance, are extensively used in 'Gerontion', 'Journey of the Magi' and *Four Quartets*), and by making parallel references to and explanatory comments on those same authors and passages in his essays (he called them 'workshop' criticism), on Elizabethan and Jacobean poets and dramatists and on Dante. And, of course, in their admiring explanations about, e.g. seventeenth-century poetic borrowings, or mysterious poets, or gathering flowers in gardens, the essays managed in passing to keep assigning the highest value to T.S. Eliot the stealing poet, the would-be impersonal writer who recalls 'the hyacinth garden', and so on.

Eliot continually tries like this to have things several ways. He deplores the dissociation of poetic sensibility, the breaking of the tradition, and yet pronounces the likelihood 'that poets in our civilization as it exists at present, must be difficult. ... The poet must become more and more comprehensive, more allusive, more indirect, in order to force, to dislocate if necessary, language into his meaning.' And in practice his best work is achieved early on, in the disjunctive, perturbed and pre-Christian 'Love Song of J. Alfred Prufrock' in *Prufrock and Other Observations* (1917) and *The Waste Land*, rather than in the smoother, liturgically sponsored approaches towards Christian assurance and reassurance that begin with *Ash Wednesday*. The early poems are never freed from the worryingly apocalyptic cities and urbanized moral despondencies they inhabit, particularly the London of sexually licentious sinners that Eliot has updated out of the pages of eighteenth-century satire, particularly Alexander Pope's (an exuberantly disgusting world the English Augustans themselves inherited from the Romans), and that Eliot only begins to tear himself free of in *Ash Wednesday*. They are preoccupied with a sense of the disjunction of the self. Prufrock is a split man, in the Romantic tradition of The Double, a good Dr Jekyll burdened by his Conradian 'Secret Sharer', a Doppelgänger self, an evil Mr Hyde. The 'Unreal city' passage of *The Waste Land*, which by dint of quotations from Dante amalgamates the City of London with Hell, even drags the reader into the narrator's Double relationship with the dead man Stetson. 'You' (in **Baudelaire's** words) 'hypocrite lecteur! – mon semblable – mon frère!'

The pervasive spiritual dryness and death, manifestations of the original sin T.E. Hulme instructed his contemporaries in, have resulted in the breaking of civilizations ('London Bridge is falling down'), the collapse of the poetry into the hard, dry imagistic bits ('These fragments ... ') that T.E. Hulme associated with Classicism, a reduction of the people to mere bits of once whole bodies and selves (this is a poetry of cut-off heads, of eyes, claws, 'butt-ends', hands, arms, fingers), a disuniting of experience into unconnectedly separate things (the typist 'lays out food in tins', her clothes are a jumble of 'Stockings, slippers, camisoles and stays'; her 'drying combinations' merely mock her fragmentedness; the narrator 'can connect/ Nothing with nothing'). And yet this world of just those rootless sinners and wretched cosmopolitans that Eliot came so strongly to

deplore in his social criticisms in *After Strange Gods* (1934) and after, the gang of flat characters thronging the earlier poems (fictions quite aware of their considerable debt to **Dostoevsky**, **Dickens**, **James** and **Conrad**), people judged to be so morally and spiritually wanting and granted, like many of Ben Jonson's or Pope's or Dickens's Londoners, not much more than a name – Fresca, Mrs Cammel, Mr Silvero, Hakagawa, Mr Eugenides, Bill, Lou, Mary – manages to be far more agreeably enticing, lives with a far more exciting energy than the tired-out penitent who narrates *Ash Wednesday*, the dutiful proletarian mouthers of churchy or anti-churchy sentiments in *The Rock* (1934), or the clutches of dulled members of the bourgeoisie who inhabit all of Eliot's plays but *Murder in the Cathedral* (1935). The later Eliot – whether composing a grindingly slow drama like those that followed *The Family Reunion* (1939), or giving one of his loftily Parnassian lectures, or just reading his poems on gramophone records – seemed scarcely even to hanker for the fire and energies of his first essays and poems. He had settled early on for tired old age.

There are isolated successes after *The Waste Land*. *Murder in the Cathedral* proved that Eliot could make temptation a dramatically engaging business. Parts of *Four Quartets* are superb, particularly the stories of ghosts (intended as vehicles for the Holy Ghost) – the ghostly children in 'Burnt Norton', the ghostly ancestors in 'East Coker', the ghostly 'double' in 'Little Gidding'. As in the earlier poems, the 'impersonal' poet is best when he is reflecting quite personally on his own sinfulness or childlessness, on his ancestor Sir Thomas Elyot or his spiritual encouragements during the Second World War Blitz on London. But when he turns to word-spinning assurances on the Lancelot Andrewes plan he becomes unconvincing. Eliot's faith is best expressed – as in 'Journey of the Magi' – doubtingly.

In '*Ulysses*, Order, and Myth' (1923) Eliot praised **Joyce** for joining in the effort of psychology, ethnology and Frazer's *The*

Golden Bough, 'to make possible what was impossible even a few years ago. Instead of narrative method, we may now use the mythical method. It is, I seriously believe, a step toward making the modern world possible for art.' Eliot's early work successfully mythicized 'the modern world', particularly the modern London Eliot had adopted as his home. When he swapped *The Waste Land*'s opportunistic mixture of ethnology, *The Golden Bough*, mythical ideas out of Jessie Weston's *From Ritual to Romance*, bits of Buddhism and Christianity, fragments of this and that reading, for a fully fledged attempt to bring an exclusive Christian myth alive, he not only (deliberately) stopped making the modern world possible for his art, he proved that his art didn't really make a convincingly possible home for his Christianity.

Further reading

Other works include: *Complete Poems and Plays* (1969); *The Waste Land: A Facsimile and Transcript*, ed. Valerie Eliot (1971). See: Hugh Kenner, *Invisible Poet* (rev. 1965); Northrop Frye, *T.S. Eliot* (rev. 1968); B.C. Southam, *A Student's Guide to the Selected Poems* (1968); *Selected Prose of T.S. Eliot*, ed. Frank Kermode (1975); Stephen Spender, *T.S. Eliot* (1975); Helen Gardner, *The Composition of Four Quartets* (1978); Peter Ackroyd, *T.S. Eliot* (1984); Anthony Julius, *T.S. Eliot, Anti-Semitism and Literary Form* (1995).

VALENTINE CUNNINGHAM

ELLINGTON, Duke

1899–1974

US jazz composer

Edward Kennedy 'Duke' Ellington, as his nickname implies, brought distinction to jazz. Partly it was social distinction, taking the American Negro's music into Carnegie Hall, Westminster Abbey and the White House, but primarily it was musical distinction: the creation of a substantial body of work that challenged comparison with that of modern European composers without losing touch with its own indigenous origins.

Ellington was a pianist who composed for the jazz orchestra he led. Born in 1899, he had a five-piece band by 1923, which attained a distinctive character with the addition of growl-trumpeter 'Bubber' Miley in 1925. Accompanying floor-shows at the Cotton Club after 1927 developed this 'jungle music' image with *Black and Tan Fantasy* and *The Mooche*, balanced by more lyrical pieces such as *Creole Love Call* and *Mood Indigo*. He began recording in 1924, and when he visited Europe in 1933 it was to find himself famous. His music was already evolving: *Reminiscin' in Tempo* (1935) showed that Ellington had begun to listen to **Ravel**, **Debussy** and Delius, with whom he had already been compared. But his compositions lost none of their excitement; by 1940 his superb orchestra had reached another peak with *Ko-Ko*, *Harlem Airshaft* and many others.

The individuality of Ellington's music lay in his adaptation of the jazz idiom to impressionist moods, and in the originality of his scoring, but he depended heavily on a long line of inventive soloists (Miley, Joe Nanton, Johnny Hodges, Cootie Williams), some of whom stayed with him for decades. In 1939 he recruited the arranger Billy Strayhorn, and a remarkable collaboration ensued until the latter's death in 1967, so that the responsibility for any 'Ellington' piece was never entirely clear.

During the second half of his career his repertoire became more extended. His stature as a Negro composer was increased by the suites *Black, Brown and Beige* and *New World A-Comin'* (both 1943), but his post-war inter-continental travels produced *The Far East Suite* (1964) and *The Latin-American Suite* (1968). There were also the three Sacred Concerts (San Francisco 1965, New York 1968 and London 1973) that were repeated all over Europe. His orchestra never abandoned its jazz character, however, and maintained a gruelling schedule of commercial engagements till within a few months of Ellington's death in 1974.

The range and originality of Ellington's music brought him worldwide acclaim.

Paradoxically, his recordings are permanent masterpieces, but their scores are neglected or lost, and in any case could not be played by another group. Despite the ambition of his concert pieces, he was most successful as a miniaturist; the suites have undeniable *longueurs*. As his great soloists aged or fell away, some of the excitement waned, but Ellington himself, disregarding post-**Parker** experiments, maintained his tireless creativity and his orchestra's unique timbre. André Previn said that whereas most arranged jazz could be analysed, 'Duke merely lifts his finger, three horns make a sound, and I don't know what it is.' Or as Ellington himself said, more simply, 'The band you run has got to please the audience. The band I run has got to please me.'

Further reading

See: *The Works of Duke Ellington* (French RCA) is a variorum edition of Ellington's recordings for Victor; *The Complete Duke Ellington* (French CBS) does the same for his work on other labels such as Columbia and Brunswick. Numerous selections have been issued. *Duke Ellington's Story on Records 1925–1945* by Luciano Massagli and others (5 vols, Milan 1966) is an exhaustive discography for the period indicated; J.G. Jepsen's *Jazz Records 1942–1965: Vol. 3 Co – E1* (Denmark 1967) provides further guidance. See also: Stanley Dance, *The World of Duke Ellington* (1971); Duke Ellington, *Music is My Mistress* (1974); Derek Jewell, *Duke: A Portrait of Duke Ellington* (1977); P. Gammond, *Duke Ellington* (1987); M. Tucker (ed.) *The Duke Ellington Reader* (1993); A.H. Lawrence, *Duke Ellington and His World* (2001).

PHILIP LARKIN

EPSTEIN, (Sir) Jacob

1880–1959

US/British sculptor

In the eighteenth and nineteenth centuries sculpture took very much a second place to painting as the medium for fine art in Europe. A renaissance of sculpture was brought about single-handedly by the French artist Auguste Rodin, during the period from his exhibition of *The Age of Bronze* in 1877 to his death in 1917. His first great successor was the Rumanian-born **Constantin Brancusi** who from 1907 onwards rapidly modified the tradition of sculpture revived by Rodin (that of Michelangelo) and gave it a new and modern form. This was in turn immediately taken up by Epstein and carried to Britain, where it found a fertile soil and led to the emergence in the 1930s of two world-class sculptors, **Henry Moore** and **Barbara Hepworth**, and to the development of a school of sculpture in Britain which has flourished mightily in the post-war period. Epstein was the father of modern British sculpture and, more generally, one of the pioneers of modern sculpture in the whole Western world, both through the force of his style and to some extent through the intense controversy aroused by his work throughout his life which firmly established in the public mind the idea of the artist as sculptor.

Epstein was born in New York, USA, on 10 November 1880 of Polish-Jewish parentage. He attended the Art Students League *c.* 1896. In 1902 the proceeds of a commission to illustrate Hutchins Hapgood's *The Spirit of the Ghetto* enabled him to go to Paris. He studied at the École des Beaux Arts and Académie Julian, then settled in London in 1905, becoming a British citizen in 1907. In the same year he received his first major commission, to carve eighteen over-life-size figures for the sides of the British Medical Association building in the Strand. These figures were later virtually destroyed because, apparently, they became unsafe, but the remnants can still be seen *in situ*. Photographs of them in their original state reveal that Epstein was still at this stage under the influence of Rodin, but they already have a highly personal expressive power as well as being fully accomplished technically. Their theme is, broadly speaking, the cycle of life with particular stress on procreation, something which remained central to Epstein's art. This theme and the emphatic nudity through which it was expressed resulted in the first of the public rows over Epstein's art, and accounts of this and later controversies can be found in Epstein's autobiography *Let There Be Sculpture* (1940).

In one respect, however, the Strand statues (as they are known) marked a break with Rodin: they were carved by Epstein himself, whereas all Rodin's marbles were carved by professionals from the master's maquettes, a not uncommon procedure at the time. Indeed, the fact that the Strand statues are carvings rather than bronzes is in itself significant. Rodin, like all nineteenth-century sculptors, was essentially a modeller in clay for eventual casting in bronze and attached no importance to carving as a creative process in its own right. The revolution in sculpture brought about by Brancusi and pursued by Epstein was in part the result of their adoption of carving and specifically *direct carving* as a means. Carving *directly*, the sculptor works on the block with his own hands and without a maquette, so that the final form of the sculpture evolves through the process of its making. In fact, Epstein did make maquettes for the Strand statues but their strength and vitality undoubtedly stem partly from having been carved by their inventor's own hand. In any case, also in 1907 Epstein made a smaller carving which appears to be fully direct, *Rom*, a head of a child based on Romilly John, son of Augustus John, now in the National Museum of Wales, Cardiff. He followed this in 1910 with a large *Maternité*, *A Sun God* and *Sunflower*. These works are increasingly simplified in form, particularly the *Sunflower* (private collection, London), and show the influence of archaic (Egyptian) and primitive (African) art which Epstein studied in both Paris and London and, in the case of African art, had also begun to collect. These influences were another vital ingredient in early modern sculpture.

In 1908 Epstein had been commissioned to produce a monument for the tomb of **Oscar Wilde** in Père Lachaise cemetery in Paris. He eventually carved it in London from a twenty-ton block of Hopton Wood stone in 1911–12 and took it to Paris for installation. The Wilde monument is a highly personal tribute to the poet, showing him in Epstein's own phrase as 'a winged demon angel' carved in high relief into the side of the massive block. This sculpture caused another major row, again because of its nudity, the cemetery authorities refusing to allow it to be unveiled until a cachesexe was provided. However, the really crucial event of this visit to Paris was Epstein's meeting with Brancusi, then in the full flood of his first maturity. The impact of his work on Epstein was profound, Epstein receiving from a greater artist abundant confirmation of the rightness of the direction he was himself already taking in some of his work. On his return to England he shut himself away in a remote part of Sussex called Pett Level and, for three years, until 1916, produced a group of carvings which constitute his great contribution to the early history of modern sculpture. The most important among them are the three groups of mating doves (second group in the Tate Gallery, London), the two large marble Venuses standing on mating birds (Baltimore and Yale University), the pregnant female *Figure in Flenite* (Epstein's term for the stone called serpentine) in the Tate Gallery and the *Mother and Child* (Museum of Modern Art, New York). During these few years he also produced one major work of a different kind, *The Rock Drill*. This was the result of the influence of the Futurism of **Marinetti** and of Epstein's brief association with the British cubofuturist group, the Vorticists, led by Wyndham Lewis. This sculpture consisted in its original state of a mechanistic plaster figure of a man mounted on a real mining drill and was undoubtedly one of the great works of Futurist sculpture. It is also important as an early contribution to that other major technique of modern sculpture besides direct carving – construction (see **Picasso**, **Gabo**). Epstein soon dismantled it and preserved only the torso which, cast in bronze, is now in the Tate Gallery.

After the hiatus of the First World War Epstein continued to produce, at regular if longish intervals, great monumental carvings on primitive and religious themes and continued to arouse controversy. However, he also began to work increasingly in bronze in a relatively naturalistic style, concentrating particularly on portrait busts of the famous and fashionable.

Further reading

See R. Buckle, *Jacob Epstein Sculptor* (1963); E. Silber, *The Sculpture of Jacob Epstein* (1986); S. Gardiner, *Epstein: Artist Against the Establishment* (1992).

SIMON WILSON

ERNST, Max

1891–1976

German/French artist

Ernst, 'the compleat Surrealist', was both the most versatile of the Surrealist artists and the one whose work was most central to the movement as a whole. He had a foot in both the main artistic tendencies within the movement, the quasi-abstraction of, for example, **Miró**, and the illusionism of, for example, **Dalí**. While the range of his technical inventiveness was exceptional, his most outstanding ability lay in the creation of images possessing an extraordinary psychological, magical and poetic power. Among his wide-ranging interests, perhaps the most prominent were those in the theories of psychoanalysis, psychology and the occult.

Much more even than with most artists, Ernst's childhood experiences were crucial for his work: for example, his obsession with birds and forests. He was born into a bourgeois artistic family at Brühl near Cologne, an area where, as he said, 'many of the important crossroads of European culture meet'. After studying philosophy at Bonn University, he took up painting just before the First World War. After the war, 'Dadamax' was the principal figure in Cologne Dada. As well as wood-reliefs, he created collages, often including mechanical imagery in bizarre juxtapositions. From 1922 in Paris, he made paintings strongly influenced by **De Chirico**, which constituted the main link between Dada and Surrealism: of

these the masterpieces were *Oedipus Rex* (1922) and *Two Children are Threatened by a Nightingale* (1924), both showing his interest in **Freud**. Ernst was in the Far East when **Breton's** *Surrealist Manifesto* (1924) was published; on his return, he experimented with a less perspectival, more textural and abstract idiom, reflecting Breton's call for 'psychic automatism' to reveal directly the workings of the unconscious. He invented *frottage* – rubbings, from surfaces like grainy wood, whose patterns provoked visions which he then worked up: a portfolio of drawings made this way were published as the *Histoire Naturelle* (1926). From this developed a series of paintings of *Forests*, recalling German artists like Altdorfer, usually with ambiguous (and alchemistic) sun/moons. Rubbings employing twine led to a series of monstrous *Hordes*, closely related to which is the sinisterly sexual *One Night of Love* (1927). Under **Giacometti's** influence, he took up sculpture seriously in the 1930s, as well as producing his most emotionally disturbing book of collages, *Une Semaine de Bonté* (1934). Among his paintings of this time were ones of mysterious cities, remnants of archaic civilizations, in the foreground of which weird vegetation flourished. The technique of *decalcomania* – using Rorschach-like blots – led to paintings with even more fantastic vegetation, suggesting insect-filled jungles or the ocean bed, among the greatest of which was *Europe After the Rain* (1940–2). In 1941 he fled to America, there meeting Dorothea Tanning, whom he married in 1946. In 1953 he returned to Paris, becoming a French citizen in 1958. With certain exceptions, his works since the war were less powerful – certainly less revolutionary – than those produced during the rise and flowering of the Surrealist movement.

Ernst's influence on subsequent art has been subtle and far from direct. He was, for example, much less relevant for the immediate post-war development of Abstract Expressionism than were the quasi-abstract Surrealists, who provided a way forward in terms of a specifically pictorial language.

Formal considerations, though important, were always secondary to him. Evident throughout his work is the mind of a philosopher-poet (he did in fact write poetry), a seeker of treasure in strange, forbidden lands. He was perhaps the most important inheritor in the first half of the twentieth century of the spirit of German Romantic art; and if this fact distinguished him, despite his centrality in the Surrealist movement, from its other leading figures, it also accounted in part for his unsurpassed success in one of Surrealism's principal aims – the pursuit of the 'marvellous'.

Further reading

Other works include: *Les Malheurs des immortels*, with Paul Eluard (1922); *La Femme 100 têtes* (1929); and *Vus à travers un tempérament* (1953). Books about Ernst include: Patrick Waldberg, *Max Ernst* (1958); John Russell, *Max Ernst – Life and Work* (1967); Uwe Schneede, *The Essential Max Ernst* (1973). See also: William S. Rubin, *Dada and Surrealist Art* (1968); Roger Cardinal and Robert Stuart Short, *Surrealism – Permanent Revolution* (1970); W. Spies (ed.), *Max Ernst: A Retrospective* (exhibition catalogue, 1991).

GRAY WATSON

F

FASSBINDER, Rainer Werner

1945–82

German film director

During his short life – he died aged thirty-seven – Fassbinder was exceptionally prolific, completing thirty-five full-length feature films, at the same time as making a substantial body of work for television, writing for and directing on the live stage, producing several films for other directors, and acting in about forty films, his own and other people's. He was probably the most prominent figure in that generation of directors, which also included **Werner Herzog** and Wim Wenders, who brought West German cinema out of its post-war doldrums into the forefront of European and world cinema in the 1970s. If, given the frantic pace of production, inevitably not all his work is of the highest standard, a remarkably high proportion is; and amongst it are to be found several undoubted masterpieces. Although, as an acclaimed auteur, he attracts intellectuals as the principal international audience for his films, much of his work was aimed at a more popular audience as well. A great admirer of Hollywood at the technical and stylistic level but with a tough and unsentimental vision informed by his leftist politics, his avowed aim was to make 'Hollywood movies, but not as hypocritical'.

He was born into a somewhat bohemian middle-class Bavarian family where he was plentifully exposed to art and literature. His childhood, however, was lonely: after his parents' divorce in 1951 he stayed with his mother, who regularly packed him off to the cinema where he sometimes watched several films a day. In 1965 he directed his first film but failed the entrance examination to the West Berlin Film and Television Academy. During the late 1960s he played a prominent role, as actor, writer and director, in radical and anarchistic theatre groups in Munich. It was from the theatre that he took over into cinema the custom of working with a consistent troupe of collaborators, both behind the scenes and on screen – Hanna Schygulla being one of his most celebrated and frequently used female leads – and it was largely the fact that he and his collaborators knew each other so well that made the high rate of production possible. His work in the theatre, together with his political outlook, also made him receptive to the ideas of **Bertolt Brecht**, whose influence is especially evident in more stylized films, such as *Effi Briest* (1972/4), but to a greater or lesser extent is present throughout. Unlike Brecht, Fassbinder was keen in the first instance to engage his spectators' emotions; but he also sought to provide them, as commercial cinema did not, with 'the possibility of reflecting on and analysing what [they are] feeling'.

In all his films, Fassbinder drew attention to historical and social context. Arranged in chronological order of the period in which they are set, they can be seen to cover almost a hundred years of German history, while also examining a wide range of social *milieux*: the Prussian upper class in the late nineteenth century in *Effi Briest*; the Berlin working class during the Weimar Republic in the thirteen-part TV series *Berlin Alexanderplatz* (1979–80); the rich manufacturing middle class during the rise of Nazism in *Despair* (1977); the intersection of the nightclub world and that of the Nazi elite from 1936 through the war in *Lili Marleen* (1980). It is typical that the first and last of these centred on the life of a woman; and this was to be the case too in his BRD trilogy which explicitly charted the development of the German Federal Republic: the immediate post-war years in *The Marriage of Maria Braun* (1978), and the 1950s in *Lola* (1981) and *Veronika Voss* (1982), the opening shot of *Lola* being a photograph of Konrad Adenauer.

In a sense, all his work can be seen as an attempt to understand the underlying dynamics of the West German society in which he lived; but for all his interest in the collective, the personal dimension was always paramount and, increasingly, seen from within the principal characters' subjective experience. In films such as *Fear Eats the Soul* (1973) he analysed the feelings of relatively powerless individuals caught up in webs of racial and other social prejudices. Largely no doubt because of his own homosexuality, several of his films depicted a homosexual milieu: *Fox and His Friends* (1974) was set in the Munich gay world; *In a Year of 13 Moons* (1978) followed the life of a transsexual; *The Bitter Tears of Petra von Kant* (1972) chronicled an upper-class female fashion designer's infatuation with a younger working-class woman. Homosexuality as such, however, was not an issue in these films: set in or only shortly before the time they were made, that was something they could take for granted. Rather, they concentrated on the painful effects of unequal power relations between the protagonists.

Fassbinder's principal theme, to which he returned again and again, was, in his own words, 'the exploitability of feelings'. His films are full of people longing for love and betrayed by the objects of their love. There is a strong autobiographical element in them, coupled with a fierce acuity of psychological and social insight. While the principal angle from which events are viewed came increasingly to be that of the weaker party, he was well aware of the complexity of the bond between victim and perpetrator and of the potential interchangeability of their roles; and he was fully ready to acknowledge how implicated he himself was on both sides. If his vision can often seem unremittingly bleak, it is also refreshingly honest. Deeply compromised in both his personal and professional dealings, he never sought to evade that fact but rather wove it into the texture of his work. His defiantly rebellious leather-clad persona was notorious, as was his wildly unhealthy lifestyle, fuelled by excessive use of alcohol and drugs, notably cocaine. His death from an overdose has sometimes been interpreted as suicide; it would probably be more accurate to say that those very demons which spurred on his prolific creativity were also the instruments of his self-destruction.

Further reading

See: Rainer Werner Fassbinder, Michael Töteberg and Leo A. Lensing, *The Anarchy of the Imagination: Interviews, Essays, Notes* (1992). See also: Tony Rayns (ed.), *Fassbinder* (1976/9); Ronald Hayman, *Fassbinder: Film Maker* (1984); Julian Lorenz et al., *Chaos as Usual: Conversations about Rainer Werner Fassbinder* (1984); Wallace Steadman Watson, *Understanding Rainer Werner Fassbinder: Film as Private and Public Art* (1996); Christian Braad Thomsen, *Fassbinder: Life and Work of a Provocative Genius* (2004). For setting him within larger historical context see: Thomas Elsaesser, *Fassbinder's Germany: History, Identity, Subject* (1996).

GRAY WATSON

FAULKNER, William

1897–1962

US novelist

William Faulkner was born in New Albany, Mississippi, and grew up in nearby Oxford. His first book – a collection of poems called *The Marble Faun* – was published in 1924. On moving to New Orleans in 1925 he met Sherwood Anderson, and it was partly as the result of Anderson's influence that he turned to fiction. His first novel, *Soldier's Pay*, appeared in 1926, and was favourably reviewed, but brought little financial reward. After writing a satire, *Mosquitoes* (1927), Faulkner returned to Oxford and began to shift his attention to his homeland. Its romantic past and present decadence were to provide the material for nearly all his major fiction. The initial result was *Sartoris* (1929), a novel in large measure based on the history of the Faulkner family. It was followed, in the same year, by *The Sound and the Fury*, whose technical inventiveness was greeted with some excitement in literary circles, but which failed to reach a wider public.

The years 1929–36 were enormously productive, and saw the publication of much of Faulkner's most important work – *As I Lay Dying* (1930), *Light in August* (1932), *Absalom, Absalom!* (1936) – together with the less remarkable *Pylon* (1935). It was *Sanctuary*, however, that in 1931 brought Faulkner popular success. A gruesome story of rape, murder and mob violence, it shocked, and aroused indignation. But sales were high, and with notoriety came the opportunity to write scripts for Hollywood. Faulkner was to work for Hollywood, if rather sporadically, for over twenty years, while continuing to live in Oxford. He wrote relatively less fiction during this time. *The Unvanquished* came out in 1938 and was followed by *The Wild Palms* (1939), *The Hamlet* (1940), *Go Down, Moses* (1942), *Intruder in the Dust* (1948) and *A Fable* (1954). *The Town* (1957) and *The Mansion* (1959) concluded the Snopes trilogy begun with *The Hamlet*. Faulkner's last novel was *The Reivers* (1962).

During the 1940s, Faulkner's reputation declined, and it was only with the award of the Nobel Prize for Literature in 1950 that interest in his work revived. His stock has remained high since. His importance as innovator has been generally recognized. His experiments with narrative chronology, and his use of 'stream of consciousness' and 'multiple perspective' techniques beg comparison with the work of contemporaries like **Virginia Woolf** and **James Joyce** – *Ulysses* was an important influence on Faulkner. But from *The Sound and the Fury* to *The Wild Palms* experimental devices serve singular ends, and Faulkner's complex, involuted prose style is likewise peculiar to him. Perhaps his most original achievement is his use of style and technique to unsettle habits of thought and perception. The vision offered by the best novels is often unfamiliar, primaeval – a disturbing refutation of the cosily humanized world of civilized man.

Faulkner's significance is partly that of a successful regional novelist. He is conspicuous as the most prominent figure in the 'Southern renaissance' of the twentieth century. Most of his novels are set in the fictional southern county of Yoknapatawpha, and from *Sartoris* onwards Faulkner's chief concern was with the South. It was a South impotent and backward, defeated in war, but inheriting a set of impossibly romantic ideals. Faulkner's attitudes to it are complicated and ambivalent, those of both critic and apologist. He attacked its intolerance and bigotry, yet his work is often coloured with the very puritanism he satirized. He cherished its legends of heroic endeavour, but he was able soberly to disengage himself from them and to demonstrate their futility. *Absalom, Absalom!*, for instance – itself a myth – is also a careful analysis of the process by which myths are born and nourished. Faulkner censured the parochialism of the post-bellum South, while finding in it the basis for a critique of the urban and commercial culture dominant in America. Hostile to views on the racial question espoused by the conservative white South, his own attitudes to the Negro, and to Negro culture, were commonly less reformist than romantic – to the point, some have complained, of evasiveness.

In his Nobel Prize address, Faulkner spoke of 'the old universal truths – love and honour and pity and pride and compassion and sacrifice'. Commentators hopeful of finding consoling faiths in Faulkner's work have affirmed his allegiance to such truths. Others have suspected that it is only endurance that he can recommend with conviction. But the novels cannot be reduced to a simple ethic. Possibly more fundamental to Faulkner is a deep-seated and pessimistic distrust of human unruliness. For Faulkner, it is at best precariously subject to the limits of law and the constraints of civilization.

It was in France that Faulkner's novels first met with a reception that was appreciative and intelligent, and they exerted an acknowledged influence on developments in French fiction after 1930, from André Malraux to Claude Simon. His impact on American writing came somewhat later, but has been felt in the work of writers as various as **Norman Mailer**, **Thomas Pynchon** and John Hawkes, as well as post-war southern fiction (William Styron, **Truman Capote**). No writer of importance, however, has followed him in blending modernist experiment with the evocation of a circumscribed but densely imagined provincial world, and a disabused and penetrating quality of insight.

Further reading

Other works include: *A Green Bough* (1933) is a collection of poems; *These Thirteen* (1931), *Doctor Martino and Other Stories* (1934) and *Knight's Gambit* (1949) are collections of stories; *New Orleans Sketches* (1958) is a collection of short pieces first published in the New Orleans *Times-Picayune* in 1925; *Requiem for a Nun* (1951) is a play with narrative interludes. On Faulkner: J. Bassett (ed.), *William Faulkner: The Critical Heritage* (1975); J.L. Blotner, *Faulkner, A Biography* (1974); C. Brooks, *William Faulkner, The Yoknapatawpha Country* (1964) and *Towards Yoknapatawpha and Beyond* (1978); Michael Millgate, *The Achievement of William Faulkner* (1966); Olga Vickery, *The Novels of William Faulkner* (1959); Joel Williamson, *William Faulkner and Southern History* (1993); Philip M. Weinstein (ed.), *The Cambridge Companion to William Faulkner* (1995).

ANDREW GIBSON

FAURÉ, Gabriel Urbain

1845–1924

French composer

Gabriel Fauré was the youngest of six children. His father was first a schoolmaster and then the director of a teachers' training college in the southern *département* of Ariège. At the age of nine Fauré was sent to the Niedermeyer School in Paris, where the teaching was more thorough and comprehensive than that at the Conservatoire, with its traditional bias towards opera. Among Fauré's teachers, Saint-Saëns did much to encourage his early efforts in composition. Fauré was to spend much of his life as an organist, but in 1896 he was appointed to a professorship of composition at the Paris Conservatoire when his influence on a whole generation of French composers started to bear fruit. He became director of the Conservatoire in 1905, the administrative duties of which left him less time for composition. Unfortunately, increasing deafness led to his resignation in 1920, and his final years were spent in semi-retirement. His last work, the String Quartet, was completed only two months before his death in November 1924.

As with many composers, Fauré's work can be divided into three periods, with the inevitable consequent overlapping. The most characteristic music of Fauré's earlier years (to *c.* 1884) is undoubtedly the chamber music, particularly the First Violin Sonata (1875–6) and First Piano Quartet (1876–83). Their originality is due to the fact that Fauré had very few French models to serve as a guide, save for the earlier chamber works of Saint-Saëns. The continuity of the accompanimental figurations show Fauré's indebtedness to Baroque movements of the single *Affekt* type, rather than to the Romantic sonata where a single movement will often unfold several 'new chapters' during its course. The clarity of the textures and the quiet inevitability of the music are astonishingly assured. Of Fauré's hundred or so songs, thirty-five date from this period; while a few add little to their Gounodesque models, the best of them (particularly *Après un rêve, c.* 1875, and those set to the sensitive poetry of Sully-Prudhomme) display a subtle correlation between poetry and music which has remained a model in French song-writing. Apart from the ambitious *Ballade*, Op. 19 (1879), Fauré's earlier piano works, while beautifully written, are more derivative: particularly the first four Nocturnes and the first three Impromptus, where Fauré's model was Chopin. The first two Barcarolles, however, are more Fauréan in their sensuousness, the composer preferring to utilize his own vivid imagination of this most romantic of musical genres rather than depend on the more elaborate *Barcarolle* of Chopin.

The second period (*c.* 1885–1900) saw the consolidation of Fauré's techniques as a composer. Gone are the occasional reminiscences of Gounod in the songs, and Chopin in the piano works. In particular, the songs demonstrate that the exquisite poetry of **Paul Verlaine** all but belongs to Fauré's music: the *Five Venetian Songs* (1891) and the nine songs of *La Bonne Chanson* (1892–4) scale the peak of Fauré's art in this form. In both, the subtle employment of thematic transference from one song to another, along with the sensitive treatment of voice and piano and the sheer fertility of Fauré's musical invention, make these cycles a landmark in the history of French song. The *Requiem* (1886–90), intimate, restrained and already showing that austerity and tenuity of texture which was to be a hallmark of the music of Fauré's third period, is still the best known of his large-scale works. The Sixth and Seventh Nocturnes for piano (1894 and 1898) are an enormous advance on the earlier Nocturnes: the latter is particularly interesting in its interrelation of material from one theme to another, and in the bold employment of passing notes in contrapuntal textures. The *Dolly Suite* (1893–6) for piano duet shows in its cheerfulness and lightness of touch a different side to Fauré. The almost unknown Second Piano Quartet (1886) is even finer than its predecessor with its large-scale opening Allegro, an almost barbaric Scherzo, a long nocturne-like slow movement, and a finale which again looks ahead harmonically and texturally to Fauré's final period. The First Piano Quintet (1890–4 and 1903–5), mostly composed in the 1890s as a projected third piano quartet, was first performed in Brussels in 1906, and belongs spiritually to the last period. As in all but one of the late chamber works, there are only three movements: the gravely beautiful first movement is remarkable for a recapitulation 'so varied as to take away all feeling of repetition' (**Aaron Copland**); while the ternary slow movement, beginning in 12/8 time, gradually mixes it with 4/4, in which time signature the movement ends. The free variation form of the finale is perhaps the least successful part of the quintet.

The production of the lyric drama *Prométhée* in 1900 marks the start of Fauré's final period. He had gradually been moving towards the ultimate refinement of his art, the paring down of all inessentials, resulting in limpid textures whose frequently contrapuntal lines had brought a new and unique quality of sound to music. The last four song cycles have never been popular either with singers or audiences, for this is essentially intimate music. The same is true of much of the piano music from this period. The almost unknown *Nine Preludes* (1909–10), the elegiac Eleventh Nocturne (1913), the tortuous harmonies of the middle of the Fourth Impromptu (1905), the surprisingly dissonant accented passing notes of the stormy Twelfth Nocturne (1915), all these epitomize the enormous variety even of Fauré's later piano music, which as a whole in both quality and quantity is in every way comparable with that of Chopin, **Debussy** or **Ravel**. But it is in the last six chamber works that one can see the most complete picture of the composer. The Second Violin Sonata (1916–17) contains one of Fauré's most powerful and compelling first movements; the glory of the Second Cello Sonata (1921) is the noble lyricism of its central movement; while the large-scale Second Piano Quintet (1919–21) provides the most comprehensive view of every facet of Fauré's genius.

Comparing the idiom of the earliest song with that of the String Quartet of over sixty years later, one can see immediately the enormous strides made by Fauré over this period: the two pieces seem almost to suggest two different composers. And yet by proceeding chronologically from one piece to the next, it is evident that his development was perfectly logical, indeed inevitable. The influence of the Niedermeyer School on his employment of modal techniques has been somewhat overstressed: the First Piano Quartet and the *Requiem* use modal themes, but they are works which have become popular to the exclusion of many others which do not. Harmonically Fauré was in fact a late Romantic, but in other respects he was very different from his contemporaries. He was one of the first to pare down the non-essentials of music at a time (*c.* 1890) when in general music was at its most opulent; and thus, like Debussy, he forestalled the Neoclassicism of the 1920s. He took considerable trouble over accompanimental figures, where often tunes will emerge against the main melody almost in a contrapuntal manner. Like Beethoven, his fondness for contrapuntal and canonic devices increased as he grew older. Fauré was particularly skilful in his employment of thematic metamorphosis, usually accomplished in a quiet way, displaying that reticence and refinement which is so characteristic of much French music in general and of Fauré in particular. He suppressed several of his early orchestral pieces, but his interest in orchestration was greater than is often imagined. When writing his only opera, *Pénélope* (1907–12), he wrote to his wife: 'The orchestration ... will be a pleasure, a relief and a relaxation.' Unlike his pupil Ravel, Fauré never 'searched for new harmonies'. His technique of moving rapidly from one chromatic chord to another was a favourite one, but his aim was never to subvert the tonal system. He often 'looks at' rather than 'states' a new key; and thus it is not so much the language which is new, it is rather the syntax, the order of words. In this respect he was a potent force for the twentieth century.

It is unlikely that Fauré will ever be as popular as Debussy, in France or elsewhere. Fauré's music never imposes itself by brute force, and therefore it will probably be always to a minority that his work will appeal. Nevertheless, like Rameau, he remains one of the great underrated figures in French music.

Further reading

See: Charles Koechlin, *Gabriel Fauré* (1945); Norman Suckling, *Fauré* (1946); Jean-Michel Nextoux, *Fauré* (1972); Vladimir Jankélévitch, *Fauré et l'inexprimable* (1974); Robert Orledge, *Gabriel Fauré* (1979); J.-M. Nectoux, *Gabriel Fauré: A Musical Life*, trans. R. Nichols (1991); T. Gordon (ed. and trans.), *Regarding Fauré* (1999).

J. BARRIE JONES

FELLINI, Federico

1920–93
Italian filmmaker and scriptwriter

Fellini left his home town, the provincial seaside resort of Rimini, for the metropolis of Rome in 1939, throwing himself into the community of cartoonists and gag-writers supplying material for satirical magazines, the variety theatre, the radio and film scripts. By now an established screenwriter, Fellini was taken up by Rossellini, first for *Roma città aperta* (*Rome Open City*, 1945), and then both as writer and assistant director on *Paisà* (1946), much of which was elaborated by the two of them on the spot during shooting. For that alone, Fellini is part-creator of one of the finest films in the history of cinema, and he revered Rossellini as his master. His first sole directorship was on a comedy, *Lo sceicco bianco* (*The White Sheik*, 1952), unappreciated at the time, but now recognized as a jewel of the genre, contrasting the 'true' life of fantasy (found in photo-comics) with the banality of reality. His reputation was affirmed with *I vitelloni* (1953), a mordant but affectionate portrayal of shallow, aimless provincial adolescence. His narrative style was by now firmly established as episodic, circular in the case of the road-movie *La strada* (1954 – earning Fellini the first of several Oscars), in which the base materialism of a circus performer was contrasted with the spiritual purity and innocence of his simple girl assistant Gelsomina, alluding to the Virgin Mary. Gelsomina was played by Giulietta Masina, the director's wife, who then played Cabiria, the victimized but undaunted pure prostitute of *Le notti di Cabiria* (*Nights of Cabiria*, 1957), set among Rome's sub-proletariat. *La strada* was internationally recognized for its poetry, while being viewed by many on the left in Italy as a mystificatory betrayal of the rational, socialist realism of the neo-realist movement from which Fellini had grown.

Rejecting the narrative logic bequeathed to classical cinema by literature, Fellini assembled his cinematic artefacts from fragments, evolving from the episodic towards what he once called a 'Picassian decomposition' (reminiscent of collage) in the film which announced his magisterial middle-period, *La dolce vita* (1960). His fragments were invariably bearers of cultural allusions (from popular culture, tradition, religion, history, school, the circus, cinema and the variety theatre), so that Silvia, in *La dolce vita*, is an assembly of ancient Roman pagan goddess, the Virgin of the Catholic Church, Hollywood sex-symbol and fertility idol. The film watches a provincial young man, recently established in Rome, encounter the shallow hedonism and spiritual emptiness of an Italy uprooted from traditional values by the 'economic miracle', and led astray by the media.

The worldwide success of *La dolce vita* gave Fellini a production freedom shared by scarcely any other major director to make his masterpiece, *8½* (1963). Blocked himself, unsure of his inspiration, he portrayed his own bewilderment in a film director unable to shoot his film (which is the film we eventually see), besieged by dreams, memories, fantasies and guilts which are embodied in the characters who float before the camera – conflicting figures in a **Jungian** landscape of the unconscious, eventually resolving in an integration of the psyche (an acceptance brought about by a variety theatre illusionist) represented by a parade around a circus-ring. The freedom and subtlety with which Fellini assembled his cinematic artefact in what is a comedy, enormously complex and yet never obscure, astonished filmmakers, for whom it was a revelation of the poetic possibilities of cinema. Using for a change the cinematographer Gianni Di Venanzo, master of shadow and strong contrasts, outrageously overexposing the film at times, and exploiting Nino Rota's music and Piero Gherardi's designs to the full (we shall probably never know what the narrative owed to Ennio Flaiano's writing), Fellini endowed the film not only with expressive power but also with extraordinary beauty and enchantment.

The films of Fellini that stand out from the fourteen which followed develop an autobiographical, satirical vein and often play with documentary, as in the case of *I clowns* (*The Clowns*, 1971, made for television), an investigation into the tradition of circus clowns; or *Roma* (1972), where he investigates, by means of collage, what Rome means to an Italian, and recreates affectionately and comically the arrival in the pre-war city of the youth from the provinces, a brothel and a popular variety theatre; or a mock interview with himself, *Intervista* (1987). The most successful of the later films was *Amarcord* (1973), a comic portrayal of family life in Rimini, structured around funny stories and local characters remembered from his past, and containing a devastating satire of the vacuous rhetoric of the fascist regime. *E la nave va* (*And the Ship Sails On*, 1983) is a paean to the gratuitousness of art, comically following an ocean liner, full of opera devotees united to scatter at sea the ashes of a revered diva, into the jaws of the First World War.

Fellini had dark and depressed moments, in which he savaged the moral and spiritual shallowness of the modern world, as in the episode *Toby Dammit* of a portmanteau film (*Histoires extraordinaires/Tales of Mystery and Imagination*, 1968); in his allegory of authoritarian politics, *Prova d'orchestra* (*Orchestra Rehearsal*, 1978); in his transformation of Petronius's fragmentary novel *Satyricon* (1969) into a psychic underworld of decadence; in his disturbing portrait of *Casanova* (1976); and in his condemnation, in *Ginger e Fred* (*Ginger and Fred*, 1986), of the triviality of television, which was replacing nobler and more authentic theatrical and cinematic forms. His last film, *La voce della luna* (*The Voice of the Moon*, 1990), returns to his provincial homeland and its popular culture, where the mad and the simple are the only people sane enough to hear the whisperings of the soul, to record a poetic and pessimistic plea for a 'quieter' world in which true communication might be possible.

Fellini gave many (and conflicting) accounts of his own art. His advice to a budding filmmaker was 'to make a beautiful film'. He once described his aim as an artist as that of overcoming modern man's condition as an isolated, lonely 'monad'. He consistently proclaimed the human value of the imagination. His death in 1993 was received by Italians as a national tragedy.

Further reading

See: Tullio Kezich, *Fellini* (1996). Criticism: Peter Bondanella, *The Cinema of Federico Fellini* (1992).

CHRISTOPHER WAGSTAFF

FITZGERALD, Francis Scott Key

1896–1940

US writer

Although his merit as a short-story writer had been shown in *Tales of the Jazz Age* (1922), it was not until the publication of *The Great Gatsby* (1925) that F. Scott Fitzgerald was revealed as a serious novelist. The titles of his earlier best-selling novels, *This Side of Paradise* (1920) and *The Beautiful and Damned* (1922), give some indication of their contents. Their theme is romantic disillusion, and their tone a strange mixture of sophistication and naïveté. With *The Great Gatsby*, however, the style tautened

and the angle of vision changed. It became apparent that, warring with the romantic dream, there was a sharp critical intelligence.

Fitzgerald's fourth novel, *Tender is the Night* (1934), his most ambitious and in some ways his best, shows him even more firmly at grips with the problems of the Jazz Age, the inner tragedy of which he understood as well as anyone. By the time it appeared, however, America had moved into the 1930s, and the Depression. Violence and crudeness became the order of the day, and it is possible that Fitzgerald's bewildered attempts to comprehend *Tender is the Night's* lack of success in this alien atmosphere hastened his early death. Fitzgerald had to be the toast of the town; he found it difficult to work at his art alone and to be ignored, like **Melville** in his later years. It is this flaw – if flaw it be – which makes him at once so pathetic and so sympathetic.

He was born in St Paul, Minnesota, the son of Edward and Mary McQuillan Fitzgerald, and was christened Francis Scott Key after the author of 'The Star-Spangled Banner', to whom he was distantly related. After two years at the Newman School in New Jersey, he went to Princeton a year before the outbreak of the First World War. There he led a busy social life, becoming a member of the Triangle Club, writing an operetta in his freshman year, contributing to the student magazines, and collaborating with his fellow student Edmund Wilson. In 1917 he joined the army, was commissioned, and became aide-de-camp to General J.A. Ryan at his staff headquarters in the South. The war ended before he was sent overseas, but into this period he managed to cram a great many social activities. He also wrote his first (unpublished) novel, *The Romantic Egoist*, and became acquainted with Zelda Sayre, whom he married in 1920.

Beneath the bright surface of Fitzgerald's life, however, there was practical ability and a shrewd grasp of affairs. While working as an advertising copywriter, from 1919 to 1920, he wrote his first short stories and revised *The Romantic Egoist*. With the publication of this revised version as *This Side of Paradise* he became an immediate success. He settled on Long Island, the scene of *The Great Gatsby*, and continued writing stories, mainly for the *Saturday Evening Post*. During the next four years he published *The Beautiful and Damned* and *Tales of the Jazz Age* and wrote an unsuccessful play, *The Vegetable*. He mixed with the rich, whose lives fascinated him, and tried to live up to their standard. In one year he is reputed to have spent $36,000 which, although no large sum compared with the extravagance of the bootleggers and gamblers, is high enough for a writer who has nothing but his wits to live on. His wits, in fact, were Fitzgerald's fortune. He had the ability both to charm his contemporaries and to sum them up in a single apposite phrase. He could not spell, but he wrote like an angel.

In 1924, he moved with his wife and small daughter to Paris and the Riviera. After a few years, his drinking and social activities became more desperate. The high-spirited charmer of Long Island and New York became a sordid brawler. The ugly scene in *Tender is the Night* when Dick Diver is arrested by the French police has the ring of truth. Out of this period, however, came his best work: *The Great Gatsby, All the Sad Young Men* (1926) and finally, after a long gap, *Tender is the Night*.

After the publication of *Taps at Reveille* (1935), Fitzgerald went to work in Hollywood, where he wrote the unfinished *The Last Tycoon*. For varying periods he managed to stop drinking, but he was an ill man, and although a hypochondriac by nature had incipient tuberculosis and a heart ailment. Zelda had finally succumbed to the schizophrenia which had been latent but unsuspected when Fitzgerald married her, and, added to this worry, there was his constant fear that his talent was drying up. The last disastrous episode of his life, his visit as a film scriptwriter to Dartmouth College, is recounted by Budd Schulberg in *The Disenchanted*. These last years are also touched on in Sheilah Graham's *Beloved Infidel*, and are documented in Fitzgerald's own words, with a memoir by Edmund Wilson, in *The Crack-Up* (1945). He died on 21 December 1940 in Hollywood.

Unlike Sinclair Lewis, Fitzgerald never wrote directly of Minnesota in his novels, and only occasionally in his short stories. His life was in the East and it was in a sense his misfortune to be romantic about great wealth. His remark in *The Rich Boy*, 'Let me tell you about the very rich. They are different from you and me,' is reported to have led **Ernest Hemingway** to reply, 'Yes, they have more money.' But Fitzgerald's star-struck infatuation has validity, for all the cynical light that Hemingway's comment casts upon it. His preoccupation with the life and status which great wealth can bring is the American equivalent of the English novelist's preoccupation with rank and manners, and had a special appeal in an age when American society was in a stage of transition.

In his career as a novelist, Fitzgerald mirrored his kind and his period as clearly as Jane Austen mirrored hers, and in his defeat ('There are no second acts in American lives') he summed up a peculiarly American failure: the inability to stay the course. But Fitzgerald was more than a writer of documentaries. He had an extraordinary ear for conversation and for the nuance of social behaviour. It is not 'good characterization' in the old-fashioned sense, but something much more intimate, a power of conveying verisimilitude through – as he says of Dick Diver – 'a trick of the heart'. His phrases are very fine, and have a poetic as well as a descriptive quality. Delicate, sensitive, with his finger on the pulse of the life which flowed around him, Fitzgerald's sensibility was of the Jamesian type. What he lacked, however, was **Henry James's** range and, finally, the deadly seriousness of the dedicated artist which comes from putting art before life. Whatever disguise he wears, it is almost always himself that Fitzgerald writes about. And for this reason, if for no other, a shadow is cast over the work of a writer who had the potentiality of a great novelist. As in the case of Hemingway, it is only in his short stories that he was able to make form and subject fuse into a perfect whole, and it is perhaps significant that the novel which comes nearest to achieving this is his shortest, *The Great Gatsby*.

Further reading

See: Arthur Mizener, *The Far Side of Paradise* (1951); Alfred Kazin (ed.), *F. Scott Fitzgerald: The Man and His Work* (1951); James E. Miller, *The Fictional Technique of F. Scott Fitzgerald* (1957); A. Turnbull, *Scott Fitzgerald* (1962); W. Goldhurst, *F. Scott Fitzgerald and His Contemporaries* (1963); Joan M. Allen, *Candles and Carnival Lights: The Catholic Sensibility of F. Scott Fitzgerald* (1978); John B. Chambers, *The Novels of F. Scott Fitzgerald* (1989); Robert L. Gale, *F. Scott Fitzgerald Encyclopedia* (1998); Ruth Prigozy (ed.), *The Cambridge Companion to F. Scott Fitzgerald* (2001).

GEOFFREY MOORE

FLAHERTY, Robert Joseph

1884–1951

US documentary filmmaker

The American filmmaker Robert Flaherty is most often associated with the anthropological strand or travelogue genre within early documentary film, although he also collaborated on American and British studio fiction film. Flaherty's documentary films chronicled diverse and exotic cultures and attracted both critical acclaim and box office success. The renowned British documentary filmmaker John Grierson coined the term 'documentary' to describe Flaherty's early films, which were often organized around the theme of man's survival in unforgiving environments, whether that be the Inuit Eskimos surviving in the Arctic wastes as portrayed in *Nanook of the North* (1922), or the small fishing community pitted against the unforgiving seas off the west coast of Ireland in *Man of Aran* (1934).

Flaherty's fascination for the wilderness and challenging natural environments stems from his own background. He was born in Michigan, the son of a mining engineer. As a boy he spent much of his young life with his family living in isolated mining communities, and rarely went to school. He later attended the Michigan College of Mines. After leaving college he accompanied his father on exploratory trips into the wilderness, and later worked as an explorer and surveyor for several mining companies. It was while undertaking a survey on behalf of the Canadian railroad builder William McKenzie that Flaherty first encountered and befriended the Inuit Eskimos. In 1920 he determined to return to film the Inuit for posterity, having secured financial backing for a film project from the French fur company Revillon Frères. He went on to have his first major success with *Nanook of the North,* a study of Eskimo life.

Flaherty was a lyrical and poetic filmmaker who returned time and again to key themes such as conflicts between man and nature, community traditions and family, the dignity of man, and nobility gained through struggle in harsh but beautiful natural landscapes. His early box office success with *Nanook of the North* attracted the attention of the large American and British film studios. With financial backing from Jesse Lasky of Paramount Studios, Flaherty and his wife Frances Hubbard – his lifelong collaborator – were able to undertake their next film project, which was to record the traditional culture of Samoan village life on the island of Savai'i. While *Moana: A Romance of the Golden Age* was popular with film audiences, it did not quite repeat the huge success of *Nanook of the North.* In 1929 the Fox Film Corporation hired Flaherty to make a film about the Acoma Indians of New Mexico, but this project never came to fruition. While in Hollywood Flaherty collaborated with the prestigious German film director Franz W. Murnau to make the film *Tabu* (1931), about a Tahitian pearl fisherman and his forbidden love for a beautiful young woman. Although Flaherty co-scripted the film with Murnau, he left the film in mid-production due to differences in opinion with Murnau as to how their script might be realized on screen.

Flaherty's foray into both documentary and fiction film continued in Britain. Grierson, as head of the Empire Marketing Board, commissioned Flaherty to shoot *Industrial Britain*

(1933), a short film about the relationship between British craftsmanship and an emerging more highly industrialized age. While working in Britain Flaherty received financial backing from Michael Balcon to make *Man of Aran*, which with its backdrop of tumultuous seascapes is often perceived as Flaherty's greatest masterpiece. From this success Flaherty went on to work with producer Alex Korda on an adaptation of **Kipling's** book *The Elephant Boy* (1937). However, this return to a studio collaboration was again to prove difficult, with Flaherty having to relinquish control over the way the film was finally edited to Korda.

While Flaherty has received great acclaim for his documentary films there has also been much criticism. Criticism has tended to focus round his observational film style and proposed recording of 'found stories', a documentary aesthetic that in its most ethical form attempts to portray everyday events as they occur with minimum intervention from the filmmaker. However, Flaherty was a filmmaker unconstrained by actuality. He often staged scenes to help develop the dramatic narrative within his films, that was truthful to his vision of the people and cultures he filmed, if not to actuality. *Moana* in particular was harshly criticized by later documentary filmmakers for the staging of a ritual tattooing scene. There, Ta'avale – the young Samoan islander who played Moana – was actually tattooed in traditional style, a practice which had diminished within his community at the time of filming. Ta'avale, like other protagonists in Flaherty's films, had been paid to take part.

However, it is the way in which Flaherty demonstrated a consistent talent for invoking a powerful and emotive poetic realism to record the lives of the people and communities that he filmed for which he is best remembered, from his earliest work through to his last film, the highly acclaimed *Louisiana Story* (1948), which was awarded the Venice Film Festival's International Prize for its lyrical beauty.

Further reading

See: Robert Flaherty, in collaboration with Frances Hubbard Flaherty, *My Eskimo Friends 'Nanook of the North'*, (1924); F.H. Flaherty, *The Odyssey of a Film-maker, Robert Flaherty's Story* (1960); P. Rotha, *Robert J. Flaherty: A Biography* (1983); R. Barsam, *The Vision of Robert Flaherty: The Artist as Myth and Filmmaker* (1988).

PAT COOK

FLAUBERT, Gustave

1821–80

French novelist

'Flaubert, creator of the "modern" novel, stands at the crossroads of all our literary problems of today,' wrote **Sartre**. Few nineteenth-century writers command the attention and status accorded Flaubert today, yet it is anything but the complacent status of a fixed, classified reputation. It has more to do with anxiety and questioning, and Sartre rightly stressed the problematic aspect of Flaubert's example: not only as a creator of modern fiction but as a pioneer in the modern problematics of writing in general. Even his influence is contradictory and diverse. Each generation finds it own Flaubert: a sign of greatness, but a disturbing greatness.

No doubt this vocation to disturb has its origin in the estrangement at the heart of Flaubert's own experience. The second son of a prestigious Normandy doctor, he was painfully aware of his position in the family: his elder brother was destined by the family structure to succeed the father, while Gustave, the unneeded child, experienced his existence as superfluous. 'We are superfluous, we workers in the field of art,' he would write in 1870. This sense of superfluity Sartre saw as the *leitmotif* of Flaubert's whole life, and the cause of his early problems with language, experiencing words as alien, non-natural. Later this would take the form of his anguished difficulty in writing, the protracted agonies of style so amply documented in his letters.

His adolescent writings were wholly in the Romantic mode; in them recurred the theme of the absent God, the resentment of creature against Creator, of 'monstrous' child against the sadistic parent who has created it for nothing. The pessimism was not merely conventional: it expressed what was to be a lifelong sense of passivity, an estrangement from praxis and a deep resentment against the world of social success, the world of the bourgeois. At the age of twenty-three, Flaubert underwent a nervous seizure, and experienced it as a significant rite of passage, cutting him off from ordinary life and leaving him with the world of art, the ivory tower of passive, ironic observation of reality, the struggle to transform that observation and that irony into language: 'my poor life, in which sentences are the only adventures'.

Not that his retreat was total – in 1849–50 he undertook a journey through Egypt, Palestine, Syria and the Lebanon. On his return began the long ordeal of *Madame Bovary*, as charted in his letters to Louise Colet, so rich in reflections on the problems of fiction. The novel's publication in 1856 created a scandal not unlike that of **Baudelaire's** *Fleurs du mal*, a notorious trial for obscenity, ending in acquittal. Thereafter, apart from the brief episode of a second trip to Africa, Flaubert's life was one of anguished, never-satisfied dedication to his art. Each successive work was a long labour, involving heroic – sometimes disproportionate – feats of documentation to be transmuted into fiction: *Salammbô* (1857–62); *Sentimental Education* (*L'Éducation sentimentale*, 1864–9); the final version of *The Temptation of Saint Anthony* (*La Tentation de Saint Antoine*) was published in 1874, the *Three Tales* (*Trois contes*) in 1877. On his death Flaubert left unfinished the major work of his last years, *Bouvard et Pécuchet*.

Few works fascinate yet resist criticism as much as these novels: above all, they show the hopeless inadequacy of the label 'realist' that contemporaries pinned on Flaubert. Though in his later years he came to be regarded as a master by Maupassant and **Zola**, the implications of his work defy labelling altogether, and evoke only doubt.

The theme of his novels is the difficulty of interpreting experience: aptly, the reader is brought up against the problem of interpreting the novels themselves. They are singularly lacking in authorial guidelines – 'Stupidity consists in drawing conclusions,' Flaubert was fond of repeating. The ideal he strove for was the impersonality of a Shakespeare, works giving such an illusion of autonomy that he hoped the reader would be astounded by them, wondering how they had come into being. Yet the profound irony of Flaubert's creative intelligence is everywhere, a destructive, vengeful force, undermining and devaluing the lives of his characters; constantly he seeks out the grotesque, 'that ridiculousness intrinsic in human life itself'.

Madame Bovary is an epic of frustration, a deeply unconventional novel about someone who tries to live her life as a conventional novel: the country doctor's wife who, like Don Quixote, sees the world through the prism of literature. Her mind is full of the bric-à-brac of Romantic illusions and stereotypes, so much so that her aspiration away from the desperately humdrum world of provincial respectability – the world of the bourgeois – can express itself in no other, more authentic way. The cycles of disillusionment are charted with pitiless irony, through marriage, adultery, up to her horrible, clinically observed death by poisoning. Cycles indeed: the overwhelming impression is one of lack of progression, as Emma inevitably fails to find an authentic language for her aspiration. She does not speak, but *is spoken* by the clichés of her culture; she is a victim of those 'received ideas' which Flaubert delighted in collecting as a vengeful gesture against the world. The writing itself embodies a sense of non-progressive nihilism: he reduces the importance of dramatic events, exploits the imperfect tense with striking originality to freeze action into *tableaux*, to emphasize the static at the expense of the dynamic. Flaubert saw his study as critical, even anatomical, but ironic detachment is only half the picture. The effectiveness of the novel depends on his ability to feel himself into his character (what

Henry James would call 'the creative effort to get into the skin of the creature'), to become Emma Bovary in the very movement, the almost physical vibration of her sensibility and her illusions, by an amazing power of empathy that allows him to capture the near-inexpressible texture of experience. The technique he enlists is that of the mobile point of view, dramatizing consciousness through description of what is perceived in a way that strikingly prefigures the modern 'phenomenological' novel. Narrative perspective is decentralized to such a degree that a sense of relativity reigns, perfectly embodying the phenomenon of non-communication with which the novel deals. Flaubert's style is, then, a constant tension between irony and empathy, detachment and intimate narrative involvement. The irony is all the more devastating for being held in tension with the uncanny ability to become the sensibility that is the object of that irony. If Flaubert saw the artist as God, it is God simultaneously as ironic observer and pantheistic penetration into the whole of creation.

Flaubert saw his own personality as a tension between two contrasting tendencies – the lyricist and the critical realist-observer. Critics once made much of the oscillation in successive works between apparent predominance of one tendency or the other: this was misleading, as the basic method is always the tension itself. While writing *Bovary* he railed against the banal subject-matter, expressive of the modern world he despised, and dreamed of a mode more 'natural' to him; to this he turned in the sumptuous exoticism of *Salammbô*, only to find just as much labyrinthine difficulty in the writing as he had experienced over the earlier work. This story of the struggle between ancient Carthage and the mercenary armies, centring on the passion of the barbarian Mathô for the priestess Salammbô, was in a sense sheer self-indulgence, allowing Flaubert to indulge his love of documentation and his quasi-sadistic taste for descriptions of cruelty, violence and lingering death – to the extent that the reader who enjoys the novel must question his own

motives for doing so. Ambivalence is everywhere: the violence shades into eroticism, Salammbô's mysticism is also sexual, and Flaubert typically wrote that the book would be both 'dirty and chaste, mystical and realistic'. Yet for all the over-richness of detail, he had the experience, faced with his longed-for subject, of confronting a void; and the effect left by the novel is that of an unnervingly petrified world in incongruous contrast with the violence of passions and action. The narrative surface remains oddly impenetrable and places obstacles in the way of interpretation: when, we ask, is Flaubert being ironic? The characters are constantly 'bewildered', 'dumbfounded' in the face of experience, and this mirrors the position of the reader faced with the text. In this respect it is strikingly unlike the normal run of historical novels in the nineteenth century.

If *Salammbô* left many contemporary readers nonplussed, Flaubert's return to the modern world in *Sentimental Education* met with almost universal incomprehension. He conceived the novel as a revenge against his age, and this story of a young man's illusions and the mediocrity of his existence in a world fated to mediocrity makes disquieting reading indeed. Such pusillanimity and anti-heroism were shocking enough in themselves (and Henry James criticized Flaubert's concentration on 'abject human specimens'), but in addition the work reads as an 'anti-novel' in that the very concept of 'plot' seems inappropriate to it. Events arise and disappear without sense of causality or purpose, so that in spite of constant agitation, nothing appears to happen. The twenty-seven years of the narration are twenty-seven years of anti-climax. In the devastatingly ironic epilogue, after a stunning 'blank' in time, the whole of the novel is, as it were, short-circuited out of existence as the 'hero' evokes his youth, 'the best times we ever had', situated before the opening of the novel itself! The historical dimension receives the same pessimistic treatment: Flaubert portrays the 1848 Revolution from the periphery, and sees it, too, as a non-event, a vicious circle of envy, greed and misplaced idealism. The overall effect of the novel for the modern sensibility is absurdist; it subverts the structures of significance of conventional fiction, constantly frustrating expectation in a way that will inspire much twentieth-century writing.

For all the difference in subject, *The Temptation of Saint Anthony* is an equally bewildering work, though less effective in that it does not even appear to fall into the category 'novel' and so never raises expectations to be frustrated. Part narrative, part drama, it owes much to Goethe's *Faust*, and again shows Flaubert at his most self-indulgent, one 'hermit' creating another, revelling in temptations, exotic varieties of religious experience, the ambivalence of mystical and sexual, grotesque and sublime. Ambiguity is its keynote – especially when the Saint utters his final wish to 'be matter': are we to interpret it as ironic nihilism or ecstatic pantheism, a religious equivalent of Flaubert's own aesthetic method? Similar questions face the reader of the exquisitely wrought *Three Tales*, stories of destinies biblical, medieval and modern with a narrative surface of such blank impersonal perfection that the reader can never be sure when – and how much – irony is being directed at the subject. For all the variety in setting, in each story we find the same tendency to freeze action into *tableaux*, the unique process of petrification.

In *Bouvard et Pécuchet* Flaubert faced an almost impossible task, problematic in its very conception. It was to extend and eventually include the 'Dictionary of received ideas', and to represent his most extreme onslaught on bourgeois culture. The two retired clerks who undertake an absurd quest for knowledge, working haphazardly and platitudinously through subjects as vast and various as medicine, archaeology, literature, philosophy, are no doubt grotesque, but not simply grotesque; for they, too, come to experience the doubts that were Flaubert's own, and he himself was obliged to read the books (1,500 of them!) that they absorb in their quest, duplicating their folly in one of the strangest and most paradoxical enterprises in the history of literature. Here Flaubert came as near as he could to his ideal of 'a book about nothing', whose unity and essential subject-matter would be language itself.

Writing in the post-1848 world, when social upheavals had cast doubt on the values and permanence of the bourgeois order, Flaubert more than any contemporary expressed that doubt, but not by adopting – like Zola – the optimistic role of social reformer or revolutionary (indeed, he was a victim of the received ideas of his class when it came to alternatives to the bourgeois order); instead, he allowed that doubt to infect the very structure of the main organ of bourgeois culture – the novel; producing texts that defy causal patterning, resist summary or reductive labelling. They are books that force us to question the nature of reading, the operation of language, the business of interpretation. Not for nothing is Flaubert seen as one of the fathers of modernist awareness, a subversive force within his own culture.

Further reading

Other works include: *Correspondance* in *Oeuvres complètes* (1974). See also: V. Brombert, *The Novels of Flaubert* (1966), *Flaubert par lui-même* (1971); J. Culler, *Flaubert: The Uses of Uncertainty* (1974); J.-P. Sartre, *L'Idiot de la famille* (1972); R.J. Sherrington, *Three Novels of Flaubert* (1970); E. Starkie, *Flaubert: The Making of the Master* (1967), *Flaubert the Master* (1971); A. Thibaudet, *Flaubert* (1964); Geoffrey Wall, *Flaubert: A Life* (2001); Timothy Unwin, *The Cambridge Companion to Flaubert* (2004).

DAVID MEAKIN

FLEMING, Ian Lancaster

1908–64

British thriller writer

'The scent and smoke and sweat of a casino are nauseating at three in the morning.' So began the most famous sequence of twentieth-century thrillers as Ian Fleming's James Bond burst on to the scene in 1953. That first book, *Casino Royale*, was followed by eleven more full-length Bond novels and two collections of short stories. Like **Conan Doyle's** Sherlock Holmes, James Bond has floated free of his creator and become an iconic figure, enduring yet curiously flexible as – in his film incarnations at least – he adapts to the spirit of each changing decade and is differently interpreted by a string of stars. Again like Holmes, Bond has continued to appear in stories written by authorized successors to Fleming, including Kingsley Amis (*Colonel Sun*, 1968).

The son of a Conservative member of parliament, Ian Fleming had a conventional upper-class upbringing. Eton and Sandhurst were followed by stints at Reuters and as a stockbroker before he joined Naval Intelligence at the outbreak of World War II. He always claimed that he started writing at the comparatively late age of forty-four in order to take his mind off the 'horrific prospect' of marriage (to Anne, ex-wife of Esmond Rothermere, the newspaper proprietor). Fleming's motives were more complex than a desire for distraction. His service in Naval Intelligence, during which he had been involved in some creative espionage/propaganda exploits, as well as his own literary tastes, inevitably propelled him towards the thriller genre. In addition, there was rivalry with his brother, the travel writer Peter Fleming (1907–71), who had achieved early success with *Brazilian Adventure* (1933), as well as competitiveness inspired by the fact that Anne Rothermere was moving in a smart 'literary' set where Fleming did not always feel comfortable. In the event, Fleming eclipsed everybody else in terms of popularity and sales.

Despite his longevity, Fleming's Bond is very much a creation of his time. Having their genesis during the first phase of the Cold War, most of the novels involve the hero in a battle against supervillains who are also indirect agents of SMERSH (the antiespionage section of the Soviet KGB). Bond's patriotism is simple and ruthless. He is a killing machine, acting on behalf of his country. Any delicacy or refinement in his character is directed towards knowing the best hotels to stay at, the right food and drink to consume. This *savoir-faire*, in a landscape only recently emerging from wartime rationing and restrictions on travel, was undoubtedly one of the reasons for the early success of the novels. Another is Fleming's expertise in a variety of fields, either ones that he pursued himself (gambling, skiing, golf) or ones that he assiduously researched (diamond smuggling, the gold trade). Fleming was attracted to closed, elitist worlds – of which the secret service may stand as an exemplar – and he instinctively understood that the majority of readers like to be informed as well as entertained. Perhaps the most highly spiced parts of the formula were those elements of sex and sadism which were explicit by the standards of the time and which attracted useful negative publicity. Bond is regularly and ingeniously tortured by the criminal masterminds in the 'Pressure Room' or the 'Question Room'; just as regularly he seduces a succession of girls with proud breasts and beautiful mouths.

The narratives have the traditional quest form of a romance. Following clues and traces, Bond tracks the mastermind to his fortified lair. There is a final confrontation during which the villain explains his philosophy – he is invariably a Napoleon of crime – before condemning Bond to a painful death. The hero's escape, together with the destruction of the villain and his lair, are crowned by the bedding of the heroine. The author's considerable imaginative powers are poured into nearabsurd scenarios such as the robbery of Fort Knox or the creation of villains like Dr No, Goldfinger and Ernst Stavro Blofeld (Fleming's Moriarty). These twisted figures are brilliantly clever, physically grotesque and prone to aphoristic asides which give Bond the time to plot his getaway.

Fleming had a genuine gift for rapid, suspenseful narrative, as well as the ability to evoke place and describe action. He influenced a generation or more of spythriller writers and films, and his impact can be seen in writers of the later 1960s such as **John le Carré** and Len Deighton, if only in their determination to break the somewhat reactionary mould which he had created. There was a falling-off in his later work but the best of Fleming's novels – *From Russia with Love* (1957), *Dr No* (1958), *Goldfinger* (1959) – have already lasted almost fifty years and look good for their second half-century.

Further reading

See: John Pearson's *The Life of Ian Fleming* (1966) and Andrew Lycett's *Ian Fleming* (1995); see also Kingsley Amis's admiring discussion of the Bond phenomenon in *The James Bond Dossier* (1965)

PHILIP GOODEN

FORD, Henry

1863–1947

US industrialist

Possessed of a minor local reputation in Detroit as a racing driver and dabbler in motor manufacturing, Ford vaulted into national prominence in 1901 as a result of his exploits on the racing circuit. Soon relegating to second place his concern with racing and racing cars, he had by 1903 founded the Ford Motor Company and had turned his attention to the production of vehicles for the commercial market. Early on he expressed his intention to produce a car 'so low in price that no man making a good salary will be unable to own one'. Introducing the famous Model 'T' on 1 October 1908, he sold a million cars within the next seven years and 15 million before the end of 1927. The extent to which he had realized, and even exceeded, his dreams was nowhere more eloquently, if poignantly, revealed than in the poverty-induced but motorized migrations of the Depression decade of the 1930s. Despite his displacement as the major automobile manufacturer in the United States, the Ford brand name still today has a worldwide recognition rivalled at all closely only by that

of Coca-Cola. He, above all, personifies the Automobile Age.

It was not only the car but the manner in which he produced it which invests Ford's career with such significance. His business success did not rest primarily upon design innovations, although the Model 'T' was innovatory in many respects. Indeed, he was in the 1920s and 1930s to lose his domination of the market in part because he was not sufficiently innovatory. His engineering creativity found a different kind of expression: in the mobilization of existing practices, techniques and knowledge to produce a concentrated attack upon the manufacturing process. To all intents and purposes the inventor of the continuous assembly line, a line increasingly automated and running ever faster, Ford made possible the high-volume, low-unit-cost production needed to create and satisfy a mass market. This concept involved also the recognition that in a consumer-oriented society production and marketing were equal partners. Just as he had rationalized the production process so Ford sought to rationalize marketing. He created highly sophisticated dealer networks, promoted massive advertising campaigns, and made well-timed price-cutting an essential element of his strategy. He encouraged public tours of his many factories, especially of the massive Highland Plant in Michigan which was opened in 1911. The public came in large numbers to marvel at the success with which this sorcerer's apprentice appeared to have harnessed the many forces unleashed by recent advances in technology.

Ford's almost heroic stature as one who served rather than exploited the consumer had first emerged during his court struggles over the Selden Patent. The Selden Patent allegedly covered vital elements in the manufacture of internal combustion engines and, if enforced, it appeared to threaten the free and rapid development of an important new area of technology. Many of Ford's rivals had succumbed to the claims of the controllers of the patent and had entered into licensing arrangements; Ford refused to do so and embarked upon a long battle in the courts which, after initial setbacks, he won in 1911. He was hailed as the defender of the small man, the entrepreneur and individualist against the evil machinations and ambitions of big business and monopoly. His marketing strategies reinforced that image and so, at least until the 1930s, did his labour practices. In 1914 he startled the business community, not just within the United States but around the world, by introducing the five-dollar day in his plants. More than doubling the pay of his workers, and leaving his competitors far behind, Ford thereby squared the circle by completing the system, the chief advocate of which he was to become, of high wages, high productivity and low prices. That system promised an effective alternative to socialism by holding out the prospect of harmonizing the interests of manufacturer, employee and consumer, their mutual antagonism dissolved in the solvent of universal prosperity.

Most highly esteemed by the public and at the peak of his powers between 1914 and 1927, Ford's eminence remained significant through the Second World War and into the late 1940s. But his reputation had become somewhat tarnished as his public persona began to reflect the ambiguities and ambivalences of his more private personality. Sharp financial practices in the 1920s, his virulent opposition to labour unionization in the 1930s, his manifest anti-semitism, and his opposition to the Second World War, all combined to lessen but not to destroy his public standing. An enigmatic character, Ford coupled ruthlessness in business with a gentle and loving marriage; anti-semitism with liberal employment practices with respect to black people; a commitment to high wages with hostility towards unions and their practices; a hostility to tradition ('History is more or less bunk') with the founding of a major museum of Americana. Yet, however complex the man and however apparently inconsistent his behaviour, it is not difficult to isolate Ford's major contributions to the culture of the modern world.

Mass-production and consumer-oriented societies have been made possible by the wide application of the techniques he pioneered. Even today, however, despite the extension of those techniques to other industries, automobile manufacturing lies at the heart of many advanced economies. Social organization in both its physical and cultural aspects has, moreover, been powerfully shaped and coloured by wide ownership and operation of motor vehicles. For many years few doubted the liberating nature of those developments. Although their essential benevolence has recently been brought into question, they still represent the aspirations of a major portion of the world's inhabitants. If any one man can be said to have played a vital role in generating those aspirations and in holding out a realistic promise of their universal attainment, whether for good or ill, then that man was Henry Ford.

Further reading

See: Henry Ford and Samuel Crowther, *My Life and Work* (1922); Allan Nevins and Frank Ernest Hill, *Ford* (3 vols, 1948); William Greenleaf, *Monopoly on Wheels: Henry Ford and the Selden Automobile Patent* (1961); David L. Lewis, *The Public Image of Henry Ford. An American Folk Hero and His Company* (1976); Keith T. Sward, *The Legend of Henry Ford* (1948); Ray Batchelor, *Henry Ford, Modernism and Design: A Twentieth Century Cultural Phenomenon* (1994); Neil Baldwin, *Henry Ford and the Jews: The Mass Production of Hate* (2001); John C. Wood and Michael C. Wood (eds), *Henry Ford: Critical Evaluations in Business and Management* (2002).

DUNCAN MACLEOD

FORD, John

1895–1973

US film director

A succinct pointer to the significance of John Ford's career is that in 1973 he received the first Life Achievement Award given by the American Film Institute. This suggests both the longevity of that career (director credit on over 130 films between 1917 and 1965) and its absolute, quintessential Americanness.

The most obvious sign of the latter is the vital link between Ford and the Western, *the* American genre, of which Ford's work virtually constitutes a history. From silent two-reelers, through *Stagecoach* (1939) and *My Darling Clementine* (1946), via the John Wayne cavalry trilogy of *Fort Apache* (1948), *She Wore a Yellow Ribbon* (1949) and *Rio Grande* (1950), to the melancholy, sometimes bitter, tones of *The Searchers* (1956) and *The Man Who Shot Liberty Valance* (1961), within the rockscapes and desert of Monument Valley Ford made nonsense of the false division between genre and 'art'. This achievement alone would guarantee Ford's pantheon status.

But the Westerns can be located within a wider-ranging version of American history which encompasses the 'biography' of *Young Mr Lincoln* (1939), the Revolutionary War in *Drums along the Mohawk* (1939), the Okie dustbowl setting of *The Grapes of Wrath* (1940) or the Second World War naval drama of *They Were Expendable* (1945). History here is never simply people rather than events, but the exploration of dynamic oppositions around three basic points: the individual (often the loner, the outsider), the group (family, community, society) and all that lies outside (Indians, the wilderness). Also, Ford's history is rarely jingoistic celebration; more often it is, despite his own disclaimers, a poetic vision of defeat.

Ford's style evolves towards simplicity. This is significant. His critical reputation resulted from rather Europeanized films like *The Informer* (1935) and even *Stagecoach*, which now seem burdened by Dudley Nichols's literary, overly symbolic scripts and a portentous 'Expressionist' visual sense. It now seems extraordinary that, as a result, Ford was valued as an 'artist' who worked within, and transcended, the Hollywood 'system'. Critical recognition of that system's virtues, i.e. the virtues of mainstream, generically based American popular cinema, enables Ford to be located, without

disparagement, alongside other Hollywood 'professionals', such as **Howard Hawks** and Raoul Walsh, whose filmographies tread similar paths. Ford's later work is characterized by a classical economy of expression, centring on performance, milieu and narrative. This economy finds its perfect counterpart in the acting styles of Henry Fonda, James Stewart and, above all, John Wayne. Wayne has come to signify what he does largely through his performances for Ford.

Two other factors deserve note. First, Ford's silent era work remains largely uncharted territory. He went to Hollywood in 1913, and worked for several years on shorts and serials with his brother Francis. Between 1917 and 1931 he was a contract director, first with Universal, then Fox, making comedies, melodramas, adventure films and Westerns. Before *The Iron Horse* (1924), the best known of his silent films, he had already directed over thirty-five features. Second, Ford was born into a large Irish émigré family. *The Informer*, *The Plough and the Stars* (1936), *The Quiet Man* (1952) and *The Rising of the Moon* (1957) all share an Irish setting, and Ford himself has been characterized as an Irish-Catholic conservative. Certainly a sense of Irishness vitally inflects the distinctive strain of humour which runs through his work.

Jean-Luc Godard wrote of the dilemma facing the critic who confronts the powerful emotional pull of Ford's work but is distanced from its investment in a traditional, conservative American ideology. One hates John Wayne for McCarthyism, but loves him when he lifts up Natalie Wood at the end of *The Searchers*, says Godard. Paradoxically this is perhaps why progressive developments in film theory are often marked by returns to Ford's work at crucial points. Thus Peter Wollen's structuralist version of auteurism in *Signs and Meaning in the Cinema* (1969) took Ford as one focal point. *Cahiers du Cinéma*'s 1970 rereading of *Young Mr Lincoln*, their attempt to expose the cracks and contradictions in its apparently seamless ideological stance, constituted perhaps the single most important example yet of filmic textual analysis. One can virtually trace the history of film criticism through responses to Ford, the championing of different periods of his work by groups of critics at various times. Ford's oeuvre is so embedded in, almost synonymous with, the institution of classical American cinema, that any attempt to understand that institution cannot really avoid Ford. **Orson Welles** made this point when asked which American directors most appealed to him: 'the old masters. By which I mean John Ford, John Ford, and John Ford.'

Further reading

See: Peter Bogdanovich, *John Ford* (1970); Andrew Sinclair, *John Ford* (1979).

STEVE JENKINS

FORSTER, Edward Morgan

1879–1970

English novelist

E.M. Forster is one of those writers who have suffered to some extent from the reputation which admiring readers and friends have forced on them. The Cambridge and Bloomsbury circles in which he moved dearly wanted him to be an intellectual, and his public, helped by his last incarnation as the revered honorary fellow of King's College, subscribed to this idea. Yet anyone who opens *Aspects of the Novel* (1927) in expectation of lucid insights based on broad and objective reading is likely to be disappointed. Much of the apparently 'intellectual' content of the novels is no more than the diluted ethic of that Edwardian homosexual and philhellene milieu in which Forster himself matured.

Edward Morgan Forster was reared, like others of the Bloomsbury group, in a family with strong evangelical traditions and a connection with the Clapham Sect. The spectres of guilt, duty and a general atmosphere of sternness in conflict with levity are thus never wholly absent from his work. He was educated at Tonbridge School and at King's College, Cambridge, where the somewhat romanticized hellenism of Goldsworthy Lowes Dickinson offered a powerful appeal.

The experience of travel in Italy produced two good novels, *Where Angels Fear to Tread* (1905) and *A Room with a View* (1908), both of them expressing what was to become a favourite theme with him, the need for strong and fulfilling human relationships summed up in the slogan 'Only connect'. His attack on narrow-mindedness, intolerance and philistinism was carried still further in *Howard's End* (1910), generally accepted as his finest artistic achievement. Despite its heavily charged plot and diffuseness of interest, it is infinitely more successful than *The Longest Journey* (1908), with its powerfully evangelical overtones and unconvincing analyses of marital experience.

Most absorbing of all Forster's works, and by far the most ambitious, is *A Passage to India* (1924), based on his visits there in 1911 and 1921. The novel is both an extended comparison of English colonial attitudes with those of the Indians themselves, and an account of the complex relationship of Dr Aziz to Fielding and Mrs Moore. The search for mutual understanding colours the entire novel, which closes with gestures ultimately symbolic of failure. Forster's liberal humanist message is not, however, overstated, and his brilliant ear for cliché and for second-hand phraseology tinges the book with a welcome vein of comedy.

The fact that his interests and preoccupations may nowadays seem rather too obviously attached to a particular era, and the likelihood that his homosexuality may have slanted or even distorted his viewpoint, need not blind us to his real merits as a writer. The posthumous publication of *Maurice* (1971) and a clutch of ungathered stories, principally on homosexual themes, did little either to enhance or diminish a reputation based, like that of Jane Austen, on a mere handful of novels. Still more telling, perhaps, is the fact that his literary fame owed practically everything to works written during the first forty years of his life. He is not a profound thinker or an original critic, but as a writer who continually demolishes cant and humbug, asserts the validity of tenderness and sympathy, and shows a sincere devotion to his craft, he holds a secure place in the history of the modern novel.

Further reading

Other works: stories, *Collected Tales of E.M. Forster* (1947); essays, *Abinger Harvest* (1936) and *Two Cheers for Democracy* (1951). See: Lionel Trilling, *E.M. Forster: A Study* (rev. 1965); Wilfred Stone, *The Cave and the Mountain* (1966); P.N. Furbank, *E.M. Forster* (2 vols, 1979); Lionel Trilling, *E.M. Forster* (1967); M. Lago and P.N. Furbank (eds) *Selected Letters of E.M. Forster* (2 vols, 1983–5); Nicola Beauman, *E.M. Forster: A Biography* (1993). See also: Michael Haag, *Alexandria: City of Memory* (2004).

JONATHAN KEATES

FOSTER, Norman Robert (Lord)

1935–

English architect

Norman Foster was born in Manchester and educated at Manchester University School of Architecture and at Yale University. He worked at first with his wife, Wendy, and Richard and Su **Rogers** as Team 4, a double husband-and-wife team, and they made the headlines in 1967 with their factory at Swindon for Reliance Controls Ltd, a design that had a strong visual impact just from the elegance of the structural bay, braced with tensioned diagonal crosswires.

In the same year he founded Foster Associates in London, and quickly established his name with two buildings in East Anglia: the Headquarters for Willis Faber Dumas in Ipswich, and the Sainsbury Centre for the Visual Arts at the University of East Anglia. The first was a three-storey building on an irregular amoebic plan whose continuous glazed facades reflected the surrounding old buildings, and whose flat roof contained a swimming pool for the use of the workers. The second was a long shed, in which the metal panels of the flat roof curved down into the walls without a break, and the recessed ends looked like massive porticos, except that they showed the metal trusses of roof and walls and so looked uncompromisingly modern. The cladding panels developed faults and had to be replaced, but as they were manufactured to a performance specification the cost was not felt by either architect or client, and the architect thus showed his astuteness from the beginning.

During the 1980s Foster Associates began to establish an international reputation, with Stanstead Airport, the Renault Distribution Centre, and the Hong Kong and Shanghai Bank in Hong Kong. These were all commercial buildings. Then in the 1990s he carried out new work at the Royal Academy in London, the Sackler Galleries (1991) and the Carré d'Art at Nîmes, a mediatheque facing the famous Maison Carré dating from Roman times. These showed that he was capable of rising to a cultural challenge, and from then on his success became extraordinary.

During the 1990s he bought and developed a site on the Thames, the Riverside Apartments and Studio, moving into a large studio there in 1990. Other works that caught the public eye were the Century Tower, Tokyo (1991), the Torre de Collserola (a communications tower in Catalonia, 1992), the Business Promotion Centre at Duisburg, Germany (1993), extensive work on the Bilbao Metro (1995), the Faculty of Law at Cambridge University (1995), the American Art Museum at Duxford (1997) and the Commerzbank Tower, Germany (1997).

But the most striking success of the 1990s will have to be the new dome he put on the Reichstag in Berlin: too tall to be read as a classical dome, this is a transparent tower open to the public, from which the members can be seen debating the laws of the nation. Nothing was so effective at showing that the Germans were now a bulwark of democracy and open to inspection at the heart of government: it must have been an emotional moment when Norman handed over the keys to Chancellor Schroeder.

The roster of his works is too massive to be repeated here: but mention must be made of the Hong Kong International Airport at Chek Lap Kok (1998), seen by many travellers, and the Great Court at the British Museum (2000). The latter solved a problem of access and circulation; by clearing out a mass of store rooms, it became possible to see all four walls of the internal courtyard, and their porticos, as well as the cylindrical core, restored to all its glory as a nineteenth-century icon. This was achieved by roofing the court, around the central domed structure, with glass held in a light metal mesh resting on the four walls without intermediate structure: magically, rain no longer falls into the court, and it can serve as general circulation for the building.

While **Le Corbusier** revolutionized modern architecture by praising engineering design, he never undertook any actual engineering. From 1993 Foster was engaged on a work of engineering, and this was unveiled finally in 2005: the viaduct at Millau, carrying a motorway over the gorge of the Tarn. This is a work of breathtaking beauty, describing a long curve high above the valley bottom, so high that the supports are often wreathed in mist. From a line of steel towers the road is carried on a series of cables, making it appear quite ethereal.

Foster pioneered high-tech architecture that depended on standardization, using the repetition of industrialized modular units manufactured in the factory. When **Frank Gehry** showed that the computer could control this manufacturing and allow irregular shapes to be made, Foster was not to be left behind: both the new City Hall in London and the Tower for Swiss Re in St Mary Axe (known as the Gherkin) have fantastically curved profiles that make them stand out as landmarks. In both, the control over architectural detail is impeccable.

Norman Foster was awarded the RIBA Royal Gold Medal in 1994, and the RIBA Trustees' Medal in 1990 for the Willis Faber Dumas Building. In that year also he was knighted. He won the Gold Medal of the American Institute of Architects in 1994, and the Pritzker Prize for Architecture in 1999. He was made a peer in 1996.

In the course of the television coverage of the 2005 Stirling Prize, Foster was interviewed descending from his helicopter, which he pilots himself, and asked why all his buildings were grey. 'I like it,' he said, 'and I shall do many more.' People also like it: his design for McLaren Technologies, which the judges passed over, was the winner by popular acclaim.

Further reading

A six-volume catalogue raisonné of *Norman Foster: Works* edited by David Jenkins and Kenneth Powell began appearing in 2003. Norman Foster, *Catalogue* (2005), presents a more selective overview of the architect's work. Other books by Foster include *More with Less* (1979); *On Foster ... On Foster*, ed. David Jenkins (2000). See: Stephanie Williams, *Hongkong Bank: The Building of Norman Foster's Masterpiece* (1989); Ian Lambot, *Buildings and Projects: 1985–1991 (Norman Foster)* (1989); Martin Pawley, *Norman Foster: A Global Architecture* (1999); Malcolm Quantrill, *The Norman Foster Studio: Consistency Through Diversity* (2000); Philip Jodidio, *Sir Norman Foster* (2000).

ROBERT MAXWELL

FOUCAULT, Paul Michel
1926–84
French philosopher

Michel Foucault was born in Poitiers, in France, in a family that boasted numerous physicians. He studied at the École Normale Supérieure in Paris, a nursery of philosophical talent, where he befriended one of his teachers, Louis Althusser. He held positions in high education in France, Sweden and Tunisia before being appointed to the Collège de France in 1970, where he lectured until his untimely death from AIDS. Foucault also at one time held a chair at the experimental department of Paris University at

Vincennes, established in the wake of the 1968 student rebellion, the so-called 'events'.

Setting aside his one book devoted to literature, a reflection on Raymond Roussel, an idiosyncratic forerunner of surrealism (*Raymond Roussel*, 1962, translated as *Death and the Labyrinth*, 1986), Foucault's works constitute a systematic inquiry into the representation and management through power structures of otherness or the condition of being 'different', from the one profile a particular society at a particular time defines as 'normal' or, as he often characterized it himself, the 'bourgeois'.

As his inquiry culminated with a study of sexuality, it became increasingly clear that, in parallel with an imposing epistemological endeavour, Foucault's intellectual pursuit amounted also to a personal quest (*La Volonté de savoir. Histoire de la sexualité Vol. I*, 1976; translated as *The History of Sexuality Vol. I: An Introduction*, 1978; *L'Usage des plaisirs. Histoire de la sexualité Vol. II*, 1984, translated as *The Use of Pleasure: Volume 2 of The History of Sexuality*, 1985). As the years went by he became increasingly open about the underlying personal dimension to his writings, and once said in a conversation, 'There will be no civilization as long as marriage between men is not accepted' (in Didier Éribon, *Michel Foucault*, 1989, trans. 1991). He held a hypothesis as to why homosexuality had become an 'issue' in the eighteenth century after centuries of social and cultural tolerance: 'once friendship disappeared as a culturally accepted relationship, the issue arose, "What is going on between men?"' (ibid.).

The steps in Foucault's investigation on the fate reserved to the 'other' were:

1 The reading of illness on the body of the sick to distinguish the pathological from the normal and the constitution of a matrix of therapeutics corresponding to the signs, visible and invisible, of the ailment. Opening the body in an autopsy so as to 'gaze' at the differences in appearances which illness has caused to the flesh represented a historical turning point for medical understanding (*Naissance de la clinique. Une archéologie du regard médical*, 1963, translated as *The Birth of the Clinic: An Archaeology of Medical Perception*, 1973);

2 The madman is defined as possessed by un-reason being equated with the amount of intellectual disorder a society cannot tolerate at any point in time among its members. The management of exclusion of the madman expresses by the forms it takes the measure of revenge that a particular society believes it needs to exert on those who reveal the relative arbitrariness of the divide between 'reason' and 'un-reason' (*Folie et déraison. Histoire de la folie à l'âge classique*, 1961, translated as *Madness and Civilization: A History of Insanity in the Age of Reason*, 1965);

3 The punishment and control of any disrupter of the social order evolved in modern times from the exemplarity of repression characterizing the periods when he was seldom caught, to his contemporary callous storage in the most economic and efficient bureaucratic manner (*Surveiller et punir. Naissance de la prison*, 1975, translated as *Discipline and Punish: The Birth of the Prison*, 1977). Foucault here turned activist, being one of the founders and most vocal representatives of the GIP (Information Group on Prisons);

4 The birth of biological taxonomy which allowed sorting out of the world and gaining control of it through the refinement of the notions of 'resemblance', where 'kind' ceased to indicate a loose association between 'sorts' to refer to one-directional inclusion, and of 'influence', where 'signs' were from then on split between causal relations and mere meetings in time and space (*Les Mots et les choses. Une archéologie des sciences humaines*, 1966, translated as *The Order of Things: An Archaeology of the Human Sciences*, 1970);

5 The exclusion of 'man' from his own world when his collective behaviour ceases to be explained by the exercise of his will to be accounted for instead by objective factors. So, for example, in the transition from 'political economy' to 'economics': while Adam Smith evokes the trader's sales tactics, Léon Walras will only speak of 'supply and demand'. But the individual agent becomes as well dissolved in (structural) anthropology and psychoanalysis, being distributed over the structures that meet in him and so constitute him. Thus the time is nearing when man will vanish as a specific object of knowledge (also *Les Mots et les choses*).

Although queasy about the extent of his indebtedness to Georges Canguilhem, Foucault's writings can be regarded as a systematic expansion of his mentor's own masterwork on *Le Normal et le pathologique* (1943). In a letter to Canguilhem, Foucault wrote, 'my method ... and especially, my counterpositions ... are possible only on the basis of what you have done ... Actually the *Clinique* and what follows it derive from this and, perhaps, are completely contained within it.'

As with **Lévi-Strauss's** and Althusser's structuralism, history for Foucault does not unfold as a progressive process but consists of alternative rearrangements of the same elementary building blocks (structuralism revives in this respect the anti-historicist theme of the 'eternal return' introduced in philosophy by Socrates and expanded in modern times by **Nietzsche**). What makes sense of the world at a particular time and at a particular place is an *episteme*: a mode of representation combining the meaningful questions as to knowledge and the legitimate ways of answering them. The pursuit of the historian is consequently an archaeological one where he uncovers the strata of the various *epistemes* that have replaced each other over time (*L'Archéologie du savoir*, 1969; translated as *The Archaeology of Knowledge*, 1972).

One constant thread in humankind's methods of social management is cruelty. The social order emerges as a *consequence* of man's need for cruelty: that is, cruelty is a cause, not an unfortunate side-effect, and otherness is the pretext found by man to exercise it.

Freud defined a number of personality types, among them the 'perverse', which he characterized as the subject toying with the question: 'How much do regulations that apply to everyone apply to me as well?' Or, from a practical standpoint: 'What can I personally get away with?' Foucault's writings asked related questions: 'Why must deviance be punished?' And if so, 'Why the utmost cruelty of the punishment?'

The answers that Foucault's self-centred quest uncovered were different from those the libertarian attains about the minimum amount of repression that prevents the social order from collapsing under the pressure of deviant trends. Michel Serres wrote perceptively about *Folie et déraison* that 'this is the book of every solitude'. He added that 'Michel Foucault's book is to classical tragedy (and more generally to classical culture) what the Nietzschean approach was to Hellenic tragedy and culture' (*Éribon*).

Each man needs to find for himself a survival strategy in the minefield of repression; Nietzsche's 'superman' found the guiding principle in a disillusioned 'dandyism' anchored in the superiority that lucidity provides, leaving each man to his lonely destiny. That Foucault located himself as one of Nietzsche's 'supermen' rather than as a libertarian was confirmed by his unflinching support for the fundamentalist Islamic revolution in Iran. To the puzzlement of many of his disciples, his glee at the downfall of the Shah's structured order blinded him as to the birth in its wake of an even more oppressive alternative.

The theme of the 'eternal return', the accent on man as the 'sick animal' (displaying cruelty as a constant of his behaviour), the modern 'superman' burrowing his separate tunnel within a regulated social universe, as well as his nihilistic fascination for the collapse of order in Iran, combine together to make of Michel Foucault the most prominent Nietzschean thinker of the twentieth century.

Further reading

Other works include: *Language, Counter-Memory, Practice: Selected Essays and Interviews* (1977); *Power/Knowledge: Selected Interviews and Other Writings 1972–1977* (1980). See: David Hoy (ed.), *Foucault: A Critical Reader* (1986); James Bernauer, *Michel Foucault's Force of Flight* (1990); Didier Éribon, *Michel Foucault* (1991); David Macey, *The Lives of Michel Foucault* (1993); Gary Gutting (ed.), *The Cambridge Companion to Foucault* (1994); Arnold Davidson (ed.), *Foucault and His Interlocutors* (1997); Béatrice Han, *Foucault's Critical Project* (2002); Thomas Flynn, *Sartre, Foucault, and Historical Reason, volume 2: A Post-structuralist Mapping of History* (2003).

PAUL JORION

FREUD, Lucian Michael

1922–

English painter

Freud, a grandson of **Sigmund Freud** and the son of an architect, was born in Berlin but, being Jewish, was brought to England in 1933. After various art schools and a spell in the merchant navy during World War II, he toyed with Surrealism but soon settled into his mainstream, elaborate, intense, even laboriously and certain slowly executed studies of the human face and figure. While there are occasional group portraits – for example *Large Interior W11 (After Watteau)* of 1981–3– the majority of his important pictures are of individuals, usually shown in interiors of considerable and ramshackle squalor. The beds on which his nudes lie are rarely clean, walls show lath and plaster, floors are streaky and dirty, figures sit, lie or stand by piles of grubby rags. Prettiness is abhorred and beauty other than erotic beauty is eschewed.

There are certain people whom he has painted many times when they have combined the roles of model and sitter. These include a female local government official, the Benefits Supervisor, of whom there are several nude studies of her massive amplitude, the gay performance artist Leigh Bowery, a quite mountainous man, also shown nude, and the artist's mother.

The paintings of his mother are the only portraits to exhibit a sense of compassion, of human warmth and sympathy. For the most part his nudes are, while undoubtedly erotically highly charged, with the women frequently displayed in vulnerable, sometimes almost pornographic postures, nonetheless emanations of a coldly clinical talent. Even when they look immediately postcoital the flesh tones, rendered in exquisite details, are fundamentally chilly. You feel that most of these women, no matter how invitingly sprawled, are cold to the touch.

Insofar as Freud was influenced by other artists, apart from his principal teacher Cedric Morris, these would appear to be the English neo-Romantic painter John Craxton, with whom Freud spent a few months on the Greek island of Poros, the German Otto Dix and the Austrian Egon Schiele. From Dix he acquired that harsh, cold searchlight of truth about flesh and from Schiele his instinct for posing his female nude models in the most provocative, intimate and vulnerable positions.

He has been accused of hobnobbing only with the rich and famous, which is unfair. Many of his most interesting portraits are either of his large family or of humdrum West London neighbours and artisans. He has, however, been decorated with both the C.H. (Companion of Honour) and the O.M (Order of Merit), and, in 2001, painted the small and singularly unflattering oil portrait of Queen Elizabeth II which, whether at his or her behest – the record is unclear – was not shown as part of his eightieth-birthday retrospective exhibition at Tate Britain.

Freud is also a considerable etcher and a brilliant, if unflattering, portraitist at the service of the very rich. They cannot get accepted by Freud solely on their wealth; they have to interest him as well and, once accepted, appear to have little say either in how they are depicted or in what their portraits are called. At least two very interesting pictures are entitled, simply, *Man in a Chair*. If one happens not to know what Lord Rothschild or Baron Thyssen looks like, one will be quite puzzled by the images, intrinsically interesting as they undoubtedly are. The portrait of the billionaire industrialist and art collector Thyssen shows a deeply unhappy man, sitting on a velvet chair next to a pile of rags and wearing a singlebreasted suit with two jacket buttons done up so that the jacket is crumpled at the front and rucked up at the back, making this enormously powerful man look not only miserable but physically uncomfortable as well. One cannot but sense that Freud is the master here, the one in control, just as he is with all those naked women. Freud is equally hard on himself in the nude self-portrait but he has also given us the best portraits, the ones by which we largely know the sitters, of his fellow artists and friends John Minton and **Francis Bacon**.

Perhaps one should simply accept him as a supreme virtuoso of portrait and figure painting; completely uncompromising in the former and, in the latter, highly erotic without giving the viewer much by way of sensual pleasure.

Further reading

See: Lawrence Gowing, *Lucian Freud* (1982); Bruce Bernard (ed.), *Lucian Freud* (1996).

T.G. ROSENTHAL

FREUD, Sigmund

1856–1939

Austrian founder of psychoanalysis

Sigmund Freud was born on 6 May 1856 in Moravia, in the present-day Czech Republic, and relocated with his family to Vienna, Austria four years later. There he remained for the majority of his life, becoming world famous for the creation of psychoanalysis and for establishing psychotherapy more generally in the Western world. Freud and his immediate family fled Nazi-controlled Austria only in 1938. After a lengthy battle with cancer of the jaw, Freud died in north London, England, on 23 September 1939.

Freud, a polyglot, was a gifted student and excelled in his studies. First he imagined for himself a career in politics or the law, and then in science – in particular the field of neurology. At the University of Vienna, Freud stretched out his studies from five years to eight, taking personal interest courses in philosophy and conducting extensive laboratory research. For example, under the direction of Carl Claus and his Institute of Comparative Anatomy, Freud in 1875 dissected and examined under microscope the testes of 400 eels. And in 1876 Freud began a six-year stint as a researcher at Ernst Brücke's Institute of Physiology. There he worked on the spinal cords of the brook lamprey, the nerve cells of the crayfish and the nervous system of the freshwater crab. On a holiday in 1878 the very keen young Freud also conducted research on the salivary glands of dogs in Salomon Strickler's experimental pathology laboratory. Finally, in 1881, Freud took his examinations for the doctor of medicine degree, after which time he put in another three years of residency at the Vienna General Hospital.

Freud continued to conduct research at the hospital. In 1883 he worked with Theodor Meynert in the hospital's psychiatry department, and took up neuroanatomy – eventually publishing articles in the field. Then in 1884 Freud took up his infamous studies of cocaine, a drug he used himself, promoted to friends and professional colleagues, and about which he published gushing reports.

A year later Freud became lecturer in neuropathology at the University of Vienna, and in that capacity won a grant to study at the Salpêtrière in Paris with the famous neurologist Jean-Martin Charcot. There he studied hysteria and hypnosis with the man he always considered his 'master'. However, advancement as a university researcher was largely barred to even secular Jews, like Freud, who refused to convert to Christianity. So in 1886, freshly married to

Martha Bernays, Freud the neurologist reluctantly embarked on a career treating 'nervous' illness. Freud, though, never abandoned his dream of becoming a recognized scientist, and from the beginning viewed clinical practice as laboratory research by another name.

During the so-called pre-psychoanalytic period of research, roughly 1887–97, Freud sought to bridge the fields of neurophysiology and psychology. Often exchanging new speculations with his close friend, the Berlin ear, nose and throat specialist Wilhelm Fliess, Freud wrote in 1895 *The Project for a Scientific Psychology* (no German title, 1895). Invoking nineteenth-century science and speculative nature philosophy, Freud postulated ideas that would influence him, at first covertly and then explicitly, for a lifetime. That Freud never completed or published the *Project* does not therefore mean that he forgot it. On the contrary, many ideas first discussed there return in the late texts. For example, the early and late Freud argued the following: that repetitive behaviours once associated with railway and war traumas can be explained by invoking the theory of recapitulation and the inheritance of acquired characteristics; that existence itself is determined, if not undercut, by the theory of constancy, the idea that all living systems seek rest as their natural state; that emotional trauma can be explained in quantitative or economic terms as the overflowing of affect into the interior of a delicate psyche; and, more generally, that life is governed by reality and pleasure principles.

From this period Freud is better known for his contribution to *Studies on Hysteria* (*Studien über Hysterie*, 1895). Freud had lobbied a very reluctant Josef Breuer, a mentor and well-regarded Viennese physician, to collaborate on this book, which is remembered for the theoretical claims that strangulated affect causes hysteria; that talking is efficacious; and, more incredibly, that through such talk one can uncover layers of repressed memories leading back to some sexually charged traumatic event or 'seduction'. Freud essentially came to believe that these memories were buried underneath the defensive mechanisms of the psyche, and that psychology, like the exciting and relatively new science of archaeology, needed new methods and theories with which to reveal them.

Freud and Breuer's sophisticated critics of that time were not convinced. Above all, they warned that the repeated, recovered, or 'abreacted' memories central to the 'talking cure' were almost certainly artefacts of the method, and pointed to Charcot's example and to the recent history of medical hypnosis to make their case. Freud, characteristically, rejected their warnings even though he privately began to realize that the patient 'memories' he reported were indeed false. Freud's response to this crisis – that his published findings were in fact wrong; that his reputation, already compromised by his advocacy of cocaine, could now be ruined – was nothing less than the creation of psychoanalysis proper.

Although problematic, Freud's own retrospective accounts of the abandonment of the Seduction Theory and birth of psychoanalysis are clear enough. What Freud had already called 'psychoanalysis' in 1896 was after 1897 rejigged as the analysis of the emotional rapport or 'transference' between patient and physician. Moreover, this rapport was now understood to be infused with sexual fantasy, itself a repetition of inner turmoil based on unresolved, repressed and unconscious sexual conflicts. Freud claimed to have dropped hypnosis altogether from his practice, thus supposedly evading the problem of suggestion, and of discovering the ubiquity of childhood sexuality and the doctrine of polymorphous perversity. His revised claim: hysteria and the neuroses are psychologically conditioned and are not caused by abuse. And so while Freud had been fundamentally right to dig deep for some repressed and unconscious meaning at the heart of mental illness, he was wrong to have accepted the reports of his early patients. He had mistaken their fantasies of abuse as actual abuse.

Never again would Freud risk the future of his science, and of his reputation, on the objective (and therefore verifiable) reality of past events. At its best, psychoanalysis took refuge in the fantasy life of the individual neurotic, if not in the self-analysis of Freud's own dreams and neuroses, which were not just objectively knowable but were in principle universally true of all people and cultures. At its worst psychoanalysis dictated the conclusions it purported to find, brazenly manipulating case studies to reflect the ever-changing theoretical and political exigencies of the day. Such was the case 'Anna O'. We now know that this patient, Bertha Pappenheim, not only failed to recover from hysteria as claimed, but was at the end of her treatment with Breuer addicted to morphine and institutionalized in a Swiss sanatorium. Her new doctor's surprising diagnosis: hysteria. A year later Breuer confided he wished Pappenheim would die to 'release' her from suffering. Yet at Freud's urging they presented this utter failure of the talking cure as the foundation of the *Studies*.

Psychoanalytic methodology is no less a quagmire than its theory. For Freud failed to say exactly what psychoanalysis was until years after its birth, only publishing his 'Papers on Technique' between 1911 and 1915. In fact, until the *Three Essays on Sexuality* (*Drei Abhandlungen zur Sexualtheorie*, 1905), readers were left to assume that by psychoanalysis Freud still meant the recovery of actual memories of childhood sexual abuse. In other words, although Freud dropped the seduction aetiology in a private letter to Fliess in 1897, readers wouldn't know this for another eight years. Freud kept busy, just the same, publishing works of 'psychoanalysis' – most notably his lengthy self-analysis conducted in the wake of his father's death in 1896, *The Interpretation of Dreams* (*Die Traumdeutung*, 1900).

Later on Freud would claim that his early work had been routinely ignored or misunderstood, and wouldn't shrink from diagnosing the cause of this apparent resistance on the part of society and of his critics. This was the time of his 'splendid isolation'. But this was merely a romantic pose, a retrospective fiction behind which Freud spun his own legend, since he was hardly ignored in his own time. Indeed, on the strength of his publications and the claims of efficacy drawn therein, Freud in 1902 was able to gather around himself a small group of loyal adherents for 'Wednesday Evening Meetings', precursor of the Vienna Psychoanalytic Society of 1908. This diverse group met weekly to discuss Freud's work and learn about psychoanalysis from the master himself. Indeed, this was the primary activity required of people wanting to become analysts in the early days.

Freud's fortunes brightened further, in 1907, when the Swiss psychiatrist **Carl Jung** became a follower. For not only would Jung's involvement bring psychoanalysis into contact with a respected research institute and discipline, but it would take analysis out of the Jewish milieu wherein Freud and his adherents, themselves largely Jewish, lived and practised. In other words, Jung's very presence would lend weight to the claim that psychoanalysis was a science.

Jung did his part advancing psychoanalysis as a theory and movement. For example, it was Jung who introduced to Freud the Zurich experiments in word association, which became a core idea of psychoanalytic practice: the injunction for patients to 'free associate', that is, to speak freely about whatever ideas pop into their heads, often in relation to a dream or fantasy. Jung also championed more institutional rigour amongst those who called themselves Freudians, arguing that all prospective analysts be analysed, an idea that would soon become a key feature of institutional psychoanalysis.

However, as in his past relationships with Fliess and Breuer, Freud demanded strict adherence to his ideas and was intolerant when people wavered on key points of doctrine or turned psychoanalysis against his own person. And so Freud, although once desperate to see Jung as his successor, broke with him in 1912. Freud's *Totem and Taboo* (*Totem und Tabu*, 1912), a fantastical work about the prehistorical origin of guilt and conscience in a presumed act of parricide, would be the first in a series of blows and counterblows between the two men.

Psychoanalysis nonetheless prospered. By this time psychoanalysis was developing its own journals, publishing house and training institutions, and enjoyed a growing international presence. Well-placed Freudians included Ernest Jones in London, Karl Abraham in Berlin, Sandor Ferenczi in Budapest, and Otto Rank in Vienna. When World War I came along, psychoanalysis quickly spread as a possible method for treating intractable war traumas and neuroses. In turn, medically trained followers increasingly surrounded Freud and a core group of disciples, the 'secret committee', who together established psychoanalysis throughout the Western world.

It was in the midst of this upswing that Freud, recommitting himself to the dualism he always favoured, announced in *Beyond the Pleasure Principle* (*Jenseits des Lustprinzips*, 1920) that the theory of sexual fantasy needed a counterpart, a theory of the death drive. However, few of his adherents, less and less of whom shared Freud's breadth of learning or intellectual curiosity, accepted this new view. Fewer yet understood why he would complicate a perfectly good, and by then well-accepted, theory of sexuality. To explain *Beyond*, some therefore pointed to his own well-known pessimism and misanthropy; to the death of a favourite daughter; to the events of World War I, in which two sons served; to unresolved emotional conflicts; and even to boredom during the inter-war period.

In fact, even now insufficient attention is given to the connection between Freud's new 'meta-psychology' of 1915–20 – of which the death-drive theory is the crowning achievement – and the oldest, pre-psycho-analytic ideas of the 1880s and 1890s. But once the connection is made it is impossible to ignore the entirely wrongheaded aspects of Freud's own scientific worldview, including the intricate bio-logic that underwrites the enterprise. For example, in the wake of **Mendelian** genetics in 1900, few serious

scientists could believe in the inheritance of acquired characteristics. Freud did, however, figuring this was a problem for others. As he plainly admits in *Moses and Monotheism* (*Der Mann Moses und die monotheistische Religion*, 1939), much to the embarrassment of his followers, 'I cannot do without this factor [i.e. Lamarkian inheritance] in biological evolution.'

Freud's retrograde biologism is all the more ironic in that his final 'cultural' works, all made possible by his biologically determined theory of the death drive, are nowadays considered among his most famous and classical. These include *The Future of an Illusion* (*Die Zukunft einer Illusion*, 1927), wherein he reduces religion to an infantile attachment to Daddy, and *Civilization and Its Discontents* (*Das Unbehagen in der Kultur*, 1930), wherein he analyses the persistent discomforts of civilized existence. Similarly, it is not well appreciated that Freud's late turn towards 'ego psychology' in *The Ego and the Id* (*Das Ich und das Es*, 1923), and along with it the shift from the conscious/unconscious model of mental functioning to that of the famous superego/ego/id, was conditioned by this old biology. Unfortunately, Freud's explicit biological statements in these late works have been downplayed or simply ignored in favour of his more acceptable, if trite, conclusions about the repressed, guilt-ridden individual of modern society. According to the sanitized view of Freud's late work, society often requires too much deferred satisfaction and repression of individuals. As a compensation, the lucky few 'sublimate' their discomfort with civilization into art and science, while the mob is consigned to infantile submission to God and/or neuroses. But Freud's vision is actually darker and more complex. For he claimed, perversely, that human beings are driven to death by biology, one acquired and inherited over millennia. Consequently, the shape of human achievement – art, science, religion – is an aberration, however glorious, along a path to non-existence. The upshot: psychoanalysis can do very little about our historically inevitable, biologically acquired neuroses. As he said in 1927, human progress is best measured not in hours, months or even years, but in geological time. Psychoanalysis is therefore *unendliche* or 'interminable', as Freud admitted in 1937, thus putting the unmistakable stamp of therapeutic pessimism on the entire endeavour.

After his death in 1939 Freud's influence continued to spread throughout Western society, from medicine, psychiatry and psychotherapy to literature, criticism, philosophy and postmodernism more generally. A medicalized psychoanalysis prospered in the United States, at least until the late 1960s, while a more humanities-based psychoanalysis flourished in the 1970s and, energized by French theorists like **Jacques Lacan** and **Jacques Derrida**, spread throughout the Western world. But today, after the advent of drug therapies and the decline of postmodernist theory, psychoanalysis seems to have run its course. Naturally Freud remains one of the undisputed giants of twentieth-century thought. But his legacy has been radically undermined as critics continue to debate the scientific foundations of his work, including the theories of repression and of the unconscious; his clinical method, or lack thereof; the efficacy of his practice and of therapeutic talk generally; the ethics of his life and work; and the internecine politics of the psychoanalytic movement. Indeed, aside from motivated holdouts with reputations to lose, it is now widely conceded that psychoanalysis as a viable theory and practice is dead.

Further reading

Most of Freud's works are translated and collected in the *Standard Edition of the Complete Psychological Works of Sigmund Freud* (1953–74). One recommended volume that Freud wrote but never published, and which is missing from most collections, is *The Phylogenetic Fantasy* (1987). For the origins of his thought see *The Complete Letters of Sigmund Freud to Wilhelm Fliess, 1887–1904* (1985) and also Mikkel Borch-Jacobsen, *Remembering Anna O.* (1996). For a biography see Ronald Clark's *Freud: The Man and the Cause* (1980). For psychoanalytic politics see Ernest Gellner, *The Psychoanalytic*

Movement (1985) and, in the French context, Sherry Turkle, *Psychoanalytic Politics* (1992). For Freud and biology see Frank Sulloway, *Freud: Biologist of the Mind* (1977). For the death-drive theory, see Todd Dufresne, *Tales from the Freudian Crypt* (2000). And finally, for an abridged reader of essential Freud criticism, see Frederick Crews, *Unauthorized Freud* (1998).

TODD DUFRESNE

FRIEDAN, Betty
1921–2006
US feminist

Born in Peoria, Illinois, population 100,000, the symbol of the conservative heartland of America, Betty Friedan more than any other struck the spark that started the 1960s and 1970s women's revolution in the United States. Daughter of a housewife and jeweller, Mirian Horowitz Goldstein and Harry Goldstein, she remembers most from her youth the influence of her mother's thwarted professional ambition and her own refuge in books to compensate for exclusion for being a Jew. It must have been a grand personal victory when, after speaking to countless huge audiences and leading marches that she had by then rallied to feminist causes in the United States and throughout the world, she went back to Peoria in 1978 as a celebrity to lead a torchlight parade of feminists supporting the Equal Rights Amendment to the US Constitution (which failed in 1982).

Friedan's first contribution to the renewal of American feminism was her book *The Feminine Mystique* (1963). At the time of its publication, feminism had been dormant in America for forty years. Yet the book stirred highly charged responses from thousands of women, many reporting for years beyond its first publication that reading it changed their lives. Friedan identified 'the problem that has no name' among women as that of writing 'occupation: housewife' on the census form. The 'feminine mystique' is that there is but one way to be authentically a woman in the American controlling mythology and that is to be a housewife-mother. Everything that does not conform to this mystique of submission, domesticity and relationship is perceived in myriad subtle ways as deviant in women. Friedan documents this conclusion with abundant evidence from popular literature, psychology, the history of feminism, social science and educational theory. All conspire to keep women subordinate and in the home, she argues. Her solution to the mystique is self-supporting work for women outside the home.

Friedan had been a working freelance journalist before the publication of *The Feminine Mystique*, but her own personal dominant identity she claimed had been as a housewife. She had been married to Carl Friedan, whom she divorced in 1969. They had three children, Daniel, Jonathan and Emily. Educated at Smith College, she studied further at the University of California, Berkeley, and at the University of Iowa, but she gave up a professional direction in psychology for marriage and family.

Following the impact of *The Feminine Mystique*, Friedan took a leading role in organizing the first new American feminist group, the National Organization for Women (NOW), and was its first president from 1966 to 1970. That organization has continued to be the most highly visible and widely respected of the American feminist associations. Through NOW, the National Women's Political Caucus which she also helped found, and the National Abortion Rights Action League (NARAL), Friedan advocated and worked for an enormous range of issues on behalf of women, issues such as sex desegregation of want-ad jobs advertising in newspapers, sex desegregation of institutions, the right of women to abortion, fairness for women in divorce, entry of women to educational institutions and professions, equal pay for women, and the Equal Rights Amendment. She was constantly in the vanguard of all phases of women's movement activity, and she grew more radical along with the movement in the 1970s. In 1975, she organized a counter-demonstration at the Mexico City United Nations meeting for International Women's Year, insisting that the United Nations meeting was a co-optation of women rather than one genuinely attending to women's issues.

In 1976, she published a second book, writings collected from a decade of women's movement involvement, *It Changed My Life*. On her fiftieth birthday, she was quoted as saying, 'I celebrate putting it all together, finally, this half century that is me … the net I've cast for "herstory" … it is a lot of fun making a revolution.'

After 1980 she published three more books: *The Second Stage* (1981), about the status of the women's movement up to that time; *The Fountain of Age* (1993), on a psychology of old age in which she looked at the way gender and aging connect in social awareness of aging seen as diminishment, 'the aging mystique', she calls it; and a memoir, *Life So Far* (2000). She has also held appointments in several universities, including the University of Southern California, New York University, George Mason University and Mount Vernon College.

Betty Friedan died 4 February 2006, her 85th birthday, of congestive heart failure at her home in Washington, DC.

Further reading

Much has been published about Friedan, including two scholarly books: Judith Hennessee, *Betty Friedan: Her Life* (1999) and Daniel Horowitz, *Betty Friedan and the Making of the Feminine Mystique: The American Left, The Cold War, and Modern Feminism* (2000).

GAYLE GRAHAM YATES

FRIEDMAN, Milton

1912–2006

US economist

Milton Friedman – unquestionably the preeminent economist in the Western world since **Keynes** – was born in New York of Hungarian Jewish stock. He attended Rutgers and Chicago universities before taking a PhD at Columbia in 1946. In the same year he was appointed Professor of Economics at Chicago University, in which position he remained until 1976, when he became Senior Research Fellow at the Hoover Institute, Stanford. A staunch and dedicated libertarian who acted as an adviser to President Reagan, he was most usually associated with the 'Chicago School' of economics, which in turn is identified with monetarist economic theories and policies. During a long working life Friedman advocated several contentious causes, including the decriminalization of prostitution and such recreational drugs as marijuana. In 1975 he was widely criticized for lecturing in Chile, then ruled by the right-wing military dictator Augusto Pinochet. He cocked a snook at his detractors, however, by soon afterwards delivering the same lectures in communist China, and was later able to claim that his views led to a relaxation of at least some political constraints in both countries.

Friedman's influence has partly been a reflection, and partly a cause, of the shift in the priorities of economic policy pursued by the governments of the advanced industrialized countries, and in the methods of such policies, in recent decades. His ideas found particular favour with Margaret Thatcher, who, frequently invoking his name, embarked on a radical programme of privatization and deregularization as British prime minister.

Keynesian economics – both the theory and the policies derived from it – was born in the Great Depression of the 1930s, and was a major factor in the remarkable levels of employment, output and economic growth which the Western world enjoyed for very nearly three decades after the war. But throughout this period and throughout the world, the general level of prices had been rising too, admittedly at varying rates in different countries, without a break. By the early 1970s the rate of inflation had accelerated to an uncomfortable speed, and many Western politicians, whether in or out of office, sensed that electorates were as worried, even frightened, by rapid inflation as their parents were by widespread unemployment.

Keynesian economics had emphasized that economies dominated by private enterprise had no natural stabilizing forces. Stability at any level of output and employment, let alone at maximum output and full employment, could be achieved only by fiscal policy, i.e. changes in taxation and government spending. This so-called 'fine-tuning of the economy' was alone unlikely to produce price stability as well as high employment. Indeed, many economists and politicians feared that these were incompatible. A choice – or to use the jargon a 'trade-off' – existed between high employment and rapid, perhaps accelerating, inflation, and governments must and could make that choice.

Some governments and many economists held that we could enjoy the best of both worlds by arguing that prices rose because prices were raised. Prices were raised because costs rose – but costs were mainly wages, which rose because the cost of living, i.e. consumer prices, rose. The wages–prices–wages spiral could be halted. If unemployment was unacceptable, governments must intervene directly in the wage-setting and price-setting processes.

Governments of both left and right experimented with prices and incomes policies of differing forms, complexity, duration and success. Such policies were found irksome by and were unwelcome to both managers and unionists, the major beneficiaries of high employment who are arguably least harmed by (moderate) inflation.

Thus a divide in political economy opened up between the expansionists who were necessarily interventionists, and the non-interventionists who wanted to minimize the economic role of governments. The intellectual power-house of such *laissez-faire* theorizing has long been the Chicago School of economists. The core of this school's theories of inflation, which centre on both the analytical and the statistical work of Friedman, is quite simply that inflation is always and everywhere a monetary phenomenon. To Keynesians (although not Keynes himself) who argued that 'money does not matter', Friedman retorted that 'money matters most' or even (and certainly his disciples argued) that 'only money matters'.

The origins of this view lie in the distant past of economic theorizing, certainly in the eighteenth-century writings of the Scottish philosopher David Hume. He argued that the general price level is simply the rate of exchange of a flow of goods and services against a stock of currency. If any commodity becomes more abundant, it becomes cheaper relatively to all other things. Hence if the stock of money increases, the value of each unit of money in terms of goods and services – its purchasing power – will fall, i.e. the general price level will rise. This view was translated by Irving Fisher (a nineteenth-century American economist) into an instantly memorable formula – $M.V = P.T$ – called the Fisher 'quantity theory of exchange'. It is by definition true that the total value of expenditure (the amount of money, M, times the number of occasions an average unit of currency changes hands, or its velocity of circulation, V) is identically equal to the total value of purchases (the number of transactions, T, times the average price level, P). It was argued that the number of transactions was constant over short periods, and the velocity of circulation is determined by such institutions as payment periods and banking habits. Hence any change in the price level must be caused – or at least accompanied by – a proportionate change in the stock of money. In his massive *A Monetary History of the United States 1867–1960* (with Anna J. Schwartz, 1963) Friedman sought to establish statistically that all the major economic fluctuations in the US over this period were not inherent in the workings of advanced capitalism, but were due to monetary mismanagement.

His conclusion was not, as might be expected, that governments should intervene by using discretionary monetary policy more wisely: he doubted that anyone knows enough, soon enough, in order to 'fine-tune' the economy successfully by monetary policy

(which is too potent), let alone by fiscal policy (which, apart from its monetary side-effects, is impotent). He further claimed to have established that even monetary changes work only with a long (over two years) and variable time-lag. Money supply changes are therefore positively dangerous in the short run, and a further source of instability. For discretionary policy, he wanted to substitute a 'money-supply rule' whereby the monetary authorities, i.e. the national central bank, would expand the stock of money at the same rate as the growth of productive capacity. The average price level would thus *become* stable, since any general rise or fall in prices would set up contractionary or expansionary forces to return to stability.

As with all schools of thought, there are fanatical believers, worldly wise practitioners, and sceptical, even cynical, opponents. Friedman undoubtedly succeeded in restoring monetary management to the centre of economic policy in many Western countries. In particular, his theories appealed strongly to Conservative politicians in the UK, particularly during the Thatcher administration, and to right-wing parties elsewhere. This may be partly due to their political overtones and implications, e.g. a major factor in the growth of the money supply is the level of government borrowing. This can most usefully be limited by reducing government spending. Equally, the policy makes direct intervention in prices and incomes unnecessary.

Crude 'monetarism' which argues that 'control of the money supply alone is necessary and sufficient' has not yet been tested in an advanced industrialized economy with large areas of monopoly power in both product and labour markets, enjoying a high level of employment.

Friedman was awarded the Nobel Prize for Economics in 1976. He was a prolific author in the fields of economic and political theory, and in popular economic debate, and was a formidable public speaker, none more so than when he voiced his opposition to the use of trade embargoes and economic sanctions against dictatorial regimes, including at one time apartheid South Africa. He often worked closely with his wife: among their co-authored books are *Free to Choose* (1980) and *Tyranny of the Status Quo* (1984), both based on television series presented by Friedman, and also *Two Lucky People* (1988).

Further reading

Other works include: *Essays in Positive Economics* (1953); *A Theory of the Consumption Function* (1957); *Capitalism and Freedom* (1962); *Price Theory* (1962); *Inflation, Causes and Consequences* (1963); *A Programme for Monetary Stability* (1969); *The Optimum Quantity of Money and Other Essays* (1969); *A Theoretical Framework for Monetary Analysis* (1971); *There's No Such Thing as a Free Lunch* (1975); *Bright Promises, Dismal Performance* (1983); *Money Mischief* (1992). See: Eamonn Butler, *Milton Friedman* (1985); J. Daniel Hammond, *Theory and Measurement: Causality Issues in Milton Friedman's Monetary Economics* (1996).

ROGER OPIE
(REVISED AND UPDATED BY THE EDITOR)

FROST, Robert

1874–1963

US poet

Robert Frost was born in San Francisco. At the age of ten, however, he was taken to New England, the home of his forebears. There, but for three years in Britain (1912–15), he remained all his life, mostly in New Hampshire and Vermont. In 1892 he entered Dartmouth College, but left before graduating to work at various jobs. In 1895 he married, and in 1897 entered Harvard where, for two years, he studied the classics.

Never one for much formal education, Frost left Harvard as he had done Dartmouth, and began on a career of farming, supplemented by teaching. He had a book of poems, *Twilight*, privately printed in 1894 and some more of his poems were published in magazines. Despairing of a favourable reception in America, however, he took his wife and family to England. There, the 'Georgian' poets were his friends, and it is possible that he influenced them, particularly Edward Thomas, as much as they influenced him. His first two books, *A Boy's Will* (1913) and *North of Boston* (1914), were published in England and reprinted in America through the representations of **Ezra Pound** to Harriet Monroe, the editor of *Poetry*. Frost returned to America to find his reputation made. From 1916 to 1938 he was 'poet in residence' at Amherst College and, as an honoured public figure as well as an outstanding poet, lectured widely. He died on 29 January 1963.

The best of Frost's work may be found in *North of Boston, Mountain Internal* (1916), and *New Hampshire* (1923). Here are the great dramatic poems 'Home Burial', 'The Death of the Hired Man' and 'The Axe-Helve', as well as brilliantly observed and realized lyrics like 'Mending Wall' and 'Birches', which, as with all Frost's best poems, are profoundly philosophical for all their homely diction. The later books, from *West-Running Brook* (1928) to *Steeple Bush* (1947), reflect what is also found in the blank-verse plays, *A Masque of Reason* (1945) and *A Masque of Merch* (1947): namely, a more abstract interest and a more public manner.

Some critics have felt that Frost professionalized his earthy charm and homely philosophy. Louise Bogan said that he

> began early by imperceptible degrees to slip over from bitter portrayal of rural facts into a romantic nostalgia for a vanished way of life ... Frost's final role – that of the inspired purveyor of timeless and granitic wisdom – has proved acceptable to all concerned, including the poet himself.

That there is an element of the conscious cracker-barrel philosopher in his work is undeniable, and that he knew very well what he was about is suggested by the following lines from 'New Hampshire':

> I choose to be a plain New Hampshire
> farmer
> With an income in cash of say a thousand

(From say a publisher in New York City).
It's restful to arrive at a decision,
And restful just to think about New
  Hampshire.
At present I am living in Vermont.

Of his own work he said, 'To me, the thing that art does for life is to clean it, to strip it to form' and, in the Preface to his *Collected Poems* (1930), 'like a piece of ice on a hot stove, a poem must ride on its own melting. A poem may be worked over once it is in being but may not be worried into being.'

In critical retrospect Frost's poetry is undeniably deeper and tougher than it seems. The simple language, the conversational manner and the near whimsy of some of the observations tend to obscure the fact that he was no pantheistic romantic. Death and despair loom large. As Randall Jarrell put it in *Poetry and the Age*, 'The limits which existence approaches and falls back from have seldom been stated with such bare composure.' The wry humour which endeared him to a wide audience masks a pessimism which is akin to E.A. Robinson's. Like so many other New Englanders, he saw the skull beneath the skin, and his mind turned easily to metaphysics and symbolism. In this respect he was of the company of Emerson, **Thoreau** and **Emily Dickinson**, a true Yankee, gnarled, aphoristic and − for all the seeming directness of his manner − essentially oblique in his comments. Local in reference, he is universal in implication. It may well be, as F.O. Mathiessen said in his Introduction to *The Oxford Book of American Verse*, that 'When the history of American poetry in our time comes to be written its central figures will probably be Frost and **Eliot**.'

Further reading

See: Lawrance R. Thompson, *Fire and Ice: The Art and Thought of Robert Frost* (1942); Robert A. Greenberg and James G. Hepburn (eds), *Robert Frost: An Introduction* (1961); James M. Cox (ed.), *Robert Frost: A Collection of Critical Essays* (1962); John R. Doyle Jr, *The Poetry of Robert Frost: An Analysis* (1962); Elizabeth Isaacs, *An Introduction to Robert Frost* (1962); Reuben Brower, *The Poetry of Robert Frost: Constellation of Intention* (1963); Radcliffe Squires, *The Major Themes of Robert Frost* (1963); John F. Lynen, *The Pastoral Art of Robert Frost* (1964); Lawrance R. Thompson, *Robert Frost* (1964); Philip L. Gerber, *Robert Frost* (1966); Richard Thornton (ed.), *The Recognition of Robert Frost* (1970); Katherine Kearns, *Robert Frost and a Poetics of Appetite* (1994); Nancy Tuten and John Zubizarreta (eds), *The Robert Frost Encyclopedia* (2000); Robert Faggen (ed.), *The Cambridge Companion to Robert Frost* (2001).

GEOFFREY MOORE

FULLER, Richard Buckminster

1895–1983

US architect, engineer, philosopher and inventor

Buckminster Fuller was born into a nonconformist family in Milton, Massachusetts. Popularly known for his geodesic domes, these and other inventions are only a particular manifestation of his philosophy and approach to design. It is arguably the radical nature of the thinking process leading to his inventions and his global approach to design problems which will prove to be of the greatest value to mankind.

His early rejection of conventional thinking led to his being expelled from Harvard in 1914. After a brief but important experience in the US navy he worked for a while on a building system invented by his father-in-law. The death of his first child in 1922 and the loss of financial control of the building company in 1926 led him to rethink fundamentally the direction of his activities and he resolved to treat his whole life as an experiment. As at other points of crisis he turned outwards from personal problems to face global issues. A critical year was 1927, in which he privately published *4D*, attacking the stagnation of the building industry, pleading for a global approach to energy and resource problems and proposing lightweight mass-produced housing (the 'Dymaxion house') for delivery by air. There followed further Dymaxion housing proposals (1929), the building of a prototype Dymaxion car (1933), a mass-produced Dymaxion bathroom unit (1937) and a soft-tool version of the Dymaxion house (1945).

He maintained a chronofile documenting his life's experiment. This preoccupation with his own experience is central to Fuller's thinking (see *No More Second Hand God*, 1962). In a letter to John McHale in 1955 he described the significance of his childhood experiences of boat-building and fishing technology and his interest in logistics in the navy. These experiences are reflected in his research into synergetics, where the whole is greater than the sum of the parts, and led to patents for the geodesic dome (patent applied for 1951), the octet-truss (1956) and tensegrity structures (1959): these latter, maximizing the efficient use of tension, created some of the strongest and lightest clear span structures ever devised. Following the successful and widely reported building of the Ford Motor Company dome in 1953, there was a global epidemic of geodesic structures leading to the US pavilion for Montreal's Expo 67, and Fuller's efficient principles of construction are still used worldwide in structures by other architects. Fuller's interest in developing efficient structures was not aesthetic but was focused on minimizing the use of materials and energy in the context of a diminishing world availability of resources

His concern about world energy and resource problems first reached a wider audience with the publication of *Nine Chains to the Moon* (1938). He regarded making the world work as a design problem rather than a political responsibility and in an attempt to involve design students Fuller founded the World Design Science Decade in 1961. He argued that specialization was ineffective as well as socially and environmentally irresponsible and urged a comprehensive generalist approach through 'comprehensive design science'. There followed a series of publications including an *Inventory of World Resources, Human Trends and Needs* (1963) and the

Ecological Context (1967). What Fuller refers to as 'comprehensive anticipatory design science' was to be employed to reform the environment rather than man, and this was to be accomplished by employing the principle of 'synergy' to achieve more with less resources. World resources and patterns were to be modelled using a 'World Game' based on the game theory of Von Neumann. Having observed that 'spaceship Earth' had come without an instruction book, Fuller provided the *Operating Manual for Spaceship Earth* (1969).

Fuller came to enjoy worldwide recognition and honours including the Charles Eliot Norton Professorship of Poetry at Harvard (1962) and the Royal Institute of British Architects' Gold Medal (1968), 150 other awards and eighty honorary degrees and fellowships. However, Fuller's philosophical and political views are still generally misunderstood and frequently misrepresented. Some of his published works (twenty-seven books) are unedited transcripts of talks often lasting four hours and delivered without notes. Other publications are carefully written, employing a private code of precise meaning which is more easily understood when printed as verse (see *Untitled Epic Poem on the History of Industrialization* (1962); *Intuition* (1970)). Recurrent themes and preoccupations of Fuller are set out as forty strategic questions and fourteen dominant concepts in *World Design Science Decade Document 5: Comprehensive Design Strategy*, (1967); more accessibly *Utopia or Oblivion* (1969). While his inventions are well documented by others, his philosophical ideas have yet to receive the quality of critical comment and elucidation that they deserve. *Synergetics* (1975) is the seminal work.

Fuller influenced two generations of students. Richard Rogers cites Fuller as an influence, as do **Ken Yeang**, **Cedric Price** and Archigram. **Norman Foster** collaborated with Fuller on several projects and was assisting in the design of a geodesic autonomous house for Fuller himself. His vision of education (*Education Automation*, 1962) is enacted through the internet and his views on ecologically responsible design anticipate current thinking on sustainability. His lectures involved the audience in the sense that they were participating in a wider vision and part of a global human family responsible for the stewardship of Spaceship Earth. But Fuller's formidable legacy has spread far beyond influencing architectural students to make impacts in the worlds of science and economics. Typically the carbon 60 molecule (C60), having a geometrical derivation in common with a geodesic dome, was named the 'Buckminsterfullerene' ('Fullerene' or 'Bucky ball') in his honour.

Further reading

Other works include: *Ideas and Integrities* (1963); *Critical Path* (1981); *Inventions: The Patented Works of R. Buckminster Fuller* (1983); and *Cosmography* (1992). See also: Robert W. Marks, *The Dymaxion World of Buckminster Fuller* (1960); John McHale, *R. Buckminster Fuller* (1962); *The Buckminster Fuller Reader*, ed. James Mellor (1970); Amy C. Edmondson, *A Fuller Explanation: The Synergetic Geometry of R. Buckminster Fuller* (1987); Lloyd Steven Sieden, *Buckminster Fuller's Universe* (1989); *Your Private Sky: R. Buckminster Fuller, the Art of Design Science*, ed. Joachim Krausse (1999); *Your Private Sky: Discourse; R. Buckminster Fuller*, ed. Joachim Krausse (2001).

JOHN HAMILTON FRAZER

G

GABO, Naum

1890–1977

Russian/US artist, sculptor

Born Naum Neemia Pevzner in Bryansk, Russia, Gabo became a central figure of international Constructivism in the 1920s contributing significantly to the development of creative thought and work in Russia, Germany, England and the United States of America. Gabo's early training was scientific. He enrolled at the University of Munich in 1910 as a medical student and subsequently studied natural sciences and engineering in Munich. During 1911–12 Gabo also attended Wölfflin's lectures in the history of art and became increasingly interested in creative work. His first constructions, figurative works with a Cubist flavour to them, followed in 1915. Subsequently his art, progressing as a process of meticulous investigation, led to constructions that displayed all the precision of an engineer in the distribution of modern materials (metals, glass, plastics), yet the function of the structures devised by Gabo was aesthetic and not mechanical usefulness, reflecting, embodying and exemplifying instead the concepts of space and perception outlined in Gabo's essays and in his book *Of Divers Arts* (1962) in particular.

Creative work, for Gabo, was not a stylistic consideration; rather, it was the exploration of modern materials, of spatial concepts and relationships, and ultimately an investigation of the nature of creativity. In many ways these attitudes brought Gabo into line with

Russian Constructivists of the early post-Revolutionary years. When, in 1920, Gabo together with his brother Anton (Antoine) Pevsner exhibited constructions on the Moscow Tverskoy Boulevard and published their *Realistic Manifesto*, their closeness to Tatlin, the Stenberg brothers and other sculptors was apparent yet limited. Gabo did not share other Constructivists' belief in the necessary subjugation of individual creativity to political ends (the position expounded by Rodchenko), nor indeed the evolution of construction from purely material and no longer aesthetic criteria. Gabo believed in intuitive investigation that led to the manipulation of modern materials according to predetermined aims. He studied form in terms of structure and studied the structure of perception itself. As a result certain themes have recurred in his constructions, which more than once he compared to flowers, trees and to other organic structures. For example, his works often evolve outwards from a central axis or core that is mathematically precise and determined by the intersection of flat or curving planes. Materials provide a means of articulating empty space although every allowance is made for their inherent qualities. In so far as constructions emerge from a central core, their outer edge may be established at differing points so that relationships rather than ultimate positions or masses are what is defined. Similarly their engineering precision reveals Gabo as a supreme craftsman, yet a sign of this is the degree to which his constructions escape the confines of personal style and may be reproduced, some of them on different scales or in different materials, without damage to the spatial concept embodied in the original.

In 1922 Gabo left Russia for Berlin where a number of his works were exhibited at the First All-Russian Exhibition at the Van Diemen Gallery. He continued to live in Berlin until 1932 when he moved to Paris. His constructions included stage works, notably for *La Chatte* which Gabo designed with Pevsner for **Diaghilev's** Ballets Russes in 1926–7, and architectural projects both for monumental sculptures to stand in an architectural context (leading ultimately to the Bijenkorf monument erected in Rotterdam in 1957), and for buildings themselves in Gabo's designs for the Palace of the Soviets competition of 1931.

Gabo was a member of the Abstraction-Création group from 1932 to 1935 and after settling in England in 1935 he collaborated with **Ben Nicholson** and Leslie Martin on the book *Circle* (1937). He moved to New York in 1946 and two years later exhibited with Pevsner at the Museum of Modern Art there. He became a professor at Harvard University Graduate School of Architecture in 1953 and an increasingly renowned figure internationally.

In Gabo's work self-expression gave way to investigation of the nature of space and the manipulation of materials. Empty space is, in fact, the precise material of his constructions and his distribution of plastics, glass and metals a system of articulating and elucidating that space. There is, inherent in Gabo's achievement, an example of scientific and creative thought simultaneously at work: engineering and mathematics were not alien to Gabo's work. There is a vision, too, of a further unity, between the constructions of man and the structures of nature.

Further reading

See: Herbert Read and Leslie Martin, *Gabo* (1957); Teresa Newman, *Naum Gabo – The Constructive Process* (1976); *Naum Gabo* (exhibition catalogue, 1987).

JOHN MILNER

GALBRAITH, John Kenneth

1908–2006

US economist

J.K. Galbraith was an economist for the man-in-the-street. He became Professor of Economics at Harvard in 1949, and published his first book – *The Theory of Price Control* – in 1952. But in the main he wrote, and prolifically, to and for the layman. His wit and irony and his capacity to coin a telling phrase made him probably the most-quoted economist after **Marx** and **Keynes**. 'The Affluent Society', 'private affluence and public squalor', 'countervailing power', the 'new industrial state and its technostructure' became the common currency of informed day-to-day debate.

He was born in Ontario, Canada, in 1908. After graduating in agriculture from Toronto University, he took a PhD in California and became a research fellow at Cambridge (England). His professional life was spent as Paul M. Warburg Professor of Economics of Harvard until he retired in 1975. In addition he spent many years in public service – work which has both shaped and reflected his approach to economics. From 1941 to 1943 he was in charge of wartime price control at the US Office of Price Administration, an experience which has crucially affected his attitudes to, and explanation of, the causes and nature of and the cures for inflation in an advanced and highly concentrated economy. In particular it gave him insights into the process by which large corporations set their goals and consequently their prices.

He became for the next five years an editor of *Fortune* magazine, work which both extended his acquaintance with industry into peacetime and which importantly influenced his writing style. He was Director of the Office of Economic Security Policy in the State Department at the end of the war.

Politically a Democrat, like so many American academic economists, he was an influential adviser to the Democratic Party over the years, and a key member of the **Kennedy** presidential campaign. When Kennedy became president, however, Galbraith was thought to be too controversial a figure to remain in Washington as a senior government adviser and was instead sent in 1961 as US Ambassador to India. Directly responsible for the largest American overseas effort in economic development, he wrote a colourful *Ambassador's Journal* (1969) and started to analyse the problems of developing countries as sharply and wittily as he had those of the advanced economies.

Galbraith made his impact by addressing himself to the layman and by engaging in public and political controversy. In this arena, his weapons were a caustic wit, a devastating sense of irony, and a literary style that seems to produce a telling phrase on every page. He was a leading exponent of an institutionalist approach to political economy rather than the mathematical approach to economics. He wrote, remarkably in a subject so widely regarded as 'dismal', a number of world-wide best-sellers, not least *The Great Crash: 1929* (1955) which was a hilarious, biting history and analysis of the Wall Street boom and financial crisis that ushered in the Great Depression.

The main line of his thinking can be traced from his *Theory of Price Control*, based on his reflections on his wartime experience, to *American Capitalism: the Concept of Countervailing Power* (1952) to *The Affluent Society* (1958) to *The New Industrial State* (1967). The central theme is methods by which and the extent to which the typically large industrial, commercial and financial enterprise has freed itself from all outside control. Shareholders and non-executive directors were long ago made unimportant by the widening spread of share-ownership, and the concentration of power in the hands of technically trained professional managers. The increasing concentration of power within corporations was matched by a similar concentration of power by those corporations over the markets and hence over the whole economy.

All was not gloom and despondency. Galbraith demonstrated that these monopolistic enterprises, whose conduct departed so widely from the textbook norms of competition, were the most advanced and most rapidly advancing sectors of capitalism, whereas the text-book 'competitors' – industries composed of large numbers of small firms – were typically technically backward, earning low profits and paying low incomes. In any case, large corporations tended to generate 'countervailing power' amongst their suppliers or their customers. Big buyers led to big sellers, and vice versa.

This theme is developed to analyse the omnipotence of the managerial and technical elite in advanced enterprises. It matters not who owns the enterprises – 'the technostructure of the new industrial state' sets the goals, takes the decisions, distributes the rewards, according to its own judgements of its own best (long-term) interests. Its power inevitably and naturally spreads from the enterprise to the markets in which it buys and sells. Market forces, far from being autonomous, independent, anonymous and finally decisive, turn out to be other managers pursuing their own (even if competing) interests.

The technostructure's success, and hence its ethos, has spread to provide the yardsticks for judging economic performance. 'Private affluence amid public squalor' is as much the mark of successful advanced capitalism as 'poverty in the midst of plenty' was the mark of the failed capitalism of the Great Depression. Galbraith's scathing analysis of the supremacy of 'market values' has become an important ingredient in the thinking of environmentalists and the anti-growth schools, by undermining the very criteria of economic advance, viz. the level and growth and content of 'national product'.

Galbraith, as a Keynesian, had no doubts that capitalist economies can be stabilized at high, even full, employment: the rate of growth of output has been and can continue to be spectacular. He questioned not how much they can produce, but the *content* of that output – and he doubted that prices will ever stop rising, unless sellers are stopped from raising them.

Further reading

A Life in Our Times (1981) is Galbraith's auto-biography. Other works include: *Journey to Poland and Yugoslavia* (1959); *The Liberal Hour* (1960); *A Contemporary Guide to Economics, Peace and Laughter* (1971); *Economics and the Public Purpose* (1974); *Money* (1975); *The Age of Uncertainty* (1976), based on an acclaimed television series; *The Anatomy of Power* (1983); *The Culture of Contentment* (1992); and *The Good Society* (1996). See also: Peggy Lamson, *Speaking of Galbraith: A Personal Portrait* (1991).

ROGER OPIE

GALLUP, George Horace

1901–84

US pollster and public opinion statistician

Prior to the arrival of George Horace Gallup, predicting public opinion had been a scatter-gun affair. Newspapers and politicians relied on crude straw polls drawn created randomly from such repositories as telephone direc-tories, which skewed results according to background and affluence. Gallup's system uses a small representative group of people, sometimes as small as 1,500 to 3,000 people in the USA and 1,000 in European countries, to predict the opinions of a larger population. But Gallup did more than bring the world an accurate polling system. His work put politics and commerce in touch with the public and made government and markets much more attuned to their whims.

It has been said that the belief in the cross-representativeness of small communities, on which many of Gallup's subsequent polling ideas were based, owes much to his upbring-ing as the son of farmland speculator in rural Iowa. But Gallup also saw how difficult it was to supply a demand if you could not accurately gauge what it was that people wanted. As editor of the campus newspaper *The Daily Iowan at the University of Iowa*, Gallup was very aware of the importance of readership satisfaction, and in a summer at the D'Arcy Advertising Agency canvassed the opinions of readers of the *St Louis Post Dispatch*. Gallup's 1928 journalism PhD dis-sertation *A New Technique for Objective Methods for Measuring Reader Interest in Newspapers* was to be the springboard that launched his interest in public opinion research.

By now married to newspaper publisher's daughter Ophelia Smith Miller, Gallup became head of the journalism department at Drake University in Des Moines (Iowa) and then taught journalism and advertising at Chicago's Northwestern University. In 1932 he joined the advertising agency Young & Rubicam and moved to New York to be the company's director of research, becoming vice president in 1937. Gallup tested poten-tial radio programmes, books and films on sample audiences and one of his studies was a key factor in **Walt Disney's** decision to make *Alice in Wonderland*.

In 1935 Gallup set up the American Institute of Public Opinion with Young & Rubicam partner Harold Anderson and began regular polling of American public opinion, publishing the results in a regular column *America Speaks* syndicated to news-papers across the USA. But the accuracy of Gallup's polling method was not shown to the world until the following year when the Gallup Poll predicted the victory of **Franklin D. Roosevelt** in the 1936 presidential election.

The Literary Digest poll for the same elec-tion had tipped Roosevelt's rival, Alf Landon, after a postal ballot of people whose names were drawn from telephone directories and automobile registrations. But in 1936 a con-siderable number of Americans either did not have a car or did not have a phone, making the LD poll wide of the mark. Gallup's polls accurately predicted the outcome of every subsequent presidential election save two (1948 and 1976).

Gallup bequeathed what he himself described as 'one of the most useful instruments of democracy ever devised', but, some critics argued Gallup's polls wielded too much influence on political leaders and could be used to manipulate public opinion. Gallup himself never accepted these criticisms, arguing in his 1972 book, *The Poll Watcher's Guide*, that 'polling is merely an instrument for gauging public opinion' and that political leaders who followed polls closely were 'paying attention to the views of the people'.

Further reading

See: Rena Bartos, 'George Gallup: Mr Polling', *Journal of Advertising Research*, Vol. 26, No. 1 (February/March 1986).

TOM WILLIAMS

GANCE, Abel

1889–1981

French film director

Born in Paris, Abel Gance was to rise from complex social origins to become one of the greatest pioneers of silent cinema in Europe. The illegitimate son of a working-class mother and a Jewish doctor, he eventually took the name of the chauffeur/mechanic whom his mother later married, although his natural father continued to provide for him and for his education. Briefly a law clerk, his emerging literary and theatrical ambitions attracted him elsewhere. By his early twenties he had become a professional actor, formed a film production company and directed his first short film, the one-reel costume drama *La Digue*. In the era of 'primitive' cinema, between 1910 and 1915, he wrote some twenty-five short films and directed over half of these.

The outbreak of World War I prevented the production of Gance's verse play *Victoire de Samothrace* (written 1912–13), intended as a star vehicle for Sarah Bernhardt, but led to his first collaboration with cameraman Léonce-Henry Burel, with whom, in *La Folie du Docteur Tube* (1915), he explored the optical capabilities of distorting mirrors in a short film starring his future Napoleon, Albert Dieudonné. Weakened by tuberculosis, Gance served as a member of the French army's film corps, and also as a stretcher bearer, encountering the horrors of slaughter and the effects of poison gas. He returned to filmmaking in 1916–17 with his first feature films, exploring the genres of melodrama and the thriller: *Les Gaz maudits, Barberousse, Le Droit à la vie, La Zone de la mort* and, most notably, *Mater dolorosa* and *La Dixième Symphonie*. Influenced by the editing style of **D.W. Griffith** and introducing a range of visual and stylistic innovations, these films established Gance's reputation as a major new director of 'society drama'.

His major films were to follow in the postwar years. *J'accuse* (1919), his first epic, was a powerful indictment of the horrors of war. The film, a melodramatic love triangle involving two soldiers and the woman they both love back home, was shot at the front. The sequence involving ghosts of the war dead featured men who were indeed later to die in battle. But after his young second wife Ida Danis died of TB on the last day of filming, Gance took *J'accuse*, rapidly becoming a major European hit, on a lengthy trip to the US. The film was screened to an audience including Griffith and the Gish sisters, but it was mangled by distributors for its American release and its anti-war message subverted.

In 1922 Gance completed *La Roue*, a mythically and symbolically inspired sentimental family melodrama which starts with a quotation from Victor Hugo about the great wheel of creation, creative and yet crushing. Centring on the relationships between a railroad engineer – who runs the 'wheels' of modern technology – his young son and their adopted daughter/sister, and shot on location in the railway yards at Nice and in the Alps, the film displays many of the hallmarks of Gance's characteristically vivid exploration of cinematic language: optical experimentation with the image, and rapid montage effects. The restored 1980 version runs at around five hours, but it is most commonly seen today in the 1924 general release version of just over two hours. The film was critically acclaimed, but its high budget, lengthy running time and delayed release inevitably affected its profitability. Not so with Gance's perennially popular comic short *Au secours!* (1923), Max Linder's last film before he committed suicide.

Gance's undisputed masterpiece is *Napoléon* (1927). The first of a planned series of films in which Bonaparte would gradually drift away from his revolutionary ideals, the privately financed *Napoléon* portrayed him as an idealistic romantic hero. Central amongst a sprawling cast of some forty major roles, Albert Dieudonné starred as Napoleon, with Gance himself as the Jacobin leader Saint-Just and Antonin Artaud as Marat. The visionary and dynamic historical sweep of *Napoléon* is expressed through sensational farragoes of handheld camerawork and rapid cutting. The film involved a special wide-screen process (which Gance called 'Polyvision') which created a series of explosive triptychs involving three screens and three projectors. Launched at the Paris Opera in 1927, Gance's original version of *Napoléon* ran for some six hours, but over the years it was cut down dramatically for wider distribution. In 1933, at his own expense, Gance made a further version using 'sound perspective', a multi-channel sound system he had developed with André Debrie. The figure of Napoléon was to haunt him down the years as he returned to re-figure this historical moment, and his original film material, on several occasions in his later career.

Gance's subsequent Polyvision disaster movie, *La Fin du monde* (1931) was taken over by the producers and cut down to size as costs soared. His budgetary excesses had made him an expensive and risky investment, and the arrival of sound had hampered some of his inclination to visual inventiveness. He was nonetheless prolific in the 1930s, even if never again to scale the dizzy heights of his 1920s masterpieces. He made a total of fourteen feature films in this decade, including sound remakes of *Mater dolorosa*, *J'accuse* and of *Napoléon* itself. His other projects of the era were largely adaptations of fashionable stage dramas or popular novels, in which romance and family melodrama predominate: *Le Maître des forges*, *Poliche*, *La Dame aux camélias*, *Le Roman d'un jeune homme pauvre*, *Jérôme Perreau*, *Lucrézia Borgia*, *Un grand amour de Beethoven*, *Le Voleur des femmes*, *Louise*, *Paradis perdu*. By his own admission these are on the whole lesser works.

Following his early 1940s love stories *Vénus aveugle* and *Le Capitaine Fracasse*, the 'Jewish' Gance left for Spain in 1943 after a short-lived accommodation with Vichy. He did not direct again for more than a decade. Between 1953 and 1967 he made only a handful of films, which invariably saw him returning to the further reaches of French history, and to the literary legacy of Dumas and Hugo, in such works as *La Reine Margot*, *La Tour de Nesle*, *Austerlitz*, *Cyrano et d'Artagnan*, *Marie Tudor* and *Valmy*. His interest in remote historical dramas found him out of favour with the freewheeling, modernist philosophy of the emerging *Nouvelle Vague*, but while still harbouring fantasies of bringing to completion his 1939 project on Christopher Columbus he persevered in making, in 1971, his final, much reduced, edit of *Napoléon*, entitled *Bonaparte et la révolution*.

As Gance aged and his output diminished, his 1920s reputation as a major pioneer began to be acknowledged once again, largely thanks to the efforts, from the mid-1950s onwards, of the young British film historian and director Kevin Brownlow. Lovingly assembling bits and pieces of *Napoléon*, Brownlow almost single-handedly re-established Gance's reputation for formal innovation within the confines of epic historical drama. This was the Gance who had pioneered montage cinema before **Eisenstein**, stereo sound before **Disney**, and wide-screen technology a quarter of a century year in advance of Cinemascope and Cinerama. In 1981 **Francis Ford Coppola** supported a major 70 mm reconstruction, reducing Brownlow's latest version to just under three and three-quarter hours, complete with a score by Coppola's father, Carmine Coppola. Coppola sold his rights to Universal during the 1980s, while Brownlow has continued to find superior sources and extra material which have led to new releases in London since 2000 with music by Carl Davis. His latest version runs for some five and a half hours, but apparently this may not be the end of the story. Committed to the shorter 1981 version, Coppola now contests the fuller versions of *Napoléon* in deference to the score composed by his late father. In his book on the film Brownlow tells the passionate, complex and comic story of the restoration – which had numbered as many as nineteen versions as early as 1983, and he has added more since then himself.

Further reading

See: Richard Abel, *French Cinema: The First Wave, 1915–1929* (1984); Kevin Brownlow, *Napoléon: Abel Gance's Silent Classic Film* (1983); Abel Gance, *Napoléon* (1990); Roger Icart, *Abel Gance: Ou, le Prométhée Foudroyé* (1983); Roger Icart (ed.), *Abel Gance: un soleil dans chaque image* (2002); Nelly Kaplan, *Napoléon* (1995); Norman King, *Abel Gance: A Politics of Spectacle* (1984); Steven Philip Kramer and James Michael Welsh, *Abel Gance* (1978).

PHILIP DRUMMOND

GANDHI, Mahatma (Mohandas Karamchand)

1869–1948
Indian politician

A politician, saint, social and economic reformer, an originator of *satyagraha* (holding on to truth), a non-violent form of popular agitation and struggle, and an early advocate of 'small is beautiful', Mohandas (son of) Karamchand Gandhi left a lasting impression on the political culture of the Indian sub-continent, and accelerated the pace of socio-religious reform among the Hindus of the sub-continent. He dominated Indian politics for nearly three decades, from 1919 to 1948; and yet he described himself as 'a man of religion in the garb of a politician'. While his opponents knew him to be a clever tactician and shrewd negotiator, the masses revered him as a spiritual figure, a Mahatma: Great Soul.

He was born in 1869 of a middle-class *bania* (trading caste) family in Porbandar, a small port in the western state of Gujarat. A shy and diffident boy, he had an arranged marriage at thirteen to Kasturba, a girl of the same age. At eighteen he went to London to study law, and was called to the bar two years later. His strict vegetarianism brought him into contact with such leading British vegetarians of the time as the playwright **George Bernard Shaw** and theosophist Annie Besant. They introduced him not only to the works of **Ruskin**, **Tolstoy** and **Thoreau**, but also to the Bhagavad Gita, an important Hindu scripture. These early influences were at the root of what was later to emerge as Gandhism – a set of socio-economic theories which, if practised to the full, would re-create the world of the past, inhabited largely by self-sufficient village communities.

After an unsuccessful attempt to practise law in India, he went to South Africa in 1893 as a clerk with an Indian firm in Durban. Here he fought for the rights of the Indian settlers, established the weekly *Indian Opinion* (1903), and put into practice some of the concepts advocated by Tolstoy and Ruskin by founding a co-operative farm at Phoenix near Durban (1904). He synthesized the Hindu tactic of *dharna* (squatting in front of a house/office to draw attention) with the ideas contained in Thoreau's essay 'Civil Disobedience', and forged the tool of *satyagraha*, which combined passive resistance against and non-cooperation with the authorities. He initiated the *satyagraha* movement against the racist laws of South Africa in 1907 and struggled on, sporadically, until the government agreed to compromise, six years later.

On his return to India in 1915 he helped the British in their war effort. He settled down at an *ashram* (retreat) near Ahmedabad, and did not play a leading role in nationalist politics until after the Amritsar massacre in April 1919. Then, as a leader of the Indian National Congress, he gave a call for non-cooperation with the British government. This meant boycotting all the official institutions and refusing to pay taxes. Tens of thousands of people followed his lead, and were imprisoned. The consequences of this movement went beyond politics. The collective courting of jail by a group of people, often with a petty-bourgeois urban background, banished the fear among the populace of being imprisoned for a just cause. The participation of many women in the movement, actively encouraged by Gandhi, gave an impetus to women's emancipation in general. These actions inspired novelists and poets to inject social and political themes into their works – an unprecedented phenomenon.

In the mid-1920s, Gandhi turned his attention to the practice of untouchability among Hindus. He tried to break taboos against the Untouchables, the Outcastes, by having them serve food to the caste Hindus, and by encouraging the latter to sweep streets, a job traditionally performed by the Outcastes. He gave a lead by doing the menial tasks, associated with the Untouchables, at the *ashram* near Wardha, in Maharashtra, that he established in the early 1930s. Here he founded the English weekly *Harijan* ('Children of God'), a name he coined for the Untouchables. In addition he undertook a series of 'fasts unto death' either to pressurize the orthodox Hindu leaders into softening their attitudes towards the Outcastes, or merely to 'persuade' his political opponents. This practice continues. Vinobha Bhave, one of his disciples, undertook a 'fast unto death' in 1979 to force the Indian government to outlaw cow slaughter throughout the country, an irrational demand.

Although a pacifist, Gandhi did not remain neutral when wars broke out. During the Second World War he opposed **Hitler** and Nazism. But he insisted that if the Allies were really fighting for democracy and freedom then Britain should grant independence to India immediately so that an independent India could then join the war against Nazism. When this demand was turned down he launched the 'Quit India' movement against the British in August 1942.

By the end of the next five years the British had departed, leaving behind a sub-continent partitioned into the independent states of India and Pakistan. The inter-religious rioting that took place before and after the partition in August 1947 heightened the historic animosity between Hindus and Muslims. It was in this atmosphere of feverish communal tension that Gandhi, an advocate of Hindu–Muslim amity, was shot dead by a Hindu fanatic, Nathuram Godse, in Delhi on 30 January 1948.

A prolific writer, Gandhi expressed himself simply and directly in both Gujarati and English. He used the three weeklies that he edited (*Indian Opinion, Young India* and *Harijan*) as vehicles to guide his followers and expound the various theories and causes that he came to propagate. These ranged from nature cure to *brahmacharya* (celibacy) to home rule to *ahimsa* (non-violence) to opposition to industrialization and urbanization and the corporate state, and his yearning for a world peopled by communities living in self-sufficient villages.

Further reading

See: Gandhi, *The Story of My Experiments with Truth* (2 vols, 1929); *The Collected Works of Mahatma Gandhi* (90 vols, 1958–84). About Gandhi: C.F. Andrews (ed.), *Mahatma Gandhi: His Own Story* (1930); L. Fischer, *The Life of Mahatma Gandhi* (1950); J. Eaton, *Gandhi, Fighter without a Sword* (1950); D.G. Tendulkar, *Mohandas Karamchand Gandhi* (8 vols, revised edition, 1963); J.V. Bondurant, *Conquest of Violence: The Gandhian Philosophy* (1965); E.H. Erikson, *Gandhi's Truth: On the Origins of Militant Non-violence* (1969); H. Alexander, *Gandhi Through Western Eyes* (1969); G. Woodcock, *Gandhi* (1972); J.M. Brown, *Gandhi: Prisoner of Hope* (1990); Yogesha Chadha, *Rediscovering Gandhi: The Definitive Biography* (1997).

DILIP HIRO

GARCÍA MÁRQUEZ, Gabriel

1928–

Colombian novelist

Probably the best-known Spanish-American contemporary novelist. His early short stories, written partly under the influence of **Faulkner**, are abstract and rather artificial.

However, in *Leaf Storm and Other Stories* (*La hojarasca* 1955, trans 1972), he created the township of Macondo around which much of his later work gravitates. It eventually came to be seen as a microcosm of Colombian society and, more broadly, that of Latin America as well as in some ways of the West in general. In this first novel, as well as in *No-one Writes to the Colonel* (*El coronel no tiene quien le escriba*, 1958, trans. 1971) and *In Evil Hour* (*La mala hora*, 1962, trans. 1980) which constitute the first phase of his production, the emphasis is on moral corruption, social decay and political oppression, relieved by individual acts of resistance to the depressing conditions under which the characters live. However, these works mark a break with the preceding pattern of social protest in the Spanish-American novel, not only because they reach out to a more universal plane of meaning (*Leaf Storm*, for instance, is modelled on Sophocles' tragedy *Antigone*) but also because of their often ambiguous presentation of reality, their unusual symbolism and their occasional inclusion of elements of fantasy and humour.

'Big Mama's Funeral' ('Los funerales de la Mamá Grande') in *No-One Writes to the Colonel* constitutes another giant stride forward in the Spanish-American novel which until the emergence of García Márquez had, with few exceptions, tended to reject humour as incompatible with the high civic responsibilities of writers who saw their first duty as that of stirring the conscience of their readers. The theme of the novella is a traditional one: the immense power and influence of the landed oligarchy in Latin America. But instead of mounting the usual frontal attack on the rural landowners for their exploitation of the peasantry and their manipulation of the local authorities, García Márquez ridicules them, adapting for the purpose techniques of grotesque exaggeration and comic enumeration which he had learned from Rabelais. The result is a carnivalesque satire, written without bitterness or aggressiveness, but which never allows the reader to forget the author's basic aim. The difference between 'Big Mama's Funeral' and *One Hundred Years of Solitude* (*Cien años de soledad*, 1967, trans. 1970), García Márquez's acknowledged masterpiece, lies in the fact that the former is based essentially on a hilarious deformation of observed social conditions, while the latter moves much further away from observed reality towards created reality and unbridled fantasy. No general consensus about the meaning of the work, which chronicles the fortunes of several generations of the Buendía family, the founders of Macondo, has emerged. One feature of the novel is its tendency to blur the distinction between the real and the imaginary and to undermine the confidence with which we differentiate the one from the other. In this sense a theme of the novel is fiction itself.

One Hundred Years of Solitude is also a metaphor of the human condition. The iron determinism which governs the lives of the characters, the solitude, the incest, the violence and the curse under which the Buendías labour, all illustrate García Márquez's underlying tragic vision. At another level, the story of Macondo becomes a metaphor of Latin America's historical development, at first idyllic and primitive, then with a rudimentary social organization imposed from without (as in the colonial period); next succumbing to the civil strife of nineteenth-century Latin America; finally falling victim to the economic imperialism characteristic of our day. The circularity of time in Macondo implies an attempt to escape from history seen as dynamic linear progress. The biblical parallels, especially with Genesis and Exodus, indicate a Fall, but no Redemption follows. Yet this is a very funny book. Its serious themes are enveloped in an atmosphere of fantasy, of magical and miraculous events and playful, often erotic, humour. The method produces a blend of tones which is completely original and unique in Spanish American fiction, where is sometimes known as Magical Realism.

After *Innocent Irendira and Other Stories* (*La increíble y triste historia de la cándida Irendira y de su abuela desalmada*, 1972, trans. 1978), an ironic parody of the conventional fairy-tale love story, García Márquez published *The Autumn of the Patriarch* (*El otoño del Patriarca*, 1975, trans. 1976) in which he caricatured the archetypal Latin American military dictator, mythicized, almost deified, yet at the same time comic and even pathetic. García Márquez has asserted that solitude is the opposite of collective solidarity and some critics have stressed the lack of social cohesion and harmony among the villagers in Macondo as part of the author's critique of his fellow Latin Americans. This becomes a central theme in *Chronicle of a Death Foretold* (*Crónica de una muerte anunciada*, 1981, trans. 1982). It is based on a true story, in which a young man's murder is partly connected with the theme of adverse fate, which since Romanticism has been used to express the collapse of belief in Divine Providence, but more concerned with the utter failure of the townspeople to intervene and to assume any civic or human responsibility for what is going on in front of them. In addition the novel brings out the unintelligibility of human behaviour: we know how the murder happened and who committed it, but we never learn the underlying facts and motivations.

García Márquez's fiction underwent a fresh development in 1985 with *Love in the Time of Cholera* (*El amor en los tiempos del cólera*, trans. 1988), later followed by *Of Love and Other Demons* (*Del amor y otros demonios*, 1994, trans. 1995) which may contain a response to the shift in Spanish-American fiction after the Boom began to run out of steam in the middle 1970s. A prominent feature of Boom fiction was the almost total absence of love (though not of sex) as a source of fulfilment and happiness. Although in both García Márquez's novels love is treated ambiguously at best, its sudden emergence as a major theme marks a shift away from the mainstream of Boom narrative. In between these two novels García Márquez published his main contribution to the New Historical Novel in Spanish America *The General in His Labyrinth* (*El general en su laberinto*, 1989, trans. 1990) on the last period of the life of Simón Bolívar. Like other novels in this category, it is designed to undercut the 'official' historical account of the General's last days and presents him as having fought so many wars in vain.

After a ten-year interval, García Márquez published in 2004 a new short novel *Memoria de mis putas tristes*, the story of a ninety-year-old journalist who finds love and happiness with a fifteen-year-old girl. Written without sentimentality, it situates the extraordinary affair in the context of a life dominated by trashy newspaper work and recourse to cheap prostitutes. In contrast to the end of *One Hundred Years of Solitude* it seems as though at last, in García Márquez, love is not accompanied by a curse.

Further reading

See: B. McGuirk and R. Cardwell, *Gabriel García Márquez: New Readings* (1987); G. Bell-Villada, *Gabriel García Márquez, The Man and His Work* (1990); D.L. Shaw, *A Companion to Modern Spanish American Fiction* (2002). In Spanish: Mario Vargas Llosa, *Gabriel García Márquez, historia de un deicidio* (1971).

D.L. SHAW

GATES, Bill (William Henry)
1955–
US computer scientist and entrepreneur

Bill Gates was for some years the World's Richest Man – until the computer 'dot com' bubble of the late 1990s burst and technology stocks in general took a dive, reducing him for a time to second richest. Co-founder of Microsoft Corporation, and at the time its CEO and largest shareholder, he piloted the company (and his personal worth) to unparalleled success through building a computer operating system and set of applications that promoted, then became, the unquestionable concept of 'industry standard'. Gates and Microsoft promoted the (at the time novel) view that the computer hardware (platform) was of no interest so long as it matched the specification on which different software, particularly the operating system that provides the framework for all other programs, would run.

This became possible as a result of IBM's conversion to the personal computer. A latecomer to the personal computer revolution, IBM launched its PC (personal computer) in 1981 with a famous series of **Charlie Chaplin** adverts. Crucially, the PC had an open architecture (the basic design of the machine was made freely available). Although some years behind the successful development of the Apple II (and other) computers, the blue-chip IBM brand provided the insignia of approval the business community wanted. The upstarts of Apple Computer, **Steve Jobs** and Steve Wozniak (whose roots were among the hippies and geeks of California's Homebrew computer club) did not. As a result, the personal computer transformed from the enthusiast's and scientist's cult object to a serious, then ubiquitous business tool. The office computer revolution began, fuelled by software solutions originally developed for the Apple II (e.g., the original spreadsheet, VisiCalc) but given exposure and a mass market by the IBM PC. It was IBM's success with the PC that allowed the emergence of this 'industry standard', with its concomitant to remove competition and flatten the market. Apple's Mac remains the only significant competitor to the vast range of PCs manufactured by many companies but all based on IBM's original design.

Gates emerged as an extremely talented programmer and businessman. Workers at Microsoft remark that when he visits their coding efforts, his ability to understand and improve them is extraordinary. 'Genius' is the word used. But Gates was also lucky: he won the contract to provide the operating system ('DOS' – Disk Operating System) for the IBM PC with a system he and his founding partner Paul Allen had just bought and modified. The success of the PC and its unprotected design meant there was an almost unlimited market, all depending on Microsoft's operating system, which Microsoft set about controlling with great determination, often sailing uncomfortably close to the wind, ethically speaking.

Although it is the dominance of Microsoft's operating system (developed from DOS into 'Windows', a clone of Apple's Macintosh operating system) – and more recently its web browser 'Internet Explorer' – that is the basis of the Microsoft monopoly, Gates has overseen the development of a vast range of other software that has also become *de rigueur*, as Microsoft has achieved a blue-chip reputation such as allowed IBM to make the PC acceptable to business. In particular, his suite 'Office', almost all of which was initially developed on the Mac platform, has acquired a position so dominant that users have virtually no choice: Microsoft has removed the inspiration of competition, leading, some claim, to a joyless uniformity. This *de facto* monopoly leads to antagonism and the stream of litigation in which Microsoft attempts to defend its practices – in spite of Microsoft's mission which (to use the company's words) has been to continually advance and improve software technology, and to make it easier, more cost-effective and more enjoyable for the vast majority of us who have no technical background to use computers.

Gates and Microsoft would probably like to be thought of as having brought cheap and friendly computing to the world, countering the commonly held idea that they have put a stranglehold on computing and software development because of the lack of choice. In fact both views have a deal of truth. The universality of Gates's Microsoft products, and the power (albeit clumsy) of Windows gives them a critical and major position in the contemporary world.

Allen ceased active involvement with Microsoft in order to fund innovative projects (e.g. the first privately funded orbital vehicle, SpaceShip One). Gates remained, but eventually retired as CEO and became Chairman and Chief Software Architect following a rough court battle which he didn't come out of too well. Microsoft continues to battle anti-trust and similar suits brought by the US and state governments, as well as by other corporations.

Gates and Microsoft, while almost universally respected, are not greatly loved, perhaps a harsh judgement that comes from a big ideological difference between 'hacker' values and computing for profit, and a 'little guy' dislike of the large corporation. Yet Gates has supported Apple computer (he needs at least one nominal rival company to counter charges of being a monopoly). He has also attempted to share his business thoughts and practices through two books – *The Road Ahead* (1995, with N. Myhrvold and P. Rinearson) and *Business @ the Speed of Thought: Using a Digital Nervous System* (1999). 'How you gather, manage and use information,' he writes, 'will determine whether you win or lose.' His software is intended to help us in these tasks.

Born in Seattle (Washington State), William H. Gates III comes from a family with a history of success and social standing. After an exclusive education he dropped out of Harvard University in 1975 to pursue his passion for computing, co-founding Microsoft after writing a BASIC language (used for writing programs) for the ground-breaking Altair 8800 – the 'World's First Microcomputer Kit to Rival Commercial Models'. Typically, Gates and Allen sold this BASIC to Altair as ready to run before a line of code had been written.

In 1994 Gates married Melinda French. They and their children live in a wired house intended to indicate Gates's vision of a future of ubiquitous, lifestyle computing, above the lake that separates Redmond (home of the Microsoft campus) from Seattle. In 2000, they amalgamated two charities into the Bill and Melinda Gates Foundation, endowed it with $27 billion of assets (to date), and appointed Gates's father William S. Gates Sr as chairman, with the mission of 'Bringing Innovations in Health and Learning to the Global Community'. While cynics downplay the foundation as an attempt to buy credibility and affection, in his mixture of rampant capitalism and idealistic philanthropy Gates can less churlishly be seen to be following a great American tradition – *vide* (for instance) Andrew Carnegie.

Further reading

See: James Wallace and Jim Ericson, *Bill Gates and the Making of the Microsoft Empire* (1992); and *Overdrive* (1997) by the same authors.

RANULPH GLANVILLE

GAUDÍ, Antoni (Antonio)
1852–1926
Spanish-Catalan architect

One of the most innovative and best-loved architects of any age, Antoni Gaudí was born near Reus, a small town to the south of Barcelona, capital of Catalunya, an autonomous region of Spain with its own language and traditions. His father was the last in a line of coppersmiths, a craft Gaudí eschewed in preference to attending university in order to study architecture. He emerged in 1878 after a lacklustre performance to commence a career that spanned forty-eight years. While prolific in the sense of the effect and reach that his work had then and continues to have today, in number he produced relatively few buildings during his lifetime. Almost all are in or near Barcelona, and of these many were commissioned by the same patron, Count Eusabi Güell.

Typically, Gaudí's success is accounted for by a consummate originality manifested by an uninhibited experimentation with, initially, composition and colour, and latterly form, structure and construction; he complemented artistry with technical virtuosity in terms of both structural performance and the actual fabric and construction of his buildings. Although Gaudí's major work coincided with Art Nouveau, Jugendstil, Fin de Siècle, Liberty Style and other contemporary art and culture movements from the late nineteenth century, it went much further, and it is the distance that he travelled in his own time both philosophically and practically that placed him ahead of his peers then, and locates him very much in our time now.

Gaudí was at his most active during Catalunya's *Modernisme* period, which embraced everything considered ultra-modern, though this had grown out of the *Renaixença*, a movement in which Catalans reasserted their quest for political independence from Bourbon Spain through the rebirth and reassertion of their own traditions. As a kind of cultural schizophrenia, Barcelona's bourgeoisie promoted the spirit of progressiveness by the deliberate invocation of systems and values from the past. Modernity via *Modernisme* ultimately transitioned into a volte-face reactionary fallback to classicism, *Noucentisme* ('new century'), commencing in 1906 with the publication of several key texts. The same well-to-do champions of *Modernisme* now promoted a classical revival: no longer looking backwards and inwards to Catalan cultural identity, they looked instead to an equally historic Mediterranean rim collective identity. If *Modernisme* was characterized by an overt eclecticism, albeit with a distinct Moorish (*Mudéjar*) edge referencing Spain's particular history, *Noucentisme* was characterized by a desire for Catalan art and culture to acknowledge its Mediterranean roots through an essentially stripped classicism.

Gaudí's career coincided with these and other developments affecting Catalan architectural procedures. But while it is tempting to contextualize him within successive chauvinist, modernist and neo-classical movements in Barcelona, to which he undoubtedly contributed, that would undervalue his ability to transcend what went on around him, and so misunderstand his actual achievement. He was both a Catalan, through and through, and an 'internationalist' at a time when Barcelona itself enjoyed a reputation as a European cultural capital to rival Paris. Among exogenous influences detected in his work have been (for instance) the English art historian **John Ruskin**, the designer **William Morris** and the French architect Viollet-le-Duc.

Even so, we can find examples of projects in Gaudí's portfolio that demonstrate his alignment to each of the periods in question. During the late *Renaixença*, for example, Casa Vicens (1883), Finca Güell Pavilions (1887) and Bellesguard (1902) all make unequivocal reference to a rich but relatively localized architectural legacy. Moorish technical finesse and decorative appeal are abundant in Casa Vicens, as is overt reference to the formal structure of physically defensive Catalan manorial homesteads and the unique Catalan building technology in Bellesguard. From this, architectural historians might conclude that Gaudí was working in a manner entirely consistent with his peers, but there are other important critical criteria. The Finca Güell Pavilions, for instance, tell a story well beyond an obvious evocation of San Jordi (Saint George), who, as the patron saint of Catalunya, is represented by the incredible dragon gate between the two pavilions, and defensive entrance to Güell's out-of-town estate. But much more is present than a relatively trite evocation of the heroic foundation of Catalan nationhood and identity. The pillar from which the dragon gate hangs terminates high above in a metallic branch bearing apples. A more detailed scrutiny reveals that the featured dragon is guarding the tree of golden apples in the Garden of the Hesperides, recalling Jacint Verdaguer's epic poem *L'Atlantida* (1877), which equated Hercules' epic struggles directly to those of Columbus's epic journey (sponsored only in part by Catalan capital), leading to the discovery of the Americas.

More than one reading within a single work is paralleled by more than one reading across works. Two buildings completed at the same time seem to indicate quite different personae: Palau Güell and Las Teresianas convent school (both from 1890).

Gaudí spared no effort providing Güell with a townhouse of palatial proportions, rich both in abundant cultural allusion and in the generous use of costly materials – ivory and ebony abound, as does a selection of opulent stones and other timbers, with craftsmanship and invention to match. Yet despite such innovations as the naturally ventilated basement stables, an open-plan succession of public to private spaces, layered collimated façades of columns and the magical roofscape with chimneys covered in colourful *trencadis* (broken tile, plate and glass mosaics), the building itself is dark, funereal and distinctly odd. Characteristically sinuous curves and surfaces abruptly end in sharp and pointy, almost aggressive, details; voluptuous column capitals are strangely held hostage within woven filigree metal bondage. If Palau Güell is a conspicuous display of wealth, it also questions Gaudí's relationship with his client; and it is telling that Güell's family preferred not to reside in the building.

The convent is as stark a contrast as can be imagined. While sharing aspects of spatial innovation with Palau Güell, it was built on a very low budget using only the most modest of materials – predominantly random rubble; but where the townhouse is gloomy and foreboding, the convent is light, airy, optimistic.

Already evident in these and other early works is a complex, even enigmatic cultural personality that sets Gaudí apart from more senior *Renaixença* architects such as Domenech i Montaner and Puig i Gadafalch. But, as *Renaixença* gave way to *Modernismo*, so Gaudí too entered a new phase, when the freedom of expression courted by him is increasingly complemented by an equivalent experimentation in form and (particularly) structure. Having won the prize for the best building in Barcelona in 1900 with his relatively restrained retro-baroque Casa Calvet (from 1898 to 1900), he set about three projects that are sometimes regarded as the zenith of his output: the Colònia Güell Church (1898–1916), Casa Milà (aka La Pedrera 1906–10) and Park Güell (1900–914).

The Colònia Güell Church was conceived as part of a settlement sponsored by Güell for workers at the corduroy factory he owned outside Barcelona. After nearly two decades of design and construction work was abandoned with only the crypt completed, but even so it represents a mature composition. Instead of relying on drawings and plans, Gaudí constructed a model (on a scale of 1:10) for the proposed building, and then hung it upside down in a shed next to the site. His reason for doing this was to assess the optimum expression of structural loading in a building by letting nature have free expression through gravity: the form that the building assumed through gravitational tension would be the equivalent but opposite in compression. Photographs of the suspended model were rotated so as to give the 'correct' orientation. A century before the animation and image-manipulation software that aids today's digital design became ubiquitous, Gaudí had proposed an analogue design method that abandoned the paradigm of plans, sections and elevations that otherwise characterize the architectural profession.

The swirling, almost fondant façades and interiors of Casa Milà added to the playfulness and iconoclasm applied to the complex infrastructure for Park Güell, though again neither project was completed. Park Güell, intended to become an entire hillside garden suburb, was abandoned in 1914, with only two of a planned sixty houses finished. Allowing, in theory at least, Gaudí to indulge his twin passions for natural forms and social responsibility, it was, or would have become, his most ambitious project. But just a few years into the twentieth century, architectural fashion had again changed, as *Noucentisme* arrived on the scene, and Park Güell became yesterday's excitement.

The retrospective success of the only partly realized designs of Gaudí's middle period too easily mask a personal crisis, induced by, among other factors, stinging attacks issued by Eugeni d'Ors – writer, critic and principal instigator of *Noucentisme*. After spending some months in the Pyrenees recovering from a breakdown in his health, Gaudí returned to Barcelona and set about completing his designs for the church of the Sagrada Família, aka the 'cathedral of the poor'. Representing the third and final phase of his career, it too was woefully incomplete at his death, but has become (since work on constructing the Sagrada Família continues to the present) publicly the best known of all his projects.

The Sagrada Família was not commissioned by the church, but was advanced through public subscription, and shortage of funds was an abiding problem. Again Gaudí preferred to create models rather than drawings, and it is these, made from gypsum plaster and wire, that most fully incorporate Gaudí's genius, characterized by form, structure, environmental sensitivity, economy of means, constructional logic, transcendentalism and colour – and, above all, covert rationality. Using unorthodox arrangements of myriad hyperbolic geometry, in one move Gaudí proposed a *modus operandi* that makes complex curved surfaces astonishingly simple to achieve, a feature that is not apparent except to the trained eye. Through his modelling, he developed both a codex and a schema for the Sagrada Família that have provided his successors with a way forward long after his death. Had he not entered this third and final phase, a period in his oeuvre that is best aligned to the (International) Modern Movement (still two years from being declared at the first CIAM held in 1928), efforts to complete his *magnum opus* would have been utterly frustrated.

Gaudí died in 1926, struck down by a tram. Two years later, he would have seen the completion of the Barcelona Pavilion by **Mies van der Rohe** – a modernist icon that came and went, and came again. The minimalism of the pavilion seems to contrast markedly with the profusion of form and colour of the Nativity Façade spire finials at the Sagrada Família – the last constructed work in Gaudí's time – yet the two projects have more in common than first appears. Gaudí's legacy, however, is arguably the greater. Three-quarters of a century on, the Sagrada Família still poses questions that not even the most sophisticated computer computation has so far managed to answer.

Further reading

See: Cristina Montes and Aurora Cuito, *Gaudí: Obra Completa/Complete Works* (multilingual, 2003). See also: J.J. Sweeney and J.L. Sert, *Antoni Gaudí* (1960); J.M. Richards and N. Pevsner, *The Anti-Rationalists* (1973); Luis Permanyer, *Gaudí of Barcelona* (1997); Juan Bassegoda Nonell *et al.*, *Antonio Gaudí: Master Architect* (2000); Ignasi de Sola-Morales, *Antoni Gaudí* (2003); Juan José Lahuerta, *Antoni Gaudí* (2003).

MARK BURRY

GAUGUIN, Paul
1848–1903
French artist, ceramist and writer

Although born in Paris, Gauguin spent his early childhood in Peru. Later, as a youth, he travelled extensively as a merchant seaman and in the navy, before starting to paint in 1873 at the age of twenty-five. Working at first purely as an amateur, Gauguin, like his guardian Gustave Arosa, was able to collect paintings, amongst which were works by the Barbizon school and by Pissarro, with whom Gauguin painted during three summers. During this time he met the other Impressionist painters and adopted their style, which was just reaching the high point of its development.

Gauguin also gave up his career in banking and concentrated upon his painting. He began to feel, as he worked more intensely, that a realistic or naturalistic style such as that of either the Barbizon school of Courbet and Corot or of the Impressionists was sufficient in some measure. Aware of the preoccupation with volumetric structure with which **Cézanne** was struggling, Gauguin also experimented with these ideas as a way of avoiding pure description of the visual world as practised by **Monet** and **Renoir**.

In 1885, having visited England and probably aware of **Whistler's** interest in Japanese art, Gauguin produced an important work for the development of his style. This was *Still Life with Horse's Head*. The subject-matter of this painting combines a Japanese doll with the plaster cast of a horse's head from the Elgin Marbles seen at the British Museum. A letter to his friend Schuffenecker that year expresses Gauguin's realization that for him art must have some inexplicable content and convey more than a rationalist approach to ideas of sensation. These conclusions signify a rejection of the positivist tendencies of

Impressionism for a more subjective, emotional and imaginative art.

The following year this trend continued. As a result of seeing Kate Greenaway's book illustrations, the forms in Gauguin's painting became less volumetric and considerably flattened. The effect was decorative and more abstract. Areas of canvas were covered with a single rich colour, whereas his Impressionist style had been composed of a myriad multi-coloured marks.

There still remained to be solved the problem of the relationship of volume and light to decorative abstract elements. To attempt a synthesis Gauguin made some ceramics and applied the simple peasant patterns he had seen while visiting Brittany to the swelling forms of his ceramics. However, dissatisfied with the situation in Paris, Gauguin's increasing restlessness led him briefly to Martinique. As a result his painting gained a still brighter colour intensity, and spatial qualities were produced by the superimposition of layers of flat shapes one upon another.

Gauguin returned to Brittany to live amongst a group of artist friends, and his work became prolific as he moved towards a fuller synthesis of the many ideas and influences that engaged him. Aware of the new Symbolist poetry, exemplified by the writings of **Mallarmé**, in which the 'feeling of the thought' or 'the Idea' was more important than the subject-matter, Gauguin responded by making his work evocatively allusive.

At this time the ideas of Émil Bernard became particularly necessary to Gauguin. Bernard had worked out a style of painting which he termed '*cloisonnisme*'. This blending of flat richly coloured shapes with a simplified linear definition in something of the manner of stained-glass windows fulfilled Gauguin's need for an art form which was both ideal and exotically primitive.

The important painting which first fully incorporated the symbolist aesthetic and produced the complete synthesis he required was *The Vision after the Sermon* produced during the summer of 1888. The subject of Jacob wrestling with an angel is a recurrent theme in European art. Gauguin presented it in a unique manner. The two wrestling figures which form the vision are seen small in the right half of the painting against a brilliant flat red field. The work is divided into two diagonally by a serpentine tree trunk. On the left in the foreground is a group of Breton peasant women in traditional white bonnets. Only the heads and shoulders of these peasants are included and turned away from the person viewing the painting, who is therefore in the position of joining the crowd watching the visitation.

To Gauguin, who identified strongly with the simple, impoverished and religious peasants amongst whom he was living, the wrestling man and spirit symbolized not only the struggle of the peasants but also his own on two levels. In the first instance Gauguin was also poor and trying to succeed in a life away from the increasing materialism of urban civilization. In the second he was struggling in his art with a number of difficulties, in particular that of empirical naturalism which seemed to him opposed to spiritual abstraction. The painting of the Vision therefore demonstrates two main preoccupations that dominate the remainder of Gauguin's life, the relationship of innocence to knowledge and of primitivism to sophistication.

It was through Bernard's introduction that the painter Sérusier met Gauguin and was instructed how to paint the work now known as the *Talisman* of 1888. While Sérusier was sitting in front of the landscape, painting, Gauguin demanded of him, 'How do you see that tree? It's green? then choose the most beautiful green on your palette – And this shadow? It's more like blue? Do not be afraid to paint it with the purest blue possible.' Upon his return to Paris, Sérusier's little painting met with much interest from the younger painters at the Académie Julian, who later formed a group known as the Nabis. Sérusier commented upon the *Talisman* that it was 'Thus we learned that every work of art was a transposition, a caricature, the passionate equivalent of a sensation received.'

Shortly after this instruction to Sérusier, Gauguin who had corresponded and exchanged portraits with **Van Gogh** throughout the summer, journeyed south to Arles. However, although fruitful in terms of painting for both men, the few months they were together proved unhappy and ended in the tragedy at Christmas of Van Gogh's first phase of insanity. Gauguin returned north and exhibited his work in the Café Volpini at the Paris Expo Universelle.

Although financially unproductive these new paintings again caused excitement amongst younger artists. Gauguin, however, felt himself to be a failure and subsequent paintings in Brittany of the *Yellow Christ* and *Christ at Gethsemane* are the equivalents for his sense of loneliness and persecution.

At last, because of continuing disregard by the art establishment in Paris, Gauguin auctioned his paintings and left for Tahiti in 1891. The works produced there were at first questioning and pessimistic in mood. Nonetheless, the form and aesthetic were still developing so that volume became more obviously synthesized with the decorative elements. The native people, painted with a simple monumentality, are directly expressive. It was not until after a return to Paris to collect more money, and an unsuccessful suicide attempt when back in the South Seas that Gauguin's art achieved its final serenity, which appears to have been maintained until his death in 1903.

Faa Ihe Ihe of 1898, in the Tate Gallery collection, is the first of these more optimistic paintings of a primitive life. It is a work that is long horizontally and shallow vertically, giving the effect of a frieze. The trees and Javanese figures stand singly and unevenly spaced along the length with an almost musical sense of rhythm to the spacing, echoed by the lyrical undulations of branches and outlines of figures. These are set against a unifying golden yellow background. The title means 'to adorn', the kind of beautifying that precedes a feast or celebration. The central goddess figure appears as a motif and derives from a photograph in Gauguin's possession

depicting a frieze in the Buddhist temple of Barabadour. This central motif reappears in a similar fashion to the dog derived from a Courbet painting in his guardian's possession and the horse and rider in other works. Memory, imagination and reality mingle to produce a Garden of Eden on earth in which man is joyously united with both art and nature.

Gauguin's influence throughout Europe was extensive. Indeed, it may well be that, of all the artists in the latter half of the nineteenth century, Gauguin, as the foremost artist of the key Symbolist movement that was the turning point for the development of art in the twentieth century, was the most important.

In France alone his ideas were propagated by a number of disciples who lived with him in Brittany. Many of these continued to work there, and people from all over Europe visited the north of France to meet them and to absorb the atmosphere of those rural surroundings that Gauguin had projected in his paintings. Rather later, the Fauves and Cubists, in particular **Matisse**, **Braque** and **Picasso**, drew upon Gauguin in their speculations concerning primitivism. This interest was manifest in England and artists of the avant-garde, many of them connected with the Slade prior to the 1914–18 war, paid great attention to Gauguin's work.

While Cubism was developing in France, Expressionism was gaining ground in Germany and the Brücke in particular, in their drives towards a primitive outdoor lifestyle and a preoccupation with the raw technique of woodcuts, also saw themselves as following in Gauguin's footsteps. Primitivism, simplicity and subjective concerns with imaginative vision and memory abound in the first years of the twentieth century, and in the visual arts they draw their strength in large measure from Gauguin.

Further reading

Other works include: *Self Portrait with Cherries* (1888); *Where Do We Come From? What Are We?*

Where Are We Going? (1897). See: John Rewald, *Gauguin* (1938); Ronald Alley, *Paul Gauguin* (1961); Marete Bodelson, *Gauguin's Ceramics* (1964); Alan Bowness, *Gauguin* (1971); H.R. Rookmaaker, *Gauguin and 19th Century Art Theory* (1972).

PAT TURNER

GEHRY, Frank Owen (Ephraim GOLDBERG)

1929–

US architect

Frank Gehry has been at the forefront of those seeking to liberate architecture from the straitjacket of the arbitrary formalism of the rectilinear geometry and the jingoistic tedium of the dictum that 'form follows function' that dominated the modern movement of the twentieth century. Early pioneers of this reaction included **Gaudí** with his remarkable complex geometries at the Sagrada Família at the beginning of the century that were contemporary with some of the most extreme icons of modernism, such as **Mies van der Rohe's** Barcelona Pavilion (1928). Engineers such as Pier Luigi Nervi and Santiago Calatrava favoured flowing structural forms for rationalized structural reasons. Other architects attempting to sculpt the whole shell of a building include Jorn Utzon with the Sydney Opera House, **Le Corbusier's** flirtations with boat-like forms at Ronchamp and much of the oeuvre of **Aalto**, which rejoices in curving surfaces and details. However, Gehry's contribution was to link his predilection for curves derived from bending pieces of cardboard to advanced computer modelling and fabrication techniques. He thus liberated a whole new generation of architects from the excuse of the supposed rationality of the dull and the sensible and reintroduced a colourful baroque flair and whimsy, usually on a vast scale.

Gehry's later projects, from 1990 onwards, are characterized by a contrast between relatively orthogonal elements and flamboyant curves in bent titanium. Much of this curvature is achieved by using developable surfaces derived from the smooth bending of stiff card, articulated with occasional parts of complex curvature to create more crease-like attenuations of the surface. Powerful computer techniques ensure economic construction by maintaining the economic formability and optimization of the surfaces and direct links to computer-controlled machinery which ensure faithful reproduction of Gehry's concepts. But for Gehry 'fast card' in his hands and judged by his eye always is the preferred design technique and come before the computer is engaged to ensure constructability.

The award of the Pritzker Prize for a lifetime of achievement as early as 1989 is interesting because it pre-dated most of the buildings on which his international reputation now rests. He had, though, already achieved a number of exceptional Californian houses including the Winton Guest House (1982–7) and the Schnabel Residence (1986–9), while his trademark Fishdance Restaurant in Kobe (1986–7) does anticipate his later work; but at the time of the award the extant sketches of the Disney Concert Hall (Los Angeles) appeared relatively conventional and only the Vitra International Furniture Manufacturing Facility and Museum (1988–94) projected a clear vision of what was to come.

The construction of another large fish (160 feet long and 100 high) for the Olympic Village in Barcelona (1989–92) signalled not a repeat of Kobe, but a radical use of advanced computer techniques introduced by his partner James Glymph which allowed the accurate yet economic construction of these vast complex curved forms. The Guggenheim Museum in Bilbao (1991–7) used the fish-scale motif and the same computer technology to construct flowing curved surfaces, again on a large scale, and at a pivotal point in the city to the delight of both the public and architectural critics. The last of the pro-modernist critics were silenced by a building so blatantly at odds with the dictates of function and where the free form external shapes of shining sheet titanium are almost totally unrelated to the more conventional exhibition spaces within, leaving unexpected and utterly delightful spaces between. Then the design of the Disney Concert Hall project dating from 1989 was radically redesigned to finally open in 2003, spectacularly celebrating a flamboyantly baroque exterior on a scale unseen or unthought-of before, again with between spaces of enchanting and even confusing circulation and encounter.

This vocabulary was extended into other building types such as offices with the Nationale-Nederlanden Building (Prague, 1992–6) leading to the Stata building at MIT (2004) where, in the artificial intelligence laboratory, even the robots express delight at their new environment. By contrast the Experience Music Project for Seattle (1996–2000) pushes the limits of entirely free-flowing curves realized in spectacular colour; and the Museum of Tolerance in Jerusalem (due to open 2008) includes a dramatic new structural and spatial turbining element.

Alongside these large-scale dramatic signature buildings, sometimes criticized for ignoring situation and function, there have been a series of smaller buildings displaying remarkable sensitivity to location and purpose such as the Maggie Centre (Dundee, 2003), created as a cancer care home in memory of Maggie Jencks, a close friend of Gehry's and wife of architectural historian Charles Jencks.

Born Ephraim Goldberg in Toronto, Canada, Gehry lives and practises as a naturalized American citizen in Los Angeles. He studied at the University of Southern California School of Architecture and the Harvard Graduate School of Design. Unlike a majority of modern architects, he is widely known and liked by the public and a household name, even featuring in an episode of the cult TV cartoon series *The Simpsons* in 2005. Such buildings as the Guggenheim in Bilbao are so well known that other cities are striving to commission landmark buildings for the 'Bilbao effect' – a clear visual symbol of the city in the tradition of the Sydney Opera House or the **Eiffel** Tower. Gehry's notoriety for breaking the rules (typically featuring iconically in Apple's 'Think Different' campaign) has been associated with his lifetime enthusiasm for ice-hockey. His professional success has been recognized with major awards including, besides the Pritzker Prize, the Fredrick Kiesler Prize (1998), the Gold Medal of the American Institute of Architects (1999), the Gold Medal of the Royal Institute of British Architects (2000) and the Gold Medal for Architecture, American Academy of Arts and Letters (2002).

Whenever it has come his way, Gehry has also thrived on adverse publicity and questionable criticism, ranging from those committed to a rationalist architecture who see his work as mere caprice or self-indulgence to those who wish to position him in some clear tradition such as postmodernism or as part of the deconstructivist school. But Gehry's development does not easily lend itself to typecasting. While his reputation is already assured by the influence he has on younger architects, Gehry has also created a Digital Practice Ecosystem committed to changing the building industry and has made the specialized computer software on which the successful realization of his projects depends available to the whole profession. Post-1995, Gehry projects under development are starting to use photovoltaic cells integrated into curving glass skins. Gestures such as this towards a sustainable and energy-responsible architecture may emerge as his most significant contribution.

Further reading

See: Francesco Dal Co and Kurt W. Forster, *Frank O. Gehry, The Complete Works* (1998); Mildred Friedman (ed.), *Gehry Talks: Architecture + Process* (2003); Frank Gehry, *Symphony: Frank Gehry's Walt Disner Concert Hall* (2003); Mark Rappolt and Robert Violette (eds), *Gehry Draws* (2004). See also: Coosje van Bruggen (ed.), *Frank O. Gehry: Guggenheim Museum* (1997); Jason Miller and Susan Lauzau, *Frank Gehry* (2003); Nancy Joyce, *Building Stata* (2004).

JOHN HAMILTON FRAZER

GENET, Jean

1910–86

French poet, novelist, dramatist

Genet's father was unknown, his mother a prostitute who abandoned him to be brought up by the state. When his foster parents caught him stealing and called him a thief, he decided to turn this insult into a virtue and to make a career as a thief. Much of his childhood was spent in reform schools, where his first homosexual encounters took place. He escaped and joined the French Foreign Legion, only to desert soon afterwards. Living off theft and prostitution, he wandered from one part of Europe to another, often in prison or on the run from the police.

His first novels were written in prison: *Our Lady of the Flowers* (*Notre-Dame des Fleurs*) at Fresnes in 1942 and *Miracle of the Rose* (*Miracle de la Rose*) at the Santé prison in 1943. These are novels of homosexual eroticism written in sumptuously poetic prose. They are theatrical novels in the sense that they portray people constantly preoccupied with appearances, both their own and others'. Even more, they suggest an almost mystical belief in the sudden transformation of outward appearances in such a way as to reveal another reality visible only to the eye of the believer. *Miracle of the Rose* contains a celebrated account of a scene in the courtyard of Fontevrault prison in which a notorious bandit steps out from the condemned cell and suddenly his chains are transformed into a garland of roses.

In 1947 Genet's reputation was established with the publication of two more novels and the performance of *The Maids* (*Les Bonnes*) produced by Jouvet in a double bill with a play by Giraudoux. His last novel *The Thief's Journal* (*Journal d'un Voleur*) appeared in 1949, which was also the year when he produced his own play *Deathwatch* (*Haute surveillance*). Subsequently Genet wrote three major plays: *The Balcony* (*Le Balcon*, 1956); *The Blacks* (*Les Nègres*, 1958); and *The Screens* (*Les Paravents*, 1961), and nothing more.

In the 1960s and 1970s he championed the causes of various urban terrorist groups including the Black Panthers, the Fedayeen and the Baader-Meinhof gang. He described himself as 'a black whose skin happens to be pink and white' and his early identification with the criminal classes shifted to an identification with the oppressed, the dispossessed and the coloured.

Genet's life presents an extraordinarily consistent attempt to turn bourgeois morality on its head. He is at least partly the creation of **Sartre** who, when asked to write a short introduction to Genet's work, produced a 600-page essay explaining the phenomenon that was Jean Genet in Existentialist terms. This appeared as Volume I of Genet's complete works. For Sartre, Genet aspired to a kind of saintliness by his single-minded devotion to evil and his systematic reversal of received moral codes.

Genet's writing style is different from that of Sartre, being poetic rather than discursive, baroque rather than austere. Although he has written about social outcasts, it is difficult to extract a socialist message from his works. In fact he has expressed admiration for an SS torturer and regret at the closure of the Cayenne convict settlement. But his work has always been seen as subversive by the Establishment. His first novels were not available to open sale; performances of his plays all provoked some degree of protest, and the production of *The Screens* at the Odéon in 1966 led to demonstrations and street battles.

By his own definition, his method is to draw the reader or the spectator into imaginative sympathy with a character or attitude which turns out to be diametrically opposed to his normal assumptions or standards. But neither in fiction nor on the stage does Genet match the crude extremes of, say, **Burroughs** or Fernando Arrabal. His work has a greater range and depth, commenting on social, political and spiritual aspects of life. His plays embody a very brilliant interplay of different levels of illusion which suggest both the interdependence and the potential treachery of all social roles, stressing the links between the power and theatricality. They also point to the inadequacy of common notions of reality. In many ways they approach the ideals of Antonin Artaud, being characterized by an absence of traditional psychology, ritualized movements and actions, interchanges of identity and a carefully worked contrast between the sumptuousness of poetic dialogue and the sordidity of dramatic situation. They also demand an exploitation of the whole theatre space and aim for a powerful, disturbing effect on the audience. Genet has expressed contempt for most Western theatre because it offers entertainment instead of communion. He has expressed admiration for the Roman Catholic Mass and for children's games.

His plays provided opportunities for directors like Roger Blin and Peter Brook to put the theories of Artaud to the test and resulted in some very brilliant productions. But he was an uncomfortable figure: the Left never quite forgave him for writing a panegyric of Nazi killers; the Right will never forgive him for casting dirt on the French army in Algeria. He remains an unclassifiable figure, but a challenging one.

Further reading

Other works include: *Oeuvres complètes* (from 1951). Many of his works have appeared in English translation published by Faber. See also: Richard Coe, *The Vision of Jean Genet* (1968); Philip Thody, *Jean Genet: A Critical Appraisal* (1968); Jane Giles, *The Cinema of Jean Genet* (1991) and *Criminal Desires: Jean Genet and Cinema* (2002); Edmund White, *Genet: A Biography* (1993); Stephen Barber, *Jean Genet* (2004).

DAVID BRADBY

GERSHWIN, George

1898–1937

US composer

George Gershwin was an American composer no less remarkable for historical significance than for intrinsic ability. Born in 1898 of Jewish parentage, in the heart of New York, he was a natural who flourished in what might have seemed a musical desert. Nurtured off Broadway, he first made a living by plugging other people's songs at the piano in music emporia, and found himself creating his own numbers almost fortuitously. It never occurred to him that distinctions might be drawn between making songs and selling them; and intuitively he was right in believing that, although commercial art operates in order to make money, it will do so best if the dreams it proffers bear some relation to people's emotional needs. The musical comedy numbers of Gershwin, especially those for which his brother Ira wrote such witty lyrics, accept the clichés of Tin Pan Alley while imbuing them with an irony – a recognition of 'other modes of experience that may be possible' – that makes them at once comic and deeply moving. 'The Man I Love' (1924) can stake a claim to being the most affecting pop song of the jazz era because, starting from the adolescent moon-June cliché, it admits that the dream, though true to the cravings of the human heart, isn't likely to be true in fact. What happens in the music makes the girl grow up; and we grow with her. The music tells us that, though she won't find her Prince Charming, she'll almost certainly find a guy she mistakes for one; and that the mistake matters less than the fallible aspiration.

The memorability of Gershwin's tunes has ensured that no show-biz composer has created so many tunes so widely known to so many people; at the same time the subtlety of the composer's melodic and rhythmic structures and the often quite complex ambiguities of his harmony and tonality have ensured that the tunes are 'news that *stays* news'. There's enough art in Gershwin's commercial numbers to explain why it was possible for his career to climax (in 1935) with a large-scale work, *Porgy and Bess*, which starts from the conventions of the Broadway musical yet becomes a fully fledged and genuinely grand opera. Part of Gershwin's talent was to have recognized in Dubose Heyward's novel his own essential theme: for the book is a parable about alienation, oppression and the inviolability of a radical innocence of spirit, even in a corrupt world. Gershwin was not, like Porgy, a Negro, nor, in the material benefits of life, was he in any way deprived. He was, however, a poor boy who made good: an American Jew who knew about spiritual isolation and had opportunities enough to learn about corruption. He was not, like Porgy, a physical cripple; he was, however, an emotional cripple, victimized by the nervous maladjustments typical of his generation, and by the usual escapes from them. So, in his opera, he sang with honest strength of the malaise inherent in the twentieth-century pop song itself: telling of the impact of the world of commerce on those who once led, would like to have led, the 'good life', based on an intimate communion between man and nature. Significantly the veracity of the pentatonic roulades and painful false relations of the Negro blues is endemic in Gershwin's melody and harmony; and comes to terms both with the commercial clichés of Tin Pan Alley (as represented by the beguiling numbers of the light-skinned villain, Sportin' Life), and also with the operatic conventions of 'Western' art, which seek a synonym for Order and Civilization.

The pervasiveness of the black blues within Gershwin's white music bears on the fact that he has been so important a figure in the evolution of jazz as an urban folk art; *Porgy and Bess* has itself spawned jazz-improvised composition of extraordinary intensity, from the versions of Ella Fitzgerald and **Louis Armstrong** to those of **Miles Davis**, Cleo Laine and Ray Charles, and Oscar Petersen. Yet Gershwin did not regard the 'folk' aspects of his work as alien to his aspiration towards 'art'; and it's a fact that his early success (initiated by Paul Whiteman) as a composer of 'concert' music abetted his later triumphs in the pop field. Academic musicians are still apt to say that, whereas the tunes in *Rhapsody in Blue* (1924) and the *Concerto in F* (1925) are marvellous, they're not improved by the synthetic symphonic treatment. There must be something wrong with this argument, for after more than fifty years these 'synthetic' pieces continue to be frequently performed whereas literally hundreds of (often critically lauded) piano concertos composed during the period have gone the way of all flesh. Gershwin himself, who wrote the concerto in 1925 while working on the musical *Tiptoes* (1925), didn't think it odd that the first movement, which 'represents the young, enthusiastic spirit of American life', should be both in Charleston rhythm and in sonata form. The structure of the concerto proves as durably 'organic' as that of *Porgy and Bess;* and there are affinities between the two experiences, in that the finale of the concerto recaptures the gaiety of a (Porgy-like) child, while the blue sevenths of the haunting slow movement are nostalgic for a lost Eden. One of the names Americans of the 1920s and 1930s gave to that Eden is 'Paris': as is evident in the nocturnally bluesy section of Gershwin's most mature concert work, *An American in Paris* (1928), which earned the 'artistic' accolade of performance at the International Festival of Contemporary Music.

Intrinsically Gershwin matters because he was a genius, and there aren't many of them in any society. Historically he matters because he was the first, and remains the most potent, composer to fuse the vital *instinct* of black jazz as an urban folk art with the more will-dominated *creativity* of Western art music and with the *production* of an industrial technocracy. Such an achievement is basic to our future, if we are to have one. The pity is that Gershwin died before he attained forty.

Further reading

Other works include: *Lady Be Good* (1924); *Oh Kay!* (1926); *Strike Up the Band* (1927); *Funny Face* (1927); *Girl Crazy* (1930); and *Of Thee I Sing* (1931). Other works include: *Second Rhapsody for Orchestra and Piano* (1932); *Cuban Overture* (1932). See also: Wilfrid Mellers, *Music in a New Found Land* (1964); Charles Schwartz, *The Life and Music of Gershwin* (1973); R. Greenberg, *George Gershwin* (1998); William G. Hyland, *George Gershwin* (2003).

WILFRID MELLERS

GIACOMETTI, Alberto

1901–66

Swiss sculptor and painter

Alberto Giacometti was born in Borgonovo and spent his childhood in Stampa, both near the Italian border. His father, Giovanni, was a painter, and it was from him that Alberto first learnt the art of drawing. In 1919 he enrolled at the École des Beaux Arts in Geneva, but left after three days to attend the École des Arts et Métiers instead. In 1922, having travelled for two years through most of Italy with his father, he arrived in Paris, where he attended the classes of the sculptor Antoine Bourdelle at the Académie de la Grand-Chaumière, and where he settled for the rest of his life. For a period between 1929 and 1935 he joined the Surrealists, but he was never a man to be easily identified with a particular school or group – a characteristic that in time became transformed into a legend of personal integrity. Separating from the Surrealists he concentrated for five years on the study of nature. In 1937 he abandoned painting in favour of drawing and sculpture – only to resume it again after the war, most of which he had spent back in Geneva working from memory on sculptures which grew smaller and smaller until they were barely an inch high. But he continued to sculpt, and the figures he now produced – increasingly tall, but uncompromisingly thin, and extra-ordinary in their eerily erect dignity – are the ones that have come to stand for his name. From 1949 he also began the series of sculpted groups, conceived first as separate figures, but later joined on a solid base. His international recognition was established in the 1960s, when he won the Carnegie Foundation Award (1961), the Grand Prix at the Venice Biennale (1962) and the Guggenheim International Award (1964). He died at Chur, in Switzerland, of heart disease.

The upright oblong format is present in most of Giacometti's work, both painting and sculpture. Depending on the height of the piece in question, and the distance from the viewer, the emphatic verticality could suggest either intricate intimacy, as in the stick-like figurines, or monumental sparseness, as in the later public commissions (for example, *Standing Women* in the Chase Manhattan Plaza in New York, 1960–5). The artist's choice of elongation, partly derived from

Etruscan tomb statuettes, was less the application of a specific theory, more the result of a painstaking search for truth. Giacometti's work evolves around several ambiguously related ideas: the Surrealist notion of objective chance, projection of desire, silent disruption of the continuities of space and time. In addition he perhaps inherited, from the Cubists, the idea of the confrontation of opposites, and the concept of the transparency of sculpture. But his relations to formal theories are curiously mirrored by his own stylistic idiosyncrasy: the idea of distance as part of the object, and the onlooker's active role in the composition of the piece.

Thematically his work consists of still-lifes, landscapes, portraits, animals, nudes, arms, legs, heads and abstract objects. But beyond question his central pursuit is the representation of the *presence* (not the simple likeness) of a human being; and it is this quest that leads him to explore a new ground, between the fixity of conventional figurative sculpture, and the fluidity of abstraction. And indeed Giacometti's career began with a fascination for two opposing traditions: the strictly mimetic and the magically evocative. He was not alone in his generation in this respect, but he is perhaps the only artist who successfully refused to accept a solution to the dichotomy based on a preference for either of its poles. The peculiarly tortured aspect of much of his best work is perhaps a result of this. 'Art and science,' he said, 'mean trying to understand. Failure or success play a secondary role.' Like all great artists he sought to grasp reality, but sought to grasp it in the hardest place – the face; as he wrote in a poem, *Le Rideau brun* ('Brown Curtain', 1922), 'the more one looks at it, the more it closes itself off and escapes by the steps of unknown stairways'. Typically he loved the elusive *Madonna with Angels* of Cimabue, because it came 'closest to truth'.

Early works, represented by *Torso* (1925), *The Spoon Woman* (1926) and *The Couple* (1926), were abstract 'objects' with no indi-cation of what was to come. His first con-certed attempt to free himself from that manner was the deployment of the cage to envelop an object or figure in a frame that sets it off from the real world, as in *Man* (1929) or *Suspended Ball* (1930–1). The ball, suspended by a wire in an actual cage, adds the rhythm of movement to the rhythm of forms if set in motion, thus confronting measurable time with moving form. This strategy was developed through a series of pieces (*Caught Hand*, 1932, *The Palace at 4 a.m.*, 1932–3, *The Nose*, 1947) which explore the possible effects of separation and recombination. *Caught Hand* also introduced the theme of torture, as a symbol of existence, which led to *Point to the Eye* (1932) and *Woman with the Throat Cut* (1932). At the same time Giacometti was experimenting with other forms of movement. In *Man, Woman and Child* (1931), *Circuit for a Square* (1931) and *No More Play* (1932–3) he introduced tracks on boards with small horizontal or vertical figures, inviting the viewer to alter the composition by moving the form. *Circuit*, in which a ball cannot reach the hole which lies next to its path, can be seen as a metaphor for paradise lost (Hohl). But perhaps the most obviously Surrealist sculpture is the *Disagreeable Object* (1931), a smooth worm-like form spiked at one end.

Giacometti's separation from the Surrealists cost him friends and art dealers, but it was necessary if he was to pursue the theme that engaged him for the rest of his life: the perception of an Other through the distance which is part of that Other. If the terminology echoes **Sartre**, that is no accident, for it was Sartre who became his champion and in two important essays – 'The Search for the Absolute' (1948) and 'The Paintings of Giacometti' (1951) – provided a key to the artist's 'difficulty'. Above all, in his mature work, Giacometti confronts the inaccessibility and solitude of his subjects as a psychological phenomenon; or, as Sartre observed, 'Distance, to his eyes, far from being an accident, is part of the innermost nature of the object.' This summarizes the meaning of the great sculptures – *City Square* (1948), *Three Men Walking* (1949), *The Forest*

('Composition with Seven Figures and a Head', 1950), *Figure from Venice I–IX* (1956) and *Tall Figures* (1960). Here the distance is no longer achieved by artifice, as in the 'cage' period, but emanates from the pieces themselves. Because it is a psychological emanation, it is untraversable. It is a distance which only the spoken word can cross, as Giacometti himself put it on one occasion, or, on another, a gleaming floor that cannot be trodden. His faces are characteristically pointed dead ahead, without the least trace of visible humour. The severity of the long curving jawbones, which continue to encompass generally reduced crania in a single line, is to a degree contrasted by the deliberately unpolished surfaces, which allow for a subtle movement of light if the viewer himself moves but fractionally, and which perhaps account for an unexpected tenderness.

Sartre also drew attention to Giacometti's dual existence as a painter as well as sculptor, showing that when he sculpts he confers on his statues an imaginary and fixed distance, whereas when he paints he uses the space between a figure and the frame as a true void. Giacometti himself referred to the fluidity between the two media when, apropos the *Nine Figures* (1950), he said: 'I had very much wanted to paint them last Spring' – but modelled them instead.

Further reading

See: R.J. Moulin, *Giacometti Sculptures* (1962, trans. 1964); Jean Genet, *Alberto Giacometti* (1962); P. Selz, *Alberto Giacometti* (1965); M. Leiris, *Alberto Giacometti* (trans. 1971); J. Lord, *Alberto Giacometti: Drawings* (1971); R. Hohl, *Alberto Giacometti* (1972); D. Sylvester, *Looking at Giacometti* (1994).

SLAVKA SVERAKOVA

GIDE, André-Paul-Guillaume

1869–1951

French writer, intellectual, moralist

Born into a Protestant upper-middle-class family and dominated by a puritanical mother, André Gide, always a highly strung youth, sought consolation in the pleasures of botany, music and imaginative literature. From an early age he saw himself as the product and victim of contradictory and conflicting tensions – religious, social and moral. The strictness of his religious upbringing stands in contrast to the Dionysiac fervour of his sexual emancipation in North Africa in the mid-1890s. He was then, after a brief flirtation with Catholicism in 1905 and a further religious crisis in 1915, to develop a form of liberal humanism, which itself underwent a brief Communist phase. His social and moral ideas were generally more consistent – from the modish nonconformism of his Symbolist youth, he pursued his Romantic revolt against the bourgeoisie while refusing to underwrite the Dadaists and early Surrealists. Championing homosexuality in the 1920s, he became a fellow traveller in the early 1930s, only to reassert his independence and individualism in *Return from USSR* (*Retour de l'URSS*, 1936, trans. 1937). Never the darling of the French literary establishment, he remained on the fringe until his death in 1951, four years after being awarded the Nobel Prize for Literature.

Gide's commitment to his art was absolute. His range was considerable, beginning with his rather self-conscious exploration of Symbolist themes in his early works and the lyrical fervour of *Fruits of the Earth* (*Les Nourritures terrestres*, 1897, trans. 1949) and moving to the more tightly controlled classicism of his *récits* and the burlesque humour and irony of his *soties*. He experimented with every genre – poetry, plays, prose poems, moral treaties, literary criticism, social and political journalism and, above all, novels. In addition, the long correspondences with many leading literary figures add a further dimension to his self-portrait. All of this is seen in fragmentary form in his diaries, and reconstructed in his autobiographical works.

Gide's reputation rests mainly with his three *récits, The Immoralist* (*L'Immoraliste*, 1902, trans. 1930), *Strait is the Gate* (*La Porte étroite* 1909, trans. 1924) and *La Symphonie pastorale* (1919, trans. 1931), recognized by many as models of the genre. These spare, unilateral monodies are all ironical works which dramatize extreme attitudes in a critical fashion. '*L'oeuvre d'art, c'est une idée qu'on exagère*' ('the work of art involves the exaggeration of a single idea'). Each of the heroes, Michel, Alissa, the pastor, is deliberately presented as a logical extreme. In the light of their hubris, or lyrical excess, Gide hopes to convey psychological depth and illustrate significant moral dilemmas. All these works employ the first-person narrative mode and are an idiosyncratic amalgam of melodrama, understatement, discreet irony and, in addition, the patterning and rhythm of classical tragedy.

But it is in his polyphonic mode that Gide is perhaps least appreciated – by Anglo-Saxon readers, at least, who sometimes dub his novels as cerebral, desiccated and stylized in the extreme. Indeed, Gide read long and hard in other literatures in his search for a new novel form. His wide experience of the nineteenth-century French novel – Stendhal, Balzac, **Flaubert**, Barrès, **Zola** – was complemented by his study of **Tolstoy** and **Dostoevsky**, the nineteenth-century English novel from the Brontës to Stevenson and **Conrad**, but more significantly perhaps by his new look at the eighteenth-century picaresque tradition. Gide, in association with his protégé Jacques Rivière at the *Nouvelle revue française* (founded in 1908), was a leader in the movement to revitalize the novel form. In *The Vatican Cellars* (*Les Caves du Vatican*, 1914, trans. 1925) he crossed the picaresque adventure novel and the detective novel with Molièresque farce and produced in the process a deconstruction of the Balzacian realist novel – decentralized in form. His only full-scale novel, *The Counterfeiters* (*Les Faux-monnayeurs*, 1926, trans. 1927), is even more open-ended, the amalgam of many different novel-types and the focal point of many dramas. He shows his preference for Dostoevsky over Tolstoy in what close analysis reveals to be a strange conglomerate, but which in fact, due to its technical brilliance, possesses an ease of manner and a sense of natural growth. Praised somewhat stintingly by most critics (see **E.M. Forster**, *Aspect of the novel*), this novel is a major achievement of twentieth-century fiction.

Admired by the Symbolists in the 1890s, wooed by the Catholic Claudel and the materialist Gourmont before 1914, and briefly idolized by the Dadaists, Gide became in the 1920s the public champion of homosexuality and the apostle of youth, who 'discovered' the iconoclastic *Les Caves du Vatican* and the neo-**Nietzschean** song of songs, *Les Nourritures terrestres*.

Following his interest in social problems, he associated himself in the early 1930s with the Communist Party. However, the intellectual honesty and the anti-Stalinism of his *Retour de l'URSS* had reverberations in French intellectual life up to 1939. Always on the fringe of any establishment, appalled by the demands of '*le grand nombre*' ('the many'), his heart went out to '*le petit nombre*' ('the few'), the young and the oppressed.

His contribution to intellectual life was fully acknowledged by the generation of Malraux, **Sartre** and Camus. His reappraisal of the novel complements the work of **Proust**, **Joyce** and Dos Passos and conditioned the theories of the French new novelists, Sarraute, Robbe-Grillet and Claude Simon. Steeped in European culture, seeing life as a long voyage through books, men and countries, Gide is heir to a long humanist tradition – a latter-day Montaigne, by Nietzsche out of Racine.

Further reading

Other works include: *Journal, 1899–1939* (1939), *Journal, 1939–49* (1954, both vols trans. 1953); *Souvenirs* (1954, containing the autobiography *Si le grain ne meurt*, 1926, and *Voyage au Congo*, 1927); *Thésée* (1946, 'Theseus' in *Two Legends: Oedipus and Theseus*, trans. 1950). See: K. Mann, *André Gide and the Crisis of Modern Thought* (1948); J. O'Brien, *Portrait of André Gide* (1953); G. Brée, *Gide* (1963); G.W. Ireland, *André Gide – A Study of His Creative Writings* (1970); Christopher Bettinson, *Gide: A Study* (1977); Alan Sheridan,

André Gide: A Life in the Present (2000); Roger Martin Du Gard, *Notes on André Gide* (2005).

CHRISTOPHER BETTINSON

GILBERT & GEORGE

(Gilbert PROESCH 1943– and George PASSMORE 1942–)
English artists

Gilbert (born in the Dolomites, Italy, 1943) and George (born Devon, England, 1942) were the first collaborators to take the next step and define themselves as a single artist with a single oeuvre. Art co-opting the double act of the music hall and the singular authority of the post-Renaissance artist: this seemed very strange at the time but has since been imitated, most notably by Pierre et Gilles in France. Indeed, binary creativity should come as no surprise in the computer age and has a long history in other fields. Gilbert has said 'We are not Siamese twins, we are not a couple, we are two complete individuals, and that is part of our strength.'

The two met in 1967 at St Martin's School of Art, London, where they studied Advanced Sculpture under Frank Martin and Antony Caro and were encouraged to enlarge enormously the vision of what sculpture might be. They first came to notice for their living sculptures: the Long Walk, the Short Walk, Underneath the Arches, the Lecture Sculpture, and many others. These were one of the earliest and most systematic explorations of what later came to be called performance art, which itself had emerged when the happening bifurcated into the performance and the installation, although Gilbert & George, who have always been highly vocal in their own description and who use words perhaps more than any other living artist, rejected the label 'performance art' on account of its banality. They also extended performance or pose into their daily life, dressing identically in a fixed stylization of the ultra-conventional Englishman, including photographs of themselves in most of their pictures, and living in London's East End in an eighteenth-century house which has more in common with an installation than a home.

The elements of cabaret, humour and irony which play about their early work are made more subversive and disorientating by Gilbert & George's outright rejection of such terms. But the success of the living sculptures threatened to overwhelm them in modish transience and they soon found themselves wanting to work in the harder form of the picture. The initial result of this was a series of pictures made from repeating postcards. Lighthearted and attractive, they gave no indication of the coming seriousness, of what are now called the *Dirty Words* pictures (1977). This breakthrough series, both severe and warm in black and white and red, came out of their engagement with their immigrant, working-class district. At the time the pictures were thought to be political. It would be better to describe them as visceral.

Almost from the beginning they worked with photographic images, and most of their pictures are classified as photo-pieces and are very large. They would soon arrive at an immediately identifiable form from which they have hardly deviated since: a grid of regular panels which allows the picture to be seen as it were behind black horizontal and vertical bars: classical order symbolically imposed upon romantic flux. The picture itself would be built up collage-like from black-and-white photographic images, processed and coloured. Sometimes drawn features are incorporated and occasionally constitute the entire work, as in the penis extravaganzas of 1982. The palette is chemically vivid, even more so than **Warhol's**, and the pictures often voluptuous. One might expect the grid overlay to jar, but since it is always there the viewer accepts it as integral to the art and it enhances the gorgeousness of the imagery. Vital to their content is the human male, including its bodily functions (they consider the female overused in art), and the sense of place (they are the quintessential artists of late twentieth-century London, the world's most cosmopolitan city yet always recognizably itself). Lately they have been using computer graphics as an ingredient of their compositions.

Further reading

See: *The World of Gilbert & George* (film, the Arts Council of Great Britain, 1981); *Gilbert & George: Intimate Conversations with François Jonquet* (2005).

DUNCAN FALLOWELL

GINSBERG, Allen

1926–97

US poet

Though Allen Ginsberg once claimed that he wrote 'Howl' for his 'own soul's ear and a few other golden ears', it quickly became (and remains) one of the most widely read American poems of the last century. With its publication in 1956 (in *HOWL! & Other Poems*), Ginsberg would emerge as a public spokesperson for the seemingly unspeakable: obscenity, homosexuality, despair, disease. Once an iconoclast who railed against the hypocritical mores and corrosive values of social institutions, he is now an icon, an enduring symbol of the beat generation. The poet himself was evidently little troubled by the prospect that his persona could overtake his poems, as he made a career of outrageous public appearances: repeatedly uttering the word 'fellatio' on conservative host William F. Buckley's typically staid television programme, reading William Blake on the witness stand as ostensible support for the defence of the Chicago Seven, expounding on his acid trips in *Playboy*.

Ginsberg's poetics (and his politics) sought to overturn both external censorship and internal inhibition so that 'there [would] be no distinction between what we write down and what we really know [as] we know it every day, with each other'. Writing 'what we really know' implies a commitment not only to the whole truth, but to a near-spontaneous transcription of the poet's consciousness in motion. While he evidently did revise his work, Ginsberg's stated goal was to 'scribble magic lines from [his] real mind'.

The results were mixed. Once the smoke cleared, some of these spontaneous emissions emerged more ridiculous than magical, like the leaden lines from 'Paterson' (1950): 'Reality is a question/of realizing how real/the world is already.' American poet James Dickey once famously complained that Ginsberg made it seem as if anybody could write poetry. Ginsberg evidently agreed, telling an interviewer: 'All you have to do is think of anything that comes into your head, then arrange in lines of two, three or four words each.'

But Ginsberg's admirers would see in some of the best poems – 'Howl' and 'Kaddish' (from *Kaddish & Other Poems*, 1961), in particular – poetry's renewal. At their best, some of Ginsberg's 'scribblings' were as electrifying as the rawest riffs in jazz, another highly improvisational American art. Moreover, they brought to poetry the intensity of political resistance.

More bard than scholar, Ginsberg broke from the intellectual and somewhat antiseptic preoccupations of high modernism to remind readers of poetry's communal roots. Unlike later poets like Sharon Olds who would certainly find inspiration in Ginsberg's candour, Ginsberg saw himself following in the tradition of Blake, **Whitman** and William Carlos Williams, each of whom saw individual experience as the base of civic engagement.

Ginsberg met **Jack Kerouac** and **William Burroughs**, the other seminal members of the 'Beats', while he was a student at Columbia University. Once he moved to San Francisco, Ginsberg's circle grew to include poets Robert Duncan, Gregory Corso and Gary Snyder and critic Kenneth Rexroth. As a whole, the Beats, whose name Kerouac coined from the root of 'beaten-down' and 'beatific', explored previously forbidden topics in language that was deliberately vernacular, deliberately vulgar.

The Beats drew national attention with the publication of 'Howl' and the subsequent (and ultimately unsuccessful) prosecution of publisher Lawrence Ferlinghetti for obscenity. The first of 'Howl's' three parts chronicles the anger and despair of social outcasts, most famously in its opening lines: 'I saw the best minds of my generation destroyed by/madness, starving hysterical naked,/Dragging themselves through the negro streets at dawn/looking for an angry fix.' The next two parts move from anger to love and, even, transcendence.

If 'Howl' is Ginsberg's most famous poem, 'Khaddish' is the most critically praised. The traditional Jewish prayer for the dead, the five-part 'Khaddish' explores Ginsberg's deeply conflicted feelings for his mother, Naomi. Their history was certainly tumultuous: while he was a child, Ginsberg saw his mother, who suffered from schizophrenia, slash her wrist and, another time, set fire to their house in Paterson, New Jersey. But even in his mother's madness and bodily suffering, Ginsberg saw wider – civic – significance. In the manifesto that opens the poem, he claims: 'I saw my self my own mother and my very nation trapped desolate.'

Though 'Howl' and 'Khaddish' are Ginsberg's most important poems, the 'bearded American fairy dope poet', as he called himself, proved to be a remarkably prolific author, publishing over forty collections of poetry in all.

Further reading

Other collections include: *White Shroud: Poems 1980–85* (1986); *Snapshot Poetics* (1993); and *Cosmopolitan Greetings: Poems 1986–92* (1994). Ginsberg's *Indian Journals* were published in 1970. See: Jame Kramer, *Paterfamilias: Allen Ginsberg in America* (1970); Eric Mottram, *Ginsberg in the 60s* (1972); James Campbell, *This is the Beat Generation* (2001).

JODI CRESSMAN

GLASS, Philip

1937–

American composer

Philip Glass has been a pioneering figure in the development of the mechanical repetitive music known as minimalism and brought it to a large international public through opera and film. Like his colleague Steve Reich – also a composer-performer – he built on the foundations laid by American composers such as La Monte Young and Terry Riley, and in the early days Reich and Glass played in each other's ensembles. Glass has described himself as a theatre composer, and it is in a wide range of collaborations that he has found his most characteristic expression in a new non-narrative technique.

Glass was born in Baltimore in 1937 where his father had a record shop. His own instruments were the violin and the flute and he started composing at twelve. Only three years later he went to the University of Chicago, where he studied mathematics and philosophy, and then attended the Juilliard School in New York. At this time his own music resembled that of his teachers, William Bergsma and Vincent Persichetti, but he later lost interest in all these works. Glass pays tribute to the rigorous traditional grounding he received during two years of intensive study in Paris with Nadia Boulanger. He also worked with the Indian sitar player Ravi Shankar, transcribing his music for a film, founded the Mabou Mines Theatre Company and began to write pieces in a new style with very limited resources. Fellow musicians found this perplexing so when Glass returned to New York in 1967, after travelling in North Africa and India, he realized he would have to set up as a performer himself with the Philip Glass Ensemble. He took his studies in Indian music further with the drummer Alla Rakha and, through his sound engineer Kurt Munkacsi, the ensemble began to record. The only way to do this at the time was for Glass to form his own record company, Chatham Square Productions.

Works for the ensemble from this period included the ascetic process studies *Music in Contrary Motion*, *Music in Fifths*, *Music in Similar Motion* (all 1969).

The group had its own sharply defined sound based on amplified keyboards and woodwinds sometimes with voice or a stringed instrument. At this stage most of Glass's performances were in lofts, art galleries or museums rather than concert halls and his music was played almost exclusively by his own group until the late 1970s. The performing materials were restricted to the ensemble, which Glass initially supported by taking odd jobs since he was unable to obtain foundation grants until later. Michael Riesman joined the group in 1974 and became its conductor.

In that year Glass took New York's Town Hall to present his group in *Music in Twelve Parts* (1971–4) and he recognized that this was a new kind of music 'placed outside the usual time-scale, substituting a non-narrative and extended time-scale ... where nothing "happens" in the usual sense ... the music as a "presence" freed of dramatic structure, a pure medium of sound'. However, two years later the Metropolitan Opera mounted his five-hour *Einstein on the Beach*, a collaboration with Robert Wilson. Glass found that 'theatre became the catalyst for musical invention' and the ensemble gave him 'the instrument and the opportunity to develop ideas'. So from this point onwards, impressed by the partnership between **John Cage** and the **Merce Cunningham** Dance Company, he worked largely with theatre, film and dance. Subsequent operas were commissioned by the world's leading opera houses – *Satyagraha* (1980), with a text in Sanskrit after the Bhagavad Gita and using a full orchestra rather than Glass's own ensemble; *Akhnaten* (1983); *The Making of the Representative for Planet 8* (1988) and *The Marriages between Zones Three, Four and Five* (1997), both based on Doris Lessing; and he returned to the Met in 1992 with *The Voyage* (David Henry Hwang), celebrating the 500th anniversary of Columbus' landing in the Americas.

Glass has worked with pop musicians such as Laurie Anderson, David Byrne, Paul Simon and Suzanne Vega, who provided texts for *Songs from Liquid Days* (1986), and his film scores have gained many awards. He has also gone well beyond his own ensemble in writing a quantity of concert music including symphonies and string quartets. Two of his symphonies are based on music by David Bowie and Brian Eno, and they in turn have acknowledged his influence on their work in a cross-over situation which distinguishes Glass from his earlier minimalist colleagues and has often angered critics in the classical sector. But it has not affected his position in the early twenty-first century as one of America's most successful composers.

Further reading

See: P. Glass, *Music by Philip Glass*, ed. R.T. Jones (1987); K.R. Schwarz, *Minimalists* (1996); K. Potter, *Four Musical Minimalists: La Monte Young, Terry Riley, Steve Reich, Philip Glass* (2000); R. Kostelanetz (ed.), *Writings on Glass: Essays, Interviews, Criticism* (1996).

PETER DICKINSON

GODARD, Jean-Luc

1930–

French film and video maker

Born in Paris, son of a doctor, Jean-Luc Godard was educated in Switzerland and at the Sorbonne. While still a student he developed his passion for the cinema, frequenting the Left Bank ciné-clubs, writing reviews and articles (many for the short-lived *Gazette du cinéma* which he co-founded with Eric Rohmer and Jacques Rivette) and making occasional tiny appearances in the amateur films shot by his friends. Back in Switzerland in the early 1950s he made his first two shorts, *Opération béton* (1954), a twenty-minute documentary about the building of the Grande-Dixence dam, on which he worked for a while as a labourer, and *Une femme coquette*, shot in Geneva in 1955 from a Maupassant short story: a woman decides to deceive her husband with the first man she meets in the park.

On his return to Paris, Godard's career took on a new importance as he established himself as a major film critic with articles and reviews in the magazines *Cahiers du cinéma* and *Arts* and made three further short films in which the characteristic preoccupations of his subsequent features are already apparent: *Tous les garçons s'appellent Patrick*, *Charlotte et son Jules* and *Une histoire d'eau* (all 1957–8). This intense activity was part of the necessary preparation for Godard's participation in the eruption of young French talent and originality, journalistically named the New Wave, which startled the film world at the Cannes Film Festival in 1959.

During the period 1960–7 Godard worked within the French commercial film industry and in a context of enormous international publicity to make fifteen full-length feature films of his own and to contribute episodes to seven collective works. In this series of works, ranging from the affectionate gangster film parody *À bout de souffle* (1960) to the virulent *Weekend* (1967), all the problems of language and communication (both verbal and filmic) are probed in an increasingly jagged and aggressive elliptical style. Throughout this masterly sequence of films Godard explores simultaneously his own relationship to his chosen medium of expression, the social and emotional inter-connnections of his characters among themselves and also the fundamental alienation of the individual within modern urban society. In the early films *Vivre sa vie* (1962), *Le Mépris* (1963), *Une femme mariée* (1964) and the exuberant *Pierrot le fou* (1965) – where there is always the possibility, however tenuous, of some resolution through love – the visual style is lively and full of little surprises and incidental delights. But when, in subsequent films, an analogous investigation is made into the possibilities offered by political commitment, the mood darkens, whether the ostensible subject is the predicament of the French Left (*Made in USA*, 1966), **Mao's** teachings (*La Chinoise*, 1967) or Black Power (*One Plus One*, 1968). Even in his most resolutely political films of this pre-1968 period Godard retains, however, more than a trace of romantic idealism, and political issues are still formulated in simplistic terms (as in his celebrated definition of political filmmaking as 'Walt Disney with blood'). The tone of these films remains unmistakably personal, but the despair imposes itself ever more strongly from the joyful vivacity of *Une femme est une femme* (1962) to the bleak hopelessness of *Masculin féminin* (1966).

The events of May 1968 in Paris brought a new political focus and commitment to Godard's work and, for the next four years, he made a series of films which are radical in both form and content. Paradoxically he financed most of these by using his personal renown as a key figure in the European art cinema, while simultaneously playing down his own role as a film *auteur* and eventually submerging his identity in the anonymity of the 'Dziga Vertov Collective'. During this period he had the unique distinction of making films financed and subsequently rejected by four successive national television institutions: *Le Gai Savoir* (France, 1968), *British Sounds* (Britain, 1968), *Lotte in Italia* (Italy, 1969), *Vladimir und Rosa* (West Germany, 1970). The most notable films completed and given some kind of showing at this time – though hardly at all in France – are the Czech-made *Pravda* (1969) and *Vent d'est* (1969), co-scripted with a key figure of May 1968, Daniel Cohn-Bendit.

In 1972 Godard and his prime collaborator in the Dziga Vertov Collective, Jean-Pierre Gorin, made a brief return to the commercial cinema with *Tout va bien* (1972), but during this phase of his career Godard largely disappeared from the wider public's view. To the critics it seemed he had lost interest in audiences, just as audiences had begun to lose interest in him. In reality, Godard was regrouping, exploring the potential of video as opposed to celluloid filmmaking, often in collaboration with Anne-Marie Miéville. Two major works emerged from the little-seen video material produced at Grenoble between 1973 and 1977 – *Numéro deux* and *Ici et ailleurs* (both 1975), but it was not until the appearance of *Sauve qui peut (la vie)* in 1980 that audiences were reminded of Godard's continuing activity. Yet the Godard who re-emerged during the 1980s was different from

the Godard who had gone before. About *Sauve qui peut (la vie)* – a study of prostitution – and several of the films that followed there is a melancholy and sensitivity that had been absent before, even if he could, on occasion, return to overtly political filmmaking, notably in *For Ever Mozart* (1996), an idiosyncratic but effective rumination on the atrocities that occurred in Bosnia during the break-up of the Yugoslav federation.

The triumph of Godard's later career is *Histoire(s) de cinéma*, a vastly ambitious video work begun in 1988. Lasting four hours and twenty minutes, and divided into eight parts, this undertook nothing less than a critical appraisal of the whole evolution of the cinema, including what Godard regarded as missed opportunities, contextualized within, but not wholly bound by, a parallel unfolding of twentieth-century history. Exploiting to the full a new tranche of techniques made available by its chosen medium, *Histoire(s) de cinéma* is more than anything a monument to the art of montage, in its adroit manipulation of carefully chosen sounds (snippets of music, snippets of dialogue) as well as its eclectic, multi-paced plundering of visuals. By some it has been compared to **Joyce's** *Finnegans Wake*, such is its phantasmagoric fragmenatation and range of allusion.

If nothing else, *Histoire(s) de cinéma* demonstrates Godard's passionate and lifelong commitment to the cinema in its broadest definition. It remains the case, though, that much of his later work remains overlooked, or at the least is yet to be assimilated within the recent mainstream. Partly he has been a victim of his own success. One of the most influential of the directors to come out of the 1950s and 1960s, his innovations became so widespread that his early films may appear conventional now. Some of his contemporaries, such as **Alain Resnais**, were equally radical, but whereas a film like *L'Année dernière à Marienbad* (1961) still looks avant-garde, a film as revolutionary in its time as *À bout de souffle* seems to resemble a routine made-for-television gangster film in its cutting techniques and throwaway style. Godard's productivity has also been no guarantee of consistent quality, while persistent experimentation has sometimes led him into the realms of pretension. But such films as *Une femme est une femme, Pierrot le fou* and *Weekend* retain their power to surprise and delight us.

Further reading

Other works include: *Le Petit Soldat* (1960); *Les Carabiniers* (1963); *Bande à part* (1964); *Alphaville* (1965); *Deux ou trois choses que je sais d'elle* (1966); *Lettre à Jane* (1972); *Six fois deux, Sur et sous la communication, France, tour, détour, deux enfants* (all 1975–7); *Prénom Carmen* (*First Name Carmen*, 1983); *Je vous salue Marie* (*I Salute Thee Marie/Hail Mary*, 1985); *Détective* (1985); *King Lear* (1987); *Soigne ta droite: une place sur la terre comme au ciel* (1987); *Nouvelle vague* (1990); *Allemagne année 90 neuf zéro* (*Germany Year 90 Nine Zero*, 1991); *JLG/JLG: Autoportrait de décembre* (1994); *L'Origine du XXIème siècle/Origin of the 21st Century* (2000); *Notre musique* (2004). See: Jean-Luc Godard, *Introduction à une véritable histoire du cinéma* (1977) and *Jean-Luc Godard par Jean-Luc Godard, tome 2: 1984–1998*, ed. Alain Bergala (1998). See also: Ian Cameron (ed.), *The Films of Jean-Luc Godard*; Tom Milne (ed.), *Godard on Godard* (1972); James Roy MacBean, *Film and Revolution* (1975); Kaja Silverman and Harun Farocki, *Speaking about Goddard* (1998); Michael Temple and James S. Williams (eds), *The Cinema Alone: Essays on the Work of Jean-Luc Godard 1985–2000* (2000).

ROY ARMES
(REVISED AND UPDATED BY THE EDITOR)

GOLDING, (Sir) William Gerald

1911–93

English novelist

William Golding's international reputation is based on a single novel, *Lord of the Flies*, published in 1954. Translated into thirty languages and selling over ten million copies during his lifetime, the book was avidly read by both adults and children, becoming something of a cult in the USA during the 1950s and clinching his nomination for the Nobel Prize in 1983. Such a narrow focus of popular attention is undeserved. The author's later works, while not necessarily matching the success of *Lord of the Flies*, are comparably

original in addressing specifically twentieth-century obsessions. Existentialism, for example, partially inspired *Pincher Martin* (1956) and *Free Fall* (1959), while *The Inheritors* (1955) drew on neo-**Wellsian** views of human development and species evolution.

Certain of the interests reflected in Golding's fiction were directly inherited from his father, a sternly rationalist science master at Marlborough College. Young William, on leaving the school for Oxford, began the Natural Science course but soon abandoned this for English Literature. After false starts as a poet and dramatist (he had some experience as an actor) he too became a teacher, first at Maidstone Grammar School and then at Bishop Wordsworth's School in Salisbury, outside which he settled with his wife Anne Brookfield in the Wiltshire village of Bowerchalke. During World War II Golding served in the Royal Navy, emerging from the conflict with a deeply pessimistic view of human nature and its capacity for evil.

Such fatalism underpins *Lord of the Flies*, his first published novel following several earlier rejections. Essentially an ironic reinterpretation of R.M. Ballantyne's Victorian adventure story *The Coral Island*, it outlines the development of a sinisterly adult hierarchy among a group of schoolboy survivors from a plane crash during a wartime evacuation. As the thin coating of order and discipline cracks, primitive tribal impulses begin to emerge among the children. Jack's choirboys swiftly turn into the myrmidons of a fascist dictator, against whom the moral scruples and discernment of the former elected leader Ralph, the intellectual Piggy and the prophet and sacrificial victim Simon are all unavailing.

The book's triumphant critical reception encouraged Golding to embark on further novels in the same genre, a type of modern fable heavily reliant on symbol and archetype, designed to highlight the conflicts and aspirations at the heart of all human existence. After the publication of *The Pyramid* in 1967, a tragicomic interlocking of three distinct narratives, he appeared to fall silent, having already retired from teaching with the help of continuing royalties from *Lord of the Flies*. Golding's re-emergence in 1979 with *Darkness Visible* seemed like a return to his earlier manner, but *Rites of Passage*, issued the following year, made further advances into the new territory marked out by *The Pyramid*. The story of a young man's voyage to Australia in 1815, it gained the writer a fresh public and won the 1980 Booker Prize. Not originally intended as part of a trilogy, the novel was quickly followed by its sequels *Close Quarters* and *Fire Down Below* (in 1991 the three were issued in a single volume entitled *To the Ends of the Earth*).

Golding duly received the Nobel Prize in 1983 and was subsequently knighted. Some years earlier he and his wife had moved to Cornwall, where he died of a heart attack in 1993. His literary achievement has been widely debated. Critical objections are often rooted in his manipulation of symbolism, especially in works such as *The Spire* (1964), one of his most dense and sombre fictions, based on the completion of Salisbury Cathedral's mediaeval spire. In contrast, Golding's admirers have underlined his consistent originality in choice of subject-matter and his all-embracing vision of an errant and bewildered humanity. Among the immediate post-war generation of British novelists he is surely the least parochial.

Further reading

Other works include: *Poems* (1934) and *The Paper Men* (1984). See: M. Kinkead-Weekes and I. Gregor, *William Golding* (1968); H.S. Babb, *The Novels of William Golding* (1970); A. Johnson, *Of Earth and Darkness: The Novels of William Golding* (1974); P. Crawford, *Politics and History in William Golding: The World Turned Upside Down* (2002).

JONATHAN KEATES

GORBACHEV, Mikhail Sergeevich

1931–

Russian leader

Rarely is the question of evaluating success and failure so sharp an issue as when we analyse Gorbachev's leadership. During his term in office as General Secretary of the Communist Party of the Soviet Union (CPSU) (March 1985–August 1991) the country that he led disintegrated, the political system dissolved, and the external hegemony of the country over a recognizable bloc of states evaporated. Nevertheless, the manner in which these epochal events took place and Gorbachev's commitment to a set of normative goals, above all his commitment to peaceful change, means that his rule can in fact be considered relatively successful in terms of outcomes, if not in the framework of the goals that he set himself.

Born into a peasant family in the Stavropol region of southern Russia on 2 March 1931, the young Gorbachev lived through the after-effects of **Stalin's** traumatic collectivization of the agriculture. Both his grandparents suffered from Stalinist repression in the 1930s, although his maternal grandfather went on to chair a collective farm. During World War II his village, Privolnoe, was under German occupation from August 1942 to January 1943, something that in the post-war era might well have had a negative effect on his career. In the event, Gorbachev proved to be an assiduous and talented school pupil, and at the same time a model agricultural worker, for which he was awarded the Order of Red Banner of Labour at the age of seventeen. It was this that helped propel this village boy to the Law Faculty of Moscow State University in 1950. His five years in Moscow University were to be a crucial formative influence on his intellectual development. One of his fellow students was Zdenek Mlynár, who became one of the architects of the 'Prague Spring' in 1968. Mlynár wrote the Action Programme of the Czechoslovak Communist Party that called for the transformation of the party into a genuinely accountable and democratic body at the head of a popular movement to build a humane, democratic socialism. Aspirations for a reformed communism were crushed by Soviet tanks in August 1968. Gorbachev's advanced education would later distinguish him from his peers in the top Soviet leadership.

It was while at university that Gorbachev married Raisa Maksimovna Titorenko, who was to be Gorbachev's intellectual companion – she was a notable sociologist in her own right – and mother to two daughters. The couple lived in Stavropol region from 1955 to 1978. Gorbachev swiftly moved up the career pole as a party functionary, first in the regional Komsomol (Communist League of Youth) organization, which he came to head by 1958, and then in the Communist Party organization from 1962. By 1966, at the remarkably early age of thirty-five, he was First Secretary of the Stavropol city organization of the CPSU, by 1968 the Second Secretary for the entire region, and in 1970 First Secretary of the regional party organization. With the latter post came membership of the national Central Committee in 1971. As well as advancing his career, Gorbachev became part of what are called the *shestidesyatniki*, the children of the 1960s, whose views were shaped by Nikita Khrushchev's de-Stalinization campaign launched at the Twentieth Congress of the CPSU in 1956. The thaw of the 1950s and early 1960s, however, turned to disappointment and stagnation in the later years of Leonid Brezhnev's leadership (1964–82). As head of the Stavropol region, Gorbachev experimented with ways of achieving greater worker involvement, notably through the 'link' system of granting greater autonomy to groups of workers, something he later sought to give the whole country.

In November 1978 Gorbachev was elected a Secretary of the Central Committee, and thus began his swift rise in the national leadership. As the youngest by far (he was forty-seven) amid a gerontocratic elite he was clearly a contender for top office. Granted candidate membership of the Politburo in 1979 and full membership in 1980, he was one of the nation's top figures when Brezhnev died in November 1982. Following the brief leadership of Yurii Andropov until March 1984, the Brezhnevite Konstantin Chernenko managed to claw his way to power for a brief period despite his obvious infirmities, with

Gorbachev effectively acting as second in command. Chernenko's death in March 1985 finally allowed a new generation to assume the reins of leadership.

It would be wrong to suggest that Gorbachev came to power with a clear set of policies; but he did have a certain orientation towards change to which he remained loyal. Gorbachev had become convinced that the old system could not continue in the old way, and he intended to oversee the modernization of the Soviet system. One of his first acts was the attempt to achieve economic change through a misconceived policy of acceleration (*uskorenie*). This was accompanied by an anti-alcohol campaign that deprived the country of nearly one-third of tax revenues. Soon after came the first glimmers of glasnost ('openness'), intended at first only to expose corruption and to strengthen the Soviet system, but which soon became a devastating search for the truth about Leninist and Stalinist repression. Gorbachev's own views about the past were filtered through a romantic Leninism, and his attempt to return to some purer source of the revolution before being allegedly hijacked by Stalin was doomed to end in disappointment.

By the end of 1987 democratization had come to the fore, with the gradual introduction of multi-candidate elections. Gorbachev's own views at this time were eloquently developed in his book *Perestroika: New Thinking for Our Country and the World* (1987), in which he talked of perestroika ('restructuring') as a revolution from both above and below. By this time the country was swept by a wave of civic activity in the form of what was known at the time as the 'informal' movement.

The process of change inaugurated by Gorbachev began to outrun his hopes that a humane and democratic socialism could replace the moribund system that he had inherited. The high point of Gorbachev's definition of perestroika was undoubtedly the Nineteenth Party Conference in 1988, where he outlined a programme of democratic political change and a new role for the USSR in the world. Soon after institutional and constitutional changes sidelined the Communist Party, losing its constitutionally entrenched leading role in March 1990. At that time Gorbachev was elected by the new Soviet parliament (the Congress of People's Deputies) to the new post of president of the USSR, but his failure to stand in a national ballot is often considered one of his major mistakes. Lacking a popular mandate, he was displaced by those who did. The early debates of the parliament riveted the nation, as problems were openly discussed for the first time in decades.

It was at this time that what was called the 'nationalities question' began to threaten the integrity of the country. Although Gorbachev was responsive to calls for greater autonomy by the USSR's fifteen union republics, he had no time for any talk of independence. Through an increasingly desperate attempt to negotiate a new Union Treaty Gorbachev hoped to transform what was in effect a unitary state into a genuinely confederal community of nations. These hopes were dashed by Lithuania's declaration of independence in 1990, followed by that of Georgia and other republics in 1991. In foreign affairs Gorbachev advanced the idea of 'new political thinking', based on the notion of interdependence and a new co-operative relationship with the West. In the European arena he talked of the establishment of a 'common European home', but it was not clear what form this would take. By 1989 the Eastern European countries in the Soviet bloc took Gorbachev at his word when he called for change, and in the autumn of that year one after another the communist regimes fell. Gorbachev played a constructive role in the unification of Germany, although he is much criticized for failing to guarantee in treaty form the demilitarized status of the Eastern part of the new country.

At home, resistance to his aims and his policies grew to the point that a group prepared to seize power in a coup. The specific issue was the planned signing of the new Union Treaty on 20 August 1991, but the plotters were also concerned about economic disintegration and the loss of political control. For three days in August (19–21) Gorbachev was isolated in his dacha in Foros in the Crimea, while his nemesis, Boris Yeltsin, emerged as the new national leader in Russia. Yeltsin had been popularly elected president of Russia in June 1991, and in the days following the coup the Communist Party was banned in Russia. Gorbachev's hopes for a reformed democratic socialism lay in tatters. The pressure for increased sovereignty for republics grew into demands for independence, and despite Gorbachev's attempts to save the union, in December of that year the USSR was declared defunct. Gorbachev formally resigned as president on 25 December 1991, and went on to head his Gorbachev Foundation dealing with historical and social science research.

Gorbachev's reform of the Soviet system had led to its demise. The debate over the reformability of the Soviet system continues, but Gorbachev's reforms clearly showed its evolutionary potential. Debate also continues about whether the failure of Gorbachev's aspirations was the result of structural factors inherent in the system established by **Lenin**, or whether contingent factors such as declining economic competitiveness and a hostile international environment, including retreat from Afghanistan, brought the whole system crashing down. What forever will stand as Gorbachev's achievement is his role in making possible the relatively peaceful transcendence of the communist system, the dissolution of the alliance system that had become fossilized in the conventions of the Cold War, and the passage of the USSR's fifteen republics to sovereign statehood. All of this is highly contested, with many today regretting the demise of the Soviet Union, and those at the sharp end of violence in Tbilisi and Baku in 1990 and the Baltic republics in January 1991 will not consider it peaceful. Gorbachev, however, remained remarkably consistent in his commitment to a humane democratic socialism. We now know the answer to the question about whether the Prague Spring, which shared these ideals, had come twenty years too early or perestroika twenty years too late. It was Gorbachev's tragedy that he missed the generation that may have supported his vision of a reformed communism; but it was his triumph that he remained loyal to what he saw as its values while the vision itself unravelled.

Further reading

One of the best works on Gorbachev's personal development and ideals is Archie Brown, *The Gorbachev Factor* (1996). Richard Sakwa's *Gorbachev and His Reforms, 1985–90* (1990) gives good coverage of the intellectual context of the time. Books by Jerry F. Hough, *Democratization and Revolution in the USSR, 1985–91* (1997) and Gordon M. Hahn, *Russia's Revolution from Above, 1985–2000: Reform, Transition, and Revolution in the Fall of the Soviet Communist Regime* (2002) review much of the memoir literature that has emerged since to give balanced analyses of the period. For Gorbachev's own views, see the text mentioned above, *Perestroika: New Thinking for Our Country and the World* (1987), his memoirs *Zhizn' i reformy* ('Life and Reforms', 2 vols 1995), a later book expounding his ideas, *Razmyshleniya o proshlom i budushchem*, translated as *Gorbachev: On My Country and the World* (2000). The theoretical basis of his thinking vividly emerges from Mikhail Gorbachev and Zdenek Mlynár, *Conversations with Gorbachev on Perestroika, the Prague Spring, and the Crossroads of Socialism* (2002).

RICHARD SAKWA

GORKY, Maxim (Aleksey Maximovich PESHKOV)

1868–1936
Russian writer

He was born in Nizhny Novgorod, since renamed Gorky, on the Volga; his father died when he was four and he was brought up in his mother's family. His grandfather was the owner of a small dye works, a tight-fisted, domineering man who subjected the young Gorky to frequent beatings. His grandmother was a kindly, protective influence, from whom the boy first learned a fondness for folk tales and acquired his first taste for literature. The greed and feuding which marked the relations between the grandfather and his sons, the 'uncles' of Gorky's brilliant autobiographical picture of his early life, *My Childhood (Detstvo, 1913)*, were symptoms of the financial crisis about to overtake the family and turn them into paupers. Gifted though he was with a phenomenal memory, Gorky had barely any formal schooling and when, at about eleven years of age, he was 'sent out to work' – see *My Apprenticeship (V lyudyakh, 1916)* – he had no accomplishments save a largely self-taught ability as a reader and a memory crammed full of his grandmother's stories. His young life then became an untidy saga of apprenticeships, lengthy trips on the Volga and journeyings over southern Russia and the Ukraine – the years and experiences which he later bitterly entitled *My Universities (Moi universiteti, 1922)* and formed the final part of his famous autobiographical trilogy. In the 1890s, when his wanderings were over and he took his first steps as a writer, he chose to remember his father's name, Maxim, and to proclaim the bitterness of his early years by adopting the pseudonym Gorky ('bitter'), so that his fame as a writer has become international and assured under the harsh soubriquet of 'Maxim the Bitter'.

His first story 'Makar Chudra', was published in Tbilisi in 1892. It combined realistic setting and portraiture with a romantic internal narrative and set the tone for many other similar types of tale Gorky published during the decade. The realism, though often poetic in its evocation of the natural scene, derived from his experiences during his years of footloose wandering, but the romanticism sprang both from his respect for such eccentric, freedom-loving figures as gypsies or vagabonds and his conviction that humankind needed a romantic ideal in order to escape from the squalor and indignity of capitalist society. In verses, allegories and short stories Gorky celebrated humankind's aim to be free from acquisitiveness and poverty, but his was a vision of freedom with **Nietzschean** overtones. It also proclaimed a Promethean heroism, exemplified in Danko who sacrifices his heart in order to lead his people to free-dom, or, like the hero of 'Chelkash' (1895), it proclaimed a repudiation of bourgeois stand-ards in the name of freedom. If Gorky's pic-ture of the 'barefoot' migrant workers (the *bosyaki*, as they were known) was often depressing, it also depicted in manifold ways a society undergoing the initial strain of moving from an agricultural to an industrial, urban economy.

Through the portrayal of many victims of social and economic change, of which the most remarkable instances in his stories of the 1890s were 'Konovalov', 'Former People' ('Byvshiye lyudi') and 'The Orlov Couple' ('Suprugi Orlovy'), Gorky extended his search for a positive hero from among the *bosyaki* to the dissident bourgeoisie in the hero of his first novel *Foma Gordeyev* (1899) and the talkative bourgeois intellectuals of his first play *Smug Citizens* (*Meschane*, 1902). This last work contained, for the first time in Gorky's work, the figure of a young pro-letarian hero whose defiance appeared to be based on the revolutionary political con-sciousness of his class. Though his second and most famous play *The Lower Depths* (*Na dne*, 1903) explored the disillusionment and degradation of human beings at the bottom of society who are misled by a Christ-like figure's message of comfort, his most famous novel *Mother* (*Mat'*, 1906) emphasized by contrast the revolutionary potential of the working class through achieving political consciousness and leadership. The crude didacticism of the work, modified though it was in later editions, alienated the intelligent-sia of the period and brought a decline in Gorky's popularity. Between 1906 and the First World War he lived outside Russia, mostly on Capri, devoting himself to chronicle-type studies of Russian provincial life (*The Life of Matvey Kozhemyakin*, 1911–12) and his autobiography, but also writing a minor masterpiece, *A Confession* (*Ispoved'*, 1908), an interesting short novel on the theme of 'God-building'.

During the October Revolution and the Civil War, though a supporter of the Bolsheviks, Gorky did much to help fellow-writers regardless of their political affiliations. His quarrel with **Lenin** over the question of the technical intelligentsia and poor health combined to send him into a second exile on Capri and it was there that he remained for a dozen or so years, despite his triumphant official return to Soviet Russia in 1928. The final years of his life as a writer were noteworthy for probably his best novel *The Artamonov Affair* (*Delo Artamonovykh*, 1925), two outstanding plays *Egor Bulychov and Others* (1932) and *Dostigaev and Others* (1933), and his most conspicuous failure, the unfinished chronicle novel, *The Life of Klim Samgin*. He died in mysterious circumstances in 1936.

In the Soviet Union and throughout the Communist world Gorky became known as the father of Socialist Realism. As the first Russian writer to depict the struggle of the factory proletariat, especially in his novel *Mother* and his play *Enemies* (*Vragi*, 1906), he deserves this title, but neither by origin nor by experience was he strictly speaking a member of the industrial proletariat. His strengths as a writer derived from the fresh-ness and brilliance of his visual powers, the fecundity of his characterization and the compassion that he brought to his portrayals of humanity in the lower depths of society. Long-windedness, formlessness and a lack of intellectual interest were his principal weak-nesses. The Volga and its major cities pro-vided the setting for his greatest work, and commitment to that world rather than to a specific political attitude was the mainstay of his achievement. The merchants and the rich mercantile life of the Volga, the intellectuals, mostly of bourgeois origin, who protested vainly at the mercantilism of the period – these types figured almost as prominently in Gorky's work as did the 'former people' and other victims of capitalism.

Gorky's is by and large a world divided between the grasping, Old Testament ethos of his grandfather and the compassionate New Testament idealism of his grandmother. The vision of a world transformed owes much in his work to the imagery of folk tale and legend which he first received from his grandmother. In this, as in so many other ways, the durability of his reputation has come to rest upon the autobiographical element in his writing, just as the image of the man himself, Maxim Gorky, has transcended the literary images with which he is associated. His advocacy of the transforming power of work, so appropriate to a Soviet Union in the throes of the First Five-Year Plan, turned him towards the end of his life into a Soviet establishment figure, but this statuesque, official version of his reputation has yielded to a more lasting version based on the roguish nonconformism and bitter vitality of his power as a writer.

Further reading

Other works include: *Three of Them* (1905); *Twenty-six Men and a Girl and Other Stories* (1928); *Reminiscences of Tolstoy, Chekhov and Andreyev* (1934); and *Untimely Thoughts: Essays on Revolution, Culture and the Bolsheviko* (1970). About Gorky: an early biography is among the best, A. Kaun, *Maxim Gorky and His Russia* (1932). General introductions are offered by F.M. Borras, *Maxim Gorky the Writer: An Interpretation* (1967); R. Hare, *Maxim Gorky: Romantic Realist and Conservative Revolutionary* (1962); and D. Levin, *Stormy Petrel* (1967). Some detailed analysis of his work is offered in I. Weil, *Gorky: His Literary Development and Influence on Soviet Intellectual Life* (1966). Bertram D. Wolf provides a good account of Gorky's relationship with Lenin in *The Bridge and the Abyss* (1967). More recent digests of Gorky's life and work include G. Habermann, *Maksim Gorki* (1971); Tovah Yedlin, *Maxim Gorky: A Political Biography* (1999); A. Roskin, *The Life of Maxim Gorky* (2003).

RICHARD FREEBORN

GOULD, Stephen Jay

1942–2001

Paleontologist, evolutionary theorist, popularizer of science

Gould was born in New York. He was an undergraduate student at Antioch College, and a graduate student at Columbia University, New York. He received his PhD in 1967, and the same year took up an appointment at Harvard University. He remained at Harvard for all his professional career.

Gould contributed important scientific ideas to the theory of evolution, and also was influential in a wider culture through his work as a popularizer of science. Within the scientific community, his first major publication was in 1972. He co-authored a paper with Niles Eldredge (of the American Museum of Natural History, New York), in which they argued for a theory they called 'punctuated equilibrium'. The theory is concerned with the rate at which evolution proceeds in the fossil record. Eldredge and Gould argued that paleontologists (that is, scientists who study fossils) had, since **Darwin**, tended to see evolutionary change as proceeding in many small stages, gradually and slowly. Instead, they argued that evolution proceeds in fits and starts: it proceeds rapidly when new species arise, but once a new species has evolved it tends to stay the same until it goes extinct.

The theory of punctuated equilibrium has stimulated masses of research, in which paleontologists have measured the rate of evolution within series of fossils. In many cases, evolution does proceed in a 'punctuational' mode; but examples have also been found in which fossils evolve in a more gradual manner. Many paleontologists now think that evolution can proceed in several modes. The punctuational mode is one of them, but whether it is the most important remains controversial. However things turn out, Eldredge and Gould have the credit for inspiring the field of research.

For Gould, punctuated equilibrium also mattered for its theoretical implications. Punctuated equilibrium suggested to him that the standard Darwinian mechanism for evolution – natural selection – could not account for evolution on the large scale. He published a series of radical papers from 1972 to 1982, suggesting that the importance of natural selection had been exaggerated and that other mechanisms drove major evolutionary changes, including the origin of new species and the origin of new major kinds of life (including humans and their large brains).

From the early 1980s, Gould's theoretical ideas provoked a major controversy. Evolutionary theorists picked over Gould's ideas; some were supportive, others critical. Crudely speaking, there were two schools of thought. According to one, natural selection is overwhelmingly the most important theory for understanding life. Everything else (punctuated equilibrium included) is almost trivial in comparison. For Gould and his followers, natural selection is only a minor process, and punctuated equilibrium showed it up as such. The controversy between these two schools of thought was one of the liveliest features of scientific culture between about 1985 and 2000, and beyond. Gould's last word on it was his fat book *The Structure of Evolutionary Theory* (2002).

Gould was known to the general reader through his popular writings. These appeared in many places, but particularly in a monthly column, which Gould wrote for twenty-five years, in the magazine *Natural History*. The essays range over a huge variety of topics, but often excel in the way they connect a general theoretical idea with a striking example from natural history. For instance, he wrote a famous essay on the panda's 'thumb'. All bony animals that live on land (mammals, birds, reptiles, and amphibians) have hands and feet with five digits – as humans do. This constancy suggested to Gould that something other than natural selection was at work. Some constraint, due to the way bodies develop from egg to adult, prevents all these creatures from having anything other than five digits. The panda, however, has evolved a new digit. Gould looked into the details, and found that the new digit was not built from the same bones as the five standard digits. Even in the panda, some constraint still prevented the evolution of extra conventional digits. The apparently exceptional panda's 'thumb' in a sense confirmed Gould's view that digit numbers are constrained.

Gould was a larger-than-life figure who made science exciting. He was not always fair to his opponents, and did not appeal to those who admire modesty. It is too early to say whether the alternatives that he offered to the Darwinian theory of natural selection will stand the test of time. But his essays will be a permanent monument in general culture. Moreover, biologists and paleontologists will always appreciate his inspiration. Before Gould, fossils were rarely used to test, let alone challenge, big theories about evolution. 'Paleobiology' has now come to refer to just that activity, and it is a flourishing discipline. Gould did more than anyone else to put paleobiology on the map.

Further reading

Gould's popular essays, including those in *Natural History* magazine, were collected in a series of books: *Ever Since Darwin* (1977), *The Panda's Thumb* (1980), *Hen's Teeth and Horse's Toes* (1983), *The Flamingo's Smile* (1985), *Bully for Brontosaurus* (1991), *Eight Little Piggies* (1993), *Dinosaurs in a Haystack* (1996), *Leonardo's Mountain of Clams and the Diet of Worms* (1998), *The Lying Stones of Marrakech* (2000) and *I Have Landed* (2002). Other important books by Gould include: *Ontogeny and Phylogeny* (1977), which is about the relation between developmental change within an organism and evolutionary change over longer time periods, and *The Mismeasure of Man* (1981), which is about (the abuse of) measurements of human intelligence.

MARK RIDLEY

GRAHAM, Martha
1894–1991
American dancer/choreographer

Immensely influential as a dancer, choreographer and teacher, Martha Graham studied with two of the major innovators in American modern dance, Ruth St Denis (1879–1968) and Ted Shawn (1891–1972) from 1916 to 1923. By 1920 she was attracting critical attention for her intensely emotional performance in Shawn's *Xotchil* where she played an Aztec woman who is the victim of a sexual assault.

Such intensity of emotion was to become a hallmark of her work after she left Denishawn in 1923, first to work in the Greenwich Village Follies (1923–26) and then with her own company, with whom she gave her first performance in 1926. Initially Graham's work owed much to Denishawn in its exoticism and orientalism, but she gradually stripped away these aspects as she sought to find a starker way of working.

St Denis and Shawn, like other dance pioneers, such as Isadora Duncan (1877–1927) and Rudolf von Laban (1879–1958), were developing dance as an art form in opposition to ballet. But Graham felt that Duncan and St Denis were still too concerned with lyricism and flow and, like classical ballet, were failing to find a form for extreme human passions. Graham chose to work with angularity and disjunctive movement and rhythms in order to be able to present people, usually women, in situations of emotional extremity.

In *Lamentation* (1931), Graham sat on a bench dressed in a long tube of material as a second skin and explored the limits of her movement. Rather than attempting to tell a story of a grieving person, she explored the boundaries of grief as movements within this skin. Graham recounts how a woman who had been unable to cry for the loss of her son was moved to tears by the first performance.

The transmission of emotion from stage to audience was important for Graham and she looked to develop ways of increasing the emotional intensity of her dancers' bodies. A fundamental aspect of Graham's approach was the use of a dynamic of contraction and release centred on the pelvis. The dancers' ability to generate an appropriate level of intensity was important if the dance was to be the primary art and not be overwhelmed by music or reduced to an interpretative role.

Louis Horst (1884–1964) encouraged her to work with contemporary composers rather than drawing on a more traditional repertoire. Horst himself composed the music for *Frontier* (1935), a solo evoking the experience

of women pioneers, which also marked Graham's first collaboration with the sculptor Isamu Noguchi (1904–88).

The American theme in *Frontier* is also to be found in works such as *Primitive Mysteries* (1931) and *Appalachian Spring* (1944). The latter, with music by **Aaron Copland** (1900–90), and another Noguchi set, is considered one of her strongest works.

There is also a powerful strand of Greek mythology in Graham's work to be found in such pieces as *Cave of the Heart* (1946), *Night Journey* (1947) and *Clytemnestra* (1958). Her investigations, however, always centre on the woman's experience.

Graham continued to dance until 1970 and to choreograph and teach for the rest of her life. There is some debate as to whether or not she created any work of significance after the early 1950s, but her legacy is immense and many key figures in American dance worked or trained with her, including: **Merce Cunningham**; Erick Hawkins (1909–94); Paul Taylor (1930–); Anna Sokolow (1910–2000) and Twyla Tharp (1941–).

Further reading

See: Martha Graham, *Blood Memory: An Autobiography* (1992). See also: Barbara Morgan, *Martha Graham: Sixteen Dances in Photographs* (1980); Dorothy Bird and Joyce Greenberg, *Bird's Eye View: Dancing with Martha Graham and on Broadway* (1997); Russell Freedman, *Martha Graham: A Dancer's Life* (1997); Alice Helpern, *Martha Graham* (1999); Marian Horosko, *Martha Graham: The Evolution of Her Dance Theory and Training* (2002).

FRANC CHAMBERLAIN

GRASS, Günter Wilhelm

1927–

German writer

Günter Grass advanced from the small, but influential, German literary scene around the Group '47 to international recognition with Ralph Manheim's translation into English in 1961 of *The Tin Drum* (*Die Blechtrommel*,

1959), receiving both extravagant praise and expressions of disgust. Most amazing about this success was that most reviewers were able to unite on very little about his novel other than that it was dazzling though not yet quite understandable. Serious critics were still not sure that obscenity, vulgarity and, simply, childishness had a place in serious literature. However, there was no denying that the publication of his first novel was both a literary and a historical event, for Grass was of the generation of the Hitler Youth. In 1945 he was a teenage prisoner of war, later a black marketeer, a stone-cutter chiselling tombstones and a jazz timpanist on snare and washboard. At the end of the otherwise quiet 1950s, his voice seemed loud and disturbingly alone in Germany, making 'wicked' insinuations about the character and continuity of his native country's recent history.

That Grass was born on 16 October 1927 in Danzig (now Gdansk, Poland) is more than biographical incident; often mischievous autobiography is a central element. When he wrote about that era and area he fulfilled the highest critical expectations: that is to say, when his novels moved to post-war West Germany his genius ebbed. An admirer of **James Joyce** and **Marcel Proust**, he likewise rose above sentimentality in feeling exiled from place and time. His characters in the 'Danzig trilogy', *The Tin Drum, Cat and Mouse* (*Katz und Maus*, 1961, trans. 1963) and *Dog Years* (*Hundejahre*, 1963, trans. 1965), were the little people, the lower middle class who filled the ranks of **Hitler's** following. Capably reproducing their dialects, Grass made his picaroons mouth the 'Great Ideas' of that time with ignoble unpretentiousness.

Grass's father was a grocer in the lower-class Danzig suburb of Langfuhr, his mother a Kaschubian, an exotic tribe that filters into his writings and recipes. Grass never finished school, a fact, he remembers, 'that kept me from getting a job as a night-time radio programme director and from putting my writings on a shelf somewhere, to gather dust'.

After serving in the armoured infantry, he worked as a farm labourer and in a potash mine. He studied painting and sculpture at the Art Academies in Düsseldorf and Berlin, had some minor glory at exhibitions and he still designs the dust-jackets for his books. He met his wife, a ballet dancer, while hitch-hiking through Switzerland. They moved to Paris in 1956 where he finished writing *The Tin Drum*.

Grass returned to Berlin (where he still lives with his second wife). He has had to fend off innumerable attempts by right-wing groups to have his books banned for their earthiness and grotesque caricatures of Germans. The Bremen Senate refused him the city's literature prize (already awarded to him by the Art Committee) because they felt his book was a disgrace – specifically, they took offence at the blunt descriptions of sex. In 1960 he received the Berlin Critics' Prize. For a while he worked as consultant and speechwriter for Willy Brandt's mayoral campaign. Later, he would drive up and down Germany in a Volkswagen bus making speeches for the Social Democrats. A French panel in 1962 selected *The Tin Drum* as the best foreign language book of the year.

The hero of Grass's picaresque first novel begins by saying: 'Granted: I am an inmate of a mental hospital.' He relates the story of his decision to stop growing at the age of three. He remains a three-foot dwarf until 1945, when he grows another eleven inches but is then cursed with a hunch-back. Often, Oscar Matzerath thinks he is Jesus of Nazareth (the two names rhyme in German). He is a little tyrant, always able to have his way because he has the rare talent of being able to shatter glass with a stupendously shrill voice. Oscar always has his tin drum at his side with which he can conjure up spirits and even throw political rallies into confusion by drumming a different beat. At one level, this is Oscar the resistance fighter and, at another level, it is an allusion to the epithet given to Hitler, the drummer (in the German sense of rabble-rouser). During the war, Oscar is able to combine his two extraordinary talents and joins a troupe of midgets, part of a propaganda company entertaining the troops at the front. His size evokes pity. After the war, neither the Soviets nor the Americans even think of holding little Oscar responsible for anything that has happened.

Grass has a peasant's instinct for the tangible, earthy image and craftsman's sense of conservative style. Oscar and Danzig are both a microcosm and a macrocosm of Germany and Central Europe. The novel is packed with historical allusions, e.g. Germans refusing to grow up to the responsibilities of democracy in the Weimar Republic or not bearing their guilt after the Holocaust. With seeming ease Grass parodies German propaganda, philosophy and literature, exposing the penchant for inscrutable abstractions. Oscar hangs his drum around a statue of Jesus, begging Him for a little miracle in these hard times under Hitler. But Jesus remains still. The implication is that the churches never played a significant tattoo of protest when they were called upon to do so.

In *Local Anaesthetic* (*Örtlich betäubt*, 1969, trans. 1970) a teacher in a dentist's chair tries to decide what to do about one of his brightest pupils. The young man is plotting a public immolation of his pet dachshund to protest against the use of napalm in Vietnam. 'But why a dog?' his teacher asks. 'Because Berliners love dogs more than anything else.'

In *The Flounder* (*Der Butt*, trans. 1978) the reader is carried through Baltic culinary and sexual history, exploring the themes of male/female domination, as a mythical omniscient fish is placed on trial before a feminist tribunal.

Other novels have followed, notably *Ein Weites Feld* ('A Broad Field', 1995), a wide-angled take on German reunification, to which Grass had long been opposed. His later books, however, increasingly concerned with the minutiae of post-reunification German politics, have largely failed to entice the international readership Grass gained with his early *Danzig* trilogy, though that did not prevent his being awarded the Nobel Prize for Literature in 1999.

In Germany itself Grass, once regarded as a literary gadfly, has slowly but surely become a cultural institution. His favoured audience – the young non-orthodox left – have come to see him as a reformer not always in touch with their latest aspirations. In 1965 he was awarded the Federal Republic's most prestigious literary accolade, the Georg Büchner Prize. A plaster bust of him can be found in the Regensburg Memorial Temple, Valhalla. He has been elected to the German Academy of Arts (as well as to the American Academy of Arts and Sciences), and from 1983 to 1988 he was President of the Berlin Academy of Arts.

Grass himself is aware of his image as a 'committed writer' and as the 'conscience of the nation', descriptions which he has reformulated as a 'literary court jester' – a creature whose powers must serve such many-sided interests (political, aesthetic, personal) that the contradictions in those roles must deflect and limit effectiveness. If he is sceptical about the political force of one individual's attraction, he is hopeful about the influence of art and artists as such: 'Something we must get through our heads is this,' he has written: 'a poem knows no compromise, but men live by compromise. The individual who can stand up under this contradiction and act is a fool and will change the world.'

Further reading

Other novels: *From the Diary of a Snail* (*Aus dem Tagebuch einer Schnecke*, 1972, trans. 1973); *The Meeting at Telgte* (*Das Treffen in Telgte*, 1979, trans. 1981); *The Rats* (*Die Ratten*, 1987, trans. 1987); *The Call of the Toad* (*Unkenrufe*, 1992, trans. 1992). Plays include *The Wicked Cooks* (*Die bösen Köche*, 1957, trans. 1967) and *The Plebeians Rehearse the Uprising* (*Die Plebejer proben den Aufstand*, 1965, trans. 1966). Poetry: *Selected Poems* (trans. 1966); *New Poems* (trans. 1968). See: W. Gordon Cunliffe, *Günter Grass* (1969); John Reddick, *The Danzig Trilogy of Günter Grass* (1974); K. Miles, *Günter Grass* (1975); Richard H. Lawson, *Günter Grass* (1985); Julian Preece, *The Life and Work of Günter Grass* (2001).

FRANK STEELE
(REVISED AND UPDATED BY THE EDITOR)

GREENE, Graham

1904–91

English novelist

After an education at Berkhamstead School (where his father was headmaster) and Balliol College, Oxford, where he read history, Graham Greene was for a time a sub-editor on *The Times* and film critic for the *Spectator*. During World War II he was involved in intelligence work in West Africa. In the autobiography of his early years, *A Sort of Life* (1971), Greene comments on the affinities between the spy's trade and the writer's. An insight into this author's temperament can be found in the same book, where he describes how he played Russian roulette as an antidote to boredom. He continues,

> It was the fear of boredom which took me to Tabasco during the religious persecution, to a léproserie in the Congo, to the Kikuyu reserve during the Mau-Mau insurrection, to the emergency in Malaya and to the French war in Vietnam.

Greene was unusual among the English novelists of his time in both the range of his settings and his political sense, the two drawing together in the list above. But the key component of his work is its religious dimension (Greene himself was received into the Catholic Church in his twenties). There were and are other English Catholic novelists, like **Evelyn Waugh** and David Lodge, but none has made such capital out of spiritual doubt and despair. Often the religious consciousness serves only to heighten the certainty of damnation. Indeed the landscape – 'Greeneland' – of his books can be hellish. One of the characters in the lurid *Brighton Rock* (1938) misquotes slightly from Marlowe's Dr Faustus, 'Why, this is Hell, nor are we out of it.' It was a claim that Greene seemed determined, sometimes wilfully, to substantiate.

The squalid locales, such as Haiti in *The Comedians* (1966) or the Latin American states in *The Power and the Glory* (1940) and *The Honorary Consul* (1973), are matched by the frayed despotisms that rule over them. The two latter novels, their publications separated by more than thirty years, both feature priests who have lapsed from the church, one into a literal fatherhood, the other into revolutionary action. The erratic courses they trace while trying to escape the demands of their creeds are presented as preferable to the arid piety enjoined by a rich and reactionary church. Greene's 'damned' heroes are closer to salvation because of their doubt, self-abasement and unorthodoxy, certainly closer than the bishops who dine with the generals.

Greene provided the category 'entertainments' for some of his books, and so differentiated them from the more serious work. The distinction was a matter of labelling rather than anything else, but there is no doubt that in the later stages of his career Greene perfected a sardonic, urbane style and a lightness of touch which were not so evident in the earlier novels. As examples, see the anecdotal *Travels with My Aunt* (1969), the parodic spy story *Our Man in Havana* (1958) or the short stories in the collection *May We Borrow Your Husband?* (1967).

Throughout his writing life Greene's interest centred 'on the dangerous edge of things', a phrase from **Robert Browning** that he chose as 'an epigraph for all the novels I have written'. From this came his concern with spies, murderers, men fallen from grace. For all its topicality – and occasional prescience, as in *The Quiet American* (1955), which dealt with American meddling in Vietnam a decade before the war – Greene's oeuvre was consistent in its interests and anxieties. In later years his popular reputation grew to a degree unusual for a serious novelist, although he sometimes seemed to be working the same ground with a conscious self-parody. His last novel of real significance, *The Human Factor* (1978), was set in the town of his childhood and dealt with the ambiguities of loyalty, a constant of his work, as for example in the novella and screenplay *The Third Man* (1950).

Further reading

Other works include: *Stamboul Train* (1932); *The Heart of the Matter* (1948); *The End of the Affair* (1951); *A Burnt-out Case* (1961). Interest in Greene in the years since his death has grown rather than diminished and his critical status remains high. In addition to memoirs such as Shirley Hazzard's *Greene on Capri* (2000), there have been several biographies, notably the exhaustive life by Norman Sherry (*The Life of Graham Greene*, 3 vols, 1989, 1994, 2004). See also Michael Shelden, *Graham Greene: The Man Within* (1994), offering a more critical account of the man and his work.

PHILIP GOODEN

GREER, Germaine

1939–

Australian writer, journalist and feminist

The eldest of three children of a conservative, middle-class Melbourne family, Germaine Greer had an intensely unhappy childhood marked by her mother's persistent violence towards her and her father's frequent absence, as chronicled in her 1989 book *Daddy, We Hardly Knew You*. After attending the Star of the Sea Convent, Melbourne, she went to the University of Melbourne, graduating in 1959 in English and French. A year later she started graduate work at the University of Sydney, obtained an MA in English and continued work in that department as a senior tutor. In 1964 a Commonwealth Scholarship to Newnham College, Cambridge, offered the opportunity to leave Australia. A successful PhD thesis on Shakespeare's early comedies led to her appointment as a lecturer in English at the University of Warwick, specializing in Elizabethan and Jacobean drama – a position she held intermittently between 1967 and 1973. In 1979 she was appointed Director of the Center of the Study of Women's Literature at Tulsa University (Oklahoma). Between 1989 and 1996 she returned to Newnham College as a special fellow, but left in controversial circumstances after being accused by fellow feminists of exposing Dr Rachel Padman as a transsexual.

During the late 1960s Greer became actively involved with the London 'underground' scene, writing for papers like *It* and *Oz* and co-founding *Suck*, a radical pornographic paper published from Amsterdam, as well as contributing to more conservative weeklies like the *Spectator* and the *Listener*. The combination of her dazzling appearance, erudition and fondness for sharp repartee made her an obvious choice for mass media, as a TV personality, broadcaster and popular journalist.

Greer's relatively late entry into the feminist arena in 1970 arose from a suggestion by her agent that she write a book on the failure of women's emancipation. Although Greer was associated with radical activity, *The Female Eunuch* (1970) is not in the political tradition of English feminism or in keeping with its emphases on collective action and non-hierarchical structures. More aligned with American feminism, *The Female Eunuch*'s highly autobiographical, anarchic nature, wit, pace and apparent controversiality made it attractive and accessible to both women and men – it sold by the million and was translated into twelve languages.

Greer's central thesis is that society symbolically castrates women, perpetuating their status as consummately inferior beings, and thus maintains a state of oppression which enslaves men as well as women. An exercise in individual 'consciousness-raising', Greer follows the dictum of the personal as political, with liberty and communism being possible through individual intervention, without revolutionary strategy.

The book divides into sections, 'Body' and 'Soul' examining how the stereotype of the 'Eternal Feminine Woman' has been created. Greer argues that the negation of the female libido – sexual and life-giving energy – is the product of conditioning. Women are conditioned by the basic assumptions male-orientated society makes about the female body, mind and sexuality and the way these are reinforced – by rearing and status in the nuclear family, education, the under-valuation of women's work and the pressures of capitalist consumer society. On 'Love', Greer considers that love is essentially narcissistic (self-esteeming), and that the castration of women has been carried out in terms of a masculine–feminine polarity, in which women have been systematically deprived of their narcissism and men have usurped their power and energy, thus reducing all heterosexual contact to a sadomasochistic pattern. What passes for love in our society are perverted forms of mutual dependence, reinforced by 'Altruism', 'Egotism' and 'Obsession' and upheld by 'Romance', 'The Middle Class Myth of Love and Marriage' and the 'Family', each distortion or fantasy being treated separately. Using examples from history, literature and popular culture, Greer traces how society arrived at these present forms of sanctified oppression. Criticizing the nuclear family and the institution of marriage, Greer views the isolated mother–child relationship as the model for exploitative, possessive adult relationships, suggesting alternatively a structure similar to the preindustrial extended family. Examining male–female antagonism in the section on 'Hate', Greer regards their polarized positions as creating circular systems of oppression. She argues that female conformity to stereotyping is the prime motivator for female self-loathing as well as for men's hatred towards them. Equally men's violence, both physical and psychological, to women is counteracted by women's psychological oppression of men, to which Greer sees parallels in some aspects of the Women's Liberation Movement.

Greer's anarchic position on feminism and her cultivated media persona made her both identified with and alienated from the women's movement. Although none of her writings since *The Female Eunuch* has attracted similar sales, Greer has continued to pursue her individualistic polemics with courage and outspokenness while perpetuating a colourful, at times definably bohemian, lifestyle. In *The Obstacle Race* (1979) she highlighted the usually adverse fortunes of women painters and their work – a historical and sociological survey from the Middle Ages to the twentieth century. *Sexual Destiny: The Politics of Human Fertility* (1984) offered a critique of specifically Western sexual values and the enshrining of the so-called 'nuclear' family as a normative cultural and social goal. Opting to favour the alternative values of 'developing' countries, Greer caused controversy when she equated female circumcision with breast enlargement. In *The Change: Women, Ageing and the Menopause* (1991) she attacked the practice of hormone replacement therapy among older women, arguing that HRT is both a means of satisfying male expectations and an affront to natural processes.

Never pretending that men and women are or can be the same, Greer has consistently sought space for a radically revised understanding of what a woman is and can become. *The Female Misogynist* and *The Whole Woman* (both 1999) showed the pitfalls of what may happen when women endeavour to challenge men on the latter's terms. For her pains, in April 2000 Greer was briefly held hostage in her own home by a feminist extremist, Karen Burke. As provocatively, and returning to art history, in *The Beautiful Boy* (2003) Greer advocated aesthetic abandonment in the pursuit of the ideal young masculine form. But if in part her intention here was to satirize conventional age patterns between heterosexual lovers, critics taunted that she had merely replaced one set of pin-ups with another.

Always robust in her delivery, Germaine Greer has never been shy to simultaneously exploit and confront the media. In 2000, to the delight of the press, she participated in the UK 'reality TV' show *Celebrity Big Brother*, only to quit after five days. Accusing the programme's producers of being manipulative and bullying, Greer herself was accused of having been designedly naïve. For some, she is a principal egotist *de ses jours*; for others a brilliant example of what may be achieved by feminine forthrightness.

Further reading

Other writings include: *Shakespeare* (1986); *The Madwoman's Underclothes: Essays and Occasional Writings* (1986); *Libraries* (2003); *Whitefella Jump Up: The Shortest Way to Nationhood* (2004). See: Christine Wallace, *Germaine Greer: Untamed Shrew* (1997).

MONICA PETZAL
(REVISED AND UPDATED BY THE EDITOR)

GRIFFITH, David Wark

1875–1948

US film director

When D.W. Griffith joined the Biograph film company in 1908 the narrative fiction film was essentially 'theatrical' in two ways. First, the plots of most films were lifted from stage melodramas. Second, in terms of form, the action was filmed with a single static camera, placed in a centre orchestra position, with each shot corresponding to a complete scene. It is generally accepted that between 1908 and 1913, in the (approximately) 450 one- and two-reel shorts he directed for Biograph, Griffith defined the elements which have, ever since, constituted the 'syntax' of narrative cinema, and which broke the formal theatrical tie. The Griffith films of this period contain close-ups, longshots, fade-outs, iris shots, soft-focus, back lighting, moving camera and, perhaps most important, rapid cutting and parallel montage. While he was definitely not the first to use many of these devices (despite his claims to the contrary) he was certainly the single figure most responsible for developing their usage in terms of dramatic and psychological effect. However, it is also significant, as regards Griffith's later career, that the plots and characters of these films remained almost entirely rooted in the conventions of the nineteenth-century stage melodrama.

Griffith wanted to make longer, more spectacular pictures to rival contemporary Italian productions and, after overspending problems on the four-reel biblical epic *Judith of Bethulia* (1913), he left Biograph. Under conditions of greater independence he made *The Birth of a Nation* (1915) and *Intolerance* (1916), the two films which, in conventional cinema history, massively overshadow in importance any other works in his filmography. The former, a Civil War drama, is, in its blending of the personal and the epic, the summation thus far of Griffith's art of narrative construction, and effectively established him as the cinema's first 'director as artist'. It is also a profoundly reactionary work, a racist celebration of the Ku Klux Klan, and a vision of the Old South as a model society (Griffith was born and raised in Kentucky, the son of a Confederate officer). *Intolerance* interweaves four narratives (stories set in the present, Judaea at the time of Christ, sixteenth-century France and ancient Babylon) in 'A Drama of Comparisons', supposedly illustrating the 'theme' of intolerance through the ages. Parallel montage is here developed to link events occurring within disparate narratives. The massive spectacle of the Babylonian sets is still impressive, as are the fine female performances, but the central idea justifies **Eisenstein's** claim that Griffith's 'tender-hearted film morals go no higher than a level of Christian accusation of human injustice'.

Despite its later enormous critical reputation and significance, *Intolerance* was a financial disaster. Griffith's subsequent work, up to the mid-1920s, can be characterized as melodrama and romance on a smaller and simpler scale. Relationships may be set against a larger historical background – the First World War in *Hearts of the World* (1918), the French Revolution in *Orphans of the Storm* (1921), the War of Independence in *America* (1924) – but there is no sense of the latter interest swamping the former. Events and numbers of characters are pared down in rural dramas like *True Heart Susie* (1919) and *Way Down East* (1920), and in *Broken Blossoms* (1919), set in a foggy, atmospheric re-creation of London. The results, despite occasional lapses into bathos and unsubtle humour, seem more impressive now than the 'monumental' qualities of the epics.

Several of the above titles were produced by United Artists, founded in 1919 by Mary

Pickford, Douglas Fairbanks, **Chaplin** and Griffith, with a view to producing and distributing 'quality' product, but Griffith's career from approximately 1925 onwards is basically a tale of alienation from the Hollywood system and its values. He directed eight movies between 1925 and 1931, but reassessment has so far rescued from critical oblivion only *Sally of the Sawdust* (1925, with W.C. Fields), and his two sound films, *Abraham Lincoln* (1930) and *The Struggle* (1931). The latter title is a particularly powerful study of a descent into alcoholism. Otherwise Griffith's essentially Victorian sensibility seems hopelessly at odds with the kind of Jazz Age material he was forced to deal with, particularly at Paramount.

However, rather ironically, recent critical interest has centred precisely on aspects of this 'Victorianism'. His cultivation of the 'childwoman' image, with actresses such as Lillian Gish, has obvious historical importance *vis-à-vis* Hollywood's investment in, and cultivation of, female stereotypes. And, most important, Griffith's work can be seen as the vital link between the nineteenth-century roots of melodrama and the absorption and development of that mode throughout the whole history of the American cinema.

Further reading

See: Paul O'Dell, *Griffith and the Rise of Hollywood* (1970); Robert M. Henderson, *D.W. Griffith – His Life and Work* (1972); Joyce Jessonowski, *Thinking in Pictures: Dramatic Structure in D.W. Griffith's Biograph Films* (1987); Tom Gunning, *D.W. Griffith and the Origins of American Narrative Film* (1990).

STEVE JENKINS

GROPIUS, Walter

1883–1969

German architect

Alongside **Frank Lloyd Wright**, **Le Corbusier** and **Mies van der Rohe**, Walter Gropius is one of the great 'Modern' architects. He helped to evolve an architectural style for the twentieth century which, after rejecting nineteenth-century historicism, derived its inspiration from the contemporary world of mechanization and mass-production. This pursuit of a new aesthetic idiom, combined with a burning interest in a new form of visual education which sees the arts as a totality headed by architecture, characterizes Gropius's contribution to the twentieth-century environment. In particular he is remembered as the prime mover of the Bauhaus.

Born in Germany in 1883, Gropius's early architectural theories reflect the ethical and aesthetic goals of **William Morris** and the English Arts and Crafts Movement – ideas which were transported to Germany by Herman Muthesius and expressed in his book *The English House* published in Germany in 1906. After studying architecture at the universities of Berlin and Munich, Gropius worked as Chief Assistant to Professor Peter Behrens in his Berlin architectural practice from 1908 to 1910. These years coincided with the early existence of the Deutscher Werkbund – an institution set up to encourage links between art and industry and to replace nineteenth-century ideas about standardization and anonymity. Behrens's work for the A.E.G. company reflected totally these new concerns and undoubtedly influenced Gropius in his search for a new architectural language. The traditional brick walls and pitched roofs of his designs for housing for farm workers of 1906 are soon replaced, in his famous Fagus Shoe-Last Factory of 1911 (built in collaboration with Adolf Meyer), by a flat roof, and a steel-frame structure supporting large panes of glass. This was the first true use of a curtain wall; through the use of the frame construction, the wall became simply a screen stretched between the upright columns. The visual effect is one of transparency and weightlessness bestowing a new significance to the built structure. The Werkbund Exhibition Model Factory, built in Cologne in 1914, displays the same concerns and contributes the first rounded glass wall surrounding a circular staircase to the growing architectural syntax of the International Modern Movement.

On his return from the Western Front in the First World War, and following a brief involvement with a German Expressionist group in Berlin in 1918–19, Gropius was summoned, at the urging of Van der Velde, to Weimar to become director of a new art school called the 'Staatliches Bauhaus Weimar' which was formed from two existing institutions – the School of Applied Art and the Academy of Art. It was during this period, until his resignation from the Bauhaus and his resumption of private practice in Berlin in 1928, that Gropius consolidated his theories of architecture and of art education and designed one of his most important buildings – the Bauhaus at Dessau.

In 1919 Gropius wrote a Manifesto for the Bauhaus which was accompanied by a woodcut by the German painter Lionel Feininger – one of the several expressionist artists (who also numbered **Paul Klee** and **Wassily Kandinsky**) to be employed by Gropius at the Weimar Bauhaus. In this piece of polemical writing he set out his ideas about architecture being the queen of the arts and about the necessity of all designs for mass production being based in the crafts. These ideas dictated the structure of art education at the Bauhaus. This consisted of a foundation course which encouraged experimentation in basic form, colour and composition, followed by time spent in a materials workshop – wood, metal, etc. – in which results learnt from the earlier course could be applied to the design of three-dimensional objects which were seen as prototypes for mass production. Well-known names among the staff and students at the Bauhaus included Moholy-Nagy, Mies van der Rohe, Josef Albers and Marcel Breuer.

Gropius never succeeded in establishing an architectural school at the Bauhaus during his reign – this was left to his successor, Hannes Meyer. The Bauhaus building which was constructed in Dessau in 1925 is the high point of Gropius's early architectural career. Built on a reinforced concrete frame, it is a simple, flat-roofed building housing both work and residential facilities for the students and is characterized internally by an extreme flexibility. Other designs by Gropius during the Bauhaus period include the Sommerfeld Residence of 1921, the Chicago Tribune Building of 1922, the Municipal Theatre of 1922, the Törten development of 1926–8, the prefabricated house for the Werkbund Housing Exhibition of 1927, the Total Theatre of 1927 and the Megastructure of 1928. All contribute unique features to early twentieth-century architecture. In 1930 Gropius designed a car called the Adler Cabriolet.

During the years leading up to the Second World War and the expansion of Nazism in Germany, Gropius came first to England, working in partnership with Maxwell Fry (1934–7), and then in 1937 went to the USA to become Professor of Architecture at Harvard University. This marks the beginning of the final stage of his career, during which time he worked for a while with Marcel Breuer and with the 'Architects' Collaborative' which he formed in Massachusetts in 1945 and which was responsible for the Harvard Graduate Center. He continued to design right through the period, concentrating on private residences and academic centres. Some of his larger projects include the Pan Am Building in New York (1958–63), the US Embassy in Athens and the Gropiusstadt in Germany (1959–71). The aesthetic idiom for all these buildings is either a reworking of his early forms or an extension of them into high-rise structures which combine all the technical and aesthetic discoveries of the 1920s. Above all Gropius's work is characterized by a strong consistency which has had an enormous influence upon the twentieth-century architectural environment.

Further reading

Other works include: *The New Architecture and the Bauhaus* (trans. 1936) and *Scope of Total Architecture* (trans. 1956). See also: Sigfried Giedion, *Walter Gropius, Work and Teamwork* (1954); James Marston Fitch, *Walter Gropius* (1960); Hans M. Wingler, *Bauhaus – Weimar – Dessau – Berlin*

(1969); Wilfred Nerdinger (ed.), *The Walter Gropius Archive* (1990); Reginald Isaacs, *Gropius: An Illustrated Biography of the Creator of the Bauhaus* (1991).

PENNY SPARKE

GUEVARA, Che (Ernesto GUEVARA DE LA SERNA)

1928–67

Argentine revolutionary

Che Guevara became the archetype of a modern revolutionary hero. His image still adorns T-shirts and posters; his death provoked two films shown simultaneously around the world. Yet his political philosophy is as little known as his face and beret are Familiar.

Guevara was an Argentine, born to a middle-class radical family. He completed a medical course at Buenos Aires University, interspersing his studies with travels around the continent. His very severe asthma put few constraints on his mobility; he travelled under all conditions, taking a series of jobs from mine guard to bookseller.

Growing up in an Argentina dominated by Peronism, there was no political channel for his obvious discontent. He was uneasy with Peron's demagoguery and there was in Argentina no mass socialist alternative. Perhaps his stay in Guatemala was a more definitive experience. Having seen Bolivia in the wake of its 1952 Revolution, Guevara was in Guatemala when the radical democratic regime of Jacobo Arbenz was overthrown by force of arms – arms supplied directly by John Foster Dulles's US State Department. That experience reinforced Guevara's conviction that, faced with a well-armed adversary supported by imperialism, revolutionaries must be prepared for armed struggle.

From Guatemala he went to Mexico, where his wife Hilda Gadea introduced him to the Cuban exiles of the 26 July Movement. He was among the eighty-two people who landed on Cuban soil from the *Granma* in December 1956. Ambushed by Batista's army, only twenty survived; Guevara was among them, and joined the guerrilla army in the Sierra Maestra.

The experience of that struggle is documented in Che's *Reminiscences* and his *Guerrilla Warfare*. According to Fidel Castro, Che was a courageous fighter, distinguished by his 'resolute contempt for danger', and it was he who led the victorious 26 July Movement into Havana on 2 January 1959.

As a theorist of revolutionary guerrilla warfare, Che has few equals. *Guerrilla Warfare* is a response to – and a reaction against – a theory of socialist change which emphasized the need to pass through a series of prior stages of development before reaching the socialist revolution. This theory, sustained by the Communist parties since the late 1930s, had few attractions for Che – especially after the Guatemalan experience. Like so many Latin American revolutionaries, Che had emerged from a period dominated by a populism whose ambiguities and compromises offered no solution to Latin America's central problem – its subordination to the interests of imperialism. In his view, their vague commitment to 'creating the conditions for change' only postponed the inevitable struggle indefinitely.

In Che's view, where the conditions for revolution did not exist, it was the vanguard (an *advance* guard in his terms) which would by its actions create the conditions; the guerrilla group, or *foco*, was to provide a catalyst for revolution. It is in this sense that Che is a theorist of revolutionary war, and not merely a tactician.

This aspect of Che's life and work is well known in the West – particularly through the work of Regis Debray. Yet in the controversies that developed in post-Revolutionary Cuba, Guevara evolved and argued for an alternative strategy whose implications were more far-reaching and contentious than his theses on guerrilla war. For in the economic debates, on the question of the relationship with Russia, and the nature and implications of Third World solidarity, Che's position (for all its idealism) did challenge received ideas about socialist construction and the excessively mechanical perceptions of the model of economic development.

In late 1959, Che was appointed Director of the Cuban National Bank; eighteen months later, as Minister of Industry, he was to play a key role in the major debates on economic policy and its political consequences.

In the immediate aftermath of the Revolutionary victory, Cuba's response to economic problems had been essentially pragmatic; the largely American-owned sugar estates were nationalized, the essential services taken into state ownership, wage levels raised and unemployment eliminated. While this took up the slack in the economy, it did nothing to attack the fundamental *structural* problems that best Cuba; and it became clear, especially after the imposition by the United States of an economic blockade from late 1960 onwards, that the expansion of the economy was no substitute for a development policy. The search for a planning policy moved the Cuban government closer to the Russian model of economic growth and its Cuban advocates – the Cuban Communist Party.

By 1963, however, the Cuban government's disillusionment with Russia over the Missile Crisis, coupled with a growing dependency on Russia, provoked a new debate over development strategies. In the course of that discussion, Guevara emerged as the spokesman for an alternative strategy linking the economic and the political levels.

In brief, the Cuban Communists had argued that the central planning should operate on the principle that each individual enterprise or branch of the economy should raise its level of productivity and maintain its profitability. To achieve that, it would be necessary to introduce work quotas and combine them with material incentives to encourage productivity. At the same time, this would involve a reintroduction of some market mechanisms (particularly in commerce) and a growing differentiation within the workforce.

Against this, Che argued a model that was closer to the Chinese than the Russian experience. Market relations, he believed, should be eliminated. The economy should be treated as a single unit within which resources were distributed according to need, and the society as a whole should take collective responsibility for accumulation and economic development.

The political implications were profound, and related closely to Che's rejection of the concept of a revolution by stages. As he had insisted in his famous essay 'Man and Socialism in Cuba', the socialist transformation of Cuban society should occur simultaneously with its economic development. As an instrument of this policy moral incentives (social solidarity, revolutionary commitment, 'moral' rewards) should replace material recognition, as money was progressively eliminated.

If the Communist plan involved a *de facto* integration into the Eastern European bloc, Che's strategy required the creation of a Latin American – indeed a Third World – structure of mutual support and exchange. Hence the call for 'one, two, three, many Vietnams', a policy expressed in the period between 1963 and 1968 in the concept of Latin American Solidarity (OLAS) and the firm commitment to the export of the Cuban revolution which flowed into support for those pursuing the guerrilla struggle throughout Latin America. In this Che, as the theorist of the Cuban revolutionary *method*, became a key figure.

The debate over moral and material incentives reflected two concepts of revolutionary change – in Che's case, a still not fully evolved theory of permanent revolution which was both a political position ('Man and Socialism') and a response to scarcity, through its socialization. By contrast, the acceptance of differentials involved an implicit concept of revolution by stages to which Che's theory and practice had been consistently opposed.

It was perhaps inevitable that Che should follow the logic of his own position and return to the armed struggle, first in the Congo and later in Bolivia, which, he had argued, was ripe for revolutionary change.

Tragically, Bolivia (and Che's *Bolivian Diary*) demonstrated the limitations of Che's politics, his tendency to overstate the catalytic role of the vanguard and to underestimate the importance of a mass vanguard organization which was itself the product of struggle. Typically, too, his concept of the guerrilla *foco* rested on peasant support, and said little of the role of the working class. In Bolivia the limited support of the peasantry and the failure to establish a clear link with the workers, and in particular the militant and highly organized miners, led to the isolation of the guerrillas. In what became an exclusively military confrontation between the guerrillas and a Bolivian army trained in counter-insurgency by the United States, the outcome could not be long in doubt. In October 1968, Che was trapped and captured; rather than attempt to hold a prisoner who would rapidly become a symbol of the continuing struggle against imperialism, his captors killed him on the spot.

Che's death closed finally that alternative course for revolutionary construction. His epitaph, sadly, was the Venezuelan guerrilla leader Douglas Bravo's criticism (in 1970) of the Cuban regime. Cuba, he said, had abandoned the guerrilla struggle. It was undoubtedly true. For it had become clear by then that the guerrilla strategy had failed. And perhaps Che, while he had raised key questions about the transformation of the consciousness of the masses through struggle, and himself led an exemplary life, had forgotten **Lenin's** dictum that the emancipation of the working class must be the act of the workers themselves.

Further reading

Other works include: Che Guevara, *Reminiscences of the Cuban Revolutionary War* (trans. 1968); *Guerrilla Warfare* (trans. 1967); *Bolivian Diary* (trans. 1969); *Venceremos*, ed. John Gerassi (1968). See: R. Debray, *Revolution in the Revolution* (1968); M. Lowy, 'The Marxism of Che Guevara', *Monthly Review* (1973); Jon Lee Anderson, *Che Guevara: A Revolutionary Life* (1997).

MIKE GONZALEZ

GYATSO TENZIN, 14th Dalai Lama

1935–

Tibetan religious and political leader

In mid-April 1959 scores of journalists and photographers descended on the town of Tezpur on India's north-east frontier region to meet a living legend: the 14th Dalai Lama, reincarnation of his predecessor and manifestation of Avalokiteshvara, Buddha of Compassion and protector of Tibet.

To the disappointment of the world's press the god king turned out to be an exhausted young man in glasses who had nothing to say about his dramatic escape from Tibet. A statement was read on his behalf thanking the Indian people for the promise of asylum and he was then conveyed into guarded exile at the Himalayan hill-station of Mussoorie. To many observers it appeared then that the remarkable phenomenon of Tibetan Buddhism, of which the Dalai Lama was the living symbol, was destined for swift extinction.

Born into a peasant family in north-eastern Tibet, the reincarnation of the late 13th Dalai Lama (d. 1933) was identified in the summer of 1937, when he was two years old. The equivalent in today's prices of over a million US dollars had to be paid to the local Chinese authorities before the boy and his family were allowed to proceed to Lhasa, where he was proclaimed the 14th Dalai Lama and renamed Tenzin Gyatso (Ocean of Wisdom). In March 1940 he was enthroned in the Potala Palace as temporal ruler of Tibet and head prelate of the Geluk, largest and most powerful of the several schools of Vajrayana Buddhism followed in Tibet. A year later he began to receive instruction as a Buddhist monk under the then Regent of Tibet – a process that continued for the next nineteen years, culminating in a final examination conducted in Lhasa's Jokhang Temple days before the events that precipitated his flight from Lhasa in March 1959.

Nine years earlier the fifteen-year-old Dalai Lama had been forced to set aside his religious studies and assume full temporal powers when Chinese troops invaded Tibet to 'reclaim it for the Motherland'. After failing to win the support of the United Nations the Dalai Lama's representatives signed a seventeen-point agreement that acknowledged Tibet's 'return to the big family of the Motherland' while guaranteeing the established powers of the Dalai Lama and the 'religious beliefs, customs and habits of the Tibetan people'. However, it soon became apparent that the occupying Chinese had no intention of honouring the treaty. Despite talks with the Chinese leadership in Beijing in 1954 matters grew worse, with widespread human rights abuses. In 1956 the Dalai Lama was permitted to go on a religious pilgrimage to the Buddhist holy places in India but found the Indian prime minister unable to suggest any political strategy other than peaceful negotiation. He himself took the same line when approached by Khampa rebels bent on armed resistance against the Chinese. By mid-1958 this resistance movement had became a national revolt, leading to the Lhasa uprising of 10 March 1959 and the Dalai Lama's departure from Tibet. It is said that when Chairman **Mao** heard of his escape he declared, 'In that case we have lost the battle.'

Over the next decade more than 100,000 Tibetans followed the Dalai Lama into exile. In 1960 the hill-station of Dharamsala became the seat of a Tibetan government in exile as the Dalai Lama set about keeping alive the issue of Tibetan self-determination while preserving Tibetan identity and culture in the meantime. The Dalai Lama's subsequent efforts to reach a peaceful accommodation with China along the lines of the Beijing accord of 1951 achieved little beyond winning the sympathy of the international community, culminating in the 1989 presentations to the Dalai Lama of the Nobel Peace Prize and the Raoul Wallenberg Congressional Human Rights Award.

Over this same period the fortunes of the Tibetan community in exile, initially impoverished, scattered and seemingly doomed to cultural absorption, were transformed. This change was due in large measure to the Dalai Lama's skill in finding a balance between preserving the essential elements of traditional Tibetan culture while at the same time leading his people into the twentieth century, a process made possible as much by his personality as by the extraordinary degree of veneration accorded to his person by all Tibetans. This allowed him to challenge the feudal establishment within the exile community and begin a process of democratization based on access to education.

At the same time scores of monastic centres were established to preserve the teachings of the many schools of Tibetan Buddhism and to pass these on to future generations. Here, too, the Dalai Lama was a powerful instrument for change by making the esoteric intricacies of Tibetan Buddhism more accessible, not least to non-Tibetans. In 1967 he began the first of a many international tours that helped establish him as a major world figure and as a teacher of Buddhism. In doing so he kept Tibet on the international agenda but, perhaps more significantly, helped transform Vajrayana Buddhism into one of the fastest growing religions of our time.

Further reading

The Dalai Lama's first autobiography, *My Land and My People* (1962) was later followed by *Freedom in Exile* (1999). His many published expositions of Vajrayana teaching include *An Introduction to Buddhism* (1965) and *Ancient Wisdom, Modern World* (1999). See: Heinrich Harrer, *Seven Years in Tibet* (1953); Roger Hicks and Ngakpa Chogyam, *Great Ocean: An Authorised Biography* (1984); and Tsering Shakya, *The Dragon in the Land of Snows: A History of Modern Tibet Since 1947* (1999).

CHARLES ALLEN

H

HARDY, Thomas

1840–1928

English poet and novelist

Thomas Hardy was born near Dorchester on 2 June 1840. His birthplace in Higher Bockhampton was a substantial cottage, at the end of a lane and on the edge of a piece of heath-land. His father was a builder and mason working on his own but, by the time Hardy was twenty, employing half a dozen men; his mother was a cook and serving-maid. The marriage took place less than six months before the child was born. Thomas Hardy the elder was said to have got more than one village girl into trouble, but Jemima's mother was more than a match for him. She was the disowned daughter of a yeoman farmer, left to a widowhood of great poverty with seven children. These social ramifications are of some importance, because Hardy's work, like the man himself, was strongly marked by his origins. He was a delicate child, after a difficult birth. He went to the village school and then, for seven years, to a school in Dorchester which he left at the age of sixteen with a knowledge of Latin. He was articled to an architect and church-restorer, a man for whom his father had done building work. During this time he continued his education with the help of Horace Moule, the son of a local clergyman, and did some reading in the Greek dramatists. There was a spell with an architect in London, from 1862 to 1967; Hardy then went back to his original employer in Dorchester. He married Emma Gifford, whom he met while on an architectural assignment in Cornwall, and shortly afterwards gave up architecture to write novels. Emma was of a clerical family and the marriage seems to have confirmed Hardy's sensitivity about his social position; his wife died in 1912. In 1914 Hardy married Florence Dugdale, with whom he conspired to write *The Early Life of Thomas Hardy* (1928 and 1930), published under her name after his death – a book designed to conceal from posterity all he did not want people to know about himself, and in particular whatever he regarded as inadmissible about his family. In his later years Hardy seems to have been obsessed with the notion that the family had gone down in the world, from gentle origins.

If Hardy's social life has its elements of rather depressing comedy, there are few writers who have so long and consistent a record of unselfconscious devotion to their work. His first surviving poem, 'Domicilium' – which describes the cottage where he grew up – was written before 1860. When Hardy died in 1928 he was preparing the volume which appeared posthumously as *Winter Words*, and although the volume concludes with a poem called 'He resolves to say no more', his introductory note says merely that this is 'probably' his 'last appearance on the literary stage'. So we have nearly seventy years of writing by a man who, even at eighty-eight, had not definitively given up. The whole corpus of his work is made up of 947 poems, besides a huge dramatic epic, *The*

Dynasts (1904–8), and a score of novels and volumes of short stories. Hardy's work stretched well into the twentieth century, and was accepted by the new century as by the old. His reputation has grown and his readership continued to spread so that his works are still a valuable property in the paperback market. His poems, the high value of which was recognized early in the present century by such figures as Ford Madox Ford and **Ezra Pound**, have been a living influence on poets after the Second World War and indeed up to quite recent times.

For the nineteenth century, Hardy was a novelist almost exclusively. Yet he is on record as saying that he would never have written a line of prose if he could have made a living by poetry. It was not until 1898 that the first and only volume of verse he published during the nineteenth century, *Wessex Poems*, appeared, but all his volumes contain, in revised if not in the original form, poems he wrote in the 1860s. The reception of both the volume of 1898 and of its successor of 1902 – *Poems of Past and Present* – was grudging. By then Hardy had long established himself, in two continents, as a major novelist. After what might be regarded as false but – to the author – no doubt instructive starts with an unpublished story called *The Poor Man and the Lady* and with *Desperate Remedies*, the publication of which he paid for himself, Hardy found his true *métier* with *Under the Greenwood Tree* (1872). The essential elements of this novel were provided by the scenes of Hardy's childhood and the persons and traditions of his immediate family and acquaintance. It was in this novel that Hardy began the creation of a 'Wessex' which corresponded in remarkable detail with the geography and manners of Dorset and the bordering lands; for many readers the fictional names are more familiar than the real ones. Hardy's own parish came to enjoy, as Mellstock, a fame it had never known as Stinsford. There is a touch – but no more – of Shakespearian comic dialogue about some of the talk in *Under the Greenwood Tree*; for the most part Hardy was making an adaptation of the dialect familiar to him as a child. Indeed, although Hardy shows a more practised hand in several of the later novels, the language of *Under the Greenwood Tree* is exemplary, showing nothing of the occasional stiltedness which marks Hardy's forays into cosmological reflections or into the social milieux which, for all his later dinners in London and membership of a London club, were never close to his imagination.

Under the Greenwood Tree was published anonymously, but its considerable success gave Hardy confidence to launch his further works under their author's name. *A Pair of Blue Eyes* followed in 1873, then in 1874 what may be regarded as the second of the essential books in the Hardy canon, *Far from the Madding Crowd*, with its memorable picture of sheep-farming in old Dorset. The third is *The Return of the Native* (1878), more sombre in tone, with its evocation of Egdon Heath which is, so to speak, a presiding spirit in the book. *The Trumpet Major* (1880) introduces a new historical element; it is set in the days of the Napoleonic wars, which interested Hardy deeply and which later provided the subject-matter of *The Dynasts*. In *The Trumpet Major* the local scene is still central and, once again, crucial characters such as Sergeant Troy seem to have been drawn from life – Troy himself apparently from the husband of Hardy's aunt – one of those whom, with the social pressures of marriage and his own aspirations, he came to regard as socially ineligible. *The Mayor of Casterbridge* (1886), probably the greatest of Hardy's novels and a tale of great tragic force, with its roots in the immediate past of Dorset and in what Hardy had learned of its inhabitants, is on a scale which lifts plot and characters far out of any merely local interest. The scene is set in the town in which fate had set Hardy himself only because it is through the local minutiae that Hardy is best able to present the universalities of human nature – as Dante, it might be said, sees so much of the destiny of man in the streets of Florence. *The Woodlanders* (1887) is an altogether less powerful book, but presents aspects of the picture, or myth, of Wessex not to be found else-where. *Tess of the D'Urbervilles* (1892) not only does that but gives us the second of the great tragic characters of Hardy's novels – Tess herself, whose mythic force is not les-sened by the portentous epitaph with which Hardy saw fit to end her history. Hardy's final novel – *The Well-Beloved*, though pub-lished the year after, was written earlier – was *Jude the Obscure* (1896). It is a book in which the Wessex landscape, though still sig-nificantly present, becomes a muted back-ground to a plot which evolves almost entirely out of the interaction and final explosion of the interlocked characters.

From the first, Hardy felt the drive to include in his novels elements of social and in particular sexual relationships which the ethos of the times was inclined to suppress. He remained preoccupied by then 'modern' ideas and absorbed a good deal of the ration-alism of **Darwin**, **Mill**, **Spencer** and **Huxley**. He was 'churchy', as he said, and soaked in the language of the Bible and the Prayer Book, but from an early age without religious belief, as Jude himself became. With *Jude* he ran into dramatic – though, it must be said, comic – trouble. Poor Emma was scan-dalized; in the United States Mrs Oliphant deplored the outrage to morality. It has often been said that Hardy gave up writing novels because of these troubles; it is more likely that he now found that his novels were doing so well that he could devote himself to poetry, his great work in prose being anyhow in a sense completed.

The enduring importance of Hardy is cer-tainly not in any set of abstract ideas – 'enlightened' or otherwise – which may have attracted him more or less as they attracted many of his contemporaries. It is in the imaginative body of his work where life is presented with a closeness of observation possible only to a man working within a milieu he knew intimately and from the cradle. There are romantic excesses which sometimes amount to absurdities, but the great novels remain solid in spite of them and these faults hardly touch the poems. Many

reasons combine to give Hardy's work not only significance but popularity in our own day. One is that he was a genuine provincial, and the importance of that is being realized at last by a world in which local differences are threatened with extinction. The reality he saw is a very solid one. He speaks on behalf of a class – what might be called the lowest middle class of the countryside, below any pretension to gentility – which had scarcely made its voice heard in literature before. It is the very class from which he had tried to distance himself socially. He lived through immense changes, in the economy as in the social life of the countryside, and the impact of urbanization, now worldwide, was per-ceived by him in a manageable local setting. Finally, whether in prose or verse, he could tell a good story.

Further reading

The Complete Poems of Thomas Hardy were pub-lished in 1978. There were numerous printings of the earlier *Collected Poems*, and there is an excellent *Selected Poems*, ed. David Wright with introduction and notes (1978). See: Mervyn Williams, *Thomas Hardy and Rural England* (1972); Robert Gittings, *Young Thomas Hardy* (1975) and *The Older Hardy* (1976); F.B. Pinion, *Hardy Companion* (1968); K. Brady, *The Short Stories of Thomas Hardy* (1982); J. Gibson, *Thomas Hardy* (1996); R. Morgan, *Women and Sexuality in the Novels of Thomas Hardy* (1988).

C.H. SISSON

HAVEL, Václav

1936–

Czech writer and statesman

Václav Havel was born in Prague into an affluent family which identified with the ideals of the First Czechoslovak Republic, and he absorbed the democratic humanism of Czechoslovakia's first president, Thomas Masaryk. Although these beliefs seemed uto-pian during the Nazi occupation and the post-1948 Stalinist terror, they shaped Havel's later views. His role as a playwright and social critic began during the 1960s, as the regime slowly distanced itself from Stalinism. Havel urged literary independence, both before and during the 'Prague Spring', and encouraged resistance after the Soviet invasion of 1968, for example signing in 1969 a petition against suppression of freedom. However, it was during the 1970s and 1980s, the period of repression, conformity and public apathy he labelled 'post-totalitarianism', that Havel became a prominent critic of the regime. His plays were banned in Czechoslovakia, but performed abroad.

As a playwright Havel reflected the prevailing politics, from his first co-authored play written as an army conscript in 1959 – *You've Got Your Whole Life Ahead of You* – to his semi-autobiographical 1984 play about the crises of a dissident intellectual, *Largo Desolato*. One of his best-known critiques of the Communist regime is *The Memorandum* (1965), ridiculing the bureaucratic invention of a 'strictly scientific' meaningless language. Literary influences included **Franz Kafka** and Jaroslav Hašek, author of *The Good Soldier Schweik*, and he acknowledged debts to **Beckett** and Ionesco. Havel avoided a specific political message, encouraging the audience to recognize the absurdity of everyday reality. The Prague Theatre on the Balustrade, which developed a Czechoslovak version of the theatre of the absurd, produced his plays, starting in 1964 with *The Garden Party*, which follows a young man's career in the 'liquidation office'.

Havel became well known as a campaigner for human rights when he played a key role in launching Charter 77, which called on the government to honour its human rights obligations under the Helsinki Declaration. He was arrested several times, and then imprisoned in 1979. After he fell seriously ill in early 1983 he was released, but subjected to continuing police harassment. Havel's essays and letters, originally circulated underground, were translated and published abroad. *Living in Truth*, for example, marking the award of the Erasmus Prize in 1986, reprinted six of Havel's texts, including his open letter of 1975 to President Gustav Husak condemning the devastation of culture, hypocrisy and corruption created by 'stabilization'.

Unlike many intellectual dissidents, Havel was never a **Marxist**, and during the Prague Spring he argued the necessity of an official opposition party to buttress political freedoms. But he never supported extreme anti-communism. Indeed, influenced by **Heidegger**, he was highly critical of the consumerism and dehumanizing technological trends within Western capitalism. *Letters to Olga*, written to his wife from prison, combine personal anxieties with reflections on philosophy and morality.

Havel also became sceptical about competitive party politics. Instead, he espoused the sense of solidarity, moral responsibility and citizenship generated by initiatives like Charter 77, which transcended ideological labels. His 1984 essay 'Politics and Conscience' took up from other dissenters the concept of 'anti-political politics' to celebrate the evolution of a civil society from below. This was expressed through alternative trade unions (as in Poland), and in alternative forms of communication, culture and education, for example the 'flying university'.

His best-known and frequently reprinted essay is the 1978 'The Power of the Powerless', which contributed to the dialogue between dissident intellectuals in Czechoslovakia, Hungary and Poland, inspired many in these countries, and stimulated Western social theorists, as well as later on the prominent exponent of non-violent resistance Aung San Suu Kyi. Havel analysed the nature of post-totalitarianism, and argued that individuals could begin to erode the dominant regime and ideology by refusing to co-operate, so 'living in truth'. He created the well-known image of the greengrocer who unreflectingly puts the slogan 'Workers of the World Unite' among the vegetables in his window, but could begin a chain of resistance by refusing. The essay also looked forward to the future emergence of a co-operative political and economic life based on self-management: 'post-democracy'.

When the Velvet Revolution brought down the Communist regime, Havel was at the centre of planning and negotiations. Backed by the newly formed Civic Forum, he was elected president by the Czechoslovak Federal Assembly in December 1989. Briefly, the 'anti-political' ideals of Civic Forum, which formed the first post-Communist government, suggested the possibility of an alternative to the Western political and economic model. But although Havel's early speeches and essays as president, published in *Summer Meditations* (1991), held out the hope of a highly decentralized and pluralist society, Havel soon came to terms with the reality of competitive party politics. He also endorsed the market, but continued to criticize consumerism and corruption and to argue for the importance of civil society. After 1992 he opposed the neo-liberal ideology of the new government under Vaclav Klaus. Havel also used his role as president to condemn the nationalism creating havoc in parts of Europe and to appeal for a sense of global responsibility.

Following his greatest setback, the exodus of Slovakia from the Federation in 1992, he was re-elected president of the Czech Republic in January 1993, and re-elected again, though with significantly reduced support, in January 1998. He left office in January 2003, widely respected abroad but regarded more cynically at home. Havel tried to uphold the moral values he proclaimed as a dissident, but began to look like other power-seeking politicians. However, despite serious ill-health, he remained central to politics in post-Communist Europe longer than any other prominent intellectual dissident, and achieved his goal of seeing the Czech Republic integrated into the European Union.

Further reading

Havel's major plays are available in *Selected Plays 1963–83* (1992) and *Selected Plays 1984–1987* (1994). In addition to political writings mentioned in the text, see *Disturbing the Peace* (1990) and *Open*

Letters: Selected Prose 1965–1990 (1991). John Keane, *A Political Tragedy in Six Acts* (1999) is a critical biography.

APRIL CARTER

HAWKING, Stephen William
1942–
English theoretical physicist

Born on the 300th anniversary of Galileo's death, 8 January 1942, Stephen Hawking took a first degree in natural science at Oxford University before moving to Trinity Hall, Cambridge, to study for a PhD in cosmology. Made a Fellow of the Royal Society in 1975, he had earlier become a fellow of Gonville and Caius College, and was appointed Lucasian Professor of Mathematics at Cambridge in 1980 – a post once held by, among several distinguished others, Sir Isaac Newton. It was, however, during his last year as an Oxford undergraduate that, aged twenty-one, Hawking was diagnosed with the disorder that has given him, in the public mind at least, near-iconic status: amytrophic lateral sclerosis (ALS), a type of motor neuron disease that has confined him to a wheelchair. Given no more than three years to live, he startled everyone by his capacity to survive, despite further physical setbacks. In 1985, following an attack of pneumonia and a tracheostomy, he lost the power of speech except with the aid of an electronic voice synthesizer that lends his utterances an unearthly, metallic frost curiously appropriate to his best-known subject-matter: outer space.

A few more years, and Hawking was barely able to move any part of his body. Yet the crafting of a computer attached to his wheelchair has enabled him to lead if not a normal life – though he has had two wives and three children – then a remarkably productive one. As well as continuing to write scientific papers of high calibre, he has authored a series of popular expositions, among them *A Brief History of Time* (1988), a challenging survey of modern astrophysics that, translated into thirty languages and more, became a runaway best-seller. That the man who, more than any other, has dared address the mysteries of the universe in language the layman may, with a little effort, understand should also be chronically disabled has proved an irresistible combination for the media. Among many celebrity forays, his synthetic voice has featured on an album by the Pink Floyd rock band, and in *The Simpsons*, the American cult cartoon series in which Hawking appears as one of the characters. By some he is perceived as the unlikely embodiment of the Good Scientist, his gallantry and childlike wonder at the phenomena he investigates a welcome redemption of a profession whose reputation has become increasingly tarnished by the discovery and invention of a succession of processes and artefacts inimical to human well-being, most obviously weapons of mass destruction and the various agents of global warming.

Hawking's own reputation as a serious scientist is keyed to his work on theoretical cosmology and quantum mechanics, from the time he was a post-graduate at Cambridge. In 1965, following a lead provided by Roger Penrose, he offered a mathematical proof that **Einstein's** Theory of General Relativity necessitates the 'big bang' explanation of the origin of the known universe – an idea originally floated by Edwin Hubble in 1929. Such an event was described by Hawking as a 'singularity', a point where the known laws of physics do not pertain. Another singularity is the 'big crunch', when, having ceased expanding, the universe will finally collapse back in on itself. Parallel work on 'black holes', which Hawking saw as lesser singularities generated by certain types of collapsed stars, brought him face to face with apparent inconsistencies between General Relativity and quantum theory, in particular **Heisenberg's** 'uncertainty principle', which posits that at the sub-atomic level predictability (hitherto the touchstone of valid science) fails. Much of Hawking's subsequent work has been dedicated to the elusive search for an overarching theory that will reconcile the two, seemingly incontrovertible main currents of

modern physics, and therefore, in his own words, 'explain everything'.

A gifted mathematician, Hawking has often been prepared to revise his own theories and findings, while sometimes allowing a fecund imagination to stimulate speculation. Thus, early on, while subscribing to the conventional view that black holes are sealed lacunae in the observable universe, he was prepared to discuss the possibility that they may contain 'wormholes' that might give access to 'alternative universes'. But from around 1974 he began promoting a revised understanding of black holes. Drawing on quantum mechanics, he suggested both that they may emit a form of radiation (which previously had been denied), and that their mass may contract, even to the point of extinction – a theory known as 'the Hawking process'. Then, at the 17th International Congress on General Relativity and Gravitation, held at Dublin in 2004, he went one step further: it might after all be possible to understand what goes on in a black hole, once its disordered gravitational emissions are decoded.

Hawking's purely scientific output is highly technical, and not all his peers have managed either to keep up with him or to agree with his theoretical positions. No other contemporary physicist, however, has had a greater impact on the popular imagination. His is a world packed with such imponderables as 'event horizons', 'dark matter', 'imaginary time', 'super-strings' and 'p-branes', as well as black holes themselves. Famously, in *A Brief History of Time*, he wrote that to fully understand the universe might be to 'know the mind of God', although he has rejected any belief in a 'personal' deity and has tended instead to the view that any concept of the divine is irrelevant to the pursuits of scientific knowledge. Rather, with all its many hypotheses, the extraordinarily ambitious cosmogony he strives for may be seen as, in part, a product of the secularist culture he inhabits, just as secularism itself is in part a product of the sort of theoretical science he practises.

In 1989 Hawking was made a Companion of Honour – one of scores of honours that have been heaped upon him, though (to date) no Nobel Prize. Despite his disability, he is also recognized as an able and inspiring teacher. His eventual legacy is likely to rest in the hands of the many post-graduates who have come under his supervision.

Further reading

Hawking's other publications include: *The Large Scale Structure of Space-Time* (with George Ellis, 1975); *Black Holes and Baby Universes* (essays, 1993); *The Large, the Small and the Human Mind* (with Roger Penrose *et al.*, 1997); *The Universe in a Nutshell* (2001); *On the Shoulders of Giants: The Great Works of Physics and Astronomy* (2002). See: John Gribbin and Michael White: *Stephen Hawking: A Life in Science* (1992); G.W. Gibbons and E.P.S. Shellard (eds), *The Future of Theoretical Physics and Cosmology: Celebrating Stephen Hawking's 60th Birthday* (2003).

JUSTIN WINTLE

HAWKS, Howard Winchester

1896–1977

US film director

Of all the directors brought into the limelight by French cinema critics in the 1950s, Howard Hawks is the one whose work most deserved acclaim and most repays close scrutiny. Ironically, for a director of popular and often profitable films, his oeuvre has the kind of thematic coherence that is more usually associated with literature or classical music, with a similar self-inspiring sense of irony, and a comparable formal purity.

Howard Winchester Hawks began his career in the props department of Mary Pickford's film company, after serving as an airman in the First World War. Rising through the editing department, he became a scriptwriter in his mid-twenties and directed his first feature (*The Road to Glory*) in 1926. A series of uneven silent features followed, though with *A Girl in Every Port* (1928) he brought to life one of the cinema's greatest actresses, Louise Brooks (who was subsequently cast in Pabst's screen classic, *Pandora's*

Box). Despite studio misgivings, he directed his first sound film in 1930, and two years later shot to prominence with *Scarface* (1932), a *succès de scandale*, and the definitive example of the gangster cycle which it spawned. This was also the first of Hawks's many successful collaborations with hardbitten ex-journalist and screenwriter Ben Hecht – *Scarface* was reputedly written in ten days.

Hawks's career in the 1930s is characteristically varied, but in every case betrayed an eye for talent that had little to do with the studio system: **William Faulkner's** first screen script (*Today We Live*, 1933) was for Hawks. And the decade culminated in three extraordinary collaborations with the mercurial Cary Grant: *Bringing Up Baby* (1938), *His Girl Friday* (1940), *Even Angels Have Wings* (1939). What is so hard to conceive, and remains a distinguishing feature of his career, is the diversity of the projects – in this case a screwball comedy, a headlong farce and a semi-tragedy. This last (*Even Angels*) reveals Hawks's central strength, an optimism (improbable in this tale of loneliness and courage among airmen) born of looking into the dark heart of things, and an irony (intimated by the title) which is anything but glib.

Strangely enough, the comparison that springs constantly to mind is that of Shakespeare's mature comedies, for Hawks's heroines have a comparable seriousness beneath their life-enhancing resilience, and his heroes the same complex instinct towards self-knowledge and integrity. Thus *To Have and Have Not* (1945), spawned by the war propaganda effort and adapted (by Faulkner, admittedly) from one of **Hemingway's** most garrulous and least engaging novels, is an almost tragically intense moral text: Humphrey Bogart (an apolitical and apparently cynical gunrunner) grimly maintains the fine line between 'right' and 'wrong' despite the immense conflicting demands of private loyalty, nationality and survival. In *The Big Sleep* (1946) which, because of its dark stylistic skill and Lauren Bacall's performance, is probably Hawks's best-known film, the Bogart character faces a choice so internal that it is virtually metaphysical – whether to acknowledge *to himself* that the woman he loves is herself part of the night-living corruption against which he is struggling.

Doubt and self-doubt; respect and self-respect; Hawks's emphasis is committedly humanist, ambivalent and incapable – despite the apparent stylistic ease – of simplification. What matters is choice, because right choices make for integrity and self-respect; and integrity in turn permits right choices. Only the will-power of the individual, a constant struggle, permits the inner freedom that is essential to making real choices. What distinguishes will-power from an over-weaning will *to* power (and what is so lacking in Hawks's close colleague and polar opposite **Ford**) is a caustic wit. Humour in Hawks goes with humanity and, surprisingly (in view of the way he has been attacked for chauvinism), with *women*. From the aggressive Katharine Hepburn in the 1930s, to the laconic Bacall in the 1940s, to the ironical Angie Dickinson in *Rio Bravo* (1959), Hawks's women (or, more abstractly, their freewheeling sexuality) put at risk the most rigid social and sexual roles. Cary Grant in *I was a Male War Bride* (1949) is forced by an obstructive bureaucracy into adopting a female persona to win his wife; and in *Red River* (1948), one of the great traditional Westerns, it is the irruption of a woman (Joanne Dru) which saves the film from Oepidal tragedy as John Wayne and Montgomery Clift prepare to fight to the death.

Though the eleven-year period 1938–49 was perhaps the fertile peak of his career, Hawks's work in the 1950s bristles with inspired moments and ideas, like his first venture into science fiction in 1951, *The Thing* (on which he is credited as producer only, but seeing is believing). And in 1959, with *Rio Bravo*, Hawks (aged sixty-three) married comic and tragic themes wholesale for the first time. A Western? A comedy? A drama of inner growth? *Rio Bravo* is all these things, a film which humanized the rigid self-assurance of John Wayne as thoroughly as the earlier *Red River* had implicitly criticized it.

Hawks 'discovered' (among others) Louise Brooks, Carole Lombard, Lauren Bacall and Montgomery Clift. It is surely no coincidence that the three actresses were so much more than the pretty comediennes Hollywood at the time required, nor that Clift was one of the most spiritual and tragically self-aware actors the cinema has seen. Hawks was a great director of actors; a master of genres; a man sensitive to good scripts and to the ideas of others. But above all, in an art where so much tends to artifice, the cinema of Howard Hawks is unique for never faking: there is never an unnecessary close-up to signal emotion; never an arbitrary cut to hasten the action; never, even in his failed films, a sense of portentous self-indulgence. It is an extraordinary record in an art form which is also an industry.

Further reading

See: Robin Wood, *Howard Hawks* (1960); David Thomson, in *A Biographical Dictionary of the Cinema* (1975); Joseph McBride (ed.), *Hawks on Hawks* (1996); Jim Hillier and Peter Wollen (eds), *Howard Hawks: American Artist* (1997).

CHRIS AUTY

HEANEY, Seamus
1939–
Irish poet

In a 1972 essay titled 'Belfast', Seamus Heaney writes revealingly of his early reading of both the Gaelic literature of Ireland and of the literature of England. Since that time, he claims, he has maintained a notion of himself as 'Irish in a province that insists that it is British'. Although he counts such powerful influences as Wordsworth and **Hopkins** among the voices of his education, his development as a writer has in many ways been shaped by his resistance to English literary modes, and by a determination to write out of his own distinctive and complicated sense of place and tradition. It has been both a continual challenge and a vitally enabling realization that 'the English tradition is not ultimately home'.

Heaney's first major book of poems, *Death of a Naturalist* (1966), is deeply rooted in the rural life and labour of Co. Derry, where he grew up on a farm. The title poem suggests the abandonment of a naïve identification with the natural world, though (like other poems in the book) it is effective precisely because it so vividly recreates a world of childhood innocence. The opening poem, 'Digging', has come to be regarded as the signature piece of Heaney's poetic vocation, neatly balancing his fidelity to the land and physical labour on the one hand and a commitment to the life of the imagination and the intellect on the other. *Door into the Dark* (1969) shows a marked development in Heaney's interest in Irish history and geography. 'Requiem for the Croppies' links successive stages of political conflict through the potent image of the barley that sprouted from the pockets of Irish rebels killed in the rebellion of 1798, while 'Bogland' explores the mythological potential of the Irish equivalent to the American prairie. *Door into the Dark* was published as sectarian violence became more widespread and intense in the aftermath of the Catholic civil rights marches, and the book was to mark a political, as well as a psychological, threshold in Heaney's career.

In the summer of 1969, in the context of increasing political violence, Heaney felt it imperative to reconsider the nature of his vocation. One of the urgent questions he asks about the role of poetry is prompted by Shakespeare's Sonnet 65: 'How with this rage shall beauty hold a plea/Whose action is no stronger than a flower?' He answers, appropriately, with a line from **William Butler Yeats's** 'Meditations in Time of Civil War'. The poet, he suggests, must find 'befitting emblems of adversity'. Heaney was to find those appropriate images and symbols in the work of the Danish archaeologist P.V. Glob, whose studies of Iron Age sacrificial victims preserved in peat bogs suggested a terrifying parallel with the victims of ritualistic killings in Northern Ireland. Glob's vivid account of the discovery of the Tollund man and the Grauballe man in *The Bog People* (1969) was the inspiration for Heaney's compelling series of bog poems in *Wintering Out* (1972) and *North* (1975).

Several poems in *Wintering Out*, including 'Servant Boy' and 'Bog Oak', declare their solidarity with those who have suffered oppression in Ireland's long political and religious struggles. There is also a striking new interest in the politics of language, especially in the semantic history of anglicized Gaelic place names like 'Broagh' and 'Anahorish' (the riverbank and the place of clear water). His confrontation with the political tumult of the 1970s is much more explicit in *North*. There is a chilling starkness in the poems that constitute Part I of the book, as with the description of the dead in 'Funeral Rites': 'their eyelids glistening,/their dough white hands/shackled in rosary beads'. Part II draws on a more conversational idiom, especially in the 'Singing School' sequence, but the tension is unabated: 'Have our accents/Changed? "Catholics, in general, don't speak/As well as students from the Protestant schools."/Remember that stuff?'

Field Work (1979) is a sober reassessment of the poet's commitments and responsibilities after ten years of political antagonism in the north. It shows a strong and continuing interest in the land itself as a source of inspiration and sustenance, both in its title and in the sonnet sequence deriving from a new attachment to Glanmore, Co Wicklow, where Heaney and his family had settled in 1972. The book also mourns the deaths of fellow artists, friends and relatives, including those who were the victims of sectarian violence in the 1970s. In *Station Island* (1984), Heaney follows the penitential rites of pilgrims visiting an island closely associated with St Patrick and the coming of Christianity to Ireland. The meditative nature of the quest produces a poetry that is strongly self-questioning, and he begins to test the adequacy of lyric modes of writing against the competing claims of narrative, dramatic poetry. The shade of **James Joyce** affirms for Heaney the need to trust in his own poetic instincts: 'What you must do must be done on your own.'

Heaney's continuing belief in the possibilities of lyric form is given ample expression in *The Haw Lantern* (1987), especially in the exploration of grief and loss in the elegiac sonnets titled 'Clearances', dedicated to his mother after her death in 1984. *Seeing Things* (1991) initiates a more reflective and visionary mode in Heaney's poetry and a general lightening in mood, both of which are marvellously captured in the sonnet 'Fosterling': 'Time to be dazzled and the heart to lighten.' A tentative note of optimism prevails in *The Spirit Level* (1996), the first collection of poems to appear after the ceasefire in 1994, and in *Electric Light* (2001), both of which revisit places and themes associated with Heaney's earlier work.

Heaney's work has continued to grow in stature and appeal since his appointment as Professor of Poetry at Oxford in 1988 and his acceptance of the Nobel Prize for Literature in 1995. Among his later achievements are his versions of Sophoclean tragedy, *The Cure at Troy* (1991) and *The Burial at Thebes* (2004), and his much-admired translation of *Beowulf* (1999). Like Yeats before him, Heaney has held fast to the idea of poetry as a potentially redemptive act, continually revising his own procedures and daring to believe that 'the end of art is peace'.

Further reading

A wide-ranging selection of Seamus Heaney's poetry can be found in *Opened Ground: Poems 1966–1996* (1998), and a generous selection of his essays is available in *Finders Keepers: Selected Prose 1971–2001* (2002). The following critical studies offer detailed and illuminating analysis of the poems: Neil Corcoran, *The Poetry of Seamus Heaney* (1998), Blake Morrison, *Seamus Heaney* (1982), Andrew Murphy, *Seamus Heaney* (1996; 2000), Bernard O'Donoghue, *Seamus Heaney and the Language of Poetry* (1994) and Michael Parker, *Seamus Heaney: The Making of the Poet* (1993).

STEPHEN REGAN

HEIDEGGER, Martin
1889–1976
German philosopher

Though condemned as a purveyor of literal nonsense by men as eminent as Rudolf Carnap and **Karl Popper**, Heidegger's influence has been pronounced in fields ranging from theology to psychotherapy. Furthermore, a much used and sometimes abused 'existentialist' vocabulary of 'authenticity', 'anguish' and man's 'being unto death', though popularized by the work of **Sartre**, derives from Heidegger's early but most influential book *Being and Time* (*Sein und Zeit*, 1927, trans. 1962). The heyday of existentialism passed with the 1950s but the direct influence of Heidegger has continued.

The radical intellectual impact of Heidegger's work stands in marked contrast to the external quiet of a life passed in study and teaching in southern Germany. The philosopher was born into a Catholic family at Messkirch in the Black Forest. He attended school at Constance and at Freiburg and, from 1909 to 1916, studied theology and philosophy at Freiburg University. The presentation of his dissertation on Duns Scotus qualified him to teach and in 1922 he became an associate professor at Marburg. *Being and Time* appeared in 1927 with a dedication to Edmund Husserl, whom Heidegger succeeded as Professor of Philosophy at the Albert-Ludwig University in Freiburg the following year. In 1933, following **Hitler's** appointment as Chancellor, Heidegger became Rector of the university. Though he resigned the rectorship in February 1934, the period of tenure was marked by a number of statements in which the characteristic vocabulary of *Being and Time* was blended all too easily with the 'blood and soil' jargon of Nazi ideology. Disillusion with the regime came swiftly, but following Germany's defeat the Allied authorities forbade Heidegger to teach until 1951. Neither the war nor the teaching ban interrupted Heidegger's single-minded philosophical quest, to explore the meaning of that most problematic and ubiquitous term, Being. Throughout the post-war years, which he spent living in the Black Forest, Heidegger published a series of works, mostly in the form of brief essays. Their subjects were various (the Pre-Socratics, the nature of the work of art, poetry and the significance of technology) but the dominant theme remained the same, a concern with the meaning of Being and with language as a speaking of the truth of Being.

Though Husserl was the major philosophical influence on the young Heidegger, his interest in ontology contrasted from the beginning with the older man's concern with the analysis of consciousness. In *Being and Time* he uses the phenomenological approach to shed new light on central ontological issues, first raised by the earliest Greek thinkers but, according to Heidegger, lost from sight in the over-formalized terminology of later metaphysics. Thinking about Being must consist in concrete phenomenological analysis of *how* beings are and not *what* or *why*, and in *Being and Time* he analyses man's particular mode of being in the world, *Dasein* (literally 'being-there'), as an approach to the understanding of Being itself.

Dasein is that being for whom its being is a problem. Uniquely *Dasein* is aware that sometime he will die and cease to be. He is a temporally bound being and the horizon of being in time is death. Heidegger conceptualizes the relationship between *Dasein* and other beings not as one of knowing subject and known object but as a multifarious involvement summed up in the notion of 'care'. *Dasein* cares about his existence. He is also beset by 'anxiety' (*Angst*). Anxiety must not be confused with fear, for fear is fear of some particular object while anxiety arises from being in the world as such and, in particular, the consciousness of mortality. In anxiety, '*Dasein* finds itself face to face with the nothing of the possible impossibility of its own existence.' The essence of man is to exist in a particular way that uniquely exposes him to awareness of the truth of Being and the horizon of death. But man can shield himself from such awareness. Language which might articulate the truth can become a veil that hides it. When this happens, *Dasein* is living inauthentically, cut off from the true problems and mysteries of his existence.

Such themes were readily integrated in the literature of an insecure age, but the analysis of *Dasein* did not satisfy its author. In his later works Heidegger turns to a less human-centred approach to ontological issues. To Sartre's statement: 'We are precisely in a situation where there are only human beings', Heidegger replies: 'We are precisely in a situation where principally there is Being' and the path to the understanding of Being is one that seems to bypass the concerns of humanism. Man, at most, is the 'shepherd of Being', who articulates its truth through language, but only in so far as language remains in contact with engendering experience.

It is Heidegger's relentless concern with avoiding the abstractions of traditional philosophy that accounts for much of the difficulty of the later arcane texts. He seems to many, admirers and critics alike, to be entering an area that falls outside the limits of what can be thought or said. Yet in the very effort to transgress these limits Heidegger revitalized central questions of philosophy and the human sciences, and this is likely to remain his most significant contribution to modern culture.

Further reading

There is a useful bibliography of Heidegger's vast output in Walter Biemel, *Martin Heidegger: An Illustrated Study* (1977), while *Martin Heidegger: Basic Writings* (1977) makes available several of his key essays. See also: Michael Gelven, *A Commentary on Heidegger's 'Being and Time'* (1970); George Steiner, *Heidegger* (1978); C. Guignon (ed.), *The Cambridge Companion to Heidegger* (1993).

DAVID J. LEVY

HEISENBERG, Werner

1901–76

German physicist

The founder of quantum mechanics and the inventor of the uncertainty principle, Werner

Heisenberg was born in Würzburg and brought up in Munich, where he entered the university in 1920 to study physics under Arnold Sommerfeld. After a brief stay at Göttingen University he took his doctorate in 1923 with a dissertation on turbulence in fluid streams. In 1924 he returned to Göttingen as assistant to Max Born. Later that year he moved to Copenhagen to pursue research under Niels Bohr and remained there until 1927.

After 1913 the Quantum Theory made considerable progress, but by 1924 it was running out of steam, largely owing to its lack of a coherent and systematic mathematical foundation: it consisted largely of a set of piecemeal modifications to classical physics that took account of the quantum of action. What was needed was a new mechanics, a quantum mechanics that would be valid for the microphysical, as well as for the macrophysical, realm. In the summer of 1925 Heisenberg discovered the foundations of just such a mechanics. His theory was rapidly developed by Max Born, Pascual Jordan and P.A.M. Dirac to form matrix mechanics, the basis of which is a non-commutative algebra in which observable physical quantities are represented by matrices, i.e. sets of numbers arranged in rows and columns. In 1926 Erwin Schrödinger invented wave mechanics which, though very different from matrix mechanics, led to the same results.

In the spring of 1927, while a lecturer at Bohr's institute, Heisenberg followed up his great work with his discovery of the uncertainty relations, $\delta q \, \delta p = h/2\pi$ and $\delta E \, \delta t \, \delta h$, which are of central importance in quantum mechanics. Heisenberg took these relations as an expression of a fundamental limitation on the accuracy with which position and momentum (q and p) and energy and time (E and t) can be simultaneously measured: simultaneous measurement of these quantities must always involve an inaccuracy at least as great as the value of the quantum of action h. This is Heisenberg's *uncertainty principle*.

The exact physical significance of the uncertainty relations is still a controversial question. Most physicists, though by no means all, believe that the uncertainty principle provides the correct interpretation of the uncertainty relations. The basis of the uncertainty principle, however, is itself a disputed question. Heisenberg believed that the uncertainty is due to the unavoidable disturbance of the object by the process of measurement. All observation involves an interaction between the object and the instrument of observation. For macrophysical objects this interaction is usually negligible, but for microphysical objects it generally involves a considerable disturbance.

In a penetrating analysis Bohr showed that the uncertainty is due not simply to the unavoidable measurement disturbance, as Heisenberg had thought, but to the fact that the amount of the disturbance cannot be accurately ascertained. Although Heisenberg accepted Bohr's analysis, there are certain differences in their views. Heisenberg sees quantum mechanics as being concerned not with nature as it is but with nature as exposed to our methods of questioning. He stresses the fact that observation of the microphysical world is possible only at the expense of interfering with it. For Bohr, however, the disturbance involved in observation is of secondary importance. The central point for Bohr is logical rather than epistemological: the concepts of exact position and exact momentum, he thinks, are, though equally indispensable for quantum mechanics, strictly speaking incompatible in that they presuppose mutually exclusive conditions for their meaningful applicability – they are in that sense complementary.

The consequence of the uncertainty principle is clear, viz. the statistical character of quantum mechanics: we cannot predict the behaviour of micro-physical objects, since we cannot obtain sufficiently accurate information about their exact simultaneous position and momentum. The philosophical significance of the uncertainty principle is, however, far from clear. Some are inclined to the view that the principle restricts only the simultaneous observability of exact position and exact momentum; microphysical objects, for all we know, may *have* an exact simultaneous position and momentum and a causally determined behaviour. Others, including Heisenberg, who are influenced by the philosophy of positivism, hold that since exact position and exact momentum cannot be simultaneously measured, microphysical objects cannot be said to have an exact simultaneous position and momentum, for the positivistic reason that what cannot be observed cannot meaningfully be said to exist. Whether the behaviour of microphysical objects is causally determined is, on this view, a meaningless question. Bohr too held that an object (even a macro-physical object) cannot meaningfully be said to have a definite simultaneous position and momentum, not for the epistemological reason that no such property is observable, but for the logical reason that the concept of such a property is basically incoherent.

Heisenberg was awarded the Nobel Prize for Physics in 1932 for his contribution to the development of quantum mechanics. He continued to make important contributions to physics, particularly in the fields of ferromagnetism, nuclear theory and elementary particle theory. In the 1950s he strove to develop a unified field theory based upon an equation reflecting a set of basic mathematical symmetries that would account for all the dynamic properties of matter.

He was Professor of Theoretical Physics at the University of Leipzig from 1927 to 1941. Although privately unsympathetic to the Nazi regime, he remained in Germany throughout the Second World War, seeing it as his duty to work for the preservation of German physics and its future reconstruction. From 1941 to 1945 he was Director of the Kaiser Wilhelm Institute for Physics at Berlin, where he worked with Otto Hahn on the development of a nuclear reactor. After the war he became Director of the Max-Planck Institute for Physics, first at Göttingen and later at Munich. After the war he played a prominent part in the promotion of scientific research in Germany. He married Elisabeth

Schumacher in 1937; they had three sons and four daughters.

Heisenberg played an important part in twentieth-century thought: the notion of uncertainty or indeterminacy which he introduced is, like **Einstein's** concept of relativity, one of the major ideas of the century; it has changed not only physics but our entire world picture.

Further reading

Other works include: 'On the Quantum-Theoretical Re-interpretation of Kinematic and Mechanical Relations' ('Über quantentheoretischen Umdeutung kinematischer und mechanischer Beziehungen'), *Zeitschrift für Physik*, Vol. 33 (1925), and 'On the Visualizable Content of Quantum-Theoretical Kinematics and Mechanics' ('Über den anschaulichen Inhalt der quantentheoretischen Kinematik und Mechanik'), *Zeitschrift für Physik*, Vol. 43 (1927). See also: *The Physical Principles of the Quantum Theory* (1930), and the collections of his essays, *Philosophic Problems of Nuclear Science* (1952); *Physics and Philosophy* (1959) and the semi-autobiographical *Physics and Beyond* (1971); Patrick A. Heelan, *Quantum Mechanics and Objectivity* (1965); Max Jammer, *The Conceptual Development of Quantum Mechanics* (1966).

D.R. MURDOCH

HELLER, Joseph

1923–99

American author

Joseph Heller authored some of the funniest American fiction of the twentieth century. He is less in the tradition of **Mark Twain** the humorist than in the tradition of Twain the satirist: in their best work, closely observed absurdity incites an ironic response, almost as a reflex, but one with moral power to address, if not redress, inhumanity and irrationality. Heller's style is of its era, its fragmented, time-shifting narrative yielding stark dramatic moments and steep surreal flights and pratfalls. But even more than most storytellers, tellers of funny stories must have a talent for narration, for voices, and Heller's gift for dialogue and narrative prose rhythms approaches genius – when he has something to say.

For more than two decades after its publication, *Catch-22* (1961) was one of the most praised and popular American novels, and it is still important, controversial, and hilarious. World War II, a 'good war' if there ever was one, is deconstructed and found to be folly, waged by eager madmen – or worse, a commercial enterprise managed by incompetents and monomaniacs. The cast of characters is sprawling, but if that means many are caricatures they are sharply drawn and precariously placed, so we know who they all are but have no idea what might happen to them. The book is full of jokes and shocks, and Heller's service as a bombardier in the war gives them specificity and authenticity. When Yossarian, Heller's anti-hero, deserts at the end of the novel, he became an archetype for the generation raised during the Vietnam War, and he joins Huck Finn as an archetypal outsider in the ranks of American fiction.

The perils of writing a masterpiece for a first novel played out over the rest of Heller's career. He took thirteen years to publish his second novel, *Something Happened* (1974), which – longer, less funny, set in a corporate world seemingly mundane in comparison to a world at war – disappointed expectations. But it was no less serious a work, and Heller's skill at spinning out elliptical narrative and his assured writing style served his chilly tale of personal anomie and social entropy well. The dissociation of reality from self-rationalizing representation as the means to power, and the further degradation of representation by mindless repetition as the expression of power, remained his central themes, but this time the result was not dissension but the dissolution of self.

Good as Gold (1979) seems to extend the author's methods and central themes to the battlefields and business practices of academia and government. But, though Bruce Gold, professor and pundit, moves in circles of the intellectual elite and politically powerful, that movement, like the endless missions of Yossarian's bomber squadron or the corporate career of Bob Slocum, the protagonist of *Something Happened*, ends up going nowhere. The true setting of the novel is where Gold, like Heller, is *from*, Brooklyn, and his extended family and enduring friendships in the old neighbourhood provide most of the most successful characters the author ever created. While friends and family are no easier on the identity than the obsessed oligarchs of government, they stand in bold relief as verbal portraits, voices from home. Heller's Connecticut Yankees are Coney Island Jews, and King Arthur's Court, the seat of irrational power, is the military, the corporate culture, the patrician halls of Washington.

Over the rest of his writing life, Heller turned to memoir and returned to the novel, revisiting themes and extending method. *God Knows* (1984) explores the roots of politics in the reign of David, King of the Jews, lover of famous women, father of a dysfunctional family, and narrator of the weary-hearted yet comic novel. *No Laughing Matter* (1986) recounts, in a narrative shared with the author's friend and care-giver Speed Vogel, Heller's struggle with Guillan-Barre syndrome. The variety of voices in *Picture This* (1988) speak for and about some of the most canonical figures in Western civilization – Socrates, Plato, Aristotle, Rembrandt – but they speak to America approaching the millennium, meditating, lecturing, joking on issues of art, history and commerce. *Closing Time* (1994) imagines a millennial apocalypse as it re-imagines characters from *Catch-22*, including Yossarian, while adding some Brooklynese and corporate angst from earlier fiction. And it is back to Brooklyn for *Now and Then* (1998), a memoir of Heller's Coney Island boyhood, with glosses on his young adulthood at war and in business, crowned with authorship and acclaim. Like his plays and screenplays, none of Heller's later fiction and non-fiction meet the standards of his first three novels, in comic invention or prose rendering, but few works for four decades of American literature did.

Further reading

See: Robert Merrill, *Joseph Heller* (1987); David Seed, *The Fiction of Joseph Heller* (1989); Sanford Pinsker, *Understanding Joseph Heller* (1991).

DENNIS PAOLI

HEMINGWAY, Ernest

1899–1961

US novelist and storywriter

Time was when modern American literature looked to Hemingway, alongside **William Faulkner** and **Scott Fitzgerald**, as one of its great presiding voices, a writer, a man, as it seemed, for all seasons. If modernism had pronounced God dead, the universe indifferent or absurd, and war the despoiling condition of things, Hemingway had held on to his own coded vision of heroism. Mankind was to endure against odds, *nada*, and, in one of his signature phrases, aspire to 'grace under pressure'. This also came with style to match, the celebrated declarative prose idiom at once spare, enactive, necessarily shorn of all frill and elaboration. From the best-known early writing of *The Sun Also Rises* (1926) to *The Old Man and the Sea* (1952) and the Nobel Prize in 1954, his art and life would become the stuff of legend, the writer as existentialist, be it in the guise of war reporter, soldier, safari hunter-sportsman, fisherman or, notably, aficionado of the bullring. Whether through his own real enough bravery, or the one or another scrape, or the four marriages (to Hadley Richardson, Pauline Pfeiffer, Martha Gellhorn and Mary Welch) and amours like that with Marlene Dietrich, or the international magazine and film-star celebrity, or even the several times prematurely reported death, few US authors can have quite so held sway, a literary figure close to cult.

Without suggesting a complete volte-face, and all the more so since his suicide in 1961, this version of Hemingway has undergone radical revision. 'The closet everything' observed a waspish **Truman Capote**. Was not Hemingway simply a macho fossil, some anachronistic self-parody, full of undeclared anxiety and sexual self-doubt, a man whose depressive temperament not inappropriately would end in Mayo Clinic treatment and his own fatal shot to the head? As to the writing, did not that more bespeak pseudo-style than true style, a formula, as critics like Leon Edel alleged? Read against the canon of **Henry James** or **Joseph Conrad**, Stendhal or **Flaubert**, he was to be thought provincial, minor league. His women, and not only under feminist critique, were hopeless, accommodating fantasies, silhouettes rather than flesh and blood. For those, latterly, given to the postmodern turn, **Becket** to **Nabokov**, or an American gallery to include **Thomas Pynchon** or **Kurt Vonnegut**, he also was to come under the hammer as lacking reflexivity, the quite larger challenge and resonance of self-referential fashioning and play. A due estimate of Hemingway cannot but take note of this changed profile.

Born in Chicago's affluent Oak Park suburb, his father Clarence E. Hemingway an MD, he was quick to progress from high school athlete to fledgling writer. The career has become its own legend: cub reporter on the *Kansas City Star* (1917); Red Cross ambulance-driver in 1918 on the Italian front where he suffered the first of his many wounds; foreign correspondent for the *Toronto Star* and *Star Weekly* (1921) and reporter of the Greco-Turkish war (1922); and the author of the story vignettes of in our time first published in Paris in 1924 and in the US in 1925 as *In Our Time*.

It was, however, with *The Sun Also Rises* (1926) that Hemingway made his mark. A tale of two cities, Paris and Pamplona in the 1920s, it offers a canvas of post-World War I ennui, loves lost, values shattered. Told in the laconic reporter-voice of Jake Barnes, 'technical Catholic', wounded and sexually impotent lover and necessary cuckold to the ruined (and ruinous) Lady Brett Ashley, it offers up a cast of expatriate disaffiliates to include Robert Cohn as would-be writer, his increasingly desperate fiancée Frances Clyne and the be-medalled and preposterous Count Mippipopolous. If Paris is all drift, bars and prostitution, Pamplona is figured in the bull-fighter Pedro Romero, into whose hitherto unspoiled art of life over death, the *corrida de toros* during San Fermín, Brett, Cohn and the rest bring their own despoilation. The novel remains Hemingway's landmark, easily the greater sum of its parts, his impressive and abiding cautionary tale.

The career, thereafter, novel or story, reportage or discursive work, would have to contend with the public persona, the vaunted Papa Hemingway relished by the headlines. There was also a pattern of shifting residence: Key West, Florida, from 1928 to 1938, the Finca Vigía in pre-Castro Cuba from 1939 to 1958, and the Sun Valley house in Ketchum, Idaho, from 1959 until his death. Within these were the ongoing visitations to Civil War Spain, World War II Normandy and Paris, then the East Africa of his different safari expeditions. Throughout, and whatever his depressive bouts or the drinking, he kept to a demanding schedule of authorship, not only the fiction but also a vast gallery of reporting, journalism and letters.

The principal short-story work would appear in a series of key collections, the symptomatically named *Men Without Women* (1927) which contains vintage Hemingway like 'The Undefeated', 'In Another Country' and 'Hills Like White Elephants' and a reprinting of 'The Killers'; *Winner Takes Nothing* (1933) with its 'A Clean, Well-Lighted Place' as one of his classic vignettes of stoicism; and *The Fifth Column and First Forty-Nine Short Stories* (1938) which draws from the previous collections and sees the first publication of 'The Short Happy Life of Francis Macomber'. This safari story, told in flashback, and in which Macomber's relationship with his wife Margot, hers in turn with the hunter Wilson, and the shooting of Macomber, yields a parable of good and bad faith, has become as well known a story as any Hemingway wrote.

The longer work, likewise, would continue. *A Farewell to Arms* (1929), his novel of the Italian front in which the doomed love of Frederic Henry, American volunteer, for Catherine Barkley, the English nurse who will die in childbirth, offers its own five-act dark shadow to Romeo and Juliet. It serves as Hemingway's bleak epitaph to war, a parable of the death of love, though for some also his inveterate love of death. *Death in the Afternoon* (1932) gives his classic account of the ritual and etiquette of bullfighting, not to mention a figural version of the art of writing itself. It has a postscript in the posthumous *The Dangerous Summer* (1985), parts of it serialized in *Life* magazine (1960), and the account of the 1959 bullfighting season's rivalry between Spain's then best-known matadors Antonio Ordóñez and Luis Miguel Dominguín. *To Have and Have Not* (1937) has long been thought to do Hemingway few favours, the near bathetic tale of the life and death of Harry Morgan as Key West smuggler and one of the 'have nots' at the bottom of the Depression-era economic ladder.

With *For Whom the Bell Tolls* (1940) Hemingway attempts **Tolstoyan** scale, the Spanish Civil War as epic told as the life of Robert Jordan, American loyalist volunteer against Franco's fascist army. Its considerable political coverage, the Aristotelian economy of its three-day span, and its play and counter-play of locale once earned it high esteem, even if there were always doubts about its heroine figure María. *Across the River and into the Trees* (1955), its protagonist the US army officer Richard Cantwell stationed in Trieste in 1948 and caught up in a triangle with Barone Alvarito and the young woman Renata, for many again bordered on unintended pastiche. *The Old Man and the Sea* (1952) served as the last major work Hemingway would see into print in his lifetime. Its story of Santiago as Cuban ancient mariner, his eighty or so days at sea, and final resolve to land a 1,500-pound marlin, is pitched to suggest heroism over defeat, the dream of stoic dignity over all compromise and death-in-life.

Since Hemingway's own death a formidable amount of posthumous work has surfaced. *A Moveable Feast* (1964) recalls the expatriate and so-called lost generation of 1920s Paris, from Hemingway's own early struggles as a writer to his often tetchy recollections of the literary milieu which included Gertrude Stein, **Ezra Pound**, Ford Maddox Ford and Scott Fitzgerald. *Islands in the Stream* (1970), set in Cuban and Caribbean waters and Hemingway's would-be Conradian 'sea-tale' as he termed it, has its centre in Thomas Hudson, father to lost sons and 1940s American spy against German submarines. If, overall, an uneasy performance, its interaction of memory, setting and event also recalls some of the best of Hemingway. *The Nick Adams Stories* (1972), a dozen in total and never previously collected as sequence, notably includes 'A Way You'll Never Be' as Nick's experience of shell shock and the Michigan-sited 'Big Two-Hearted River' (parts 1 and 2) with its portrait of Nick's resort to Nature as recovery from trauma. *Garden of Eden* (1986) and *True at First Light* (1999), the former with its Mediterranean setting and obsessive, knotted androgynous triangle, and the latter a last safari story based on Hemingway's time in Africa in 1953–4, both of them likely far from finished, give witness in the face of vexatious and depleting health to his sheer staying-power.

'Use short sentences. Use short first paragraphs. Use vigorous sentences.' These, and similar touchstones from the *Kansas City Evening Star*, give a departure point for the style by which Hemingway continues to be remembered. Taken with his resolve to aim for 'one true sentence' and 'never to write a phony line' or his well-known passage in *Death in the Afternoon* about the writer's craft being one of calculated omission ('The dignity of movement of an iceberg is due to only one-eighth of it being above water'), it underlines Hemingway's unyielding will to authentic and serious authorship. His star undoubtedly has faded, but that should not distract a contemporary readership from recognizing an American literary career of wholly singular historic consequence.

Further reading

See: Michael Reynolds, *Hemingway: The Final Years* (1999), *Hemingway: The 1930s* (1997), *Hemingway: The American Homecoming* (1992), *Hemingway: The Paris Years* (1989), *The Young Hemingway* (1986); Charles M. Oliver, *Ernest Hemingway A to Z* (1999); Mark Spilka, *Hemingway's Quarrel with Androgyny* (1990); *Ernest Hemingway: Six Decades of Criticism* (1987), ed. Linda W. Wagner; *Ernest Hemingway on Writing*, ed. Larry W. Phillips (1984); A. Robert Lee (ed.), *Ernest Hemingway: New Critical Essays* (1983); Carlos Baker (ed.), *Ernest Hemingway: Selected Letters, 1917–61* (1981); Mary Welsh Hemingway, *How It Was* (1977); Edmund Wilson, *The Twenties: From Notebooks and Diaries of the Period* (1975); Carlos Baker, *Hemingway: The Writer as Artist* (1973); Philip Young, *Ernest Hemingway: A Reconsideration* (1966); Morley Callaghan, *That Summer in Paris* (1963); Robert P. Weeks (ed.), *Hemingway: A Collection of Critical Essays* (1962); George Plimpton, 'Ernest Hemingway: The Art of Fiction XXI', *The Paris Review*, Spring (1958); Lillian Ross, *Portrait of Hemingway* (1950, 1961).

A. ROBERT LEE

HENDRIX, Jimi

1942–70
American virtuoso electric guitarist

Many consider Jimi Hendrix's four years of international fame from 1966 to 1970 to have been the zenith of twentieth-century guitar-based popular music. His instrumental skill had been developed at an early age in Seattle by listening to records, as well as by observing and jamming with visiting guitarists, while his flamboyant clothing and stage gimmicks were learned when on tour in the backing groups of figures such as Little Richard. Promising performances in New York's Greenwich Village inspired a British manager to bring Hendrix to England in 1966. There, the Jimi Hendrix Experience was formed with two British musicians whose driving bass and percussion provided solid foundations for his elaborate guitar sounds. This trio was immediately successful, not least because Hendrix's looks and image were perfectly suited to the newly fashionable 'hippie' look. Their repertoire drew upon

American blues, British pop and experimental psychedelic sounds – all enhanced by a desire to expand the range of the electric guitar with the help of new electronic effects and studio technology. Hendrix wrote and played many songs that lacked a direct connection to the blues, and performed striking versions of songs by **Bob Dylan**, but an intimate knowledge of the blues remained at the heart of his music.

The *Experience* soon conquered Europe and America, where Hendrix's popularity was increased by appearances at rock festivals, notably Monterey in 1967. By the time of Woodstock in 1969 he was experimenting with larger groups of musicians, and recording sessions had become noted for their duration and complexity. The Woodstock performance included an astonishing deconstruction of 'The Star Spangled Banner', played with an intensity reminiscent of John Coltrane. However, film of this performance illustrates the growing conflict between his creative ambitions and his audience's demand for familiar songs and stage antics.

What is Hendrix's place in the history of popular instrumental music? Brass and woodwind instruments dominated the first half of the twentieth century, and some virtuosi – for example clarinettist Sidney Bechet or trumpeter **Louis Armstrong** – attracted wider attention. The saxophone became dominant in the hands of **Charlie Parker** and Coltrane from the 1940s to the 1960s, but complex 'bebop' led jazz away from a mass audience. As a cheap and portable alternative to the piano, the guitar was popular in the music of poor minorities, from Spanish flamenco to American 'folk blues' and 'country' music. Although a skilled player could pick out melodies, the acoustic guitar was normally a background instrument whose rhythms and chords accompanied singers or other instruments. Guitarists in American big bands experimented with amplification during the 1930s, and Charlie Christian (1919–42) shot to fame between 1939 and 1941 through performances and recordings with the 'King of Swing', Benny Goodman. Christian's solos exploited the electric guitar's ability to produce sustained notes and phrases, and informal live recordings made in 1941 preserve extended improvisations in a style that retained a blues inflection but anticipated bebop. Many 'urban' blues musicians adopted electric guitars in the 1940s, and amplification encouraged riffs and solo lines. The electric guitar became the leading instrument in rock 'n' roll in the 1950s, and guitar-based 'groups' have been prominent in popular music ever since – although few have approached the intensity and range of the Jimi Hendrix Experience.

Hendrix died in 1970 at the age of twenty-seven. What direction would his career have taken had he lived longer? Recordings of live performances reveal constant reworking of his material in the manner of a jazz musician. He inspired **Miles Davis** to make comprehensive use of electric keyboards and rock-influenced guitarists, and the results influenced a new generation of jazz, soul, funk and rock performers. At the time of his death Hendrix was scheduled to collaborate with Gil Evans, who had created orchestral settings of **Gershwin's** *Porgy and Bess* and Rodrigo's *Concierto di Aranjuez* to show off the full range of Miles Davis's trumpet playing. Large-scale arrangements of Hendrix compositions recorded by the Gil Evans Orchestra in 1974 underline the strength and adaptability of his music. Beyond jazz and rock, the violin virtuoso Nigel Kennedy has attempted to reproduce the energy of Hendrix's improvisations, while the Kronos Quartet's frequent performances of *Purple Haze* made it sound like something by **Bartók**. Despite epitomizing the late 1960s, interest in Hendrix, both as an innovative guitarist and as an enigmatic person, has endured – fortunately sustained by a rich legacy of studio and live recordings.

Further reading

Charles Shaar Murray, *Crosstown Traffic: Jimi Hendrix and Post-War Pop* (2nd edn, 2001) cuts through romantic mythology and places Hendrix into a wide cultural context; K. Shadwick, *Jimi Hendrix: Musician* (2003) is an intricate musical biography. Key recordings: *Are You Experienced?* (1967); *Electric Ladyland* (1968); a collection of short radio appearances (*The BBC Sessions*, 1998) captures the vitality and excitement of early live performances. Film: *Jimi Hendrix* (Warner, 1973) is a documentary with plentiful concert footage, while *Jimi Hendrix at Woodstock* (MCA, 1999) illustrates his technical virtuosity but shows a muted reception for his elaborate playing. Hendrix compositions played by other musicians: *The Gil Evans Orchestra Plays the Music of Jimi Hendrix* (1974); *Purple* (2002), by Nguyên Lê, a French/Vietnamese jazz guitarist who incorporates elements of Asian and African 'world music'.

KEVIN GREENE

HENZE, Hans Werner

1926–

German composer

The period immediately after the Second World War was one of great change in German music, for suddenly scores became available which had been suppressed by the Nazis and the music of **Schoenberg**, **Stravinsky** and others could at last have an influence on German composers. Henze was one of the first to take advantage of the new freedom. He attempted to combine Schoenberg's serialism with Stravinsky's neoclassicism in such works as his First Symphony and First Violin Concerto (both 1947). Equally important to his subsequent development, however, was the close association with the theatre which he began in 1948 by taking an appointment at the Deutsche Theater, Konstanz: within the next five years he had completed four ballets and four operas, the latter including a version of the Manon Lescaut story as *Boulevard Solitude* (1951).

During the same period Henze was briefly attracted by the rigorous serial methods being developed by **Boulez** and **Stockhausen**. In his second quartet (1952) he came close to their concerns, but the next year he took the decision to free himself and settle in Italy. He broadened his style to embrace a rich flood of lyrical melody and colour, expressed most abundantly in his opera *König Hirsch* (1953–5), which was later revised as *Il re cervo* (1962). During the next few years he continued to produce music of nostalgic Mediterranean warmth – the Hölderlin cycle *Kammermusik* for tenor, guitar and eight instruments (1958) is typical – but he could range also as far as the militarist world of his Kleist opera *Der Prinz van Homburg* (1958) or the romantic waterscapes of his full-length ballet *Undine* (1956–57), which was choreographed by Frederick Ashton.

The early 1960s saw the culmination of Henze's 'southern' manner, with its roots in early nineteenth-century Italian opera as much as in the German tradition. Apart from his Fifth Symphony (1962) he wrote little abstract music at this time but instead concentrated on operas and cantatas, the latter including ecstatically lyrical settings of **Rimbaud** in *Being Beauteous* for soprano, harp and four cellos (1963), Tasso in *Ariosi* for soprano, violin and piano duet (also 1963) and Virgil in *Musen Siziliens* for chorus, two pianos, wind and percussion (1966). The operas of this period include the satirical comedy *Der junge Lord* (1964) and two works to librettos by **W.H. Auden** and Chester Kallman: *Elegy for Young Lovers* (1959–61), a tragedy of art and love in an alpine setting, and *The Bassarids* (1965–6). The latter, a reworking of *The Bacchae* as a continuous two-hour, symphonically modelled structure, sustains a crucial creative engagement with the expressive and formal procedures of Mahler and Berg

After completing *The Bassarids*, Henze became dissatisfied with his role as a purveyor of new operas for essentially bourgeois audiences in Germany: his psychological conflicts are recorded in his second piano concerto (1967). In 1968, following in the wake of worldwide student unrest, he declared himself on the side of revolutionary socialism and began, with the oratorio *Das Floss der Medusa* (1968), a series of works attacking bourgeois convention and eulogizing sons of the oppressed. He found a sympathetic environment in Cuba, where in 1969 he composed his Sixth Symphony, heavily indebted to the rhythms and sounds of Cuban music, and where he found the materials for his *El cimarrón* (1970), the story of a runaway slave in songs for baritone and three players.

The opera *We Come to the River* (1974–6), to a text by Edward Bond, has more in common with these works of commitment than with Henze's earlier operas. However, he had departed somewhat from the intransigent political stance taken in every work of 1968–70: there had been, among other things, two big symphonic poems, *Heliogabalus imperator* (1971–2) and *Tristan* (1974), both of which show his fertile orchestral invention and his dazzling eclecticism. The latter work, which includes a virtuoso solo piano part and music on electronic tape, is an important reappraisal of the **Wagner** legacy (a deeply ambivalent one for the composer) and an evocation of the processes of mourning.

After *We Come to the River* Henze went back to chamber music, which he had neglected since the early 1950s: a set of three Quartets, Nos 3–5, was finished in 1976. However, with the ballet *Orpheus* (1979), again a collaboration with Bond, he returned to the theatre. This work, part of a series exploring the Orpheus myth, continues Henze's investigation of the process of mourning. The *Requiem* (1990–2), written in memory of Michael Vyner, was another large-scale statement of grief. In his recent symphonies this sombre tone is often sustained, as part of an engagement with the Germanic symphonic tradition. Henze described his Ninth (1995–7) as a 'single long nightmare' dealing with suffering and death in the concentration camps. There is also a search for some form of affirmation, and the Tenth (1997–2000, commissioned by Paul Sacher and premiered by Simon Rattle with the Berlin Philharmonic in 2002) has a central Hymn surrounded by horrific storms and dreams.

In 2003, with *L'Upupa und der Triumph der Sohnesliebe*, Henze turned to opera for what

he declared would be the last time. By contrast with the high-profile literary collaborations of earlier operas, this was a setting of the composer's own text. It is a magical, fairy-tale conflation of Arabian and Persian myths exploring differing types of love, with acknowledged parallels to Mozart/Schikaneder's *Die Zauberflöte* and obvious stylistic debts to **Berg**.

Further reading

Selected other works: *Apollo et Hyacinthus* for contralto, harpsichord and eight instruments (1949); *Nachtstücke und Arien* for soprano and orchestra (1957); *Novae de infinito laudes* for soloists, chorus and orchestra (1962); Double Concerto for oboe, harp and strings (1966); Double Bass Concerto (1966); *Der langwierige Weg in die Wohnung der Natascha Ungeheuer*, music theatre (1971); Violin Concerto No. 2 (1971); *La Cubana*, music theatre (1973); *Voices* for mezzo-soprano, tenor and chamber orchestra (1973); *The English Cat* (1983); *Das verratene Meer* (1986–9); *Venus and Adonis* (1993–5); Violin Concerto No. 3 (1996); *Sechs Gesänge aus dem Arabischen* (1997–8). See: Hans Werner Henze, *Music and Politics: Collected Writings 1953–81* (trans. 1982), *Bohemian Fifths: An Autobiography* (trans. 1998). About Henze: Klaus Geitel, *Hans Werner Henze* (1968); Guy Rickards, *Hartmann, Hindemith and Henze* (1995).

PAUL GRIFFITHS (REVISED AND UPDATED BY STEPHEN DOWNES)

HEPWORTH, (Dame) Jocelyn Barbara

1903–75

English sculptor

Barbara Hepworth was one of a small group of artists – the most important of whom were herself, the painter **Ben Nicholson** and the sculptor **Henry Moore** – whose combined achievements during the 1930s were largely responsible for giving British art a central place in the modern movement, despite public indifference amounting at times to hostility. After the Second World War she went on to become an abstract sculptor of international reputation.

She was born at Wakefield, the eldest child of H.R. Hepworth, a civil engineer and later

County Surveyor to the West Riding of Yorkshire, whom she would sometimes accompany on his motor tours through the Pennine landscape – journeys which she later recalled made a deep impression upon her. Responsiveness to natural form remained a rich source for the making of her sculpture and can be sensed most powerfully in those works which she carved in wood or stone. At the age of sixteen she won a scholarship from Wakefield Girls' High School to Leeds School of Art, where Moore was a fellow student. In 1921 both artists transferred to the Royal College in London. In 1924 she travelled to Italy on a West Riding Scholarship, where she met the sculptor John Skeaping, a scholar at the British School in Rome. The couple were married in Florence in May 1925. They returned to London in 1926 and exhibited together at the Beaux-Arts Gallery in 1928 – her first important exhibition.

Throughout this period, Hepworth, like Moore, developed a strong preoccupation with 'direct' carving, a practice which had been revived in the decade or so before the First World War by **Brancusi**, **Epstein**, Gaudier-Brzeska and others. The doctrine of 'truth to materials' – of respecting the intrinsic properties of different types of stone or wood – was central to the work of Hepworth and Moore up until the 1950s, when both artists began to cast extensively in bronze – though Hepworth always insisted that she was primarily a carver. Her earliest surviving carvings, which date from the late 1920s, are on the whole stylized treatments of the human figure which also reflect an interest in primitive art. During the early part of the 1930s her work became freer and more abstract, though still based loosely on the human anatomy. The white alabaster *Pierced Form* of 1931 (destroyed during the war) was the first sculpture to explore the relationship of solid to void and of exterior to interior by incorporating in it a hole. From this sensuous, organic phase, which has close affinities with Moore's work of the same period, Hepworth progressed in about 1934 to a completely abstract sculpture of elementary geometric – or, as she described them, 'constructive' – forms.

Hepworth's meeting with Nicholson in 1931 (they married two years later, after her divorce from Skeaping) marked the beginning of one of the most mutually beneficial relationships in the history of British art. Together they visited Paris, where they made pilgrimages to the studios of **Picasso**, **Braque**, Brancusi, **Mondrian** and **Arp**. The purity of Brancusi's sculpture, with its reliance on simple archetypal shapes, profoundly affected Hepworth. In 1933 she and Nicholson joined *abstraction-création*, an association of artists of all nationalities dedicated to the promotion of non-objective art through exhibitions and an annual review (1932–6). Such contact with the Parisian avant-garde was one of the main reasons for that renewal of communal artistic activity in England which began in 1933 with the formation of the group Unit One and continued through various publications and organizations, some more politically committed than others, until the outbreak of war. Further impetus was provided by the presence in London from about 1935 of certain refugee artists and architects from the continent, amongst whom were **Gropius**, Moholy-Nagy, **Gabo** and later Mondrian. The progressive ideals of these artists are embodied in the publication *Circle* (1937), subtitled 'International Survey of Constructive Art', in which abstract art takes its place in a broad aesthetic and social programme embracing technology and architecture – in short, the 'constructed' environment. *Circle* was edited by Nicholson, Gabo and the architect Leslie Martin; Hepworth was closely involved in its preparation and contributed photographs of her work and a statement of her beliefs.

Shortly before the outbreak of war, Hepworth, Nicholson and their triplets (born in 1934) moved to St Ives in Cornwall, where they were soon followed by Gabo and his wife. For a variety of reasons, including the scarcity of material for sculpture, Hepworth's output during the first half of the war was limited to making geometrical abstract drawings in pencil and gouache in which she worked out ideas for a sculpture using both colour and strings – ideas which were later realized in a series of hollowed-out wooden ovoids of extraordinary clarity and perfection of shape. Some of these – for example, *The Wave* (1944) – are equivalents for natural rhythms, a reaction to the new environment of caves, wide curving bays and the sea. The megalithic landscape between St Ives, Penzance and Land's End became the inspiration for a number of major sculptures executed over the next thirty years, culminating in the two monumental bronze groups *Family of Man* (1972) and *Conversation with Magic Stones* (1973). The relationship of figure to landscape was an important theme in her post-war work.

However abstract, Hepworth's sculptures nearly always suggest a human presence or a relationship of one person to another. Her interest in the human figure can be seen in the beautiful series of Operating Theatre drawings which she made in 1948–9. In 1949 she also moved into the studio at St Ives where she worked permanently from 1951, after the dissolution of her marriage to Nicholson, until her death in a fire in 1975.

Further reading

See: *Barbara Hepworth, Carvings and Drawings*, ed. Herbert Read (1952); *Barbara Hepworth: Drawings from a Sculptor's Landscape*, ed. Alan Bowness (1966); *A Pictorial Autobiography* (1970); *The Complete Sculpture of Barbara Hepworth 1960–69*, ed. Alan Bowness (1971). See also: J.P. Hodin, *Barbara Hepworth* (1961); *Barbara Hepworth* (Tate Gallery catalogue, 1968); *Barbara Hepworth: Late Works* (Edinburgh International Festival, 1976).

RICHARD CALVOCORESSI

HERZL, Theodor

1860–1904
Zionist leader

The founder of political Zionism and of the World Zionist Organization, Theodor Herzl was born in Budapest. He grew up in a culturally assimilated, middle-class family, and studied law at Vienna University, where he took a doctorate in 1884. Pursuing a literary and journalistic career, he spent some years writing plays which, though performed, enjoyed little success, before becoming Paris correspondent of the Vienna *Neue Freie Presse* in 1891.

Up until the Dreyfus affair Herzl believed that the only answer to the Jewish question was the complete assimilation of Jews within the countries of their residence. During 1894, however, he witnessed at first hand the vicious, anti-Semitic behaviour of the Paris mob, and his views changed dramatically. The emotional shock of what it was his responsibility to observe resulted in the famous pamphlet *Der Judenstaat* ('The Jewish State'), published in 1896. In this he identified two major factors – one external, one internal – that would always militate against the possibility of successful assimilation. The first, anti-Semitism, would never be eradicated as long as Jews lived in abnormal social and economic conditions: 'If they let us alone for just two generations . . . But they will not let us be. After a brief period of toleration, their hostility erupts again and again.' And the second factor, Herzl now perceived, was a will amongst Jewish people to survive as a separate nation. The true solution, therefore, would be to establish a Jewish state. This could only be accomplished with the help of existing states, and so Herzl argued for international support, to be won through political action. In particular, since Palestine was chosen as the new homeland, it would be necessary to obtain a charter from the Sultan of the Ottoman Empire, and to this end every other activity should be subordinated. To achieve this end Herzl envisaged two necessary institutions: a 'Society of Jews', providing political leadership and legal representation (and forming, eventually, the sovereign body of the proposed state); and a joint-stock 'Jewish Company', providing finance for the immediate diplomatic moves, and eventually coping with the practicalities of migration and resettlement.

Although a liberal, Herzl saw that decision-making, at least initially, must be entrusted to the upper strata, 'to our intelligentsia'. While stressing the necessity of equal and non-discriminatory treatment of all citizens, irrespective of race and creed, and opposing religious interference in any matter of state, he nevertheless foresaw that, at the local level, it would be the rabbis who would provide direction. Beyond these prescriptions, *Der Judenstaat* offered little or no coherent social programme, but was rather a rag-bag of analysis and liberal principles. Thus, while advocating work as the right and duty of everyone, he envisaged a national flag composed of seven stars in a white field, symbolizing the seven hours of the working day – at a time when the eight-hour day was still an unachieved ideal throughout most of Western Europe.

Before Herzl's 'conversion' to Zionism, Jewish settlements were being founded in Palestine, and a movement (*Hoveve Zion* – 'The Lovers of Zion') advocating a return to Zion was already active in Eastern Europe. But its policy was simply to continue the practical work without waiting for official recognition. This Herzl opposed. Pursuing the programme he had set out in the *Judenstaat*, he laboured instead on three fronts: diplomacy, to achieve the charter; the creation of the 'Society of Jews'; and publicity. He proposed that in exchange for the payment of Turkey's foreign debts, the Sultan should allow Palestine to become a Jewish dependency. Negotiations in Constantinople in 1896 were inconclusive, but left Herzl with sufficient confidence to embark on stage two. Despite opposition from *Hoveve Zion*, and from a majority of rabbis who denounced his views as a distortion of Judaism, the first Zionist Congress assembled in Basle in August 1897, and the World Zionist Organization was founded soon after. Most importantly, the Congress adopted Herzl's recipe for its own programme: 'Zionism seeks to secure the Jewish people a publicly recognized, legally secured home in Palestine for the Jewish people.'

'In Basle I created the Jewish state,' Herzl wrote in his diary: 'In Basle I created the abstraction which, as such, is invisible to the great majority.' Since the state itself did not yet exist, the abstraction had to be kept alive – through publicity. *Die Welt*, first published a few months before the Congress, now became the organ of the World Zionist movement, and Herzl himself was mainly responsible for the decision to hold a World Zionist Congress annually. At the same time he worked indefatigably, though with rather fewer results, to sustain diplomatic and financial activities. Following an unsuccessful attempt to enlist the support of the Kaiser (Palestine would become a German protectorate), he turned once more to the Sultan, who granted him several audiences in 1901 and 1902, but still no charter. These were followed by meetings with Joseph Chamberlain, but after an abortive plan to allow a Jewish settlement in Wadi el Arish, a Sinai valley near Palestine, and a rejected alternative suggestion, made by Chamberlain, to create a Jewish state in Uganda, the territorial objective remained unaccomplished at Herzl's death. And the Jewish Company, though registered in the form of 'The Jewish Colonial Trust' in London in 1899, fared little better. In three years it succeeded in selling only £250,000 worth of shares, and in 1902 its main functions were transferred to the Anglo Palestine Company.

Notwithstanding these setbacks, Herzl's ideal remained intact, as can be seen in the utopian *Altneuland* (trans. *The Old New Land*, 1960), his one serious novel, published in 1902. Here he described life in a future Jewish state in Palestine in 1923. Steering a middle road between capitalism and collectivism, almost all economic activities are conducted within a co-operative framework ('mutualism'). All land is publicly owned, but leased for periods of fifty years. There is complete sexual equality, and every inhabitant is covered by a general social insurance which includes sickness, old age and life. Punishment has been replaced by re-education, and, since both parties profit from the flourishing state, antagonism between Jews and Arabs is non-existent.

In this, as in most of Herzl's political thinking, there was little that was new: indeed it was almost the standard production of a late nineteenth-century West European liberal, and in some quarters the book met with fierce criticism precisely because of its seeming divorce from Jewish culture and traditions. Even the *Judenstaat* had very little new to offer when compared with Leo Pinsker's *Autoemanzipation*, published in Berlin in 1882. And yet the fact remains that Herzl's contribution to the Jewish national revival was greater than anyone else's. It was his perseverance, dynamism and above all his personal charm and charisma that led to the transformation of small groups of East European Jews into a mass movement that finally succeeded in bringing about the establishment of the Jewish state. 'If you will it, it is no legend': these words he had attached to *Altneuland* as the book's motto; and they became one of the most popular slogans of the Zionist movement.

Further reading

A translation of *The Complete Diaries* was published in 1960. See: A. Bein, *Theodor Herzl* (1957); D. Stewart, *Theodor Herzl* (1974); and W. Laqueur, *A History of Zionism* (1972).

DAVID DINOUR

HERZOG, Werner

1942–

German film director

Herzog first achieved international acclaim with *Aguirre – Wrath of God* (1972) and *The Enigma of Kaspar Hauser* (1974), at which time he was seen as part of the emerging New German Cinema, along with **Rainer Werner Fassbinder**, Wim Wenders and others. However, narrative feature films such as these account for only a part of his large oeuvre, a significant proportion of which consists of 'documentaries' on a wide range of subjects including mountain-climbing (*The Dark Glow of the Mountains*, 1984; *Scream of Stone*, 1991), ski-jumping (*The Great Ecstasy of Woodcarver Steiner*, 1974), religious fanaticism (*God's Angry Man* and *Huie's Sermon*, both 1980), the excesses of the mad dictator Jean Bedel Bokassa (*Echoes from a Sombre Empire*, 1990), and the burning of the Kuwaiti oil fields (*Lessons of Darkness*, 1992). Hardly documentaries in the conventional sense, these highly poetic and richly visual films go well beyond a mere recording of facts and aim at uncovering deeper levels of existential and metaphysical truth; on occasion they incorporate fictional or scripted elements to that end, just as his predominantly fictional narrative films sometimes incorporate elements of non-fictional 'reality'.

Almost all his films investigate human experience at its extremes. They present the extraordinary, bizarre and strange with little or no comment or explanation, leading to a sense of bemusement and wonder. It is as if he is pointing to the utter strangeness of life and the pointlessness and inadequacy of attempting to understand it by rational means alone. Nowhere is this more true than in *Fata Morgana* (1970), set mostly in the Western Sahara, where the line between fiction and non-fiction is blurred entirely: early sequences showing us the eerie majesty of the desert landscape increasingly give way to melancholic images of the detritus of Western, technological civilization and then to satirical scenes such as that of the German scientist in wetsuit and flippers holding a vast turtle of whose biological functions he is giving an inanely pedestrian account. Here, as in Herzog's work as a whole, we are given a sense of the vastness of nature and the universe, the puniness of humankind and the deep questionability of the notion of 'progress'.

Born in Munich with the legal name Werner Stipetic, Herzog was brought up in a remote Bavarian mountain village singularly untouched by modern technology: he was seventeen when he made his first phone call. However, he won a scriptwriting competition at fifteen and made his first film at nineteen, using money he had earned working the night shift as a welder in a steel works. At eighteen he visited the Sudan and since then he has travelled extensively, making films in, amongst other places, Greece (*Signs of Life*, 1968), Mexico (*Even Dwarfs Started Small*, 1970), Peru (*Aguirre* and *Fitzcarraldo*, 1982), several African countries (*Fata Morgana*, *Echoes from a Sombre Empire* and *Herdsmen of the Sun*, 1989), Australia (*Where the Green Ants Dream*, 1984), Ghana, Colombia, Brazil (*Cobra Verde*, 1987) and Pakistan and Patagonia for his two mountain-climbing 'documentaries'. Yet for all his travels, there is a sense in which he remains firmly rooted in his homeland. He has not, like most German directors of his generation including Fassbinder, made films specifically about German history and society; but his vision is deeply impregnated with the spirit of German Romanticism. It is consistent with this that landscape plays a massively important role in his films; and it is significant that the kind of travelling he likes best, provided it is for a genuine purpose, is on foot. Famously, he walked from Munich to Paris to see the great film critic Lotte Eisner, who was dying; and he walked across the Alps to the border of Slovenia to propose to his future wife.

His life and his work are inextricably intertwined and in both there is an obsessiveness bordering on lunacy. The dangers to which he has exposed himself and his collaborators are legendary, one example being the making of the 31-minute *La Soufrière* (1977) which involved his going to the island of Guadeloupe, after experts had predicted a volcanic eruption with the force of 'five or six atomic bombs' and the inhabitants had been evacuated, in order to meet an elderly peasant who had refused to leave, and to share the sense of impending catastrophe. The making of the big-budget feature *Fitzcarraldo*, about an Irish rubber baron obsessed with building an opera house in the Amazonian jungle – Herzog has himself directed around twenty opera productions – largely paralleled the difficulties and perils

encountered by its subject, most famously the episode of hauling a boat over a mountain. The star of that film, Klaus Kinski, brought to his role an air of dangerous madness, as he did in other Herzog films including *Aguirre*, *Cobra Verde* and *Woyzeck* (1979); one incident in their well-documented love–hate relationship was when Kinski threatened to leave the set of *Aguirre* and Herzog pulled a gun on him.

Despite the sardonic eye with which he views the folly and sometimes destructiveness of much human endeavour, Herzog shows sympathy and admiration for those who at least try to transcend the limitations of social conventions; and through the eyes of outsiders and 'holy fools' he sees the possibility of approaching a deeper truth, even if it is one which they themselves may be unable to reach. His whole life and work can be seen as a continuing quest for what he has called 'ecstatic truth' and, for him as a filmmaker, the principal means he has at his disposal are the creating and poetically right ordering of images. He has said that the lack of significant images is as great a threat to our civilization as the recognized ecological and nuclear threats. His single-minded devotion to rectifying that lack is at least as heroic as the obsessive quests of some of the protagonists of his films.

Further reading

See: P. Cronin (ed.) *Herzog on Herzog* (2002). There is a great deal of worthwhile material on the Internet, and Herzog's own website http://www.wernerherzog.com is very informative.

GRAY WATSON

HESSE, Hermann

1877–1962

German novelist and poet

Born in the Black Forest into a family with a tradition of missionaries and scholars in India, Hesse lived sporadically in his youth in Basel, where he also worked in a bookshop for three years. He made a trip to India in 1911 and took up permanent domicile in Switzerland a year later. During and after the Great War he underwent psychoanalytic treatment for nervous collapse by **Jung** and his pupil J.B. Lang. In 1919 Hesse moved to Montagnola in the Ticino, which was to be his home until his death. He married three times but shunned the business of the literary world, its groups and movements, preferring – like his heroes – an existence of voluntary withdrawal, embarking on journeys into his self, discovering hidden layers of the personality through dreams and engrossed contemplation.

Hesse's thought was influenced by men like Kierkegaard and Jakob Burckhardt, and especially **Nietzsche**. The latter, together with other 'visionaries' like Blake and **Dostoevsky**, are seen as key 'loners' in modern culture by Colin Wilson in *The Outsider* (1956) where a chapter, 'The Romantic Outsider', is devoted to Hesse. His relations with fellow-writers were cordial and often of close affinity (e.g. with **T.S. Eliot** and **Thomas Mann**) and his already high reputation – he received the Nobel Prize for Literature in 1946 – was given a fresh and unexpected boost when his work became posthumously the gospel of the West Coast 'hippie' cult, **Timothy Leary** to the fore, in the late 1960s. Hesse's ascetic, withdrawn lifestyle reinforced the myth, and this notoriety fed renewed interest in his writings in Europe.

Hesse's search for individual ways of achieving a harmonious personality appealed to a young generation rebelling against the consumerist conformist values of their elders. The attainment of a higher state of being does not occur overnight; it is a long, painful, though evolutionary process of shedding preconceptions and outer 'skins' and proceeding through organic stages to ultimate harmony. Hesse's own life and writings were a blue-print for this journey into the interior or 'inner way', starting with his early phase of Romantic restlessness where his vague yearnings, sensitive reactions and aesthetic ambitions were projected on to his heroes. In *Peter Camenzind* (1904, trans. 1961) the

wandering outsider figure, the footloose vagabond in flight from society, appears. Already evident, too, is a recalcitrant dissatisfaction with and isolation from the establishment and its cultural values, particularly – from bitter personal experience – its stultifying educational system; Hesse ran away from school in Maulbronn, an event still powerful enough to inspire *Under the Wheel* (*Unterm Rad*, 1906, trans. 1958).

This hallmark of the young Hesse, the desire for experience untrammelled by the inhibitions of institutionalized society, elicited a liberation of thought and behaviour in personal responses, love and sexual matters. On the face of it this may appear as a licence for 'permissiveness', but it actually expressed Hesse's urgent need to break out of the constrictions of accepted morality to open the way for the development of a healthier, balanced personality. The rejection of worn-out morals coincided during the First World War with the infiltration into Hesse's life and work of the psychoanalytic techniques of **Freud**, Stekel and others. From Nietzsche came the idea of the lost God and empty worldly values, from his trip to India (prompted by 'sheer inner distress') the burgeoning study of Indian and Chinese thought, and from his own life the nervous illness of his first wife and the breakdown of their marriage that had serious repercussions on Hesse's mental state. The protracted treatment he received from his friend Dr Lang contributed to the transmutation of psychoanalysis into literature in *Demian* (1919, trans. 1923), a novel documenting the stages in the emergence of a reborn personality. Emil Sinclair, the hero, is guided by his mentor Demian along the way to discover his own self in a contemplative search that entails – as in most of Hesse's novels – the investigation of the individual psyche and the neglect of action and external reality.

Despite his absorption with the individual and inner problems Hesse was by no means abstracted or publicly reticent during the Great War. Vigorously pacifist, he kept up a stream of political essays, open letters and hortatory calls to the warring nations, and worked especially hard on behalf of prisoners of war. His ideas had a notable influence on Eliot's assessment of Western culture in *The Waste Land*, and the warnings of cultural doom Hesse voiced are transformed in his most famous work, *Steppenwolf* (*Der Steppenwolf*, 1927, trans. 1929), into the desolation of the lone hero, Harry Haller, whose discontent with a stifling and neurotic bourgeois society leads him to shun it. But Haller's real agony is internal, in his struggle to balance his 'wolfish' and 'human' psyches, his instincts and ideals. The depiction of his anguish that leads him through despair to a release in a symbolic death reflects imaginatively the stages of a therapeutic psychoanalytic cure. Hesse stressed that the story certainly recounted 'sufferings and distress, but was by no means the story of a despairing man, but one full of hope'. The rebirth of Haller's identity is brought about in the incidents of the climactic Magic Theatre, the door to which is opened by the use of drugs and in which metaphors from the armoury of psychoanalysis – mirrors and images, violence and murder, sexual bipolarity, music and art – are played out until Haller emerges from his mental and emotional chaos to a new potential for balance and serenity.

Serenity ('*Heiterkeit*') becomes the key word in the mature Hesse. Around 1930 a fresh dimension in his thought came with his renewed interest in the inward-turning, contemplative spirit of the East which gave a new and precise focus to what had always preoccupied him, namely personal religious experience. Stirrings of this Eastern attitude are evident in *Siddhartha* (1922, trans. 1951), a novel highly regarded by Henry Miller, and *The Journey to the East* (*Die Morgenlandfahrt*, 1932, trans. 1956), which showed how Hesse had moved beyond conflict with society into a sort of secular mysticism. Hesse's engagement with Eastern thought culminated after eleven years of gestation in his last major work, *The Glass Bead Game* (*Das Glasperlenspiel*, 1943, trans. 1970), which

recounts the life of the *magister ludi*, Josef Knecht, in the pedagogic province of Castalia. Here a secularized religious order seeks through teaching and example to instil in its young charges the 'search for wholeness' that, if successful, leads to an 'awakening' ('*Erwachen*'), a true understanding and a tranquillity transcending the arbitrary values of the world that only clog the personality. The path that leads both upwards and inwards to this fulfilment is in three stages, reflecting again the themes that dominate Hesse's whole output: the innocence of the child (*Peter Camenzind*) is followed by the guilt and despair of the man (*Steppenwolf*), leading in turn either to downfall or to life itself, the latter exquisite state achieved through abnegation and self-denial, overcoming yet accepting the world. The disintegration of the self into innumerable personae, already adumbrated in *Steppenwolf*, is a prerequisite for this progression that contains many echoes of the Bhagavad Gita, the *Upanishads* and the practice of yoga.

In addition to search, the motifs of 'play' and 'service' are other essential elements in this process; although the pedagogic province is the home of the spirit ('*Geist*') and the desired awakening occurs through meditation at moments of intense feeling and insight, Hesse nevertheless seems to recognize that this state of felicity can also end in impotence, rigidity and lifelessness. The model of perfect attainment postulated in Castalia is therefore one where a symbolic unity of the *vita contemplativa* and the *vita activa* is achieved by Josef Knecht, the supremely serene sage and teacher of the young, who drowns after following his star pupil into a glacial mountain lake.

Like Goethe's Faust, Hesse's hero too finds ultimate fulfilment, even salvation, in service to humanity. In articulating the total dedication to the search for awakening, in harmony with one's fellow-men and eschewing strife, Hesse opened up a path that could lead to wisdom, serenity and happiness for many troubled individuals.

Further reading

Other works include: *Knulp* (1915, trans. 1971); *Klingsor's Last Summer* (*Klingsors letzter Sommer*, 1920, trans. 1970); *Narziss and Goldmund* (*Narziss und Goldmund*, 1930, trans. 1959); *If the War Goes On* (*Krieg und Frieden*, 1946, trans. 1970). See also: Hugo Ball, *Hermann Hesse: Sein Leben und Werk* (1947); Theodore J. Ziolkowski, *The Novels of Hermann Hesse* (1965); Mark Boulby, *Hermann Hesse: His Mind and Art* (1967); Walter Sorell, *Hermann Hesse. The Man who Sought and Found Himself* (1974); Ralph Freedman, *Hermann Hesse: Pilgrim of Crisis. A Biography* (1979).

A.V. SUBIOTTO

HIRST, Damien

1965–

English artist

The celebrity status enjoyed by Damien Hirst is unprecedented. If his studio entourage compares with **Andy Warhol's** factory, and his bluff, screen-friendly personality with that of fellow Yorkshireman **David Hockney**, Hirst surpasses both in the speed with which he engaged, and continues to engage, the headlines. In the early 1990s, his ready-made sculptures made notorious use of a 14-foot tiger shark, cased and preserved in formaldehyde. Then followed dissected cows, sheep and pigs, and flies breeding on the carcass of a cow's head. All packed a visual punch with powerful, unsettling images. Their iconographic memorability caught the imagination of a wide public. With his animal pieces in particular, Hirst can be credited with creating a popular taste for art that shocks. As winner in 1995 of the controversy-led Turner Prize he seemed an obvious choice. Not all his work has been exceptional or sensational – his spot and spin paintings, for example – but his diverse activity has fed an appetite for surprise, encouraged by media attention.

It could be said that Hirst made his name with his controversial early work and rested on the laurels he earned in the early 1990s. Financially, this would be true, as he himself has stated publicly. But it would hardly do justice to an artist who at the time of writing is forty and, therefore, still in mid-career. At most we can plot his phenomenal sweep to fame and fortune in specific cultural circumstances, and attempt to assess its already legendary significance.

There is an element of national pride attached to this legend. Hirst's success built on the youthful image and experimentation of the new British sculptors of the 1980s, who generated excitement around British art with their unconventional use of discarded materials, or 'rubbish'. With his *Natural History* series Hirst developed Marcel Duchamp's concept of the ready-made further by transforming reality into art both metaphorically with his suggestive titles, and by a natural process of metamorphosis, as with the fly and the butterfly. Other contemporaries shared his ideas, but his was the most exciting and energetic voice in British art. As such he was acknowledged leader of a young British art movement emanating from Goldsmiths College, which lifted Britain into the international vanguard. Despite strong doubts on both sides of the Atlantic, that perception holds. But the critical question persists: are we celebrating the man or his art? For the buzz around Hirst has been as much to do with his 1990s, fun-loving lifestyle, his drinking and drug-taking, as with the provocatively morbid characteristics of his art. Hirst has further confounded the question 'What is art?' by conflating his star status with his production. Rather than have a work judged as sculpture or painting, he wants it valued for its brand name, Damien Hirst.

Hirst absorbed art market tactics early. His generation were educated in an age of professionalization and private business patronage for the arts. It was his enterprise in mounting *Freeze*, a show of work by fellow students, which drew him in 1988 into the limelight. Since then he has stage-managed his career, prompting comment that the content of his art would be considered negligible were it not for its presentation. His success has soared in a culture which confuses aesthetic values with those of advertising, fashion, pop and the media, and in which the investment value of art overrides its personal appreciation. Hirst's career was founded on the patronage of advertising mogul and collector Charles Saatchi, who exhibited Hirst in his West London gallery in 1992, launching the collective name Young British Artists. Without the backing of Saatchi, and of the British and American dealers Jay Jopling and Larry Gagosian, Hirst could not have sustained production of the technically complex and very expensive sculptures which fuel his reputation.

Hirst's relationship with the fine art establishment has been cautious. Given his enormous early success and the manipulative nature of his *modus operandi*, it is not surprising that, in the later 1990s, he decided to work outside its parameters on other projects, such as restaurants, the design of a golf course and book covers. He refused to stand for election to the Royal Academy of Arts, 'a stuffy, old, pompous institution'. Although in 1992 the British Council showed Hirst as national representative at the third International Istanbul Biennial, in 1997 he reportedly turned down its invitation to represent Britain in the Venice Biennale, the leading international forum for contemporary art. His gesture of independence was brief, as he saw the need to re-establish his career as a fine artist. Nevertheless, he has been reluctant to exhibit alone under a national spotlight. Having won the Gold Medal at the Ljubljana Biennial of Graphic Arts in 2001, entered by the British Council, he accepted its invitation for a drawing retrospective in 2003. However, for his first retrospective exhibition in 2004–5 he chose the Naples Archaeological Museum, explaining in the catalogue that at forty and on the wagon it was a moment to reflect on his career, but not to give it closure, as critical scrutiny by a national institution might do.

The unpredictable nature of Hirst's art makes him hard to categorize. More than **Picasso**, Gerhard Richter and those of his own generation, he has made a feature of diversification, working in discrete series of animal sculptures, vitrines, installations and paintings, and even edging into film, book illustration and production, and restaurant design.

His continual self-invention as an artist falls back constantly on his obsession with death, and he has not escaped the charge that his work is derived from one idea, *memento mori*, and that his thoughts on the meaning of life are truisms presented with teasingly weighty titles. He disarms criticism with ingenuous replies, saying of his famous title for the shark sculpture, *The Physical Impossibility of Death in the Mind of Something Living* (1992), that to call it 'It's hard to imagine death while you are alive' would be patronizing. Like **Francis Bacon**, Lucian **Freud** and others, Hirst's aim is to make his art more real. Whether he is curating an exhibition, putting together an installation or painting a photo-realistic picture, everything for him is collage, an assembly of objects selected from the real world. They provide the starting point for getting nearer the truth about life, and for waking the public up to it. From Bacon and Bruce Nauman, as much as from advertising, he absorbed the need for a visual shorthand to communicate his message, letting its deeper meaning resonate with the onlooker. To this end he uses traditional reminders of death, such as the skull or the butterfly, or modern ones such as cabinets of pills and gleaming surgical instruments, stub-filled ashtrays or fly-blackened surfaces titled *Holocaust*, *Genocide* or *Aids*. He reworks popular icons, such **Degas'** bronze sculpture of a ballet dancer, and makes photo-realistic pictures derived from newspaper images, in order to tackle war, violation and other issues that concern him.

Hirst's early originality lay in his presentation of objects to startling effect. His later work often appears bland, but his religious pieces of 2004, in which, for example, Jesus was represented as a naked woman, with a crucifix hung over her genitals on a string of sausages, demonstrates that he still has the ability to shock. Commercially, he is one of the most successful living artists, lending obvious motivation for maintaining his celebrity profile. Whether the Damien Hirst trademark will keep its value, and how art historians will finally assess his contribution, it is probably too soon to predict.

Further reading

The most complete visual record of Hirst's work to the late 1990s, with brief commentaries in his own words, is his artist's book, Damien Hirst, *I Want to Spend the Rest of My Life Everywhere, with Everyone, One to One, Always, Forever, Now* (1997). For the most up-to-date appreciation of his work, including a long interview with the artist, and a full bibliography, see *Damien Hirst. The Agony and the Ecstasy: Selected Works from 1989–2004* (exhibition catalogue, Museo Archaeologico Nazionale, Naples, 2004).

JUDITH BUMPUS

HITCHCOCK, (Sir) Alfred Joseph

1899–1980

British/US film director

Alfred Hitchcock's career in cinema is in many ways unique: no other British director established himself so securely in Hollywood, and few others of any nationality have earned a descriptive tag ('The Master of Suspense') or become such a familiar public figure. Born in London, he began working in the customary minor capacities in the early 1920s, designing title cards, serving as assistant director and art director, all the while acquiring a fascination with the mechanics of cinematic illusion. By 1925 he was a full-time director: his material was mostly drawn from popular stage plays, yet he quickly and effectively mastered the grammar of silent cinema. *The Manxman* (1928) remains a stunning example of storytelling through the manipulation of visual symbols. And in *The Lodger* (1926), with stage matinée idol Ivor Novello as a suspected Jack the Ripper, he showed his early interest in crime and the harassment of the innocent.

In *Blackmail* (1929) Hitchcock pounced on sound as another tool to convey mood and propel the plot imaginatively. Then in 1934,

with *The Man Who Knew Too Much*, he began a run of six solid thrillers for Gaumont-British, which have retained all their pungency. *The Thirty-Nine Steps* (1935) has many key Hitchcock ingredients – an innocent hero pursued by both police and enemy spies all over Britain, handcuffed for some of the way to a resentful heroine (Hitchcock always treated male/female relationships somewhat icily). And *Sabotage* (1936), derived from **Conrad's** novel *The Secret Agent*, is quite the equal of its Hollywood successors in its power to generate audience jitters and deep unease.

Rebecca (1940) was his first American film, and Hitchcock luxuriated in the superior technical facilities Hollywood could offer. Yet there were losses as well as gains – none of his American films had that quirky response to everyday life found in his earlier work. Hitchcock took some time getting acclimatized. *Shadow of a Doubt* in 1943 found him beginning to explore small-town manners, but elsewhere he marked time with propaganda-slanted entertainments like *Lifeboat* (1943) or the bizarre melodrama of *Spellbound* (1945).

Then in 1951 came *Strangers on a Train*, in which an unhappily married tennis champion becomes ensnared in a psychotic's murderous trap: Hitchcock's use of Washington society and character psychology was ingenious and unerring. His best films were now probing deeper into fears and motivations: *I Confess* (1952) was a bleak study in tormented conscience, while *Rear Window* (1954) and *Vertigo* (1958) provided a sexual dimension to the problems faced by James Stewart's two heroes – a voyeur who discovers a murder through a neighbour's window, an ex-detective hounded by his love for a neurotic girl he failed to save from death. Even *North by North West* (1959) contained worried reflections of depersonalized modern life beneath its surface escapades.

In *Psycho* (1960) Hitchcock's love of teasing his audience reached a spectacular consummation. This deeply deceptive story of Norman Bates (played by Anthony Perkins),

HITLER, Adolf   349

his motel and his beloved mother was told with fiendish skill. The vicious murder of a woman taking a shower, immaculately pared through precision editing, has spawned countless imitations. In *The Birds* (1963) Hitchcock had a field day manipulating the mysterious attacks of massed birds, though the film's technical daring interfered with its emotional resonance. His subsequent output received mixed responses: what some interpreted as laxity and slipping standards others kindly regarded as the relaxed approach suitable to old age. *Marnie* (1964), *Torn Curtain* (1966) and *Frenzy* (1972) certainly have superior sequences, yet their narrative momentum is erratic. But Hitchcock's reputation remains unassailable: no one has ever used the elements of cinematic storytelling so artfully or so disturbingly.

Further reading

See: Howard Maxford, *The A–Z of Hitchcock* (2002); Patrick McGilligan, *Alfred Hitchcock: A Life in Darkness and Light* (2003); Charlotte Chandler, *It's Only a Movie: Alfred Hitchcock – A Personal Biography* (2005); Robert Kolker (ed.), *Alfred Hitchcock's 'Psycho': A Casebook* (2004); Murray Pomerance, *An Eye for Hitchcock* (2004); Richard Allen and Sam Ishii-Gonzales (eds), *Hitchcock: Past and Future* (2003).

GEOFF BROWN

HITLER, Adolf

1899–1945

Austro-German politician

Adolf Hitler was born in Braunau on the Inn as a national of the Austro-Hungarian Empire. He died, as Reich Chancellor of Germany, on 30 April 1945, in a bunker beneath the rubble of Berlin. He had been Germany's leader since 1933. Originally he had wanted to become an artist but two rejections from the Vienna Academy of Fine Arts changed his mind. In 1913 he left Austria for Munich where the following year he volunteered for a German regiment and went into the First World War. He was twice

decorated for bravery and, in 1918, was wounded in a British gas attack. While in hospital he learned that the Kaiser's Germany had been defeated and that Socialists now ruled the land. Hitler, who had gone into the war a dreamer and a drifter, emerged from it as a highly politicized demagogue.

After recovering, Hitler was employed as a political instructor by his old regiment and it was in this post that he first came across the small Fascist Party, which he joined and then led. His success was the result of his skill in politics, for he combined a polished demagogic style with an easy political logic, one which made a new and complex world situation seem the simple result of a Jewish–**Marxist** conspiracy. Indeed, it was from this concept that the subsequent history of the Third Reich was to flow even though the road to power was not easy.

In the Fascist manner Hitler first tried to ape the March on Rome tactic of his forerunner and idol Mussolini. But Hitler's attempt at a putsch ended in a nine-month gaol sentence and the need to rethink strategy. Since Weimar Germany was a democracy, the Nazi leader reasoned, power had to be won by methods which were appropriate to it: the party would have to become a mass movement and democratic privileges might be exploited to the point of illegality. In addition, Nazis would have to peddle a coherent ideology, and Hitler himself set about trying to provide the latter. In fact his intellectual contribution was minimal, for *Mein Kampf* (1924) was no more than a rambling account of his own version of the Social **Darwinism** and anti-Semitism of others badly glued to an attempt at making his own life appear a suitable symbol for a future Germany. His spoken ideas were generally banal although they could, on occasions, seem remarkably apposite.

Hitler came to realize that in an era of mass communication the communicator-politician supported by dedicated followers could flourish, and so, within ten years, he became Germany's dictator. He was helped by the Nazis' open use of political terrorism (which nonetheless never won for him the majority of Germans) and the world economic crisis of 1929. Once in power, he dismantled the achievements of the Weimar: he banned all parties except his own, he transformed the economy and he institutionalized the violent intimidation of all opposition. Indeed, the spiritual site of the Third Reich was not located, as popular myth would have it, in **Wagnerian** idylls or licentious excess but in the concentration camp and the Gestapo cell.

A special part in all this was played by Hitler's persecution of the Jews. It enabled him not only to prove his ruthlessness but also to fabricate a kind of national identity. So-called Aryan Germans (and Europeans in general) were invited to define themselves as those who did not have to wear yellow stars, resettle themselves in ghettos and vanish suddenly to the east and its gas chambers.

To suggest that the reality of the Third Reich was very different from the image its leadership tried to create is, however, to fail to explain adequately why the Nazis' own image proved so strong. For Hitler appeared to have abolished class conflict, to have enabled the Germans to go back to work, to have provided law and order at home and stood up for Germany in international affairs. Equally, the Nazis' desolation of German cultural life, not least by their elimination of the Jews, seems less significant than their support of obvious bourgeois art and traditional values of propriety and rural harmony. One answer is simply that Hitler and his henchmen possessed such understanding of the nature of mass communication and such mastery of its techniques that any myth they chose to create was bound to be effective. The very notion that National Socialism was a German phenomenon rather than a straightforward variety of European Fascism is a case in point. Nazi attitudes were, more often than not, Fascist ones, originating from a response to the overthrow of the old world by the Great War and its aftermath by those who contrasted the glory of comradeship under arms and patriotic death to the chaos of Marxist revolution.

Hitler's individual impact was very different from what it seemed and has been made to seem. He was but a figurehead in most areas of politics, convinced that the correct appearance would always be taken as the correct action and that its consequences would be attributed to something for which he could not be held responsible. Hitler's most important offering, then, was that he realized that in the new politics of Nazism, propaganda or the interpretation of reality was interchangeable with leadership, or the shaping of reality. That the results would one day catch up with him was exemplified by his death. For to commit suicide by shooting himself in the mouth was to destroy himself through the same organ that had brought him his fame, the source of his demagogic appeal. Hitler verbalized the intentions of the Nazis and they intended him to be their leader and run their affairs. This is the cause of the exaggeration of his personal role.

The Thousand Year Reich, that figment of Nazi imagination, lasted a little over twelve years. National Socialism did not create a new Germany for it brought only the destruction of an existing alternative one, based on Fascist ideals of violence, anti-Marxism and racial exclusiveness. Indeed, the destructive power of Nazi policies, which was a result of the dynamism inherent in the movement, led directly to war and defeat. Each Nazi campaign was designed to engender another campaign, another struggle, another test. There was only one exception, of course: the final solution of the so-called Jewish problem, perhaps the most consistent Nazi aim and one to which all real strategic goals were subordinated.

Hitler was remarkable as a violent demagogue, the leader of a political movement which imposed on human lives an unrealizable set of policies. He could no more be appeased than Germany become a nation of blonde blue-eyed giants. Claiming to uphold German nationhood, he in fact destroyed it; pretending to be close to the German people, he in fact prescribed their destruction since their defeat by the Allies would render them valueless. Hitler and his state are a monument not to the values he maintained he was promoting but rather to a more abstract and frightening truth: political manipulation by a violent movement with a violent leadership outpaced humankind's comprehension of the extent to which political reality was being fabricated.

Further reading

See: H.R. Trevor-Roper (ed.), *Hitler's Table Talk* (1953); Ernst Nolte, *The Three Faces of Fascism* (1965); George Mosse, *The Crisis of German Ideology* (1966); Alan Bullock, *Hitler* (1971); Ian Kershaw, *Hitler, 1889–1936: Hubris* (1998) and *Hitler, 1936–1945: Nemesis* (2000).

ANTHONY GLEES

HOCKNEY, David

1937–

English artist

From *enfant terrible* to golden boy of the colour supplements and now probably one of the world's most popular artists, Hockney's career has been a brilliant success story. Arriving in London in 1959 from his native Bradford, he achieved public notice while still a student at the Royal College. Like many of his generation, he reacted against the dominance of abstraction; critics were misled, however, in taking the inclusion of certain motifs, for example tea-packets, in his work as justification for labelling him a Pop Artist. His concerns have, rather, always been personal and autobiographical – in a sense, very traditional. At first, he felt very strongly the need to reconcile this with the main tenets of modernist painting, especially flatness. Much of his work explored, with great wit, the contradictions between the two-dimensional surface and three-dimensional illusion: this underlay his playing with several 'styles', for example the Egyptian – as in *The First Marriage* (1962). Such explorations helped him to develop, with remarkable consistency, towards the smooth, somewhat photographic

style which characterized his painting in the later 1960s and early 1970s. The year 1964 represented a watershed: in that year he began to use acrylic paint and he discovered California. The geometry of Californian architecture provided his paintings with a strong, slightly graphic, construction which did not conflict with a naturalistic reading. He frequently painted swimming pools, partly because the depiction of water, like glass and other transparent substances, posed a fascinating challenge, and partly because they were a convenient setting for his principal interest, the male human figure.

Arguably Hockney's greatest contribution to cultural change has been his frank avowal of homosexuality well before this became commonplace, in that it is hard to think of any reputation which did more to liberalize public opinion on this matter before the late 1960s. His influence in the specific sphere of art, by contrast, has been essentially conservative or, better, conciliatory. Not much in sympathy with the aims of avant-gardism, he is above all a superbly talented practitioner of recognized skills. His graphic works, including several small books, are of a very high quality. Particularly evident is his talent as a draughtsman: he has produced many drawings, some in coloured crayon, which capture the atmosphere of certain situations and the characters of several close friends (as well as his parents) with extraordinary accuracy and feeling. A painting with a similar quality is *Mr and Mrs Clark and Percy* (1970–1). In some ways, it is a quality shared with good short-storytelling; nor would the literary analogy be offensive to Hockney. Much admired worldwide, there is nevertheless something about his art which is very English and in particular Yorkshire. From that county no doubt derives his plentiful common sense, enabling him to be straightforward about what matters to him and cynical about what he believes to be pretentious in many of the modern art world's attitudes.

His avowed hedonism, however, sets him apart from his background, and is one of the reasons that in 1978 he settled in the Hollywood Hills. His painting *Nichols Canyon* (1980) marks another stylistic change; there followed several colourful landscapes done in a less naturalistic, more magical style somewhat reminiscent of good book illustration. In 1982 he began making composite pictures made up from polaroid photographs, moving on to photocollages made with regular 35 mm photographic prints, which made up a 'complete' picture of a scene from a large number of individually photographed details, as in the several versions of *Pearblossom Highway* (1986). During the 1980s he experimented with colour photocopiers, fax machines and computers. A major retrospective in 1988 was followed by another in 1995–6 at the Royal Academy, London.

A lover of opera, he has designed a number of sets, including for *The Magic Flute* at Glyndebourne in 1978. Already in 1983 there was a large touring exhibition, *Hockney Paints the Stage*, of his designs for opera and ballet; since when he has designed sets for a **Stravinsky** triple bill at the Metropolitan Opera, **Wagner's** *Tristan und Isolde* in Los Angeles, **Puccini's** *Turandot* in San Francisco, and **Richard Strauss's** *Die Frau ohne Schatten* at Covent Garden. Tragically, given his love of music, he has been afflicted with deafness.

His book *Secret Knowledge: Rediscovering the Lost Techniques of the Old Masters* (2001), in which he argued that Old Masters including Van Eyck, Leonardo, Velazquez and Ingres had made use of various optical devices in the creation of their paintings, caused controversy. He continues to paint in his Hollywood Hills studio and in a small house he purchased more recently in Malibu.

Further reading

Other works include: *David Hockney by David Hockney* (1976); *That's the Way I See It* (1996) with Nikos Stangos; *Hockney on 'Art': Conversations with Paul Joyce* (2002). See: Peter Clothier, *David Hockney* (Modern Masters Series, Vol. 17) (1995); Paul Melia, Ulrich Luckhardt and David Hockney, *David Hockney: Paintings* (2000); Gregory Evans and David Hockney, *Hockney's Paintings: The Definitive Retrospective* (2004). Hockney is the subject of the film *A Bigger Splash* (director Jack Hazan, 1974) and there are two more recent videos, *Behind the Scenes with David Hockney* (1992) and *David Hockney: Pleasures of the Eye* (1997).

GRAY WATSON

HOLABIRD, William and ROCHE, Martin
1854–1923; 1855–1927
US architects

It was in Chicago that the first skyscraper appeared in 1885, built by William Jenney whose office was to produce two of the most influential of the Chicago skyscraper architects, Holabird and Roche. Possibly it might have been thought that New York would be the first city to build a ten-storey building; however, in the 1830s Chicago became the more important commercial centre due to railways and increases in the Great Lakes traffic. When in 1871 a fire decimated the city there was an opportunity for experimental building. The increase in the cost of land meant that clients pressured architects for maximum usage of the site and therefore building heights started to rise. However, skyscrapers only became possible with the new technology which provided for steel-framed buildings that were strong enough to carry the weight of curtain walls that were not self-supporting. This was an improvement on the original frame buildings which were of weaker construction, being made of cast and wrought iron. It was an Englishman, Henry Bessemer, who invented the process which produced mild steel beams which first appeared in the United States in the 1880s.

Holabird and Roche in 1888–9 were able therefore to build the Tacoma building, thirteen storeys high with projecting bay windows from the first floor to the roof. For lightness most of the curtain walling is window glass. By 1894 the two architects had produced the far simpler flat-faced fifteen-storey Marquette building, with slight recessions for the windows which are horizontally stressed, leaving the vertical emphasis to the piers which shoot dramatically from the bottom to the top. However, compared with their next design, the Marquette building appears heavy and rather rustic in style.

This next, only nine-storey, skyscraper, known as the McClurg building of 1899–1990, displays a fully modern twentieth-century style. The glass expanse is far larger and piers and mullions are narrow and linear, leaving the horizontal load-bearing frame to be expressed by the greater width. It is a particularly fine example of an early skyscraper and the pattern for many more that follow.

Perhaps the most well-known skyscraper architect was **Louis Sullivan**. He worked for a time in Chicago with various architects including Holabird and Roche. He produced the frontage for a frame designed by the latter at No. 18 South Michigan Avenue in 1898–9. This is the third frontage section of three adjoining frame buildings produced by the partnership; Sullivan's third is similar to theirs in style in terms of weight and proportion and his windows are as long horizontally but not so high. In addition, the cross-beam frontage has a typical although restrained repeat decoration set at wide intervals on the horizontals and a veritable flourish of plant forms at the top of the two dividing piers. The whole of Sullivan's frontage is clad with terracotta moulding, and the effect is rather richer and more subtle than the adjoining two buildings.

In general the 'Chicago style' was to become more severe and express a more open appearance than skyscraper building in New York.

Further reading

See: W.A. Starrett, *Skyscrapers and the Men who Built Them* (1928); C.W. Condit, *The Chicago School of Architecture* (1964); H.R. Hitchcock, *Architecture: Nineteenth and Twentieth Centuries* (1971); Robert Bruegmann, *The Architects and the City: Holabird & Roche of Chicago, 1880–1918* (1997).

PAT TURNER

HOMER, Winslow

1836–1910
US painter

Homer's biography and motivations are frequently obscure. After an apprenticeship to John Bufford, a Boston lithographer, he became a freelance illustrator. Contributions to *Harper's Weekly* continued for eighteen years. In 1859 he moved to New York, attended a drawing school in Brooklyn, then the National Academy of Design, and in 1861 decided to paint, helped by Frédéric Rondel. For twenty years he spent summers in the country, collecting material, and winters in New York, painting. Two journeys were crucial – ten months in France (1866–7) where he exhibited at the Exposition Universelle, and two visits to Teignmouth in Devon (1881, 1882) when he exhibited at the Royal Academy in London. No proof exists that Homer ever saw a Japanese print or an Impressionist painting, even in France. Despite strong similarities with **Monet**, he was less intent on questioning the solidity of the three-dimensional world than his French counterparts. At this time, in pictures such as *Croquet Scene* (1866), rituals of polite behaviour served as excuses to study the emotional resonance of gestures, glances or simply empty space. Unusual compositions and irresolute perspectives foreshadowed the style of **Edward Hopper**, an admirer of Homer's 'weight'. A temporarily high-keyed palette (1868–9), evident in paintings such as *Long Beach, New Jersey*, has been explained as a reaction to French painting. A period of more severe classicizing followed (1871–5); *Waiting for Dad* of 1873, in which a Gloucester wife and two children await a fisherman's return, has been compared to Piero della Francesca. Commonplace themes abounded. The flippant yet amazed manner of **Henry James's** criticism in 1875 barely concealed a sense that Homer's task resembled his own as seen in the early study of Hawthorne – to colonize America as a subject for art.

At the height of his fame as an illustrator Homer unaccountably stopped. Henceforth his new medium, watercolour, would occupy as much of his attention as oil on canvas. While staying in Teignmouth he abandoned his genteel, sunlit themes for grey seas and heroic figures. In 1883 he moved to Prout's Neck, Maine, where he lived alone, concentrated on the elements and embarked on another new medium, etching. The late work was strongly post-Darwinian. Human beings disappeared almost completely; only a dynamic play of natural forces mattered. *The Fox Hunt* (1893) shows a flock of starving crows attacking a fox during a bleak Maine winter.

From the 1890s onwards Homer spent part of each winter in a hotter climate. Together with one or two of his etchings, the late Bermudan watercolours seemed to him to represent his finest work. Sensuous, harmonic, joyous, translucent, *Rum Cay* (1898?) or *The Turtle Pound* (1898) are oddly reminiscent of Greek art. Homer died alone at Prout's Neck aged seventy-four.

In his lifetime Homer transformed genre painting into a means of conveying subtle emotion and produced masterpieces of woodblock engraving as well as watercolours, etchings and oil paintings. Subjects included Negro life, the Civil War, hunting, fishing, children, sport and nature. Yet these were utilized for their possibilities for formal invention. It is difficult to describe Homer's technical brilliance as an artist. Barbara Novak has argued that his career in general demonstrates a duality which combines 'indigenous conceptualism with a perceptual realism that was developing with teleological authority in the Western world at that moment'. Perhaps the struggle between eye and idea, 'making' and 'matching', the conflicting demands of innate classicism and *plein air* observation account for much in his art. It is as good a definition as we are likely to get of the historical significance of the talent of the greatest painter of nineteenth-century America.

Further reading

See: Lloyd Goodrich, *Winslow Homer* (1973); Lloyd Goodrich, *The Graphic Work of Winslow Homer* (1968); Barbara Novak, *American Art of the* *Nineteenth Century* (1969); H. Cooper, *Winslow Homer Watercolours* (1986); Nicolai Cikovsky *et al.*, *Winslow Homer* (1995).

STUART MORGAN

HOPKINS, Gerard Manley

1844–89

English poet

Gerard Manley Hopkins was born in Stratford, Essex, on 28 July 1844, the first of eight children of an affluent Victorian couple: his father, Manley, worked in shipping, wrote poetry, published a book on Hawaii (whose Consul-General in London he became in 1856) and practised a tolerant Episcopalianism; Gerard's mother, Kate, was a doctor's daughter, a conscientious Christian, and a lover of music and literature. The family moved to Oak Hill, Hampstead, in 1852 and, two years later, Gerard went as a boarder to Highgate School. There he won the poetry prize for his Keatsian set-piece 'The Escorial', courageously resisted the sadistic authority of the headmaster, earned the nickname 'Skin' (Hop*kin*s anagrammatized to suggest his skin-and-bones physical frailty), attracted attention by his nightly devotion to the New Testament, and won an exhibition to study classics at Oxford.

In 1863 Hopkins arrived at Balliol College and delighted in the theologically charged intellectual atmosphere of Oxford. He became friendly with fellow undergraduate Robert Bridges and fell under the influence of Edward Bouverie Pusey who, after the defection of John Henry Newman to the Church of Rome in 1845, was the leader of the High Church Party (or Puseyites). Hopkins was not content to adhere to the Anglican *via media* for long, however, and on 28 August 1866 wrote to Newman telling him, 'I am anxious to become a Catholic'; two months later Newman received him into the Roman Catholic Church. The following year Hopkins, the 'star of Balliol', took a first in Greats and seriously contemplated his religious future. On 30 May 1868 he was accepted as a novice by the Society of Jesus and began his nine years' training for the Jesuit priesthood.

Although he had chosen a life of dedication and strict discipline, Hopkins continued to take an interest in aesthetics and the outside world. From 1868 he began to develop his own theory of natural beauty; he used the word 'inscape' to describe the quintessential, intrinsic character of natural things; and 'instress' to denote the dynamic energy that informs the 'inscape'. He was so distressed by the social conditions prevailing in Victorian England that he wrote to Bridges on 2 August 1871:

> Horrible to say, in a manner I am a Communist ... it is a dreadful thing for the greatest and most necessary part of a very rich nation to live a hard life without dignity, knowledge, comforts, delight, or hopes in the midst of plenty – which plenty they make.

In fact, Hopkins was a man who took art and life very seriously indeed, and he discussed his philosophical development in his journal and his fascinating correspondence.

While the philosopher officially approved by the Jesuits was St Thomas Aquinas, Hopkins preferred to read the medieval Franciscan philosopher Duns Scotus. In 1872 Hopkins read the *Scriptum Oxoniense super Sententiis* and excitedly endorsed the Subtle Doctor's principle of individuation and his conviction that Christ was motivated more by love than filial duty. Hopkins adored Christ as a supreme creator, a great artist: in a sermon of 1879 he described Christ as 'the greatest genius that ever lived ... nowhere in literature is there anything to match the Sermon on the Mount'.

In 1874 Hopkins was sent to St Beuno's College, North Wales, to study theology: he also studied the Welsh language and the complexities of classical Welsh prosody. As a Jesuit he had renounced the writing of poetry 'as not belonging to my profession' and this self-denial was typical of Hopkins (who, on

reading R.L. Stevenson's *Dr Jekyll and Mr Hyde*, said, 'My Hyde is worse'). He was obsessed by the idea of sacrifice: Christ's sacrifice, his own sacrifice of the flesh in cultivating the Jesuit spirit, the sacrifice of his artistic gifts. On 7 December 1875 another sacrifice occurred, when five Franciscan nuns were drowned after the iron-vessel *Deutschland* was wrecked in the sands of the Kentish Knock. The rector of St Beuno's remarked that the subject was worthy of a poem and Hopkins accordingly produced *The Wreck of the Deutschland*, his first great poem and his most sustained imaginative effort.

For some time Hopkins had been formulating a new theory of poetry. Instead of the ding-dong predictability of traditional English iambic verse, he substituted what he called 'sprung rhythm' which, as he explained in a letter of 5 October 1878 to R.W. Dixon, 'consists in scanning by accents or stresses alone, without any account of the number of syllables'. Hopkins was, temperamentally, an ecstatic poet dogmatically attached to the notion of self-discipline. He felt an obligation to justify his poetry by an elaborate theory, so he coined the term 'sprung rhythm', invoked labels like 'reversed feet' and 'counterpoint rhythm', insisted on the use of 'outriding half-feet or hangers', and generally attempted to hide his spontaneity behind a front of pedantry.

What Hopkins's sprung rhythm amounted to, in action, was a combination of oral rhythm and literary style; he wanted his poems to sound right and told Bridges on 21 May 1878, 'You must not slovenly read ... with the eyes but with your ears.' He used alliteration, internal rhymes and enjambment to create a rich verbal texture, and his poetry reads as if the torrential flow of inspiration could hardly be contained by technical means. This section from the eighth stanza of *The Wreck of the Deutschland* indicates his method, with each burst of sound provoking its own echo:

> How a lush-kept plush-capped sloe
> Will, mouthed to flesh-burst, Gush! – flush
> the man, the being with it, sour or
> sweet

Brim, in a flash, full! – Hither then, last or
    first,
To hero of Calvary, Christ's feet – Never
    ask if meaning it, wanting it, warned of it –
    men go.

Hopkins offered *The Wreck of the Deutschland*
to the Jesuit journal the *Month* but, in his
own words, 'Though at first they accepted it,
after a time they withdrew and dared not
print it.' Thereafter Hopkins felt free to
write, though without any hope of publication. Although resigned to lack of recognition he took an ambivalent attitude to poetic
celebrity: on 13 June 1878 he told R.W.
Dixon, 'The only just judge, the only just
literary critic, is Christ'; yet he ended one of
the sombre sonnets of 1885 by saying, 'to
hoard unheard,/Heard unheeded, leaves me a
lonely began'. These late sonnets (especially
when contrasted with the early sonnets in
celebration of a world 'charged with the
grandeur of God') show how Hopkins
experienced, in an agonizing way, acute
spiritual crises:

O the mind, mind has mountains; cliffs of
fall Frightful, sheer, no-man-fathomed.
Hold them cheap May who ne'er hung
there. Nor does long our small Durance
deal with that steep or deep. Here! creep,
Wretch, under a comfort serves in a whirlwind: all Life death does end and each day
dies with sleep.

In 1889 Hopkins contracted typhoid fever
and, after the onset of peritonitis, died on 8 June.
His last words were: 'I am so happy, so happy.'
His *Poems*, edited by his lifelong friend and
correspondent Robert Bridges, were posthumously published in 1918 and his astonishingly fresh work helped change the shape and
nature of modern prosody. Though chronologically a Victorian, he was one of the most
influential figures in twentieth-century poetry.

Further reading

The poetry is collected in *Poems* (1970), ed. W.H.
Gardner and N.H. Mackenzie; the prose in *The*
Correspondence (2 vols, 1935), ed. C.C. Abbott;
Further Letters (1956), ed. C.C. Abbott; *The*
Journals and Papers (1959), ed. Humphry House
and Graham Storey; and *The Sermons and*
Devotional Writings (1959), ed. C. Devlin; the life
of the poet is discussed in W.H. Gardner, *Gerard*
Manley Hopkins (2 vols, 1944–9). See also:
N. White, *Hopkins* (1992); J.G. Lawler, *Hopkins*
Re-constructed (1998).

ALAN BOLD

HOPPER, Edward
1882–1967
US artist

Perhaps the finest of all those American artists
labelled 'realists' for convenience, Edward
Hopper was, like his near contemporary
Norman Rockwell, essentially a New Yorker
who received some of his training at the
Chase School of Art and who worked as an
illustrator to help pay his bills. Unlike
Rockwell, though, he maintained a fierce
distinction between commercial practice and
what he considered his important art. At the
New York School of Art he fell under the
influence of Robert Henri (1865–1929),
who, encouraging his students to record particularly urban life as closely and faithfully as
they could, became the acknowledged
inspiration of the so-called 'Ashcan' school of
realism. Significantly, although between 1906
and 1910 Hopper made several journeys to
Paris and other European centres specifically
to study Post-Impressionism and the early
stirrings of Cubism, he remained ostensibly
unaffected by whatever he found there.
Similarly, he steadfastly refused to be perturbed by Abstract Expressionism and other
modernist art movements that flourished in
America during his lifetime. Rather, he was
the inheritor of a tradition of demandingly
technical figurative painting that has at its
apex the examples of Diego de Velásquez and
Jan Vermeer.

It would be wrong, however, to think of,
let alone dismiss, Hopper as a conservative or
traditionalist. 'What I wanted to do,' he once
famously said, 'was to paint sunlight on the

side of a house,' and in all his mature work there is an uncompromising ability to make the rendering of light textures and their contrasts integral to his sense of composition and structure, so that his paintings have a rare quality of apparently non-contrived unity. Nor is Hopper's deployment of light naturalistic in a photographic way, despite the assertions of some critics. Rather, light is painstakingly modulated to give his typical subject-matters – a filling station, a chop suey parlour, an isolated house in the countryside close to a deserted railroad – a low-level but pervasive sense of unearthliness.

Humanity is often absent from a Hopper picture – which is paradoxical, since so many of his settings are deliberately and obviously urban; and where people can be found, they seem to exist entirely independently of each other. In his most celebrated composition – *Nighthawks* of 1943 – a handful of non-communicative eaters sit at the counter inside a late-night diner. The diner, boxed in by plate glass, is viewed from the outside, the inferred desolation of its inmates underscored by the cold, artificial but powerful electric light of the interior, while outside the drab darkness of the city street creates an enveloping tomb. For all that Hopper's technique is so categorically non-impressionistic, the effect of the picture is mesmeric, and finally overwhelming. It is at once just an ordinary scene from the bleaker side of urban living, and a vision of hell, however subtle and understated. As well as Velásquez, the artist seems to owe something at least to Breughel.

Nighthawks is a masterpiece of American art, modern or otherwise, a mystery painting made mysterious precisely by its surface refusal to admit mystery of any kind, either in its thin narrative or in its Spartan imagery. In a sense, Hopper foreshadows the minimalist school of art, where to say less is to say more, and matters of taste are necessarily set aside. In his own lifetime, recognition came relatively late. Only in 1919 was he first accorded a one-man exhibition, and it was only after 1923, following a successful sale of watercolours, that he was able to abandon commercial art and concentrate on what mattered most to him. But in 1933 he was given the unexpected distinction of a retrospective at the Museum of Modern Art in New York, since when his standing in America has seldom been challenged. It was not until 2004, however, that his international reputation was finally assured by an exhibition of his work that toured Europe, attracting tens of thousands of visitors at London's Tate Modern gallery.

In the latter part of his life Hopper worked out of a studio in New York's Washington Square, shared with his wife and fellow artist Josephine Nivine, who, after his death, arranged for a substantial proportion of his work to be bequeathed to the Whitney Museum.

Further reading

Other works include: *House by the Railroad* (1925) and *Gas* (1940). See: *Edward Hopper: A Catalogue Raisonne*, ed. Gail Levin (1995); Edward Hopper, *Edward Hopper: A Journal of His Work* (with Deborah Lyons and Brian O'Doherty, 1997). See also: Lloyd Goodrich, *Edward Hopper* (1993); Gail Levin, *Edward Hopper: An Intimate Biography* (1995); Sheena Wagstaff, *Edward Hopper* (2004); Avis Berman, *Edward Hopper's New York* (2005).

SAMANTHA GOAT

HUGHES, Ted (Edward James)
1930–98
English poet

Hughes was born in Mytholmroyd, in the Calder Valley, on the Yorkshire side of the Pennines. Although he left his birthplace at the age of seven, it was a vital formative influence: growing up with a harsh, vigorous, non-standard form of spoken English, and close to some of the wildest country in England, shaped his poetic voice and his vision. Until the age of seven he used to accompany his much older brother on shooting expeditions on the moors, a time he later described as 'paradise'. The family moved to Mexborough in south Yorkshire, his brother joined the RAF and later emigrated to Australia. Many years later Hughes wrote that he felt 'orphaned' by this. He was educated at Mexborough Grammar School in south Yorkshire and Pembroke College, Cambridge, where he changed from English to Anthropology after a dream in which a burnt fox told him that academic literary study was 'killing us'. Hughes came to believe that the poetic temperament is akin to that of the shaman, and he would certainly have regarded this dream as a shamanistic vision. The choice of a discipline that took him beyond his own civilization was a significant pointer to the imaginative range of his later work. An abiding early influence was *The White Goddess* by Robert Graves.

In 1956 he married the American poet **Sylvia Plath**. In 1961 they settled in Devon with their two children. In this period his first two volumes, *The Hawk in the Rain* (1957) and *Lupercal* (1960), were published. He was immediately recognized as a powerful new voice. Some reacted as if English poetry had been invaded by a barbaric, primitive force. His language, though highly literate, was harsh, physical, aggressive and energetically mimetic. It related to tradition via **Dylan Thomas** and **Gerard Manley Hopkins**, by-passing the dominant urbane and ironic mode of modern English poetry. His subject, of which this style was the natural expression, was, and remained, the continuity, broken in consciousness and culture but affirming itself in the biological and unconscious self, between humanity and the natural world beyond. This entailed a particular stress upon and empathy with predatory violence – in such poems as 'The Jaguar', 'Pike' and above all 'Hawk Roosting'. At the same time, for example in 'The Thought-Fox', 'Pike' and 'The Bull Moses', he showed great delicacy and subtlety, and there is a deeply meditative quality in much of his best work. 'Violence' is a word that has always bedevilled Hughes criticism. He has said that his work is about not violence but vitality, and that what his critics call violence is an integral quality of great poetry, to be found in Shakespeare, Homer, Aeschylus and the Bible. His third book, in 1961, was *Meet My Folks!*, the first of fifteen books of verse and prose for children. Writing for, and encouraging writing by, children was a lifelong commitment.

In 1962 Hughes began an affair with Assia Wevill. He and Plath separated and in 1963 Plath committed suicide. The reverberations of these events shaped the rest of his life and writing career. For some time he wrote no poetry and his next major volume, *Wodwo*, did not appear until 1967. This contains some of his best nature poems, such as 'Skylarks' and 'Gnat-Psalm', and also some more overtly ambitious metaphysical poems, of which the best are perhaps 'Pibroch', 'Stations', 'The Green Wolf' and 'Wodwo' itself. 'Full Moon and Little Frieda' is one of his most tender poems. The book also contains five stories and a play. Many of the poems express a darker, less celebratory view of nature, and a profound preoccupation with death.

With *Crow* (1970) he began a new phase of connected, mythical work. It is his harshest book, a sequence of poems, many of them narrative in form, linked by Crow, a protean figure influenced by American Indian Trickster mythology, and the antagonist of the Christian God. *Crow* severely divided Hughes's critics. His admirers saw it as a bold attempt at unillusioned poetry, with a new energy and simplicity of language; his detractors found it crude and nihilistic. Unfortunately Hughes confused matters by speaking of its 'super-simple, super-ugly' style, which does scant justice to its subtlety and variety. He originally conceived *Crow* as an 'epic folk-tale' in prose and verse, and drafted a large number of prose episodes. He abandoned the project in 1969, when Assia Wevill committed suicide, taking with her their daughter Shura. The book, published in 1970, is a selection of the Crow poems. Some critics have regretted that the project was not completed, but the fragmentary and unfinished quality of the published volume has a distinct imaginative power that could be foreclosed as much as enhanced by the narrative frame.

In 1970 he married Carol Orchard and in 1971 collaborated with Peter Brook on *Orghast*, a drama written in a language invented by Hughes. Two major 'mythical' works followed *Crow*. *Gaudete* (1977) is a narrative poem about Dionysiac disruption in a beautifully and powerfully evoked English countryside, combined with a collection of lyric poems addressed to the Goddess, that are the most overtly religious of Hughes's works. *Cave Birds* (1978) is a more connected sequence than *Crow*, with drawings by the American artist Leonard Baskin. A drama of psychic rebirth, it demonstrates a renewed richness and complexity of language, and a more hopeful view of the human condition.

Simultaneously with these two ambitious texts, Hughes worked on *Season Songs* (1975), a sequence of lyric poems partly but not exclusively addressed to young readers, and *Moortown* (1979), which is most notable for a powerfully direct sequence about farming, later published as *Moortown Diary*. In 1973 Hughes had bought a farm on which he raised cattle and sheep with his father-in-law, the farmer Jack Orchard. These collections were followed by *Remains of Elmet* (1979), a sequence about the Calder Valley, with accompanying photographs by Fay Godwin. This was a very successful collaboration, but Hughes was dissatisfied with the book, and later published a revised, more auto-biographical version as *Elmet* (1993). *River* (1983), which contains some exceptionally fine poems that draw on the spiritual connection with the natural world that Hughes experienced when fishing, is also a collaboration with a photographer, but in this case the photographs are a distraction from rather than a complement to the poems.

In retrospect, *River* represents the end of a long and remarkable period in which Hughes consistently and prolifically produced original poetry of outstanding quality. His subsequent volumes, *Flowers and Insects* (1986) and *Wolfwatching* (1989), though they contain

some fine poems, are comparatively thin. In 1984 he was appointed Poet Laureate in succession to John Betjeman. This was a task that he took more seriously than any poet since **Tennyson**. Hughes believed in the Crown as the symbol of the spiritual unity of the people, and he revived the ostensibly anachronistic practice of writing poems for royal birthdays. His Laureate verses are collected in *Rain-Charm for the Duchy* (1992). Written in elaborate and archaic forms such as the Ode and Masque, with the exception of the title-poem they have little of Hughes's energy and vision, but they provide a fascinating insight into his essentially religious conception of society.

Most of Hughes's energy in the last fifteen years of his life went into prose and translation. He wrote a number of very successful theatre translations, notably of Euripides's *Alcestis* (a story that bears on his relationship with Plath) and Racine's *Phèdre*. *Tales from Ovid* (1997) won considerable acclaim and sparked a revival of Hughes's critical fortunes. His major prose work is *Shakespeare and the Goddess of Complete Being* (1992). This lengthy book interprets the whole of Shakespeare's oeuvre from *As You Like It* in the light of his early narrative poems, as a response to the religious crisis through which Shakespeare lived. Inevitably it casts as much light on its author as on its subject, especially the imbrication of religion, sexuality and gender in Hughes's sensibility; but, despite its excessive length and obsessive detail, it is a bold and challenging synoptic interpretation, and contains much brilliant commentary on Shakespeare's language. *Winter Pollen* (1994) collects most of Hughes's important occasional prose, and is an indispensable volume.

For most of his life Hughes was opposed to the direct use of autobiography in poetry. The unjustified vilification to which he was subjected, in the press, in the more unscrupulous Plath biographies, and sometimes at public readings, made him even more reluctant to make his first marriage directly a subject for poetry. Nevertheless, from the mid-1970s onward, he began to write poems about his relationship with Plath. When the majority of these were written is unclear, but they were finally published as *Birthday Letters* and the limited edition *Howls and Whispers* in the year of his death. Some critics saw this publication as self-serving, but predominantly it further enhanced Hughes's reviving reputation, both as a poet and as a man. Whether this is owing to the intrinsic merits of the poems is doubtful; their value as a biographical record is equally uncertain. But, as a text in which one major writer engages with both the personality and the work of another, with whom he was intimately and tragically connected, and as a record of the ongoing burden of guilt and loss, *Birthday Letters* will surely remain a classic. Perhaps more than anything, this notoriously private poet won the public's affection at the end of his life by an act of vulnerable self-exposure. He died believing that the latter part of his career and life had been blighted by his earlier failure to expose himself in this way.

Further reading

Other works include: *Collected Poems* (2003) contains all Hughes's collected poetry for adults, with the exception of the narrative of *Gaudete*, including numerous limited editions, and nearly all his uncollected poems. Other works for children: *How the Whale Became* (1963); *The Earth-Owl and Other Moon-People* (1963); *Nessie the Mannerless Monster* (1964); *The Iron Man* (1968); *The Coming of the Kings and Other Plays* (1970); *Moon-Whales* (1976); *Under the North Star* (1981); *What is the Truth?* (1984); *Ffangs the Vampire Bat and the Kiss of Truth* (1986); *The Cat and the Cuckoo* (1987); *Tales of the Early World* (1988); *The Mermaid's Purse* (1993); *The Iron Woman* (1993); *The Dreamfighter and Other Creation Tales* (1995). Prose: *Poetry in the Making* (1968). Fiction: *Difficulties of a Bridegroom* (1994); Translations: *Seneca's Oedipus* (1969); *Spring Awakening* (1995); *Blood Wedding* (1996); *The Oresteia* (1999). See also: A.C.H. Smith, *Orghast at Persepolis* (1972); Keith Sagar, *The Art of Ted Hughes* (1975, revised 1978); *The Laughter of Foxes* (2000); (ed.), *The Achievement of Ted Hughes* (1983); (ed.), *The Challenge of Ted Hughes* (1994); Ekbert Faas, *Ted Hughes: The Unaccommodated Universe* (1980); Stuart Hirschberg, *Myth in the Poetry of Ted Hughes* (1981); Terry Gifford and Neil Roberts, *Ted Hughes: A Critical Study* (1981);

Leonard M. Scigaj, *The Poetry of Ted Hughes: Form and Imagination* (1986); (ed.), *Critical Essays on Ted Hughes* (1992); Janet Malcolm, *The Silent Woman: Sylvia Plath and Ted Hughes* (1994); Paul Bentley, *The Poetry of Ted Hughes: Language, Illusion and Beyond* (1998); Nick Gammage (ed.,) *The Epic Poise: A Celebration of Ted Hughes* (1999); Lucas Myers, *Crow Steered, Bergs Appeared: A Memoir of Ted Hughes and Sylvia Plath* (2001); Elaine Feinstein, *Ted Hughes: The Life of a Poet* (2001); Diane Middlebrook, *Her Husband: Hughes and Plath – A Marriage* (2003); Joanny Moulin (ed.), *Ted Hughes: Alternative Horizons* (2004); Neil Roberts, *Ted Hughes: A Literary Life* (2006).

NEIL ROBERTS

HUXLEY, Aldous Leonard

1894–1963

British novelist

Grandson on his father's side of **T.H. Huxley**, eminent Victorian champion of the new biology; on his mother's side the great-grandson of Dr Thomas Arnold of Rugby; the great-nephew of **Matthew Arnold**; the nephew of Mrs Humphrey Ward, novelist and reformer; the third son of Leonard Huxley, editor of *Cornhill Magazine*, and Julia Arnold Huxley, founder of Prior's Field, a school for girls; youngest brother of Julian Huxley, the biologist – few writers indeed can lay claim to a legacy of such learning and distinction as that into which Aldous Huxley was born.

His childhood was spent at Laleham, near Godalming in Surrey. While at Eton he contracted a serious eye ailment (*keratitus punctata*) that rendered him nearly blind and ended his plans to pursue a career in biology. His older brother Trevenan took his own life in August 1914, an event which affected Aldous deeply. His first publications were poems (collected in *The Burning Wheel*, 1916) written while he was an undergraduate at Balliol College, Oxford. In the next few years he worked intermittently as a schoolmaster at Eton, was a frequent guest of Lady Ottoline Morrell at Garsington, and became an editor on the *Athenaeum* under John Middleton Murry.

During the 1920s Huxley's keenly witty and urbane novels earned him a vast and ardent following, and like his American counterpart, **F. Scott Fitzgerald**, he became identified with the era whose hysterical nihilism roused in him both fascination and revulsion. The earliest novels, *Crome Yellow* (1921) and *Antic Hay* (1923), were country-house farces in the Peacockian manner brought up to date. These works involve a cast of grotesques, constituted largely of predators and their all-too-eager victims, who assemble to pursue their respective lusts: for power, learning, sexual conquests, diversions of all kinds. Whether or not the pursuits are successful, there is a general air of futility about it all, and an underlying loneliness that belies the festive occasion. 'Parallel straight lines,' muses a character in *Crome Yellow*, 'meet only at infinity ... Did one ever establish contact with anyone? We are all parallel straight lines.' The remark typifies the satirical vantage point of these works, which proved influential upon younger novelists such as **Evelyn Waugh**, Henry Green and Anthony Powell.

Huxley's view of the contemporary world darkened considerably near the end of the decade. *Point Counter Point* (1928) is a devastating portrait of the utter baseness and hollowness of modern life. Technically it marked an important advance in his fiction. Where the 'parallel lines' of the earlier novels were embodied in characters whose ideas, and attempts at communication, failed to connect, here the same image governed the very structure of the novel, through a sustained contrapuntal arrangement of several plots, intercalated with entries in the journal of the novelist-surrogate, Philip Quarles. One of these entries, manifestly an apologia for Huxley's works to date, is worth noting:

> Novel of ideas. The character of each personage must be implied, as far as possible, in the ideas of which he is the mouthpiece ... The chief defect of the novel of ideas is that you must write about people who have ideas to express – which excludes all but about .01 per cent. of the human race. Hence the real, the congenital novelists

don't write such books. But then, I never pretended to be a congenital novelist.

Of all the novel's characters produced according to this recipe, the most important – if also the least convincing – is Mark Rampion, who was modelled after Huxley's close friend **D.H. Lawrence**. The novel was written during a period in which Huxley was much influenced by Lawrence's vitalist-cum-primitivist creed, and Rampion was intended to be the lone 'life-worshipper' in a gallery of death-obsessed hedonists, charlatans and fanatics.

Brave New World (1932), despite its veneer of comic–satiric fun and its verbal play ('Ford's in his flivver, all's well with the world'), marked the culmination of Huxley's 'dark' period. Thrown off perhaps by the book's deceptively light anti-utopian beginning, some have professed bafflement at its abruptly tragic ending. In fact, the suicidal, guilt-ridden despair of John 'the Savage' is an index of the author's own state of mind at a time when, after the death of Lawrence, he cast about for something to believe in and came up empty-handed.

The 1930s amounted to the crossroads of Huxley's career. He had already begun to turn away from 'pure' satire and from the kind of novel in which ideas were juxtaposed for their own sake, towards the more explicitly didactic novel, the moral apologue, which would become the dominant mode of all his subsequent fiction. In the later, more affirmative novels such as *After Many a Summer Dies the Swan* (1939), *Time Must Have a Stop* (1944) and especially *Island* (1962), the play of diverse ideas gave way to the exposition of Huxley's own ameliorative creed – a kind of rationalist mysticism – as the answer to the world's ills. Few of these works (all written after his emigration to Southern California in 1937) satisfy as novels, and Huxley's reputation underwent a precipitous decline. A revaluation of *Eyeless in Gaza* (1936) after Huxley's death, however, has led to a restoration of Huxley's critical fortunes. Once considered the prime exhibit of

Huxley's decline as a serious writer – the common view of those readers who felt betrayed by his apparently abrupt forsaking of the 1920s ethos which, in their eyes, he had epitomized in all its contradictions – the work came to be recognized for what it is: his best and most ambitious novel.

The book recounts the conversion experience of Anthony Beavis, a world-weary, psychologically spent aesthete who, after several encounters with violent death during a trip to revolutionary Mexico (loosely based on Huxley's own journey, described in *Beyond the Mexique Bay*, 1934), discovers in himself the will to live, and the concomitant need to love and to serve his fellow men. No description of its theme, however, can do justice to the brilliance of the work's structural design, or to the emotional authenticity (unusual in Huxley) that anchors the astonishing array of ideas and experiences upon which Beavis broods as he makes his agonizing pilgrimage toward spiritual rebirth. Though he was never again to attain its heights, it is clear that this was the novel Huxley had to write if he was to survive the nihilistic despair to which his earlier works, especially *Point Counter Point* and *Brave New World*, had brought him.

Throughout a long and distinguished career Huxley also produced numerous volumes of short fiction, essays, poetry, travel books, plays and a fine biography, *Grey Eminence* (1941). These works bear ample testimony to his vast erudition and his unceasing curiosity about science, art, politics, economics, religion and many other subjects. All are of interest. But it is for his novels that Huxley will be best remembered, and of these *Eyeless in Gaza* is his one major achievement.

Further reading

Other works include: *Those Barren Leaves* (1925) and *Ape and Essence* (1949), both novels; *Collected Short Stories* (1957); *Leda* (1920), *Limbo* (1920) and *The Cicadas* (1931), collections of poems; *The Genius and the Goddess* (1955) and *The Giaconda Smile* (1948), both plays; *On the Margin: Notes and* *Essays* (1923), *Do What You Will* (1929), *Music at Night* (1931), *The Olive Tree* (1936), *Ends and Means* (1937), *The Art of Seeing* (1942), *The Perennial Philosophy* (1945), *Brave New World Revisited* (1958) and *Collected Essays* (1959), essays and journalism; *Letters*, ed. Grover Smith (1969). About Huxley: Sybille Bedford, *Aldous Huxley: A Biography* (1973); Jerome Meckier, *Aldous Huxley: Satire and Structure* (1969); George Woodcock, *Dawn and the Darkest Hour: A Study of Aldous Huxley* (1972). See also: Ronald G. Walker, *Infernal Paradise: Mexico and the Modern English Novel* (1978); G.A. Nance, *Aldous Huxley* (1988).

RONALD G. WALKER

HUXLEY, Thomas Henry

1826–95

British biologist

T.H. Huxley was an English biologist whose work and thinking led him into public battles over Darwinism and many other leading questions of the day. Inspired as a boy to become a mechanical engineer, his career led him to study the mechanism of living bodies, and his enemies claimed that he came to treat human beings as machines. His medical studies began at Charing Cross Hospital when he was seventeen, and on graduating in 1845 he at once published a paper about the hitherto unrecognized layer on the inner sheath of hair subsequently known as 'Huxley's layer'. He was granted a commission in the Royal Navy and set out on board the *Rattlesnake* to make a prolonged survey voyage to Australia, arriving in Sydney in 1848.

There he fell in love with Anne Heathorn and at the age of twenty-two proposed to her. She accepted in the full knowledge that years must pass before a struggling and almost penniless scientist could marry her. Success came early but did not make marriage any easier. His first important paper, 'On the Anatomy and the Affinities of the Family of Medusa', was printed by the Royal Society in its *Philosophical Transactions* (1849) and to his surprise at the very early age of twenty-six he was elected a Fellow of the Royal Society. Within a few years he began exchanging papers with many leading scientists and corresponded regularly with men of the calibre of **Charles Darwin**.

During his first interview with Darwin, who was to publish his great book *The Origin of Species* in 1859, Huxley expressed his belief in the sharpness of the line of demarcation between natural groups and was disconcerted when Darwin received the statement with a smile. When he married Anne Heathorn in 1855 Darwin said to him: 'I hope your marriage will not make you idle: happiness I fear is not good for work.' The warning was unnecessary. Mrs Huxley sometimes levelled against her husband that age-old cry from the wives of dedicated men that he was not only as much married to his work as to her but that his work often came first.

Huxley's most important published work at this time was the Croonian lectures, *The Theory of the Vertebrate Skull* (1858), in which he developed the principle he was to follow all his life of not hazarding any statement beyond those revealed by the facts. Employing this inductive method in the Croonian lectures, he successfully demolished the idealistic views of the origin of the skull held by the leading comparative anatomist, Richard Owen. Incapable of the flexibility required to qualify orthodox thinking, Owen asserted that man was clearly marked off from other animals by the anatomical structure of his brain. Huxley undermined if not destroyed this approach and summed up his view in *Man's Place in Nature* (1863).

By 1860 Huxley was defending Darwin's theory of evolution against the attacks of Bishop Wilberforce. His brilliant polemic not only resulted in a victory for science over obscuranticism; it made scientific theorizing respectable in a way it had never been before. Wilberforce had challenged Huxley: 'If anyone were willing to trace his descent through an ape as his grandfather would he be willing to trace his descent through an ape on the side of *his grandmother*?' Huxley replied:

If the question put to me is 'would I like to have a miserable ape for a grandfather or a

man highly endowed by nature and possessed of great means and influence and yet who employs these faculties and that influence for the mere purpose of introducing ridicule into a grave scientific discussion,' I unhesitatingly affirm my preference for the ape.

Huxley's attitude to religion changed over the years. At one period he was quoting an eighth-century BC Hebrew prophet: 'And what doth the Lord require of thee but to do justly, to love mercy and to walk humbly with God.' Two years later he stated: 'There is no evidence of the existence of such a being as the God of the theologians.' On purely philosophical grounds he considered atheism untenable and adopted a brand of agnosticism which subordinated belief to evidence and reason. His personal creed gradually developed into a kind of scientific Calvinism.

In 1876 he visited America where his favourite sister already lived. America seemed more prepared than England to receive his agnosticism, scientism and full-blooded belief in empirical investigation as the only means of establishing real truth.

Over the years his scientific work continued unabated, concentrating on palaeontology, and his many studies of fossil fishes established far-reaching morphological facts. Among other publications, *Elementary Physiology* (1866) and *Anatomy of Vertebrate Animals* (1871) were masterpieces of lucidly ordered exposition.

From 1870 onwards public duties drew him away from scientific studies and between 1862 and 1884 he sat on no fewer than ten royal commissions. From 1871 to 1880 he was secretary of the Royal Society, from 1883 to 1885 president of the Royal Society and in 1870 to 1872 a member of the newly constituted London School Board, where he wielded wide influence and propounded relatively revolutionary ideas. A man dedicated to work, his values were otherwise highly unconventional. He was against the theological conception of God, conventional religion, privilege, elite education and normal university teaching, and had serious doubts even about royalty.

His appearance was described by Professor Osborn of Columbia College: 'His eyes were heavily overhung by a projecting forehead and eyebrows, and seemed at times to look inward. His lips were firm and closely set.' Late photographs show a formidable person – brooding, disillusioned, given to stern discipline.

His working habits could be erratic: 'He was not one of those portentously early risers who do a fair day's work before other people are up,' his son wrote. There were royal commissions, committee meetings, lectures and research but 'the greater part of the work by which the world knows him best was done after dinner'.

His early resilience and energy eventually gave place to tiredness and bouts of depression. Aspects of his life remain a mystery. What did he mean, for instance, when he said: 'Few men have drunk more deeply of all kinds of sin than I'? Despite this, person after person was struck by what they referred to as his domestic happiness.

Illness troubled him from 1885, when indeed he nearly died, and his last years were plagued with the usual troubles of old age. Challenged whether – in the face of death – he still did not believe in God, he said that if there was a God waiting for him he hoped he would turn out to be Darwinian and believe in hard work.

Since his day the mind–body problem has undergone revolutionary re-examination in depth but two schools are still divided, the mechanistic believing that mind is little more than a function of brain, and the dynamic that psychological concepts like intentionality remove the whole question from such reductionist simplicity.

Huxley is remembered as a great scientific teacher, a brilliant expositor and a man who made the scientific approach to human nature and social affairs not only respectable but desirable.

Further reading

See: *The Scientific Memoirs of T.H. Huxley* ed. Michael Foster and E. Ray Lankester (5 vols, 1898–1903); Leonard Huxley, *The Life and Letters of Thomas Henry Huxley* (1900); Cyril Bibby, *T.H. Huxley: Scientist, Humanist and Educator* (1959); Cyril Bibby, *The Essence of T.H. Huxley* (1967); Cyril Bibby, *T.H. Huxley on Education* (1971); Cyril Bibby, *Scientist Extraordinary: The Life and Scientific Work of T.H. Huxley* (1972); Mario A. Di Gregorio, *T.H. Huxley's Place in Natural Science* (1984); Adrian Desmond, *Huxley: Evolution's High Priest* (1997); Paul White, *Thomas Huxley: Making the 'Man of Science'* (2002).

VINCENT BROME

I

IBSEN, Henrik

1828–1906

Norwegian dramatist

Ibsen was born into the family of a rich merchant in the southern Norwegian town of Skien in 1828. He spent his early childhood in large houses filled with the sound of laughter and entertainment. By 1833, however, his father's business empire had collapsed, and the family was obliged to move out of town and eke out a miserable existence in an isolated country property. The years of bitterness and recrimination that followed left an indelible scar on Ibsen's consciousness. Repeatedly in his mature work, he returned to the formative experiences of these years, tracing out the politics of family life within the context of an aggressively competitive capitalist world.

After an apprenticeship lasting six years as an apothecary's assistant in the small coastal town of Grimstad, followed by an unsuccessful attempt to pass the matriculation exam for university study in the capital city Christiania in 1850, Ibsen worked as a resident playwright and director in the newly founded Norwegian National Theatre in Bergen between 1851 and 1857. In 1857 he returned to Christiania to take over the post of artistic director of the Christiania Norwegian Theatre. This decade of theatrical work gave him invaluable experience as a playwright, but also left him with mixed feelings towards the contemporary theatre. It was the start of a love–hate relationship he

never managed to resolve. Ibsen's ambitious plans to offer an exciting and challenging repertoire in Christiania were thwarted by cash-flow problems and the indifference of the theatre-going public. By 1862 he was completely demoralized. He began drinking heavily and neglected his work, which provoked hostile comment from the press and his own staff. In May 1862 the theatre was forced to close, leaving Ibsen almost destitute. For the next two years, he somehow managed to provide for his young wife and son, acting as a poorly paid literary adviser to the rival Christiania Theatre. But it was with a sense of relief that he left Norway in 1864, armed with a small travel grant and the donations of a few well-wishers, to begin a period of exile that was to last for twenty-seven years.

Ibsen's first play *Catiline* (*Catilina*) had attracted very little attention when it was published under a pseudonym in April 1850. A few months later, his second play, *The Warrior's Barrow* (*Kæmpehøjen*), was accepted for performance by the Christiania Theatre and was given its successful première in September 1850. For the remainder of the 1850s and until his departure from Norway in 1864, he wrote a steady flow of plays: *St John's Night* (*Sankthansnatten*, 1852); a revised version of *The Warrior's Barrow* (1854); *Lady Inger of Østråt* (*Fru Inger til Østråt*, 1855); *The Feast at Solhaug* (*Gildet på Solhaug*, 1856); *Olaf Liljekrans* (1857); *The Vikings at Helgeland* (*Hærmændene på Helgeland*, 1858); *Love's Comedy* (*Kærlighedens Komedie*, 1862); and

The Pretenders (*Kongs-Emnerne*, 1863). In almost all of these plays, there were characters and themes that were to recur in his later work. But there was also a gulf, an incommensurateness, between form and content. Romantic melodrama and the Scribean intrigue play proved to be an inadequate base from which to undertake a probing exploration of human aspirations and human interaction. Even in *The Pretenders*, by far the most ambitious work of this early period, there is no real balance in the play between the dynamics of the spiritual exploration (centred on the theme of vocation) and the remorseless pace of the complex Romantic intrigue.

Ibsen's poems from the 1850s and 1860s take up similar themes to those explored in the plays, examining the nature of the poet's vocation and the clash Ibsen felt between the demands of art and life. Generally the poems suffer from Ibsen's all too quick facility for rhyming verse: the shape, the highly patterned structure of his verse forms, inhibiting the relaxed development of complex themes. But in a few poems, notably in *The Miner* (*Bergmanden*, 1851) and *On the Heights* (*På vidderne*, 1859–60), there is a muscular precision in the verse and imagery that impresses.

When Ibsen left Norway in 1864, he travelled to Rome where he was to make his home for the next four years. The landscape, the architecture, the impact of new friendships had a liberating effect on him. He worked now at a furious pace, publishing within a very brief space of time two magnificent verse plays that were to establish his international reputation as a writer: *Brand* (1866) and *Peer Gynt* (1867). *Brand* was a play that challenged the religious and political orthodoxies of the contemporary world. It explored the demands and the limits of human will-power, posing a number of crucial questions for Ibsen and his readers. How can one fulfil oneself with a heritage of guilt? How does one reconcile will-power and a sense of vocation with love? How can one oppose the crass limitations of accepted social and political doctrines without being driven

to extremes? *Peer Gynt* brought an exuberant treatment of a similar complex of themes. Structured like a morality play, it explored images of selfhood in a fanciful kaleidoscope of scenes: selfishness and selflessness are juxtaposed dialectically until the dialectical triad is resolved in the notion that 'to be oneself is to slay oneself'. Where *Brand* was lean and rugged in texture, *Peer Gynt* was effervescent and sparkling.

Ibsen marked this turning point in his career as a writer by changing both his style of handwriting and his style of dress. Casting aside his earlier Bohemian image, he adopted a neat, dapper façade behind which he took refuge from the memory of the bitter failures and humiliations that had marked his earlier career. There were still difficult years ahead of him, but from now on his social and financial position became increasingly stable. In 1868 he moved with his family to Dresden; he was to remain in Germany for ten years, in order to ensure that his son had suitable schooling.

After settling in Germany, he wrestled with the problem of finding a dramatic form more in tune with the increasingly naturalistic temper of the age. His first steps towards modern prose drama were hesitant and tentative. A popular political comedy, *The League of Youth* (*De Unges Forbund*, 1869), was followed by a somewhat turgid philosophical work in two parts, *Emperor and Galilean* (*Kejser og Galilæer*, 1873). It was not until 1877, when he completed *Pillars of the Community* (*Samfundets Stotter*), that he began to achieve that mastery of modern prose dialogue for which he was to become famous. *Pillars of the Community* was a witty and devastatingly accurate reckoning with the ruthless entrepreneurs who were spearheading the advance of industrial capitalism in Norway. In the figure of Consul Bernick, Ibsen exposed the personal and social lies that lay behind the forging of an industrial and mercantile empire. Two years later, after leaving Germany for Rome, he completed *A Doll's House* (*Et Dukkehjem*, 1879), an equally devastating reckoning with contemporary bourgeois marriage. Nora, the main character in the play, rejects her role as a bank manager's wife, in which she is reduced to the status of a mere commodity, and leaves her husband and children to discover her own identity.

In his next play, *Ghosts* (*Gengangere*), written in Sorrento in 1881, Ibsen painted a sombre picture of what happens when a woman who has left her husband is forced, by social pressure, to return. In a classically taut form, Ibsen reveals the horrifying details of Mrs Alving's marriage and fleshes out in the action a chain of events that leads inexorably to the madness of her son Osvald. The play provoked a storm of abuse when it was published. In openly attacking the sanctity of marriage, Ibsen was threatening the very basis of patriarchal society and was duly savaged for his temerity. His response was to write an ironic riposte in *An Enemy of the People* (*En Folkefiende*, 1882), where Dr Stockman declares that the strongest man is the one who stands alone.

Two years later, when he completed *The Wild Duck* (*Vildanden* 1884), his passionate involvement with social and political issues had mellowed. He now concentrated his attention on the politics of family life, showing how easily a fragile nexus of family relationships in the Ekdal home is disturbed by the clumsy intervention of a neurotic outsider, Gregers Werle. There are numerous echoes in the play, in terms of character and setting, of Ibsen's own childhood experiences. In its use of overt symbolism and its blending of tragicomic effects, the play also marked a new, and for many a puzzling, departure.

In 1885 Ibsen moved from Rome to Munich. Before doing so, he visited Norway. It was a visit that prepared the way for his eventual return home to his native land in 1891. The immediate effect of the visit was to influence the mood and setting of his next two plays, *Rosmersholm* (1886) and *The Lady from the Sea* (*Fruen fra Havet*, 1888). Both plays are set in a small town in western Norway, clearly reminiscent of Molde where

Ibsen spent two months in the summer of 1885. Both also explore complex states of mind, particularly in respect of the two main women characters, Rebecca West and Ellida Wangel. Rebecca West and her platonic lover, John Rosmer, act out in *Rosmersholm* a lethal drama of thwarted and diseased love and passion that ends with their suicide in the mill race. Ellida Wangel, by way of contrast, rejects her longing for freedom and emotional fulfilment, encapsulated in the mysterious figure of a seaman to whom she was once betrothed, and commits herself to her loyal but unexciting husband. There is a distinctly elegiac, late-summer feel to the happy ending of the play.

The mood of *Hedda Gabler* (1890) is decidedly autumnal. Here the major character, a general's daughter, finds herself trapped in a conventional bourgeois marriage and decides, quite literally, to shoot her way out. A strong sense of black comedy runs through the action right up to the very last line when Judge Brack reacts to Hedda's suicide with the comment, 'But, good God! People don't do such things.'

Ibsen's last four plays reflect an increasingly icy soulscape. In *The Master Builder* (*Bygmester Solness*, 1892), Solness the main character fears the threat of youth and, in failing at the end of the play to climb successfully the high tower he himself has designed, expresses something of Ibsen's own fears of artistic and personal impotence. *Little Eyolf* (*Lille Eyolf*, 1894) is dominated by themes of vibrant but thwarted eroticism. Much of the play explores a sustained incestuous fantasy involving Asta and her supposed half-brother Alfred Allmers. By the end of the play, it is only in renouncing overt sexuality that the main characters can achieve any form of mental equilibrium. In *John Gabriel Borkman* (1896) the winter landscape mirrors expressionistically the spiritual state of the protagonists. Borkman is a former industrial magnate who overreached himself and had to serve a lengthy prison sentence for speculating with money and shares belonging to others. He also ruthlessly sacrificed the woman he loved for the sake of personal ambition, for the power and the glory. There are many echoes in the play of *Pillars of the Community*. Borkman is like an ageing Bernick who has fallen victim to his dreams. *John Gabriel Borkman* was Ibsen's final reckoning with the destructive values of contemporary capitalist society and, at the same time, an oblique criticism of his own commitment to art in preference to a life of emotional fulfilment.

Finally, in *When We Dead Awaken* (*Når vi døde vågner*, 1899) Ibsen returned yet again to the clash of art and life, vocation and personal happiness. It was the major theme that had preoccupied him throughout his creative life. An ageing sculptor, Rubek, is confronted by the woman he rejected when he was a young and aspiring artist. Irene was his youthful inspiration. But he rejected her for the sake of artistic and material advancement. He now discovers that what he lost in rejecting her was the only thing that matters: complete authenticity of response. It is too late to live his life again, but in the final scene of the play he commits himself to Irene irrevocably, passionately, in a *Liebestod* that achieves mythical stature. In this final play, there is an expressionist blend of myth and reality.

Ibsen often shocked and bewildered his contemporaries. The daunting complexity of his work baffled critics who were unwilling or unable to probe below the surface detail of his plays to seek out the hidden patterns of meaning beneath the dialogue, the hidden poetry. Many failed to see that his vision of life was ultimately life-affirming, despite the sombre tonality of his work. But there were some, notably **George Bernard Shaw** and Georg Brandes, who understood and appreciated the scope of his genius.

The impact of Ibsen's work on modern theatre has been enormous. Directors have explored approaches to his plays ranging from the naturalist to the expressionist, while playwrights as diverse as **Harold Pinter** and **Arthur Miller** have been influenced by his ideas. Critics have made good their initial rejection of his work and have explored his plays from almost every conceivable angle:

historical-biographical, **Freudian**, new critical, **Marxist**, sociological, existentialist. If one accepts Longinus's definition of literary merit, namely that which pleases 'all men at all times', then it is clear that Ibsen fully deserves his status as a modern classic.

Further reading

Other works include: *Samlede verker, hundreårsutgave* (22 vols, 1928–58); *The Oxford Ibsen* (8 vols, 1960–77). Biographies: Halvdan Koht, *The Life of Ibsen* (2 vols, 1931): Michael Meyer, *Henrik Ibsen* (3 vols, 1967–71). Critical: John Northam, *Ibsen's Dramatic Method: A Study of the Prose Dramas* (1953); James McFarlane, *Ibsen and the Temper of Norwegian Literature* (1960). For a Freudian interpretation see Hermann J. Weigand, *The Modern Ibsen* (1925), and for a Marxist interpretation Horst Bien, *Henrik Ibsens Realismus* (1970). See also: *Contemporary Approaches to Ibsen*, Vol. 4, ed. Daniel Haakonsen (1979), essays; Maurice Valency, *The Flower and the Castle: An Introduction to Modern Drama* (1963); Robert Ferguson, *Henrik Ibsen: A New Biography* (1996); J.W. McFarlane (ed.), *The Cambridge Companion to Ibsen* (1994).

DAVID THOMAS

IVES, Charles Edward

1874–1954
US composer

The son of a former Civil War bandmaster, Charles Ives came from a New England Puritan background and spent his early years in Danbury, Connecticut. His relationship with his father George Ives was both emotionally and intellectually satisfying, for Ives senior not only gave his son instruction in practical and academic musicianship but also encouraged an interest in more experimental ways of employing the tools of sound, texture and timbre, in order to construct a new kind of music. Taking harmony and counterpoint of the German romantic tradition as a departure point, Ives composed with the materials that he had grown up with, namely the sounds of the marching band, barn dance, revivalist hymn and 'nigger minstrelsy', liberally sprinkling his scores with quotations from these home-grown sources. His arrival at Yale University in 1894 proved a great cultural shock, for his tutor was to be the Leipzig-trained Horatio Parker, one of the nation's most respected composers and pedagogues. Parker appears to have contributed little to his pupil's musicality other than consolidate what Ives had already thought to be the case, that the whole of American musical society was dominated by a German academicalism which had little to offer to the making of a specifically indigenous musical style. However, his time at Yale was not wasted for he found part-time employment as a church organist and choirmaster, stood in as a bar pianist at beer-halls and frequented the local theatres; thus he could add choral music, early ragtime and popular song and dance to his musical experiences.

At the turn of the century a career as a professional musician was considered precarious and, in Ives's milieu, unrespectable. Accordingly, on his departure from Yale he entered the insurance business as a broker and within a short space of time had teamed up with a partner to form one of the most successful independent agencies in New York, eventually to become the Mutual Life Insurance Company. A succession of heart attacks caused him to retire early from business practically a millionaire.

Ives was influenced, as his father had been, by the pragmatic philosophy of the Transcendentalists and was well acquainted with the prose and poetry of America's major authors. Though not politically active, he was a strong believer in American democratic principles, and besides drawing up draft amendments to the Constitution held protracted correspondence with prominent senators and two presidents as well as writing political pamphlets for distribution to those who expressed any interest. Such was Ives's passionate ardour for all that occurred around him, coupled with an intellectual conditioning steeped in the Puritan aesthetic, that they provided the stimulus not only for spiritual and emotional conflict in Ives's personal life but also for the unique creativity which was an attempt to resolve this dilemma.

Ives's musical output spans the years 1888 to 1927, although after 1921 he virtually ceased composing. The 141 songs not only cover the whole of his creative life but also demonstrate every facet of his compositional style. His choice of texts is eclectic: it not only covers the English and American Romantic poets but also French and German verse of the same period as previously set by Schubert, Schumann, **Brahms** and others; neither was he averse to setting the contemporary poetry of Brooke, **Kipling**, Vachel Lindsay and even epithets from newspaper columns. The psalm settings for chorus of 1894–1901 reflect his early preoccupation with experimental rhythmic and harmonic textures, reaching a peak of complexity in the *Harvest Home Chorales*. Such innovations were continued in the chamber pieces *Central Park in the Dark* and *The Unanswered Question* (both 1906), where independent rhythmic textures in different sections of the orchestra are heard simultaneously. To a much greater extent this also occurs in the later pieces for full orchestra collectively entitled *New England Holidays* (1904–13), in the two orchestral sets (1903–15) and especially in the massive Fourth Symphony (1909–16), which requires two conductors for a successful performance. Besides producing four violin sonatas, two string quartets and many smaller experimental works for chamber groups and theatre band, the composer has endeavoured to express the aesthetic of the Transcendentalist writers in the second piano sonata entitled *Concord 1840–1860*; its four movements are called 'Emerson', 'Hawthorne', 'The Alcotts' and 'Thoreau'.

During his composing life Charles Ives worked in complete isolation from contemporary European developments and as a result had to wait thirty years for national recognition. However, since his death both his innovative techniques and his individual aesthetic stance have exerted a major influence on experimental composers of the post-war period in America and Europe.

Further reading

Other works include: *Essays before a Sonata, The Majority, and Other Writings by C.I.*, ed. H. Boatwright (1970); *Charles E. Ives: Memos*, ed. J. Kirkpatrick (1971). See also: F.R. Rossiter, *Charles Ives and His America* (1976); H. and S. Cowell, *Charles Ives and His Music* (reprint 1974); R.S. Perry, *Charles Ives and the American Mind* (1974); D. Wooldridge, *From the Steeples and the Mountains* (1975); *An Ives Celebration*, ed. H. Wiley Hitchcock and V. Perlis (1977); H. Wiley Hitchcock, *Ives* (1977); *Charles Ives Remembered*, ed. V. Perlis (1976); J.P. Burkholder (ed.), *Charles Ives and His World* (1996); J. Swafford, *Charles Ives: A Life with Music* (1996); Stuart Feder, *The Life of Charles Ives* (1999).

MICHAEL ALEXANDER

J

JAMES, Henry
1843–1916
US novelist

It is entirely typical of Henry James that he should belong to nowhere in particular. An abundant solitude haunts both his life history and his fiction, and in this respect he appears like a kind of belated avatar of the Romantic exile or the doomed wanderer so familiar as a cultural cliché in the early decades of the nineteenth century. The fact that the wanderings and the exile were both self-imposed and eminently comfortable is beside the point: it is his role as the lonely, half-alien observer which gives shape and vividness to his creations, and the direction of much of his early life seems to have tended towards the successful achievement of such a stance. His works continue to exhale an air of half-intimated confidence which is central to our appreciation of his unique viewpoint. 'A work of art that one has to *explain*,' he told a friend in reference to *The Awkward Age* (1899), 'fails in so far, I suppose, of its mission.' Both the italicizing and the subjective qualifier in this sentence are characteristic of its author's retreat into the kind of verbal labyrinth which anticipates the monumental inarticulateness of twentieth-century English, with its host of qualifiers and its mass of unfinished sentences. That there was something both intensely understood and supremely inexpressible in fiction was an idea to which James gave prominence in several stories, including the archetypal 'The Figure in the Carpet', in which the hidden meaning conveyed in the work of Hugh Vereker perishes in obscurity. Interest in James's writing has so far recovered from a preoccupation with his stylistic obliquity (all too easily parodied – see, for example, **H.G. Wells's** *Boon* and the squibs of Max Beerbohm) as to accept this aspect of his later novels as one of the most consistently rewarding.

It matters little, in the last analysis, whether he is or is not an American novelist (he became a naturalized Englishman a few months before his death). That markedly eccentric and almost too careful use of English which has characterized the American novel from its beginnings down to our own day, and which is seen at its most mannered in the writings of **Melville**, Hawthorne, James Fenimore Cooper and others of their period, undoubtedly bit deep into the Jamesian style, for better or worse. American too is his mingled reverence and censure of England and the English, revealed at its strongest in the correspondence of the early 1890s and in the curious sense of challenging menace conveyed in *English Hours* (1905) and stories such as 'The Turn of the Screw' (1898). In the end his preoccupations do not label him as either particularly American or especially Anglicized. More obviously and intractably than any novelist of either tradition, he belongs (if indeed he has to be made to belong anywhere) to currents altogether more emphatically European.

Europe, or at any rate the notion of it, played a significant part in his spiritual development from the beginning. His father, Henry James senior, the wealthy son of a millionaire, gave his children a broadly based education within the lively milieux of mid-century New York and New England. He himself was an amateur theologian of an eccentrically Swedenborgian cast and was keen to encourage his family to think for themselves and to shun pattern and system. In 1856, when Henry junior was thirteen, his father removed them to Europe 'to absorb French and German and get a better sensuous education than they are likely to get here', as he told Emerson, but the boy had already based his earliest memory on sight of the column in the Place Vendôme when he was two years old.

A more fruitful experience of the Old World − indeed, it may be said the crucial encounter with it − took place in 1869 when James set sail for England. He was already a published American author, his first story, 'A Tragedy of Error', having appeared in 1864 and his first review being issued in the *North American Review*. He had begun to contribute stories to the *Nation* and the *Atlantic Monthly*, whose editor, William Dean Howells, was a friendly and beneficial influence upon his style and his career. In addition, as has been convincingly suggested, the fact that he had *not* fought in the American Civil War was something which both affected his future detached and critical attitude towards America and determined his posture of passivity. The mention of an 'obscure hurt' sustained in manipulating a rusty fire-engine has prompted some absurd speculations designed to connect James's apparent remoteness from sexual contact with some sort of castration. There is no evidence for this, any more than there is evidence for a pronouncedly homosexual bias, and his life in this respect retains its secrets to the last.

He, was, however, deeply attached to the idea, as much as to the substance, of his cousin Minnie Temple, the news of whose death he received while undergoing treatment at Great Malvern for his recurring constipation. His letters suggest that the emotional upheaval created by Minnie's death, experienced amid landscapes whose threatening loveliness is memorably portrayed, created for him that sense of brilliance and liveliness being crushed by acquisitiveness and greed which is at the heart of some of his greatest work. Certainly it may be said that Isabel Archer in *The Portrait of a Lady* (1881) and Milly Theale in *The Wings of the Dove* (1902) derived significant inspiration from Minnie Temple herself.

The richness of James's experience of England, France and Italy during the 1870s is almost without a parallel in the history of the growth of creative personality, and to read it through the medium of his incomparable letters, probably the best in English after Byron's, is to feel a profound envy, mingled with inevitable admiration. In London he dined with **Ruskin** and met **George Eliot**; in Paris he enjoyed the company of **Flaubert**, Maupassant, Daudet and the Goncourts, as well as making the acquaintance of Turgenev; and in Italy he made good friends among the American expatriate circles of Rome, Florence and Venice. It is as well to mention here that important, though frequently overlooked, sense of place which manifests itself in works such as *A Little Tour in France* (1884) and *Italian Hours* (1909) and surprises those who think of James purely as a 'psychological' novelist, devoid of any interest in the visual. After settling in England in 1876 James had few serious thoughts of returning to live in America, and though his view of Europe and Europeans was significantly modified in later years he already perceived the extent of the inspiration both offered to the exercise of his talent.

The novels and stories of the late 1870s and early 1880s play to the full upon what their author called 'the international situation', the idea of the moral confrontation of cultivated Americans with the Old World. In *The Europeans* (1878) this takes place in America itself, but his fullest and most magisterial exploration of the theme appears in *The Portrait of a Lady*, often taken to be his finest work. Of the mass of short stories based on this idea the best is probably 'Daisy Miller' (1878), in which the essential vitality of an American girl is overwhelmed by the stuffiness of censorious Roman society and symbolically extinguished by a fever caught during a louche moonlight escapade in the Coliseum. It was a subject which, in varying forms, he was to return to in his last great period during the early 1900s.

An increasing absorption with the severe contrasts presented by London society both rich and poor, and by the English in general, found reflection in *The Princess Casamassima* (1886), James's most ambitious book and the nearest he ever came to the type of French realism practised so thoroughly by his friends Alphonse Daudet and Paul Bourget. *The Tragic Muse* (1890), begun two years later, mirrors his continuing amazement at the depths of English philistinism, in an analysis of the confrontation between the artist and the world.

It was to be this very philistinism which brought to an abrupt close the most confused and agonizing period of James's literary career, when, during the early 1890s, he dabbled extensively in writing for the stage. He was not, *pace* even his most fervent admirers, a good playwright, and his naive belief that he could dazzle the hidebound London theatrical public with the sophistications of French boulevard drama *à la* Sardou was rudely shattered by the spectacular failure of *Guy Domville* in 1895, one of the most memorably disastrous first nights in English stage history. He returned with relief to fiction and produced in rapid succession *The Spoils of Poynton* (1897), *What Maisie Knew* (1897), *The Awkward Age* and 'The Turn of the Screw', a series of works firmly concentrated on English backgrounds and situations.

In 1896 he moved from London to Lamb House at Rye in Sussex, where he was to remain for the rest of his life. Even if his readership had never been of a 'popular' extensiveness and despite complaints as to his increasing stylistic obfuscations, he was a highly regarded figure in England, and a naturally sociable manner had won him the friendship of Robert Louis Stevenson, **Rudyard Kipling**, Edmund Gosse and other distinguished men of letters. His growing inability to express himself in any but the most parenthetical of utterances became legendary, enshrined within the reminiscence of friends such as the novelist Edith Wharton and the various small children who were taken to tea with him. During his residence in England he had remained on comparatively good terms with his family: thus the death of his sister Alice was another in the series of catastrophic blows to serenity at that time. A return to America in 1904 was an experience both vivid and horrifying, which produced *The American Scene* (1907), a travel document of fascinated revulsion.

James's last great burst of creative energy brought forth *The Wings of the Dove, The Ambassadors* (1903) and *The Golden Bowl* (1904), novels which powerfully revive several of his earlier thematic concerns in new ways. He wrote little of importance thereafter, beyond a handful of short stories and an unfinished novel, *The Ivory Tower*, abandoned owing to his sense that the First World War had effectively destroyed the world celebrated by the book. He returned to London and immersed himself in charitable work connected with the British war effort, becoming a naturalized subject in 1915 and receiving the Order of Merit on his deathbed a few months afterwards. He was buried in Chelsea Old Church, where a plaque commemorates him as a 'lover and interpreter of the fine amenities, of brave decisions and generous loyalties'.

He was finely prophetic in supposing that the Great War had annihilated his world, and it is difficult to imagine what he could have made of that which succeeded it. Interest in the whole nature of his work becomes enhanced by the tension sprung within it between the deliberate rhythms of a nineteenth-century life and the sense of barely suppressed hysteria authentic to the twentieth. A story like 'The Turn of the Screw', nowadays groaning under the weight of post-**Freudian** analysis of its unnamed governess's sexual traumas, is archetypally the creation of the man who had gone 'reeling and moaning' among the monstrous horse-drawn equipages of Papal Rome in its last days and who was to whirl through Italy as a delighted passenger in Edith Wharton's motor car. His stories and characters need and are given their due of expansiveness.

James's fiction falls very loosely into a series of moments related to his various journeyings and preoccupations. During the late 1860s and early 1870s it is still heavily marked by the influence of Nathaniel Hawthorne, and a distinctively Jamesian stance only properly emerges in his first major novel, *Roderick Hudson* (1875), which expresses his 'international' theme in fairly simple terms through the story of an American sculptor's love for a cosmopolitan beauty, Christina Light (subsequently to return as the Princess Casamassima). The nature and role of artists, indeed, dominates many of James's novels and tales during this and the following decade, but its supreme articulations in his work are not to be found until the later 1880s, when stories such as 'The Author of Beltraffio', 'The Real Thing', 'The Lesson of the Master' and the wryly comic 'The Death of the Lion' act as finely wrought pendants to our understanding of the flawed brilliance of *The Princess Casamassima* and *The Tragic Muse*.

Related to his interest in the threats and challenges of art is James's concern with the notion of innocence, not only among his wandering Americans who, like Isabel Archer in *The Portrait of a Lady*, gather wisdom through experience, but as embodied by children. His treatment of childhood is unique among nineteenth-century writers for its singularly penetrating comprehension of the child's vision of the adult world. Startling as a work like *What Maisie Knew* may at first appear through imposing the machinery of mature analysis upon a little girl's view of her mother's sexual adventures, it persuades by the overwhelming consistency of its method. The theme was to be resumed in *The Awkward Age*, a novel of marmoreal perfection in its technical finish, but perhaps the

most successful of James's briefer explorations of the subject is the short story 'The Pupil', in which the sophisticated perceptions of a small boy are contrasted with the surprised naivety of his tutor.

The corruption which menaces such innocence is better suggested by James than by almost any other contemporary writer, and underpins the triumph of a work such as *The Wings of the Dove*, in which greed and sexual intrigue drive Merton Densher and Kate Croy to prey upon the goodwill of the dying Milly Theale. James's art, distancing him from the fictional traditions to which he was heir, is to suggest the extent and inclusiveness of such corruption through his minute disclosure of viewpoints rather than through a series of gestures and vicissitudes. None of his novels better demonstrates his complete understanding of evil than *The Bostonians*, whose failure in 1886, though it shocked him, was in part due to the severity with which he had caused his readers to scrutinize the characters surrounding his heroine Verena Tarrant.

'She wasn't born to know evil. She must never know it,' cries Fanny Assingham of Maggie Verver in *The Golden Bowl*. In at least one respect, all James's major works can be seen as concentrating upon the conflict between living and knowing, between energy and consciousness, a dangerous duality encapsulated at its best in the famous boating scene in *The Ambassadors*. The completeness and refinement of his moral apprehensions, and his singular and obsessive determination that we should grasp the nature of their truth in its entirety, give his work, both in statement and expression, a pre-eminence whose dignified solitariness is wholly typical of James himself.

Further reading

Other works include: *A Small Boy and Others* (1913); *Notes of Son and Brother* (1914); and *The Middle Years* (1917). James's *Notebooks* (1947) were edited by F.O. Matthiessen and K.B. Murdock. Four volumes of a new edition of James's *Selected Letters*, ed. Leon Edel (from 1978) have so far appeared. Leon Edel, *The Life of Henry James* (5 vols, 1953–72) is the standard biography. See: F.O. Matthiessen, *Henry James: The Major Phase* (1944); F.R. Leavis, *The Great Tradition* (1948); Dorothea Krook, *The Ordeal of Consciousness in Henry James* (1962) and *Henry James: A Collection of Critical Essays*, ed. Leon Edel (1963); I.F.A. Bell, *Henry James and the Past* (1991); R. Salmon, *Henry James and the Culture of Publicity* (1997).

JONATHAN KEATES

JAMES, William

1842–1910

US psychologist and philosopher

The first son of Henry James Sr, William absorbed the religious, philosophical, and humanistic concerns of his father and his father's friends. Domiciled in Paris, James developed the ambition to become an artist. To enable him to study under William Morris Hunt in Newport, Rhode Island, the whole family returned to the United States. Within a year James transferred to the Lawrence Scientific School in Harvard to take up chemistry. A further move, this time to medicine, came in 1864, and led to his medical degree in 1869.

Under the spell of Harvard's great zoologist Louis Agassiz, James had looked forward to a career in biological research. The opportunity to test his enthusiasm came in 1865 when he joined Agassiz's Brazilian expedition, the experience of which seriously undermined his resolve. Instead he turned to physiology; once again interrupting his medical studies in Harvard, he spent eighteen months in Germany (1866–8); in Berlin he attended the lectures of the great Du Bois-Reymond; he visited but did not tarry in Heidelberg where Wundt and Helmholtz worked. More important, he read Hermann Lotze's *Medizinische Psychologie* and Griesinger's *Pathologie und Therapie der psychischen Krankheiten*, was introduced to the philosophy of Charles Renouvier, and, freed from the influence of Agassiz, he became a decided **Darwinian**. In Germany James's health had been poor despite frequent visits to Teplitz

for medical treatment. Returned to America he suffered three further years of depression before he accepted the position of instructor in anatomy and physiology at Harvard in 1873. Two years later he added a graduate course on 'The Relations between Physiology and Psychology'. In the undergraduate course on physiological psychology which he introduced in 1876 he used Herbert Spencer's *Principles of Psychology* as the text. Like Spencer his approach to psychology was biological but in contrast to that great synthetic philosopher James worried about the steps in an argument, the use of analogies, the precision of terms. On every count he found Spencer wanting. Spencer's one virtue, he remarked, was his belief in the universality of evolution. His one thousand crimes were 'his 5000 pages of absolute incompetence to work it out in detail'. James's published critique of Spencer began with 'Remarks on Spencer's Definition of Mind as Correspondence' in the *Journal of Speculative Philosophy* in 1878. Here he stressed what was to become a central feature of his psychology – the active role of the mind in contrast to the passive mirror-image model of Spencer. Mind did not simply *correspond* to external relations; by its own activity it transformed those relations. To mind belonged spontaneity and creativity.

In 1879 James started a course on 'The Philosophy of Evolution', in which he tackled Spencer's *First Principles* (1862); he criticized Spencer's famous law: 'Evolution is an integration of matter and concomitant dissipation of motion; during which matter passes from an indefinite, incoherent homogeneity to a definite, coherent heterogeneity.' James reformulated the statement as: 'Evolution is a change from a no-howish untalkaboutable all-alikeness to a somehowish and in general talkaboutable not-all-alikeness by continuous stick-togetherations and something-elseifications.' Nor did Spencer's conception of the 'unknowable' find favour with James. Spencer had relegated all attainable knowledge to that which is relative. The absolute, not being relative, was therefore unknowable. James saw that such a negative view offered no satisfaction to our emotional needs and theistic beliefs. It was, he said, as if a watchmaker were to say: 'Your watch is relative. Here is an absolute one that will not go at all.'

From 1877 onwards James's teaching on psychology was transferred to the philosophy department, and in 1880 the subject title of his post was altered from physiology to philosophy. Having introduced the new physiological psychology to the American academic world and given laboratory instruction in experimental techniques, James was able to hand over such instruction to the young Freiburg psychologist Hugo Münsterberg, whom he attracted to Harvard in 1892. Together with his pupil Stanley Hall, James was thus a central figure in the introduction to the United States of the new psychology so successfully developing in Germany. To teach the subject successfully, he told the college president, called for the union of the two disciplines of physiology and psychology in one man, a tradition set by Lotze in Göttingen and Wundt in Heidelberg.

James's work is difficult to summarize because it covered so many fields, psychological, philosophical and theological. In addition to the early articles in *Mind* and the *Critique philosophique* James edited his father's posthumous essays in 1885. He respected the deep theological aspects of his father's Swedenborgian system but he wanted to see it fashioned into a more articulately scientific form. He had long been familiar with Swedenborg through his father's studies and his own reading of this mystic author. James's subsequent preoccupation with the central role of the will, the function of belief, the existence of the supernatural, the rejection of determinism, and the espousal of moral freedom show the conformity of his fundamental concerns with those of his father. All James's subsequent writings can be viewed as contributions towards the elaboration of a philosophical position incorporating these features.

This position lay midway 'twixt the two extremes which James labelled the tender- and the tough-minded. The former were rationalists devoted to abstract and eternal principles, to monism, free will and religion. The tough-minded were empiricists devoted to facts, to pluralism, fatalism and irreligion. As examples of the tender-minded rationalists he had in mind philosophers of the school of Hegel such as McTaggert and T.H. Green in England and Josiah Royce in Harvard. James found the rationalists' search for the real world, one infinite folio – that *édition de luxe* of all the finite distorted editions of the world – suffocating in its 'infallible impeccable all-pervasiveness'. It was discouraging that in this absolute world 'where all that is *not* is from eternity impossible, and that *is* is necessary, the category of possibility has no application'. He called this the 'through-and-through universe' and it stifled him emotionally.

Hegelian philosophy had taken root in the English-speaking world late in the nineteenth century owing to the entrenched position of British empiricism. James was therefore reacting to a contemporary movement. Equally his opposition to the tough-minded empiricists was a reaction to positivism in the materialist and evolutionary form in which T.H. Huxley, W.K. Clifford and Herbert Spencer presented it. These positivists, James opined, had an impoverished view of the extent and variety of truth because they ruled out of court all knowledge that was not reducible to the factual data of experience, and they cautioned against belief in unproved statements. To Clifford's 'duty' not to believe, Spencer's doctrine of the unknowable and Huxley's agnosticism, James replied with his famous address granting the 'will to believe' that for which we lack adequate empirical evidence. The positivists' dependence on the empirical data of science led to a materialistic and depressing vision. What was higher was explained by what was lower. In Herbert Spencer's hand the world's history became a redistribution of matter and motion; in the writings of Ernst Haeckel God became a 'gaseous vertebrate'. The course of evolution was in Spencer's synthetic philosophy as inevitable as the Hegelians' conception of history. Social changes were for Spencer impersonal; they were due to environment, i.e. physical geography and the like. Man's mind developed in a fatalistic, passive manner, moulded by its experience of the 'outer relations'. This philosophy of evolution, James declared, was a metaphysical creed. Against this Spencerian predestination of all human actions James put the Darwinian conception of spontaneous variations, due to 'internal molecular accidents'. The cycle of influences which acted upon the germ to cause such variations was not directly deducible from the visible external conditions of the environment. We could not therefore predict the emergence of given variations, including those geniuses which became the great men of history. Their existence was a given datum for the social philosopher just as spontaneous variations were for the biologist. James concluded that history was not an inevitable process determined in advance but the result of many unpredictable events.

James's *Principles of Psychology* (1890) was deliberately positivistic and non-metaphysical. His acceptance of the empirical parallel between states of consciousness and brain processes was, he declared, no more than a 'mere admission', but we may note its conformity with his pluralistic ontology. Central to his conception of mind was its place in the basic structure of behaviour. Although he criticized Spencer's formulation of the essence of mental life as 'the adjustment of inner to outer relations', he approved the way it pictured minds inhabiting environments 'which act on them and on which they in turn react'. The *Principles* was also crucially dependent upon the facts of immediate experience as revealed by introspection. This is particularly evident in James's theory of emotion and the ideomotor theory of will. In the former he identified emotion with the sensation of the bodily changes which follow perception of the exciting fact. We are not afraid and tremble, he declared, but tremble and are afraid. Emotion is then the mental

correlate of bodily responses, not the cause of such responses. According to the ideomotor theory, introspection reveals to us that in addition to the element of consent or fiat the only psychic state which precedes our voluntary acts is an anticipatory image of the sensorial consequences of the movements which that act will involve.

In both these theories physiological processes played an important part, but the most important physiological element in *Principles* was the reflex arc. As early as 1881 in an address to Unitarian ministers entitled 'Reflex Action and Theism', James claimed that the most fundamental conclusion to be drawn from physiological research was that our will dominates both our thought and our feeling. The reflex was a triad made up of incoming impressions, contemplation or thinking, and outward discharges. Thinking was thus a place of transit, 'the bottom of a loop', the ends of which were applied to the external world. The purpose of thinking was to bring about action. The theorizing faculty, he declared, 'functions *exclusively for the sake of ends* that do not exist at all in the world of impressions we receive by way of ourselves, but are set by our emotional and practical subjectivity altogether'. It effected a transformation of sense data 'in the interests of our volitional nature'. Hence the subjugation of thinking to willing, and the fallacy of considering thought in isolation from action. Anticipating the doctrine of pragmatism which he was later (1898) to define, James claimed that 'if two apparently different definitions of the reality before us should have identical consequences, those two definitions would really be identical definitions, made delusively to appear different'.

James considered two further aspects of the physiological reflex – the automaton theory and the concept of instinct. The former was included in his lectures at Johns Hopkins University in 1878 and appeared in print in *Mind* a year later entitled 'Are We Automata?' Here he rejected T.H. Huxley's claim that consciousness was a mere epiphenomenon like the whistle of a steam engine and that no state of consciousness caused any change in the motion of the organism. In the state of psychology at the time, James considered this theory an 'unwarrantable impertinence'. If, as Spencer asserted, our actions are determined by our consciousness of pleasure and pain, then it was easy to see how, by the principle of selection, those individuals whose pleasures were derived from actions conducive to their survival would predominate. Consequently consciousness, by playing a causal role in steering a nervous system grown too complex to regulate itself, played a vital part in the evolution of man. This was only possible, however, if our will could act on our body. Without such causal influence, consciousness could have played no such role. James's treatment of instincts was also evolutionary. They all conformed to the general reflex type; they were present in all animals including man. He listed thirty human instincts and declared that 'no other mammal, not even the monkey, shows so large an array'. He sided with Darwin against Spencer in believing that instincts originated by spontaneous, heritable variations and were not acquired from acts originally executed intelligently. This was in line with James's general distrust of the alleged inheritance of acquired characters. His long list of instincts was later severely pruned by the behaviourists, who gave a prominent role to the **Pavlovian** conception of conditioned reflexes. James merely allowed for the modification and inhibition of reflexes due to experience, leading to the development of a variety of habits which might displace the original instinct entirely.

Two aspects of James's treatment of consciousness deserve comment. The first concerns its evolution, the second its continuity. He criticized the vagueness of Spencer's representation of the emergence of consciousness by the term 'nascent' and the analogy of the ultimate unit of consciousness with the nervous (mental) shock. James rejected any such atomistic hylozoism, and he found the assumed self-compounding of mental units 'logically unintelligible'. It just

was not true that the roar of the sea was compounded in our minds from the perceptions of many little waves. Nor was it admissible to distinguish unconscious from conscious mental states. To allow this would be to turn psychology from becoming a science into 'a tumbling-ground for whimsies'. The least objectionable view was to admit the soul 'as a medium upon which the manifold brain-processes combine their effects'. Since consciousness was unitary and integral from the outset, there was no need for the self-compounding of separate feelings.

James emphasized the continuity of consciousness in the metaphor 'the stream of thought'. He denied that anyone ever had a simple sensation by itself. Each sensation was accompanied by relations both spatial and temporal to other sensations. We do not hear thunder *pure* but 'thunder-breaking-upon-silence-and-contrasting-with-it'.   Thought was like a bird's life made up of flights and perchings. The perchings were the substantive parts, and the flights were the transitive parts of the stream of thought. Our words and images might appear discrete and our thoughts divisible into substantive elements, but in reality they were 'fringed' with the 'overtones' of their relations with each other. James went on to underline the quality of wholeness which characterized thinking. Like the Gestalt psychologists twenty-three years later, James urged that 'whatever things are thought in relation are thought from the outset in a unity'.

We have noted that the basic strands of James's philosophical thinking were present in the *Principles*. His functional view of thought and its subservience to will also marked his more mature exposition of pragmatism in 1898. Equally. his discussion of perception of time and space in the *Principles* contained the essence of his later development of radical empiricism. Against the rationalists he argued that we have no intuition of space and time. Empty time and empty space meant nothing to us. Against Hermann Lotze he raised objections to the doctrine of 'local signs' as cues to the spatial location of sense data. There was no independent entity known in our minds as space into which spaceless sensations could be dropped. The sensations themselves brought space and duration with them; they were the psychic fringes. Thus the rhythmic repetition of our heartbeat, our pulse and our breathing gives us a sensation of duration when all else is still. Likewise our bodily sensations carry an element of varying degrees of 'vastness' or 'voluminousness' which 'is the original sensation of space, out of which all the exact knowledge about space that we afterwards come to have is woven by processes of discrimination, association and selection'.

Although the most consistent target of James's criticism was the school of Hegelian rationalists, we have seen that he attacked the crudities of the old associationist psychology. As for the elaborate, technical development of psychophysics, he reckoned its proper psychological outcome was nothing. Yet he welcomed the signs of a return to a revised empiricism in philosophical circles, for he sought to promote what in 1897 he had called 'radical empiricism', of which he gave a systematic account in *The Meaning of Truth* (1909).

In his latter years James gave a fuller, more explicit development of his philosophical position, stressing pluralism, pragmatism and anti-intellectualism. Pluralism denied that there was any one entity – the absolute – embracing all reality, but admitted that 'the constitution of reality is what we ourselves find empirically realized in every minimum of finite life'. It was reality 'in distributive form', the 'strung-along unfinished world in time'.

James defined pragmatism as a method for attaining clarity of thought:

> To attain perfect clearness in our thoughts of an object . . . we need only consider what conceivable effects of a practical kind the object may involve . . . Our conception of these effects . . . is then for us the whole conception of the object.

Theories, then, become instruments, not answers to the enigmas of nature. But pragmatism also constituted a theory of truth. Just as scientists were coming to recognize the provisional character of all scientific laws and theories – 'a conceptual shorthand . . . in which we write our reports of nature' – so pragmatists held that all our ideas and beliefs 'become true just in so far as they help us to get into satisfactory relation with other parts of our experience'. Purely objective truth lacking any such function did not exist. In so far as theological beliefs did prove of value in concrete life they were to be considered true.

James admitted willingly that his views were anti-intellectual in the sense that the role he allowed for logic was severely limited. Against the Hegelians he urged that logic cannot help us to become acquainted 'with the essential nature of reality'. There was no objective fixed reality waiting to be discovered; it was in the making. Truth might happen to an idea. Faith in a fact could help create the fact. Thus did James fuse together in pragmatism his evolutionary, religious and positivist concerns, creating thereby a strong current in the anti-intellectualist thought in America at the beginning of the twentieth century.

Further reading

See: *The Origins of Pragmatism* (1968). On Darwin's influence on James see Philip P. Wiener, *Evolution and the Founders of Pragmatism* (1949). The definitive biography is Ralph B. Perry, *The Thought and Character of William James* (2 vols, 1935, reprinted 1974). James's influence upon American thought is discussed by Morton White, *Pragmatism and the American Mind* (1975). See: Kim Townsend, *Manhood at Harvard: William James and Others* (1997); Linda Simon (ed.), *William James Remembered* (1999); Howard F. Feinstein, *Becoming William James* (1999).

ROBERT OLBY

JANÁČEK, Leoš Eugen
1854–1928
Czech composer

The son of a Moravian schoolmaster and organist, he was a boy chorister at the Abbey of St Augustine in Brno (1865–9), which was then directed by Pavel Kížkovsky, a noted composer of church music. Janáček continued his education at the Brno Teachers' Training College (1872–4) and at the Prague Organ School (1874–5). He also went for brief periods of study to the conservatories of Leipzig (1879) and Vienna (1880), but found the German approach unsympathetic.

By this time Janáček had already begun to make a local reputation in Brno as a composer of choral music in the Kížkovsky tradition. In the 1880s he began to widen his scope, and in 1887 he produced his first opera, *Šárka*, though this was not staged until 1925. In it he treated a mythical theme in a manner close to that of **Dvořák**, whose influence is also clear in the set of *Lachian Dances* for orchestra (1889–90). However, his second opera, *The Beginning of a Romance* (1891), makes a more direct use of the Moravian folk music which he had been collecting since 1885, abandoning the Dvořákian effort to civilize such material within a symphonic style.

Janáček progressively refined his method of using folk elements in the cantata *Amarus* (1897) and in his third opera, *Jenůfa* (1894–1903), a passionate tale of love and jealousy set in a Moravian village. This was several times revised before its Prague première in 1916, which belatedly brought its composer national and soon international recognition. In a sense this event marked the beginning of his career, at the age of sixty-one. Another opera, *Fate* (1903–4), had been completed soon after *Jenůfa*, but this was not performed until 1934, and the great majority of Janáček's finest works came in the twelve years after the Prague performance of *Jenůfa*.

Among those works are the orchestral rhapsody *Taras Bulba* (1915–18), based on episodes of love and death from Gogol's treatment of the Cossack hero, and the *Sinfonietta*, boldly scored for an orchestra including twelve trumpets (1926). There was also the powerful *Glagolitic Mass* for soloists, choir, organ and large orchestra (1926), as well as a variety of chamber pieces, including two string quartets, both of a private, auto-biographical character: the first (1923–4) is subtitled 'Kreutzer Sonata' in reference to **Tolstoy**, the second 'Intimate Letters' (1928). In other works of this period Janáček disregarded conventions of form and genre, especially in the *Diary of a Young Man who Disappeared* for tenor, contralto, female voices and piano (1917–19), in the set of *Nursery Rhymes* for voices and instruments (1925–7), and in two miniature piano concertos: the Concertino for piano and six instruments (1925) and the Capriccio for left-hand piano and eight wind (1926). But then all of these late compositions are highly individual, sometimes even quirky, being based on short, irregular phrases of modal character and strong personality.

Janáček used the same features of style in the five operas he wrote after 1916, and these show also the full fruits of his research into Moravian folk music. That research, coupled with the work he had done in noting down the pitch inflections and the rhythms of speech in Moravia, had provided him with the material upon which he could build an operatic style suited to his own language, as **Mussorgsky** had done. It was no longer necessary for him to justify his procedures by using a local setting, as he had in *Jenůfa*: the Moravian elements had been thoroughly absorbed into a vigorous personal style. His five late operas are widely varied in dramatic tone and location, but they all show his ability to follow the words (usually his own) naturally yet with high intensity, in a manner that benefits from folk models but by no means sounds picturesquely ethnic.

These operas also demonstrate Janáček's unerring skill in depicting his characters and their emotions by means of swift, imaginative strokes, and in achieving potent dramatic effects through his very original use of the orchestra, involving, as in his contemporary orchestral and chamber works, stark sonorities and the rapid development of pungent motifs. Again, like other compositions of the same period, they display his relish of the bizarre and unusual. *The Excursions of Mr Brouček* (1908–17), Janáček's only comedy, is a fantasy which finds a commonplace man transported to the moon in the first act and to the fifteenth century, the time of the Hussite wars, in the second. *The Cunning Little Vixen* (1921–3), which benefited from the composer's keen ear for animal sounds, is a quite unpatronizing story of woodland creatures. *The Makropoulos Case* (1923–5) reveals the empty fate of a woman who has magically prolonged her existence for three hundred years, and *From the House of the Dead* (1927–8), which was left unfinished, is an austere setting of incidents from **Dostoevsky's** prison-camp novel. Yet despite all these examples of a taste for the extraordinary, Janáček was stimulated above all, as *Katya Kabanova* (1919–21) eloquently proves, by the inner lives of real human beings and by the tragedy of their destinies, and it was in this version of Ostrovsky's play *The Storm* that he produced his greatest achievement.

Further reading

See: Jaroslav Vogel, *Leoš Janáček: His Life and Works* (1962); Hans Hollander, *Leoš Janáček: His Life and Work* (1963); Erik Chisholm, *The Operas of Leoš Janáček* (1971); Michael Ewans, *Janáček's Tragic Operas* (1977); P. Wingfield (ed.), *Janáček Studies* (1999); Michael Beckerman, *Janáček and His World* (2003).

PAUL GRIFFITHS

JOBS, Steven

1955–

US computer entrepreneur and digital animation technologist

Steve Jobs is one half of the team who, in 1976, invented the personal computer as we recognize it. The other was Steve Wozniak. Put too simply, Wozniak was the computer designer, Jobs the entrepreneur. Wozniak's genius was to design a computer on one board (the original Apple I) and then to develop it to the mould-breaking Apple II. He and Jobs met at the Homebrew Computing Club in California, a group of enthusiasts from whom so much that has happened in computing stemmed, including the personal (desktop) computer, the Well computer community, and virtual reality. Jobs had access to his parents' garage, and the two Steves sold their cars and began assembling their computers there. Wozniak was infected by the idealism characteristic of so many of these pioneers and eventually left an active involvement in what had become Apple Computer to work with schoolchildren, introducing them to the wonders of computing.

Jobs, a computer enthusiast who had designed games for Atari, had an entrepreneurial streak and a vision that extended beyond the desktop – and even computing as it was then known – towards universality and entertainment. It was he who recognized the value of the work carried out by Doug Englebart and others at Xerox's Palo Alto Research Centre (PARC) which led to the first popular computer that used windows and a mouse. Jobs obliged Apple to produce what evolved into the Macintosh (Mac) computer – the origin of the ubiquitous 'what you see is what you get' (WYSIWYG), 'look and feel' and 'plug and play' of modern computer operating systems since imitated by others, most notably **Bill Gates's** Microsoft Corporation's Windows. The Mac was introduced in 1984 with a legendary advert based on breaking free from Big Brother: an image Apple would still like to believe of itself.

Thus, Jobs had a major role in both the type of computer that now appears in a majority of the relatively affluent households of the world, and the type of operating system that allows the computer to be used with a minimum of fuss and difficulty as a result of it being designed for the user rather than the computer scientist. This considerable achievement remains embodied in Apple's unique insistence on being sole provider of both the Mac operating system and the Mac computer it runs on.

Jobs's vision of computing is essentially different from other leading figures in Silicon Valley, as became apparent after he left Apple. He founded NeXTstep, a computer company reflecting his criticisms of and desired extensions to the Mac operating system. And he co-founded Pixar, the animation company that revolutionized cartoon-making and has brought him and his partners a second fortune. By 2004, Pixar had won several Oscars and grossed more than $2 billion. Jobs remains CEO.

Both Pixar and Apple are assessed by leading businessmen as among the most highly innovative companies ever, with Jobs winning accolades as most innovative CEO. For Jobs, though, computing is not so much about calculation, or even being useful. He did not lose the initial inspiration of the Homebrew Computer Club: computers are for fun (i.e. entertainment). To replace hobbyist computer construction, he imagined pleasure resulting from the marriage of computing to entertainment. An early manifestation is the Apple Fellows programme, where outstanding computer scientists were invited to play with Macs. It is demonstrated by the early inclusion of CD players in Apple's machines and the pioneering development of the media-rich QuickTime format that allows easy handling of time-based material such as film and music. The most recent manifestation is Apple's combination of personal music library and online music store that culminates in the trend-setting iPod personal music player attached to the iLife suite of entertainment/lifestyle programs. Such is the influence and success of this device that an update to the iMac computer has been built 'in the style of the iPod'.

The i-prefix is an Apple branding relating to machines that are designed to link easily to the Internet: as with everything Apple does, ease of use (transparency verging on invisibility) is the key: Apple's special gift is to make the difficult much easier, and to do so in an elegant and stylish manner. Apple's success comes from the quality of the machines; from the effectiveness of the Mac operating system; and from the extraordinarily high quality of Apple's design department under Jonathan Ives: Apple produces extremely desirable objects.

Orphaned at an early age, Jobs was adopted by Paul and Clara Jobs in California (he subsequently traced his blood sister, the novelist Mona Simpson). Married since 1996, both he and his wife are vegans. In 2004 he was diagnosed with a rare cancer, but seems to have made a full recovery after surgery. He is sometimes described as having a difficult temperament. This led to him being given the opportunity of leaving Apple not long after the launch of the Mac by John Scully, brought in from Pepsi Cola to be Apple CEO by Jobs himself. In 1997, when Apple's fortunes were at their lowest, he was invited back as CEO. He had earlier sold NeXT to Apple, providing them with much of what was needed for the revamped Mac operating system.

Jobs (and through him, Apple) has also sustained a long and ambiguous relationship with Microsoft's **Bill Gates**. In 1987, Gates proposed that Microsoft license the Macintosh operating system. Apple, some would say typically, refused. Mac users like to wonder about how the world would have been had Apple not been so recalcitrant. Ten years later, however, Jobs brokered a non-voting investment in Apple by Microsoft. The constantly challenging, awkward child, Apple, is, paradoxically, vital to the survival of Microsoft: its continuing (though niche) success allows Microsoft the claim that it is not a monopoly. Apple Computer, and the traumas it carries with it, looks set to run and run, providing Steve Jobs is there to keep on kicking it.

Further reading

See: Steven Levy, *Insanely Great: The Life and Times of Macintosh, the Computer that Changed Everything* (1995).

RANULPH GLANVILLE

JOHNS, Jasper

1930–

US painter

Born in Augusta, Georgia, Johns studied at the University of Southern Carolina. In 1949 he served in the US Army in Japan, then moved to New York where from 1952 to 1958 he worked in a bookstore and, with **Robert Rauschenberg**, as a window display artist for Tiffany's. Painting with little outside influence Johns chose flags, targets, alphabets and numerals – 'Things the mind already knows,' he explained. Johns was making painting serve philosophy, yet in no sense illustrate ideas or arguments. Nor was the sensuous side of painting neglected. The subtlety of inflection of encaustic – painting into wax – was a constant reminder of the distance between signifier and signified, language and reality. Work for the 1958 one-man show at Castelli was made in three years; in 1954 Johns had destroyed all but a few of his pieces. Their preoccupations were to remain with him throughout his career: the play between different ways of looking; the defences of art–objects not only against visual ransacking but also against their innate expressivity; the paradoxical dialectic between recognizable, *a priori* structures, icons which become increasingly strange as the mind fails to encompass them, and the brute *Dinglichkeit* of illusions, or rather of objects as springboards for illusions. In an early interview Johns said:

> I am concerned with a thing's not being what it was, with its becoming other than what it is, with any moment in which one identifies a thing precisely and with the slipping away of that moment, with at any moment seeing or saying and letting it go at that.

The first crisis in Johns's career occurred when his stock of 'flat' images was exhausted. But in 1959 he was introduced to **Marcel Duchamp** and from 1961 onwards began reading **Wittgenstein**. Both affected his work in the 1960s, typified by a broad painterly style, suspended objects and names of subjects and colours stencilled on to the canvas. A consuming interest in process and change overtook not only the new paintings but also the procedure of the career itself, with motifs pursued, rehearsed and ransacked in an act of ceaseless redefinition. After denying the rampant individualism of Abstract Expressionism – 'I worked in such a way that I could say it's not me,' Johns remarked – then moving through an intensification of that irony and *maniera* inherent in American 1960s art, he arrived at that complex obsession with exhaustion which prepared the ground for the mathematical systems of 'epistemic' post-minimalism. Like the lives of Duchamp or **Joyce**, whose artistic decisions resemble a cultural equivalent of military strategies, Johns seemed to have cleared an area in which he could enrich his chosen form. The cross-hatched motif of *The Barber's Tree*, *The Dutch Wives* and *Weeping Women* was remembered from a brief but vivid experience. 'I was riding in a car ... when a car came in the opposite direction ... covered in these marks ... I only saw it for a moment ... but I immediately thought that I would use it for my next painting.' All of Johns's major themes are present in the finished pictures – a Puritan mistrust of the mendacity of visual forms and a counterbalancing, defensive desire to employ them, a concern with beginnings and endings of events and the arbitrary but blinding effect of a shifted point of view. Like the mature style of **Henry James** or Milton, Johns's manner, which *is* the painting, is both an approach and a tool for understanding that approach. Johns is not recording the existence of anything but locating his subject, sensing its presence, then registering it by providing a visual parallel to the act of permitting it to impinge on his consciousness. In his monograph on Johns, the novelist Michael Crichton seriously suggests a biological reason for his lateral thinking. Perhaps they amount to the same thing, an originality so powerful that the very foundations of the art they are using are exposed, questioned and miraculously rearranged. Jasper Johns himself has said: 'I don't know anything about art.' And on another occasion, 'I'm just trying to find a way to make pictures.'

Alongside Rauschenberg, **Warhol** and **Lichtenstein**, Johns is regarded as a master of Pop Art, but this sits uncomfortably with the depth and scope of his output. His later work especially displays a phenomenal range of reference – to fugitive texts as well as to other artists, from Grünewald and Holbein to **Picasso** and **de Kooning**. Preoccupied with reconfiguring the space between the figurative and the abstract, Johns's career has become an odyssey that is as 'cultured' as it is idiosyncratic.

Further reading

See: Leo Steinberg, *Jasper Johns* (1963); Max Kozloff, *Jasper Johns* (1969); Richard Field, *Jasper Johns: Prints 1960–1970* (1970) and *Jasper Johns: Prints 1970–1977* (1978); Michael Crichton, *Jasper Johns* (New York, Whitney Museum/New York Graphic Society, 1978); Kirk Vanedoe, *Jasper Johns: A Retrospective* (Museum of Modern Art catalogue, 1996). See also: O. Tilman, *Pop Art* (1999).

STUART MORGAN
(REVISED AND UPDATED BY THE EDITOR)

JOYCE, James Augustine

1882–1941

Irish writer

Criticism has long cast Joyce as a supreme practitioner of international modernism in literature who just happened to come from Ireland. This effectively deracinated him, and left his work open to an unlimited range of interpretations. In recent decades, he has been claimed by myth critics, structuralists, post-structuralists, **Marxists**, feminists, gays, Deleuzeans and postmodernists, to name but a few. But Joyce was in fact a profoundly Irish writer. In the first instance, his work was always and everywhere concerned with Irish history, politics and culture. Its modernism was an expression of a specifically Irish-centred agenda. The cosmopolitan and global

Joyce was an expression of the Irish one, not a release from him.

James Joyce was born into a middle-class Dublin Catholic family in 1882, just as Charles Stewart Parnell and the cause of Home Rule in Ireland were beginning to pick up momentum. His family were strongly Parnellite. They had ties to the Liberator, the great Irish proponent of Catholic Emancipation in the early nineteenth century, Daniel O'Connell, and even to the clandestine and sometimes violent nationalism of the Fenians. Their allegiances made them both hostile to British rule and fiercely anti-clerical. Joyce shared what he called 'the inherited tenacity of heterodox resistance' in his family, but turned it into great Irish art. His radicalism and his opposition to the politics of the British and Roman Catholic *imperia*, and the cultural formations on which they pervasively left their mark, poke up irrepressibly from every nook and cranny of his work.

The Parnellite cause failed. In the 1890s, the Irish turned away from politics and invested their energies in culture. The decade saw the birth of the Revival, both Gaelic (Hyde, Pearse) and Anglo-Irish and literary (**W.B. Yeats**, Moore, J.M. Synge, **Russell**). Joyce found the Gaelic Revivalists slavishly obedient to the church and intellectually unambitious. But he was also separated from the Anglo-Irish by long-lived, deep-rooted questions of race, class difference, possession and dispossession. He would discover his own form of Irish self-assertion that would finally surpass them all. Changes in the culture helped. Between 1898 and 1903, legislation gave unprecedented rights to the Catholic Irish. In 1898, Joyce started at University College, Dublin. He soon found himself to be that strange new special creature, a modern dissident Irish Catholic intellectual. He proclaimed his loss of faith and started writing criticism. The critical writings 1898–1903 are very much concerned with Ireland, its history and prospects, its politics and culture, its relation to the church and the colonial power, and the place of art in it. They are a portent of the work that would follow them.

By 1903, Joyce's alienation from the Irish literary scene had deepened. The political scene was still stagnant. The English had evidently used Catholic empowerment to kill off the prospect of Home Rule. Joyce met Nora Barnacle, the woman he was to live with for the rest of his life, and who was a constant source of inspiration. In October 1904, he quit Dublin, winding up in Trieste. Thereafter, he lived the life of exile, as he thought of it. Later, his friend and collaborator **Samuel Beckett** would make the same choice. In Joyce's case, however, in the great tradition of Irish saints, scholars and political refugees, exile was paradoxically an expression not of disloyalty, but of attachment to locality, home and people, about which Joyce never stopped writing. In *Exiles* (1918), his play of 1914–15, what is crucial to the hero is that he rise superior to Ireland's dispossessors and the fact of dispossession. In effect, the play provides a Joycean logic of exile. So too does Joyce's collection of short stories *Dubliners* (1914), which he finished in Trieste. It is about the Dublin Joyce left, and helps to explain why he left it. 'It is high time,' Joyce wrote, 'that Ireland finished once and for all with failures.' He meant both personal and political failures. Again and again, Ireland had failed successfully to resist the conqueror and blaze its own way to independence. While nationalists fulminated unceasingly against British rule, Catholic Ireland remained blithely willing to accept the continuing hold of Rome on its soul. *Dubliners* is full of personal failures. But Joyce places these failures in a context of historical disaster and political inertia and collapse. The stories in *Dubliners* are about the ineluctable failure of the psyche under the conditions of a colonial politics and economy. In the scientific spirit of the French realists Joyce so admired, the volume anatomizes the pathological structure of a colonized culture. In the great last story, 'The Dead', Joyce indicates that the pathology at stake is also post-traumatic, the consequence of the Irish Famine of the 1840s.

In Trieste, Joyce repeatedly came up against a set of stereotypes of the Irish. He became vividly aware that the source of the images of the Irish in circulation in the world at large was English, not Irish. His work as a whole between 1907 and 1922 was to some extent powered by an intense desire to rectify this state of affairs, beginning with his Triestine journalism and lectures of 1907–12. He also had practical battles to fight. He could not get *Dubliners* published without revisions (omissions of expletives, changes to anti-royalist and sexually suggestive passages) that he refused to make. Then, in 1913, **Ezra Pound** took over his literary affairs. Pound was becoming an extraordinary catalyst, champion of modern art and generous supporter of new writing. He offered Joyce a chance to cut straight through the twisted knots that were troubling him. Joyce could continue to write the moral history of his country and to serve the cause of its liberation. Henceforth, however, he would pursue his project under other auspices. The world would call those auspices modernism.

Pound arranged the publication of the novel Joyce was finishing, *A Portrait of the Artist as a Young Man* (1916). Joyce had begun an autobiographical novel as early as 1904. He needed to grasp the specific character of the historical forces that had been formative for him. For to understand them was also to recognize their historicity, how they might have been different, how Ireland might have been different, too. *A Portrait* is a late exemplar of the nineteenth-century tradition of the European *Bildungsroman*, the novel concerned with the development and formation of a young man. Exceptionally, however, the young man in question grows up in a culture that is both European and colonial. Three kinds of personal development are at stake: first, *Bildung* itself, the 'official' formation of a young man in a particular stratum of colonial society. Joyce shows us very clearly how far the two imperial masters are responsible for this formation. *Bildung* takes place in specific institutions, family, school, university, church. It is also a product of cultural institutions, and a question of language, discourse, habits of thought that are verbal habits, too.

Second, there is *Entbildung*, the coming apart or dismantling of formations. For Joyce, a novelist of a colonial society little more than a decade from independence, *Entbildung* also implies the third kind of development, counter-formation. Counter-formation comes about as a result of counter-discourses (rebellious, anti-colonial, anti-clerical). *A Portrait* handles the relationship between *Bildung*, *Entbildung* and counter-formation with immense subtlety and an extraordinary awareness of hidden ironies. Joyce picks a precise and delicate path through issues that have become extremely complex for him. In particular, he is painfully but pitilessly conscious of how far counter-formations can seem to oppose established ones while actually turning out to consolidate them. The irony at the expense of his hero, the young Stephen Dedalus, is often correspondingly exacting. Stephen is characterized by his declarations of independence. However, he finds himself repeatedly caught in complicity. Joyce's project was, massively, libertarian. But he was also everywhere conscious of the immensely problematic character of any definitive conception of Irish freedom. On this point, he very clearly distinguished himself from all his Irish republican and nationalist contemporaries.

When war broke out, the Joyces went from Trieste to Zürich. It was here that the greatest novel of the twentieth-century, *Ulysses*, took on solid bulk. Joyce knew that an emergent new Ireland needed its epic. He was also well aware of later nineteenth- and early twentieth-century Irish debates about the form this epic should take. Anglo-Irishman Standish O'Grady had even presented his *History of Ireland* as a modern Irish equivalent of Homeric epic. Joyce, too, was interested in a modern Irish version of Homer. This eventually became *Ulysses*, for which the *Odyssey* served as a structural foundation. At the same time, more than any other novel, *Ulysses* is saturated in a sense of a particular place (Dublin) at a particular time (16 June, 1904). Joyce begins, again, with Stephen. Stephen is obsessed with and cast down by Irish history. It is 'a nightmare' from which he is 'trying to awake'. The novel hugely extends his effort. The trouble is that, in Joyce's phrase, 'Stephen has a shape that can't be changed'. Enter the modest and unpretentious figure of Leopold Bloom.

No one has evoked the complexity of an ordinary life, of a basically cheerful, sane, resilient, unremarkable city-dweller's mind, better than Joyce does in Bloom. But Bloom is also both Joyce's modern Irishman and an indication of how far Joyce's Ireland still has to go to reach modernity. Bloom is a Dublin Jew. He is therefore both familiar with and foreign to the Dublin culture fashioned by the two imperial masters, but has neither the intimacy nor the complicity with it that stems from historical disaster and profound hostility to the conqueror. This means that he can serve as an extremely subtle and flexible instrument of critique of and imaginative liberation from contemporary Ireland. Having set this process in motion, however, Joyce doubles it, notably with the extraordinary styles that dominate the second half of the novel. Here the struggle for freedom becomes a linguistic and discursive struggle. But *Ulysses* is also very much about resignation, acceptance, settling for things. This emerges above all in the last chapter, which Joyce said was about 'the end of all resistance', and is wholly made up of the thoughts of Molly Bloom as she lies in bed, early in the morning of 17 June.

Ulysses is Joyce's national epic. The novel is saturated in a consciousness of Irish history. But it is also sophisticated and subversive in a way that makes it very much of its time. Joyce arrived in Paris in July 1920. *Ulysses* was published in 1922. Paris was a city of avant-garde artists and intellectuals. Here, in a post-war climate distrustful of stuffy old tradition and eager for innovation, the modernist *Ulysses* was born. Joyce became a luminary and iconic figure. In March 1923, he embarked on the work that finally became *Finnegans Wake* (1939). The *Wake* was composed in a very different fashion to Joyce's earlier work. For Joyce was by now a celebrated modern genius surrounded by admirers. He used the situation to his advantage. It allowed him to create a book like an Irish megalith: massive, strange, cryptic, sometimes decorated with unreadable hieroglyphs, and a prodigious testimony to the life and history of a people. The *Wake* is both an encyclopaedia and a memorial. But if Joyce wanted to commemorate a subjugated culture, he also wanted to write a sense of its historical invisibility into the commemoration itself.

If there are characters, events, scenes, landscapes and cityscapes in the *Wake*, they are consistently Irish at root. Its range of reference to Irish materials – Irish topography, geography, mythology, lore and literature and historiography – is mind-boggling. Its range of non-Irish material is also vast. But that material is drawn into an Irish orbit and made to signify in an Irish context. The *Wake* is a monument, but of a very unusual kind. Joyce combines Irish history with a thought about actual and possible change in Ireland and an Ireland open to the world. The title *Finnegans Wake* suggests remembrance, commemoration, a testimony to the past. It also suggests an injunction to the Irish to make a new start. Like *Ulysses*, the book is a work of liberation, but a cautious, sceptical, even perverse one. It insists on the importance of escaping repetitive historical patterns, but refuses to quite escape them itself. This is reflected in its language, which is a composite of more than sixty languages, but with English as its recognizable base. Joyce's linguistic practice in the *Wake* is inseparable from his declaration of cultural war. He desecrates one of the conquerors' most precious shrines. He sprays it with foreign matter. Yet the more Joyce proclaimed his struggle with England, the more he announced his continuing tie to it. He himself was acutely aware of the paradox: hence the fact that, in his work, radical resistance and acceptance co-exist.

Joyce's later life was scarred by ill-health, misfortune and family troubles. Yet his dedication was, beyond all bounds, unstinting. His task was to transform if not reverse a historical structure that had conferred immense significance on one of two adjacent cultures, at the massive expense of the other. He undertook this task with his eyes wide open, in full acknowledgement of its labyrinthine complexities. He died in Zurich in 1941, having fled there after the outbreak of war. By then, he had produced an oeuvre that matched those of the very greatest English writers, and inscribed itself in the select pantheon of European masterworks.

Further reading

Other works include: *Chamber Music* (1907); *Pomes Penyeach* (1927); *Stephen Hero* (1944); *Letters* (3 vols, 1957–66); *Giacomo Joyce* (1968); *Occasional, Critical and Political Writing* (2000). Richard Ellmann's *James Joyce* (revised edn, 1982) remains the definitive biography. See also Vincent Cheng, *Joyce, Race and Empire* (1995); Thomas J. Hofheinz, *Joyce and the Invention of Irish History: 'Finnegans Wake' in Context* (1995); Emer Nolan, *James Joyce and Nationalism* (1995); Len Platt, *Joyce and the Anglo-Irish: A Study of Joyce and the Literary Revival* (1998); Derek Attridge, *Joyce Effects: On Language, Theory, History* (2000) and, with Marjorie Howes (eds), *Semicolonial Joyce* (2000); Gregory Castle, *Modernism and the Celtic Revival* (2001); Andrew Gibson, *Joyce's Revenge: History, Politics and Aesthetics in 'Ulysses'* (2002) and *James Joyce: A Critical Life* (2006).

ANDREW GIBSON

JUDD, Donald

1928–94

US artist

Donald Judd called his art 'specific'. His three-dimensional stacks, wall progressions, boxes and other objects differ from most of what we see in the world, which we treat as general rather than specific. Drinking straws, for instance, are general. We learn through repeated experience to anticipate and ignore the illusion of a broken straw in a glass of water since, time and time again, it is intact when we lift it out. By casually assuming that new things look like and are like familiar things, we save ourselves the trouble of having to stop and study them. And our hunch usually ends up being right. But we have no reliable backlog of seeing Judd's objects. He declared in a 1966 interview that 'Art is something you look at.' One can only look harder as materials like motorcycle lacquer, enamel, plexiglass, copper, aluminium and galvanized iron confound expectations. Some pieces do not appear heavy yet weigh hundreds of pounds. Other works' surfaces are highly reflective and seem to dematerialize when properly lit. Interiors glow. Edges flicker. While most of us think better than we see, cursory scans and mental shortcuts fail with objects so specific.

Born in Missouri, Judd attended William and Mary College (Virginia), Columbia University and the Arts Students' League, New York. His university studies of pragmatism and empiricism provided philosophical grounding for his art. He claimed in a 1983 lecture that:

> A person lives with a little solid knowledge, a great deal of fragmentary knowledge, a lot of assumptions, and many provisional solutions and reactions made from day to day. Most people have some philosophical ideas. Almost none live by one of the grand systems, only by their fossil fragments. Neither is art at the present based on a grand system.

Judd relied on sensory perception for knowing the world and on vision in particular for knowing his art. There were consequences. Representations of actual things, references to the human body, evidence of handicraft, and framing elements like pedestals prevented one from seeing an art object for itself. After eliminating these distractions, pieces by Judd and other socalled Minimalists seemed rarefied and puritanical. Judd rejected these characterizations and claimed he had removed only what was extraneous. He believed there were ideas that art could and

could not – and, therefore, should and should not – investigate. The artist wrote in 1981, 'Since I leapt into the world an empiricist, ideality was not a quality I wanted.' There was to be no metaphor by which meaning could drift from his specific objects to generalities about politics, love, or god. Meaning consisted in what a piece of art could legitimately demonstrate for an empiricist – its own material attributes as perceived by a viewer.

Judd's art criticism, for *Arts Magazine* and other publications, demonstrated philosophical and aesthetic principles similar to those guiding his own art. Looking closely at objects, he began reviews with a blunt account of what was where before examining metaphorical content. Judd was uncompromising when he thought work weak, but he praised many artists unconcerned with Minimalism, including Lee Bontecou, John Chamberlain, Ed Kienholz, **Claes Oldenburg**, Lucas Samaras, George Segal and H.C. Westermann. In addition to 'specific', Judd used words like 'single', 'definite', 'particular', 'individual', 'polarized' and 'separate' to define his main aesthetic criterion. An object's various properties, like its material, hue and scale, were to remain distinct. Adjusting one attribute to suit another made the specific object a vague and general amalgamation. Judd thought such art promised less compelling visual experience coupled with dependence on ideality for meaning. He found both indefensible.

You come to know Judd's pieces bit by bit – a slow process of prolonged and repeated viewing. Most exhibitions were inadequate since temporary. In 1986, Judd organized the Chinati Foundation for the permanent installation of his and other artists' work in the big sky country of west Texas. Changes in light from the local weather, seasons and time of day transform how his one hundred milled aluminium boxes appear. One sees cast reflections of the sun, clouds, prairie grass, glass walls and other boxes (and those works' reflections). By turns, each object gives material form to light and then itself seems to dematerialize. These aluminium works complement the immense outdoor concrete pieces at Chinati, which look surprisingly different at sun up, high noon and sun down. Their uncomplicated form and neutral grey hue emphasize the rich effects of natural light that we ignore in most art.

Customary ways of looking at art entail traditional meanings, and vice versa. The primacy of seeing in Judd's work was new. By trying to eliminate interpretative readings of his objects, he did not make viewing them easier. It was just the opposite. When seeing takes priority over thinking, one cannot glance over a piece and begin explaining allusions, translating symbols and unpacking metaphors to find meaning. In everyday experience of the world, we usually lack the time or energy to look hard. Judd's art required it.

Further reading

See: Brydon Smith, *Donald Judd: Catalogue Raisonné of Paintings, Objects, and WoodBlocks, 1960–1974* (1975); Donald Judd, *Complete Writings, 1959–1975* (1975, 2004) and *Complete Writings, 1975–1986* (1987). The best critical writings about Judd are Barbara Haskell, *Donald Judd* (1988); Richard Schiff, 'A Space of One to One', in Richard Schiff, *Donald Judd* (2002); Nicholas Serota (ed.), *Donald Judd* (2004); and David Raskin, 'Donald Judd's Skepticism', an unpublished dissertation (University of Texas at Austin, 1999)

ADRIAN KOHN

JUNG, Carl Gustav

1875–1961

Swiss psychiatrist

C.G. Jung was an original thinker who made notable contributions to the understanding of the human mind. Jung was born in Kesswil, Switzerland, on 26 July 1875. His father was a pastor in the Swiss Reformed Church. He remained an only child for the first nine years of his life, and, since he was far ahead of his contemporaries at the village school to which

he was first sent, remained somewhat isolated emotionally during most of his childhood. At the age of eleven, he went to school in Basel, and later became a medical student at the university there. He had almost decided to specialize in surgery when he came across a textbook of psychiatry written by Krafft-Ebing. Reading this book made Jung decide that he must specialize in psychiatry, which at that time was a poorly regarded branch of medicine. In 1900, he obtained a post in the Burghölzli mental hospital in Zürich. In 1905 he was appointed lecturer in psychiatry at the University of Zürich. In 1907 Jung first encountered **Freud**, with whom he actively collaborated for the next six years. In 1909 Jung gave up his hospital appointment in favour of his growing private practice; and, in the same year, travelled with Freud to the United States to lecture at Clark University, Massachusetts. Increasing divergence between the two men led to Jung's withdrawal from the psychoanalytic movement; and in April 1914 Jung resigned his position as president of the International Psychoanalytical Association. He also gave up his academic post at the University of Zürich, feeling that he could not continue to teach until he had more clearly formulated his own, individual point of view. Henceforth he devoted himself to his practice and to research. Jung's psychology became known as 'Analytical Psychology' in contrast to Freud's 'Psychoanalysis'. As the eighteen volumes of his *Collected Works* attest, Jung was an indefatigable writer. The rest of his long life was outwardly uneventful. From time to time, after he became world-famous, his routine was interrupted by travels to India, Africa, the United States and other parts of the world; but for the most part he continued to live and work at his home in Küsnacht, by the lakeside of Zürich. Jung died at the age of eighty-five on 6 June 1961.

When Jung started work in the Burghölzli hospital, associationist theories of mental functioning held the field. Jung transformed the tool of word-association tests from a means of investigating contrast, contiguity and so on into a way of uncovering personal problems and emotional preoccupations. In using the tests in this way, Jung provided experimental support for Freud's concept of repression; for his subjects were often unaware that their hesitations in response to stimulus words revealed their inner life. It was this work which led to Jung's introduction of the word 'complex' into psychiatry. It also led to correspondence with Freud, whose first surviving letter to Jung acknowledges the latter's paper 'Psychoanalysis and Association Experiments'.

In 1906, Jung published *The Psychology of Dementia Praecox* which was the first notable attempt to apply psychoanalytic interpretation to the phenomena of insanity. He sent the book to Freud, who promptly invited Jung to visit him in Vienna. It was Jung's research into schizophrenia which led to his conception of a 'collective unconscious': that is, a deeper layer of mind, common to all people, which lay beneath the merely personal. Jung was widely read in history and also in comparative religion. His efforts to understand the bizarre delusions and hallucinations of the insane led him to compare them with the myths and religious beliefs of primitive people. He found many parallels. In Jung's view, this myth-making substratum of mind could not be explained in terms of the personal vicissitudes of childhood, as were the neuroses described by Freud. The child was not born into the world with a mind like a blank sheet of paper upon which anything could be inscribed. The child was already predisposed to feel and think along the same lines as had his ancestors since the beginning of time. The unconscious was not just a part of the mind to which unpleasant experience was banished: it was the very foundation of our being and the source not only of mental disturbance but also of our deepest hopes and aspirations.

At least part of the divergence between Jung and Freud was the result of their different clinical experience. Freud did not work in a mental hospital and had little experience of insanity, whereas Jung continued to be interested in schizophrenia throughout his life. Jung concluded that the delusional systems of schizophrenia served a positive function. First, delusional systems were explanatory devices which served to make sense out of the sufferer's experience and to preserve his self-esteem. An obvious example is the familiar type of paranoid system, which explains the individual's plight as the consequence of the machinations of others, thus relieving the sufferer from responsibility while attributing to him an undeserved importance. Second, delusional systems often contained material which resembled myth and to which parallels could be found in various forms of religious belief, even though the patient might never have encountered any such parallel. Jung concluded that the collective, myth-creating level of mind, in both normal persons and in the insane, had the function of making sense out of the individual's experience and giving meaning to his existence. In later life, Jung concluded that the real cause of much mental suffering was the fact that the individual had become alienated from this level of mind, with the result that he lost any sense of significance in his life. In this way, Jung anticipated the point of view of the existentialist analysts. In a letter to Freud in 1910, discussing the possibility of joining a new ethical society, Jung wrote:

> What sort of a new myth does it hand out for us to live by? Only the wise are ethical from sheer intellectual presumption, the rest of us need the eternal truth of myth ... 2000 years of Christianity can only be replaced by something equivalent.

In 1912, just before his break with Freud, Jung published *The Psychology of the Unconscious*, later to become known as *Symbols of Transformation*. This was the first major work in which his own distinctive point of view was made manifest. During the next few years, Jung went through a period of profound upheaval which is vividly described in his autobiography. He described himself as being 'menaced by a psychosis'.

This 'midlife crisis', as it would now be called, proved to be very important for his subsequent development. The self-analysis which he was forced to pursue during the years of the First World War shaped the whole course of his subsequent psychological theorizing, and also influenced his technique of psychotherapy. He wrote: 'The years when I was pursuing my inner images were the most important in my life. In them, everything essential was decided.' He managed to retain his hold on reality, partly because he was supported by his wife and family, and partly because he learned to objectify his own fantasies by painting them and writing about them. In later life, he encouraged his patients to use the same techniques in coming to terms with their own psychopathological material.

Emerging from this period of mental turmoil, Jung started to reflect upon how it was that such men as Freud, Alfred Adler and himself could study the same psychological material and yet come to such different conclusions about it. These reflections led to the theme of his next major work, *Psychological Types* (1921), in which his concepts of Extraversion and Introversion were delineated. Jung saw that men approached the study of the mind, and life in general, from different basic attitudes. The extravert was primarily interested in the world of external objects; the introvert in what went on within his own mind. Both attitudes were necessary for a full comprehension of reality; but people were usually one-sided, and tended to one or other extreme. From his concept of types sprang Jung's idea that neurosis arose from a one-sided development of the individual, and his valuable conception that the unconscious compensated for the one-sided development of consciousness. Neurotic symptoms were not always residues of childhood experience, as Freud supposed, but were often attempts on the part of the mind to correct its own lack of equilibrium, and therefore pointers to a new and more satisfactory synthesis. This point of view is in accord with modern ideas on cybernetics,

and with the recognition by physiologists that the body is a self-regulating entity. It follows from this conception that there must be an ideal state of synthesis or integration towards which the human being is striving, even though it may never, in practice, be attained. In Jung's view, this search for integration or wholeness was characteristic of the second half of life; and it is in dealing with the problems of older people that Jung's psychological ideas have proved most effective.

Many of Jung's patients were successful people who did not fall into the conventional categories of neurosis, but who complained that life no longer held any meaning for them. Jung treated such people by encouraging them to pursue the products of unconscious fantasy, whether these manifested themselves in dreams or day-dreams. He encouraged them to enter into a state of reverie in which consciousness was not lost, but in which judgement was suspended. His patients were urged to write or paint the fantasies which came to them while in this condition, a technique which became known as 'active imagination'. In this way a process of psychological development was initiated which Jung named the process of 'individuation'. This might be described as a kind of Pilgrim's Progress without a creed, aiming not at heaven but at integration and wholeness, a condition which his patients expressed in paintings resembling the patterns known as Mandalas which are used in the East for meditation. Although individuals might differ very widely from one another, the paths they pursued in their exploration of the unconscious shared some landmarks in common. In the course of analysis, patients would encounter various typical, 'primordial images' which Jung named 'archetypes'. These images are the same kind of figures which are familiar in myth and fairy story: heroes, heroines, demons, witches, gods and goddesses. A characteristic encounter is with the Shadow: that is, with a personification of the least acceptable parts of human nature, often symbolized by a sinister, dark 'other' who is felt to be terrifying or alien. The primordial image of the opposite sex is named Animus in women, Anima in men. A typical anima figure is Rider Haggard's 'She'. 'She' is not only spectacularly beautiful, but also an immortal priestess with access to arcane wisdom. She is clearly not an actual woman, but an image of Woman, a distilled essence of all that is most fascinating and seductive about women for men. Jung maintained that, in order to attain integration, the individual must recognize and differentiate himself from the immensely powerful influence of such archetypal images which, all too often, are projected upon actual people in the external world.

The greater part of Jung's later work is concerned with the process of individuation. Having formulated the idea, Jung set about looking for parallels from the past. Jung believed that man's essential nature did not alter much in the course of centuries, and that there must therefore be evidence that the men of old were looking for the same integration as were his patients in the present. He found his main parallel in alchemy.

Alchemy is interesting psychologically just because there is nothing in it scientifically. The alchemists were looking for something (the philosopher's stone) which had no real existence, but which, for them, was of extreme importance. The symbolism in which the alchemists expressed their search was found by Jung to be remarkably similar to that produced by his patients, and he chronicles much of his research in this field in *Psychology and Alchemy* (1953).

In his later years, Jung became interested in the problem of time. He came to the conclusion that events were linked, not only in a causal sequence but also by their simultaneous occurrence. Throughout his life, Jung was interested in what he called 'meaningful coincidences'; and he finally came to believe that there was an acausal principle of equal importance with causality which he named 'synchronicity'. This aspect of his work has not been generally accepted.

In spite of the fact that Jung became something of a cult figure amongst the young of the Western world during the 1960s and 1970s, his work has never been very widely appreciated. Moreover, some of his contributions have been taken over by others without acknowledgement, or perhaps without realization of their origin. This is especially true of the so-called Neo-Freudians. For many years Jung was reluctant to allow his teaching to become formalized within an institutional framework; but centres at which analysts are trained in his methods exist in Zürich, London, various cities in the USA, and some other European countries. His impact upon psychiatry has been small; but his influence upon the practice of psychotherapy has been greater, particularly as regards a more flexible approach than that of orthodox Freudian analysts, together with the use of painting, modelling and writing as adjuvants to talk. Jung's emphasis upon the spiritual, as opposed to the physical, is a valuable counterbalance to Freud's insistence upon the body. Distinguished people from spheres other than psychiatry and psychotherapy have paid tribute to Jung's influence. Among them are the writers **Hermann Hesse** and J.B. Priestley; the historian Arnold Toynbee; the physicist W. Pauli; the art historian Sir Herbert Read. Jung is certain of a place in history; but the ultimate significance and impact of his ideas are as yet undetermined.

Further reading

See: *Collected Works* (18 vols, 1953–71); *Memories, Dreams, Reflections* (1963); C.G. Jung, Marie-Louise von Franz, J.L. Henderson, Jolande Jacobi and Aniela Jaffe, *Man and His Symbols* (1964); and William McGuire (ed.), *The Freud/Jung Letters* (1974). About Jung: Frieda Fordham, *An Introduction to Jung's Psychology* (1953); Raymond M. Hostie, *Religion and the Psychology of Jung* (1957); Anthony Storr, *Jung* (1973); Antonio Moreno, *Jung, Gods and Modern Man* (1974); Marie-Louise von Franz, *C.G. Jung; His Myth in Our Time*; Volodymyr Walter Odajnyk, *Jung and Politics* (1976); Vincent Brome, *Jung: Man and Myth* (1978); Ronald Hayman: *Jung: A Biography* (1999); Deirdre Nair, *Jung: A Biography* (2003); Sonu Shamdasani, *Jung and the Making of Modern Psychology: The Dream of a Science* (2003).

ANTHONY STORR

K

KAFKA, Franz

1883–1924

Austrian novelist

The timid, reticent son of a robust self-made businessman, Kafka was born in Prague, and educated at the German Gymnasium and then the German University, where he read law. After receiving his doctorate he worked from 1908 until 1922 for the Workers' Accident Insurance Institute, where his duties were to write reports concerning the dangers of various trades and recommending methods of accident-prevention. Until 1915 Kafka lived with his parents, helping in their shop during his spare time, a fact which, combined with the exigencies of his profession, left him with little time for writing. He was thus compelled, to the eventual detriment of his health, to do his writing at night, and in 1909 and 1910 published a number of short prose pieces in literary journals. Through his close lifelong friend the writer Max Brod, in August 1912 Kafka met Felice Bauer, a young woman from Berlin with whom, for the next five years, he pursued a troubled relationship involving him in profound vacillation. Twice engaged to Felice, Kafka found himself torn between reluctance to bear life alone and the fear that marriage would involve a threat to the solitude which he saw as a necessary precondition of his art. In the event, Kafka never married, although in addition to Felice a number of women played an important part in his emotional life, including Dora Dymant with whom, towards the end of his life, he lived for

a short time in Berlin. But the quickened development of tuberculosis, which had been diagnosed in 1917, caused him to return to Prague and thence to a sanatorium in Vienna where he died in 1924, leaving instructions to Max Brod that his unpublished writings should be burned. Brod disobeyed, thus rescuing from oblivion the three unfinished novels, *America* (*Amerika*, largely written 1911–14, trans. 1949), *The Trial* (*Der Prozess*, 1914–15, trans. 1937), and *The Castle* (*Das Schloss*, 1922, trans. 1930, rev. 1969).

During his lifetime, Kafka published only a proportion of his shorter fiction in various collections. Late in 1912, he wrote the two stories which are generally regarded as his first mature achievement, *The Judgment* (*Das Urteil*, trans. 1928) and *The Metamorphosis* (*Die Verwandlung*, trans. 1961). Each is the history of its hero's regression from the confident certainties of 'normal' life to a state of overwhelming psychic bewilderment and finally death: in the first story the protagonist unquestioningly accepts the death sentence passed upon him for his dishonesties and inadequacies by a spectacularly rejuvenated father; in the second, the hero is transformed overnight into an enormous beetle while retaining a lucid human consciousness as ironic accompaniment to his physical degradation. In both cases – and this is a recurrent feature of much of Kafka's work – the punishment unconsciously incurred by the protagonist seems monstrously disproportionate to any ascertainable crime. Yet the works transcend the status of mere paranoid fantasies by virtue of two factors: the meticulous lucidity of the writing and the gain in metaphoric range occasioned by the disconnection of effect from cause. The described effect thus acquires the status of free-standing or unascribed metaphor, so that the area of suggestivity which radiates from the central situation is vastly enlarged.

In the relatively immature novel, *America*, Karl Rossmann's emigration to the USA is in itself a punishment, inflicted by his parents: so that in the bizarre adventures which ensue (in which the hero is on a number of occasions actually or implicitly brought to trial) the causes of events, no matter how grotesquely refracted, are at least dimly perceptible. But in Kafka's most famous work, *The Trial*, the protagonist, Josef K, is suddenly arrested for no apparent reason, and finds himself plunged into a world in which absurd appearances correspond to no ascertainable reality, where explanations make a mockery of logic and where the individual is subject to a power whose mechanisms are obscure and whose ultimate nature remains wholly inscrutable. Josef K, a victim of the ineluctable force known simply as The Law, is both constrained and attracted by it. Armed only with the hopelessly inadequate powers of human perception and language, he seeks unsuccessfully to establish the nature of his guilt and, though still questioning, submits passively to a grotesque execution.

In *The Castle*, the hero, here called simply K., has in common with his namesake in *The Trial* the fact that he undergoes, *vis-à-vis* an oppressive authority, a progression from defiant arrogance to a relative humility. At the beginning of the work K. has arrived at a nameless village in order to take up a post as land-surveyor. More hindered than helped by the intricate network of bureaucracy which is the castle's representative presence in the village, K. finds that in effect no conscious exercise of will or intention can in any way advance his aims. His position in the village, he is told, is paradoxical: he has been appointed land-surveyor, but none is needed. Officials whom K. tries to contact for clarification of his position prove elusive, even fugitive; the two assistants assigned to him seem to K. childish to the point of imbecility; and, humiliated by being given a menial position as school caretaker, K. is, in effect, left to fumble his own way through the maze of irrationality that constitutes the life of the village. Thus the world into which he enters unremittingly challenges his expectations, his will, his entire sense of himself. Any achievement, he is told in a crucial interview with the official Bürgel, would be inadvertent: having accidentally slipped through the castle's protective net, he would find himself able to command all he wished. But this information – which is in any case couched in a plethora of cautious subjunctives (for Bürgel is in effect describing theoretically the position in which K. actually finds himself at this point) – comes ironically at a moment where K. is too drugged and fatigued to make use of it: unable, that is, to enforce a will which he has by this time effectively abandoned. Shortly after this, the novel breaks off, unfinished: but a note communicated by Max Brod roughly summarizes Kafka's intended ending – at the moment of K.'s death a message arrives from the castle with the ironic information that K. has no official right to live in the village, but will 'in view of certain peripheral circumstances' be permitted to do so. The nature of these 'peripheral circumstances' is, of course, not clarified: but it is a reasonable negative inference that the circumstances are peripheral to anything which K.'s assertive ego, or his ego-related perceptions, may be capable of establishing.

The hallmark of *The Castle* then, as of Kafka's work as a whole, is ambiguity. The castle itself is no more an image of Divine Grace than it is of ultimate Evil: it is a symbol whose range of implication encompasses both these possible extremes. More importantly, the central feature of the novel is less the castle itself *qua* symbol than the castle *as apprehended by K*. But to what extent is K. possessed of a consciousness adequate to the task imposed upon it? Is consciousness itself, refracted and distorted by the pressures of immediate vicissitudes and the clamorous demands of self-interest, an adequate instrument for the apprehension of the world in which we find ourselves? Conversely, does the castle itself, in concrete actuality, exist at all? – or is it no more than the focal point of a web of errors, half-truths and conflicting assertions?

Kafka's work raises far more questions than it ever answers. ('To ask questions is the main thing,' Josef K is told by his advocate.) Not surprisingly, then, Kafka has been more widely and more variously interpreted than almost any other modern author. His fascination has remained undiminished by any changes in literary fashion: and it is perhaps a wholly appropriate irony that Kafka's work should have proved, in its very elusiveness, more relevant to the bewilderments of twentieth-century man than that of many writers who speak with louder voices and more confident tones.

Further reading

See: *Gesammelte Schriften*, ed. Max Brod and Heinz Politzer (1945–7). Translations of the novels are by Willa and Edwin Muir. See also: *The Complete Stories*, ed. Nahum N. Glatzner (1971); *Letters to Felice*, ed. Erich Heller and Jürgen Born, trans. James Stein and Elizabeth Duckworth (1974). About Kafka: H. Politzer, *Franz Kafka. Parable and Paradox* (1966); A. Thorlby, *Kafka: A Study* (1972); R. Gray, *Franz Kafka* (1973); R. Sheppard, *On Kafka's Castle* (1973); E. Heller, *Kafka* (1974); F. Kuna, *Kafka: Literature as Corrective Punishment* (1974); Ronald Hayman, *Kafka: A Biography* (1981); Julian Preece (ed.), *The Cambridge Companion to Franz Kafka* (2002); Ritchie Robertson, *Kafka: A Very Short Introduction* (2004); Richard T. Gray (ed.), *The Franz Kafka Encyclopedia* (2006).

CORBET STEWART

KANDINSKY, Wassily (Vasilii Vasilievich)

1866–1944
Russian painter

Kandinsky was among the pioneers of Abstraction in twentieth-century Western European art. The evolution of his work comprised a step-by-step investigation of the expressive powers at the disposal of the painter. The changes of form and technique that characterize his development reveal his sensitivity to the innovations and achievements of contemporaries, yet the driving force of his evolution remained an ultimately spiritual search, for which painting provided Kandinsky with a means of expression that he was able to manipulate with brilliance and originality. He became committed to painting relatively late after studying law and economics at the University of Moscow. In 1895 a painting by **Monet** of *Haystacks*, which Kandinsky saw in Moscow, impressed him with the force of a revelation. In addition recent travels into northern Russia had brought Kandinsky into close contact with a vigorous folk-art tradition. As for many Russian painters active in the 1890s, the simultaneous impact of a vital indigenous Russian tradition and a new awareness of the brilliant colour and virtuoso handling of French Impressionist and Post-Impressionist painting led to vigorous painting that reflected Russian themes in a welter of rich colour. Kandinsky's early studies reflect this, echoing too the decorative swirls of the *Jugendstil* which was evident both in Moscow, particularly in the works of the architect Shekhtel, and also in Munich where Kandinsky entered the studio of the painter Anton Ažbé in 1897. Russians excited by vigorously handled strong colour had preceded him: Igor Grabar, Alexei von Jawlensky (Yavlensky) and Marianne von Werefkin (Verefkina) comprised a group there. Kandinsky remained until 1899 producing brilliantly coloured evocations of garden scenes and Russian folk stories that were often fantastic. However, he brought to these works a sense of an allegory of conflicting forces, at first distinctly medieval but subsequently a timeless battle between colossal opposing elements. This theme recurred throughout Kandinsky's life. Kandinsky also painted directly from observation. While in Munich he was prolific in both kinds of painting. His observed works flourished in particular in his period at Murnau with the painter Gabriele Münter. Colour became increasingly assertive and painterly conventions were steadily broached to expressive ends. His expressive colour was comparable in its saturation and its dynamic application to that of the French Fauve painters. Like them, Kandinsky exhibited at the 1905 Salon d'Automne in Paris. While he appears never to have abandoned depiction entirely, he investigated with increasing daring and success the extent to which colour and line could be made to sustain an expressive and an emotive role: the purpose was to embody spiritual experience and make it communicable through painting.

His first major text upon painting concerns precisely this (*Über das Geistige in Der Kunst*, 1912; translated as *Concerning the Spiritual in Art*, 1914). He was necessarily acutely aware of his material means in order to employ them to provide a spiritual, expressive and emotional resonance. This attitude made Kandinsky a central figure of the Expressionist movement in Germany. His articulate theories led him to group ventures in publishing as well as exhibiting: with **Klee**, **Marc**, Macke and others he was a vital force of the Blaue Reiter group (from 1911) and its almanac (1912). He also became a theorist in the field of art education and believed that the psychological and spiritual power of the painter's means could be studied systematically and communally. His awareness of the Theosophical Society is perhaps reflected in this. The First World War caused Kandinsky's return to Russia. The Bolshevik Revolution of 1917 raised Kandinsky to a position of power concerning the establishment of new kinds of museum and new art education in Russia. His conviction that artists were the discerners, and even the moulders, of the forms appropriate to their age, poised upon the verge of widespread application in Russia before Kandinsky abandoned his post at the Institute of Artistic Culture in Moscow, was the psychological bent of his ideas and painting as opposed by

Constructivists like Tatlin, and in 1921 he accepted the invitation of **Walter Gropius** to put his principles into practice at the Bauhaus in Weimar.

Kandinsky's second major theoretical book *From Point and Line to Plane* (*Punkt und Linie zu Flache*, 1926; trans. 1947) reflects his teaching there. His investigation of the painter's means was meticulous and thorough: it led him to publish his theories and to devise teaching systems. Yet its aims, its goal at the time of his death in Paris in 1944, remained a spiritual evolution through the clarity of his means: he still sought the forms appropriate to the unfolding future, convinced of a spiritual ascent for humanity within which the painter, the creative man, played a vital and progressive role.

Further reading

See: Wassily Kandinsky and Franz Marc, *The Blaue Reiter Almanach* (1974); Will Grohmann, *Wassily Kandinsky – Life and Work* (1959); V.E. Barnett, *Kandinsky at the Guggenheim* (1983).

JOHN MILNER

KAWABATA YASUNARI
1899–1972
Japanese writer

Kawabata Yasunari was born near Osaka in 1899. He was orphaned in infancy, and soon lost his grandparents and only sister as well. He finished primary and middle school near Osaka, and went on to the elite First Higher School in Tokyo, and to Tokyo Imperial University, from which he graduated in 1924. His earliest publications were in student magazines. The story that brought him fame, 'The Izu Dancer' (*Izu no Odoriko*), was published in 1926.

The years after his graduation from the university are known as his 'Izu period', the best of his early writings being about the Izu Peninsula, south of Tokyo. The Izu period was followed by an Asakusa period, when his chief interest was the Asakusa district of

Tokyo, the liveliest of the plebeian entertainment centres. Just before the outbreak of the Second World War came his 'snow-country period', when he was fascinated with the snowy regions on the western slope of the main Japanese island.

He wrote little during the war. After the war he was for some years president of the Japanese P.E.N. The post-war years might be called his Kamakura period. He lived in and wrote about Kamakura, an old political and cultural centre south of Tokyo. In 1968 he became the first and thus far the only Japanese Nobel laureate in literature. He died on 16 April 1972. The usual view is that he killed himself, although some hold that his death was accidental.

In his early years he was much under the influence of avant-garde European literature. The influence on some of his writings is overt. The best of it, however, such as 'The Izu Dancer', is delicately lyrical, putting him firmly in the Japanese tradition, in which lyric verse and the lyrical mode in prose have been dominant. The looseness of form, the abrupt transitions, and the frequent difficulty in establishing the relation between successive statements may be ascribed to a surrealist influence. They may as well be ascribed, however, to Japanese antecedents, most particularly the linked verse (*renga*) of the Middle Ages.

Snow Country (*Yukiguni*, trans. 1956), written sporadically over several years, with revisions, from 1935 and completed in 1947, is widely held to be his best novel, and certainly it illustrates as well as any his themes and methods. It is essentially about loneliness and the impossibility of love. A Tokyo dilettante has a desultory love affair with a 'snow-country' geisha; presently he stops visiting her, and that is that. The inconclusive ending is characteristic of Kawabata, and so is the looseness of form. It is often difficult to know whether or not one of his works is in fact finished, and the list of his unfinished works is impressive. A sketch or tableau would form the nucleus of a story, which might or might not be expanded into a novel. If it did become a novel, the movement from episode to episode was most commonly by a process of flexible but controlled association, as with a *renga* sequence.

Kawabata's great achievement was a fusion of the traditional and the modern so complete that it is difficult to assign elements to either source. The looseness of form suggests the modern rebellion against the well-plotted novel, but it also suggests *renga* and the discursive lyrical essay, a form held in high esteem by the Japanese for almost a millennium. So too it is with the themes, loneliness and lovelessness, and cold, wasted beauty set off by shocking ugliness – they are modern and ancient as well. Kawabata's characterization tends to be so delicate that the characters, almost wraith-like, are constantly on the point of fading back into the natural background, which sometimes seems the principal concern, the real reason for the story.

Further reading

Kawabata's complete works, in fifteen volumes, were published in Tokyo (1969–74); a new edition, in thirty-five volumes, was planned from 1980. A partial translation of 'The Izu Dancer' appeared in *Atlantic Monthly* (January 1955). Other English translations: *Thousand Cranes* (*Sembazuru*, 1959); *House of the Sleeping Beauties* (*Nemureru Bijo*, 1969); *The Sound of the Mountain* (*Yama no Oto*, 1970); *The Master of Go* (*Meijin*, 1972); *The Lake* (*Mizuumi*, 1974); *Beauty and Sadness* (*Utsukushisa to Kanashimi to*, 1975); *Old Capital* (*Koto*, 1988). See: Edward Seidensticker, 'Kawabata Yasunari' in *This Country* (1979); M. Miyoshi, *Accomplices of Silence* (1974). See also: M. Ueda, *Modern Japanese Writers and the Nature of Literature* (1976); J. Rimer, *Modern Japanese Fiction and Its Tradition* (1978); Y. Hisaaki, *The Search for Authenticity in Modern Japanese Literature* (1978).

EDWARD SEIDENSTICKER

KEATON, 'Buster' (Joseph Francis)

1895–1966

US filmmaker

Buster Keaton's great tragedy was to be making films at the same time as **Charlie Chaplin**, whose shadow obscured Keaton's genius during their own time and in the following decades. Only with the rise of the importance of the director has Keaton taken his rightful place as one of the major 'auteurs' of the twentieth century, far superior to his comic rivals such as Mack Sennett, Harold Lloyd, and even Chaplin in his visual eye and other directing skills.

Keaton, like so many other early American show-business greats, was almost literally 'born in a trunk', performing for the first time with his vaudevillian parents at the age of three, and his only real education was that earned in the school of hard falls of his parents' acrobatic act which moved from medicine shows to burlesque to vaudeville. When his father's drinking made the act too dangerous, Keaton joined Roscoe 'Fatty' Arbuckle's company, making fifteen films with the notorious film comedian between 1917 and 1919. When Arbuckle's career collapsed, Keaton starred in almost two dozen shorts for Joseph Schenck, many co-directed with Eddie Cline. They included some of Keaton's best work, such as 'Cops', 'The Haunted House', 'The Electric House', and others.

Keaton gradually assumed total control of his film unit and eventually began to make feature films beginning with *The Three Ages* in 1923. MGM distributed his first seven features with Keaton in full control as producer, co-director and star, the best of many superb comedies probably being *Sherlock Jr* and *The Navigator*. In 1926 he joined United Artists where he made his masterpiece *The General*. His last silent film was *Spite Marriage* for MGM. The sound revolution is generally credited with destroying his career, though personal problems culminating in a year in a psychiatric clinic in 1937 undoubtedly contributed. His talkies were mostly commercial failures and he clung for the rest of his life to the fringes of the film industry, making brief appearances in anything from Billy Wilder's *Sunset Boulevard* and Chaplin's *Limelight* to Stanley Kramer's *It's A Mad, Mad, Mad, Mad World* and other real circuses. Ironically, at the end of his life his talent and his comic persona were again being more fully recognized by his appearance in *A Funny Thing Happened on the Way to the Forum* and a short film expressly written for him by **Samuel Beckett**.

While many silent comedy stars were justly famous for their physical grace and athletic ability, Keaton always took special pride in his acrobatic skills and grace. Keaton not only almost never used a double or stunt man, he often did other characters' stunts, even literally 'breaking his neck' in the process. From driving a speeding motorcycle while seated on the handlebars to diving into a net from a suspension bridge 75 feet high, Keaton always astonished his audience; but his best stunts were also integral to his character and plot, perhaps the most astonishing and beautiful being the one in *The General* where the forlorn Johnnie Grey, in despair over his lost love, rides off emotionlessly oblivious on the driving bar of his engine.

While his shorts are as acrobatic and cinematically inventive as the best work of their time, Keaton's real genius can be seen most clearly in the ten feature films that he either directed or co-directed. Unlike many of his comic rivals, Keaton strove for logical progression in his narrative rather than a series of seemingly improvised anecdotes connected by the presence of the comedian. The structure of *The General* illustrates this perfectly. Keaton is able to use the whole panorama of the Civil War for his hero's efforts to win the woman he loves. The two train chases (one going north, the other returning south) provide the visual and narrative centre for the film. Everything that happens in the first chase recurs with subtle twists in the second, making the second chase not only new but at the same time organically related to the earlier part of the film. In *Seven Chances* Keaton is pursued by two different kinds of crowds: the first a gaggle of prospective fortune-hunting brides, the second 1,500 studio-made rocks that he accidentally dislodges. The two separate chases are united when the avalanche dissipates the racing women, and then, after

Keaton successfully eludes rocks ranging in size from bowling balls to giants 8 feet in diameter, a last-minute little stone drops him in his tracks just as he will be caught by the late-arriving heroine at the end of the film. Keaton's instinctive love of form worked all this out at the last minute, since the avalanche was a last-minute addition to the film. A certain passion for order and balance thus always prevails in Keaton.

Order and balance also contribute to the lack of sentimentalism in Keaton's persona and stories. The Keaton persona, often outnumbered by villains and fate, always prevails through sheer movement and stubbornness. Even women are never sentimentalized as marital love objects. The heroine of *The General* is stuffed into a burlap bag and tossed into a freight car, among other indignities, and finds herself totally out of place in the engine cab trying to use a broom or throwing away firewood because it has a knot-hole in it. When she proudly hands Keaton a small woodchip for the fire, in reasonable anger he reaches out to strangle her and changes the gesture to a quick kiss – one of Keaton's most effective demonstrations of his humanity without excessive sentiment. His large, expressive eyes said far more than the most frenetic twistings of facial muscles of other stars of the silent era, for Keaton knew how important eyes were in film. And while those eyes expressed the pain and bewilderment of his condition, his body whirred constantly to avoid disaster, and to set things right.

Further reading

Other works: *My Wonderful World of Slapstick* (1962); see: R. Blesh, *Keaton* (1966); D. Moews, *Keaton: The Silent Features Close-Up* (1977); Donald McCaffrey, *Four Great Comedians* (1968); David Robinson, *Keaton* (1969); J.-P. Lebel, *Buster Keaton* (1967); E. Rubenstein, *The General* (1973); A. Sarris, *Interviews with Film Directors* (1967); K. Brownlow, *The Parade's Gone By* (1968); Robert Knopf, *The Theater and Cinema of Buster Keaton* (1999); Edward McPherson, *Buster Keaton: Tempest in a Flat Hat* (2004).

CHARLES GREGORY

KENNEDY, John Fitzgerald

1917–63

US president

John F. Kennedy was born on 29 May 1917 in Boston, New England, and he was assassinated on 22 November 1963 in Dallas, Texas, as the 35th President of the United States. His killing created an indelible political trauma not simply because it was never satisfactorily explained but also because it put a new perspective on what he had achieved in his brief career. It seemed that a young idealist had been sacrificed to the atavistic violence of old America, a progressive slain to appease anti-Communist, anti-Black illiberal adventurers. Kennedy himself denied highmindedness: 'Never fight on principle,' he declared, 'fight the other candidate.' Yet, as he once confided to his wife Jacqueline, he was 'an idealist without illusions' and so it is possible that even if his murder made his presidency seem more idealistic than it was, he was nonetheless one of the great political reformers of modern politics.

He was the second son of a very rich Irish American whom **Franklin Roosevelt** had made Ambassador to Britain before the Second World War. The family had strong roots in the Democratic Party and politics were a family profession. At first it had been intended that the eldest son Joe Jr should go for high office, but his death in the war caused his mantle to pass to the more thoughtful and introspective JFK.

Kennedy attended an exclusive school, followed by study at Harvard, Princeton, Stanford and the London School of Economics. It was an education intended to enhance his chances of social leadership which were, in any case, very good ones on account of his father's wealth. In the Second World War JFK volunteered for active service despite an earlier back injury. Here he showed considerable bravery when his boat was cut in half by a Japanese destroyer. He swam to safety through burning seas pulling a severely injured shipmate with him.

His health was badly undermined by this experience and he remained a sick man. He suffered from a major internal complaint and was often in pain. This, added to a number of tragic deaths within the Kennedy family, gave him a detached view of his own existence, an advantage for any politician.

JFK's political success was both dramatic and rapid. He became the youngest Congressman in the House, and, in 1952, he was elected to the US Senate as a Senator for Massachusetts. Only four years later he came close to gaining the Democratic Vice-Presidential nomination and four years after that he was elected President. He defeated the then Vice-President, Richard M. Nixon, by no more than 120,000 votes (out of an electorate of 49 million) after a campaign which the Kennedy staff had planned brilliantly, laying special emphasis on good media relations.

Two factors had caused many Americans to be wary of the JFK image. The first was his Roman Catholic faith: during the campaign Kennedy was repeatedly asked to pledge that, were he elected, he would not take orders from the Pope, or allow Catholic views of morality to influence legislative measures. Second, Kennedy was young. At the age of forty-three he would be the youngest President of the United States and a stark contrast to the sitting tenant, Eisenhower, who was the oldest. Yet JFK managed, thanks to a combination of wit, eloquence and intelligence, to capitalize on his youth, to indicate, in the words of his striking inaugural address, that 'the torch has been passed to a new generation'.

Kennedy and his supporters claimed they would offer America a 'new frontier'. New perspectives would be given to domestic politics (although at this stage a fair deal for Blacks was not emphasized) and also to American ambitions throughout the world where a greater readiness to face up to the Soviet challenge was promised. 'Softness' towards the Russians had allowed them to infiltrate a number of hitherto neutral areas including, of course, outer space, where the USSR's satellites had altered the strategic balance between the two powers.

Superficially, then, what Kennedy promised appear to have little to do with liberal or radical thinking. Rather, he promised to do more effectively what others had tried to do before. But this was not what came to pass, for both at home and abroad the young President was forced to respond to challenges more hazardous than had been anticipated, challenges that ultimately helped change America and the world. The first came from the USSR. There can be no doubt that Khrushchev, the Soviet leader, hoped to exploit the President's inexperience in order to strengthen the Russians' position in all areas. After an early skirmish over Berlin, Khrushchev tried to install nuclear missiles on Cuba in 1962. Kennedy, however, refused to accept such a move and, in the autumn of that year, he demonstrated an absolute willingness to take the world to war in order to maintain the status quo. This show of force, perhaps ironically, impressed the Russians so that peace was kept intact and the prospect for later agreement became much better.

The second challenge was a domestic one. It came from Black Americans who were now demanding with some force the same civil rights enjoyed by Whites. Kennedy had initially been unconcerned by the grave injustices done to the Blacks. But the courage they demonstrated in seeking equality in all spheres of public life and the exceptional leadership provided by **Martin Luther King** encouraged Kennedy to face up to his responsibilities. He used the full authority and power of his office to establish Black rights in education, housing and in politics generally. Blacks had to risk their lives to gain his support but once gained they could count on it. It was not insignificant that Dr King was destroyed in the same way as his white colleague.

Kennedy had by November 1963 changed a number of things, but his 'new frontier' appeared less new and less inspiring than many had hoped. There was growing concern at American interference in the politics of South-East Asia which appeared sinister. He seemed to act only when forced to by others and to avoid fighting for principles, however noble. But that day in Dallas showed this judgement was too simplistic to account for the impact he was to have. America now seemed to be on the side of the young and of change; the fathers had yielded to their sons. Although he had been rich and successful he had nonetheless established that the underprivileged and unemployed had social rights too. Kennedy the man may have been the product of old America. But Kennedy the President stood for something new. When, in front of millions, he was killed, it had seemed as if the most reactionary forces in politics would be his heirs. In fact, however, this was not so. What he had managed to do, and what had happened to him for doing it, showed how much he had actually accomplished. To be an idealist without illusions was not only a fitting aim for a President, it now appeared the only honourable response to the dangerous world of the 1960s.

Further reading

Other works include: J.F. Kennedy: *Why England Slept* (1961); *Profiles in Courage* (1965). See also: T.H. White, *The Making of the President* (1960); A.M. Schlesinger Jr, *A Thousand Days* (1965); T.C. Sorensen, *Kennedy* (1965); Pierre Salinger, *With Kennedy* (1966); Robert Dallek, *An Unfinished Life: John F. Kennedy, 1917–1963* (2003); Michael O'Brien, *John F. Kennedy* (2005).

ANTHONY GLEES

KEROUAC, Jack

1922–69

US writer

Jack Kerouac was born in the industrial town of Lowell, Massachusetts. Educated in Catholic schools, he reached Horace Mann school and Columbia University, New York, largely through his football prowess. Apart from brief spells in the Merchant Marine and army, he lived by his writing. The early years

are dramatized in *The Town and the City* (1950), *Doctor Sax* (1959), *Maggie Cassidy* (1959) and *Visions of Gerard* (1963). Subsequent life in New York, at sea, in Mexico, Tangier, France, London and San Francisco is the material of *On the Road* (1957), *The Subterraneans* (1958), *The Dharma Bums* (1958), *Tristessa* (1960), *Big Sur* (1962), *Desolation Angels* (1965), *Sartori in Paris* (1966) and *Vanity of Duluoz: An Adventurous Education 1935–1946* (1968). Most of this work comprises what Kerouac came to call *The Duluoz Legend*, a huge **Proustian** compendium of reminiscences and transformations of memory. Concurrent with these fictions, Kerouac published a number of supplementary works including *Lonesome Traveller* (1960, travel sketches), *Book of Dreams* (1961, a record of his imaginative resources), the poetry in *Mexico City Blues* (1959), *Rimbaud* (1960), *Pull My Daisy* (1961) and *Scattered Poems* (1972), and a number of uncollected pieces on jazz and the writing process. A number of recordings testify to his gifts as a reader and singer of his own works. Within this large lifetime's creativity stands his masterpiece, *Visions of Cody* (written in 1951–2, published in 1973; a very shortened version appeared in 1960).

Vanity of Duluoz (written in 1967) draws on his life as school and college football star and wartime serviceman, and on early intuitions and realizations of a literary career. It records his first published novel, *The Town and the City* (written 1946–9) which creates the Martin family out of his own family and that of friends (see his note in Ann Charter's *A Bibliography of Works by Jack Kerouac*, 1975), a work in the traditions of Sherwood Anderson and **Thomas Wolfe**, fictions of small-town experience and regional location, and the youthful hero's necessary departure for the city where ambition may be realized. *Doctor Sax* records in brilliantly inventive style the complex fantasy life of himself and his boyhood friends in Lowell, a first intimation of the interplay of fiction and day-to-day life for his creative imagination, before the severe realization that writing is a discipline. *Vanity* *of Duluoz* records his abrupt experience that professional sport is part of a corrupt system which includes military coercion. The autobiographical hero's discharge from the military service in 1943, after acting mad by the standards of the officers, is a main instance of Kerouac's responses to the stupidities of the Establishment. The 'lost dream of being a real American man' through the open road tradition – 'an adventurous education, an educational adventurousness' – is the core of *On the Road* (written in 1951), whose plot generates, through Sal Paradise's writer and intellectual's relationship with the proletarian and petty-criminal life of Dean Moriarty, ways of release from bourgeois consciousness. Their automobile mobility in search of freedom of action and speech is written in a free-wheeling associative style, later theorized in 'Essentials of Spontaneous Prose' (*Black Mountain Review*, No. 7, 1957; reprinted in *A Casebook on the Beat*, edited by Thomas Parkinson, 1961). This essay delineates the origins of Kerouac's methods in the breath-lengths of speech and jazz, and the notational ideas in the poetry of William Carlos Williams, as well as certain states of consciousness which release the writer from censor of inherited forms.

The 'Beat Generation' of writers (essentially Kerouac, **Allen Ginsberg**, Gregory Corso and **William Burroughs**) were part of a resistance to the years of civil repression under the Eisenhower–**Kennedy**–Johnson–Nixon regimes, what Kerouac described as 'a potboiler of broken convictions, messes of rioting and fighting in the streets, hoodlumism, cynical administration of cities and states, suits and neckties the only feasible subject, grandeur all gone into the mosaic mesh of Television'. But for Kerouac, resistance had to be gained against his bourgeois-Catholic upbringing. From Burroughs he learned of Spengler's history of Western decadence and barbarism (the rejuvenating *fellahin* are as constant in Kerouac as in another of his masters, Gary Snyder). He recognized Céline's bitter criticism of America and the West, the aristocratic integrity of **Renoir's**

La Grande Illusion, **Tolstoy's** peasant rejuvenators, the vision of the *poète maudit* in **Rimbaud** and Cocteau, **Gide's** *acte gratuite* as 'abandonment of reason and return to impulse', and much more, as he inherited the responsibilities of the artist in the European great tradition. The *élan vital* principle fuses with **Emerson's** 'self-reliance' to become 'a holy idea [of] "self-ultimacy"'. His friend Neal Cassady, the Moriarty of *On the Road*, exemplifies a liberated anti-bourgeois life, which Kerouac rejoined by working with him as a railroad brakeman for a time. But he needed to research his Breton origins as well (*Sartori in Paris*) to 'redeem this runaway slave of football fields'.

To summarize his experience he conceived an American *Forsyte Saga* – the Duluoz saga – as 'a lifetime of writing about what I've seen with my own eyes, told in my own words . . . as a contemporary history record for future times to see what really happened and what people really thought'. But his perspective is the Buddhist void as given in *The Scripture of the Golden Eternity* (1960); the boyhood Catholicism (*Visions of Gerard*) and the mobile search for IT in *On the Road* are modified by the vision of an oriental stillness within motion, of the artist's creativity taking place in a meaningless universe. The search for IT – the force which sustains exuberant spontaneity and charisma – is challenged from an alternate tradition which has had a profound effect on American culture at least since the nineteenth-century Transcendentalists (Kerouac gained much of his Buddhist insight from Gary Snyder, the poet and orientalist who features as Japhy Ryder in *The Dharma Bums*).

Kerouac died the year after publishing *Vanity of Duluoz*: an abdominal haemorrhage had been aggravated by a general condition from his alcoholic life. This last book contains a lament for human life over 'a million years on this planet'. Our lives are 'sacrifices leading to purity in the after-existence in Heaven as souls divested of that rapish, rotten, carnal body'. The 'Beat' natural joy in 'digging everything', whatever the doomed melancholy of artists, is lived out in *karma*, the inescapable contingencies of existence and 'the mental garbage of "existentialism" and "hipsterism" and "bourgeois decadence"'. 'Wars as social catastrophes arise from the cruel nature of bestial creation, and not from "society".' Writing is born from damnation. Kerouac had come a long way from his earlier confidence, but within his 'serious exuberance' (his phrase for jazz) and the loving records of boyhood and adolescence, there had always existed the threat of death and disease in *Tristessa* and *Visions of Gerard*, and passing love and friendship in *Maggie Cassidy* and *Desolation Angels*. Neither sexual nor religious experience gave him much happiness beyond initial satisfactions. The stylistic invention of earlier work declined into a sober flatness concomitant with his later vision. But *Visions of Cody* remains, a fine and large collection of his best achievement, written – as Allen Ginsberg says in his prefatory essay, 'The Great Rememberer' – out of 'tender brooding compassion for bygone scene & Personal Individuality oddity'd therein ... a giant mantra of Appreciation & Adoration of an American Man, one striving heroic soul'. In Kerouac's words: 'I struggle in the dark with the enormity of my soul, trying desperately to be a great rememberer redeeming life from darkness ... this record is my joy.' The marvellous prose emerges from a rich experience of life, of the twentieth-century masters, of drug-transformed consciousness, and of transcribed tapes of energetic speech. Ginsberg accurately places it in the mainstream of American arts between 1940 and 1960, which include Abstract Expressionism, 'projective verse' and Frank O'Hara's 'personism', but also within that 'Disillusionment with all the heroic Imagery of U.S.' arising out of Kerouac's 'experience on the street with Nationalist Imagery of previous generations, & his familiarity, sympathy & Disillusionment with the American myth'.

By 1952 the 'beat writers' were 'lonely at wit's end with the world & America – the "Beat" generation was about that time formulated, the Viet Nam War was just about to begin its U.S. phase, the exhaustion of the planet by American Greed & Lust'. Kerouac's last writing, an essay called 'After Me, the Deluge' (*Washington Post*; reprinted in *Sixpack*, nos 3/4, 1973) parades a regret for responsibility for the 'Beat' antecedence of 'hippies' and 'yippies', and a rejection of the 'shiny hypocrisy' of both the radicals and the Establishment, both the North Vietnam leaders and the American military-industrial complex:

> I think I'll drop out. Great American tradition – Dan'l Boone, U.S. Grant, Mark Twain – I think I'll go to sleep and suddenly in my deepest inadequacy nightmares wake up haunted and see everyone in the world as unconsolable orphans.

Further reading

Other works include: *Pic* (novel, 1971). See: John Clellon Holmes, *The Beat Boys* (*Go*, 1952) and *Nothing More to Declare* (1968); 'Jack Kerouac at Northport' (interview) in *Athanor*, nos 1–111 (1971–2); Bruce Cook, *The Beat Generation* (1972); Ann Charters, *Kerouac: A Biography* (1974); John Tytell, *Naked Angels: The Lives and Literature of the Beat Generation* (1976); Barry Gifford and Lawrence Lee, *Jack's Book: An Oral Biography of Jack Kerouac* (1979); Regina Weinreich, *The Spontaneous Poetics of Jack Kerouac: A Study of the Fiction* (1987); Carolyn Cassady, *Off the Road: My Years with Cassady, Kerouac and Ginsberg* (1990); Gerald Nicosia, *Memory Babe: A Critical Biography of Jack Kerouac* (1994); E. Ambern, *Subterranean Kerouac: The Hidden Life of Jack Kerouac* (2000); Paul Maher and David Amram: *Kerouac: The Definitive Biography* (2004).

ERIC MOTTRAM

KESEY, Ken
1935–2001
US novelist

Kesey spent his youth in Oregon timber country, became a wrestling champion at the University of Oregon, and at Stanford University, California, attended writing classes under Malcolm Cowley and Wallace Stegner. Working in a mental hospital he became sympathetically involved with the patients, organizing parties, loaning them his car for a night out, and, when an attendant refused to stop bullying a catatonic patient, threw him through a shower-room door. Kesey was discharged with the label: 'Not interested in patient welfare.' During the 1960s he wrote two novels, became a cult figure in the hippie sub-culture of drug and high-decibel communities in the San Francisco Bay area, and set up a pot-smoking, LSD-partying community in Palo Alto. Arrested in 1965, he managed to vanish via a faked suicide, but was hounded from the country, re-arrested, and imprisoned in 1966. His pop status increased, then waned severely, following which he made fairly well-publicized reappearances.

Through Cowley, *One Flew Over the Cuckoo's Nest* was published in 1962, and became a best-seller over the decade. With the royalties, and money from the Broadway version (and later a film), Kesey has lived well. In the 1960s he bought a bus, painted it in fashionable psychedelic designs, employed Neal Cassady (the manic driver in **Kerouac's** *On the Road* of the previous decade), and drove across the country, apparently abandoning fiction. But his first novel deals with the techniques of possible survival and escape from an oppressively enforced society which reduces varied life to the routines required by authority – in this case, the boss, Big Nurse, and her lunatic asylum staff. The narrator, Chief Bromden, escapes to tell the tale of how the red-headed Irish protestor McMurphy succeeds in wrecking the establishment before he is forcibly lobotomized by the Combine. At least he has enabled the patients to enjoy themselves, however briefly. Kesey's second novel, *Sometimes a Great Notion* (1964), had little of the success of the first, but it, too, concerns a violent break for individual freedom against majority coercion. Using the large-scale manner of Thomas C. Wolfe, it tells of the two Stamper brothers' lurch towards independent manhood by acting against a strike in the timber industry. They float their logs downstream, a social confrontation with the community which ends in a sort of victorious and deathly defeat. The huge book is propelled by a compulsive necessity and massive *macho* energy, but it remains a bulky high adventure story of masculinity in a traditional family, pastoral setting.

Meanwhile, Kesey shot 60,000 feet of film and set up his pleasure dome at La Honda, south of San Francisco, calling himself the Navigator and giving light and music shows infused with LSD. He organized the 'Acid Test', a psychedelic discotheque, in the 1964–5 years when acid became popular on the West Coast – spiked punch was served, it is said, to unsuspecting 'squares' who 'freaked out'. He also used his camera and tape-recorder continually, with drug aids: 'To discover something new, you have to put yourself in a position when an accident can happen to you.' Once acid became trite, he moved on. In prison – or rather, in the San Mateo sheriff's honour camp, in the redwood forests – he painted, wrote his notebooks, and planned a book on justice. His earlier aim, to form an exemplary mobile family group called the Merry Pranksters, appeared in the documentary fiction *The Electric Kool-Aid Acid Test* by **Tom Wolfe** in 1968. Travelling across America in a bus called 'Further', he enacts one more version of 'the open road' obsession, attempting to incorporate the current transformations of both **Timothy Leary** and the Hell's Angels – without their concurrence. As Wolfe wrote in the *New York Times Book Review* in 1968, Kesey's bus was totally American – a family car, an '18-foot gleaming dreamboat' in which to achieve 'all the freedom, the free time, the gadgets, the TV, the movies, tapes, sound systems' denoting the good life, and the effort at ecstasy against the inherent boredom of the conformist society of labour and sobriety.

In 1973, *Kesey's Garage Sale* offered a retrospective presentation of his ideas and beliefs in a broadly ecological context – one section was *The Last Supplement to the Whole Earth Catalog*. Another section concerned the myth of how he wrote his first novel. A section of letters is followed by an interview with Paul

Krassner (editor of the *Realist*, an abrasive satirical journal of the period). The book's form combines print and picture information, characteristic of methods put forward by **McLuhan** and others in the 1960s.

When Kesey's visit to New York was reported in 1979, he turned out to be a married man with four children and living on a dairy farm near his Oregon boyhood home, finding Wolfe's book and his early reputation 'a nuisance', but looking forward to riding at the head of the local Rhododendron Festival parade as Grand Marshal, on a white Harley-Davidson motorcycle. In the aftermath of the 1960s Kesey showed little slow-down. The flight to Mexico to evade drug charges, his jail time and the move to his farm at Pleasant Hill, Oregon, with his wife and Jed, Zane and Shannon Kesey and where the 1939 Harvester bus of the Pranksters is still parked, led to an unflagging continuation of writing, film and performance activity. In *Demon Box* (1986) he assembled stories given over to counter-culture memory, Oregon as coastal and forest west, travel pieces on China and Egypt, a fictional memoir of John Lennon, and excerpts from a US picaresque novel in which the alter ego narrator of Devlin E. Deboree presides. *The Further Inquiry* (1990), short essays and fictions, with photography by Ron Bevirt, offers more retrospect. *Sailor Song* (1992), set in the fishing port of Kuinuk, Alaska, where a Hollywood team comes to film, reveals him in classic comic-baroque mode with the twin major figures, Alice Carmody, indigenous woman, and Ike Sallas, ex-ecoterrorist, at the centre. The movie ostensibly being made, *The Sea Lion*, replete with its cast of studio actors and local extras, becomes Kesey's platform for exploring ethnicity and the media control of 'minority' image. In *Last Go Round* (1994), with Ken Dobbs, he offers a story-collection set at the Pendleton Round Up, an Oregon gathering-place in which rodeo, horse-riding and other associated western fare opens into yet further portraiture of black, Native, Asian and white stereotype along with a focus on women's gender roles in the West in general.

Further reading

Two useful and composite Kesey perspectives are to be found in Paul Perry, Michael Swartz and Neil Ortenberg, *On the Bus: The Complete Guide to the Legendary Trip of Ken Kesey and the Birth of the Counterculture* (1990), with photography by Ron Bevirt, and contextual (and greatly admiring) forewords by Hunter S. Thompson and Jerry Garcia; and *Spit in the Ocean #7* (2003), edited by Ed. McLanahan, a fond homage and last issue, fittingly, of Kesey's own magazine. See also: Tony Tanner, *City of Words* (1971); Bruce Carnes, *Ken Kesey* (1974); Barry Leeds, *Ken Kesey* (1981); Stephen L. Tanner, *Ken Kesey* (1983); Gilbert Porter, *The Art of Grit* (1982); Peter O. Whitmer, *Aquarius Revisited: Seven who Created the Sixties Counterculture* (1987).

ERIC MOTTRAM (REVISED AND UPDATED BY A. ROBERT LEE)

KEYNES, John Maynard

1883–1946

English economist

A.C. Pigou, one of Keynes's tutors at Cambridge, once said of him that 'he was, beyond doubt or challenge, the most interesting, the most influential and most important economist of his time' (Pigou, *John Maynard Keynes*, 1949). Indeed the revolution in economic theory, the break with the 'classical' tradition, that he brought about is thought to be the only theory change in the social sciences that comes close to **Kuhn's** theory of scientific revolutions. Possibly more important, however, and certainly more important to him, was his influence on post-war governmental economic policy throughout the whole of the Western world. In fact the post-war boom, the most sustained period of rapid expansion in history, is often referred to as the 'Keynesian Era'.

It is impossible to tell to what extent this was due to Keynes. His theory certainly dominated economic thought and government policy for the thirty years from 1945 to 1975. It was his 'Demand Management' which had substituted small and short wobbles in economic activity for the classic cycles. This led many to believe that Keynes's dream of regulated capitalism had come true and at last continuous growth could be assured. Ironically, it was this total victory of the 'Keynesian Revolution' which contributed a great deal to its downfall. Keynesianism dominated the policy of both Labour and Conservative governments in Britain for the thirty-year period. It was government commitment to full employment and trade unionists' 'proven' conviction that it was here to stay that finally brought the era to an end.

John Maynard Keynes was born in Cambridge to John Neville and Florence Ada Keynes. He was educated at Eton and won a scholarship in mathematics and classics to King's College, Cambridge, where he graduated as 12th Wrangler in mathematics. After his degree he studied economics under Alfred Marshall for the Civil Service entrance examination. The young Keynes was profoundly influenced by Marshall, especially by his conviction that in order to explain booms and slumps monetary economics should be separated from the rest of economics. He decided to specialize, at Marshall's prompting, in money and banking.

Marshall was sufficiently impressed by Keynes's ability that he expressed hopes that Keynes might become a professional economist. However, in 1906 Keynes entered the Civil Service and requested to be posted to the then small and intimate India Office. There he became especially interested in Indian currency and finance, which formed the basis of his first book in economics – *Indian Currency and Finance* (1913). In 1908 Marshall offered him a lectureship in economics at Cambridge, which he accepted. In 1912 Keynes became editor of the *Economic Journal* through which he was able to exercise great influence over younger generations of economists.

Soon after the outbreak of war Keynes was invited to join the Treasury, and by 1917 he was head of the External Finance Department. In early 1919 he was sent to Paris as principal representative of the Treasury at the Peace Conference. However, he found himself in fundamental disagreement with the terms in the Treaty dealing with reparations. In June he resigned, returned to England and wrote *The Economic Consequences of the Peace* (1919). This book, which brought him immediate and international recognition, made him unacceptable to British official circles for nearly two decades.

During his undergraduate days Keynes became a member of a small intimate group, including **Leonard Woolf** and Lytton Strachey, called 'The Apostles', which later formed the Bloomsbury Group. Although closely connected with the Webbs, **Shaw** and other socialists, he remained almost wholly ignorant of **Marx**. Indeed, he proclaimed that, as an 'immoralist', 'The class war will find me on the side of the educated bourgeoisie.' However, he was a profound and effective critic of unregulated capitalism, writing in 1924, 'Capitalism in itself is in many ways objectionable' (*The End of Laissez-Faire*, 1926). He recognized that capitalism possessed enormous expansive powers and it was his wish to save capitalism from itself.

It was through the Bloomsbury Group that he met many of the great artists of his time. His love of art and his anxiety that it should reach an audience as wide as possible, as well as his lifelong friendship with the painter Duncan Grant, led him to be instrumental in the creation of the Arts Council.

In 1925 he married Lydia Lopokova, a famous dancer with the Imperial Ballet of St Petersburg and later in **Diaghilev's** company. 'Oh, what a marriage of beauty and brains, fair Lopokova and John Maynard Keynes,' it was said at the time. However, Keynes soon lamented to Lytton Strachey, himself brilliant but hideous, that beauty and intelligence were rarely combined, and that it was only in Duncan Grant that he found such a satisfying combination.

The cornerstone of what Keynes described as 'Classical Theory' was Say's Law (formulated by the French economist Jean-Baptiste Say, 1767–1832), which states that supply creates its own demand. In other words, all income is spent. Money withheld from expenditure on consumer goods is saved but not hoarded. No rational householder would hold idle balances which yield no income. Instead, he would use the accumulated balance directly, or lend it to others to use in order to purchase capital goods, i.e. to invest. The flow of savings and the flow of investment which are the supply of and the demand for 'loanable funds' are brought into balance, as in any other market, by changes in price, in this case in interest rates.

In 1935 Keynes wrote to George Bernard Shaw, 'I believe myself to be writing a book on economic theory which will largely revolutionize – not, I suppose at once, but in the course of the next ten years, the way the world thinks about economic problems.' Keynes's first task in his *General Theory of Employment, Interest and Money* (1936) was to show that in certain circumstances hoarding of money would take place; he argued that money was not only a medium of exchange but also a store of value available for the 'speculative' purpose of buying assets at some future unknown date.

Because of the reciprocal relationship between interest rates and the capital value of paper assets, Keynes argued that at low rates of interest (when it was generally thought that they would rise) people would prefer to hold money balances rather than risk a capital loss, since in any event they were not forfeiting much interest-income. In other words, surplus speculative balances will be willingly held, in what Keynes christened the 'Liquidity Trap', without driving down the interest rate to a market-clearing level. Furthermore, this same trap could very likely render monetary policy aimed at raising expenditure, output and employment ineffective. Thus it could be said that Keynes's *General Theory of Employment, Interest and Money* put forward a general theory of unemployment based on a new theory of the working of interest rates derived from a different view of money. It was a theory of *unemployment* to the extent that it could explain the level of employment, which was a function of an ever-changing cycle of total spending.

It was Keynes's abhorrence of the effects of unregulated capitalism and the human waste of unemployment that spurred him towards finding a method by which state intervention could leave intact the great expansive powers he recognized in capitalism, while at the same time forestalling its anarchic effects.

Once he had analysed money and freed saving and investment from their neoclassical identity, it was essential to discover their determinants. Savings, Keynes argued, were simply the residue of income after consumption. But as income rose consumption would not rise as much. Thus savings would rise in absolute terms and also as a proportion of income. Investment, on the other hand, was to some degree determined by interest rates as the neo-classicists had argued, but more important by far was the entrepreneurs' anticipated future return from that investment. Such expectations are volatile and self-reinforcing.

At the time the *General Theory* was published, the cause of the Depression was held to be too high wages, which prevented any fall in prices, and too high interest rates, which prevented any rise in investment. His analysis had shown why interest rates would fall no further and also that such a fall was not effective in raising investment. He also demonstrated that a fall in money wages would reduce consumer demand even further, which would make entrepreneurs even less willing to invest.

However, it was only by using Richard F. Kahn's recent invention of 'the multiplier' that Keynes was able to demonstrate the logic of what many people, including Lloyd George in the UK and **F.D. Roosevelt** in the USA, had argued intuitively, viz. that the state itself should carry out investment. The multiplier is the ripple-effect that any increase in investment will have on the level of total economic activity. A proportion of the income generated first by the purchase of extra capital goods will in turn be spent on consumer goods, and that income too will be spent in part, thus generating more income than the initial outlay. Therefore the state could, even by simply employing people to dig holes and fill them up again, generate more income in the economy than the initial expenditure and by so doing induce business-men to invest. By this method, Keynes argued, it would be possible to raise the economy to stable full employment. Conversely, if expansion were too vigorous, fiscal policy could damp down demand by cutting government expenditure and, through higher taxes, private expenditure as well. This practice of government interven-tion has in recent years come to be known as 'Demand Management'. Thus in opposition to Say's Law, Keynes postulated that demand will create its own supply.

Keynes, through his *General Theory*, had provided a theoretical justification for the sort of state intervention in the economy that many people had arrived at through common sense. However, it was the practical experi-ence of the economic effects of rearmament expenditure and even more those of total war which persuaded post-war governments as well as academic theorists to embrace the Keynesian analysis as well as the politics.

In 1940 Keynes was invited by the Chancellor of the Exchequer to become once again an adviser to the Treasury. He was chiefly responsible for a new concept of policy instituted in the Budget of 1941, aiming to prevent inflation by raising taxation enough to equate civilian expenditure to the goods and services available. In 1943 Keynes began to turn his attention to the problems of peace and in 1944, as leader of the British delegation at the International Conference at Bretton Woods, was the main architect of the International Monetary Fund and the International Bank for Reconstruction and Development. In May 1944 the coalition government published a White Paper on employment policy. Although Keynes con-tributed little in person to this document, its publication, together with a peerage awarded him in 1942, showed that his ideas had become acceptable to the British Establishment.

Keynes first suffered from heart trouble in 1937. Between the autumn of 1944 and early 1946 he was chief negotiator of the 'Lend-Lease' aid programme from the USA. But when he finally returned in April 1946 he was near collapse and died a few days later on Easter Sunday, 12 April 1946, at his home in Sussex.

Keynes, through his *General Theory*, essen-tially achieved his aim in that liberal Western capitalism was given a new lease of life. Evidently it was not all his doing in that Western capitalism was due for a period of expansion after fifteen years of slump and a world war. However, his policy prescriptions certainly helped to spawn the strongest and longest expansion of the Western economies in history. Through rising living standards and full employment, social tensions were eased, such that a peaceful intellectual revo-lution was substituted for a bloody one.

His triumphant professional life was not enough to engage his talents to the full. As well as his prolific writings in theoretical and applied economics he wrote innumerable articles and published some in *Essays in Persuasion* (1931) and *Essays in Biography* (1933). He speculated actively in commodi-ties, currencies and the Stock Exchange. He was a brilliantly successful bursar of his college, chairman of an insurance company and later a director of the Bank of England. He was a lifelong bibliophile, a lover of the ballet, chairman of the National Gallery, and founder of the Arts Theatre in Cambridge. He was a supreme example of the Universal Man.

Further reading

Other writings include: *A Treatise on Probability* (1921); *A Revision of the Treaty* (1922); *A Tract on Monetary Reform* (1923); *A Short View of Russia* (1925); *A Treatise on Money* (1930); *How to Pay for the War* (1940). *The Collected Writings of John Maynard Keynes* ed. Sir Angus Robinson and D.E. Moggridge (24 vols, from 1971) is now published by Palgrave. See also: Sir R.F. Harrod, *The Life of John Maynard Keynes* (1951); Michael Stewart, *Keynes and After* (1974); *Essays on John Maynard Keynes*, ed. Milo Keynes (1975); *The End of the Keynesian Era*, ed. R. Skidelsky (1977); and

E.S. and H.G. Johnson, *The Shadow of Keynes* (1979); John Cunningham Wood (ed.), *John Maynard Keynes: Critical Assessments* (1994) Charles R. McCann (ed.), *John Maynard Keynes: Critical Responses* (1998); Will Hutton, *The Revolution That Never Was: An Assessment of Keynesian Economics* (2001); Robert Skidelsky, *John Maynard Keynes 1883–1946: Economist, Philosopher, Statesman* (2003).

ROGER OPIE

KHOMEINI, Ruhollah Musavi

1902–89

Iranian religious–political leader

Born into a religious Shia family in Khomein, Ruhollah Musavi (Mustasaddi, his original surname) Khomeini was educated in theology at a religious school run by Ayatollah Abdul Karim Hairi-Yazdi in Arak. When Hairi-Yazdi moved to Qom in 1922, Khomeini went with him. Three years later Khomeini graduated in the Sharia (Islamic law), ethics and spiritual philosophy. Over the years he related ethics and spirituality to contemporary issues, and taught his students to regard the addressing of current social problems as part of their religious duty.

In 1941 he published a book anonymously in which he attacked secularism. Four years later he graduated to the clerical rank of hojatalislam (Arabic: 'proof of Islam'), which allowed him to collect his own circle of disciples, who would accept his interpretations of the Sharia. In 1961, urged on by his students, Khomeini published a book entitled *Clarification of Points of the Sharia*. It secured him promotion to ayatollah (Arabic: 'sign of Allah'). This enabled him to assume the leadership of the radical clergy.

In 1963 he combined his criticism of the White Revolution – a socio-economic reform package, consisting of agrarian reform, votes for women and profit-sharing in industry – with a personal attack on Muhammad Reza Shah Pahlavi (r. 1941–79), Iran's autocratic monarch. His arrest on 5 June 1963 triggered a countrywide uprising. The Shah used the army to crush it,

reportedly causing the death of thousands. Pressured by clerics, the Shah released Khomeini two months later and put him under house arrest in a Tehran suburb.

After his release in April 1964, Khomeini resumed his oppositional activities. In November he was expelled to Turkey. After living in the Turkish city of Bursa for a year, he moved to the Shia holy city of Najaf in Iraq. From there he kept up his campaign against the Shah – an enterprise that the leftist Baathists, who seized power in Iraq in July 1968, found convenient since they too were opposed to the pro-American Shah.

In 1971 Khomeini condemned the celebrations of 2,500 years of unbroken monarchy in Iran, a claim made by the Shah that lacked historical evidence. That year his book, *Hukumat-e Islam: Vilayet-e Faqih* (Persian: 'Islamic Government: Rule of the Faqih'; *Faqih* = 'Islamic jurisprudence'), based on a series of lectures, was published. In it Khomeini argued that an Islamic regime required an Islamic ruler who is thoroughly conversant with the Sharia, consisting of the Koran and the Hadith (the 'Doings and Sayings' of Prophet Muhammad) – and is just in its application. He should be assisted by jurisprudents at various levels of legislative, executive and judicial bodies. The function of a popularly elected parliament, open to both lay believers and clerics, is to resolve the conflicts likely to arise in the implementation of Islamic doctrines. However, judicial functions are to be performed only by jurisprudents since they are the ones conversant with the Sharia. Such jurisprudents also oversee the actions of the legislative and executive branches. The overall supervision and guidance of parliament and judiciary rests with the Just Faqih, who must also ensure that the executive does not exceed its powers.

Instead of prescribing dos and don'ts for believers, and waiting passively for the return of the last (Twelfth) Hidden Imam, the Shia clergy must attempt to oust corrupt officials and repressive regimes and replace them with ones led by just Islamic jurists, Khomeini urged in his highly original book.

In 1972, unhappy at the mistreatment of Shia clerics by the secular Baathist regime in Iraq, Khomeini sought – but was denied – permission to leave for Lebanon. Three years later, Khomeini attacked the Shah's inauguration of a single ruling party, the Rastakhiz, and this resonated well with many Shia clergy and theological students, who were disenchanted with the Shah's pro-Western, secular rule.

As a result of a rapprochement between Iraq and Iran in the wake of the Algiers Accord of March 1975, the number of Iranian pilgrims to the holy cities of Najaf and Karbala rose sharply. This made it easier for Khomeini to guide his followers in their anti-Shah campaign through smuggled tape recordings.

These audio tapes became all the more important as the revolutionary process, consisting of massive and repeated demonstrations and strikes, gathered momentum through successive stages, from February 1977 to October 1978, when Khomeini was exiled to France by the Iraqi government.

The turning point in the movement had come in January 1978, when a scurrilous attack on Khomeini in a Tehran-based pro-government newspaper inflamed popular feelings and placed the initiative in the ongoing struggle firmly with him. He made astute use of Shia history and Iranian nationalism to engender and intensify anti-royalist militancy among a rapidly growing circle of Iranians. He showed considerable shrewdness in uniting various disparate forces, Islamic and secular, along the most radical demand – the deposition of the Shah – and in causing the disintegration of the 413,000-strong military of the regime, starting with the soldiers refusing to fire on the protesting demonstrators in Tehran and other cities.

By November 1978, operating from Neuphle-le-Château, a Paris suburb, Khomeini had put the Shah on the defensive, and the economy, crippled by the stoppage of vital oil exports due to an indefinite strike by oil workers, was in a tailspin. On 13 January 1979, three days before the Shah's final departure from Iran, Khomeini appointed the Islamic Revolutionary Council (IRC) to facilitate the formation of a provisional government to produce a constitution for an Islamic republic in Iran.

On his return to Tehran on 1 February 1979 Khomeini appointed Mahdi Bazargan, an IRC member, as prime minister. Following a referendum, based on universal suffrage, Khomeini announced the establishment of the Islamic Republic of Iran on 1 April. In August an elected Assembly of Experts began debating the draft constitution, based on the *Vilayet-e Faqih* ('Rule of the Just Jurisprudent') doctrine propounded by Khomeini, and adopted it in December. It named Khomeini as the *marja-e taqlid* (Arabic: 'source of emulation') and Leader of the Revolution.

Khomeini first isolated and then repressed all non-Islamic forces that had backed the revolutionary movement. He was equally hostile to the Mujahedin-e Khalq (Persian: 'People's Mujahedin'), which combined Islam with **Marxism**. Khomeini turned against non-clerical Abol Hassan Bani-Sadr, the first directly elected president of the Islamic Republic, when the latter tried to foster a constituency outside Khomeinist circles. Having brought about Bani-Sadr's dismissal, constitutionally, in June 1981, Khomeini later endorsed only those candidates for the presidency – Muhammad Ali Rajai and Ali Khamanei – who were his proven acolytes.

In the early crisis-ridden years of the Islamic Republic, Khomeini provided strong leadership and showed ruthlessness in crushing opposition, bent on either staging a military coup against the regime (the monarchist strategy) or triggering a civil war (the Mujahedin-e Khalq strategy).

Convinced that Iran could never be truly independent until it had excised American influence from all walks of Iranian life, Khomeini kept up his campaign against the United States, the prime source to him of moral corruption and imperialist domination, describing it routinely as the 'Great Satan'. Engaged in a cold war with the Soviet bloc, the United States considered the 'loss' of Iran, sharing a long border with the Soviet Union, as the biggest international blow in its post-World War II history.

Khomeini was pleased when, following the storming of the US Embassy in Tehran in November 1979 and taking of its fifty-two diplomats as hostages, Washington cut off its diplomatic links with Iran. Conversely, he was incensed when, after Iraq invaded Iran in September 1980, neither the United Nations (UN) nor the Islamic Conference Organization (ICO) condemned the Iraqi action. However, Iraq's aggression helped him rally Iranians on a patriotic platform, and make his fractious supporters sink their differences on how to run the country, especially the economy. Conscious of the cementing effect of the Iran–Iraq War, Khomeini repeatedly rejected offers of mediation and a ceasefire.

Khomeini's attempts to export Islamic revolution to the neighbouring countries failed. The Gulf States' monarchs, all of them Sunni Muslim, managed to sideline Khomeini by successfully portraying him as the Shia leader of a non-Arab country. The only success Khomeini had in this regard was among the Shias of Lebanon.

At home Khomeini managed to keep together the moderates and radicals within the ruling establishment by intermittently favouring one side and then the other. When he realized that the governing Islamic Republican Party had become incurably faction-ridden, he ordered its disbandment in 1987.

Khomeini's radicalism did not blind him to reality. The military setbacks suffered by Iran in its war with Iraq in the spring of 1988 made him realize that if he did not stop fighting, the Islamic Republic would disintegrate; and that led him to accept the UN-brokered ceasefire in July 1988. Nonetheless, this was a bitter blow, described by him as 'taking poison'.

He died within a year of taking that decision – on 3 June 1989. He left behind an Iran with its territorial integrity intact, its Islamic regime well entrenched, but its economy shattered.

Further reading

See: *Islam and Revolution: Writings and Declarations of Imam Khomeini,* trans. Hamid Algar (1981); Baqer Moin, *Khomeini: Life of the Ayatollah* (2000)

DILIP HIRO

KING, Martin Luther, Jr
1929–68
US racial leader

Born in 1929, Martin Luther King Jr was only twenty-six years old when the Montgomery Bus Boycott thrust him into the midst of America's civil rights struggle. A little over a year later he achieved fame – the cover of *Time* magazine, the Spingarn Medal for his contributions to race relations, and a flurry of honorary degrees. In 1964 he became the youngest winner in the history of the Nobel Peace Prize.

Success at an early age could not have been completely unexpected. King had graduated from Morehouse College at nineteen, finished divinity school at the head of his class at twenty-two, and completed his PhD degree at Boston University at twenty-six. When black residents of Montgomery, Alabama, began their spontaneous boycott of segregated buses, however, King was nothing more than the young, rather shy pastor of the largest black Baptist church in the city. He was not an activist seeking an occasion; the occasion sought him. Before taking a public stand, King had to convince himself, and for this reason it would be easier for him to convince others. King was schooled in theology and philosophy, but he had prepared himself to be a minister. He had no programme and no commitment to a theory of change. Beginning with a strong Christian faith in the power of love and a black American tradition of non-violent protest against white oppression, Martin Luther King also came to appreciate the example and teachings of **Mahatma Gandhi**. Before the Montgomery Boycott was successfully concluded, King had articulated a philosophy of non-violent direct action whose spirit, he said, came from Jesus and whose technique came from Gandhi. King, however, was never an organizer, planner or administrator. In January 1957 he and some sixty other black leaders, mostly preachers, met in Atlanta to form the Southern Christian Leadership Conference (SCLC) in an attempt to co-ordinate the many civil rights efforts and ambitions spawned by the success in Montgomery. The SCLC would be Martin Luther King's official organization throughout the remainder of his thirteen-year career, but it never controlled or directed the civil rights movement. King became *the* civil rights leader and a man of immense national and international prestige, but his influence and contribution were predominantly spiritual.

Almost all the civil rights campaigns of the late 1950s and 1960s began as local campaigns, led by established local leaders and manned by local blacks, especially students. Rarely could these campaigns win success, however, unless they achieved national awareness. Here was the critical role of Martin Luther King. Only he had the prestige and influence to elevate a local crisis to the attention of the news media and the federal government. Only he could attract sufficient white support to provide the stamp of 'legitimacy'. His devotion to non-violence, his emphasis upon love, and his openness to compromise made him appear responsible and moderate and, therefore, respectable. But King's role as a symbolic and spiritual leader meant that he often had little power to control the movement he represented. The inability of the SCLC to define a coherent programme of action in the late 1950s, for example, led to impatience among many black students and thus to the birth of the sit-in movement in 1960. King endorsed the sit-ins and for a time brought the Student Non-violent Coordinating Committee (SNCC) under the loose umbrella of the SCLC. In this way, he maintained his important position, but as one observer commented, 'It was not leadership but agility that put him there.' The popularity of the student sit-in movement

among local black communities put great pressure on King. Expectations had been raised, and blacks looked expectantly to Martin Luther King. His instincts, agility and prestige served him well, but on occasion, as with the demonstrations in Albany, Georgia, in 1961–2, they failed. In Albany, a lack of planning and background information had caused King to step into a virtually impossible situation. His prestige slipped, particularly among more aggressive civil rights groups such as SNCC and the Congress of Racial Equality (CORE).

If King and the SCLC had a tactical civil rights plan, it was to maintain tension on the South's caste-like system of segregation and discrimination. Unless pressure was applied, there was no impetus to change. By 1963 King needed a productive crisis. Dissent was growing among black activists, and civil rights legislation was making little progress in Washington. Consequently, King turned his attention to a massive demonstration assault on Birmingham, Alabama, perhaps the most segregated city in the South. For two months marches confronted the forces of white resistance. Violence flared and eventually over 2,400 civil rights demonstrators, including King, were jailed. The two sides finally reached a compromise in Birmingham, but not before the full weight of **John F. Kennedy's** presidency was thrown into the fray. In addition, the crisis renewed Kennedy's support for a comprehensive new civil rights law and also raised recognition of Martin Luther King's leadership to new heights. In an eloquent and widely publicized 'Letter from Birmingham Jail', King had defended his direct action tactics and articulated his goals in a fashion that contrasted dramatically with the harsh and primitive measures of his segregationist opponents. In the sensitive months following Kennedy's assassination in November 1963, Martin Luther King's prestige reached its peak – the passage of the Civil Rights Act of 1964 and the awarding of the Nobel Peace Prize.

Still, however, there was tension within the ranks of the civil rights movement. On the one hand, many SNCC and CORE workers continued their criticism of King's willingness to compromise short of his declared objectives, and they turned more and more away from co-operation with whites in favour of various brands of 'black power'. On the other hand, King was being pressured to give attention to the ghettos of the North where violence and the black nationalism of Malcolm X were on the rise. Furthermore, he was also beginning to feel the pull of a growing anti-Vietnam War movement. In effect, many blacks had come to feel that the accomplishments associated with King's leadership had not sifted down to the black masses. King responded to these pressures by taking his non-violent programme to Chicago in an effort to force improvement in inner-city housing and employment practices. He attained little success and his prestige suffered. Advocates of protest violence and black power gained voice and urban rioting increased. Meanwhile, in April 1967, King had reluctantly taken a public stance against the war in Vietnam – a position he had maintained privately for many months. The decision to go public further diminished his leadership role in the increasingly fragmented civil rights movement. Conservative black workers in the National Association for the Advancement of Colored People (NAACP) and National Urban League criticized King sharply, and he lost his once considerable leverage with the Lyndon Johnson administration.

By 1967 Martin Luther King's approach to bringing meaningful social change in the United States showed the strains of his twelve-year struggle. In *Where Do We Go From Here?*, published in that year, King had embraced a modified version of black power. But while he was no longer the shy, rather naive young black minister who had been drawn into the Montgomery Bus Boycott, he still relied heavily upon Christian oratory and clung hopefully to his belief in Gandhian non-violent techniques. King began to put together plans for what he hoped would be a massive 'Poor People's March' on Washington

in the summer of 1968. Many advisers warned him of the probability of violence in such a march, but King rejected their advice and pushed ahead in what seemed an almost desperate effort to re-establish the viability of non-violent demonstrations. While planning was going on, however, a plea came from striking Memphis, Tennessee, garbage workers. They wanted King's support. Here was an opportunity to re-establish his own sagging prestige and, therefore, to enhance the chances for success of his Poor People's March. It was in Memphis on 4 April 1968 that Martin Luther King Jr fell victim to an assassin's bullet. In addition to a floundering and fragmented civil rights movement, King left his wife, Coretta Scott King, and four children. His personal prestige was still huge, but his special capacity as an effective spiritual leader had deteriorated significantly from its peak in 1964.

Further reading

Other works include: *Stride Toward Freedom* (1958); *The Measure of a Man* (1958); *Strength to Love* (1963); *Why We Can't Wait* (1964); *The Trumpet of Conscience* (1968). See also: David L. Lewis, *King: A Critical Biography* (2nd edn, 1978); C. Eric Lincoln (ed.), *Martin Luther King, Jr: A Profile* (1970); James A. Colaiaco, *Martin Luther King, Jr: Apostle of Militant Nonviolence* (1993); James Ralph Jr, *Northern Protest: Martin Luther King, Jr, Chicago, and the Civil Rights Movement* (1993); Stephen B. Oates, *Let the Trumpet Sound: The Life of Martin Luther King, Jr* (1994); David J. Garrow, *The FBI and Martin Luther King, Jr* (2005).

LESTER C. LAMON

KIPLING, Joseph Rudyard
1865–1936
English writer

Rudyard Kipling was born in Bombay, the son of Alice and Lockwood Kipling (who later became curator of the Indian Museum and director of the Art Institute at Lahore). After an idyllically happy early childhood he was sent 'home' at the age of six to England with his sister, and spent six bitterly wretched years at a foster-home in Southsea which he later called 'The House of Desolation'. In 1877 he was sent to the recently founded United Services College at Westward Ho!, Devon, on which the stories of *Stalky & Co.* (1899) were later based. At sixteen Kipling left school and rejoined his family in India to work as a journalist. The next seven years, at Lahore and Allahabad, stimulated some of his finest early work and remained a continuing inspiration for much of his writing life. Beginning with the witty light verse of *Departmental Ditties* (1886) he wrote many of his classic short stories. The first collection of these to be published in England – *Plain Tales from the Hills* (1888) – was immediately acclaimed, and in 1889 Kipling left India to pursue a literary career in London. His success was quickly assured, but he soon learnt to dislike the metropolitan literati. Throughout his life he was to maintain the stance of a plain experienced man of action, despite unquestioned dedication to his art. His friendships included Stanley Baldwin, Lord Milner and Max Aitken (later Lord Beaverbrook), but few fellow writers.

The years between 1890 and 1902 were the zenith of Kipling's popularity. During this time he published three superb collections of mainly 'Indian' short stories: *Life's Handicap* (1891), *Many Inventions* (1893) and *The Day's Work* (1897), which included his finest fable 'The Bridge Builders'. These were followed by *Kim* (1901), his only full-length romance, the story of a boy who moves within the 'daylight' world of the British in India, and the dark, rich, friendly world of the native Indians, equally at home with the 'Great Game' of spying for the British and with the mysticism of the Buddhist lama whose disciple he becomes. The same period also witnessed Kipling's children's classics: *The Jungle Book* (1894), *The Second Jungle Book* (1895) and the brilliant fables of *Just-so Stories* (1902). In verse he published *Barrack Room Ballads* (1892 and 1896), 'vernacular' poems inspired by his knowledge of military life in India and by the London music-halls, of their

kind unsurpassed in the English language. In addition, Kipling established himself as a public spokesman on behalf of a Tory populism characterized by the ideals of patriotism, the glory of the Empire, and the value of hard work and dedication to one's duty in all classes. Of particular note in this context are the hymn 'Recessional' (1897, published in *The Times* for Victoria's Diamond Jubilee), warning Britons against pagan pride in their inevitably transient Empire, and the song 'Absent-Minded Beggar', which raised £250,000 for the wives and dependants of soldiers fighting in the Boer War.

In 1892 Kipling married the American Caroline Balestier, and after a world tour settled with her in their Vermont house 'Naulakha', where their daughters Josephine and Elsie were born, until a family row and lawsuit drove them to England. By 1897 Kipling was settled in Sussex. Here his son John was born, and here he remained for the rest of his life apart from occasional spells of foreign travel, principally to South Africa where he and his family spent nearly all their winters between 1898 and 1907, and once to New York in 1899 (a disastrous trip on which Kipling became critically ill with pneumonia and, most cruelly, his beloved Josephine – 'Best Beloved' of the *Just-So Stories* – died of the same illness: a blow from which he never fully recovered).

During the Edwardian period Kipling became if anything even more firmly identified with the English ruling class, although he steadfastly refused official status, declining both the Laureateship and the Order of Merit. His fiction of this 'middle period' deals less with alien cultures and more with the apparently mundane English world of solid, hard-working non-intellectuals, with the problems of administration, but also with the new technologies of communication that always fascinated him: newspapers, cinema and air transport. 'Below the Mill Dam' (from *Traffics and Discoveries*, 1904) and 'The Mother Hive' (from *Actions and Reactions,* 1909) are his most skilful political fables, while other stories, such as 'They' and 'Mrs

Bathurst' (from *Traffics and Discoveries*), 'The House Surgeon' (*Actions and Reactions*) and the coldly terrifying 'Mary Postgate' (*A Diversity of Creatures*, 1917), brilliantly combine surface commitment to modern actuality with profound explorations into the recesses of the psyche.

During the First World War Kipling threw himself passionately into German-hating propaganda (his war verses have a rage and shrillness unparalleled elsewhere in his writing), but he was also deeply disillusioned by the sordid waste of life after his son John was killed at Loos in 1915, and embittered both by the conduct of the war and by its aftermath. In the sense that his later fiction is concerned more with suffering, and less with the action of his earlier work, the spiritual damage was permanent, yet it moved him to write important works of mourning: in poetry the 'Epitaphs of the War', including the famous, self-accusing epigram 'Common Form'('If any question why we died/Tell them, because our fathers lied'), in prose the tautly written *History of the Irish Guards in the Great War* (1925, 1926), commemorating the suffering and achievement of his son's regiment, and many short stories touching on the harsh experience of civilians, especially bereaved parents, as well as shell-shocked soldiers. War is often the background and partial cause of the suffering in his late stories (as with 'The Janeites' and 'The Gardener', in *Debits and Credits*, 1926); but, at least as often, pain is treated simply as an inevitable part of the human condition as with 'The Wish House', in *Debits and Credits*, or 'Dayspring Mishandled' in *Limits and Renewals* (1932). At the same time Kipling's interest in historical settings, of the kind that he had used in the children's books *Puck of Pook's Hill* (1906) and *Rewards and Fairies* (1910), was rekindled in stories like 'The Eye of Allah' and 'The Church that was at Antioch'.

Many of Kipling's late stories are masterpieces of technical narrative complexity, and serve to remind one of their author's versatility, energy and mastery of form: qualities that are apparent in nearly everything he wrote. What is less consistent in Kipling's work, however, is the *persona* behind it. The more one reads of him, the more elusive his character becomes. His stories frequently employ a narrating 'I' (just as many of his poems are best read as dramatic monologues) – yet this 'I' has a whole range of personalities and its only regular qualities are that it is invariably possessed of an 'insider's knowledge' about whatever world it narrates, and that it is (usually) compassionate. The kind of difficulties Kipling offers his interpreters are exemplified in the story 'Mary Postgate', in which a middle-aged governess, in revenge for the wartime death of her pupil, watches the death agony of a German pilot, refusing to help him and taking an unmistakably sexual pleasure in the experience. This can be seen as the vilest kind of war propaganda or as a masterly piece of compassionate psychological realism.

Not surprisingly, in the light of this, responses to Kipling have been extreme, and, despite the technical brilliance of his writing, his importance has been cultural rather than literary, at least among English-speaking writers, though he was admired by **T.S. Eliot**, who drew on his light verse for *Practical Cats* and edited a selection of his poems in 1941, and by **W.H. Auden**, who parodied him and imitated him, and has visibly influenced the poets Tony Harrison and Wendy Cope; outside England, he was admired by **André Gide** and by Alain Fournier, author of *Le Grand Meaulnes*, while **Brecht**, who translated *Barrack Room Ballads* into German, and **Jorge Luis Borges** both acknowledged his influence. To the conservative middle classes, whom he celebrated while often implicitly criticizing their narrow outlook, he embodied the pieties of patriotism and tradition; while to liberals and the progressive left he stood for everything they hated: reactionary politics, jingoism, brutality and cultural philistinism. One reason for this simplistic caricature of a complex man is the intertwining of 'Kiplingesque' values with the (assumed) ideology of the English public schools. The

English intellectual Left of the 1930s were much affected by public school experience, values and mythology, a parodic and partially distanced version of which the poets made their own; which meant that to the extent that these values continued to affect them, their outlook was inversely shaped by Kipling. The jibe of **Orwell** (in *The Road to Wigan Pier*) that Auden was 'a sort of gutless Kipling' is typical: the comparison is intended as a deliberate insult, and yet not only is Kipling a landmark for both writers, but the word 'gutless' reproduces the very 'Kiplingesque' values which are ostensibly rejected.

Further reading

Other works include: *The Light that Failed* (novel, 1890); *The Naulahka* (novel, 1892, with Wolcott Balestier); *Captains Courageous* (novella, 1897); *Something of Myself* (autobiography, 1937); *The Verse of Rudyard Kipling* (definitive edn, 1940). See also biographical studies: Charles Carrington, *Kipling: His Life and Art* (1955); Angus Wilson, *The Strange Ride of Rudyard Kipling* (1977); Andrew Lycett, *Rudyard Kipling* (2001); David Gilmour, *The Long Recessional: The Imperial Life of Rudyard Kipling* (2002); and Harry Ricketts, *The Unforgiving Minute: A Life of Rudyard Kipling* (1999). See also: J.M.S. Tompkins, *The Art of Rudyard Kipling* (1959); A. Rutherford (ed.), *Kipling's Mind and Art*, including essays by Orwell, Edmund Wilson and Lionel Trilling (1964); Sandra Kemp, *Kipling's Hidden Narratives* (1988); Zohreh T. Sullivan, *Narratives of Empire: The Fictions of Rudyard Kipling* (1993); Janet Montefiore, *Rudyard Kipling* (2006).

JANET MONTEFIORE

KITAJ, Ronald Brooks

1932–2007

American painter and printmaker

R.B. Kitaj was born in America. In late 1957 he went to England, returning in 1997 to Los Angeles. During an almost forty-year sojourn in Britain he completed his art education, and made his name and reputation with great critical acclaim. In the 1960s the import of Kitaj's work rivalled that of **Francis Bacon**,

heralding a new future for painting. Thirty years later, following his Tate retrospective in 1994, critics were so harsh in their attacks, not just on the abstruse nature of his art but on his artistic ability, in particular his draughtsmanship, that he felt hounded out of Britain. The fact that he was an artist in exile, an American and, above all, a Jew, was initially a cultural asset but later, as he came to believe, prejudicial to his acceptance. His Jewish identity, particularly his intellectuality, which concerned him increasingly from the 1970s, became an insuperable difference as criticism turned hostile.

At the start of Kitaj's career in Britain it was his difference that attracted attention and gained him national, quickly followed by international, recognition. The fundamental importance he attached to drawing, his handling of colour, and the introduction to painting of a meaningful, if obscure, narrative, were received positively in the prevailing climate of abstraction. Although some critics voiced concern that the literary bias in his work, supported by explanatory texts, outweighed its visual qualities, Kitaj was more generally extolled for re-establishing a balance between the formal significance of art and a representational subject–matter, which was imaginative rather than mimetic. To the art world in the early 1960s he brought an intelligence to picture making and its experience, which crystallized a radical trend towards a new figuration. In 1963, Kitaj prefaced the catalogue of his first one-man exhibition with a translation of Horace's words, 'As in painting, so it is in poetry', declaring his ambitious intention to revive a rich classical tradition for the twentieth century. In paintings such as *Kennst du das Land?* (1962), he aspired to do for painting what **T.S. Eliot** and **Ezra Pound** had achieved in modern poetry, to compose visual poems from meaningful fragments. The references he exploited were impressive. His intellectual interests ranged from literature, political history, philosophy and iconographic studies inspired by his encounter with the scholar Professor Edgar Wind, and by the esoteric imagery he found in the *Journal of the Warburg and Courtauld Institutes*. His pictorial conjunction of these disparate elements round a central idea exploited the technique of collage, jumping between seemingly incongruous images and snatches of text in different styles and on different scales, rather like a personal scrapbook or a stream of thoughts in his diary. Kitaj saw himself as leader in a movement to rehumanize art after Abstract Expressionism. He succeeded besides in expressing this sense of tradition in a contemporary voice by virtue of his eclectic painting techniques: drily worked surfaces, for example, taken from Bacon, expressive brushwork from **Robert Rauschenberg** or **Willem de Kooning**. The Tate sealed his triumphant start by purchasing *Isaac Babel Riding with Budyonny* (1962).

Various factors contributed to Kitaj's success, not least his experience of life, army and travel, and the consequent maturity he brought to his early pictures. He was twenty-five, and married, when he was accepted at the Ruskin School of Drawing and Fine Art in Oxford under the educational terms of the American G.I. Bill. He continued there before taking a two-year, post-graduate diploma at the Royal College of Art. Compared to younger students, Kitaj came to his education with an ambitious sense of purpose, which he demonstrated in pictures such as *Tarot Variations* (1958), painted in Oxford, and *The Murder of Rosa Luxembourg* (1960), one of his Royal College works. The personal basis for his work, his independence of mind and his assurance explained his role as mentor to younger contemporaries, who saw the failure of American Abstract Expressionism to engage directly with everyday life, and wanted to replace it with a new figurative content. Among these so-named Pop artists were Derek Boshier, Allen Jones, Peter Phillips, **David Hockney** and Patrick Caulfield, who, rather than follow Kitaj's erudite aesthetic, began to experiment with imagery taken from their urban environment. They shared his wish to make an art which was relevant and accessible to the public, but in his pictures the visual impact, though intended to have popular appeal, was always in tension with his scholarly obsessions. Even the erotic attraction of a much later pastel drawing *Communist and Socialist* (1977), which showed a man with an erection lying in bed beside a woman, relied on its audience understanding his titular allusion to the political catch-phrase 'reds under the bed'.

As Kitaj's confidence grew in the 1970s, criticism of his studied approach hardened. Appraisal of such pictures as *The Autumn of Central Paris (After Walter Benjamin)* (1972–74), which relied on knowledge that its title was that of Anthony Sutcliffe's book on the rebuilding of Paris in the nineteenth and twentieth centuries, made unfavourable comparison with Kitaj's earlier work. Some observers questioned whether his paintings were better read than looked at. Although he ceased attaching explanatory texts to his exhibition catalogues, suspicion grew that his learned references might be more suggestive than meaningfully coherent.

With Hockney as his ally, Kitaj shifted his attention to championing the cause of figurative art, and making a case for a return to life drawing. The exhibition he assembled in 1976 called *The Human Clay* had a huge resonance. It was in effect a manifesto on behalf of artists concerned with the human condition. Kitaj's one-man exhibition the following year was evidence of his concentration on the drawing techniques of old and modern masters. Art historical references appeared in paintings of 1975–6, such as *If Not, Not*, with its allusion to Giorgione. Mantegna was referenced in the head of the dealer James Joll, in *From London*, a double portrait with Joll's partner, the painter and art historian John Golding. In 1980, the exhibition he selected from the National Gallery's collection, *The Artist's Eye*, confirmed his mission, and included examples of his own drawing interest in **Degas**.

Kitaj's enthusiasm for the cause generated heated debate in the art world, bringing him unwanted publicity. It was during this unsettling period that he explored Jewish history and his own identity with greater concentration. In America Kitaj, in common with many Jews, became part of the general culture. Yet, even his early work, notably *The Murder of Rosa Luxembourg*, was charged with Jewish connotations. In England his attitudes were informed by an intellectual and artistic milieu inhabited by European Jews, whose lives were deeply affected by the Holocaust. The Israeli–Arab wars of 1967 and 1973 revived their fears of a final solution. Kitaj's second wife was Jewish, and from the 1970s the issue of being a Jew became central to his work and more dramatically focused. His *If Not, Not*, dominated by a gatehouse at Auschwitz in incongruously idyllic scenery, was significantly one of the first paintings to articulate an experience that had been harboured by the Jewish community for thirty years. The surge of literature on the Jewish Holocaust did not emerge until the 1980s, and Kitaj's *First Diasporist Manifesto*, which reflects on his Jewishness, was published in 1989, four years after a solo exhibition at Marlborough, in which he had evidently come to terms with recent Jewish history and its human repercussions. His painting *Cecil Court, London WC2 (The Refugees)* (1983–4) was a very personal expression of his and other European refugees' predicament. *The Jewish Rider* (1984–5), a portrait of the art historian Professor Michael Podro riding in a train through the landscape of the Holocaust in the stance of Rembrandt's *Polish Rider*, represented a powerful configuration of Jewish and art historical preoccupations. In 1990, a major London survey of twentieth century Jewish art, *From Chagall to Kitaj*, assigned him a place in the modern pantheon.

Kitaj's leading position as a confessional painter and the high regard with which his work is held in America and Europe seem at odds with his appraisal in Britain. In 1995 he was awarded the Golden Lion at the Venice Biennale of International Art for his outstanding achievement. In Britain, by comparison, the art world remains strongly divided. There are those who, like their Continental counterparts, are ready to find a pedestal for the intellectual artist, and others who find his art pretentious and literary.

Further reading

See: *R.B. Kitaj* (1985; *Kitaj*, 3rd rev. edn, 1999), including the artist's texts, a list of his writings, and bibliography; see also his *R.B. Kitaj: Portrait of a Hispanist* (exhibition catalogue, Museo de Bellas Artes, Bilbao, 2004). *R.B. Kitaj. A Retrospective*, ed. Richard Morphet (exhibition catalogue, Tate Gallery, 1994), includes full bibliography and the artist's texts; Jane Kinsman, *The Prints of R.B. Kitaj*, with afterwords by R.B. Kitaj (1994). For new art-historical interpretations, see James Aulich and John Lynch (eds), *Critical Kitaj: Essays on the Work of R.B. Kitaj* (2000). Andrew Lambirth, *Kitaj* (2004), includes a conversational exchange with Kitaj conducted by e-mail.

JUDITH BUMPUS

KLEE, Paul

1879–1940
Swiss–German artist

Born near Berne in Switzerland, Paul Klee hesitated for a long time as to whether to be an artist, a poet or a musician; he finally left home to study at an art school in Munich. He soon felt the urge to shed the strict training of the hand which classical art studies entail, and entered upon a lifelong practice of experimentation, trying out dozens of fresh techniques and styles, some inspired by the artless drawings of children or the insane, others by the work of such artists as **Van Gogh** and Ensor. The scratchy, fantastical manner of his early drawings reflects a talent straining away from all orthodoxy. 'I want to be as though new-born,' reads an entry in his diary.

In 1901 Klee had visited Italy and busied himself with relatively out-of-the-way attractions such as Byzantine mosaics, the Pompeii frescoes and a marvellous aquarium in Naples, whence sprang an enduring fascination with the dim forms of marine life. His travels were always occasions to gather primary impressions which he then allowed to germinate in their own time, eventually to surface as artistic forms. After a period back in Berne, Klee married in 1906 and returned to Munich, where he became a member of the Blaue Reiter circle with **Kandinsky** and **Franz Marc**. Already a virtuoso draughtsman and watercolourist, Klee now came to contemplate the suggestive potential of graduated tones of colour, revealed most dramatically upon his discovery of **Cézanne** in 1910. He was beginning to grasp that the art of painting might be based on fidelity to the palette itself rather than to any pre-existing subject-matter.

A visit to another great colourist, Robert Delaunay, in Paris was followed in 1914 by a journey to North Africa. Lasting less than a fortnight, this journey was to be the climax of Klee's quest for the full understanding of his artistic orientation. The town of Tunis manifested itself as the perfect model for a vision of painting in which architectonic shapes could be synthesized with orchestrated zones of luminous colour. The harmonic vibrancy of the place created an impression which was to radiate throughout Klee's subsequent work. The mosaic patterns made up by the cubes and cupolas of the Arab buildings, the textures of parched earth and hot walls, the lush oases, the moon rising over the desert sands – these elements of an exotic reality nourished a language of shapes and colours which was to become Klee's native idiom. 'It is all sinking so deeply and calmly into me,' he recorded in his diary. 'Colour has taken possession of me. That is the significance of this happy hour: colour and I are one. I am a painter.'

By 1920 Klee was an artist of repute and was engaged by **Walter Gropius** to teach at the Bauhaus in Weimar, along with the painters Lyonel Feininger, Oskar Schlemmer and Kandinsky, the latter already an intimate friend and co-explorer in the realms of pure colour and form. Klee's work with students encouraged him to systematize his intuitions concerning the construction of forms and the relationships of line, tone value and colour. The *Pedagogical Sketchbook* (*Pädagogisches Skizzenbuch*, 1925, trans. 1953) is a résumé of his teaching on graphic procedures and deals with the dynamics of the dot, the line, the spiral, the square and so forth. Pedagogic practice merely confirmed Klee's ingrained habit of self-scrutiny, of making conscious that which was primarily instinctive. In this Klee came close to the Surrealists, with whom he exhibited in Paris in 1925: but against their unbridled 'psychic automatism' he favoured a mode of 'psychic improvisation' whereby the spontaneous gestures of pen or brush are studied, interpreted, even supervised by a purposive, lucid intelligence.

In the 1930s, Klee came up against antagonisms at the Bauhaus and in Germany at large, and in 1933 decided to move back for good to Switzerland. The Nazis in due course suppressed all his works in public galleries after derisively showing Klee in their 1937 exhibition of 'degenerate art'. Re-settling in Berne, the artist fell victim to a malignant skin condition but continued to produce at a phenomenal rate: during 1939 he completed 2,000 works. He died in 1940 in a clinic near Locarno.

Klee left behind an extraordinary oeuvre of some 9,000 works, primarily watercolours, drawings and oil paintings, in a great range of styles. Most of his pictures are on a diminutive scale, neat miniatures in which daring experimentation is almost hermetically sealed. Each image is the tiny encapsulation of a happy solution to a particular aesthetic question.

Klee's approach was markedly different from that of his Expressionist contemporaries. He was drawn to a type of abstraction in which identifiable shapes from the real world – his favourite motifs are birds and fishes, trees, parks and cities, human figures and faraway landscapes – are rendered in spidery lines that suggest a kind of kabbalistic picture-writing. It is an idiom of intellectual signs rather than of emotions, and is indeed based on Klee's understanding of the conceptual rather than expressionistic mode of child art. Some works are self-conscious displays of verbal signs: *Villa R* (1919) and *Vocal*

Fabric of the Singer Rosa Silber (1922) present letters from the alphabet as visual configurations in their own right. At one time Klee did a series of 'inscription pictures' in which poetic texts are rendered in capitals upon ribbons of colour to create a lilting synthesis of word and image. *Leaf from the Town Records* (1928) depicts a manuscript whose 'text' consists of interlinked runic figures suggesting turrets, flags, domes and city walls; the title of the work underlines the draughtsman's claim to equate the pictorial with the written sign. In due course Klee adumbrated a set of simple figures – squares, triangles, dots, squiggles, arrows – which were the letters of his personal alphabet.

Another analogy which asserts itself in the context of Klee's semi-abstract paintings is that with the set of notes which are arranged and rearranged in a musical composition. *Highway and Byways* (1929) presents a wide road stretching to the horizon across a plain built up to either side in rich ochre, pale green and purple strips, some thick, some thin. Inspired by a visit to Egypt, this landscape is in transition from being the transposition of a real spatial experience to being a prodigiously organized exercise in the polyphonic combination of colour tones and geometric shapes across the picture surface.

Klee's conception of Nature springs from the notion that the artist is himself a fragment of the totality of things: 'The artist is a man, himself nature and a part of nature, within nature's space.' His task is therefore not to reproduce idly what he sees, but to attune himself to natural processes and translate these formative energies into the idiom of aesthetic signs. The artist should not linger over surface perceptions: after all, 'the visible is only an isolated case'. His picture must be the record of a meditation upon deeper, invisible truths; he fashions not a mirror of natural creation but its emblem. 'He transcends reality, dissolves it, in order to reveal what lies behind and inside it.'

The canvas *Blossoming* (1934) consists of a framework of irregular multi-coloured squares, their tonal values meticulously graded so that the eye is first drawn to the brilliance at the centre, then out to the surrounding areas of progressive darkness. The movement of the viewer's eye, from brightness to darkness, from centre to circumference, corresponds to the dimly sensed motion of natural growth. The picture is a geometrical allegory of blossoming rather than a direct representation of any flower. Similarly *Untamed Waters* (1934) shows us not literal turbulence but an ideogram in which lines of flow are stylized into intertwined ribbons of blue, turquoise, rust and pink: the literality of water in motion is transcended in an image of thrusting currents held in suspense, convulsive lines soothed by calm watercolour hues.

Klee's art often seems to drift away from all immediacy. Thus the wistful portrait of the *Man in Yellow* (1921), with its caricatural reduction of facial features to a few slickly curled lines and the breathless way Klee floats this yellow figure on to the green depths of the background, evokes a presence which is remote, unreal. *The Tightrope Walker* (1923) is a vaguely comic portrayal of a spotlighted manikin with bird-like face easing his way silently along a thin rope with a balancing pole; fussy paraphernalia – rope-ladder, safety-net and the like – dangle irrelevantly beneath. The black lines representing these are inscribed over an unearthly pink ground, a typical combination for Klee, who loved to draw in spiky transparent configurations over an initial wash of glowing watercolour. The effect of this little image is to evoke a feeling of diminished gravitational pull: the tightrope walker is like Klee himself, delicately stepping from the world of substance on to the higher plane of art. This sure-footedness, this discretion, this cool remoteness seem characteristic: they place Klee in the lineage of a Mozart rather than of a Beethoven, and can make some of his pictures come across as things to be peeped at, quaintly seductive windows on to a fantasy world, rather than the solemn repositories of the semi-mystical teachings of the theoretical writings.

Klee was active in so many different styles and his example has been so subtly pervasive that it is impossible to pin down the exact range of his artistic influence: there are touches of Klee in the work of artists as disparate as Bissier, Wols, **Dubuffet**, De Staël and Hundertwasser, to name but a few. And perhaps because Klee never relinquished the child-like manner, his images have also been among the most popular in twentieth-century art, doing much to accustom a reluctant public to the formidable modernist proposition which the artist once formulated, simply yet boldly, in the aphorism: 'Art does not reproduce the visible – it makes visible.'

Further reading

Other works include: *Tagebücher* (*Diaries*, 1957); *Notebooks*, Vol. I *The Thinking Eye* (*Das bildnerische Denken*, trans. 1961) and Vol. II *The Nature of Nature* (*Unendliche Naturgeschichte*, trans. 1973); *On Modern Art* (*Über die moderne Kunst*, trans. 1948). On Klee: C. Giedion-Welcker, *Paul Klee* (1952); W. Haftmann, *The Mind and Work of Paul Klee* (*Paul Klee: Wege bildnerischen Denkens*, trans. 1954); W. Grohmann, *Paul Klee* (1954); G. di San Lazzaro, *Klee* (1957); J.S. Pierce, *Paul Klee and Primitive Art* (1975); E.-G. Guse (ed.), *Paul Klee: Dialogue with Nature* (1991).

ROGER CARDINAL

KLEIN, Yves

1928–62

French artist

In 1946, lying on the beach at Nice, Klein made a 'realistico-imaginary' voyage and signed his name on the other side of the sky. From that experience dated his ambition to express the infinite in art. The pure cloudless sky was for him not only the symbol of 'existential space' but also of the 'immaterial' and of 'absolute freedom'.

Klein's vision was optimistic and Utopian, believing as he did in a future technological Garden of Eden. But to achieve this it was first necessary to transform the sensibility of humankind and this was the central purpose of his art. Such a transformation did not entail, as it has for most avant-gardistes, a total break with the past. On the contrary, all existing traditions contained truths which could be used. His own creative development was facilitated by the practice of judo: 'Judo has helped me to understand that pictorial space is above all the product of spiritual exercises.' Nevertheless, as 'an Occidental, a right-thinking Christian', he did not believe that the answer lay in the wholesale espousal of Eastern systems. The principal answer which he proposed was: pure colour. From 1956 he produced his monochrome paintings. Finding that differently coloured monochromes hung together were seen comparatively and hence polychromatically, he limited himself principally to one colour – a deep ultramarine which he later (1960) patented as International Klein Blue (IKB). Despite their resonance, however, his blue paintings were not in themselves finished artworks but 'only the title-deeds' proving him to be an artist. His real art, the transformation of sensibility, consisted also of his many activities. His *anthropométries*, for example: in 1960 he directed three nude models as they imprinted IKB paint on to canvases before an audience while twenty musicians played his one-note *Symphonie monotone*. In the same year, Klein threw himself off a first-floor parapet, injuring himself in so doing, to create *A Man in Space*; this action was recorded in his *Newspaper of a Single Day, Sunday* (27 November 1960). Fascinated by air, he was also fascinated by fire, creating in 1961 a gas-fuelled *Fire Fountain* and *Fire Wall*, as well as numerous *Fire Paintings*. His involvement with the elements was alchemistic. Not surprisingly, therefore, he executed a number of works in gold, the 'monogolds'. But the metal must be abandoned for its 'immaterial' equivalent, as demonstrated in Klein's sale, for gold, of *Immaterial Pictorial Sensitivity Zones* (1959–62); while he threw away or destroyed half the gold, the 'buyer', was obliged to destroy the receipt if his proprietorship was to be validated. In 1962 Klein began work on a project intended to contain IKB-coloured plaster-casts of his friends against gold backgrounds with, in the centre, a gold plaster-cast of himself against an IKB background: its completion was prevented by his early death.

The posthumous reputation of 'Yves, le Monochrome' has been complicated, and greatly enhanced, by the rise of Conceptual Art and Performance Art, both of which he prefigured to a remarkable degree. Perhaps no artist of his generation had a clearer understanding than he of the direction in which art needed to develop if it were to fulfil its properly investigative and didactic function.

Further reading

See: Pierre Restany, *Yves Klein, le monochrome* (1974); also the catalogues to his exhibitions at the Jewish Museum, New York (1967), and the Tate Gallery, London (1974). See also: S. Stich, *Yves Klein* (1995).

GRAY WATSON

KLIMT, Gustav

1862–1918

Austrian artist

Born at Baumgartner in 1862, Klimt became the leading figure in the dynamic and forceful decorative art that characterized late nineteenth-century Vienna. He was not, however, simply a painter of murals, for his easel paintings were equally decorative; they in turn were informed by the grave and erotic personal preoccupations that provided a driving force for the portraits, landscapes and subject paintings evolved in his studio. Indeed, Klimt was to be active in many fields scarcely distinguishing between art and design, uniting the visionary themes of Symbolist art inspired by Moreau, Toorop and Khnopff with the rhythmically lavish decorations of international Art Nouveau and Jugendstil. He designed clothes, posters and publications as well as paintings.

Klimt's initial artistic impetus came from his father, the Bohemian engraver Ernst

Klimt. He studied at the School of Arts and Crafts of the Austrian Museum in Vienna, and his early commissions included decorative panels, amongst which were spandrels for the Kunst-historisches Museum in Vienna executed in deliberately archaic styles. Klimt's tastes were subsequently to embrace many cultures from Byzantine mosaics to the asymmetrical clarity of Japanese prints. He shared with the Post-Impressionists a love of paint as pigment and employed dense firm colour, yet immense professional and academic facility ensured the continuing importance of line and drawing in his painting. All of these diverse elements were combined with great vigour in stylized compositions that were as evidently talented and competent as they were daring, for Klimt was, above all, a virtuoso of consummate skill.

His subjects owed much to the Symbolist movement that spread throughout Europe in the 1880s and into the 1890s, an introspective and fantastic art that evoked the images of imagination more often than it reflected the world of visual observation. This background permitted Klimt to revitalize allegorical painting in Austria reinforcing its themes with personal expressive force and ravishing effects of decoration. Klimt synthesized the myriad tendencies and tastes of his day, but his art, not least as a result of sheer talent, was wholly his own.

Music (1895) exemplifies these qualities. A decisively contemporary Viennese girl plays a stylized version of an ancient lyre. Greek sculptures are depicted at either side, while behind the figure a riot of curling organic patterns spread out across the flat surface of the board on which Klimt has painted, appearing not simply to decorate the background wall but to spill across the painting as embodiments of sound, a symbol or equivalent of music itself. The work is at once expressive and decorative: the two were never separate in Klimt's art where design and emotion combine.

Allegory was used by Symbolist painters and writers as a vehicle for emotional expression. Klimt seized upon this to embody his own meditations upon life, love and death. Frequently morbid and erotic themes combined and made his most public works intelligible and disturbing to a wide public, projecting his fears and longings beyond the confines of personal preoccupations on to a level of public awareness that made Klimt a key figure in the cultural life of late nineteenth-century Vienna.

He was an unapologetic artist whose every mark, including abstract decorations, was informed by suggestions of the wealth and the frailty of life. *Hope* (1903) depicts with an unprecedented and immodest directness the profile of a naked contemporary and heavily pregnant young Viennese girl, who stares frankly at the viewer, with flower-studded hair, against a background of anguished figures, a large fish and a skull. The theme of fecundity and hope confronting death is extended to flat and decorative motifs. This is allegory but is also shocking in its emotionally expressive directness, at once beautiful and intensely sinister.

In 1897 Klimt became president of the newly formed Vienna Secession (Vereinigung Bildender Künstler Österreichs), the designer of its first poster and a regular contributor to its square-format periodical *Ver Sacrum*. The Vienna Secession under Klimt embraced design and architecture as much as painting, establishing a brilliant and distinctly Viennese contribution to Jugendstil.

Major undertakings by Klimt during the Vienna Secession period included murals for the Great Hall of Vienna University (*Philosophy*, 1899–1907; *Medicine*, 1900–7; *Jurisprudence*, 1903–7) which caused a scandal, and the *Beethoven Frieze* designed around Max Klinger's polychrome sculpture of the seated Beethoven displayed at the Vienna Secession in 1902, Klimt's frieze attempting a visual equivalent of Beethoven's music and a homage to the composer whose imagination inspired so many Symbolists.

His last major decorations were no exception. In 1908 he collaborated with the architect Josef Hoffmann at the Palais Stoclet in Brussels, enclosing its dining room in a frieze that extended the tendrils of a tree of life in curling branches round the entire room, catching in their flow two embracing lovers in precious robes so densely linked and inter-twined as to be visually inseparable, a single unit, allegorical, expressive and decorative.

Klimt travelled widely and received many honours. He was an honorary professor at the Academies of Munich and Vienna in 1917. He died the following year.

Further reading

See: Fritz Novotny and Johannes Dobai, *Gustav Klimt* (1956); Werner Hofmann, *Gustav Klimt* (1972); F. Whitford, *Artists in Context: Gustav Klimt* (1993).

JOHN MILNER

KOONING, Willem de

See: DE KOONING, WILLEM

KOONS, Jeff
1955–
US artist

Jeff Koons became infamous in the 1980s for his appropriations of commodity objects and images, having others make his artwork, and, later, his extensive self-promotional campaigns. Koons was initially grouped with other artists exploring commodification and simulation in art and culture as an alternative to the emergence of neo-expressionist painting in the early 1980s. In his early works, Koons appropriated the everyday consumer object with the intention of exposing the ways in which it posited a classed subject. He increasingly became interested in those objects he understood to be directed at the middle and lower classes (that is, kitsch) and elevating them to the status of finely crafted art objects.

Beginning in late 1987, Koons shifted his strategy from appropriating consumer objects to the more ephemeral commodity of celebrity itself. He began to cultivate an image of the artist as rock star – a parallel often made by critics and journalists in the booming art market of the 1980s. Koons's new attitude and posturing manifested themselves most infamously in a series of art magazine ads in 1988. These full-page advertisements featured him attended by bikini-clad women, snuggling a pig, or teaching a class of small children. Though criticized as mere self-aggrandizement, the art magazine advertisements take on, as their object of appropriation and transformation, the ideal persona of the artist. These advertisements announced a series of kitsch-inspired works which consisted of large-scale porcelain sculptures of the Pink Panther, Michael Jackson, St John the Baptist, and others. One of the works in the exhibition also resulted in a major legal battle when a greetings card photographer sued Koons for unattributed use of his work for the sculpture *String of Puppies* (1988). With far-reaching implications for artistic license and appropriation, Koons's translation of the photograph into a polychromed statue was deemed plagiarism.

His next series, *Made in Heaven* (1989–91), further pursued his focus on his self-image. Beginning as a collaborative project between Koons and his wife at that time Ilona Staller, *Made in Heaven* initially encompassed film, sculpture, advertisements and painting. Though the film was never made, controversy erupted over the sexually explicit polychromed wood and porcelain sculptures and oil-ink paintings (mechanically printed from photographs on to canvas so they would have the status and durability of painting). Prior to her involvement with Koons, Staller (also known as 'La Cicciolina') had been an erotic performance artist (appearing in a number of pornographic films) as well as a member of the Italian parliament.

In response to the lukewarm critical reception of the *Made in Heaven* series, he created his monumental *Puppy* (1992) – arguably one of Koons's most successful works. The 37-foot-tall topiary dog encapsulates Koons's interests in making heroic those objects normally excluded from the high art context. Koons embraced the sweetness of kitsch with *Puppy* but, as with all of his earlier work, did not affect an ironic posture. *Puppy* is both monumental and cute, grandiose and humble. Though rooted in the long tradition of garden design, the medium of topiary has come to be degraded as *faux opulence* – that is, kitsch. *Puppy* capitalizes on this to create a triumphant celebration of the warm, the fuzzy and the cute that provides an alternative to the ennui and angst that characterize modern definitions of art, public sculpture and the artist. After a hiatus, Koons has continued to create larger, even monumental art with works such as over-sized shiny metal balloon dogs that dominate even large gallery spaces. In all of these works, the fragile childish object takes on the scale and presence normally associated with geometric abstract sculpture from the 1960s and 1970s.

The most discomforting element of Koons's art and persona has consistently been his lack of irony. Modern art has often exploited kitsch to disparage popular culture, but by affecting earnestness Koons breaks with the assumptions connected with high art. Instead of attempting to dissolve the artificial distinctions between high or low in art or assume a traditionally avant-garde posture through the ironic substitution of bad taste for good art, Koons effects the much more radical and disconcerting intervention of naively embracing it all.

Further reading

The clearest instance of Koons's self-fashioning is *The Jeff Koons Handbook* (1992). That same year there were simultaneous international retrospective exhibitions of Koons organized by the San Francisco Museum of Modern Art, the Aarhus Kunstmuseum and the Stedelijk Museum, Amsterdam. In addition to the catalogues for those exhibitions, see also Angelika Muthesius, *Jeff Koons* (1992). For more recent work, see *Jeff Koons: Easyfun-Ethereal* (2000), *Jeff Koons* (Kunsthaus Bregenz, 2001), and *Jeff Koons: Pictures 1980–2002* (2002).

DAVID J. GETSY

KROPOTKIN, Petr Alekseyevich

1842–1921

Russian anarchist

Born in Moscow to a wealthy aristocratic family, Kropotkin's education in the Corps of Pages was intended to make him either a courtier or a soldier. His brief period as a page to Alexander II left him sceptical of the emperor's liberal reputation. From 1862 to 1867 Kropotkin served in the army in Siberia, where he took a great interest in natural history and geology. He then studied mathematics at St Petersburg University and pursued his scientific investigations with such distinction that in 1871 he was invited to become secretary to the Imperial Geographical Society. He declined the post on the grounds that he had no right to such pleasures when others were struggling for a scrap of bread.

This was a crucial decision. Kropotkin now devoted himself to political activities and joined a socialist propaganda circle; he was duly imprisoned in 1874. After escaping to Switzerland in 1876 he won a reputation as the leading exponent of European anarchism. His activities led to expulsion from Switzerland and imprisonment in France. In 1886 he settled in England where he made a living by writing and speaking, principally on anarchism. Following the February Revolution of 1917 in Russia, Kropotkin was able to return to his native land. Although on good terms with Kerensky, prime minister of the Provisional Government, Kropotkin declined a ministerial post on principle. After the October Revolution his relationship with **Lenin's** Communist dictatorship was distinctly uneasy until his death in 1921.

Kropotkin was unrelenting in his opposition to the power of the state. His own strength was as a peaceful propagandist, though he could have been more prompt to condemn bomb-throwing by other anarchists. The decision of 1871 was indeed crucial but it was not a turning-point. Kropotkin had been distressed for some time at the misery of others less distinguished and privileged than himself. He was influenced by Herzen, Proudhon and Bakunin. **Marx's** emphasis on conflict and his attempts to reduce human behaviour to pseudo-scientific laws had little appeal for Kropotkin, who had an acute insight into the totalitarian potential of Marxism. To this extent he aligned himself with Bakunin against Marx; but Kropotkin's positive cast of mind distinguishes him from Bakunin, whose frivolous bellicosity led him to concentrate primarily on destruction.

Kropotkin's central doctrine was mutual aid, or a constructive refutation of sociological Darwinism. He respected **Darwin** for his *Origin of Species* (1859) and did not deny that the struggle for existence was an element in evolution. However, he thought that some of Darwin's followers, notably **T.H. Huxley** in the late 1880s, were excessively preoccupied with the struggle. Still more unsound, in Kropotkin's judgement, was the application of this evolutionary principle to society: as a counterbalance he cited the way in which animals protect each other and drew a sociological parallel with the co-operation among groups of peasants and tribesmen which he had observed in Siberia. Kropotkin was also strongly influenced on a visit to Switzerland by the craftsmen's guilds of the Jura watchmakers which he regarded as living proof of the possibility of co-operative activity without state intervention.

Private property would, in Kropotkin's system, be abolished so that both products and the means of production could be shared. Equal rewards for all would replace wages, regardless of the contribution to society made by the recipient. Although division of labour destroyed the human spirit, industrialization was to be welcomed: the machine would provide men with sufficient leisure to recoup their spiritual energies in agricultural exertions. It will come as no surprise in this context that Kropotkin was friendly with **William Morris** and admired by **Tolstoy**. The only form of organization envisaged by Kropotkin was the spontaneous federation of those directly involved to make practical arrangements for their work and daily life. These federations would collaborate with others to make larger groupings. The structure would start from the bottom and work upwards to avoid creating a state, socialist or otherwise, which would always intervene from on high in the individual's affairs.

Though neither a Marxist nor a Leninist, Kropotkin was a communist in his own way. If his trust in goodwill (doubtless stemming from his own benevolent nature) was naive and Utopian, his humane reflections are still a valuable corrective to the usual viciousness of Russian radical thought.

In his time Kropotkin was an important figure in European radical circles, though more on account of his character than his ideas. He was later to influence **Gandhi** and to enjoy something of a cult revival among youth movements of the left in the 1960s and 1970s.

Further reading

See: Kropotkin: *Memoirs of a Revolutionist* (1971); *Mutual Aid* (1972); *The Conquest of Bread* (1972); *Selected Writings on Anarchism and Revolution*, ed. Martin A. Miller (1970); *The Essential Kropotkin*, ed. Emile Capouya and Keitha Tompkins (1976). About Kropotkin: George Woodcock and Ivan Avakumović, *The Anarchist Prince* (1950); Martin A. Miller, *Kropotkin* (1976); P. Avrich, *The Russian Anarchists* (1967); Andrzej Walicki, *A History of Russian Thought from the Enlightenment to Marxism* (1980); George Woodcock, *Peter Kropotkin: From Prince to Rebel* (1998); S. Mukherjee and S. Ramaswamy, *Prince Peter Kropotkin: His Thoughts and Works* (2002).

R.M. DAVISON

KUBRICK, Stanley

1928–99

US/UK filmmaker

Kubrick was one of the most stylish, influential and controversial directors of the twentieth century. *Paths of Glory* (1957) was banned in France for nearly twenty years, while he withdrew *A Clockwork Orange* (1971) from UK circulation in 1974, a situation prevailing till after his death. That he had this power over his film's distribution showed the exceptional position he developed in the film industry, an artistically independent director with the full backing of Warner Brothers.

He was truly a maker of modern audio-visual culture. Like **Godard**, Kubrick left an indelible personal imprint on the wide range of genres he negotiated, while never becoming typecast. Kubrick's narratives mixed sardonic humour (*Dr Strangelove*, 1964), mordant social critique (*Clockwork Orange*, *Full Metal Jacket*, 1987), adventurous combinations of timeframes (*The Killing*, 1956; *2001: A Space Odyssey*, 1968) and an almost fundamentalist **Freudianism** (*Lolita*, 1962), *Eyes Wide Shut*, 1999). Across screen history, Kubrick super-intended some of the most enduring images (the airborne primeval bone transformed into a space station in *2001*), performances (Malcolm McDowell in *Clockwork Orange*, Peter Sellers' multiple roles in *Dr Strangelove*, and his dialogue with James Mason in the opening sequence of *Lolita*) and sounds. He continues to influence directors beyond their homages (*Paths of Glory* in Jeunet's *A Very Long Engagement* (2004) and sundry allusions in Becker's *Goodbye Lenin* (2003), not forgetting **Spielberg's** completion of Kubrick's unfinished project, *A.I.: Artificial Intelligence*, 2001).

He pushed pre-existing music, both popular and classical, in new directions on the soundtrack. His symbiosis between image and sound, above all with his use of Ligeti (*2001*, *The Shining* (1980), *Eyes Wide Shut*), is on a par with Bresson, **Welles** or the Tavianis. Accompanying this assuredness was an instinct for choreography, of camera movements, of human figures and, in *2001*, of weightlessness. In *Barry Lyndon* (1975), music functions as a sustained courtly dance, animating human remoteness and cultivated natural splendour. When the **Rolling Stones'** *Paint It Black* begins over the end credits to *Full Metal Jacket*, it is the signature-tune of this artist, capable of Baroque grotesqueness but also of a deadly surreal logic (both in this film, polar opposite of the contemporaneous *Platoon*, and in the unfadingly contemporary *Dr Strangelove*).

Kubrick's range no doubt owed partly to his spanning both sides of the Atlantic, like

Losey, with his roots in the US and a move to the UK, the reverse of **Hitchcock's** trajectory. This mix further melts down nationalism and national cinema as categories: *Clockwork Orange*, not least its use of Beethoven's Ninth, is unsettling as a gloss on Western civilization, certainly not just British or German society. A constant irritant to the mainstream, Kubrick is considered by his critics to be masking deficiencies in characterization by his technical wizardry and logic (candlelit scenes in *Barry Lyndon*, which minimize depth of field, elsewhere matching a luminous painterly quality, the whole contextualized by a zoom lens functioning like the iris out of silent cinema). Females are often absent, rarely three-dimensional. His particular use of voice-over does not reveal psychology, but compounds enigmas.

The richness and the pitfalls of his films are synthesized in *Eyes Wide Shut*, a longstanding project. Here stylistic mastery diverges ever more from content, as Kubrick takes up the wider challenge to film of conveying psychological processes through an illusion of realism. Via his revered model Max Ophüls he transposes a Schnitzler Novelle to a millennial setting, attempting to translate its heavily Freudian influence into more general fantasms of the gaze, and the mind's fevered gaze. But a couple celebrated by Hollywood, the loneliness of the nuclear family, and non-specific Christmas trappings lack the social anchoring of Schnitzler's carnevalistic hall of mirrors, the iridescent decadence of Viennese class-based society, and rituals steeped in theatricality. The satirical undertow of **Shostakovich's** waltz, and Ligeti's ominous repetition of two adjacent notes, like this couple going nowhere, again prove inspired musical choices. But the secret society episode, an evocation of a misunderstood pre-Christian sex rite (see *The Da Vinci Code*, 412), becomes a protracted, cold orgy without historical roots. The film combines the preoccupations, narrative and stylistic, of an intense career, while its question marks also apply to film's place within modern culture. Kubrick's oeuvre assures his prominent place in modern film culture, which he at once unmade and remade.

Further reading

Filmography, beyond films mentioned above: *Fear and Desire* (1953); *Killer's Kiss* (1955); *Spartacus* (1960); Biography: John Baxter, *Stanley Kubrick: A Biography* (1997); Tony Pipolo, 'The Modernist and Misanthrope: The Cinema of Stanley Kubrick', *Cinéaste*, Vol. 27, No. 2 (Spring 2002) (survey of recent books and DVDs).

ROGER HILLMAN

KUHN, Thomas Samuel

1922–96

US historian and philosopher of science

Born in Cincinnati, USA, Thomas Kuhn set his sights originally on a career as scientist, and after taking his degree at Harvard he worked for a time in the Radio Research Laboratory. But life in a large laboratory fell far short of his youthful idea of a research career. He was hampered on the one side by intellectual constraints, on the other side by social pressures. Professional science was more frustrating, less interesting than he had imagined. He escaped, becoming a junior fellow of Harvard in 1948, and a member of the Faculty of the History of Science in 1951. By 1961 he was a professor in the history of science at Berkeley, and in 1964 he moved to a similar chair at Princeton, before finishing his career at the Massachusetts Institute of Technology.

The fruit of his years of research and reflection on the role of science in the development of human cognition was his book *The Structure of Scientific Revolutions* published in 1962. It was an intellectual *tour de force*: a new voice; a new viewpoint on science at once unique, wide-ranging and devastatingly near the truth. Although it is a book 'about' science, rather than 'of' science, it has probably done as much to colour our awareness of the meaning of science as any single scientific event in the period since World War II.

Until Kuhn produced his essay, it was customary for philosophers and historians to treat the development of science with a certain amount of idealization. Science, it was agreed, represented a systematic attempt to marshal rational thought and purposive experiment to the task of understanding the physical and the biological. It was natural, therefore, to think of science as itself being a systematically rational enterprise. But Kuhn showed that, when examined in detail, step by step, science was a far less rational exercise than had previously been supposed. Science and scientific communities, he argued, are as much structured to resist breakthroughs as they are to compel them. Any scientific theory functions as a 'paradigm': a point of view (and a method of analysis based on that point of view) which is thought to be worth following. But why is it thought to be worth following? On what grounds does the credibility of a particular paradigm ultimately rest? The official, pre-Kuhnian view was that credibility rested on the balancing of empirical evidence and the fielding of logical argument. But Kuhn showed that, to a surprising extent, the leading paradigms which have been followed in science have not been, initially, very satisfactorily grounded *either* in evidence *or* in deductive argument. They have been, rather, imaginative leaps: hunches, which have given people the feeling 'that something like this must be true'. In a word, scientists have adopted paradigms for reasons which they have been unable fully to render into the public discourse.

Similarly, relationships between scientific schools of thought seem to have been frequently less than satisfactory. Kuhn introduces the idea of the 'incommensurability' of old and new scientific points of view: there is no common ground, he argues, between paradigms. If paradigms were fully rational, there would be such common ground; but as they are not, there is none. And education does not escape Kuhn's witheringly accurate glance. Typically the insights and methods of a particular paradigm are transmitted in the classroom by the primitive pedagogy of 'Do it this way and follow me!'

Nor is the life of science quite what previous theorists thought it was. Kuhn distinguishes 'normal' science from 'revolutionary' science. Normal science, Kuhn suggests, operates in an hierarchical way, defensively, with some complacency. It consists, not in any earth-shattering intellectual adventure, but in the patient application of existing paradigms to new cases, and to new variations of old cases. Most normal science is successful. Most science is normal science.

Kuhn's book, then, has altered the vocabulary, the perspectives, the frontiers, of our whole conception of science, of science's contribution to knowledge, of science's place in society. Kuhn perceived what previous theorists had overlooked; but it is, in the end, his unique blend of theoretical generalization and historically accurate particularity which creates the total impact. And Kuhn's theory can be applied, with minimum modification, to almost any field.

Kuhn's philosophy of science has the unfortunate characteristic that the more successful it is, the more it creates the preconditions for its own reversal. Once it has been widely perceived that science has operated irrationally in the past, the chances that it will continue to do this inevitably diminish. Scientific education is only one area where scientists have tried to remedy the unsatisfactoriness revealed by Kuhn. Some scientific empires (e.g. Barrow's) have been given up without revolution. This does occasionally happen, as it does in the political arena (India, French Africa). And there is mathematics. Kuhn overlooked the Peircean interpretation of mathematics as 'the science of hypothesis', the science whose role is, in effect, to be unimpressed by paradigms.

It is a measure of the importance of Kuhn's thought that it has shaken scientists' belief in their own rationality. Science will never be quite the same again; scientists have become more self-critical; more on their guard against the irrational bewitchments of a paradigm. This is less than satisfying for Kuhn, but healthier for science.

Further reading

Other works include: *The Copernican Revolution: Planetary Astronomy in the Development of Western Thought* (1957); *Sources for the History of Quantum Physics* (1967). See: Thomas Nickles (ed.), *Thomas Kuhn* (2002); Keay Davidson, *The Death of Truth: Thomas S. Kuhn and the Evolution of Ideas* (2006).

CHRISTOPHER ORMELL

KUROSAWA, AKIRA

1910–98

Japanese film director and screenplay writer

Born in Tokyo, Kurosawa studied art before joining the Photo Chemical Laboratory (PCL) in 1936. PCL was soon to form part of a merger that formally became the Tōhō Studios in 1937. At Tōhō, Kurosawa worked as an assistant director and scriptwriter, ultimately becoming principal assistant director to Yamamoto Kajirō on, among other films, the 1941 production *Horse* (*Uma*), before making his directorial debut *Sanshiro Sugata* (*Sugata Sanshirō*) in 1943. In keeping with the wartime ethos, this judo saga, based on a popular novel of the time, emphasizes the ultimate supremacy of the spiritual over brutish physical force. This film was followed in 1944 with the docu-drama *The Most Beautiful* (*Ichiban utsukushiku*) based on the lives of a group of young women working in a munitions factory during the latter stages of the war.

In the immediate post-defeat period, under the auspices of the Allied Occupation Forces, Kurosawa went on to direct five films which further enhanced his reputation; these included *No Regrets for Our Youth* (*Waga seishun ni kuinashi*, 1946), *Drunken Angel* (*Yoidore tenshi*, 1948), and *Stray Dog* (*Norainu*, 1949). These films, all characterized by strong individuals who struggle against uncompromising social odds, ultimately asserting their will over social forces that would destroy weaker characters, brought together the actors who would form the core company (including Mifune Toshirō and Shimura Takashi) for many of Kurosawa's post-occupation productions. While Kurosawa achieved recognition and acclaim for his screenplays and films in Japan during this period, it was in 1951 with his esoteric adaptation of the two short stories by the Japanese novelist Akutagawa Ryūnosuke that brought Japanese cinema to international attention when *Rashomon* (*Rashōmon*, 1950) was awarded the Golden Lion at the Venice Film Festival. Set in pre-modern Japan, the plot questions the subjective nature of 'truth' as four people recount the events of a murder. There followed a series of international successes throughout the 1950s which firmly established Kurosawa as Japan's best known *auteur* – the Berlin Film Festival 1954 *Living* (*Ikiru*, 1952) and 1959 *The Hidden Fortress* (*Kakushi toride no sanakunin*, 1958), and the Venice Film Festival in 1954 *Seven Samurai* (*Shichinin no samurai*, 1954).

Always considered within critical writings as Japan's most 'Western' of film directors, Kurosawa adapted classical Western texts to the Japanese *mise-en-scène* – **Dostoyevsky's** *The Idiot* (*Hakuchi*, 1951), **Maxim Gorky's** play *The Lower Depths* (*Donzoko*, 1957), Shakespeare's *Macbeth* became *Throne of Blood* (*Kumonosujō*, 1957) and *King Lear* became the historical epic *Ran* (1985). However, it was in the 1960s with the release of *Yojimbo the Bodyguard* (*Yōjinbō*, 1961) and its sequel the following year *Sanjuro* (*Tsubaki Sanjūrō*, 1962) that Kurosawa challenged the defining conventions of the post-war Japanese period drama (*jidaigeki*). Through the innovative incorporation of Western cinematic and narrative devices, Kurosawa linked the *jidaigeki* to the Hollywood cowboy film, which in turn inspired Hollywood remakes; *Seven Samurai* became *The Magnificent Seven* (John Sturges) in 1960, and *Yojimbo the Bodyguard* was remade as *A Fistful of Dollars* (Sergio Leone) in 1964. In terms of industry collaboration, this cross-fertilization resulted in the joint Tōhō and 20th Century Fox production *Kagemusha* (1980).

Within Japanese historiography, *Yojimbo* and *Sanjuro* are linked to the emergence of the 'cruel' (*zankoku*) period film. These films are characterized by a shift from stylization to 'realism' through a return to black-and-white filming, an emphasis on depth of field, and a realistic display of blood (or in the case of *Yojimbo* the sound of swords being plunged into bodies) in dynamic action sequences. Kurosawa's adaptation of Western-style montage linked this display of violence to speed of action, thus breaking with the conventions of classic Japanese *jidaigeki* derived from the kabuki and noh theatrical forms. Through these devices, Kurosawa's period films directly challenged the sensibility of nostalgia central to the genre of the 1950s as 'scruffy' *rōnin* (masterless *samurai*) sporting 'designer stubble' roam aimlessly around windswept, dusty streets.

Allied to the inclusion of blood and realistic sound effects was a reconsideration of the value of violence in the genre. Reflecting the moral ambiguities of the 1960s, the ethical distinctions between characters become increasingly blurred in these films. The hero of *Yojimbo* (Mifune Toshirō) intervenes in the town politics, not out of any altruistic sense of restoring justice for the commoners but because the situation 'seems interesting' (*omoshirosō*). The final confrontation between Sanjuro (Mifune Toshirō) and his adversary (Nakadai Tatsuya) is not a contest between 'good' and 'evil' but a quarrel between two equals.

At the time of Japan's re-entry into international politics and economics after the disasters of World War II, Kurosawa bridged an ideological divide between a Western individualist sensibility epitomized by the priorities of the occupation film policy and an earlier Neo-Confucian derived worldview. Throughout his oeuvre, both in his adaptations of Western texts or through a Westernization of Japanese genre films, he presented a humanist vision that transcends geographical borders. To try to trace the genealogy of his filmmaking to specific influences is perhaps futile, as he clearly drew from a broad range of classical Japanese theatrical and literary forms, and was also influenced by the Russian classics as well as the John Ford cowboy films of the Hollywood tradition. What is perhaps more profitable to reflect on is the breadth of his vision, a vision that encompassed cinema as a communicative medium on a truly universal scale – a vision recognized in 1985 in Japan where he received the Order of Culture and in 1990 when he was awarded a special honorary Oscar for his lifetime achievements.

Further reading

See: Donald Richie, *The Films of Kurosawa Akira* (1984); David Desser, *The Samurai Films of Kurosawa Akira* (1988); Stephen Prince, *The Warrior's Camera: The Cinema of Akira Kurosawa*, (1991); James Goodwin, *Akira Kurosawa and Intertextual Cinema* (1994); Mitsuhiro Yoshimoto, *Kurosawa* (2001); Isolde Standish, *A New History of Japanese Cinema: A Century of Narrative Film* (2005).

ISOLDE STANDISH

L

LACAN, Jacques

1901–81

French psychoanalyst

In the second half of the twentieth century, Jacques Lacan was the psychoanalyst who perhaps did most to confirm the importance and the utterly revolutionary character of **Freud's** discovery of the unconscious. If, despite all of the controversies surrounding its allegedly unscientific character, psycho-analysis is today still widely practised and if its theory continues abundantly to influence many academic disciplines, this is to a great extent due to Lacan's multi-faceted ability to update both Freudian clinics and conceptual models by means of the most recent elaborations of structural linguistics (**Saussure**, Jakobson), structural anthropology (**Lévi-Strauss**) and post-Hegelian philosophy (Kojève, **Heidegger**).

Lacan was born in Paris to a prosperous, middle-class Roman Catholic family, studied medicine and then specialized in psychiatry; his doctoral thesis on self-punishing paranoia, published as *De la psychose paranoïaque dans ses rapports avec la personnalité* (1932), enjoyed a great success in avant-garde literary circles for its treatment of human knowledge as essentially paranoiac and resulted in Lacan's becoming a contributor to the surrealist journal *Le Minotaure*. In the same years, he also began his psychoanalytic treatment with Rudolph Loewenstein and assiduously attended Alexander Kojève's influential lectures on Hegel together with other French intellectuals such as Georges Bataille and Raymond Queneau. He made his first appearance on the psychoanalytic scene as early as 1936 when he presented a paper on the so-called 'mirror stage' of a child's development at the 14th Congress of the International Psycho-analytic Association. Although his articles from the 1930s and 1940s were already highly original contributions to Freudian theory (see among others, 'Le temps logique' and 'Propos sur la causalité psychique', now in *Écrits*, 1966), as well as 'Les complexes familiaux dans la formation de l'individu', now in *Autres écrits*, (2001), it was nevertheless only in 1953, with the beginning of his famous 'seminar' – which he held uninterruptedly until 1979 – and his first rupture with the psychoanalytic establishment, that his controversial thinking captivated the intellectual world of the time.

The fact that Lacan's principal published work – provocatively entitled *Écrits* ('Writings') – mostly consists of written re-elaborations of earlier lectures suggests that his teaching was first and foremost oral. In the 1970s he assigned his son-in-law the task of establishing the text of his annual seminars on the basis of existing shorthand notes, but so far only eleven volumes have been published in French and only six of these have been translated into English; this means that the transmission of Lacanian psychoanalysis continues to rely principally on the circulation of unauthorized transcripts. What clearly transpires from both the openness of the work-in-progress of the seminars and the notoriously cryptic recapitulations offered by the *Écrits* is the fact that Lacan's systematic 'return to Freud' is never finally settled but is constantly subjected to the most radical critical scrutiny.

While it is crucial to emphasize that Lacan tends to rehabilitate every 'old' theory within the framework of a 'new', increasingly complex elaboration, it is nevertheless possible to divide his work into three consecutive stages.

The first is characterized by a predominant interest in the order of the Imaginary. This is the realm of instinctual life which presides over animal sexuality and should be regarded as fundamentally disrupted in human beings. An animal is instinctively predisposed to recognize the image of the body of another animal of the same species; on the other hand, man identifies himself with the completeness of the image of another human body, and thus alienates himself in it, in order to compensate for his original helplessness – a baby cannot walk and is absolutely dependent on adults to carry out every one of its basic vital tasks. These considerations led Lacan to consider the ego as a paranoiac construction made up of a succession of alienating identifications with the image of the other: thus, at this stage, the role of psychoanalysis is to disalienate the subject's unconscious desire from these identifications. In this way, Lacan stood diametrically opposed to mainstream post-Freudian theories which understood psycho-analytic treatment as a means of enabling the ego to 'colonize' the unconscious and consequently aimed at assisting the patient's adaptation to society. Lacan scrutinizes these topics in articles such as 'The Mirror Stage as Formative of the Function of the I' (1949) and 'Aggressivity in Psychoanalysis' (1948), as well as in *The Seminar. Book I* (1987).

The second stage in Lacan's development began in the early 1950s, as he devoted himself to a more precise discussion of the Freudian unconscious and proposed that its nature is essentially symbolic. Not only does the subject undergo an imaginary alienation but is also (unconsciously) 'spoken' by language understood as a structure. The unconscious is structured like a language: hence, far from simply being identifiable with sheer irrationality, it follows a specific logic which manifests itself in phenomena such as dreams, bungled actions, slips of the tongue and psycho-somatic symptoms. In his seminal article 'Function and Field of Speech and Language' (1953), Lacan suggested that alienation in language could be overcome; this overcoming would in turn enable the subject to overcome his imaginary alienation. At this stage, Lacan thus appeared to believe that unconscious desire can fully be realized: it is enough for it to be recognized by the Other (subject) through psychoanalytic treatment, since desire is basically the desire to be desired by the Other (subject). The key reference for Lacan here was Hegel's dialectical notion of desire as propounded by Kojève. On the other hand, a few years later, in his article 'The Agency of the Letter in the Unconscious' (1957) – as well as in *Le Séminaire, livre IV* (1994) and *Le Séminaire, livre V* (1998), from 1956 to 1958 – Lacan realized that alienation in language is unsurpassable. The subject's individual desire is irremediably subjected to the universal field of language and to its laws. Here Lacan's key reference – which allowed him to rethink the Freudian notion of the Oedipus complex in structural terms – was Saussure's linguistics (largely in the form of Jakobson's re-elaboration).

Although Lacan's name is often associated with the movement of structuralism and although the notion of structure undoubtedly played a significant role in his theories, we should remember that, in opposition to structuralist and post-structuralist talk of a 'death of the subject', for Lacan the notion of subjectivity was an essential precondition of psychoanalytic experience. The impossibility of reducing his thought to structuralism becomes clearer if we take into consideration the work that he carried out in the 1960s and 1970s in which the order of the Real acquires increasing pre-eminence. This pre-eminence characterizes the third stage in Lacan's development. Here the unconscious structure – and, similarly, language *tout-court* – is considered as inherently limited by a non-assimilible non-symbolic remainder which is at the same time a prerequisite for the very functioning of the unconscious. Lacan identifies this 'real' dimension with the psycho-sexual pleasure-in-pain of enjoyment (*jouissance*): this notion results from a reworking of Freud's idea – rejected by many of his followers – that human tendencies also include a masochistic death drive. The aim of psychoanalysis is now to allow the subject to adopt a different stance in relation to his unconscious enjoyment. During this period, the clinical and theoretical study of enjoyment obliges Lacan to examine the ethical and political implications of psychoanalysis: he carries out these investigations most thoroughly in *The Seminar. Book VII* (1992) – held in 1959–60 – and *Le Séminaire, livre XVII* (1991) – held in 1969–70.

It is indubitably Lacan's work on the Real which today dominates Lacanian practice and has had the most profound repercussions for the most advanced formulations of philosophy and political theory (including Alain Badiou), as well as cultural studies and film theory – especially through the pioneering comparative readings of Slavoj Žižek who is also largely responsible for Lacan's recent academic fortune in the Anglophone world.

While Lacan remains more widely known for his theoretical achievements, it is nevertheless important not to underestimate a series of innovations that he introduced to the conception and conduct of psychoanalytic treatment: (1) the lack of distinction between 'training analysis' and 'therapeutic analysis': analysands who enter analysis in order to become analysts should not be treated differently from analysands who enter analysis with a view to being cured of a given symptom; (2) the institution of the 'passe': an analysand logically ends his analysis only when he is able convincingly to transmit the meaning of what he has achieved within it; (3) the variable length of the sessions; (4) the reformulation of the transference–countertransference phenomenon in terms of the relationship established between the demand of interpretation that

the analysand presents to the analyst – whom he sees as a 'subject supposed to know' – and a complementary 'desire of the analyst' which is a desire without object.

Further reading

Other works include: *Écrits: A Selection*, 1977, retranslated with major changes in 2002; articles mentioned above whose title is translated into English appear in this selection while those whose title is left in the original French do not. Those of Lacan's seminars which have been published in book form and are not mentioned above are the following: *The Seminar. Book II* (1988); *The Seminar. Book III* (1993); *The Seminar. Book XI* (1977); *The Seminar. Book XX* (1998); other seminars which have been published in French but remain as yet untranslated are *Le Séminaire, livre VIII* (1991) and *Le Séminaire, livre X* (2004). The most popular account of Lacan's life remains Elisabeth Roudinesco's *Jacques Lacan* (1997). Bruce Fink's volumes *The Lacanian Subject. Between Language and Jouissance* (1995) and *A Clinical Introduction to Lacanian Psychoanalysis* (1997) are good general introductions to Lacanian theory and practice.

LORENZO CHIESA

LANG, Fritz
1890–1976
German/US film director

Lang, the most important film director to make a successful transition from the German silent cinema of the 1920s to Hollywood in the 1930s, was born into a bourgeois Catholic family in Vienna in 1890. His early studies in architecture, encouraged by his father, a municipal architect, conflicted with his own interests in the visual arts, particularly the work of **Klimt** and Schiele, and in 1911–12 he left home to globe-trot before settling in Paris in 1913. Here he scraped a living as a commercial artist and became interested in the new art of the cinema. With the outbreak of the Great War, Lang escaped home to Vienna, where he joined up, was promoted to officer, and was wounded and decorated on more than one occasion. In military hospital he began to write film scenarios – three of them known to have been brought to the screen by Joe May during 1917 – and as an actor came to the attention of Erich Pommer's company Decla, which Lang joined in Berlin in 1919. Here he read and wrote scripts and also did some editing and bit-part acting before moving promptly into direction with *Half-Caste* (1919). In this first year with Decla Lang also directed *The Master of Love*, *Hara-Kiri*, *The Wandering Image* and the two-part adventure melodrama *The Spiders*, his first surviving work of the period. In 1920, rapidly emerging as a major young director, Lang married the writer Thea von Harbou, with whom he was to write the majority of his German films, and who also turned several of their scripts into successful novels.

Following *Four Around a Woman* (1920, now lost) Lang directed eight films before fleeing **Hitler's** Germany in 1933. Two of these deal with historical fantasy and legend. *Destiny* (1921) tells its stories of lovers separated by the Angel of Death through a triptych of flashbacks – to the Arabian Nights, to Renaissance Venice, and to Imperial China – while an epic German version of *The Niebelungen* is retold in Lang's two-part film, *Siegfried* and *Kriemhild's Revenge* (1924). Two of Lang's silent films of the 1920s deal on the other hand with futuristic fantasy in the science fiction genre. The spectacular and costly *Metropolis* (1926) recounts the story of a workers' revolt in a visionary city of the future, while *Woman on the Moon* (1928) presents a comic-strip account of a rocket trip to prospect for lunar gold. The other four films of the period draw from the contemporary world of criminality and post-war angst. The two parts of *Dr Mabuse* – *Dr Mabuse the Gambler: A Picture of the Times* and *Inferno: Men of the Times* (1922) – enact the exploits of an unscrupulous master criminal with skills in hypnotism and disguise. His talents are later transferred to his psychiatrist in *The Last Will of Dr Mabuse* (1932–3). Lang's other two chief criminals of the period are the master spy in *The Spy* (1928), and the pathetic child-murderer hunted down by

both police and criminals in Lang's first sound-film, *M* (1931).

The Last Will of Dr Mabuse, drawing links between criminality, dictatorship and mind-control, was immediately banned by Goebbels, but Lang was nonetheless offered charge of the Nazi film industry on the basis of Hitler's admiration for *Metropolis*. Fleeing overnight to Paris, Lang was once more hired by fellow émigré Pommer, now with Fox, to make his only French film, *Liliom* (1933), a tragi-comic fantasy of fairground life starring Charles Boyer. Espoused to National Socialism, however, Thea von Harbou remained in Germany, and divorced Lang. After *Liliom* Lang joined the central European exodus to the United States, where he joined MGM. Here, on the basis of sophisticated work in the popular genres, he was rapidly to become established as one of the leading Hollywood directors and as one of the key *auteurs* discovered by emerging generations of film critics in the 1950s and 1960s in America and Europe.

The bulk of Lang's twenty-two Hollywood films are crime thrillers. These commence with the anti-lynching drama of his first American film, *Fury* (1936), and his drama of the consequences of wrongful conviction, *You Only Live Once* (1937), and then re-emerge in the middle and later 1940s with his celebrated murder dramas in the *film noir* style, full of narrative and visual panache and complexity and frequently reworking some of his German themes such as the 'guilty innocent' and the *femme fatale*: *The Woman in the Window* (1944), *Scarlet Street* (1945), *Secret Beyond the Door* (1948), *House by the River* (1949), *The Blue Gardenia* (1952), *The Big Heat* (1953), *Human Desire* (1954), *While the City Sleeps* (1955) and *Beyond a Reasonable Doubt* (1956).

In the 1940s Lang also directed a group of films dealing with the experience of war – *Man Hunt* (1941), from Geoffrey Household's novel *Rogue Male*, *Hangmen Also Die* (1943), co-written with **Brecht**, a version of **Greene's** novel *Ministry of Fear* (1941), *Cloak and Dagger* (1946) and *An American Guerrilla* *in the Philippines* (1950). He made only three Westerns – *The Return of Frank James* (1940), *Western Union* (1941) and *Rancho Notorious* (1952). His more off-beat work in Hollywood included the anti-realist musical romance with music by Weill, *You and Me* (1938), his version of Clifford Odets's fishing melodrama, *Clash by Night* (1951), and *Moonfleet* (1955), a smuggling yarn set in Britain, his first film in Cinemascope and one of his rare films in colour.

Lang's career as a director ended, as it had begun, in Germany, and consisted of a return to some of his early German themes. *The Indian Tomb* (1958) remade the two films written by Lang for Joe May in the early 1920s – *The Tiger of Bengal* and *The Indian Tomb* itself. His last film, *The Thousand Eyes of Dr Mabuse* (1960), similarly, extends the 1920s Mabuse theme to the contemporary world of industrial intrigue. In 1963, signalling his importance for filmmakers of the new European cinema, the patriarchal Lang appears as himself in **Godard's** film industry love-tragedy, *Contempt*.

Further reading

See: Siegfried Kracauer, *From Caligari to Hitler* (1947); Peter Bogdanovich, *Fritz Lang in America* (1967); Paul M. Jensen, *The Cinema of Fritz Lang* (1969); Lotte H. Eisner, *Fritz Lang* (1976); Steve Jenkins (ed.), *Fritz Lang* (1981); Patrick McGilligan, *Fritz Lang: The Nature of the Beast* (1997); Tom Gunning, *The Films of Fritz Lang* (2000).

PHILIP DRUMMOND

LARKIN, Philip Arthur

1922–85

English poet

Poet and novelist, born in Coventry, educated at St John's College, Oxford – in a generation *mirabilis* that included also John Wain and Kingsley Amis – who has deliberately embraced an ordinary, provincial life (working as a university librarian in Belfast, then in Hull) and cultivated a principled provincialism of outlook and practice in his writing. His two novels, *Jill* (1946, rev. 1964, written in 1943–4 when he was only twenty-one) and *A Girl in Winter* (1947), both rightly rejected by their author as juvenilia, are of little interest now except as early indicators of Larkin's sense of the provincial self (*Jill* is about a northern working-class boy up at Oxford) and of the stimulus the bleaker, wintrier aspects of English life grant him. The poems of *The North Ship* (1945), a juvenile *mélange* soon as toughly denigrated by their author as his novels, indicate rather more clearly Larkin's maturer direction. For among the soothing echoes of the earlier **W.B. Yeats** and odd hints of a young poet too overpowered by **Dylan Thomas** there appear clearly the formal polishings of Robert Graves and the adjectival precisions that come from having attended carefully to **W.H. Auden**:

> Who can confront
> The instantaneous grief of being alone?
> Or watch the sad increase
> Across the mind of this prolific plant,
> Dumb idleness?

Larkin's emerging personal voice, however, only achieved its complete definition much later, with *The Less Deceived* (October 1955) and *The Whitsun Weddings* (1964). Larkin lacks, of course, the prolific output frequently associated with major poets, and there is a marked levelling-out in his *High Windows* volume (1974), but *The Less Deceived* and *The Whitsun Weddings* poems have achieved for him a central, even *the* central position, among English poets of the middle twentieth century.

Larkin's mature style is consciously in an English tradition. His poetry was considerably inspirited by his discovery (he dates it 1946) of **Thomas Hardy's** poetry, his realization of the possibilities of the best Georgian poets, particularly (though no doubt Georgianism was also filtered through Robert Graves and William Empson) **Edward Thomas**. Larkin has rejected influences from overseas. He points to the failure of authors who 'change countries' ('Look at Auden'). He believed the styles and fashions imported and popularized by **Pound** and **Eliot** to be regrettable intrusions into the English tradition. Modernism of all kinds – in painting and music as well as in literature – he rejected (see his volume of jazz reviews, *All What Jazz*, 1970, whose Introduction is his major anti-modernist tract). He blamed the academic industry of literary study for supporting much pretentious literary and critical nonsense (see, for example, 'Posterity' in *High Windows*).

Larkin has been accused of standing for the impoverished achievement, the cowardly practice of a retreating islanded minimalism. His *Oxford Book of Twentieth-Century English Verse* (1973), with its carefully garnered harvest of the provincial and minor, its large welcome to the likes of Hardy, Betjeman and Walter de la Mare, was seized on to illustrate the meagreness of his stand. Admittedly, Larkin's modernist targets are the very largest ones ('whether ... **Parker**, Pound or **Picasso**: it helps us neither to enjoy nor endure'). Granted, too, that the pervasive negativism so frequently noticed by his readers (his fondness, for example, for words beginning with *un-, in-* and *dis-*) settled in *High Windows* into a sometimes dismaying drizzle of envious hostility towards the young and freer ('They fuck you up, your mum and dad'; 'Sexual intercourse began/In nineteen sixty-three/(Which was rather late for me)'). But the gains for his poetry purchased by Larkin's dedicated hostility to the modernistic macrocosm were impressively positive. He became the laureate of the common bloke, the unheroic man in bicycle clips (see 'Church Going' in *The Less Deceived*), the quiet narrator of life in back-street digs on Saturday afternoons as seen from the railway train ('An Odeon went past, a cooling tower,/And someone running up to bowl': lines from 'The Whitsun Weddings' sometimes hailed as the essence of the so-called 'Movement' of the 1950s), the voice of the ordinary chap who would rather stay at

home, listen to his Sidney Bechet records and ponder death (see 'Vers de Société' in *High Windows*). 'I love the commonplace,' he said, 'I lead a very commonplace life. Everyday things are lovely to me.' This means accepting ordinariness – the truth of 'a real girl in a real place' that he celebrates in 'Lines upon a Young Lady's Photograph Album' (*The Less Deceived*). It entails paying attention to the vernacular of 'Mr Bleaney' and his landlady (*The Whitsun Weddings*), to people who like bottled sauce, do the football pools, go to Frinton in the summer and have sisters in Stoke. It's an impressive refusing not to face our common mortality (see, for example, 'Dockery and Son' in *The Whitsun Weddings*). And its success depended on a lovingly close regard (and Larkin wrote some very fine love-poems) for the intransigent stuff of the day-to-day – a quotidian reality that Larkin's language constantly animates as it unflaggingly presents us with toughly bitten-off metonymic gobbets of it for our continual delight and illumination.

Further reading

See: Anthony Thwaite (ed.), *Selected Letters of Philip Larkin 1940–85* (1992); David Timms, *Philip Larkin* (1974); Blake Morrison, *The Movement* (1980); Andrew Motion, *Philip Larkin* (1982); D. Salwak, *Philip Larkin: The Man and His Work* (1989); Anthony Thwaite (ed.), *Further Requirements: Interviews, Broadcasts, Statements and Reviews, 1952–85* (2002); A.T. Tolley (ed.), *Early Poems* (2005); Richard Bradford, *Then Fear: The Life of Philip Larkin* (2005).

VALENTINE CUNNINGHAM

LAWRENCE, David Herbert

1885–1930

English novelist, poet, playwright and artist

The reputation of D.H. Lawrence has suffered many vicissitudes but he is now placed among the greatest English writers. Condemned as a reactionary in the Marxizing 1930s, he became a major influence on

English writing during the regionalist revival of the 1950s, largely on the strength of his third novel, *Sons and Lovers* (1913). This therapeutic venture into psychological realism, admired now for its exploration of adolescent sexuality, vivid dramatization of family conflicts (influenced by **Freud**), the scrupulous authenticity of its local colour (the mining country of Nottinghamshire and Derbyshire where Lawrence grew up), and the new intensity it imparted to the genre of the *Bildungsroman*, earned Lawrence abuse as well as praise from his contemporaries, whose repeated accusations of 'formlessness' derived, as Lawrence well knew, from class resentment and sexual prudery. Much rewritten and in many places painfully confessional, *Sons and Lovers* is the record of a personal struggle between the son and the (bourgeois) mother and (working-class) father in a style which Lawrence himself criticized almost immediately as 'hard and violent' and 'full of sensation and presentation', no doubt referring in this way to the moral over-determination of certain episodes. The novel represented, however, a major artistic and personal breakthrough for its author, being much less self-consciously literary than his two earlier novels, *The White Peacock* (1911), a technically insecure work, the main interest of which lies in the way it prefigures the key motifs of his last novel, *Lady Chatterley's Lover*, and *The Trespasser* (1912), a **Wagnerian** mythological romance with a **Dostoevskian** finale, the product of an intense artistic sensibility working with second-hand materials.

Only when Lawrence had exorcized the 'cultured' mother and come to terms with his psychological problem, which he was able to do in *Sons and Lovers* with the help of Frieda, wife of his German tutor at Nottingham University College, with whom he eloped in 1912, could he mature as man and artist. A prolific poet, influenced by **Whitman** and praised by **Pound** for his 'modernity' of image and movement, Lawrence, whose poems were very personal right up to the posthumous *Ship of Death* (1933), recorded his sense of liberation in the significantly entitled collection *Look! We Have Come Through!* (1917), his third volume of verse. This maturation coincided with the First World War and a growing sense of disintegration and disorientation in European civilization. In 1913 he began writing *The Sisters*, a work of epic proportions charting the evolution of a family generation by generation from a mythic Genesis to an Apocalypse corresponding more or less with the war. In the first part of this work, *The Rainbow* (published in 1915 and suppressed at once as immoral on sexual and political grounds), Lawrence builds up a massive cyclical interpretation of history in which the organic rhythms of the life of a farming family within a rooted community are shown responding and reacting to the pressures of industrialization, with a consequent intensification, atomization and individuation of consciousness as well as growing ideological conflicts. The emergence of a recognizably 'modern' (i.e. sharply individuated and explicit) expression of sexual desire and sexual anxiety, the search for a sexual identity, embodied above all in the novel's ultimate protagonist and heroine, Ursula, are accompanied by experimentation in the presentation of character which Lawrence, in a famous letter of 1914, compared to the techniques of the Italian Futurist poets and painters. F.R. Leavis's high praise of the novel helped to establish it as a classic in direct relation to the English 'great tradition'; but it has more in common with Emily Brontë than with **George Eliot** and should in any case be read in relation to its 'sequel' (the continuation of the projected *Sisters* novel) *Women in Love* (1921), in which the intricately woven 'rainbow' of history and myth is unwoven, painfully and obsessively, and discontinuous, fragmentary, imagistic 'illuminations' take the place of God's covenantal bow in the clouds as the correlatives of modern consciousness, if and when this elusive entity can be discovered. The moralized landscapes of Lawrence's earlier work have receded (there are apocalyptic visions instead), together with *The Rainbow's* apparatus of Victorian interpretation explicitly derived from Ruskin and others, though the quest for the sources of life persists, especially in the characters of Ursula (recognizably continuous with the Ursula of *The Rainbow*) and Birkin (a new, deliberately intermittent and 'unfinished' character). Through Birkin's anguished and self-contradictory scrutinizing of himself and others, and his complex theory of the two rivers, of 'life' and of 'dissolution', a 'polarization' of male and female principles is advanced as the antidote to the neurosis of the modern world.

As Keith Sagar remarked, marriage might seem to have been the end of the quest, and many critics have taken this to be the case: but the novel itself makes this reading impossible, as do those which follow. Virtually an exile, Lawrence gave his wanderings literary form in a sequence of works (novels, short stores, travel writing, poetry) which constitute a loose synthesis of genres: journalistic commentary and travelogue go arm-in-arm with political philosophy and poetic descriptive writing, while through the whole runs a bitterly satirical note, often (as in *Women in Love*) implicating living persons. Italy engendered *Aaron's Rod* (1922), Australia *Kangaroo* (1923), and Mexico *The Plumed Serpent* (1926). Seldom have geographical exploration and literary improvisation gone so closely together. In the course of this 'third' phase of his career Lawrence returned to painting, the rudiments of which he had mastered as a boy and which he often wrote about, brilliantly if idiosyncratically. He regarded his own paintings as improvisations; influenced by **Cézanne**, whom Lawrence greatly admired and tried to 'rescue' from English art historians in his *Introduction to These Paintings*, they celebrate, in bold colours and forms, what Lawrence liked to call the 'phallic', which might be understood as a veneration for sexual desire and sexual tenderness liberated from dictatorial will.

Lawrence's last novel, *Lady Chatterley's Lover*, unpublishable in England during Lawrence's lifetime, is wholly shaped by the 'phallic' faith of the now impotent and ill Lawrence (the rejected title of his late story 'The Man who Died', which was originally 'The Escaped Cock', makes explicit the connection between resurrection and the phallus). All three versions of the text are characterized by an intense eroticism (though Lawrence himself characteristically eschewed this word). In the later rewritings, however, the political and naturalistic elements of the earlier are restructured as myth and symbol in close touch with folklore and fairy-tale. **W.B. Yeats** spoke of the use of dialect by the aristocratic lady and her gamekeeper lover (a device related to the use of the infamous 'four-letter words') as 'a forlorn poetry uniting their solitudes, something ancient, humble, and terrible'. The national scandal of the prosecution of Penguin Books in 1960 for finally publishing the uncensored text in England was a major cultural event. *Lady Chatterley's* victory signalled a new 'permissiveness' in life and letters, and for a time Lawrence became a cult hero of sexual liberation. This misrepresents him to the extent that the context of Lawrence's phallic religion is an apocalyptic radical Puritanism (Bunyan and Blake are among his forebears), and the apocalyptic eroticism of *Lady Chatterley's Lover*, which defied literary and moral convention, is consistent with Lawrence's essentially religious veneration for the act of love as the core of what, for want of a better word, he called 'Life'.

Lawrence's output was as large as it was diverse. His short stories alone would have commanded a reputation. In recent years increased attention to his writings on art and his paintings, his plays (very effectively staged), his poetry, his very distinguished literary criticism, as well as the philosophizing he self-deprecatingly called 'pollyanalytics', has gone hand-in-hand with a new awareness of the dominant place he occupies in what is now called Modernism. The immensely rich and complex *Women in Love*, for example, now looks no less impressive and central in its way than **Joyce's** *Ulysses*.

Further reading

Other works include: Novels: *The Lost Girl* (1920); *St Mawr* (1925); and *The Virgin and the Gypsy* (1930). Short stories: *The Prussian Officer and Other Stories* (1914); *England, My England and Other Stories* (1922); *The Ladybird* (1923); *The Woman Who Rode Away and Other Stories* (1928). *The Collected Poems* (2 vols) were published in 1964. His *Letters* (ed. Aldous Huxley, 1932, and again in two vols by Harry T. Moore, 1962) are indispensable. Critical studies include: F.R. Leavis, *D.H. Lawrence: Novelist* (1955); Graham Hough, *The Dark Sun* (1956); Julian Moynahan, *The Deed of Life* (1963); H.M. Daleski, *The Forked Flame* (1965); George H. Ford, *Double Measure* (1965); Keith Sagar, *The Art of D.H. Lawrence* (1966); Colin Clarke, *River of Dissolution* (1969); Frank Kermode, *Lawrence* (1973). The standard biography is Harry T. Moore, *The Priest of Love* (1975), although the earlier three-volume *D.H. Lawrence: A Composite Biography* (1957–9) remains important. See also: J. Worthen, *D.H. Lawrence: The Early Years, 1885–1912* (1991); M. Bell, *D.H. Lawrence: Language and Being* (1992); A. Fernihough, *D.H. Lawrence: Aesthetics and Ideology* (1993); D. Ellis, *D.H. Lawrence: Dying Game, 1922–1930* (1998).

G.M. HYDE

LE CARRÉ, John (David John Moore CORNWELL)

1931–

English novelist

John le Carré's writing career is now in its fifth decade, a remarkable achievement for a writer ostensibly working in a genre (the spythriller) which is seen both as inherently second rate and as having lost its *raison d'être* with the end of the Cold War. Where his early novels, particularly *The Spy Who Came in from the Cold* (1963), were initially seen as a reaction against the macho glitz of **Ian Fleming's** James Bond or the classless cool of Len Deighton, le Carré's subsequent work has shown a capacity to transcend genre limitations and a sheer perseverance which ally him to Eric Ambler or **Graham Greene**.

Like Greene, le Carré has always cultivated a somewhat mysterious persona. By his own account, his father was a charming con man whose rackety life and associates inspired several of the dubious figures who populate his novels, for example *A Perfect Spy* (1986). Born David Cornwell, he was educated (unhappily) at Sherborne School and later at Berne University and Lincoln College, Oxford, where he read Modern Languages. He taught at Eton before joining the Foreign Office and serving in Bonn, which provides the backdrop for *A Small Town in Germany* (1968). Le Carré – the writing pseudonym was necessary because of his simultaneous diplomatic career – is rather cagey about the extent of his involvement with the intelligence services but the presumed association has always given his books their apparent authenticity.

His first two novels, *Call for the Dead* (1961) and *A Murder of Quality* (1962), were fairly standard mysteries, but *The Spy Who Came in from the Cold* catapulted le Carré into bestsellerdom and enabled him to leave the Foreign Office and write full time. More importantly, *Spy* announced the arrival of a distinctive new voice in espionage fiction, one that was unheroic and unillusioned. The central figure, British agent Alec Leamas, is treated as a pawn by his own side in a complex game of betrayal and dissimulation. At ground level, in the grey world of moles and double agents, there did not seem to be that much difference between the freedom-loving West and the duplicitous East.

Le Carré's most enduring and endearing character was introduced on the first page of *Call for the Dead*. George Smiley is utterly unremarkable or, more properly, unremarked – in a characteristic flourish the author describes him as travelling 'without labels in the guard's van of the social express' – and so ideally suited for undercover work. Smiley, memorably played by Alec Guinness for television, is the central figure in a trilogy of novels, most famously *Tinker, Tailor, Soldier, Spy* (1974), in which he is given the task of unmasking a double agent at the heart of the 'Circus', the author's name for the Secret Service. Smiley sifts through files, listens to the tales of superannuated spies and arrives at the truth through an unshowy display of patience. In the next two books, *The Honourable Schoolboy* (1977) and *Smiley's People* (1980), Smiley brings about the defeat and defection of his opposite number at 'Moscow Centre', a shadowy figure known as Karla. In the duel between the two there is a touch of other, more sensational fictional confrontations – one thinks of Holmes and Moriarty, or of Bond and Blofeld – although le Carré's attitude is one of weary ambivalence.

A similar contradiction marks le Carré's treatment of the British establishment, always a central factor in his work. On the one hand, there is a grudging relish for the mores of the commonroom and the club. Single-handed, the author created a lexicon of spying terms ('control', 'lamplighters', 'scalphunters') reflecting his attraction to closed, secretive societies. On the other hand, there is his impatience with the snobbish obstructions and evasions of the intelligence hierarchy, and above all with Britain's post-imperial delusions and its dependance on the USA. In a sense the greater part of le Carré's work can be interpreted as an attempt to open the reader's eyes to the 'reality [which is] a poor island with scarcely a voice that would carry across the water' (*Tinker, Tailor*). It is revealing that *Absolute Friends* (2003), a kind of résumé of the later stages of the Cold War and the beginnings of the so called War on Terror, should climax with the betrayal and death of the central character at the hands of American special forces.

Recent events may have given an angry zest to le Carré's work but in the years which followed the crumbling of the Berlin Wall (always a key location in his work) he produced a series of novels, such as *The Night Manager* (1993) or *The Constant Gardener* (2001), which showed a switch of focus from traditional espionage to the murkier areas of business and industry. Le Carré is in for the long haul and it is always interesting to see where this author, with his global concerns and his insider's touch, will next direct his attentions.

PHILIP GOODEN

LE CORBUSIER (Charles-Édouard JEANERET)

1887–1965
Franco-Swiss architect and painter

Of all the great architects of the Modern Movement, Charles-Édouard Jeaneret (Le Corbusier) had, perhaps, the most unlikely origins. He was born in La Chaux-de-Fonds, which as he liked to point out is over 1,000 metres above sea level, the centre of the Swiss Jura watchmaking industry. His mother was a musician and his father, a stalwart of the town industry, had Jeaneret apprenticed at the age of thirteen as a watchmaker and engraver. However, he detached the retina of his left eye by drawing at night and his resulting bad eyesight (enshrined in his uniform of heavy glasses) prevented him pursuing this vocation: at the age of seventeen he gave it up to study building (in the local technical school) and to undertake some minor architectural commissions.

Early in the twentieth century he set out on a series of apparently aimless but serendipitous tours: to Budapest, Vienna and Berlin, and later to Greece and Turkey, where the architecture profoundly impressed him. In Vienna and Berlin, his *wanderlust* paid off when he found work with the Vienna Werkstätte and in Peter Behrens's office, where **Mies van der Rohe** and **Walter Gropius** were his contemporaries.

In between these two trips he worked in Paris with that great pioneer in concrete, the engineer-contractor and family friend Auguste Perret, and then in northern France designing houses, sluice-gates and other waterway architecture for the local Waterways Board. Jeaneret was always rather proud of his lack of conventional architectural training, and, in later years, was one of the only three 'unqualified' architects licensed to practise in France.

In 1919 he moved to Paris, where he lived the rest of his life, and set up a small office with his cousin, Pierre Jeaneret, who had undergone a more conventional architectural training. Perret introduced him to Fernand

Léger and Amedée Ozenfant and the transformation from Jeaneret to Le Corbusier had begun. The name 'Le Corbusier' Jeaneret chose under the direction of Ozenfant to distinguish clearly his new architectural self from the old. It refers to an annual task undertaken in the Middle Ages by the Jeaneret family of cleaning the crows' nests out of the local church steeple, probably their only previous architectural connection. With its adoption came a rigorously maintained lifestyle (painting and 'visual researches' before lunch, then a role change to the besuited, bespectacled after-lunch architect), and a complete change in his persona, for before this time he had never painted, and his architecture had generally been of little interest with the exception of the Dom-Ino concrete housing system (1914), where six columns, arranged as on a domino tile, support flat concrete slabs, thus allowing a special freedom of spatial division.

On Le Corbusier the painter and visual artist (as he now was), Léger's work left a profound mark. Le Corbusier painted, and later sculpted and designed murals and tapestries, within the 'Purist' style of post-Cubism, broadening his approach and using brighter, plainer colours and strong, almost crude forms, sometimes with a particularly symbolic intention (e.g. his frequent use of the open hand). His painting is not particularly significant except in regard to his architecture. Indeed, it is almost as though his paintings, failing to live in two dimensions, take on life and vitality in the three-dimensional world of the built form, where the concrete realization of the crude forms and bright colours could flourish as massive monuments.

Le Corbusier's work as an architect may be divided into three categories: his building; his town-planning projects; and his theorizing. One of the earliest and clearest theoretical statements he made of his intentions was in a manifesto he composed with his partner-cousin (who is usually, and quite inexplicably, neglected) in 1926, and called *Almanach de l'architecture moderne* (translated as *Almanac of Modern Architecture*). In this, they call for five 'principles' in the new architecture: free supports, that is to say a column structure which lifts the building off the ground ('pilotis'); roof gardens, i.e. using the new flat roof as a resource and a viewing platform; a free plan (as in the Dom-Ino house, where the walls may move freely within the space without being confined by the structure); horizontal windows, which 'express' the non-structural character of the external walls; and the free design of the façades of the building. (These five principles became Le Corbusier's operations manual and, together with his early experience of concrete and industrial buildings, essentially account for his architecture.) The five principles, and Le Corbusier's other theoretical works of the 1920s – he also wrote several other manifesto-type statements, especially in the magazine *L'Esprit nouveau*, and many justifications of his ideas and buildings – constituted a revolutionary architectural statement, a realization in architecture of a new aesthetic of particular honesty and utility which had its origin in the fragmented picture plane of the 'Cubists', and the novel consequent interpretation of the concept of transparency and thus spatial definition. Its effect was profound: it was almost as though Le Corbusier had single-handedly invented the Modern Movement – particularly that part of it we now call the Heroic Period of the International Style – and his importance and influence were enormous. Indeed, it was through his work that the foundation of the Congrès Internationaux d'Architectes Modernes (CIAM), the formative architectural association of the century, came about, in which internationalist group of architects Le Corbusier was the energetic and highly esteemed flag-bearer.

He also wrote several books, the earlier statements of architectural theory being very polemical, as in *Towards a New Architecture* (*Vers une architecture*, 1923, trans. 1946), which espouses the 'Machine Aesthetic', and *When the Cathedrals were White* (*Quand les cathédrales étaient blanches*, 1937, trans. 1947). In later years, his theorizing became somewhat more ascetic and less polemical, culminating in the publication of *The Modulor* (*Le Modulor*, 1949, trans. 1954), an account of his proportional system. This book had a wide influence among architects in the 1950s, but was founded on a most peculiar view of mathematics and absolute size standards. Nevertheless, its Fibonacci series of related lengths did provide variety in the somewhat sterile environment of the post-war pre-fab.

His building work can be assembled in four groups: the first consists of individual villas which he built for rich clients and in which he could explore some of the spatial freedom demanded in the *Almanach*, using free-standing walls and double volume spaces, and experimenting with roof gardens, an exploration that gave play to his machine aesthetic and which generated his famous aphorism 'A House is a Machine for living in'. (His meaning of Machine was more Platonic than ours, and his comment is mainly about aesthetics.) Of these, the villas Vaucresson (about which he said, 'Until the house at Vaucresson, he [i.e. Le Corbusier] had no creative ambitions of any kind'), La Roche, Stein and Savoye (now a French national monument), all built in the 1920s, are the most interesting. For these houses he also designed his famous furniture, some of it still in production.

The second group, social housing, actively involved Le Corbusier for most of his life-span. Here he tried to express his vision of the contemporary city and lifestyle of what Reyner Banham has called the 'First Machine Age'. Essentially he developed the large housing block, containing the street in the sky and the vertical street. These blocks were developed from about 1930, starting with the Pavillon Suisse in Paris and including his Salvation Army building, finding their most exact form in the 'Unité d'Habitation' built in Marseilles and duplicated elsewhere. These schemes almost all had strong town-planning overtones.

The third group includes the projects in what may be thought of as urban composi-tions (as opposed to town-planning). Le

Corbusier had a megalomaniac streak, which not only led to a massive self-righteousness but let him enjoy designing the largest of urban buildings. The first of these, in the 1920s, was the project for the League of Nations which, he tells us, was the competition jury's preferred scheme but was disqualified because it was not drawn in Indian ink. He followed this with the (unbuilt) Palace of Soviets which included an auditorium for 14,000, which he claimed rather simplistically 'was acoustically faultless (tested by light-waves)'. Other schemes include a sports stadium project, the Ministry of Education in Rio de Janeiro, and the initial planning of the United Nations building in New York: but the most celebrated is the new provincial capital Chandigarh in the Punjab, where Le Corbusier designed and built the whole administrative and juridical complex around a vast pool of water.

The final aspect of his building is a number of extremely individualistic one-off jobs. The most impressive of these (and they are superb) are the pilgrimage church at Ronchamp in the Vosges mountains, noted for its scrolled roof and windows puncturing the massive walls; the Dominican Training Monastery at La Tourette with its randomly articulated façade; and the Philips Pavilion built for the Brussels World Fair, the home of one of the world's first 'total art' shows. (These last two were largely designed by Iannis Xenakis, better known as a composer for his stochastic music.)

One cannot conclude an account of Le Corbusier without discussing his town-planning projects. It was largely he who put forward and developed the ideas adopted by CIAM for the contemporary city. His was the driving force behind the vision of the vast separated blocks in the Elysian Fields that was the modernist's dream. These ideas he devel-oped through various projects, for 'La Ville contemporaine' – the initial design as an iso-lated new town for three million people – to proposed applications involving large-scale rebuilding of several distinguished towns, including Paris (the Plan Voisin), Stockholm and Barcelona. None of these schemes was built, much to his chagrin, for they aroused great public anger; but they had an enormous influence on architects and planners and their effects can be seen in the vandalized tower blocks situated in seas of asphalt that are all too familiar nowadays. However, it is hardly fair to Le Corbusier to judge his ideas on these realizations, for they are not only unpleasant and extraordinarily bad buildings, they are also appallingly executed travesties of his ideas. Whether such ideas, attacked by some as megalomaniac and totalitarian, could ever work, we are unlikely now to find out.

Le Corbusier built himself a pair of small 'primitive huts' on the Mediterranean coast where he went for privacy and contemplation. It was while there, swimming, in 1965 that he had a heart attack and drowned. He was married but had no children.

Further reading

See: C. Jencks, *Le Corbusier and the Tragic View of Architecture* (1973); C. Blake, *Le Corbusier* (1964); Carol Palazzolo and Riccardo Vio (eds), *In the Footsteps of Le Corbusier* (1991). W. Boesiger, *Le Corbusier* (1999) is an eight-volume chronological record of Le Corbusier's work.

RANULPH GLANVILLE AND SAM STEVENS

LEAN, (Sir) David
1908–91
English film director

David Lean made only fifteen films as sole director, but they include a half-dozen that deserve inclusion in any history of the cinema as an expressive art form. One of the few British filmmakers to realize the potential of film as both a narrative and a visual medium, Lean was responsible for some of the most memorable moments in cinema history: the poignant railway-station farewell of *Brief Encounter* (1945), the rain-lashed Gothic orphanage that opens *Oliver Twist* (1948), the parched desert panoramas of *Lawrence of Arabia* (1962) and the snowy vistas of revolutionary Russia in *Doctor Zhivago* (1965). Yet for all his

accomplishments, Lean has been criticized for an obsessive perfectionism that meant his oeuvre was small in comparison with those of Britain's other two greatest film talents, **Alfred Hitchcock** and Michael Powell.

Lean was born in South Croydon, London, the son of staunchly Quaker parents whose disapproval of picture houses as 'dens of vice' did nothing to dampen his youthful ardour for the cinema. He followed the usual apprenticeship for a budding filmmaker by working his way up through the British studio system of the 1930s from tea-boy, messenger and clapper-loader to editor. It was the combination of his technical proficiency and his intuitive understanding of film narration that by the outbreak of the Second World War had earned for Lean the reputation as the best editor in the industry. Having turned down opportunities to direct supporting features, Lean's entry into direction came in 1941 when Noël Coward asked him to act as co-director of Coward's patriotic naval flag-waver *In Which We Serve* (1942). The success of this film marked the beginning of a four-picture collaboration between Lean and Coward. *Blithe Spirit* (1945) was a lightweight supernatural fantasy in the style of René Clair, but it was Lean's sensitive direction of *This Happy Breed* (1944) and *Brief Encounter* that demonstrated his ability both to represent realistic social environments on screen and to draw moving, understated performances from his actors.

Lean came to prominence at a time of unprecedented artistic creativity and cultural visibility for British cinema. *This Happy Breed* and *Brief Encounter*, especially, were prominent examples of what contemporary critics referred to as 'the quality film', praised for the realism and emotional restraint that differentiated them from the tinselled melodramas of Hollywood. This was a time when a genuinely British national cinema can be seen to have emerged and Lean was one of the directors whose films were, to quote Roger Manvell, 'bound to the national life of Britain'.

It was also a time when the Rank Organization was investing heavily in films that were the antithesis of either economic or cultural conservatism. Lean's two **Dickens** adaptations were part of an ambitious attempt by Rank to open up the American market for British films, though in the event *Oliver Twist* was released in a truncated version in the United States due to perceived anti-Semitism in its characterization of Fagin. Nevertheless, these two films represent probably the peak of Lean's visual powers and narrative skill. The opening sequence of *Great Expectations* (1946) on the Essex marshes, for instance, includes a bravura example of suspenseful editing that owes much to the montage principles of **Sergei Eisenstein**.

Lean's critical standing declined in the 1950s, when his films, like so many products of the British film industry during that period, were more workmanlike than artistic. His first colour film, the romantic drama *Summertime* (1955), shot on location in Italy, indicated that Lean was ready to leave the drab austerity of British cinema behind. It was the acclaimed prisoner-of-war drama *The Bridge on the River Kwai* (1957) that restored Lean's reputation (he won the first of his two Academy Awards for Best Director) and set him on the path of expensive, visually sumptuous epics. *Kwai*'s narrative of intense psychological drama against the background of war was repeated to even greater effect in *Lawrence of Arabia*, garnering Lean's second Academy Award, while his adaptation of **Boris Pasternak's** *Doctor Zhivago* was the biggest box-office success of his career.

Lean's meticulous working methods meant that the periods between his films became longer. The inevitable critical backlash came with *Ryan's Daughter* (1970), an over-long love story set during the Irish Uprising of 1916, though its reputation as a sincerely acted pastoral drama has since improved. It was fourteen years until Lean directed his next, and last, film, a literate and well-received adaptation of **E.M. Forster's** *A Passage to India* (1985). Lean was honoured in his later years by a knighthood (1984) and by the American Film Institute's Lifetime Achievement Award (1990). At the time of his death in 1991 he was working on an unrealized film of **Joseph Conrad's** *Nostromo*.

The career of David Lean highlights issues that are central to any assessment of film as an art form rather than a mere entertainment medium. That, for most of his career, he enjoyed relative creative autonomy free from the philistinism of studio executives would seem to lend substance to the *auteur* theory which sees the history of film in terms of its visionary directors. Certainly Lean experienced little of the disruption that blighted **Orson Welles's** career. That so many of his most successful films, however, were literary adaptations (Coward, Dickens, Pasternak, Forster) might call into question the autonomy of film from other art forms. Lean always had a strong visual sense, though his later films were criticized for their overly pictorialist style and languorous pace. Nevertheless, as a director whose films won both critical and popular acclaim, Lean deserves to be regarded as one of cinema's outstanding talents.

Further reading

Other works include: *The Passionate Friends* (1949), *Madeleine* (1950), *The Sound Barrier* (1952) and *Hobson's Choice* (1954). See: Roger Manvell, *Film* (1946); Alain Silver and James Ursini, *David Lean and His Films* (1974; rev. 1991); and Kevin Brownlow, *David Lean: A Biography* (1996).

JAMES CHAPMAN

LEARY, Timothy

1920–96

US cult figure

Born in Springfield, Massachusetts, Leary rejected the parental insistence of being trained at West Point military academy, studied psychology in the University of California at Berkeley, served in an army hospital in the Second World War, became assistant professor of psychology at the San Francisco School of Medicine, and finally lectured in psychology at Harvard University.

While he was working in the Center for Research in Personality, Harvard sacked him in 1963; the faculty discovered he had become the leader of a group of researchers and volunteers working with psilocybin, a chemical derived from a mushroom sacred for many centuries to certain Amerindians. Leary had taken the mushroom at the behest of a University of New Mexico scientist at Cuernavaca in 1960, and the experience changed his attitudes towards consciousness and religion. Then, he began to concentrate research on the uses of lysergic acid (LSD), and other drugs, towards forms of expanded consciousness, psychedelic experience and religious illumination.

During the 1960s Leary became one of the most powerful influences on American youth, particularly those of the campuses deeply engaged in critical action against the official imperial and domestic wars into which they had grown up. Leary's psychedelic messianism became part of American cultic life, contributing strongly to the breaking up of fixed inherited patterns of behaviour. In the mid-1960s, the LSD 'trip' was featured in every newspaper and magazine. In 1963, *Esquire* ran an article on the work of Leary and Richard Alpert at Harvard, quoting the former's beliefs that drugs provided the consumer with 'transcendence of space–time, of subject–object relations, and the ego or identity'; they were thought to be 'mental vitamins, or mental health foods'. The first issue of the *Psychedelic Review*, organ of the International Foundation for Internal Freedom, appeared the same year, and Leary's Center was investigated by the Food and Drug Administration. *Playboy* magazine published a panel discussion on the issues, whose members included **William Burroughs**, Leslie Fiedler, Alan Watts and Harry J. Anslinger, for thirty-three years commissioner of the Bureau of Narcotics. By 1966, two thousand people could pack a New York theatre for Leary's 'Psychedelic Celebration No. 1', presented by the League for Spiritual Discovery. At the same time

Leary's centre at Millbank, New York, was raided. Subsequent charges, however, were dismissed. In his 'Death of the Mind Service', Leary preached 'the biochemistry' of the body bringing about 'a state of grace', and followed this up with 'The Reincarnation of Jesus Christ' and an 'LSD Mass', a performance in which he proclaimed, 'I am here to lead the broken-hearted', and so on, in Christ-like style. The same year he told a Senate subcommittee on juvenile delinquency that the use of LSD had run out of control and that a third of the nation's college students were experimenting with it. His slogan 'Turn On. Tune In. Drop Out' (in an article syndicated by a widely distributed underground press organization) appeared everywhere – he intended good advice: 'Do not routinely and blindly expose yourself to stupor-producing, symbol-addicting environments.'

In 1968, the state declared him 'a menace to the community'. A year later he said a kind of farewell at the Village Gate Theatre in New York, backed by **Allen Ginsberg** and Paul Krassner, among others. In 1970 Leary was sentenced to ten years' imprisonment (Lawrence Ferlinghetti's City Lights press published his 'Memorandum' for bail), but escaped through the Weatherman Underground, and issued a statement from hiding calling on Americans to resist the Third World War waged by the government against its own people (he had been arrested an estimated fourteen times on drug charges). In 1971 his *Jail Notes* appeared with a preface by Ginsberg excoriating both the narcotics laws and Harvard University.

Leary next turned up in Beirut in 1970, hoping to contact Al Fatah, and then emerged in Algiers in 1971, hoping to ally with Eldridge Cleaver there, but the Black Panther leader arrested him as a dangerous influence on the black revolt – 'we cannot afford to jeopardize our work toward revolution in Babylon', and in any case Leary's mind 'has been blown by acid'. In 1973, after a spell in Switzerland and Afghanistan, Leary was back in jail in Los Angeles.

His cult status is best described by Ginsberg: 'a hero of American consciousness'. He began as a sophisticated academician, he encountered discoveries in his field which confounded him and his own technology, he pursued his studies where attention commanded, he arrived beyond the boundaries of public knowledge.' This is indeed the basis of his messianic politics, extended in jail to the necessity for 'worldwide ecological religious warfare'. *High Priest* (1968) speaks of the need to break fixed, trained motivation, attitude and preconception by transformation in personal consciousness. The book is a record of 'a psychedelic scholar-politician', a contribution to 'the psychedelic revolution ... a religious renaissance of the young', and he includes important meetings with Charles Olson and Arthur Koestler, Ginsberg and **Burroughs**, and other highly influential figures. The change came for him in 1961 when, under acid, he had to confront the stereotypical pointlessness of his family's life, and then, under an overdose, to realize the void in his own life and his own responsibility for change. He concluded later that 'psychedelic research is experimental philosophy, empirical metaphysics, visionary science ... The discovery of LSD is as important to philosophy and psychology and religion as the discovery of the microscope was to biology.' In 1962, after a trip in a Vedānta *ashram* in Boston, he began 'the slow invisible process of becoming a guru, a holy man'. The Harvard project became 'an ontological conspiracy' – 'the course of social conflict is usually neurological. The cure is biochemical.' Such is his basis for 'the religious, scientific quest', 'the great plan', through which we are to find courage to recognize new forms of energy (*The Politics of Ecstasy*, 1969). The notorious 'generation gap' is in fact 'an evolutionary lurch ... a species mutation'. The LSD lesson was to mean you have to re-enact the evolutionary drama, 'go through the *whole* sequence yourself'. Leary admitted to over three hundred acid trips in order to 'suspend' social conditioning (but, he adds, Herman Kahn had taken acid, so that there is no guarantee of any radical identity change for the better ...). Leary's faith lay with the young: 'No one over the age of fifty should be allowed to vote' and 'voting should be by the extended family ... We must return – advance to – the tribal unit of society.' The prelude to a better society is to be found in 'the retracing of genetic memories back down through the myriad, multi-webbed fabric of RNA-DNA memories'. Freedom from symbol systems addiction comes through 'cellular wisdom'. Leary's advice to the youthful reformer is 'become your own priest ... your own doctor ... your own researcher on consciousness', and to 'love God and every living creature as thyself'. In addition, he claimed, in the famous *Playboy* interview (reprinted in *The Politics of Ecstasy*), that 'LSD is the most powerful aphrodisiac ever discovered by man' – a highly disputable assertion, apparently. He totally denied that LSD led to any harmful effects on the body–mind system – again a disputed claim. Reviewing both these books in the *New York Times Book Review* in 1969, Rollo May, the American psychotherapist, observed that it was not surprising that hallucinogenic drugs should appeal to a younger generation 'beset with malaise and apathy'; and 'when the prospect of discovering God is combined with the joy of escape that drugs promise, you have a power whose attraction is great indeed'. May concludes that while drugs do 'clear away debris, the false faiths, the conventional hypocrisy', you still have to 'move on to something more complete'. Leary himself seems never to have discovered that condition beyond the *ashram*.

Leary's last two decades before his death of prostate cancer at his Beverley Hills home were eventful in another way: he became a yet more prolific writer and lecturer. After arrest in Afghanistan in 1973, and parole after three years, the books poured from him, prominent among them *What Does Woman Want?* (1976), *Exo-Psychology* (1977), *The Game of Life* (1979), his detailed and illuminating autobiography *Flashbacks* (1983), *Chaos and Cyber-Culture* (1994) in which his preoccupation with death as integral to life is explored, and a run of posthumous collected work to include *Design for Dying* (1997) and *The Delicious Grace of Moving One's Hand: The Collected Sex Writings* (1998). Throughout this period he flirted with the Libertarian Party; worked a highly lucrative lecture circuit with G. Gordon Liddy, the Watergate burglar who had once arrested him in Texas; ran a Multimedia Show called *How to Operate Your Brain*; and even made his own dying into a cyber-performance in which his last moments were telecast. As the figure Richard Nixon once called 'the most dangerous man in America' and **Ken Kesey**, not unironically, a 'psychedelic wiseman', he observed of his cancer, 'I am looking forward to the most fascinating experience in life, which is dying.' Vintagely loved and hated, the guru and the ogre, yet always a true counter-culture name, it may be appropriate that his very last words were 'Why not?'

Further reading

See: Leary, with R. Metzner and R. Alpert, *The Psychedelic Experience* (1964); Leary, G.M. Weil and R. Metzner (eds), *The Psychedelic Reader* (1965); Leary, *Psychedelic Prayers* (1966).

ERIC MOTTRAM
(REVISED AND UPDATED BY A. ROBERT LEE)

LENIN (Vladimir Ilyich ULYANOV)

1870–1924

Russian revolutionary, statesman, publicist and theoretician

Lenin was born in 1870 at Simbirsk in the heart of Russia. He came from an educated and enlightened family: his father was a schoolteacher and so too was his mother for a while. Lenin was the second son in a family of six children and received the usual middle-class schooling of his time. Lenin's elder brother, Alexander, was a romantic revolutionary; he was executed for plotting to murder the then Tsar. Lenin was seventeen then and the execution left a deep impression

on him. Lenin's elder sister, too, was active in the revolutionary movement. Soon after his brother's death Lenin enrolled as a law student in the provincial university of Kazan. His university career, however, did not last for long; he was sent down and confined to his mother's estate for playing a leading role in a demonstration against the government regulations to which students were subject. Lenin did eventually qualify as a lawyer but only to practise for a year or so. Throughout his life he remained a professional revolutionary.

Lenin embarked on his eventful political career by joining in the revolutionary groups which had started to develop all over Russia. After a couple of years of political activities in provincial towns he moved to St Petersburg, then the capital of Russia – also the main industrial city and naturally the hub of anti-government political activities. It was there that Lenin in 1894 published his first major political work: *Who the Friends of the People Are and How They Fight the Social Democrats* (*Chto Takoye 'Drusya Naroda', kak oni voyuynt protiv Sotsial-Demokratov?*, trans. 1946). The tract is a blistering attack on the Narodniks (populists in Russian) and has all the features which characterize Lenin's voluminous writings: written by way of a political intervention with a view to drawing specific conclusions to guide political activity. Lenin's style is to combine didactic arguments with withering polemics.

Lenin was not allowed to remain free to participate in political activities for long. After a year of imprisonment he was exiled to Siberia for three years; it was there that he married a fellow revolutionary, Krupskaya. Lenin used his period of imprisonment and exile to write his monumental *Development of Capitalism in Russia* (*Razvitiye Kapitalizma v Rossi*, 1899, trans. 1956). Though the work is scholarly in content as well as in style, it is nonetheless political. It is, like most other pre-1900 writings of Lenin, directed against the Narodniks.

To start with, Narodism covered a heterogeneous group opposed to the autocratic political and economic order in Russia. But by the 1890s the label came to be applied exclusively to non-**Marxists** who saw in the village commune the foundation of the future Russian society. They regarded capitalism – large-scale manufacturing industry and modern farms – as an alien import grafted on to Russian society.

What Lenin argued against the Narodniks was that capitalism was not only firmly implanted but also rapidly growing, both in the Russian cities and in the countryside. The village commune which was to serve as the foundation of the Narodniks' future Russia, Lenin demonstrated, was no longer a community of equal individuals. On the contrary it was stratified; a small minority of richer peasants (*kulaks*) prospered while the rest were becoming progressively poorer and forced to work for wages. From this Lenin drew the political conclusion that Russia, contrary to the Narodnik thesis, would not follow a path of economic and social changes radically different from the one already traversed by Western European countries. The implication was that in Russia, as in the rest of Europe, the leading political force was the working class and the appropriate form of political organization a Social Democratic Party, similar to those which had already developed in Western Europe.

From 1900 onwards one may divide Lenin's life and activities into three phases: (1) the period up to 1907; (2) the period of exile from 1907 to 1917; and finally (3) the period of revolution and the establishment of the Soviet Union from 1917 till his death.

The Social Democratic Party was founded when Lenin was still in Siberia, and it grew very rapidly in size and influence soon after its formation. During the period 1900–7 the question of differences between Marxism and Narodism was no longer important. The two main issues which occupied Lenin during this period were, first, the nature of the impending revolution, and second, the aim and the organization of the Social Democratic Party.

Lenin was convinced of the imminence of revolution and so too were other Russian revolutionaries. There was a nationwide uprising again the Tsarist autocracy and feudal lords in 1905 – an event which Lenin later termed the full dress rehearsal of the 1917 revolution. In his *Two Tactics of Social Democracy* (*Dve taktiki Sotsial-Demokraty v demokrat icheskoy revolyutsi*, 1905, trans. 1935) Lenin argued that the impending revolution would be bourgeois rather than socialist in character. For, according to him, the working class and the Social Democratic Party, because of conditions specific to Russia could not carry through the revolution to victory on its own and thus realize a socialist economy. That, Lenin went on to argue, did not mean that Social Democrats could not play a leading role in the impending revolution; on the contrary, it was necessary for them to do so in order to make sure that all vestiges of autocracy and feudalism were wiped out. Thus for Lenin, though it may seem paradoxical, the impending bourgeois revolution was to be led by the socialist party rather than by bourgeois parties.

Within five years of its establishment the Social Democratic Party split into two factions, the *Bolsheviks* (majority, in Russian) and the *Mensheviks* (minority) – the labels which later came to designate two separate socialist parties. Lenin became the leader of the former and it was the Bolsheviks who led the October Revolution of 1917. The immediate cause of the split was the difference of opinion on the nature of the party, its internal organization and the condition of its membership. Lenin argued for the establishment of a tightly knit party led from the centre, and which restricted its membership to only those who actively participated in its activities. The Mensheviks, in contrast, wanted the Russian party to develop like other European Social Democratic parties – a mass political party covering a wide political spectrum which was willing to admit a variety of individuals ranging from active participants to sympathizers. Lenin managed to win over the majority by a very slim margin. His conception of the party has become a legacy of the communist movement and it came in for criticism from diverse quarters, including Trotsky and Rosa Luxemburg.

The 1905 revolution shook the existing political and economic order but did not overthrow it. It led to the persecution of leading revolutionaries; Lenin like other Russian revolutionaries was driven abroad. He left Russia in 1907 to return to it in 1917 and spent most of his exile in Switzerland.

The Tsarist government, shaken by the 1905 uprising, tried to introduce a modicum of reforms: the commune was abolished and there was a half-hearted attempt on the part of the government to grant more power to the feeble assembly of elected representatives. The outbreak of the First World War soon put a stop to the process of economic and political reforms, and it was that which was decisive in shaping the course of events up to the October Revolution.

The outbreak of the war confronted the European socialist movement with the awkward problem of what attitude to adopt towards the war. Earlier, the Second International, as the socialist movement was then named, had decided that in the event of a war it would stand aside, leaving the ruling classes of belligerent countries to fight it out. This was not, however, what the majority of socialists did when the war was declared. In Germany the majority of Social Democratic members of parliaments voted funds for the war. The war split the socialist movement and put an end to the Second International.

Lenin argued that socialists should stand aside and refuse to take any part in the conduct of the war. For, as he explained, the war was an imperialist war – by that he meant that it was not the national boundaries of the leading European combatants but the division of Africa and Asia into colonies which was the main issue in the war. Therefore the war was not worthy of support by socialists for patriotic reasons. Lenin's theses on imperialism, publicized in his pamphlet *Imperialism* (*Imperializm*, 1917, trans. 1933), had a dual political significance. Apart from indicating to socialists the right attitude towards the war, they were based on the postulate that

imperialism was a particular stage of capitalism. He analysed imperialism as a product of the internal dynamics of capitalism and went on to argue that imperialism had turned the whole world into a unified and interdependent system. From this Lenin drew the political conclusion that revolutions could no longer be regarded as just national affairs; and that socialist revolutions in advanced capitalist countries, bourgeois revolutions in semi-capitalist countries like Russia and the struggles of national liberation in colonized regions were all interlinked. This was an important innovation; because till then the prevalent conception was that socialist revolution would first take place in advanced capitalist countries like Germany and then later in other countries, depending on the development of capitalism in those countries.

The war, which was opposed by all sections of Russian Social Democracy, sapped the Russian state of all its power. In February 1917 – when Lenin was still in Switzerland – an almost bloodless revolution ended the Tsardom. The political power then passed into the hands of not one but two governments: one formal in the shape of the provisional government (dominated by conservative and liberal parties), the other informal and founded on the Soviets – a revolutionary council of workers' representatives. Of them the St Petersburg Soviet was the most important; such assemblies had been established before, during the 1905 revolution.

Lenin arrived in Russia in April of 1917 and he argued for the transfer of all power to the Soviets, thus ending the situation of dual power which existed then. At that time it was not the Bolsheviks but the Mensheviks and the Social Revolutionaries (heirs of the Narodniks) who dominated the Soviets. With the two governments the political situation was balanced on a knife-edge. It was the attempt by a General Kornilov to capture political power which finally shifted the balance in favour of the Soviets, because it was they who frustrated the attempted *coup d'état*. By the beginning of October 1917 the leadership of the Soviets had passed into the hands of the Bolsheviks. It was then that Lenin called for an immediate seizure of power. Lenin's call was initially opposed by the majority of Bolshevik leaders, but, as in so many other situations in 1917, he managed to have his way. Thus within a year Russia went through two revolutions: one bourgeois democratic (the February Revolution) and the other socialist (the October Revolution).

After the October Revolution, Lenin became an undisputed leader of Russian socialism and also of a substantial section of the European socialist movement. The centre of revolution shifted from Germany to Russia; Lenin went on to establish the Third International (the international organization of communist parties) to replace the already fissured and demoralized Second International.

The new Soviet state had to fight a civil as well as an external war against Germany. It survived both of them, but at a very heavy cost. The war lasted for two years and it was the period of what was then termed War Communism – meaning a strict regimentation of citizens and the direct administrative control of industrial production and of distribution. The war and the War Communism led to a near collapse of the Russian economy. In order to avert that, Lenin boldly suggested rolling back the frontiers of the communist economy. This he did by proposing what has come to be known as the New Economic Policy. Lenin did not live long enough to see the construction of the first socialist economy in the world. He died after being bedridden for a year and a half.

The significance of Lenin and the Russian revolution are intertwined; both of them left a decisive imprint on the politics of the twentieth century. The Leninist political legacy consisted of three main elements: his conception of the revolutionary party, his refinement of the art of political calculation, and his conception of the state.

It could almost be said that Lenin spent all his political life determining what is possible and calculating what is needed to realize the chosen possibility. It was Lenin who made revolutions objects of calculation; it was in this respect that he added an entirely new dimension to Marxist politics.

Lenin's ideas on the state are elaborated in his famous *The State and Revolution* (*Gosudarstvo i revolyutsiya*, trans. 1919) which he wrote in the midst of revolution in 1917. In it he treated democracy and dictatorship as complements rather than as mutually exclusive alternatives. He argued that parliamentary democracy of capitalist countries was, nonetheless, a dictatorship of the capitalist class. Further, that the aim of a socialist revolution was to replace the dictatorship of the capitalist class with the dictatorship of the proletariat – a phrase which acquired an ominous meaning during the mass purges of the **Stalin** era.

Further reading

See: *Collected Works* in forty-five volumes (English translation, Moscow 1960–70); the three-volume *Selected Works* (1967). See also: Adam B. Ulam, *Lenin and the Bolsheviks* (1965); Robert Conquest, *Lenin* (1972); Neil Harding, *Lenin's Political Thought* (1977); Christopher Hill, *Lenin and the Russian Revolution* (1978); Robert Service, *Lenin* (2000); Christopher Read, *Lenin: A Post-Soviet Re-evaluation* (2005).

ATHAR HUSSAIN

LEVI, Primo

1919–87
Italian writer

When Primo Levi committed suicide, many refused to see this as simply the last desperate act of a man in the throes of profound depression and dogged by physical illness. Two of his most distinguished contemporaries among Italian writers, Natalia Ginzburg and Alberto Moravia, believed that it was the enduring memory of his years in the concentration camp at Auschwitz which had finally overwhelmed him. Several close friends, on the other hand, attributed his profound gloom to worries as to the health of his mother, to whom he was profoundly – some felt abnormally – attached. Others feared the effect of hostile criticism directed at his complex response to the Holocaust, of which he was so eloquent a survivor.

If, for some of these detractors, Levi had never seemed sufficiently Jewish, this was because the community into which he was born in 1919 appeared more assimilated than others throughout Europe at the time. Primo's parents belonged to the prosperous bourgeoisie of Turin, one of northern Italy's fastest-growing industrial cities, which welcomed **Mussolini's** 1922 seizure of power as a guarantee of social stability. Levi was encouraged to join the Fascist youth movement, becoming an enthusiastic skier and mountaineer, passions which later enabled him to survive the bitter winters of Auschwitz. School and university studies, focused on science, were threatened by the issue, in 1938, of the notorious Racial Laws, under which Jews were excluded from public education and barred from state employment.

Managing, with the help of sympathetic Gentile professors, to circumvent restrictions on Jewish students, Levi was able to complete a chemistry course at Turin university, gaining first-class honours. After the fall of the Fascist government in 1943 and the subsequent German occupation of Italy, he joined the Resistance, but was taken prisoner, along with a group of Jewish fugitives, at an inn near Aosta and sent to an internment camp before being transferred to Auschwitz. By no particular irony, Levi's scientific expertise made him too valuable to be exterminated forthwith, and he became a 'specialist slave' working in the IG Farben chemical laboratory close to the camp. His luck held when an attack of scarlet fever confined him to an isolation ward just before the Germans evacuated Auschwitz in January 1945, as Russian armies advanced into Poland. Eight months later, via several Russian transit camps and a journey across Romania and Hungary to the Italian border, Levi returned to Turin, to find his mother and sister still alive, though one-fifth of Italy's Jewish population had fallen victim to the Nazis.

The trauma of Auschwitz was exorcised for him, if only partially, by the writing of his memoir *If This is a Man* (*Se questo è un uomo*, trans. 1959). On its publication in 1947 the critics were puzzled by the notable avoidance of vindictiveness and accusation in its overall tone, as well as by an elegance of style unfashionable in post-war Italy. Temporarily abandoning his literary ambitions, Levi resumed work as an industrial chemist. It was another twenty years before genuine critical recognition greeted him on publication of *The Truce* (*La Tregua*, 1963, trans. 1987), an account of his experiences between leaving Auschwitz and returning to Italy. The book was widely translated, film rights were sold, and the writer gained several major Italian prizes.

Levi soon retired from his job at a Turin enamelling plant and began a writing career in earnest.

The Periodic Table (*Il sistema periodico*, trans. 1984), a remarkable sequence of portraits, sketches and stories all inspired by the various chemical elements and their properties, appearing in 1975, confirmed his status among Italy's major authors. Less successful was *If Not Now, When?* (*Se non ora, quando?*, 1981, trans. 1985), an attempt at novel-writing to which Levi's talents were unsuited. In *The Drowned and the Saved* (*I sommersi e i salvati*, 1986, trans. 1987) he returned to the subject of Auschwitz via a series of essays more gloomy and questioning in tone than any of his earlier work.

The delayed impact of his wartime ordeal now made itself felt both physically and mentally. Levi's depressions, exacerbated by his mother's illness from cancer, were made worse by attacks on his integrity, whether as a Jew, an anti-Fascist or a writer, launched in the American press. Increasingly haunted by memories of the concentration camp and outraged by revisionist historians who sought to diminish its significance, Levi equated his mother's suffering with 'the faces of men stretched out on their Auschwitz plank-beds'. On 11 April 1987 he left his apartment to throw himself down the stairwell.

Primo Levi remains the most admired and effective of all writers on the Holocaust, not simply for his dignity of utterance but for his refusal to deal in blanket condemnations, sentimental rhetoric or crude demands for revenge. He himself observed, in his introduction to the German edition of *If This is a Man*, that his only clear aim was 'to bear witness, to have my voice heard'. If the horrors of Auschwitz contributed in the end to his self-extinction, they had also, by no special irony, shaped his purpose as a literary artist.

Further reading

Other works include: *The Wrench* (*La chiave a stella*, 1978, trans. 1987) and *Other People's Trades* (*Altrui mestiere*, 1985, trans. 1985). See: Mirna Cicioni, *Primo Levi: Bridges of Knowledge* (1995); Myriam Anissimov, *Primo Levi: Tragedy of an Optimist* (1999); Carole Angier, *The Double Bond: Primo Levi: A Biography* (2002); Ian Thomson, *Primo Levi: A Life* (2003).

JONATHAN KEATES

LÉVI-STRAUSS, Claude

1908–

French social anthropologist

A central exponent of Structuralism, Claude Lévi-Strauss was born in Brussels. His secondary education was acquired in Paris at the Lycée Janson de Sailly. In 1931 he graduated in law and in philosophy. After two years as a philosophy teacher in small country towns he left France for Brazil, where he lectured at the University of São Paulo (1934–9). During his stay he became interested in social anthropology and started travelling in the Matto Grosso and the Amazon. He returned to France in 1939, but left again after the settling of arms in 1940, this time for the USA. In New York, Lévi-Strauss lectured at the New School for Social Research, then, with other exiled French intellectuals, founded the École Libre des Hautes Études de New York. After a brief return to Paris at the end of the war he became Cultural Counsellor at the French Embassy in Washington (1945–8). Back in Paris he was appointed Associate Curator of the Musée de l'Homme (1949),

Director of Studies at the École Pratique des Hautes Études (1950–74), and, from 1959, Professor of Social Anthropology at the Collège de France. A member of the Académie Française since 1973, Professor Lévi-Strauss is the recipient of many awards, and a member of British, American, Dutch and Norwegian Academies.

Lévi-Strauss's remarkable autobiographical travel account, *Tristes Tropiques* (1955, translated as *A World on the Wane*, 1961, and as *Tristes Tropiques*, 1973), is littered with references to overcrowding and congestion of every sort. Time and again he exposes 'those outbreaks of stupidity, hatred and credulousness which social groups secrete like pus when they begin to be short of space'. The cardinal virtues Lévi-Strauss appreciates are discretion and good manners. Only Buddhism is allowed to qualify as an acceptable moral and intellectual system, although Amerindian myths share his own concern for privacy: they regard the world as overcrowded as soon as a man has got a brother or a woman a sister. For 'as the myths explain, a brother can be a hardship ... his social function being usually limited to that of potential seducer of their sibling spouse.' This establishes Lévi-Strauss's claimed affinity with Rousseau, who wrote: 'The ancient times of Barbarity were the Golden Age, not because men were united, but because they were separated.'

Although Lévi-Strauss does not propose a global system of interpretation of the world, there is a remarkable consistency in his approach to widely different domains of human culture. His epistemological framework can be briefly described. Recent interpretations of the fate of the human race hesitate between two explanatory schemes: either the human environment, natural and cultural, is shown as a near-perfect clockwork wherein any part of the system is strictly constrained by the others and every event occurs necessarily; or constraints are shown to be few and human cultures have repeatedly to face choices between various alternatives. Sociobiology and the other varieties of cultural materialism belong to the first scheme, while Lévi-Strauss's system belongs to the second. However, to him the great diversity of human culture is not arbitrary; it exhibits combinations which result from the interplay of two types of constraints: the constraints which lie in the outer world and the constraints of the inner world, what Lévi-Strauss calls '*l'esprit humain*', the human mind. The human mind is not a metaphysical entity, it is a material object: man's nervous system. Cultures result from the interplay between the outer world and the possibilities of man's nervous equipment. This is why Lévi-Strauss regards structural anthropology as a variety of psychology: anthropology is necessarily 'cognitive' anthropology.

Although Lévi-Strauss has sometimes claimed to be a **Marxist**, his conception of history is essentially anti-historicist. To him there are no laws to history: history is a probabilistic process which he compares to roulette; favourable sets of throws will allow some cultures to engage in cumulative sequences, while unfavourable throws will mean for others stagnation or cultural regression. The presence of culturally variegated neighbours acts here as a stimulus towards added sophistication; isolation, on the contrary, entails a risk of cultural regress. But as history is unpredictable it is therefore capital to keep a record of it, as accurately as circumstances allow. History provides the only experiments the anthropologist has at his disposal. This is one of the differences between the '*Sciences de l'homme*' and the other natural sciences. Another difference is that the natural sciences restrict their level of apprehension to that of *explanation*, while a Science of Man cannot do so without tackling also the level of *understanding*, otherwise it would be meaningless. But very seldom does the anthropologist know whether he is dealing with *explanation* or with *understanding*. Therefore the Sciences of Man cannot state propositions which are falsifiable like propositions in physics. Lévi-Strauss distinguishes, however, the Sciences of Man from the social sciences (law, economics, political science, social psychology, etc.), which are 'in cahoots' with their object.

A hypothesis which pervades most of Lévi-Strauss's work is that of exchange, or rather of gift and counter-gift as it was defined by Marcel Mauss. Humankind is constituted of a collection of groups socially defined in kinship on the basis of natural reproduction. To a large extent the social tissue results from these groups refraining from using for their own sake their own women, their own words and their own commodities.

The Elementary Structures of Kinship (*Les Structures élémentaires de la parenté*, 1949, trans. 1969) rests on 'the structuralist hypothesis ... that in every society, even where marriage seems to result only from individual decisions dictated by economic or emotional considerations foreign to kinship, definite *types* of cycles tend to get constituted' (D. Sperber, *Le Structuralisme en anthropologie*, 1973). Elementary structures appear in societies where men refrain from marrying their own women (incest prohibition) for the benefit of other men who belong to other groups but are nevertheless traceable kinsmen of a particular kind, e.g. the bridal pair is of cross-cousins, children of siblings of different gender. Lévi-Strauss introduced as a conceptual tool the opposition between 'restricted' and 'generalized exchange'. In restricted exchange, two exogamous groups exchange women, the men of A marry women of B, while men of B marry women of A. In generalized exchange, men of A marry women of B, while men of B marry women of C, etc. Another contribution of *The Elementary Structures* and later texts is the emphasis on the 'atom of kinship'. Kinship can only be analysed if the unit considered is not the nuclear family (parents and children) but an atom where the wife-giving group is taken into account. The representatives of the wife-giving group might be one mother's brother, but also any other suitable representatives (e.g. the mother's mother's brother in a society where men marry their mother's mother's brother's daughter's daughter).

The Elementary Structures is a vast survey of the societies where prescriptive marriage with definite kin is in force. Many critics have discovered inaccuracies in the ethnography whereon Lévi-Strauss's argument rests; others have insisted that formalization in such matters leads to a neglect of essential sociological features of the marriage systems described: for instance, alternative choices or infringements on the rules. Whatever the case, *Les Structures élémentaires* became a reference book of Anglo-Saxon anthropology long before it was translated into English, a rare achievement.

The exchange scheme is visible in other spheres of social life: some gift-cultures of the Pacific have established a kind of exogamous economy – I give all I have produced and I only consume what I have been given. In many ways verbal taboo is also giving my 'words' for others to use. Lévi-Strauss shows the exchange scheme as having a high operational value; castes appear, for instance, as reversed totemic groups: castes keep their women for themselves but exchange goods and services, while totemic groups exchange women but consume their own products (*La Pensée sauvage*, 1962, trans. as *The Savage Mind*, 1966).

Lévi-Strauss's near fascination for the formal properties of his object of enquiry has often upset his critics. Indeed, once he has established the possible combinations, the 'group of transformations', of a particular social phenomenon, not only is he not much concerned in determining why this possibility has been chosen preferably to others (this is related to his probabilistic view of history), but he is not prepared to privilege empirical actuality over mere logical possibility. His reply to critics in a slightly different context on this latter point is disarming:

What does this matter? For if the final aim of anthropology is to contribute to a better knowledge of objectified thought and its mechanisms, it is in the last resort immaterial whether in this book the thought processes of the South American Indians take shape through the medium of my thought, or whether mine take place through the medium of theirs.

(*Le Cru et le cuit*, 1964; translated as *The Raw and the Cooked*, 1969)

If in his enquiry of kinship Lévi-Strauss was preceded by anthropologists like L.H. Morgan or W.H.R. Rivers, this is not the case for mythology; only the Russian formalist Vladimir Propp can be regarded as a forerunner of the French anthropologist's approach. The four volumes of *Mythologiques* (1964–72; *Introduction to a Science of Mythology*, 1969–79) constitute the illustrative programme, on Amerindian myths, of Lévi-Strauss's method of analysis. Myths are not to be deciphered, there is no latent message lurking behind their manifest meaning. Rather, the meaning of a myth resides in the fact that there are other myths. The myths of a particular culture constitute a mythological system, and it is possible to discover the rules that account for the transformation of one myth into another. Similarly, there are rules which account for the differences between two versions of the *same* myth in different cultures. The existence of such rules explains why for Lévi-Strauss there is no authentic version of a myth: the set of all possible versions constitute a group of transformations. Any version is as good as any other as long as it is felt by the native listener that 'it tells properly the same story': 'Therefore, not only Sophocles, but **Freud** himself, should be included among the recorded versions of the Oedipus myth on a par with earlier or seemingly more "authentic" versions' (*Anthropologie structurale*, 1958; *Structural Anthropology*, 1963). The function of a myth is neither to be a charter – Lévi-Strauss regards this idea as a platitude – nor to *explain* the origin of things. It is true that myths often mention when such and such an animal or plant appeared for the first time, but this is not the function of the myth. Plants and animals are actors in myths, not the things to be explained. The function of myths – if there is any such thing – is to account for categories. The world seems to be torn apart by the contradiction between irreducible opposites like near and remote, right and left, up and down, nature and culture, etc. Myths are a reflection on the conceptual puzzles and attempts at mediation. Mediation might succeed, for instance by showing that it is possible to bridge the opposition by 'stuffing' the conceptual gap with intermediaries, or it might fail, 'either that the mediator joins one of the two poles and gets completely disjuncted from the other (and then not always from the same one), or that it gets disjuncted from both'. Although Lévi-Strauss's venture in *Mythologiques* is undoubtedly impressive critics have been very embarrassed at appraising it. His reading is obviously consistent, but as his own method entails, it is but one among many. Moreover, the limitations of the method show conspicuously when it is used by anthropologists less gifted than Lévi-Strauss himself.

It is tempting to locate Lévi-Strauss in a straight line of descent from **Durkheim** via Mauss, but as he himself repeatedly stressed, he owes much more to Anglo-Saxon social anthropology than he does to the French school of sociology. In particular, Durkheim's 'attempt to use sociology for metaphysical purposes' is not congenial to him. Time and again Lévi-Strauss praised Rivers's, Radcliffe-Brown's or Robert Lowie's contributions to anthropology. But most of all he has underlined his personal debt towards **Boas**. This particular assertion of filiation does not seem to have been taken seriously by most reviewers, probably because of the discrepancy between Lévi-Strauss's theoretical achievements and Boas's conspicuous unpretentiousness in theoretical matters. But as Lévi-Strauss noted, it is Boas's excessive demands towards theory which prevented him from contributing decisively to it. The development of anthropology during the fifty years which separate Boas's and Lévi-Strauss's works might explain their different attitudes to theory.

But Lévi-Strauss's most decisive contributions seem to have resulted from outer influences, especially those of structural phonology (Jakobson) and cybernetics (Wiener) with which he became familiar through personal contact during his New York days. Later writings reveal his constant concern of keeping in touch with the latest developments in the natural sciences, particularly with neurophysiology.

Lévi-Strauss's influence on recent anthropology is so considerable that it is difficult to evaluate it properly. Among the anthropologists who have best understood Lévi-Strauss's lesson and have applied it to other objects in their own way are, in Britain, Edmund Leach and Rodney Needham; in France, Pierre Bourdieu and Dan Sperber; and in the United States, Marshall Sahlins.

In the early 1960s in France, Lévi-Strauss's works became very fashionable. *The Savage Mind* in particular was read by a large public of laymen. A trend called Structuralism flourished then before it receded dramatically after the May 1968 'events' which resulted in a renewed interest in Marxist studies. Not all the stars of Structuralism were noticeably influenced by Lévi-Strauss. **Jacques Lacan**, the psychoanalyst, borrowed the concept of 'symbolic function', and constituted his own topology of 'The Real', 'The Imaginary' and 'The Symbolic'. **Roland Barthes** found some inspiration in Lévi-Strauss's approach to myth, especially visible in his *Système de la mode* (1967) and *S/Z* (1970). **Foucault's** '*épistème*', the spirit of the time in natural and human sciences, functions much like a Lévi-Straussian 'group of transformations'. **Jacques Derrida** discovered in Lévi-Strauss's reading of Rousseau matter for his reflection on the role of writing in the constitution of modern metaphysics (*De la grammatologie*, 1967).

Aiming to bridge C.P. Snow's 'two cultures', Lévi-Strauss has managed to combine the talent of an acclaimed writer with the skills of a properly scientific mind, mesmerized by the human endeavour's infinitely kaleidoscopic nature. Often impatient with mathematical formalization, which he regards as de-humanizing and simplistic, he has shown time and again his own aptitude at grasping underlying structures in a quasi-algebraic fashion. Lévi-Strauss's students were struck by the contrast existing between the severe style of his lecturing, self-absorbed and rarely if ever turning towards the audience, and the captivating manner of his chairing of the seminar he led at the Collège de France. Respectfully interrupting the invited speaker, he would often bring order to the chaos of his guest's original account with his own definitive and glowing abstract

Lévi-Strauss's original work is often seen as the disincarnated report of a coroner. But such interpretations miss altogether what is probably one of the distinctive qualities of his work: the very ethical premises whereon his whole approach rests. His sympathy for Buddhism is everywhere endemic, and his use of the conceptual opposition of nature and culture can only be understood in the light of his play 'L'Apothéose d'Auguste' (Chapter 37 of *Tristes Tropiques*). The true meaning of his work appears clearly in his reply to the question: what should be deposited in a coffer for the benefit of archaeologists in the year 3000?:

> I will put in your time-vault documents relative to the last 'primitive' societies, on the verge of disappearance; specimens of vegetable and animal species soon to be destroyed by man; samples of air and water not yet polluted by industrial wastes; notices and illustrations of sites soon to be ravaged by civil or military installations.
> (*Anthropologie structurale 2*, 1973; trans. as *Structural Anthropology 2*, 1976)

Further reading

Other works include: *Race et histoire* (1952); *Le Totémisme aujourd'hui* (1962, translated as *Totemism*, 1969); *Du miel aux cendres* (1966, translated as *From Honey to Ashes*, 1973); *L'Origine des manières de table* (1968, translated as *The Origin of Table Manners*, 1978); *L'Homme nu* (1971, translated as *The Naked Man*, 1980); *La Voie des masques* (1975); *Le Regard éloigné* (1983, translated as *The View from Afar*, 1985); *La Potière jalouse* (1985, translated as *The Jealous Potter*, 1988); *Regardez, écouter, lire* ('Look, Listen, Read!', 1993); *Saudades Do Brasil. A Photographic Memoir* (1994, 1995). See also: Edmund Leach, *Lévi-Strauss* (1970); Catherine Clément, *Lévi-Strauss* (1970); E. Nelson Hayes and Tanya Hayes, *Claude Lévi-Strauss: The Anthropologist as Hero* (1970); Raymond Bellour and Catherine Clément, *Claude Lévi-Strauss* (1979); R.A. Champagne, *Claude Lévi-Strauss* (1987).

PAUL JORION

LICHTENSTEIN, Roy

1923–97

US painter

Fascinated by American popular mythology and by the language of mass visual communication, Lichtenstein was central to the American Pop Art movement of the 1960s – even if it was **Warhol**, not he, who was its most celebrated exponent. His pre-war paintings had frequently depicted a certain side of his native New York: jazz musicians, Coney Island, etc. In 1949–50 his favoured subjects had been cowboys, Indians and all aspects of the Western myth. But it was only in 1961 that his painting style, hitherto mostly loose and expressionistic, changed into the impersonal, hard-edged look for which he is famous and which was the perfect tool for his ironic semantic analysis.

His first properly called Pop paintings were of **Walt Disney** characters but he soon switched for his material to comic books like *Armed Forces at War* and *Teen Romance*, whose subject-matter was more emotionally charged. With deliberate humour he exploited the powerful narrative impact of such images. At first sight, his paintings appear merely as massively enlarged reproductions; only then does the difference appear between his purpose and that of the 'originals'. Rather than storytelling, his aim is the creation of a unified work of art, in an almost Classical sense. From his student days at Ohio State University, he learned the central importance for art of 'organized perception'. What one happens to be looking at is far less important than 'building a unified pattern of seeing'. His work testifies that this is possible even from the most unpromising material and in so doing opens up hitherto unsuspected perspectives on that material, in terms of both technical and wider social factors.

Particularly successful is his painting *Whaam!* (1963), whose overt subject is aerial combat but whose real subject is the exploration of one sign-system by means of another. Like many of Lichtenstein's pictures, this features an explosion, the attraction of which lies in the contrast between the amorphousness of the phenomenon and the concreteness of its conventionalized representation. He even made solid sculptures of explosions. In the same spirit, he produced paintings of Expressionistic brushstrokes in which the calm deliberateness of their making gently mocked the convention by which wild brushstrokes were taken as evidence of creative spontaneity and authenticity; again later concretizing this in three dimensions, for example in the aluminium sculpture *Brushstrokes in Flight* (1984). Almost his trademark was the Benday dot, the commercial printing technique for simulating halftones, to whose artificiality attention is drawn by its being transferred, in his work, to a vastly larger scale than that for which it was intended.

It was his use of comic book imagery which made Lichtenstein famous but already in 1963 he had painted *Woman with Flowered Hat* (1963) parodying **Picasso**; and after 1965 he turned primarily to pastiches of high art, especially various Modernist styles, including Cubism and Futurism, as well as both German and Abstract Expressionism. Without aggressively negating the significance of earlier styles of art, he nevertheless drew attention to their abstract and formal properties at the expense of their content. A natural semiotician, he stressed the importance of the signifier rather than the signified. Thus, as Robert Hughes pointed out in an obituary, he can be seen as 'a postmodernist before the term got going'. While underneath the cool exterior of Warhol's work it is not hard to discern an element of turmoil and pain, emotional as well as existential anxiety is entirely absent from Lichtenstein's, even if, as he himself once

pointed out, the cool 'lack of sensibility' in it does perhaps relate to that 'kind of brutality' and 'aggressiveness' which he believed characterized the 'world outside largely formed by industrialism or by advertising'.

Further reading

See: Lawrence Alloway, *Roy Lichtenstein* (Modern Masters Series, Vol. 1, 1983); Janis Hendrickson, *Lichtenstein* (2001); and his own book *Roy Lichtenstein: All About Art* (2004), published posthumously. There is a celebrated video (also DVD in USA and Canada) *Roy Lichtenstein* (1991) directed by Chris Hunt.

GRAY WATSON

LINCOLN, Abraham
1809–65
Sixteenth president of the United States

Born on 12 February 1809 in Kentucky, Lincoln arrived in Illinois at the age of twenty-one, having lived the previous fourteen years in Indiana. The northwest, and Illinois in particular, was growing more rapidly in population and in the means of producing wealth than was any other region in the United States. It was a good location for an able and ambitious man. Engaging in a variety of occupations before making his reputation as a lawyer, Lincoln entered politics as a Whig: that is, as a member of the political party most committed to the idea of a strong central government in a nation defined by its regional and sectional diversity. By the time he entered national politics in the 1840s it was sectionalism and its associated problem of slavery which dominated the national political scene, and Lincoln's own political career was shaped by it and was ultimately dedicated to the search for a reconciliation between the needs of the nation and the diversity of its components.

After serving a single undistinguished term in Congress during the Mexican War Lincoln was thrust into the political wilderness by the partial eclipse of the Whig Party in Illinois. He returned to the fray with renewed enthusiasm in 1854 as a result of the Kansas–Nebraska crisis. Douglas's plan for the settlement of Kansas and Nebraska attempted to take the associated issue of the expansion of slavery out of national politics by making it a matter for local self-determination. Pro- and anti-slavery forces hastened to confront each other in the new Territory and the continued turmoil in Kansas became a reference point for the emergence of a new set of political alignments. The Republican Party, opposed to the spread of slavery, replaced the Whig Party in the North while the Democratic Party, purged of its northern anti-slavery elements, and reinforced by southern Whigs, upheld the equal rights of slavery. Over the course of the next six years Lincoln emerged as the leader of the Republican Party, and it was the positions he took which came to define the central ground within that party. Those positions will best be understood, perhaps, when contrasted with those of his principal opponent, Stephen A. Douglas.

Both Lincoln and Douglas were nationalists but their nationalism differed. Douglas equated nationalism with expansion and democracy; the latter he conceived of in terms of the spread of American democratic institutions and of popular sovereignty: that is, local self-determination. Lincoln was less expansionist because he recognized that in the context of the mid-nineteenth century it involved less the expansion of the nation than that of its sections. His commitment to democracy was, moreover, more complex than that of Douglas. It was never for him merely a matter of majority rule and certainly not one of local majorities. It was the content of politics which mattered, not merely its operations. The American Union was defined for Lincoln by its commitment to certain goals and principles. These had been enshrined in the Declaration of Independence at the moment the nation was conceived. It was the moral content of American democracy which concerned Lincoln, and at the centre of a web of moral propositions was the idea of equality. He refused to contemplate the implication of Douglas's position that slavery and freedom shared an equal moral status depending upon the whims of local majorities. He also refused to contemplate the abdication of the central government from a determination of national issues in the interest of political quiet. Lincoln's sense of the past, his insistence that the Constitution be read in the light cast upon it by the Declaration of Independence, was complemented by a sense of history as an ongoing process. American ideals were belied by American practice but Lincoln conceived of a nation in which they would converge.

The slavery issue was a crucial test of the national commitment to such a vision. Arguing that the Founding Fathers had been prepared to compromise their principles with respect to slavery only because they assumed its inevitable demise, Lincoln denied the possibility that the nation could survive on the basis of a permanent co-existence of slavery and freedom. Yet the course of events in the 1840s and 1850s pointed towards a commitment in the South to the permanence of slavery and, indeed, towards a vigorous promotion of its interests. Lincoln's response was to invoke the Declaration of Independence on behalf of black as well as white Americans. Equality was a universal right. His concept of the meaning of equality was narrow when compared to that prevailing in the late twentieth century, and even when compared to some radical spirits in his own day, but it was well in advance of the majority of his compatriots. His ability, after coming close to defeating Douglas in the 1858 senatorial contest, to make his own position that of the centre of his party testifies to his political skill. It was around his ideas that the Republican Party coalesced, and fought and won the presidential contest in 1860 which sparked off the secession of the South from the Union. What Lincoln posited, in essence, was the interpendence of white and black freedom. Pressing Congress in 1862 to agree to his scheme of voluntary and compensated emancipation in the loyal states, he insisted that 'in *giving* freedom to the slave, we *assure* freedom to the free'.

It was his recognition that the future of the Union, as he conceived it, and the future of slavery were inextricably linked that enabled Lincoln to embark upon a political course that always carried with it the risk of civil war. It was only because the Union contained a profound moral quality that the risk was worth taking. Lincoln clearly underestimated the risk, and he equally clearly had no conception of the cost of the struggle to preserve the Union, but even with greater foresight he might have been willing to pay the price to preserve the 'last, best hope of earth'.

Lincoln's extraordinary political skill was exhibited during the Civil War in his ability to maintain the integrity of his administration, and the commitment of his party to the war, in the face of fierce opposition and of continued and severe reverses on the battlefield. The eventual collapse of the Confederacy ensured the final abolition of slavery. Lincoln's assassination, only days after Lee's surrender, on Good Friday 1865, left the even more difficult task of reconstruction in other hands, but Lincoln's work was done. In great part through the force of his own character and determination he had preserved the Union, thereby guaranteeing the unity and great power of a major part of the North American continent. He had played an important role in the release from servitude of some four million human beings. Above all, perhaps, his commitment to an American purpose, to the idea of the United States as embodying certain principles, had a decisive effect, if only because of its association with the Civil War, in moulding a continued sense of American idealism. Often crass, but sometimes noble, that commitment has had a profound effect upon subsequent world history.

Further reading

The literature on Lincoln is enormous. Larger biographies include: Carl Sandburg, *Abraham Lincoln: The Prairie Years* (2 vols, 1926) and *The*

War Years (4 vols, 1939); and James G. Randall, *Lincoln the President* (4 vols, 1945–55). The best one-volume biographies are: Benjamin Thomas, *Abraham Lincoln* (1952); and Stephen B. Oates, *With Malice Toward None: The Life of Abraham Lincoln* (1977). His speeches and letters can be found in Abraham Lincoln, *Collected Works*, ed. Roy P. Basler (9 vols, 1953–5). See also: David Herbert Donald, *Lincoln* (1996); Joshua Wolf Shenk, *How Depression Challenged a President and Fueled His Greatness* (2006).

DUNCAN MACLEOD

LISZT, Franz

1811–86

German/Hungarian composer and pianist

One of the foremost musicians of the Romantic period, Liszt was born into a German-speaking family, being the son of a steward on the Esterhazy estate where Haydn had previously served as *kapellmeister*. As a youth he received piano tuition from Carl Czerny and composition lessons from Salieri, the teacher of Beethoven and Schubert. After his first public appearance at the age of eleven, which met with high critical acclaim, he gave up lessons and embarked on a course of self-instruction lasting five years. Afterwards he lived exclusively on his earnings as an international virtuoso pianist until early retirement in his mid-thirties. In 1823 he settled in Paris, though during the next decade he travelled extensively, visiting Russia, Portugal and Turkey as well as England and the rest of Europe. In 1848, having abandoned most of his performing activities, he took up permanent residence at the court of Weimar as musical director. By now he had all but given up the concert stage and instead applied himself to the task of composing orchestral works and directing operatic music. His friendship with **Wagner** at this time produced piano transcriptions of *Tannhäuser*, *Lohengrin* and new scores by Berlioz, whose music he had always championed. These performances realized a lifelong ambition to publicize the many unrecognized compositions of his contemporaries;

however, he eventually clashed with the court authorities and resigned his post in 1859. Soon afterwards Liszt moved to Rome where in 1865 he took up orders as a minor canon of the church. From then on until his death in 1886 his time was divided travelling between Rome, Weimar and Budapest, where he spent his remaining years both as a teacher and promoter of new music.

Aptly described as a truly international artist, Liszt had a unique musical style which reflects a vast interest in the literary eclecticism of the Romantic period: such philosophical inquiries were frequently expressed in the formal and harmonic experiments within his works. Though the composer himself wished to be thought of primarily as a Hungarian with strongly nationalistic traits, his early training in Vienna brought him in touch with more classical concepts via the music of Bach and Beethoven, which during the 1820s was considered out of favour. However, his move to Paris added the new dimension of Romantic thought to the conception of his compositions and concert performances. This new exposure led him to meet not only the writers Victor Hugo, Lamartine, Sainte-Beuve and George Sand, but also the painter Delacroix, whose creations were the embodiment of Romantic imagery. Liszt's early interest in the church can be traced to this period, when he was to study the spiritual writings of Lamennais and Saint-Simon whose philosophies of Christian socialism and the advocation of art as a means of attaining moral perfection were to colour the composer's religious attitudes in later life. Such influences explain the strongly programmatic and spiritual elements in most of his output.

Besides these literary considerations, more musical influences must also be taken into account. Liszt's meeting with Berlioz, Chopin and Paganini in the early 1830s offered new opportunities for experiment in his many piano works of the period. The recent success of Berlioz's *Symphonie fantastique* caused Liszt to transcribe it for piano solo and also enabled him to champion the Frenchman's later works, many of which rarely met with the public's approval. The programmatic elements of Berlioz's scores together with their frequent use of a cyclic musical thread of *idée-fixe* did much to shape Liszt's own thinking in terms of a similar 'thematic metamorphosis' within his own larger compositions. It was Chopin who offered Liszt new approaches to the treatment of sonority and pianistic effect together with singing melodic lines derived from the lyrical operatic arias of Bellini. Liszt assimilated these characteristics into his own style by further extending their emotional content via more rubato, dynamic range and rhythmic interest. The addition of folk rhythms from central Europe, advanced chords and particularly distant modulations to unrelated keys made him the most daring of composer-performers.

During this period the development of orchestral instruments lagged well behind that of the piano, and this is the main reason why Liszt preferred a medium over which he had total personal control. Probably the greatest contribution to his art was that of Paganini, whose violin recitals he attended in Paris in 1831. Though much less a composer than a performer, Paganini gave the young musician the impetus to study and perfect a kind of showmanship and extroversion unknown during this period and yet so typical of the Romantic spirit. Liszt was not only impressed with the violinist's daring performances but was determined to emulate this method of musical sorcery, both with the inception of a new kind of pianistic virtuosity and by way of its presentation.

Liszt's compositions spanned seventy years, and though a large proportion are original works for piano, he also made many transcriptions and arrangements of songs, orchestral works and symphonies for the medium. Added to this there are over a dozen symphonic poems, the programmatic *Faust* and *Dante* Symphonies (1856), concert pieces and two piano concertos (1856, 1861), together with many choral compositions and songs. The mature piano works are well represented in the *Études d'exécution transcendante* (1851), many of whose titles convey the particular technical device or mood to be exploited. Of less difficulty are the three sets of short pieces called the *Années de pèlerinage* (Vols 1 and 2, 1850; Vol. 3, 1867–77) and reflect his impressions as a visitor to Switzerland and Italy. The brilliant Sonata in B minor (1853), an extended movement on four interrelated themes, exploits the process of thematic metamorphosis by subjecting the material to constant variation in tempo, texture and mood as it unfolds: similar procedures are to be found in the piano concertos and in many of the symphonic poems. These descriptive works, though generally rather short, exploit a similar cyclic use and follow the train of thought in some work of poetry or painting that provided the creative inspiration: their essentially programmatic nature is displayed in such titles as *Les Préludes* (1848), *Mazeppa* (1851), *Hamlet* (1858) and many others which like *Hungaria* (1854) are strongly nationalistic. Similar preoccupations can be seen in the nineteen *Hungarian Rhapsodies* written between 1846 and 1886: these are again free in conception, taking the czardas as their formal basis, and contrast many sections of tempo changes, melodic variations and virtuoso devices.

Although Liszt gave up a virtuoso career at the age of thirty-five he continued to write for the piano until his death. These late works were only heard by a close circle of friends and pupils who appeared reluctant to reveal their existence. Their availability now shows that Liszt was constantly paring down his musical materials to a minimum and that his experiments were to be responsible for shaping the outlook of many composers at the beginning of this century. This process of economy invariably mixed with advanced chromatic treatment appears in the early *Années de pélerinage* and in the *Malédiction* for piano and strings sketched as early as 1830. Similar practice with roving harmonies and obscure key centres can be seen in the two great organ works *Fantasia and Fugue on Bach* (1855) and in his Meyerbeer arrangement on

the choral *Ad nos, ad salutarem undam* (1850): both works foreshadow the heavy chromaticism of **Richard Strauss** and Max Reger by nearly fifty years. Though the above mentioned are rather severe in style, many of the lighter piano pieces also look to the future as in the four *Valses oubliées* (1881–6), the three *Mephisto Waltzes* (1860, 1881, 1883) and especially the *Fountains of the Villa d'Este* (1877) which strongly influenced the Russian school of pianists and the impressionist works of **Debussy** and **Ravel**. The majority of these late works reflect the composer's obsession with his own mortality, though their melancholy feeling can often be explained by Liszt's increasing use of exotic scales derived from folk song: good examples of this effect can be seen in the *Czardas obstiné* (1884), *Czardas macabre* (1882) and the little-known *Hungarian Portraits* (1885). The aphoristic style of these piano pieces, together with the *Lugubre Gondola* (1882), *R.W. – Venezia* (1883) and *Am Grabe Richard Wagner's* (1883) memorial fragments were to be a major influence on the harmonic experiments of Busoni and **Bartók**. Many were just sketches conceived for optional performance as chamber music for solo strings with harmonium or piano accompaniment, as can be seen in the enigmatically titled *Dark Star, Sleepless, Sinister* or *Grey Clouds*: their economy of melodic and rhythmic material may well convey the composer's spiritual disappointment and resignation to the 'idle uselessness that frets me'. Likewise, other strange essays of this period reflect a similar state of mind: the meditation *Via Crucis* for chorus and organ (1878) and the final symphonic poem, *From the Cradle to the Grave* (1881–2).

The position of Liszt as a composer of major importance went unrecognized in his own time, and for a long while Wagner was considered to be the sole prophet of new developments in twentieth-century music. Though both men were fully involved with a creative means of expression which encompassed traits of nationalism and Romanticism in the nineteenth century, it befell Liszt to anticipate the importance of a later internationalism in music of the future.

Further reading

See: C. Wagner, *F. Liszt* (1911); E. Newman, *The Man Liszt* (1934); H. Searle, *The Music of Liszt* (1954); B. Szabolcsi, *The Twilight of Liszt* (1956); *Franz Liszt, the Man and His Music*, ed. Alan Walker (1970); A. Walker, *Liszt* (1974) and *Reflections on Liszt* (2005).

MICHAEL ALEXANDER

LONDON, Jack (John Griffith)

1876–1916

US novelist

The illegitimate son of an astrologer, Jack London was born in San Francisco and brought up by his mother and step-father, keeping the latter's name. Throughout his adult life he worked hard, like **Hemingway** after him, to create a myth of himself and the short episodes experienced as an adolescent: working as an oyster pirate and on the Fishery Patrol, joining Coxey's Army in its march of protest on Washington against unemployment, going to the Arctic on a sealer, or to the Klondike rush for gold. These experiences became exaggerated into the major episodes in his life, and out of them emerged an ambitious writer of short stories and novels who worked in short bursts and spent the rest of the time with his friends and hangers-on, accumulating debts which had to be paid for by hackwork. The myth he clung to and disseminated was that of the self-made man, rising from drudgery and criminality to a hard-living outdoor man, traveller and intellectual, absorbing all the latest theories and combining radical socialism with evolutionism and determinism.

The fusion of the ideas of Herbert Spencer, **Marx** and **Nietzsche** with the stylistic influences of **Kipling** and R.L. Stevenson produced vivid adventure stories riddled with philosophizing, wildly inconsistent and yet hauntingly revealing of the dilemmas and nightmares of the time. Captain Wolf Larsen in *Sea Wolf* (1904) is a Nietzschean superman, immensely strong, resourceful, intelligent and articulate, who propounds a belief in the supremacy of power as the only meaning in the universe, and yet is defeated by a brain tumour and a bourgeois greenhorn whom he kidnaps. Similarly, in the semi-autobiographical *Martin Eden* (1909), the seaman hero becomes a successful author only to reject the possibility of marriage into the middle classes and instead, in disgust and despair, he commits suicide. Such self-defeat suggests that evolution, conceived as a competition to find the fittest, is a metaphor inadequate to our life as a species, and that the elitism it entails is empty because it is nihilistic; there is no obvious purpose in power except the exercise of it.

London's best writing works by undercutting itself and hence suggesting further depths. His renowned animal stories, *The Call of the Wild* (1903), in which a pet dog becomes a sledge-dog and thence the leader of a wild pack, and *White Fang* (1906), in which a wild dog enters into a close but ambiguous relationship with a man, explore his ambivalent attitude towards predatory and aggressive drives. This takes the form of both an admiration for them and a fear of the ruthless and unstable consequences. Closer to contemporary problems, his documentary account of the poverty of the East End of London, *The People of the Abyss* (1903), alternately sees the inhabitants as social victims and as dregs, the evolutionarily unfit; *The Iron Heel* (1907) is a distopic vision of the future of Chicago under a totalitarian dictatorship. The underlying contradictions of London's time emerge here with a commitment to competitive individualism and also a fear of centralized power. Even the socialism of the time stressed the efficiency of nationalization and centralization, and yet London could only conceive this as the result of individual initiative. This is illustrated in *The Dream of Debs* (1914) or the posthumously completed *The Assassination Bureau* (1963), where socialist millionaires use force and violence to bring about universal peace and justice.

The underlying despair, most clearly visible in London's account of his alcoholism, *John Barleycorn* (1913), where an inner 'white logic' argues against all purpose or meaning, seems to have underpinned most of his life, and his death was at least partially caused by his own indulgence in drink and drugs.

Further reading

See: *The Son of the Wolf* (1900), *Children of the Frost* (1902), *South Sea Tales* (1911) and *The Scarlet Plague* (1915). Other novels include: *Before Adam* (1907); *The Valley of the Moon* (1913). See also: Dale Walker and James E. Sisson III, *The Fiction of Jack London: A Chronological Bibliography* (1972); Charmian London, *The Book of Jack London* (1921); Joan London, *Jack London and His Times* (1939); Irving Stone, *Sailor on Horseback* (1938); Earle Lubor, *Jack London* (1974). James I. McClintock, *White Logic* (1976) is a critical study of the stories.

DAVID CORKER

LORCA, Federico García

1898–1936

Spanish poet, dramatist

Born in Fuente Vaqueros, Granada, Lorca achieved mythic status as a symbolic sacrificial victim of fascism with his murder in 1936. His work, status and worth have been buried under layers of interpretation and exegesis; his versatility and difficulty have attracted every sort of criticism – the reason for his murder (his homosexuality, his politics, his notoriety?) being a good example of this.

Lorca was a mercurial figure in whose enigmatic work several different elements can be identified. Central to all was the theatrical, sometimes histrionic but always dramatic nature of his life and work. He wrote many experimental plays from folk tragedies to surrealist farces, from puppet plays to almost naturalistic dramas and can be considered Spain's foremost twentieth-century playwright: he incorporated children's songs and games, surrealist devices, symbolic scene settings in his main plays from *Mariana Pineda* (1925) to *When Five Years Pass* (*Así que pasen cinco años*, 1931), *The Public* (*El público*, 1933) to the celebrated trilogy *Blood Wedding* (*Bodas de sangre*, 1933), *Yerma* (1934) and *Bernarda Alba* (*La casa de Bernarda Alba*, 1936). He was at the height of his skill as a ceaselessly inventive dramatist when he was killed. His poetry could also be anecdotal and dramatic (with events and characters), even self-dramatic, as in the posthumously published *Poet in New York* (1940). A narrative thread links his famous *Gypsy Ballads* (*Romancero gitano*, 1928), binding the brilliant images together. Lorca loved declaiming his verse aloud.

Lorca was also a painter (he exhibited in Barcelona in 1927) and was an early friend of **Salvador Dali**. His naive, colourist and whimsical paintings underline the power of his poetic imagery by drawing attention to their visual, plastic and sensual basis. For Lorca the image was at the origin of all language; the image was a transposition of the senses, the poet being the 'teacher of the five body senses'. This points to the emotionally vivid way his writing deals with the external world.

A friend of the composer Manuel de Falla, Lorca was also a proficient musician; he collected folk songs and possessed an acute ear for rhythm and sound, which, allied with visual acuity, underscores all his writing. He often incorporated lullabies, popular songs, *cante jondo*, into his work.

Lorca's receptivity to the aural, visual and dramatic was the mainspring of his art. Although he began a formal education (law at Granada University) he never graduated. He was a humorous, provocative and deliberately childish anti-intellectual (he avoided self-analysis, explanation, definitions of poetry), though his critical effort in his generation's revival of Góngora is revealing. Lorca had a strong sense of craft and tradition but always experimented.

By 1927 (with *Book of Poems*, *Poem of the Cante jondo*) he was already considered as a major poet. But his famous *Romancero gitano* (1928) brought him the kind of instant popularity usually denied to modern poets. In these updatings of medieval ballads (*romances*)

Lorca used the gypsy (the romantic outcast, primitive, still tied to elemental forces) as a myth on which to bind his often difficult and private but always sensual images in poems dealing with fundamental passions (sex, death, violence, pain). The following year Lorca left Spain (for the first time) for New York (part failed love affair, part escape from popularity) where the extreme culture shock produced Lorca's most difficult poems (*Poeta en Nueva York*). He hated Anglo-Saxon culture, but found sympathy with the blacks and **Walt Whitman**. It is from these explosive, private and surrealistic poems that Lorca started out on another burst of creativity. He founded a student drama group (La barraca) to bring theatre back to the people in the villages (he was always a populist). In 1935 he published his moving and beautifully controlled *Lament for Ignacio Sánchez Mejías (Llanto por I.S.M.)*, a bullfighter friend killed, and his last collection heralding yet another direction, the *Diván del Tamarit* (1936).

His sudden violent death seemed to many to be the death of a certain kind of carefree artist-child; a quality that most witnesses to Lorca's life selected as essential to his personality (his charm, spontaneity, his mimetic qualities). As a poet it is the literally enchanting way in which Lorca makes the reader participate in the work, combining seductivity with a pressure to communicate. Lorca's identification with the gypsy as persecuted outcast, with the sterile mother, with doomed passionate lovers, with passion, death and violence, could all be metaphors of his own life, but that would be to psychologize his gift, his fertility, what he called the *duende* (the magical, dionysiacal source of art, close to 'blood', 'death' and found in music, dance and oral poetry).

Further reading

See: *Obras completas* (1963). Best translations include *Poet in New York*, trans. Greg Simon and Steven F. White (1988); and Christopher Maurer (ed.) *Selected Poems* (1997). There are numerous translation of the plays, See also: *Selected Letters* (1984); Leslie Stainton, *Lorca: A Dream of Life* (1988); Ian Gibson, *Federico García Lorca. A Biography* (1989); C. Brian Morris, *Son of Andalusia: The Lyrical Landscapes of Federico García Lorca* (1997).

JASON WILSON

LORENZ, Konrad Zacharias
1903–89
Austrian ethologist

Konrad Lorenz's father was an eminent surgeon who invented a method of curing a congenital hip disorder, as a result of which he was proposed for (but did not receive) the Nobel Prize. Konrad himself graduated in medicine at Vienna University, but was already more interested in animal behaviour (ethology). He did his best work at the family home in Altenberg during the 1930s. His first major academic post was a chair of philosophy at Königsberg which he held for a year until conscripted. After being a prisoner of war in Russia until 1948 he worked mainly at Buldern. In 1956, together with his geese, he moved to Seewiesen, where he stayed until retiring back to Altenberg in 1973, in which year he shared the Nobel Prize with Niko Tinbergen and Karl von Frisch.

Although **Darwin**, among others, had made important observations of animal behaviour, Lorenz is aptly referred to as 'the father of ethology' because it was he (and Tinbergen) who first formulated many of the problems of ethology and who, both directly and through his many students, inspired much subsequent work. His naturalistic approach is apparent from the descriptions of jackdaws, geese and other animals in his ever-popular *King Solomon's Ring* (*Er redete mit dem Vieh, den Vögeln und den Fischen*, 1949, trans. 1952). Lorenz recognized that behaviour, just like anatomy, is organized into units, such as distinct sequences of movements. He called these units 'fixed action patterns' and studied their function and evolution by comparing them in different species. His 'theory of instincts' explained how fixed action patterns are 'released' in response to stimuli ('releasers') or sometimes occur spontaneously.

Lorenz tended to dichotomize animal behaviour into the innate and the learned. This was strongly criticized because 'innate' behaviour is demonstrably dependent on the environment during its development, though in different ways from learning. In his *Evolution and Modification of Behaviour* (1965), Lorenz said that he meant the dichotomy to apply to the animal's 'sources of information' about its environment, not to development. Lorenz also stressed that learning is adaptive and so cannot be independent of the genes (i.e. there must be 'innate teaching mechanisms').

After 1960 Lorenz increasingly concentrated on human behaviour. Much human behaviour, he argued, is the product of evolution ('phylogenetically acquired'). For example, in *On Aggression* (*Die sogenannte Böse*, 1963), he argued that aggression is 'instinctive' in humans and in many other animals; aggression will appear spontaneously in humans unless 'redirected' to some less destructive pursuit. The subsequent controversy was exacerbated by his bold, assertive literary style which makes him liable to misrepresentation. In *Civilized Man's Eight Deadly Sins* (1974), in addition to rehearsing the themes of environmentalism, Lorenz repeated his fear that civilization causes genetic deterioration. (He had previously written on this in a paper of 1940 replete with Nazi jargon later on retracted; a mistranslation led to Lorenz's being falsely accused of racism.) His fear that civilization is dysgenic may have been aroused by his father's work on congenital disorders.

In addition Lorenz was interested in the consequences of evolutionary theory for epistemology; early in his life he identified his idea of 'innate' with Kant's a priori. *Behind the Mirror* (*Die Rückseite des Spiegels*, 1973) further explores this theme.

Further reading

Other writings include: *Man Meets Dog* (*So kam der Mensch auf den Hund*, 1950); *Darwin hat recht gesehen* ('Darwin Has Seen Correctly', 1964); *Motivation of Human and Animal Behaviour* (*Antriebe tierischen und menschlichen Verhaltens Gesammelte*

Abhandlungen, 1968); his collected papers, *Studies in Animal and Human Behaviour* (2 vols, London 1970 and 1971); *Vergleichende Verhaltensforschung* ('Comparative Ethology', 1978). See also: R.W. Burkhardt, *Patterns of Behavior: Konrad Lorenz, Niko Tinbergen, and the Founding of Ethology* (2005); F.M. Wuketits, *Konrad Lorenz: Leben und Werk eines grossen Naturforschers* (1990); *Konrad Lorenz: The Man and His Ideas* (1975), ed. R.I. Evans; A. Nisbett, *Konrad Lorenz* (1976).

MARK RIDLEY

LOSEY, Joseph Walton

1909–84

US film director

Born in La Crosse, Wisconsin, into a middle-class family of declining wealth and influence, Joseph Losey abandoned his medical studies at Dartmouth College on the eve of the Depression and the New Deal in order to pursue an interest in the theatre. In a classical reaction against an upbringing in which culture and liberalism were offset by snobbery and prejudice, he worked throughout the 1930s almost exclusively on Leftist plays or such agit-prop ventures as 'The Living Newspaper'.

In Hollywood, from 1948 to 1951, Losey made five feature films, which included a charming fantasy designed as a call to peace (*The Boy with Green Hair*, 1948), a powerful but conventional indictment of racial intolerance (*The Lawless*, 1948 – *The Dividing Line* in the UK), and a classic thriller in the *film noir* mode (*The Prowler*, 1951). It was during this period, troubled by a sense of uselessness and by the anomaly of his position in Hollywood, that Losey joined the Communist Party. As a result, he was obliged to go into exile, in anticipation of being blacklisted for 'un-American activities'.

In England, from 1954 until *The Servant* brought him worldwide recognition in 1963, there ensued a long and difficult period in which Losey was forced to work on subjects which held little interest for him, over which he did not exercise control, and to which he was initially prevented by the blacklist from signing his name. The result was the birth of what has been called Losey's baroque style, evident in the symbolic role played by explosive camera movements and Goya's painting of a bull in characterizing the tyrannical father in *Time Without Pity* (1957), or in the systematic use of mirror images and serpenting camera movements to suggest the ebb and flow of a marital relationship in *Eve* (1962).

Although frustration led to some over-elaboration while Losey was re-establishing his reputation, this 'baroque' style was brought under perfect control from *The Servant* onwards. Essentially it derives from two complementary factors at the root of all Losey's work. First, a theatrical conception of character – pre-rehearsal before filming begins enables the actors to work in depth, while the pursuing camera allows them to develop characterization in continuity – and second, an acute awareness of the role played by settings as reflectors or elucidators of behaviour.

First with the animator John Hubley in America, then with the artist Richard MacDonald in England, Losey established a method of 'pre-designing' his films: with the aid of sketches, details of setting, lighting and movement were pre-planned so that the filmed images would yield *only*, and *precisely*, the impression required by the director's conception. In *The Prowler*, for example, a policeman enviously eyes the spacious archways and elegant white walls of a rich man's Spanish-style house to which he is summoned to investigate reports of a prowler; but as he becomes sexually involved with the lady of the house and contemplates murder for gain, one begins to see the house itself somewhat differently, as a cheap and shoddy imitation, a snare for consumers of the American dream. An even more striking example occurs in *Blind Date* (1959), where the same room looks entirely different when viewed first through the eyes of a young man in love, then again when he is beginning to suffer disillusionment.

It is this exactness of perception which made masterpieces of later Losey films like *The Servant*, *Accident* (1967) and *The Go-Between* (1971), all three superbly scripted by

Harold Pinter. Here, the roles played (respectively) by the town house foundering into decadence as the master is taken over by his servant, by the dreaming spires and Oxford lawns where the academics are faced with their own inadequacies, by the country mansion bathed in endless summer which tempts a boy to venture disastrously out of his social depth, are absolutely crucial to the barbed analysis of a lingeringly moribund English social system.

The Servant, cold, calculating and glitteringly witty, was generally hailed as the insight of an outsider casting an acidly dispassionate eye on an alien society. But the warmth, the nostalgia even, that infuses *Accident*, *Secret Ceremony* (1968), *The Go-Between* and much of *Mr Klein* (1976) suggests that in these films Losey was also coming to terms with his own background, one of wealth and privilege remarkably similar to the Middle Western family whose past grandeurs and present decadence are chronicled with a bittersweet mixture of malice and regret in **Orson Welles's** *The Magnificent Ambersons*.

Further reading

Other works include: *M* (1951); *The Sleeping Tiger* (1954); *The Gypsy and the Gentleman* (1957); *The Damned* (1962); *King and Country* (1964); *Modesty Blaise* (1966); *Boom* (1968); *Figures in a Landscape* (1970); *The Assassination of Trotsky* (1972); *A Doll's House* (1973); *The Romantic Englishwoman* (1975); *Les Routes du Sud* (1978); *Don Giovanni* (1979); *Steaming* (1984). See: Tom Milne (ed.), *Losey on Losey* (1967); James Leahy, *The Cinema of Joseph Losey* (1967); Michel Ciment (ed.), *Le Livre de Losey* (1979); David Caute, *Joseph Losey: A Revenge on Life* (1996); Colin Gardner, *Joseph Losey* (2004); James Palmer and Michael Riley, *The Films of Joseph Losey* (1993).

TOM MILNE

LOVELOCK, James Ephraim

1919–

English chemist and environmentalist

James Lovelock, inspired by the first images of the earth from the moon, proposed the hypothesis of 'Gaia', the living earth, which has engendered controversy ever since. Contrary to his popular image as an environmentalist visionary, he began his professional career as a chemist. Brought up in Brixton, London, Lovelock was 'repelled by formal schooling', but read avidly and found a school-leaver's job as a laboratory assistant. He then enrolled as an evening student at Birkbeck College, and completed his studies in Manchester during World War II, when he registered as a conscientious objector.

A chemist among biologists, he spent twenty years at the National Institute for Medical Research, London, working on subjects as diverse as clotting in blood, protecting cells from freezing, and the common cold. It was here Lovelock began developing inventions such as his 'electron capture detector', which could determine the presence of a chemical in minute quantities (such as a femtogram, a thousand million millionth of a gram). This device helped provide insight into pollution levels, detecting, for example, PCB pesticides and chlorofluorocarbons (CFCs) in the natural environment. It also generated a good income as Lovelock visited labs advising on its use, and enabled him to come into contact with many diverse scientists to discuss his ideas on Gaia. In 1963, Lovelock came back to the UK after a spell in the USA, to devote himself to his research as an independent scientist.

Always a lateral thinker, Lovelock proposed while working as a consultant for NASA that rather than going all the way into space, he could determine the likelihood of life on Mars by observing its atmosphere from the earth using data from an infra-red telescope. Living creatures, by adding and subtracting gases, tend to alter the balance of the earth's atmosphere away from what would be expected by chance. If Mars had life, its atmosphere might be expected to show such a property.

He then took a leap of thinking to suggest that these alterations on earth were due to the behaviour of the living earth as an organism, regulating conditions to make them optimal for life. The influence, for example, of marine shoreline algae on the global sulphur cycle; the balance of oxygen in the atmosphere held at exactly the right range, above which living beings would spontaneously ignite, below which they would be unable to respire, breathe and therefore live. Something, Lovelock urged, must be regulating the oxygen at exactly the right quantities. These ideas were incorporated into various papers and eventually three books: *Gaia: A New Look at Life on Earth* (1979), *The Ages of Gaia* (1988) and *The Practical Science of Planetary Medicine* (1991), followed by the autobiographical *Homage to Gaia: The Life of an Independent Scientist* (2000).

The idea of the earth having an overriding regulatory system was enthusiastically greeted by new age hippies and many in the environmental movement who felt at last a scientist had lent credence to their sense of wonder and unity of the earth. The downside was that for scientists, in the words of Margulis and Sagan (see over), Gaia can seem like 'the latest deification of the earth by nature nuts'. Throughout, Lovelock's greatest conundrum has always been his quest for scientific credibility, contradicted by his success as a guru for new age 'Mother Earth' worship.

The original Gaia hypothesis, that life controls planetary processes, became known as the 'strong Gaia'. Few scientists are willing to support it. Among notable objections are: first and most widespread, experiments can't be designed to test it. Second, Lovelock's use of the term 'Gaia' and the idea of the earth maintaining a global optimal environment for life, guarding her offspring benignly and consciously planning, has been difficult to reconcile with current evolutionary thinking. **Darwinian** biologists, notably Richard Dawkins, archproponent of the Selfish Gene concept, have suggested that if the earth is an organism and she falls within current biological paradigms, she must exist as part of a reproducing population of planets, or how did she evolve? These and many other concerns remain.

Gradually though, a form of the Gaia hypothesis has achieved scientific credibility. Further research has firmly established as true Lovelock's brilliant insight that life influences planetary processes. This idea has become known as the weak (or influential) Gaia hypothesis. Most scientists support this notion, which forms the basis of a new 'earth systems science' (what Lovelock refers to as geophysiology). The late and brilliant evolutionist William Hamilton compared Lovelock to Copernicus, the astrologer who suggested that the earth moves round the sun. He had a big idea that others found hard to accept, and was waiting for his Newton to explain how it could all work.

James Lovelock is the author of approximately 200 scientific papers on medicine, biology, instrument science and geophysiology. He has received many awards and accolades for his work among them: Fellow of the Royal Society of Science (1974); the Amsterdam Prize for the Environment (1990); the Volvo Prize for the Environment (1996); the Blue Planet Prize (1997). He has also received many honorary doctorates, and was made a Companion of the British Empire in 1990.

Further reading

See: L. Margulis and D. Sagan, *Slanted Truths: Essays on Gaia Symbiosis and Evolution* (1997); J. Turney, *Lovelock and Gaia, Signs of Life* (2003).

SASHA NORRIS

LOWELL, Robert

1917–77

US poet

The scion of an old Boston family, Lowell was descended from the poet James Russell Lowell and related to the Imagist ('Amygist') Amy Lowell. After entering Harvard, he left to study under John Crowe Ransom at Kenyon College, Ohio, where he also came under the influence of the poet Allen Tate. The move was a symbolic one, a reaction against the suffocating civilization of money he had inherited in New England which he sought to correct with the classicism and decorum of the Southern tradition. While growing up, as he himself said, as 'Northern, disembodied, a Platonist, a puritan', he grew to despise the values of his forefathers. In 1943 Lowell served five months in prison for refusing military service, and during the 1960s was an active spokesman in both the Civil Rights Movement and in the campaign against the war in Vietnam.

His work shows a three-part movement, as the critic Thomas Parkinson puts it, 'from Roman Catholicism to general Christian piety to a kind of agnostic existentialism'. He in fact entered the Catholic Church in 1940 and seceded from it in 1950. *Land of Unlikeness* (1944), *Lord Weary's Castle* (1946) and *The Mills of the Kavanaughs* (1951) contain studied poems, sometimes clotted with allusiveness and rigid with metaphor, burdened with his sense of the war and a profound alienation from traditional Christian consolations. His principal subject, as he himself glossed it, was 'struggle, light and darkness, the flux of experience'. Another chief theme he found in his personal antagonism towards Boston as a city representative of commercialism. He associated the notions of dread and death and materialism as sterile misconceptions of spirituality, engrossed himself in the works of Hawthorne, **Melville**, Bunyan, Hooker and Jonathan Edwards, and accordingly took the stance of an anti-Calvinist. In an Introduction to *Land of Unlikeness*, Allen Tate pin-pointed the concern with a 'memory of the spiritual dignity of man now sacrificed to the mere secularization and a craving for mechanical order'. A number of the early poems are in a sense spoiled by being forced towards a position of religious affirmation. Though some end with strident, rhetorical appeals for divine intercession in the affairs of humankind, however, perhaps most of them succeed in expressing Lowell's keen apprehension of religious vacuity, desolation and determinism. We must allow in the early work for two strains: the spirit of violence and doom which he loathed in Calvinism, and the sense of grace he perceived as a possibility of his Catholicism. The best-known of the early works is 'The Quaker Graveyard in Nantucket', a powerfully achieved elegy for his cousin Warren Winslow who was killed at sea.

After losing his faith, it was eight years before Lowell brought out another volume, *Life Studies* (1959). A sequence which Stephen Spender has cruelly but pertinently called Lowell's 'Family Album', *Life Studies* has likewise been inappositely labelled 'Confessional' verse, although the volume was assuredly a new departure towards loose verse forms detailing the poet's feelings of dispossession. The prevailing mood is one of pathos: Lowell defines himself through an ironic inspection of his memories and impressions of childhood and close kin. He discovers both destitution, sometimes comic and ineffectual, and new dignity. Subdued, conversational, and yet strictly controlled in form despite their apparent looseness, the poems can be affectionate and indulgent, as in the close of 'My Last Afternoon with Uncle Devereux Winslow', or directly satirical, as in the portrait of his father 'Commander Lowell'. More emphatically personal is 'Man and Wife', though perhaps the most important and exciting poem is 'Skunk Hour', which moves from satire, through sardonicism, to what Lowell himself called 'affirmation, an ambiguous one'. Throughout *Life Studies*, in fact, there runs an ambiguous statement of personal integrity; the affirmation of human affections ironically characterizes the remainder of Lowell's work.

For the Union Dead (1964) is in many ways more painful than *Life Studies*: a volume of post-Christian poems largely concerned with the failure of personal relationships, its tone is self-condemning. Although the poet is no less morally alert, the poems seem to lack morale and a substitute for the Christian sanction which suffused the earlier work.

Near the Ocean (1967) contains a number of translations, but precedes them with a group of fine poems about the ambiguous moral order Lowell has ascertained. They combine wistfulness with a sense of theological disease; their uncanny poise of tone is undercut by a terrifyingly severe indictment of a land which has lost spiritual values, as in 'Waking Early Sunday Morning' where the earth is figured as 'a ghost/orbiting forever lost/in our monotonous sublime'. The tenor of the poems veers between bitterness at Man's estate and a growing faith in existential consolation.

History (1973) consists of serried blank-verse sonnets. The volume reworks, expands and puts into chronological order an earlier volume called *Notebook* (1969) and is presumably modelled on *Les Trophées* (by José-Maria de Heredia), a sequence which, just like Lowell's, attempts to chart and evoke the foci of succeeding civilizations, from Greece through Rome and the Renaissance to the landscapes and impressions of its own times. Lowell found the period from 1967 to 1972, during which he seems to have written mainly unrhymed sonnets, a time of happy reversion to his ideal of 'formal, difficult' poetry.

The Dolphin (1973) represents perhaps the happiest marriage possible between the studied, formal and evasive mode that he indulged for so long in *Notebook* and *History* and a treatment of personal experience that he had cultivated earlier. Exploring a symbol of succour, lovingness and constancy, *The Dolphin* makes available the best devices that may be recovered from the Symbolists, raising personal emotion to a level of suggestiveness and immutability.

Day by Day (1977) represents a wilful regression to free verse, 'a way of writing I once thought heartless'. Although these last verses continue Lowell's serial autobiography, they lack the proven fierce rhetoric and syntax of his earlier decades. The prevailing mood is elegiac, rehearsing old friendships and mismanaged love, and indeed the rue and melancholy of certain poems about lost relationships often have an intense poignancy. The finest poems continue to illustrate Lowell's porcelain sensitivity. Lowell clearly regretted leaving behind the grand and formal manner. His last poems demonstrate contemplation and achieved art, though the evidence of fresh insight is disconcertingly weak. Tender-hearted, enduring without demanding, several poems do still touch to magic moments, whimsies, a sense of transience, and the pathos and incorrigibility of the poet's own life.

Further reading

Other works include: *Phaedra* (1961); *Imitations* (1961); *The Old Glory* (1965); *Prometheus Bound* (1969); *For Lizzie and Harriet* (1973). The *Collected Poems* were published in 2004 and *The Letters of Robert Lowell*, ed. Saskia Hamilton, in 2005. See: John Crick, *Robert Lowell* (1974); Hugh B. Staples, *Robert Lowell: The First Twenty Years* (1962); Jonathan Price, *Critics on Robert Lowell* (1974); Patrick Cosgrave, *The Public Poetry of Robert Lowell* (1970); and Alan Williamson, *Pity the Monsters: The Political Vision of Robert Lowell* (1974); Steven Axelrod and Helen Deese (eds), *Robert Lowell: Essays on the Poetry* (1996); Peter Davison, *The Fading Smile: Poets in Boston from Robert Lowell to Sylvia Plath* (1996); Ian Hamilton, *Robert Lowell: A Biography* (1998).

JOHN HAFFENDEN

LUTOSŁAWSKI, Witold

1913–94

Polish composer

As with Chopin and Szymanowski, the two other indisputably great art music composers to have emerged from Poland's molten cultural topography, Witold Lutosławski's life and work appear inextricably intertwined. He was born in Warsaw in 1913, and his early years included episodes of unquestionably stark drama – visiting his father Józef in a Moscow prison just hours before his execution by the Bolsheviks in 1918, escape from the Wehrmacht as a prisoner of war during World War II, brushes with the Nazis during the occupation of Warsaw. Later on,

Stalinism, Communism and Poland's struggle for democracy all impinged on his artistic consciousness, and Lutosławski never entirely denied the impact on his work (albeit unwanted and perhaps unconscious) of life's often tragic intrusions. As a latter-day romantic humanist, however, he viewed his music as an attempt to transcend the turmoil of everyday existence, designing his works to open channels of communication between individuals in an ideal world of sound.

Lutosławski's first great achievement was a unique modernist voice. Rather than embracing abstractionism, and not too self-absorbed to countenance fresh takes on established musical conventions, he fashioned a stylistic continuum ranging between the riches of contemporary compositional thinking and deeper currents of expressivity. Consequently, his post-1960 music is justly prized for its harmonic riches (Lutosławski was one of the twentieth century's masters of harmony), its animation of texture through carefully delimited chance procedures, and its distinctive take on large-scale musical forms. But it must also be celebrated for its gestural verve, expressive shaping and masterly control of atmosphere. Even the evolution of his original voice, however, pivoted around politically mediated circumstances – the brief thaw in Polish cultural life during the late 1950s, which permitted art music to surge into experimental territories forbidden to most other artists under the post-war Stalinist then Communist regimes. Beforehand, Lutosławski had worked within the constraints of Poland's robustly pungent take on musical neo-classicism. His soundworld at this stage was inspired by **Debussy**, **Ravel** and early **Stravinsky**, but in the 1930s the course on classical forms taught at the Warsaw Conservatory by his teacher Witold Maliszewski encouraged a spirited fusion of French–Russian sonorities with Austro-German symphonism. The inventiveness, panache and punch of his early music – whether in the assured Symphony No. 1 (1941–7), countless songs, suites, dance tunes and didactic works, or magnificent Concerto for Orchestra (1950–4), the finest Polish composition to admit traces of socialist-realist ideology through its symphonic treatment of folk materials – marked him out as the outstanding Polish composer of his generation.

Lutosławski's post-1960 output is generally split into middle and late periods, although there was no further evolution comparable to the one separating his neo-classical and modernist styles. Indeed, in his post-1979 'late' style, increasingly transparent textures permitted a revitalizing of melody that, fascinatingly, brought his modernism stylistically parallel to his earlier neo-classicism. For instance, the linguistic and expressive similarities between the *Poco adagio* of his First Symphony and 'La Belle-de-Nuit', the first song in *Chantefleurs et Chantefables* (1989–90), a delightful cycle of Robert Desnos settings for soprano and chamber orchestra, are as arresting as the differences. So wit, energy and invention are traits of the later music too. They shine through the pathos of his Symphony No. 3 (1981–3), the drama of which revolves around its material's search for a unified melodic voice (perhaps the work's most compelling claim to being connected, albeit obliquely, to the emergence of Solidarity), and are abundant in both *Chain 2* for violin and orchestra (1984–5), which the always modest Lutosławski considered to be his least imperfect work, and the enchanting Piano Concerto (1987–8). His crowning late achievement, however, Symphony No. 4 (1988–92), brought the often lighter tone and textures of the later works into conflict with a darker mood more prevalent in the music of his middle period.

All of Lutosławski's works of the 1960s contain riches, particularly his String Quartet (1964) and *Paroles tissées* (1965), a setting of Jean-François Chabrun poems for tenor and chamber ensemble. But the chain of works inaugurated by *Livre pour orchestre* (1968) and including the Cello Concerto (1969–70), *Les Espaces du sommeil* (1975–76) and *Mi-parti* (1976) are Lutosławski's finest triumphs. On the one hand, these are his most ravishing sonic tableaux. Few composers could match the exquisiteness of *Livre*'s iridescently textured opening sonorities, *Les Espaces du sommeil*'s central dreamscape of luminously refracting harmonies, or *Mi-parti*'s infinitely poised and poignant close. On the other hand, they reveal a mastery of musical plotting filtered through a modernist's gift for subverting conventional expectations. Almost operatic in their initially tragic impact, in each of these works a catastrophic rupture releases, in turn, transcendence – elegiac in the codas of *Livre*, *Les Espaces* and *Mi-parti*, defiant in the Cello Concerto's Petrushka-like resurrection of its protagonist after the soloist's battle with an oppressive orchestra. Lutosławski himself was no puppet of contemporary events, still less of political regimes, and his music will always resist crude allegorical readings. Yet it will also continue to electrify and intrigue, as much for the multivalent resonances of its dramatic symbolism as for its rarely surpassed sonic beauty.

Further reading

See: recordings directed by Esa-Pekka Salonen and Antoni Wit are highly commendable, alongside the composer's own readings. See Charles Bodman Rae, *The Music of Lutosławski* (1999) for an accessible and cogent survey of Lutosławski's entire life, stylistic evolution and oeuvre.

NICK REYLAND

M

MACHADO DE ASSIS, Joaquim Maria

1839–1908

Brazilian writer

Unanimously reckoned as the foremost name in Brazilian literature and one of the very greatest masters of fiction in Portuguese, Joaquim Maria Machado de Assis was born a poor mulatto on a Rio hill, where his parents lived under the protection of the widow of an empire grandee. He was brought up by a kind stepmother, a negress. Still in his teens, the self-taught boy, who learnt French from the Gallic bakers of the Court district, S. Cristóvão, was helped by a Dickensian figure, the printer and bookseller Paula Brito, to enter the world of journalism and of the belated Latin-American Romanticism; he spent most of his twenties as a drama critic, a translator (notably of Hugo and **Dickens**) and a parliamentary reporter deeply attached to liberal causes. His status improved at thirty, when he became a government official and when he married Carolina, the mature and learned sister of his friend, a minor Portuguese poet named Faustino Xavier de Novaes. A tough social climber, he turned his back on everything connected with his humble past, including his stepmother. Machado had suffered for long from epilepsy, though of a milder kind than **Dostoevsky's**. Shortly before he was forty, a major crisis forced him to a protracted convalescence in a mountain resort near Rio. The result was a baffling transformation of the outlook of his work, issuing in the unique prose works which earned him his enduring glory. By the closing years of the century, he led, with the critic José Verissimo, the group of the Revista Brasileira, cradle of the Brazilian Academy, whose chairmanship he was offered by general consensus. Remote as he was to everything smacking of edifying literature, he died as the living symbol of institutional fine letters, widely acclaimed yet scarcely understood. The subsequent heroic age of the avant-garde entailed further misunderstandings; the noisy Dionysiac nationalism of 'modernismo' was indeed a far cry from the subtle shadows of Machadian art.

Machado first reached consistent literary quality as a poet. In *Americanas* (1875) he added moral probing to the staple Romantic subject-matter of *indianismo*; the *Ocidentais* (written *c.* 1880) yield philosophical musings in impeccable Parnassian technique. The beginnings of the storyteller were also romantic. Like the founder of Brazilian novel, José de Alencar (1829–77), who befriended him, Machado was alive to the dialectic of love, money and ambition in well-to-do urban settings of mid-century Brazil; on the other hand, he still sticks to the Victorian versions of values such as honesty, self-sacrifice and the work ethic. But he shows remarkable skill in drawing female characters and eventually, in his fourth novel, *Iaiá Garcia* (1878), eschews melodramatic language for the sake of natural dialogues and deeper psychological analysis.

Yet it was the short story that harboured his final break with Romanticism. The novelette 'The Alienist', a masterpiece where Swiftian humour is enhanced by anachronism, portrays the toils of Dr Simon Bacamarte, a paragon of moral and scientific integrity who, having started a thorough research on human folly as 'an island lost amidst the ocean of reason', fatally begins to suspect it is rather like a continent. Madness, and especially madness *qua* vice, is universal; man is most often a predatory animal, and men slaves to opinion. Coming back to one's senses actually means coming back to *others'* senses, says the story, which theorizes about selfhood as the 'external soul'.

The significance of Machado's later novels lies in their ability to project this wry cast of mind on the formal level. Thus *Epitaph of a Small Winner* (*Memórias póstumas de Brás Cubas*, 1881, trans. 1952), originally entitled 'Posthumous Memoirs of Brás Cubas', technically amounts to a wilful return from **Flaubert** to Laurence Sterne – a Sterne purged of sentimentality. This odd book, written 'with a mocking pen and melancholy ink', re-enacts an old genre: the Menippean satire, the comic-fantastic brand of philosophical narrative. Machado is a modern Lucian who put the Menippean within the crazy autobiographical framework of a 'dead author', Brás Cubas, a wealthy, selfish *fainéant* with a few amours and much spleen, who deems nature a plague and history a catastrophe. The background of his erratic memoirs discloses the misery and sadism of slave-owning elites ever hankering after lust and power. Machado writes as a disillusioned French moralist well acquainted with Schopenhauer, who cannot help caricaturing philosophical optimism ('humanism') as sheer nonsense. Nevertheless, unlike other late nineteenth-century pessimists, he is by no means a determinist, and does not seem to hold too tragic a view of humankind. Instead, he keeps a sense of *lusus naturae*, and defines man as 'a thinking erratum'.

Most of Machado's later *contos* (short stories) are in keeping with this poetics of disillusion. Although he was also an excellent *conteur à la* Maupassant, as well as a master

of the apologue, Machado's favourite focus fell on the painting of characters in the La Bruyèrean sense: taken together, his *contos* present a magnificent moral pageant, rendered with a command of narrative technique unsurpassed in the Iberian countries until Borges. Machado's characters are not, like those of Naturalism (which he opposed), *described* – rather, they *betray* themselves, caught, as it were, in the net of nimble sentences fraught with witty, revealing tropes.

The *Epitaph*'s sequel, *Philosopher or Dog* (*Quincas Borba*, 1891, trans. 1954), is also told in short chapters, but in the third person and with the humorous authorial interventions made more organically related to the plot. The anti-hero, Rubião, far less eccentric than Cubas, is a humane fool, a *loco cuerdo* enriched by an inheritance and – as a victim of megalomania – an easy prey to the cupidity of those he helped or saved. With *Dom Casmurro* (1899, trans. 1953), Machado returned to the first-person novel, but this time with fewer characters. Dom Casmurro – 'the Brazilian Othello', as an American critic described him – is an unsocial widower trying to relive the green paradise of youthful love. He is obsessed with Capitu, the sensuous brunette who embodies the 'life is treason' theme, not the least because their son grows into a startling resemblance of the couple's best friend. The 'impregnation' motive – the idea that a woman can lend her child the looks of her beloved even though the latter has not fathered it – was already present in Goethe's *Elective Affinities* (1809) and at the centre of young **Zola's** *Madeleine Férat* (1868); but Machado tackles it with a wonderful, truly **Jamesian** impressionistic sensibility, particularly apt at grasping the feeling of time.

The novels of maturity are crowned by *Esau and Jacob* (1904, trans. 1966), again in the first person, but with a positively self-effacing narrator, the retired diplomat Ayres. Allegory prevails throughout, especially around Flora, a Botticellian beauty who proves foreign to the world of passion and appetite (and the rivalry of two brothers) because she is in love with the absolute. Since the action of *Epitaph for a Small Winner* harks back to pre-Independence Brazil, and *Esau and Jacob* comments on the first decade of the Republic, with a novel like *Iaià Garcia*, set in the days of the war with Paraguay, in the middle, one might say that Machado's chronicle of Brazilian life covers the whole of his century. In spite of his conscious avoidance of 'social' fiction, no other novelist provides more insight into the national mind of the age. In an oblique way, Machado often showed the huge gap between progressive bourgeois ideology and the grim realities of Brazilian class structure. His book-length farewell to fiction, *Counsellor Ayres' Memorial* (*Memorial de Aires*, 1908, trans. 1973), goes beyond misanthropy in the purest music of Machadian prose. Some see in his language – a faultless balance of high and low, old and new usage – his most precious bequest to Brazilian literature; its expressive powers also shine in a modest but most popular genre, the *cronica*, which was established by Machado. Perhaps the biggest paradox about Machado de Assis is that such a profound writer, in whose hands Brazilian letters outgrew the age of naive consciousness, should also be the least solemn of authors.

Further reading

Other works include: *The Psychiatrist and Other Stories* (trans. 1963). Important studies include: Augusto Meyer, *Machado de Assis* (1958); Eugenio Gomes, *Machado de Assis* (1958); Helen Caldwell, *Machado de Assis: The Brazilian Master and His Novels* (1970); Dieter Woll, *Machado de Assis – die Entwicklung seines erzaehlerischen Werkes* (1972); Roberto Schwarz, *Ao Vencedor as Batatas* (São Paulo, 1977); R. Magalhães Jr, *Vida e Obra de Machado de Assis* (4 vols, 1981); Maria Luisa Nunes, *The Craft of an Absolute Winner: Characterization and Narratology in the Novels of Machado de Assis* (1983); Maria Manuel Lisboa, *Machado de Assis and Feminism* (1996); Roberto Schwarz, *A Master on the Periphery of Capitalism: Machado de Assis*, trans. John Gledson (2001).

J.G. MERQUIOR

MACKINTOSH, Charles Rennie
1868–1928
Scottish architect and designer

Standing halfway between the English Arts and Crafts Movement and European Art Nouveau, Mackintosh is a unique figure, part of both the nineteenth and the twentieth centuries. He combines, in his designs for architecture, interiors and furniture, extreme decoration with extreme functionalism, evolving an aesthetic idiom which is very much his own.

Born in Glasgow in 1868, Mackintosh's first love was for two dimensions and he spent much time up until 1900 and again in the last decade of his life with decorative graphic work – pencil sketches and watercolours – producing designs, in the early period, which are reminiscent of **Aubrey Beardsley** and the Dutch symbolist painter Jan Toorop. Simplified stylizations of natural forms, particularly flowers and their stems, appear in these designs and recur throughout his career. Mackintosh's architectural training was broad, and in the same year as he was articled to the Glasgow architect John Hutchins (1884) he signed on as an evening student at the Glasgow School of Art to study painting and drawing. He moved in 1889 to the firm Honeyman and Keppie as a draughtsman but left temporarily in 1891 to travel to Italy on the scholarship he had won. It was at Honeyman and Keppie that he met another draughtsman, Herbert McNair, who was to introduce him to two sisters, Margaret and Frances MacDonald. The group soon became known as 'The Four' publishing their graphic designs in periodicals at home and abroad.

In the late 1890s Mackintosh began designing furniture for various tearooms in Glasgow with simple, stylized pieces of furniture. He is best known for the high-backed ladder chairs and white painted chairs with an abstracted rose motif. The interiors were total environments with the same shapes and motifs echoed throughout. In 1898 Mackintosh started work on his design for a new building for the Glasgow School of

Art – his best-known piece of architectural work. The form of the building, completed in 1909, is dictated entirely by its internal function and plan, and the large, unembellished windows look forward to the Modern Movement.

Other architectural projects of the following decade reflect the same progressive attitude combined with attention to detail and a smattering of controlled decoration. In 1899 Mackintosh designed Windyhill and, in 1902, Hill House. His reputation abroad grew when a design for a room was exhibited at the 1902 Turin exhibition and in the same year he was commissioned to design a music room in Vienna. Links with the Vienna Sezession group were strong, particularly with Josef Hoffmann.

After 1910 Mackintosh's work declined rapidly and in 1914 he moved with his wife, Margaret MacDonald, whom he married in 1900, to Suffolk and subsequently to the south of France, where he returned to watercolours for the last five years of his life. Although Mackintosh's designs are few in number they are striking in their originality and have influenced many designers who came after him both in Britain and in Europe.

Further reading

See: T. Howarth, *Charles Rennie Mackintosh and the Modern Movement* (1952); R. Macleod, *Charles Rennie Mackintosh* (1968); Alan Crawford, *Charles Rennie Mackintosh* (1995); William Buchanan, *Mackintosh's Masterwork: The Glasgow School of Art* (2004); J. Macaulay, *Charles Rennie Mackintosh: A Biography* (2005).

PENNY SPARKE

MAGRITTE, René-François-Ghislain

1898–1967
Belgian artist

The Belgian surrealist painter René Magritte may be said to have cultivated a career of minimal incident, electing to spend most of his life in a neat house in the suburbs of Brussels with his wife and a succession of pet Pomeranian dogs. Out of this unimpeachably respectable existence – typified by Magritte's perennial bowler hat and businessman's suit – came forth some of the most disquieting images in modern painting.

Magritte's premise is that 'the world is a defiance of common sense'. Our everyday surroundings are fraught with mystery – a mystery as potent as it is, in essence, banal. Where other Surrealists go to great lengths to document complex dream versions of reality, Magritte worked from the things around him in an unruffled, deadpan style, pursuing a few fundamental ideas in the manner of a speculative philosopher. Painting was for him a medium in which to explore intellectual puzzles, and his work as a whole represents a kind of elegant treatise on certain problems of consciousness.

In particular, Magritte was fascinated by questions of perception and conception, the ways in which our sightings of phenomena and our images thereof are oddly disjunct. *Familiar Objects* (1927–8) portrays five men with blank stares, each with a different object suspended before his eyes – a lemon, a sponge, a pitcher, a knotted ribbon, a seashell in which may be discerned the form of a naked female body. Are these to be interpreted as obsessional delusions? It may be that Magritte is simply dramatizing the hypothesis that at any given moment our perception of a material object turns into a mental concept, the object proper being emptied of its corporeality: we unconsciously seek to project this phantom form from conceptual space back into the external world.

In thus addressing himself to the gap between the mental and the material, Magritte established that 'there is little relation between an object and that which represents it'. Our conventional sign-systems, whether verbal or pictorial, are inadequate to the task of truly isolating what is singular in the object, since 'whatever its manifest nature may be, every object is mysterious'. Magritte often went about a picture by asking himself in what way a given object might be represented so as to demonstrate this intrinsic mystery. Each object, he thought, possesses just one property or aspect which will, if exposed, illuminate its singularity. Rejecting the usual Surrealist practice of arbitrary association, Magritte purported to calculate *exactly* the one correct answer to 'the problem of the object'. 'He has a thirst for precise mysteries,' commented his friend Louis Scutenaire.

Magritte's calculations led to the invention of a whole set of devices to defamiliarize the object and so force the spectator to witness it under the bright light of visual surprise. In *Homesickness* (1941), a recumbent lion poses next to a gentleman with wings leaning against a parapet, lost in thought. Neither protagonist appears concerned about the bizarreness of the arrangement. In *The Heart of the Matter* (1928), Magritte offers an enigmatic collocation in the manner of **de Chirico**, evoking a lingering sense of profundity shorn of explanation: a burly woman with a cloth over her face stands beside a tuba and a closed suitcase. A clue to this image derives from one of the few details in Magritte's bland biography: one night his mother was drowned and her body recovered from the local river with her nightgown wrapped round her head. But the tuba and the suitcase remain a perfect mystery.

Elsewhere the artist tampers with the rules of physical plausibility. In *The Listening-Room* (1952), he shows us an apple so huge as to occupy all the space in a room. He paints a sky built of solid azure cubes, a petrified lightning-flash, a granite bird on the wing, a cloud slumped to the ground, a door key which bursts into flames. In *Not to be Reproduced* (1937), a man with his back to us stands before a mirror in which he is reflected not full-face, but *still* with his back to us. Hybrid forms – a chair with a tail, a mountain shaped like an eagle, a carrot turning into a bottle, a cigar-fish (or fish-cigar!) – enact propositions about the compatibility of alien entities. All this is done with a perfectly cool sense of logic. Thus the creature depicted in *Collective Invention* (1935) is an anti-mermaid – a woman's lower body with

the upper body and head of a fish. It is a typical example of Magritte's system: he has taken the proposition *mermaid* and scrupulously reversed its terms. In so doing he has not created something counter-mythical, but rather something *doubly* unreal. Nevertheless the soberly academic paintwork encourages the feeling that this chimera is somehow 'a matter of fact'.

These paradoxical images, with their deliberately unhelpful titles, have done much to imprint a certain image of Surrealism upon the popular consciousness. While Magritte has had an influence on the visual arts, notably on painters in the orbit of Pop Art such as **Oldenburg**, Dine and **Johns**, his deepest impact has been in the field of commercial art. An American television network adopted as its emblem Magritte's image of an eye with the iris composed of a section of sky with clouds (*The False Mirror*, 1929); the publicity brochure of an international airline exploits his image of a soaring cut-out bird superimposed on a seascape (*The Large Family*, 1947). The repertoire of Magrittian devices of surprise is regularly exploited in magazine ads across the globe. Their inventor, who himself once worked for an advertising agency, designing illustrations for a furrier's catalogue, might have been amused by this further paradox of an idiosyncratic approach to the 'problem of the object' being made into a 'collective invention' – though it must be said that the products Magritte advertised in his paintings are rather less congenial than those promoted by commercial pastiche.

Further reading

Other works include: *Manifestes et autres écrits* ('Manifestos and Other Texts', 1972). On Magritte: P. Nougé, *René Magritte ou Les Images défendues* ('René Magritte or The Forbidden Images', 1943); P. Waldberg, *René Magritte* (1965); D. Sylvester, *Magritte* (1969); S. Gablik, *Magritte* (1970); A.M. Hammacher, *Magritte* (1974); H. Torczyner, *Magritte: Ideas and Images* (1977); D. Sylvester, *Magritte* (1992).

ROGER CARDINAL

MAHLER, Gustav

1860–1911

Austrian composer

The second of fourteen children, Mahler studied music at the Vienna Conservatoire under Robert Fuchs and Franz Krenn and at the University of Vienna with **Anton Bruckner**. He began his career as a conductor at Linz in 1880 and returned to the Linz Opera as one of its two chief conductors in 1886, having spent the intervening years as conductor at the Cassel Opera, the Prague Opera and elsewhere. The First Symphony (1888), the *Lieder eines fahrended Gesellen* (1884) and *Das klagende Lied* (1880) belong to this early period of his creative career.

In 1888 Mahler was appointed director of the Budapest Opera and in 1891 the chief conductor of the Hamburg Opera. For the ten years from 1897 to 1907 Mahler was conductor and general director of the Vienna Opera and also occasional conductor of the Vienna Philharmonic. In 1901 he married Alma Schindler. During these years as conductor of the Vienna Staatsoper he composed Symphonies 4–8 and the *Rückert Songs*.

Following his resignation from the Vienna Opera in 1901 Mahler left Europe to take up a post in America as conductor of the Metropolitan Opera and the New York Philharmonic. He returned to Europe in the early months of 1911 and died in Vienna in May of that year.

Despite the bitter controversy surrounding his appointment and tenure of office as the director of the Vienna Staatsoper – a controversy which eventually led to his leaving Vienna – Mahler was generally acknowledged to be one of the finest conductors of his generation. Composing was almost entirely confined to the summer months, when the opera was closed, with what little free time was available during the rest of the year being devoted to copying and scoring the works.

Apart from a number of songs for voice and piano or voice and orchestra, Mahler's creative output consists entirely of symphonies.

Mahler's symphonies can be conveniently divided into three chronological and stylistic groups: (1) the first four symphonies, all of which employ material from Mahler's settings of poems from the *Das Knaben Wunderhorn* collection of German folk poetry (Symphonies 2, 3 and 4) or from the *Lieder eines fahrenden Gesellen* song cycle (Symphony 1). With the exception of the First Symphony all the works in this group employ voices: a single soprano voice in the Fourth Symphony; soloists and a large chorus in Symphonies 2 and 3; (2) the three purely instrumental middle period symphonies (Nos 5, 6 and 7); (3) the works of the final years including the vast Symphony No. 8, the so-called 'Symphony of a Thousand' (the performance of which requires a double mixed chorus, a children's chorus and eight solo voices as well as a large orchestra), *Das Lied von der Erde*, a 'symphony' for tenor and alto soloists and orchestra, the instrumental Ninth Symphony and the unfinished Tenth Symphony.

In many respects Mahler's symphonies can be seen as the final products of the tradition of the Austro-German symphony during the Romantic period. Like most nineteenth-century German composers, Mahler felt that Beethoven had established the symphony as the supreme musical form and consequently regarded it as being the only form suited to the expression of sustained, serious musical-philosophical thought. Many of the characteristics of Mahler's musical style are a logical extension of the features to be found in the work of his immediate predecessors. Thus, for example, Mahler's time scale springs from that of the **Wagnerian** music drama, his use of large choral and instrumental forces in a symphony from the example of Beethoven's Choral Symphony, his fondness for simple folk-like melodies and for folk dances such as the Ländler from Schubert and Weber and his discursive and frequently leisurely developmental technique from Schubert. On a less purely musical level many of those features that appear to be peculiarly Mahlerian – his love of the grotesque, the demoniacal and the sinister, his view of the artist as an individual isolated from society, his feeling for nature and for natural sounds and his occasional triumphant visions of the possibility of redemption – are equally typical of much of the artistic work and thought of the German Romantics. Although Mahler expanded both the time scale of the individual movements and the number of movements in a work, his formal designs are those traditionally employed in the German symphony, the weight of the musical argument being concentrated in the sonata form first movement and in the last movement of the work (which may also be a sonata form), with the central movements (often, in Mahler, a collection of three or four short movements) forming a lighter, more relaxed episode.

Alongside such traditional and characteristically late-Romantic elements, however, can be found many techniques and an aesthetic outlook that now strike us as peculiarly modern and forward-looking. Like Berlioz, the other great virtuoso composer-conductor of the nineteenth century, Mahler had an unerring ear for instrumental timbre. By employing his large forces less to create big 'massed' effects than as a means of obtaining a wide variety of instrumental colour, Mahler created a new 'unblended', chamber music-like texture (achieved by bringing together clearly differentiated solo timbres) that was to have a great influence on those composers who followed him. To some extent this handling of the orchestra was a result of Mahler's equally forward-looking conception of music as being essentially polyphonic, the harmonies resulting from the coming together of a number of separate melodic lines. In the Ninth and Tenth Symphonies the individuality of the parts, coupled with the large leaps and the extreme chromaticism that spring from the desire for maximum emotional expression, creates a harmonic structure that frequently borders on the edge of atonality.

Equally significant as a pointer to future musical developments are the aesthetic implications of Mahler's style. In Mahler's works intensely emotional and deeply felt passages exist alongside music which seems deliberately to question and undermine this emotional ardour; the folk songs give way to tortuous chromatic lines, the simple dance melodies to biting dissonance, the naive to the sardonic, the noble and elevated to the banal and trivial. The characteristically late-Romantic yearning is, thus, coupled with a bitter acceptance of the impossibility of recapturing the tonal and moral innocence towards which much of the music seems to reach. It is this emotional ambiguity, the ironic detachment which enables Mahler to confront his own emotional response and his own illusions, that makes him such an influential figure in the development of twentieth-century music. A typically Mahlerian use of the cheap and trivial can be found in works as different as **Berg's** *Wozzeck*, **Britten's** *Peter Grimes* and **Vaughan Williams's** Fourth Symphony as well as in much of the music of **Shostakovich** and **Peter Maxwell Davies**. To the extent that Mahler's irony is also a means of creating a music which questions its own premises – a means, that is, of creating a music about music – Mahler's work not only looks forward to the themes of such apparently antithetical works as Berg's *Lulu* and **Stravinsky's** *The Rake's Progress* but anticipates one of the basic concerns of much twentieth-century art.

Further reading

See: *Mahler, Memoirs and Letters*, to Alma Mahler, ed. Donald Mitchell (1973); *Selected Letters of Gustav Mahler*, ed. Knud Martner (1979); Bruno Walter, *Gustav Mahler* (1941); Donald Mutchell, *Gustav Mahler; The Early Years* (1958) and *Gustav Mahler; The Wunderhorn Years* (1975); Henry-Louis de la Grange, *Mahler* (Vol. 1, 1974); Natalie Bauer-Lechner, *Recollections of Gustav Mahler* (1980); J. Carr, *The Real Mahler* (1997); D. Mitchell and A. Nicholson (eds), *The Mahler Companion* (1999); Stuart Feder, *Gustav Mahler: A Life in Crisis* (2004).

DOUGLAS JARMAN

MAILER, Norman

1923–2007

US novelist

Mailer was born in New Jersey, but his family moved to Brooklyn, New York, when he was four. He graduated from Harvard in 1943 and married for the first time in 1944, shortly before being drafted into the army to serve in Leyte, Luzon and Japan. In his long and uneven career as a novelist, commentator on the American political scene, poet and film writer/producer, the central theme of his work has always been to relate the large-scale economic, political and institutional events of the national to the inner spiritual condition, the lifestyles and the choices of individuals, in their sexual bodily existences.

In his first novel, the highly successful *The Naked and the Dead* (1948), the army is an organism which feeds off the repressed and channelled energies of those it has swallowed. The soldiers' thoughts are predominantly about sex and money, and yet these seemingly private realms are the very sources of the competitive masculine energy which will ensure that they conform, outperform each other, and excel in courage or control of others. Even the general, Cummings, finds the battle won in his absence, so that we see that his personal weight and authority derive from the army and not from his will. The ambiguous hero-figure, Hearst, is a liberal whose beliefs in high-mindedness and detachment are impotent to intervene in the situation, to control it, or to prevent his death.

Mailer's second novel, *Barbary Shore* (1951), similarly translates the struggle between **Marxist** and capitalist ideologies into personal terms, as the again ex-communist, McLeod, tries to atone for his own bloody past yet to reaffirm his own relationship to ideals of justice and progress. His adversary, the FBI agent Hollingsworth, is, by contrast, an adolescent figure who keeps his role at a distance from his personality, and thereby grants to authority an empty zombie.

Clarifying his ideas under the influence of Wilhelm Reich's psychology with its equation of political and sexual repression, and various existentialist ideas. Mailer produced a volume of fragments and essays. *Advertisements for Myself* (1959), with its key essay 'The White Negro', an attempt to define authentic behaviour without involving morality or sanctions. This line of speculation was continued in *Cannibals and Christians* (1966) in the essay 'Metaphysics of the Belly', where he explores the idea that the soul can die, indeed that it lives only by those of our acts which nourish it, and that, having died, only empty forms of spirits exist. Even the way we eat, digest and excrete are indicative of our acceptance or avoidance, the guilt, fear or courage with which we face our lives. The clearest fictional expression of these ideas is his *American Dream* (1965) in which the hero, Rojack, war hero, television personality, ex-Senator and academic, finally rejects the swollen image from which he derives his status by killing his wife. The divorce of his true and false selves started in the war, when, by shirking the challenge in the eyes of those he was killing, he chose to identify himself with an image of bravery and success. He and his father-in-law, Kelly, become materially successful by identifying with and allowing themselves to be used by those institutionalized forces which run the country. This is seen as a form of black magic, selling one's soul in return for material power, and in the process becoming larger than life, bloated with non-human, social power.

The other side of the coin is explored in *Marilyn* (1973), a rather weak account of Marilyn Monroe's tragic attempts to come to terms with the enormous power she wielded as the nation's sex-queen, tapping the energy from the fusion of personal beauty and generalized desires.

Much of Mailer's critique of American society stemmed from his belief that the leaders in particular, and the population at large, refuse to perceive these collective energies even though they identify with them and consume them via the media. This refusal to see he called 'the plague' or 'totalitarianism', and was recreated in a concentrated form in *Why are We in Vietnam?* (1967), in which the hip-talk of a bear-hunting disc-jockey embodies all the psychoses and aggressions pent up in the American psyche. *A Fire On the Moon* (1970), on the other hand, laments the effect of this blindness in totally depriving the moon-shot of any human significance or poetry, making it into a piece of technological common sense.

At one point in the **Kennedy** administration, Mailer thought that decisive leadership could awaken the nation to the struggle for the possession of its own souls, and he cast Kennedy in that role in *The Presidential Papers* (1963), but Kennedy's death and the Vietnam War placed Mailer on the side of the protesters, and in *The Armies of the Night* (1968, Pulitzer Prize winner for non-fiction) he champions the power of those marching on the Pentagon to outflank the embedded military mind by acting in a spontaneous and natural way. His own image in these books, however, is that of a muddled and puzzled participant, somehow left behind the march of events in a way reminiscent of Henry Adams in *The Education of Henry Adams* (1918).

In 1969 Mailer's failure to be elected mayor of New York City heralded what seemed at the time a decline in his writing abilities. Not until *The Executioner's Song* (1979, Pulitzer Prize winner for fiction) – a 'non-fiction novel' about Gary Gilmour, the first man to be executed in the USA in twenty years – were his immense powers as a natural journalist not afraid to resort to raw aggression seen to revive. From then on this prolific, but also at times wearingly prolix, author seldom laid aside his pen, for all that he simultaneously attempted to sustain his career as a film director. *Ancient Evenings* (1983) is a big novel set in Egypt of three thousand years ago, followed quickly by a conventional thriller, *Tough Guys Don't Dance* (1984). In the same year he visited the Soviet Union, which he percipiently reported not as a commensurate antagonist in the Cold War, but as an underdeveloped place unlikely to last much longer. Then in the following decade appeared arguably Mailer's most ambitious novel, *Harlot's Ghost* (1992), a chronicle of the CIA set against a backdrop

of the Cold War, followed by *Oswald's Tale* (1995), another 'non-fiction novel' that reconstructs the life of Kennedy's assassin, Lee Harvey Oswald, including the two years he spent in Russia.

Nothing on the same scale or of the same quality followed. *The Gospel According to the Son* (1997) is an idiosyncratic life of Jesus. *The Time of Our Time* (1998) is a compendium of previously published writings, while *The Spooky Art* (2004) gives Mailer's version of the writer's craft. Lacking the finesse of his literary contemporary **Gore Vidal**, the self-consciously virile Mailer is likely to be considered a heavyweight for a while to come, for all that he was sometimes regarded as a master of the importunate. That he also led an entertaining life has sustained his reputation: six wives, one of whom (Adele Morales) he attacked with a knife, in 1960; arrest as a peace protestor during the Vietnam War; and an unfortunately successful campaign to gain the release of a convicted murderer, Jack Abbot, in 1980. Not long afterwards Abbot murdered someone else.

Further reading

Mailer published over forty books. Other titles include: *The Deer Park* (1955); *Deaths for the Ladies* (1962); poems, *The Idol and the Octopus* (1968); *Miami and the Siege of Chicago* (1968); *The Prisoner of Sex* (1971); *On the Fight of the Century* (1971); and a film script, *Maidstone: A Mystery* (1971). See: Donald L. Kaufman, *Norman Mailer: The Countdown* (1969); Richard Poirier, *Mailer* (1972); H. Mills, *Mailer: A Biography* (1982); Nigel Leigh, *Radical Fictions and the Novels of Norman Mailer* (1990); J. Michale Lennon, *Critical Essays on Norman Mailer* (1986); Barry H. Leeds, *The Enduring Visions of Normal Mailer* (2002).

DAVID CORKER
(REVISED AND UPDATED BY THE EDITOR)

MALEVICH, Kazimir
1878–1935
Russian artist

Initiator of Suprematism (a radical 'hard-edged' abstractionism in painting), and generally one of the pioneers in twentieth-century art, Malevich developed his talents and theories slowly, not reaching the climax of his evolution until his late thirties. In this he resembles **Kandinsky** – the other internationally famous abstract innovator in modern Russian art – though in almost every other respect their ideas and careers make an instructive contrast.

Born near Kiev of humble parents (many of the leaders of the Russian 'modern movement' were provincials), he lived successively in Kursk, from 1902 in Moscow (where he managed to get some art education), in Vitebsk (from 1919) where he joined the art college headed by **Chagall** – whom he quickly ousted and superseded – and finally (from 1922) in Petrograd/Leningrad. His earliest surviving works, from the first decade of the century, have Art Nouveau elements; after *c.* 1908 his style evolves rapidly through several well-defined stages. Heavily outlined, powerful, lumbering peasant figures characterize a primitivistic phase in which curvilinear rhythms dominate the canvas; subsequent developments take him close (though not derivatively so) to Italian Futurist methods, to geometricized figures reminiscent of Legér, to a Cubist dissection of the object: always his bold colour sense plays a primary role in the organization of the composition. By *c.* 1913 the 'alogism' that was to form a main plank of his aesthetic theory is discernible in works (e.g. the famous *Englishman in Moscow*) that outstrip any Western European analogues in their anti-rational daring and fragmentation.

Malevich was close to other representatives of the second (post-Symbolist) phase of modernism: notably to the literary Futurists, who similarly developed the concept of *sdvig* (dislocation) as a prime element of their aesthetic. He illustrated various Futurist books, and designs for the Futurist opera *Victory over the Sun* (1915) opened the path to Suprematism. Suprematist paintings were first shown late in 1915, and caused a furore within the avant-garde (notably a violent quarrel with Vladimir Tatlin). Unlike Kandinsky's – though with no less spiritual

verve – his abstractionism 'liberated' the painting from any connection with representationalism, creating a universe of free-floating, geometrically simple monochrome shapes against a white background suggestive only of limitless space. Though a vigorous controversialist, his aim was not shock for its own sake, but a breakthrough on behalf of the autonomy and cognitive status of art, informed by an intense awareness of beauty as an independent category.

From *c.* 1920 painting occupied him less, and he devoted himself more and more to educational endeavours, to writing and – with his disciples (notably El Lissitzky) at the art group Unovis – to devising ideal architectural models (*planity*), whose lack of functionalism emphasizes how remote his concerns were from the post-Revolutionary Constructivists, on whom his innovations nevertheless had an impact. In 1927 he travelled to Germany with a substantial exhibition of his works; these remained in the West and are the source of the major public collection at the Stedelijk Museum, Amsterdam. His short book of the same year, *The Non-Objective World,* was influential at the Bauhaus and beyond. However, the atmosphere in the USSR was already turning against his approach to art, and his last years (though he remained a focus for modernist endeavours in Leningrad) were passed in obscurity. The paintings and drawings of this period, sometimes unjustly impugned as a 'sell-out', are extremely interesting: Suprematist elements are combined with a pervasive cross motif in a 'classicizing' return to recognizable subject-matter, notably the transcendentally simplified human figure.

When Malevich died and was buried in his Suprematist-decorated coffin, the anti-modernist reaction in the USSR (even indeed outside it) was in full swing. For years his heritage was publicly ignored; only in the 1970s did Western and Soviet scholarship begin tentatively to explore it and a small proportion of the works to emerge from museum store-rooms. It lived on, however, not only through the force of his example on his many followers, but as a crucial formative element in much modern design, and above all as one of the noblest modern expressions of an anti-utilitarian, anti-romantic justification of the autonomy and spiritual purpose of art.

Further reading

Other works include: *The Non-Objective World, Essays in Art,* ed. T. Andersen (1968 onwards). See: C. Gray, *The Russian Experiment in Art* (1971); S. Compton, *The World Backwards: Russian Futurist Books 1912–16* (1978); T. Andersen, *Malevich* (Stedelijk Museum, Amsterdam, 1970); W. Simmons, *Malevich: Black Square* (1981); G. Demosfenova (ed.) *Malevich: Artist and Theoretician* (1990); C. Douglas, *Malevich* (1994); J. Milner, *Kazimir Malevich and the Art of Geometry* (1996).

ROBIN MILNER-GULLAND

MALINOWSKI, Bronislaw Kaspar

1884–1942

Polish/British anthropologist

Bronislaw Malinowski, one of the most influential scholars in modern British social anthropology, was born in Cracow and died in New Haven, Connecticut. He obtained his PhD at Cracow University in 1908 in physics and mathematics, but illness prevented him from pursuing these subjects. While convalescent he turned to the study of anthropology, notably Frazer's *Golden Bough*, and, after studying at Leipzig, he came to London as a postgraduate student at the London School of Economics. His publications on the Australian Aborigines (1913) and the Mailu of New Guinea (1915) earned him a DSc degree in 1916, but a major breakthrough in his career had already occurred in 1914, when, with the support of Professor C.G. Seligman, he attended the meeting of the British Association for the Advancement of Science in Australia. He then undertook fieldwork in New Guinea for much of the next four years. It was his fieldwork in the Trobriand Islands which was decisive in shaping his approach to what he conceived, in effect, as a new discipline, social anthropology.

Malinowski was closely linked with the LSE from 1920 to 1938. He was appointed Lecturer in Social Anthropology for 1922–3, becoming Reader in 1924 and Professor of Anthropology in 1927. By 1938 his health was not good and he went to the USA for a sabbatical year. Following the outbreak of the Second World War he became a visiting professor at Yale until 1942, when he was appointed to a permanent professorship, an appointment cut short by his death. In the relatively short period of intense academic work between the wars Malinowski, more than any other individual in Britain, changed the leading ideas and fieldwork strategies of his subject away from preoccupations with comparative ethnology and cultural evolution towards the study of contemporary non-Western societies. His influence was notable in three main areas: fieldwork, theory and methods of teaching.

Malinowski's fieldwork was characterized by its depth, care for detail, a balance of quality against quantity, and a concern for the apparently inconsequential imponderabilia of life – collected as far as possible in the vernacular. This gave his ethnography a richness unusual for his time, which enabled him to demonstrate the close contextual (i.e. functional) interrelationship of many aspects of social behaviour. He was not, of course, the first functionalist in British anthropology, but in his hands functionalism became an analytical tool at several levels of abstraction. First, the function of an institution was seen in terms of its effects on other institutions, from which principles of social organization could be induced. Second, the study of function included 'an analysis of the effects of an institution on the maintenance of specific relationships and the achievement of specific ends as defined by the members of a particular community' (Kaberry, in Firth, 1957). Third, Malinowski saw function 'as the part played by an institution in promoting social cohesion and the persistence of a given way of life or culture in a given environment'

(Kaberry, ibid.). Thus his insistence on the need for prolonged and detailed fieldwork was the concomitant of his championing of the functionalist theory. In a series of books on aspects of his Trobriand fieldwork published between 1922 and 1935 these concepts were elaborated and refined. Concurrently he was developing a theory of needs which he defined as follows:

> By need, then, I understand the system of conditions in the human organism, in the cultural setting, and in the relation of both to the natural environment, which are sufficient and necessary for the survival of group and organism. A need, therefore, is the limiting set of facts. Habits and their motivations, the learned responses and the foundations of organization, must be so arranged as to allow the basic needs to be satisfied.
> (*A Scientific Theory of Culture*, 1944)

Malinowski's seminars at the LSE have acquired an honoured place in the history of anthropology, partly because they attracted many able students who subsequently attained positions of importance in the discipline and developed many of his ideas. The seminars were notable for their scope, rigour, polemical character and wit. Indeed, the manuscript of *Coral Gardens and Their Magic* (1935) was there subjected to page-by-page scrutiny. Many of his students have testified to the stimulation, sense of inspired leadership and strong affection which Malinowski gave them. Not surprisingly, there were elements of messianic dedication in his teaching and research which stamped the character of social anthropology for many years after his death. His writings retain an important place in anthropological literature and show no sign of being consigned to 'history'. On the other hand, his work has inevitably generated much criticism, aspects of which must be mentioned briefly.

The functional concept is self-evidently limited in analytical value. Moreover, despite his debt to **Durkheim**, Malinowski used it more for the study of culture than of society.

His empiricism led him to this position. But to give the study of culture the central place in anthropological theory was, in the eyes of many scholars, to preclude an effective comparative study of social institutions regardless of their particular empirical character. Similarly, these theoretical constraints limited his studies of economics, magic and religion.

Malinowski's work, because it was so clearly directed against accepted prevailing attitudes within anthropology, bears plainly the marks of his time. But if one discounts these, there is still an enormous amount of ethnographic information and analysis in his writings worthy of careful study. As a fieldworker he remains a major exemplar, and as an analyst his insights can still stimulate, while an understanding of his career is necessary to appreciate the character and interests of British social anthropology.

Further reading

Other works include: *Argonauts of the Western Pacific* (1922); *Crime and Custom in Savage Society* (1926); *Sex and Repression in Savage Society* (1927); *The Sexual Life of Savages in North-Western Melanesia* (1929). See also: R. Firth (ed.), *Man and Culture: An Evaluation of the Work of Malinowski* (essays, 1957); M.W. Young, *The Ethnography of Malinowski: The Trobriand Islands 1915–18* (1979); M.W. Young, *Malinowski: Odyssey of an Anthropologist, 1884–1920* (2004).

PETER GATHERCOLE

MALLARMÉ, Stéphane
1842–98
French symbolist poet

Mallarmé trained as a teacher of English and settled in Paris in 1871, where he led a Jekyll and Hyde existence as a conscientious if unenthusiastic *lycée* teacher by day and, by night, a toiling insomniac passionately devoted to the construction of a revolutionary poetic language which remains his distinctive and monumental contribution to poetry. His uneventful public life was chequered only by four brief visits to England. Yet Mallarmé lived cocooned rather than secluded. He took seriously his role as the head of a family and valued greatly the company of the fellow-artists who came to pay him court at his famous Tuesday-evening gatherings in the rue de Rome. The rarefied and often ritualistic character of Mallarmé's social encounters (it is reported that he would allow the reading of poetry to begin only after the room was saturated with cigar smoke) perhaps represents a psychic compromise struck between a fear of loneliness and a Baudelairean abhorrence of 'real' life: 'The proper occupation of any self-respecting man is to contemplate the blue sky while dying of hunger.'

If this unlusty outlook needs an explanation more specific than that afforded by the general nature of poetic sensibility, then it is probably attributable to the series of bereavements and separations which punctuated Mallarmé's life. His mother died when he was a child, as did his beloved sister, Maria; and his own son died at the age of eight. But whatever their origins in his personal experience, the notions of 'nothingness' and death came to loom large in the mature poet's thinking about the creation and the mode of being of the poetic universe: 'I found nothingness, then I found beauty.' He held that the imitation of death in life was a prerequisite for the evocation of the spiritual realm to which poetry must aspire; and the conjuring up of this realm presupposes the linguistic destruction of the detail of the real world, in order that its 'pure notion' be released into the fall-out atmosphere of the world's 'vibratory disappearing', and sensed in or through the musical quasi-substantiality of the destructive language itself. Death, which 'speaks' in this language, is thereby defeated, by being not cancelled out but transvalued. Poetry redeems when it demonstrates that it is 'nothingness which is the truth': it is the brother who, as a living person, is in a deficient state of being relative to the dead sister, so that his biological death holds out hope of reunion with her in the truth of non-being, which for Mallarmé is

not a void but the impersonal 'silent music' revealed and guaranteed by poetic language.

Mallarmé was never tempted to transpose this aesthetic credo into a religious faith, but the ease with which this could have been done attests to the literalness with which he believed, with **Proust**, that art alone effects salvation. His daily devotion to art, moreover, may be properly described as religious, for Mallarmé laboured endlessly and anxiously over a relatively small poetic output which, in a deathbed gesture of characteristic perfectionism, he instructed, unavailingly, to be burned.

The first phase of his output consists in poetry written in a lyrical-descriptive Parnassian vein between 1857 (the year of his sister's death) and 1862. These technically conventional juvenilia, in which the influence of Poe, Banville and Gautier is apparent, show a marked talent for the kind of lyrical composition which Mallarmé soon came to regard as facile, but which continued to tempt him throughout his later striving to develop the austere 'cerebral' poetry to which he owes his fame and influence. The first batch of this mature poetry appeared in the *Parnasse contemporain* of 1866, and thanks mainly to the publicizing efforts of **Verlaine** and of Huysmans, Mallarmé came to prominence in the mid-1880s as the leader of the Symbolist movement. By this time his oeuvre was becoming increasingly hermetic, a tendency which culminated in the seeming obscurantist hocus-pocus of his typographical poem 'Un coup de dés jamais n'abolira le hasard', which attempts to emulate the capacity of music to express meanings simultaneously rather than in the linear sequence enforced by typographical conventions.

This notorious hermeticism has two aspects. The first, which may be described as the 'obscurity' of the poetry, arises mainly from his philologically erudite use of words and, more bewilderingly, from a private symbolism, the origin and development of which is not made clear in its context of use, as it is in Proust. The words 'wing', 'window', 'glory', 'dream', among others, simply appear on the page bearing meanings that lie outside the fields of normal semantic connotation and even 'sophisticated' cultural association. It has been pointed out that the meanings attributed to those words in the complex poems may be made clear by studying their use in simpler contexts. Thus L.J. Austin says that 'the aim must be to make the utmost use of the documents available – earlier versions, parallel texts in prose, correspondence'. But it might well be felt that poetry loses its vitalizing cultural function when it becomes the preserve of scholars in possession of the necessary documents.

The other, more justifiable aspect of Mallarmé's hermeticism may be described as the 'difficulty' of the poetry, and this is distinct from its obscurity both in that it results from formal complexities and in that these largely do yield to sustained analytical and imaginative attention. For the most part, this difficulty is intrinsic in the new poetic language which Mallarmé spent his life developing. It is accordingly more pervasive and obstructive of easy understanding than the elements of obscurity. The difficulty of this language is organically connected with its aesthetic productivity: it is contrived to yield to pressure and not to yield univocally. But what is new and exquisite is that the residual indeterminacy appears as the mystery of the reader's process of *creating* meaning rather than as a background of missing intelligibility against which assimilated meaning is set. The result is the 'bright darkness' of the poem, the glimpsing of the darkness that the process of dispelling darkness is for itself.

The purpose of Mallarmé's language was to express what he variously called his Dream, the Idea, the Ideal, or Literature, although it is perhaps his description of poetry as the 'musician of silence', or of reading it as a 'solitary silent concert', which best conveys the flavour of the aesthetic experience to which these abstractions refer. Language must be made to create or present a universe envisaged as a dynamic or musical system of analogic relations accessible to the imaginative intelligence rather than to the senses. For

Mallarmé 'Poetry ... is Musique *par excellence.*' Where for **Baudelaire** the system of universal analogy was still material, and apprehended in synaesthesia, with Mallarmé it is refined into pure spiritual structure or 'silent' music. He was dogmatically convinced that this spiritual music can be played only by poetry, and that it is 'more divine', by reason of its silence and pure form, than the 'public or symphonic expression' given by the orchestra. 'It is not from the elementary sonorities of the brass, string or wood instruments, but from the intellectual word that ... Music, as the totality of relations existing in the universe, must result.' The suggestion seems to be that it is the *propositional* structure of language, present in poetry as in prose but absent from music, which, suitably cast and effectively interacting with patterns of word-music (rhythm, assonance and alliteration), supplies the vital ingredient that makes poetry alone capable of expressing the music of the spheres.

Be this as it may, propositional meaning is an essential part of Mallarmé's poetic language. This fact is important, first because it implies that the syntax of the poems was meant to be and can be understood, although understanding here is usually a matter of winning from the syntax a dialectic of tentative proposals as opposed to a set of mutually confirming confident propositions. Second, the ballast given by ordinary propositional meaning prevents the aesthetic meaning of the poem from being monopolized by word-music, in the manner of some Surrealist poetry. His method is not to allow word-music to take over from propositional meaning, but to produce silent music by bringing the two into suggestive modes of contact through the 'artifice of dipping words by turn in sonority and in sense'. The sound-system, instead of being merely confirmatory, inflects, deflects and even contradicts the acquisitions of the propositional (syntactical) system; a word or phrase will change colour when 'dipped' in some dimension of the sound-system, an effect which acquires a special poignancy in a poetry that playfully treads the tightropes of philosophical dilemmas (do Platonic Ideas exist objectively or only in the imagination?) relevant to the nature and aspirations of literary creativity. Syntactical commitments entered into in the penultimate tercet of a sonnet condemn an anticipated object not to exist. Inexorably the syntax snakes its way down to the final line of the poem where it names and annihilates its victim: a rose indwelt by night. But the protective isolation in which this image is placed by the short octosyllabic line, allowing room for it and for not a syllable more, reinforced by the self-sufficient beauty of the image, confers on the rose a kind of absolutism which liberates it from the control of the ambient negative forces that logically ought to destroy it. Audio-visual effects afford the fleeting illusion of the rose blossoming at the moment of its obliteration by syntax. The same sonnet begins with the title-line 'Surgi de la croupe et du bond', a literally meaningless phrase which strikes the reader as a garbled version of the more plausible 'Surgi de la coupe et du fond'. But this is as Mallarmé intends: the printed line causes the reader to follow through with his mind's eye the movement of a vase springing into being, while the more plausible line implants spectral submeanings which later reveal their connections with the declared themes of the poem. This interplay of meaning-systems accounts for a pervasive and distinctive characteristic of Mallarmé's poetry: the disproportion between tininess of linguistic cause and colossalness of metaphysical effect.

The immediate obstacle confronting the reader of a Mallarmé poem is its contorted syntax, which is rich in suggestivity quite apart from its transactions with the sound-system. Without actually dislocating it, Mallarmé bends and twists syntax, pulls it out of true and recasts it with about the same degree of deviation from the norm as **Cézanne** imposes on the contours of surfaces. Ambiguities are courted, expected affirmations tortuously deferred, linear developments give way to vertical imbrications of syntactical units, by means of long parentheses, contrapuntal contrivances and far-flung appositions. A given stretch of words often belongs to more than one syntactical pattern. The result is a multiplicity of meanings 'flickering' among themselves, and the emergence of the poem as an autonomous linguistic world in which meaning constantly makes and unmakes itself. The sound-system is contrived to the same end. Mallarmé likes to think of verbal sounds as facets of precious stones exchanging reflections and refractions. His use of words in oblique senses evoking strange but revealing associations is also a factor here. But for the main it is ordinary language which these techniques transform into a keyboard. The guiding intention is to ensure that the reader 'no longer receives the impression of anything external'; by their play of verbal mirrorings, words 'no longer appear to have their own colour, but to remain only as the transitions of a gamut'.

Mallarmé's syntactical convolutions have led many people to describe his poetry as 'intellectual'. Others, more impressed by its phonetic qualities, see it as pure musical substance. The first of these emphases is inadequate because it neglects the sensuous quality of the poetry, the second because it assumes that this sensuous quality consists in word-music alone. But it lies just as much in visual imagery imported from the real world. This imagery is 'poetic' in so far as it is 'unreal', and to purify it of real denotation is the function of the referential aspect of his language. The problem of reference, and so of sensuous imagery, may be stated as follows: on the one hand, the creation of a poetry in which the unworldly Dream might seem to be realized calls for a language where meaning is separated from existential reference, since this ties meaning to the real world: on the other hand, words which did not *somehow* refer to the real world would have no value as bearers of images, forming a trivial realm of analytical discourse. (What would absent flowers be without real flowers?) It follows, therefore, that the only relation which Mallarmé's language can tolerate with the world is one in which reference is restricted to distilling the spiritual structure of sensuous experience. Things are referred to (inevitably), but in a way which yields up their latent spiritual content by means of obscuring their real existence – a kind of verbal equivalent of Husserl's transcendental reduction. Poetry practises the art of suggestion when its language simultaneously combines these positive and negative functions. It must 'paint, not the thing but the effect it produces'. The negative condition of the poem's being able to capture the inwardness of things is that it should never name them. 'To name a thing is to destroy three-quarters of the pleasure of the poem.' And in order to suggest without naming, Mallarmé dispenses with titles, spins elaborate periphrases, besets his terms with privations and restructions, keeps his metaphors implicit, all of which adds to the difficulty of the poetry.

'My art is an impasse.' Mallarmé's prophetic words explain and correctly predict the scope of his influence. The limits of intelligibility had been reached. The literary contingent of the flock of artists who came to his 'Tuesdays' are today nearly all great names, including Proust, **Gide**, Verlaine, Maeterlinck, Claudel, yet wisely none of them attempted to emulate him. But his *ideas* on poetry have had a profound and far-reaching impact, immediately and personally through his illustrious friends and subsequently through the established position he now occupies in the theory of poetry. He was the major impetus behind the emergence of the short-lived Symbolist Theatre in France; however, it is as a poet and poetic theorist that his international stature has steadily grown, casting its shadow over all future innovators. Perhaps the most revealing reflection on Mallarmé's existence is that Verlaine, his admiring fellow-poet, should have almost equalled him, with the sonorous joys of a new simplicity.

Further reading

Other works include: *Oeuvre*, collected in the Bibliothèque de la Pléiade edition (1945), edited and annotated by Henri Mondor and G. Jean-Aubry. Most of Mallarmé's mature poems are collected in *Poésies* (1965). An English edition of *Poésies* in the original French, accompanied by translations, is A. Hartley, *Mallarmé* (1965). See: J. Seherer, *L'Expression littéraire dans l'oeuvre de Mallarmé* (1947); G. Davies, *Les Tombeaux de Mallarmé* (1950); G. Delfel, *L'Esthétique de Stéphane Mallarmé* (1951); L. Cellier, *Mallarmé et la morte que parle* (1959); K.G. Kohn, *Towards the Poems of Mallarmé* (1965); Emilie Noulet, *Vingt Poèmes de Stéphane Mallarmé, Exégèses* (1967); M. Bowie, *Mallarmé and the Art of Being Difficult* (1978); Richard Pearson, *Unfolding Mallarmé: The Development of a Poetic Art* (1996); Michael Temple (ed.), *Meetings with Mallarmé* (1998); Rosemary Lloyd, *Mallarmé: The Poet and His Circle* (1999).

ROGER MCLURE

MANDELA, Nelson
1918–
South African statesman

Nelson Mandela, born in a remote Xhosa village in South Africa's Transkei, became quite simply one of the most famous people in the world, and not just famous but near-universally admired, respected and, by many, loved. He was president of South Africa from 1994 to 1999 after spending twenty-seven years of his life in the apartheid jails of white-supremacist South Africa. It was he who was responsible more than anyone for leading his country not just to majority rule but, even more important, achieving this while averting racial conflict and possibly civil war in what Archbishop Desmond Tutu had dubbed 'the rainbow nation'.

Although he came from a royal Xhosa family his childhood was modest – he herded cattle, underwent the tribal initiation, and fled his clan when his guardian arranged an unattractive marriage. He went to Johannesburg and eventually became a lawyer, with his life-long friend Oliver Tambo.

He joined the African National Congress and quickly became dissatisfied with the quietism of its older leaders at a time when the National Party government was institutionalizing apartheid. Convinced of the hopelessness of the plight of the African majority, he embraced civil disobedience, was 'banned', arrested, imprisoned, banned again. At the 'Treason Trial' in Pretoria, 1959–61, he and his colleagues were eventually found not guilty, but after the Sharpeville Massacre in 1960 he went underground and became a 'Black Pimpernel', travelling in disguise for a year. He had reluctantly agreed that non-violence was a futile policy and that he had no option but to agree to an 'Armed Struggle' in which he was commander-in-chief of Umkhonto we Sizwe, the ANC's military arm. His sentence to five years' jail in 1962 was overtaken by the 'Rivonia Trial' (1963–4) of most of the Umkhonto leadership.

Sentenced to life imprisonment, Mandela delivered one of the most memorable speeches of the century:

> During my lifetime I have dedicated myself to this struggle of the African people. I have fought against white domination, and I have fought against black domination. I have cherished the ideal of a democratic and free society in which all persons live together in harmony and with equal opportunities. It is an ideal which I hope to live for and to achieve. But if needs be, it is an ideal for which I am prepared to die.

He was sent to South Africa's Alcatraz, Robben Island, off-shore from Cape Town, where he was forced to break rocks in a quarry. But as the years passed, conditions were slowly improved a little, as Mandela won the allegiance of his fellow prisoners and even the respect of some of the warders. The government gradually realized that these very years of the Island were giving Mandela a charisma, at home and also abroad, where the 'Free Mandela' campaign gathered momentum.

It was a secret at the time but the government, from the mid-1980s, began to make tentative approaches to him. He had been moved to the mainland, to much better, even comfortable, conditions. He kept his negotiations secret even from his own party-in-exile, and later said that 'it was time to talk'. The breakthrough came in February 1990 when the new white president, F.W.

de Klerk, bravely decided to release the ANC prisoners and Mandela emerged to worldwide acclamation.

The ANC suspended its Armed Struggle. Mandela, determined on a reconciliation between South Africa's racial groups, agreed to a Government of National Unity in which he associated himself with the National Party which had imprisoned him for so many years. These years had succeeded in destroying his marriage to the flamboyant Winnie Mandela, who had tended the flame while he was in prison. They separated in 1992 and he later wrote, 'She married a man who soon left her, the man became a myth, and then the myth returned home and proved to be just a man after all.'

President Mandela was sworn in on 10 May 1994, saluting the courage of F.W. de Klerk. The two men had shared the Nobel Peace Prize in 1993. As president, he deliberately held back from the minutiae of Cabinet government: his overwhelming concern was to promote reconciliation in his nation. He made many gestures of forgiveness and friendship to the whites who had near-destroyed his life. In this he had a great gift for what can only be described as public relations – most famously when South Africa won the World Cup rugby competition in 1995, the traditional game of the country's Afrikaners, and he went on to the field wearing a Springbok jersey and embraced the (white) captain. Most South African whites became convinced that they were fortunate that he had emerged as their leader.

He always understood that the first five years of majority rule would be critical for future multi-racial harmony, but he stuck to his plan to step down at the first election, in 1999. In these years he was often candid to admit the failures and shortcomings of his administration – with the exception of the country's horrifying AIDS epidemic which, he afterwards admitted, he had been slow to acknowledge and publicize. He made up for this in retirement, when he did not hesitate to confront his successor, Thabo Mbeki, who was turning a blind eye on the scourge. His ghosted autobiography, *Long Walk to Freedom* (1994), was a brilliant success, a worldwide best-seller.

In old age Mandela was extraordinarily active, particularly on the international stage, where his reputation was unique and where his diplomatic skills were in constant demand. No longer the official leader of his own country, he had in effect become the single most respected elder statesman of the developing world.

There was a final achievement of a normal life when 'Madiba', as he was known at home, in 1998 at the age of eighty married Graca Machel, widow of the late president of Mozambique. In his homes in the Transkei and in Johannesburg the world's best-known political prisoner is approaching his end surrounded by a large extended family. His beaming smile, his fancy shirts and his curious, rather high-pitched voice had become famous throughout the world, symbols of his iconic status.

Further reading

See: Anthony Sampson, *Mandela: The Authorised Biography* (1999).

J.D.F. JONES

MANET, Edouard
1832–83
French painter

Although he was a reluctant rebel, Manet played a leading role around the middle of the nineteenth century in formulating a new and modern style of painting in opposition to the outworn conventions of academic painting. He was a friend of **Monet** and **Degas**, but while his innovations were to have a decisive influence on the Impressionists he refused to be associated with the group and never contributed to their exhibitions. It was Manet's ambition to achieve success within the official art establishment, but ironically his work was repeatedly rejected by the Salon and castigated by the critics, even after he had established a reputation as the leader of the modern school.

Manet was the son of a magistrate and it was only after twice failing the entrance examinations to the Naval Academy that his father permitted him to enrol, in 1849, at the École des Beaux Arts, where he studied under Thomas Couture. From his master he imbibed a love of Venetian art and a vigorous painterly technique. But the pupil's methods were too radical for the teacher, and after quarrelling with Couture, Manet left his studio in 1856 to complete his education by copying in the Louvre and travelling in Italy, Germany and Holland. His first entry for the Salon, in 1856, *The Absinthe Drinker*, was rejected, in spite of Delacroix's support, but in 1861 a portrait of his parents and *The Spanish Guitar Player* were shown at the Salon and he was at once hailed by young painters and progressive critics as a leader. During the next decade the pattern continued, with major works being rejected or creating scandal in the press, but with such writers as Astruc, **Baudelaire** and **Zola** rallying to his defence. At the Café Guerbois, artists and critics gathered to hear Manet speak, and his Paris studio became a meeting place for artists. In Fantin-Latour's painting of 1870, *A Studio in the Batignolles*, Manet is shown surrounded by **Renoir**, Monet, Bazille, Zola, Scholderer and Maître, at work on a portrait of Astruc.

Manet was surprised at the official response to his work since he regarded himself as a traditionalist. He greatly admired the Spanish masters, and his broad handling and rich, dark colouring, with a liberal use of black, are derived from Velazquez, Ribera and Goya. A number of his early works also treat Spanish themes, such as bullfights and Spanish dancers. His chief entry for the Salon of 1863, *Le Déjeuner sur l'herbe*, was rejected and created a scandal at the special Salon of rejected works – the so-called 'Salon des Refusés'. It derives its composition from an engraving by Marcantonio Raimondi after a lost Raphael painting, and transposes into a modern idiom the arcadian idyll of Titian's early *Fête champêtre* in the Louvre. But critics were appalled by the sight of naked women beside men in contemporary dress, and, furthermore, attacked

Manet's style. In looking back to the example of Velazquez, Manet rejected the detailed finish, polished surface and laborious modelling of academic painting for a rapid execution and bold colouring. In order to preserve the vitality of his visual impressions he simplified what he saw, encompassing figures in bold outlines and eliminating the carefully modulated halftones favoured by the academic masters.

Manet daringly applied this radical technique to contemporary themes. In 1863, at an exhibition of his work at the picture dealer Martinet's, he showed a painting of fashionably dressed Parisians, among them his friends, parading in a park. *A Concert in the Tuileries Gardens* is a landmark because it treats modern life in a spontaneous style, in a composition that is apparently so unpremeditated as to be almost haphazard. At the Salon of 1865 Manet caused yet another scandal with his *Olympia*. The picture is a reinterpretation of Titian's *Venus of Urbino*, but the reclining female nude is defiantly modern, so much so that she outraged the public. The model, as in *Le Déjeuner sur l'herbe*, was Victorine Meurend, but here she is more abrasively erotic, brazenly staring at the spectator, naked except for a pair of slippers and a black velvet lace around her neck.

It is impossible to determine how much of the air of worldliness and vulgarity in *Olympia* is intentional. Manet denied that he intended to shock, but in transposing a Renaissance Venus into a nineteenth-century boudoir she became a prostitute, and Manet's intuition and honesty as an observer prevent him from denying the fact. He is the painter of modern life *malgré lui*, and it is precisely his keen sense of the flavour of modern life that earned him the admiration of Baudelaire and Zola.

Not until 1865 did Manet in fact visit Spain and encounter the work of Velazquez and Goya in quantity, and in 1867 he painted a large picture of *The Execution of the Emperor Maximilian*, inspired by Goya's *Third of May*. That same year he exhibited some fifty paintings at the Exposition Universelle but with little success. During the Franco-Prussian War he served as a staff officer in the National Guard, but under the Commune of 1871 he retired to the country with his family. He travelled in Holland in 1872 and *Le Bon Bock*, which was a great success at the Salon of 1873, shows the strong influence of Frans Hals.

The next phase of Manet's career shows him turning increasingly to modern themes, and even, under the influence of the Impressionists, painting out of doors. It was through Berthe Morisot, his pupil since 1868, and one of the models for *The Balcony* (Salon 1869), that he became intimate with Monet and Renoir. During the summer of 1874 he joined Monet at Argenteuil and painted river scenes and regattas in a lively Impressionist technique. Such pictures as *Boating* (1874) and *Monet Painting in His Floating Studio* (1874) are more brilliant in colour and more loosely painted than his earlier work, but still retain some touches of the black of which he was so fond.

The association with the Impressionists did nothing for Manet's reputation, and he suffered more Salon rejections in 1876 and 1877. Nor did his paintings of modern life help. From the mid-1870s he began a dazzling series of pictures, close in spirit to the work of his friend Degas, of bars, concert-halls and prostitutes which includes *Nana* (1877) and *La Servante de Bocks* (1878, two versions), and culminates in the masterful *Bar at the Folies-Bergère* (1881). This late work, completed less than two years before his death, defines the type of the modern female, in her glance, her pose, her dress, and in her habitat, the brash, noisy and mysterious world of the café-concert reflected in the mirror behind her.

In the summer of 1879 Manet first began to feel the effects of the illness (*locomotor ataxia*) that was to lead to his death. Over the next four years he retreated increasingly to the seclusion of the country around Paris, to Bellevue, Versailles and Rueil. In semi-retirement his work took on a lighter and more domestic character, with paintings of women sitting in his garden, and pastel portraits of such lady friends as the actress Méry Laurent. Even his chief Salon exhibits of these years, *In the Conservatory* (1879) and *At*

Père Lathuille's (1880), are like vignettes of modern life, comedies of manners in a light, romantic vein. From this period also date many of Manet's still-lifes. It was above all in this genre, in small canvases of peonies or asparagus, that he displayed his keen colour sense and virtuoso brushwork.

Manet's influence in his own lifetime and since has been enormous. His early disciples included Monet, Berthe Morisot and Eva Gonzales, but his process of bold simplification of form was to determine the approach of most of the Post-Impressionists, as well as the early **Picasso** and **Matisse**. But he also created the genre of contemporary social themes which was taken up by **Toulouse-Lautrec**, and also debased by many fashionable painters of the latter part of the century, such as Boldini, Carolus-Duran and Émile Blanche. The aspect of Manet's achievement that is most often neglected is his psychological insight. Because his understanding of the modern human animal is so much more subtle than Renoir's, for example, he avoids the latter's excesses of sentimentality. In his pictures of men and women meeting, conversing, at a bar or a ball, over lunch or dinner, he creates a drama which, though calculated understatement, evokes with great intensity the spirit of the era.

Further reading

See: Julius Meier-Graefe, *Edouard Manet* (1912); Etienne Moreau-Nelaton, *Manet raconté part lui-même* (2 vols, 1926); George H. Hamilton, *Manet and His Critics* (1954); Pierre Courthion, *Manet* (trans. 1962); Anne Coffin Hansen, *Edouard Manet* (1967); Pierre Schneider, *The World of Manet* (1968); K. Adler, *Manet* (1986).

MICHAEL WILSON

MANN, Thomas
1875–1955
German novelist

Son of a prosperous north German grain merchant and a mother of partly Brazilian origins, Thomas, younger brother of Heinrich Mann, was born in Lübeck. He began writing early and was fortunate enough, on leaving school, to be able to devote most of his time to it. In 1893 Mann left Lübeck for Munich, which became his home for the next forty years. His marriage to Katia Pringsheim in 1905 resulted in six children, a number of whom were to become distinguished in their turn as writers or scholars. In 1929 Mann was awarded the Nobel Prize; in 1933 the rise of Nazism forced him and his family into exile, first in Switzerland, then in the USA where he was held in high honour, his home in Pacific Palisades, California, becoming something of a place of pilgrimage. After the war he returned to Switzerland and settled there for the remainder of his life.

At the age of only twenty-six, Mann achieved immediate success with his first novel, *Buddenbrooks* (1901, trans. 1924). This surprisingly mature work is the history of four generations of a family of grain merchants from prosperity and full integration into the Hanseatic community in which they live to final alienation and decline. The single-minded vitality of the Buddenbrook clan is able, in its great days, to assimilate and control its rogue members with their dangerous traits of fecklessness or lethargy: but these elements are gradually reinforced by a more powerful and complex strain – that of the imagination with its tendency to question and even subvert the stolid self-assurance of the practical life. In proportion as imagination, art and the probing intellect assert their claims, the Buddenbrook hold on life diminishes until, in the musically gifted but physically feeble Hanno, the last of the line, it disappears altogether.

The tendency, supported by Mann's reading of Schopenhauer, to view the imagination as a force essentially hostile to the crude vitality of life is one which fuels much of Mann's earlier fiction, notably the novellas *Tonio Kröger* and *Tristan* (1903), both in their different ways studies in the predicament of the writer. In Mann's possibly most famous work, *Death in Venice (Der Tod in Venedig,*

1911; translated in *Three Tales*, 1929), the protagonist, Gustav von Aschenbach, is a mature and renowned writer who has subjugated the moral dubieties of the imagination to the demands of a classicizing art of intransigent ethical and aesthetic rigour. But Aschenbach's (in Nietzsche's term) Apolline solutions are undermined and finally obliterated: on a journey to Venice he encounters the Polish boy Tadzio whose almost perfect beauty, though seeming at first a confirmation of Aschenbach's classical ideals, gradually tempts him into sensual indulgence, Dionysian disintegration and finally death. *Death in Venice*, then, is concerned with the essential paradox of the artistic endeavour: the ethical and aesthetic realms which Aschenbach has thought to reconcile with one another prove in the end to be warring elements: and the story itself, which is constructed with consummate artistry, thus implicitly calls its own very virtuosity in question.

The Magic Mountain (*Der Zauberberg*, 1922, trans. 1927) was originally conceived as a comic pendant to *Death in Venice*, but grew to a novel of considerable length. It is, ironically, a *Bildungsroman*: ironically because its hero, the innocent young Hans Castorp, is educated to life not, like the traditional hero of the German novel of education, via life itself, but in the hermetically sealed environment of a Swiss tuberculosis sanatorium whose entire *raison d'être* is disease and death. Does disease heighten the sensibilities, ennoble the personality? Hans Castorp is at first romantically disposed to think so, but finds himself disenchanted by the relentlessly trivial preoccupations of most of the sanatorium's denizens. More deeply demanding are the claims on his consciousness of a small number of characters who act as educators or at least as perpetrators of particular, exclusive viewpoints: Hans Castorp's cousin Joachim, devoted to a Prussian ethics of duty; Settembrini, an Italian rationalist and humanist; Naphta, a Jew turned Jesuit turned Marxist, advocate of a reviving terror; Dr Krokowski, adherent of psychoanalysis; Claudia Chauchat,

bearer to Hans Castorp of the darkly irresistible attractions of Eros in a diseased body; and Mynheer Peeperkorn, the aged and tragically impotent apostle of vitalism. Hans Castorp, representative of Germany, pays respectful heed to all these mentors, but does not unequivocally decide for any of them. History, in the shape of the First World War, erupts into his timeless dream and precipitates him on to the fields of Flanders: perhaps, the narrator reflects in the book's final sentence, Love will rise from this universal carnage. Both here and in his earlier vision in the chapter entitled 'Snow', Hans Castorp rejects the enticing darknesses of experience in favour of health and life: but it is possible to feel that Castorp's options remain somewhat abstract, unrealized and in context unrealizable against the author's obvious enthralment by the forces of decay.

In addition to other preoccupations, *The Magic Mountain* is much concerned with the problem of time, and in particular with the disjunction between consciousness and chronology. Mann's next major work, the tetralogy *Joseph and His Brothers* (*Joseph und seine Brüder*, 1933–43, trans. 1934–44), extends this theme further to probe the relationship between time and myth and to investigate the patterns formed by a mythic appropriation of history – many of the characters in the first volume, *The Tales of Jacob* (*Die Geschichten Jakobs*), are prone to see themselves as types in whom time-bound particularization is of far less importance than their mythical status. But Joseph, the story of whose rejection by his brothers, slavery and rise to favour and administrative genius in Egypt is the subject of the other three volumes, is of a more modern, sophisticated turn of mind: unabashed by his knowledge of his place in the scheme of things, he adapts this knowledge to his own ironic purposes, seeing myth in terms of psychology and highly conscious of the fact that he is 'in a story'. The young Joseph, handsome, gifted, egoistic and something of a rogue, undergoes a long process of education in which he is twice cast into the pit and twice resurrected to become finally adviser to Pharaoh and provider during the great famine; as in Genesis, he is ultimately reconciled with his father and brothers. Like *The Magic Mountain*, the Joseph tetralogy is a kind of *Bildungsroman* depicting the progress both of its protagonist and also, as Mann himself indicated, of the human race as a whole to arrive at a point where myth becomes fruitfully integrated into history and egoism gives place to responsibility.

The writing of the Joseph tetralogy was almost exactly contemporaneous with the rise and fall of the **Hitler** regime, and it was part of Mann's intention to oppose to the crude racist mythologizing of the Nazis a treatment of myth which should be light, lucent and ultimately humanistic. In *Doktor Faustus* (1947, trans. 1948), however, the light mood disappears to make room for Mann's fullest treatment of the suspect and demonic nature of the imagination. The devil grants to Mann's Faust, the composer Adrian Leverkühn, the traditional twenty-four years of heightened existence, at the end of which he shall succumb, via the syphilis he has already contracted, to the hell that awaits him. Leverkühn's creativity shall be intensified and he shall find, in his music, the true passion which, according to this highly sophisticated devil, can, at this late stage of men's culture, inhere only in ambiguity and irony. But a clause is attached to the pact – the eschewal of love. Hence, Leverkühn's genius, the devil goes on to say, will be that of sickness, a type of genius which life loves far more than the plodding progress of health. But Leverkühn's story is transmitted to the reader via a narrator for whom the composer's genius, however great its fascinations, is essentially suspect: the scholar Serenus Zeitblom, a representative of the humanistic tradition submerged and silenced during the Nazi era. Zeitblom writes his account of Leverkühn's life during the last two years of the war, ending as the Allied troops are marching into Germany: and he develops during the time of that narration from a bumbling, slightly absurd figure into a figure of moving dignity as he laments the fate of his country. Above all, Zeitblom is a *decent* man; and although Mann attempts no crude equation between Leverkühn's career and the course of Nazism, he does, by setting the decent against the damned, limited order against creative chaos, achieve the effect of a dialogue between the forces at work in the German – and, indeed, the human – psyche. Mann reverts here to his early theme of the contrast between the man of imagination and the man of the practical life – but the contrast here is far more subtly differentiated and has a far greater resonance.

In *Confessions of Felix Krull* (*Bekenntnisse des Felix Krull*, begun 1911, resumed 1951, published 1954, translated 1955), however, the man of imagination makes his last and most light-hearted appearance. The long line of Mann's artist figures, stretching from Hanno Buddenbrook and Tonio Kröger via no less a figure than Goethe (in *Lotte in Weimar*, 1940) to Leverkühn, culminates in Felix Krull, the artist as illusionist. Blessed with a combination of extreme good looks, quick wits and a flawless acting technique, Krull in effect makes his life his material, rising from obscure beginnings to the pleasures of assumed aristocracy and justifying his roguery with a paradoxical evaluation of himself as a practitioner of high moral self-discipline. In comic form, the novel is concerned with the moral dubiety of the aesthetic enterprise. But Mann only completed the first half of this parodistic exercise in the picaresque: completion in the traditional pattern would have had to involve Krull in some form of remorse and penitence – as it is, he leaves us in the full flush of triumph.

And this, perhaps, has its own appropriateness. Mann's ultimate stance is that of the humanist, concerned to explore those forces by which the health of life is threatened. Yet many readers have felt that the health of life fails to engage the full weight of Mann's creative interest, but is merely implicitly posited somewhere outside the text, theoretically deferred to but never imaginatively realized. Other serious disagreements have arisen: is Mann's famous irony an expression of balance and mature judgement or does it too often function as a means of evading the issues involved? Does his frequent play with paradox result in revealing perceptions or only in a kind of higher glibness? Are his novels over-schematized? These are problems which continue to be discussed: but discussed in the context of the realization that Mann's commanding stature as a novelist – his range, creative energy and sustained technical mastery – can hardly be seriously questioned.

Further reading

See: *Gesammelte Werke* (12 vols, 1960). Other translations include: *The Holy Sinner* (1951); *The Black Swan* (1954); *Stories of Three Decades* (1936). See also: E. Heller, *The Ironic German* (1958); R. Gray, *The German Tradition in Literature* (1965); T.J. Reed, *Thomas Mann: The Uses of Tradition* (1974); T.E. Apter, *Thomas Mann: The Devil's Advocate* (1978); Nigel Hamilton: *Brothers Mann: The Lives of Heinrich and Thomas Mann* (1978); Herbert Lehnert and Eva Wessell (eds), *A Companion to the Works of Thomas Mann* (2004).

CORBET STEWART

MAO ZEDONG (MAO TSE-TUNG)

1893–1976

Chinese leader

'Chairman Mao', as he was known during the later stages of his career, was by any measure a world-historic figure. With the exception of Taiwan (then called Formosa), which fell into the hands of his arch-enemy Jiang Jieshi (Chiang Kaishek), and some other, smaller islands, he re-unified a vast nation-empire containing a sixth of humankind that, following the final collapse of the last imperial dynasty, the Qing, in 1912, had endured thirty-seven years of uncertain progress, exacerbated by Japanese occupation. Yet the brighter future that seemed implicit in Mao Zedong's proclamation of a People's Republic in 1949 did not eventuate. Instead, Mao instituted a tyranny that culminated in the notorious, but at the time little understood, Cultural Revolution – launched in

1966, and only 'officially' ended ten years later with his demise. Yet such was Mao's charismatic reputation, both among portions of China's population and among developing nations in Asia, Africa and Latin America, that he was widely perceived as a force for the good. In the aftermath of World War II, when Europe's colonial empires were palpably past their sell-by date, but when the USA was emerging as an interventionist superpower, Mao, who coined the very term 'third world', was the undisputed champion of anti-imperialism, to the extent that his image was cherished as an icon by left-wing students and other radicals, in both Europe and America.

Based on a much firmer knowledge of the quarter-century period of his rule in China, Mao has since been subjected to fierce and unflattering re-appraisal, anecdotally supported by revelations of megalomania, sexual depravity and physical decline contained in *The Private Life of Chairman Mao* (1994), a grotesquely intimate memoir written by Mao's long-serving personal physician, Zhisui Li. While the sheer numbers of those who perished as a result of Mao's ill-conceived policies, running into tens of millions, are sufficient in themselves to bespeak a despot, it is also clear that Mao's impact on China's economy was ruinous. Even so, the concept of Mao as founder of the modern Chinese nation, of Mao the 'great helmsman' in the parlance of the self-propaganda he assiduously promoted, sticks. In the great, 4,000-year sweep of Chinese history, he may even be seen as a traditionalist as much as a revolutionary. Towards the end of his life he increasingly extolled the virtues of Qin Shihuangdi, the 'first' emperor who established the imperial throne in 221 BC on the back of a narrow 'legalist' ideology that, countervailing the paternalist precepts of Confucianism, insisted on the observance of draconian laws. For all its overt debts to **Marx**, **Lenin**, **Stalin** and other communist ideologues, communism as redefined by Mao amounted to a refashioning of an abiding strand in Chinese affairs, its necessity and success, temporary or otherwise, a reflection of the innate difficulties in furnishing an entity as populous, culturally diverse and geographically extensive as China with any sort of centralized government at all; and it has been claimed that Mao's actual achievement was to found a new 'dynasty', based on the one-party state, with the difference that, unlike all previous dynasties, succession is determined not by heredity, but by opaque power-struggles at the apex of a distinctly pyramidal and authoritarian power structure in which cadres, apparatchiks and politburo members have merely replaced the old and equally hierarchical mandarinate.

What is seldom questioned is Mao's formidable political skill, ultimately self-serving though it became. During his rise to supremacy over the nascent Chinese Communist Party (CCP) he repeatedly faced the censure of comrades, but each time toughed it out to consolidate his position.

Born in Shaoshan village in the central province of Hunan, Mao entertained a strong dislike for his father – a 'rich' peasant who profiteered from hoarding grain and whose kind became earmarked for persecution by a government largely moulded by his son a half century later. The family's relative wealth, however, enabled Mao to acquire an education. In 1911 he enrolled at a secondary school in Changsha. Between 1913 and 1918 he attended a teacher training course at Hunan's Fourth Normal School, but although he organized evening classes for workers and contributed to the radical *Xin Qingnian* ('New Youth Magazine'), edited by the future founder of the CCP, Chen Duxiu, it was not until he accepted a post as an assistant to Li Dazhao, the librarian of Beijing University, that Mao found his true political direction.

Under Li's tutelage Mao was introduced to the core tenets of Marxism-Leninism, while also learning about such anarchists as Proudhon and **Kropotkin**. As importantly, Li stressed the validity of fomenting a revolutionary spirit among the agrarian classes, and brought Mao to the attention of Chen. Mao was not, however, a founding member

of the CCP, which, with the backing of the Soviet Comintern (Communist International), was secretly inaugurated in Shanghai in 1920. By then, Mao had returned to Hunan as a junior school teacher. His commitment to communism was evidenced both by a Marxist study group he set up in Changsha, and by his vociferous support for a boycott of Japanese goods in the wake of the May Fourth Movement of 1919, when Chinese students confronted a Republican government which had acquiesced in Japan's acquisition of German concessions in Shandong province, in accordance with the provisions of the Treaty of Versailles. Only in the following year, 1921, did Mao join the CCP's inner circle, attending its First Congress in Shanghai and becoming Party Secretary for Hunan.

Initially the CCP was dependent on the USSR, to the extent that its policies were directed by Moscow through a succession of political 'agents'. These agents demanded that Chinese communists follow the Russian model by building support among China's urban proletariat, and that they co-operate with the Guomindang, the Chinese Nationalist Party which, under the leadership first of Sun Yat Sen, and from 1925 Jiang Jieshi, endeavoured to restore Chinese unity after the Republic had fallen foul of contending warlords following the death of its first president, Yuan Shikai, in 1916. Such policies did not appeal to Mao, who, although a pragmatist when he had to be, sought a communist state on Chinese terms; and it was because of this, as well as a string of personality clashes, that he frequently fell out with his associates in the years before 1935, when Mao succeeded in stamping his authority on the Party.

From as early as 1923, when he became a Central Committee member, Mao consistently argued that only by mobilizing the peasantry would communism triumph in China. In February 1927 he summarized his views in a 'Report on the Peasant Movement in Hunan', knowing that it would be strongly criticized by the Comintern agent, and in September orchestrated the 'Autumn Harvest

Uprising', an attempt to set up a rural soviet in his home province. The failure of this, and of a similar uprising in southern Guangdong, led by Peng Pai, meant that Mao was temporarily excluded from the Party's top echelon. But if Moscow insisted that the CCP co-operate with the Guomindang, the Guomindang, also supported by the USSR, was unminded to co-operate with the CCP, and Jiang was ruthless in liquidating communists in Shanghai and other central cities.

It was against this background that Mao's views began to prevail. A decision was taken to support 'base areas' in the deep country-side. The most significant of these was created by Mao and Zhu De in 1928 in Jinggang, a mountainous region of Jiangxi province, adjacent to Hunan. In effect, Mao and Zhu established a local but autonomous communist government in opposition to Jiang's republican government. Jiang respond-ed by ordering the encirclement of Jianggangshan, in a bid to flush the rebels out. By now, however, the Guomindang had also to contend with growing Japanese militarism – in 1931 Japan, on the slenderest of pretexts, seized Manchuria in the north-east – and it was not until the summer of 1934 that a fifth encirclement campaign looked likely to achieve Jiang's objectives.

Seemingly trapped, Mao and Zhu auda-ciously led their force of 100,000 ill-equipped men through Guomindang lines in October – the beginning of the Red Army's legendary but also desperate 'Long March' through southern China to Yunnan, and then north to Shaanxi province, where, having lost all but 6,000 of his troops, Mao set up a new base area centred on Yanan. But if the Long March reflected the lowest ebb of the CCP's fortunes, it also made Mao. At a cru-cial meeting of the communist leadership held at Zunyi (Guizhou province) in February 1935, he persuaded a majority of his associates that the Comintern's strategy was suicidal. Although Mao still faced opposition from Zhang Guotao and other 'Chinese Bolsheviks', henceforth his ascendancy was secure.

In Shaanxi, far from the Guomindang capital at Nanjing, Mao was able to put his theories into practice. Playing his own nationalist card, he also insisted that the communists should take the lead in resisting the Japanese. To this end he extrapolated in full his concept of 'people's war', combining guerrilla tactics with main offences while conducting an unremitting propaganda cam-paign to win over the populace. By blending in with a well-disposed civilian population, communist guerrillas could operate deep inside enemy lines. It was not until the Allied defeat of Japan in 1945, however, that Mao could realistically contemplate gaining con-trol of all China. For a year, the communists and the Guomindang, now backed by the USA, uneasily shared power, but in June 1946 the inevitable civil war broke out. At first the better armed Guomindang prevailed, but without decisive popular support their cause was stymied. In 1948 the People's Liberation Army (PLA), as the Red Army now called itself, began inflicting defeat on Guomindang forces in open battle. Beijing was taken in January 1949, followed by the capture of Nanjing in April and Shanghai in May. The People's Republic was proclaimed, by Mao himself, in Beijing's Tiananmen Square on 1 October; two months later Jiang fled to Taiwan, to establish a far smaller Chinese republic.

Despite much slimmer resources, it was the Taiwanese, not the communist, republic, that prospered. In mainland China, as else-where, the communists' skills were well suited to managing a war, but not peace. The CCP's neo-Stalinist recourse was to insti-tute a totalitarian style of government that, among the totalitarianisms of the twentieth century, ranked as one of the most bloodily repressive. For this, Mao was largely responsible. Using the 'mass-line campaign' as his favoured political instrument, he tar-geted all the main elements of Chinese society, beginning with capitalists and reac-tionaries, but extending to elements within the government itself and to Mao's hallowed peasantry.

Initially the People's Republic of China (PRC) reached out to the global socialist movement at large. New laws were introduced granting women access to divorce courts, among other rights, and in December 1949 Mao visited Moscow to express solidarity with Stalin. Thereafter, however, he went determinedly his own way, severing remaining links with the USSR in 1960. As in imperial times, officials were graded according to twenty-four ranks, and by the end of 1950 the first of many purges was in full swing. Not only were former Guomindang followers hunted down, but, as China entered the Korean War against America, so too were 'foreign sympathizers'. This was followed in 1951 by a 'Five Antis Campaign', aimed against China's 'business class'. Landlords and intellectuals were Mao's next victims, followed by rich peasants. At the same time, the PRC reasserted China's historic hegemony over Tibet, and also the huge western territory of Xinjiang, then mainly inhabited by Uighur and other Muslims. In 1952 the first steps were taken towards 'collectivization' – in effect the abolition of small land-holdings to be replaced by state-run 'co-operative' farms. In 1953 grain markets were closed, and a state monopoly in agricultural produce enforced. Farmers in Guangdong and other southern provinces protested violently, and were violently suppressed. In 1955, during the 'Little Leap Forward', full collectivization was instituted and the last vestiges of private property abolished. In 1956 a system of 'internal passports' was introduced, bringing urban migration and other types of movement under tight government control.

But all this was as nothing compared to what ensued. Some of Mao's Central Committee colleagues, notably Liu Shaoqi and **Deng Xiaoping**, had begun voicing doubts as to the desirability of some of Mao's policies. Mao's response was to launch the 'Hundred Flowers Campaign' of 1957 – on the face of it a gesture at liberalization, since it encouraged intellectuals and others to express their opinions, but in reality a ploy to entice Mao's critics into the open, where they could then be persecuted. At the same time an 'Anti-Rightist Campaign' inaugurated a policy of banishing alleged dissidents from the cities to rural labour camps for 're-education'. Then came the wholly extraordinary 'Great Leap Forward' of 1958, Mao's attempt to drive economic development at such a pace that China would swiftly overtake not only the USSR but also Britain.

By any reckoning the Great Leap Forward was catastrophic. While rural and industrial collectivization was replaced by vast 'people's communes', one instruction was for everybody to increase steel production by melting down everyday metallic objects in 'backyard furnaces'. Another was for the planting of grain seed in a way no rational agriculturalist could conceivably have condoned. As a result an estimated thirty million died of starvation, and Chinese industry sank to its knees. Yet even though Mao himself was among the last to learn of the actual consequences of his initiative – such was the kowtowing that surrounded him that no one until Defence Minister Peng Dehuai in August 1959 dared submit an adverse report – the political fallout was considerable. Although Peng was speedily replaced as Defence Minister by the hardliner Lin Biao, and although Mao launched yet another anti-rightist campaign, purging many middle-ranking cadres, Mao felt it expedient to stand down as head of state, while continuing as Chairman of the Party. By 1962 it was apparent that, on a day-to-day basis at least, Mao was no longer in supreme control.

Liu Shaoqi, the new head of state, and others on the politburo had prevailed. But a Mao so constrained was a Mao at his most lethal. As early as July 1962 he began his counter-offensive. Backed by Lin Biao and the state's security apparatus he launched an attack on 'right revisionists', emphasizing the enduring importance of class struggle. Then he introduced his estranged fourth wife, the malevolent and hypochondriac former Shanghai actress Jiang Qing, on to the public stage. In 1963 he upped the ante by mounting a 'Socialist Education' campaign, with Liu in its sights, while Lin published *Quotations from Chairman Mao*, a slim but hugely effective anthology of Mao's pronouncements that became universally known as 'The Little Red Book'. For the next two years Mao maintained the pressure, adroitly manipulating the *People's Daily* and other media, until a bursting point was reached. Then, using Jiang Qing as his mouthpiece and students as his henchmen, in May 1966 he floated the 'Great Proletarian Cultural Revolution', aimed at the entire class of administrators and professionals.

Within weeks 'Red Guards' – schoolchildren as well as students – ran rampant through the streets of Beijing and other cities, waving copies of the Little Red Book and photographs of Mao. No one, least of all politburo members, was immune from their acrimonious attentions. Teachers, doctors, factory managers and politicians were forced to make abject confessions of their errors in public, during so-called 'struggle sessions'. Massed rallies and 'big character' posters followed. As turbulence spread through China, Liu and Deng were castigated as 'capitalist roadsters'.

This, though, was only the first phase of the Cultural Revolution, which claimed a million lives or more. Although Mao swiftly achieved his personal objectives – the overthrow of Liu (who died in ignominious circumstances in 1969), and the removal of Deng (hounded into internal exile) – the forces he had unleashed threatened to spin out of control after the Red Guards began factionalizing and fighting among themselves. To restore order, in September 1967 Mao authorized the PLA to open fire on radicals 'in self-defence'. The following year 'revolutionary committees' packed with army-men began taking control of schools, hospitals and factories, and increasing numbers of Red Guards were themselves deported to the deep countryside for lengthy spells of re-education, giving rise to the phenomenon of China's 'lost generation'.

The Cultural Revolution – which in essence made a political process based on manufactured class antagonisms itself the goal of political activity – threw other problems Mao's way, in particular the rivalrous ambitions of Lin Biao and Jiang Qing, at the head of her notorious 'Gang of Four'. Both were disgraced, Lin dying in an air-crash while attempting to flee. But by relying on the loyalty of his perennial and popular foreign minister Zhou Enlai, as well as rehabilitating the supremely able Deng, Mao continued to manipulate those around him with apparent ease. Further, in February 1972 he stunned everyone by welcoming President Nixon to Beijing. Designed to infuriate the USSR, Mao's about-turn in Sino-American relations profoundly affected the geopolitical balance at the height of the Cold War.

Mao died on 9 September 1976, following a run of heart attacks. He bequeathed his successors, Hua Guofeng and Deng Xiaoping, an unenviable inheritance. By promoting anarchic dystopia in place of the conventional utopianism of communism, Mao fostered a deep mistrust, as well as a fear, of politics and politicians in China; by regularly deploying such terms as 'left deviationist' and 'right opportunist' against his personal enemies regardless of the substance of such accusations, he consolidated his own power-base only at the cost of debasing political discourse; and by his repeated purges of officialdom, he inhibited the confidence and self-esteem of the new political elite itself. Mao, however, seems to have been impervious of the effect he had. His character was that of a traditional strongman who finally had no sentimental attachment towards anyone or anything other than his own survival. In his polemical writings, directness of purpose and expression yielded some of the best-known maxims of the last century – 'Political power grows out of the barrel of a gun', for instance, or 'A revolution is not a dinner party'. Yet Mao's was also a complex personality, as the calligraphy of such poems as he wrote reveals: an untutored and unkempt hand, but startlingly determined.

Further reading

Other works include: *Selected Writings of Mao Tse-tung* (1961–77) and are still available from the Foreign Languages Press of Beijing, which also publishes his *Poems* (1976). Good biographies include Stuart Schram, *Mao Tse-tung* (1967); Dick Wilson, *Mao: The People's Emperor* (1979); P. Rule, *Mao Zedong* (1984); and, especially, Philip Short, *Mao: A Life* (1999). See also: Edgar Snow, *Red Star Over China* (1937); Roderick MacFarquar, *The Origins of the Cultural Revolution* (3 vols, from 1974); Harrison Salisbury, *The Long March: The Untold Story* (1986); J.K. Fairbank, *The Great Chinese Revolution 1966–1982* (1987); Stuart Schram, *The Political Thought of Mao Tse-tung* (1989); Dick Wilson, *China's Revolutionary War* (1991); and Jasper Becker, *Hungry Ghosts: China's Secret Famine* (1996), exposing the full horror of the Great Leap Forward.

JUSTIN WINTLE

MARC, Franz

1880–1916

German painter

Marc was one of the leading painters of the German Expressionist movement. 'Expressionism' was a term coined by critics, not by artists, in an attempt to indicate that after a period when the French had led modern painting with their Impressionism, German art had taken the next step. Marc, whose mother was a native of Alsace and who had been influenced, on visits to France, by Impressionist, Post-Impressionist and eventually by Cubist painting, did not subscribe to the nationalism which marked some German artists of the time, not least because his closest artistic contact was the Russian **Kandinsky**, with whom he created Der Blaue Reiter ('The Blue Rider') movement in Munich in 1911, a movement and grouping of artists with an international membership. Kandinsky himself later recalled this second Expressionist movement (after *Die Brücke*), for all those who participated in its exhibitions, in these terms: 'we were two'. French, Russian and Italian Futurist influences there were, but the international flavour of the modern movement had also to

co-exist with Marc's awareness of his own national identity. In a letter of 1915, written from the battlefield, he said:

> I am myself ... so wholly German in the old sense, one from the land of German Dreamers, Poets, and Thinkers, the land of Kant and Bach of Schwind [a Romantic painter of whose work he was particularly fond], of Goethe, Hölderlin and **Nietzsche** ... [that I wonder uncomfortably] whether the Slavs, especially the Russians, won't soon take over the Spiritual leadership of the world, while Germany's spirit grows worse and worse, involved in business and war matters. But any thought always leads me back to my good little Deer!

Marc's idealist and religious spirit was present in the letter – he had begun a study of philosophy and theology – but the mention of deer leads us to the work for which he has always been best known – as a painter of animals. There were indeed many paintings of deer, some of which he liked to keep in his garden at Sindelsdorf to the south of Munich, but the painting for which he became most famous, and with which he conquered even conventional spirits, was called *Der Turm der blauen Pferde* ('The Tower of Blue Horses') of 1913. The painting has been lost, as have many modern works which were considered by the Nazis to represent what they called *entartete* ('degenerate') art, but photographs show a large painting, vertical in format, where four horses, their heads rising one above another, are set in a landscape whose forms, like those of the horses themselves, bear traces of geometrical simplification in a sub-Cubist manner close to that of Henri Le Fauconnier, one of whose works had been exhibited with the Blaue Reiter group and illustrated in their *Almanac* (1912). Marc's painting was provided with a summit – a rainbow – in neo-Romantic manner.

The Tower is a leading work from Marc's 'middle period', if such a term is applicable to a career which, juvenilia excepted, lasted a bare four years. He had studied at the Munich Academy from 1900 (his own father was a competent landscape painter working in the current tonal manner of Lenbach). His very first paintings were similarly naturalistic. But in 1910 he painted his well-known *Three Red Horses*, followed in 1911 by *The Large Blue Horses*. As can be seen from these titles, naturalism was now abandoned, partly encouraged by the Post-Impressionist works he had seen in Paris and in Munich and furthered by his own belief in the spiritual value of colour. He had no precise and consistent language of colour, nor even the synaesthetic beliefs of Kandinsky, but a belief that art should speak to the soul on an intuitive level. Another aspect of this style is evident in the linear rhythms created both by the horses themselves and in their relationship with their landscape setting. The curvilinear forms seem to owe something to *Jugendstil* (German Art Nouveau) and the holism implied here in morphological terms where horses and setting are seen in unified terms was soon, through the influence of Robert Delaunay, to be supplemented by a colouristic holism. Marc, with his friend the Rhenish painter August Macke, visited Delaunay in Paris in 1912. The Frenchman's 'Orphism' was a 'Pure Painting' (both terms were coined by Apollinaire) which dispensed with the object. This art, with Kandinsky's, was enough to encourage Marc and Macke to turn toward a non-objective art. Marc appreciated, too, **Tolstoy's** belief that art should have a purpose, and reconciled this seemingly all too functional belief with his own spirituality by seeing the purpose of art not in social but in ontological terms. After a period of seeking the 'animalization' of painting (which was itself a substitute for the 'impurity' of the human form) this philosophical artist came eventually to find something 'hateful' in all nature and found the abstract form (though not wholly devoid of empathetic implications) to be a purer substitute in both moral and aesthetic terms. Thus in 1914 he painted his *Hot, Playing, Fighting* and *Fragmented Forms*.

This process seems to be summed up in an unintentionally ironically titled drawing (ironic because he was in the artillery) which he made while at the front and titled *Arsenal for a Creation*. Two of his most important works had been painted in 1914. These were *Tirol* and *The Fate of Animals* (*Tierschicksale*), which were both works which could be considered prophetic. *Tirol* was the successor to a painting of 1913 called *Armes Land Tirol* ('The Unhappy Land of Tirol'), a mountain landscape with a graveyard and some skinny horses. *Tirol* itself is far more abstract, and only with reference to its predecessor can a mountain landscape where the light of sunrise and darkness do battle be deduced. No animal is present, but Marc softened these jagged forms by adding as an afterthought a form based on that of a primitive Bavarian wood-carving of the Virgin. Marc had chosen *The Book of Creation* as his subject for a projected series of Bible illustrations, to be undertaken by himself, **Paul Klee**, Alfred Kubin, Erich Heckel of Die Brücke and Kokoschka. He was not himself a Catholic, but this Virgin seems to bless the darker side of the landscape. All 'Blue Rider' artists admired primitive art forms, many of which were illustrated in their *Almanac*. Marc himself made some experiments with the Bavarian technique of *Hinterglasmalerei* (painting behind glass). He also made some sculptures of his own, including a *Tiger* which is very powerful and expressive.

The Fate of Animals, which can now be seen in Berne, had an alternative title written on the back by Marc: *Und alles Sein ist flammend Leid* ('All Being is Flaming Suffering'), a quotation from the Vedas. Marc was said by Klee to have considered yet another title: 'The Trees Show Their Rings, the Animals Their Veins.' The effect created is as of a forest fire from which beasts, not least deer, are fleeing. The painting was itself damaged by fire soon after execution and was carefully restored by Paul Klee. Its style is similar to *Tirol* but it is larger and may be considered Marc's masterpiece.

Marc was above all important as a painter whose work quickly became popular and which made 'modernism' accessible to a wide public. He cannot be said to have exerted a strong influence on the specific style of any other artist, but was important as one whose work demonstrated the viability of non-objective values in painting.

Further reading

Other works include: *Briefe 1914–1916 aus dem Felde* (1938) and *August Macke – Franz Marc Briefwechsel* (1964). His 'Aphorisms' can be found in *Franz Marc: Briefe, Aufzeichnungen und Aphorismen* (2 vols, 1920). Alois Schardt's catalogue of the works (1936) is now outdated, but has not been succeeded. See Klaus Lankheit, *Franz Marc* (1950); M. Rosenthal, *Franz Marc* (1989).

BRIAN PETRIE

MARCONI, Guglielmo

1874–1937

Italian technologist

Marconi was born in Bologna in 1874 and by the end of the century he was famous. A year later, in 1901, his name entered the history books; by 1909 he had won the Nobel Prize. It was a remarkable rise. Marconi subsequently lived to the threshold of the Second World War, an institution rather than a man. He sustained his success: he pushed the technology ahead with nerve and flair; his companies prospered while most of his rivals fell by the wayside. He became rich, fêted, friend of the grand and the powerful.

Marconi was the 'Father of Wireless Telegraphy'. It was Marconi who, against the most weighty scientific opinion of the day, showed first that the 'wireless' could work, second that it could become a reliable system, and third that it could broadcast to the world. Marconi was a single-minded technologist, who worked incessantly to perfect and to develop his wireless system. Marconi's early success was a product of his independence of mind, tenacity, imagination, thoroughness. That he became widely known was partly, no doubt, because his demonstrations *worked*; but also because the press found Marconi's exploits irresistible. The communicators

were always interested in developments in communications; they were also interested in this unlikely figure: bi-lingual, Anglo-Italian, well-connected, handsome and a ladies' man. This was a far cry from the typical image of the boorish technologist/unkempt inventor. But Marconi *was* a dedicated technologist: he worked long hours and never shrank from working in conditions like heaving seas, the cabin awash with seawater, while he kept going determinedly with his transmissions. It was Marconi, more than anyone else, who, by the exercise of imagination and willpower, technical dexterity and flair, practical and commercial judgement, turned the world into an electronic village.

To appreciate Marconi's achievement it is necessary to bear in mind the kind of world into which he was born and in which he grew up. It was a world of new-found communications. Telegraphy was triumphant, with lines criss-crossing Europe and a substantial number of underwater cables linking continents. In 1866 **Brunel** had laid the transatlantic cable, a feat of olympian proportions. Everywhere messages were being carried on *wires* by the agency of this remarkable electricity.

It was in 1887 that Heinrich Hertz discovered radio waves or 'Hertzian waves', as they were known at first; but they were little more than a laboratory trick. They were weak, indiscriminate in wavelength, and could only be detected at distances of a few metres. Physicists such as Hertz himself, Oliver Lodge, Bose in India, Righi in Bologna, found them interesting because they confirmed the theoretical predictions of James Clerk Maxwell, but the interest was mainly in the phenomenon as a phenomenon, not in what it might be made to do.

Hertz died in 1894 and the young Marconi, then twenty, read an obituary notice about Hertz while holidaying in the Italian Alps. Suddenly the idea came to Marconi that it might be possible to use 'Hertzian waves' to convey messages around the world. He said later: 'In those mountains of Biellese I worked it out in my imagination.'

Suddenly Marconi, whose boyhood had been listless, divided and awkward – bullied at school in Florence, a failure in exams at Leghorn – saw his role in life. He had long been addicted to all things electrical and had infuriated his father with his constant experimenting with scientific toys. Now, however, he had an aim.

Back home at the Villa Grifone he set up his laboratory in the attic. He repeated the basic Hertzian experiments; he devised improvements; he lengthened the range, first to the door of the attic, then down the stairs, then on to the terrace, and finally out into the estate. By chance he discovered the efficacy of combining an aerial with an earth. He tried every permutation of arrangements, always searching for improved efficiency, and always using a minimum of theory. By 1895 his 'range' was over half a mile. He came to England with his talented Anglo-Irish mother to seek resources to go further. On Salisbury Plain his range was four miles, by 1897 nearly nine miles, and in 1899 he sent messages across the Straits of Dover.

Then Marconi staked his reputation and that of his company on sending messages across the Atlantic. It was considered a preposterous idea by the scientific opinion of the day, for the Hertzian waves were like light and would surely travel in straight lines, passing far above Marconi's Newfoundland kite-carried aerials! When, in December 1901, Marconi finally heard the three dots of the morse 'S' faintly audible behind the crackle of transatlantic static, he knew it was the start of a new era. From this beginning it took Marconi several years to perfect his transatlantic service, but he stuck at it and finally got it right.

When Marconi began on the research in 1894 there were three monumental reasons why his work *seemed* to be ill-advised: (1) it was not needed; telegraphy on wires was a proven, reliable, heavily capitalized system; (2) it was hard to see how 'wireless' could be financed; who would be induced to *pay* for information thrown indiscriminately to all and sundry? (3) the range would be very short, at best a hundred miles or so.

Many years later the *Electrician* commented that Marconi had two pieces of striking luck: his talented, well-connected, doting mother, Annie Jameson, and the existence of the ionosphere! It was the ionosphere which bounced his transmissions back to earth and confounded the scientific opposition. It was his mother who kept him going during 1894 and 1895, when he was considered an eccentric fool and the foundations of his triumphs were being laid.

Further reading

See: Address by Marconi to the Institution of Electrical Engineers, *Journal of the Institution of Electrical Engineers*, Vol. 28 (1899); Degna Marconi, *My Father Marconi* (1962); W.P. Jolly, *Marconi* (1972); Gavin Weightman, *Signor Marconi's Magic Box: The Invention that Sparked the Radio Revolution* (2003).

CHRISTOPHER ORMELL

MARINETTI, Filippo Tommaso
1876–1944
Italian writer

Marinetti was born to a wealthy lawyer living in Egypt. He studied briefly in Paris and made the city his cultural home, soon writing for and editing literary periodicals which attempted to introduce French Symbolist poetry to Italy. His own poetry, of which there was much, was in French until 1912, Symbolist, but with a violent idealist-anarchistic character. In 1909 he published the 'Futurist Manifesto' in *Le Figaro*. It exalted the machines, the violence and the competition of the modern world, and demanded that art abandon conventional subjects and styles, and glorify the present.

The Manifesto was generally interpreted as an iconoclastic tirade in favour of modernism. In fact it went much further, as other manifestos by Marinetti himself and by the painters Boccioni and Carrà and the 'musician' Russolo showed. Futurism wanted art not to *signify* life – least of all 'arty' life – but to *be* life. Conversely, it saw everything in social life as having meaning, as being a language, even food, clothes and gait, and sought to exploit the expressive power of every conceivable medium. War was the perfect aesthetic event.

Marinetti was probably more consciously aware of the impact of what he was proposing than most of the Futurist artists (with the exception of Boccioni). Art was to be part of the competition of modern life rather than an alternative to it. He held 'serate' – soirées – in theatres where Futurist poetry and music and politics were declaimed. He travelled frenetically, promoting Futurism, organizing exhibitions of painting, paying for the publication of books, and cajoling one artist after another into audacious innovation. By 1914 he was vigorously agitating for Italy's entry into the Great War.

He was a staunch supporter of Fascism – one of the first; indeed, **Mussolini** borrowed much from Futurism – though personally too anarchist to accept corporativism, and too intelligent to stomach the party's imperialist xenophobia. But he never ceased to look after the interests of the Futurist movement, and so tried to keep it in the good graces of the regime.

He made an art of the literary manifesto, bringing to it lyricism, rhetoric and a concise, punchy clarity of diction. He pioneered visual poetry, in which syntax all but disappears, and in which the graphic element of calligraphy and typography played as important a role in the expression as the meaning of the words themselves, mingling writing with drawing and abstract shapes. The influence of these innovations, from Apollinaire to the concrete poets and beyond, is incalculable. Marinetti wrote a large number of books which mixed memoir and political and artistic polemic, as well as novels, one of which brought him prosecution for obscenity. His prose style was sharp and simple, but degenerated into empty verbosity later in life. His plays and theoretical writings on the theatre were enormously influential: he proclaimed the abolition of polite, highbrow theatre, which was to be fused with music hall and

vaudeville; he destroyed the barrier between stage and audience; he pioneered very short ('synthetic') plays – in one of which only the actors' legs and feet were visible. He wrote abstract aural pieces for radio in the 1930s, and helped make a futurist film.

Marinetti's credit has been low in academic circles because of his fascist associations. Among artists, however, he has had so profound an influence that scarcely any artist in any field can have entirely escaped it. The whole twentieth-century avant-garde owes much of its general audacity and willingness to ignore the past, as well as a number of its detailed innovations, to Marinetti personally and to his Futurist movement. His personal creative works, however, only have real stature for their formal qualities and for their energy. Marinetti does not express profound feelings and thoughts; he can be brash and frivolous. For this reason, though his importance to culture of the last century will grow ever more apparent, his works will always have a limited emotional appeal.

Further reading

Some major works: *Mafarka le futuriste* (1909); *La Ville charnelle* (1908); *Zang Tumb tuuum* (1914); *Les Mots en liberté futuristes* (1919); *L'alcova d'acciaio* (1921). Contained in collections and anthologies are his theatrical writings: *Teatro*, ed. G. Calendoli (1960); and theoretical writings: *Teoria e invenzione futurista*, ed. L. De Maria (1968); *Selected Writings*, ed. R.W. Flint (1972). For his visual poetry, see *Tavole parolibere futuriste*, ed. S. Caruso and L. Martini (1977). See also: Cinzia Sartini Blum, *The Other Modernism: F.T. Marinetti's Futurist Fiction of Power* (1996).

CHRISTOPHER WAGSTAFF

MARLEY, Bob (Robert Nesta)

1945–81

Jamaican musician

Robert Nesta Marley was the archetypal hero, a man from humble beginnings who conquered the world, a man whose legend shows no sign of diminishing in the years since his death.

He was one of the most charismatic musical performers of his time, the first global superstar to emerge from the Third World, but to describe Bob Marley as simply a singer and songwriter who fronted a Jamaican reggae band is to seriously understate his impact. He was a pop culture phenomenon; or, as Judy Mowatt of the I-Threes, his vocal backing group, put it: 'Bob was a musical prophet.'

There was something Messianic about Marley. He has been described as a natural mystic and soul rebel: his work was inspirational and life-changing. In the Third World he's revered as a saviour, in the first world – East and West – he remains an idol.

Marley's strong Rastafarian beliefs were the foundations upon which he built the vision he embodied of 'One World, One Love' – a vision which suffused his music. In the words of Timothy White, author of the biography *Catch a Fire: The Life of Bob Marley* (2000): 'His music was pure rock, in the sense that it was a public expression of a private truth.' His art had, still has, the power to cross all barriers – country, class, language, culture, religion and race. The last Bob Marley and the Wailers tour in 1980 attracted the largest audiences at that time for any musical act in Europe.

Marley was born in Jamaica, into that country's heady racial mix, the son of a middle-aged white father, Captain Norval Marley, and his eighteen-year-old black wife, Cedella. His birthplace was the rural north, not, as many later assumed, the slums of Trenchtown made famous in his song 'No Woman No Cry'. Marley only moved to Kingston as a teenager in the late 1950s, eventually settling in the outlying Trenchtown shanty. He seldom saw his father as he grew up. Norval provided financial support, but constant family pressure kept him away.

Marley's musical ambitions took root in Trenchtown where, with his friend Bunny Livingston, he took his first steps into that world with lessons from famous singer Joe Higgs. It was at one of Higgs' sessions that they hooked up with Peter Tosh in the early 1960s. Bunny, Peter and Bob became the original Wailers, their music tough and urban, taking its cue from the slums.

Cedella, Marley's mother, meanwhile remarried and moved to the United States, sending money for her son to join her. But before he moved in 1966, Marley met and married Rita Anderson. He stayed all of eight months in the USA before returning to his roots. It was at this point that he became increasingly drawn to the Rastafarian faith, as much a militant stand in those days as a blend of both Judaism and Christianity, as Rastas were far from embraced by Jamaican society. By 1967 Marley's music was reflecting his new beliefs. He re-formed the Wailers, signing in 1971 with Chris Blackwell's Island Records, their first rung on the ladder to international fame.

Uncompromising and outspoken, Marley was no stranger to danger in the violent political landscape of 1970s Jamaica. He survived an assassination attempt in 1976 and moved to London to record *Exodus* – the album that put the seal on the band's international status – before returning to his troubled homeland to play the 'One Love' peace concert in front of the prime minister, Michael Manley, and the leader of the opposition.

With lyrics of revolution and revelation, religion and politics resonate passionately throughout Marley's music, but to him there was little distinction. To him it was a way of being and it won him the United Nations' Medal of Peace in 1978. His ninth album, *Survival*, was a statement of pan-African solidarity and precursor to the event that the Wailers considered to be their greatest honour – playing at Zimbabwe's independence celebrations in 1980.

That same year, Marley started his final battle with cancer, first diagnosed three years before in his toe. He had refused to have the toe amputated, which allowed the cancer to spread, but he was determined not to die. He did not believe in death. Once he had accepted that his alternative treatments in Germany had failed, he left for home, where the government had just awarded him the Order of Merit. He never saw Jamaica again – only his body finished the journey.

Bob Marley was thirty-six and the father of nine children when he died in Miami, Florida, on 11 May 1981. He had dodged the bullets but still his fate was to die young, all in the very best rock tradition.

Further reading

See: Roger Steffens and Leroy Jody Pierson, *Bob Marley and the Wailers: The Definitive Discography* (2005). See also: Cedella Marley and Gerald Hausman, *56 Thoughts from 56 Hope Road: The Sayings and Psalms of Bob Marley* (2002); Dennis Morris, *Bob Marley: A Rebel Life* (2003); Jeremy Collingwood, *Bob Marley* (2005), Rita Marley and Hettie Jones, *No Woman No Cry: My Life with Bob Marley* (2005). The official Bob Marley website is: http://www.bobmarley.com.

JOAN BIRD

MÁRQUEZ, Gabriel García,

see: GARCÍA MÁRQUEZ, GABRIEL

MARX, Karl Heinrich

1818–83

German historian, economist and revolutionary

Marx was born in Trier on 5 May 1818, the son of a prosperous Jewish lawyer. He studied at the Universities of Bonn and Berlin between 1835 and 1841; in Berlin he associated with the 'Young Hegelians', who constituted the radical wing of Hegel's followers. When the reactionary Friedrich Wilhelm IV came to the Prussian throne in 1840, the government became increasingly hostile to the Young Hegelians, and Marx had to give up all hope of an academic career. Instead, he turned to journalism, and in October 1843 he moved to Paris to take up the editorship of a new journal. His stay in Paris, which lasted until February 1845, was of great importance in his life. It was in Paris that he first met Friedrich Engels, who was to become his lifelong friend and fellow-worker; it was there, too, that he began a serious criticism of Hegel's philosophy. He

was at first influenced in this respect by the German philosopher Ludwig Feuerbach, but by 1845 he was criticizing Feuerbach too and was well on the way towards his own distinctive doctrines. Expelled from France in 1845, and later from Belgium and Germany, Marx arrived in London in August 1849. He continued to live in London until his death on 14 March 1883.

Marx's doctrines are of great range and power, and their influence has been enormous. But there have been, and still are, fierce disagreements about the exact nature of the Marxism of Marx. Argument has centred around the problem of whether one is to see his thought as an organic whole, developing in an orderly way, or whether there was a sharp break in his thought. However, there is no reasonable doubt that the main lines of Marx's thought were fixed by 1848, the year in which he and Engels published their *Manifesto of the Communist Party* (*Manifest der Kommunistischen Partei*). This is probably their most influential work, and is certainly a masterpiece of polemical literature – compact, wide-ranging and forcibly argued. Though *The Communist Manifesto*, as it is now commonly called, was a joint production, Engels insisted that its basic idea belonged to Marx alone. This basic idea, commonly known as historical materialism, is a thesis about human history, and according to Engels it did for the study of history what **Darwin's** theory had done for the study of organic nature. Very briefly, it asserts the fundamental importance of class struggles, both in the present and in the past, and it claims to explain their nature and inevitability. Section I of *The Communist Manifesto* begins with the assertion, 'The history of all hitherto existing society is the history of class struggles.' This is important both for what it denies and for what it asserts. If you are to understand human history, says Marx, you must not see it as the story of great individuals; you must not even see it simply as the story of states and their conflicts. You must see it as the story of social classes and their struggles with each other. Social classes have changed in the course of time, but in the middle of the nineteenth century the most important classes, Marx argued, were the bourgeoisie and the proletariat. By 'the bourgeoisie' is meant the class of big capitalists, who own the factories and the raw materials which are processed in them. The members of the proletariat, on the other hand, are completely property-less. They do not even own hand-looms or their own small plots of land, as small-scale manufacturers used to do between the sixteenth and the eighteenth centuries. All that they have is their power to work, and this they sell to the bourgeoisie. These two classes are not merely different from each other, but also have opposite interests. Here we reach the heart of the Marxist position. The struggles between bourgeoisie and proletariat, and the struggles between classes which existed before them, are not a chance affair. They are necessary and, like the existence of the contending classes themselves, they can be explained.

In his explanation, Marx distinguishes between 'productive forces' and 'production relations'. Productive forces include not only tools and machines, but the human beings who make and use them; that is to say, human labour is a productive force. As to relations of production, Marx points out (*Wage Labour and Capital*, 1849) that production is a social matter. When human beings produce things they enter into relations with each other, and only in the context of these social relations does production take place. What is called a 'society' is these relations of production taken as a whole. So far, there have been three main types of society: ancient, feudal and bourgeois. These types of society involve social classes of distinctive sorts − e.g. slaves in ancient society, serfs in feudal society, the proletariat in bourgeois society − so the relations between classes belong to the relations of production. Marx adds that productive forces and production relations, besides being unable to exist in isolation from each other, also influence each other. In *Wage Labour and Capital*, Marx says that production relations 'will naturally vary according to the character of the means of production'. For example, on the introduction of fire-arms − a new instrument of warfare − 'the whole internal organization of the army necessarily changed'. Again, as Marx said in *The Poverty of Philosophy* (*La Misère de la philosophie*, 1847), an attack on the French socialist Proudhon, 'The hand-mill gives you society with the feudal lord; the steam-mill, society with the industrial capitalist.' But production relations can also influence the development of productive forces. For example, the bourgeoisie, in the early stages of its history, helped to develop productive forces, creating (as *The Communist Manifesto* puts it) 'more massive and more colossal productive forces than have all preceding generations together'.

We now reach a very important part of Marx's theory. Corresponding to productive forces of any given sort, Marx thinks, there is a set of production relations that fits those forces. More than this: these fitting production relations will come into existence. Feudalism provides an illustration. At a certain stage in the development of the means of production, feudal property relations ceased to be compatible with the productive forces that had already been developed. In the words of *The Communist Manifesto*: 'They had to be burst asunder; they were burst asunder.' According to Marx, there is a parallel situation in the nineteenth century, but now it is bourgeois society that provides the fetters, in that bourgeois production relations no longer fit the new and powerful forces of production. 'For many a decade past,' says *The Communist Manifesto*, 'the history of industry and commerce is but the history of the revolt of modern productive forces against modern conditions of production, against the property relations that are the conditions for the existence of the bourgeoisie and of its rule.' Marx argues that this revolt will have an inevitable outcome. Just as feudal society was burst asunder, bourgeois society will suffer the same fate.

The detailed defence of this thesis forms an important part of the first volume of Marx's chief work, *Capital* (*Das Kapital*; Vol. 1 was published by Marx in 1867; Vols 2 and 3 were edited by Engels and published in 1885 and 1894). The bulk of this work concerns economics, and its two major principles are the labour theory of value and the theory of surplus value. The latter, according to Engels, was Marx's second great discovery, worthy to be set beside his new conception of history. Marx started from the thesis (which he derived from Adam Smith and David Ricardo) that labour is the source of all value. He then asked how this can be reconciled with the fact that the workers receive only a part of the value that they create, and have to surrender the rest to the owners of the means of production. In other words, Marx set out to explain the exact nature of what he saw as the exploitation of workers by capitalists, and his theory of surplus value is central to this explanation. So much is clear; but whether Marx succeeded in his aim – whether, as he would claim, the labour theory of value and the theory of surplus value have the status of scientific laws – is far from clear. Certainly, these theories have not had the wide influence enjoyed by Marx's theory of history, and some Marxists go so far as to argue that Marxism can do without the labour theory of value. But the real power of *Capital* lies in the chapters of volume 1 that describe, with burning passion, the rise of capitalism, the misery that it creates, and its future downfall. These culminate in a famous passage, in which the clash between productive forces and production relations is clearly stated:

> The monopoly of capital becomes a fetter upon the mode of production, which has sprung up and flourished along with and under it. Centralization of the means of production and socialization of labour at last reach a point where they become incompatible with their capitalist integument. This integument is burst asunder. The knell of capitalist private property sounds. The expropriators are expropriated.
> (Ch. 24, trans. Moore and Aveling)

To sum up: the relations between hitherto existing social classes – and these are hostile relations, struggles between classes – have to be seen in the light of the development of productive forces, and the way in which this is helped or hindered by the relations of production. But it is also Marx's view that history so far essentially *is* the story of class struggles. In the preface to his *A Contribution to the Critique of Political Economy* (*Zur Kritik der politischen Ökonomie*, 1859) Marx put his point in the form of a metaphor. The passage in question is very condensed, and its precise interpretation is disputed, but Marx's main point is usually taken to be this: that the material productive forces and the relations of production, which together constitute the 'mode of production of material life', form a 'basis', a 'real foundation', on which there arises a 'superstructure' of law, politics, religion, art and philosophy. Marx also asserted that this superstructure is 'determined by' the economic basis. 'It is not,' he says, 'the consciousness of men that determines their existence, but their social existence that determines their consciousness.' So the conflict between the forces of production and the relations of production is of fundamental importance for human history as a whole. Hegel, too, had (in his own way) recognized the importance of conflict within reality, and it may have been this aspect of Hegel's thought which Marx found attractive, and which led him to proclaim himself 'a disciple of that great thinker' (postscript to the second edition of *Capital*, 1873). Hegel, said Marx, had some idea of the true nature of dialectic – i.e. of the basically contradictory nature of reality – but he 'mystified' it by turning the thought process into an independent subject. But there is a rational kernel within the wrappings of mystification, and this can be discovered if one turns Hegel's dialectic the right way up. This seems to mean that we should regard matter (in the shape of the economic basis) as prior to mind, instead of regarding matter as a form of mind, in the way that Hegel did. The extent of Marx's debt to Hegel is hotly disputed. Perhaps the truth is that the way in which Marx presented his views in *Capital* owed something to

Hegel's philosophy; but it is unlikely that the *content* of his thought would have been fundamentally different if he had never read a word of Hegel.

Marx's theory of the relations between basis and superstructure, and between the components of the basis itself, is a form of historical determinism. Marx's version of determinism is sometimes called 'the economic interpretation of history'; here, attention is drawn to the determination of the superstructure by the basis as a whole. Sometimes it is called a 'technological determinism', where the emphasis is on the fundamental role played within the basis by the forces of production. But however it is described, Marx's determinism may seem to involve a paradox. On the one hand, Marx speaks of law, politics, etc. as being determined, i.e. necessitated; on the other, Marxists have always been extremely active politically, and behave as if the outcome of historical development were not a foregone conclusion. The problems of human freedom exercised Engels, but Marx seems to have paid little attention to them. An often-quoted remark from Marx's *The Eighteenth Brumaire of Louis Bonaparte* ('Der achtzehnte Brumaire des Louis Napoleon', 1852), a study of events in France leading up to the seizure of power by Louis Napoleon in 1851, states that 'Men make their own history, but they do not make it just as they please; they do not make it under circumstances chosen by themselves, but under circumstances directly encountered, given and transmitted from the past.' This seems to allow some freedom of action to human beings, but only within certain limits. The same view is presented in the preface to *Capital*, in which Marx says that the discovery of the laws of the movement of society cannot alter the necessary phases of development; it can at best shorten and lessen their birth-pangs. What is certain is that for Marx there can be no question of the proletariat sitting back and letting events take their course; the proletariat's struggle is itself a part of events, a factor in the historical process. Marx emphasizes, too, the practical importance of a comprehension of the nature of historical development. Such a comprehension is not a purely theoretical affair, restricted to a scholar's study; it is itself a factor in the transformation of society. Theory, Marx wrote in an early critique of Hegel (1843), 'becomes a material force as soon as it has gripped the masses'. Marx's term for theory-based revolutionary activity, a union of theory and practice, was 'revolutionary praxis'. The term 'praxis' played an important part in Western Marxism, where it often had a much vaguer sense than that which Marx gave it; for some modern Marxists it seems to mean no more than 'revolutionary activity'.

When he explains the nature of the superstructure in his preface to *The Critique of Political Economy*, Marx makes use of another important concept, that of ideology. He says that law, politics, etc., are so many 'ideological forms' in which men become conscious of the conflict within the basis and fight it out. Just as we do not assess individuals by what they think about themselves, so our judgement of a historical epoch ought not to be based on what it thinks about itself, i.e. on its consciousness of itself. Rather, we should explain this consciousness, which belongs to the superstructure, in the light of conflicts occurring within the economic basis. An ideology, then, is not just a set of ideas; it is not even just a set of false ideas. Rather, it is a set of ideas which mask their true dependence on the economic basis: ideas that involve (to use a phrase employed by Engels) a 'false consciousness'. The ideologist believes, falsely, that his thought is autonomous; he fails to recognize the real forces that impel him.

Marx's thesis about the dependence of the ideological superstructure on the economic basis is a sweeping generalization, the detailed justification of which is beyond the power of any single man. Many Marxists have tried to confirm this thesis in the realms of law, religion, art and philosophy; Marx himself, in his investigations of the dependence of the superstructure on the basis, paid most attention to politics. His account of the nature of the state may serve as an illustration of the character of his arguments, and is also important in its own right. The state, according to Marx, does not exist for the benefit of the community as a whole; it exists to serve a class interest. 'The executive of the modern state,' says *The Communist Manifesto*, 'is but a committee for managing the common affairs of the whole bourgeoisie', and more generally, 'Political power is merely the organized power of one class for oppressing another.' However, Marx has to qualify this. The theory expounded so far may be called 'instrumentalist', in the sense that it regards the state as just a means by which an exploiting class maintains itself in its dominant position. But Marx had to recognize that this was not always the case. In *The Eighteenth Brumaire of Louis Bonaparte* he described a situation in which there was a balance of social forces, which led to the emergence of a state which was relatively autonomous, in the sense that it was not in the service of any specific class-interest.

Marx's view of the state as a means of class oppression had, as he saw, important implications for the future. With the triumph of the proletariat and the disappearance of the bourgeoisie as a class, there will no longer be a class society, in the sense of a society in which one class opposes another. So the state, as an instrument for the oppression of one class by another, will cease to have a function and will disappear, as a useless part of the body disappears in the course of evolution. As Engels put it, in a famous phrase, 'The state is not "abolished", it withers away.' This does not mean that a future classless society will be without any organs of control. *The Communist Manifesto* says simply that 'the public power will lose its political character', which implies that a public power will still exist. But this power will be exercised by society as a whole and not by one social class over another.

But between the overthrow of the bourgeois state and the establishment of a classless society there will be an interim period. The transition to a classless society, Marx thought,

was unlikely to be peaceful. He came to think that a peaceful transition is possible in some countries (England was one); in the main, however, he thought that the overthrow of bourgeois rule would be by means of violent revolution. This being so, there will be a period during which the victorious proletariat and the defeated and resentful bourgeoisie co-exist, and during this period it will be necessary for the proletariat to maintain their dominant position by force. There must be, in other words, what Marx called a 'class dictatorship of the proletariat', as 'the necessary transit point to the abolition of class distinctions generally' (*The Class Struggles in France, Die Klassenkämpfe in Frankreich*, 1850). In his book *The State and Revolution*, written just before his seizure of power in 1917, Lenin laid great emphasis on this part of Marx's political theory. Lenin's 'dictatorship of the proletariat' turned out to be a dictatorship of the Communist Party, and writers on Marxism often point out that Marx and Engels did not have this in mind. According to *The Communist Manifesto*, the Communists are the most advanced section of the working-class parties of each country, but they do not form a separate party. This does not mean that Marx and Engels would have disapproved of **Lenin's** methods; he was operating under conditions that were very different from those envisaged in *The Communist Manifesto*. But they would not have regarded Lenin's idea of a separate, rigidly disciplined Communist Party as necessarily applicable to all epochs and all countries.

It is natural to ask, 'How did Marx envisage the future classless society?' The new society will of course be a communist one, but Marx refuses to speculate about its precise nature. In his view, the elaborate pictures of a new society painted by some socialists and communists, such as Fourier and Robert Owen, are mere Utopias. What is clear is that *The Communist Manifesto* emphasizes, not the abolition of private property as such, but the abolition of *bourgeois* property; it does so because such property is 'the final and most complete expression of the system of producing and appropriating products that is based on class antagonisms'. Earlier, in the so-called *Economic and Philosophic Manuscripts* ('Ökonomisch-philosophische Manuskripte aus dem Jahre 1844', written in Paris in 1844, but not published until 1932), Marx related his ideas about the abolition of private property to what he called 'alienation'. Marx recognizes no fewer than four kinds of alienation in capitalist society. First, the worker is alienated from his product, in that he sees the product as foreign to him, and indeed as dominating him. Second, the worker is alienated from himself; only when he is not working does he feel truly himself. Third (and more obscurely) the worker is alienated from man's 'species life'. Marx seems to start from the position that labour is fundamental to human beings, i.e. that man is by nature a producer. It follows that, to the extent that the produce of his labour is taken from him by the capitalist, the worker is less of a human being. Finally, in capitalist society man is alienated from man; that is, in a competitive society a man is set against other men. One might expect Marx to say that alienation is produced by private (or, more exactly, bourgeois) property. Curiously, he says that private property is initially the *product* of alienated labour; only later does private property become a cause of alienation. For Marx, the solution to the problem of alienation is communism. But not what he calls 'crude communism' – not, that is, a form of communism which is based on general envy and aims at a levelling-down. Communism of this kind still regards possession as the ultimate end; for Marx, on the other hand, communism is 'the real appropriation of the human essence by and for man'. One may take this to mean that communism is not concerned with what a man has; it is concerned with the fulfilment of his potentialities as a human (and that means as a *social*) being. Communism of this kind, says Marx, is humanism.

Although Marx's theory of alienation had great influence on Western radical thought

after the Second World War, Marxists disagreed about its importance in Marx's thought as a whole. It is noteworthy that the term 'alienation' occurs most frequently in works that Marx himself did not publish – in the *Economic and Philosophic Manuscripts* of 1844, and in the so-called *Grundrisse*, a rough draft of *Capital* written in 1857–8. True, Marx always emphasized the miserable lot of the proletariat under capitalism, but the view of alienation that he expounded in 1844 covers much more than that. The dispute has been sharpened by the fact that the Marx of 1844 is often regarded as having a fundamentally different worldview from that of the later Marx. The early Marx, it is argued, saw communism as a moral ideal; the later Marx saw it as a scientific doctrine. Some Marxists see this as introducing a contrast where none exists. Marx, they argue, never drew a sharp distinction between fact and value, and so between the fields of science and morality. If this view of Marx is correct, then the development of his thought from the 1844 manuscripts to the works of his maturity may be regarded as a unified whole. But it cannot yet be said that the problem has been resolved.

Further reading

Although there have been very many editions and translations of the works of Marx and Engels, there is as yet no complete edition. Publication of the complete works in the original languages was begun in Moscow in 1927 but abandoned after 1932; a fresh start was made in 1975 (*Karl Marx/ Friedrich Engels, Gesamtausgabe*, Berlin). In 1975 publication was also begun of a fifty-volume edition in English of *Marx and Engels: Collected Works*. The literature about Marx is enormous. The following books give lucid and critical accounts: Isaiah Berlin, *Karl Marx: His Life and Environment* (1st edn 1939, 4th edn 1978); D. McLellan, *Karl Marx: His Life and Thought* (1973); J. Plamenatz, *Karl Marx's Philosophy of Man* (1975); L. Kolakowski, *Main Currents of Marxism*, Vol. 1, *The Founders* (1978). Of the many defences of Marx's doctrines, one of the most able is G.A. Cohen, *Karl Marx's Theory of History: A Defence* (1978). See also: Terrell Carver (ed.), *The Cambridge Companion to Marx* (1992); Sidney Hook and Christopher Phelps, *From Hegel to Marx: Studies in the Intellectual*

Development of Karl Marx (1994); Frank E. Manuel, *A Requiem for Karl Marx* (1995); Terry Eagleton, *Marx* (1999); Francis Wheen, *Karl Marx* (1999).

G.H.R. PARKINSON

MATISSE, Henri

1869–1954

French painter, sculptor, print-maker, illustrator and designer

Henri Matisse was born at Le Cateau Cambrésius in France. As a student he first studied law, then in 1890 turned seriously to painting. For a while he attended classes at the École des Beaux Arts in Paris under the tuition of the Symbolist painter Gustave Moreau.

Later Matisse was to use elements from the work of several contemporary artists in order to formulate an original and vibrant style of his own that rapidly became influential as far afield as Moscow and New York. The teachings of Moreau resulted in Matisse taking an imaginative rather than a naturalistic look at the world. At the same time the primitivism of both Puvis de Chavannes and of **Gauguin** interested him deeply. Besides these concerns he also appreciated the search for simplicity of structure undertaken by **Cézanne**. In addition Matisse continually endeavoured to increase the brilliance of colour in his painting. For these experiments he found Paul Signac's theories based on **Seurat's** colour perceptions vital.

By 1905 Matisse's art had become sufficiently developed to attract a number of followers including Derain, Vlaminck, **Rouault** and Marquet. The art critic Louis Vauxcelles, when reviewing the Parisian exhibition at the Salon d'Automne in that year, referred to a number of paintings there as those of wild beasts, Les Fauves. This term (Fauvism) remained to designate the work produced by Matisse and his group during the next few years. Their revolutionary style, until the Cubists became more influential, was considered the most avant-garde in Europe.

Besides drawing and painting in the brilliant sunlight of southern France, Matisse visited Spain, Morocco and Italy between 1907 and 1913. These journeys, viewing other cultures and periods besides his own, confirmed for Matisse that rules in art had no existence outside individuals. His aesthetic belief was akin to that of the philosopher Henri Bergson. Each work of art should be the result of artistic intuition which is expressed through that work. Matisse's painting and sculpture in fact became an equivalent of his own individual sensibility's response to the visual world. It was not, therefore, a naturalistic representation of objects as seen by the artist. He practised essentially what was to become known as French Expressionism. This should not be confused with its more pessimistic counterpart, German Expressionism.

Except for one haunting grey war year in 1915, Matisse's constant theme was the joy of life. He felt this as a glorious pantheism, 'a nearly religious feeling' that he had towards man and nature. Mostly naked people, dancing and making music, perhaps relaxing in sunlit landscapes or richly coloured interiors, were his commonest subjects.

Using a dynamically flowing line to control the forms and single colours to give shape a brilliancy, in his mature work Matisse dispensed with tonal variations to suggest the three-dimensionality of an object. This in turn emphasized the flat surface of the canvas and reduced spatial recession.

Matisse's desire to synthesize his imaginative identifications with his subject-matter in the art work led to progressive simplification. In the series of reliefs known as *The Backs* the last one is almost a complete abstraction. The single standing nude female becomes a powerful unity of strength and serenity.

This idea of serenity was important to Matisse. He aimed to avoid depressing subject-matter. In his writings he proposes that his art should be an appeasing influence on tired working people, a mental soother that should 'like a good armchair rest the weary from fatigue'.

In the years immediately before his death, while sick and bedridden Matisse continued to produce his art. By tearing and cutting brightly coloured paper into large shapes he was able to form compositions by giving the pieces to assistants to assemble under his instruction. When attached to walls these shapes seem to float reflectively or energetically in space, reanimating the themes from former years when Matisse painted the murals for the Barnes Foundation at Merion in the USA in the early 1930s, and from 1945 to 1951 decorated the Chapel of the Rosary at Vence not far from his last home. As a superb designer, whether illustrating with etchings **Mallarmé's** poetry and working on a small scale or producing larger designs for sets to **Diaghilev's** ballet *Le Rossignol*, Matisse, through his unification of the sensual and imaginative, informed his best work with a vibrant lyricism and delightful harmony.

Further reading

Other works include: *Woman with the Hat* (1905); *Joy of Life* (1905–6); *Le Luxe II* (1907–8); *Harmony in Blue* (1908); *Dance* (1909–10); *Lady in Blue* (1937). Book illustration: mainly in the 1940s and mostly of poetry including Baudelaire's *Les Fleurs du Mal* and James Joyce's *Ulysses*. See also: 'Notes d'un peintre' published in *La Grande Revue*, December 1908. About Matisse: A. Barr, *Matisse, His Art and His Public* (1951); W. Liebermann, *Matisse, 50 Years of His Graphic Work* (1956); Hilary Spurling's two-volume biography, *The Unknown Matisse: A Life of Henri Matisse* (1998) and *Matisse the Master* (2005).

PAT TURNER

McLUHAN, Herbert Marshall

1911–80

Canadian culturologist

Born in Alberta, Canada, McLuhan studied at Manitoba University but took his PhD in Thomas Nashe at Cambridge University. He taught in American and Canadian universities (Catholic institutions or branches of them),

and worked from his Centre for Culture and Technology, University of Toronto. He became a Catholic in 1937 and this sense of the universe as a purposeful system of incarnate energies impregnates his vision. His main value lies in his exploration of the interfaces set up between traditional genre studies, and his methods lie nearer to those of Alfred Korzybski and **Roland Barthes** than to the separatism of sociology, literary criticism or pure semantics. In fact, his excellent literary criticism repeatedly refers to the cultural and technological context of writing – **Mallarmé** and **Joyce** in relation to newsprint, **Tennyson** to optics, Coleridge to 'radial' thinking, Pope to print technology, and so on. These approaches stem partly from Cambridge attitudes towards literary studies, and partly from the teachings of H.A. Innis, of which he writes in the introduction to a 1964 edition of the latter's *The Bias of Communication*. Innis belonged to the Chicago University school of the 1920s which included, in its field of teaching and reference Robert Ezra Park, **Max Weber**, John Dewey and Thorstein Veblen. From Park, Innis learned 'how to identify the control mechanisms by which a heterogeneous community yet manages to arrange its affairs with some degree of uniformity', and how technological devices 'have necessarily modified the structure and functions of society'. McLuhan developed these assumptions into a radical investigation of how 'the extensions of man' change both the external and the internal environments (the concept of an internal environment draws on the work of the Canadian experimental psychologist Hans Selye, whose *Stress* and *The Stress of Life* appeared in 1950 and 1956). In 1953 McLuhan founded, with the distinguished anthropologist Edmund S. Carpenter, the journal *Explorations*, a major vehicle for environmental and cultural studies. The selection in *Explorations in Communication* (1960) indicate the distinction of its contributors, who included Northrop Frye, Siegfried Giedion, Fernand Léger, David Riesman, Robert Graves and Gilbert Seldes. The semantic category of these studies is indicated in the introduction which speaks of exploring 'the grammars of such languages as print, the newspaper format and television', 'revolutions in the packaging and distribution of ideas and feelings', the 'switch from linear to cluster configuration' in order to understand the 'almost total subliminal universe' of the modern form of 'preliterate man' living within the circuitry of electric media in 'the global village'. The new outlook is 'tribal'. The danger is not merely illiteracy but mediocrity, a society anti-individualistic in its repudiation of the previous print-media culture which still lingers on in a predominantly visual, tactile, oral and aural environment. (Although *Explorations* ended in 1959, an abbreviated version appeared as a supplement to the University of Toronto *Graduate* magazine through the 1970s.)

The warnings implicit in *Explorations* are explicit in *The Mechanical Bride* (1951), a brilliant analysis of advertising and propaganda methods subtitled 'Folklore of Industrial Man' (McLuhan was always concerned to expose contemporary mythology), and designed to show how the media of magazines, newspapers and films control consumption and self-definition in the capitalist state. In fact, the state emerges as a malign work of art (a concept partly derived from Jakob Burckhardt's analysis of Machiavelli). The mechanization of choice moulds human life caught in 'a radical separation between business and society, between action and feeling, office and home, between men and women'. McLuhan believed that these divisions cannot be healed until their fullest extent is perceived. Popular culture, therefore, must be studied to understand the full effect of the media. The historical implications of changes caused by the shift from script to print to electric technology – the major media transition – is documented in *The Gutenberg Galaxy* (1962) from a large variety of texts, selected to elucidate changes towards 'social change which may lead to a genuine increase of human autonomy'. McLuhan's principle is:

If a technology is not understood either from within or from without a culture, and if it gives new stress or ascendancy to one or another of our senses, the ratio among all our senses is altered ... The result is a break in the ratio among the senses, a kind of loss of identity.

William Blake on the 'perceptive organs' and James Joyce's multilingual *Finnegans Wake*, as a spatial involvement of the whole body–mind system, are presented with a wide range of social, psychological and scientific analysis in 'a mosaic pattern of perception and observation', 'the mode of simultaneous awareness' which is the basis of a culture, its practical and observable 'tribal or collective consciousness'. Media hypnosis is to be restricted by understanding the means and arts of communication. The artist functions primarily in this 'new clairvoyance' of the state's design, a prophetic necessity since 'the new electric galaxy of events has already moved deeply into the Gutenberg galaxy', causing 'trauma and tension to every living person'.

Understanding Media (1964), which gained McLuhan international fame and a cult status in America, examines the grammars of communication technology, encouraging the student of 'integral patterns' to 'live mythically and in depth' in order to comprehend 'the medium is the message' – that is, how the grammars of environment afford major clues to present and future. 'The machine turned Nature into an art form', and our own 'proliferating technologies have created a whole series of new environments', with the arts functioning as 'anti-environments' or 'counter-environments': 'art as radar acts as "an early alarm system"', 'the function of indispensable perceptual training rather than the role of a privileged diet for the elite'. McLuhan's political and religious attitudes appear in his presentation of 'the revulsion of our times against imposed patterns' and of 'a faith that concerns the ultimate harmony of all beings'. Without social awareness in depth, patterns will be dictated: 'electric technology is within the gates'. One instrument of resistance, which entered the popular jargon of the 1960s, is to recognize 'hot' media – 'low in participation' – from 'cool' or requiring 'completion by the audience', which is therefore actively engaged rather than passively manipulated.

After 1964, McLuhan found himself in demand to analyse, predict and advise. His aphoristic ability to harness slogan or advert methods to penetrating social analysis of surprising sources found favour with the business world (as much as it was suspiciously loathed by the academic fraternity) and his *Dew-Line Newsletter* supplied the information culture controllers needed. In spite of this ambivalence in political action, he continued to function as an early warning system. *The Medium is the Message* (1967, with the designer Quentin Fiore) is a print and picture collage of media criticism composed with considerable wit and humour, a probe (a favourite term of action in his writings) into 'the environment as a processor of information', and therefore as a virulent propaganda system. *War and Peace in the Global Village* (1968, with Fiore) is 'an inventory of some of the current spastic situations that could be eliminated by more feedforward'. At this stage, McLuhan had come to believe that technologies are 'self-amputations' rather than the extensions of the body. 'Mosaic vision' is still necessary to combat 'corporate decision-making for creating a total service environment on this planet'. *Counter Blast* (1969), acknowledging the methods of Wyndham Lewis's *Blast* (1914) and incorporating design and typography techniques partly explored in *Explorations 8* (reissued in 1967 with the Joycean subtitle, *Verbi-Voco-Visual Explorations*), probes book, film, videotape, etc. as shapes of our consciousness, and therefore as the form of contemporary myth in which human energies are incarnated (another of his recurrent terms):

The electronic age is the age of ecology ... The Age of Implosion in education spells the end of 'subjects' and substitutes instead the structural study of the making and learning process. Software replaces

hardware ... In the Age of Information, the moving of information is by many times the largest business in the world.

Much of the history and theory of these later works is contained in one of McLuhan's most substantial books, *Through the Vanishing Point* (1968, with Harley Parker), a challenge to perception restricted to the 'rear-view mirror' point of view by analysing the history of space design in the arts, including the origins, images and effects of perspective and 'multi-level space' – necessary, since 'civilization is founded upon the isolation and domination of society by the visual sense'. *From Cliché to Archetype* (1970, with Wilfred Watson) is a fascinating discourse on language through such categories as 'Author as Cliché (Book as Probe)', 'Cliché as Breakdown' and 'The One and the Mini'. The range of examples is, once again, extraordinary, and the vivacity of McLuhan's perceptions unmatched. *Culture is Our Business* (1970) returned to his old obsession, American advertising as mythology – 'a world of festivity and celebration' which indicates 'a flip in American society from hardware to software' and how 'advertising provides the corporate *meaning* for the experience of the private owner ... complex social events and "meanings" minus the experience of the commodities in question'. McLuhan's warning now extended to criticism of the USA's war in Vietnam as part of 'the electric infamy environment'.

Needless to say, his beliefs, techniques and conclusions aroused both controversy and downright hatred. (The best criticism of McLuhan's work remains Sidney Finkelstein's *Sense and Nonsense of McLuhan*, 1968.) But McLuhan himself separated his personal intentions from his emphatic style, particularly in an excellent interview in *Playboy* magazine (No. 64, 1969):

I'm making explorations ... my books constitute the *process* rather than the completed product of discovery; my purpose is to employ facts as tentative probes, as means of insight, of pattern recognition, rather than to use them in the traditional and sterile sense of classified data, categories, containers. I want to map new terrain rather than chart old landmarks. But I've never presented such explorations as revealed truth. As an investigator, I have no fixed point of view, no commitment to any theory – my own or anyone else's.

Further reading

See: Gerald E. Stearn (ed.), *McLuhan Hot and Cool* (1968); Harry S. Crosby and George R. Bond (eds), *The McLuhan Explosion* (1968); Donald F. Theall, *The Medium is the Rear View Mirror: Understanding McLuhan* (1971); G. Genosko, *McLuhan and Baudrillard: Masters of Implosion* (1999); Paul Levinson, *Digital McLuhan: A Guide to the Information Millennium* (1999); Richard Cavell, *McLuhan in Space: A Cultural Geography* (2002); Janine Marchessault, *Marshall McLuhan* (2004); G. Genosko (ed.), *Marshall McLuhan: Critical Evaluations in Cultural Theory* (3 vols, 2005).

ERIC MOTTRAM

MEAD, Margaret

1901–78

American anthropologist

Born into a New England academic family, Margaret Mead took a BA at Barnard College and higher degrees in anthropology at Columbia University. Here she was greatly influenced by her teachers, **Franz Boas**, the father of modern American anthropology, and Ruth Benedict, whose interest in the relationship between 'culture' and 'personality' was to provide the central scientific preoccupation of Margaret Mead's career.

In 1925 Mead carried out her first field-study, in Samoa, becoming one of the first women to do anthropological field-research and one of the few American anthropologists of her generation to work outside the Americas. She took into the field a problem posed by Boas: whether adolescence was a culturally specific experience, which happened to occur in modern Western societies, or (as the Western folk-view had it) whether

adolescence was the symptom of profound biological changes which inevitably manifested themselves in disruptive behaviour. The relaxed, sexually free, responsible Samoan maidens were presented to the American public, in *Coming of Age in Samoa* (1928), as the resolution of that particular argument, and the book became a best-seller.

Her next study, of early childhood in Manus (*Growing Up in New Guinea*, 1931), was less explicitly directed towards the testing of a hypothesis, but her description of how another culture raised its children was directly relevant to educational debates then in progress in the United States – particularly since the Manus employed the free-and-easy techniques in favour in avant-garde European kindergartens. The real problem suggested by the book was left unexplored, namely the contrast between the expressive and indulged Manus infants and the driven adults they were later to become.

The theme of these early works remained the leitmotif of Mead's work. 'Human nature' is plastic; cultural conditioning and environment are more vital than biological factors in determining what kinds of people are found in different societies. Perhaps the most radical version of this argument is to be found in her *Sex and Temperament in Three Primitive Societies* (1935), in which the contrasting male and female types in three New Guinea societies were analysed to show that there is nothing natural or universal about particular 'masculine' or 'feminine' role expectations. Scepticism was aroused at the time by the fortunate coincidence that her fieldwork happened to occur among three societies which formed such a perfect contrast for her purposes, but if the impressionistic descriptions cannot be accepted without reservations, the broad lines of her reports, and the conclusion drawn, have proved reasonably acceptable.

During the Second World War Mead was active in a team which made 'national culture' studies of allies and enemies for the US government, and even after the war she produced significant academic studies, notably her *Continuities in Cultural Evolution* (1964). She also remained for the greater part of her professional life on the staff of the American Museum of Natural History. Nonetheless she increasingly devoted herself to public or popular activities, which she saw as an essential product of her anthropological studies. As she wrote in her autobiography, *Blackberry Winter* (1972): 'I have spent most of my life studying the lives of other peoples, faraway peoples, so that Americans might better understand themselves.' The point of view she propagated was liberal and optimistic, and perhaps characteristically American in its emphasis on cultural malleability, providing a sort of academic blessing for the melting-pot. An intelligent, sophisticated and religious person, she escaped the intellectual vulgarization which her popularizing role might have implied, retaining a sense of the complexity of social issues and an openness to new ideas. *Margaret Mead: The Complete Bibliography 1925–1975* (ed. Joan Gordon, 1976) lists over 1,400 items, bearing witness to a passion for communication which was rewarded by the attention and interest of millions both inside and outside the social sciences.

Further reading

See: Jane Howard. *Margaret Mead: A Life* (1989); Derek Freeman *The Fateful Hoaxing of Margaret Mead: A Historical Analysis of Her Samoan Research* (1999): Hilary Lapsley, *Margaret Mead and Ruth Benedict: The Kinship of Women* (2001); Steven Pinker, *The Blank Slate: The Modern Denial of Human Nature* (2002).

ADAM KUPER

MELVILLE, Herman

1819–91

US writer

'I love all men who *dive*' – so, in part, runs Melville's reaction on hearing a lecture in Boston in 1849 by Ralph Waldo Emerson. It was generous acclaim, for Melville thought Emerson's Transcendentalism largely a fraud, a well-meant but facile credo of optimism and spiritual good cheer which failed to acknowledge the tragic currents in man's condition, his especial vulnerability to pain, war, evil and illusion. But in designating Emerson a 'diver', Melville as aptly might have been speaking of himself. For in nearly all his fiction and poetry, and in his lively correspondence and several reviews, he confirms his own deep probing energies of mind, the writer-diver in search of the elusive, absolute condition of things. This irresistible 'diving' for truth, a lifelong, unslackening curiosity which finds expression through the intelligent playfulness and vitality of his style, situates him, with Emerson, Hawthorne, **Whitman** and **Thoreau**, at the centre not only of the mid-nineteenth-century 'American Renaissance' but the American literary tradition at large, a restive, major imagination whose powers come best into focus in his whaling epic, *Moby-Dick* (1851), stories like 'Bartleby, The Scrivener' (1853) and 'Benito Cereno' (1855), his 'Ship of Fools' allegory, *The Confidence Man* (1857) and the posthumous novella *Billy Budd* (1888–91). The scale of Melville's 'curiosity' – 'his ontological heroics' as he describes matters in his correspondence – has rarely been better perceived than in the diary entry made in 1856 by Hawthorne, then American Consul in Liverpool, after he and Melville spent an afternoon in discussion on the Southport sands:

> Melville, as he always does, began to reason of Providence and futurity, and of everything that lies beyond human ken ... He can neither believe nor be comfortable in his unbelief; and he is too honest and courageous not to try to do one or the other.

The reputation that once attached to Melville, and which the revival of his critical fortunes, begun in the 1920s, still has not entirely dislodged – that of the compelling but artless teller of sea-stories – has nevertheless given way to a growing awareness of how layered his writing was from the outset.

So, at least, from differing angles, fellow-authors like **D.H. Lawrence**, Cesare Pavese, **Albert Camus** and Charles Olson have borne impressive witness. Paradoxically for a writer at one time thought only an American-Victorian purveyor of 'adventure', and whose career dissolved into obscurity after *Moby-Dick*, Melville has increasingly been taken for a prophet of 'modern' consciousness, a wary, sceptical, knowingly ironic voice of resistance to every manner of human ruling illusion. Whether recognized for his arts of narrative, or for the fine ambition of his thought, Melville has justly entered the American literary pantheon. Few of his writings are entirely free of fault, but his essential 'depths', as Hawthorne remarked of *Mardi* (1849), Melville's least gainly book, 'compel a man to swim for his life'.

Melville alleged that his life only 'began' when he wrote his engaging first work, *Typee* (1846). Yet his beginnings were auspicious, if not necessarily for a literary career. He came of two socially eminent American families, the Melvilles of Boston and the Dutch-descended Gansevoorts of Albany, New York. One grandfather, Major Thomas Melvill (sic), took a leading part in the Boston Tea Party; the other, Peter Gansevoort, fought as a general in the War of Independence. This patrician stock was an important source of pride in Melville, the basis of high personal expectations. He grew up, one of eight children, in a busy, well-connected and convivial home, in New York City. In *Redburn* (1849), *Pierre* (1852) and parables like 'Bartleby' and 'The Two Temples' (1854), Melville would reveal himself as a writer of the city as much as the sea. The unexpected bankruptcy, then delirium and death of his father, Allan Melville, an 'Importer of French Goods and Commission Merchant' and a seemingly prosperous member of New York's commercial middle class, in the recession of 1832, brought profound family reverses. For Melville it inflicted a trauma he would try to re-confront in the writing of *Pierre*. In the short run, it made for a series of abrupt personal false starts.

First, in 1834–6, he clerked in an Albany bank, and in the summer of 1835 worked on his uncle's farm at Pittsfield. Fifteen years later, he himself bought a farm in Pittsfield, drafted the early versions of *Moby-Dick* and, following the publication of his essay, 'Hawthorne and his Mosses' (1850), discovered the author of *Mosses from an Old Manse* for his neighbour in nearby Lenox. In 1837, he tried teaching in a country school. The same year he made his writing début in the correspondence columns of a local paper, and then as the author of a two-part Gothic story fragment. In late 1838 he studied engineering in hopes of working on the Lake Erie canal system. In June 1839, he sailed down the Hudson to New York, and secured a place to Liverpool and back as a deckhand on the packetship, *St Lawrence*. His encounters with the brute equations of Victorian sailor and city life he portrays, in some irony, in *Redburn*. Once back in New York, and again jobless, he tried another spell of teaching, and in 1840 took off to Illinois, where he saw and travelled the Mississippi, experience put in store and re-worked in his canny 'metaphysical' satire, *The Confidence Man*.

In near desperation, in January 1841, appropriately the turn of a new year, he sailed out from New Bedford as a whalerman and harpooner aboard the *Acushnet*, the beginning of four years of Polynesian and whaling adventure. His journeys into the South Seas, on the *Acushnet* and two subsequent whalers, took him to a multitude of ports and sailor haunts, and specifically to the Marquesas, Tahiti and Honolulu. Later he would visit ocean outposts like the Galápagos, where he found the inspiration for his cycle of island portraits, 'The Encantadas', as **Darwin** had for his *Origin of Species*. His litany of adventure includes jumping ship and his vaunted 'stay mong the cannibals' (which yielded *Typee*), a spell of detention in the local 'calaboose' and various intervals of beachcombing of which he makes use in *Omoo* (1847), even temporary managership of a bowling-alley, and his eventual return to Boston in 1844 via the Horn and Latin

America as an enlisted seaman aboard the frigate *United States*, on which his fifth book, *White-Jacket* (1850), is based. On his reunion with his family, he could look back to these years, life lived dangerously and at full throttle, as a seasoned ex-mariner, the one-time patrician for whom a whaler (as he testifies in *Moby-Dick*) had been his 'Harvard and Yale', and who knew from the inside the testing, male, enclosed ship-world of the common sailor, and that toughest of forcing-grounds, the Pacific whale-fisheries. It is this dense, energetic personal history, and more, that Melville gives imaginative expression to in the fiction which culminates in *Moby-Dick*.

His early writing, in sequence *Typee, Omoo, Mardi, Redburn* and *White-Jacket*, centres upon a young, usually ingenuous, 'isolato', a quester embarked for adventure, and even outright 'truth', whose eventual incarnation will be Ishmael in *Moby-Dick*. Each narrative, thus, Melville conceives as a journey-out, a remembered diary of events either on land or aboard different types of ship. In *Typee*, Melville's setting is Nuku Hiva in the Marquesas, and a concealed inland 'cannibal' valley to which Tommo, the narrator, and his companion flee, only to become prisoner-guests, two fugitive consciousnesses from the West set down amid the arcana and totemic mysteries of Typee culture. Despite its surfaces as 'adventure', Melville, as he says, 'varnishes' his facts at every turn, playing one ambiguity off against another, and hinting of darker other worlds beneath the affable outward show of the valley. The zest of the telling, and the story's lavish, contrapuntal play of detail, make for an astonishing first effort. *Omoo* continues the saga, Melville's most free-wheeling volume, genuinely light of touch and funny, almost South Seas picaresque. With *Mardi*, he begins as before, another jumping from ship and the promise of Polynesian derring-do. Less than a third along, however, the story changes radically in temper, and for the worse. For into this third narrative, Melville poured an avalanche of recent reading, from Plato and Montaigne, Spenser and the Elizabethans, from the major

European Romantics, and even from Victorian books of flower symbolism. The results are painful, a cluttered would-be 'philosophical' travelogue in which Taji, the hero, and his retinue pursue an ethereal albino princess across a mythic archipelago of sixteen islands. *Mardi* with justice can be taken as a dummy-run for *Moby-Dick*, but one which outran Melville's control. Stung by the criticism aroused by *Mardi*, Melville spoke of returning to the 'cakes and ale' world in *Redburn*. Based on the Liverpool journey he made at eighteen, and a subtler effort than he allowed, it tells the rite-of-passage endured by Wellingborough Redburn, youthful confrontations glossed and teased by an older, far wiser head. The stark scenes of sailor DTs, death, malignity in the person of the sailor Jackson, and the observation of Liverpool penury and human suffering and of the plague which breaks out among emigrants in steerage, make for vivid, dramatic narration. In *White-Jacket*, also told as first-person narrative, Melville depicts the hierarchic, man-of-war world of the frigate, a compendious account of American navy custom and life seen from his customary fo'c's'le stance. In the shedding of the narrator's emblematic white coat, as Redburn's before, Melville projects a sea-version of the fall from innocence, the awakening of a deeper, 'ocean' state of knowing.

By the time he published *Moby-Dick*, Melville had married (in 1847) Elizabeth Shaw, daughter of the Chief Justice of Massachusetts; read like a novice possessed the works of Shakespeare; and, having published in *The Literary World* (1850) his admiring account of *Mosses from an Old Manse*, met and began his astonishing correspondence with Nathaniel Hawthorne. His 'whale-book', large, striking in canvas and reach, represents him at full imaginative stretch. Ostensibly the story of the *Pequod*'s search for the definition-eluding white whale, it quickly yields many other levels of quest – for self-meaning, community, 'light', and again, overwhelmingly, 'truth'. Defined one way, then another – by Ahab as evil, by Starbuck as a 'dumb beast', by the Parsee counter-crew as a god, by Queequeg as a hieroglyphic mystery, the whale dominates the narrative, incapable of being 'caught' and fixed by any single meaning. Melville declares the organizing principle of *Moby-Dick* to be 'careful disorderliness', an appropriately flexible mode of narrative able to contain, and actually discipline, the book's abundance, both the cetology and the epic flights of speculation. Whether read as a simple whale adventure, or metaphysics, or as 'modernist' self-reflexive narration, *Moby-Dick* offers Melville's central legacy, an essential landmark of American literary history.

With *Moby-Dick* behind him, Melville turned his imagination inland, and in *Pierre or The Ambiguities* attempted a portrait of a heroic 'Fool of Truth' ultimately entombed by his endeavour to redeem his father's abandonment of a mysterious, illegitimate daughter, the hero's half-sister. Within its apparent Gothic labyrinths lies a profound drama of sexual feeling, and Melville's own 'inside narrative' of the writer's life. Between 1853, when he tried to secure a consular appointment, and 1857, he turned to the short story, publishing in 1856 his *Piazza Tales*, five pieces (with an introduction) from the fourteen he had issued in *Putnam's Monthly Magazine* and *Harper's New Monthly Magazine*. These stories are now rightly taken to rank among his best efforts. In 'Bartleby' he tells a parable of Wall Street, an account of liberal capitalism's impact on the human spirit redolent of **Kafka**. In 'The Encantadas' he depicts a version of hell, a bleak landscape of island volcanic ruins to complement the saddest and worst of human isolation and loss. In 'Benito Cereno', a story almost **Conradian** in its hints of ineffable corruption, he makes an act of slave-insurrection his occasion, a bleak, violent portrait of the moral blindness slavery requires for its very existence. These, and his other stories of the 1850s, and *Israel Potter* (1855), a satire of American national heroes, prepared the way for his blackest chronicle of illusion, *The Confidence Man*. If literary kin could be claimed for *The Confidence Man*, it would include **Dostoevsky's** *Notes from the Underground*, **Mann's** *Felix Krull* and Kafka's *The Castle*. A Mississippi river story, begun and ended on April Fool's Day aboard the steamer *Fidèle*, it sets about the gullibility and panacea-seeking of latter-day American 'pilgrims' with Swiftian incision. The instrument is an apparent master confidence-man, a 'metaphysical scamp', whose different avatars mock and ensnare the unvigilant. Within its onslaught on different American shibboleths, it contains key clues to Melville's overall theories of fiction (especially chapters XIV, XXXIII and XLIV). Neither the tone, nor the precise direction of Melville's satire, can always easily be pinned down, but his idiom is never less than vigorous, brilliantly alert and inventive.

By 1856, Melville was approaching nervous collapse. He sailed for the Levant as an attempt at recuperation; visited Hawthorne in Liverpool; and in 1857, after his trip to the Holy Land, landed back in America a month after the publication of *The Confidence Man*. In 1858–60 he tried lecturing on the Lyceum circuit; sailed with his brother Tom to San Francisco in 1860; sold the Pittsfield farm in 1862–3 and, dismayingly for a man who had written *Moby-Dick*, in 1866 was obliged to take employment as a minor Customs Inspector in New York, a post he discharged with resigned diligence for nineteen years. His times saw little improvement. His volume of Civil War poems, *Battle-Pieces and Aspects of the War* (1866), and the later *Clarel* (1876), a massive Victorian work of doubt and faith longer than *Paradise Lost*, barely gained a readership. In 1867, his son Malcolm died, a probable suicide, to be followed in 1886 by the second Melville son, Stanwix. Only two further works were published in Melville's lifetime, both privately, the poems in *John Marr and Other Sailors* (1888) and *Timoleon* (1891). The work which first saw light in 1924, however, *Billy Budd*, after a confused textual history, has come to be recognized for Melville's final masterpiece. A fable of 'iniquity' and sacrificial innocence, it explores the triangulation of three 'phenomenal' men, Captain Vere, the master-at-arms John Claggart, and 'welkin-eyed' Billy Budd – hanged for alleged murder aboard a British warship during the Napoleonic Wars and in the wake of the risings at Nore and Spithead. Whether read as Melville's testament of 'acceptance', or 'rebellion', or as more complex dialectical drama, it underscores the enduring, radical strengths of his art. Melville ended his career as he began, an unyielding 'diver' for truth.

Further reading

See: F.O. Matthiessen, *American Renaissance: Art and Expression in the Age of Emerson and Whitman* (1941); Leon Howard, *Herman Melville: A Biography* (1951); Jay Leyda, *The Melville Log: A Documentary Life of Herman Melville, 1819–91* (2 vols, 1951); Newton Arvin, *Herman Melville* (1957); Charles Olson, *Call Me Ishmael* (1958); Warner Berthoff, *The Example of Melville* (1962); *Melville: A Collection of Critical Essays*, ed. Richard Chase (1962); Edgar A. Dryden, *Melville's Thematics of Form: The Great Art of Telling the Truth* (1968); *Studies in the Novel*, Herman Melville special number, Vol. 1, No. 4 (Winter 1969); *New Perspectives on Melville*, ed. Faith Pullin (1978); Robert S. Levine (ed.), *The Cambridge Companion to Herman Melville* (1998); Hershel Parker, *Herman Melville: A Biography* (2 vols, 2002–5).

A. ROBERT LEE

MENDEL, Gregor

1822–84

Austrian botanist, founder of genetics

As the son of a peasant in the Silesian village of Heinzendorf (Hynčice), Mendel showed promise at the village school and was selected for academic studies in Leipnik and Troppau. When he left the *Gymnasium* at Troppau in 1839 he entered the Philosophy Institute at Olmütz. There financial worries and overwork dogged his progress so that it was with relief that he entered the Augustinian Monastery at Brünn (Brno) in 1843. This was the centre of intellectual life in the area. Several of the monks taught in the local schools, as did Mendel from 1849 until he

became abbot of the monastery nineteen years later.

In addition to his work as teacher and cleric Mendel was an active member of the Natural Science Society (Naturforschende Verein in Brünn), he was on the central board of the local agricultural society (K.K. Mährisch-schlesischen Gesellschaft zur Beförderung des Ackerbaues, der Natur – und Landeskunde), and he was known locally as a plant breeder, apiculturist and meteorologist.

Despite Mendel's academic ability and excellence as a teacher he twice failed to pass the teachers' examination in the natural sciences. The time which he spent at Vienna University (1851–3) preparing for re-examination proved invaluable for his subsequent researches into plant hybridization, although it did not lead to success in the teachers' exam. Mendel's hybridization experiments – with the edible pea – lasted from 1856 to 1863. His study of the Hawkweed (*Hieracium*) was completed in 1871 by which time his duties as abbot took almost all his time. These latter years were marked by controversy over the new ecclesiastical tax on monastery property which Mendel obstinately refused to pay. His funeral in 1884 was a major event in Brünn, but it was another sixteen years before his researches in plant hybridization became generally known and identified as the foundation stone of the modern conception of heredity.

When Mendel studied science at Vienna University the subject of the fixity of species was under discussion. The adherents of *Naturphilosophie* had pictured life as developing progressively under the direction of an inherent, non-material agency of 'world soul'. Species therefore had been changed or transmuted, albeit gradually. The old dogma of the constancy of species had already come under attack in the eighteenth century and Linnaeus had weakened his hard line on the subject when he suggested that many species had originated from the hybridization of a few original types, the generic forms. This claim was greeted with scepticism. It was pointed out that hybrids were frequently sterile, and when they yielded progeny these tended to 'revert' to one or other of the originating species. Debate over this 'hybridization theory' of the origin of species, however, continued and prizes for essays on the subject were offered by the Dutch Academy of Sciences in 1830 and the Paris Academy in 1860.

Mendel recognized that the debate over the hybridization theory would only be settled when a systematic and extensive series of experiments had been carried out in which the transmission of each differing trait united in the hybrid had been followed through successive generations in a large population of its offspring. Between 1856 and 1863 Mendel raised some 28,000 plants, involving crosses between varieties differing in one, two and three hereditary traits.

In all cases where the parents differed in one trait, such as seed shape – round or wrinkled – the seeds produced by the resulting hybrids were either round or wrinkled, never intermediate between the two forms. Moreover, the proportion of round to wrinkled seeds approximated to the ratio 3:1. This proved to be the case for all the seven traits he studied. Further studies revealed that the round seeds were of two types, one breeding true, the other yielding both round and wrinkled seeds. The latter were twice as numerous as the former, so the ratio of 3:1 was really 1:2:1, the middle term representing the hybrid forms, the first and last terms the true-breeding forms.

With his training in mathematics Mendel realized that the 1:2:1 ratio corresponded with the terms of the binomial series: $(A + a^2 = A^2 + 2Aa + a^2)$. Mendel pictured the two letters in the binomial as representing the two contrasted forms brought together in the hybrid. The fact that the offspring yielded by sexual reproduction mirrored the binomial expansion in their statistical relations suggested to Mendel that sexual reproduction involved a process equivalent to the multiplication of the terms A and a. Evidently the forms A and a became separate from each other, then they united in all possible combinations with equal frequency. Since each fertilized egg cell was produced by the

fertilization of one female germ cell by one pollen grain, it must be in the formation of these cells and grains that the separation of types A and a occurred. These gametes were hence either of type A or type a and their union in fertilization gave the forms A, Aa and a.

Mendel went on to show that where more than one pair of contrasted characters was involved, the hereditary transmission of each was independent of the other. Thus in the case of two pairs of contrasted characters brought together in a hybrid the offspring showed all possible combinations between the two pairs. These combinatorial forms corresponded in their relative frequencies with the terms in the expansion of *two* binomial series. When dominance was involved the resulting ratio was 9:3:3:1.

These statistical regularities, which have become known as Mendelian ratios, were Mendel's empirical discovery. The explanatory hypothesis which he advanced to account for them is generally known as germinal or Mendelian segregation. Today these achievements tend to be regarded in terms of the light which they have thrown upon the nature of inheritance, a subject which lacked a sound theoretical foundation until Mendel's work became generally known. For Mendel, the significance of his work lay in a different direction. He had set out to throw some light upon the hybridization theory of the origin of species and the conflicting reports of plant hybridists thereon, and it was to their work that he devoted the concluding section of his paper. He urged that the unit of analysis was not the species but the hereditary characters. The results obtained by hybridists therefore depended upon the number of such characters which differed in the originating forms. According to the binomial theorem, if this number was n then the number of different types of hybrid offspring would be $3n$. If n was 7 the reappearance of either of the originating types would be likely to occur only once in 16,000 hybrid offspring, whereas if n was 1 the expected frequency would be 1 in 4. That previous hybridists using different species arrived at different results was hardly surprising. Nor was it a matter for surprise that hybrids showed a wide range of variability, for this again was a function of the number of differing characters crossed. There was no need to postulate the existence of species or of characters with varying degrees of constancy. It sufficed to distinguish hybrids in which germinal segregation occurred, whose progeny followed the example of the edible pea, and those in which it did not occur, where permanent hybrids were formed which represented new combinations of characters from the originating species.

Although Mendel's papers were referred to a number of times in the nineteenth century their importance was not recognized. Thus the standard bibliographical review of W.O. Focke merely noted Mendel's numerous hybridization experiments and added somewhat sceptically that Mendel 'believed he had found constant numerical ratios between the hybrid types'. When in 1900 three botanists, Hugo de Vries, Erich von Tschermak and Carl Correns, rediscovered Mendelian ratios and read Mendel's paper the Mendelian theory was finally launched. Six years later the term 'genetics' was introduced for the subject whose theoretical foundation had been furnished by Mendel.

Further reading

The best biography of Mendel is still that of Hugo Iltis, *Life of Mendel* (trans. E. and C. Paul, 1932; reprinted 1966). A translation of Mendel's paper and associated documents will be found in C. Stern and R. Sherwood, *The Origin of Genetics: A Mendel Sourcebook* (1966). For a discussion of the context of Mendel's research see R.C. Olby, *Origins of Mendelism* (1966).

ROBERT OLBY

MESSIAEN, Olivier Eugene Prosper Charles

1908–92

French composer

One of the most gifted French composers of any age, Messiaen attended the Paris Conservatoire from 1919 to 1930, where his teachers included Paul Dukas (composition), Marcel Dupré (organ) and Maurice Emmanuel (history of music). In 1931 he took up the post of organist at the Église de la Sainte Trinité in Paris, a position he held for life. Together with Andre Jolivet and others he formed the group 'La Jeune France' in 1936. This was dedicated to restoring a sense of seriousness to French music, then dominated by the anti-romantic aesthetic of the composers of 'Les Six'. During the war he was interned by the Germans in Stalag VIII, where he performed for the first time his apocalyptic *Quatuor pour la fin du temps* (1941) before the entire assembly of prisoners in icy conditions. Upon his release, he resumed teaching duties in Paris, becoming in 1947 Professor of Analysis, Aesthetics and Rhythm at the Conservatoire. His radical experiments with musical language in the early 1950s attracted some of the outstanding young composers of the day to his classes, including **Pierre Boulez** and **Karlheinz Stockhausen**. After the death of his first wife in 1959, he married his former pupil Yvonne Loriod for whom he had written many of his piano works. In 1966 he became Professor of Composition at the Conservatoire and travelled and taught extensively throughout the world.

Any discussion of Messiaen's music must take as its starting point his artistic personality, which offers an intensely private and individual response to the traditional concerns of Christianity, nature and human love. The astonishing power and commitment of his work derived in some measure from his unquestioning acceptance of the diverse influences of his childhood, while its attraction resides in the integration of a radical reappraisal of the elements of musical language with an aesthetic that derived unashamedly from **Richard Wagner** and the French Symbolists.

Many of these features are present in the early works of the late 1920s and 1930s. If the titles of the piano *Préludes* (1928) reflect an obvious **Debussyism** (*Les Sons impalpables du rêve, Un reflet dans le vent*, and so on), their forms by contrast are constructivist. The same is also true of the subsequent organ pieces that stand in the line of César Franck and Jehan Alain and show a characteristic commitment to sacred subjects: *Le Banquet céleste* (1928), *L'Ascension* (1933) (which also exists in an orchestral version), *La Nativité du Seigneur* (1935) and *Les Corps glorieux* (1939). In the 1940s this line was extended by *Visions de l'amen* (1943, for two pianos), *Vingt regards sur l'enfant Jésus* (1944, for piano), and *Trois petites liturgies de la Présence Divine* (1944, for women's choir and orchestra). That these pieces mainly comprise short descriptive movements points to a lifelong preference for episodic forms, with simple but sharp internal contrasts, rather than for the integrated, developing forms of the Austro-German tradition. The imaginative stimulus to using even sacred texts in this way, Messiaen suggested, arose out of his childhood delight in the fantastic elements in Shakespeare (Ariel, Puck); in manhood he created comparably fantastic tableaux illustrative of the 'truths' of Catholic dogma, whose range embraces the extremes of peace and violence, reverence and penitence.

In the 1930s, he had also composed two song cycles for Wagnerian voice to his own surrealistic texts (he derived his literary bent from his mother, a writer). These celebrated his marriage (*Poèmes pour Mi*, 1936) and the birth of a child (*Chants de terre et de ciel*, 1938). In the 1940s he pursued the themes of secular love in three works devoted to the Tristan and Isolde myth: *Harawi* (1945, for voice and piano), *Turangalîlâ-Symphony* (1948, for orchestra), and *Cinq rechants* (1949, for twelve solo voices). These works represent the summation of the first part of his life. In the Symphony especially, the remarkable new eroticism is projected on the one hand through a glittering rhythmic brilliance, and on the other hand through a spaciousness in repose that had already been adumbrated by the timeless contemplations of the early organ music.

In all these works, there had been technical innovations: still working within a tonal framework, he had devised a number of pitch modes ('of limited transposition') characterized by internal symmetries that he used in various combinations; in response to the disassociation of pitch and rhythmic functions in *The Rite of Spring* of **Igor Stravinsky**, he approached purely rhythmic thought from several standpoints: he derived small cells from a Hindu treatise (*Sharngadeva*), employed Greek rhythms based on conventional ideas of the poetic foot, used prime numbers to determine large proportions, and built multi-levelled rhythmic structures out of canons and ostinati. Increasingly he came to prefer the 'free, unequal durations' he found in nature to what he considered to be the artificial metric regularity of traditional music. These concerns came to a head in a number of experimental, and highly influential, keyboard pieces: the *Modes de valeurs et d'intensités*, *Neumes rythmiques* and *Cantéjodjayâ* of 1949; the *Île de feu I et II* of 1950; and the *Livre d'orgue* of 1951. These works, in part or in whole, reflected the obsessive contemporary desire for a high degree of ordering in all the simply identifiable musical dimensions – a desire to a certain extent fostered by post-war analyses of the music of **Anton Webern**. In pitch terms, although Messiaen used the twelve-tone scale modally more often than serially, he here developed mechanistic permutational patterns in a spirit he viewed as redolent of the Middle Ages. In rhythmic terms, he measured note-lengths as additions of durational values which he then permutated according to 'interversion' procedures. Comparable methods were applied to dynamic values and to different modes of articulation. Although twelve-tone, these means embodied nothing of the 'organic' processes found in the music of **Arnold Schoenberg** and his school, and, indeed, were crude to a degree. Nevertheless, they undoubtedly ushered in a new phase of European music, and their fruits are, to a certain extent, still with us today.

Immediately after these works, however, there was a dramatic change. For personal reasons he turned to a contemplation of nature – something he knew well from his boyhood in Grenoble – in which he saw, if not a solace, then certainly a refuge from the world. His principal concern was to transcribe the melodies, rhythms and timbres of birdsongs for conventional instruments, and to intersperse the results with musical passages descriptive of the birds' natural habitats. In this he considered he was extending the nature music of Wagner and Claude Debussy. While there had been elements of birdsong in his earlier works, three pieces were now entirely given over to it: the *Réveil des oiseaux* (1953, for piano and orchestra), which like the later *Chronochromie* (1960, for orchestra) includes an elaborate dawn chorus; *Oiseaux exotiques* (1956, for piano and orchestra), a fantasy combining birdsongs from all over the world; and *Catalogue d'oiseaux* (1956–8, for piano) a richly imaginative inventory in seven volumes.

The works after 1960 showed once again a profusion of concerns: there was the consolidation of nature imagery (*La Fauvette des jardins*, 1970, for piano, and *Des canyons aux étoiles*, 1971, for orchestra); a return to sacred subjects (*Couleurs de la Cité Céleste*, 1963, for piano and small orchestra, *Et expecto resurrectionem mortuorum*, 1964, for orchestra, *La Transfiguration de notre Seigneur Jésus Christ*, 1963–9, for choir, seven soloists and orchestra, and *Méditations sur le mystère de la Sainte Trinité*, 1969, for organ); and an extension of his interest in exotica (*Sept Haïkai*, 1962, for piano and orchestra, which includes an imitation of Sho, the Japanese mouth organ). Here, Messiaen's lifelong concern with musical colour achieved a new prominence, especially in the selection and juxtaposition of chords and textures. The sonorities were more brittle and relied particularly on the 'mysterious' resonances of greatly expanded percussion sections. All these features achieved their greatest synthesis in his only opera, *St-François d'Assise* (1975–83) a work of huge proportions written for the Paris Opera that reinterpreted in sacred terms the awe and terror of the Kantian sublime. The late works broke new territory by diversifying his ensembles: *Un vitrail et des oiseaux*

(1986) and *La Ville d'En-haut* (1987) were for piano, brass, wind and percussion; *Concert à quatre* (1990–1) was for piano, flute, oboe, cello and orchestra; and *Pièce pour piano et quatuor à cordes* (1991) was for piano and string quartet. His last work *Éclairs sur l'au dela*, like *Un sourire* (1989), was for orchestra alone and astonished audiences at its first posthumous performance for its poignant mastery.

While the elements of the Messiaen legacy are in themselves clear enough – and none has been more influential than his concern with the formation of musical language, as testified by his idiosyncratic writings *Technique de mon langage musical* ('Technique of My Musical Language', 1942) and *Traité de rhythme, de couleur, et d'ornithologie* (1949–92) – it is the power of his innate gifts that has proved persuasive: even those whose aesthetic and musical attitudes are quite other than his have acknowledged him as a modern legend.

Further reading

Most of Messiaen's works are published by either Durand or Leduc (Paris). See: Robert Sherlaw Johnson, *Messiaen* (1975); Claude Samuel, *Conversations with Olivier Messiaen* (1976 and 1994); Paul Griffiths, *Olivier Messiaen and the Music of Our Time* (1985); and Peter Hill, *The Messiaen Companion* (1995).

CHRISTOPHER WINTLE

MIES VAN DER ROHE, Ludwig
1886–1969
German/US architect

Mies van der Rohe and **Le Corbusier** are the most important architects of what has been called the Heroic period of modern architecture, the period between the two world wars when the theories and style of the new architecture were first demonstrated. The double challenge that the architects of this time took upon themselves was to derive a form of building which could exploit the new manufacturing technology, which could make use of machine-produced parts, and more importantly create an undecorated architecture, an intention first suggested by Adolf Loos's essay 'Decoration and Crime' published in 1908. Through this latter ambition the pioneer architects identified themselves with the urgency of modernism, the desire to break once and for all with the irrelevancies and encumbrances of the past. Although recent reassessment has often been directed towards finding parallels between the works of this period and the more distant past, notably the comparison by Colin Rowe of the villas of Le Corbusier and Palladio, and although a more detailed analysis of Mies might show an unbroken line from the German neoclassicism of Schinkel, received through Behrens with whom he worked at a formative time, the spirit of the early modern movement was obsessively, to borrow Moholy-Nagy's phrase, the New Vision.

In his later work, Le Corbusier displayed a huge and varied talent, whereas Mies held to the same aims – the desire for clarity and purity, expressed through a strict rectilinear geometry and careful detailing – throughout his long career. These qualities were characteristics of all his mature works, from first to last, and this consistency of effort and inspiration explains why his influence is so pervasive, and why he can be considered above all others as the father of steel and glass architecture. The prophetic nature of his abilities can be judged by the models of the glass tower blocks, done between 1919 and 1921.

Mies's mature style found its first clear expression in the design of the German Pavilion for the 1929 International Exhibition in Barcelona. In this small one-storey building can be found the essence of what was to inform the rest of his life's work, demonstrated with complete authority. The characteristics of the style were the building placed upon a pedestal, the use of opulent materials, treated as pure clear-cut rectilinear horizontal and vertical surfaces, spaces within and without treated as overlapping and interlocking, transparent external walls, and a separation of the structure from the walls, using non-load-bearing partitions around a regular placing of load-bearing columns, allowing for a free composition of the plan. This approach allowed him to compose the plan unrestricted by the demands of support and gravity, as a painter might compose an abstract painting. The similarity between the plan of the Barcelona Pavilion and the contemporaneous Dutch de Stijl school is notable. It has been pointed out elsewhere that this freedom of the plan was achieved at the cost of a much more rigid, stratified section than is usual with traditional load-bearing wall buildings.

For the Pavilion, Mies designed a chair, a stool and a glass-topped table, examples of which were carefully placed within the buildings to further structure and enhance the clear geometrical organization of the space. The deep transparency of the building conveys a sense of space that flows through and beyond the Pavilion, as if this were some local organization within a universal continuous system, which was capable of consistently organizing the placing of furniture and the relationship of one building to another. Thus from this one building he was able to realize a total vision that would allow him confidently to tackle any scale of work, from the layout of a large campus to the design of other exquisite single transparent pavilions.

Apart from the few pieces of furniture, the Barcelona Pavilion only contained a statue by Georg Kolbe placed on a pedestal in a pool. As with all his best work, the beauty of the composition is best appreciated when empty, devoid of the random casualness of everyday life.

The ideal of continuous space which he was to serve in later buildings, notably in Crown Hall on the Illinois Institute of Technology (IIT) campus, by stopping the internal partitions short of the ceiling, allows for no clear demarcation of one space from another, and explains why clearly defined doors and isolated windows, the ancient items that mark one space from another, and inside from outside, are an anathema to Mies.

His career divided between the work in Germany, which he left in 1937, and the work of the rest of his life in America. Apart from the Barcelona Pavilion his major achievements include the organization of the Weissenhof exhibition in 1927 at which the major architects of the new style, including Le Corbusier, **Walter Gropius**, J.J.P. Oud and Hans Scharoun, at his invitation contributed buildings to a master plan by Mies, producing a unique assemblage of seminal buildings of the Modern Movement; the Turgendhat house in Brno, Czechoslovakia, in 1930; and the model house for the 1931 Berlin Building Exhibition. These latter two buildings were adaptations of the style of the Barcelona Pavilion to the requirements of a dwelling.

In 1930 he was appointed director of the famous design school, the Bauhaus, on Gropius's recommendation, and remained so until, by his own decision, the school was closed in 1933. His cool courage at this time in the face of considerable harassment by the Fascists was unwavering. He left for America in 1937.

Soon after arriving he was appointed Director of Architecture at what was to become the Illinois Institute of Technology, consequently coming to live in Chicago, the city where he was to remain for the rest of his life, and which was to come to contain the greatest concentration of his buildings. In the 1940s and 1950s there developed a deep empathy between his work and the work of the native American architects.

In his inaugural address at IIT he gave a rare and illuminating insight into his philosophy. Education, he asserted, consisted of leading the student from materials, through function, to creative work. He then, with great passion, expounded the virtues and beauty of primitive building methods. In this was an echo of neo-classicism, of the belief that the Greek temples were a refined development from the first primitive hut, from Adam's first house in Paradise.

He was a man of few public utterances, unlike Le Corbusier who was to the end a tireless polemicist. His two most famous typically sparse statements were 'less is more'

and 'God is in the details'. These two, however, when read against his buildings, are as revealing as all the volumes produced by Le Corbusier.

There is an interesting divergence in the work in America of the two newly resident pioneer architects and past directors of the Bauhaus, Mies and Gropius. Gropius after the Second World War, working with Konrad Wasehumann, undertook to develop a system for mass-producing housing, called the General Panel house. Mies started at about the same time the design of a house for a close friend, Dr Edith Farnsworth. The house was to take six years to reach completion. Two more opposed uses of the new techniques and materials of building would be difficult to imagine. In retrospect the seeds of difference are evident in the work done by the pioneers of pre-war Europe, but the early enthusiasm still allows the work to be read as a concerted effort. Mies's differences with much of other Modernist orthodoxy began to become clearer in the post-war period. The early edict that form follows function he gently and firmly inverted, stating that as the function of building was liable to change during its lifetime, then the only permanent quality is beauty. This problem of the subservience of the function to the beauty of the building he resolved in many of his schemes by dropping the necessarily enclosed offices and rooms beneath the pedestal, upon which he then placed the familiar beautiful transparent uncluttered pavilion. This he did with the design for the Bacardi Company in Santiago, which was not built, and with his final building, the National Art Gallery in Berlin. Similarly, truth to materials with Mies became love of materials; thus it was love and not truth that informed how he was to treat particular parts of his buildings.

The site for the Farnsworth House was wooded and rural. He produced his most refined example of the steel and glass transparent structure placed upon a pedestal, albeit the latter was a cantilevered slab. As an object to be looked at and from, the house is the clearest expression of a beautifully made object which relates through its transparency the architecture and its setting. The building allowed him to realize the quality suggested by the drawings for the unbuilt Resor House of 1938, which was his first commission in America. The comment still applies that the beauty depends to a large degree on a sense of emptiness. Once marked by occupancy the nature of transparency becomes something quite different from an agent of an open continuous system. When occupied it is more likely to provoke extremes of privatization in at least two ways: first, not having a dark depth into which to withdraw, to avoid the eyes that see all too well, the window walls are liable to be obscured with total curtaining, or as an alternative one needs to own or at least to control the landscape into which the structure is placed.

The designs for court houses that he experimented with throughout his life were less than urban solutions to this paradox.

In 1940 Mies undertook his largest commission, the overall design of the IIT campus in south Chicago and the design of the individual buildings. This was to be the best opportunity to express the idea of a universal building, of the subservience of function to the form. The buildings were designed with the same skeletal steel structure holding to the same set of dimensions into which the variety of uses, chapel, offices, design studios, were then fitted. The overall plan can be seen as an abstract composition, as with the Barcelona plan, but it lacked the dynamics of interpenetration of the earlier plan, seeming to move towards a more regular, symmetrical organization. Many have seen a spirit of Renaissance planning in the final plan, but it might be that it falls rather uneasily between the continuous, interlocking spaces of the earlier work, and the Renaissance genius of place, the concern for focus and forming of particular spaces.

His work included several tower blocks, some for flats, some for offices, and although they are all distinguished by an unequalled clarity of resolution, they are rather more expected than his glass and steel pavilions.

Probably the most famous tower is the Seagram Building in Park Avenue, New York, completed in 1958. The building was set back from the line of the avenue, allowing for the setting out of a plaza, the building and the plaza being related by a clear symmetry. The plaza undoubtedly provided an open public space, but more importantly it acted as a pedestal, a device that allowed the finely detailed, symmetrical tower to be viewed, at the cost of breaking the line and identity of the avenue.

His influence as an educator was enormous, his most faithful and successful ex-students being perhaps Skidmore Owings and Merrill.

The final building was the National Gallery in Berlin, completed after his death in 1969. Thus Mies's mature work is begun and finished by two steel and glass pavilions, placed on pedestals, both commissioned by a German government. Their dissimilarities show a move from asymmetry to symmetry and paradoxically, because of his lifelong neo-classical interest in universal solutions, a lessening of concern for context. Their similarities and the consistency of his life's work are striking, and a monument to his unwavering genius.

Further reading

See: Peter Blake, *Mies van der Rohe* (1966); Philip Johnson, *Mies van der Rohe* (1953); F. Schultze, *Mies van der Rohe: A Critical Biography* (1986); E.S. Hochman (ed.), *Architects of Fortune: Mies van der Rohe and the Third Reich* (1989).

FREDERICK SCOTT

MILL, John Stuart

1806–73

British thinker and essayist

Mill is a giant among modern thinkers. Nearly all subsequent political philosophers, economists, sociologists and writers on culture and society have started from Mill, whether following, amending or reacting against him. Any student can be taught to find contradictions in parts of him, but no thinker has surpassed him when taken as a whole. For a long time he was thought of as the very model of a fully systematic thinker (or at least an acceptable one: Bentham with feelings). But studies of his whole output, made possible by the reprinting of his scattered major essays, reveal a more complex, contradictory but stimulating thinker than the 'saint of rationalism', 'the prince of utilitarians' or the 'king of the philosophic radicals'. He always strove for conclusions relevant to policy or personal conduct, but finally the red thread running all through his life and works appears as a dedication to free-thinking or to the character-forming process of thinking freely itself: the 'free-spirit' outlasts the 'social-engineer'.

His father was James Mill, a disciple and friend of Jeremy Bentham who, although employed by the East India Company, taught John Stuart himself, in the early mornings and evenings, using the Benthamite principle of didactically associating 'the good' with pleasure and evil with pain. He began Greek at three and by six was reading the great Latin authors. Walking with his father he was questioned ceaselessly on what he had read and prepared during the day. By fifteen, after massive doses of economics, history and philosophy, he was ready to be introduced to Bentham's works themselves: almost at once he understood them as a unifying principle to be applied to all political, social and moral life, the great 'Felicific Calculus', always to calculate the 'greatest happiness of the greatest number' according to 'our two sovereign masters, Pleasure and Pain'. As he wrote in his *Autobiography* (1873): 'I now had opinions; a creed, a doctrine, a philosophy; in one of the best senses of the word, a religion.' Rarely can a child, except in a strictly religious household (like his father's Calvinistic, Scottish youth), have been brought up so seriously, so ideologically, so solitary and so joyless. At seventeen he became a corresponding clerk with the East India Company, but very soon articles began to flow forth

promoting the Benthamite cause, and he was active in forming discussion groups and debating societies with other talented young men, all advocates of reform and, in varying degrees, disciples or admirers of Bentham and James Mill.

In 1825 he performed an awesomely complex and taxing editorial labour for Bentham, reducing to one coherent book three early and varying manuscript versions of his great *Rationale of Judicial Evidence*. The following year he fell into a depression and became obsessed with the pointlessness of activity and the meaninglessness of life. Reading by chance a literary passage about the death of his father, tears flowed, natural feelings or sensibility began to return or to grow and he found that the poetry of Wordsworth and the ideas of Coleridge spoke to him, whom previously he had had to read as bad examples of the Benthamite 'fallacy of the feelings'. Articles at this time showed not repudiation but a subtle and cautious modification of the utilitarian doctrine: there were true *higher* pleasures, such as poetry; ultimately it was better/happier to be 'Socrates unhappy than a pig happy'.

In 1829 Macaulay made a savage attack in the *Edinburgh Review* on James Mill's *Essay on Government*, and when John Stuart came to help his father compose a reply for the *Westminster Review* he dispassionately discovered that, apart from the tone, he was much in agreement with Macaulay: the sum total of self-interest did not add up to the general good or the social interest; good government did not always need an identity of interest between rulers and ruled, one could occasionally know what was best for other people; and the idea of model institutions derived from pure reason needed tempering to custom, culture, different levels of understanding and the relativity of circumstances. But only after Bentham's death in 1832 and the trauma of his father's death in 1835 did he openly attack the limitations of Benthamism in his famous essays on Bentham and on Coleridge which keep him still read by (in our far more culturally fragmented times) students of literature as well as by political philosophers. Mill did not abandon reason and the spirit of the French *philosophes*: rather, he argued that Bentham and his father were wrong to look for a single principle from which rules of legislation and personal conduct could be deduced: there were many such principles of society compelling respect and understanding, and they all had to be adapted to circumstances sociologically and compromised together politically. For a period Mill became so unassertive, so unlike the young Benthamite missionary, that some people thought that he was turning Wordsworthian or Coleridgean Tory; and the myopic Carlyle actually believed that Mill was becoming his disciple, simply because he listened and high-mindedly strove to find some truth in all that sage's early blather. But he read Comte, Saint-Simon and Tocqueville as well.

Tocqueville was especially congenial to Mill. His *Autobiography* admits that it was reading Tocqueville that made Mill understand that even democracy needs 'a necessary protection against its degenerating into the only despotism of which, in the modern world, there is real danger – the absolute rule of the head of the executive over a congregation of isolated individuals, all equal but all slaves'. Yet Saint-Simon's speculations on co-operativism and Comte's on necessary cultural stages of society also remained with him.

Amid so much mental change, small wonder that he found in this period 'a perfect friendship'; rather, he fell desperately in love in 1830 with a married woman with three children. Harriet Taylor was the wife of a prosperous, radical merchant and her mind was forceful, bold, energetic but rather vain and mediocre. To Mill she was a perfected human type. In his *Autobiography* Mill wrote that 'it was years ... before my acquaintance with her became at all intimate and confident'. He painted a picture of a high-minded Platonic friendship, a spiritual love which **George Bernard Shaw** was to take as a dramatic model and which some have seen as the forerunner of that alleged 'sacerdotal

celibacy' that some of the first generation of married dons at Oxford professed to practise. But it was untrue. Whether or not there was actual sexual intercourse, their letters reveal that the twenty years before her husband's death were full of the most painful and romantic storm and stress, of which her tolerant husband quickly tired, setting her up on her own where Mill was free to visit her, indeed to take her and her children on holiday together while all the time pretending to live at home with his sisters.

His *A System of Logic* (1843) was his first book and the last uninfluenced by Harriet. It dominated British philosophy in the nineteenth century and Book 6, on the method of the social sciences, is of lasting value. While his insistence on inductive method is now generally rejected, as in **Karl Popper's** argument that science begins with hypotheses to be tested and refuted, not with observations made from a *tabula rasa* mind, Mill himself is surpassingly rich in fertile hypotheses, whether or not he thought they were derived from pure reason (deduction) or pure observation (induction). His *Principles of Political Economy* followed in 1853 and he claimed that the 'qualified socialism' of the last chapter on 'The Probable Futurity of the Working Classes' was 'entirely due to her'. Scholars once thought that these were the pietistic words of a besotted lover, but correspondence between them shows this to be all too true: his scepticism was swept away by her idealism and bullying, at the expense of flagrant contradictions in the text. It was the least successful of his major works. Apart from Harriet's socialism, he went back to what his father had taught him in the 1820s, ignoring twenty years of subsequent economic theory.

There is now no reason to doubt that *On Liberty* (1859) was a truly collaborative work, written together after his retirement from the East India Company. But this greatest work was fortunately on a theme on which they had both always basically agreed. He was to speak of the young Benthamites as having had 'an almost unbounded confidence in the efficacy of two things: representative government, and complete freedom of discussion'; only the young Benthamites would not have even appeared to value eccentricity for its own sake, or for example to conformists, but only if it led to the truth. And the essay does contain some criteria for limitations on liberty, which Mill inserted but which Harriet mercifully glossed over, not greatly stressed, but then a famous writer has some right to assume that people knew where he stood already: that there can be *utilitarian* grounds of public order for limiting individualism, but never absolute moral grounds. 'You may not do this because it is not convenient to most of us' at least leaves more in place than the absolute prohibition, 'That is wrong.'

If he enjoyed his great public fame, it must have been somewhat marred by Harriet's quarrelling with nearly all his celebrated friends during their seven years of marriage before she died unexpectedly in Avignon in 1859. Mill moved there with her daughter Helen, bought a house and installed in it the entire furniture and fittings of the hotel room in which she had died. The rationalist shared the Victorian cult of the dead. But gradually his old ways resumed: friendships and publications, and even three years in the House of Commons as Radical Liberal member for Westminster, though unsuccessful in re-election because of his support on principle for the atheist Bradlaugh, a man he disliked personally. *Considerations on Representative Government* appeared in 1861, a subtle discussion of the relationship of the idea of democracy to types of institutions and circumstances. Democracy was universally possible, but only with universal compulsory education and, moreover, its forms would vary greatly. So strong was national feeling, for instance, that he doubted if representative government was possible in a multi-national state (a view that Lord Acton regarded as 'uncivilized'). So an historical relativism had come to temper the old rationalism, and the idea of an open, educated, cultivated and rational elite (open to all eventually, but eventually) tempered the old Millite

utilitarians of each actual opinion counting as one. He even advocated, somewhat tentatively, that while each person should have a vote, votes should be weighted according to education. But he noted that the politicians were indeed interested in a property, not an educational franchise. So proportional representation became his last piece of Benthamite institutional advocacy.

The last years were extraordinarily fruitful. The year 1861 saw his final attempt, still intellectually impressive, to synthesize Bentham and Wordsworth, in *Utilitarianism*. During the American Civil War he attacked pro-Southern writers strongly and influentially. In 1871 came *The Subjection of Women*, an emancipatory tract in which, if Harriet's influence is obvious, he was also returning to his first serious criticisms of Bentham and his father, both of whom were somewhat half-hearted in their acceptance of women as equally mankind. He came to terms with his own intellectual development in his *Autobiography*, published in 1873 soon after his death. Though austere and solely concerned with the intellect, it is impressive and moving. Only a few pages were removed by Helen Taylor (now recovered). His last words were: 'You know that I have done my work.' An unseemly public controversy broke out as to whether such a great man who was a sceptic should or could be buried at Westminster Abbey. The wily Gladstone hedged on the issue. But Mill had insisted on being interred alongside Harriet at Avignon. His bust appeared in secularist and Unitarian meeting houses until very recently, and every free-thinking intellectual until 1914 had his portrait on the study wall.

Further reading

See: *Collected Works of J.S. Mill*, ed. J.M. Robson et al. (33 vols, 1963–91). A good modern selection from both the political and the cultural essays is *Essays on Politics and Culture* ed. Gertrude Himmelfarb (1962). See also: F.A. Hayek, *John Stuart Mill and Harriet Taylor* (1951); Michael St John Packe, *The Life of John Stuart Mill* (1954): Joseph Hamburger, *Intellectuals in Politics: John Stuart Mill and the Philosophic*

Radicals (1965); A. Ryan, *J.S. Mill* (1974); C.L. Ten, *Mill On Liberty* (1980) and S. Collini, D. Winch and J. Burrow, *The Noble Science of Politics* (1983).

BERNARD CRICK

MILLER, Arthur

1915–2005

US playwright

After **Eugene O'Neill**, Arthur Miller is the most talented and significant playwright America has produced. His theories of drama are provocative; his plays rich and varied.

Miller was the son of a prosperous manufacturer hit hard by the Depression; and one of the ironically creative results of that terrible period in American history was the compassion that it bred in Arthur Miller ('The icebox was empty and the man was sitting there with his mouth open', *The Price*, 1968). It made him realize how adverse circumstances could diminish man's self-respect and dignity; it made him especially critical of men who by their own acts diminished themselves and other people; it made him cherish those individuals who sought above all to preserve their integrity. 'I am Willy Loman,' says the hero of *Death of a Salesman* (1949); 'Give me my name,' says John Proctor in *The Crucible*, 1953. The Depression contributed importantly to Miller's sense that the duty of the dramatist is to deal with the moral problems of the day. As a democrat and American he feels that he has a contribution to make to both the theory and practice of the drama. 'The Common man is as apt a subject for tragedy in its highest sense as kings were,' he has written, and has gone on to define tragedy as 'the consequence of a man's total compulsion to evaluate himself justly' (*Tragedy and the Common Man*, 1949). His 'Introduction' to *Collected Plays* (1957), his essays 'On Social Plays' (1955) and on 'The Family in Modern Drama' (1956) are of profound merit and illuminate the reading and viewing of his plays.

His first successful play, *All My Sons* (1947), was a reproach to the capitalist ethic which led manufacturer Joe Keller to market faulty aircraft parts and thus cause the death of a number of pilots, including one of his sons; his second and greatest play, *Death of a Salesman*, lovingly chronicled the last days of Willy Loman, an insignificant man in terms of his career, but a significant human being who fights to the last against unsympathetic employers, an unhelpful wife, self-centred sons and his own weakness in order to salvage something worthwhile from his life. Willy Loman is, to Arthur Miller, a tragic hero. But Miller's plays are not merely about human potential and its abuse; they are about families. Miller is a moralist who believes that self-realization can only come through helping others; man is a social and caring animal and must show himself as such in his most immediate context, the family unit. But while Miller believes in man's potential for good and happiness he also finds evil and misery wherever he looks. The Lomans live together yet barely understand each other; the great love in the family of immigrant Italians proves a jealous and destructive emotion (*A View from the Bridge*, 1955). Even in the play in which the protagonists are able to articulate precisely how they felt about each other as children, adolescents and adults – *The Price* – there is no real coming together of the brothers Victor and Walter Franz. The play begins with the Victrola playing Gallagher and Shean; it ends with the sound of the laughing record. Miller seems finally to despair of answering the questions he has asked in play after play. 'How may a man make of the outside world a home?' ('The Family in Modern Drama') and how may a man make a nominal home a real one? *The Creation of the World and Other Business* (1973) indicates his despair – it depicts God as an inept old man, dependent on Satan for breathing life into creation.

Miller is often compared with **Ibsen** – he adapted *An Enemy of the People* (1950) – and there is something of Ibsen's fatalism in Miller's *The Crucible*, which used the seventeenth-century Salem witch trials to point out the true nature of McCarthyism and implied the continuity of evil and persecution. Two plays which deal with the Second World War,

Incident at Vichy (1965) and *After the Fall* (1964), also sound a note of pessimism as the protagonists attempt to evade the responsibility for chaos which is truly theirs. Rare indeed is Leduc in *Vichy*, who admits: 'Each man has his Jew: it is the other', and John Proctor in *The Crucible*, who manages finally to be true to himself, his family, his society and his God.

Sensitivity, humour, an effective use of Jewish grammatical inversion – 'Attention, attention must be paid' to Willy Loman – a strong sense of dramatic confrontation and an ability to exploit such scenes to the full characterize Miller's work as a playwright. If nothing is too commonplace to be tragic, nothing is too private to publish, as is evident in the self-critical portrait Miller painted of his relationship with his second wife, Marilyn Monroe, in *After the Fall*. His novel *Focus* (1945), about a non-Jew who looks Jewish and feels he discharges a moral debt by pretending to be Jewish, and his short story/screenplay *The Misfits* (1961) suggest that Miller could have been effective as a novelist, had he so chosen. But he is committed to 'the fated mission of the drama', for 'within the dramatic form [lies] the ultimate possibility of raising the truth-consciousness of mankind to a level of such intensity as to transform those who observe it' ('The Family in Modern Drama').

Further reading

Other works include: *Playing for Time* (1981); *Danger: Memory!* (1987); *The Ride Down Mount Morgan* (1991); *The Last Yankee* (1992) and *Mr Peter's Connections* (1998). See: Dennis Welland, *Arthur Miller* (1961); Edward Murray, *Structure, Character and Theme in the Plays of Arthur Miller* (1966); Leonard Moss, *Arthur Miller* (1967); Robert Martin (ed.), *The Theatre Essays of Arthur Miller* (1978); N. Carson, *Arthur Miller* (1982).

ANN MASSA

MILLETT, Kate (Katherine Murray)

1934–

US feminist

Born in St Paul, Minnesota into an Irish Catholic family, Kate Millett was the daughter of an insurance saleswoman and a contractor who left the family when she was fourteen. She went to parochial school in St Paul, and then just across the Mississippi River to the University of Minnesota in Minneapolis as an undergraduate. She subsequently attended St Hilda's College, Oxford, and Columbia University for her PhD. Her PhD dissertation, much to her surprise, became the best-selling feminist treatise *Sexual Politics* (1970). The book established her as the premier theorist for the newly rising women's movement and for a time put her at the forefront of public attention in the radical, liberationist and lesbian faction of 1970s American feminism.

Before this Kate Millett was successful as a sculptor, exhibiting in the Judson Gallery in Greenwich Village and in the Miniami Gallery in Tokyo. From 1961 to 1963 she was resident in Japan, where she met her future husband, the Japanese sculptor Fumio Yoshimura. Subsequently they shared a Bowery loft apartment, the bisexual Millett saying of their relationship that they were 'friends and lovers'. They were divorced in 1985.

In contrast to Millett, the other leading early 1970s American feminist theorist, **Betty Friedan**, essentially advocated economic independence and social and political leadership for women, a reformist position. Far more sweeping in what she advocated, Millett articulated a theory of patriarchy and conceptualized the gender and sexual oppression of women in terms that demanded a sex role revolution with radical changes of personal and family lifestyles.

The clash between these two women was the dividing line between two approaches to the movement and was epitomized in their differing attitudes towards lesbianism. Having identified sexuality per se as the root of masculinist domination of women, Millett consistently sought to affirm lesbianism as part of her programme for the recognition of woman's freedom of sexual expression in general. Friedan, on the other hand, had opposed affirming lesbianism – at least up until the 1977 Houston National Women's

Conference. There she announced: 'I've had trouble with this issue. But we must help women who are lesbians in their own civil rights.' Friedan's and the Convention's acceptance of lesbian practice as one of their public policy proposals was seen by most commentators as a vindication of Millett's position.

Intellectually important, *Sexual Politics* was an instant best-seller. Its central ideas are that all power relationships are rooted in gender, that men belong to a 'caste of virility' and exercise what they, women and society, as well, believe to be a birthright power over women in every arena of human life. Patriarchy (male power) is the dominant mode of Western culture, and women are the victims of submission to it in the family, religion, politics, technology, education, economics and psychology. 'Patriarchy,' Millett says, 'decrees that the status of both child and mother is primarily or ultimately dependent on the male.'

Patriarchy also sets woman against woman ('whore and matron/career woman and housewife') in the confines of seeking status and security through men. Women, Millett says, are separated and subordinated by men's control of institutions, production and access to information. While men invent and manufacture technologically advanced machines, women are not allowed to have the power of knowledge of their design and production, though they may be allowed to operate them. The central institution of male hegemony, however, is the nuclear family. The significant symbol for it is sexual intercourse with the man 'taking' the woman. This leads Millett to document, in a somewhat scattered way, what has come to be called sexism. She provides its historical context, together with four literary examples: the works of **D.H. Lawrence**, **Henry Miller** and **Norman Mailer** exhibiting sexual politics, and **Jean Genet** through his male homosexual queen illustrating an empathetic possibility with the oppression of women.

While *Sexual Politics* was Millett's most widely read book, she sought to move beyond the theory expressed there towards understanding its implications. *Three Lives* (1971) is a film that candidly reveals the actual lives of three women told in their own voices. An equivalent technique informs *The Prostitution Papers* (1971), a book that is divided into four voices, or chapters: two prostitutes, a woman lawyer who specializes in defending prostitutes, and the author's. While Millett did not invent the vocal reproductive form, her use of it is particularly intense, allowing her subjects to pour out the life and observation of prostitution without any apparent editorial interference. In *Flying* (1974) the mode is extended into her own autobiography. Abolishing privacy, a scrupulous transparency is implied as, in a succession of self-revealing details, she describes her relations with lesbian lovers and the subsequent creativity generated through relationships. *Sita* (1977), styled by one critic as a 'ticker-tape account', is even more explicit in its picture of the demise of a love affair, to the point where even her admirers wondered in print whether the public wants to know quite so many moments in the life of Kate Millett.

In 1971, with proceeds from her book sales, Millett bought fields and buildings near Poughkeepsie, New York, and established Women's Art Colony Farm, a place to provide space and community for women writers and artists. This project has continued more than three decades.

By the end of the 1970s, not having been very interested in organizing and promoting for feminism, and not being very effective in public appearances, Millett saw her influence diminish and interest in her work wane. She continued to produce as a visual artist and she continued to write, though her later work got little attention, and *Sexual Politics* was out of print by 1995. Her later books include *The Loony Bin Trip* (1990), an attack on psychiatry and the mental health system after her personal experience with mental health treatment; *The Politics of Cruelty* (1994), a study of state-sanctioned torture in many countries; *A.D.: A Memoir* (1995), an account of her beloved Aunt Dorothy's negativism about Millett's lesbianism and thus their alienation; and *Mother Millett* (2001), a memoir around her mother's dying.

In 2000, a university press re-issued *Sexual Politics* and some of Millett's other writings, paying tribute to the 'groundbreaking nature of her writing, art, and activism'.

Further reading

A feminist scholarly volume, *Women's Autobiography: Essays in Criticism*, edited by Estelle Jelinek (1980) contains two essays about Millett's work: Suzanne Juhasz, 'Towards a Theory of Feminist Autobiography: Kate Millett's *Flying* and *Sita* and Maxine Hong Kingston's *The Woman Warrior*'; and Annette Kolodny, 'This Lady's Not for Spurning: Kate Millett and the Critics'.

GAYLE GRAHAM YATES

MIRÓ, Jóan

1893–1983

Spanish painter

Jóan Miró was born in Barcelona. Though his father was a prosperous goldsmith in that town, Miró's antecedents were farmers and the landscape and peasant traditions of rural Catalonia were an important part of his early artistic and emotional life. In his late teens he studied at the local art school and in 1919, fully committed to being a painter, he made his way to Paris.

After a relatively short time there he made contact with the leading personalities of French art and almost immediately found himself at the centre of the Surrealist movement. By 1922 he had met, through André Masson, the poet Louis Aragon and the 'pope of Surrealism', **André Breton**, and later, in 1927, he became a close neighbour of the painters **Max Ernst**, **Hans Arp** and **René Magritte**. But despite this ideological barrage Miró, who returned to his native countryside every summer, retained a measure of independence. In works like *Self Portrait* (bought by **Picasso**) and *The Farm* (bought by **Hemingway**) he continued to preserve the identities of well-loved domestic objects

realistically intact inside a decorative Cubist structure, but with *The Ploughed Field* (1923–4) reality becomes more scrambled until in *Harlequin's Carnival* (1925–5) human figures, animals, plants, etc., were completely replaced by clusters of new symbols, so laying the foundation of his particular personal style. Between 1925 and 1927 he experimented with the sources of creativity by working spontaneously in self-induced states of hallucination and impaired consciousness producing paintings, like *The Birth of the World* (1925), which departed further and further from the appearance of the common-sense world.

He married in 1929 and from then on, with the exception of an unsettled period during the Spanish Civil War and the 1939–45 conflict, he worked in Paris and Spain in a relatively consistent style over a wide variety of media. His paintings have been exhibited worldwide, especially in America where he had his first one-man show in New York as early as 1930, and his vast output also includes designs for the theatre (for Massine and **Diaghilev**), sculpture, ceramics and murals, notably in the Guggenheim Museum, for Harvard University and in 1957 for the UNICEF building in Paris.

Though linked historically with the Surrealists, and though he himself distrusted the term 'abstract', his particular use of signs and symbols is an important contribution to the development of non-figurative painting. While other pioneers more inclined to theory, like **Kandinsky** or **Mondrian**, compared non-representational art to music or mathematics, Miró, no doubt prompted by his interest in poetry and involvement with the mainly literary preoccupations of the Surrealists, instinctively chose the equally fruitful analogy of poetic language. But he also placed as much stress on the essentially visual aspects of painting such as colour, line, composition, etc., which the academic, illustrative artists such as Magritte or **Dalí** tended to neglect.

He cultivated this attitude to form from the start and the works in his first one-man exhibition of 1919 show that he was fully conversant with the latest pictorial advances made by **Matisse** and Picasso and had learned to use bright colour, simplifications and perspective distortions. But this sophistication was not complete. In his landscapes and still-lifes, depictions of vegetables, animals, fruit, foliage and utensils were highly detailed and unschematic and this almost naive particularization carried through into the hieroglyphs which populate the later works. The groups of symbols in *Catalan Landscape* (1923–4), for instance, can be given precise collective and individual interpretations. When placed against lushly painted backgrounds, suggesting interiors or landscapes, they conjure a typically strange non-naturalistic world, entered by the imagination rather than the senses, from which the laws of physical anatomy and gravity are missing. But they are not anarchic daubs. They are formally sound and they relate to a valid if fugitive variety of human experience.

It is precisely in this combination of opposites, combining freedom and control, an excess of form with an excess of content, introspective depth with an original system of public signs which accounts for Miró's continuing reputation. His influence in the 1940s is understandable. The Abstract Expressionists, particularly **Pollock**, and **Rothko**, derived forms directly from Miró's earlier work, but it is a more unexpected tribute to the balance he achieved that he was just as admired in the 1960s when ideas of meaning, expression and psychology were out of favour.

Further reading

See: Clement Greenberg, *Jóan Miró* (1949); Jacques Dupin, *Jóan Miró; Life and Work* (1962); Roland Penrose, *Miró* (1970); C. Lanchner, *Joan Miró* (1993).

DAVID SWEET

MISHIMA YUKIO (HIRAOKA KIMITAKE)

1925–70

Japanese writer

Mishima Yukio is the most versatile, and some consider the best, modern Japanese writer. He committed suicide by *harakiri* after calling on Japan's Self-Defence Forces to rise up against the values of the country's post-war democracy. Some right-wing nationalists regard him as their hero, but in his lifetime politics mattered less to him than the desire to 'conquer the world' by his pen.

Mishima Yukio is the pen-name of Hiraoka Kimitake. In his childhood he was much influenced by his grandmother, a strong-willed and aristocratic woman who kept him apart from other children. The dark romanticism of his imagination is already obvious in his early poems and stories. 'A Forest in Full Bloom' ('Hanazakari no Mori', 1944), his first published story, was written at the age of sixteen. Set in a romantic past, it identifies the author as having a privileged destiny. Its theme is the longing for an absolute ideal of beauty, and the consummation of that longing in death.

The war made a deep impression on Mishima. He later described the period 1944–5 as 'a rare time when my own personal nihilism and the nihilism of the age and the society corresponded perfectly'. He was rejected as unfit for active military service, but exulted in the idea of a glorious death on the battlefield. He found himself completely at odds with the left-wing, egalitarian mood of the post-war years in Japan.

He graduated in law from Tokyo University and was a civil servant for a short time. In 1949 his first major work, *Confessions of a Mask* (*Kamen no kokuhaku*, 1949, trans. 1958), was acclaimed by the critics as a masterpiece. It is an autobiographical novel which describes the author's discovery of his own latent homosexuality, and the 'masquerade of reality' he constructs in order to come to terms with the world outside. The book displays a strong streak of narcissism, and explores a private world of sado-masochistic images – especially that of St Sebastian pierced with arrows – to which Mishima often returned in his later writings.

Over the next twenty-one years Mishima produced an astounding quantity of poetry, drama, essays and fiction, including forty

novels and eighteen plays. *Forbidden Colours*
(*Kinjiki*, part I 1951, part II 1953, trans. 1968)
depicts the mentality and milieu of homo-
sexuals in Tokyo. *The Sound of Waves*
(*Shiosai*, 1954, trans. 1956) – the only
straightforward love story Mishima ever
wrote – brought him great popular success.
Many people regard *The Temple of the Golden
Pavilion* (*Kinkakuji*, 1956, trans. 1959) as his
best novel. It is about a young Zen Buddhist
monk perversely obsessed with the beauty of
the temple (one of Japan's finest architectural
treasures) who finally burns it to the ground.
Its theme is characteristic: the sense of an
insurmountable barrier between the self and
others (the young monk here suffers from a
ridiculous stutter) which is only assuaged by
an act of wilful destruction. But Mishima also
observed contemporary Japanese society with
a keen eye. *After the Banquet* (*Utage no Ato*,
1960, trans. 1963), for example, is a vivid
satire on the world of politics and patronage.

In 1966 Mishima produced the first part of
The Sea of Fertility, the tetralogy which he
intended to be his crowning achievement.
The four successive novels, *Spring Snow* (*Haru
no yuki*, 1966, trans. 1972), *Runaway Horses*
(*Honma*, 1968, trans. 1973), *The Temple of
Dawn* (*Akatsuki no tera*, 1969, trans. 1973) and
The Decay of the Angel (*Tennin gosui*, 1970,
trans. 1974), embrace the whole sweep of
Japan's twentieth-century history up until the
time of their composition. The central figures
in each book are connected by a cycle of
reincarnation. But in the final book the
awaited sign fails to appear to confirm the
thread of destiny, and the whole logic of the
narrative is put in question. Mishima wrote
this conclusion after making detailed plans for
his own death, and it is a clear statement of
his lifelong obsession with the impossible
quest for some transcendent truth.

Mishima Yukio had an extraordinary zest
for life, and thirst for every kind of human
experience. In his late twenties he began a
rigorous programme of bodybuilding and
martial arts, including *kendo* (swordsmanship)
and karate. This played an essential part in his
personal philosophy of the 'unity of thought

and action', a concept with its antecedents in
Zen. It also gave him the stamina to keep
up a regular routine of writing through
every night. At the age of thirty-three
Mishima had an arranged marriage, which
was successful. He later became the father of
two children.

His romantic concern with the role of the
Emperor and with *bushido*, the way of the
warrior, recurs often in his writing. In 1965
he acted the central role in a film version of
his own short story, 'Patriotism', about a
young officer who commits *harakiri* at the
time of the abortive military uprising in 1936.
In 1968 Mishima founded the Shield Society,
a 'private army' of one hundred unarmed
youths who trained with the Self-Defence
Forces. Four of the group's members were
with him at the military headquarters in
Tokyo where he made his appeal for a return
to pre-war nationalist ideals, and one of them
died with him.

Mishima's suicide profoundly affected
the Japanese people, but had no direct
political consequences. His action was widely
condemned within Japan, and it prejudiced
some critics' assessment of his literary
achievement. There is an artificial and
morbid strain in some of his work. But he
portrayed Japanese life and society in a multitude of aspects with skill and assurance. He
used his sure command of classical language
and tradition to effect in his modern
Noh plays and throughout his novels. The
novels are untypical of much Japanese fiction
in being consistently well structured, and
this makes them accessible to Western
readers. **Kawabata Yasunari** described
Mishima as 'a writer with the kind of exceptional talent which appears only once
every two or three hundred years in Japan's
history'.

Further reading

Other works include: *Thirst for Love* (*Ai no kawaki*,
1950, trans. 1969); *The Sailor Who Fell from Grace
with the Sea* (*Gogo no Eiko*, 1963, trans. 1966). His
plays include: *Five Modern Noh Plays* (*Kindai*

Nogakushu, 1956, trans. 1957); *Madame de Sade* (*Sado koshaku fujin,* 1965, trans. 1968); 'My Friend Hitler' (*Waga tomo Hittora,* 1968). See also: Henry Scott Stokes, *The Life and Death of Yukio Mishima* (1975); and John Nathan, *Mishima, A Biography* (1974); Marguerite Yourcenar, *Mishima,* trans. A. Manguel (1986); Roy Starrs, *Deadly Dialectics: Sex, Violence and Nihilism in the World of Yukio Mishima* (1994).

WILLIAM HORSLEY

MIZOGUCHI KENJI

1898–1956

Japanese film director

Kenji Mizoguchi was born on 16 May 1898 and died on 24 August 1956. During his lifetime, the cinema went from its infancy as a curious hybrid of vaudeville and mechanical peep show to the quintessential storytelling form in a technological age. In 1898, Japanese culture, still rooted in the social and religious hierarchies nurtured by generations of chosen isolation, regarded itself superior to other Asian societies, and the decadent West as well. By the time of Mizoguchi's death from leukaemia, Japan had suffered the humiliation of World War II, forcing a re-examination of her social and political assumptions, including the brutal system of class and gender roles that set the context for his thirty-four year career as a filmmaker.

Though born into a family of the samurai class, Mizoguchi's early life in Tokyo was splintered by his father's financial failure, which impoverished his family and triggered a series of events that shaped Mizoguchi's attitudes towards family and, especially, women. His sister was given up for adoption and later sold as a geisha. Young Kenji's schooling was interrupted and he was sent away to apprentice as a pharmacist. When he returned home his father refused to send him back to school and he began work designing patterns for kimonos, a job his sister found for him, beginning a dependency on her emotionally and financially. At the age of seventeen he entered the Aiobashi Institute to study painting; here he began his immersion

in the Japanese literature of the day, as well as the works of Maupassant, **Zola**, **Dostoyevsky** and **Tolstoy**. Through acquaintance with a young actor, Mizoguchi got a job as a set decorator at Nikkatsu Studios, then the premiere film studio in Japan. With the onset of a strike in 1922, he was given his first opportunity to direct, at the age of twenty-four. *The Resurrection of Love,* now lost, demonstrated early his gift for innovation. Of the approximately eighty feature films Mizoguchi directed between 1922 and 1956 (the records are inconclusive), only thirty are extant.

After the great Tokyo earthquake of 1923, he was moved to Nikkatsu's Kyoto studio where his 'perfectionist' tendencies in working with scriptwriters and set designers began to manifest themselves. In 1925 he was attacked by a jealous prostitute with whom he was living, and suffered razor slashes on his back; this event seems to have focused his concern on the plight of women and, perhaps, led to his famous ambivalence in portraying women as either suffering victims of the social structure or desperate rebels defying convention.

The upheaval of the Great Depression and Japan's rising militarism sharpened Mizoguchi's social conscience and led to his direction, in the early 1930s, of a series of successful but controversial 'tendency films' (*keiko eiga*), influenced heavily by **Marxist** ideology. During this period, he began to experiment with his now-famous *mise-en-scène* technique of 'one shot – one scene' which came to full maturity in the post-war years. **Josef von Sternberg's** luminous images and fluid camera moves were a lasting influence, as were the pre-war films of **John Ford** and William Wyler. Also characteristic of his mature style (which he shared with **Akira Kurosawa**) was his insistence on historically realistic, detailed sets – a demand, Mizoguchi argued, that enabled his actors to perform with a heightened sense of authenticity. To avoid the draft and keep working during World War II, Mizoguchi claimed he was forced to direct four propaganda films, including the competent, but dull, samurai film *The Loyal Forty-Seven Ronin of the Genroku Era* (1941–2). Following the war, and subject to the Allied censors, he was granted permission to work in the banned genre of the 'period film' (*jidai-geki*), resulting in *Utamaro and His Five Women* (1946), and opening the door to his final decade and greatest cinematic achievements.

With the triumph of Kurosawa's *Rashomon* at the Venice Film Festival in 1951, Mizoguchi followed by winning the Silver Lion in 1952 for *The Life of Oharu*, in 1953 for *Ugetsu Monogatari*, and again in 1954 for *Sansho dayu*. This recognition brought him belated international acclaim and the devotion of French New Wave directors **Jean-Luc Godard**, Jacques Rivette and Eric Rohmer, as well as the critics of the influential *Cahier du Cinema*. In these three masterpieces, Mizoguchi's great themes find their culmination: the bitter logic of moral and social descent in *Oharu,* the transcendence of death by love in *Ugetsu,* and the will-to-power redeemed by sacrifice in *Sansho*: with women in all their incarnations at the centre. These three films represent a mature genius whose mastery of camera, performance and filmic structure stand at the summit of cinematic achievement, and yield a heartbreaking beauty and grace that, as his cameraman Kazuo Myiagawa said, 'unroll seamlessly, like a scroll'.

Like Shakespeare's *The Tempest,* or the late string quartets of Beethoven, Mizoguchi's final films are at once a summation and transcendence of the struggles that defined his personal life and the cultural life of Japan. The tension between sacred tradition and arrogant modernity, his longing for the ideal of the cohesive family, the redemption of love by sacrifice, and the rejection of worldly desire found their purest expressions in these late works. Though some critics have lamented the lack of moral consistency across his career, including his political confusions and shifting attitudes towards women, in the final analysis, Mizoguchi created films, as Gilbert Adair has remarked, 'for whose sake cinema exists'.

Further reading

A thorough exploration of the relationship of Mizoguchi's life and work can be found in Audie Bock's *Japanese Film Directors* (1978); a feminist perspective in Joan Mellen, *The Waves at Genji's Door – Japan through Its Cinema* (1976); a general view of his place in Japanese film in Donald Richie, *Japanese Cinema: Film Style and National Character,* (1971). Recent assessments include Andrew Dudley and Carole Cavanaugh's monograph *Sansho Dayu* (2000) and Alexander Jacoby's excellent Internet survey at *Senses of Cinema,* Great Directors: A Critical Database (2002), http://www.sensesofcinema.com/contents/directors/02/mizoguchi.html.

STERLING VAN WAGENEN

MODIGLIANI, Amedeo
1884–1920
Italian artist

Modigliani was born in Livorno, Italy. In 1898 after a severe attack of typhus he was forced to abandon his academic studies in classics. From this point in his life his health was always bad, with a tendency to tuberculosis from which he eventually died; it was this affliction which helped to earn him the title of '*peintre maudit*'. As he showed great promise as a painter his parents sent him to study under Guglielmo Micheli, a pupil of the Macchiaoli painter Giovanni Fattori.

After a serious relapse in 1900 Modigliani travelled throughout Italy attending briefly courses at the academies in Rome, Florence and Venice. During this period he was particularly influenced by the new developments of the Sezession and Art Nouveau artists. It was above all the sculpture of Elie Nadelman which, along with his reading of **Ruskin** on the Italian Primitives and D'Annunzio's ideas on aestheticism, led to Modigliani's first elegant attempts at carving in stone. From the beginning of his career his main concern was with the expressive possibilities that might be found in the human face and figure.

In 1906, dissatisfied with the parochial nature of contemporary Italian art, Modigliani moved to Paris where, financed by his mother, he entered the Académie

Colarossi and began to work seriously as both painter and sculptor. He quickly befriended leading avant-garde painters like Vlaminck, Utrillo and **Picasso** and critics like André Salmon. His poor health and nervous disposition led him at this time to excesses of narcotics and alcohol which contributed as much to the linear tensions and dissonant colours of his art as to his untimely death.

In 1908 Modigliani showed five works at the Salon des Indépendants. The most important in terms of his future development was probably *Le Juive* of 1907 which shows a range of influences encompassing those of **Cézanne**, **Gauguin**, Picasso and **Matisse**. His sculpture of this period shows the influence of African tribal art as well as that of his close acquaintance **Brancusi**. Both media interacted upon one another positively, and from 1910 to 1913 Modigliani's sculpture noticeably shows how far his interests in either were complementary. He attempted to discover formal values by largely disregarding naturalistic modelling and instead developing a synthetic resolution of planes. In this he was of course in step with the experiments of other Parisian artists. To this community of interest he brought a sinuous and rhythmic framework of line bounding his planes and bringing unity to the whole. In his painting these concerns are seen in the use of colour constructively rather than mimetically. Zones of colour bounded by a free and varied line create a simple harmony reminiscent of African and other primitive styles. Before 1914 one of the greatest influences on his work was the large Cézanne exhibition at the Galérie Bernheim. In particular he admired Cézanne's *Young Man with Red Waistcoat*, which first showed him how far the painter can use his subject to expressively distort a human image in the service of a lyrical vision. By 1914 both his painting and his sculpture can be said to have reached their maturity and the rest of his brief career was dedicated to the perfection and refinement of this personal style. The *Portrait of Paul Guillaume* (1916) is a typical example of his work at its best. The tendency to expressive distortion coupled with the peculiar mixture of refinement and primitiveness, in some respects a formula initiated by **Degas**, are resolved in a remote almost hieratic image. Despite Guillaume's casual pose and the picture's disregard for a smooth finish, the final image is one of mask-like detachment and even emptiness.

The physical facts of Modigliani's life in Paris during the war and until his death in 1920, described very evocatively in his daughter's critical biography of 1959, are of illness and poverty. He cared little for money, and even during the harsh years of the war he was to be found selling his drawings in cafés for trifling sums. This lifestyle and dedication to art were virtually lost after the war and Modigliani's personal reputation rests partly on his aristocratic disdain for worldly success and his image of doomed martyr. It should perhaps be mentioned that for some time after his death he received very little acclaim in his native country.

In many respects the varied critical response to Modigliani's work reflects the stylistic uncertainties typical of all early twentieth-century art. His drawing, usually executed swiftly and with little pentimenti, has received praise as psychologically astute and formally terse and subtle. On the other hand critics as diverse as Wyndham Lewis and Anthony Blunt have accused his work of being expressively shallow and inventively weak. These are ultimately questions the spectator must decide for himself by comparing his oeuvre with those of other figurative artists of the period struggling with the possibilities offered by recent experimentation in pictorial expression. There can be no doubt, however, that the later series of nudes, often depicting his mistress Jeanne Hebuterne (e.g. *Reclining Nude*, 1919), represent a unique and powerful contribution to the work of the Paris School. This power stems from a severity of line and richness of colour-matching which directly express his haughty, elegant and possibly nostalgic personality. He exerted virtually no influence on his contemporaries but, in the same way as **Rouault**, showed those working in Paris how an expressionist tendency could enrich purely formal interests. He was not an intellectual nor a didactic artist and his work never veered towards neo-classicism or urbane cubism as did that of so many of his colleagues in Paris after 1914.

Further reading

Other works include: *Note e ricordi* (1945). See: J.T. Soby, *Modigliani* (1951); F. Russoli, *Modigliani* (1958, trans. 1959); J. Modigliani, *Modigliani: Man and Myth* (*Modigliani senza leggenda*, 1959, trans. 1959); W. Schmalenbach, *Modigliani* (1990).

RICHARD HUMPHREYS

MONDRIAN, Piet

1872–1944

Dutch artist

Piet Mondrian, born in the small country town of Amersfoort into a strictly Calvinist family, became an early painter of Pure Abstraction. Of all the Abstract painters he might be considered the most widely influential and significant. In the early 1880s he studied at the Amsterdam Academy following a traditional Dutch landscape style of dark, almost monochromatic forms against light skies. An awareness of the work of the Dutch Symbolists added to Mondrian's painting the violently twisted and decorative line of Art Nouveau. By 1907–8 he had rejected dark tones for the brilliant colours of the Fauves and fine lines for the broad brush-work of the Post-Impressionists. In *The Red Mill* (1910–11) there is considerable simplicity of shape coupled with strong strokes of vivid red.

During 1909 Mondrian became absorbed in Theosophy, the quasi-religious movement that held the central notion that a great 'New Spiritual Epoch' was at hand. During this era the metaphysical realities which in the past had only been available to a few privileged souls in the form of sacred mysteries would be appreciated by increasing numbers of people as their sensibilities became more refined. Like **Kandinsky**, Mondrian believed that the artist, as seer, could through his art help produce this new state of being.

In 1911 Mondrian arrived in Paris and from a welter of artistic influences meeting in this foremost centre of the art world he chose Cubism as the most relevant. For him the unemotional scaffolding of Analytical Cubism structure pointed the way to increasing simplification of form. The famous tree and also church series were then carried out, whereby Mondrian severely reduced and gradually abstracted the linear structure of both organic and architectural subjects.

After meeting a fellow Theosophist, Dr M.H.J. Schoenmaekers, in 1915 Mondrian formed an artistic group in Holland with his compatriot Theo von Doesberg. Much influenced by Schoenmaekers's neo-Platonic ideas on the relationship of beauty and mathematical proportion they produced a magazine called *De Stijl* and wrote the theory of Neo-Plasticism. This proposed that art had to hold an equal balance between two oppositions, the artist's desire for 'direct creation of universal beauty' and 'the aesthetic expression' of himself. These polarizations they saw as objective and subjective, the one that thinks and the one that experiences, and they wished to marry the two. Ultimately for Mondrian this form resolved itself into the basic opposition of vertical and horizontal, made more dynamic by the use of pure primary colours in solid blocks.

During the 1920s and 1930s, living in an all-white studio in Paris, Mondrian worked simultaneously over long periods on a number of canvases, intuiting the correct balance for his grid forms and colours. The steady progression of this period was from a work such as *Composition Grey Red Yellow and Blue* of around 1920 to *Composition Red Yellow and Blue* of 1937–42. The former is composed of large rectangles of the four colours interlocking and separated only by a narrow line. The latter replaces grey with a white ground that sparkles between the now important and heavier black line grid. Only four rectangles of colour exist in the work. The greater restraint at the same time gives an increased dynamic intensity of contrast.

At the request of **Ben Nicholson**, who visited him in Paris, Mondrian went to England in 1938, and then moved to New York in 1940. Fascinated by the rhythms of urban life, of American jazz and the incessant energies of the 'Big City', he painted his celebratory and perhaps most dynamic work, *Broadway Boogie Woogie* (1942–3). In it the now small multiple blocks of bright colour seem to chase each other down the tracks of the grids and pre-empt with their dazzling colour and tonal oppositions the Op Art movement of the 1960s.

Further reading

See: Essays: *Plastic Art and Pure Plastic Art 1937 and Other Essays* (1945) and *Circle*, ed. B. Nicholson and N. Gabo (1937). See also: Michael Seuphor, *Mondrian* (1957); Frank Elgar, *Mondrian* (trans. 1968); H.L.C. Jaffé, *Mondrian* (1970); J. Joosten and R. Welsh, *Piet Mondrian: A Catalogue Raisonné* (1996).

PAT TURNER

MONET, Claude

1840–1926

French artist

The most important member of the Impressionist group, Monet was born in Paris, the son of a wholesale grocer. At the age of five he moved with his family to Le Havre and lived there until adult. A physically strong and self-willed boy, Monet deeply loved the sea and its shore in all its moods: fierce, stormy or gentle and limpid. No doubt this continuing early fascination provided the basis for much of his art.

He was fortunate to have met in Le Havre, by the age of eighteen, the painter Boudin, among the first to realize that painting carried out in the open air in front of the depicted subject contained an immediacy and vitality lacking in studio work. Boudin's paintings have a delightful freshness and, although more than sketches, retain something of the sensuous excitement to be found in such preliminary work. Monet wrote later that after he had tried Boudin's method he continued to paint *en plein air.* 'It was as if a veil had suddenly been torn from my eyes. I understood. I grasped what painting was capable of.'

While enduring a short term in the army Monet worked with the Dutchman Jongkind, a more dramatic painter than Boudin but one who also worked out of doors. By 1862 the young Monet was in Paris, shortly to study at Gleyre's studio and to see **Manet's** exhibition at the Galerie Martinet, Salon des Refusés. Manet's paintings at this time were not acceptable to the official jury members. Monet was greatly impressed by Manet's work but was soon to diverge from the older man's view of painting, over the question of shadows.

In France during the nineteenth century a number of people were investigating the optical laws of vision and of colour. Chevreul had published *The Principles of Harmony and Contrast of Colours, and Their Application to the Arts* in 1839. This book made clear the theory of negative after-images whereby a colour becomes surrounded faintly after a moment or two by its complement or opposite. This negative effect modifies the surrounding colour so that green which has a patch of yellow in its centre will appear slightly brown because of the mauve after-image superimposed upon it by the eye. Colour complements or oppositions of primary to secondary colours had been known before the nineteenth century. However, Chevreul also discovered that two small areas of colour close together will, when seen at a distance, merge and produce a neutralizing effect. Later the Post-Impressionists realized that, by contrast, when the two complements are used in larger areas, they intensify each other.

The difference between the Impressionism of Monet and Manet lay largely in the treatment of shadows. Manet claimed that to paint sunlight there had to be a sudden change and strong contrast from light and dark. It is as though he imagined not only the artist's eye moving to survey sunshine and shade but the whole person walking into it and being surrounded by sudden shade. Monet took a more objective, distanced and less dramatic view so that the eye could move back and forth, comparing and becoming aware of the effects of refraction and reflection within both light and shade. He sought not the oppositions but the similarities, thus unifying his painting.

When first exhibited, Impressionism seemed strange to the public. Not only was the work produced in the open air, it dealt with contemporary subject-matter rather than historical myths or events, which were the usual province of the painter until Courbet broke with that tradition. He met Monet in 1865 when the younger man was already rapidly moving towards the finest period of Impressionism, that of the 1870s.

By 1869 Monet, his friends **Renoir**, Pissarro and Bazille were producing highly accomplished works in the new style and seeking a means of exhibiting them. A typical work of this period by Monet was *La Grenouillère* of 1869. It depicted his great love, water, a bathing and boating area of the River Seine on the outskirts of Paris. Manet and Monet painted a similar view of the same place and the comparison is instructive. Monet's version shows a small island connected by wooden planking to the river bank and to the bathing station. On it people sit or stand. A few bathers, chest-deep in water, look across to the far bank of the river where a mass of variegated yellow greens suggest a line of trees in sunlight. In the foreground the trees are painted in blue greens for they, like the people and boats, are all in the shade. The painting of the water is the most striking effect. Strong short strokes of various colours form the shadow side of lively curving ripples and almost pure white the crests. The work is brilliantly alight and alive, and compared with Renoir's softer version of the same year is crisply and sharply seen. Manet's *River at Argenteuil* (1874) differentiates little between the greens in the foreground and on the far bank. Distance is emphasized by the controlled use of black bonnet ribbons near to, slightly less dark boats in the middle distance and a grey structure even further away.

It was *Impression: Sunrise* of 1872, produced while Monet was in England during the German attack upon Paris, that gave the Impressionist movement its name. The fogs of nineteenth-century industrial London afforded Monet great delight. They had the effect of both unifying the view and dissolving the forms of buildings and structures so that he is left with a mass of reflecting and refracting colour. The Thames was a major source for subject-matter during these visits.

One work of 1878 by Monet, called *Rue Montorgueil Decked Out with Flags*, foreshadows **Jackson Pollock's** *Blue Poles* of 1953. The New York Abstract Expressionists of the gestural kind, such as Pollock, have admitted a great debt to Monet. Certainly the Monet scene, with tricolours by the hundred fluttering in the quick morning air above an enormous crowd winding down the street, is almost an abstraction of large and small strokes which express an immense hedonistic pleasure in being alive and part of the day's activities. However much Monet attempted to be no more than 'an eye', his sturdy temperament makes itself felt, sometimes with extreme sensitivity as in the painting of his dying and beloved wife Camille.

Gradually he came to realize along with many of his contemporaries, both writers and artists, that 'realism' as it was often termed was not in itself sufficient for great art. For Monet this meant a greater search for colour structure. He rejected **Seurat's** Pointillisme of the 1880s because of its deliberate slow technique and static hieratic effect upon form. Monet, used to painting 'fleeting moments of time', understood movement and change.

He once more became interested in choosing an object and painting it several times under different lighting conditions. In 1891 he produced the *Haystacks* series and the *Poplar on the Epte* variations which he himself prized greatly. The Tate Gallery version shows a dramatic curve and counter-curve of dancing tree tops, from top right-hand corner of the work to bottom left-hand. The wide swinging brush strokes of leaf clusters follow the curve across the row of parallel thin trunks which are set against a brilliant blue sky with swirling small white clouds. It is a painting produced with confidence and panache.

Then follows the exquisite *Rouen Cathedral* series while Monet is building his water gardens at Giverny. The result of this endeavour are the glorious views of these gardens with bridge and water-lilies, works known as the *Nymphéas*.

In 1908, after an illness, Monet visited Venice for the first time and while staying with a friend in a house on the Grand Canal painted views of that city, rising above and reflected in the waterways. The paintings are quieter in mood although intense but unified in colour.

Among his last works are the water-lily decorations (1916–23) in the Musée de l'orangerie, a small palace in Paris. Here, 'subject, sensation and pictorial object have all become identical'. By that Monet means that the picture is an equivalent sensation for that which the eye experiences; an eye, however, constantly on the move but rejecting an entirely intellectual or imaginative appraisal of the visual world.

Further reading

Other works include: *Westminster Bridge* (1871); *Gare St-Lazare* (1877). See: Daniel Wildenstein, *Monet* (biography and catalogue raisonné, 3 vols, 1974–9); Joel Isaacson, *Claude Monet* (1978); John House, *Monet* (1981).

PAT TURNER

MONTY PYTHON

*(Graham CHAPMAN 1941–89,
John CLEESE 1939–, Terry GILLIAM 1940–,
Eric IDLE 1943–, Terry JONES 1942–
and Michael PALIN 1943–)*
*(Mostly) British writers, actors, directors
and comedians*

The BBC television show *Monty Python's Flying Circus*, which ran in four series between 1969 and 1974, was the comic voice of the generation that did its growing up in the two decades after the Second World War.

It was largely the creation of five writer-performers who had emerged in the mid-1960s from the thriving, competitive world of English undergraduate revue. Graham Chapman, John Cleese and Eric Idle had been at Cambridge (they had overlapped, but were not exact contemporaries), Terry Jones and Michael Palin at Oxford. The symmetry is inconsiderately spoiled by Terry Gilliam who is American, and who also differs from the others in possessing a talent that is not primarily verbal; he is a cartoonist and animator who subsequently blossomed into a notable movie-director.

It was Gilliam who created the animated logo – a giant foot, crunching down down, crushing everything in its path – which started every Monty Python programme and defined the tone of the whole enterprise: savage whimsy. The shows themselves weren't *that* savage, but that they certainly had an appetite for destruction. They were also subversive, without taking on any named satirical targets, and unflinchingly literate. In all this, they suggested a graduate version of the Marx Brothers, probably the greatest force in twentieth-century comedy (who themselves derived, whether they knew it or not, from **Lewis Carroll**, the greatest ever). But more immediate influences, from the two British generations immediately preceding the Pythons', were the 1950s BBC radio series *The Goon Show*, whose non-stop anarchic humour communicated a distrust of all authority without actually saying so, and *Beyond the Fringe*, the Oxbridge graduate revue that made wonderful jokes, in public, about people and things that had previously been thought untouchable. Idle, seeing it as a teenager, 'had never laughed so hard in my life', and he spoke for most of his contemporaries.

Beyond the Fringe sparked off the British 'satire boom' – basically, saying rude things on television about politicians – and the Pythons, before they became the Pythons, came in on the tail-end of it; some of them wrote material for David Frost (who in those days was still a comedian, or just about).

There was a feeling, even then, that that had been done; and when it came to Monty Python, the group stopped doing it. They were interested in a more poetic kind of comedy: Peter Cook, in *Beyond the Fringe*, had impersonated Harold Macmillan: John Cleese created the Minister of Silly Walks, who seems at least as real and whose ministry, once its peculiar premises are accepted, seems a textbook example of the workings of bureaucracy.

The six Pythons broke down into a series of smaller writing-groups who would then meet and pool their ideas with, at least in the earlier years, remarkable amicability. They changed the structure of the TV comedy show; they weren't sitcom, they were sketch-comedy but with a difference. Accepting that the hardest thing to write is a punch-line they let each item merely blend into the next, as incongruously as possible, and as unexpectedly. (Nobody ever expects the Spanish Inquisition.) Or they would simply call a halt and change the subject. The Ministry of Silly Walks shows this process at its most refined. It begins as an absurd film-clip, apparently there for its own sake, then reveals its true and logical nature. Later in the same show it makes a momentary, and killingly funny, reappearance. The effect, a crucial element in the show's enduring cult status, is that of a self-contained comic universe.

If there was an individual comic genius in the group, it was Cleese. His capacity for suggesting upstanding (approximately six foot three) English middle-class respectability with madness in its heart is encapsulated in the two legendary numbers in which he plays an outraged consumer, opposite Palin's imperturbably disobliging shopkeeper: the Dead Parrot Sketch ('this is an ex-parrot!') and the Cheese Sketch. (Cleese's family name would have been Cheese if his father hadn't changed it, which is intriguing if irrelevant.) He wasn't in the last of the TV series, and it shows.

The sextet reunited, however, for a series of movies: *And Now For Something Completely Different* (1971), highlights from the TV shows with enhanced production values: *Monty Python and the Holy Grail* (1974), about King Arthur; *Monty Python's Life of Brian* (1979), about Christianity; and *Monty Python's The Meaning of Life* (1983), about everything. Of these, *Brian* is regarded by the team themselves, and by most others, as their masterpiece. It is not, they insist, a satire on Jesus (of whom they all became fans) but on the things done in his name – and in those of all other beliefs, religious and political. Chapman gives a sublime performance as the accident-and-crucifixion-prone Brian. He was always the group's straight man. Though he was in fact gay. He also differed from the others in being an alcoholic. And, now, dead.

The five survivors have all had successful subsequent careers. Cleese, though he always claimed comedy was only a part-time interest for him, has nevertheless achieved the most in the genre. His TV series *Fawlty Towers* (1975, 1979) raised situation comedy to the level of classic farce and allowed Cleese, as a manic hotelier, to perfect the art of being victim and bully at the same time; the film *A Fish Called Wanda* (1988) went some way to re-kindling the spirit of Britain's post-war Ealing comedies. Idle, who has always been the most concerned with keeping the Python name alive (or, as he might cheerfully admit, exploiting it) and is also the most musical of the bunch, co-wrote and co-composed *Spamelot* (2004), a hugely successful Broadway adaptation of the Holy Grail movie.

Further reading

See: The Pythons with Bob McCabe, *The Pythons' Autobiography* (2003).

ROBERT CUSHMAN

MOORE, (Sir) Henry

1898–1986

English sculptor

The most celebrated British sculptor of the twentieth century underwent an orthodox training at Leeds School of Art and then at the Royal College of Art in London. But from an early stage his sources of inspiration were extra-curricular. Roger Fry's *Vision and Design* led him to Paris to experience the work of **Cézanne**; and at the British Museum he was deeply impressed by the sculpture of 'primitive' civilizations in pre-Columbian America, the Near East and Archaic Greece. It became clear to him, as he wrote in 1941, that 'the realistic ideal of physical beauty in art ... was only a digression from the main world tradition of sculpture, while, for instance, our equally European Romanesque and Early Gothic are in the main line'. But a tour of Italy ensured that the Renaissance tradition also left its mark on Moore's work – as many of his Reclining Figures testify.

Moore's sculpture of the 1920s and 1930s is extremely diverse. Passing references to **Picasso** and **Hans Arp** are to be found, and to Mexican and African statuary; Moore's experiments with various media culminated in the late 1930s in a series of 'stringed figures', in which parallel threads of string or wire are set against the flowing curves of the sculptured mass. Several of his 'heads' and 'helmets' carry a surrealist flavour, and in 1936 Moore was a contributor to the International Surrealist Exhibition. But he never saw himself as a Surrealist; and although he was closely associated with **Ben Nicholson** and **Barbara Hepworth** in the same decade, Moore did not campaign on behalf of any specific attitude or theory. He was, however, always an articulate analyst of his own work, and in 1937 he seems to have seen his role clearly. **Brancusi** has made us shape-conscious, he wrote, by his simple, polished forms, which cast off the superficial excrescences that had overgrown European sculpture since the Middle Ages. But this 'one-cylindered' approach might no longer be necessary: 'We can now begin to open out, to relate and combine together several forms of varied sizes, sections and directions into one organic whole.' Moore's figures followed this course with mounting boldness, splitting into two, three or four components. Bronze became his favourite medium, and he undertook an increasing number of large sculptures for exterior locations, where they might become an element of city architecture or (preferably) of natural landscape. Some of Moore's later works are so 'open' that the spectator is able, and indeed encouraged, to walk through them.

Moore advised that 'the sensitive observer must learn to feel shape simply as shape'; many of his own designs have been furnished by the uncomplicated forms of bones and pebbles. But it is the human figure which, above all, has occupied Moore's imagination. As an official War Artist he depicted groups of men and women huddled in air-raid shelters, their faceless immobility suggesting an eternal capacity to endure. In both sculpture and drawing he developed the subtle potentialities of forms to suggest emotional states or qualities, in particular those of maternal or sexual attraction, which animate Moore's 'archetypal' themes of the reclining woman and the mother with child. The power of his *Sheep Piece* (1971–2) lies not only in the physical conformation of the two massive structures, but also in the psychological overtones of warmth and protectiveness which their relationship suggests.

Moore's international reputation was established after the Second World War through major exhibitions in New York, Venice, São Paulo, Toronto, Florence and Zürich. His eightieth birthday was marked in London by an exhibition in Kensington Gardens, largely of recent work, which displayed an undiminished grandeur and vitality.

Further reading

Other works include: *Henry Moore On Sculpture* (1966), ed. Philip James. See: Herbert Read, *Henry Moore: A Study of His Life and Work* (1965); John Russell, *Henry Moore* (1973); Alan G. Wilkinson, *The Drawings of Henry Moore* (Tate Gallery catalogue, 1977); David Finn, *Henry Moore: Sculpture and Environment* (1977); *Henry Moore 2: Sculpture and Drawings* (4 vols, 1957–77), eds David Sylvester and Alan Bowness; W. Packer, *Henry Moore* (1985); R. Berthoud, *Henry Moore* (1987).

PATRICK CONNER

MOORE, Marianne Craig

1887–1972

US poet

For her last two decades, Marianne Moore was considered 'the greatest living woman poet' in America, a neat little niche which has, on the whole, constrained the understanding of her poetic accomplishment. Sometimes considered eccentric, limited, 'whimsical' (i.e. what one might assume a woman poet to be), Moore has also been placed, wrongly, as a disciple of the Imagist movement. In fact, her deliberate complex poems develop far older traditions of emblem poetry and moral wit, formed according to her own version of modernism: collage-like overlays of the ordinary, the bizarre, and the quoted fragment which are expressed by a syllabic but strongly cadenced metre organized into stanzaic units of sense.

Marianne Moore lived a relatively quiet life, devoted to her mother and brother. After childhood in Carlisle, Pennsylvania, Moore moved to New Jersey and then (with her mother) to New York, where her almost sixty-year 'sojourn in the whale' ended with her being treasured as a kind of cosmopolitan regional poet. At Bryn Mawr College, Moore majored in biology (1905–9), which may partly account for the moral value her poetry puts on precise natural description. At Bryn Mawr, Moore's strong ethical sense was certainly sharpened by the blue-stocking's proud intellectual isolation. In her 'serial' poem 'Marriage', Moore rejected the institution which required 'all one's criminal ingenuity/ to avoid!' 'Eve: beautiful woman' is 'the central flaw' in the 'crystal-fine experiment' of pure Adamic existence, too powerful for Moore: 'each fresh wave of consciousness/is poison'.

Many of Moore's early poems, which appeared from 1915 in the little magazines *Poetry*, the *Egoist* and *Others*, assume both an inner enemy in the poem's object of satire and an outer enemy in a hostile or absent audience. Although Moore's poetry never needs recourse to *persona* to veil the writer's presence in the poem, it displaces her articulate anger by coolly addressing emblematic animals or modes of behaviour. 'You crush all the particles down/into close conformity,' she writes in 'To a Steamroller' (1915), attacking the materialist's destructive attempts to achieve 'impersonal judgement'. In the much-anthologized 'Poetry' her audience's philistinism is taken for granted. 'I, too, dislike it,' she begins, and then pretends to be 'Reading it ... with a perfect contempt for it' until she discovers its capacity for the 'genuine'.

With the publication of *Poems* (1921) and *Observations* (1924) Moore established herself as an important American poet, a position confirmed by the *Selected Poems* of 1935. Scofield Thayer, editor of the long-established arts magazine the *Dial*, accepted many of Moore's poems and reviews, and from 1925 to 1929, when the magazine ceased publication, Moore did most of the *Dial*'s editing and wrote many articles for it. As an editor Moore intelligently publicized the modern movement, even if her tendency to tinker with work and censor it gave offence to **James Joyce** and Hart Crane, among others. In her perceptive 1931 essay on **Pound's** *Draft of XXX Cantos* Moore took Pound to task for not distinguishing 'between Calvin the theologian and Calvin the man of letters'. Moore defended Calvin because, like the Prophets, Blake, Sir Thomas Browne or the natural historians and Elizabethan explorers she prefers to quote, his writing forms a traditional Protestant version of experience which Moore, uniquely of the modernists, was prepared to accept and use.

If Pound's Imagist poetic was a flight from abstraction, Moore's poetry used the material world as a means to describe abstractions. She was interested in exotic or mythical animals as borderline cases of the real, not escapes from it. 'The Jerboa', 'The Plumed Basilisk', 'The Frigate Pelican', 'Sea Unicorns and Land Unicorns', 'The Pangolin', 'The Arctic Ox' all tend towards essence because our habit hasn't blunted their 'natural' capacity for imposed meaning. 'The Jerboa', subtitled 'Too Much', with his 'shining silver house/of sand' is an emblem of humility, almost Blakean in its radiance.

The Romantic and modern terror at the gap between subject and object does not exist in Moore's poetry, where everything is already related. The mind's meditative play merges with the object, a deliberate wit which is expressed formally by Moore's stanzas. The first stanza is 'expedient' following the necessity of the subject, the rest turn the arbitrary pattern of the first into an order, the same within each poem, different from poem to poem. Moore's playing upon a curiously malleable 'real' recalls **Wallace Stevens**, who wrote admiringly that for Moore 'Reality is not the thing, but the aspect of the thing.' At first reading, Moore's poem 'He "Digesteth Harde Yron"' has an extraordinarily factual appearance. But it is, after all, an abstraction.' Xenophon's 'camel-sparrow', who, Lyly asserted, ate iron, 'was and is/a symbol of justice', according to historian Bernard Laufer, not merely a stupid bird. Moore assembles her emblem through facets which compact into a kind of quiddity or *gestalt* without ever stabilizing visually.

> he
> whose comic duckling head on its
> great neck revolves with compass-needle
>   nervousness
> when he stands guard.

'He' is equidistant from the encyclopaedia ostrich and the meaning he dramatizes, a meaning which shifts from justice to the heroic solicitude in the course of Moore's interlocked stanzas. For a parallel to this imputed natural value one must look back in American poetry to Edward Taylor's 'Upon a Spider Catching a Fly' or forward to Elizabeth Bishop's 'The Man-Moth'. Moore was not, however, a puritan. She takes too much pleasure in assigning her meanings, and she doesn't believe in original sin. In 'In the Days of Prismatic Color' Eve's gift is rather to make obliqueness ambivalent so that now 'Truth is no Apollo/Belvedere, no formal thing', however much one may long for that inaccurate ideal.

After the Second World War Moore felt more sure of her audience, and permitted her ethical views direct expression. In 'The Arctic Ox (or Goat)', the title poem of a 1964 collection, one quotation suffices. The poem ends with hortatory wit: if we can't use the wool which the musk ox generously produces, 'I think that we deserve to freeze.' From 1945 to 1953 Moore translated the *Fables* of La Fontaine. Since Moore undertook translating long after her style was fixed, and she paraphrases rather than imitates, the *Fables* are interesting mainly as Moore's homage to a kindred spirit (though she is actually more like Molière). Moore's *Collected Poems* (1951) and her mistitled *Complete Poems* (1967, 1968) edit and omit many important earlier poems. 'Omissions are not accidents,' says Moore's one-line Preface to the *Complete Poems*. In the end Moore's belief in values such as 'Humility, Concentration, and Gusto' (the title of a 1948 lecture) and her hard-won power to show 'Feeling and Precision' operating together to reveal truth seemed certainties so alien to her society that it became easier to simply call her eccentric. Perhaps now her readers will find it easier to accept a modernism which isn't based upon despair.

Further reading

See: Jean Garrigue, *Marianne Moore* (a University of Minnesota pamphlet, 1965); Charles Tomlinson (ed.), *Marianne Moore* (1969); Laurence Stapleton, *Marianne Moore: The Poet's Advance* (1978); Joseph Parisi (ed.), *Marianne Moore: The Art of a Modernist* (1990); Charles Molesworth, *Marianne Moore: A Literary Life* (1991); Jeanne Heuving, *Omissions are Not Accidents: Gender in the Art of Marianne Moore* (1992); E. Gregory, *The Critical Response to Marianne Moore* (1993); Cristanne Miller, *Marianne Moore: Questions of Authority* (1995); Elisabeth W. Joyce, *Cultural Critique and Abstraction: Marianne Moore and the Avant-Garde* (1999).

HELEN MCNEIL

MORRIS, William

1834–96

English writer and designer

As poet, translator, painter, designer, craftsman, socialist, Morris has rightly been described as a pivotal figure of his age. A rebel against his own time, he was yet deeply of his time, deeply Victorian, and this is only one of the many fertile paradoxes that make his manifold activity so fascinating.

Morris was born into a wealthy bourgeois family (enriched by speculation in copper) which ensured him a handsome private income. In 1853 he went up to Oxford and formed a lasting friendship with the future painter Burne-Jones. Their High Church zeal was soon ousted by literature (**Tennyson's** Arthurian legends, medieval chronicles and romances), then, after a visit to the gothic cathedrals of France and Belgium, by art and architecture. Deeply impressed by Carlyle and **Ruskin** – especially the latter's *Stones of Venice*, in which gothic architecture is presented as the supreme example of creative joy in labour under a harmonious, pre-commercial social order – they conceived the ideal of a quasi-medieval fraternity, only then to discover the existence of the nascent Pre-Raphaelite Brotherhood. In 1856 Morris began work for the architect G.E. Street, but was seduced away from architecture to painting by **D.G. Rossetti**. In 1858 a first volume of verse, *The Defence of Guenevere*, was published. Morris's artistic interests extended further into the field of practical designing and in 1861 he founded the 'Firm' (Morris, Marshall, Faulkner & Co., later to become Morris & Co.) which, with help from Burne-Jones and others, would produce fine quality stained-glass, furniture, wallpaper, chintzes, tiles, carpets and tapestries, and in which Morris, with Philip Webb, was to take a major designing role.

The year 1867 saw a first long epic poem, *The Life and Death of Jason*, followed in 1868 by the first volume of the massive *Earthly Paradise*. A period of pessimism – due in part to the failure of his marriage with the Pre-Raphaelite beauty Jane Burden – was countered by the discovery of Norse literature: Morris found its vigorous stoicism a good corrective to 'the maundering side of medievalism'. Not only did he publish 'translations' of Icelandic sagas but also his own

Sigurd the Volsung (1876), probably his most effective epic.

In 1877 Morris, enraged by examples of inept restoration, founded 'Anti-Scrape' (Society for the Protection of Ancient Buildings); subsequently he was to help found the Art Workers' Guild and, through his lectures on the 'lesser arts' in the 1870s and 1880s, to inspire not only the Arts and Crafts movement but the socialist movement as well. For Morris was drawn increasingly into political activity as a necessary extension of his ethical-aesthetic vision. Disillusioned by the opportunism of the Liberals, he joined the Democratic Federation in 1883 but left the following year to found the Socialist League, dedicated to safeguarding the pure principles of socialism. He was to give generously of his income and his energy to the movement. Active in street demonstrations, he also edited the periodical *Commonweal* and published in 1885, after his *Chants for Socialists*, the political poem *The Pilgrims of Hope*. The year 1886 saw the historical prose romance *The Dream of John Ball*, based on the peasant revolt of 1381, while 1888 saw the collection of lectures *Signs of Change*. The romance *The House of the Wolfings* (1888), like *The Roots of the Mountains* (1889), portrays struggles against tyranny in the fifth century, while the important utopian romance *News from Nowhere* (1890) embodies much of Morris's nostalgia, aspiration and vision in the dream of a harmonious, post-revolutionary but curiously neo-medieval England of the twenty-first century. That same year, Morris's Hammersmith Branch split off from the Socialist League, which had become dominated by anarchists. His final years were as creative as ever: in 1891 he founded the Kelmscott Press, to resurrect the art of fine printing, and subsequently published the unhistorical romances *The Wood beyond the World* (1894), *The Well at the World's End* (1896) and, posthumously, *The Water of the Wondrous Isle* and *The Sundering Flood* (1897).

If at first one is struck by the variety of Morris's activities, in the end it is the deeply felt moral unity beneath them that ensures his stature. A true Victorian rebel against commercial and industrial civilization in the lineage of Carlyle and Ruskin, he had a keener historical understanding than either. It is said that he sought to reconcile Ruskin and **Marx**: certainly his vision begins with architecture and the vital question of the nature of work, and is completed and enriched by the insight into commercialism and the historical process he derived from his reading of *Capital*. This saved him from the repressive work-ethic of Carlyle and the equally repressive neo-feudal authoritarianism of Ruskin's late writings. His understanding is best expressed in the lectures on art and society: 'The Art of the People', 'How We Live and How We Might Live', 'The Aims of Art', 'A Factory as it Might Be', etc. Always he returns to his ideal of art 'made by the people and for the people, a joy to the maker and the user' – something that can never be achieved in an inorganic society founded on competition and the search for profit.

Examining Morris's achievement in the individual spheres of his work, we realize that his greatness lies in no particular field *per se*: in each there are contradictions and inadequacies, though also evidence of his influence on succeeding generations. The activities of the Firm offer clear examples of paradox, not least that of a capitalist (albeit paternalistic) enterprise run by an ardent socialist. Morris's own designs, notably for wallpaper and textiles, have kept an astonishing freshness, but the fact remains that his gift was especially for repeating patterns which demanded of the printer a monotonous handwork remote from his ideal of joyous, creative labour. Ironically, these patterns are admirably suited to machine-production, whereas in theory Morris wanted to give precedence to handicrafts over industrial methods. While in his writings he railed against the division of labour, the Firm practised it, often separating designer and 'hand'. His ideal was 'simplicity of life begetting simplicity of taste', but he and his collaborators were, willy-nilly, under the influence of Victorian taste, and the Firm's interiors were rich and elaborate (though a development towards lightness and relative simplicity is apparent in later work).

Little of what the Firm practised was wholly original – the architect and designer Augustus Pugin had preceded them in many fields, and the medieval revival was very much a feature of the age – but the overriding concern was for quality of design and execution. Throughout, the enemy is clear: 'It is a shoddy age. Shoddy is king. From the statesman to the shoemaker, all is shoddy.' But this gives rise to another paradox: quality of this order was expensive, and for all Morris's democratic principles, his products were available only to the privileged few.

While he never designed a building, his influence on the approach to architecture and planning is real through his writings. He was a pioneer of environmentalism in his insistence on the need to clean the land of pollution, his concern for a more organic environment safeguarding the ideal of community. On industrial architecture and the whole concept of the workplace he had much of lasting importance to say, arguing the need for garden factories combining, in an ethical fusion vital for Morris, daily work with culture and education.

If Morris painted little, finding he had no gift for human figures (his genius in the visual arts was above all for the stylization of natural forms, their transformation into pattern), on the other hand he wrote at enormous length, and his poetry suffers from this prolixity. His verse lies firmly within the Romantic tradition, and is severely limited by it, even though as a thinker and activist he was able to step beyond Romanticism. This is especially apparent in late committed verse, *Chants for Socialists* and *The Pilgrims of Hope*, where the Romantic diction can conflict with the revolutionary subject-matter. His own literary tastes were inflexibly Romantic, and despite the blood and guts in some of his epics, his mode is not the realist one that dominated literature in the second half of the century. His first verse was promising: *The Defence of Guenevere* expresses, through the medieval subject, a sense of loss and nostalgia captured in the hesitant, flexible rhythm. This Keats-like quality will later give way to the monotony of rhythmic competence; already in *The Earthly Paradise* the pessimistic nostalgia is diluted in verbiage. More positive in tone, *Sigurd* wields greater force with its stoic theme of steadfast courage in the face of eternal recurrence. The prose romances are also frequently hampered by ornamental archaic diction, the final ones being especially self-indulgent and largely forgotten, though an age that enthuses over **Tolkien** may well discover a taste for them. However, the best of the romances, *John Ball* and *News from Nowhere*, appear as something more than escapism into a remote past or imagined future; for they embody a tension between reality and dream, thanks to the presence within the work of a narrator-dreamer who, belonging to the modern world, can movingly contrast with its inadequacies his vision of apocalyptic change or of the perfect community. Thus a work like *News* is not merely a charming fantasy but a deeply committed work which forces recognition of Morris's political importance generally. Though acknowledging that his work was 'the embodiment of dreams in one form or another', he was anxious that the new socialist theories should not be 'left adrift on the barren shore of Utopianism'. Yet he had little talent for politicking, and the intransigence of the Socialist League tended to cut it off from the 'wearisome shilly-shally of parliamentary politics'. He feared and denounced the tendency for socialism to sink into compromise and palliatory reform, offensive to his total ethical vision. Only in his final years, uncompromisingly styling himself a communist, did he come to accept the educative value of local struggles, while always insisting that these should be catalysts for total change. Engels scorned Morris, yet in the end this is a judgement on Engels' own narrow, deterministic outlook. A socialism that can comprehend Morris – in all his variety and all

his unity – is more open and human than one that cannot. If vision is now recognized as 'the education of desire' then not only his best work in particular, but above all the example of the man's thought and activity as a whole, have almost unequalled force in this respect.

Further reading

See: N. Kelvin (ed.), *The Collected Letters of William Morris* (4 vols, 1984–96). See also: E.P. Thompson, *William Morris: Romantic to Revolutionary* (1967); P. Henderson, *William Morris: His Life, Work and Friends* (1967); P. Thompson, *The Life and Work of William Morris* (1967); R. Watkinson, *William Morris as Designer* (1967); J. Lindsay, *William Morris* (1975); I. Bradley, *William Morris and His World* (1978); F. MacCarthy, *William Morris* (1994).

DAVID MEAKIN

MORRISON, Toni
1931–
US novelist

Few if any writers have dramatized and penetrated the African–American experience on a larger scale or more consistently than Toni Morrison. However, while her early books were sometimes dismissed as 'village literature', and regarded as suitable only for black female readers, she has with growing fame and skill reached a secure position as a novelist representing not merely a race or sex, but a nation. Interestingly, Morrison's first novels are sometimes re-interpreted in the light of her present image. Today she is routinely compared to **William Faulkner** and, because of her lyrical style, to **Virginia Woolf**. Unlike many American authors, Morrison emphasizes questions of social class, apart from gender and racial issues.

Born as Chloe Anthony Wofford (according to herself) or Chloe Ardelia Wofford (according to recent scholarship), she belonged to a respectable working-class family. Among her childhood interests were literature and classical ballet, and her first ambition was to become a ballerina. Morrison went to Howard University where she studied

English, and later to Cornell, obtaining an MFA. She taught at both universities, then married the Jamaican architect Harold Morrison, by whom she had two sons.

Toni Morrison worked in New York for Random House, the publishing company, divorced her husband, and wrote her first novel, *The Bluest Eye* (1971). This is a disturbing story about a girl whose self-respect and very existence are destroyed by racism. In 1973, *Sula* followed; it depicts two parallel lives, those of an African–American young woman who simply marries and has children, and another who leaves her home town, studying and roaming the United States freely. These heroines may be interpreted as aspects of, or possibilities for, the same person. *Song of Solomon* (1977) centres on a middle-class man who explores his roots among rural African–Americans, and thus achieves self-knowledge. Black politics during the post-war years play a significant part in the novel, which gained Morrison a National Book Critics Award.

In *Tar Baby* (1981), a couple of white protagonists are introduced; the rest of the cast are black. Set in a Caribbean island, the narrative can partly be read as an allegory of colonialism. There are some suitable allusions here to Shakespeare's *The Tempest*. A mother kills her baby girl, rather than allow her to be turned into a slave, in *Beloved* (1987), a colourful but gruesome novel about the legacy of slavery. *Jazz* (1992) presents love as well as murder in the 1920s against a Harlem backdrop. Formally, the story is said to illustrate a jam session.

Morrison's later books include *Paradise* (1997), with a modern kind of witch-hunt, and *Love* (2003), where many aspects of love, and a black Aphrodite, figure. The highly original *Playing in the Dark: Whiteness and the Literary Imagination* (1992) is a critical study of 'Africanism', seen as a threatening dark presence, and physical whiteness (not necessarily of anyone's skin), another menace, in fiction by white Americans.

In addition, Morrison has written many children's books, a play called *Dreaming Emmett* (premiered 1986), a song cycle, *Honey and Me*

(with André Previn, 1992) and the opera libretto *Margaret Garner* (2003).

On her enormous canvas where history, folklore and dreams intersect, Morrison employs magical realism resembling that of **Gabriel García Márquez** and **Salman Rushdie**. There is no questioning her popularity and moral seriousness. But some critics feel that she should be called successful rather than great, and that she is not more than a middlebrow writer who has benefited from being politically correct in several ways. She has also been criticized for relying overmuch on violence and other crude or obvious plot devices.

During her career, Morrison has been 'first' in a number of contexts. She is the first writer to have received both the Nobel Prize for Literature (1993) and a Pulitzer Prize (for *Beloved*). And she was the first African–American Nobel laureate, and the first black woman to hold a named chair – that of Robert F. Goheen, Princeton – at an Ivy League university.

Further reading

See: Marc C Conner (ed.), *The Aesthetics of Toni Morrison: Speaking the Unspeakable* (2000); and Missy Dehn Kubitschek, *Toni Morrison: A Critical Companion* (1998).

SUSANNA ROXMAN

MUNCH, Edvard
1863–1944
Norwegian painter

The naturalistic description of appearances in painting reached its culmination in Impressionism. Munch was a leading figure in transcending this, creating an art of the archetypal and symbolic. Born in provincial Norway, he became, through his assimilation of French art and especially that of **Gauguin**, one of Europe's principal artists at the turn of the century. The undulating lines of contemporary Art Nouveau, normally essentially decorative, provided him with a vehicle for profound psychological revelations. His principal themes were sex, love, loneliness, illness and death.

Many of his paintings originated in emotionally painful memories, for example his earliest masterpiece *The Sick Child* (1885–6) recalling the death of a sister. The intensity of this painting was largely achieved through prolonged scratching away of layers of paint, the novelty of which method caused contemporaries to condemn it as 'unfinished'. The pain of loss is accompanied by the pain of isolation, as in *The Death Chamber* (*c.* 1894–5), where members of the bereaved family stand stiffly, each wrapped in his own incommunicable thoughts. In Munch's work, individuals are isolated not only from each other but also from nature, including their own nature, which becomes a threatening 'other'. Nature, furthermore, is symbolically equated with Woman. Munch was profoundly mistrustful of sexual love, sensing union with a woman as a kind of death, as can be seen most obviously in *The Vampire* (1894), but also in his many versions of *The Kiss*. This was not simply misogyny – see, for example, his sympathetic treatment of a young girl's anxiety in *Puberty* (1894) – but something much deeper: the fear of the destruction of the creative ego through its (desperately desired) union with natural forces. The flowing lines in many of his landscapes are the same as those of the hair in his ambivalently sexual *Madonna* (1893–4). In *The Scream* (1893), probably his most famous painting, the form of the screaming creature in the foreground is echoed in the forms of the landscape beyond and the swirling blood-red sky above: anxiety is raised to a cosmic level.

Despite his emphasis, however, on the more painful aspects of life, Munch was aiming at a broad synthesis of all fundamental aspects of human experience, balancing the dark against the light. In 1902 he exhibited, under the title of *The Frieze of Life*, a series of pictures which between them were intended to show 'life in all its fulness, its variety, its joys and its sorrows'. Close parallels exist between his art and the drama of Strindberg,

of whom he painted several portraits, and Ibsen, for whose *Ghosts* he designed the décor in Max Reinhardt's 1906 production. Like them, he raised contemporary themes, acutely observed, to a more universal plane, infused with a partly tragic, partly mystical vision.

In 1908–9, Munch underwent a nervous breakdown. With certain notable exceptions, his work after that date seldom achieved the dramatic intensity of his early work nor was it any longer revolutionary in art historical terms. He had already, however, by then had the profoundest influence on European art, having become famous in Germany during the 1890s, somewhat helped by a fortunate art-world scandal. Technically, his paintings and graphic work, especially his woodcuts, directly influenced such German Expressionists as Nolde and Kirchner. But in a deeper sense, too, it could be claimed that he was the single most important spiritual precursor of Expressionism. He combined the traditional mysticism and anxiety of Northern art with a specifically modern awareness of the predicament of the individual cut adrift from the restrictions, and the securities, of a socially sanctioned system of values.

Further reading

See: J.P. Hodin, *Edvard Munch: Norway's Genius* (1945); Hannah B. Muller, *Edvard Munch: A Bibliography* (1951); Otto Benesch, *Edvard Munch* (1960); Werner Timm, *The Graphic Art of Edvard Munch* (1969); Reinhold Heller, *Edvard Munch's 'The Scream'* (1972); John Boulton Smith, *Munch* (1977); Ketil Bjornstad, *The Story of Edvard Munch* (2005); Sue Prideaux, *Edvard Munch: Behind the Scream* (2005).

GRAY WATSON

MUSSORGSKY, Modest Petrovich

1839–81

Russian composer

The most original composer of the 'Mighty Handful' was educated privately and then at the Cadet School of the Guards in St Petersburg. He served in the Preobrazhensky Regiment of Guards and was later employed in the civil service. His interests shifted from the traditional pursuits of Guards officers to some of the most advanced ideas of the time. He claimed to have been drawn to music through folk art rather than art music, and despised the rules and conventions of the latter. In 1857 he encountered for the first time Balakirev, Stasov and Dargomyzhsky. The first-named attempted to guide him along his customary musical path, Stasov eventually became a lifelong friend, and Dargomyzhsky pioneered some of the ideas and techniques which Mussorgsky later embodied in his own compositions. From 1863 or so his music begins to show his deep interest in folk art and his attachment to truth rather than beauty as an artistic ideal. His projected opera *The Marriage* (1868) is the laboratory in which he experimented with modelling vocal lines on the inflections of (Russian) speech, an idea recently tried out in Dargomyzhsky's *The Stone Guest*. His avoidance of grandiose cosmopolitan subjects, his concentration on various aspects of Russian life, treated realistically, and his taste for caricature draw him close to the utilitarian ideas of the time and to the group of painters known as the 'Itinerants'. But his talent for vivid representation through highly unorthodox musical devices put his works beyond the comprehension of the majority of his contemporaries, even of many musicians sympathetically disposed to him. In his case bouts of alcoholism compounded the inability, characteristic of many Russian composers of this period, to bring projected compositions to completion, and his works were much altered after his death in the name of turning them into performable material.

Ever an enemy of routine and convention, Mussorgsky did not really try to make a successful career as a composer by the lights of the time. Particularly in its first version (1868–9), but to some extent also in the second (1871–2, performed in 1874), the opera *Boris Godunov* was not tailored for

immediate success. Its very subject made it liable to censorship troubles. It was deficient in opportunities for the expected vocal display and ballet, and it was short of love interest and comedy. Yet it is a masterly work, in its own terms, in which Mussorgsky's gift for characterization is brought to bear on the psychological development of Boris himself, and in which the stark and sombre music magnificently reflects and communicates the events and atmosphere of the time. The 'time of troubles' in the early seventeenth century which preceded the beginning of the Romanov dynasty's rule provided the composer with a serious subject from the Russian past which gave him scope for musical depiction of a wide variety of characters, including nobles, peasants, clergy, Polish aristocrats and Jesuits. His knowledge of Russian folk music determined the character of the greatest part of the Russian scenes. **Rimsky-Korsakov's** version, which for long kept out Mussorgsky's original, has smoothed out and made 'grammatical' what in the original was more striking and novel, while its orchestration has often substituted conventional tinsel for what the composer had coloured with greater discrimination and sensitivity.

With *Khovanshchina*, on which Mussorgsky worked from 1872 until his death, it is more defensible to use Rimsky-Korsakov's version of 1883, given the incomplete and rather unsatisfactory state in which the composer left it. Once more the subject is a troubled period of Russian history – the 1680s, when the Princes Khovansky tried to overthrow the ruling Romanovs. The former personify the old feudal class and the latter more modern ideas. An important part is played by Old Believers, who remained faithful to details or Orthodox ritual after these had been changed by Patriarch Nikon in 1653. It is probable that Mussorgsky intended to close the opera (in good *grand opéra* style) with their mass suicide by fire. The precise course of the action was not worked out in advance, and the plot is sprawling and over-elaborate. Like *Boris*, it is concerned not so much with the interaction of individuals as with the unfolding of a national tragedy. There is much fine music in it.

Still less was written of *Sorochintsy Fair* on which the composer worked between 1874 and his death. This opera, based on a short story by Gogol, was more humorous in tone but still allowed Mussorgsky to use his gift for graphic characterization. He was handicapped, however, by his failure to work out a scheme to begin with and by an inadequate immersion in the Ukrainian language and background of the proposed opera. *Pictures from an Exhibition* (1874) is a series of short piano pieces, each 'representing' a work by the artist Victor Hartmann, linked by a 'walking' theme ('Promenade'). Each is a brilliant miniature which seizes on some aspect of the picture's content and translates it into sound.

Mussorgsky's particular talent for characterization is made clear in his nearly fifty songs, plus three cycles. The vast range over which this talent extended, together with the development of the composer's style and technique, is also shown in the songs. 'Where Are You, Little Star?' (1857) has strong references to the modes, harmony, cadences and ornamentation of folk song. *Kalistrat* (1864), *The Peasant Lullaby* (1865), *Hopak* (1866) and *Eryomushka's Lullaby* (1868, dedicated 'to the great teacher of musical truth, A. S. Dargomyzhsky') follow on from it in still more rigorous style. *Gathering Mushrooms* (1867) and the first song of the *Nursery* cycle (1868–72) exemplify the composer's attempts to capture speech inflections while using a single note-value (the crotchet) for the vocal part. The cycle shows his ability to penetrate the thought processes of a child, and his readiness to encapsulate them in musical language of unprecedented empiricism.

In *Svetik Savishna* (1866) Mussorgsky depicts an unhappy idiot declaring his love for a girl while acknowledging that his condition deprives him of everything including love. The music is 'realistic' in the sense that it most cleverly reflects the manner of voice and gesture of the scene; from such songs we might well deduce that the composer was a mimic of considerable talent. *The Seminarist* (1866) shows a student learning Latin nouns and indulging simultaneously in amorous reflections. *The Classicist* (1867) is a lampoon of a critic who had attacked the 'modernism' of Rimsky-Korsakov's *Sadko*. A subjective lyrical vein and a more conventional handling of musical figures are revealed in the cycle *Sunless* (1874). The bold graphic quality of many other songs is here replaced by a degree of stylization. The *Songs and Dances of Death* (1875–77) sum up the most important features of Mussorgsky's songs. Vivid yet structured, inventive yet disciplined, speech-inflected yet generating lyrical melody – this cycle is one of the composer's best works. Each song shows the intervention of death in an area of human life – taking a sick child from its mother, serenading a sick girl, dancing with a drunken peasant, and on the battlefield – and treats each subject like a miniature *scena*.

When he had characters and dramatic situations to stimulate him, Mussorgsky could respond with music of wonderful truth and imagination. Song and opera offered greatest scope, and it is in these forms that Mussorgsky's splendid marriage of music with drama succeeded most consistently. His influence was felt most strongly after his lifetime – by **Debussy**, **Stravinsky**, **Prokofiev** and **Shostakovich**.

Further reading

See: Jay Leyda and Sergei Bertensson, *The Mussorgsky Reader* (1974); M.D. Calvocoressi (completed and revised by Gerald Abraham), *Mussorgsky* (1974); A. Orlova (ed.), *Remembering Mussorgsky* (1991); R. Taruskin, *Mussorgsky: Eight Essays and an Epilogue* (1992); Carl Emerson, *The Life of Mussorgsky* (1999); David Brown, *Mussorgsky* (2004).

STUART CAMPBELL

N

NABOKOV, Vladimir Vladimirovich

1899–1977

Russian/US novelist

Nabokov was a writer (primarily a novelist) who wrote in two languages (Russian and English), had two literary careers (as an émigré under the pen-name of Sirin and as a major American author), and whose art is preoccupied with worlds within and beyond other worlds. Born in St Petersburg, the son of a well-known liberal politician, he left Russia with his family after the Revolution of 1917. After taking a degree in French and Russian at Cambridge, he settled in Berlin, where he became a prominent and distinguished member of the Russian émigré literary world (the name Sirin is an obscure homage to the Russian publishing house which brought out Andrey Bely's modernistic novel *Petersburg*, much admired by Nabokov). His first novel, *Mashenka*, was published in Russian in 1926 and translated into German two years later (translated into English as *Mary*, 1970). Its theme of exile, loss and erotic yearning, as well as its comic and parodistic elements, and its self-conscious illusionism, foreshadow later and greater works, especially those which hold up distorting mirrors to a distorted reality, like *Despair* (1936/66), *Invitation to a Beheading* (1935/60), and *Bend Sinister* (1947). The erotic strain in *Mashenka* foreshadows *Lolita* (1955), while the element of fictitious biography is developed in *Glory* (1932/71) and *The Defence* (1930/64) as well as two

novels which, with *Lolita*, may be considered his crowning achievement, *The Gift* (1937/63) and *Pale Fire* (1962), the former a sophisticated revaluation (by means of parody) of the Russian literary tradition, the other a novel lying hidden among the references and cross-references of a misleadingly erudite commentary to a limpid and lengthy pastiche poem in the manner of **Robert Frost** (with more than a dash of **Wallace Stevens**). The writings and rewritings of biography/autobiography, doubtless an artistic transformation of personal insecurity, also lie behind Nabokov's first novel in English, *The Real Life of Sebastian Knight* (1941).

Nabokov, who married in 1925 and had one son, Dimitri, in 1934, continued to live and work in Berlin, where his father had been assassinated by right-wing extremists in 1922, until history (a nightmare from which, like **Joyce's** Stephen Dedalus, he could not awake) forced him to move to Paris, and thence, in 1939, to the USA. His peregrinations are recorded, very subjectively, in his 'real' autobiography, *Speak, Memory*, but his full bitterness at the horrific turn of historic events is evoked (always by way of parody and mockery, never direct commentary) in *Invitation to a Beheading*, a Kafkaesque work uninfluenced by **Kafka**, and *Bend Sinister*, a kind of carnivalesque *1984* in which European totalitarianism is grotesquely garbed in the banalities of American comic strip. In America, in addition to a fairly obscure academic career, Nabokov enjoyed some small repute as a lepidopterist, until his life was transformed by the overnight notoriety of a novel which 'respectable' publishers would not handle, *Lolita*, now recognizably one of the seminal works of twentieth-century American fiction. Suddenly the émigré academic (not unlike his own creation, *Pnin*, 1957) became a best-seller. He moved with his wife to Montreux in Switzerland, and continued to live there in a hotel until his death, publishing regularly.

Lolita has been considered variously as a story of true love and as forming part of the 'literature of exhaustion', and there is no doubt that part of its fascination lies in its power of appealing at different levels. The love of the obscure émigré, Humbert Humbert, for the nymphet Lolita (both household words since Nabokov) is both text and pretext in a symbolic journey in the American tradition (and loaded with Americana past and present): part flight, part quest, where innocent desire plays a deadly game with retributive lust, the latter being embodied in the character of one Clare Quilty, C.Q. the pursuer, the avenging angel or the devil in disguise. Quilty is (like Emerald in *Pale Fire*) simply, on another level, the novelist playing chess with his protagonist, or the mechanism of 'plot' with its ineluctable ending. On the moral plane, he is an emanation of Humbert's guilty conscience, and when Humbert kills him in a mock-Hollywood shoot-up, Humbert is a lost soul. 'Decadent' as the subject-matter of *Lolita* may be, the centre of attention in the novel is not morbid psychology but the creative potentialities of language itself: Nabokov's wit plays over a wide range of narrative modes and devices, exploring in particular the tensions of memory and desire, the quasi-erotic longing for a symbolic order.

The exceptional awareness of the limits of literary conventions, born of Nabokov's peculiarly 'extraterritorial' (to use George Steiner's term) situation, has led critics to emphasize his kinship with such writers as **Borges**, **Robbe-Grillet** and **Pynchon**, at the expense of his Russianness and the direct relationship of his art to such writers as Pushkin and **Chekhov** via Bely. Nevertheless, just as Nabokov influenced American fiction, so it influenced him: his work became more labyrinthine and mannerist, while remaining beneath the surface profoundly personal, even plangent. The crazed commentator of *Pale Fire* is a sado-masochistic double of the scholarly Nabokov, who edited and translated – very brilliantly – Pushkin's *Eugene Onegin* (1964); the family chronicle of *Ada* (1969), strikingly combining motifs from American and Russian culture, is a kaleidoscope of statelessness as well as an exercise in translation; while the strangely brief *Transparent Things* (1972) and *Look at the Harlequins* (1974) are respectively the fictionalized epilogue and the index-cum-bibliography to Nabokov's life's work, as if death might coincide, by a higher authorial logic, with 'the end' on the page. Although occasionally hinting at new stylistic departures, these late works are nostalgic and solipsistic, suggesting that the mandarin stance Nabokov assiduously cultivated in his later years preyed, in the end, on his talent.

Further reading

Critical studies of Nabokov include: Page Stegner, *Escape into Aesthetics* (1966); L.S. Dembo (ed.), *Nabokov: The Man and His Works* (1967); Andrew Field, *Nabokov: His Life in Art* (1967); Karl Proffer, *Keys to Lolita* (1968); Julian Moynahan, *Vladimir Nabokov* (1971); Alfred Appel, *Nabokov's Dark Cinema* (1974); John O. Stark, *The Literature of Exhaustion* (1974); H. Grabes, *Fictitious Biographies* (1977); G.M. Hyde, *Vladimir Nabokov: America's Russian Novelist* (1977); Vladimir E. Alexandrov (ed.), *The Garland Companion to Vladimir Nabokov* (1995); Kurt Johnson and Stephen Coates, *Nabokov's Blues: The Scientific Odyssey of a Literary Genius* (2001); Jane Grayson, *Nabokov's World* (2 vols, 2001); Stanley P. Baldwin, *Vladimir Nabokov: His Life and Works* (2004); Julian W. Connolly (ed.), *The Cambridge Companion to Nabokov* (2005).

G.M. HYDE

NEEDHAM, Joseph

1900–95

Anglo-Scottish biochemist, historian and sinologist

As Arthur Waley worked indefatigably to bring the riches of oriental literature to the attention of Western readers through his translations of Chinese and Japanese classics, so Joseph Needham, in his monumental and posthumously ongoing *Science and Civilisation in China*, mounted a sustained campaign to destroy a widely held assumption that 'science' is a Western preserve. In so doing, he adumbrated an 'ecumenical' theory of world civilization which, while being broadly evolutionist, addressed such issues as the volume and reciprocity of technological transfer between civilizations – India and Islam as well as China and the West – as well as the apparent reasons for success and failure in scientific advancement at specific times in specific places. Never content merely to document the mechanical and theoretical achievements of non-European cultures, especially China's, he sought to demonstrate how social, economic and, particularly, religious and ideological variables can act as either local enhancers or local inhibitors in the fulfilment of what he conceived as a truly global undertaking: a final (though still far distant) rapprochement between humankind's spirituality and its thirst for manipulating the physical world in which it finds itself embedded.

Such a protean, inclusive vision of history only coalesced when Needham was well into his middle age and had already made a name for himself as a biochemist. Born in London, he was the only child of bickering Scottish parents. From Oundle School he progressed to Gonville and Caius College, Cambridge University, where he took a first degree in medicine, then, in 1925, a doctorate in biochemistry. Specializing in embryology and morphogenesis, he published scores of papers, leading to the publication of *Chemical Embryology* (3 vols, 1931) and *Biology and Morphogenesis* (1941). Excellence and productivity in his chosen field secured him a fellowship at Caius, and, much later, the college mastership, from 1966 to 1976. But although Needham continued to teach biochemistry until 1966, from early on in his career he sought to promote the history of science as a discrete discipline.

Like many intellectuals of his generation Needham was drawn towards **Marxism**, although at Cambridge he also contemplated a religious life, for several years attending the Oratory of the Good Shepherd, an Anglo-Catholic brotherhood. But the event that finally determined his future course was the arrival in Cambridge of three biochemistry students from Nationalist China in 1936, among them Lu Gwei-djen, who helped Needham learn to read and write Chinese, and whom he eventually married in 1989, following the death of his first wife, Dorothy Moyle. Fired by a passion for China, Needham secured for himself the directorship of the wartime Anglo-Chinese Science Co-operation Office, based in Chonqing, between 1942 and 1946. There he met the historian Wang Ling, later to become the most important of Needham's many research collaborators.

After the war Needham headed up the Natural Science division of the newly created UNESCO, before returning to Cambridge in 1948 to begin work on *Science and Civilisation in China*. Although from the outset this project was conceived on the grand scale – Needham soon mapped out seven volumes, the first being published in 1954 – it expanded beyond even his expectations, and was unfinished at his death, though work on it continues under the auspices of the Needham Research Institute, founded in 1989.

Until Needham began publishing his findings, it was acknowledged by some that a handful of key inventions, among them printing, gunpowder and the magnetic compass, may have originated in China. Not only did *Science and Civilisation* confirm such speculation, but added vastly to the number of historic Chinese inventions and discoveries, among them (in chronological sequence) the iron ploughshare (sixth century BCE), sunspots, cast iron, the double-action piston, the kite, the collar-harness, the rotary fan, the seed drill, steel, circulation of the blood, the parachute, endocrinology, the armillary ring, deep drilling for salt and gas, the belt-drive, the wheelbarrow, sliding callipers, decimal fractions, the square-pallet chain pump, the suspension bridge, the stern rudder, the seismograph, tear gas, the fishing reel, the metal stirrup, porcelain, the umbrella, chess, the paddle boat, solar wind, the segmental bridge, the mechanical clock, playing cards, immunology and, in the tenth century, phosphorescent paint.

To provide detailed, scholarly accounts of each of these and many other developments, *Science and Civilisation* is divided up by field. Thus Volume V, running to thirteen parts and itself published as three separate volumes, is subtitled 'Chemistry and Chemical Technology'. Each volume too, while always bearing the stamp of Needham's approach and authority, benefits from the collaboration of other researchers. But if the net effect is to provide overwhelming evidence that, during the Sui, Tang and Song dynasties certainly (589–1279), China was unquestionably the most advanced civilization anywhere, at least in material terms, the very success of Needham's advocacy posited a fundamental problem, often referred to as 'Needham's Grand Question': if the Chinese were so spectacularly good at 'science', then why did it befall Europe, for so long so backward, to achieve the breakthroughs needed for 'modern science'?

Needham recognized this dilemma from the outset, and the scope of his response, informing the entire project, is what makes *Science and Civilisation* a landmark investigation. Volumes I and II specifically set out to describe the myriad circumstances in which Chinese science both flourished and stagnated. If he recommends that the close-to-nature, anti-authoritarian, experimental, holistic character of Daoism was the most consistent driving force, he also allows Confucianism's promotion of scholarly

learning a place, while examining such other traditional Chinese philosophies as Legalism and Mohism. Equally, he elaborates China's trading relations with other parts of Eurasia, as well as its own internal social and productive requirements. Brilliantly, he demonstrates how an advanced hydraulics emerged out of China's need to manage its water resources to keep both people and empire alive. What inhibited further advances was the period of Mongol rule (1289–1368), followed by the distinctly conservative Ming Dynasty (1368–1644).

Although Needham is at pains to point up the contiguities of science as practised in different parts of the Eurasian landmass over a stretch of time far exceeding the twelve centuries of Edward Gibbon's *Decline and Fall of the Roman Empire* (1766–88), he acknowledges the qualitative difference of European science as it began emerging in the sixteenth and seventeenth centuries. Essentially, in Needham's view, the new European science was mathematically axiomatic in a Euclidean way, and it was this, combined with an ultimately religious belief in immutable laws of nature the unity of which is supposedly guaranteed by God, that gave it its radical edge.

Needham's account of the success of European (later American) science in the modern period is generally considered less persuasive than his account of Chinese science. He undervalued both the questioning fomentation of the European Reformation and the role played by such centralizing scientific bodies as the Royal Society, and perhaps allowed too little room for the unpredictability of individual genius. Yet his larger thesis – that 'science' is a human universal – remains intact, borne out by an increasing incidence of discovery and invention outside the magic circle of Euro-American laboratories.

Notwithstanding his unrivalled achievements as a historian and promoter of Western respect for Chinese ingenuity, Needham has not been without his critics, quite apart from contentious issues surrounding his Grand

Question. Chinese science owed more to an influx of such primary technologies as weaving, the wheel and probably bronze-making via the central Asian 'steppe corridor' from the Black Sea region in the late Neolithic Age than Needham seems prepared to concede, and the structure of *Science and Civilisation in China* reflects Western, not indigenous, scientific categories. Conversely, a rose-tinted attitude towards Marxism ('the only possible moral theology'), and towards **Joseph Stalin** as well as **Mao Zedong**, sometimes cast Needham in a too determinedly anti-Western light. Unwisely, in 1954 he supported unfounded Chinese claims that the USA had used biological weapons during the Korean War. As a consequence he was blacklisted by the US State Department, though this did not deter him from protesting America's actual use of chemical weapons during the Vietnam War in the following decade.

Further reading

To date thirteen volumes of *Science and Civilisation in China* (from 1954) have been published. Robert Temple, *The Genius of China: 3000 Years of Science, Discovery and Invention* (1986) furnishes a somewhat slapdash but authorized resumé of Needham's findings. Other books by Needham include: *Chinese Science* (with Dorothy Moyle, 1945); *The Grand Titration: Science and Society in East and West* (1969); *Science in Traditional China* (1982). Needham's biography has yet to be written, but, for an overview of his philosophy, see Maurice Cowling, 'Joseph Needham & the History of Chinese Science', in *The New Criterion* Vol. 11, No. 6 (February 1993).

JUSTIN WINTLE

NERUDA, Pablo (Neftalí REYES)

1904–73
Chilean poet

Parral, central Chile, where Neruda was born, and Temuco where he was brought up by his train-guard father (his mother died early on), is the source of much of his basic imagery – a wet, misty, forested area (rain, river, sea – all natural elements). He adopted

the pseudonym Neruda (from a nineteenth-century Czech writer) for fear of ridicule from his 'humble' companions. Neruda always saw himself as a natural, born poet. He linked poetry with the vitalistic elements and natural energies, although the myth of facility and spontaneity has camouflaged the careful craftsman behind the exuberant images. From the start Neruda assumed the role of bard.

Neruda was a very successful poet. His second book, *Twenty Love Poems* (*Veinte poemas de amor y una canción desesperada*, 1924), became one of the best-known collections in Spanish. These poems deal with Neruda's move from his provincial roots to the capital Santiago in terms of two contrasting love affairs in a dense and moody language based on symbols and images taken from nature. The poet's *persona* is that of a melancholic anarchist at odds with the world.

But popularity was a trap and Neruda sought a diplomatic post (rather than train as a schoolteacher) to enrich his experience. From 1927 to 1943 he lived outside Chile, in the Far East (Rangoon, Colombo, Java), Spain and Mexico. This was the central (and best?) phase collected in the three volumes of his *Residence on Earth* (*Residencia en la tierra*, 1925–47). The first two *Residencias* (1925–35) are magnificent crisis poems dealing with Neruda's confusion and loneliness as a foreigner 'abandoned' abroad in terms of the breakdown of his literary and Romantic *persona*.

The borrowed surrealistic devices are moulded into his vision in hermetic poems working out shifting and obsessive emotional knots almost as therapy. But it was the Spanish Civil War, and his friend **Lorca's** murder, that shocked Neruda out of his private spiritual anguish. His *Spain in My Heart* (*España en el corazón*, 1937) reflects this change of responsibility in a more conscious, controlled poetry, based on anger, indignation. His years in Spain confirmed his reputation as one of the foremost poets of his age.

Neruda was not converted to **Marxism** but found in it an answer to his own dark emotions: it was an ordering and granting of purpose to his life. Neruda's best political poems barely differ from his earlier ones with the same luxuriant, sensual language, a 'daylight' poetry of visual, tactile things. The year 1943 was crucial in the development of Neruda's Latin American consciousness: from a visit to Machu-picchu (the Inca fort) he began elaborating his dream of writing an epic combining his commitment to his *pueblo* (people) with a poetic re-vision of Latin American history. Paralleling this, in 1945 he was elected senator and began a long career in politics that ended with being a presidential nominee (1970, standing down for his friend Allende). Political persecution and exile (1947) pushed him to complete the *Canto general* (1950), a poetical, political history of his continent. He aimed to create a new sense of identity based on his belief in his role and identity with his land and people where the poet interprets the silent masses. In 1951, with **Picasso**, he won the **Lenin** Peace Prize.

This change towards an earthy simplicity – a constant in his poetry – led to his *Elemental Odes* (*Odas elementales*, 1954) celebrating tomatoes and fallen chestnuts and so forth. From here to his death Neruda was to combine all his phases, using long or short lines with a Protean freedom; the best books being: *Estravagario* (1958); *Memorial de Isla Negra* (1964); the posthumous *La rosa separada* (1973) and *El mar y las campanas* (1973).

Through this diversity Neruda remained a Romantic poet, the *registro sensible* (sensitive register); his best poems are always personal (great erotic and nature poems). Neruda exploited the sensuality of words, the body of the world. He was an amazingly popular public reader and he enjoyed this prestige. He moved through many relationships and places, but his best biography is his poetry (see Monegal). In his personal response to experience Neruda avoided introspection, self-analysis, philosophizing in favour of a poetry of love for the world, objects, women and physical sensations.

From 1970 to 1973 Neruda was Allende's ambassador in Paris. In 1971 he won the Nobel Prize for Literature. He died soon after

his friend Allende fell. As a sensitive witness to his age, Neruda condensed in his work the history of Chile and of his continent; what unites his work and makes it Nerudian are the basic responses to nature and the self learned in Parral and childhood, the need to establish a poetic identity with his own working-class roots and his craftsmanship. Neruda was a poet who sought a responsible social function that fused his personal anguish (the misery of being isolated and unloved) with the need to forge a new myth (based on solidarity) as a way to deal with the individual's death. He was both innovative, modern and anachronistic, prolonging the Romantic/symbolist tradition.

Further reading

Other works include: *Obras completas* (1999), and his *Memoirs* (1978). Good biographies are Volodia Teitelboim, *Neruda: An Intimate Biography* (1991) and Adam Feinstein, *Pablo Neruda. A Passion for Life* (2004). A good anthology is Robert Pring-Mill, *Pablo Neruda. A Basic Anthology* (1975). Good criticism: René de Costa, *The Poetry of Pablo Neruda* (1979); John Felstiner, *Translating Neruda: The Way to Macchu Picchu* (1980); Manuel Durán and Margery Safir, *Earth Tones: The Poetry of Pablo Neruda* (1981); and Christopher Perriam, *The Late Poetry of Pablo Neruda* (1989).

JASON WILSON

NICHOLSON, Ben

1894–1982
English artist

Born into a family of extravert artists, Ben Nicholson studied for a brief period at the Slade School of Art, but then moved rapidly away from the mainstream of Edwardian painting. During the 1920s, during which he worked closely with his first wife Winifred Dacre, his still-lifes became increasingly more schematic, employing the pared-down profile of a bottle, a glass or a guitar, and sometimes scraps of newspaper or lettering. He travelled frequently on the Continent, where he was inspired by the work of **Cézanne**, **Picasso** and **Braque**, and in the following decade by **Mondrian**.

In the mid-1930s Nicholson's work became abstract to a more radical and controversial degree. He experimented with rarefied colour and, significantly, with carved surfaces; in 1934 his first white reliefs were exhibited in London. In the same year he married the sculptor **Barbara Hepworth**. Well aware of the close relationship of his own painting to other forms of art, he became in the mid-1930s an active member of 'Unit One', a group of British painters, architects and sculptors which spread the concept of a 'modern movement' in Britain. With **Naum Gabo** and the architect Leslie Martin, moreover, he edited *Circle – International Survey of Constructive Art* (1937); among the contributors were Mondrian and **Le Corbusier**, and *Circle* firmly identified the work of Ben and Winifred Nicholson, **Henry Moore** and Hepworth with the School of Paris and with an 'international modern' style.

Nicholson's art was not restricted to austere geometrical forms; he remained fascinated by the outlines of household utensils, the coastal curves and rooftops of Cornwall (where he lived during the 1940s and most of the 1950s), and the contours of the lakes and hills of Switzerland. In his view abstraction represented not a withdrawal of the artist from 'reality', but a means of bringing art back into everyday life, and a liberation of form and colour. The constant features of his work are delicacy, precision and a readiness to explore new textures and configurations. Towards the end of the 1950s he began to increase the scale of his productions, a development which led in the 1960s to his 'relief projects' for free-standing walls. Nicholson enjoyed international recognition from the 1950s; a major retrospective exhibition of his work toured the United States in 1978–9.

Further reading

The artist's statements and reminiscences are collected in *Ben Nicholson*, a *Studio International* special issue, ed. Maurice de Saumarez (1969). Exhibition catalogues: Tate Gallery (1969); and *Ben Nicholson: Fifty Years of His Art* (Albright-Knox Art Gallery, Buffalo, NY, 1978). See also Herbert Read, *Ben Nicholson, Paintings, Reliefs, Drawings* (Vol. I, 1948; Vol. II, 1956), and *Ben Nicholson, Drawings, Paintings and Reliefs 1911–68* (1969); J. Lewison, *Ben Nicholson* (1991).

PATRICK CONNER

NIEMEYER, Oscar
1907–
Brazilian architect

In 1930 Niemeyer began his architectural studies at the National School of Fine Art in Rio de Janeiro, and in 1934 joined the office of the influential Lucio Costa who at that time was responsible for much of the restoration of Brazil's historic buildings. Costa, who tried to dissuade Niemeyer because of the limited amount of work he could offer such a promising young man, became one of the two major influences in his life. The other was the important European **Le Corbusier**, who paid a brief visit to Brazil in 1929 and returned for a spell of three months in 1936 to work on his plans for the campus of the University of Rio de Janeiro and a new building for the Ministry of Education. Niemeyer worked directly under Le Corbusier and as a result of this fruitful and exciting experience produced his designs for the Athletic Centre in Rio and the Aeronautical Training Centre at São José dos Campos. Like Le Corbusier he saw architecture as a fine art and continued to associate with painters and sculptors, believing that a successful environment can only be achieved if all those concerned with the total design are closely involved with the project right from the start, and like Le Corbusier in this respect he was something of an elitist.

In 1939 he built the Brazilian Pavilion for the New York World Fair in conjunction with Lucio Costa, with whom he was later to be associated on a far grander scale in his most dramatic contribution to modern design at Brasilia.

The dominant style in Brazilian architectural history is the extremely flamboyant and richly decorative Portuguese Baroque which came to a full colonial flowering in a country which offered an equally rich and exotic natural environment for its undoubted excesses. A somewhat mundane functionalism followed, but after the Second World War Brazil became one of the leading countries in the development of the ideas of the Congrès Internationaux d'Architecture Moderne (CIAM) culminating in 1957 with the concept of Brasilia.

Brasilia was conceived as a bureaucratically controlled city of superblocks and functional zoning. Luca Costa drew up the Utopian plans and Niemeyer was appointed Architectural Adviser to Nova Cap, the organization instituted to create the brave new capital. Later he was made Chief Architect.

Though we may have second thoughts as to the wisdom of the scheme, bearing in mind the bleak living conditions of the majority of Brazilians at the time and bearing in mind that Brazilian political systems are far from stable, it can be argued in Niemeyer's defence that he did see the project as an architectural challenge, and did approach each individual building with care and attention to functional rightness.

He designed the Hotel in 1958 and later the same year the President's Palace. He built the Law Courts and the Cathedral and the whole scheme was based on a policy of rapid urbanization. Despite the urgency, Niemeyer's forms have a grace and refinement and his solutions to the varying problems set by the diverse requirements are novel and wholly satisfying. The result is a kind of super-modern Baroque reduced to a crisp geometric formal arrangement which well answers the needs required of it.

Niemeyer's first really personal contribution to modern architecture was the Church of St Francis which he built at Pampulha outside Belo Horizonte in 1942 and, though not without its critics, it has a rightness and simplicity of form well suited to its modest scale.

The house he built for himself outside Rio de Janeiro in 1953 reflects his understanding of Le Corbusier's civilized thoughts on how to live well, and it seems that it is at this scale that Niemeyer is at his best, and not in the vast impersonal scale of Brasilia. Like Le Corbusier he has often been tempted to overreach himself. Yet, during a career lasting seventy years, Niemeyer has consistently surprised with his inventiveness, too often confined to sketches of unrealized projects.

Further reading

See: Oscar Niemeyer, *The Curves of Time: Memoirs* (2000); and *The Work of Oscar Niemeyer*, Foreword by Lucio Costa (1950); Charles Jencks, *Modern Movements in Architecture* (1973); David Kendrick Underwood, *Oscar Niemeyer and the Architecture of Brazil* (1994).

JOHN FURSE

NIETZSCHE, Friedrich
1844–1900
German philosopher

Nietzsche was born in 1844 in Saxony, then a part of Prussia. His lifelong intellectual war with Christianity was tied to his having come from a male line of Lutheran pastors and his father having died when Nietzsche was only four, a traumatic event for the young boy, who thereafter grew up in a household of women. At the extraordinarily young age of twenty-four Nietzsche was appointed to the Chair of Classical Philology in Basel, a position he held for ten years until failing health forced his resignation. From the age of twenty-seven his life was to be a persistent struggle with torturing migraine, stomach complaints and various other illnesses. Commentators have related his poor health to syphilis, which he may have caught as a university student. The one strong influence on Nietzsche's thought had both an intellectual and a personal side. For most of the Basel years he was a close friend of **Richard Wagner**, to the point that he virtually became a member of the family. Through Wagner he was also influenced at this time by Schopenhauer's work.

From 1879 when he left Basel, Nietzsche spent ten years travelling alone, from single room to single room, from Genoa to Sils Mania to Turin, living out of one suitcase, reading little, rarely meeting friends and then briefly, his notebooks his only steady companions. No philosopher has ever lived in such intimate contact with his work – these years saw him write most of his important work, above all *The Gay Science (Die Fröhliche Wissenschaft,* 1882, trans. 1974), *Thus Spake Zarathustra (Also Sprach Zarathustra,* 1883–5, trans. 1954), *Beyond Good and Evil (Jenseits von Gut und Böse,* 1886, trans. 1968) and *The Genealogy of Morals (Zur Genealogie der Moral,* 1887, trans. 1968). In Turin in 1889, after running across a square to protect a horse that was being cruelly whipped, Nietzsche collapsed into madness. He lived until 1900 in an increasingly catatonic state, mainly in the care of his mother.

Nietzsche's importance is predominantly in two spheres, as a theorist of culture and as a psychologist. His theory of culture is put most profoundly in his first book, *Die Geburt der Tragödie* (1872, translated as *The Birth of Tragedy,* 1968). He argues that culture is in essence *mythos* – the classical Greek conception exemplified in its tragedies, in which the 'Dionysian' forces of power-mania, lust and sadism, which underpin human existence, are balanced by an ordering and rational 'Apollonian' principle, which in turn provides individuals with beautiful illusions that give meaning to their lives. The great destroyer of culture was Socrates, who attacked the tragic perspective as barbaric, replacing it with a rationalist optimism that has dominated the West ever since. Nietzsche identifies Socrates with the view that through thinking we can become both better and happier people – in effect, that reason can reform being. For Nietzsche this is the great turning point in the history of the West, and the death of culture.

Nietzsche is the first psychologist in the sense that we who live after Freud now use that term. He was the first man to go intensively and across a broad frontier into the question of motives, of why people do what they do. There are thousands of Nietzsche's aphorisms that explore the complicated relations between impulses and desires, fantasies and rationalizations – and how they influence what we do. Typical of the content and style of his aphorisms is: '"I have done that," says my memory. "I cannot have done that," says my pride, and remains inexorable. Eventually, memory yields.'

The focus of Nietzsche's psychologizing is over morality. His starting point is the query as to whether morality itself does not present the greatest danger to human society. Perhaps what has hitherto been praised as 'good' is 'a seduction, a poison, a narcotic, through which the present was possibly living at the expense of the future'. According to Nietzsche's history of morality there was originally an aristocratic age in which the terms 'good' and 'bad' were employed to describe noble, high-spirited, self-affirming action, and alternatively that which was plebeian, uninspired and utilitarian. Only late in human history did the relationship of the noble to the common become moralized. Simultaneously the egoist–altruist dichotomy took possession of human consciousness. The early product of, and in turn catalyst for, this transition was the priest; with him emerged the reactive type, he who, in the absence of spontaneous passions to direct his actions, applies his intellect to create a network of moral, religious and metaphysical rules to guide his conduct. The reactive emotions – pity, compassion and humility – are endowed with supreme virtue; altruism is established as the moral yardstick for social interaction. Finally, a second type of reactive emotion – vengeance, envy and resentment – takes root at a deeper level, and erodes the remaining capacities for impulsive, expressive action: 'the slave revolt in morals begins by "resentment" turning creative and giving birth to values.'

Nietzsche maintains that it was in a desperate attempt to avoid pain, to evade the cruelty and hostility of his neighbour, that man was driven to sharpen his wits, to extend his memory – to think. But this same struggle to reduce tension also gave birth to morality; thereby it provided community with its most powerful nexus, its most resilient self-preserving bond. Nietzsche is led finally to differentiate the universe of human action into two broad classes: the one aristocratic, powerful, hedonistically vital, later egoistic, creative, irreligious, and asocial; the other structured and rationalized according to a strict moral code, Christian, utilitarian, reactive emotionally, and community-centred.

However, the history of morality is not simply a malign one. European culture, and with it the highest achievements of civilization, have been nurtured in the same soil, that of the slave's attempt to master his hostile environment: the priest with his evil introduced the seeds out of which the individual grew 'interesting', 'complex' and 'deep'. The quality of a philosopher's thought, for instance, is directly related to the levels of instinctual repression under whose burden he struggles. Ultimately Nietzsche does not criticize the slave morality itself, but a society in which the priest has gained too much power, where the creative forces of the master are in danger of becoming completely repressed. It is this advance of the naive conception that morality and social constraint, and the instinctual renunciation that they enforce, are fully ameliorable that prepares the way for Freud's insights into the psychological nature and necessities of civilization.

Nietzsche's lifelong wrestling with the problem of morality drove him ultimately to choose the beautiful rather than the good. Thus it is that his central socio-historical concern is with *Kultur;* thus it is that he scorns ethical commitment to individual happiness and social melioration; and thus it is that he singles out the politically optimistic philosophies of liberalism and socialism as mutilating human reality through their ideals. Nietzsche's qualms about humanist ethics stem from his fatalist conviction that the human individual does not have the power, by means of conscious choice or application, to improve the quality of his or her life. 'Quality' is an aesthetic concept, and the 'beautiful',

whether in the form of a human creation or of an exemplary individual, is supra-historical – it can neither be predicted nor prepared for. Man is more than an animal only in finding expression for the beautiful. Additionally, it is significant merely that he may recognize and praise that beauty which moves him. The ugliness of the ideological and the political lies in their legitimating the pursuit of the trivial: they have no rapport with the essence of beauty, nor with its elusive origins.

In terms of the status of philosophy and knowledge Nietzsche was a sceptic. He argues that philosophers have placed an unwarranted trust in concepts, they have absurdly overestimated consciousness. He poses the question again and again of whether the whole of conscious life is not a reflected image, of whether thought and belief bear any relation to active life other than that of providing it with an *ex post* signature.

This querying of *homo sapiens'* cardinal assumption about himself intensifies Hegel's reflection that the owl of Minerva takes flight at dusk, that the time for philosophy is when the action is over. Nietzsche's sounding of knowledge is potentially far more radical, and self-annihilating, than **Marx's** contention that hitherto philosophy had failed to change the world. Nietzsche, in addition, questions the very assumptions of our thinking, calling the principle of causality at best a useful fiction.

Nietzsche identifies philosophy as being like tragedy, one of the high arts of living. At its best, philosophy is the means used by one type of exceptional individual to represent himself, to tell his tale with the uncompromising honesty which renders it hauntingly beautiful. The reflective process is in this case vindicated:

> Gradually it has become clear to me what every great philosophy so far has been: namely, the personal confession of its author and a kind of involuntary and unconscious memoir; also that the moral (or immoral) intentions in every philosophy constituted the real germ of life from which the whole plant had grown.

Nietzsche implies that the search for knowledge conducted on any other basis, for example that of positivist science, is not fundamentally serious.

Nietzsche called himself the philosopher with a hammer. His psychology and his scepticism fuse in his model for philosophy, or thinking. All modern individuals are infected with slave morality, and as a result bad conscience and half-heartedness. Zarathustra mimics the modern decadent: 'One has one's little pleasure for the day and one's little pleasure for the night: but one has a regard for health. "We have invented happiness," say the last men, and they blink.' The slave morality's leading symptom is idealism, the fact that humans need to tell themselves what they *ought* to do, and whom they *ought* to be. Nietzsche sets up his philosophy as a method of self-criticism, of individuals putting their own ideals into question. 'Self-overcoming' is the first task of thinking. Nietzsche describes himself as taking a tuning fork to the ideals of the time, including his own, and tapping them to hear how hollow they sound.

Nietzsche is famous for his proclaiming the 'death of God'. He meant to command and to warn, for once God is truly removed there are no moral markers left to tell humans what to do. Only those with an undertow of driving, Dionysiac instincts will survive, if there are such people left. With characteristic ambivalence Nietzsche places nihilism as the cardinal modern disease, and at the same time advocates a mode of thinking guaranteed to make humans less confident in their moral attachments.

The Anglo-Saxon world in particular has often condemned Nietzsche as one of the founders of Nazi ideology. In fact, Nietzsche loathed anti-Semites and the Nazi movement itself would have appalled him. Nevertheless there are parts of his political philosophy, and his ideal of the 'superman', that have affinities with the later ideas of Nazism. But essentially Nietzsche was an unpolitical man: as Thomas Mann suggested, his political views are the fantasies of an inexperienced child, anticipating rather than creating fascist ideology.

It is more important to recognize, in conclusion, that much of Nietzsche's own life, like his politics, was disturbed. To take him at his own instruction, to judge the work in terms of the man, should make us wary of his philosophy, and perhaps turn to his great French precursor, La Rochefoucauld, a sane and engagingly urbane character who produced a similar psychology, and also in the form of maxims. However, that would be to deny the brilliance of Nietzsche's insights, the uncanny accuracy and pungency of much of his prophecy, and especially his theory of culture; all of which makes him one of the handful of great thinkers of the nineteenth century. Freud several times said of Nietzsche that he had a more penetrating knowledge of himself than any other man who ever lived or was ever likely to live.

Further reading

Other works include: *Unzeitgemässe Betrachlungen* (4 vols 1873–6, translated as *Thoughts Out of Season*, 2 vols 1909); *Menschliches Allzumenschliches* (1878, translated as *Human All-Too-Human*, 1911); *Götzendammerung* (1889, translated as *Twilight of the Idols*, 1968); *Der Antichrist* (1895, translated as *The Antichrist*, 1968); *Nietzsche Contra Wagner* (1895, trans. 1954); *Ecce Homo* (1908, trans. 1968). See: Arthur C. Danto, *Nietzsche as Philosopher* (1965); Karl Jaspers, *Nietzsche* (1965); Walter Kaufman, *Nietzsche: Philosopher, Psychologist, Antichrist* (1968); Alex McIntyre, *The Sovereignty of Joy: Nietzsche's Vision of Grand Politics* (1997); Thomas Heilke, *Nietzsche's Tragic Regime* (1998); Rüdinger Safranski, *Nietzsche: A Philosophical Biography* (2002).

JOHN CARROLL

NOBEL, Alfred Bernhard

1833–96

Swedish industrialist and philanthropist

Nobel was brought up in Stockholm and, from 1842, St Petersburg where his father, a failed architect, moved in 1837 after being declared bankrupt in Sweden. He was tutored privately and before joining his father's munitions business in 1853 travelled widely in Europe and the United States. A further bankruptcy in 1859 forced the family back to Sweden.

Success appeared to have come to Nobel's father at last when, in 1862, he seemed to have worked out a reasonably secure method for the large-scale production of nitroglycerine. This powerful explosive was discovered by the Italian chemist A. Sobrero in 1846 by nitrating glycerine but, despite the attempts of several chemists to develop its commercial potential, it had proved far too unstable to handle in any quantity. In 1864 the family factory, starkly called Nitroglycerin Inc., was opened at Heleneborg outside Stockholm. Hardly had production begun when a serious explosion destroyed much of the factory and killed Nobel's brother Emil. Clearly much more needed to be done.

It was Alfred Nobel three years later who made the crucial step permitting the full commercial development of the new explosive. He mixed the oily nitroglycerine with an inert earth known as kieselguhr able to absorb some three to four times its own weight. Exploded by the mercury fulminate detonator developed by Nobel in 1863 the new explosive, known as dynamite, became one of the great forces of change, allowing feats of construction to be executed which would not have been even considered earlier in the century.

Dynamite, patented by 1867 in Sweden, America and Britain, used throughout the world by the civil engineer rather than the military, was the basis for Nobel's vast fortune. A further advance was made in 1875 when he developed blasting gelatine. More powerful, less sensitive to shock and with greater resistance to moisture, the new explosive opened up additional markets, including the safe-cracker, under the more familiar name of gelignite.

Despite his fortune Nobel's life was far from idyllic. His offer of marriage to his secretary Bertha Kinsky was rejected and in later life he suffered from angina. He wrote of himself: 'When at the age of 54 one is left so alone in this world, and a paid servant is the only person who has so far showed one the most kindness, then come heavy thoughts, heavier than most people imagine.' There were also business disputes and legal battles in his later years which added to his general gloom.

In his will Nobel left most of his fortune of 33 million kroner to set up a fund, the income of which would be used to award annually five prizes. Specifically, prizes were to be awarded in the fields of physics, chemistry, and medicine and physiology for 'the most important discoveries or inventions made during the previous year', in literature for 'the most outstanding work ... of idealistic tendency' and the peace prize for 'the best work for fraternity among nations'.

The prizes were first awarded in 1901 and have since continued, despite several minor crises of confidence, to hold an unchallenged esteem in both the popular imagination and the world of learning. The conjunction of peace prize and explosives manufacturer added precisely the right degree of paradox to guarantee its uniqueness.

Further reading

Nobel wrote one book, *On Modern Blasting Agents* (1875). See also: E. Bergengren, *A. Nobel, the Man and His Work* (1962); and H. Schück and R. Sohlman, *The Life of A. Nobel* (1929). Details of the Nobel Foundation and its operations can be found in *Nobel, the Man and the Prizes* (1962), edited by the Foundation itself, and sociological aspects of the prizes are dealt with in H. Zuckermann, *Scientific Elite* (1977).

DEREK GJERTSEN

NUSSBAUM, Martha Craven

1947–

US philosopher

Noted for her richly illuminating readings of Western and especially classical literature, Martha Nussbaum has been a distinctive and important voice in contemporary moral philosophy. Against the increasing academic tendency to retreat into the safety of narrowly specialized disciplines, she has opened

NUSSBAUM, Martha Craven 567

up new possibilities for the mutual enrichment of the philosophical and the literary domains. She was trained in classical philology at Harvard, and her first major work was a critical edition and translation of Aristotle's *Motion of Animals* (1978). There followed *The Fragility of Goodness*, published to great critical acclaim in 1986, which remains her most influential work.

The book is an exploration of the relation between luck and ethics: it unravels a dominant preoccupation of ancient Greek ethical thought – that the good life for human beings is crucially dependent on factors outside our control. Through detailed analyses of the works of the great tragedians (including Aeschylus' *Agamemnon*, Sophocles' *Antigone* and Euripides' *Hecuba*), intertwined with philosophical examination of the ethical theories of Plato and Aristotle, Nussbaum offers a compelling account of the precariousness of the human condition: 'we need to be born with adequate capacities, to live a fostering natural and social circumstances, to stay clear of abrupt catastrophe, and to develop confirming associations with other human beings'; yet all these needs and achievements are hostages to contingency or vulnerable to potential loss. A classic philosophical response is to advance an ideal of ethical self-sufficiency (found in some of Plato's writings, and much later deployed, in a different guise, in Kant's notion of a domain of moral value immune to the assaults of luck). But the 'aspiration to make the goodness of a good human life safe from luck through the controlling power of reason' cannot be achieved without a cost, as Nussbaum argues in her subtle account of the various ways in which Plato's and Aristotle's theories of the good life struggle with the problem of human vulnerability – the 'fragility' of her title.

The overall vision to emerge from the book is a sombre one: 'that an event that simply happens to me may, without my consent, alter my life; that it is equally problematic to entrust one's good to friends, lovers or country, and to try to have a good life without them' are 'not just the materials of tragedy but everyday facts of lived practical reason'. A secondary theme explored in *Fragility* concerns the internal as opposed to external risks to our attainment of the good – the frequent power of our own appetites, feelings and emotions to upset the settled deliverances of reason on how we should live. These issues are taken up in Nussbaum's subsequent collections of essays, *Love's Knowledge* (1990) and *The Therapy of Desire* (1994), the latter providing a critical examination of the ancient Stoic account of the danger of the emotions and their need for philosophical control. In *Love's Knowledge*, whose range extends beyond the classical world to **Proust**, **Henry James**, **Beckett** and others, Nussbaum provides a powerful defence of the role of the feelings not merely as human impulses that need to be accommodated in any plausible philosophical recipe for well-being, but as themselves constitutive of a certain kind of understanding. Here as in all her writings, Nussbaum shows how much our moral awareness can be developed not via abstract analysis alone, but through the particular examples and the specific forms of expression found in the great dramatists and novelists and poets.

In her latter career Nussbaum has applied herself to a variety of political and social issues, including problems of inequality, for example in *Sex and Social Justice* (1998). But her more lasting influence on moral philosophy is likely to be her conception of the subject as one which engages with our grasp of the human condition on all levels, emotional as well as intellectual, literary as well as narrowly philosophical. In writing with such insight and honesty about the nature of the good for humankind, she not only illuminates, but exemplifies, that commitment, fraught with risk, that is at the heart of the moral enterprise.

Further reading

Other works include: *The Therapy of Desire* (1994); (ed.), *The Poetics of Therapy* (1990); *Upheavals of Thought: The Intelligence of the Emotions* (2001). See also: D. Statman (ed.), *Moral Luck* (1993); G.W. Harris, *Dignity and Vulnerability* (1997).

JOHN COTTINGHAM

O

OATES, Joyce Carol

1938–

US author

Given the hundred or more titles of fiction, poetry, drama, anthology work, essays and discursive writing, and whose span runs from the stories of *By the North Gate* (1963) through to her working personal credo and *compte rendu, The Faith of a Writer: Life, Craft, Art* (2003), it can little surprise that Joyce Carol Oates immediately stirs cavils. Is this not a writer in over-drive, at risk of being thought a one-woman paper mill? Has she not long ago traded quality for quantity?

However best regarded, the author raised in rural upstate New York, which she pointedly names Eden County in several of her novels, and to a family marked by the Depression and with its own history of traumatic death, cannot be thought other than singular. Educated at Syracuse and Wisconsin Universities, with professorships to follow in Detroit and Windsor, Canada, for three decades she has led the amiable, if busy, life of writer-in-residence at Princeton University where she continues to edit the *Ontario Review: A North American Journal of the Arts* which she and her husband, Raymond Smith, co-founded in 1974. In art as in life she has been nothing if not one of American literature's genuine distance-runners.

A genuinely sustained craftsmanship, moreover, underwrites her stories of an America off-tilt, shadowed in violence and psychological blight, and whether to be met with in family, suburbia, the professions, gangs, guns or drugs. She has made an especial forte of exploring damage in the lives of adolescents and women. New Gothic has been one kind of shorthand for her writing, Oates's intricately observed America of township and country the equivalent of **Faulkner's** Yoknapatawpha or Flannery O'Connor's Georgia. But talk of Gothic serves only to an extent.

An extraordinary range of interests and command of detail mark out her work, be it the pathology of murder in *Expensive People* (1968), family collapse in *Wonderland* (1971), case law as against moral law in *Do With Me What You Will* (1973), the power-play of evangelism with its anticipation of the Jim Jones massacre in Jonestown, Guyana, in *Son of the Morning* (1978), dynastic revenge in *Angel of Light* (1981), or America as staging-ground of gender contests and claims with dips into vampirism, mysticism and the nineteenth century in her strategically feminist trilogy *Bellefleur* (1980), *A Broadsmoor Romance* (1982) and *Mysteries of Winterthurn* (1984). Women's friendship, intense, affirming and unmediated by male intrusion or gaze, lies at the centre of *Solstice* (1985). Boxing, an interest from childhood as borne out in her friendship with Mike Tyson and the reportage of *On Boxing* (1987), plays a role also in the **Jamesian** chronicle of generational time-and-change she creates in *You Must Remember This* (1987). Race as America's perennial haunting, its historical secret sharer, lies at the heart of the 1950s black–white love affair of *Because it is Bitter and Because it is My Heart* (1990).

Few of her writings have quite shown the finesse of *Black Water* (1992) as drawn from the Senator Edward Kennedy–Mary Jo Kopechne scandal, a woman's violent drowning reconstructed as both visionary nightmare and identity lost inside the totemism of media and politics. Later fiction reworks the Jeffrey Dahmer case, for all its macabre sexuality a deliberately de-theatricalizing story of cannibalism and lobotomy, in *Zombie* (1995); rape and its ambient middle–class family repercussion in her best-selling *We Were the Mulvaneys* (1996); and Marilyn Monroe as America's ultimate, near transcendent icon of the beauty-myth, and what it refracts about the culture-at-large, in her epic fiction of fact *Blonde* (2002).

Most of Oates's best strengths, her grasp of character psychology and setting, the control of rhythm and viewpoint, are to be found in her short stories. Few work to keener or more representative effect than 'Where Are You Going, Where Have You Been?' which Oates based on the so-called Pied Piper murders in Tucson, Arizona. The encounter of pretty, boy-struck Ellie, fifteen years of age, with the chill, beguiling Arnold Friend, their back-and-forth talk, and the denouement of her teenager's final sexual sacrifice to save her family from murder even as he dawdles over her with talk of 'My sweet little blue-eyed girl', depends upon a surest gathering pace. It bears the winning hallmarks of the craft she calls for in her writer's manual and autobiographical essay-collection *(Woman) Writer: Occasions and Opportunities* (1988).

Further reading

See: Greg Johnson, *Understanding Joyce Carol Oates* (1987), *Joyce Carol Oates: A Study of the Short Fiction* (1994) and *Invisible Writer: A Biography of Joyce Carol Oates* (1998); Linda W. Wagner (ed.), *Critical Essays on Joyce Carol Oates* (1979); Ellen G. Friedman, *Joyce Carol Oates* (1980); Eileen Teper Bender, *Artist in Residence* (1987); Nancy Ann Watanabe, *Love Eclipsed: Joyce Carol Oates's Faustian Moral Vision* (1988); Lee Milazzo (ed.),

Conversations with Joyce Carol Oates (1989); Joanne V. Creighton, *Joyce Carol Oates: Novels of The Middle Years* (1992); Brenda Daly, *Lavish Self-Divisions: The Novels of Joyce Carol Oates* (1996).

A. ROBERT LEE

ŌE KENZABURŌ

1935–

Japanese author

When Ōe Kenzaburō was awarded the Nobel Prize for Literature in 1994, the accompanying citation referred specifically to the 'poetic force' that the author deploys in his literature to 'create an imagined world where life and myth condense to form a disturbing picture of the human predicament today'. The comment is incisive: Ōe's oeuvre, while always challenging and often shocking, retains a focus on the difficult moral questions of the day, as it attempts to question the evolving meaning of being Japanese, initially as the nation sought to come to terms with defeat, nuclear devastation and the need for rapid economic regeneration and, thereafter, with the search for spiritual direction among Japan's disaffected youth.

Born in a small mountain village in Shikoku, the smallest and most rural of Japan's four main islands, Ōe's literary considerations of the human condition can be seen as premised on his own experience of life on the periphery; indeed, some of his most memorable protagonists are themselves marginal figures attempting to make sense of the dictates of mainstream society. For Ōe, moreover, this divide was brought into sharper focus, first by his experience of primary school education under the relentless scrutiny of Japan's military authorities and subsequently by his decision to relocate to Tokyo to study French literature.

The majority of Ōe's early protagonists are typical post-war males. Secular individuals, torn between personal desires and an awareness of wider responsibilities to society, many find themselves confronted by a series of seemingly impossible choices over which they struggle to exercise their own free will. Here, too, echoes of Ōe's own personal experience are never far beneath the surface, leading several critics to portray Ōe as a natural successor to the pre-war generation of *shishōsetsuka* ('I-novelists'). The comparison may be expedient, but it masks a complexity in the relationship between author and his creations – and a sharply ideological intent – not identified with the traditional 'I-novel'.

The autobiographical element is particularly prominent in Ōe's early work, with 'Prize Stock' ('Shiiku', 1958, trans. 1981), the early story for which Ōe was awarded the prestigious Akutagawa Prize for fiction, a prime example. Here, the unremarkable life of a small Shikoku village is disturbed by the arrival of an African-American soldier captured during the intense fighting towards the end of the war. Initially, the villagers 'adopt' the soldier, whom they come to see as a 'beautiful animal'; and when the order comes from above that he is to be killed, a scuffle ensues in which the father of the young protagonist succeeds in severing his son's hand along with the soldier's head. The allegory is rich, as the broken relationship that ensues between father and son is equated with the loss of the father figure, the Emperor, following renunciation of the latter's divine status after defeat in the war.

Another issue introduced here and pursued in more detail in Ōe's subsequent writing is that of mainstream society's inhuman treatment of the disempowered – and this theme lies at the heart of the three works, written during the 1960s, with which Ōe secured his international reputation. The first, *A Personal Matter* (*Kojinteki na taiken*, 1964, trans. 1968), was penned in the aftermath of the birth, with a severe brain hernia, of Ōe's son, Hikari. Reduced to desperation at the sight of his son, the protagonist, Bird, initially seeks solace in the sexual embrace of a former girlfriend, and the two contemplate abandoning the baby to the whims of a neighbourhood quack doctor and escaping to Africa. Eventually, however, Bird is obliged to confront reality – and the responsibilities of fatherhood – and, although the ending has been much criticized for its incongruity with the savagery that has preceded it, the work helped secure Ōe's reputation as a masterful portrayer of the human psychological drama. Shortly after publication of this work, Ōe, already a noted activist for several left-wing causes, made a trip to Hiroshima where his interviews with several *hibakusha* (A-bomb victims) resulted in *Hiroshima Notes* (*Hiroshima nōto*, 1965, trans. 1982), his second work dealing with those struggling on the margins. Before long, however, these enquiries led Ōe to a consideration of Japan's often awkward political position *vis-à-vis* the outside world – and the result was *The Silent Cry* (*Man'en gannen no futtobōru*, 1967, trans. 1974), a lengthy novel which, in its depiction of Takashi attempting to foment a revolution in a rural Shikoku village in order to reinstate a pre-modern Japanese sense of community, evokes the arrival of Commodore Perry in Yokohama Bay a century earlier as well as the US–Japan Security Treaty riots of the 1960s. Here as elsewhere, however, the more Ōe explores the tensions and contradictions between centre and periphery, the more he discerns there, not so much a straight inequality, but rather a genuinely symbiotic relationship.

In 1970, Ōe was as stunned as the rest of Japan by the death by ritual disembowelling of his literary nemesis **Mishima Yukio**, and in the years that followed he proceeded to write a series of novels, epitomised by *The Day He Himself Shall Wipe My Tears Away* (*Waga namida o nuguitamau hi*, 1972, trans. 1977) in which he sought to critique what he saw as the latter's romanticized, single-minded fanaticism towards the emperor system. At the same time, in works such as *The Game of Contemporaneity* (*Dōjidai geemu*, 1979), he frequently resorted to inspiration from the folklore and legends of his native Shikoku as an antidote to the pernicious influence of the myths that Mishima and others had sought to weave around the imperial institution.

In all of this, there is an increasingly spiritual tenor to Ōe's more 'mature' writing, this being particularly evident in *The Burning Green Tree* (*Moeagaru midori no ki*, 1993–5), the work often cited as his 'lifework' and which best betrays the oft-cited influence on his work of the likes of **Norman Mailer** and Flannery O'Connor, as well as **Yeats** and Dante. Here, Ōe's lifelong social focus leads to an exploration, through the image of the 'church of the green tree', of the frustration evidenced by a segment of Japanese youth at the lack of an obvious viable future, their lack of clear purpose resulting in the contemporary boom in the 'new, new' religions. Ōe's concern here is with the messianic and often apocalyptic messages spawned by these cults, the decision of those involved to embrace destruction subtly contrasted with the quiet yet desperate optimism he had earlier encountered in the *hibakusha*.

Following receipt of the Nobel Prize in 1994, Ōe vowed to renounce literature. It was not long, however, before he returned to his tried and trusted vocation, his 1999 novel, *Somersault* (*Chūgaeri*, trans. 2003), offering novel treatment of many of his earlier concerns.

Further reading

After Ōe received the Nobel Prize, there was a boom in translations of his work into a number of languages. Most of his major work is now available in translation. For critical discussion of Ōe's work, see Susan Napier, *Escape from the Wasteland: Romanticism and Realism in the Fiction of Mishima Yukio and Ōe Kenzaburō*, 1991; and Michiko Wilson, *The Marginal World of Ōe Kenzaburō: A Study in Themes and Techniques*, 1986.

MARK WILLIAMS

OLDENBURG, Claes

1929–

US artist

'Everything I do is completely original – I made it up when I was a little kid.' Born in Stockholm, Oldenburg was brought up in Chicago from 1936. Slightly an outsider, he created an imaginary island, Neubern, a coherent parallel reality worked out in minute detail, which contained the germs of most of his later work.

After interdisciplinary studies at Yale, he worked as a crime reporter while attending night classes at the Art Institute of Chicago. Arriving in New York in 1956, it was the life of the slums that inspired his exhibition/environment *The Street* (1960). Next year he set up *The Store*, in which were exhibited parodies of clothes, food and other objects, for example *Blue Shirt, Striped Tie* and *Slice of Yellow Pie* (both 1961). The splashed paintwork on this pseudo-merchandise was a recognition of Abstract Expressionism, then the dominant style in avant-garde painting. But Oldenburg's involvement with vulgar, everyday reality was in deliberate opposition to abstract art's hermeticism. Inspired by Kaprow's idea that **Pollock's** actions were more significant than the finished product, he staged several Happenings at The Store and later elsewhere.

An important exponent of Happenings, Oldenburg became, with **Warhol**, one of the principal figures of American Pop Art. Invited to exhibit uptown, he continued to make parodies of consumer goods, but glossier and more commercial-looking than before, and without the splashes. He played with textures, creating a hard, geometrical *Bedroom Ensemble* (1963) and, by contrast, 'soft machines', for example the *Soft Typewriter* (1963) and *Soft Dormeyer Mixer* (1965). He also played with scale, as in the *Floorburger (Giant Hamburger)* (1962) and *Giant Pool Balls* (1967). The interest in scale led on to designs for colossal monuments, of which to begin with very few were executed. Unrealized proposals from the 1960s include a *Teddy Bear* (1965), at least the size of the surrounding buildings, for Central Park, New York, and a *Ball* (1967) for the River Thames, London, like a vast lavatory cistern, rising and falling with the tide. The first large-scale project that was realized was *Lipstick (Ascending) on Caterpillar Tracks* (1969–74) for Yale University, a symbol of love rising from death made in the context of the Vietnam War.

Since 1976 Oldenburg has collaborated with Coosje van Bruggen, whom he married in 1977. They have concentrated on making sculptures for specific outdoor urban sites in which familiar objects are vastly magnified, simultaneously parodying and extending the monumental tradition. These include: *Clothespin* (1976) for Philadelphia; *Flashlight* (1981) for Las Vegas; *Dropped Bowl with Scattered Slices and Peels* (1990) for Miami; *Inverted Collar and Tie* (1994) for Frankfurt-am-Main; *Saw, Sawing* (1996) for Tokyo; and *Cupid's Span* (2002), a vast bow and arrow, for San Francisco. Sometimes the sculptures interact with a building, as in *Knife Slicing through Wall* (1986) in Los Angeles, and *Dropped Cone* (2001), a massive inverted ice cream cone on top of a building in Cologne. The work most fully integrated with architecture is *Binoculars* (1991) which forms the central segment of a building designed by **Frank Gehry** in Venice, California. These works constitute a major contribution to public art.

Oldenburg has always wanted to be fully involved with the real world, to touch and be touched. The tactility in his work is therapeutic both for himself and for society, especially American society. As an immigrant, he was fascinated by everything typically American and in his creative-destructive alter ego, Ray Gun, he semi-ironically fused himself with American maleness. He continues to celebrate the democratic aspiration to freedom but, through his humour, undermines the repressions of a culture both puritanical and phallic, proposing instead a more complete, childlike, tactile freedom, related to **Freud's** concept of 'polymorphous perversity'. Satirical and mystical, realistic and fantastic, personal and public, Oldenburg's complex art aims at a synthesis completely human.

Further reading

Other works include: *Injun and Other Histories* (1966), *Notes* (1968) and *Raw Notes* (1973). The classic text on his early work is Barbara Rose,

Claes Oldenburg (1970). *Claes Oldenburg: An Anthology* (1995), published by the Solomon R. Guggenheim Museum, with texts by Oldenburg and others, is very useful, as is Germano Celant (ed.), *Claes Oldenburg, Coosje van Bruggen* (1999). See also: Richard Morphet, *Claes Oldenburg and Van Bruggen* (2002).

GRAY WATSON

O'NEILL, Eugene Gladstone
1888–1953
US dramatist

To all intents and purposes modern American drama began with Eugene O'Neill. The son of a famous actor father, he began writing in a tuberculosis sanatorium where he spent six months in 1912. His first produced play, *Bound East for Cardiff*, staged by the Provincetown Players in the Wharf Theatre in 1916, marked a sharp break with a theatre which for the most part had simply exchanged the melodrama of action for a melodrama of character, in replacing the sentimentalities of nineteenth-century popular art with a naturalism which O'Neill rejected as the mere 'holding of the family Kodak up to ill-nature'. He wished to transcend 'the banality of surfaces' and in his early sea plays he offered tone poems, lyric portraits of marginal characters straining to make sense of a life whose dominant mood was one of loss and whose central need was for a sense of belonging.

In part this sense of alienation was a product of social divisiveness, a division between the classes, which he dramatized in *The Hairy Ape* (1922), and between races, which he presented in *All God's Chillun* (1924). But this merely concealed a more fundamental sense of abandonment.

Accused of pessimism, he insisted that he was concerned with the tragic spirit, for 'to me, the tragic alone has that significant beauty which is truth. It is the meaning of life – and the hope.' And tragedy, for him, emerged essentially from the gulf between human aspirations and their consistently denied fulfilment – transcendence deriving from the greatness of the dream and the persistence with which it is pursued. But the same gulf which could generate tragedy could equally create a fierce undertow of absurdity, and in fact it is this rather than any sense of tragic transcendence which really typifies his work.

For the transfiguring Apollonian vision, the dream designed to aestheticize life and give it the shape which in reality it lacked, devolved all too often into simple self-deception. More often than not his plays are not about a glorious struggle against fate, an heroic pursuit of the unattainable. They are concerned with the desperate illusions which are the acknowledgement of defeat. It is difficult, indeed, to think of any of his plays which adequately expressed this potential. In *Beyond the Horizon* (1920) the visions are wilfully abandoned, as fate intervenes to deflect the aspiring mind into simple irony. *The Emperor Jones* (1920) is an account of the collapse of illusion and character alike. *Anna Christie* (1921) pitches wilful sentimentalities against determinism. Yank, in *The Hairy Ape*, is ironically transfigured but his vision is hopelessly naive and self-destructive in a way which has very little to do with the tragic. Even *Desire Under the Elms* (1924) and *Mourning Becomes Electra* (1931) offer psycho-pathology in the place of tragic fatalism.

But his talent lay elsewhere. He was a determined experimenter. In *The Emperor Jones*, for example, he mobilized the *mise-en-scène*, making it an active element in a play which concerned itself with the deconstruction of character and language. Brilliantly original, it dramatized a personal and racial reversion to archetype. In *The Great God Brown* (1926) he used masks to dramatize the public and private selves of his characters and in *Strange Interlude* (1928) breathed life into the dramatic aside, seeing this as an apt symbol of the conscious and unconscious self.

Few of his plays were without flaws. His enthusiasms were seldom less than total, whether it be for such devices as those identified above or for the work and ideas of Schopenhauer, **Nietzsche**, **Strindberg**,

Freud and **Jung**. Their mark is clear on his work. Too often, indeed, character became a function of idea and subject deferred to method. But he was a writer of genuine originality and energy. His range was phenomenal and in his last plays, plays written as he wrestled with disease, he created some of the most powerful works of modern drama.

The Iceman Cometh (1939) is set in Harry Hope's New York bar. In many ways we are apparently offered an absurdist vision. A group of individuals are suspended in a timeless void, cut off from past and future. Their vulnerability, the irony of their situation, seems simply exacerbated by action. Thus they pass the time sitting motionless, using drink to deny the consciousness which is the source of their pain. Virtually all of them are betrayers. They have failed the causes which they have served, the people they have loved, the world which in their youth they had perceived as opportunity but which now they regard as a lost cause. Their drunkenness, their retreat into self, into unreality, is a protection against knowledge of that imperfection. And yet there is a crucial connection between their imperfection and the compassion which is equally generated by despair and which becomes a primary value.

The Iceman Cometh was, O'Neill suggested, a denial of any other experience of faith in his work and it was so primarily through his acceptance of that progression identified by **Albert Camus** when he asserted that 'The end of the movement of absurdity, of rebellion, etc. . . . is compassion . . . that is to say, in the last analysis, love.' Certainly his dedication to his greatest play, *Long Day's Journey into Night* (1939–41), speaks of a 'faith in love' inspired by his marriage to Carlotta, which enables him to face his dead in a play written 'with deep pity and understanding and forgiveness'. It is a play which re-creates his own painful family experiences. Set in 1912, the year of his own attempted suicide, it is an attempt to understand himself and those to whom he was irrevocably tied by fate and by love. It is the finest and most powerful play to have come out of America.

Further reading

See *The Plays of Eugene O'Neill* (3 vols, 1951). The principal biographies are by Arthur and Barbara Gelb (1974) and by Louis Sheaffer (1968). See also: Stephen Black, *Eugene O'Neill: Beyond Mourning and Tragedy* (1999); Travis Bogard, *Contour in Time: The Plays of Eugene O'Neill* (revised edn, 1988); Michael Mannheim (ed.), *The Cambridge Companion to O'Neill* (1998).

C.W.E. BIGSBY

ONO, Yoko

1933–

Japanese artist

While Yoko Ono is known throughout the world as John Lennon's widow (The **Beatles**), she is to be regarded as an artist in her own right, working in a number of different media, including performance art. As the most celebrated Japanese woman of her era, who has deliberately and successfully broken with the traditions and customs that conventionally constrict the Japanese female, she has, too, made a startling contribution to feminism, albeit through implicit rather than explicit means. Her advocacy of peace, on the other hand, is explicit, and has been fully articulated through her work.

Ono was born in Tokyo, the oldest of three children. After surviving World War II and the bombing of the Japanese capital, she moved with her family to New York State. Studying music in New York City, and writing her first compositions, she mingled freely with avant-garde composers, soon marrying Toshi Ichiyanagi. Already, though, she was turning her mind to art, and her downtown apartment on Chambers Street became something of a *salon*. Inevitably, perhaps, she was drawn to, and became associated with, the Fluxus art group (George Maciunas), encouraging her to further widen the means of her own creative expression, which now for the first time included early versions of some of the 'performances' which later gained her notoriety.

The fun-loving but haphazard aesthetics of Fluxus, together with its connection to the American composer **John Cage**, and its commitment to beneficial social change, struck deep chords with Ono. In 1961 she exhibited a series of 'instruction paintings' at the AG Gallery, part-owned by Maciunas. These consisted of proto-minimalist canvases that bore sometimes ironic injunctions to the viewer on their use, and established Ono's artistic credentials. To underscore that the instructions embodied ideas and did not function as aesthetic or graphic representations, she insisted that they were typed. Later, after the AG Gallery had closed and Fluxus had become internationalized, she removed the artwork from the paintings, and presented the instructions as objects, thus overturning the traditional relationship between object and commentary.

Shortly after Ono divorced Ichiyanagi and briefly returned to Japan, marrying Tony Cox, a musician and film producer by whom she had a daughter, Kyoko, in 1963. In 1964 she returned to New York, rejoined Fluxus, and redoubled her productivity, adding poetry-writing to the lengthening list of her accomplishments. In 1966 she visited London to attend a symposium for the 'Destruction of Art', and there performed for the first time *Cut Piece*. In this Ono, still a young woman, knelt on the stage as members of the audience were invited to remove pieces of her clothing with pairs of scissors. Thirty-eight years later, and approaching seventy, she returned to London for a repeat performance, consciously substituting her known iconic status for a lost youth.

The original performance of *Cut Piece* resulted in Ono being invited to mount an exhibition of her work at London's Indica Gallery, and it was at the preview of this show that she met an admiring John Lennon, seven years her junior.

In 1969 Ono and Lennon married, following a second divorce. A mutual interest in each other's work led to collaboration in recordings, performances and events.

Famously they spent their honeymoon in a hotel room in New York, staging a 'Bed-In for Peace' attended by the press and media, partly in protest against the Vietnam War, but also against the proliferation of nuclear weapons during the Cold War.

Ono's conceptual activities fed Lennon's desire to make a more conceptual kind of music, and her influence is present in much of his later solo work. Together they released new albums, made films and generally confounded their respective audiences, along the way forming the Plastic Ono Band. Conversely, their close relationship, viewed by outsiders as cloying, was held responsible by an ungenerous public for the break-up of the Beatles, with Ono being obliged to bear the brunt of media censure.

Fans of the 'Fab Four' never forgave her, even though in the 1970s Lennon produced much of his best work. Resilient by nature, Ono too continued with her own work, publishing a book, *Grapefruit*, in 1970, and releasing her own solo album, *Approximately Infinite Universe*, in 1972. Press and media attention did, however, get to them both, and in part explained a temporary separation. But in 1975 Ono gave birth to a son, Sean Lennon, and the couple were 'together' until Lennon's murder outside their home in New York in December 1980.

Ono had now to contend with her husband's followers, as well as her own grief. Steadfast in her values, she has, ever since, adroitly managed Lennon's legacy while sometimes exhibiting new works of her own, turning her apparent isolation into an ambiguous art object in itself.

Further reading

Other works include: *Yes Yoko Ono* (2000) is a comprehensive catalogue of Yoko Ono's output published in conjunction with a major retrospective of her work mounted by the Japan Society of New York in the same year. See also Barbara Haskell, *Yoko Ono: Arias and Objects* (1991).

ANNE K. SWARTZ

OPPENHEIMER, J. Robert

1904–67

US nuclear physicist

While the development and first use of the nuclear bomb was a collaborative effort between America's political administration, its military and a large group of scientists, it is J. Robert Oppenheimer who must forever bear the stigma of being its principal architect. Whether or not he quoted a verse from the Baghavad Ghita – 'I am become death, the destroyer of worlds' – after his atom bomb was successfully tested in New Mexico is doubted: he may just have said 'It worked!' But no other words could have been more appropriate. Science, the handmaiden of warfare throughout history, had finally revealed its potential to ruin just about everything; and the man best placed to prevent the bomb's deployment preferred instead to watch the deadliest of research programmes reach fruition.

It is perhaps an irony that Oppenheimer came of Jewish German stock, in an era when the Jewish people suffered the Nazi Holocaust. His father was a wealthy New York textile merchant, his mother a painter. As a child and as a student he was exceptionally clever, graduating *summa cum laude* in chemistry at Harvard University. Immediately his attention turned to theoretical physics, and he packed off to England, where, aged just twenty-two, he gained a doctorate at Cambridge University's Cavendish Institute, under the supervision of J.J. Thomson and the influence of Ernest Rutherford.

He next attended the University of Göttingen, in Germany, to study quantum theory under Max Born, with whom he developed the 'Born–Oppenheimer approximation', which distinguished nuclear from electron motion. Returning to America in 1927 he temporarily became a staff member at Harvard before joining the California Institute of Technology (Caltech), a department of the University of California at Berkeley. There he remained nineteen years.

Something of a scientific gadfly, he broadened his interests to include, as well as nuclear physics, spectroscopy and astrophysics – he was among the first, if not *the* first, to posit the existence of black holes in deep space. At Berkeley, Oppenheimer became intimate with Ernest O. Lawrence, who had established the Radiation Laboratory that was already attracting the attention of the US army, and which provided a link to Washington. As early as 1939 President **F.D. Roosevelt** created the Uranium Committee specifically to investigate ways of utilizing nuclear physics for military purposes. Out of these circumstances was born the Manhattan Project, tasked with fast-tracking the production of a nuclear bomb, headed up by General Leslie R. Groves – who also oversaw the building of the Pentagon – with Oppenheimer as its science director.

Oppenheimer assembled a team of front-line scientists, whose members eventually included, *inter alia*, Hans Berthe, Enrico Fermi, Edward Teller, Victor Weisskopf and Robert R. Wilson. At first research was carried out at various academic departments across America, but for the sake of expediency, and also security, a secret centre was built at Los Alamos in New Mexico.

Impetus for the Manhattan Project came from intelligence reports that **Hitler's** Germany was pursuing the same goal. The first nuclear bomb, nicknamed 'Trinity' by Oppenheimer, was exploded at Alamohardo on 16 July 1945, almost two months after Germany had finally capitulated, and in the knowledge that the German nuclear programme was stillborn. Less than a month later, on 5 August, a uranium bomb ('Little Boy') was dropped on Hiroshima. On 8 August a second, plutonium bomb ('Fat Boy') was dropped on Nagasaki, almost directly above the largest Christian community in Japan. All told, as a result of both the immediate blasts and long-term radiation sickness, several hundred thousand non-combatants died.

During the lead-up to these deployments fierce arguments had raged at Los Alamos: would a nuclear explosion ignite the whole of Earth's atmosphere? would it not be better simply to intimidate Japan by dropping the

bombs away from civilian centres? On both counts, as project leader, Oppenheimer argued passionately in favour of the actual outcome.

Oppenheimer showed some, but not overwhelming, remorse for what he had achieved. After the Pacific War ended, he became chief consultant to the Atomic Energy Commission, set up to regulate the further use and development of nuclear technology, and thereby hoping to stop the USSR from acquiring a nuclear capability. For a while he opposed production of the greatly more destructive hydrogen bomb, but in 1951 political pressure made him acquiesce, particularly after Russia acquired the capability it sought and the nuclear arms race had become a reality. In Oppenheimer's own words, the hydrogen bomb was 'technically so sweet'.

By then Oppenheimer had moved to Princeton University. There was, however, a fly in his ointment. In the 1930s Oppenheimer's circle had included several communists, and although he never joined the party himself, it was thought he had been a sympathizer. In 1953 he fell victim to Senator Joe McCarthy's anti-communist witch-hunt. Although he was not arraigned before the infamous Un-American Activities Committee, President Eisenhower revoked his security clearance, and Oppenheimer, while remaining academically employed, took no further part in military research.

Still in his middle age, Oppenheimer became increasingly reclusive, spending much of his time on a beach in the Virgin Islands. A partial rehabilitation came in 1963, when **J.F. Kennedy** bestowed upon him the Enrico Fermi Award for his contribution to theoretical physics. Four years later he died of cancer of the throat.

As a man, Oppenheimer was unstable. Given to depressions, he once attempted to strangle a friend – Francis Ferguson – in Paris. But like many depressives, he had a crusading energy; and like many crusaders, he was unable to take a rounded view of the likely consequences of what he did.

Further reading

See: Peter Goodchild, *J. Robert Oppenheimer: Shatterer of Worlds* (1981); Ken Bird and Martin J. Sherwin, *American Prometheus: The Triumph and Tragedy of J. Robert Oppenheimer* (2005); David C. Cassidy, *J. Robert Oppenheimer and the American Century* (2005). See also: John Hersey, *Hiroshima* (1946).

JUSTIN WINTLE

ORWELL, George

1903–50

English essayist and novelist

Orwell's real name was Eric Blair and he was born in India, the son of an official in the Opium Service, and was brought to England by his mother at the age of three. He gained a scholarship to St Cyprian's, a fashionable preparatory school where Cyril Connolly was among his contemporaries. His family were of what he called 'the lower-upper middle class', that is the 'upper-middle class without money'. He was crammed for a scholarship to Eton but did little work there, already being something of an odd man out and against the system. His most brilliant contemporaries went on to Cambridge, but he entered the Burma police, a very unprestigious part of the Imperial Civil Service. He endured it for five years but resigned in 1927, having come to hate the social pretentiousness of the British in Burma and their indifference to Burmese culture. All this comes out in his first published novel, some say his best pre-war novel, *Burmese Days* (1935).

Burmese Days is often taken to be socialist because it is anti-imperialist. But between 1927 and 1934 Orwell often called himself, when other young writers asked 'Where do you stand?', simply 'a Tory anarchist'. He was first an individualist who resented one man or one culture imposing its values on another; and though he was familiar with socialist arguments about economic exploitation, he did not fully agree with them until 1935 and 1936. Immediately after his return from Burma he tried to write novels, which have not survived, and published a few essays, poems and book reviews. Searching for material and wondering whether English working men suffered like the Burmans, he began spasmodic but intense spells of living among tramps. He taught some poorly paid jobs in awful private schools and knew poverty. He ran out of money while spending a year and a half writing in Paris, worked as a dishwasher, and lived in a Parisian slum, all of which experience led to his first and characteristic published book, *Down and Out in Paris and London* (1933). Victor Gollancz published it and had great faith in Orwell as a writer, especially as a novelist, though political differences finally led to a rupture. He suggested the theme of *The Road to Wigan Pier* (1937) to Orwell, who wrote it as a brilliant account of how the unemployed live, adding an eccentric but provocative section announcing both his conversion to socialism and the indifference to freedom of most socialist intellectuals.

He went to Spain to fight, not to write, but *Homage to Catalonia* (1938) resulted. It sold badly at the time but is now seen as both a classic and an honest description of war, and as one of the shrewdest of polemics against the **Stalinist** attempt to dominate both the Spanish Republic and the whole international Left. For a brief period until 1939 he was militantly anti-war, close to pacifism, a member of the Independent Labour Party, often mistakenly called – like his new publisher Frederic Warburg – **Trotskyite**, because they were strongly left-wing, egalitarian and both anti-Labour Party and anti-Communist. Gollancz continued to publish his novels, *A Clergyman's Daughter* (1935), *Keep the Aspidistra Flying* (1936) and *Coming Up for Air* (1939). Only the latter, written in the middle-brow tradition of **Dickens** and **H.G. Wells**, came up to the now extraordinarily high standard of his documentaries and his essays. The war had a great influence on him. He saw the need to defend even a shoddy and hypocritical democracy against Fascism, but thought, as in *The Lion and the Unicorn* (1941), that a socialist revolution was taking place in the ranks of the British army. He rescued patriotism from its identification with nationalism, trying to show that its roots were radical as much as Conservative. Being tubercular, he was not accepted for military service and wasted two years in the BBC's Far Eastern Service before becoming literary editor of *Tribune*, a wholly congenial post with Aneurin Bevan as the editor. He was an 'English Socialist' of the kind of Michael Foot and Bevan: libertarian, egalitarian, but quite untheoretical, almost anti-theoretical. Early in the war he conceived a grand design for a three-volume novel of social analysis and warning which would deal with the decay of the old order, the betrayal of the revolution and what an English totalitarianism would be like if it ever came to power. This design never came to be, but the pre-war novels have some such connection with his masterpiece *Animal Farm* (1945) and his most famous work, *1984* (1949). *Animal Farm* is a story of the good revolution of the animals betrayed by the (Stalinist) pigs. It is not a parable of the impossibility of revolution; and *1984* is *not a prophecy* of what will happen but a satiric warning of what could happen if power is pursued for its own sake – despite some right-wing American critics reading him in a contrary sense. His values remained those of a left-wing socialist until his early death from tuberculosis; only his hope of seeing 'the Republic' emerge in our times declined.

There is so much more in Orwell than his books. Some critics plausibly see his genius as an essayist. 'A Hanging' and 'Shooting an Elephant' are both ambiguously short-story or personal recollections, but both didactic or moral writing of great stature. His *Tribune* 'As I Please' column virtually invented mixed column journalism, polemical and discursive. Rich humour is found in nearly all his essays, as when he would mock the fierce readers of *Tribune* by describing the mating habits of a common toad or the virtues of a sixpenny Woolworth's rose, all of which would form part of the good life, even in the classless society.

He wrote major essays on censorship, plain language, the social beliefs of boys' magazines, and on pornography and violence: he believed passionately in liberty, but also in condemning the bad both morally and aesthetically. Literary criticism would be the less without his seminal essays on Dickens, Swift and in 'Inside the Whale' on the failings of the intellectuals in the 1930s. The *Collected Essays, Journalism and Letters* (4 vols, 1968), edited by his second wife and widow, Sonia Orwell, together with Ian Angus, though not in fact 'complete', for the first time enabled the remarkable range of his essay writing to be appreciated. Unfortunately by 1968 many distinguished critics had committed themselves to positions based on little more than reading his books. Almost certainly he is the greatest English polemical writer since Swift, and a master of simple prose, someone whose style has had more influence than any over his contemporaries: plain, easy, colloquial, yet precise and capable of great variations between the formal, the informal, the leisurely and the excited. He always distinguished between good writers and bad men; he insisted against the Left that **Pound** and **Eliot** were great writers, though he condemned them as moralists. Those who admire Orwell's plain speaking against Communism may need reminding that his values became and remained Socialist through and through.

He wrote well on national character and is rightly seen, for his style, his common-sense philosophy, his simple way of living and love of the countryside, and his somewhat eccentric preoccupations with little things as well as great moral issues, as essentially an English writer. Above all else, he said of himself that he was 'a political writer', with a hatred of 'totalitarianism' and a love of 'democratic Socialism'. But in the phrase 'political writer', the integrity of each word is of equal value.

Further reading

See: Richard Rees, *George Orwell: Fugitive from the Camp of Victory* (1962); George Woodcock, *The Crystal Spirit* (1966); William Steinhoff, *George Orwell* and the Origins of 1984 (1975); George Orwell: The Critical Heritage, ed. Jeffrey Meyers (1976); Bernard Crick, George Orwell: A Life (1980); J.R. Hammond, A George Orwell Companion (1982); M. Shelden, Orwell (1991); P. Davison, George Orwell (1996).

BERNARD CRICK

OWEN, Wilfred
1893–1918
English poet

Brought up in the back streets of Birkenhead and Shrewsbury, where his father was assistant superintendent of the railways, Wilfred Owen first became aware of his poetic calling at the age of ten or eleven. The dominant presence of his childhood was his devout and adoring mother, who hoped he might eventually enter the church. It was as a result of her influence that, having failed to win a scholarship to London University, he accepted an unpaid post as lay assistant to the vicar of Dunsden, Oxfordshire, in return for board, lodging and coaching towards a second attempt at a university scholarship. Fifteen months in the vicarage convinced him that his belief in evangelical religion was less strong than his allegiance to poetry, and he left in 1913 to teach English in France, first at a Berlitz school, and subsequently as a private tutor. For more than a year after the outbreak of war he could not decide whether or not to join up, but in September 1915 returned to England and enlisted in the Artists' Rifles. Plunged into the battle of the Somme in January 1917, he was involved in heavy fighting and in May was found to be suffering from neurasthenia, or shell-shock, and invalided back by stages to Craiglockhart War Hospital, near Edinburgh. There he met Siegfried Sassoon and, largely as a result of the older man's encouragement and practical criticism, abandoned the sub-Keatsian luxuriance of his early style in favour of the disciplined sensuality, the passionate intelligence characteristic of the poems written during the fourteen months that remained to him. Sassoon's influence is discernible in the shock

tactics, and especially in the explosive colloquialisms, of such of Owen's first 'war poems' as 'The Dead-Beat' and 'Dulce et Decorum Est', but he soon found his own more meditative and resonant voice.

The ten months following his discharge from Craiglockhart in November 1917 were the most creative of his life. He was based in Scarborough and Ripon and spent a succession of leaves in London, where he was introduced to a wider circle of literary acquaintance that included Arnold Bennett, **H.G. Wells**, Robert Ross, Osbert Sitwell and Charles Scott Moncrieff. The last three and certain of Owen's other friends were homosexual, and the extent to which he came to acknowledge and indulge his own latent homosexual tendencies at this time is a matter of speculation. What is certain, however, is that he wrote more eloquently than other poets of the tragedy of young men killed in battle because he felt that tragedy more acutely.

He was being considered for a home posting when Sassoon returned wounded to England, and Owen decided that his duty as a poet lay in taking his friend's place as a witness to the suffering of the troops. He crossed to France in September 1918, was awarded the Military Cross some weeks later, and seven days before the Armistice was killed.

He lived to see only five of his poems in print, but the selections edited by Sassoon (1920) and Edmund Blunden (1931) were a potent influence on the left-wing poets of the 1930s, who hailed him as hero and martyr for his stand against 'the old men' responsible for the conduct of the war, against whose successors they were themselves in revolt. Owen's use of pararhyme (*escaped/scooped, groined/ground*) was widely emulated; the fragmentary Preface to his poems became one of the most famous of literary manifestos; and the compassion, learnt among the poor at Dunsden and expressed in his poems from the Western Front, reached an international audience as the basis of **Benjamin Britten's** *War Requiem* (1962).

Further reading

See: C. Day Lewis (ed.), *The Collected Poems of Wilfred Owen* (1963) and Harold Owen and John Bell (eds), *Wilfred Owen: Collected Letters* (1967). About Owen: D.S.R. Welland, *Wilfred Owen: A Critical Study* (1960, revised 1978); Harold Owen, *Journey from Obscurity* (3 vols, 1963, 1964, 1965); Jon Stallworthy, *Wilfred Owen: A Biography* (1974); Dominic Hibberd, *Wilfred Owen* (1975); M. Williams, *Wilfred Owen* (1993); D. Kerr, *Wilfred Owen's Voices* (1993).

JON STALLWORTHY

P

PALMER, Samuel

1805–81

English painter

Palmer's present reputation rests overwhelmingly on the works he produced between 1825 and 1832 at Shoreham, Kent, some of which are among the finest jewels of English landscape painting.

He was born and brought up on the still rural edges of London and Kent. Although his parents were Baptists, Palmer's liking for tradition and ritual led him to join the Church of England. He acquired very early a love for poetry, his favourites being Virgil and Milton, both of whom could endow familiar country scenes with spiritual significance. His older friend John Linnell perceptively steered him away from contemporary landscape painting, which had little to offer him, towards the early Italian, Flemish and German old masters, especially Dürer. In 1824, Linnell introduced him to William Blake, whose ideas on art, poetry and religion were to be crucial to Palmer throughout his life; and it was in the same year that he first visited Shoreham. From 1825 dates a series of works in sepia, including *The Valley Thick with Corn,* which depict nature in all its fecundity and possess an almost hallucinatory intensity. Palmer went to live in Shoreham, which he called the 'Valley of Vision', in 1826 and was joined there by a circle of like-minded friends calling themselves the 'Ancients', who were united by their admiration for Blake.

Palmer's Shoreham paintings combine an accuracy of detail with an extraordinary imaginative freedom. The compositions make use of a somewhat flattened, Gothic perspective and a high horizon line, above which a large moon sometimes dominates, as in *Coming from Evening Church* (1830); there is always a 'mystic glimmer behind the hills'. The hills, which are rounded and breast-like, are complemented by trees and church spires and, although Palmer would have been shocked by a sexual interpretation of his symbols, it seems to modern eyes that they may well derive part of their power from this source; nevertheless, the erotic charge is doubtless the greater for not being explicit. In typically Romantic fashion, his landscapes usually (but not always) contain at least one person, which aids the viewer's participation in the scene: such is the role of the figure walking through the twilight with his large staff in *Cornfield by Moonlight with the Evening Star* (*c.* 1830). If the contemplative mood of this picture is tinged with melancholy, the same, though less obviously, is true of nearly all Palmer's many depictions of harvest, even though they are first and foremost celebrations of God's plenty. For his love of the harvest was linked to his High Church and Tory love of tradition: an appreciation of things that have come to glorious fruition, made more poignant by the knowledge that their passing away is imminent. Although the Shoreham years were the most fulfilled of Palmer's life, he was never even then free from bouts of despair; these had first been brought on by his mother's death when he was thirteen and were later to become worse with the early death of two of his three children. This disposition to a pessimistic view of life fuelled his horror at the unpoetic and secular quality of advancing industrialism; a horror which accounted for his semi-feudal views and his tendency, somewhat corrected later in life, to romanticize the condition of the rural poor, with whom at Shoreham he was on amicable but never intimate terms. No doubt this made it easier for him to paint, as he did, in the pastoral tradition. His paintings, many of which depict shepherds and/or shepherdesses with their flocks or similarly tranquil bucolic scenes, re-create an earthly paradise. But if his aims were not realistic, nor were they idealizing in the manner of Claude. Suffused with emotion and the desire for redemption, Palmer's Shoreham land-scapes fulfilled his ambition of revealing the divine behind the natural.

In 1834, partly for financial reasons and partly from personal disappointments, Palmer returned to London. The vision faded. Several tours in the British Isles produced work which was little more than topographical. In 1837 he married Linnell's daughter and toured Italy with her for two years. It is true that in a sense this experience broadened his art but it also diluted it, robbing it of almost everything that had made it special. Financially dependent as he was on his increasingly tyrannical father-in-law, Palmer fell ever more victim to the mediocrity which the Linnells in practice forced on him, even to the extent of living in a vulgarly mock-Tudor villa in Redhill, Surrey, the antithesis of everything in which he believed. His art never recovered to the level of the Shoreham period but he did master a new medium, that of etching, in which in the last years of his life he produced some out-standing work. In 1865, he began a series of etchings illustrating Milton, of which *The Lonely Tower* and *The Bellman* are particularly fine examples. From 1872 he worked on a series of etchings illustrating Virgil, although these were less successful – doubtless because

Palmer's genius and feeling for landscape were firmly anchored in the North European tradition, a fact which he did himself a great disservice by ignoring so often. His influence was not felt until the twentieth century and then, characteristically, it surfaced in the work of two thoroughly English painters: Paul Nash and Graham Sutherland.

Further reading

See: Geoffrey Grigson, *Samuel Palmer: The Visionary Years* (1947); Carlos Peacock, *Samuel Palmer: Shoreham and After* (1968); David Cecil, *Visionary and Dreamer* (1969); James Sellars, *Samuel Palmer* (1974); R. Lister, *Catalogue Raisonné of the Works of Samuel Palmer* (1988).

GRAY WATSON

PAOLOZZI, (Sir) Eduardo

1924–2005

British sculptor, decorative artist and printmaker

Eduardo Paolozzi's mission as an artist is to give permanent expression to the ephemeral and neglected in popular culture in order to enhance the visual experience of modern life. His work is as likely to be found in a shop-ping mall or an airport as in the Tate Gallery. In scale it ranges from a postage stamp to the monumental bronze sculpture *Newton* in the courtyard of the British Library. Whether decorating Tottenham Court Road under-ground station with images from the street, making sculptures for the passer-by on the banks of the Rhine in Cologne, or designing stained glass for a cathedral in Edinburgh, Paolozzi brings an internationalism to art which transcends the limitations of the avant-garde by which he was first known.

Born in Edinburgh to Italian parents, trained in London and inspired by living in Paris, he played a major role in the develop-ment of pop art in London in the early 1950s. In 1952 he represented Britain at the Venice Biennale, and from 1958 to 1969 exhibited widely in Europe and America and was regularly awarded international prizes for sculpture and prints. Unlike many post-war artists whose modernism became increasingly reductive, Paolozzi adopts an inclusive agenda, by embracing 'low' and 'high' art, philosophy and literature, music and the cinema. He has done much to bridge the 'two cultures' of which C.P. Snow wrote; and the relationship between man and machine is a subject he has made his own. Paolozzi's ironic sculpture of robots and machine intelligence, and his variations on Duchamp's readymades, have also influenced younger artists in Britain. The garden shed, bicycle wheel and other odds and ends in the *This is Tomorrow* exhibition of 1956 was the first time such humble everyday things had been seen in a British art gallery. Paolozzi's work is based on collage, a technique that owes much to Dada and Surrealism, some of whose practitioners, including **Arp** and **Giacometti,** Paolozzi knew in Paris. By cutting up images and recombining them, Paolozzi suggests the schizophrenic experience of urban living which he expressed in 1960 as 'the golden ability of the artist to achieve a metamorphosis of quite ordinary things into something wonderful and extraordinary'.

In the 1960s Paolozzi pioneered screen-printing and explored relationships between language and picture-making with twelve prints based on the life of the philosopher **Ludwig Wittgenstein**. Although initially attracted by the glamour of consumerism, on which he passed sardonic comment with some brilliantly coloured screenprints, Paolozzi's love affairs with America waned before the end of the Vietnam War. In 1970 he severed his connections with the USA and concentrated on abstract relief sculpture with a practical function which was incorporated into architecture as in the *Cleish Castle Ceiling* (reinstalled in the Dean Gallery, Edinburgh) and the *Hunterian Art Gallery Doors*, Glasgow University (but now a room divider). This in turn gave way to figurative sculpture which reflected his concern for the waste and pollution that threatens the future of the planet. In the 1980s he began a series of expressionist heads illustrative of what he perceived as 'the

madness of modern life'. His last series of prints was dedicated to the life and work of the great twentieth-century cryptologist **Alan Turing**.

Paolozzi was Her Majesty's Sculptor in Ordinary for Scotland (1986); was Professor of Sculpture at the Munich Academy of Fine Art (1981–91) and recipient of the Goethe Medal (1991). A permanent display of his art, presided over by his two-storey-high figure of *Vulcan*, is in the Dean Gallery, Edinburgh.

Further reading

See: Eduardo Paolozzi, *Writings and Interviews*, ed. Robin Spencer (2000), and *Lost Magic Kingdoms* (exhibition catalogue, 1985). See also: Diane Kirkpatrick, *Eduardo Paolozzi* (1970); Winnfried Konnertz, *Eduardo Paolozzi* (1984); Fiona Pearson, *Eduardo Paolozzi* (1999); Robin Spencer, *Eduardo Paolozzi Recurring Themes* (exhibition catalogue, 1984); Frank Whitford, *Eduardo Paolozzi* (exhibition catalogue, 1971).

ROBIN SPENCER

PARKER, Charles Christopher, Jr (Bird)
1920–55
US jazz alto saxophonist, composer

Charlie Parker embodied the popular stereotype of the jazz musician as an inspired, self-destructive genius. From a man whose personal and professional life was a chaos of narcotics, alcohol and abused personal relationships flowed an endless stream of inventive and passionate improvisation performed with astounding virtuosity. Whereas early jazz and swing had been multiracial and intimately linked with light-hearted entertainment, bebop, the music of Parker, was predominantly for black people, played by black people (at first), and it was serious. Although it grew out of swing, it deliberately broke with tradition, and this break was significant for black Americans.

Parker was a self-taught musician who, at the age of nineteen, was playing alto saxophone with the Jay McShann band. He soon dropped out and went to live in New York, taking on casual jobs and sitting in with the bands that played in the clubs of 52nd Street, where the new style of Parker, Dizzy Gillespie (trumpet), Thelonius Monk (piano) and Kenny Clarke (drums) was being worked out. Clarke was moving the accents from the first and third beats of the bar to the second and fourth. Gillespie and Parker were developing the melodic and harmonic aspects of the music, at first independently of each other.

Their music avoided the simple harmonies of earlier jazz, added chords to the sequences of the tunes they played, and filled out major and minor triads with the higher intervals. In their melodic improvisations they tended to make great use of these higher intervals, and of alterations to the standard intervals – the characteristic sound of Bird and Diz has lowered fifths and ninths, often accented at the end of a phrase on the second quaver of the first beat in the bar (the name 'bebop' is in imitation of this). Their phrases were not tailored to the conventional two- and four-bar lengths, and would cross the junctions between the sections of the song that they were playing, making it quite difficult for non-musicians listening to follow the solo. This obscurity was partly offset by the fact that Parker often chose either the chord sequence of *I Got Rhythm* or of the twelve-bar blues – naturally with added harmonies.

Slam Slam's Blues (1945) has Parker and Gillespie standing out from the other, more conventional, swing players for the rhythm, phrasing and harmonic structure of their solos. In 1943 Parker and Gillespie were in the Earl Hines and then the Billy Eckstine big bands, and in 1945 recorded together in sessions that have become classic. Parker's erratic behaviour led to a break with Gillespie (who rarely played with him after that), and **Miles Davis** joined the Parker quintet for a series of recordings for the Savoy and Dial labels.

Three types of Parker solo can be mentioned here: very fast quaver runs, spiced with triplets, syncopation and great variety of accent on *Ko Ko* (1945); blues such as the slowish *Parker's Mood* (1948) where rhythmic variety and melodic agility are combined

with intense emotional expression; and ballads (*Embraceable You*, 1947) where Parker embroiders on the melody with flurries of semi-quavers and demi-semiquavers through added passing chords.

Parker's health and constitution began to give way under the strain of heroin, alcohol and disordered living, and his usefulness as a musician suffered when he could not be counted on to turn up for engagements. He went through a number of marriages (the first at the age of fifteen), and was hospitalized. He recorded with strings (*Just Friends*, 1949), toured with various organizations and bands, and played in a justly famous concert in Toronto in 1953. He became more and more down and out, and finally died while watching television in the apartment of a friend.

Parker's unedifying life fuels the legend of the artist sacrificing himself to his art, and that of the black man oppressed by the American system. But the music he played is not a matter of legend. It laid the basis of the language of jazz improvisation for the next twenty years, turned jazz towards the cult of the solo improviser, and offered an example of supreme cultural achievement to two generations of black Americans.

Further reading

Parker's recordings have been reissued on LP records by Savoy, Spotlite, Verve and many other labels. Transcribed solos can be found in *Charlie Parker Omnibook* (1978). See: Robert Reisner, *Bird: The Legend of Charlie Parker* (1962); Ross Russell, *Bird Lives* (1972); Leonard Feather, *Inside Bebop* (1949, republished as *Inside Jazz*, 1977); C. Woideck, *Charlie Parker: His Music and Life* (1997); C. Woideck (ed.), *The Charlie Parker Companion: Six Decades of Commentary* (1998).

CHRISTOPHER WAGSTAFF

PASOLINI, Pier Paolo

1922–75

Italian filmmaker, writer

The brutal murder of Pier Paolo Pasolini on a piece of waste ground on the outskirts of Rome on 2 November 1975 brought to a hideous end the most spectacular artistic career in Italy since the Second World War. Known outside Italy mainly as a filmmaker, Pasolini was also a novelist, poet, essayist and journalist and a public figure of some notoriety. His early novels – *Ragazzi di vita* (1955) and *Una vita violenta* (1959) – established him as a linguistic innovator. His poetry – *Le ceneri di Gramsci* (1957), *La religione del mio tempo* (1961) – managed to combine public content with a highly distinctive speaking voice, in sharp contrast to the prevailing poetic tradition in which a largely private content was expressed from a somewhat impersonal stance.

He began his film career as a scriptwriter for a number of generally undistinguished films about the Roman underworld. The first film he directed himself, *Accattone* (1961), also had an underworld and subproletarian setting (as indeed do his novels), but its treatment was very remote from the kind of 'low-life picturesque' favoured by his contemporaries. With *The Gospel According to Matthew* (1964) he took a further step away from the debased heritage of neo-realism, but laid himself open to a different misconstruction – this time as 'Catholic-Marxist'. In fact he was neither (though he was both religious and politically left-wing) and the appellation only makes sense to the extent that Catholicism and **Marxism** are the two great rival orthodoxies in Italy whose influence it is impossible to escape. Pasolini, however, was a heretic in relation to both, constantly and self-consciously at odds with every form of either Marxist or Catholic orthodoxy. His political heterodoxy was most clearly revealed in 1968, when he published a poem 'Dear Students, I Hate You', which was instantly read as an attack on student radicalism and a defence of the riot police. It re-emerged around 1973 when he took up position against the campaign to liberalize the abortion law. It was also in the course of this debate that Pasolini 'came out' on the question of his own homosexuality. Meanwhile, his religiosity became increasingly pagan. While never losing his respect for what he called the '*sacrale*' (sacredness), he came to locate this

sacredness further and further away from the world of organized religion, particularly as organized by the Vatican and Christian Democracy. What he did retain, however, was a sentimental attachment to the religion of the poor, to be defended against lay intellectuals and prelates alike.

Pasolini's later films, beginning with *Oedipus Rex* (1967), are distinguished by an overt fascination with primitivism and by an underlying structure through which he sets out to affirm values antithetical to those of modern capitalist society. The values he opposes are those of technology, capitalism, patriarchy, heterosexual monogamy, conformity and repression. Against those negative but all too real features of the modern world Pasolini sets up various imaginary alternatives. Most of his films are set in the past – in the Middle Ages or in prehistory. When set in the present – as with *Theorem* (1968) or *Salò* (1975) – they show bourgeois society as a network of corruption and repression from which only a few innocents can escape. In all the films there is a search for lost innocence, which is always regressive, coupled with a recognition that recovery of this innocence is difficult if not impossible. Knowledge always comes too late, and takes the form of a knowledge of being already guilty.

Stylistically, these films are chiefly remarkable for the role they ascribe to the image. Whereas most films consist of a series of shots whose meaning is established either through contrast or continuity with other shots composing the narrative, in Pasolini's films narrative continuity is weak and each shot stands on its own, evocative of a meaning which is not always decipherable in narrative terms. The result is to enhance the imaginary character of the films, since not only is the intellectual content predicated on a negation of contemporary reality, but the presentation of it is hallucinatory and dream-like. Whereas in his essays Pasolini is explicit in his denunciation of the modern world, but unable to envisage any realistic alternative, the films do offer an alternative – but only to the extent that the world they portray is avowedly imaginary. That this imaginary journey might bring one closer to a psychic 'real' that ordinary reality denies is a dialectical possibility not to be dismissed.

Further reading

Other works include: *Uccellacci e uccellini* (1966); *The Decameron* (1970); *The Arabian Nights* (1974). Books include: a volume of essays, *Empirismo eretico* (1972); a collection of journalism, *Scritti corsari* (1975); and his last work *La Divina Mimesi* (1975). See: Oswald Stack, *Pasolini on Pasolini* (1969); P. Willemen (ed.), *Pier Paolo Pasolini* (1977); Enzo Siciliano, *Vita di Pasolini* (1978); Naomi Greene, *Pier Paolo Pasolini: Cinema as Heresy* (1990); Patrick Rumble and Bart Testa (eds), *Pier Paolo Pasolini: Contemporary Perspectives* (1995); Robert S.C. Gordon, *Pasolini: Forms of Subjectivity* (1996).

GEOFFREY NOWELL-SMITH

PASTERNAK, Boris Leonidovich

1890–1960

Russian poet and novelist

Boris Pasternak grew up in a highly cultivated Moscow environment; his father Leonid was an important painter and his mother a former concert pianist. Much influenced by Scriabin, Pasternak at first wanted to become a composer; it was only in 1912, after some months as a philosophy student in Germany, that he committed himself to poetry. After the Revolution he remained in Russia, and in 1922 published his best-known book of poems, *My Sister Life* (*Sestra moya – zhizn*, 1922). This was followed soon afterwards by *Themes and Variations* (*Temy i variatsii*, 1923). In the 1920s Pasternak occupied a somewhat isolated position in the Soviet literary world; he was a poet of great prestige, but many regarded him as at best a lukewarm friend to the new regime. Various writings of this period show his attempt to come to terms with the Revolution, both long poems such as *Lofty Malady* (*Vysokaya bolezn*, 1924) and *Lieutenant Schmidt* (1926–7) and the volume of lyric poetry *Second Birth* (*Vtoroe rozhdenie*,

1932), which also reflects the break-up of his first marriage and his love for the woman who was to become his second wife.

From early on Pasternak had also been writing prose and he came to place more and more emphasis on it as a means of doing justice to his own experience and that of his country. In 1931 he published the autobiographical *Safe Conduct* (*Okhrannaya gramota*) and in the 1930s he began work on his novel *Dr Zhivago*. This was the great work of his last two decades, though he also produced several remarkable sequences of verse and a large number of memorable translations, in particular of Shakespeare. *Dr Zhivago* was rejected by the journal *Novy Mir* in 1956, but at the end of the following year it was published in Italy and in 1958 Pasternak was awarded the Nobel Prize for Literature. This gave rise to a violent campaign of denunciation in the Soviet Union; Pasternak was expelled from the Writers' Union and forced to decline the prize in order to remain in his native country. Greatly shaken by this experience, he died near Moscow in 1960.

For most non-Russian readers, Pasternak is above all the author of *Dr Zhivago*, and this is as he would have wanted it. For many Russian readers, however, his finest work is to be found in his early collections, particularly *My Sister Life*. In the pre-Revolutionary period he had been associated with the Futurist movement and his early poems show a verbal inventiveness (and sometimes obscurity) which matches that of Mayakovsky. But Pasternak was not interested in verbal experiment for its own sake. His conception of poetry was essentially expressive; in his words, 'focused upon a reality that has been displaced by feeling, art is a record of this displacement'. In his poems figures of speech, sound orchestration and rhythm all serve to render the vivid feeling of life. One of the dominant themes is renewal or transfiguration, often conveyed through images of weather, wind, rain and storm. The starting point is personal experience – *My Sister Life* is constructed round a love affair – but Pasternak characteristically brings together the great and the small, the universe and the detail. He later interpreted the excited consciousness of *My Sister Life* as reflecting the heightened vitality of the year of revolutions, though it is worth noting that the poems which compose it were written between February and October 1917.

My Sister Life brought Pasternak an outstanding reputation, but he later turned against the 'frills and fancies' of his early verse, aiming for what he once described as an 'unheard-of simplicity'. This is opposed rather to official jargon than to obscure poetry; what he was interested in was a realistic art that would 'contain' the world (**Chekhov** and Chopin were models), and this did not necessarily involve writing poems of banal accessibility. Even so, his late poems are certainly easier for the average reader. At their best (and above all in the poems which make up the final chapter of *Dr Zhivago*) they show the same concern for life as the early work, together with an increased emphasis on ethical and historical questions. All of this is well seen in one of Pasternak's most famous poems, 'Hamlet'. At times, however, and particularly in his last collection *When the Weather Clears* (*Kogda razgulyaetsa*, 1956–9), there is something of a decline into banality.

Dr Zhivago (trans. Max Hayward and Manya Harari, 1958), although hailed by some Western reviewers as a novel in the **Tolstoyan** tradition, is very much a poet's novel, a highly personal view of the destiny of modern Russia as experienced by a young doctor-poet to whom Pasternak attributes some of his own best poems. Many of the themes of the early collections are present in the novel, together with their author's intense awareness of the life of the world. The book is permeated by a symbolism which is accentuated by the poems of the final chapter; it expresses Pasternak's faith in traditional ethical and religious values and his hope for a future in which the best features of the Revolution (seen here largely in negative terms) and of the old intellectual tradition would be reconciled. One may feel that the novelist is too close to his hero and

does not always avoid a certain sentimental idealizing, but it can hardly be denied that *Dr Zhivago* is a major novel of the last century. At the same time, it should not be allowed to overshadow the marvellous achievement of the early poems.

Further reading

Other works, including *Dr Zhivago*, are in the three-volume Russian edition by G.P. Struve and B.A. Filippov (1961). Other translations include: *Fifty Poems* (trans. Lydia Pasternak Slater, 1963); *Poems* (trans. E.M. Kayden, 1959); *The Poetry of Boris Pasternak* (trans. G. Reavey, 1959); *Collected Prose*, ed. C. Barnes (1977). On Pasternak see: H. Gifford, *Pasternak* (1977); D. Davie and A. Livingstone (eds), *Pasternak: Modern Judgments* (1969); V. Erlich (ed.), *Pasternak: A Collection of Critical Essays* (1978); Christopher Barnes, *Boris Pasternak: A Literary Biography* (2 vols, 1989–2004).

PETER FRANCE

PAVLOV, Ivan Petrovich
1849–1936
Russian physiologist

As the eldest of the ten children of the family of Pyotr Dmitrievich, a member of the lowest priesthood in the provincial town of Ryazan, Pavlov knew poverty and unremitting toil. Following in his father's footsteps he entered the theological seminary in Ryazan where contact with scientific and philosophical literature kindled in him an enthusiasm for science. George Lewes's *The Physiology of Everyday Life* (Russian translation 1861) and I.M. Sechenov's *Refleksy golovonogo mozga* (1863) left a deep impression upon him. These authors who expounded the empiricist stance and experimental method in physiology, and championed mechanism and objectives as against vitalism and subjectivism, found a ready disciple in Pavlov. The popular writings of the radical intellectual, Dmitri Pisarev – his conviction of the progressive character of natural science – and especially his enthusiastic account of **Darwin** also influenced the young Pavlov.

Although no revolutionary activist Pavlov had hopes for the ameliorating impact of science upon society. Leaving the Ryazan seminary before completion of his studies he enrolled in the natural science section of the faculty of physics and mathematics at St Petersburg University. By 1874 he had made physiology his major subject. The next year M.I. Afanasiev and he were awarded a gold medal for their study of the enervation of the pancreas. Physiology was but a young science in Pavlov's student days; those who had fought for its status as an experimental science belonged to the nineteenth century. Russia, though considered backward in relation to other European countries, had a galaxy of outstanding scientists in St Petersburg, the physiologists I.M. Sechenov and E.F. Cyon, the clinician S.P. Botkin, and the chemists Mendeleyev and Butlerov. Sechenov had founded Russia's first school of physiology at St Petersburg before he resigned his post there in 1870. In 1890 Pavlov wisely chose to stay in St Petersburg and accept the Chair of Pharmacology offered him by the Military-Medical Academy rather than go to the new University of Tomsk in Siberia. He remained in or near St Petersburg for the rest of his life.

Pavlov's researches can be divided into three phases: his study of blood circulation between 1874 and 1888, his research into the physiology of digestion from 1879 to 1902 for which he was awarded the Nobel Prize in Physiology and Medicine in 1904, and his investigations into the conditioned reflex and higher nervous activity from 1902 to the end of his life. All this work was marked by a conscious concern over method. When he moved on to the higher mental processes, thus entering the field of psychology and psychiatry, he remained true to his physiological upbringing and relied upon the objective methods of that science. Like a later generation of behaviourists in America, Pavlov described in his Nobel lecture how he and his co-workers tried to discipline their thought and speech 'in order to completely ignore the mental state of the animal'. Unlike the behaviourists, however, they 'desired to remain

physiologists instead of becoming psychologists'. All three phases of Pavlov's work were also marked by recognition of the leading part played by the central nervous system in all physiological processes. This was Botkin's doctrine of 'nervism'. It was a recognition of the integration of physiological processes by the centripetal nerves and of the action of the *whole* organism in relation to its surrounding environment. This relation was subtle and adaptive, and to investigate it successfully called for great care in surgical treatment so that the animal remained healthy and normal. Both in his studies of physiological and of psychical secretion he developed chronic as opposed to acute surgical treatment which left the animal functioning normally and with a reasonable life expectancy. Some of the greatest achievements of nineteenth-century physiology were in the field of digestion. Beginning with the studies of an open-stomach wound described by William Beaumont in 1833, physiologists used surgery to produce a duct or 'fistula' from the digestive glands to the exterior. Glandular secretion could then be studied. Unfortunately such fistulas tended to close up, or the normal pattern of secretion disappeared; often the animal died soon after the operation. After a period of study under Rudolf Heidenhain, hitherto the most successful practitioner of the fistula, Pavlov and his co-workers overcame these problems by modifications of technique and skilful surgery. Pavlov described these problems and his solutions to them in his famous *Lectures on the Work of the Principal Digestive Glands* (*Lektsii o rabote glavnukh pishchevaritelnykn zhelez*), publication of which in 1897 brought their author international recognition.

Pavlov's studies of the digestive glands had impressed him with the remarkable powers of adaptation of the organism to changes in its diet. On a carbohydrate diet the intestinal digestive juices were weak in proteolytic enzymes but strong in such enzymes for a protein-rich diet. Likewise, a dry diet stimulated a copious secretion of saliva, a moist diet only a slight secretion. Also striking was the power of the stomach to start secretion after the animal had been 'sham-fed', i.e. food from the mouth was diverted by surgical modification from the stomach. Evidently it was not the direct contact with food that caused gastric secretion but a more remote 'signalling' system. Likewise salivary secretion was stimulated by the sight or smell of food before the food made contact with the lining of the mouth. Pavlov referred to this production as 'appetite juice' or 'psychical secretion'. In his address to the International Congress of Medicine in Madrid in 1903 Pavlov recalled how he and his co-workers 'had honestly endeavoured to explain our results by fancying the subjective condition of the animal. But nothing came of it except unsuccessful controversies.' Rejecting subjective explanations, Pavlov turned instead to the physiological theory of the reflex. The result, he told his audience, was the opening of 'a second immense part of the physiology of the nervous system'. The first part had concerned the relations within the organism, the second concerned its relations with the surrounding world.

In that there was a definite stimulus or signal and a response, psychic secretion did not differ from physiological secretion. The difference lay in the distance of the stimulus and the 'unessential' even accidental property of the stimulus. In a physiological reflex the property of the stimulus was 'essential', i.e. intimately connected with the physiological role of the glandular secretion. Furthermore, he noted a striking contrast between the constancy or *unconditioned* nature of physiological secretion and the inconstancy and apparent capriciousness of psychic secretion. The latter he therefore called a *conditioned* reflex. Its performance was conditional upon its association with the stimulus to the unconditioned reflex. The more frequently this association was made the stronger the conditioned reflex became. It was in his Madrid lecture that Pavlov described his efforts to discover the laws governing conditioned reflexes based upon the experiments on the dog carried out by his co-worker,

F. Tolochinov. To the English-speaking world he gave a more developed version of the subject in his **Thomas Huxley** lecture in London in 1906. Not until the translation of his *Lectures on Conditioned Reflexes* in 1929 by his American co-worker, W. Horsley Gantt, however, did the riches of the Pavlovian experimental programme become fully appreciated in the Western world.

In the first phase of these studies Pavlov had used 'natural' conditioned reflexes – those formed by the 'natural association' between, for example, the sight of food and eating it. Later work concentrated on 'unnatural' conditioned reflexes, such as the sound of a bell before presenting food. Such reflexes could be rendered exact, were easily controlled and varied, and they opened up a vast field for research. Both types of conditioned reflex showed law-like behaviour. Repeated without the unconditioned stimulus – e.g. food – the conditioned stimulus evoked progressively less response until it was completely extinguished. Left unstimulated for a few hours the animal's conditioned response was spontaneously restored. Restoration was also achieved by presentation of the conditioned stimulus with the unconditioned stimulus. Such a procedure could be repeated to reinforce it, but coupling the unconditioned stimulus with another signal inhibited the original conditioned response. It was the temporary nature of these reflexes which allowed the organism to be delicately adapted to its changing environment.

Further studies showed that the power to make conditioned reflexes was associated with the cerebral hemispheres, and stimuli could only be effective if the centre in the cerebral cortex to which the sense organ in question was connected remained intact. Pavlov looked upon these centres and their associated sense organs as 'analysers'. They acted as a signalling system since they gave the animal signals for its needs. The number of potentially significant signals for food were legion, but with repeated presentation of a given stimulus with food the conditioning became more narrowly limited to this signal.

This was possible because the analysers decomposed the mass of signals from the animal's surroundings. In 1932 Pavlov suggested that in addition to this first signal system there was in man a second signal system which generalized and analysed the multitude of signals from the first system. The most important signals for this second system were those from the kinaesthetic stimulations of the speech organs; its functions were abstraction and speech. It marked 'the very last attainment in the evolutionary process'.

In the earlier phase of his study of conditioned reflexes Pavlov was distinctly hostile to psychologists. When he became familiar with the work of Thorndike and later with those of the early behaviourists he modified his position, but he criticized E.R. Guthrie and K. Lashley. To the school of Gestalt psychology he was vehemently opposed. Köhler especially he viewed as a serious threat to objective research, and in one of his 'Wednesday' meetings he declared 'We are at war with him. This is a serious struggle against psychologists.' Pavlov was not a crude materialist but he believed in the need for objective methods and denigrated what he considered were the subjective methods of psychology. Yet he looked forward to a time when 'the physiological and the psychological, the objective and the subjective will really merge, when the painful contradiction between our mind and our body ... will either *actually* be solved or [will] disappear in a natural way'.

The theory of the conditioned reflex had a considerable impact upon psychology. In the nineteenth century the reflex had been a prominent element in Herbert Spencer's psychology and it was the dominant element in I.M. Sechenov's treatment of higher mental processes, but it was the incorporation of the *conditioned* reflex into behaviourist literature around 1915 that introduced it to the mainstream of twentieth-century psychology. Many of the numerous instincts attributed to animals in the literature of comparative psychology were then banished and their place taken by conditioned reflexes. Shorn

of the special surgical difficulties associated with Pavlov's fistula technique, conditioning experiments became a major feature of behaviourist research.

Further reading

The best collection of extracts from Pavlov's writing is *I.P. Pavlov: Selected Works*, ed. K.S. Koshtoyants, trans. from Russian by S. Belsky (1955); his best-known work is the *Lectures on Conditioned Reflexes* (2 vols, 1928 and 1941). There are many biographies, the most readily available of which is E.A. Asratyan, *Ivan Petrovitch Pavlov, Work* (1953, latest edn 1979). See also: Jeffrey A. Gray, *Pavlov* (1979).

ROBERT OLBY

PENDERECKI, Krzysztof
1933–
Polish composer

An astonishing stylistic volte-face a third of the way through Krzysztof Penderecki's output to date – severe even by the protean norms of twentieth-century compositional practice – indicates one of the reasons why he is the most fascinating Polish composer of his generation. For there are two Pendereckis to consider, both of whom have connected to impressively large audiences beyond the contemporary art music ghetto. One is the young Polish firebrand whose hyper-expressionistic 'sonorism' scores of the 1960s marked him out as one of the avant-garde's most original voices, and whose music subsequently became known to millions through its use on film soundtracks. The other is a doyen of the more traditionally minded wing of the classical music establishment, a purveyor of grand symphonies and oratorios in possession of a neo-romantic musical voice that did not so much turn its back on the earlier Penderecki's achievements as perform a backward somersault into its late nineteenth-century idiom.

Penderecki emerged as a force on the Polish music scene in 1959 when, following studies   at   the   Music   Academy   in

Kraków (1954–8), he won all three top prizes at a national competition. This was a timely emergence for an ambitious and creatively audacious composer. In the late 1950s, the post-**Stalinist** new wave of Polish art music was seeking to process the flux of the international avant-garde. No one responded to this challenge with more panache and verve than Penderecki, who moved swiftly, via neo-classical and modernist models, to the creation of a stunningly novel soundworld. One of those triple award-winning pieces, *Emanacje* ('Emanations', 1958), which features two string orchestras tuned a semitone apart, inaugurated a swiftly expanding body of triumphs including *Tren* for fifty-two strings ('Threnody to the Victims of Hiroshima', 1960), *Polymorphia* for forty-eight string instruments (1961), which is arguably his finest essay in sound, and the electrifyingly sensuous *Capriccio* for violin and orchestra (1967). Rightly lauded for his bold approach to timbre, texture and musical time, Penderecki's sonoristic scores pushed back the frontiers of instrumental and notational technique in the service of a more primal force: forthright musical drama. Having pared modernism down to bands of evolving sonority and intensity, Penderecki was able to create scores so direct in their gestural and affective immediacy that he seemed simultaneously to sculpt his audience's emotional experience – hence at least some of his music's efficacy on horror movie soundtracks including William Friedkin's *The Exorcist* (1973) and **Stanley Kubrick's** *The Shining* (1980).

It was Penderecki's *St Luke Passion* (1963–6), however, which catapulted him to international success; and, when 15,000 people attended a performance in the courtyard of Kraków's Wawel Castle, the oratorio also became a national icon, bringing religion (a symbol of Polish resistance to oppression) to the centre of his country's musical life. Harnessing his flair for drama to the Passion story, the oratorio's singular musical impact rests on its potent fusion of sonorism, serialism and – crucially – refracted traditional resources (Polish religious songs, the B.A.C.H. motive). This stylistic continuum enabled Penderecki to move between the extremes of allusions to J.S. Bach and sonorism's obliteration of pitch and pulse. Later, Penderecki went on to make statements of a more consciously political nature, such as the *Polish Requiem* (1980–4, expanded 1993), parts of which commemorate tragedies suffered by Poles, and *Seven Gates of Jerusalem* (1996), which commemorates the 3,000th anniversary of Jerusalem's founding while addressing, through Christian allegory, the conflicts encompassed by that city's walls.

The expanded palette of the *Passion*, as well as providing a blueprint for Penderecki's operas – including the deliciously profane *Devils of Loudon* (1969) and rumbustious *Ubu Rex* ('King Ubu', 1990–1) – can also be connected to Penderecki's change of style in the mid 1970s. His Violin Concerto No. 1 (1976–7) and Symphony No. 2 (1979–80) cemented the dominant features of the new Penderecki. Increasingly tonal harmony, clearer-cut melodies, simpler rhythmic patterns and generic forms all returned to be deployed within a gestural language deeply indebted to late romanticism, and prone to veering into darkly turbulent emotional territory. A string of symphonies, concertos and choral works followed, and at their best – as in the serene *Adagio* at the centre of Symphony No. 3 (1988–95), the blazing climax of Symphony No. 5 (1992), or the desolate close of Violin Concerto No. 2 (1992–5) – this is music of impressive scope and power. Some recent works, moreover, have revealed a brightening of Penderecki's occasionally oppressive atmospheres to admit more delicate and even playful music, as in the delightful Quartet for clarinet and strings (1993). Penderecki has made some bold pronouncements concerning these later works. He has described his recent symphonies, for example, as arks designed to protect all that was important, from his current perspective, in the tradition of art music during the twentieth century. Yet although they would not be permitted to board this ark of neo-romantic values, Penderecki's earlier modernist scores may ultimately mark his most significant cultural contributions.

Further reading

Recordings of all Penderecki's major works, often conducted with accomplishment by the composer himself, are readily available on CD. Wolfram Schwinger's *Krzysztof Penderecki: His Life and Work* (1989) is a useful survey up to the *Polish Requiem*, while Penderecki's own *Labyrinth of Time: Five Addresses for the End of the Millennium* (1998) can be consulted regarding his later aesthetics.

NICK REYLAND

PICASSO, Pablo (Ruiz y)

1881–1973

Spanish/French artist

Pablo Picasso was born into a comfortable middle-class family in Málaga, Spain, in 1881. His father was a curator of a museum and teacher of painting. From an early age Picasso had shown remarkable talent which his father made every effort to foster. By 1895 the family had moved to Barcelona where Picasso's professional life began, centred around the café of El Quatre Gats. It was in Barcelona that Picasso saw Symbolist works including those of the Englishman Edward Burne-Jones, whose sad-eyed processions carried the same inward melancholy as the Continental Symbolists. Picasso's own Symbolist 'Blue' period with its subject-matter of old age, poverty and lonely clowns maintained this mood of psychological depression, but in its contemporaneity of subject-matter came closer to the poetry of Jules Laforgue.

In 1900 Picasso left Spain for the first time, visited France and decided in 1904 to settle in Paris. From then on he holidayed frequently in his native land until 1934, when he became a permanent exile. France then became his second mother country and promoted his talent to such an extent that he became a living legend as the greatest twentieth-century artistic genius of the Western world, comparable with such masters as Velázquez

and **Manet**, both of whom influenced him deeply.

It is perhaps useful to consider the vast oeuvre of Picasso in phases. The early 'Blue' period gave way to a happier 'Pink' period in Paris, while Picasso was living with Fernande Olivier. It was, for this restless man, a brief time of relative tranquillity when his work reflected a classic serenity. This was soon to be shattered.

During 1906 and 1907 Picasso painted the awkward and primitive *Demoiselles D'Avignon*, undoubtedly one of the key works of the first half of the twentieth century, when he was only twenty-five years of age. This painting set in motion the movement that later became known as Cubism, without which it is doubtful whether Pure Abstraction such as that of **Mondrian** and **Malevich** would have occurred when and in the way that it did.

Picasso's concern with primitivism as a way of seeing afresh, of connecting again with the vital creative forces of artistic endeavour that he felt had been lost to the Renaissance tradition produced the *Demoiselles*, a bold and dramatically direct statement. Five figures of nude women squat or stand showing progressive distortions and flattenings of form from left to right of the work. Space is diminished and colour limited. Picasso had become aware of African tribal carvings and early Iberian sculpture in the Trocadéro Museum in Paris. He had also seen much of the work of **Gauguin** with its primitive South Sea island subjects. He well knew also **Cézanne's** painting with its floating colour orchestrations of the structure of space and object. Both these artists had shown regularly at Paris exhibitions in the years immediately preceding 1907.

Georges Braque was introduced to Picasso at this time, saw the *Demoiselles* and understood its revolutionary significance. He himself had studied Cézanne thoroughly. Together the two painters went on 'roped together like rock climbers' to work out Cubist form which had as its central tenet the breaking of single-point perspective. Both Braque and Picasso felt that perspective had become 'a stranglehold on art', stultifying it with irrelevant rules. It was possible to remember an object from another view while seeing it in front of the eyes. Perception became multidimensional if you included existing concepts. They realized that this could form a new reality for art.

During the early analytical stage of Cubism from 1907 until 1912, objects were painted as though viewed from many angles. Simple, often rectangular, hence the name Cubist, facets of these various views were then painted flat, overlapping and parallel to the picture surface, emphasizing that surface and shutting out distance. Bright colour was abandoned to avoid an emotional impact and to focus on the restructuring of space–object relationships. Only later did rich and at times brittle colour appear during the synthetic Cubist period (1912–15). At this time also decorative patterns were used and actual paper cut-outs or pieces of objects stuck on to the canvas surface to form *papier collé* or collage. This latter technique was in part to emphasize the flatness or two–dimensionality of the canvas and therefore the autonomy of the work of art as an object in its own right, denying its role as an illusion of natural appearances. However, it was also to make concrete for the viewer the reality the artist was dealing with. Both Picasso and Braque had felt around 1912 that their myriads of small facets had become too abstract. For this reason they also added words or parts of words to the paintings – labels for the objects, in fact.

The First World War separated the two artists, for Braque, as a Frenchman, had to enlist. They did not see each other again. During the war Picasso met **Diaghilev**, master of the Ballets Russes, and worked on sets for the ballet *Parade*. He also loved and married one of the dancers, Olga. As a result of his marriage he produced many portraits and statuesque half-figures of full and fruitful women and children. These take on once more a Classical figurative appearance, at times parodying that style. A return to Classical form was common throughout

Europe after the war in many of the arts. However, in Picasso's case it was not long lasting; Dada and Surrealist ideas provided more exciting material to work with.

André Breton, the poet leader of the Surrealist movement, knew Picasso and admired his work. Picasso in turn took an interest in Breton's writings and the Surrealist journal he edited called *La Révolution surréaliste*. The year 1925 saw the first large Surrealist exhibition and it was also the date of Picasso's painting *The Three Dancers* with both Surrealist and Expressionist influences. In it Picasso utilizes again, as he had done for a year or two previously, Cubist flattening of form and lack of depth in space. Three figures, with a fourth death's head, entwine in a primitive dance of conflicting passions. The Surrealist element in the work which gives the left-hand figure its violent contortions derives from **Freudian** concerns with the erotic. The woman, both symbolically and expressively sexual, is linked with the man and the death's head on the right. Between the two and across the linked hands is a cruciform figure suggesting pain and suffering. Picasso had taken the traditional archetypal theme of love and death and added to it several personal significances connected not only with his own marital difficulties but also with the past love affair of a friend who had committed suicide.

Throughout the 1930s Picasso's work carried this double level of interpretation, the universal and the particular, with much use of visual metaphor. A hand could also look like a bird's wing and so suggest the qualities of touch as well as of vision. There is no doubt that Picasso was very physical in his approach to his art. He enjoyed sculpting and was strongly aware of volumetric form. It was this very acute consciousness that made him more especially able to visualize forms as expressive shapes.

At the time of the Spanish Civil War in 1936 Picasso had acquired facility with a great range of expressive subject–matter and formal devices. His experiments with themes of young maidens carried off by bulls or horses,

of man desiring and woman enticing, of crucifixion and fear, meant that for the greatest
theme of his life, *Guernica*, he had a vivid
repertoire on which to draw.

The war itself was a shock to Europe. For
the first time the political far left confronted
and fought fascism. The outrage of bombing
one of Spain's small and defenceless towns
with no warning meant a deepening of
Picasso's commitment to communism and
the total absorption of his dynamic personality
in the theme of war. Again the archetypal
themes of weeping women, of animals and
savagely torn bodies were given a new and
personal significance by Picasso's physical and
emotional identification with his subject-
matter.

The forms in *Guernica* and other works of
the period became sharply jagged, hard in
colour and texture, twisted and wrenched
apart with the tensions of pain and grief. Yet
at the same time a classically rhythmic structure
underlies the drawing and composition. The
twentieth-century element remains as the
degree of distortion set in Cubist space.

Faced soon with the isolation, deprivation
and hardship of Paris during the Second
World War, Picasso sculpted and painted
with whatever materials he could assemble.
The works were bleak, gaunt and at times
fragile. The *Charnel House* of 1944 competes
with *Guernica* as a great visual document of
protest against human suffering.

After the war, the joyous release gave rise
to works of warmth, wit and invention.
Picasso's sculptural interests turned more to
pottery, which he carried out at Vallauris in
the Mediterranean South. By Françoise Gilot
he produced more children, and life was
perhaps supremely zestful. However,
although great themes were not lacking, a
more literal look at war as in the painting
Massacre in Korea of 1951 did not produce
works to compare with *Guernica*.

The creativity of this period that commands the greatest respect is more personal
and self-revealing. Drawings of old age and
youth where Picasso sees himself as less than
heroically hiding behind a mask to gaze on

the beauty of his young beloved move the
viewer at the deepest levels.

Intermittently also, Picasso explored, after
the war, paintings of earlier artists. Variations
on Velázquez's *Las Meninas* are works of a
high order in their own right. As interpretations of the enclosed social milieu of court
life and its infantas they must frequently have
reminded Picasso of his own. He had from
youth been encouraged as a prince among
painters. During his mature life the world
press followed him as routinely as any member
of royalty.

In many senses for Picasso, as for **Matisse**,
intuition and expression were one, but as a
Spaniard he responded most strongly to
themes of the greatest dramatic content,
which meant ultimately to tragedy.

Further reading

See: Christian Zervos, *Pablo Picasso* (catalogue rai-
sonné, 23 vols, 1932–71); Alfred H. Barr (ed.),
Picasso: Fifty Years of His Art (1946); H. Jaffé, *Picasso*
(1964); J. Berger, *Picasso: Success and Failure* (1965);
John Golding, *Cubism* (1965); J. Crespinelle,
Picasso and His Women (trans. 1969); Timothy Hilton,
Picasso (1975); J. Richardson, *A Life of Picasso*
(2 vols, 1991–6).

PAT TURNER

PINTER, Harold

1930–

English dramatist

A surprise but wholly justified winner of the
2005 Nobel Prize for Literature, Harold Pinter
grew up in Jewish Hackney, East London.
After wartime evacuation he attended Hackney
Downs Grammar School, then the Royal
Academy of Dramatic Art for two disen-
chanting terms. In 1948–9 Pinter twice stood
trial for refusing National Service and was
fined as a conscientious objector. *Poetry
London* published two poems (1950). After a
spell at the Central School of Speech and
Drama Pinter began his acting career in
earnest by touring Ireland with Anew
McMaster's repertory company. Between

1951 and 1957 he acted, wrote poetry, married (one son), did odd jobs, and wrote an unpublished novel, *The Dwarfs*. Since 1957, though occasionally acting and frequently directing, Pinter has written for all media, including celebrated screenplays for **Joseph Losey**, and published a ***Proust*** *Screenplay* (1978), later reworked as a less than convincing stage play, *Remembrance of Things Past* (2000).

Nearly all Pinter's plays remove a wall from a domestic interior and reveal existences in process. Truth of character relationship is uncertain, unverifiable and remains unexplored by dramatic exposition. Evasion of communication exacerbates the menace of intruders – agents or victims of psychological and physical domination and dispossession. Pinter's foremost stylistic is obtrusive idiomatic naturalism heightened, almost expressionistically, by an hallucinatory atmosphere which is duplicated by patterns of structural augmentation evoking alternate laughter and apprehensive silence in the audience. The plays are powerful emotional experiences not intellectual blueprints of modern thought. Comedy is a means not an end. The complicity of laughter qualifies the audience's final recognition of a state of being: the failure or betrayal of friendship and love.

In the first plays, *The Room* (1957), *The Dumb Waiter* (1957), *The Birthday Party* (1958) and *A Slight Ache* (1959), a mundane setting is entered by something bizarre which brings blindness, betrayal and death. An incapacitated and alien bearer of identity, a blind Negro, enters the room of an elderly housewife's subservient existence with a silently dominating husband who eventually kicks the Negro to death, precipitating his wife's blindness. The two men waiting argumentatively beside the dumb-waiter of a café basement for instructions are neither workmen nor lodgers but hired gunmen. The order is that one kill the other. The birthday party is given by two strangers for the seedy bullying lodger of a seaside boarding house. Hysteria and final breakdown follow celebration and the strangers abduct the lodger. A slight ache

anticipates the blindness that occurs with the admission of a voiceless tramp matchseller to a seemingly complacent middle-class household. In all, physical disability symbolizes moral deficiency.

The year 1960 saw the first performance of four plays. *A Night Out* studies naturalistically the shifting pattern of domination from mother to son, son to prostitute, the son failing to grasp the one possibility of friendship in an otherwise jeering world. *The Caretaker* is Pinter's masterpiece of intuitive psychological insight into three damaged lives: a tramp, an ex-mental patient and his brother, warped by 'normality'. The need for mutual 'caretaking' is betrayed by alternating self-assertion, aggression, domination and rejection. In spite of critical insistence on allegorical interpretation (fostered by the symbolism of the earlier plays), the exhausting realism of *The Caretaker* established Pinter's popular reputation. *The Dwarfs*, a strained reworking from the earlier novel, are creatures of a paranoid imagination breaking down at the betrayal of friendships. In *Night School* and, later, *Tea Party* (1965), Pinter saw the danger of capitulating to mannerism which, he felt, would amount to betrayal of his characters.

A developed sense of dramatic form produced two virtuoso pieces, *The Collection* (1961) and *The Lover* (1963), concerned, respectively, with verification of the truth or otherwise of an adulterous betrayal, and the almost algebraic inversion of a pattern of erotic domination. It was as if Pinter were practising for a large-scale formal assault on the mind and senses which is *The Homecoming* (1965), a modern *King Lear*. Shakespeare explores a pagan world bereft of Christ's grace, Pinter a womanless family abandoned to animality and suburban barbarism, unredeemed by human love, tainted and tainting all.

The script of *The Basement* (1967) dates back to 1963 and both characters and structure belong to the earlier period. Sexual rivalry as an expression of combative egoism leads to a circular pattern of intrusion, betrayal and expropriation. In 1969 Pinter turned startlingly to the extremes of Beckettian austerity and attenuation in *Landscape* and *Silence*. But with *Old Times* (1971) and *No Man's Land* (1975) it could be seen that the primary concern was with double betrayal, by fallibility and disclosure, of memory, that both appropriates and rejects – in thought, image or embodied intruder, the past marooning the present, leaving Pinter's characters stranded by time as well as in place.

Betrayal (1978), focuses through retrospective time sequence on the illusory nature of assumed mutuality in love and friendship. Love can only be betrayed if it is real. The origin of all betrayals lies in fostering initial illusion. The characters are incapable of consummating true betrayal. Beneath the patterned, desultory surface there is the intensity of the later Shakespeare sonnets.

With *One for the Road* (1984), *Mountain Language* (1988) and *The New World Order* (1991), Pinter's theatre veered towards the overtly, even uncomfortably, political, torture and other human rights concerns representing a newfound subject-matter. *Celebration* (2000) – a portrait of aimless, ageing yuppies dining out in an upmarket restaurant that encroaches on the perimeters of John Osborne-land – is notable as a species of self-parody, the emptiness of its characters' lives echoing, and mirrored by, the final emptiness of the play itself. Pinter, coming up for seventy, seems in this work to have lost his touch for original ambiguity, but still makes theatre out of it. The faintly **Ibsenesque** *Moonlight* (1993) is judged by some the last authentic Pinter play: its central bedridden character, surrounded by his family, twists between a lingering appetite for control and a besetting sense of powerlessness.

Increasingly Pinter has publicly protested his political concerns, seldom missing an opportunity to express his hostility towards, particularly, US foreign policy. To the delight of the London press, in 1985 Pinter famously stormed out of a reception given to honour his fellow playwright **Arthur Miller** at the American Embassy. His private life too has come under scrutiny, following his divorce from the actress Vivien Merchant in favour of Lord Longford's daughter Lady Antonia Fraser, in 1977. His plays, particularly the earlier, are often discussed in terms of Theatre of the Absurd, Black Comedy, or Comedy of Menace. Acknowledged admiration for **Kafka** and **Beckett** might appear to support this, but the most powerful and least discussed artistic influences are the multifarious traditions of comedy absorbed through years of acting. Pinter's style and power have been copied, but rarely followed, the young Joe Orton being a conspicuous example.

Further reading

Other works include: *Revue Sketches* in *A Slight Ache and Other Plays* (1961); *Night* (1969); *Five Screenplays* (1971); *Monologue* (1973); *Poems and Prose* (1978); *The Hothouse* (written 1958, first performed 1980); *A Kind of Alaska* (1982); *Ashes to Ashes* (1996); *Conference* (2002). See also: J.R. Brown, *Theatre Language* (1972); Martin Esslin, *Pinter. A Study of His Plays* (3rd edn, 1977); Harold Bloom (ed.), *Harold Pinter* (1987); Michael Billington, *The Life and Works of Harold Pinter* (1996). Pinter's official website–http://www.haroldpinter.org–is eminently visitable.

RONALD KNOWLES
(REVISED AND UPDATED BY THE EDITOR)

PIRANDELLO, Luigi

1867–1936

Italian poet, short-story writer, novelist and dramatist

The Sicilian Pirandello was educated at the Universities of Rome and Bonn, where he wrote a doctoral thesis on his native dialect. That he wrote verse (*Mal giocondo*, 1889; *Pasqua di Gea*, 1891) was more an indication of the prestige of poetry than a recognition of his true gifts. In Rome in 1893, Pirandello was induced by a fellow Sicilian, Luigi Capuana, to write prose. His first novel, *The Outcast* (*L'esclusa*, 1908, written in 1894, trans. 1925), deals with a woman wrongly suspected of adultery, cast off by her husband,

and forced by social pressures to become what she was thought to be. The themes of Pirandello's early fiction are the contrast between appearance and reality, form and life, the tragedies of a society which values appearance and formality. Until 1910–12, Pirandello wrote novels and short stories – sketches of peasant and middle-class life, coloured by his conviction that external reality is unknowable and that we are irremediably alone. He is capable of humour, as in *The Jar* (*La giara*, short story 1909, play 1925, trans. 1928), but for the most part his laughter is either sardonic or compassionate, as he explains in the essay *L'umorismo* (1908).

Although in his first fiction Pirandello seemed the natural heir of the Sicilian naturalists, Verga and Capuana, he soon turned to the exploration of ideas. The first full formulation of his attitude to life comes in the novel *The Late Mattia Pascal* (*Il fu Mattia Pascal*, 1904, trans. 1923). The phrase 'relativity of personality' is often used to describe his belief that personality is a subjective phenomenon. Deriving from Alfred Binet and Henri Bergson, Pirandello's attitude is philosophically unsound, but expressed with lucidity and emotional conviction.

His ear for the spoken language led him naturally to cast his tales in dramatic form, with lively dialogue. He wrote his first play, *The Vice* (*La morsa*, trans. 1928) in 1908, and he was several times invited to write for the theatre. In 1916, he wrote nine plays in a year, of which the best known is *Right You Are, If You Think So!* (*Così è, se vi pare!*, 1918, trans. 1960). In this group of plays, the ideas at stake are recognizably Pirandellian, but his techniques are conventional. Contacts with avant-garde theatre groups between 1915 and 1920 helped him to clarify his ideas. He learned from Craig the importance of harmonizing all elements on the stage, and from Bragaglia the use of lighting to clarify the action. From 1920 onwards, his stage directions became much more detailed and precise, his sets less realistic, often illustrating symbolically the different levels of reality at which the action takes place.

Pirandello's 'total theatre' has its origin in the story *A Character in Distress* (*Tragedia di un personaggio*, 1911, trans. 1938), which led to the play *Six Characters in Search of an Author* (*Sei personaggi in cerca d'autore*, 1921, trans. 1923). This is often regarded as the first in a 'trilogy' which is crucial for our understanding of his contribution to the theatre, the others being *Each in His Own Way* (*Ciascuno a suo modo*, 1924, trans. 1924) and *Tonight We Improvise* (*Questa sera si recita a soggetto*, 1930, trans. 1932). He stresses that the theatre is illusion, but that it is superior to life since it has, or rather, *is* form, 'form that moves', and so has a stability missing in life, which is all flux. His plays therefore have a polemical thrust and are not concerned with pointing to an alternative set of values other than in the realm of abstract ideas. His situations are contrived, so exceptional that they can never constitute the basis of another norm. As Raymond Williams writes: 'It is, really, a mystification of demystification, since the experience ... depends on a theatrical special case.' *Henry IV* (*Enrico IV*, 1922, trans. 1923) remains Pirandello's most performed play, because it is the most imbued with deep feeling. Henry's tragedy is that the mask of madness, which he has consciously chosen to wear, is at the end of the play forced on him by the pressures of emotions outside his control. In his depiction of the loss of identity and the reduction of personality to a social role, Pirandello achieved his greatest success.

Further reading

Other works include: the novel *The Old and the Young* (*I vecchi e i giovani*, 1913, trans. 1928); and the plays *Naked* (*Vestire gli ignudi*, 1923, trans. 1924) and *The Man with a Flower in His Mouth* (*L'uomo dal fiore in bocca*, 1926, trans. 1928). See: G. Giudice, *Luigi Pirandello* (1963); A.L. De Castris, *Storia di Pirandello* (1966); R. Williams, *Modern Tragedy* (1966); John Louis DiGaetani (ed.), *A Companion to Pirandello Studies* (1991).

BRIAN MOLONEY

PLATH, Sylvia

1932–63

US poet

Sylvia Plath's suicide launched a tragic myth which was largely validated by the dramatic, intensely imaged and highly personal poems of her posthumous *Ariel* (1965). Today, Plath's life and writings are still often seen through the distorting glass of opinions about the myth of poet as female victim and rebel. In the women's movement, Plath has functioned both as an image of heroic development towards a female poetic and as a contemporary avatar of a much older type, the suicide-prone Romantic poet, sensitive to the point of madness, persecuted by family and society. While such uses of Plath involve misreadings of her total accomplishment, the ways in which a writer can be used inevitably become part of that writer's historic role. And Plath is one of the few recent poets to have had an undoubted social, as well as literary, impact.

Part of the 'personal' reading of Plath has a genuine basis in her text. One need not agree with A. Alvarez's aesthetic of death in *The Savage God* (1971) – where he argues that suicide and attempted suicide are, for the writer, existential investigations of extremes – in order to feel that Plath's phenomenal development during her short career owed much to the energies released when she began to incorporate covert, then overt, allusions to her private life in her poetry. Like many mythologized poets (Shelley, Byron, Heine), Plath made inner biographical incident and subjective images of herself into part of the poetic armoury with which she faced her audience. In *Ariel* and in some earlier poems, Plath represented herself and threats to herself through a few repeated images: moon, egg, blank-faced corpse, sack of blood. She used several *personae*: the mummy ('All the Dead Dears'), the Jew ('Daddy'), the ritual victim ('The Bee Meeting'), the resurrected corpse ('Lady Lazarus'), the cold nihilist ('Lesbos'). Often, as in 'Tulips', the speaker is assaulted by the physical world,

from which she longs to escape ('Fever 103°', 'In Plaster'). Plath's masks are convincing, their dilemmas passionately expressed, but ultimately they are fictions, more about a way of seeing than about the 'real' person seeing it. Plath began and ended as a metaphoric poet, and her literary life was highly professional.

In 'Daddy', probably her most famous poem, Plath moves from mute grief at her lost father (Otto Plath had died when Plath was eight) to rejection of Oedipal obsession with both father and husband. In this poem Plath's story fragments do seem to play a partly extraliterary role in creating sympathy for the author, while the mythic images carry the thematic burden of an archetypal truth.

> If I've killed one man, I've killed two–
> The vampire who said he was you
> And drank my blood for a year,
> Seven years, if you want to know.

The apparently casual revision of 'a year' to 'seven' has been left in the finished text to signal that the mythic vampire is Plath's real husband, English poet **Ted Hughes**, whom she had known for seven years. At first the 'daddy' addressed by the poem is an archetypal patriarch, 'Marble-heavy, a bag full of God,/Ghastly statue.' But he also comes from Germany, like Plath's father, and he is seen 'at the blackboard' like Plath's father, an entomologist who researched into the habits of bees. The poem's pressure towards a psychological resolution forces the private event over into myth, where, as myth, it can be encompassed, if not solved. Plath's father is described as a fascist, Plath as 'a bit of a Jew', biographically incorrect remarks which express the larger truth that 'Every woman loves a fascist', and woman will remain enslaved until the concept of the all-powerful 'daddy', whether father or husband, has been violently rejected: 'Daddy, daddy, you bastard, I'm through.'

Plath's first volume of poems, *The Colossus* (1960), was an impersonal, highly crafted collection of poems whose interpretable ambiguities located it firmly in the era influenced by the criticism of **T.S. Eliot** and William Empson. Plath had obviously been reading the metaphysical poets and Jacobean dramatists, as well as **W.B. Yeats** and **Emily Dickinson**. She further enlarged her vocabulary by writing with a thesaurus at hand. The *Colossus* poems are written in tightly imaged, short lines and precise stanzas. Plath's small characteristic body of images was already present: the colours white, black and blood-red. There is a threatening, even Gothic, outer world, as in 'Hardcastle Crags', and lurking, insinuating death, as in 'Two Views of a Cadaver Room'. The poet, when present, is almost bewitched by 'The Disquieting Muses' 'with heads like darning eggs' brought down on her from the cradle by her witch-like mother: 'And this is the kingdom you bore me to,/Mother, mother.'

When *The Colossus* was published, Plath had already settled in England with Hughes. In the early years of their marriage, they worked closely together, and some of Hughes's interests are reflected in Plath's use of primitivist animal imagery. Even when she was an undergraduate at Smith College in Massachusetts, Plath had deliberately taken on influences. At first she wanted to become a short-story writer like Frank O'Connor: 'I will imitate until I can feel, I'm using what he can teach.' In the apprentice pieces subsequently collected in *Johnny Panic and the Bible of Dreams* (1977), Plath aimed for the impersonal writerly craft of the 1950s. As she wrote in her diary, 'I justified the mess I made of life by saying I'd give it order, form, beauty, writing about it. The highly formed writing would then reciprocally "give me life" (and prestige to life).'

While Plath's drive for success has dismayed critics who like their tragedy pure, it meant that she strove to understand other writers in order to extend her own range. When Plath read the poetry of Theodore Roethke in the late 1950s, she adapted his use of **Jungian** archetypal image to re-work painful personal loss into poetic knowledge; Roethke's influence is almost palpable in poems like 'Maenad', 'Dark House' and 'The Beast' and in the theme of the lost father. In the summer of 1959 Plath and poet Anne Sexton visited **Robert Lowell's** poetry seminar at Harvard. Plath was deeply impressed by the 'confessional' mode of Lowell's *Life Studies*, even if her own poems do not seek to give the impression of the 'real' poet to the extent that Lowell's do. Also, Plath, unlike Lowell, read history primarily as myth. Once some – but not all – of the poems written between *The Colossus* and *Ariel* had been collected in *Crossing the Water* (1971) and some others written during the period of *Ariel* appeared in *Winter Trees* (1971), it was clear that Plath arrived at the rage and recognition of *Ariel* through poems like 'I Am Vertical', which embraces the temptations of death and release from the body:

> And I shall be useful when I lie down
> finally:
> Then the trees may touch me for once,
> and the flowers
> have time for me.

Other poems focus on specifically womanly compulsions, expressing loathing and identification: 'Heavy Women', 'The Zoo-Keeper's Wife' and 'Three Women: A Monologue for Three Voices' (1968), a 1962 BBC broadcast.

The Bell Jar (1963), Plath's autobiographical novel, begins the story of Esther Greenwood's breakdown and attempted suicide as a satiric novel of adolescence. Esther, like Plath, has won a literary prize and goes off to New York to be exploited by the women's magazine which has awarded it. Through her episodic adventures, Esther realizes that the radical hostility between men and women can't be got rid of by throwing up, taking a purifying bath, writing a scathing letter, briefly adopting a false identity, or even cynically getting herself deflowered. Destined, as a woman, for the life in the kitchen which was the 'feminine mystique' of the 1950s, Esther feels she can't write unless she has the mysterious 'experience' denied her by the banality of her aspirations. Esther stops writing, sleeping and washing: 'I could see day after day after day glaring ahead of me like a white, broad, infinitely desolate avenue.' She takes sleeping pills and crawls underground to die. Rescued (like Plath) after her suicide attempt, Esther spends months in a mental institution (quite wittily described). Helped by a friendly woman doctor, Esther sees the 'bell jar' of schizophrenic isolation rise, and she returns to the outside world. She now realizes, among other rejections, that she hates the overbearing mother whom she always tried to please. Although it lacks the metaphoric power of the poems in *Ariel*, *The Bell Jar* is an important novel, since it links its heroine's breakdown to the contradictory social demands of the age, and it does so with a lucid appreciation of complexity.

Further reading

Other works include: *Collected Poems*, ed. Ted Hughes (1982). See also: Charles Newman (ed.), *The Art of Sylvia Plath: A Symposium* (1970); Margaret D. Uroff, *Sylvia Plath and Ted Hughes* (1979); Judith Kroll, *Chapters in a Mythology: The Poetry of Sylvia Plath* (1976); Gary Lane (ed.), *Sylvia Plath: New Views on the Poetry* (1978); A. Stevenson, *Bitter Fame* (1989); Ronald Hayman, *The Death and Life of Sylvia Plath* (1991); Jacqueline Rose, *The Haunting of Sylvia Plath* (1991); Janet Malcolm, *The Silent Woman* (1994); Erica Wagner, *Ariel's Gift* (2000); Jo Gill (ed.), *The Cambridge Companion to Sylvia Plath* (2006).

HELEN MCNEIL

POLANSKI, Roman

1933–

Polish film director

For a man whose mother died in Auschwitz and whose wife was murdered, Roman Polanski makes films less graphically violent than might be supposed. He does, however, take a pointedly absurd view of the world which cruelly and implacably separates its subjects into survivors and victims. Polanski's films are essentially heartless – perfect

metaphors for the cool but troubled 1960s and early 1970s – kept buoyant by a strong curiosity and wry, bizarre humour.

Polanski was born in Paris to Polish parents who returned to Cracow when he was three. There he fended for himself from an early age after his parents were arrested by the Germans. Films, Polanski has admitted, were an escape. He began acting at the age of fourteen and appeared in the films of Andrej Wajda, notably *A Generation* and *Innocent Sorcerers*. After art school Polanski attended the Lodz Film School where his short film *Two Men and a Wardrobe* (1958) attracted considerable attention. This fifteen-minute exercise drew far more from the Polish avant-garde, particularly the Theatre of the Absurd, than from the dominant tradition of social realism. Polanski's first feature, *Knife in the Water* (1962), was also made in Poland, after a sojourn in Paris. This cool tale about a *ménage à trois* aboard a yacht develops the jaundiced view of human behaviour apparent in the short film and it introduces the intruder figure that was to become central to many of the later films. At the time *Knife in the Water* was read as about the conflict between the Polish bourgeoisie and rebellious youth, although it now looks more like the product of a fundamentally more conservative and pessimistic universal philosophy.

Polanski's next feature was made two years later at the invitation of a Polish producer working in England. Ostensibly a horror film made for a company specializing mostly in sex products, *Repulsion* (1965) in fact remains one of Polanski's most disturbing films for its treatment of a young woman's sexual obsession and mental disintegration. The presiding influence was **Luis Buñuel**, a debt acknowledged in the credits' reference to *Un chien andalou*. The fissures of Catherine Deneuve's cracking-up gain concrete form through the use of surreal images, particularly those inside her oppressive, crumbling London mansion block whose very walls split open in the end and turn against her.

Polanski's commercial astuteness enabled him to find financial backers eager for cultural prestige: Hugh Hefner of *Playboy* magazine financed *Macbeth* (1971). *Rosemary's Baby* (1968) – the first Hollywood film by a director from behind the Iron Curtain – which turned the occult into a subject for major rather than second features, was produced by William Castle, who made his reputation in low-budget exploitation films.

In a sense, Polanski's recurring explorations of sexual tensions, linked to a visceral rather than intellectual surrealism, have made the director attractive to commercial backers.

Money for Polanski's second film in England, an earlier project called *Cul-de-Sac* (1966), was forthcoming after the success of *Repulsion*. The result was a public and critical failure that nevertheless remains Polanski's personal favourite. The themes of intrusion and sexual humiliation find a broader base than before in a black comedy and satire strongly influenced by **Beckett** and **Pinter**, and reinforced by the use of Jack MacGowran and Donald Pleasence, both known foremost as actors for the respective playwrights. Polanski's next film, *Dance of the Vampires* (1967), affectionately parodied horror films and in it Polanski played a bumbling assistant that echoed his role in an earlier short film about a master–servant relationship, *Le Gros et le maigre* (1963). Sharon Tate, his wife, played one of the leading parts in *Dance of the Vampires*. She was murdered later in Los Angeles by the followers of Charles Manson. Polanski's next film, based on Shakespeare's *Macbeth*, was his bloodiest and also continued the diabolic, supernatural theme of the hugely successful *Rosemary's Baby*; it has been noticed that the only birth in the Polanski canon brings forth the child of Satan.

Polanski's style was given its freest rein in *What?* (1972), a droll and inconsequential piece of humour in which an American innocent abroad finds herself in the middle of a comedy of sex and embarrassment. Polanski again appears in the film, clearly delighted to observe such strange behaviour in rich summer villas. The wry, throwaway humour (which teases at the edges of much of his work) is the same kind that in *Chinatown* (1974) put an unglamorous bandage on the nose of its hero.

Restricted settings, like the villa in *What?*, are made much of by Polanski, who favours long takes and frugal editing to allow the cast as much space as possible and to enhance the atmosphere of the geography. Castles in *Cul-de-Sac* and *Macbeth*, apartments in *Repulsion*, *Rosemary's Baby* and *The Tenant* (1976) are all treated in an expressionistic fashion. The urban paranoia of the last three is also central to *Chinatown*, one of his least personal but most successful works. The script by Robert Towne was the first that Polanski did not have a hand in but its themes of complicity and urban corruption make it central to Polanski's cinema.

From the mid-1970s Polanski worked in France after fleeing America following a sex scandal that involved the rape of a thirteen-year old girl – a crime he acknowledged. Whether the personal pressures in his life took their toll is hard to say. *The Tenant* (1976) was a disappointing small-scale return to the territory of *Repulsion*. Polanski's leaving America forced him to give up the direction of *Hurricane*. His next large-scale project was his screen adaptation of **Thomas Hardy's** *Tess* (1979), but this was not universally applauded. During the 1980s he made only two films, *Pirates* (1986) and *Frantic* (1988), neither of which enhanced his reputation. But if critics and his admirers thought Polanski was played out, they were wrong. He rediscovered some of his form at least in the 1990s, with *Bitter Moon* (1992), *Death and the Maiden* (1994) and *The Ninth Gate*, before stunning everyone with *The Pianist* (2002), a semi-autobiographical, profoundly lyrical, though characteristically disturbing, evocation of the Holocaust in his native Poland that won Polanski both an Academy Award for direction, and the *Palme d'Or* at Cannes.

Further reading

Other works include: *Oliver Twist* (2005). See: Ivan Butler, *The Cinema of Roman Polanski* (1970); Thomas Kiernan, *Repulsion: The Life and Times of Roman Polanski* (1981); Roman Polanski, *Roman*

(1984); Pierre-Andre Boutang (ed.), *Polanski par Polanski: textes et documents* (1986); John Parker, *Polanski* (1993).

CHRIS PETIT
(REVISED AND UPDATED BY THE EDITOR)

POLLOCK, Jackson

1912–56

US painter

After the Second World War the centre of avant-garde painting switched from Paris to New York, where a revolutionary new movement, later to be called Abstract Expressionism, emerged. The principal artists of this New York School were Pollock, **de Kooning** and **Rothko**. It was Pollock who, in de Kooning's words, 'broke the ice'. It was also Pollock who probably departed the furthest – certainly further than de Kooning – from all European antecedents.

Born in Cody, Wyoming, Pollock studied in New York under the Regionalist painter Thomas Hart Benton. The old masters who interested him most were those who stressed vigorous movement; his favourite moderns were **Picasso** and **Miró**. He became interested in **Jung** and it was to a Jungian psychotherapist that he turned for help with his alcoholism. In the 1940s, in search of a personal yet universal mythology, he painted a series of pictures filled with references to archaic symbols, including *Guardians of the Secret* and *Pasiphaë* (both 1943). Deciding that these were too literal, and partly inspired by Surrealist automatism, he sought to convey the workings of his unconscious more directly through abstract marks, transforming the canvas into an 'all-over' field of energy. In 1947, he began placing the canvas on the floor and throwing or dripping paint on to it, while moving around it. The act of painting became like a ritualistic dance, involving his whole body. Complete trance-like concentration and a total psychic involvement with the picture, as it developed its 'independent life', was essential. When successful, the dense web of swirling lines conveyed a sense of liberated energy and perfectly controlled yet spontaneous movement, as in free-form jazz, which Pollock loved. The 'all-over' quality suggested an endless time–space flux. Physically very large, violent yet (increasingly) lyrical, Pollock's dripped paintings constitute his 'heroic' phase. Among the first were *Gothic* and *Full Fathom Five* (both 1947). Some, like *One* and *Autumn Rhythm* (both 1950), evoke the mood of the natural environment, specifically that of Long Island, while remaining totally abstract. Using such paints as Duco, Dev-o-Lac and (silver) aluminium, Pollock produced extraordinary colour harmonies. Nevertheless, he was a draughtsman even more than a colourist and it was the linear element which predominated. In 1951–2 he restricted himself to black and white; at the same time, strongly figurative motives reappeared. The following year, he painted what many consider his masterpiece, the massive *Blue Poles*. The dark blue poles of the title act as markers of rhythm in a frenzied field of bright, artificial colour, providing the work with its special strength and authority.

Pollock's influence on subsequent art has been immense, though in two essentially contradictory directions. Some, believing his work represents a new beginning in painting, have tackled some of the formal, pictorial problems it raises. For others, his 'action painting' has signalled the end of painting as such, pointing rather to the artist as performer or shaman. Pollock's status as a culture-hero makes it difficult to distinguish what is inherent in his paintings from what is reflected back into them from the legends woven around him. Perhaps the distinction is anyhow a false one. Pollock himself sometimes wondered, not whether he was making good paintings, but whether he was making 'paintings' at all. The ambiguity of his influence may result from the ambiguity, and hence the richness, of his life's work.

Further reading

See: Bryan Robertson, *Jackson Pollock* (1960); Francis V. O'Connor, *Jackson Pollock* (1967);

I. Tomassoni, *Jackson Pollock* (1968); Bernice Rose, *Jackson Pollock: Works on Paper* (1969); Alberto Busignani, *Pollock* (1971); C.L. Wysuph, *Jackson Pollock: Psychoanalytic Drawings* (1971); B.H. Friedman, *Jackson Pollock: Energy Made Visible* (1973); S. Naifeh and G.H. Smith, *Jackson Pollock: An American Saga* (1990).

GRAY WATSON

POPPER, (Sir) Karl Raimund

1902–94

Austrian/British philosopher

Karl Popper was born in Vienna, the son of a well-to-do lawyer. Both Popper's parents were Jewish, but were baptized in the Lutheran Church before he was born. Popper's late teens coincided with the upheaval following the First World War and the collapse of the Austrian Empire. At this time Popper was strongly influenced by socialist thought; for a short time he became a Marxist, but was soon disenchanted. His wide-ranging interests while he was a student at the University of Vienna included philosophy, psychology, music and science; after taking his PhD in 1928 he qualified as a secondary-school teacher in mathematics and physics. In the later 1920s he became involved in the internationally renowned Vienna Circle of philosophers, and he received encouragement from some of its members, notably Herbert Feigl. From the beginning, however, Popper was highly critical of the group's central doctrines, and many of these criticisms appeared in his masterpiece *The Logic of Scientific Discovery* (*Logik der Forschung*, 1934). A year before **Hitler** marched into Austria, Popper left Vienna with his wife, and took up a position at the University of New Zealand in Christchurch. Here he perfected his English, and in 1945 published the work which won him recognition in the English-speaking world, the two-volume *The Open Society and Its Enemies* (5th edn 1966). In 1946 he took up residence in England. He taught at the London School of Economics, and was made Professor of Logic and Scientific Method in 1949. He was knighted in 1972, and continued to be philosophically productive, his *Objective Knowledge* appearing in 1972.

The Logic of Scientific Discovery is a powerfully original contribution to our understanding of scientific method. When Popper wrote this book the prevailing account of empirical science was that it used 'inductive methods' – that is, inferences from particular observations and experiments to universal laws. Yet ever since Hume such inductive procedures had faced a serious problem: how can observation of a finite number of particular instances logically justify the scientist's confident belief in general laws which are supposed to hold good for all time? Popper's revolutionary suggestion was that the problem of induction was irrelevant to scientific knowledge. How scientists arrived at their theories was a matter for psychology, not logic. What was important was the *testing* of a scientific theory once proposed. And here Popper argued that strictly logical, deductive reasoning is applicable: scientific theories cannot logically be guaranteed to be true, but they are logically capable of being proven *false*. And it is this – the principle of falsification – that is the essence of the logic of science. Science thus works by a process of *Conjectures and Refutations* (the title of a later book – revised 1972 – in which Popper amplified his position). A scientific theory has the status of a tentative hypothesis which is then matched against observations; if the observations actually made are inconsistent with those predicted by the theory, then the theory is refuted and the way is open for a new conjecture.

One remarkable feature of Popper's book is that, at a time when the verificationism of the Logical Positivists was the ruling doctrine, he had already grasped the fundamental weakness that was to lead to its ultimate downfall (i.e. its inability to specify a logic for the verification of scientific law). In place of verifiability Popper's slogan was falsifiability, though, unlike the Positivists, Popper never offered his principle as a criterion of meaningfulness. Instead he suggested it as a principle of demarcation, which separated genuine science from pseudo-science. The mark of a true scientific theorist was the willingness to 'stick one's neck out': theories which did not take the risk of empirical falsification were not entitled to claim scientific status.

It would be hard to overestimate Popper's influence on the methodology of science. It is probably correct to say that the bulk of scientists practising today would accept the Popperian model of the status of scientific theories. On the philosophical front, two problems with Popper's approach are worth noting. First, it is not at all clear that the problem of induction can be disposed of as neatly as Popper supposed. Second, the work of **Thomas Kuhn** has demonstrated the extent to which entrenched scientific theories are immunized against the possibility of falsification. But even Popper's strongest critics would admit that the contemporary scene in the philosophy of science would be unrecognizable without the foundations which he laid.

There is a close link between Popper's seminal work on scientific methodology and the important contribution to political theory and sociology which he went on to produce. The scientific attitude, as defined by Popper, was one of 'critical rationalism' – the preparedness to submit one's ideas to criticism and modification. This approach, Popper proceeded to argue, was applicable not just in science, but throughout social life, and was the hallmark of what he called the 'open society'. The open society is a highly individualistic one, characterized by free critical thinking; it is a society where individuals are confronted with responsibility for their personal decisions. The closed society, by contrast, embodies the 'organic' view of the state: it is in effect a throw-back to 'tribalism', where the identity of individuals is submerged within a harmonious whole. This distinction leads to the main thesis of *The Open Society and its Enemies*: totalitarianism, with its closed society, is not, in essence, a

new movement, but is a form of reactionary primitivism – an attempt to resist the increasing expansion of the critical powers of individual man.

Popper's targets, the theorists of the closed society, are Plato, Hegel and **Marx**. His attack on Plato upset many scholars, but Popper was undoubtedly correct in arguing that the concept of justice in Plato's *Republic* is a collectivist one in which individuality is subordinated to the good of the state. Popper's most violent strictures are reserved for Hegel for his totalitarian glorification of the state, his 'bombastic and hysterical Platonism'. The triumph of Popper's book, however, is his systematic and devastating attack on all aspects of Marxist theory. In particular, Popper attacks Marx as an economic 'historicist'. The argument ties up with the companion work to *The Open Society, The Poverty of Historicism* (1957); historicism is there defined as

> an approach to the social sciences which assumes that historical prediction is their principal aim, and which assumes that this aim is attainable by discovering the 'rhythms' or the 'patterns', the 'laws' or the 'trends' that underlie the evolution of history.

Popper's position is that even in the natural sciences complete deterministic prediction is impossible; and his arguments against the possibility of determinism in the social sphere provide a powerful challenge to any sociological theory with serious predictive aspirations.

In his later book, *Objective Knowledge* (1972), Popper returned to his fundamental preoccupation – the development of human knowledge. Popper now saw his earlier notion of science proceeding by a constant process of conjecture and refutation as a special case of evolution by natural selection: the continuous production of tentative conjectures and 'the constant building up of selective pressures on these conjectures [by criticizing them]'. The evolution of knowledge is, in effect, a continuation of the 'problem-solving' activities in which all organisms are engaged. In developing this position, Popper introduced an important conceptual category which he labels 'World 3'. Most philosophers have habitually distinguished between the objective world of physical things and the subjective world of human experience; to these two categories (which he labels Worlds 1 and 2 respectively) Popper now adds a third, independent world of philosophical and scientific knowledge, of 'problems, theories and critical arguments'. This world, though the product of human activity, has a real and autonomous existence whose repercussions on us are as great or greater than those of our physical environment. Popper has made great claims for the explanatory power of this notion of a man-made yet autonomous Third World. In particular, he has proposed that the thorny problem of the emergence of self-consciousness can be solved by analysing it in terms of an interaction between the self and the objects of World 3. Though this is certainly a fascinating approach, it has yet to be satisfactorily developed; and it is not at present clear whether it will turn out to be as philosophically fruitful as Popper confidently predicts.

If his later ideas met with some scepticism among the philosophical establishment, this was nothing new to Popper, who had always been something of a rebel. In his early career he was a lone critic of the orthodoxy of the Logical Positivists; in later life he consistently condemned the dominant 'linguistic' approach to philosophy as a retreat from the 'great problems' into trivial scholasticism. Whatever the truth of this judgement, there can be no doubt about Popper's own extraordinary contribution to the 'great problems'. To categorize or neatly label this contribution is impossible, for Popper's thought ranges so widely and illuminates so many different aspects of philosophy. He was one of the truly original and creative thinkers of his century.

Further reading

Other works include: *Unended Quest* (1976, originally *Autobiography of Karl Popper*, 1974); see also: Thomas Kuhn, *The Structure of Scientific Revolutions*

(1962); I. Lakatos and A. Musgrove (eds), *Criticism and the Growth of Knowledge* (1970); R. Bambrough (ed.), *Plato, Popper and Society* (1967); Brian Magee, *Popper* (1973); Malachi Hacohen, *Karl Popper: The Formative Years, 1902–1945* (2000).

JOHN COTTINGHAM

PORTER, Cole

1891–1964

US popular composer

Of America's 'golden age' songwriters, Cole Porter is the one most fondly remembered for his particular creations – for his songs' wit, warmth, sophistication and currency as 'standards'. Because of their jazz-age titles, love-wise lyrics and harmonic breadth, 'Anything Goes', 'I've Got You Under My Skin', 'Night and Day', 'Just One of Those Things', 'At Long Last Love', 'Always True to You in My Fashion' and many other numbers have become particularly associated with black artists such as Ella Fitzgerald and led at least one reference book to state, erroneously, that Porter was African American. In his own day Harold Arlen was more concretely associated with black culture; Porter's view of the matter was that, born a white millionaire Protestant from Indiana, the secret of his success was that he learnt to write 'Jewish', apparently meaning that he exploited minor-key harmonies (though rarely through to the end of a song). Like Jerome Kern and **Gershwin**, Porter wrote the vast majority of his songs for stage entertainments (musical comedies and revues) or for musical films, and as with them, it is the songs, not the musicals, that have survived, with very few canonical exceptions, basically *Anything Goes* (1934), *Kiss Me, Kate* (1948) and perhaps *High Society* (film, 1956) and *Silk Stockings* (1955).

Anything Goes is a routine, indeed rather old-fashioned shipboard farce, but *Kiss Me, Kate*, with its multiple layers of diegesis and its incorporation of the core of Shakespeare's *The Taming of the Shrew*, was the perfect vehicle for Porter's verbal innuendo (he always wrote his own lyrics), encyclopaedic smartness (he excelled at 'list' songs) and sidelong view of love, though the music ranges curiously between antique pastiche, Broadway pizzazz and operetta romanticism. Beyond this, high society, if not the silk stockings, was exactly Porter's milieu. The image of the elderly gay man, in constant pain since a riding accident in 1937 (one leg had eventually to be amputated), predeceased by his beautiful wife, Linda, dining with his butler because he could not conceive of foregoing either the company or the formal elegance, lends his artistry a legendary dimension lacking in his contemporaries. It had always been understood that, after his Yale education, Porter would excel as a connoisseur, *bon vivant* and musical dilettante, and going to live in Paris with Linda in the 1920s seemed for a while to confirm the traditional expectation of talent and the good life cancelling each other out; but it was Porter's hard-working, determined effort to learn the Broadway and then the Hollywood trade that caused the steady, much admired rise in his reputation until the accident, after which it was expected that he would revert at most to the occasional purveying of amusement. (*Kiss Me, Kate*'s triumph came as a glorious surprise.)

At the same time the songs are undoubtedly party pieces, and it is their mixed revelation and concealment of the sexual truth that continues to bind them to the man. (Porter recorded some of them, including 'Anything Goes' with any number of encore verses, in his deadpan piano style and clipped sardonic voice, in obvious parallel to Noël Coward as a musical *raconteur*.) He had trouble with the censor, and 'Kate the Great' still sounds daring today. Given the law, it was an honestly chosen lifestyle for a sociable, wealthy man; Linda valued the protection, Cole fell for many a younger man and took it as far as he could without jeopardizing his marriage. The result was a lifelong bitter-sweet stand-off with love that he knew would find its fulfilment in the songs. In 'Begin the Beguine' he lengthened the Tin Pan Alley song's frame and enlarged its emotional scope magnificently; in 'Ev'ry Time We Say

Goodbye', the most unlettered listener can feel their heart stop at the sad 'change from major to minor' which Porter's genius effortlessly conveyed.

Further reading

Cole Porter on Broadway (1987) is a useful song anthology; there are others. *Anything Goes* and *Kiss Me, Kate* are available complete in piano/vocal score. Robert Kimball has edited *The Lyrics of Cole Porter* (1983). The definitive biography is William McBrien: *Cole Porter* (1998); see also Charles Schwartz: *Cole Porter* (1978).

STEPHEN BANFIELD

POULENC, Francis
1899–1963
French composer

Poulenc's early career was determined not so much by his formal studies with Charles Koechlin (which took place in 1921–4, after he established himself as a composer) as by his association with Jean Cocteau and with fellow-members of the group known as Les Six. Poulenc came to the attention of this circle in 1917 with his precocious and absurd *Rapsodie nègre* for voice and chamber ensemble, a work showing those qualities of cool wit and sophistication which were to mark much of his output. He followed Cocteau's demands for economy and crispness in many of the works which immediately followed the *Rapsodie*, but the musical influence of Eric Satie was gradually superseded by that of **Stravinsky**: the early wind sonatas, for two clarinets (1918), clarinet and bassoon (1922) and brass trio (1922), show this quite clearly. Inevitably his talent was noticed by **Diaghilev**, for whom he wrote *Les Biches* (1923), a suave and seductive picture of high society life.

Les Biches proved Poulenc's almost Stravinskyan ability to take alien kinds of music, whether from history or from the dance band, and make them his own. He applied this skill with capricious delight in many of his subsequent larger works, creating in his *Concert champêtre* for harpsichord and orchestra (1927–8), for instance, a knowing backwards glance at eighteenth-century elegance. The Concerto in G minor for organ, strings and timpani (1938) looks back through **Liszt** to Bach, and to a grand rhetoric which is nonchalantly coupled with music of café-style triviality. More exuberant pastiches are to be found in the Concerto for two pianos and orchestra (1932) and in the Piano Concerto (1949), which is rather rare among Poulenc's post-war works in its outgoing vivacity.

His cultivation of a more serious manner can be dated to 1936, in which year he returned to a devout Catholicism. A simple inward piety is expressed in the sacred pieces which followed, including the *Litanies à la Vierge Noire* for women's or children's voices and organ (1936), the Mass in G major for unaccompanied choir (1937) and various motets, while the larger religious works for soprano, choir and orchestra, a *Stabat mater* (1950) and a *Gloria* (1959), are in a colourful and dramatic style which shows Poulenc's continuing debt to Stravinsky. He did not, however, follow that master in taking up serialism, but instead pursued his own very French style, tuneful and diatonic, bringing it to a peak of refinement in his late sonatas for flute (1956), clarinet (1962) and oboe (1962).

Poulenc's later works also include three operas of very different character: *Les Mamelles de Tirésias* (1944), a typically witty setting of Apollinaire's play; *Dialogues des Carmélites* (1953–5), where the convent location of Bernanos's libretto gave him the opportunity for an operatic exposure of his religious manner; and *La Voix humaine* (1958), a soprano monologue of fleeting mood set to words by Cocteau. The last of these in particular shows the sensitivity to language which made Poulenc the most versatile and distinguished contributor to the repertory of French song since **Fauré**. Specially noteworthy are his song cycles to poems by Apollinaire (*Le Bestiaire*, 1919; *Banalités*, 1940; *Calligrammes*, 1948), Eluard (*Tel Jour, telle nuit*, 1936–7; *Le Fraîcheur et le feu*, 1950; *Le Travail du peintre*, 1956), Cocteau (*Cocardes*, 1919) and Carème (*La Courte paille*, 1960). Many of these were written for the baritone Pierre Bernac, with whom from 1935 he appeared often in recitals.

Further reading

Other works include: *Aubade* for piano and small orchestra (1929); *Suite française* for ten instruments or piano (1935); *Sextet* for piano and wind (1932–9); *Les Animaux modèles*, ballet (1940); Violin Sonata (1942–3, revised 1949); *Figure humaine* for chorus (1943); *L'Histoire de Babar* for narrator and piano (1940–5); *Sinfonietta* (1947); Cello Sonata (1948); Sonata for two pianos (1952–3); many solo piano pieces. Writings: *Emmanuel Chabrier* (1961); *Moi et mes amis* (1963); *Correspondance, 1915–1963*, ed. Hélène de Wendel (1967); *Journal de mes mélodies* (1964). About Poulenc: Henri Hell, *Francis Poulenc* (1958, trans. 1959); Jean Roy, *Francis Poulenc* (1964); Wilfred Mellers, *Francis Poulenc* (1995); B. Ivry, *Francis Poulenc* (1996); S. Buckland and M. Chimènes (eds), *Francis Poulenc: Music, Art and Literature* (1999).

PAUL GRIFFITHS

POUND, Ezra Loomis
1885–1972
US poet

Born in Idaho, in the American north-west, of Quaker parents, Ezra Pound moved east as a child when his father became an assayer at the US Mint in Philadelphia. He studied at Hamilton College, the University of Pennsylvania, where he met William Carlos Williams and the imagist poet Hilda Doolittle. A year of postgraduate study in Romance languages led to a small scholarship to travel and study in Europe. In Italy he published his first book of verse, *A Lume Spento*, in 1908. In England from 1909, he taught a course at the Regent Street Polytechnic which he turned into a collection of lively and original essays on *The Spirit of Romance* (1910; revised 1953), but his life in London is now better remembered for his spirited involvement in contemporary literary movements. Together with F.S. Flint, he promulgated the aesthetics of imagism, that crucial reaction against the metaphysical speculation and heavily declarative syntax of Victorian public verse. Advocating 'direct treatment of the "thing", whether subjective or objective', the pure imagist poet described objects or emotions in non-literary language, leaving explicit analysis, where necessary, to the reader.

While in London, Pound also promoted individual careers. Though **W.B. Yeats's** generous testimony to Pound's helpful advice probably overstates the effect the young American could have had on his late work, there is no doubt that Pound arranged for the publication of **Joyce's** *Portrait of the Artist as a Young Man* and some of **Eliot's** early short poems, and Pound's midwifery at the delivery of *The Waste Land* is a matter of record.

His own poems written during this period, published in various collections like *Exultations* (1909), *Canzoni* (1911) and *Ripostes* (1912), show an increasing economy of expression, and they also reflect his interest in classical and medieval subjects. It may be because the theory of imagism discourages the presence of 'subjects' that he began to turn increasingly to translation, a device by which an author can transmit ideas without overt editorial comment. Pound's version of poems by the Chinese Li Bo (Li Po), taken from Japanese transliterations and English prose translations by Ernest Fenollosa, was published as *Cathay* in 1915. Like his translation of the Old English *The Seafarer* (published in *Ripostes*) and his 'Homage to Sextus Propertius' (in *Quia Pauper Amavi*, 1919), *Cathay* contained a number of mistakes – some intentional, some inspired, and others just wrong – yet the effect of these works is of astonishing insights into the sensibilities of three entirely different cultures.

As Pound began to have more and more to say – about the war and its causes in the economics of Europe and America – imagism began to look increasingly mannered and miniaturist to him. It was at this point that he began work on a much more ambitious project for his poetry. Originally conceived as a

Browningesque dramatic monologue about the ironies of attempting to educate America in the European past, the first three *Cantos* (published in *Quia Pauper Amavi*) were later revised so as to give prominence to a reworking, in 'Seafarer' metre, of what Pound took to be the oldest kernel of the *Odyssey* story, the epic hero's visit to the underworld. Just as Odysseus had to beat back the beguiling shades of his comrades and relations (including his own mother) so as to get, from Teiresias, the facts he needed to pilot himself and his crew back to Ithaca, so Pound had to raid the past selectively in order to guide his culture back 'home' to the integral society from which he thought it had departed. The *Cantos*, which finally comprised well over a hundred separate, though related, poems, were to occupy him for the rest of his long life.

Despairing of the revolution in taste and politics which he had once hoped to further in England, Pound left London in 1920. Together with his English wife, the artist Dorothy Shakespear, he lived for a while in Paris before settling in Rapallo, Italy, four years later. His departure from the city in which his chief interests had been formed, and his poetry much firmed, was signalled in *Hugh Selwyn Mauberley* (1920), for many critics still his most admired work. An allusive, multi-faceted satire on English life and letters, *Mauberley* is also a kind of exorcism, like Eliot's 'Prufrock' and **Wallace Stevens's** 'The Comedian as the Letter C', of an aspect of the author as dilettante that he felt he had outgrown.

In Italy Pound formed an alliance with the American violinist Olga Rudge. Their daughter, Mary, born in 1925, was fostered by a peasant family in the Tyrol. But Dorothy also remained in Rapallo, and their son, Omar, was born there in 1926. By 1930 Pound had completed the first thirty *Cantos*, and he continued to produce essays on literature and economics, incorporating his ideas and discoveries into *Cantos* XXXI to LXXI. His attraction to Italian fascism, as his short book *Jefferson and/or Mussolini* (1935) makes clear, was based on his analogy between the remaking of the Italian economy under Mussolini and the work of Jefferson, Madison and Martin Van Buren in establishing the American Republic. His infamous broadcasts from Rome under the sponsorship of the fascist regime began in 1940 and continued until after the United States was at war with Italy. As he saw it, Pound never attacked the basic American principles of government, but supported the Constitution against its perversion by more recent American administrations. In 1943 he was indicted for treason by a Washington, DC, grand jury, and in 1945, near the end of the European war, was imprisoned in a US Army 'disciplinary training centre' north of Pisa. Returned to the United States later that year to stand trial, he was found to be 'suffering from a paranoid state' and unfit to advise counsel. He was subsequently committed to St Elizabeth's Hospital, outside Washington, for treatment.

In St Elizabeth's he continued to read and write, completing his translations from Confucius first made into Italian (finally published in English as *The Unwobbling Pivot and The Great Digest*, 1947) and Cantos LXXIV–LXXXIV, begun in Pisa. The *Pisan Cantos* (1948) are thought, even by critics normally hostile to Pound, to be especially sensitive evocations of his mental state as he reflected on his public and private life in his captivity. For them he was awarded, amidst considerable controversy, the prestigious American Bollingen Prize for poetry in 1949. In 1956 he completed and published the next ten Cantos as *Section: Rock Drill*. In 1958 his indictment for treason was quashed, and he was released from St Elizabeth's to join his daughter Mary and her husband in Italy. In 1959 Cantos XCVI–CIX appeared as *Thrones*, and ten years later, *Drafts and Fragments of Cantos C–CXVII*. He died in 1972.

Ezra Pound's life and work invite the adjective 'modern' not least in their perennial difficulty. Though most of his translations and shorter poems have found an uneasy place in contemporary critical esteem, the *Cantos* have been slow to be accommodated in the school and university courses that now govern the sense of a 'tradition' in English and American literature. This must be due in part to their wide range of reference to Greek, Latin, Provençal, early American and Chinese history, as well as his recollections (mainly in the *Pisan Cantos* and later) to the author's many friends and antagonists, both illustrious and obscure. Again, the *Cantos* do not tell a story, or pause – except occasionally – for moments of lyric repose, but dive restlessly into various versions of the past to find whole chunks of letters, laws, books on economics, and (more rarely) works of literature, with which to confront the wayward present. Though these documents are sometimes cited with inviting economy and almost always 'rhymed' with great subtlety, readers accustomed to the self-sufficient literary object, the 'words on the page', have been deterred by the pressure outwards into non-literary materials beyond the poet's aesthetic frame. One answer to this problem is that Pound was always more of a translator and a maker of syllabi than he was a poet in the conventional sense of the term, and that a major satisfaction of the *Cantos* is predicated in a subsequent reading of the documents towards which they gesture. But the reader is not expected to have got there before the poet, and the guilt or pique apparently felt by some critics at not having anticipated Pound's cultural 'set' is probably misplaced.

Not just the form, but also the contents of the *Cantos*, have given offence. Regular readers of poetry can accept the denunciation of usury in the much-anthologized Canto XLV as being in some general sense against nature, but Pound's more specific and contemporary advocacy, elsewhere in the *Cantos*, of the state control of credit has been criticized as too cranky, or at any rate too unliterary, a subject for poetry. Cranky it certainly was not; the economic theories of Douglas, Gesell, Alexander Del Mar and Christopher Hollis, whatever their differences, had in common a search for alternatives to monetarism, an attempt to put money back into the community and to get unemployed men and facilities back to work, without committing the taxpayer to ever-increasing charges for interest. Whether Pound managed to make poetry out of the topic depends partly on the success with which he worked it in with other themes. In the *Cantos*, at least, it was always part of his larger subject, or what might be called his one idea: that every contrivance of the human imagination, from a metaphor to a political system, may be either derived from, or imposed upon, nature. Telling the difference is the one essential discrimination, the necessary moral discipline. This idea did not originate with Pound, but it connects his earliest imagism with the most specific topics in the *Cantos*. 'Banker's Credit' is suspect, therefore, because it does not reflect the 'natural' wealth of a country's material and human resources.

But Pound's anti-semitism remains beyond accommodation. Though restricted largely to his broadcasts and other polemical pieces, and though derived ultimately from the rhetoric of the American Populists, whose economics Pound shared, his use of Jews as a shorthand for usurers showed a failure of sympathy and foresight that cannot be brushed aside by his admirers. It is hard to deny, furthermore, that elements of the paranoia and hectic self-righteousness that have accompanied the more serious forms of anti-semitism are present in Pound's work, even when he is not treating of the economy.

Ultimately Pound's reputation must rest on his life's work, the *Cantos*. He finally came to see them as a failure, because though begun as an epic on the model of *The Divine Comedy* they never get their hero (in this case, the poet himself) home to Paradise at the end. But the *Cantos* are a classic 'made new': an address to the times adducing ancient sources of a better future. In this respect they resemble millennial projections, and should put the reader in mind of that other great, unfinished apocalypse, *Piers Plowman*. Both poems keep interrupting their progress towards the empyrean to cite contemporary abuses, especially by those institutions (for Langland the monasteries, for Pound the banks) considered by the authors to be most capable of reforming the fallen society, and therefore most culpable in failing to do so. The *Cantos* are a great synthesis, a great excursion in an open field of reference.

Further reading

Other works include: *Cantos* (except nos LXXII and LXXIII) see *The Cantos of Ezra Pound* (1972). See: *Selected Poems* (1975); and *Ezra Pound, Selected Prose 1909–1965*, ed. William Cookson (1973). The standard biography is Noel Stock, *The Life of Ezra Pound* (1970). See also: Hugh Kenner, *The Poetry of Ezra Pound* (1971); *Paideuma*, a journal devoted to Pound studies (quarterly, from the University of Maine at Orono); John Tytell, *Ezra Pound: The Solitary Volcano* (1987); Ira B. Nadel, *The Cambridge Companion to Ezra Pound* (1999) and *Ezra Pound: A Literary Life* (2004); Demetres P. Tryphonopoulos and Stephen J. Adams (eds), *The Ezra Pound Encyclopedia* (2005).

STEPHEN FENDER

PRESLEY, Elvis Aaron

1935–77

US popular singer

Although the invention of rock 'n' roll is generally accredited to Bill Haley, it was Elvis Presley who transformed a new musical vogue into a social phenomenon. The son of a poor farm worker from South Tupelo, Mississippi, Presley's dangerous good looks and wonderfully expressive voice made him the first and most charismatic icon in the post-war development of an independent youth culture based on music.

In 1954 he recorded for Sun Records, Memphis, a song called 'That's All Right Mama'. Though not a national success at the time, it defines the sources of rock 'n' roll: a white country singer records a black song and for the first time, instead of eliminating black emotion and physicality, retains them in a new synthesis of country music and the blues. Colonel Tom Parker became Presley's manager soon after, and in 1955 they signed a contract with RCA Records. Most of his classic rock 'n' roll numbers were recorded the following year: 'Heartbreak Hotel', 'Blue Suede Shoes', 'Tutti Frutti', 'Lawdy Miss Clawdy', 'Shake Rattle and Roll', 'Hound Dog', etc. Presley's impact, conveyed by his records and stage appearances with their swaggering content of sex and insubordination, was amplified through films, and hysteria climaxed in 1957 with the film *Jailhouse Rock*, which many cinema managers banned when it became associated with teenage rioting.

At the end of 1957 Presley was drafted into the army and when he returned to civilian life it was without anarchic overtones. Hereafter he was simply the world's most famous pop singer. Only at his death, the victim of obesity and drugs, did he again touch the deepest emotions of the public.

Presley was not a composer, he did not direct his own career, and his only articulation was in performance. At its height his music was blamed for the rise of 'juvenile delinquency', a period catch-phrase which referred only to the negative aspect of a spectacular outburst of energy among young people. Positively, he was the inspirational figurehead in the origination of a new cultural group, with its own financial resources, between the traditional categories of childhood and adulthood – that of youth.

Further reading

Alan Harbinson, *The Life and Death of Elvis Presley* (1977).

DUNCAN FALLOWELL

PRICE, Cedric John

1934–2003

English architect

Demonstrating his concept of 'anticipatory architecture', Cedric Price placed architecture in an entirely new perspective, generating models for a future architecture as yet unrealized. The astonishing range and output of projects served to explore his generic ideas about new ways of making environments responsive to the needs and desires of their users and became the fundamental archetypes of a new deal for users – or a new 'menu' for the consumers of architecture in Price's terminology.

Born in Staffordshire, Price was to become the most provocative questioner of the architectural profession and its assumptions, rejecting traditional architectural conventions and values and challenging the social, functional and aesthetic norms. Price was extremely highly regarded and acknowledged by the leading architectural thinkers of the time, but remained an enigma to the rest of the 'sleepy profession'. At a time when architects were beginning to acquire a social conscience, Price went much further and centred his thinking on social and ethical concerns of which architecture might, almost incidentally, be a by-product. He continually challenged the preconceptions of the profession and society about the limits and social usefulness of architecture, in the process generating an astounding variety of provocative and inspirational ideas. Working always through the medium of testable propositions, his projects and ideas are extraordinarily powerful and challenging, but also delivered with a sense of mischief, fun and pure delight.

Having studied architecture at Cambridge University (1952–5) and then at the independent Architectural Association School in London (1955–7), he worked briefly for Fry, Drew and Partners and Erno Goldfinger before setting up his own practice in 1960. The catalogue of projects from his small practice is immense in quantity as well as in the quality of their thinking, but most of all was a staggering ability to 'think the unimaginable'. His projects are recognized as the seminal architectural propositions of the twentieth century.

The impresario Joan Littlewood came to Price with a project to replace the formalism of theatre and amusement facilities and reincorporate them into the everyday life of the city, a brief which resulted in the proposition to create a Fun Palace – a concept of a flexible and indeterminate space which reverberated through two generations, inspiring Piano and **Rogers'** Pompidou Centre in Paris, and being the topic of an entire conference in Berlin in 2004 which reaffirmed the visionary nature of the project. Price's concept was not a static monument, but an ever-changing environment responding to the appetites of its users. There was no façade or even formal enclosure, but cranes redeploying a kit of parts as needed and all under cybernetic control (consultant Gordon Pask). A different configuration is shown in every drawing, the conventional labels such as Elevation being replaced with titles such as 'Selection', 'Assembly', 'Movement' and 'Control', and the whole proposition is only grasped from a helicopter view at night with the roof retracted. Writing in the *New Statesman* in 1964, Reyner Banham started a public debate about the social potential of architecture by comparing the traditional frozen monumentality of the then recently completed Crystal Palace sports centre with the flexibility and new set of choices in proposed Price's Fun Palace.

Price quickly followed his radical thinking about reconfigurable places of entertainment by rethinking higher education with the Potteries Thinkbelt proposal (1963–6). At a time when new universities were still being constructed following the monastic model, Price proposed a new form of university organization which was mobile and dispersed, utilizing an abandoned rail network in the derelict potteries and mining areas of north Staffordshire. The university was conceived as a reconfigurable network of mobile classrooms and laboratories, a thinkbelt following the existing rail line. Provocatively, Price described higher education as a major industrial undertaking integrated into the community rather than a service for the elite.

Price moved on to tackle the office environment. The Generator project (1976) for the Gilman Paper Corporation located in a forest in Florida was described by Price as 'A forest facility … a place to work, create,

think and stare.' Architecture is used as an aid to the extension of the users' own interests, a series of structures, fittings and components that respond to the appetites they themselves may generate: a 'menu' of items for individual and group demands of space, control, containment and delight. However the Generator moves further than previous projects by offering a clear programme of how and why change is to be effected and what the variation in resulting environments might be like. It poses the notion of an intelligent building that learns from its own experience. The Generator is a field of reconfigurable units, a mobile crane permanently on site and a completely worked-out strategy for self-organization. Price's cybernetics consultants suggested that the site and the elements on it should have a life and intelligence of their own, and the programme would start to generate unsolicited plans, improvements and modifications in response to users' comments, records of activities, or even by building in a boredom concept so that the site starts to make proposals about changes of itself if no changes are made. Inevitably dubbed by the press as the world's first intelligent building, it was the logical conclusion of Price's thinking about interactive buildings since the Fun Palace – the new ideas included embedded intelligence in the form of a microprocessor into the reconfigurable elements of the building, and having organizational software learning from experience during use.

There followed a galaxy of spectacular projects which moved his thinking into urban environments internationally with projects such as Magnet, which proposed a series of temporary constructions for London and Tokyo that would be redeployed as magnets to attract regeneration. The ideas were rich and varied continuing the 'questioning of indisputable premises'.

Price's vast output of projects and ideas was hugely influential but largely unbuilt. However, what he did manage to construct provides insights into how his thinking might have been realized on a large scale. For example the Aviary for London Zoo 1961 (in collaboration with Lord Snowdon and Frank Newby) was designed on the tensegrity principles of **Buckminster Fuller** (with whom he also collaborated on a number of projects) which generate highly efficient minimal structures with maximum transparency and clear flying space for the birds and exemplifies his interest in lightweight ephemeral structures. The Inter-Action Trust Community Centre in Kentish Town in 1971 gave Price the opportunity to realize on a small scale some parts of the Fun Palace concept, embracing at least flexibility, and impermanence to the extent of opposing the listing of the Centre for cultural preservation and insisting on demolition. Apart from the Pompidou Centre, his ideas found their way through to other mainstream architectural designs; even the London Eye, erected to celebrate the new millennium in 2000, was originally proposed by Price in his 1984 plans for the South Bank commissioned by the then Greater London Council. His feasibility studies and proposals for British Rail for Stratford East and the Thames Gateway are now to be realized for the London Olympic Games of 2012.

Espousing no arbitrary formal allegiances, Price's process of problem-questioning thrust his projects far beyond the bounds and methods of existing architecture 'Architecture should have little to do with problem-solving – rather it should create desirable conditions and opportunities hitherto thought impossible.' Projects where functions and spaces continuously move about are understood by some to be the architectural equivalent of the preoccupations of **John Cage**, or are dismissed as formless or as being more like a permanent construction site; for others they embodied anonymous design. But certainly the work was provocative and distanced itself from the formal preoccupations of shape-making that obsesses architecture and industrial design.

Formally recognized with awards such as the prestigious Kiesler Prize (previously awarded to **Frank Gehry**), Price's influence

and status rest on the radical nature of his propositions, assisted by their wide publication, and his influence on several generations of students as a visiting critic and occasional tutor mostly at the Architectural Association in London. His acknowledged professional influence was extensive and ranges from Archigram, then **Norman Foster**, **Richard Rogers**, through to the younger generation of **Ken Yeang**, Will Allsop and Rem Koolhaus.

Further reading

Price's drawings and papers are mostly archived in the Canadian Centre for Architecture, Montreal, the Museum of Modern Art, New York or in private collections. Exhibitions included the Architectural Association (1984) and the Design Museum, London (2005); Cedric Price, *Works II* (1984), *The Square Book* (2003) and *Re: CP* (2003); Royston Landau, *New Directions in British Architecture* (1968); Neil Spiller (ed.), *Cyber–Reader* (2002), which includes the Generator project; Reyner Banham, *A Critic Writes* (1996); and Samantha Hardingham, *Cedric Price OPERA* (2003).

JOHN HAMILTON FRAZER

PROKOFIEV, Sergei Sergeievich

1891–1953

Russian composer and pianist

Born in the village of Sontsovka, the son of an agricultural engineer who managed a large estate in the Ukrainian steppe, Prokofiev was musically precocious to an unusual degree. By 1902, when he received his first formal tuition in music from the composer Rheinhold Glière, he was already the composer of two operas and numerous short piano pieces. On Alexander Glazunov's advice, he entered the St Petersburg Conservatory in 1904, where he spent a stormy and unhappy ten years. At a time of increasing political tension, the Conservatory provided a less than ideal environment for the unruly student, and his classes with **Rimsky-Korsakov**, Lyadov, Winkler and Cherepnin made less impact on his development than his contact with progressive artistic groups in St Petersburg – the 'World of Art' and the Evenings of Contemporary Music. At the height of the Scriabin cult, and in the heyday of the literary Symbolists, he was encouraged to evolve a novel style of his own, and some of his most iconoclastic and aggressive music dates from the immediately pre-war years – works like the First and Second Piano Concertos (1912 and 1913), and the piano *Sarcasms* (1912–14). The highly charged Romanticism of late Scriabin and early **Richard Strauss** also influenced him for a time, and by contrast with his piano music, his early songs, symphonic poems and the opera *Maddalena* (1911–13) are intense and strongly atmospheric works.

His career as a St Petersburg *enfant terrible* took a new turn in the summer of 1914, when, on a trip to London, he attended the season of **Diaghilev's** Ballets Russes, the heady glamour of which he found irresistible. For the first and perhaps the only time in his career, he found the direct influence of another composer inescapable: the impact of **Stravinsky's** ballets, in particular *The Rite of Spring*, is evident in many of his large works of the following years, from the ballet *The Buffoon* (1915) to the Second Symphony (1925). The occasion also marked the beginning of Prokofiev's own involvement with the Ballets Russes, which was to last until Diaghilev's death in 1929.

The first of Prokofiev's works to gain international recognition, the 'Classical' Symphony – deliberately close to Haydn in style, but with 'something new' as well – was written in the summer of 1917, as political events in Russia were reaching a crisis. With the Revolution and the ensuing civil war, it seemed to Prokofiev that his own country might, for the foreseeable future, have graver concerns than for new music. In May 1918 he left for the United States, where his reception was initially encouraging: the music of Stravinsky and the performances of Rachmaninov had set an artistic fashion for all things Russian. He was soon disillusioned, however, by both the commercialism of

concert promoters and the basic conservatism of audiences, and it was increasingly in Western Europe, particularly in Paris, that he found a more receptive audience for his music. Yet it was in these artistically and financially difficult first years abroad that some of his most characteristic and popular works were written. The music for *The Buffoon*, revised in 1920, the Third Piano Concerto (1921), the opera *Love of Three Oranges* (1919), and the Fifth Piano Sonata (1923, rev. 1953) are flights of energetic fancy, clear, incisive, and often humorous; Prokofiev's music was never more dynamic nor more whimsically imaginative.

By the end of the 1920s, the time of the opera *The Fiery Angel* (1923, rev. 1926–7) and the ballet *The Prodigal Son* (1929), Prokofiev was at the height of his composing career in the West. As a pianist, too, he was in demand throughout Europe and in North and South America. But in 1929, with the death of Diaghilev and his spirit of artistic adventure, and with the repercussions of the Wall Street collapse in Europe, the market for new music received a severe blow. Between 1932 and 1936 he received only two commissions – the Sonata for Two Violins (1932) and the Second Violin Concerto (1935) – from Western Europe. Over the same period he received seven Soviet commissions, including those for *Lieutenant Kije* (orchestral suite, 1934), *Romeo and Juliet* (ballet, 1936), and *Peter and the Wolf* (symphonic tale, 1936) – three of his best-known and finest scores. He had renewed contact with the Soviet Union during a concert tour in 1927. After some years of apparent indecision he returned there permanently in the spring of 1936.

Prokofiev's first Soviet works – works in which he was very conscious of the need for a much wider popular appeal – are the result not merely of a process of simplification in his idiom; his musical style underwent a change of emphasis. The Romanticism of his youth, never entirely absent from his works, re-emerged: in his Second Violin Concerto, *Romeo and Juliet* and *Alexander Nevsky* (cantata,

1939) it takes the form of a more serene lyricism and textural warmth. The earlier whimsy with which he juxtaposed dynamic ideas was resolved in the clarity and breadth of his later musical structures: his later symphonies and sonatas have a typically Russian 'epic' feel to them. The sardonic humour of *Love of Three Oranges* was replaced by the elegant wit of *The Duenna* (opera, 1940–1) and *Cinderella* (ballet, 1944) – though, sadly, after *Cinderella*, in the face of the Second World War and the Communist Party's strictures on the arts which both preceded and followed it, Prokofiev's music was rarely frivolous in content. The characteristic works of his later years – the Fifth and Seventh Symphonies (1944 and 1952), the operas *Semyon Kotko* (1939) and *War and Peace* (1943, rev. 1946–52), the music for **Eisenstein's** *Ivan the Terrible* (1944–8) – are 'heroic' and traditional works, serious in intent.

After 1938 Prokofiev's contact with Western Europe ceased; he gave no further concerts abroad. In 1941 he suffered the first of a series of heart attacks. His last concert appearance, as the conductor of his Fifth Symphony, was in 1945. After a bad fall that year his health deteriorated. His prodigious rate of composition slowed down in his last years, and he died of a brain haemorrhage on 5 March 1953, the same day as **Stalin** died.

The scope of Prokofiev's career, and the contradictions it embodies, are in most respects a product of the times in which he lived. Cut off from the roots of his own Russian traditions by the Revolution in 1917, he had to attempt to rediscover them in 1936, but by then he was a product of the sophisticated 1920s in the West. Yet, as a Russian, and because of his uncompromising personality, he had found it difficult to meet the West on its own musical ground, and in any case his efforts were pre-empted by Stravinsky. Outside Russia, his music, and especially the dynamic nature of his earlier piano music, has become a familiar element in contemporary concert programmes, but his overall influence has been indirect. His return to Russia had a significant impact on the course of Soviet music, however, and the flavour of Prokofiev's melodies, rhythms and turns of cadence characterized much of the music of Khachaturyan, Kabalevsky and even **Shostakovich** in the 1940s and 1950s.

Further reading

Other works include: operas: *The Gambler* (1917, rev. 1927–8); *The Story of a Real Man* (1948); ballets: *Le Pas d'Acier* (1926); *The Tale of a Stone Flower* (1948–53); symphonies: No. 3 (1928); No. 4 (1930); No. 6 (1947); concertos: for piano: No. 4 for left hand only (1931); No. 5 (1932); for violin: No. 1 (1917); Sinfonia Concerto for Cello and Orchestra (1950–52); *Cantata for the Twentieth Anniversary of the October Revolution* (1937); and nine sonatas for piano (1909–47). See: *Sergei Prokofiev: Autobiography, Articles, Reminiscences*, ed. S. Shlifstein (1956, trans. 1960); *Prokofiev by Prokofiev* (1979); Israel V. Nestyev, *Prokofiev* (trans. 1961); Victor Seroff, *Prokofiev: A Soviet Tragedy* (1968); Claude Samuel, *Prokofiev* (trans. 1971); H. Robinson, *Sergei Prokofiev: A Biography* (1987); O. Prokofiev (trans. and ed.) *Sergei Prokofiev: Soviet Diary 1927 and Other Writings* (1991).

RITA MCALISTER

PROUST, Marcel
1871–1922
French novelist

Marcel Proust was born into an upper-middle-class family of strong scientific and artistic interests that marked both the subject-matter of his future writing and the metaphors through which he was to convey his picture of the mind. His father was an eminent physician, conversant with French psychology of the day, and his mother, with whom he had the more intense relationship, a cultured and witty woman. The letters exchanged between mother and son show the ambivalent intimacy that may have been responsible for his susceptible and unhappy adult relationships, which were homosexual.

Of contemporary influences, that which most affected him during his education at the Lycée Condorcet and the École des Sciences Politiques (where he took degrees in law and philosophy) was perhaps Henri Bergson's, but to speak of this one only would be an absurdly narrow assessment of a catholic taste that had absorbed not only the finest writings of the nineteenth century in France and England but the classics of world literature, music and painting. Both direct references and metaphors in his writing show what he owed to **Baudelaire**, Nerval, **George Eliot**; to the Bible, and the Italian Renaissance; to French medieval epic, and to hundreds of other works of art. As one critic says, 'he sucked so much nourishment into his own great plant that his successors had to grow roots in other ground' (J. Cocking; see bibliography).

There has been a widely held picture of the young Proust as a dilettante: this in spite of the publication of a collection of short stories, 'portraits' and poems in his twenties (*Les Plaisirs et les jours*, *Pleasures and Regrets*, 1896, trans. 1950); the translation and annotation of some **Ruskin** in his thirties; and the discovery in the 1950s of an early unfinished novel, *Jean Santeuil* (1952, trans. 1955). Nevertheless, it is still true that, although Proust was clearly brilliant, he published nothing of major artistic importance until *Remembrance of Things Past* (the inept English title for *À la recherche du temps perdu*, 1913–27, trans. 1922–31). His previous sketches, and longer essays or fiction, show that he already had all his themes, many of his characters, a gift for imagery, and wit; but he was still groping towards a structure for these, and still often lacked complete stylistic control. It does seem that he may have had a sudden inspiration, round about 1909, comparable to that he describes for the hero of his novel, even if it was only how to use insights long held. The result was *Remembrance of Things Past*, the greatest twentieth-century French novel, and considered by some to be the greatest twentieth-century European novel.

Its influence has been huge: its unprecedentedly bold use of a subjective first-person narrator, its stress on the relativity of perception, its radical departures from linear chronology, and its ostentatious patterning by image, association and coincidence have profoundly marked the novel both inside and outside France. Even French novelists of the 1930s and 1940s like Malraux and **Sartre**, seeming to depart from Proust with novels exploring political decisions and the biological solidarity of the human species, still show their debt to Proust's psychological perceptions and his methods of creating fluid or volte-face character. Later, the French *nouveau roman* took up the lessons of *Remembrance of Things Past*, and wove them into a game more elaborate than anything since **Gide's** *The Counterfeiters* (which is, incidentally, often wrongly credited with many of Proust's narrative innovations). And in general, modern preoccupations with the interpretation of chaotic material, or with the meaning of language, had already reached perhaps their most adult expression and their most satisfactory explanation in *Remembrance of Things Past*.

Proust's novel is not an easy one; Roger Shattuck claims that it is the least read of the modern classics, and it is true that to read it with enjoyment, one must discard all habits of short-cutting. One of Proust's earliest critics, Léon Pierre-Quint, recommended that readers should start with twenty pages a day for the first week, then, slowly working up, increase this by five pages a day. Yet, like all great novels, it is its peculiar balance between simplicity and complexity that makes *Remembrance of Things Past* rewarding. The plot, for instance, can be seen as a bare and satisfying one – an odyssey of kinds. The nameless narrator, whom critics usually call Marcel, grows up longing to be a great artist, and filled with attractive but illusory notions about travel, the aristocracy, and love. He superficially fulfils his worldly ambitions, going to places he had wanted to visit, achieving outstanding social successes, and entering close relationships with three of the women he desires; but he finds that none of these experiences brings him the excitements he had hoped for, and that love can be agonizing. Above all, though his evaluation of art deepens and brings him a certain wisdom, he cannot, himself, create. Finally – in the last 200 pages of the total 3,000 – he reaches a nadir of discouragement. Nature no longer moves him; he cannot even believe in art. Then – an ending presented as quasi-miraculous – a series of physical sensations brings back to him a flood of involuntary memories, which make him both realize the richness of his own life, and, by suggesting to him the continuity of his personality – which he had mainly experienced as disparate and contradictory – give him the faith to create his work of art: a book about his life. He is approaching death, but, after this illumination, he retreats from the world with a new appreciation of ecstasy and sadness to write his work with what strength he still has.

Within this uncluttered framework, Proust plays dazzling variations on certain conceptions of time, personality, love and art – some his own, some clearly in a nineteenth-century lineage, some coinciding startlingly with those of other great contemporary thinkers whom he could not have read, like **Freud**. Those suggestions of Proust's which have disturbed the largest number of critics are the ones about love. Proust illustrates over hundreds of pages his own assertions that love is almost always unreciprocal and that we attribute to the loved one qualities and faults which issue merely from our own imaginations. We fall in love less with the beauty, kindness or intelligence of the beloved than as a result of our belief that he or she represents a world into which we wish to penetrate but from which we feel excluded. These ideas are stated baldly in *Remembrance of Things Past*, but it is still surprising that they should have seemed so controversial, since most of them had already been mooted, in one form or another, by Mme de la Fayette, Racine, Constant, Stendhal and Flaubert. Other insights of Proust's have been greeted with equally strong reactions; for instance, the fact that a large number of his characters prove bisexual has not made critics realize how heterosexually biased the novel had been before him, but has, instead, provoked

numerous accusations of partiality on Proust's part and affirmations of the critics' own orthodox sexuality.

More acceptable has been Proust's depiction of the power of involuntary memory, which he shows as able to break down habit – the great blunter of perception – and to restore our freshest impressions of years ago, both sensory responses and intimate hopes and fears of the time. And, although few critics have tackled his style in detail, all accord him the praise of being an outstanding prose stylist. Proust is a master of the short, maxim-like sentence, and of the deliberately dissonant repetition, but he is more famous for the long sinuous sentences that re-create the multilayered quality of both physical sensations and inner associations; for the metaphors and similes which have the gift of seeming simultaneously an accurate commentary and joyously extravagant; and for his handling of the generalizations about human nature that appear on almost every page, and that are couched in physical and figurative terms that make them more integrated with the fictional narrative than in many other great novels.

What, finally, also makes *Remembrance of Things Past* a work of genius is its comedy. The same early critic who recommended a gradually increasing daily quota of Proust was honest enough to admit that it was only on his second reading that he realized how amusing the novel was; the first time he was too overwhelmed by the prose-poetry and the generalizations to notice the entertainment. Proust has at his command an unusually wide range of comic talents: he is able to write, with equal success, in a vein of relaxed whimsy or one of burlesque caricature. He follows the nineteenth-century movement away from divisions of genre, rarely strictly separating darker topics from amusing ones, and often, at the gravest moments, slipping in some light-hearted aside; he also takes much further than did Flaubert, Balzac or Stendhal the exploitation of tics of speech for comic effect. There is, too, a less frequently commented-on tradition of French literature into which Proust falls: the earthy one. He treats gross subjects with such delicate irony that many commentators have been able to overlook them, and to judge the work over-refined, or 'art for art's sake'; in fact, there are physically farcical episodes, scatological diatribes, and much play on love of food. Among Proust's finest comic passages are literary parody, deliberately bathetic combinations of phrases, and embroidery on an already comic reference after an interval of pages or even chapters; and one of his most frequent sources of comedy is snobbery, which he sees everywhere: in love and even in sadism (the sadist is trying to penetrate into the circle of the glamorously wicked).

Proust's novel has been said to be rarefied, masturbatory, merely toying with political issues – this in spite of a profound thoughtfulness in its treatment of the Dreyfus Affair and anti-semitism, the First World War, the possibilities of class-mobility, and the mutual fascinations whereby the aristocracy and working classes maintain each other in rigid stereotypes. Devoted Proustians would, however, doubtless maintain that the greatest reward of reading him is the changes he effects in one's own perception of sense-impressions.

Further reading

Other works include: *By Way of Sainte-Beuve* (*Contre Sainte-Beuve*, 1954, trans. 1958). Publication of Proust's complete *Correspondance*, ed. Philip Kolb, began in 1970. See: G.D. Painter, *Marcel Proust: A Biography* (2 vols, 1959 and 1965). See also: Samuel Beckett, *Proust* (1931); J. Cocking, *Proust* (1956); G. Poulet, *L'Espace proustien* (1963); V. Graham, *The Imagery of Proust* (1966); G. Brée, *The World of Marcel Proust* (1967); J.H.P. Richard, *Proust et le monde sensible* (1974); R. Shattuck, *Proust* (1974); M. Bowie, *Proust, Jealousy, Knowledge* (1978); T. Kilmartin, *A Reader's Guide to Remembrance of Things Past* (1983); Richard Sprinker, *History and Ideology in Proust* (1994); Jean-Yves Tadié, *Marcel Proust: A Biography*, trans. Euan Cameron (2000); Richard Bales (ed.) *The Cambridge Companion to Proust* (2001).

ALISON FINCH

PUCCINI, Giacomo

1858–1924

Italian composer

Puccini was born into a family whose musical tradition stretched back several generations and included composers of sacred as well as secular music. His early training in Lucca was primarily as a church musician, but in 1876 a performance of **Verdi's** *Aida* persuaded him to pursue an operatic career. He moved to Milan to study composition with Amilcare Ponchielli, and it was there, in 1884, that his first opera, *Le villi*, was produced. *Edgar* (1889), his next work, was less successful with the public, but *Manon Lescaut* (1893) brought him an international reputation, in spite of inevitable comparisons with Jules Massenet's opera of the same title.

This success was consolidated with the next three works, all of which remain firmly in the operatic repertoire. *La Bohème* (1896) depicts a tragic love affair against the background of bohemian artistic life in Paris; the sentimentality of the plot and its blending of comic and serious elements have led many to consider it the opera in which subject-matter is most convincingly matched with Puccini's particular musico-dramatic gifts. However, *Tosca* (1900) marked a sharp change in direction. The violence and cruelty of the plot did not prevent Puccini from including several lyrical scenes, but it did perhaps encourage him to experiment with various 'modernistic' musical devices, in particular with harmony based on the whole-tone scale. *Madama Butterfly* (1904) again attempted to break new ground, this time with an exotic, oriental setting and, at least on the surface, a more refined orchestral sonority.

After *Butterfly* the pace of Puccini's creative output slowed considerably. From his published letters it seems that the major problem was that of finding suitable operatic subjects. As we can see from the last three operas discussed, he clearly disliked repeating himself in his choice of dramatic setting, presumably because the background of a work produced the initial stimulus towards composition. In every respect the comparison with Verdi's relatively unproductive period (from *Aida* to *Otello*) is striking and relevant, and can tell us much about the composers' creative processes. The breakthrough finally occurred when Puccini discovered a story set in the Californian gold-rush of 1849. *La fanciulla del West* (1910) was, in the violence and austerity of its plot, somewhat akin to *Tosca*, but it noticeably lacked the earlier opera's sections of sustained lyricism and perhaps for this reason has tended to be less popular with the opera-going public.

La rondine (1917) has been even less frequently revived, but the next work, *Il trittico* (1918), showed many interesting innovations. Three contrasting one-act operas make up the evening: a sinister melodrama (*Il tabarro*); a sentimental tragedy, entirely for female voices (*Suor Angelica*); and a pure comic opera, set in thirteenth-century Florence (*Gianni Schicchi*). Though rarely seen as a complete evening, these operas (particularly the first and third) are important documents in the development of Puccini's musical personality. The new orchestral refinements of *Il tabarro* show that the composer was less indifferent to the music of his more radical contemporaries, **Debussy** in particular, than is sometimes suggested (we might also remember that he was an attentive listener at one of the earliest performances of **Schoenberg's** *Pierrot Lunaire*). On the other hand, *Gianni Schicchi* places in the clearest possible context Puccini's debt to Verdi, and to that composer's last opera, *Falstaff*, in particular.

Puccini's final work, *Turandot* (first performed 1926), represented yet another change in dramatic direction. The fairy-tale atmosphere of the plot, and its bold mixture of various dramatic genres, initially struck the composer as a source of limitless possibilities, as a chance to supersede all his previous work; but ultimately the complicated dramatic structure created severe problems of musical continuity, and the work remained unfinished at the composer's death. It is performed today in a completed version by Franco Alfano.

In spite (perhaps, in some circles, because) of Puccini's vast popular success, he has sometimes been the target of academic/critical abuse, on both the dramatic and the musical level. Joseph Kerman, for example, described the musical texture of *Tosca* as 'consistently, throughout, of café-music banality', and eventually identifies the 'failure, or, more correctly, the triviality of [Puccini's] attempt to invent genuine musical drama'. More recently a less jaundiced view has prevailed, even though it is conceded that his mature musical language (from *La Bohème* onwards) changed little, and was only marginally affected by contemporary developments. Puccini was above all a master of the theatrical situation – his operas can be assessed realistically only in the opera house itself. There the almost fanatical precision with which he judged the pace of the drama always seems to justify itself magnificently, and even in some cases to transcend the limitations of his musical language.

Further reading

Other works include: religious music and a few choral, orchestral and chamber works, the vast majority of them written during the 1880s. Source writings: *Epistolario*, ed. Giuseppe Adami (1928, trans. Ena Makin, *Letters of Giacomo Puccini*, 1931); and *Carteggi Pucciniani*, ed. Eugenio Gara (1958). Mosco Carner, *Puccini: A Critical Biography* (2nd edn, 1974), covers all the works in detail and includes a full biography. See: M. Girardi, *Puccini: His International Art* (2000); Mary Jane Phillips-Matz, *Puccini: A Biography* (2002); Julian Budden, *Puccini: His Life and Works* (2005).

ROGER PARKER

PYNCHON, Thomas

1937–

US novelist

Born in Long Island, New York, Pynchon attended the engineering department at Cornell University, but did not graduate, instead joining the US Navy. He returned to Cornell in 1957, to complete a degree in English in 1959. Controversy surrounds whether or not he was a student of **Vladimir Nabokov** there. Although following graduation he almost immediately set about writing fiction, he joined the Boeing Corporation as an engineering assistant in 1960, drafting technical papers some of which related to nuclear arms projects, before the critical and commercial success of his first novel, *V* (1963) enabled him to set aside regular employment. Since then he has published only four further novels, but these have kept Pynchon's reputation as one of America's foremost, and arguably most interesting, novelists alive. Famously, like Nabokov, and even more like **J.D. Salinger**, he has eschewed contact with the media, telling CNN in a rare interview in 1997, 'My belief is that "recluse" is a code word generated by journalists … meaning, "doesn't like to talk to reporters".' Like **Stephen Hawking**, he has become a character in the long-running *The Simpsons* television cartoon series. That he has survived and prospered as an iconic writer secluded from the public gaze, however, is down to the undoubted quality of his work. A new Pynchon novel is always a literary event of the first magnitude.

V creates a world constituted by a bewildering variety of groups and individuals, all searching for truths to live by and emerging with an utterly fantastic variety of lifestyles; these range from the systematic sexual exploitation and extermination of an African people to the exaltation of plastic surgery or dentistry to the status of a religion. Of the central characters, Benny Profane sees himself as a *schlemiel*, at the mercy of the material world, and hence excused effort or involvement, while Stencil, searching for 'V', the object of his grandfather's quest, which is simultaneously a place, a person and a truth, treats himself as a character in a work of fiction, and hence refers to himself in the third person. References to 'V' abound in the book, but their very multiplicity undermines the quest as a whole, especially when their common element emerges as a desire to fuse with the mineral world, to become inert, stable and immortal.

Pynchon's second novel, *The Crying of Lot 49* (1966), which won a National Book Award but was denied a Pulitzer Prize when the Pulitzer committee overruled the jurors' unanimous decision in its favour, takes the heroine Oedipa Maas into a twilight zone between paranoia and the revelation of an alternative postal communication system, Trystero, which seems to offer a way of transcending alienation and of genuinely being in touch with others across space and time. The more information she gains, however, the more the plot thickens in a baroque fashion, and the closer it gets to an obsessive and insane need for there to be a parallel realm of meaning and truth to the obvious everyday world. In *Gravity's Rainbow* (1973), however, this quotidian reality has been entirely swallowed up in the nightmare of the Second World War. The hero of the book is Tyrone Slothrop who, subjected to Pavlovian conditioning in childhood, finds himself sexually aroused by the future firing of a V2 rocket, and drawn to its place of impact. This inversion of causal sequence finds many echoes in the book and picks up the earlier themes of erotic submission to the world of matter and technology. Instead of 'gravity's rainbow', a natural parabola of excitation and release, of life and death, science seeks a continuous increase of energy and power, abetted by the multinational companies which profit by war. War is the logical outcome as the greatest possible centralization of power, squandering of energy, growth of knowledge and mobilization of individuals' energy through the eroticization of violence and submission by sado-masochistic conditioning.

Around the time *Gravity's Rainbow* was published, the elusive Thomas Pynchon (sometimes dubbed 'the Greta Garbo of American Letters') was alleged to have settled in California. At any rate, his fourth novel, *Vineland*, is best described as a Californian extravaganza with serious undertones. Its central relationship, between an FBI agent and a feminist filmmaker, is used to explore as well as satirize tensions between authority and liberalism. The style and mood of the book, however, is persistently governed, or contaminated, by a welter of allusions to *Star Trek* and other Hollywood enterprises. Drugs are present, as is a subset of characters called 'Thanatoids', who, hovering somewhere between life and death, represent latter-day Transcendentalism.

At some point in the mid-1990s Pynchon returned to New York, where he married his literary agent Melanie Jackson. His fifth, and to date most recent, novel, *Mason & Dixon*, appeared in 1997. As the title suggests, it canvasses the fortunes of the cartographers Charles Mason and Jeremiah Dixon, who between them devised the eponymous Mason–Dixon Line, that divided the northern and southern states in the pre-Independence period. Insofar as Pynchon ever makes a didactic point, his message here is that man-made frontiers and boundaries are always bad news, whatever the context. On its surface *Mason & Dixon* adopts the spirit, if not always the form, of an eighteenth-century picaresque novel, but as always with Pynchon there is too much going on beneath the surface for genre classification to be of much help. Wry jokes abound: for example, an observation that sitting beneath trees may be conducive of enlightenment – Pynchon cites not only Newton and the Buddha, but also Adam and Eve. But collectively, as forests, trees are forbidding, and the novel is shot through with a lingering sense of unease as its protagonists investigate what was then 'virgin' territory.

Critics have responded variously to *Mason & Dixon*, some seeing it as the latest in a series of masterpieces, others condemning it as unwieldy and unfocused. Most, however, would perhaps agree that there is about Pynchon an enduring quality of indeterminability, which has given him at least the reputation of America's premier postmodern author. His is an entropic vision in which the accumulation and dissemination of information and the geometrical increase in usable and used energy create a condition where there is no central organizing agency or truth. This is (or can be read as) a moral insight into the ways we have brought upon ourselves by seeking to be the victims or passive objects of forces we identify as being outside ourselves. In Pynchon, however, our inner neuroses and paranoia create the history we ostensibly seek to avoid.

Further reading

Other works include: *Slow Learner*, a collection of early short stories (1984). See: George Levine and David Laverenz (eds), *Mindful Pleasures: Essays on Thomas Pynchon,* (1976); T.H. Schaub, *Pynchon: The Voice of Ambiguity* (1981); Robert D. Newman. *Understanding Thomas Pynchon* (1986); Steven Weisenburger, *A Gravity's Rainbow Companion: Sources and Contexts for Pynchon's Novel* (1988); Deborah L. Madsen, *The Postmodernist Allegories of Thomas Pynchon* (1991).

DAVID CORKER
(REVISED AND UPDATED BY THE EDITOR)

Q

QUTB, Sayyid Muhammad

1906–66

Egyptian Islamist

Born into a poor, but notable, family near Asyut in Lower Egypt, Sayyid Muhammad Qutb trained as a teacher in Cairo. Deeply interested in literature, he had literary ambitions. He joined the ministry of education as a teacher and graduated to a school inspector.

His writing covered not only essays and literary criticism but also fiction, all of which bore the stamp of his fluency in Arabic. An early autobiographical novel conveyed his disenchantment with romantic love, which was so intense that he remained a bachelor all his life.

Since Cairo was the headquarters of the League of Arab States, which declared war on the newly established Israel on 15 May 1948, Qutb could not remain immune from the political events of the region. Later that year, he ministry of education sent him to Colorado State College, Greenly, in the United States for further studies. He stayed in America for three years. The experience left him disillusioned with the US in particular and the West in general, and made him turn to his Islamic roots and Islam.

In *America as I Saw It*, his account of his travels in that country, serialized in a journal of the Muslim Brotherhood, the leading political-religious party in Egypt, he conveyed his loathing for the gross materialism, racism, sexual licentiousness and depravity, and widespread backing for Zionism, that he witnessed in the United States, and cited his personal experiences to illustrate his statements. He then expanded his thesis to include the rest of the Western world, and concluded that decadent Western civilization was following the path of ancient Rome in decline. Using Islamic terminology, he asserted that the West was turning into a *jahiliya* ('ignorant') society.

Later, in *Islam and the Problem of Civilization*, Qutb would pose a series of rhetorical questions, 'What is to be done about America and the West, given their overwhelming danger to humanity? Should we not issue a sentence of death? Is this not the verdict most appropriate to the nature of the crime?' Decades later, such views would be expressed by **Osama bin Laden** and his intellectual mentor, Ayman Zawahiri.

On his return to Egypt in 1951, the education ministry found his anti-American views so objectionable that it forced him to resign. Freed from the restrictions of the civil service, he became a religious and political activist. He joined the Muslim Brotherhood, and quickly established himself as one of its most eminent members.

Following the ban on the Muslim Brotherhood in 1954, Qutb was arrested and held in a concentration camp. Here he wrote his classic, *Maalim fi al Tariq* (Arabic: 'Signposts on the Road', or simply 'Signposts'), which is the primer for radical Islamists worldwide. It was smuggled out, and published in 1964, the year Qutb along with other Brotherhood detainees was released.

In *Maalim fi al Tariq* Qutb divided social systems into two categories: the Order of Islam and the Order of Jahiliya, which was decadent and ignorant, the type which had existed in Arabia before Prophet Muhammad had received the Word of God, when men revered not God but other men disguised as deities. He argued that the regime of Egyptian President Abdul Gamal Nasser was a modern version of *jahiliya*. This earned him the approval and respect of young Brothers and the opprobrium of the political and religious establishment.

The militant members of the (still clandestine) Muslim Brotherhood drafted Qutb into the leadership. They wanted him to avenge the persecution of the Brotherhood in the mid 1950s. By inclination a thinker, he wished to avoid violence. But when his radical followers pressed for a *jihad* to be waged against the social order he had himself labelled *jahiliya* because of its betrayal of Islamic precepts, Qutb could find no way out.

During his trial in 1966 he did not contest the charge of sedition, and instead tried to explain his position ideologically, arguing that the bonds of ideology and belief were sturdier than those of patriotism based upon region, and false distinctions among Muslims on a regional basis was an expression of the Crusading and Zionist imperialism, which had to be eradicated. In his view, *watan* (homeland) was not a land but the community of believers, *umma*.

He argued that once the Brothers had declared someone to be *jahil* (ignorant/infidel), they had the right to attack his person or property, a right granted in Islam, and that if, in the course of performing this religious duty of waging a jihad against unbelievers, a Brother found himself on the path of sedition, so be it. The responsibility for creating such a situation lay with those who through their policies had created such circumstances.

Qutb's subsequent execution turned him into a martyr in the eyes of his followers. This gained his thesis a wider acceptance in the Arab and Muslim world, infused the mainstream of Muslim thought, and helped change the age-old habits of lethargy and passivity.

Further reading

Qutb's books include an exegesis of the Koran, *Fi Zilal al-Koran* ('In the Shadow of the Koran'), being published in nine volumes (1954). English translations of his work include *Islam: The Religion of the Future* (1977); *Milestones* 1991; *Sayyid Qutb and Islamic Activism: A Translation and Critical Analysis of Social Justice in Islam* (trans. William E. Shepard, 1996); and *Social Justice in Islam* (trans. John Hardie, 2000). See also: Dilip Hiro, *War Without End: The Rise of Islamist Terrorism and Global Response* (2002).

DILIP HIRO

R

RACHMANINOV, Sergei

1873–1943

Russian composer and pianist

Born into the lesser Russian nobility at a time when the family fortunes were waning, Rachmaninov had an insecure home life, though his musical ability was recognized and encouraged from an early age. A continuation of these reduced circumstances caused the family to split up and move to a much humbler home in St Petersburg. This emotional turmoil, together with the loss of his younger sister, did much to fashion the composer's lifelong feelings of emotional insecurity and fear of death shielded by a rather subdued temperament. In 1882 he attended the local conservatoire where he received piano lessons together with a general education. Lack of self-motivation promoted a move to the Moscow Conservatoire, where tuition under the pedagogue and disciplinarian Nikolai Zverev caused him to show immediate improvement by way of a concentrated work programme involving a study of the classics and the virtuoso piano tradition of **Liszt** and contemporaries. Living in at the Zverev household, he was to meet the foremost musicians of his day including the pianist Anton Rubinstein, the composers Arensky and Taniev who were soon to become his teachers and above all **Tchaikovsky**, whom he idolized.

By 1890 Rachmaninov had sketched his First Piano Concerto and was also promoting other compositions via many public concerts.

His graduation exercise, the opera *Aleko* from Pushkin, won him the conservatoire's Great Gold Medal in 1893 and the approval of Tchaikovsky, though a later performance at the Bolshoi Ballet was only moderately successful. By 1895 he had completed the First Symphony but a disastrous première under the baton of the popular Glazunov plunged him into the depths of despair: he withdrew the work and sought the help of a psychiatrist. Under this successful treatment he produced the famous Second Piano Concerto (1901) and its companion piece, the Second Suite for Two Pianos (1901) which has become equally popular. His marriage to his cousin in 1902 brought great stability into his life and soon afterwards he released his first book of Piano Preludes, Op. 23 (1903) and another Pushkin opera entitled *The Miserly Knight* (1905).

During the early years of the twentieth century he took up various conducting posts, starting at the Bolshoi Opera where his own works were premièred, though he soon moved to Dresden where he began the beautifully lyrical Second Symphony (1906). At this time he also wrote one of his most haunting works, the symphonic poem *The Isle of the Dead* (1909) based on a Symbolist painting by Böcklin. The same year an offer to tour America resulted in the exceedingly difficult Third Piano Concerto which won him new audiences for both his piano playing and his conducting of Russian music. On his return to Europe he once more sought emotional security and purchased a large estate called 'Ivanovka' where he could work in seclusion. Indeed, this was one of Rachmaninov's most fertile composing periods for he was to pen the choral *Liturgy of St Chrysostom* (1910) and two more sets of piano pieces, the Preludes, Op. 32 and the *Études Tableaux*, Op. 33. The continuation of some conducting work did not prevent him occasionally from going abroad and it was on a trip to Rome in 1913 that he wrote his choral symphony *The Bells*, though the outbreak of war led to the cancellation of its projected performance in England.

The crisis of world events and the fact that Rachmaninov was a member of the landed gentry put him in a precarious position. Accordingly he decided to leave Russia on the pretext of a concert tour of Scandinavia. Now finding himself an exile, he emigrated to the USA, setting up home in San Francisco in 1919 and signing important contracts with recording companies. Throughout the 1920s he travelled extensively around Europe, though very few compositions were produced during this period. The poor reception of the Fourth Piano Concerto (1926), which was criticized for its lack of melodic interest, once more plunged him into a depressive state. As a result he moved first to Paris and then to Lucerne, where he wrote the highly inventive *Rhapsody on a Theme of Paganini* (1934), to be followed by the Third Symphony (1935). The final decade of Rachmaninov's life brought him international success not only because of his extensive concert tours but also because of a collaboration with the Philadelphia Orchestra which recorded most of his major works under the baton of Eugene Ormandy. These performances, together with those of solo repertoire, are both superb documents of creative insight and remarkably modern in interpretation. Already the strain of such a busy lifestyle was beginning to take its toll, though the composer, after rejecting many requests for film scores, did produce his last and probably most nostalgic Russian work, the *Three Symphonic Dances* (1940). Indeed, these are the summation of a whole life's

work and incorporate all the influences on his mature style while adding yet a new dimension of chamber scoring to the often ethereal textures of the piece. By 1942 Rachmaninov was already very ill with cancer and, after the cancellation of an important concert tour, he died the following year at the age of sixty-nine.

Rachmaninov is generally thought of as a composer in the late Romantic tradition who followed in the footsteps of Tchaikovsky. Though this is true, unlike his predecessor's, most of his compositions were conceived in terms of keyboard figuration, whether in the songs, where the vocal lines are often woven within the piano counterpoint, or in the orchestral works which were initially sketched at the piano. Like Tchaikovsky his output contains a strong vein of lyricism, melancholy tone and rhapsodic expansiveness of a kind rarely seen in the more nationalist works of **Borodin** and **Rimsky-Korsakov**. The orchestral scoring is more weighty than that of his contemporaries, being influenced by the fuller textures of **Brahms** and the German school. To this Rachmaninov adds thematic material which is exclusively Russian with melodies reminiscent of Orthodox chant and modal folk song often gravitating around one note. An early interest in Symbolist art with its dream and death imagery pervades many of his pieces: this obsession often takes the shape of the 'Dies Irae' which is hinted at in the symphonic slow movements and in the *Isle of the Dead*.

Throughout his busy life as pianist, composer and conductor there was the inevitable conflict caused by an inability to fulfil all his ambitions at once. The failure of his early works may explain why he experimented little over forty creative years. Having lost all his possessions as an exile, he was often faced with financial problems which drove him on to the concert platform all too frequently, though his recitals always met with great success especially when he played popular transcriptions of his own songs and instrumental compositions by Bach, Mendelssohn and Fritz Kreisler. Such appearances invariably detracted from the appreciation of his larger orchestral and choral compositions, as did the wholesale plagiarism of his Romantic style by Hollywood film composers. Fortunately the recent revival of interest in large-scale symphonic writing, the availability once more of Rachmaninov's expert recordings and the unbiased assessment of his music by a younger generation have shown that his performances were remarkably up to date in conception, and ensured his place in musical history as the finest pianist of his day and a composer whose music is expertly crafted and full of emotional sincerity.

Further reading

See: V.I. Seroff, *Rachmaninov* (1951); S. Bertensson and J. Leyda, *Sergei Rachmaninov: A Lifetime in Music* (1965); R. Threlfall, *Sergei Rachmaninov* (1973); P. Piggott, *Rachmaninov's Orchestral Music* (1974); G. Norris, *Rachmaninov* (1976); P. Piggott, *Rachmaninov* (1978); B. Martyn, *Rachmaninoff: Composer, Pianist, Conductor* (1999).

MICHAEL ALEXANDER

RAUSCHENBERG, Robert

1925–2008

US artist

Rauschenberg's art does not operate within fixed parameters. Heterogeneous and open-ended, it straddles boundaries both between different domains of art and between these and the outside world. The categories into which it is sometimes put, proto-Pop, neo-Dada, junk, etc., merely characterize it by certain of its aspects and do little justice to its richness and complexity.

Born and educated in Texas, Rauschenberg studied painting in Kansas and Paris before enrolling at Black Mountain College, North Carolina, under Albers, primarily for the discipline which Albers offered. On leaving, Rauschenberg produced a series of White Paintings, which he described as 'hypersensitive', registering as they did the colours and shadows of passers-by: these have been compared with **Cage's** – slightly later –

silent piece *4′33″*. Then came a series of Black Paintings with strongly textured surfaces. There are close parallels between these monochrome works and those of **Yves Klein**.

In 1953 Rauschenberg turned to red, which for him was the most difficult colour. The climax of the red series was *Charlene* (1954), in which appear photographs, newsprint, fabrics, a flattened parcel and even a functional light bulb, along with the paint. This led directly to his Combine Paintings and Free-standing Combines, operating somewhere between painting and sculpture. If the physical substantiality of paint was already stressed in the monochrome works, in the Combines it is just one substance among several others. As Rauschenberg put it: 'A pair of socks is not less suitable to make a painting with than wood, nails, turpentine, oil and fabric.' Each component of his extended 'palette' brings with it associations specific to its background. Paint brings the tradition of painting and most specifically (since it is usually splashed on) that of **de Kooning**; photographs, when included, conjure up various associations depending on their subject-matter, as well as suggesting a pin-up board; while the other objects, usually categorized as junk, far from being reduced simply to elements within a formal composition, are given a new lease of life and new meanings by being placed in this non-utilitarian context. Particularly successful Combine Paintings are *Bed* (1955), containing a real pillow, sheet and patchwork quilt, the sinister *Canyon* (1959), containing a flattened oil drum and stuffed eagle, and *Trophy I* (1959), dedicated to the dancer **Merce Cunningham**, with whose troupe Rauschenberg, like Cage, was closely associated. The most striking Free-standing Combine is probably *Monogram* (1959), whose main motif is a stuffed angora goat encircled by a rubber tyre.

In 1959–60, Rauschenberg turned to the illustration of a specific text with his complex and powerfully evocative *Thirty-Four Drawings for Dante's Inferno*. During the 1960s his paintings mainly consisted of silk-screened images, a notable example being *Estate* (1963). In these, as in his Combines, Rauschenberg creates a specifically urban poetry, largely from the detritus of technological, industrial civilization. An involvement with technology's active side came in 1966 when he co-founded EAT (Experiments in Art and Technology), evidence of his refusal to accept the confines of a specialist profession. His performance pieces of the 1960s also involved him in collaboration with others. Throughout the 1980s and 1990s he continued experimenting, especially in collage and new ways of transferring photographic images. From 1986 to 1985 he created several series of paintings on metal: the 'Shiners' series (1986–93) were almost mirror-like; less extremely reflective were the 'Night Shades' series, combining photographic imagery with gestural marks on aluminium surfaces which both absorbed and reflected light in a highly poetic way. A big retrospective of his work was held at the Guggenheim, New York, in 1997 and travelled to Houston and around Europe in 1998. Following this, Rauschenberg undertook a number of high-profile public projects as well as continuing to work in the relative seclusion of his home in Florida, where a number of younger artists became his assistants.

The triumph of Abstract Expressionism in avant-garde art circles had, by the mid-1950s, led to an impasse. Rauschenberg's art was, with that of **Jasper Johns**, the principal means by which this was overcome. By abandoning art's ivory-tower isolation and proposing all aspects of the modern world as in principle equally worthy of artistic attention, Rauschenberg not only paved the way for Pop Art but, more widely, helped create an inclusive, outward-looking aesthetic to which a great deal of subsequent art is deeply indebted.

Further reading

A classic study of Rauschenberg is Andrew Forge, *Robert Rauschenberg* (1969). See also: Sam Hunter,

Robert Rauschenberg, (2000); Robert Saltonstall Mattison, *Robert Rauschenberg: Breaking Boundaries* (2003); Branden W. Joseph, *Robert Rauschenberg and the Neo-Avant-Garde* (2003); Mary Lynn Kotz, *Rauschenberg/Art and Life* (2004).

GRAY WATSON

RAVEL, Joseph Maurice
1875–1937
French composer

Of mixed Swiss-Basque parentage, Ravel was born in the Basque region of France but grew up in Paris. In 1889 he entered the Paris Conservatoire, where he remained until 1904, studying composition with **Fauré** and others. During this period he came to know Satie, whose influence is to be felt in his earliest published work, the *Menuet antique* for piano (1895). He was also one of the 'apaches', a group of self-styled outlaw artists which also included the poet Tristan Klingsor and the pianist Ricardo Viñes: Klingsor supplied the text for one of his great vocal works, *Shéhérazade* for soprano and orchestra (1903), and Viñes gave the first performance of most of his earlier piano works, including the *Pavane pour une infante défunte* (1899, orchestrated 1910) and *Jeux d'eau* (1901).

Between 1901 and 1905 Ravel entered the competition for the Prix de Rome four times; the failure of the judges to award him the prize, despite the fact that he was already a mature and proven composer, caused a public scandal. There was also heated debate at this time about his debt to **Debussy** and Debussy's to him. Undoubtedly *Shéhérazade* owes something to the composer of *Pelléas et Mélisande*, though the work has a languid opulence which is quite foreign to Debussy's style; equally, the similarities between *Jeux d'eau* and some of Debussy's more brilliant preludes can be attributed to a shared appreciation of **Liszt** rather than to direct imitation.

In any event, Ravel was swiftly drawing away from the ambit of the older composer. In 1907 he produced two major Spanish works, the orchestral *Rapsodie espagnole* and the one-act comic opera *L'Heure espagnole*, which, while contributing to a favoured genre among French composers, strike a quite individual note. The composer's distinctive quirky gaiety is to the fore, and for all their gusto the scores show too his high regard for technical precision, for an exact matching of means to effect and for the creation of perfect musical objects. He was to return to the Spanish motif again at the end of his career in the orchestral *Boléro* (1928) and in *Don Quichotte à Dulcinée* (1932), a set of three songs for voice and piano or orchestra.

Spain was not the only country Ravel visited in his music. He was often stimulated by the prospect of applying his skills to conventional musical genres: the Viennese waltz in *Valses nobles et sentimentales* for piano (1911, orchestrated 1912) and in the dark orchestral fantasy *La Valse* (1919–20), the Baroque suite in *La Tombeau de Couperin* for piano (1917, orchestrated 1919), gypsy violin-playing in *Tzigane* for violin and piano or orchestra (1924) and jazz in the Piano Concerto in G major (1931). By using such disguises he was able to distance himself from his creation, and this tendency led him gradually to abandon the harmonic lushness and the rich colour washes of his earlier output. His ballet or 'choreographic symphony' *Daphnis et Chloé* (1909–11), commissioned by **Diaghilev**, marked the end of his impressionist period, a sustained wander through the idyllic Grecian landscape that Debussy had discovered in his *Prélude à 'L'après-midi d'un faune'*.

Daphnis was followed by a number of works in which Ravel appears to have been testing new possibilities, composing more slowly and circumspectly than hitherto. In the *Trois Poèmes de Stéphane Mallarmé* (1913), a refined and rarefied score for soprano and nonet, he reacted, though at some distance, to the experience of *Pierrot Lunaire*: there are tinges of atonality, and the instrumentation is modelled on **Schoenberg's**. The Piano Trio of 1914 has middle movements more exactingly patterned on a Malayan verse form (the pantoum) and on the passacaglia, presaging the full-blown neo-classicism of *Le Tombeau*

de Couperin. Then, in his Sonata for violin and cello (1920–2), Ravel produced an acerbic response to the bitonality and the neoclassical imitations of **Stravinsky**.

Contemporary with this last work was the best known of Ravel's orchestrations, his version of **Mussorgsky's** *Pictures from an Exhibition*. He was a masterly orchestrator, developing his technique from that of **Rimsky-Korsakov** and creating scores of crystal clarity in which every detail tells. Apart from the Mussorgsky, he also orchestrated music by Debussy, Satie, Schumann and others as well as a great many of his own piano compositions. His scoring suggests a willingness to take pains with the tiniest detail, a fascination with perfecting musical objects which is also apparent in the substance of many of his works: *Boléro*, based on the continued redecoration of one idea, is only the most blatant example.

Another facet of this concern with the small is exposed in those works in which Ravel entered the world of childhood with penetrating insight, notably *Ma Mère l'oye* for piano duet (1908, orchestrated 1911), based on Pérrault's fairy-tales, and the opera *L'Enfant et les sortilèges* (1920–5) to a libretto by Colette in which a child is hounded by the animals and household objects he has abused.

Ravel never married, nor did he accept any official position. He appeared only rarely as a pianist or conductor: he had originally intended the G major concerto for himself, but did not in the event play it (the contemporary left-hand concerto, a searching shadow of its exuberant companion, was composed specially for Paul Wittgenstein). **Vaughan Williams** was one of his private composition pupils; those influenced by his music make up a larger group, embracing Milhaud, Roussel, **Poulenc** and even **Boulez**.

Further reading

Other works include: String Quartet in F (1902–3); Sonatine for piano (1905); *Miroirs* for piano (1905); Introduction and Allegro for harp and sextet (1906); *Cinq Mélodies populaires grecques* for voice and piano (1904–6); *Histoires naturelles* for voice and piano (1906); *Gaspard de la nuit* for piano (1908); *Deux Mélodies hébraïques* for voice and piano or orchestra (1914); *Trois Chansons* for chorus (1915); *Chants populaires* for voice and piano (1910–17); *Ronsard à son âme* for voice and piano or orchestra (1924); *Chansons madécasses* for voice and trio (1925–7); Violin Sonata (1923–7). About Ravel: Vladimir Jankélévitch, *Ravel* (1959); Rollo H. Myers, *Ravel* (1960); H.H. Stuckenschmidt, *Maurice Ravel* (1968); Arbie Orenstein, *Ravel* (1975); Roger Nichols, *Ravel* (1977); A. Orenstein (ed.), *A Ravel Reader* (1990); D. Mawer (ed.), *The Cambridge Companion to Ravel* (2000).

PAUL GRIFFITHS

RAWLS, John Bordley

1921–2002

US philosopher and university teacher

John Rawls was born in Baltimore, Maryland, on 21 February 1921. He entered Princeton University in 1939 as an undergraduate. There he was first introduced to political philosophy by Norman Malcolm, a student of **Ludwig Wittgenstein**. Rawls wrote his senior thesis on the 'problem of evil'. Upon graduating in January 1943, he joined the US army as a private in the Infantry and saw active combat service in the Pacific (1943–6). He then returned to Princeton in 1946 to begin postgraduate studies in philosophy, receiving his PhD degree in 1951. In 1952–3 Rawls had a Fulbright Scholarship to Oxford University, where he was affiliated with Christ Church College. At Oxford Rawls attended, and was especially influenced by, lectures by H.L.A. Hart on the philosophy of law and a seminar on social and moral theory jointly taught by **Isaiah Berlin** and Stuart Hampshire.

From the time Rawls received his PhD degree a period of persistent tension, marked by the spectre of nuclear war, had begun between the NATO nations and the Soviet bloc. This 'cold war', as it was called, lasted until the demise of the Soviet Union in the early 1990s. In short, from the time Rawls became an adult until his retirement (in 1991) from his long-time university chair at Harvard,

an ongoing and demanding challenge – physical as well as intellectual – threatened liberal political institutions. The theoretical side of this challenge was advanced by Fascism/Nazism, on the one hand, and by **Marxism**, on the other. Though these theoretical challenges were significantly different from one another, they had certain points of agreement: they concurred in a deep contempt of parliamentary government and an intolerance for political controversy (disdaining the idea of a 'loyal opposition' or any acceptable difference of opinion from the official line); and they had no commitment to and no respect for the idea of the rights of individuals, human or constitutional.

These challenges are the wellspring of Rawls's political thinking. He believed that they were not being effectively met by utilitarianism, the dominant political and moral theory in the Anglo-American world at the time he began his reflections. In the preface to the 1999 revised edition of his *Theory of Justice* (originally published in 1971), Rawls says that he 'wanted to work out a conception of justice that provides a reasonably systematic alternative to utilitarianism'.

Where did Rawls turn for the materials for this 'alternative to utilitarianism'? To three sources mainly: to the social contract tradition, as found in the writings of Locke and Rousseau and especially Kant; to the notion of liberalism as set forth most notably in **J.S. Mill's** *On Liberty*; and to the practice and theory of democratic politics.

In the thirty or so years since the original publication of *Theory of Justice*, the dominant philosophical theorist of justice in the last thirty years of the twentieth century, certainly in the English-speaking world and in much of Western Europe, has been John Rawls. The heart of *Theory of Justice* is Rawls's idea that two principles are central to political liberalism – the principle of equal basic rights and liberties and a principle of economic justice, which stresses equality of opportunity, reciprocal benefit, and egalitarianism. What is distinctive about Rawls's arguments for these principles is that he represents them as taking place ultimately in an ideal arena for decision-making, which he calls the 'original position'. The features of the original position (in particular, the so-called veil of ignorance and the requirements of publicity and unanimity) taken together provide a setting for structuring the competition between potential governing principles (for example, the Rawlsian two principles versus various forms of utilitarianism) in a fair and objective way and then for determining a preference, if possible, for one of the candidate principles of justice over the others.

In time, Rawls came to have some dissatisfaction with this approach and he began to reconfigure his basic theory in new and interesting directions. He loosened things up in two distinct ways. First, he moved the focus away from his own two principles and towards a family of liberal principles (which included his two principles as one possible option). And second, he developed a background theory of justifying this family of principles that did not require people to come to any sort of unanimous foundational agreement. In short, people didn't have to hold one and the same basic moral theory or profess one and the same religion in order for the family of liberal principles to be conclusively justified; rather, the issue of justification could be approached from a number of different angles, and this would work out all right, he argued, if a sufficient overlapping consensus developed over time. Rawls thought that this new theory (which he developed in his second book, *Political Liberalism*, 1993, revised edition 1996) solved the main problem he had seen in his own earlier theory of justice. It did so by taking account of the fact that in a free and open society there is very likely going to be an irreducible and continuing pluralism of ultimate moral and religious beliefs.

In a third book, *The Law of Peoples* (1999), Rawls then took this new theory (which he called political liberalism) and tried to outline a constructive place for it in the international order that has emerged since the Second World War. This order

is, like the international orders that have come before it, a world of disparate peoples and of incommensurable values; but it also exhibits much more *worldwide* economic and even political integration than has ever been the case before. One notable example of this is the widespread human rights culture that has emerged since the UN's *Universal Declaration of Human Rights* (1948). The law of peoples, about which this third book is written, includes the traditional international relations view of states, that they have independence, sovereign status, territorial integrity and formal equality with other states (the old Westphalian system, in short), but adds to it certain conditions or constraints on that traditional view. All these constraints derive from the post-World War II settlement; the most important of them are the prohibition on waging war except in self-defence (or in collective defence), the idea that human rights are to be respected (and even enforced by international action in the case of grave violations), and the claim that nations have a duty to provide economic and development aid to burdened societies.

Further reading

Other works include: *John Rawls: Collected Papers*, ed. Samuel Freeman (1999); Barbara Herman (ed.), *Lectures on the History of Moral Philosophy* (2000): and *Justice as Fairness: A Restatement*, ed. Erin Kelly (2001) – based on a lecture set of 1989 of his political philosophy lectures at Harvard, as revised by Rawls in the early 1990s. See also: *The Philosophy of John Rawls*, ed. Henry S. Richardson and Paul J. Weithman (5 vols, 1999); *John Rawls*, ed. Chandran Kukathas (4 vols, 2003); *The Cambridge Companion to Rawls* (2003); *Rawls's Law of Peoples*, ed. Rex Martin and David Reidy (2006).

REX MARTIN

RAY, Man

1890–1976
US artist

Man Ray probably did more than anyone else to integrate the traditions of photography and avant-garde painting. Growing up in New York, where his family had moved from Philadelphia when he was seven, he first encountered modern art in the gallery of the photographer Stieglitz. In 1913 came the Armory Show, where Duchamp's *Nude Descending a Staircase* enjoyed a *succès de scandale*. Ray's sensibility was in many ways very close to that of Duchamp, and when they met soon afterwards they became lifelong friends. Like Duchamp's, Ray's oeuvre is unified not by a consistent stylistic development but rather by a witty and enquiring intelligence. Like Duchamp, too, Ray was quick to appreciate the central cultural importance of the machine and to incorporate it, with highly ambiguous connotations, into his painting. A work of 1920 includes cogwheels interlocking so tightly that they are unable to turn, and the word 'Dancer' which can also be read 'Danger'. Duchamp and Ray were the leading figures in the short-lived New York Dada movement, and in 1921 Ray followed Duchamp back to Paris, where he was introduced to the circle of writers and intellectuals who, believing that Dada was now outliving its usefulness, were evolving the doctrines of Surrealism. Ray created several powerfully sinister Surrealist objects, including *Gift* (1921), a flat-iron to which is attached a row of tintacks, and *Indestructible Object*, originally called *Object to be Destroyed* (1923), a metronome to which was clipped a photograph of an eye. He collaborated with the Surrealist poet Paul Eluard to produce a book of love poetry, *Facile* (1935), in which his photographs were integrated with Eluard's verse in a visually superb combination.

Photography brought Ray into the most fashionable circles in France, somewhat in contrast to his more revolutionary Surrealist connections. His film *The Mystery of the Château of Dice* (1926) was made during a house-party at the home of the Vicomte de Noailles, whose distinguished guests provided the cast. Ray produced fashion photography of the highest order as well as portraits of many of the leading artistic and cultural figures of the age. Perhaps his most original contributions in the photographic field were the inventions of new technical processes, arrived at in suitably Dada style by chance accidents. Most famous of these was the 'Rayograph', produced by placing objects directly on to sensitized paper, thus obviating even the need for a camera. He also exploited the phenomenon of 'solarization', some of his most remarkable solarized photographs being published in his album *The Age of Light* (1934).

In 1940 Ray escaped from occupied France and went to live in Hollywood, almost immediately meeting his bride-to-be, Juliet. In 1951 he returned with her to Paris, his spiritual home. With his love of girls and fast cars and his ability to mix in widely differing circles, Ray was gifted with exceptional charm as well as talent and originality. Despite several excursions into the sinister, the principal quality in his work is a commitment to freedom, individuality and happiness.

Further reading

Other works include: *Électricité: 10 Rayographes* (1931); *La Photographie n'est pas l'Art* (1937); *Man Ray* (1944); *Revolving Doors* (1972). His other films were: *The Return to Reason* (1923); *Emak Bakia* (1926); *L'Étoile de mer* (1928). On Ray: Louis Aragon, Jean Arp et al., *Man Ray: Sixty Years of Liberties* (1971); Roland Penrose, *Man Ray* (1975); Arturo Schwarz, *Man Ray* (1977); M. Foresta (ed.), *Perpetual Motif: The Art of Man Ray* (1988).

GRAY WATSON

RAY, Satyajit

1921–92

Indian film director

The most distinguished filmmaker to emerge from India, Satyajit Ray is also the one who most successfully bridged the gulf between Eastern and Western cinemas. Coming from a cultured middle-class background, Ray completed his studies of music and the arts at Santineketan, to whose founder he devoted the documentary *Rabindranath Tagore* (1961).

With a keen critical interest in film (Hollywood, **Jean Renoir**, the Italian neo-realists) but no prior professional experience, he embarked in the mid-1950s on what was to become one of the cinema's major trilogies: *The Song of the Road* (1955), *The Unvanquished* (1956) and *The World of Apu* (1959). Working in a minority language, Bengali, and in face of the indifference of the bulk of the Indian film industry, Ray succeeded in part thanks to the international acclaim which greeted his work from the very beginning.

Subsequently his subjects, mostly taken from existing Bengali stories, have ranged widely. *The Music Room* (1958) and *The Goddess* (1960) were both depictions of an upper-class society in decline, brought down by pride and superstition. The early 1960s saw several delicate studies of the difficulties faced by Indian women in rural and urban societies: *Two Daughters* (adapted from **Tagore** stories, 1961), *The Big City* (1963) and *Charulata* (1964). *Days and Nights in the Forest* (1970), a brilliantly realized portrayal of four young town dwellers out of their depths in the country just outside Calcutta, opened a fresh decade of achievement, marked by a number of films on the irreconcilable tensions created by the decline of traditional values in Calcutta: *The Adversary* (1970), *Company Ltd* (1971) and *The Middleman* (1975). Though Ray used colour as early as *Kanchanjungha*, made in 1962, most of his work has been photographed in black and white, with the camera in the hands of only two photographers, Subrata Mitra and Soumendu Roy, but colour was used for two recent oblique studies of the impact of world events on Indian rural societies, *Distant Thunder* (1973) on the famine caused by the Second World War and *The Chess Players* (1977), which depicts the annexation by the British of an Indian state. This latter film is a departure too in being made in Urdu for the mass Hindi market.

Ray was a complete film author, responsible for the direction, script and (after 1961) the music of all his films, and working closely with a constant team of actors and technicians whom he trained himself. Though he remains essentially true to his Indian, or more precisely Bengali, origins, Ray can also be seen as the greatest heir to the humanist tradition of Western filmmaking which uses a basically realistic film style and finds its European peak in the work of Renoir and the neo-realists. Though he described himself as a commercial director, Ray's work derives from a moral impulse. His statement in 1958 that 'working in Bengali, we are obliged morally and artistically to make films that have their roots in the soil of our province' set out a programme to which he remained faithful.

In 1992, the year of his death, Satyajit Ray received the Lifetime Achievement Award from the American Academy of Motion Picture Arts and Sciences.

Further reading

Other works include: *The Philosopher's Stone* (1957); *Expedition* (1962); *The Coward and the Holy Man* (1965); *The Hero* (1966); *The Zoo* (1967); *The Adventures of Goopy and Bagha* (1968); *The Inner Eye* (documentary, 1974); *Golden Fortress* (1974); *Bala* (documentary, 1976); *The Home and the World* (1984); *An Enemy of the People* (1989); *The Stranger* (1991). See: Satyajit Ray, *Our Films, Their Films* (1976); see also Marie Seton, *Portrait of a Director – Satyajit Ray* (1971); Robin Wood, *The Apu Trilogy* (1972); Surabji Banerjee, *Satyajit Ray: Beyond the Frame* (1996); Darius Cooper, *The Cinema of Satyajit Ray* (1999).

ROY ARMES
(REVISED AND UPDATED BY THE EDITOR)

RENOIR, Jean

1894–1979

French film director

The most influential of all French film directors, Jean Renoir was the second son of the Impressionist painter **Pierre-Auguste Renoir**, whose impact on him was crucial (see his book of memoirs, *Renoir, My Father*, 1962). Throughout his life Jean Renoir remained open to the influence of landscape, outside events and the personalities of others, and many of his films are examples of true collaborative effort. For years he was uncertain about his career, serving as a cavalry officer and pilot in the First World War and working for years in ceramics. Only at the age of thirty did he turn to filmmaking, inspired principally by Erich von Stroheim's *Foolish Wives*. His first films were made for his own production company, with his wife as star. From his very first film, *La Fille de l'eau* (1924), the characteristic themes of landscape and love, and an intermixing of varied styles, were apparent. His major silent film, an adaptation of **Zola's** *Nana* (1926), was commercially unsuccessful and his later silent films were commercial ventures.

In the 1930s, which were the years of his greatest successes, he achieved notable impact with *La Chienne* (1931) and *Boudu sauvé des eaux* (1932), both starring the anarchic Michel Simon. *Toni* (1935) was a major departure. Shot on location with little-known players, it shows a deepening social concern and in many ways anticipates post-war Italian neo-realism. In 1936, with Jacques Prévert, he made *Le Crime de Monsieur Lange*, in which the social optimism of the Popular Front is most apparent, and subsequently took his political commitment a stage further by making *La Vie est à nous* (1936) for the French Communist Party. But Renoir was not a man to be confined within one style or ideological approach and his work far transcends the limitation of the cinematic 'poetic realism' of the period. Subsequent films include a delicately observed adaptation from Maupassant, *Une Partie de campagne* (1936); a passionate denunciation of war, the highly successful *La Grande Illusion* (1937); a patriotic epic, *La Marseillaise* (1938); and a further adaptation of Zola, *La Bête humaine* (1938). His masterpiece is *La Règle du jeu* (1939) which, beneath surface frivolity, shows a disintegrating society on its way to self-destruction.

Renoir spent the 1940s in exile in Hollywood where he made several notable films, among them *The Southerner* (1945),

despite the alien atmosphere of the studios. After a visit to India to make *The River* (1950), he returned to Europe to direct a number of colourful meditations on art and life, among them *Le Carrosse d'or* (1953) and *French Cancan* (1955). In his later years he explored new methods of production and his last film, *Le Petit Théâtre de Jean Renoir* (1970) was shot for television.

The impact of Renoir's work and personality has been enormous. Apart from the inspiration given by his great series of works in the 1930s, he has personally influenced a large number of young filmmakers at a crucial moment of their careers: **Luchino Visconti** in the late 1930s, **Satyajit Ray** while in India in 1950, and above all the group of would-be filmmakers gathered around André Bazin and the magazine *Cahiers du cinéma* in the late 1950s – Truffaut, **Godard**, Rivette, Rohmer among them.

Further reading

Other works are: *Sur un air de charleston* (1927); *La Petite Marchande d'allumettes* (1928); *Marquitta* (1927); *Tire au flanc* (1928); *Le Tournoi dans la cité* (1929); *Le Bled* (1929); *On purge bébé* (1931); *La Nuit du carrefour* (1932); *Chotard et cie* (1933); *Madame Bovary* (1934); *Swamp Water* (1941); *This Land is Mine* (1943); *The Diary of a Chambermaid* (1946); *The Woman on the Beach* (1948); *Elena et les hommes* (1956); *Le Testament du Docteur Cordelier* (1961); *Le Déjeuner sur l'herbe* (1959); *Le Caporal épinglé* (1962). Books by Renoir, as well as his book on his father, are: *The Notebooks of Captain Georges* (a novel, 1966), and *My Life and My Films* (1974). See also: André Bazin, *Jean Renoir* (1974); Leo Braudy, *Jean Renoir – The World of His Films* (1972); Raymond Durgnat, *Jean Renoir* (1975); Christopher Faulkner, *The Social Cinema of Jean Renoir* (1992); Martin O'Shaughnessy, *Jean Renoir* (2000); Bert Cardullo, *Jean Renoir: Interviews* (2005).

ROY ARMES

RENOIR, Pierre-Auguste
1841–1919
French painter

Although he is always chiefly regarded as one of the leaders of the Impressionist group,

Renoir's career extends into the twentieth century, well beyond the Impressionist years, and his art embraces other styles and other subjects than the sunlit landscapes with which Impressionism is often associated. After the initial years of struggle and hardship, he achieved success at the Salon and found himself sought after by society as a portraitist. His output was enormous, and the greater proportion of his work dates from the last thirty years of his life, when, his reputation established, he devoted himself above all to his family, painting countless pictures of his wife, his sons, his servants and the models that posed for him at his country house near Cagnes.

However, there are consistent strands which link together his life's work. Renoir was not an intellectual painter and he was not an eager revolutionary. He was little concerned with theories of perception and of the analysis of light, and was gratified by public recognition when it came. Even while participating in the Impressionist group exhibitions, he continued to submit works to the Salon, and of all the Impressionists he had most success in official circles. He was the first of the major artists of the group to grow disillusioned with its aims and return to a more traditional idiom, and unlike **Monet** and **Pissarro** he had no interest in politics or social concerns. All this is reflected in his work, in the sustained note of charm and gaiety that permeates it. Renoir was always attracted by people, and even his landscapes are seldom without a strong human element. As an unrepentant hedonist, he gave free expression to the pleasure he found in beautiful women and pretty children. He wanted no further pretence for a picture than a lovely face or a seductive figure. When his master, the academic painter Gleyre, remarked to him 'one does not paint for amusement', Renoir is said to have replied, 'If it didn't amuse me, I wouldn't paint', words which neatly sum up his approach to painting.

It would be wrong, though, to think of Renoir as a mere dabbler, a kitten playing with coloured wool, as **Degas** spoke of him.

His origins were working class. He was born in Limoges, the son of a tailor, and in Paris, where he came as a child, he was trained as a porcelain painter. His ambition was to be an artist, and he graduated to it through painting china, fans and decorative blinds. But through this arduous apprenticeship he developed a strong belief in the importance of craftsmanship, and a sense of pride in something well done. Throughout his life he applied himself to painting in long and regular sessions, like an artisan rigorously carrying out his obligations.

In 1862 Renoir enrolled at the École des Beaux Arts and took tuition at the studio of Gleyre, where he befriended Monet, Bazille and Sisley, his fellow pupils. It was in their company that he began to study landscape painting, working in the open in the forest of Fontainebleau, and with them he shared an admiration for Courbet and Corot. It is the influence of Courbet above all that dominates his early works, such as *At the Inn of Mother Anthony, Marlotte* (1866), *Lise* (1867), *Diana* (1867) and *Alfred Sisley and His Wife* (1868). These pictures are firmly modelled, sombre in colouring and show Renoir striving towards an official manner. He had some success, exhibiting at the Salon in 1864, 1865, 1868, 1869 and 1870, but only at the expense of suppressing his own personality. Diaz had advised him to use more colour, and the effect of his advice shows in his more private work. He formed a strong friendship with Monet, and the two of them painted together at the popular bathing and boating place of La Grenouillère on the Seine near Bougival, in the summer of 1869. Renoir's paintings of the scene are light in tone and abound with life. His experience as a porcelain painter reveals itself in the high-keyed colour and delicate touch. He painted alongside Monet, but the difference in their characters already shows, in Monet's concentration on effects of light and in Renoir's delight in the holidaymakers. People are given peremptory treatment by Monet; Renoir focuses his attention on them, so that their light-hearted mood permeates the pictures. As described by Maupassant some years later, La Grenouillère was a vulgar and sordid place, but, as one of the bourgeoisie, Renoir shares in the frivolity and his paintings have more the air of an eighteenth-century *fête galante* than a nineteenth-century resort. As a porcelain painter, Renoir had copied Watteau and Boucher, and it is their spirit which infuses his scenes of modern life.

The Franco-Prussian War of 1870, in which he fought, interrupted Renoir's artistic development, but back in Paris afterwards he worked again with Sisley, and in search of inspiration undertook some free imitations of Delacroix – costume pieces with models posing as Algerians. But he was at last finding his own idiom, and the decade of the 1870s saw some of his finest productions. He maintained the light tone of the La Grenouillère pictures and applied it to a series of paintings which are modern in subject and personal in feeling – that is, they express his sense of pleasure in the sights and experiences of modern life. Amongst the earliest and most famous is *La Loge*, which he exhibited in 1874 at the first Impressionist exhibition, a picture which is charming and richly evocative of the spirit of the time. It is also more technically accomplished than anything Renoir had yet painted – subtle in colour, confident in its modelling, and yet using softly merged paintwork to give the effect of life captured in a fleeting impression. He also strove to capture the light and atmosphere of the open air. Not such a fervent apostle of *plein air* as Monet, he confined himself to subjects he loved: couples, women and children enjoying themselves in the sunshine. He could see no point in painting snow scenes or unpopulated landscapes. *The Swing* (1876) is typical of this genre. The filtering of light through trees and the colouring of the shadows are brilliantly caught, but their effect is above all to add charm to the image of the woman at a swing in the alley of a garden, a subject that might be taken from Fragonard – as indeed might the subject of one of Renoir's chief works of the 1870s, *The Ball at the Moulin de la Galette* (1876). **Manet** had

treated a similar theme in his *Concert in the Tuileries Gardens* in 1860, and thereby opened the door to paintings of modern-day entertainments, light-hearted pictures without story or moral. But Renoir's fondness for his theme makes his treatment more *galante*, in an eighteenth-century sense, than Manet's. Although the dancers are only the artists and shop-girls of Montmartre, in Renoir's eyes they are elegant and beautiful. It means that he misses the more profound aspects of the life he depicts, that note of tragi-comedy that Manet hints at in his café scenes. Renoir's people are always charming, rarely interesting or moving. But the sincerity of his vision does mean that his charm is authentic, and in the nineteenth century this is a rare commodity. His women and children are robust, healthy and endowed with a well-being which is as deep and refreshing as Renoir's own.

In spite of this, Renoir, like the other Impressionists, had difficulty in selling his works and was attacked by the more conservative elements of the press. Albert Wolff, the critic of the *Figaro* and one of the fiercest opponents of Impressionism, wrote of his *Torso of a Woman in the Sun* (1876), 'Try to explain to M. Renoir that the body of a woman is not a mass of decomposing flesh, with the green and purple spots that denote the entire purification of a corpse.' Like his friends, Renoir sold works to Père Martin and Père Tanguy for small sums, and the dealer Paul Durand-Ruel courageously bought his pictures knowing he had little chance of selling them. But gradually Renoir built up a small circle of patrons, amongst them a civil servant, Victor Chocquet (who shared with him a passionate admiration for Delacroix and whom Renoir introduced to **Cézanne**), and Georges Charpentier, the publisher, and his wife. Chocquet was a highly sensitive man (as can be seen in Renoir's touching portrait of him in the Reinhart Collection, Winterthur) and greatly appreciated Renoir's painterly art, but it was the Charpentiers who 'made' the artist. At Madame Charpentier's *Salon* he became known to visitors and intellectuals, and his large portrait of her with her daughters was a great success at the Salon of 1879.

The commissions he received from the Charpentiers released Renoir from financial constraint and for the first time in his life he was able to travel. In 1880 he visited Algiers and in 1881, after his marriage, he travelled in Italy where he discovered Raphael and the Roman frescoes at Pompeii. His Italian experience coincided with a developing discontentment with his own work and the methods of Impressionism. He confessed that he did not know how to paint, and set out to introduce greater structure and discipline into his work. There is a new clarity in his pictures of couples dancing (1883), and *The Umbrellas*, which was painted over a period of years and completed around 1884, clearly shows the change in style. The women and children on the right are painted in his earlier 'soft' manner; the girl on the left and the umbrellas in a new, linear style. Renoir stayed at l'Estaque with Cézanne too at this time and may well have derived something of this austere manner – his *manière aigre* – from the Provençal painter. The pictures of this period are more laboriously worked-up than hitherto, consciously assembled in the studio, and sometimes, like the *Grandes Baigneuses* of 1885, they are based on traditional prototypes. Renoir borrowed the composition for this work from a bas-relief at Versailles by the sculptor Girardon. The painting itself is linear and sculptural, and the colour (little more than tinting) no longer conveys the light and atmosphere of the open air.

Renoir was temperamentally unsuited to such a chaste and academic approach, and by 1890 he had reverted again to soft contours, merging colour and swelling forms. But the work of his last years is far from the naturalism of early Impressionism. His figures and landscapes are robust, warmly coloured and simply modelled, an evocation of physical well-being, an imagined golden age. The onset of arthritis caused him from about 1902 to move south to Cagnes, and there he centred his attentions increasingly on his

family, his wife, his sons Pierre, Jean and Claude, and their servant Gabrielle, all of whom regularly appear in his paintings. In Cagnes the family lived prosperously. Renoir had many commissions for portraits, bathers and decorative panels, and the dealers Durand-Ruel and, from 1894, Vollard had no difficulty placing his work. Success was accompanied by official acclaim. In 1896 six of his works, included in the Caillebotte bequest, were finally hung in the Luxembourg Museum and in 1900 he was awarded the Legion of Honour. Only the outbreak of war in 1914, when the two eldest sons were called to the front, disturbed the calm tenor of life at Cagnes, and Renoir died there in 1919, finally crippled by arthritis. But he continued to paint up to his death, in a wheelchair with brushes strapped to his hand. And he also directed an assistant to model sculptures, the three-dimensional counterparts of his painted figures. The last paintings are broad in treatment, lacking in all detail, yet rich in colour and of extraordinary amplitude, with no less a sense of the pleasure of life than the great Impressionist pictures of forty years earlier.

Further reading

See: *Catalogue raisonné de l'oeuvre peint*, ed. François Daulte (4 vols from 1971); John Rewald, *Renoir: Drawings* (1946). See also: Albert C. Barnes and Violette de Mazia, *The Art of Renoir* (1935); Jean Renoir, *Renoir, My Father* (trans. 1962); William Gaunt, *Renoir* (1962); Lawrence Hanson, *Renoir: The Man, the Painter and His World* (1968); Parker Taylor, *Renoir* (1969); B.E. White, *Renoir: His Life, Art and Letters* (1984); A. Distel and J. House, *Renoir* (exhibition catalogue, 1985).

MICHAEL WILSON

RESNAIS, Alain

1922–

French film director

A delicate child, Alain Resnais was educated at home by his mother, developing a lifelong love of literature and music. Subsequently he studied first acting and then film editing at the IDHEC (French Film School). While still in his teens he made a number of short amateur films and, later, two feature-length dramas (now lost) and a number of studies of painters, all in 16 mm format. The success of one of the latter led directly to the beginning of his professional career, with three documentaries on *Van Gogh* (1948), *Gauguin* (1950) and **Picasso's** *Guernica* (1950). In the next nine years, while planning a breakthrough into feature filmmaking, he was commissioned to direct five documentaries on a wide variety of subjects: colonization (*Les Statues meurent aussi*, 1950–3), the Nazi concentration camps (*Nuit et brouillard*, 1955), the French National Library (*Toute la mémoire du monde*, 1956), industrial safety (*Le Mystère de l'atelier 15*, 1957) and the manufacture of polystyrene (*Le Chant du styrène*, 1958). With these unlikely subjects he developed the techniques which he would use in his early features: a disregard for the synchronization of image and sound and instead a separation and new fusion of the elements of image, music and text (the latter often by a well-known literary figure, such as Paul Eluard or Raymond Queneau).

Resnais's début as a feature filmmaker came in 1959 with *Hiroshima mon amour*, from a script by Marguerite Duras. In the 1960s he followed this same pattern of work on four further features, collaborating with **Alain Robbe-Grillet** on *L'Année dernière à Marienbad* (1961), Jean Cayrol on *Muriel* (1963), Jorge Semprun on *La Guerre est finie* (1966), and Jacques Sternberg on *Je t'aime, je t'aime* (1968). All five films are marked by the use of novel formal structures: the interplay of past and present in *Hiroshima*, the refusal of chronology in *Marienbad*, and its opposite, the strict chronology of *Muriel*, the flash forward shots of anticipation in *La Guerre est finie* and the almost aleatory interweaving of levels of time and reality in *Je t'aime*. When he resumed his directing career in 1974, with *Stavisky* (from a script by Semprun) and then, in 1977, with *Providence* (shot in English from a text by David Mercer), the same technical

assurance was apparent, but also a certain shallowness beneath the immaculate surface. Subsequently his work has alternated between attempts to recapture his position as an artist of the avant-garde, and more commercial ventures.

Resnais's reputation, based on his work between 1955 and 1963, is secure, but he remains a paradoxical figure, ten years older than the New Wave directors with whom his name was once erroneously linked: a one-time amateur filmmaker whose work denies improvisatory freedom; an intellectual filmmaker whose stated preferences are for **Hitchcock**, the comic strips and pulp fiction serials; a creator of revolutionary filmic structures whose working methods seem to cry out for the controlled atmosphere of the traditional studio. His direct impact is undeniable – all four of his first writers went on to direct features – and elsewhere in modern cinema one finds a more diffuse influence as powerful but hidden as the mainsprings of his own creative imagination.

Further reading

Other works include: *My American Uncle* (1980); *La Vie est un roman* (1983); *Mélo* (1986); *Gershwin* (1992); *Smoking* (1993); *No Smoking* (1993) and *Pas sur la bouche* (2003). See: Roy Armes, *The Cinema of Alain Resnais* (1968); John Ward, *Alain Resnais, or the Theme of Time* (1968); James Monaco, *Alain Resnais* (1978).

ROY ARMES
(REVISED AND UPDATED BY THE EDITOR)

RICHARDSON, Henry Hobson

1838–86

US architect

There is only one idea of America: it is that of the New World, that of not a Utopia, but of a Paradise. The American Constitution is a programme for realizing this. Her heroes are those that have this idea central in their being; her traitors are those who attempt to emulate the values and styles of the Old

World. Thus it may often appear that the most cultured are the most philistine. The condition only becomes apparent at times of cultural crisis. The true American artist retains his nation's vision through a primitive quality in his work, and this he finds by descent.

Henry Hobson Richardson was born in 1838 on a plantation in Louisiana, of English ancestry, studied at Harvard, and received his architectural training at the École des Beaux Arts in Paris, the second American ever to do so, during the Civil War years, which delayed his return. He arrived back in New York in 1865 at the second beginning of the American Nation after the end of the Civil War, marrying his fiancée Julia Gordon Hayden from Cambridge, Massachusetts, and settling in Staten Island, the island on which were landing the waves of immigrants from the Old World.

The war effectively finished the reign of the Neoclassical 'colonial' style of architecture over American buildings. On his return, Richardson found two contesting and essentially illusory styles dominating, one with English and one with French origins: the styles of **Ruskinesque** Gothic and of the Deuxième Empire. They were, however, the mirror of his own experience, of his Beaux Arts training and of his travels and interest in England.

He established his practice with buildings in both styles, building, to begin with, two churches from 1866 to 1869 which, except for a certain wildness about the openings, would appear unremarkable in an English Victorian suburb. In 1869 he completed the Western Railway Offices at Springfield, which from above the ground floor was an equally unremarkable exercise in the Neo-Renaissance style. The lower level, however, was handled with signs of a startling vigour, the symmetrical composition formed using roughly hewn stone, more primitive than any European rustication. The dichotomy of style reached a crisis with the building of the Worcester High School in 1871, a hugely unsuccessful attempt to work in the flux

between the Classic and the Gothic. He attempted to resolve the difficulty of his task and of his path to an authentic American architecture in two important church commissions, built within sight of one another in Boston, by reversion to a working of a round-arched Romanesque style. This style had been propounded earlier as appropriate for the emergent Great Society, intuitively, perhaps attempting to avoid de Tocqueville's censure, to sustain civilization between barbarism and the decadence that great wealth and freedom constantly offer.

The first building, the Brattle Square Church of 1872, shows a newfound ease of composition using simpler, more elemental forms and openings, particularly in the design of the tower. Between this and the second church, he worked on a large lunatic asylum in Buffalo, which had an increasing assurance at elevating Beaux Arts rational planning into an early Gothic form.

Trinity Church, built as a result of his winning a limited competition, is often considered one of his masterworks, but is better seen as a summation of his achievements up to that time. The plan has a wonderful rigorous resolution which was a tribute to his Beaux Arts training, and the massing as shown in the competition drawings was as picturesque as any English Gothicist, and greater than anything he would attempt again. As is typical of the artist's progress, he learnt here not what he would have expected, which would have been some attitude to prevalent styles, but that the architecture could be changed and fully realized during the building, that the form might have a will to be independent of the drawings. This deeply absorbed illumination was crucial to his emergence.

The tower of Trinity Church as shown in the drawings caused many dissatisfactions and difficulties in the building. The story goes that he was sent a photograph of the cathedral at Salamanca and handed it to his assistant, Stanford White, who brilliantly adapted the form of the Romanesque tower for the new church. In the task of adapting the half-finished building he began a close lifelong association with his builders, the Norcross brothers. From this time onwards he increasingly distrusted drawings, except in the solving of the plan, and increasingly worked with a southern engagement, his fine mind in a powerful body competing to shape his creations as they emerged from the Arcadian earth. It has been said that often neither his assistant, clients, builders, and perhaps not he himself, could see what he was driving at until the building was finished. He required, consequently, a considerable indulgence from all parties, and, being adored, he was allowed this on enough of his major projects.

Richardson came to believe that the architect's primary responsibility was, if he saw how to improve a building, to change it even as it approached completion. Such an approach necessarily depended upon a soundness of the plan.

Building Trinity prompted him to move home to be near it. He rented a house near Boston in a landscape of rolling hills, punctuated with rock outcrops, carefully landscaped in an untamed romantic manner, thinly populated by the cultured, rich and influential. From these surroundings he was to draw out his most important clients, collaborators and friends. The most important was F.L. Olmsted, who lived within, for such large men, a stone's throw of the Richardson house; he was an established landscape designer of great vision, a man who thought in terms of whole regions, deeply concerned as he was, after Rousseau and **Thoreau**, for democratic man's place in nature. Brookline, as the estate where they lived is called, was described then, and could be now, as containing the most impressive pieces of real estate in an area of rare loveliness.

Olmsted collaborated on many projects, but more importantly he by proxy provided Richardson with the theoretical basis for his work that the architect himself never wished to articulate but which is the essential of all great architecture, and with the image of a social programme that at least all architecture since the eighteenth century has needed.

Richardson's maturity of work and life, the two symbiotically linked, began with his move to Brookline. Adjoining the house he added studios (within which he grew an intimacy with his assistants that was essential to his art) and his library (being a great lover of books and of much else).

Fittingly, many of his finest buildings are libraries. In particular the Crane library of 1883 at Quincy, Massachusetts, and the Ames Memorial library at North Easton of 1879 are both convincing examples of his mature work, of how he made the Romanesque style strange and new. Although nearly literal in many of their details, in their massing, in the organization and form of the openings, doors and windows and in the wild surface of the stone, they are completely American and his own. However massive and simple the form, in the savage treatment of the surface and the originality of the composition, the buildings have an urgent freedom about them, as if the Romanesque style had been received from books found in a cave or washed up on the shore in this other Eden.

The entrances to both libraries were huge, engulfing arches of pure geometry and rough stone. This motif he was to work repeatedly in other buildings, reaching its most elemental in the Ames Memorial Gatehouse. As Warren Chalk has said, this motif was to recur, and will recur again, in the work of all the finest American architects after him. Although he made an important contribution to what was to be called by Vincent Scully the 'shingle style' with the Stoughton House of 1883 in Cambridge, Massachusetts, quintessentially his material was stone. The question remains: if the shingle style can only make large private houses, if this is the true American style, is this then the adequate and appropriate programme?

Richardson built many of his finest works for Harvard University, notably the Austin Hall Law School, completed in 1883. His most impressive assemblage is the Allegheny County Court House and Jail of 1884 and his most charming small buildings are the commuter railway stations on the Boston and Albany Railway.

During the 1880s, the decade of his greatest successes and declining health, he undoubtedly undertook too many commissions, and the varied quality of many of the works that carry his name bears witness to this. Of all his achievements, in the end he drew pride from the Pittsburgh Court House and the Marshall Field building in Chicago, of 1887. The Field building was to be a large commercial building, what was then a new programme in a new city, with new pressures of space and money, and as such a crucial test for his art. Considered by many to be his opus, the building is in many ways away from the body of his other best work, at an extreme of his favoured methods of working. The façade, for instance, was obviously resolved through drawing. It cannot be said that in this engagement between the new programmes and an ancient art a complete harmony was achieved. The conflict was between the pressure of the utilitarian volume within the building and the use of stone for the walls. The depth of the plan required extensive daylighting, and the increasing height of such buildings depended upon a sophistication of structure that only metal could fulfil, all of which served to stretch and dilute the power of his beloved rock.

Richardson was a difficult architect to follow. His two most brilliant ex-assistants, White and McKim, working in partnership, in reaction emulated the Beaux Arts style in their most important works, and he remains today, like his contemporary Frank Furness, peculiarly undigested by American architectural thought and practice. In the grotesque refinements of the European Modern movement practised by many current American architects, purged of social relevance, there is no inheritance. The question remains: apart from the large private house and the office block, what is the appropriate programme that will revive a true American architecture, to which Richardson first gave expression?

Further reading

See: Henry-Russell Hitchcock, *The Architecture of H.H. Richardson and His Times* (1966); M.G. Van Rensselaer, *Henry Hobson Richardson* (1969); James F. O'Gorman, *H.H. Richardson and His Office* (1974); Jeffrey Karl Ochsner (ed.), *H.H. Richardson: Complete Architectural Works* (1982); Maureen Meister (ed.), *H.H. Richardson: The Architect, His Peers and Their Era* (1999); Kenneth A. Breisch, *Henry Hobson Richardson and the Small Public Library in America: A Study in Typology* (2003).

FREDERICK SCOTT

RIEFENSTAHL, Leni (Helene Bertha Amalie)

1902–2003
German film director and photographer

Born in Berlin, Leni Riefenstahl was the daughter of a rich plumbing and heating engineer. Against her father's wishes she decided at an early age to be a dancer, and was trained at the Berlin Russian Ballet School. After touring Europe for three years in various companies, she rejected Max Reinhardt's plans for her in order to take part in Arnold Fanck's film *The Holy Mountain* (*Die heilige Berg*, 1925), one of many 'mountain films' attracting large audiences in Germany throughout the 1920s and 1930s. Over the next few years she appeared in a number of similar ventures, including the highly successful *Storms over Mont Blanc* (*Stürme über dem Mont Blanc*, 1930), experience which not only developed her considerable acting ability but also exposed her to the complexities of location photography. It was against this background that, with the help of Bela Balazs, she directed her first film, *The Blue Light* (*Das blaue Licht*, 1932), which she also produced, wrote and starred in. This won the Gold Medal at the Venice Film Festival, immediately establishing Riefenstahl as a remarkably talented woman in a male-dominated industry. She was idolized in Germany, and the Nazis quickly recognized a compatibility between her style and theirs: **Hitler** himself commissioned Riefenstahl to make *Sieg des Glaubens* ('Victory of Belief',

1933), a short documentary of the Nürnberg party congress brilliantly capturing the spirit of the Nazi movement and the near deification of its leader. This was the decisive stage of her career: protected by her friendship with Hitler even from the interference of Goebbels, she enjoyed a unique advantage over other chroniclers of the Reich; but when the Reich itself collapsed, her career went with it. Although she repudiated everything to do with Nazism in 1952, she was unable to resume life as a director, and only completed one film in the years that followed the war, *Tiefland* (1954), a project begun in 1940 but abandoned then due to one of her recurrent breakdowns in health. Her natural talent, however, was not to be daunted. She re-emerged at the end of the 1960s as a photographer, producing two acclaimed studies of remote African tribal life, *The Last of the Nuba* (1969) and *The People of Kau* (1976). At the age of seventy-five she began deep-sea diving and underwater photography, which led to the equally remarkable *Coral Gardens* (1978). Surviving a helicopter crash at the age of ninety-eight, she celebrated her own centenary with the completion of her last film, *Impressionen unter Wasser* ('Underwater Impressions').

Whatever their politics, Riefenstahl's films represent a rare cinematic achievement. *Triumph of the Will* (*Triumph des Willens*, 1935) is a record of the 1934 Nürnberg party congress. From the first sight of Hitler's plane emerging from the clouds, to the pace of the triumphal drive through Nürnberg, to the Führer's appearance in one long shot amongst the rows of immaculate uniformed soldiers, walking among so many beetles to pay homage to the dead in the gigantic stadium, her genius here lies in her ability to create a mounting tension surrounding an event the outcome of which is never in doubt. This was followed by *Day of Freedom* (*Tag der Freiheit*, 1935), about the Wehrmacht, intended to redress the fancied slight of their exclusion from *Triumph of the Will*. Her masterpiece, however, was *Olympia* (*Olympische Spiele*, 1936), an epic documentary

of the Munich Games in two parts, recording athletes and sports as an evocation of human physical beauty at rest or in motion. The first part, the lyrical *Festival of the Nationals* (*Fest der Völker*), includes a mystical, languid eurhythmic display expressing the sensual aspects of physical exercise, followed by a sequence on contemporary Berlin and, inevitably, Hitler, juxtaposed with footage on Greece filmed by Willy Zielke. Part Two, *Festival of Beauty* (*Fest der Schönheit*), depicts the Olympic Village, and the main events. Apart from its brilliant photography and accompanying score by Herbert Windt, the film was a feat of organization. Riefenstahl employed thirty cameramen in special pits, on rails and hoists, often with equipment that had been specifically manufactured for her requirements. It took six months just to train the photographers of the diving sequences. But the work owes its coherence to the eighteen months' solitary editing by Riefenstahl once the Games were over, reducing 400,000 metres of film to 6,151. Of the many awards given to *Olympia*, perhaps the least expected were the diploma and Gold Medal presented to Riefenstahl by the Olympic Committee in 1948, the time when she was suffering most heavily for her Nazi associations.

Olympia was followed by *Berchtesgaden über Salzberg* ('Berchtesgarden near Salzburg', 1938), a short documentary on Hitler's mountain retreat, and in 1944 a terse, gloomy portrait of the sculptor Arno Breker.

Further reading

See: *The Sieve of Time* (1993) is Riefenstahl's autobiography. See also: Glenn B. Infield, *Leni Riefenstahl: The Fallen Film Goddess* (1976); David Stewart Hull, *Film in the Third Reich* (1969).

MICHAEL PICK

RILKE, Rainer Maria

1875–1926

Austrian poet

Born, like **Kafka**, into the German-speaking minority in Prague, Rilke suffered in his early years from enforced oscillation between extremes; from the smothering influence of his posturing, religiose mother to the rigours of a Prussian-style military academy; from the aridity of two terms at a business school in Linz to the adoption, back in Prague, of a pose of *fin-de-siècle* aestheticism. His studies, which, being subjugated to his early efflorescence as a writer, were somewhat perfunctory, took him from the universities of Prague to Munich and thence to Berlin. In Munich he had met and fallen under the influence of the remarkable Russian intellectual Lou Andreas-Salomé (who had been loved by **Nietzsche** and was later to become one of the early pupils of **Freud**). In 1899 and 1900 Rilke, who became for a while her lover, accompanied her on two journeys to Russia. On his return he joined an artists' colony in Worpswede in north Germany, where he met and married the sculptress Clara Westhoff, a pupil of Rodin. But the claims of marriage, or indeed of any demanding emotional relationship, were always, for Rilke, irreconcilable with his poetic vocation, and the couple, after the birth of a daughter, agreed to separate. Soon afterwards, in August 1902, Rilke moved to Paris.

Throughout his life, Rilke was a restless traveller and a detailed biography would therefore have to consist in large part of a conscientious account of his itineraries. Three places, however, may be singled out as the significant *loci* of his life: Russia, Paris and the Canton Valais of Switzerland. In later life Rilke himself was to point to the contrasting influences on his own sensibility of Russia and Paris. From the former he gained a sense of the inexorable and intransigent vastness of experience. In *Das Stundenbuch* ('The Book of Hours', 1899–1903, published 1905), the work most directly influenced by the Russian journeys, a humble Russian monk addresses to God utterances which can only ironically be described as prayers: for God here, far from representing the God of Christianity (which Rilke had vehemently repudiated in his Tuscan Diary of 1898), is a figure of fluctuating significance, sometimes creator,

sometimes created by the speaker, now entreated, now despised, the origin and the goal of ceaseless proliferations of metaphor. The *Stundenbuch* is an abundant and a fluent work, but in its very fluency Rilke saw signs of danger: Paris, and in particular the example of Rodin, was to provide the necessary antidote. *Das Buch der Bilder* ('The Book of Images', 1902) and, more radically, *Neue Gedichte* ('New Poems', published 1907 and 1908) are concerned essentially with the tension between perception and experience: but experience not, as in the *Stundenbuch*, on a cosmic scale, but in the form of isolated minutiae, objects or beings whose elusive significance both attracts and challenges the poet's 'shaping spirit'. The element of challenge is more intensely dramatized in the novel *The Notebook of Malte Laurids Brigge* (*Die Aufzeichnungen des Malte Laurids Brigge*, 1910, trans. 1930). The eponymous hero of this work, a young Danish poet living in Paris, is possessed of (and by) an acute and painful power of empathy; immediate perceptions, childhood memories and recollections from history and myth crowd in upon him, but Malte's sensibility is too passive for him to be able to master creatively the overwhelming multiplicity of experience. Ironically then, *Malte Laurids Brigge* is a work of art constructed out of the agonies of artistic insufficiency.

The claims of experience *vis-à-vis* the individual consciousness: this, essentially, is the theme of Rilke's two major cycles, *Duino Elegies* (*Duineser Elegien*, trans. 1939) and *Sonnets to Orpheus* (*Die Sonette an Orpheus*, trans. 1936), both completed in Muzot in the Canton Valais of Switzerland in 1922. The *Elegies*, begun at Duino, a castle on the Adriatic, in 1912, took Rilke ten years to complete and were regarded by him as his major achievement, They are a series of ten poetic meditations on a number of interrelated problems, the chief of which is that of the creative sensibility (and, by extension, the human sensibility as a whole) in a transient world; its awareness, in the light of inevitable death, of the disparate and fragmentary nature of human achievement and the imperma-nence of love; its consciousness of, but inability to emulate, figures which, through their all-consuming singleness of aim, achieve a kind of existential integrity – the hero, the saint, the child, the animal. Chief of these figures, and the poet's ultimate point of reference, are the terrible and unapproachable Angels, beings of infinite beauty and cosmic energy, whose sublime indifference to man is an implicit rejection of him. The *Elegies* move from lamentation over man's alienation to a triumphant climax in which the trans-formatory powers of man are celebrated: his ability to overcome alienation by translating outer experience into *Weltinnenraum* (world-inner-space), a realm of inner sensibility in which time, and hence transience, is over-come by being transformed into space – the infinite space of the creative imagination which can overcome even death. Orpheus, the tutelary deity of the *Sonnets*, is the singer-god who, in gentler, more conciliatory form, possesses the undivided consciousness of the Elegiac Angels and in particular their ability to move unconcernedly between the realms of the living and the dead. Polarities are reconciled not in any static synthesis, but rather in a sort of mobility of spirit which can comprehend and even emulate the fluid and the fixed, productive dynamism and significant stasis:

> Zu der stillen Erde sag: ich rinne.
> Zu dem raschen Wasser sprich: ich bin.

> (Say to the still earth: I flow/Say to the rapid water: I am.)

Rilke's work, it is perhaps fair to say, is important not so much for any particular *Weltanschauung* which may be extracted from it as for the unmistakable tone and range of utterance. Although Rilke was the most cos-mopolitan of German-speaking poets (his later work contains several cycles of poems in French) and although he assimilated influ-ences from many sources, these hetero-geneous elements are transmuted by an intensely individual poetic voice. It is a voice which has not pleased all his readers and he has been blamed by some critics for such faults as over-preciosity or a somewhat ethe-real brand of sentimentality. But Rilke's range is considerably wider than his detrac-tors admit, and extends from the most subtly delicate lyricism to the most piercing angular-ities of Modernism. Rilke is a master at dis-solving the fixed forms of the external world and reshaping them into new ones; at infus-ing everyday objects with new and vivid sig-nificance; at finding verbal correlatives for the most elusive and evanescent emotions. His poetic sensibility was at once extraordinarily fine and intensely ambitious; or, to put it another way, he had on the one hand the artist's desire for form and, on the other, an acute and anxious awareness of a vastness of experience which no formal impulse could subjugate. It is his expression of the tension between these extremes and his total dedica-tion to its resolution that places Rilke firmly in the mainstream of modern poetry.

Further reading

Other works include: *Sämtliche Werke*, ed. Ernst Zinn (6 vols, 1955–66). Other translations include: *Selected Works, Vol. I: Prose*, trans. G. Craig Houston (1954); *Vol. II: Poetry*, trans. J.B. Leishman (1960); *Selected Letters of Rainer Maria Rilke 1902–1926*, trans. R.F.C. Hull (1947). See also: E.M. Butler, *Rainer Maria Rilke* (1941); H.E. Holthusen, *Rainer Maria Rilke: A Study of His Later Poetry*, trans. J.P. Stern (1952); Frank Wood, *Rainer Maria Rilke: The Ring of Forms* (1958); H.F. Peters, *Rainer Maria Rilke: Masks and the Man* (1960); E.C. Mason, *Rilke* (1963); Patricia Brodsky, *Rainer Maria Rilke* (1988); D. Kleinbard, *The Beginning of Terror: A Psychological Study of R.M. Rilke's Life and Work* (1993).

CORBET STEWART

RIMBAUD, Arthur

1854–91

French poet

At a superficial level Rimbaud has attracted worldwide attention as a quasi-mythical figure, the archetypal rebel, the poet prodigy who abandoned poetry at the age of twenty, and eventually became a trader in Abyssinia. More significantly for modern culture, his actual work places him at the source of modernism, exercising its influence up to the present day.

Born in 1854 in Charleville in the Ardennes, he had, by the age of fifteen, gone through the stages first of pastiche and then of parody of poets such as Hugo, Leconte de Lisle and Banville, and was writing poetry which though still traditional in form was already intensely personal. Characteristically it swings between the two poles of idealism and revolt, the idealism taking the form of a passionate desire for freedom and adventure, for a oneness of body and soul, and a sublimation of eroticism into an ecstatic communion with nature: the revolt is against all constraints, in particular those of bourgeois society and religious hypocrisy. God and Napoleon III also come in for their fair share of opprobrium; but the intense disgust seems to apply to all the limitations of the human condition generally.

The best-known poems of this period are 'Dormeur du Val', 'Ma Bohème', 'Premières Communions', 'Les Assis'. He was also at this time developing ideas which have their sources in the social illuminism of earlier nineteenth-century thinkers like de Maistre and Fourier, and which unite a belief in social revolution and possibilities of a new fraternity with a mystical desire to fuse with the one dynamic, spiritual force uniforming the universe. Rimbaud's practical hopes for social change were dashed after a brief disillusioning experience of the actuality of revolution in Paris just before the tragic experience of the Commune, and with characteristic intransigence and ambition he then turned all his energies to his vocation as poet and *voyant*. The aim was nothing less than to '*changer la vie*' (the phrase that, taken out of its context, has done more than anything to make him typify the revolutionary stance). The task of the poet as *voyant* is to attain, to 'see' the spiritual unknown, and then to express his

visions in a form which will inculcate in his fellows a new sense of harmony and splendour and lead them forward to social progress. The means of attaining these visions of the unknown were to be found through the famous '*dérèglement de tous les sens*', the abuse of the body through alcohol, fasting, drugs, perversions of all kinds, in order to extend consciousness, even if these experiments might lead the *voyant* to the point of death.

These theories, first expressed in May 1871 in two short letters to a schoolteacher and to a schoolfriend, were put into practice in the deservedly famous 'Le Bateau ivre' where the dazzling imagery, the powerful rhythms, the poignant intensity of tone go some way to justifying the pretensions of the ambitious young *voyant*. This was the poem with which he hoped to take Paris by storm. With admirable generosity a group of writers headed by **Verlaine** had invited him to join them there, but Rimbaud's scandalous behaviour and in particular his passionate affair with the recently married Verlaine, eventually tried even the patience of those who admired his genius and he was sent back to the Ardennes in the summer of 1872. There he produced a fascinating, still enigmatic collection of poems, *Derniers vers*, very much under the influence of Verlaine. Indeed, these delicate, tenuous poems, expressing in simple folk melodies not only his tortured love but also the extreme states of mystical experience engendered by the physical deprivations which were leading him close to madness and even death, can also be read as part of a dialogue perhaps unique in literature, a *réplique* and already a critique of Verlaine and his *Romances sans paroles*.

In September the anguish turned to euphoria as Verlaine decided to leave his wife and go with Rimbaud first to Belgium and then to London. It was there during the winter of 1872–3 that Rimbaud began to write his extraordinary collection of prose-poems: *Les Illuminations*, which best show his revolutionary attempts to translate his visions of the 'unknown' into a form which will be organic and no longer preordained. True to their title these visions, whether of the unknown or of a childish, primitive world of fantasy and wish-fulfilment, are brilliant, dynamic, theatrical, as vivid and sometimes as frightening as hallucinations. They manage to create a total imaginary universe, with its own mythology, its own new god-like beings, its landscape and its fabulous new towns which may have something to do with London but more with Rimbaud's own New Jerusalem. Rimbaud's avowed aim as poet-voyant had been to find a language which would appeal to all the senses so as to attract the reader into his vision magnetically. Through the associative powers of the imagery, the dense musical patterns, and the hypnotic rhythms, these brilliant, breathless fragments indeed show an innovatory use of language which has been immensely fertile in its influence on the development of French poetry.

The affair with Verlaine ended abruptly and tragically. In the summer of 1873 Verlaine left Rimbaud, who, however, followed him to Brussels. Tried beyond his endurance, he actually shot at Rimbaud, wounding him slightly. The ensuing case against Verlaine was influenced by the revelation about his homosexuality and he was sentenced to three years in prison. The effect on Rimbaud was traumatic. In the autumn he completed a short prose work, *Une Saison en enfer*, which, although written out of the personal hell of a guilt-ridden and unhappy passion as well as the failure of an over-ambitious aesthetic, has also wider significance in the way in which it works through the idea of hell itself as fostered by Christianity towards a new and still ill-defined humanism, inspired by the characteristic ideas of fraternity (as opposed to dependence on a debilitating sexual passion), of a new and proud love (as opposed to Christian charity and guilt due to original sin) and a transcendence of the age-old dualism between the flesh and the spirit. Each short prose piece condenses in highly dramatic and often ironical form a stage in this rapid evolution. The progress is via a dialectic; the pull of the past, of superstition and human weakness, relived through brief, bright images, works against the visionary fragments of an impossible idealism in order to produce a third, more realistic stance, that of the sane, the independent, the possible. It is a unique work: in highly condensed form an exemplar of a whole spiritual crisis in Western society.

Rimbaud had claimed that his fate depended on this book. It was in fact not published until much later. Whether this marked the end of his literary endeavour, or whether he continued to add to the *Illuminations* during the following year when he came back to England with Germain Nouveau, became a subject of critical discussion for many years. Certainly from 1875, that is at the age of twenty-one, he showed no further sign of interest in a literary career and embarked on a quite different life of travel and adventures, eventually setting up in 1880 as a trader in Harrar, Abyssinia. He died of cancer in a hospital in Marseilles in 1891. It was due finally to Verlaine that most of the *Illuminations* were published for the first time in *La Vogue*, in 1886.

The ambivalence implicit in his life and work has continued in the nature of his influence. The topicality of problems raised by his '*dérèglement de tous les sens*' is too obvious to be stressed. Claudel is said to have been converted to Christianity after reading Rimbaud. The Surrealists used his '*changer la vie*' as their device for revolution and yet could not forgive him for having sold out. However, it is through them, and their recognition that he had found a language fit to explore and express the urges and desires of the unconscious, that his influence has been fostered. Few living French poets would deny if not a positive influence at least a deep admiration.

Further reading

Other works include: *Oeuvres complètes* (1972). For poetry in translation see: *A Season in Hell, The Illuminations*, by Enid Rhodes Peschel (1973); *Complete Works*, by Paul Schmidt (1967). The most useful critical works in English are: Wallace Fowlie, *Rimbaud* (1965); C.A. Hackett, *Rimbaud; A Critical Introduction* (1981); N. Osmond, introduction and notes to his edition of *The Illuminations* (1979). The best biographical work in English remains Enid Starkie, *Rimbaud* (1949).

MARGARET DAVIES

RIMSKY-KORSAKOV, Nikolay Andreyevich

1844–1908

Russian composer

It was into an aristocratic family with a tradition of service to the state that the composer was born. His earliest years were spent in the provinces where folk music and the gorgeous ritual of a nearby monastery made a profound impression on him. The Corps of Naval Cadets in St Petersburg provided his education from 1856 to 1862, and the musical life of that city introduced him to a wider musical world. Until 1873 he served in the navy, both aboard ship and ashore; as with many such appointments in the Russian public service, duties were not at all onerous. In 1871 he was appointed to a professorship at the St Petersburg Conservatoire, where he remained on the staff (with a brief interruption, for political reasons, in 1905) until his death. He was also at various times inspector of Naval Bands, director of the Free School of Music, and assistant musical director in the Imperial Chapel. His career encompassed teaching, conducting, editing or completing the works of others (including Dargomyzhsky, **Borodin** and **Mussorgsky**), authorship and folk-song collecting as well as composition.

The single most important event in his musical development occurred when he met Balakirev in 1861. He thus was introduced to the circle of dilettante musicians drawn 'as if by magnetism' by the power of Balakirev's personality. He exchanged ideas with likeminded young composers (Borodin, Cui, Mussorgsky) and under Balakirev's tutelage the compositional activity of all of them was

given direction and purpose. Their mentor persuaded his disciples to undertake works on a scale they would never have attempted without him, and thus they progressed from talented dabblers to serious composers. With his Conservatoire appointment, however, Rimsky-Korsakov felt an obligation to study systematically the elements of music ('practical composition and instrumentation' initially) which he was employed to teach, and he went on, by self-instruction, to acquire a greater mastery of the technical aspects of music than any of these associates ever possessed. In completing or preparing for publication the works of Mussorgsky, he at times substituted more conventional treatment for the boldly original ideas of the composer; this is notoriously the case with *Boris Godunov*. Though now regretted, Rimsky-Korsakov's work did begin to acquaint the public with that and other masterpieces.

Rimsky-Korsakov began to compose with the example of Glinka before him. Mendelssohn, Schumann, Berlioz and especially Liszt also served as models, but the composer was primarily animated by the idea of writing Russian music. In the subject-matter of his operas and orchestral music, Russian material predominates. History and folklore supply the majority of subjects, sometimes viewed through the works of Russian writers. His treatment inclines to the objective, avoids emotional excess and eschews the extremes of experiment of, for instance, Mussorgsky. He regarded opera as 'primarily a musical phenomenon', and had no sympathy with **Wagner's** ideas about musical drama. He completed fifteen operas, and some of these are his most important works.

His orchestral music is noteworthy for the brilliance of its orchestration. Acquaintance with much of it reveals a restricted melodic invention and a paucity of constructional resource. The finest works are *Sheherazade* and the *Russian Easter Festival Overture* (both 1888). The influence of the composer's orchestration may be felt not only in the work of his Russian pupils, who include

Lyadov, Glazunov, **Stravinsky** and **Prokofiev**, but also in orchestral music by **Debussy**, **Ravel** and other composers.

Serious historical topics and fantastic tales involving the supernatural are the main areas for operatic subjects. Convincing characters are conspicuous by their rarity, and the composer is happier with a ritualistic enactment of historical events or imaginary, fairy-tale figures. The real world of his own time never impinges, unless *The Golden Cockerel* (1906–7) is viewed as a burlesque of the Russo-Japanese War of 1904 and Russian government; this is a debatable interpretation, though there was no doubt at the time that the opera was near the bone. The musical representation of good and evil, or 'real' and fantastic is achieved in this opera (as in many other works) by the use of diatonic music for the former and chromatic music for the latter; this distinction, familiar from Weber's *Der Freischütz*, is exploited in Glinka's *Ruslan* and later in Stravinsky's *The Firebird*. Rimsky-Korsakov takes it further by contriving fresh arrangements of notes in non-diatonic scale patterns.

The outstanding example of an opera using folk motives is *The Snow Maiden* (1880–1). This incorporates elements from folk wedding celebrations and the Shrovetide festival, and is full of folk-like melodies and instrumental effects. The method of treating brief tunes of narrow melodic range, relying on ostinatos and pedals, is distinctive. *The Maid of Pskov* (1868–72, 1876–7 and 1891–2) is perhaps the best example of a historical opera by this composer. It deals with Ivan the Terrible's campaign of 1570, in which the inhabitants of Pskov are menaced by the same cruel treatment the tsar has just meted out to Novgorod. This fate is prevented by the tsar's discovery in Pskov of one who is his own daughter. Her lover, though, wishes to kill the tsar and rescue the 'maid of Pskov' from him. She is accidentally killed in the ensuing fight.

Further reading

Other works include: Symphony No. 2 (*Antar*, 1868, 1875, 1897); *Musical Picture – Sadko* (1869, rev. 1892); *Capriccio espagnol* (1887). Operas: *May Night* (1878–9); *Christmas Eve* (1894–5); *Sadko* (1894–6); *The Tsar's Bride* (1898–9); *The Tale of Tsar Saltan* (1899–1900); *The Legend of the Invisible City of Kitezh and the Maid Fevroniya* (1903–5). *Forty Folksongs*, a collection compiled in 1875; *Collection of 100 Russian Folksongs*, compiled in 1875–6. Rimsky-Korsakov's *Chronicle of My Musical Life* is available in a translation by J.A. Joffe (1942); his *Principles of Orchestration*, ed. M.O. Shteynberg, has also been published in English (2nd edn, 1964). See: Gerald Abraham, *Rimsky-Korsakov – A Short Biography* (1945); S.A. Griffiths, *A Critical Study of the Music of Rimsky-Korsakov* (1989).

STUART CAMPBELL

ROBBE-GRILLET, Alain
1922–2008
French novelist and filmmaker

There seems little obvious connection between Robbe-Grillet's early life and his subsequent career as the best-known and most radical figure in the group known as the Nouveau Roman. He grew up in Brittany, studied agronomy, and worked as an agricultural scientist in various parts of the world before becoming a full-time writer.

His first novel, *Un Régicide*, was completed in 1949, but was not published until 1978. It was the publication of his second novel, *The Erasers* (*Les Gommes*, 1953), which began his career as a writer of critical notoriety. With a few notable exceptions (such as **Roland Barthes**), critics were appalled first by what they saw as a pointless, detailed description of a dehumanized world, then by the apparent lack of novelistic coherence in his books, and from the late 1960s, by the blatantly sado-erotic aspect of his work. Robbe-Grillet grew up reading **Kafka**, **Rudyard Kipling**, Raymond Roussel and Queneau but without realizing that they did not represent the mainstream of conventional fiction, so that his own challenge to traditional forms of the realist novel can to some extent be seen as unwitting or involuntary. However, once he was aware of his subversive position, he continued to emphasize and refine it, and he played a significant role in the development of modern French fiction through his association with his publisher, Jérôme Lindon at the Éditions de Minuit, for whom he worked as editorial adviser for a number of years in the 1950s and 1960s. His creative work was also accompanied by an explicit interest in theoretical questions, and he published numerous essays and interviews on the novel.

In the early years, Robbe-Grillet gained a reputation as the champion of *chosisme*, the flat, meticulous description of the physical world – a tomato slice or the layout of a banana plantation. The implication is that the world can be described but not interpreted. His attacks on plot and character in the early essays (collected in *Towards a New Novel, Pour un Nouveau Roman*, 1963) were based on the view that they constitute false interpretative models for fundamentally meaningless experience: life cannot be read as narrative, nor people as characters. The detectives who appear intermittently throughout Robbe-Grillet's work illustrate (sometimes very comically) the impossibility of making sense of the factual evidence they are confronted with. Wallas, the hero of *The Erasers*, becomes so disorientated that he ends up by accidentally committing the crime he has been sent to investigate. The jealous husband whom we are invited to imagine as a possible source of the apparently narratorless *Jealousy* (*La Jalousie*, 1957), is in a similar position to the detective's, for he is tantalized by an inability to interpret appearances with any confidence. There are signs that his wife is having an affair with a friend, but he proves incapable of reading them as straightforward indications of her adultery. Like many of Robbe-Grillet's characters and narrators, he swings between purely factual observation on the one hand and obsessive, unbridled imagination on the otherhand.

With the appearance of *In the Labyrinth* (*Dans le labyrinthe*, 1959) it became clear that one can no longer even count on the unambiguous presence of the physical world in Robbe-Grillet's novels. The world represented in these later novels is self-contradictory and inconsistent. Characters change names, plots go round in circles, descriptions of reality prove to be descriptions of paintings or theatrical performances, – or vice versa. The policeman-narrator in *Recollections of the Golden Triangle* (*Souvenirs du triangle d'or*, 1978) simply invents his reports. It is not only impossible to give meaning to the world, but even confidently to represent it. For this reason one can no longer talk of realism in the traditional sense of the word. The real world is one thing, the written world of Robbe-Grillet's novels another. Or so it seems, until Robbe-Grillet goes one step further and suggests that assumptions about the real world are just a set of constructions and myths which happen to be popularly shared. It might be possible to speak of a new kind of realism in Robbe-Grillet's fiction, consisting in the representation of these collective views or the current mythology about the world. The exaggeratedly stereotyped setting and plot of *The House of Assignation* (*La Maison de rendez-vous*, 1965) in a world of prostitution, vice and drug-smuggling in Hong Kong, or those of *Project for a Revolution in New York* (*Projet pour une révolution à New York*, 1970) in a world of revolutionary conspiracy and subway violence, or the mix of gothic fantasy and spy-fiction in *Djinn* (1981), exemplify very well these new forms of such realism. Robbe-Grillet's realism consists in drawing attention to our contemporary mythology, and not necessarily in distinguishing between reality and invention, making coherent narratives, or avoiding contradictions. The sado-eroticism which invaded the novels with increasing explicitness from *The House of Assignation* onwards, is in one sense simply an extension of this representation of popular mythology and culture. His preoccupation with surface rather than meaning, writing rather than subject-matter, made this engagement with sexual issues problematic and provocative, and in 1974 his film *Glissements progressifs du plaisir* was put on trial in Italy for the offence of outraging public decency – much to Robbe-Grillet's own personal outrage. From then on, his writing began to show signs of a much greater suspicion of his reading public, including the reading public of the *nouveau roman* itself. In 1984 he published the first volume (*Ghosts in the Mirror, Le Miroir qui revient*) of his semi-autobiographical trilogy, in which he sought to confound the supporters of the very principles which he had campaigned to establish, but which by then had become widely accepted within the academic institution. The turn to autobiographical writing was a polemical gesture aimed at keeping the spirit of controversy and invention alive, and in Robbe-Grillet's hands this shows as a mix of frank confession, half-truths, fiction and overt fantasy which was continued over two further volumes, *Angélique ou l'enchantement* (1988) and *Les Derniers Jours de Corinthe* (1994).

In 2001 he published another novel, *Repetition* (*La Reprise*), set in Berlin at the end of the war, but for the latter part of his career Robbe-Grillet devoted himself more to film than to fiction, a medium in which he had less popular prestige than in the field of literature, but which allowed him to continue to explore in cinematic terms many of the same issues and problems found in his novels. His first venture into cinema was his script for a film made in collaboration with **Alain Resnais**, *Last Year at Marienbad* (*L 'Année dernière à Marienbad*, 1961). This launched him on a career as a filmmaker in his own right, which he began with *L'Immortelle* in 1963, followed by *Trans-Europ-Express* (1966, starring himself and his publisher, Lindon), and various other experimental films with limited distribution, directed by himself. This work also led to the creation of a new genre, the *ciné-roman*, halfway between fiction and film, more than the script and yet not simply the novel of the film. *L'Année dernière à Marienbad* was the first of these, and it was followed by *L'Immortelle*, and others, concluding with *C'est Gradiva qui vous appelle* (2002), whose film counterpart was never made because of lack of funding. His collected interviews on cinema appeared in English under the title *The Erotic Dream*

Machine (1992), a title which could also describe a number of his collaborations with visual artists, such as *Dreams of Young Girls* (*Rêves de jeunes filles*, 1971) and *Sisters* (*Les Demoiselles de Hamilton*, 1972), both with photographs by David Hamilton, or *Traces suspectes en surface* (1978) with lithographs by **Robert Rauschenberg**, and *La Belle Captive* (1975) using paintings and illustrations by **René Magritte**. In 1972, Harrison Birtwhistle used the text of one of Robbe-Grillet's short pieces collected in *Snapshots* (*Instantanés*) for his piece *La Plage: Eight Arias of Remembrance for Soprano and Five Instruments*.

Robbe-Grillet taught for several years as visiting professor in a number of universities in the USA, and in 2004 became a somewhat surprising new addition to the broadly establishment Académie Française. He was one of the most eloquent – if provocatively inconsistent – commentators on his own work, and a volume of collected essays, *Le Voyageur* (2003) was published to coincide with his eightieth birthday.

Further reading

Other works include: *The Voyeur* (*Le Voyeur*, 1955) and *Topology of a Phantom City* (*Topologie d'une cité fantôme*, 1976). Further film titles include, *L'Homme qui ment* (1968); and *L'Eden et après* (1970), *N. a pris les dés* (1971, an anagram version of *L'Eden et après*), *Le Jeu avec le feu* (1975), *La Belle Captive* (1983), *The Blue Villa* (*Un bruit qui rend fou*, 1995). See also: Bruce Morrissette, *Novel and Film: Essays in Two Genres* (1985), Ben Stoltzfus, *Alain Robbe-Grillet: Life, Work, and Criticism* (1987).

ANN JEFFERSON

ROCHE, Martin *see:* HOLABIRD, WILLIAM AND ROCHE, MARTIN

RODIN, François-Auguste-René

1840–1917

French sculptor

Rodin's early life was marred by two failures. First, after a period at the 'Petite École' (École

Spéciale de Dessin et de Mathématiques) under Horace Lecoq de Boisbaudran, he was refused by the 'Grande École' (École des Beaux Arts). Second, when he submitted a bust to the Paris Salon in 1864 it was rejected. Meanwhile he earned a living by taking various craftsmanly jobs, working for jewellers, stonecutters, architectural decorators and the Sèvres porcelain factory. Only by the early 1880s were financial conditions less straitened. By that time Rodin's sculptural career had begun.

In his first full-length work, *The Age of Bronze* (1876), a gesture of anguish was transformed to one of awakening – not into erotic self-awareness, like Michelangelo's *Bound Slave*, seen six months before on a visit to Italy – but into a realm of pure thought. Accustomed only to Salon suavity, his audience accused him of working from casts of his model, Auguste Neyt. *St John the Baptist Preaching* (1878–80), another full-length bronze, this time of an Italian named Pignatelli, was less stable and coolly modelled. It displayed what Rodin himself called 'progressive development of movement'; the man, speaking as he walked, had been captured in the process of shifting his weight from foot to foot. Physically, it was a study in mobility, emotionally an impression of the way a powerfully felt message could conquer hardship and derision, historically a meditation on transition, announcement, a bridge from one era to another. Both figures have the air of a manifesto; they speak of the blindness of the present and the gigantic effort needed to transcend it. Both have the qualities of all of Rodin's work – a tension between idealization, nobility, a desire to elevate the audience, and a counterbalancing appeal to reality, the hard facts of day-to-day experience. Both figures are taken beyond their merely physical existence by thought, inspiration or faith. One reviewer compared the man in *The Age of Bronze* to a sleepwalker. Indeed, thought has provided the only escape route possible. St John concerns himself with more public issues, yet lacks any evidence whatsoever. Only his

fervour can sustain him. One key issue in Rodin's art is the passionate desire to express spiritual values simply by means of physical gesture, to combine the spiritual and aesthetic. Like St John, he descended into an arena of action.

In 1880 the French Government Fine Arts Committee commissioned him to make a door. At his death *The Gates of Hell* remained unfinished. For thirty-seven years he altered over 180 figures which filled the double portal. They became an anthology of his most poignant themes and the faces and gestures he returned to most often in his life. The theme was religious, yet vital to his entire conception was a reading of **Baudelaire's** *Les Fleurs du mal*, which he illustrated. Surmounting the hosts of the damned is not God but simply a man thinking, a miniature version of his *Thinker* (1880). Of the figure he said, 'He is no longer dreamer, he is creator', an indication that once again he wished to challenge the theme of thought as an escape from the world of action. By transferring the whole of Dante into the mind of the artist he was dramatizing the divisions which most concerned him as an artist – between interiority and superficies, spirit and musculature, mind and matter – but also, perhaps, seeking vainly to heal the breach between these oppositions. The Gothic sculptors he so respected recognized no such dichotomies. Between their time and the nineteenth century some **Eliotean** 'dissociation of sensibility' had occurred, or rather some undermining caused by the 'death of God'. Rodin's religious views are obscure and possibly irrelevant. He had, however, been a member of a religious order, taking the name Brother Auguste. In his art he concerned himself with every kind of physical existence, from sanctity to high eroticism. There is an almost dogged desire to run whatever gamut the flesh could offer. Could this have concealed some search for an enabling philosophy?

The Burghers of Calais was commissioned in 1884. Taken from an incident in Froissart's *Chronicles*, it showed the sacrifice of six Calais citizens who had surrendered to Edward III during the Hundred Years' War in exchange for his ceasing an eleven-month siege of their city. One of Rodin's original plans was to fix his six statues one behind the other on the stones of the *place* outside the Calais town hall, so that they would seem to be wending their way towards Edward's camp. 'And the people of Calais of today, almost elbowing them, would have felt more deeply the tradition of solidarity which unites them to the heroes.' That proposal was rejected. Instead, the figures moved in a circle, at differing speeds and with various degrees of visible distress, united in passivity by the concordant diagonal sweep of their procession, most clearly seen from behind. As with *The Gates of Hell*, Rodin researched each of the figures fully before beginning, worked from models and made nude maquettes before clothing his characters. In *The Gates of Hell* Rodin had accepted no programme; he would work, he said, simply from his imagination. In *The Burghers of Calais* he was operating in a definable historical mode. Perhaps the need to establish and authenticate some sense of historical otherness – in Dante, in Froissart – is a familiar result of artistic estrangement in the nineteenth century. Paradoxically, if this can be seen most easily in Rodin's public, monumental pieces, it could be possible to interpret it as the indication of a deeply felt private doubt. **Bernard Shaw** reported that as he watched his own portrait being sculpted, Rodin took it through Byzantine, Mannerist and classical phases before allowing it to congeal into some final likeness. In his description we sense at once the international 'modernist' of the twentieth century, adrift in time and space. If the thinking man at the top of *The Gates of Hell* is Dante, he is also Baudelaire watching Paris being rebuilt, Tiresias or H.C. Earwicker dreaming their respective masterpieces. Are his eyes open or closed? Is he locked into history or is the whole of time his domain?

The easiest way to answer the question is by examining Rodin's greatest achievement, his *Balzac*. Honoré de Balzac had died when Rodin was ten. Working from caricatures,

photographs, details remembered by acquaintances, even tailors' records, he reconstructed the figure of the paunchy, gap-toothed writer. Even at the outset it was evident that the research methods of the two men bore striking resemblances; Rodin visited the district where Balzac was born in order to study facial types. After several full-scale experiments in which his subject stood nude, he eventually hit on the idea of radical simplification; the entire body would be covered by the Dominican friar's habit he wore when writing.

> I had to show Balzac in his study, breathless, hair in disorder, eyes lost in a dream, a genius who in his little room reconstructs piece by piece all of society in order to bring it to tumultuous life before his contemporaries and generations to come.

The press pilloried the final version of *Balzac*. And, indeed, the way the great writer had been captured almost invites such treatment; the portrait is a vivid and immediate presence such as every satirist yearns to convey. Yet it is only registered, not pushed to satirical ends. The sheer arrogance of the creative mind unaware of anything except its own imaginative process is an ultimate Romantic solution. Yet for a sculptor the means of conveying the dialogue between the self and the other differs fundamentally from that of the writer. When he made a portrait of Baudelaire, Rodin refused to create anything but a head, polished until it shone, eyes glazed, inviting ambiguous responses without providing any keys to unlock them. He defended his decision to dispense entirely with the body. 'With him the head is everything,' he replied. Balzac seems all body, and his body, as critics have since pointed out, is a man-size column reminiscent of a phallus; in his sheer fecundity Balzac has been transformed into an instrument of reproduction. Yet we cannot *see* writers in the act of creation. By some lateral legerdemain the spectator reads 'mind' for 'body', takes assertion for truth, interprets narcissism as genius. Rosalind Krauss, who has pointed out that the mature career of Rodin coincides with that of Husserl, has suggested that their attitudes may have a lot in common. The idea that meaning is synchronous with experience, the notion that if self is private and inaccessible then each of us would be two people – one to ourselves and another to others – can be paralleled in Rodin. Absence of premeditation and foreknowledge, best and most obviously proposed in an examination of the act of creation, and a total emotional dependence on the external gesture reveal Rodin's religion as a kind of paganism, total truth achieved by a realization that the self is what is manifested to others. 'Truth to materials' in his work takes the form of a record of the procedure by which the goal was accomplished. On the surface is the whole story of the bronze, its handling and casting. Rodin did not devise a solution to the problems raised by all of the dichotomies which beset him. But he did lodge himself securely between the poles of each, and *Balzac* reveals how brilliant a device that was.

After a century of academic dullness in sculpture, Rodin came and, as **Brancusi** said, 'succeeded in transforming everything'. Honoured and abused during his lifetime, he was seldom ignored. Private affairs were publicized, his technical prowess became legendary, and his work was fiercely attacked. A century later he remains an enigma. Rooted in academic models, he persisted in applying mythological and literary titles to his sculpture despite an uncanny grasp of modernist abstraction. Obsessed with the rehabilitation of monumental sculpture, his approach probably hastened its decline. Instrumental in encouraging **Degas** to experiment, he himself drew back from the course he may have advocated. Rodin's use of the fragment alone ensures him a place as a proto-modern. Yet as the Rodin expert Albert Elsen wrote:

> Like the biblical Moses, he lived only long enough to look on the Promised Land. Not his death, however, but his steadfast adherence to naturalism and certain of its traditions prevented Rodin from entering into

the new territories that were being surveyed and colonized by younger sculptors.

Further reading

See: Albert Elsen, *Rodin's Gates of Hell* (1960) and *Rodin* (1963); *Rodin, Readings on His Life and Work*, ed. A. Elsen (1965); Robert Descharnes and J.F. Chabrun, *Auguste Rodin* (1967); *The Drawings of Rodin*, ed. A. Elsen and K. Varnedoe (1972); A. Elsen, S. McGough and S. Wander (eds), *Rodin and Balzac* (1973); Victoria Thorson, *Rodin Graphics* (1975); Monique Laurent, *The Rodin Museum of Paris* (1977); R. Butler, *The Shape of Genius* (1993).

STUART MORGAN

ROGERS (of Riverside), Richard George (Lord)
1933–
British architect

Richard Rogers was born in Florence of British parents. He was educated at the Architectural Association in London and, as a Fulbright Scholar, at Yale University, where he was taught by Paul Rudolf and Louis Kahn.

His first job was a house at Creek Vean in Cornwall, for his family. He gave it white walls and large windows, and it still looks modern today. Then, in partnership with Su Rogers and Norman and Wendy Foster, a foursome working as Team 4, he designed a factory at Swindon for Reliance Controls Ltd (1967) which made its mark by the visual quality of its structural system, a row of rectangular bays stiffened by tensioned diagonal braces.

He has since then committed himself to the clarity of such structural tours-de-force. The Centre Pompidou in Paris (1971–7, with Renzo Piano) is still the most famous example of this approach. The south elevation is marked by a clear succession of bays overlaid by diagonal tension cables, in front of which an escalator mounts the facade in one continuous line. This motif has since become the logo for the Centre. The north elevation is further distinguished by the pipes and ducts displayed on the outside.

This display of the mechanisms brings architecture close to the machine, but it also endows it with a sculptural richness. There is an evident influence from the Archigram group, some of whom were employed as technicians. But it also expresses Rogers' attitude to architecture: an intellectual movement towards the 'real' sources of functional truth. As Louis Kahn proposed, the services become the essence of the building. Rogers proposes a functionalist architecture that goes beyond Kahn in an attempt to eliminate the arbitrary character of façade-making. Also important is a devotion to the principles of change and indeterminacy in use, of which the prophet was the Archigram guru, Reyner Banham.

A more balanced approach is evident in the European Court of Human Rights (1989–94) at Strasbourg. Here the elements into which the complex is broken down are not the service elements as such, but spaces of use; they stand on the ground, more expressive of human habitation, while the building takes its shape from its context on the curve of a river. This increased sensitivity towards the city is also evident in the very elegant project for the Alcazar, in Marseilles (1988), which shows a distinct sensitivity not only to an analytical idea of urban form but also to the sense of civic propriety.

Richard Rogers has been recognized as a master of modern design: he was made a Chevalier de la Légion d'Honneur in 1985, elected to the Royal Academy in 1978, awarded the Royal Gold Medal of the RIBA in 1985, knighted in 1991 and made a peer in 1996. This role enables him to influence in political and practical terms the future of architecture within Britain. He will go down to posterity as the principal author of the Millennial Dome at Greenwich, where a tent suspended from steel gantries is given the spread and authority of an immense domed space. His designs continue to exploit the cutting edge of architectural technology. Midway through the first decade of the twenty-first century he has many projects ongoing across the world, including in China and the United States.

When invited by the BBC in 1995 to give the Reith Lectures, he chose to build his lectures around the theme of the dense modern city. Although a major pollutant, it can, he believes, be modified scientifically so that it contributes to a sustainable environment, while preserving the social vivacity that makes it vital. We may hope then to see his architecture come to terms with the demands of civic space, for cities evolve through time and are not cultural entities unless they preserve as well as innovate. There *is* a sense of continuity in Rogers' designs: at Pompidou, the structural frame behind the escalators has a classic dignity and grace, and the public place which the building forms with the ancient city of Paris is positive and useful. Its shelving shape pays tribute to one of the greatest civic spaces in the world – the Campo in Siena.

Further reading

See: Richard Rogers, *Architecture – A Modern View* (1990); Kenneth Powell (ed.), *Richard Rogers* (1994).

ROBERT MAXWELL

ROLLING STONES, The

1960s British rock band

Mick Jagger (1943–), Keith Richard (1943–), Brian Jones (1944–69), Charlie Watts (1941–) and Bill Wyman (1941–) formed their musical taste on the growing number of urban black American rhythm and blues players whose work was becoming known in England in the late 1950s. This strident strutting music of heavily rhythmic guitar, harsh harmonica wails and raw vocal style offered intense emotional excitement along with a subversive challenge to white sexual and social conventions. The Rolling Stones' emergence in the 1960s as 'The Greatest Rock 'n' Roll Band in the World' was on the development and exploitation of these roots.

Their early performance repertoire and recordings consisted of material derived directly from artists like Muddy Waters, Bo Diddley, Howlin' Wolf, Jimmy Reed, Slim Harpo and Chuck Berry. This deliberate embracing of transatlantic idiom and myth was recreated and given thrilling freshness through Jagger's extraordinary voice. Early in 1962 he had bitten off the tip of his tongue in a gym mishap, which radically altered his delivery and lent extra lasciviousness to the sexual ambiguities of songs like 'I'm a King Bee' and 'Walking the Dog' (both on *The Rolling Stones*, 1964). In the still highly repressed climate of late-Tory, post-Profumo Britain, the erotic rhythmic assertiveness and unabashed suggestiveness of lyric constituted a threat to the bourgeois citadel. This was augmented by a public posture of cynicism and defiance, carefully orchestrated by Andrew Loog Oldham, the group's manager. Deliberately shunning the **Beatles'** whimsical charm, and refusing the popular music form of consolatory romantic love, the Stones marketed a mood of aggressive anger which caught a genuine feel of the times, despite being initially channelled through rural and urban Negro frustration;

With their fourth and fifth LPs (*Aftermath*, 1966, and *Big Hits (High Tide and Green Grass)*, 1966), Jagger and Richard largely turned their backs on borrowed material in favour of their own compositions. Songs like 'Satisfaction', 'Paint It Black', 'Get Off of My Cloud' and '19th Nervous Breakdown' relocated the target of a ferocious resentment firmly within experience of drugs and capitalist media neurosis. Elements of nihilism and sado-masochism were central to the group's work in the 1960s, and were to endure in its productions. Another central element was trans-sexualism. Jagger's stage act as a non-musician had always been provocatively athletic, partly from childhood agilities acquired from his physical education instructor father, partly from imitation of James Brown. Through androgynous make-up and gesture, and sexually cajoling voice distortion, he questioned the supposed rigid divide between male and female in a manner broad enough to include self-mockery. Overt transvestism,

later to be copied *ad nauseam* in the rock world, was broached with Jerry Schatzberg's publicity photograph for the single 'Have You Seen Your Mother, Baby, Standing in the Shadow?' (1966). Apocalyptic, primeval atmospheres of bacchanalian violence were projected through a version of rhythm and blues deliberately jagged, hard and flashy, with some tracks (such as 'Jumpin' Jack Flash', on *Through the Past Darkly*, 1969) partially recorded on cassette to achieve this effect.

The vast youth following for this symbolic desecration of public order produced hysterical establishment reaction. Systematic harassment of the group by media and police culminated in the arrest of Jagger and Richard, and their sentencing to imprisonment on petty drugs offences. The convictions were quashed on appeal, not without some atypical assistance from a *Times* leader ('Who Breaks a Butterfly on a Wheel?', 1 July 1967), which drew a parallel with the hounding of Stephen Ward in the Profumo affair, and suggested that the case was 'a symbol of the conflict between the sound traditional values of Britain and the new hedonism'. Further cannabis charges against Brian Jones were partially responsible for his leaving the group in 1969 and his apparent suicide that year in the swimming pool of his Sussex house, where A.A. Milne had written *Winnie the Pooh*.

Late 1960s political ferment was superficially reflected in *Beggars Banquet* (1968) with 'Factory Girl', 'Salt of the Earth' and notably with 'Street Fighting Man', taken by many as an invitation to storm the barricades, but in fact proposing rock 'n' roll as a substitute area for revolutionary action. The invitation to ecstatic participation which was a feature of music festivals of the period gave serious encouragement to a vague diabolism in the group's work. Brian Jones's fascination with the Dionysiac musical rituals of the Moroccan Bou Jeloud (*Joujouka*, 1972) was registered in *Their Satanic Majesties Request* (1967), and developed specifically in 'Sympathy for the Devil' (on *Beggars Banquet*), the number Jagger was singing at the

Altamont Speedway, California, in 1969, while below him Hell's Angels bodyguards stabbed to death a young black. This sacrificial death flowed with seeming inevitability from the demand for adulatory homage exerted by gods, devils and stars alike. It nullified the optimism of the Woodstock generation. Lucifer resurfaces in 'Midnight Rambler' (on Let It Bleed, 1969), with Jagger incorporating words from the confession of the Boston Strangler. Nevertheless, Let It Bleed presents a synthesis of the Stones' musical excellence across a range of rock, blues and country styles.

In the 1970s their politics of delinquency became increasingly dominated by camp theatricality and international drug-culture chic, purveyed through lavishly staged shows and some powerful recordings.

Further reading

Other works include: The Rolling Stones No. 2 (1965); Out of Our Heads (1965); Between the Buttons (1967); Get Yer Ya Yas Out (1970); Sticky Fingers (1971); Exile on Main Street (1972); Goats Head Soup (1973); It's Only Rock 'n' Roll (1974); Black and Blue (1976); Some Girls (1978); See: David Dalton, The Rolling Stones (1972); Roy Carr, The Rolling Stones (1976); The 'Rolling Stone' Rock 'n' Roll Reader, ed. Ben Fong-Torres (1974); P. Norman, The Stones (1984); S. Booth, The Adventures of the Rolling Stones (1985); G. Giuliano, Paint It Black (1994).

JOHN PORTER

ROOSEVELT, Franklin Delano

1882–1945

US statesman

As president from 1933 to 1945 Roosevelt radically transformed American government in policies, process and politics, while advancing a massive programme of economic reform and leading the nation to victory over totalitarian aggression. These achievements had profound long-run effects on the political order of the United States and of the world at large

Physically paralysed by polio from the age of thirty-nine, his victorious struggle with pain, depression and immobility was a spiritual rebirth, engendering in him sympathy with human frailty, serene self-assurance and a passion, as he said in his famous Inaugural of 1933, for 'action and action now'. Facing a country devastated by the great depression, he launched the New Deal, a programme of government intervention breaking sharply with the 'rugged individualism' of the past. This widening of scope led to a centralization of power in the federal government and in the presidency. FDR not only directed this nationalization of policy and process, but also evoked and masterfully led a electoral coalition which on balance kept the Democratic party in power at all levels for the next generation

In what way were these achievements the work of FDR? One can think of the New Deal as simply a string of the ad hoc reactions of an ambitious pol to group pressures, thereby inferring that he was no statesman but a wheeler-dealer and/or lucky figurehead. In the many and varied programmes of the New Deal, however, one sees certain common purposes which testify to an ideology. This outlook identified two problems which had been emerging in recent decades of industrialization. They were such economic concentration and economic deprivation as to create a severe imbalance of power and wealth between the two extremes, which FDR personalized as the 'economic royalists' and 'the forgotten man'. Accordingly the solutions attempted by the New Deal were directed at redressing this imbalance by programmes of empowerment and entitlement.

In fundamentals Roosevelt did not originate, but inherited this assessment of problems and solutions from the Progressive movement exemplified by President Theodore Roosevelt, his cousin and the idol of his youth, and President Woodrow Wilson, whom he served as assistant secretary of the navy. Progressivism, moreover, was part of a broad political movement in the Western world in the late nineteenth century away from individualism and towards collectivism. In the capitalist democracies this movement gave rise to the welfare state of the twentieth century. Usually, this reaction to the industrial economy also produced a strong socialist party. Not in the United States, however, and Roosevelt reflected this preference when he named his cause 'liberalism'. He thereby introduced this term into common use in American political discourse, proclaimed in effect that his proposals did have an ideology and distinguished it from socialism. This curious adoption of the term, which traditionally had denominated the individualist creed, Roosevelt owes to the example of the radical programme of the Liberal government of 1908–16 founding the welfare state in Britain. When one examines how the New Deal performed a similar role in the United States, the British comparison brings out the distinctively American/Rooseveltian innovations, such as the different ways of institutionalizing the principle of social insurance and the needs of organized labour. The pressures of the industrial order in general and its current collapse in particular could be perceived and confronted in different ways. Those tumultuous times generated a great array of isms. What Roosevelt called 'liberalism' defined the ends and means which his ambition needed if he was to choose among these possibilities.

In foreign affairs Roosevelt's greatest achievement was his leadership of the great victories over the Axis powers. The magnitude of the American effort in preparing for war and in four years of fighting was prodigious. In the Pacific, victory over the Japanese was won virtually alone by the Americans, climaxing in their use of the atom bomb. In the European theatre, although the Russians were almost entirely responsible for the German defeat, the American contribution was indispensable. In these achievements of American power Roosevelt's leadership was to bring a reluctant and isolationist nation to the brink of war and then to direct and invigorate its military and industrial response once it had been attacked. In the conduct of the war, he dealt with its political implications in the company of **Churchill** and **Stalin**. Their decisions were mainly concerned with the international order following the peace whose goals Roosevelt set forth repeatedly as the Four Freedoms of speech, of religion, from want and from fear, 'everywhere in the world'. This new order of peace and justice he sought to realize and safeguard by the establishment, largely under his inspiration, of the United Nations.

What are the long-run impacts of FDR's achievements? In the United States, despite swings in public policy between public choice and market choice, the political culture basically supports the institutions of the welfare state and managed capitalist economy, which were established by Roosevelt, and developed by his like-minded successors. Thanks in some degree to the success of American liberalism, socialism is no longer a serious model elsewhere in the contemporary world. On the other hand, Roosevelt's global vision has suffered severe disappointments. The Russian veto prevented the UN from coping with the great post-war conflict of the Cold War, the American policy of Soviet containment being effected thanks to the North Atlantic Treaty Organization and the nuclear stand-off. One happy survival has been 'the special relationship' between Britain and the United States which emerged during the war and has continued to this day.

Despite the failures of the UN in practice, the principles which Roosevelt intended it to serve have lived on and flourished as the powerful worldwide movement for universal human rights. When one reflects on such statements of purpose as the Four Freedoms 'everywhere in the world', the promise seems utopian and even dangerous. For here is not merely the promise of the negative rights of the old League of Nations to protect member nations against attack, but also the promise of collective action to enforce within nations the positive rights of democracy and social justice. The echo of Rooseveltian liberalism is unmistakable. But surely the mightiest of the unintended consequences of his achievements has been the emergence of the United

States as the superpower. FDR did not foresee this eventuality. But it was a massive side-effect of the enormous economic and military potential achieved and demonstrated by the United States during World War II and the Cold War. As the UN displayed its incapacity, this superpower found itself confronting those grand Rooseveltian commitments to secure human rights universally 'everywhere in the world'.

Further reading

See: James MacGregor Burns, *Roosevelt: The Lion and the Fox* (1956); Arthur M. Schlesinger, Jr, *The Age of Roosevelt* (3 vols, 1957–60); and Frank Freidel, *Franklin D. Roosevelt* (4 vols, 1952–73). The most recent major study is Conrad Black, *Franklin Delano Roosevelt: Soldier of Freedom* (2003.): superficial and grandiose as interpretation, but at 1,280 pages encyclopaedic as a compilation of facts, with a huge bibliography.

SAMUEL H. BEER

ROSSETTI, Dante Gabriel (Gabriel Charles Dante ROSSETTI)

1828–82

English painter and poet

More than that of most creative men, Rossetti's was a divided nature. At its simplest this is reflected in his Anglo-Italian background out of which came the translations from Dante (who was always an obsession, hence the transposition of his Christian names, and who was drawn, like most of Rossetti's iconography, from a not wholly imaginary time when the Renaissance overlapped the Middle Ages) and the early Italian poets (1861, revised as *Dante and His Circle*, 1874). At its deepest was an impossible conflict between the spiritual and the sensual which he attempted to overcome by transferring to art much that had previously belonged to religion and to sexual love, hence the charge of fleshliness made in poetry by Robert Buchanan (*The Fleshly School of Poetry*, 1871) and in painting by Holman Hunt, who in a letter as early as 1860 said that Rossetti's picture *Bocca Baciata* was 'remarkable for gross sensuality of a revolting kind'. The assertion of the flesh was of course an urgent need in Rossetti's day, although it is typical of his neurosis that he was never comfortable with the nude.

The ambivalence of his origins, aggravated by a patchy education in London (where he was born and where, on the whole, he lived) made Rossetti both pugnacious and socially sensitive. He was a natural leader but his confidence and powers of application were constantly undermined by an excess of self-questioning. He was lazy and brooding, and therefore came to venerate inspiration – always a woman. He was extremely vulnerable to criticism and suffered from periods of persecution mania. He disliked showing in public and stopped doing so as soon as his reputation was made, retaining the copyright of his pictures to prevent their unauthorized exhibition. He was an exaggerated Romantic, not a Decadent, because in him remorse was pitched as high as passion and he vibrated helplessly between these two points of command. The only possibility for blunting this conflict was the horrible descent into melancholy. His work is dominated by the autumnal mode, but never was this mode more vehement.

In the heyday of bohemianism in London and Paris, when the writings of **Ruskin** and **Baudelaire** had revived the romance of the artistic life, Rossetti's was as artistic as any. His was the originating genius of the Pre-Raphaelite movement. He and Elizabeth Siddal (known as 'Guggums') were the classic Pre-Raphaelite couple, imprisoned by guilt, anxiety and death. She took to veronal, gave birth to a dead child, and within two years of their marriage killed herself. Stricken by a bad conscience, Rossetti buried a manuscript of poems with her. But in 1869, seven years later, at the prompting of Charles Howell who supervised the macabre operation, the manuscript was exhumed and published as *Poems* (1870) – naturally to great acclaim. In that year Rossetti also completed his portrait of Elizabeth, *Beata Beatrix*, perhaps his greatest picture. Yet he was unable to exorcize her – on the contrary, he attempted to make contact through seances. Buchanan's attack precipitated a collapse in 1872 and Rossetti tried to commit suicide by swallowing a bottle of laudanum: his morbidity had been made insufferable by an obsession for **William Morris's** wife, Jane. But the tortured dreamer was also a hard-headed man of business. He derived a large income from the *nouveau riche* magnates of the north of England (*Astarte Syriaca*, his most ambitious portrait of Jane Morris, was commissioned by Clarence Fry for two thousand guineas) and was tough in his dealings with clients. Many of his finest pictures are now to be found in the public galleries of Manchester and Liverpool. Rossetti became addicted to chloral, taken originally for insomnia, and was helped through his last years by Watts-Dunton and finally Hall Caine.

It is understandable that a man for whom art was simply a more vivid form of life should extend his activity into literature and aesthetics generally. His poetry provides a link in the strain of mysticism which passes between Blake and **W.B. Yeats**, although in Rossetti's case this is usually expressed as 'yearning'. But it is the distinctive intensity of his visual imagination which continues to be fascinating, especially in his portraits of women where his sexuality is made ferocious by denial. The Rossetti woman was such an extreme type that she came to be fixed in the popular mind as the Art Woman, to be replaced eventually not by Isadora Duncan but by the attenuated figures of Edith Sitwell and **Virginia Woolf**. Heavy, fecund, the embodiment of a lust made drowsy with the weight of accumulated delay, but capable, when aroused by the inflictions of sado-masochism, of an overwhelming congress, she is empress-like in scale, but whether one sees her as an Amazon or a cow depends on mood because she is both (Rossetti's menagerie at Tudor House in Chelsea included a Brahmin bull because he said its eyes reminded him of Jane Morris's). These female figures, like Michelangelo's male nudes on the Sistine ceiling, border on the grotesque, even on the comic, but the laughter is uneasy and they remain very powerful presences, unlike anything else in art.

Rossetti liked to play up his English aspect but it was the infusion of his warm Mediterranean blood into the English artistic world which supplied the audacity which the other Pre-Raphaelites required in order to fulfil themselves; because the Pre-Raphaelite movement, even when it thought otherwise, was fundamentally dedicated to a reawakening of the senses in a society dulled by habits of prudery and obligation.

Millais was technically more accomplished, Holman Hunt more moral, and Burne-Jones a purer master, but it is the art of Rossetti which expresses fully that crucial moment in nineteenth-century culture when the challenge to decorum is held in a paralysis of tragic passion.

Further reading

See: Max Beerbohm, *Rossetti and His Circle* (1922); Evelyn Waugh, *A Life of Rossetti* (1928); Oswald Doughty, *A Victorian Romantic* (1949); Christopher Wood, *The Pre-Raphaelites* (1981); J. Marsh, *Dante Gabriel Rossetti* (2000).

DUNCAN FALLOWELL

ROTH, Philip Milton
1933–
US writer

Twenty or more novels on from *Goodbye, Columbus* (1959), with which he made his bow, Philip Roth occupies a simply luminous place not only in the Jewish American literary roster but in America's canon-at-large. Newark-born, educated at Rutgers, Bucknell and the University of Chicago, much resident in Europe, husband until their divorce to the actress Claire Bloom, and editor of an influential East European author-series, he has frequently been enrolled in a kind of Jewish imaginative collective along with **Saul Bellow**, Bernard Malamud, **Norman**

Mailer or Cynthia Ozick. Nor have other affinities gone unnoted, whether America's literature of manners from **Henry James** to **John Updike** or Europe's legacy of Gogol, **Kafka** and Milan Kundera. But few would deny Roth ever to have been his own man, the fierce, often comic-sardonic spilling of Jewish family secrets, the repertoire of style and irony.

His first book gave the signposts for this daring, whether *Goodbye, Columbus* as the title novella's wonderfully furtive encounter of the lower-class Neil Klugman with the affluent family of Brenda Patimkin as Jewish princess, or an accompanying story like 'The Conversion of the Jews' with the boy Ozzie Freedman's zany, precocious questioning of Rabbi Marvin Binder as to the Jews as Chosen People in an American republic of equals or God's credibility in the face of science. A shared virtuosity marks out other early fiction, whether *Letting Go* (1962), his Jamesian-Jewish anatomy of campus and suburb, *Portnoy's Complaint* (1969), his best-seller of a life literally haunted by masturbatory over authentic value and told, pilloryingly and with coruscating wit, as though from the psychiatrist's couch, *Our Gang* (1971) as his devastating send-up of Nixonism, or *The Great American Novel* (1973) which turns on baseball as obsession, at once pastime and key to American life. It little surprises that firestorms frequently have flared around him for his alleged Jewish betrayals, self-hate or derogation of women, not least among them Sophie Portnoy as Jewish mother.

Roth has also laid his claim to having written two *romans fleuve*. His 'Nathan Zuckerman' series makes a first appearance in *My Life as a Man* (1975), sexual adventuring as the mirror of a larger American gender politics. *The Ghost Writer* (1979) offers the finely nuanced New England portrait of generational literary influence and competition with its footfalls in Roth's own relationship to Bernard Malamud. *Zuckerman Unbound* (1981) unravels a chronicle of the glut, screens and false turns attendant upon literary fame. In *The Anatomy Lesson* (1983), Rembrandt's 1632 painting serves as the metaphor of Zuckerman's own medical stasis as a writer. *The Prague Orgy* (1985) uses Zuckerman's notebooks for its take on Yiddish heritage and the writer's life under Soviet rule. *The Counterlife* (1987) best can be thought a parable of art's transforming powers of life over death told as the history of the brothers Nathan and Henry Zuckerman. *Patrimony: A True Story* (1991) invokes painful son and father intimacy, the latter dying of a tumour, as fact–fiction memoir. *I Married a Communist* (1998) explores the play of writerly self and persona within the McCarthy era. With *The Human Stain* (2000) Roth puts the Clinton era under ironic purview, identity politics to latter-day class hierarchy, PC to Viagra. David Kapesh, Comp. Lit. academic and writer, serves as main figure and viewpoint in three novels: *The Breast* (1972), Roth's reflexive American adaptation of Kafka's *The Metamorphosis*; *The Professor of Desire* (1977) as the ongoing sexual-autobiographical diary of the campus as a species of shadow-life; and *The Dying Animal* (2001) with its self-mocking anatomy of male sexual libido and rapacity from professor–student affairs to phone sex.

Roth's energy has little flagged as *American Pastoral* (1997), his Pulitzer-winning novel set in the Vietnam-era of the 1960s and told one more time in the voice of Nathan Zuckerman, bears witness. Its life and times of Seymour Levov, affectionately known on account of his blond hair as The Swede, admired high school athlete and spouse to a former Miss Jersey, and of his daughter Mary and her haunting act of terrorist bombing, serves to challenge the American illusion of itself as benign New World garden. It is not hard to see why he continues to be a source of controversy. But, as he confirms in *Operation Shylock* (1993), *Sabbath Theater* (1995) or *The Facts: A Novelist's Autobiography* (1988), texts given to the writer as double-voiced puppeteer or ventriloquist while themselves full of artful feint, Roth is not to be denied. He remains a contemporary of wily, unflagging invention, if Jewish bad boy then also one of American literature's vital gamesters against life reduced to cliché.

Further reading

See: John McDaniel, *The Fiction of Philip Roth* (1974); Sanford Pinsker, *The Comedy that 'Hoits'* (1975); *A Philip Roth Reader*, ed. Martin Green (1980); *Critical Essays on Philip Roth*, ed. Sanford Pinsker (1982); Hermione Lee, *Philip Roth* (1982); *Philip Roth*, ed. Harold Bloom (1986); Jay Halio, *Philip Roth Revisited* (1992); Alan Cooper, *Philip Roth and the Jews* (1996); Stephen Wade, *Imagination in Transit: The Fiction of Philip Roth* (1996); Steven Milowitz, *Philip Roth Considered: The Concentratory Universe of the American Writer* (2000); Mark Shechner, *Up Society's Ass, Copper: Rereading Philip Roth* (2003).

A. ROBERT LEE

ROTHKO, Mark
1903–70
US artist

There were two principal streams in New York Abstract Expressionism: the gestural painting of **Pollock** and **de Kooning**, and colour-field painting, of which Rothko was probably the foremost representative.

Many of his paintings in the 1930s were of isolated human beings in cities. Early in the 1940s, inspired by Surrealist automatism and by his interest in Classical mythology, he began to paint biomorphic images, as in *The Omen of the Eagle* (1942), where he hoped to evoke 'the spirit of Myth, which is generic to all myths of all times. It involves a pantheism in which man, bird, beast and tree ... merge into a single tragic idea.' The backgrounds of these paintings were thinly washed, suggesting an atmosphere suffused with a magic light. Increasingly, these washed backgrounds ousted the semi-figurative elements, in accordance with his desire to create a general and universal symbolic image. This he finally achieved by 1950, from which time on he consistently used an arrangement of soft-edged rectangles, placed vertically above each other. Nearly all his paintings from then until

his death are in this format, the most usual variant being a vertical canvas with two or three horizontal rectangles. Because the image is symmetrical one is not encouraged to see it in relational terms, as one would with **Mondrian**, but on the contrary as holistic, an effect increased by the fact that the rectangles seem to fill the whole canvas. Rothko's paintings are usually extremely large, not because he wished to create a public art but, on the contrary, because he believed that the large scale made them more intimate. As he said: 'To paint a small picture is to place yourself *outside* your experience as a stereopticon view or with a reducing glass. However you paint the large picture, you are *in* it. It isn't something you command.' Rothko's scale is architectural, in that rather than a space being created within the painting, the painting – or group of paintings – modifies the real space of its environment. The mood generated is essentially contemplative and mystical. Although he greatly admired **Matisse**, Rothko's use of colour was never sensuous or hedonistic. Rather, it was a vehicle for transcendence of this world. The paintings made at the very end of his life were entirely grey and black. In 1970 he committed suicide. There is about his art something perhaps passive, certainly tragic and, above all, profoundly moving.

Further reading

See: Diane Waldman, *Mark Rothko* (1978); also the catalogue to his exhibition at the Museum of Modern Art, New York (1961); James E.B. Breslin, *Mark Rothko: A Biography* (1993); Diane Waldman, *Mark Rothko, 1903–1970* (2001).

GRAY WATSON

ROUAULT, Georges
1871–1958
French painter

Rouault was born in Paris of a poor family and received his first tuition in drawing from his grandfather, Alexandre Champdavoine, at the age of ten. At fourteen he became an apprentice in stained-glass decoration with the firm of Tamoni & Hirsch. He trained for five years, during which time he was engaged mostly in the restoration of medieval windows. In 1890 he became a student at the École des Beaux-Arts where, after studying for two years under Élie Delaunay, he entered the studio of the symbolist painter Gustave Moreau. He soon became the master's favourite pupil. Moreau's predilection for mystical subject-matter and style stimulated Rouault's already strong preference for religious and hieratic painting. During the 1890s he also came under the influence of the neo-Catholic writer Léon Bloy. Bloy later introduced him to the scholastic philosopher Jacques Maritain, who wrote an essay on Rouault in 1924, by which time he was acquiring an international reputation.

Rouault's first entries for the Prix de Rome, *Samson tournant la meule* (1893) and *Le Christ Mort pleuré par les Saintes Femmes* (1895), were unsuccessful and this led to a psychological crisis at the end of the decade. In 1898 he held the job of curator at the Musée Moreau for a brief period. His first exhibits at the Salon d'Automne between 1903 and 1908, having lost their explicitly religious aspects and discovered some of the recent developments in art, were to associate him in the public's mind with the Fauve painters, such as **Matisse** and Vlaminck, whose work his resembled in fierceness of form and colour, though not in spirit. The series of clowns and whores shown in 1905 caused a particular sensation on account of their almost barbaric portrayal of misery and degradation. In 1910 he received wide acclaim as a result of his first one-man show at the Galérie Druet. His fame was further advanced in 1913 when the major Parisian dealer, Ambrose Vollard, bought the entire contents of his studio. (In fact in 1947, upon the dealer's death, a large number of these canvases were returned to Rouault who burned over 300 of them.) In 1952 he was given a major retrospective in Paris and upon his death six years later he was honoured by a

state funeral. During his life he became an important, if often reclusive, representative of the modernist Catholic institution. His output was large and varied and includes oil paintings, gouaches, watercolours, tapestries, enamels and graphics executed with considerable versatility. In 1929 he designed the sets and costumes for **Diaghilev's** ballet *Le Fils prodigue.*

Rouault's art is characterized by two major themes, one formal and the other iconographic. The deep luminosity of his colours, very often sombre reds and blues, and the thick, almost primitive dark lines which enclose and highlight them, reveal an obvious debt to his experience in working on stained-glass. His deep concern for the continuing health of an expressive religious art ran parallel to this adoption of certain modern aspects of style. The colour and line are thus Fauvist in one sense but highly traditional in another. Where his art is not straightforwardly religious in content, it dwells upon the outcasts of society whom **Picasso** had introduced into his work of the 'Blue' period. Clowns, acrobats and prostitutes are portrayed with an expressionist intensity more typical of German and Scandinavian artists than of French ones – although Rouault balanced this content with scathing portraits of the more successful members of society, like advocates and judges, who are antithetically opposed to the potentially redeemed failures. His work has, thus, in its imagery of revealed despair and evil, a kinship with that of the nineteenth-century satirist Daumier. His art, very largely drawn out of the literary inspiration of writers like Bloy and Péguy, is a visual equivalent for that area of French literary culture which combines an interest in modern form with essentially conservative intellectual concepts. Jacques Maritain once described Bloy as 'Job on the dunghill of modern civilization', and this description would no doubt have suited Rouault. Man was, in this apocalyptic version of catholicism, a fallen creature facing a terrifying Old Testament deity. Of his own work Rouault once wrote that it was 'A cry in the night! A stifled sob! A laughter that chokes itself.'

In 1916 Rouault stopped painting and began to work on a series of graphic works, the most important of which were fifty-seven plates collectively entitled *Miserere et guerre*. These were commissioned by Vollard. The original composition was transferred by photo-mechanical process on to the copper plate which Rouault would then work over with a variety of engraving tools. The luminosity and strength of the finished plates are, as in the oil paintings, founded on deep colours bounded by thick expressive lines. In many respects these works echo the late canvases and prints of Rembrandt, an artist, along with Daumier, who exerted a great influence on Rouault's mature style. This can also be seen in his other major print series of the same period, *Réincarnations du Père Ubu*, *Le Cirque* and *Paysages légendaires*.

In 1929 Rouault began painting again. Although at first he struggled with his old medium he gradually overcame these problems and went on to produce a succession of masterpieces which, during the 1940s, became solely religious in content. In 1938 he was given a major exhibition of his graphic work at the Museum of Modern Art in New York and in 1945 a retrospective by the same gallery which included the large windows he had executed for the church at Assy.

Rouault was in many respects a painter apart in France. The urbanity and intellectualism common to the mainstream of the Paris school were quite at odds with the expressionist conscience he represented. He opposed an enlightenment vision of man perfected and free with his own of man fallen and bestial. His art was explicitly dogmatic and was executed from a traditional stance of the artist as scourge rather than as comforter. His contemporary, Matisse, using a related pictorial vocabulary, was aiming at an art which would function as a '*calmant cérébral*'. He wished to transcend ethical issues by ignoring or denying the religious sense of the fatality of the self's relationship with the world. He has written, 'We must learn how to discover joy in the sky, in the trees and the flowers. How to draw happiness from ourselves, from a full working day and the light it can cast into the midst around us.' Rouault believed that this missed the religious truth of *la condition humaine*.

Further reading

Other works include: *Souvenirs intimes* (1926) and *Correspondance de Rouault et de Suarès* (1960). See: L. Venturi, *Georges Rouault* (1948); J.T. Soby, *Georges Rouault* (1945); P. Courthion, *Rouault* (1962); F. Hergott and S. Whitfield, *Georges Rouault: The Early Years, 1903–1920* (exhibition catalogue, 1993).

RICHARD HUMPHREYS

ROUSSEAU, Henri ('Le Douanier')
1844–1910
French painter

After a period in the French army, Henri Rousseau worked for some years as a minor official in the Paris toll-gate service, whence the grandiose nickname he later received: 'Le Douanier', the Customs Officer. He was in his forties before he began to paint, but he at once found his idiom and gave up his job to devote himself to art, making a living from occasional private lessons in painting and music. From 1886 onwards he regularly exhibited in Paris at the annual Salon des Indépendants, his intention clearly being to gain recognition as an artist among other artists; this aim he pursued with dignity and total dedication, even though many considered his entries to be a standing joke. His reputation grew as sponsorship came from a succession of writers and artists, whose attitude seems to have evolved from tongue-in-cheek patronage to genuine, somewhat startled enthusiasm. The poets Alfred Jarry and, later, Guillaume Apollinaire had their portraits painted by Rousseau; Robert Delaunay became a sincere admirer and friend, while **Picasso** began collecting his pictures in the same spirit as he collected African tribal art –

seeing in them a significant formal stimulus and a demonstration of the power of innocent vision. Half figure of fun, half aesthetic innovator, Rousseau was to emerge as both mascot and exemplar for the avant-garde of Fauvism and Cubism; his mixture of naivety and skill fulfilled a necessary myth of spontaneity, of inventive design liberated from academic constraints.

Almost entirely an autodidact, Rousseau kept to a narrow range of favourite subjects: principally portraits, cityscapes and exotic landscapes. The portraits, usually of neighbours and their children, give the clearest indication of his untutored hand: sitters are portrayed as monumental figures with stereotyped features standing woodenly in decorative parkland. Rousseau's cityscapes record picturesque aspects of Paris and environs, often showing bourgeois families out for a Sunday stroll in the public gardens or along the river; they are characterized by the naive artist's affection for the telling detail: the distant Eiffel Tower, an ostentatiously posed fisherman, an airship as if pinned up on the sky. The impression of whimsicality mingled with painstaking literalness modulates into something more compelling when Rousseau turns to imaginary exotic landscapes; it is indeed these which have most contributed to his reputation as a naive who somehow transcends his naivety.

Rousseau's art is certainly 'naive' in the sense that it falls short of the standards of traditional mimesis to which, it appears, he nevertheless diligently sought to conform. His figures look frozen stiff rather than simply immobile; his sense of scale is aberrant, his grasp of perspective faulty. But undismayed by such deficiencies (if indeed he ever recognized them as such), Rousseau was able to compile a repertoire of compensatory virtues. His sharply outlined and flattened figures can have a strange formal seductiveness: a chestnut tree or a standing woman take on an emblematic radiance once placed within a scene. And the meticulous rendering of detail, the insistent patterning of such repeated elements as foliage, the concern for

nuances of colouring, the compulsive brushing-in of each last square inch of canvas – these symptoms of over-earnestness, of the naive's desire to produce 'the professional look' at all costs, do end up creating an idiom of intensity which has a coherence and an allurement all of its own.

Rousseau's most powerful effect – a kind of hypnotic translucency of finish – is nowhere more memorably achieved than in the series of paintings of wild beasts in exotic settings. In *The Sleeping Gypsy* (*La Bohémienne endormie*, 1897), a lion is shown nuzzling a sleeping woman beneath a desert moon. The woman, black-skinned and massive, wears a dress patterned in bright multicoloured stripes which echo the design on her pillow and the parallels of the strings on the nearby mandolin. The contrast between this visual dazzlement and the stark simplicity of the surrounding sand, hills and sky creates an effect of visual consternation and a queer mood of suspense. In *The Snake Charmer* (*La Charmeuse de serpents*, 1907), a naked negress plays her flute by the river bank. As snakes sway towards her out of the jungle, she herself remains in shadow, an inexplicable silhouette set against the gleaming water and sky: we discern only two staring eyes within the illegible blackness of her form. The impression is of hidden depths, an enigma equally suggestive of unspoken ferocity and utopian tenderness.

Several jungle paintings exploit the incongruity of setting a lady in splendid town clothes down in the middle of a profusion of tropical vegetation. Such a juxtaposition of the familiar and the extraordinary is a favourite device, and may be seen as translating Rousseau's basic project of offering us windows through which we can perceive the world in an adventurous new way. However, it cannot be claimed that the jungle pictures, with their rampant beasts of prey, eccentric birds and tropical storms, are at all naturalistic. The animals are frequently derived from such sources as illustrations in popular encyclopaedias; the plants are thought to be largely inspired by Rousseau's visits to the tropical section of the botanical gardens in Paris, the Jardin des Plantes. And whole pictures have been shown to be the result of simplified copying from undistinguished engravings. Yet by a curious reversal, Rousseau's images are at their most compelling to the extent that they are manifestly unrealistic and thus most overtly fantastical. His most sophisticated performances arise from a fine balance between the theatrics of his jungle tableaux, where leaping jaguars and flamboyant orchids appear almost to be snipped out from cardboard, and the sheer resplendence and depth of his colours – he once boasted that he had used twenty-two variants of green in a single canvas – and no less a colourist than **Gauguin** is said to have envied him his command of black tones.

Elevated by the avant-garde into a kind of cult hero for Modernism, Rousseau has a claim to being seen as a central figure in the development of twentieth-century art. His influence has been traced to Surrealism and the work of De Chirico, and to the current of Magical Realism in Germany and Austria. As a naive, Rousseau also takes his place in the specific history of neo-primitive painting. Promoted in the 1920s by collectors such as Wilhelm Uhde, who placed him with other naives like Séraphine Louis and Camille Bombois, he has since been universally acknowledged as the grand master of naive art in the last century. Meanwhile, seen within a more academically respectable perspective, his work has been considered worthy of representation in the Louvre and the National Gallery in London.

How then should Rousseau finally be evaluated? It has to be said quite bluntly that some of his pictures reveal the untutored hand at its worst; they are downright incompetent and lack any saving grace in terms of impetuous colouring or artless design. Again, several paintings have that fussy prettiness which is one of the less stimulating characteristics of naive art. But above these loom the true masterpieces, from *A Carnival Evening* (*Un soir de carnaval c.* 1886) to *The Dream* (*Le Rêve* 1910), a series of works

which remain marvellously authoritative and consistently appealing. These are paintings whose subject-matter may be palpably ridiculous or else merely trivial, yet whose technical execution lifts everything on to an entirely fresh expressive plane. In them, Rousseau is able to transcend all the ready-made categories and to assert his originality as the creator of an inimitable personal style.

Further reading

See: Ronald Alley, *Portrait of a Primitive: The Art of Henri Rousseau* (1978); Adolphe Basler, *Henri Rousseau* (1927); Roger Shattuck, *The Banquet Years* (1969); Wilhelm Uhde, *Henri Rousseau* (1921); Dora Vallier, *Henri Rousseau* (1961); Roger Shattuck, *Henri Rousseau* (1986); Gotz Adriani, *Henri Rousseau* (2001).

ROGER CARDINAL

RUSHDIE, Salman
1947–
British/Indian novelist

Son of a Cambridge-educated Indian businessman, Salman Rushdie was born into a Muslim family in Bombay in the year of India's independence. He was sent to England to be educated at Rugby School, which he disliked, and while he was there his family moved to the Islamic state of Pakistan. By now Rushdie had been a Muslim in Hindu India, an Indian in Pakistan, and an Asian at an English public school.

Rushdie worked as an advertising copywriter after graduating from Cambridge, and was responsible for the cream slogan 'Naughty but Nice'. During this time he published his first novel, *Grimus* (1975), which featured an American Indian searching for the meaning of life, but he only became well known in 1981 with his magic realist epic *Midnight's Children*. Comparable in scope to the work of **Gabriel García Márquez**, this was a humorous, allegorical, and ultimately critical novel that followed the recent history of India through the life of its narrator and one thousand other children born in the hour after the declaration of India's Independence. It won the Booker Prize and was acclaimed in both Britain and India, although it caused offence to Indira Gandhi; she won a libel suit against Rushdie shortly before being assassinated.

Rushdie then turned his attention to Pakistan in *Shame* (1983), a harsher, less humorous and far less affectionate book which was almost immediately banned in Pakistan. When General Zia-ul-Haq ('Old Razor Guts' in the book) died in a plane bomb in August 1988, Rushdie commented 'Dead dictators are my speciality ... all the political figures most featured in my writing ... have now come to sticky ends ... This is a service I can perform, perhaps. A sort of literary contract.'

Rushdie's tendency to put noses out of joint escalated to an unforeseen level in September 1988, with the publication of *The Satanic Verses*. Still concerned with post-colonial history, as well as the nature of narrative and belief, *The Satanic Verses* dealt with Islam and included a number of 'in-jokes', hardly noticed by most Westerners, such as giving the names of Mohammed's wives to prostitutes.

Many Muslims felt this calculated irreverence was an act of treachery and apostasy, and the insiderish aspect only increased the offence. In February 1989 the **Ayatollah Khomeini**, Iran's religious leader, pronounced a *fatwa* not just on Rushdie but on all those who knowingly had anything to do with the book's production: 'I call on all zealous Muslims to execute them quickly.' A million dollar bounty was offered, later increased to 2.5 million.

The *fatwa* was of questionable legality under Islamic law, but neither Rushdie's life nor his significance would be the same again. There were a number of deaths, including that of his Japanese translator, and Rushdie went into protracted hiding, protected by the British police. His virtual confinement continued for several years, during which his second marriage, to the American writer Marianne Wiggins, cracked

under the strain, and he reviewed *The Oxford Guide to Card Games* for the *Times Literary Supplement*.

Rushdie was now fully established as a *cause célèbre*, although he remained controversial in Britain: some commentators felt it was ironic that the British state (which Rushdie had earlier spoken of in the same breath as apartheid South Africa and Nazi Germany) should bear the considerable cost of protecting him. After a meeting with Islamic scholars in Christmas 1990, Rushdie affirmed the Oneness of God and the genuineness of the Prophet Mohammed's revelation, leading to his essay 'Why I Have Embraced Islam.' In 1996, however, he described this as a 'depressed and despairing moment ... a very foolish attempt at appeasing the opposition,' adding 'I have no problem with other people's religious beliefs. I just don't happen to have any.'

Rushdie was reported to have hopes of a Nobel Prize, which has not yet materialized – **Martin Amis** claimed 'Salman even knows the names of the cats and dogs belonging to the Nobel Prize judges' – but in 1993 *Midnight's Children* was awarded the Booker of Bookers. In 1994 he published a collection of short stories *East, West*, exploring the interface and interpenetration of the title, and in 1995 another major novel, *The Moor's Last Sigh*, the multi-cultural and miscegenated family history of a Jewish Indian descended from a Muslim Sultan. The book's depiction of a Hindu fundamentalist caused it to be temporarily banned in India.

Aside from their magic realism, a genre associated with post-colonial writing, Rushdie's fictions are remarkable for their supple, polyphonic, pun-packed linguistic verve, and the teeming multiplicity of their plots and inventions: reviewers variously acclaimed one book as 'several of the best novels he has ever written' (Robert Irwin) and complained that another had 'too much too muchness' (Michael Gorra). This multi-faceted abundance can itself be read as a post-colonial refusal to be categorized or forced to choose.

As well as declaring himself a citizen of Sarajevo, Rushdie was elected first Head of the International Writers' Parliament in 1994. The *fatwa* – perhaps the major landmark of the showdown between liberal globalization and Islamic fundamentalism before 9/11 – was lifted in 1998, but the literary merits and demerits of Rushdie's work have been all but overshadowed by his status as an icon of free speech.

Further reading

Other works include: *The Jaguar Smile* (1987), a partisan account of his time in Nicaragua; *Haroun and the Sea of Stories* (1990), ostensibly for children; *The Ground Beneath Her Feet* (1999), which led to a stage appearance with the rock band U2; and *Fury* (2000), a product of his later life in New York. His essays have been collected in *Imaginary Homelands* (1991), predominantly about post-colonial issues, and the more journalistic collection *Step Across This Line* (2002), which also contains his 2002 Tanner Lectures on Human Values as its title piece.

PHIL BAKER

RUSKIN, John

1819–1900

English writer on art and critic of society

John Ruskin was the only man of his century whose writings on painting and architecture were widely read outside specialist circles; and the extent of his influence in artistic matters has never been matched. He achieved this pre-eminence, however, without publicizing the trivial or immediately appealing aspects of art. On the contrary, he subjected his readers to a stern re-examination of the fundamental principles of art, and its connections with human personality and social behaviour.

The only child of a wealthy sherry importer, John Ruskin was educated privately in south London, but the seclusion of his childhood was relieved by annual tours with his parents, in Britain and abroad. By the age of twenty he had published scholarly essays on geographical phenomena, and a book-length series of articles entitled *The Poetry of Architecture*. At Oxford University he gained a reputation as a skilful watercolourist and amateur geologist. In 1843, as 'A Graduate of Oxford', he published the first volume of *Modern Painters*, boldly proclaiming 'the superiority of the modern painters to the old ones', and eulogizing above all the art of J.M.W. Turner. Ruskin was scathing in his analysis of many of the established masters of seventeenth-century painting, but won respect nevertheless for his acute observation of nature and for his lyrical evocations of Turner's art.

In 1845, on a momentous visit to Italy, Ruskin 'discovered' the work of the fourteenth- and fifteenth-century artists of Pisa, Florence and Venice. It was these artists, together with Tintoretto, who were the heroes of the second volume of *Modern Painters* (1846). Ruskin commended the sense of calm devotion which he discerned in the painting of the early Italian masters, contrasting this quality with the insipidity and self-absorption which he found in the work of Raphael and his successors of the 'High Renaissance'. These sentiments were largely shared by a group of young British artists, led by William Holman Hunt, John Millais and **Dante Gabriel Rossetti**, who formed the Pre-Raphaelite Brotherhood in 1848; and when in 1851 the Pre-Raphaelites were fiercely criticized, Ruskin defended them in the columns of *The Times*, and initiated a revival of their fortunes.

By this time Ruskin was preoccupied with architecture. In *Seven Lamps of Architecture* (1849) and *The Stones of Venice* (1851–3), he drew the attention of the public to the merits of pre-Renaissance Italian architecture, and thereby broadened the scope of the Gothic Revival in Britain; substantial evidence of his persuasive powers can still be seen in the Anglo-Venetian capitals and arches of many an English suburb – as Ruskin himself observed, and regretted, in later life. These books also exerted a more fundamental influence on Victorian attitudes to architecture. *Seven Lamps* put forward, a little clumsily, the notion of architecture as a manifestation of such moral qualities as 'truth', 'life' and 'sacrifice'. Then *The Stones of Venice*, Ruskin's *tour de force*, fully exemplified his conception that a work of art reflects the personality of its creator – and in the case of architecture, a collective personality or age-spirit, whose growth, health and decay could be traced even in the smallest details of architectural decoration.

Ruskin espoused architecture, however, at the expense of his wife, who left him in 1854. Their marriage, which in six years had not been consummated, was annulled, and she married Millais in the following year. Meanwhile Ruskin began to patronize Rossetti, and his writing proved an inspiration to **William Morris** and Edward Burne-Jones, whose enthusiasm carried Pre-Raphaelite principles into many branches of the decorative arts. They inherited from Ruskin a hostility to classical and Renaissance culture which extended to the arts and design of their own time. Ruskin and his followers believed that the nineteenth century was still afflicted by a demand for mass-production and standardization which had been initiated in the sixteenth century or even earlier. They opposed themselves to mechanized production, meaningless ornament and anonymous architecture of cast iron and plate glass – all symbolized in the Great Exhibition and Crystal Palace of 1851.

Towards the end of the 1850s Ruskin's message was significantly redirected. As he lost his faith in the Protestant Christianity of his youth, he became less confident in the correlation of artistic merit with purity of soul, and found a new respect for the 'magnificent animality' of Titian, Giorgione and Veronese. He taught drawing at the Working Men's College, and became concerned increasingly with the economic and social aspects of art. In his Manchester lectures of 1857, on 'The Political Economy of Art' (republished as *A Joy for Ever*), he emerged as an articulate opponent of capitalism and the ideology of laissez-faire. The pursuit of profit, he maintained, condemned the working man to an inhuman existence of mindless routine. Proclaiming that the principle of co-operation was superior to that of competition, he called for a return to the guild system of craftsmanship, the manufacture of articles of lasting value, and a steady wage guaranteed by a strong, paternal government.

These proposals were unacceptable to many of Ruskin's contemporaries; the fury aroused by a series of articles written by Ruskin for the *Cornhill Magazine*, attacking the libertarian principles of Ricardo and **J.S. Mill**, prompted its editor, Thackeray, to cut short the series. But in the succeeding decades these articles, reprinted as *Unto this Last*, reached a wide audience; such diverse figures as **Tolstoy, Mahatma Gandhi** and the early leaders of the British Labour movement acknowledged the powerful influence of *Unto this Last* on their own philosophy.

Conversely, those works of Ruskin's which were most popular at the time of publication – *Sesame and Lilies* (1864) and *The Ethics of the Dust* (1866) – have appealed much less to subsequent generations. These offered advice to young men and women on their proper roles in life, with (in the second work) elaborate geological and botanical allegories. Ruskin continued to revel in controversy, however, lecturing to the cadets of Woolwich Academy on the glories of war, and advising the citizens of Bradford to decorate their new town hall with pendant purses in honour of their presiding deity, the 'Goddess of Getting-on' (*The Crown of Wild Olive*, 1866).

The last decades of his life were occupied with short-lived philanthropic ventures, unrequited love for young girls, lectures delivered as Slade Professor of Fine Art at Oxford University, and debilitating bouts of mental illness, whose effects are often evident in his monthly publication commenced in 1871, *Fors Clavigera*. In these 'Letters to the Workmen and Labourers of Great Britain' he pronounced erratically on art, literature, mythology and political economy. In an early issue he launched 'The St George's Guild', a form of rural commune financed principally by himself, on which there were to be 'no steam engines ... no untended creatures ... no liberty'. The Guild gained few Companions, but much of its museum still survives.

In a later issue of *Fors* Ruskin criticized a painting by **Whistler**, *Nocturne in Black and Gold: The Falling Rocket*: 'I never expected to hear a coxcomb ask two hundred guineas for flinging a pot of paint in the public's face.' Whistler sued for libel, won a farthing's damages without costs, and was bankrupted. Ruskin was perhaps seen as the moral victor, but in retrospect this celebrated lawsuit of 1878 has come to symbolize the clash between the traditional but outmoded values of figurative art and the daring innovations of the modern movement – an ironic reversal of roles in the case of Ruskin, once the champion of the avant-garde.

Ruskin spent most of his final fifteen years as an invalid at Brantwood, near Coniston, but managed to produce one last major work: his unfinished autobiography *Praeterita*, which, although unreliable in matters of fact, is as compellingly lucid as any of the works of his prime.

Further reading

See: *The Works of John Ruskin*, ed. E.T. Cook and A. Wedderburn (39 vols, 1903–12), whose massive index volume is the single most valuable aid to the study of Ruskin. Many volumes of Ruskin's letters and diaries have been published subsequently, notably *The Diaries of John Ruskin*, ed. Joan Evans and John H. Whitehouse (3 vols, 1956–9): these are listed in *Ruskin: A Bibliography 1900–1974*, ed. H. Kirk Beetz (1977). Recent studies include: Quentin Bell, *Ruskin* (1963); Robert Hewison, *John Ruskin: The Argument of the Eye* (1976); John D. Unrau, *Looking at Architecture with Ruskin* (1978); Patrick Conner, *Savage Ruskin* (1979); Joan Abse, *John Ruskin: The Passionate Moralist* (1980); John Dixon Hunt, *The Wider Sea: A Life of John Ruskin* (1982); D. Birch, *Ruskin's Myths* (1988); Timothy Hilton, *John Ruskin: The Early Years* (1985) and *John Ruskin: The Later Years* (2000). Ruskin's artistic output is examined in Paul Walton, *The Drawings of John Ruskin* (1972).

PATRICK CONNER

RUSSELL, Bertrand Arthur William (Earl)

1872–1970
British philosopher

Russell was born into an aristocratic family; his grandfather, Lord John Russell, had twice been prime minister. When he was orphaned at the age of three, the will of his free-thinking parents was set aside with the result that he and his older brother (upon whose death in 1931 he succeeded to the earldom) were given a strict and puritanical upbringing by their paternal grandmother. When Russell entered Cambridge in 1890, he had been, apart from a period spent preparing for scholarship examinations, educated entirely at home by governesses and tutors. He entered Cambridge with a passionate interest in mathematics which he claimed (*Autobiography*, Vol. I, 1967) had been at one time all that prevented a suicidal outcome to his adolescent loneliness and despair.

Russell sought in mathematics the certainty and perfection of object he had lost when he abandoned his early religious beliefs, and was gradually disillusioned by the teaching at Cambridge, where, 'The "proofs" that were offered of mathematical theorems were an insult to the logical intelligence' (*My Philosophical Development*, 1959). His final undergraduate year was devoted entirely to philosophy and he absorbed the prevailing Hegelian idealism of the time. Study of the *Greater Logic*, however, led Russell to the conclusion that 'all [Hegel] says about mathematics is muddle-headed nonsense' (P.A. Schilpp (ed.) *The Philosophy of Bertrand Russell*, 1944) and in 1898 he was ripe to follow his friend G.E. Moore in revolt against idealism.

Moore persuaded Russell in the name of common sense to accept the existence of fact independent of experience, while Russell reinforced the rebellion by exposing the logical nerve of the argument by which the English Hegelian, F.H. Bradley, had sought to establish the impossibility of knowledge of anything which did not involve knowledge of everything. Russell saw in Bradley's argument the same mistake about relations which he previously discerned in Leibniz (in *A Critical Exposition of the Philosophy of Leibniz*, 1900), the belief that every relation requires foundation in the intrinsic properties of the objects related; these intrinsic properties turn out on deeper investigation to be properties of the whole which the objects compose. The critique of Bradley provided the foundation for the subsequent development of Russell's techniques of analysis: understanding of a complex can be achieved by an account of how its simple parts form a whole.

While the revolt against idealism was mounted in the name of common sense, there remained much in Russell's thinking not sanctioned by common sense. Maintaining that for a word to mean something it must stand for some kind of object, he was led to a belief that numerals, predicate-expressions, even the definite article must stand for non-material entities of some kind. This crude Platonism was eroded over the following decades by the successive development of logical techniques which enabled Russell to distinguish between the apparent logical form of a sentence and the true form of the proposition it expressed. The principle, that for something to be meaningful it must stand for something, could then be applied only to the true logical form.

The soil in which these techniques germinated was the philosophy of mathematics. In 1900 Russell attended a conference in Paris where he encountered the work of the Italian mathematician, Giuseppe Peano. Impressed by the rigour, and aided by the advances, in Peano's work, Russell wrote a treatise (*The Principles of Mathematics*, 1903) which, while heavy with Platonic commitment, was able to eliminate numbers as metaphysical entities in favour of similarity classes, i.e. of classes all members of which can be placed in one–one correspondence with each other. This was the first step in what became a highly influential programme for 'logical construction', the principle of which emerged in 1918 under the slogan, 'Whenever possible logical

constructions are to be substituted for inferences to unknown entities' (*Mysticism and Logic*, 1917).

Because he regarded *class* as a logical notion, the *Principles* was Russell's first defence of the 'logicist thesis': 'that all pure mathematics follows from purely logical premises and uses only concepts definable in logical terms' (*My Philosophical Development*). Russell soon discovered he had been anticipated by sixteen years in the work of the German mathematician Gottlob Frege, but it was Russell who uncovered a problem with the notion of class which threatened the logicist programme for mathematics. Known as 'Russell's Paradox', it points out that the class of all classes not belonging to themselves can neither belong nor fail to belong to itself. The paradox turned out to be one of a family of similar difficulties and could not be ignored. Frege was eventually led to abandon logicism, but Russell pressed on.

Between 1900 and 1910, Russell collaborated with his friend and former teacher at Cambridge, A.N. Whitehead, on an improved presentation of the logicist position, the three-volume *Principia Mathematica* (1913). During this period Russell was frustrated by his inability to find a satisfactory solution to the problems surrounding his paradox. Progress on another front suggested a way of eliminating classes in the same spirit as numbers had been eliminated. The progress consisted in a logical representation of sentences involving definite descriptions. Known since as 'Russell's theory of descriptions', it obviated the problems caused by descriptive expressions which purport to refer to what in fact does not exist. However, to apply a similar idea to classes in such a way as to avoid all the paradoxes ('the ramified theory of types') invalidated vital parts of mathematics and Russell was forced to resort to what many regarded as an *ad hoc* principle, the axiom of reducibility.

Principia and its problems stimulated important mathematical and philosophical work in the three decades after its publication. Among the philosophical work was that of Russell's pupil, **Ludwig Wittgenstein**, who acknowledged, in his *Tractatus*, the importance of the distinction between apparent and true logical form which had emerged with the theory of descriptions. Wittgenstein's principles of 'atomicity' and 'extension' in turn clarified further for Russell the aim and nature of analysis. Between them these principles suggest the world consists of 'atomic facts' which can be described by propositions, the truth of each of which is independent of every other atomic proposition and from which one can infer all other true propositions.

Wittgenstein's development of this idea avoided confronting questions about how human beings know or could know the world so conceived. Russell's development was alive to such epistemological questions from the start. Even before he had assimilated the influence of Wittgenstein, the theory of descriptions had suggested the outline of a sophisticated version of Hume's empiricism. Russell founded his empiricism on the principle, 'Every proposition which we can understand must be composed wholly of constituents with which we are acquainted' (*Mysticism and Logic*) and developed some of Whitehead's techniques for eliminating, by means of logical constructions, such theoretical ideas in science as points, instants and particles, with which we could not claim acquaintance (*Our Knowledge of the External World*, 1914).

Logical atomism required a purification of the notion of acquaintance. Russell wanted the constituents of atomic propositions to be known by acquaintance, but for the propositions to retain their logical independence this acquaintance had to be based on pure experience without taint of inference. To claim to be acquainted with a particular man involves inferences based on more immediate sensory experience, hence men and other material objects are notions requiring elimination by means of logical constructions. Russell even attempted (in *The Analysis of Mind*, 1921) to replace the knowing subject by a construction. He was the first to acknowledge the limitations in his analyses and the shortcomings of his logical constructions. In his last major philosophic work (*Human Knowledge, Its Scope and Limits*, 1948), he explored the extent to which what we accept as knowledge can be founded on the data of immediate experience by means of non-deductive inference.

It is difficult to gauge Russell's influence. Important though *Principia* was, it did not set the style of subsequent mathematical foundations. Mathematicians concurred with the view expressed by Gödel in 1944 that compared to Frege the logical precision of *Principia* represented 'a considerable step backward'. In philosophy the influence of Russell's epistemological theories has waned with growing doubts about the intelligibility of the immediate personal experience which Russell required for the foundation of knowledge. Where Russell's influence is still strong, it is probably so complete and pervasive it is hard to detect. Russell set new goals and problems for philosophic inquiry and demonstrated a new way of pursuing them. Anglo-American philosophy nowadays pays much lip service to the name of Frege, but the conduct of analytical philosophy remains a most sincere, if often unconscious, tribute to Russell.

Part of the explanation for the pervasiveness of Russell's influence lies in his skill as a popularizer and in the charm and accessibility of many of his important works. Addressing an audience of philosophers in 1966, Quine testified, 'I think many of us were drawn to our profession by Russell's books.' Russell's influence, moreover, extended well beyond academic philosophy. Involved directly in many social and political issues he wrote passionately about most of them. His pamphleteering on behalf of pacifism and against conscription during 1914–18 earned him at first a fine, then loss of his Cambridge lectureship, refusal of a passport, and finally six months in prison. His pacifism cost him many friends on the right, but he was not afraid to alienate his friends on the left when, after a visit to Russia, he published a prophetic attack on the communist regime in *The Practice and Theory of Bolshevism* (1920). He stood unsuccessfully for parliament as a women's suffrage candidate in 1907 and again as a Labour candidate in 1923. Interest in the education of his children led him to establish with his second wife (he was married four times) a progressive school, Beacon Hill. He lectured extensively in the United States, both on tour and in university posts. His unconventional ideas, particularly about sexual morality (see *Marriage and Morals*, 1926), led to a civil lawsuit in 1940 which successfully blocked his appointment at City College, New York.

He was awarded the Order of Merit in 1949 and the Nobel Prize for Literature in 1950. During the last fifteen years of his life, he tried to impress upon the world the threat to human survival posed by nuclear arms. He helped found the Campaign for Nuclear Disarmament in 1958 and was sent to prison for a second time (two months reduced to seven days) in 1961 for civil disobedience activity with the Committee of 100.

Further reading

Other works include: *The Problems of Philosophy* (1912); *An Introduction to Mathematical Philosophy* (1919); *The Analysis of Matter* (1927); *An Inquiry into Meaning and Truth* (1940); *A History of Western Philosophy* (1945). Collections of Russell's articles and essays: *Philosophical Essays* (1910); *Logic and Knowledge*, ed. Robert C. Marsh (1956); *Basic Writing of Bertrand Russell, 1903–1959*, ed. R.E. Egner and L.E. Dennon (1961); *Essays in Analysis*, ed. Douglas Lackey (1973). For Russell's life, see his three-volume *Autobiography* (1967–9) and R.W. Clark, *The Life of Bertrand Russell* (1975). Critical studies: F.P. Ramsey, *The Foundations of Mathematics* (1931); D.F. Pears, *Bertrand Russell and the British Tradition in Philosophy* (1967); A.J. Ayer, *Russell and Moore: The Analytical Heritage* (1971); N. Griffin (ed.), *The Cambridge Companion to Bertrand Russell* (2003).

J.E. TILES

S

SAID, Edward Wadie

1935–2003

Palestinian writer and critic

Edward W. Said was born in Jerusalem into a Christian Arab family and was educated at St George's, the Eton of Mandate Palestine. When the Saids moved to Egypt and settled in Cairo, young Edward attended Victoria College, a British-run school. Aged sixteen, he was sent for further education at Mount Hermon, a private school in Massachusetts, where he blossomed academically, finding the American attitude to learning more imaginative and stimulating than the British approach in Cairo. After a degree at Princeton Said embarked on a PhD at Harvard graduate school where he also won the Bowdoin Prize for the best scholarly dissertation written by a student – it was on **Joseph Conrad**. In 1963, he was appointed Assistant Professor of Comparative Literature at Columbia University, New York where he later became a full professor. In the ensuing years he also served as a visiting professor at Harvard, Yale, John Hopkins and Toronto Universities.

Said's writings, some of them translated into twenty-six languages, included many books and covered a range of subjects. Books such as *Joseph Conrad and the Fiction of Autobiography* (1966) and *The World, the Text, and the Critic* (1983) established Said as one of the world's leading literary theorists. But it was his 1978 study, *Orientalism*, which became his most influential and original intellectual contribution. In *Orientalism*, which is a historical examination of attitudes to the Middle East, Said wrote of how the West has stereotyped and degraded the Arab world over the centuries. Using a wide variety of texts, from eighteenth-century travellers' journals to Victorian treatises on Islam, Said shows how these had reinforced negative stereotypes of Arabs as ignorant, lazy and untrustworthy. At the same time, the 'Orient' was seen as exotic and alluring, inviting the rule of European colonial powers.

With *Orientalism*, Said single-handedly launched what later became known as Post Colonial Studies. The book also had a strong impact in enabling academics from non-Western lands to take advantage of the mood of political correctness *Orientalism* helped to engender by associating themselves with 'narratives of oppression', creating successful careers out of representing the non-Western 'other'. Said's *Orientalism* helped transform the way people looked at the Arabs, Islam and the Middle East, but it also drew much criticism and its author was attacked by literary critics, especially in England, for forcing his facts to fit into a predetermined thesis and for distorting the views of such English writers as Jane Austen.

Said was not an armchair intellectual who only theorized about the ideology of imperialism. He became one of its most articulate public opponents. It was the 1967 Middle East war between Israel and the Arabs which shocked Said to the core and stirred him to political activism as his own identity as a Palestinian, suppressed for so many years, became evident. In the 1970s, Said became the most prominent voice in the USA to defend the Palestinian struggle for justice and self-determination and to point at the fact that the Israeli–Palestinian conflict was a battle between a state, namely Israel with its 'colonial army' attacking 'a colonized population'.

Said's literary creativity also shifted to focus on Palestinian issues and in a stream of articles, opinion pieces and books, notably in *The Question of Palestine* (1979), he argued the Palestinian case with clarity and forcefulness. In his final years, however, he took a conscious decision to withdraw from political controversy and channel his energies into music: he was an accomplished pianist who gave occasional public recitals.

Further reading

Other works include: two collections of literary essays, *Beginnings: Intention and Method* (1975) and *The World, the Text and the Critic* (1983); an elegiac work entitled *After the Last Sky: Palestinian Lives* (1986); a contemporary reprise of the theme of *Orientalism* in *Covering Islam* (1981); *Musical Elaborations* (1991); *Culture and Imperialism* (1993); *The Politics of Dispossession* (1994); *Representations of the Intellectual* (1994); *Peace and Its Discontents* (1995); and *Out of Place* (1999), Said's memoirs. See also: Paul A. Bove (ed.), *Edward Said and the Work of the Critic: Speaking Truth to Power* (2000); Bill Ashcroft, Pal Ahluwalia and D.P.S. Ahluwalia (eds), *Edward Said* (2001).

AHRON BREGMAN

SALINGER, Jerome David

1919–

US writer

J.D. Salinger was born in New York City of a Jewish father and Christian mother. He graduated from Valley Forge Military Academy, then studied at New York University and Ursinus College. He never received a degree but did attend Whit Burnett's short-story writing class at Columbia. During the Second World War he took part in the D-Day landings and five campaigns. His war experiences may have had a marked effect upon his attitude towards man, as he has chosen to live in seclusion with his family in New Hampshire, granting only one interview and avoiding all contact with the public. This lifestyle, combined with lengthy gaps between appearances in print, has given Salinger an aura of mystery.

He has been one of the most popular American authors and remains an important fiction writer of the post-war period. His major work is the novel of adolescent rebellion, *The Catcher in the Rye* (1951). Holden Caulfield, the protagonist, is a twentieth-century alienated youth trying to find what he considers honesty in a materialistic and superficial post-war America. Speaking in an adolescent vernacular with a strongly black humorous tinge, he finds that the word 'phony' describes most of what he sees. One can find in this novel the major themes of Salinger's best work: the inability of man to live without love; the need for acceptance of people's shortcomings, this acceptance possibly proving to be a sign of wisdom; and the importance of children, who can provide the key to a return to emotional stability.

The movement towards emotional stability and a reintegration with human society also occurs in Salinger's best short story, 'For Esmé – with Love and Squalor' (1950). Through the influence of two children the protagonist is able to achieve a sense of peace with himself despite the horrors of war. Esmé in particular permits Sergeant X to overcome the squalor of his situation. This 'squalor' would be explored again the following year in terms of twentieth-century society in *Catcher*.

Peace is not, however, granted to Seymour ('See-more'), the poet-sage of the Glass family, whose suicide is described in 'A Perfect Day for Bananafish' (1948). Chronicling the Glass family has become Salinger's primary literary effort, and a number of the stories collected in *Nine Stories* (1953) contain various family members. Salinger's interest in Zen Buddhism is reflected in Seymour's influence upon various of the younger Glasses, who have been both aided and hindered in their development by Seymour's stress upon universal love, looking beyond externals to what lies beneath, and intense introspection. Seymour's suicide has not lessened the validity of his teachings for the younger Glasses and, one suspects, for Salinger himself.

The style in later works concerning the Glass family like 'Franny' (1955), 'Zooey' (1957), 'Raise High the Roofbeam, Carpenters' (1955), and 'Seymour: An Introduction' (1959) is, with the exception of 'Franny', verbose, lacking in focus and, unlike *Catcher*, not particularly humorous. Salinger places a heavy hand upon the narrative, which mars the effectiveness of the tales. There is a self-indulgence in 'Zooey', 'Roofbeam', and 'Seymour' which tends to blunt appreciation of Salinger's ideas.

Between 1963 and 1997, when he published *Hapworth*, a novella, Salinger fell silent, claiming in a rare interview that publication represents a 'terrible invasion of my privacy'. Instead he has preferred the life of a recluse in rural New Hampshire. An assurance that he has always continued to write, however, promises a revival of his cult standing among American readers.

Further reading

Other collections of Salinger's work include: *Franny and Zooey* (1961); *Raise High the Roofbeam, Carpenters; and Seymour: An Introduction* (1963). See also: Frederick L. Gwynn and Joseph L. Blotner, *The Fiction of J.D. Salinger* (1958); William F. Belcher and James W. Lee (eds), *J.D. Salinger and the Critics* (1962); Warren French, *J.D. Salinger* (1963); Malcolm M. Marsden (ed.), *If You Really Want to Know: A Catcher Casebook* (1963); Ian Hamilton, *In Search of J.D. Salinger* (1988).

E.A. ABRAMSON

SARGENT, John Singer

1856–1925

US painter

Sargent always retained his American nationality, although he was born in Florence and trailed all over Europe as a child by his peripatetic parents, studied art in Paris and spent most of his career in London. The mentor of his early life as an artist was the fashionable Parisian portraitist Charles-Émile-Auguste Carolus-Duran, whose studio he entered in 1874 at the age of eighteen. The cornerstones of Carolus-Duran's teaching were bold brushwork, modelling by means of strong tonal contrasts and painting *au premier coup*, without preparatory sketches or underpainting. Keenly observant and gifted with extraordinary manual dexterity, Sargent became a star pupil. He left to set up his own studio in 1879. In the same year he visited Madrid and in 1880 Haarlem, where his education in the painterly manner was filled out by a study of Velasquez and Frans Hals. Sargent had a lifelong fascination with travel and the exotic, and the most important of his early subject-pictures, *El Jaleo* (1882), was inspired by a flamboyant Andalusian dance he witnessed in Spain.

The influence of Carolus-Duran, Velasquez and Hals was augmented in the later 1880s by that of the French Impressionist painters. Curiously, it was not in France that Sargent painted his first pictures to show an assimilation of Impressionism, but England, during summer visits to the Cotswold villages of Broadway and Fladbury. Indebted above all to **Monet**, whom he knew and visited at least once at Giverny, Sargent began to show a new delight in broken brushwork, bright colour and transient effects of light. Nowhere is this more in evidence than in the masterpiece of this part of his career, *Carnation, Lily, Lily, Rose* (1885–6), a study of the two daughters of his artist friend Frederick Barnard lighting Chinese lanterns in a garden at twilight; and yet, with its relatively careful drawing, wistful mood and latent symbolism, *Carnation, Lily, Lily, Rose* stops short of the extreme objectivity and dissolution of form to which Impressionist ideas led Monet. Impressionism extended Sargent's range as a painter but, perhaps because the human figure was always his first interest, it never wholly claimed him. The most Impressionist works of his mature career were to be the oil and watercolour landscape sketches he made in large numbers, and purely for his own pleasure, on his long summer holidays abroad.

In 1886, still smarting from the ridicule levelled at his portrait of the society beauty *Madame Gautreau* when it was shown at the Paris Salon of 1884, and having found a circle of artistic friends in England far warmer and more sympathetic than anyone he knew in France (they included **Henry James** and Edmund Gosse as well as the painters Frederick Barnard and Alfred Parsons), Sargent decided to move to London; he lived in Tite Street, Chelsea, for the rest of his life. *Madame Gautreau* had been the culmination of an impressive series of portraits painted in Paris and Sargent had hoped it would establish his reputation specifically as a portraitist. In London his reputation in this field grew with almost startling ease and rapidity. By 1894, when he was elected an Associate of the Royal Academy (he became a full Academician in 1897), he was more or less universally recognized as the leading portraitist in England; and he only gave up this position at his own wish, virtually abandoning his practice around 1907 except for quick head-and-shoulders sketches in charcoal. Dubbed by **Rodin** 'the Van Dyck of our times', he enjoyed the patronage of both aristocracy and *nouveaux riches*, investing such sitters as the Duke and Duchess of Marlborough with the appropriate pomp and superiority but clearly more at home with the family of Asher Wertheimer, a Bond Street art dealer of unashamed affluence, whom he painted in a series of portraits, most of which are now at the Tate Gallery.

Sargent's technique, always the most fascinating aspect of his work, becomes ever more dashing in his London portraits, ever more that of the supremely confident virtuoso; brushwork which at the proper distance denotes some accessory or part of a dress becomes quite meaningless, though often ravishingly beautiful as a purely abstract design, when seen close to. Sitters were

struck by his way of charging at the canvas from a distance, armed with a loaded brush and muttering strange oaths, rapidly painting in an area and then retiring to contemplate the result. At his best, Sargent shows just as much flair for overall design as for brushwork, taking idiosyncratic viewpoints, inventing brilliantly original poses and, in the case of portraits including more than one sitter, groupings that suggest complex psychological relationships. He was a worthy heir to the great tradition of portraiture in Britain stretching back to Van Dyck via Reynolds, Gainsborough and Lawrence – a tradition that had languished for most of the Victorian period and has languished ever since.

In the work on a monumental scale that Sargent carried on from 1890 onwards in the form of his murals in the Public Library and the Museum of Fine Arts in Boston, he is hardly recognizable as the same artist. Tackling an elaborate symbolical programme describing the development of religious thought from paganism to Christianity in the first, and various classical themes in the second, he replaces painterly bravura with a rather routine decorative style derived largely from Italian Renaissance models. More successful than any of the murals is the large-scale figure composition entitled simply *Gassed* (1918–19), which Sargent painted to a commission from the War Artists Committee. The feeling of authenticity about *Gassed* is undeniably powerful, but set against the work of younger war artists such as Paul Nash, its realism looks just as undeniably antediluvian.

For much of the twentieth century Sargent's reputation suffered from the tendency of art history to pass over artists who are not of the avant-garde, from the too easy equation of facility with superficiality and, perhaps most of all, from the fact that his work is so closely bound up with wealth and class. Latterly the balance has begun to be righted in recent years, largely by Richard Ormond's book *John Singer Sargent* (1970) and the exhibition *John Singer Sargent and the Edwardian Age* held at Lotherton Hall in Leeds, the National

Portrait Gallery in London and the Detroit Institute of Arts in 1979 (catalogue by James Lomax and Richard Ormond).

Further reading

See: S. Olson, *John Singer Sargent: His Portrait* (1986)

MALCOLM WARNER

SARTRE, Jean-Paul

1905–80

French philosopher, novelist, playwright, essayist, left-wing militant

A traditional French educational background prepared Sartre well for a characteristic middle-class career. After the *lycée*, he went to the École Normale Supérieure, where he studied philosophy. He failed his first attempt at the *agrégation* completely, but tried it again the following year (1929) and came out first in that competitive examination. From this point, the road ahead was clear for a successful future as a teacher, first in a *lycée* and then in the university. And, indeed, following his military service, he was appointed to a teaching post in Le Havre in 1931; his teaching career subsequently took him to Laon, and then to Paris, where it eventually came to an end in 1944: his period of notoriety had begun.

We may believe Sartre when, in his autobiography, *Words* (*Les Mots*, 1963, trans. 1964), he tells us that he began writing in his earliest years. His first published text dates from 1923, when he was still only seventeen, but it was not until 1936, with the publication of two pieces of work, that he gave some solid indication of his future development. The first, *Imagination: A Psychological Critique* (*L'Imagination*, 1936, trans. 1962), is a revised version of a study of theories of the imagination from the time of Descartes on, first undertaken as a student in 1926, and includes an account of Husserl's views, with which Sartre had come into contact in the year 1933–4, when he had lived and studied in

Berlin. The second text, *The Transcendence of the Ego: An Existentialist Theory of Consciousness* (*La Transcendance de l'Ego: esquisse d'une description phénoménologique*, 1936, trans. 1957), together with an article published in 1939 under the title 'Intentionality: A Fundamental Idea of Husserl's Phenomenology' ('Une idée fondamentale de la phénoménologie de Husserl: l'intentionnalité', trans. 1970), was written during his stay in Berlin. All three are of importance, not only as evidence of Sartre's early interest in the imagination and his dissatisfaction with deterministic views of individual psychology, but also as a reminder that, contrary to what seems often to be believed, his philosophical existence did not begin only in 1943, with the publication of *Being and Nothingness: An Essay in Phenomenological Ontology* (*L'Être et le néant, essai de phénoménologie ontologique*, 1943, trans. 1956).

Indeed, the importance of Sartre's intellectual activity during the 1930s cannot be exaggerated. Publication dates give a false sense of chronology: the fact of the matter is that a whole series of works was being elaborated concurrently in the pre-war years: apart from those already mentioned, Sartre was also working on his *Sketch for a Theory of the Emotions* (*Esquisse d'une théorie des émotions*, 1936, trans. 1962, and *The Emotions, Outline of a Theory*, 1948), the stories collected in 1939 under the title *Le Mur* (1939, trans. as *Intimacy and Other Stories*, 1949, and *The Wall and Other Stories*, 1948), *The Diary of Antoine Roquentin* (*La Nausée*, 1938, trans. 1949, and as *Nausea*, 1949), in progress since 1931, *Psychology of the Imagination* (*L'Imaginaire, psychologie phénoménologique de l'imagination*, 1940, trans. 1949), the second part of *Imagination*. *Being and Nothingness* itself was the result of his philosophical reflections since the encounter with the thought of Husserl in 1933, and began to take form in 1939. By the time it appeared in print, it was already in one sense a work attached to Sartre's past rather than to his present: the notion of commitment, which began to assume importance for him in 1940, had brought about a change of emphasis in his thinking.

A change of emphasis, but not a revolution, in that his literary, aesthetic and moral preoccupations remained strong, continuing to produce tension with that part of him which aspired towards a direct involvement in the affairs of the day. *The Diary of Antoine Roquentin*, quite apart from its considerable qualities as a novel, provides clear evidence why this should be so. To the extent that the starting-point for Roquentin's diary is an anxiety to do with the nature of being and existence, the novel clearly has metaphysical resonances; Roquentin perceives the problem, however, largely in terms of his immediate environment. The awareness of his own contingency through the insistence with which the material world forces itself upon his attention is linked to the absence of relationships between him and his fellow-men. This has the advantage of making it possible for him to view the inhabitants of Bouville from a privileged, detached standpoint, and to take a highly critical view of their behaviour and of the 'values' by which they live. On the other hand, his observation of them as manifestations, among others, of the phenomenon of Existence, does nothing to relieve his anxiety: he can be no less contingent than they. It is not, therefore, surprising that he should seek an escape from an obsession with his contingency in a direction that removes him even further from other men: a work of literature, independent of the material world, having its being in the non-real universe of the imaginary, will both distance him from his fellows and place him in a situation superior to them.

The procedure is consistent with Sartre's views on the imagination and the imaginary, but it is Sartrean in other respects as well. Roquentin shares Sartre's romantic view of the privileged situation of the artist, as well as the notion that salvation may be achieved through the production of works of art: and it may well be that this one idea, more than any other, for a long while prevented Sartre from understanding that commitment implies necessarily the abandoning of any kind of individual privilege. In addition, Roquentin

illustrates the curious link between Sartre's aesthetic and moral views which will be evident in many of his characters. The work of art is absolute and non-contingent because it is imaginary; but it is the product of the imagination of the artist, who is relative and contingent. It may therefore be a source of salvation for the artist, as Roquentin sees, in that he, as a contingent existent, must transcend himself in the act of creating the non-contingent art-object. As Roquentin equally clearly sees, however, such a form of salvation may apply only to the past; it is neither a justification for the future self (which does not exist), nor a guide for living.

Others are not so clear-sighted: they, too, will seek to create an image – an image of themselves, which will therefore exist *outside* them, but which at the same time will *be* them, and with which they will attempt to coincide. The most obvious examples are those bourgeois in *The Diary of Antoine Roquentin* who actually pay painters to fix the image on canvas, in what Sartre elsewhere calls '*portraits officiels*', whose function is to 'defend man against himself'. The attempt is understandable: our existence is not justified, we have no prior definition, we create ourselves through our acts, and can be known as a complete entity only when the series of acts is complete – namely, at death. The resulting anguish is what may lead us to anticipate that moment by the creation of a self-image which, since we shall see it as definitive, will at the same time dictate our future conduct. The procedure is characteristic of the 'bad faith' (*mauvaise foi*) displayed by so many of Sartre's characters, attempting to persuade themselves that they have succeeded in the impossible task of bringing about a coincidence between the real and the ideal.

The theme is exploited throughout a large part of Sartre's career – most notably in his theatre, always concerned with action (an ambiguous term, in that the 'action' we see in a play is imaginary, and so unreal), and with his characters' attempts to escape the consequences of the need to act. The fact should not surprise us: the evidence of the autobiography is that, despite his efforts in other directions, Sartre himself remained attached to his role as a writer at least until the 1950s.

In the meantime, his growing reputation placed him in the forefront of French intellectual life, and made him a figure of international consequence. Along with a group of more or less like-minded intellectuals and artists (among them Simone de Beauvoir, with whom he had enjoyed a close relationship since 1929, and who would continue to participate closely in his varied activities), he had emerged as a significant force in the first post-war generation. The Existentialist vogue of the years immediately following the liberation of Paris, combined with his own intense activity, meant that his name was constantly before the public. It was not simply a matter of publishing novels or writing plays, but also of taking part in a great debate about the nature of Existentialism, attacked on the left as a manifestation of a bourgeois culture in the process of decomposition, and on the right as a form of mental illness. Sartre was, of course, more concerned about the attacks from the left than about the reactions of the right, and many of the articles he produced for his monthly revue, *Les Temps modernes*, which began publication in October 1945, were an attempt to present his views on contemporary issues as well as on his situation as a writer (see, for example, his *Présentation* in the first number, in which he defines his editorial line and gives his views on committed literature).

His controversial position in public life led inevitably to tension between himself and those around him. As early as June 1946, Raymond Aron left *Les Temps modernes*; a few months later a quarrel with **Camus** kept them apart for a year. The final break with Aron (along with Arthur Koestler) came at the end of 1947, and with Camus in 1952. At the same time, he was involved in the ideological differences of the post-war world, and in 1948 was a leading figure in the creation of a new – but not long-lived – political party, the Rassemblement Démocratique

Révolutionnaire (RDR). The 1950s, corresponding with the point at which he finally realized that the fact of being a writer gave him no particularly privileged position, see him more and more heavily engaged in the affairs of the day, the more so in that the Algerian war emerged as a conflict which demanded commitment. The list of the events on which he took a stand between that time and his death is very long – whether by writing, interview, public declaration or direct participation. He made pronouncements on major political and international issues, stood up for what he saw as oppressed minorities, gave his moral or material backing to struggling or harassed left-wing publications. Eventually his activity was severely restricted by the deterioration of his eyesight to a state of near-blindness.

Even before the onset of physical infirmity, however, it was clear to Sartre himself that he had never been, and was not, the kind of intellectual he would wish to be in the contemporary world – a man ready and able to put his gifts at the service of the people instead of using them as a means of perpetuating a bourgeois culture. It is true that, in this respect, he was not necessarily his own best friend. During the 1950s, he published his study of **Jean Genet**, as well as three plays; the 1960s saw the appearance of his autobiography, his adaptation of the *Trojan Women*, and a number of studies of painters; his three large volumes on **Flaubert** followed in 1971–2. All of this work is of a kind one might well expect from an intellectual of Sartre's background. And, indeed, the same might be said of his *Critique de la raison dialectique* ('Critique of Dialectical Reason', 1960), intended as a bridge-building operation between Existentialism and **Marxism**, but given relatively little attention, partly, no doubt, because many have been daunted by its 750 closely printed pages.

It is not, of course, the case that such work prevented Sartre from continuing on his more obviously political course; on the contrary, as his bibliography makes clear. Nevertheless, it is a fact that, by the age of fifty, he had become a victim of his own reputation: whatever his own wishes in the matter, his public image was already firmly fixed. The problem is well illustrated by the award to him, in 1964, of the Nobel Prize for Literature. Sartre wished to refuse the prize, both because he believed that the writer should not allow himself to be transformed into an institution, and because he had no desire for the bourgeois respectability bestowed by the Swedish Academy. But he discovered that potential recipients are not consulted as to whether or not they are prepared to accept the prize; what is more, they may not refuse it. Despite his resistance, Sartre *is* the Nobel prizewinner for 1964.

For a man who worked so energetically and so productively, Sartre left a surprising amount of work incomplete. Apart from some fragments, the Ethics promised at the end of *Being and Nothingness* did not see the light of day; the same is true of the final volume of his *Roads to Freedom* (*Les Chemins de la liberté*, 3 vols, Paris 1945–9, trans. 1947–50). The second part of the *Critique de la raison dialectique* was not written, and the fourth and final volume of the study of Flaubert was abandoned. This is not necessarily evidence of failure, but rather of the fact that changing circumstances may, for example, deprive long-term projects of their *raison d'être*. Failures there were, though, most notably in the area of bridge-building between Existentialism and Marxism: for the Sartre of the 1940s and 1950s, such an operation was unrealizable both because of the resistances of Communist orthodoxy and Party suspicion of the bourgeois intellectual, and because of his own inability to free himself from many of the middle-class, liberal, idealist and romantic assumptions of his earlier years. After 1968 – too late – he saw that the intellectual should put himself at the disposal of the proletariat whose interests he wishes to promote, while avoiding the imposition of his own categories or habits of thought. Nevertheless, his achievement was considerable – as an intellectual influence on the post-1945 generation, and, curiously, as a moral

example whose honesty and self-questioning were, in time, recognized even by those who were his enemies.

Further reading

Other works include: Plays – *The Flies* (*Les Mouches*, 1943, trans. 1946); *No Exit* (*Huis clos*, 1945, trans. 1946); *The Victors* (*Morts sans sépulture*, 1946, trans. 1949, as *Men Without Shadows* in UK); *The Respectful Prostitute* (*La Putain respecteuse*, 1946, trans. 1949); *Dirty Hands* (*Les Mains sales*, 1948, trans. 1949, as *Crime Passionnel* in UK); *Lucifer and the Lord* (*Le Diable et le bon Dieu*, 1951, trans. 1953, as *The Devil and the Good Lord* in USA, 1960); *Kean* (1956, trans. 1956); *Loser Wins* (*Les Séquestrés d'Altona*, 1959, trans. 1960, as *The Condemned of Altona* in USA, 1961); 'Existential Psychoanalysis' – *Baudelaire* (1947, trans. 1950); *Saint Genet, Actor and Martyr* (*Saint Genet, comédien et martyr*, 1952, trans. 1953); *L'Idiot de la famille: Gustave Flaubert de 1821 à 1857* ('The Idiot of the Family: Gustave Flaubert 1821–57', 3 vols, 1971–2). The most important of Sartre's periodical and occasional writings are collected in *Situations* (10 vols, Paris 1947–76). See also: *Un théâtre de situation* (1973), ed. M. Contat and M. Rybalka, who also produced the indispensable *The Writings of Jean-Paul Sartre: A Bibliographical Life* (*Les Ecrits de Sartre: chronologie, bibliographie commentée*, 1970, trans. 2 vols, 1974). On Sartre: Francis Jeanson, *Le Problème moral et la pensée de Sartre* (1947, rev. 1965) and *Sartre par lui-même* (1954); R. Laing and D. Cooper, *Reason and Violence: A Decade of Sartre's Philosophy 1950–60* (1964); A. Manser, *Sartre, a Philosophic Study* (1966); I. Murdoch, *Sartre: Romantic Rationalist* (1953); A.C. Solal, *Sartre* (1988).

KEITH GORE

SAUSSURE, Mongin-Ferdinand de

1857–1913

Swiss linguist

By virtue of one book, *Course in General Linguistics* (*Cours de linguistique générale*, 1916, trans. 1959), edited posthumously from students' lecture-notes, Saussure is commonly acknowledged as the father of modern linguistics and of the 'structuralist' movement.

Ferdinand de Saussure was the son of a prominent Genevese Huguenot family which had emigrated from Lorraine during the French wars of religion in the late sixteenth century. Ferdinand displayed a bent for language study in childhood and, after a false start reading science at Geneva University, went to study philology at Leipzig and Berlin. At twenty-one Saussure published his *Mémoire sur le système primitif des voyelles dans les langues indo-européennes* ('Memoir on the Original System of Vowels in the Indo-European Languages'), a monograph which has been described as 'the most splendid work of comparative philology ever written'; its chief theoretical conclusion, propounded by Saussure purely on the basis of logical analysis, was corroborated almost fifty years later from archaeological evidence.

Saussure lectured at the École Pratique des Hautes Études, Paris, from 1881 to 1891, before returning to a chair at Geneva, where he remained until his death. His life was uneventful; after publishing his doctoral dissertation in 1881 he wrote only some short notes and reviews, and his publications, like the bulk of his teaching, were concerned exclusively with the established discipline of Indo-European philology. Saussure resisted requests to expound his ideas on the theoretical foundations of linguistics, and finally lectured on the subject only because a colleague teaching general linguistics happened to retire in the middle of a session.

Saussure's *Course* can be seen as part of a shift from the nineteenth-century emphasis on the historical approach as the key to understanding cultural phenomena to the twentieth-century emphasis on the sociological approach. For the ordinary (non-scholarly) speaker, Saussure said, his language has no history; if we wish to describe a language as a vehicle of communication, we need to explain not how its various components came to have their present form but how they relate to one another as a system now. Saussure called this kind of non-historical description 'synchronic' as opposed to 'diachronic'. In a synchronic '*état de langue*', what matter are not the individual components but the system of relationships between them. To understand the 'value' of the English word *sheep* we need to know that it

contrasts with another word *mutton*; French *mouton* enters into no such contrast, so the 'value' of *mouton* is rather different from the 'value' of *sheep*. The units of sound called 'phonemes' are likewise defined by their contrasts with other phonemes. Saussure compares language to chess, in which the past history of a game is irrelevant to the situation reached at a given point, and the potential of any piece depends crucially on its relationships with other pieces, but not on its intrinsic properties: we could agree to replace the white queen by a lump of chalk without affecting the state of play.

It is oddly difficult to say how far Saussure has influenced subsequent thought. The idea that what matter in a system of meanings are the contrasts between elements rather than the elements themselves is axiomatic in contemporary linguistics; but this idea was already implicit in the work of **Franz Boas**, independently of Saussure. The related notion that the realms of thought and speech-sound are devoid of inherent structure, being articulated only by various languages which bring them into different arbitrary relationships with one another, was abandoned by later linguists such as Roman Jakobson (without this rejection being presented explicitly as a repudiation of Saussure). Saussure's **Durkheimian** view of language-structure as inhering in society as an organism, rather than in its individual members, has been largely ignored by subsequent linguists (and the relationship between Saussure's and Durkheim's thought has itself become a controversial question). Finally, recent work on language variation and change has suggested that Saussure's sharp distinction between synchrony and diachrony cannot be maintained, and that (contrary to Saussure's assumption) language changes may themselves be systematic in nature.

Within linguistics, Saussure became something of a cult figure whom many regard as a master but few read closely enough to appreciate how little they agree with him. Saussure's lasting influence has been primarily on the 'structuralist' movement, represented, for example, by **Claude Lévi-Strauss**, which takes its paradigm of enquiry from linguistics but applies it chiefly to other subjects.

Further reading

See: E.F.K. Koerner, *Ferdinand de Saussure* (1973); Jonathan Culler, *Saussure* (1976).

GEOFFREY SAMPSON

SCHOENBERG, Arnold Franz Walter

1874–1951

Austrian composer

It is reported that during army service in the First World War, Arnold Schoenberg was asked by an officer if he was that controversial composer of the same name, to which he replied, 'Somebody had to be, and nobody else wanted the job, so I took it on myself.' The answer neatly sums up his sense of the inevitability of his creative mission, and the belief that his personal wishes had little to do with it: he was in many ways an unwilling revolutionary, driven by the need for continual clarification of his emotional and artistic concerns.

The son of a free-thinking Jewish shoemaker, Schoenberg was born in Vienna and began composing at the age of nine. He was virtually self-taught, beyond some lessons from the slightly older Alexander von Zemlinsky; his real training derived from the practical experience of playing classical chamber music, conducting workers' choirs, and making hack arrangements and orchestrations of other composers' works. By the turn of the century he had already composed two major pieces, the string sextet *Verklärte Nacht* and the vast romantic cantata *Gurrelieder*. After an unhappy period as musical director of a cabaret in Berlin (1901–2) he returned to Vienna, where he gained the support of **Mahler** and began teaching composition privately – his earliest pupils included **Alban Berg** and **Anton von Webern**. In 1908 a personal and artistic crisis turned Schoenberg's music sharply in the direction

of extreme *Angst*-ridden subjectivity, made possible by an equally sudden and extreme transformation of its language. In such works as the *Five Pieces for Orchestra* (Op. 16, 1909) and the monodrama *Erwartung* (Op. 17, not performed until 1924) he drew near to the aesthetic ideals of the Expressionist painters, and began himself to paint in intervals when he felt composition impossible.

Failure to secure either adequate means of living or an audience for his music in Vienna led him to move back to Berlin in 1911 – via Munich, where he established contact with **Kandinsky** and became associated with the Blaue Reiter group. In Berlin he was befriended by Busoni, acquired more pupils and gained performances from London to St Petersburg, but this good fortune was cut short by the outbreak of war. He served for a time in the Austrian infantry, and in the immediate post-war years addressed himself to the problem of picking up the cultural pieces in a shattered and inflation-torn Vienna. His Verein für musikalische Privataufführungen (Society for Private Musical Performances, 1918–22) drew its performing talent from Schoenberg's ever-widening circle of pupils and admirers, presented a wide range of contemporary music in thoroughly rehearsed and repeated performances, and became the model for many later and larger Modern Music organizations in Europe and America. This activity coincided with a creative blockage, only cleared as Schoenberg developed the 'method of composition with twelve notes related only to one another' which first made its appearance in the *Serenade* (Op. 24) and piano pieces (Opp. 23, 25) composed 1921–3.

In 1925 Schoenberg returned to Berlin for the third time, as director of the Composition Masterclass at the Prussian Academy of Arts, in succession to Busoni. This period of comparative eminence (he once described it as 'the time when everybody made believe he understood **Einstein's** theories and Schoenberg's music') saw the production of such large-scale works as the *Variations for Orchestra* (Op. 31, 1926–8) and the opera

Moses und Aron (1930–2) but came to an end with the rise of Nazism: in 1933, he was dismissed from his post as part of **Hitler's** campaign to 'break the Jewish stranglehold on Western Music'. In the same year he emigrated to the USA. After a short period teaching in New York and Boston, he moved to California and taught first at the University of Southern California (1935–6) and then at the University of California in Los Angeles (1936–44). Compelled to resign from the latter post on a tiny pension at the age of seventy, Schoenberg spent his last years teaching, writing and composing, frequently in precarious health. He died in Brentwood Park, Hollywood: it is said that his last words were 'Harmony! Harmony! Harmony!'

By temperament a romantic, but intellectually committed to classical ideals of structural proportion and consistency, Schoenberg in many respects resembled his first musical hero, **Brahms**. His creative path was guided by instinct first, only secondarily by the desire for a rational explanation of what instinct had produced. His earliest characteristic music synthesized and built upon the achievements of Brahms and **Wagner**, from whom he derived two distinct but interdependent concepts: that of 'the unity of musical space', whereby the constituent elements of a composition – melody, accompaniment, harmony, rhythm – should be intimately related expressions of the same idea in different dimensions; and the principle of 'developing variation', which tended ever away from exact repetition of ideas towards their perpetual transformation as a major structural impulse. The dazzlingly quick mind and passionate urge for maximum communication which he brought to the development of these two concepts makes such a fundamentally traditional score as the String Quartet No. 1 (Op. 7, 1905) already daunting in the sheer volume of musical information which the listener must assimilate.

The emotionally and intellectually supercharged style of this and other works of the early 1900s exploded after 1908 into the music of Schoenberg's 'Expressionist' phase, where he strove to represent extreme states of mind and feeling more or less directly, without any intervening decorum of form. His ideal, he said, was a music 'without architecture, without structure. Only an ever-changing, unbroken succession of colours, rhythms and moods.' The works of this period are accordingly characterized by an unprecedented degree of harmonic ambiguity, asymmetry of melody and phrase-lengths, wide and dissonant melodic intervals, abrupt contrasts in register, texture, stasis and dynamism. All twelve notes of the chromatic scale occur with extreme frequency and consequently the harmonic language shifts away from any kind of diatonic hierarchy towards a state of total chromaticism – an 'emancipation of dissonance' which does not, however, prevent the covert and allusive operation of tonal functions and so belies the popular misnomer, 'atonality', which posterity has happily foisted on it.

In fact, Schoenberg was concerned almost at once to reintroduce principles of 'architecture' into his music, aware that the supremely intuitive, quasi-improvisational achievement of *Erwartung* was by definition unrepeatable, and that his linguistic revolution had for the moment put traditional means of large-scale organization beyond his grasp. Most of his works for the next decade were vocal, the text helping to determine the progress of the form. At the same time he began to concentrate on intensive development of the constituent tones of principal thematic ideas, and cultivated a wide range of canonic and other 'ancient' contrapuntal devices to provide structural backbone. All these tendencies are found in *Pierrot Lunaire* (Op. 21, 1912) for instrumental ensemble and *Sprechstimme* (half-sung recitation), an ironic cycle of rondel-settings with elements of Expressionist cabaret which has remained one of his best-known scores; and they reached a new intensity, and an impasse, in the unfinished oratorio *Die Jakobsleiter* (*Jacob's Ladder*, 1917–22), a fragment of a gigantic project that brought his musical, philosophical and religious dilemmas into sharp focus.

To employ a psychological metaphor: the 'Expressionist' works had brought a host of previously inadmissible musical 'traumas' into the open, harbingers of chaos and disruption which nineteenth-century tradition and theory had rigorously suppressed. Schoenberg's struggle was to accept and assimilate these 'negative' forces into the existing scheme of musical discourse, to objectify them in an enlarged musical language which he could consciously apply in further works. His solution was the development of the 'twelve-note method'. A fixed series of all the notes of the chromatic scale, derived from the initial melodic and harmonic ideas for a piece, becomes the kernel, the essence, the germinating cell of that piece's unique tonal properties. The series is developed continually through transposition, inversion, retrograde motion, in whole or in part, in melodic lines and in chords, to provide an inexhaustible and self-consistent source of invention which Schoenberg then deploys on the largest scale through a revivification of classical forms. The works of the 1920s, such as the Wind Quintet (Op. 26, 1924) and String Quartet No. 3 (Op. 30, 1927), are imbued with an almost neo-classical spirit while retaining something of the raw immediacy of the Expressionist vision.

In the 1930s Schoenberg continued to refine and develop the method, enlarging its melodic vocabulary and relaxing some of his original 'rules' for twelve-note composition to effect an accommodation with an intermittent sense of traditional tonality. He even composed some diatonically based works of his own, averring that there was 'still a lot of good music to be written in C major'. Tonal and serial resources enriched each other in the 1940s in a series of works where the old Expressionist urgency is recaptured within a sure structural control: the String Trio (Op. 45, 1946) and the 'ghetto' cantata *A Survivor from Warsaw* (Op. 46, 1947) are the peak of this development. His last works were vocal, to his own texts: he left unfinished the first of a series of *Modern Psalms* dealing with the predicament of Man (principally, but not exclusively, Jewish Man) in the Atomic Age.

During his lifetime and for twenty years after it, Schoenberg's music was generally more talked about than listened to. But his influence has been immense. Not only was he the mentor, inspirer and incarnate artistic conscience of three generations of pupils, many of whom (e.g. Berg, Webern, Wellesz, Eisler, Gerhard, Skalkottas, **Cage**) became important figures in their own right; but his compositional methods were adopted and extended by many others. Perhaps none of them has been driven to forge the twelve-note method out of his own experience by a similarly compelling need: but the basic techniques of the method are so fruitfully simple, so easily adapted to multifarious ends, that it became the cornerstone of succeeding innovations, and an integral part of the twentieth century's musical thought. Unfortunately, it also engendered in many quarters a stress on technique and abstract formal criteria at the expense of music's expressive content, the 'idea', the 'representation of a *vision*' which for Schoenberg was music's paramount *raison d'être*. Only toward the end of the century was the balance begun redressed, in the study of his own works, away from what he called 'how it is done' towards 'what it *is!*'

Schoenberg was a pithy and ironic writer whose pungent style was influenced by his friend Karl Kraus. In addition to the texts and libretti of many of his works he wrote poetry, a play, some stories and a vast number of essays and aphorisms on musical and other topics, as well as several pedagogical works. The most celebrated of these last, *Theory of Harmony* (*Harmonielehre*, 1911, rev. 1922, trans. 1978), is an idiosyncratic but often massively illuminating study of traditional harmonic principles up to the threshold of his own radical departure from them. The paradox is characteristic. He may yet be seen, not as modern music's *monstre sacré*, the composer audiences most like to hate, but as the last great custodian of the ethical (as opposed to aesthetic) values of musical Romanticism.

Further reading

Other works include: operas – *Die glückliche Hand* (1913); *Von heute auf Morgen* (1929); *Kol Nidre*, for chorus and orchestra (1938); *Das Buch der hängenden Gärten* (song cycle, 1908–9); *Ode to Napoleon*, for reciter and piano quintet (1942); *Pelleas und Melisande* (symphonic poem, 1902–3); two Chamber Symphonies (1906 and 1938); *Suite in G* for strings (1934); *Theme and Variations* for wind band (1943); concertos for Piano (1942), Violin (1935–6), Cello (1932–3), and String Quartet (1933); five String Quartets (1897, 1905, 1908, 1927, 1936); *Phantasy* for violin and piano (1949). Writings: *Style and Idea* (1950, rev. 1975); *Selected Letters* (1964), ed. E. Stein. See: J. Rufer, *The Works of Arnold Schoenberg* (trans. 1962); C. Rosen, *Schoenberg* (1975); M. MacDonald, *Schoenberg* (1976); H. H. Stuckenschmidt, *Schoenberg: His Life, World and Work* (trans. 1977); W. Frisch (ed.) *Schoenberg and His World* (1999); Allen Shawn, *Arnold Schoenberg's Journey* (2002).

MALCOLM MACDONALD

SCORSESE, Martin
1942–

US director, actor, film historian and cultural preservationist

A prolific cinéaste and a passionate cinephile, and author of a number of films which are now regarded as classics of the American cinema, Scorsese is widely acknowledged as one of the greatest filmmakers of the latter half of the twentieth century, if not of the entire history of cinema. His highly personal, distinctively styled and brilliantly crafted films have brought him the acclaim of film critics and historians worldwide and his working methods have also earned him the universal respect of actors and fellow directors. After receiving numerous prizes and international awards for his films, in 2002 he was honoured with the Directors' Guild of America Lifetime Achievement Award which placed him in the company of legendary directors like **John Ford** and **Alfred Hitchcock**. Notwithstanding his reputation and the high regard in which he is held, however, and despite being nominated five times, he has yet to receive the ultimate accolade of an Academy Award for Best Director.

Scorsese's love affair with the cinema began at a very early age. The second child of Sicilian migrants who had settled in New York's Lower East Side, Scorsese began suffering from asthma at the age of three. Unable to take part in the usual physical activities of children he spent most of his time at the movies or watching films on television. His Italian Catholic background also instilled a strong religious vocation in him, prompting him to enter a seminary at the end of high school with the intention of becoming a priest. A year later he abandoned his religious vocation in order to study film at New York University. However a sense of spiritual guilt and religious aspirations continued to haunt him thereafter, and although he would soon become famous for his gritty, street-wise studies of urban violence and social alienation, a certain religious dimension would continue to permeate his films. The realistically depicted male aggression and violent braggadocio in his first major film, *Mean Streets* (1973), for example, also carry symbolic connotations of expiation and penance in an attempt to achieve some form of spiritual redemption and sainthood. As the voice-over which opens *Mean Streets* declares: 'You don't make up for your sins in the church. You make up for them on the streets.'

It was undoubtedly Scorsese's continuing obsession with this paradoxically redemptive violence which led the now-notorious director of such parables of male aggression and urban psychosis as *Taxi Driver* (1976) and *Raging Bull* (1980) to make *The Last Temptation of Christ* (1988). Adapted from Nikos Kazantzakis' theological-existential novel, it had been a project dear to Scorsese's heart since he had read the book in the early 1970s. Although the release of the film generated enormous controversy and opposition, especially from Christian fundamentalist groups who thought it blasphemous, the film was in fact something of a pious devotion, and making it under dire circumstances in the Moroccan desert allowed Scorsese to finally square accounts with his Catholic roots. It seems significant that the distinctive religious overtones of the early 'street' films come to be absent from post-*Temptation* gangster films like *Goodfellas* (1990) and *Casino* (1995). While the theme of self-sacrifice certainly reappears in *Bringing Out the Dead* (1999), the protagonists' mission to save the human flotsam and jetsam of New York's mean streets in that film – in direct contrast with the avenging angel of *Taxi Driver* who would attempt to wash them away in a apocalyptic bloodbath – is decidedly secular and social rather than religious. And perhaps it was also this successful settling of accounts with his Italian-Catholic background that finally freed Scorsese to engage with the non-violence of Buddhism in *Kundun* (1997), a remarkably moving adaptation of the autobiography of the 14th **Dalai Lama**. He would nevertheless return to the violence of the urban jungle of Manhattan in grand style with his *Gangs of New York* (2002), a technically awe-inspiring but essentially entertaining historical epic of urban warfare shot entirely, however, in the studios of Cinecittà.

Influenced by both classic American Hollywood cinema (including its less respectable traditions of the crime film and film noir) and by the more experimental European auteur cinema – particularly **Fellini** – Scorsese brought to every one of his films a rich and audacious polyphonic style which sought to exploit all the possibilities of the camera for expressive ends. This exciting visual style, which doesn't hesitate to mix documentary realism with stylized expressionism, is complemented in all the films by a brilliant orchestration of sound and music to create a pulsating soundtrack which has itself become part of the Scorsese signature.

The other distinctive trait of Scorsese's filmmaking has been a long-standing collaboration over a number of films with scriptwriter Paul Shrader and actor Robert De Niro. The unique combination of the talents of all three was undoubtedly responsible for the artistic success of what are arguably Scorsese's greatest films, *Taxi Driver* and *Raging Bull*.

While Scorsese's fame will always rest solidly on the extraordinary artistry of his films, his contribution to modern culture has ranged much more widely than that of any other contemporary filmmaker. Drawing on his own extensive first-hand knowledge of the history of cinema he has increasingly taken on the role of film historian and popularizer: in 1994 he responded to a request from the BFI to make *A Personal Journey through American Cinema with Martin Scorsese*, providing a selective but instructive overview of American cinema from its earliest days. A few years later with the six-hour *My Voyage to Italy* (1999–2002) Scorsese made a similar pedagogic journey through his favourite Italian films, highlighting the inspiration he had drawn from the work of directors such as Rossellini, De Sica and **Visconti**. Since 1980 Scorsese has also been a passionate campaigner for more attention and effort to be devoted to film conservation. At the same time he has initiated and guided a number of group projects to conserve cultural memory such as the PBS Blues project, which brought together seven major directors to each make a one-hour documentary on a major aspect of Blues music. The most exciting venture to date, however, is *No Direction Home* (2005), a four-hour television documentary on **Bob Dylan's** early career.

Further reading

Other films include: *Boxcar Bertha (1972)*, *Alice Doesn't Live Here Anymore* (1974), *Italianamerican* (documentary, 1974), *New York, New York* (1977), *The Last Waltz* (rock music documentary, 1978), *The King of Comedy* (1983), *After Hours* (1985), *The Color of Money* (1986), *Cape Fear* (1991), *Age of Innocence* (1993), *The Aviator* (2004). Recommended reading: Michael Bliss, *The Word Made Flesh: Catholicism and Conflict in the Films of Martin Scorsese* (1995); *Martin Scorsese: Interviews*, edited Peter Brunette (1999); Ben Nyce, *Scorsese Up Close: A Study of the Films* (2004); Maria Miliora, *The Scorsese Psyche on Screen* (2004).

GINO MOLITERNO

SCOTT, Ridley

1939–

British film director and producer

Ridley Scott's background as a student at London's Royal College of Art and then as an acclaimed director of television commercials is a good pointer to the character of his films: superbly mounted in their look and design, sweeping and energetic in tempo, lavishly calculated in their effects. The jobbing nature of advertising work – although Scott long ago reached the stage where he chose only the most prestigious projects – also informs his curiously eclectic film output. Where is he most at home? Everywhere and nowhere might be the answer. His films encompass the discovery of the New World (*1492: Conquest of Paradise*, 1992); an account of obsessive adversaries set during the Napoleonic period which was derived from a **Joseph Conrad** story (*The Duellists*, 1977); a couple of efficient contemporary police thrillers (*Someone to Watch Over Me*, 1987, and *Black Rain*, 1989) as well as the protofeminist road movie *Thelma and Louise* (1991). When the Roman epic *Gladiator* (2000), the Crusade-oriented *Kingdom of Heaven* (2005) and the dystopic sci-fi classics *Alien* (1979) and *Blade Runner* (1982) are added to the mix, it becomes apparent that in terms of range Ridley Scott can only be compared with **Stanley Kubrick**, who also travelled from the Roman era (*Spartacus*, 1960) to the near future (*2001*, 1968). And there is besides in Scott's work something of Kubrick's obsessive interest in surface and a corresponding sense of the littleness of the human presence.

Scott's mainstream masterpiece is *Alien*. The story of the crew of a workaday spacecraft, one of whom is the unwitting host to a parasitic monster, it is a highly worked conflation of the haunted house thriller, space odyssey and horror film. Yet Scott both transcends and subverts the formulas. For an audience accustomed to the galactic cosiness of Steven **Spielberg** or the highjinks of George Lucas – respective directors of the hugely successful *Close Encounters of the Third Kind* (1977) and *Star Wars* (also 1977) – Scott's vision of the future was bracingly bleak, even shocking. The spaceship is a vast and near-derelict floating warehouse while the crew, bitching about their pay and conditions, are immune to the glamour of the stars. The creature is progressively revealed in glimpses through masterly direction and cutting. The single survivor, and ultimate nemesis of the monster, is a woman known only as Ripley (played by Sigourney Weaver). It's worth noting that Scott has a habit of foregrounding strong, independent women, even to a point of absurdity as in *G.I. Jane* (1997) where Demi Moore's attempt to out-macho her fellow marines seems to be the sole purpose of the picture. This latter film, together with *Black Hawk Down* (2001), also shows Scott's preoccupation with the ethos of the military.

Blade Runner was a comparative failure on its first release, although it was quickly reassessed and is the subject of continued interest and analysis. Adapted from a story by the idiosyncratic writer Philip K. Dick, the film is set in a grimly futuristic Los Angeles. As in *Alien*, Scott uses narrative devices from another genre, in this case the private-eye thrillers of **Raymond Chandler**. Deckard (played by Harrison Ford) is employed to hunt down and destroy rogue androids or replicants, and the story conforms to the traditional pattern of clues, deductions and violent confrontations. But the most impressive and influential feature of *Blade Runner* is its look and texture. The city, seemingly more eastern than western, is permanently veiled by rain and crowded with impassive inhabitants. Paradoxically the 'robots', where it's possible to distinguish them from humans, are the most sympathetic characters. All of this, together with the high-tech squalor of the interior scenes and the suggestion of control by shadowy corporations, makes for a cogent vision of the future.

Further reading

Ridley Scott's subsequent projects, like *Gladiator* or *Hannibal* (2001), show a continued reluctance to stick within a single genre. *Gladiator* was played straight, a return to the sword and sandal Hollywood spectacle of the 1950s and 1960s, with twenty-first century effects but an old-fashioned attitude to heroism. By contrast, *Hannibal*, a knowing sequel to Jonathan Demme's *Silence of The Lambs* (1991), was watchable enough but overly dependent on nudging, visceral shocks, the kind of effect which Scott deployed with greater subtlety in *Alien*.

PHILIP GOODEN

SEBALD, Winfried Georg

1944–2001

German writer

W.G. Sebald was born in 1944 at Wertach in the south of Germany, close to the Austrian Tyrol. His father was in the army. The family prospered under the Third Reich and was silenced by its defeat. Sebald graduated in German from Freiburg University in 1965. In 1966 he 'decided for various reasons' (as he wrote in *The Emigrants*) to move to England. It is typical that he should give no more detail about what was the most significant fact in his professional and artistic life. However, the Auschwitz trials were going on in Frankfurt at the time and this probably focused his discomfort in his homeland.

In 1967 he married and the couple had a daughter, but this aspect of his life does not feature in his art which is that of the lonely wanderer, shy, voyeuristic and obsessional. After three years as an assistant lecturer in German at Manchester University he flirted briefly with the idea of being a schoolmaster in Switzerland, but returned to England in 1970 to a post at the University of East Anglia where he spent the rest of his life. In 1987 he became its Professor of European Literature and in 1989 the first director of the British Centre for Literary Translation.

Though he has published academic non-fiction, his reputation rests on four novels:

Vertigo (*Schwindel, Gefühle*, 1990), *The Emigrants* (*Die Ausgewanderten*, 1992), *The Rings of Saturn* (*Die Ringe des Saturn*, 1995) and *Austerlitz* (*Austerlitz*, 2001). They were published in Germany according to the dates given, but later and out of sequence elsewhere. They are perhaps the most pensive of the numerous works by various authors which have sought to make sense of Germany's tragedy in the twentieth century. In the end he only confirms the conundrum of the relationship between civilization and barbarism, vigour and decay; in *The Rings of Saturn* (subtitled 'An English Pilgrimage' in the German edition) he views it through the prism of Britain's imperial greatness.

The above titles are called novels because they are challenging works of literary creativity, but Sebald himself was uneasy with the ascription and in German used the word *Erzählung*, meaning 'narrative'. They might almost as easily be called essays or meditations insofar as they fuse autobiography, travel, art and history in a seamless forward movement. The amount of invention or fantasy is never clear, but it is always Sebald's intention to convince us that what we are reading is actually true. *Austerlitz* is more like a novel than the others and has in consequence a greater sense of contrivance, seeming less open to the elements.

The inventor of this hybrid form is Sacheverell Sitwell in *Southern Baroque Art* (1924) and developed in his subsequent, weird prose rhapsodies, though it harks back to de Nerval, De Quincey and even Rousseau (*Les Rêveries du Promeneur solitaire*), while Sebald's moods of elegiac melancholy, lush nostalgia, game-playing and lurking paranoia link him to **Rilke**, **Proust**, **Borges** and **Kafka**.

Association is very much part of his method and yet the effect is wholly original. First, this is because of presentation. He made a weak but graceful beginning in *After Nature* (*Nach der Natur*, 1988) in which the prose is printed as lines of poetry, a mannerism he did not repeat. A novel by Sebald doesn't look like anyone else's. Facing pages of solid text are frequent, with no dialogue or paragraph indentations. The page is rendered less forbidding to the modern eye by extra space between the lines and by black-and-white photographs, often of banal or incidental subjects such as a bus ticket or restaurant bill whose function is to act as evidence of actuality. That the photographs are printed within the body of the text renders them murky, which increases the sense of mystery they are ostensibly there to dispel. They are sometimes fakes.

The second aspect of originality is in the writing itself, done in a high yet languid style of the pre-computer, indeed the pre-television age. The texts are relatively short but have the aura of full-length works because their prose unrolls with few breaks. The sentences are very long in an age which commands them to be short; seductive and intimate, moving like tentacles of exploration through the deeps of memory and imagination; and they seem to emerge from a great hush, always in a cello tone, and ask to be taken slowly. The text is literally eccentric since it develops as a fractal does, by repeatedly moving off centre.

Lastly the content. A boundary-leaping postmodernist he may be, but there is no sex, no humour, no identifiable authorial presence. Writing in the first person, he tells us exactly where he is but never who he is: a ghost among ghosts. Quite often we discover *how* he is, and mostly he isn't very well. Panic attacks, terror of flying, nervous breakdown, insomnia, stomach trouble, allergies, claustrophobia all point to a temperament repelled by modern life and which found the remote spaciousness of East Anglia therapeutic. This pathos is often moving, occasionally ridiculous.

One of Sebald's great charms is that he has never been lost to popularity. Reading him has a private beauty associated more with poetry, obscure black-and-white films, forgotten artists in old albums. His achievement is to revive the highest ambitions for prose at a time when it is everywhere being degraded by the mass market. Like Luis Cernuda and Elias Canetti when they lived in Britain,

Sebald was largely ignored by the British literary establishment until his death in a car crash at the age of fifty-seven (cf. **Camus**) gave him mythic status. The English translations by Michael Hulse are particularly fine.

Further reading

See: 'A Symposium on W.G. Sebald', *The Threepenny Review* (Spring 2002).

DUNCAN FALLOWELL

SEN, Amartya
1933–
Indian economist

The Nobel Prize-winning economist Professor Amartya Sen has achieved international renown for his pioneering work on a framework for economic analysis that focuses on individual substantive freedom rather than income and growth. Sen's distinctive blend of economic insight and ethical reflection has challenged orthodoxies and resulted in the development of important new paradigms and approaches in theoretical and empirical economics and in a range of related fields across the social sciences (including development, social policy, gender studies, political theory, philosophy and human rights). His work has expanded knowledge about critical world problems including inequality, poverty and starvation and has had a major international impact beyond academia by driving forward international debates and influencing the policies of key international organizations.

Sen was born in Santiniketan (West Bengal). His father taught chemistry at Dhaka University and he received much of his education at the school founded by the poet and writer **Rabindranath Tagore**. While being immersed in Indian intellectual life from an early age, Sen was not disengaged from the wider world. Formative experiences helped to shape his passionate commitment to making economic analysis relevant to the problems that people confront and the situations in which they live. The communal violence of the 1940s heightened Sen's awareness of diversity and difference and raised a critical question that he would pursue at the theoretical level for more than five decades: how to reconcile commitments to universal human values and substantive equity with respect for pluralism and tolerance. Early observations of the impact of entrenched inequality and gender discrimination, and of the phenomena of poverty, hunger and starvation, were also important influences. Memories of the Bengal famine of 1943 would motivate and inform later projects and helped to clarify a critical theme in Sen's work – that the socioeconomic processes by which individuals and groups fulfil their basic needs should be subjected to critical scrutiny, taking account of both the adequacy of people's opportunities, and the influences and constraints on their choices.

As an undergraduate in 1950s Calcutta, Indian philosophical and cultural traditions as well as **Marxist** thought (especially the focus on the nature of value, 'commodity fetishism' and the perspective of human need) must have fuelled the development of this idea. The debates of the day at Trinity College, Cambridge (England), where Sen completed a doctoral thesis in 1959, were another important influence. However, it was not in **Keynsian**, neoclassical or Marxist economics, but in the emergent field of social choice, that Sen's inclinations and skills found early application. Focusing on the relationship between individual values and collective decision-making, this mathematically exacting branch of welfare economics addresses a critical foundational question: given important differences between people (including differences in tastes, interests and judgements), is it possible to aggregate 'individual preferences' into a procedure for collective choice that is both theoretically robust and morally defendable? Kenneth Arrow's groundbreaking work had set the stage with its underlying message of pessimism. In *Collective Choice and Social Welfare* (1970), Sen set out to restore the possibility of social choice by addressing the informational basis of Arrow's 'Impossibility Theorem' and exploring the ways in which alternative assumptions about interpersonal comparability can influence the search for a 'reasonable' rule for collective decisions. Early emphasis on the importance of freedoms and rights was reflected in the key article 'The Impossibility of a Paretian Liberal' (1970).

These contributions in the field of social choice were followed by proposals for the measurement of poverty and inequality and by innovative analyses of the nature and causes of deprivation, hunger and starvation. *On Economic Inequality* (1973) provided a systematic analysis of the measurement of income distribution, while empirical examinations of 'excess mortality' in parts of Asia and North Africa (the phenomenon of 'Missing Women') highlighted gender discrimination and the neglect of female health and nutrition. The influential study *Poverty and Famines: An Essay on Entitlement and Deprivation* (1981) focused on the socioeconomic processes underlying hunger and starvation and helped to shift the focus of international food security policy away from aggregate food supply and towards the differential ability of individuals, groups and classes to acquire sufficient food in practice (the 'entitlement approach'). The idea that competitive market outcomes and processes of growth and development can generate very different results for individuals and groups is pivotal to Sen's work. Important empirical insights on this issue were reported in *Hunger and Public Action* (1989, with Jean Drèze). These include the finding that income and growth can be poor predictors of the quality of life and that public action and institutional conditions (including democracy and the protection of human rights) can be of critical importance in securing the fulfilment of basic needs.

The search for a more adequate metric of individual advantage is a central theme that integrates Sen's work in economics and philosophy. Sen has emphasized the limitations of traditional 'income-based' and 'utility-based' frameworks (including the 'Fundamental

Theorems of Welfare Economics' and the criterion of 'Pareto Optimality') from the perspectives of inequality, poverty, freedoms and rights. Later contributions, including the Dewey Lectures on 'Wellbeing, Agency and Freedom' (1984), *On Economic Inequality after a Quarter of a Century* (1997, with James Foster) and *Development as Freedom* (1999), have highlighted the idea that evaluative exercises concerning basic human interests should focus on individual substantive freedoms (such as the ability to avoid premature mortality, to be adequately nourished and to have access to basic health and education) rather than alternative informational focuses (such as income, growth, utility, liberty and 'primary goods'). The 'capability approach' provides an alternative 'informational focus' to both libertarianism and utilitarianism and underpins influential proposals for assessing economic processes and arrangements as well as Sen's important and innovative contributions to ethical debates about equality, freedom and human rights. The far-reaching international impact of this idea is reflected in the emergence of new paradigms and approaches across the social sciences and beyond academia (e.g. in the UN's 'Human Development Index').

Sen's career has taken him through a series of prestigious appointments at leading universities including Cambridge, the Delhi School of Economics, the London School of Economics, Oxford and Harvard. He has published prolifically, edited leading journals, presided over important societies and organizations, and received countless awards and accolades. The far-reaching influence of Sen's work on international organizations including the United Nations Development Programme, the Food and Agricultural Programme and the World Bank is widely acknowledged. He was awarded the Nobel Prize in 1998 for his contributions to welfare economics.

Further reading

Other works include: *Choice, Welfare and Measurement* (1982), *Resources, Values and Development* (1984); *On Ethics and Economics* (1987); *Markets and Freedoms: Achievements and Limitations of the Market Mechanism in Promoting Individual Freedoms* (1993); *Consequential Evaluation and Practical Reason* (2000); and *Rationality and Freedom* (2002).

POLLY VIZARD

SEURAT, Georges Pierre

1859–91

French painter

Georges Seurat was born in Paris, the youngest child of a bailiff. He was a pupil of Henri Lehmann, a disciple of Ingres, at the École des Beaux Arts, 1878–9. He studied antique sculpture, the Renaissance masters and the drawing of Ingres. While on military service at Brest, 1879–80, he began to paint landscapes. On his return to Paris he became interested in urban social subject-matter and began to develop the distinctive drawing style for which he is famous, using soft *conté* crayon on heavily textured paper. These studies with their monumental forms devoid of hard outline were prototypes for his painted figures. While working at drawing and painting Seurat read the works of Charles Blanc and Michel-Eugène Chevreul on colour contrast and harmony and Hermann von Helmholtz on physiological optics. His painting style during this period was close to that of Barbizon and Impressionist artists. In the autumn of 1884 he showed his celebrated large canvas *Une baignade à Asnières* (1883–4), which had been refused by the Salon, at the first exhibition of the Société des Artistes Indépendants, which he had founded with Signac, Redon and other radical artists. In 1886 he exhibited the other very large canvas for which he is renowned, *La Grande Jatte* (1883–5), at the last Impressionist exhibition. This was his first major attempt at what became known as 'pointillism' or 'neo-Impressionism'. A number of Symbolist writers and critics, like Felix Fenéon and Gustave Kahn, rallied round Seurat and also Paul Signac, in defence of their art and theories. Painters like Cross, Angrand, Lucien Pissarro and Luce became 'neo-Impressionists' and **Van Gogh**, who met Seurat this year, incorporated some of the latter's ideas into his own work. Seurat died quite suddenly of infectious angina in 1891. He produced seven large canvases, sixty small ones, 160 very small wood panel studies and nearly 500 drawings.

Seurat's art, developed in a little over ten years, grew from a number of 'scientific researches' into physiological optics, colour theory and the affective qualities of colours, lines and forms, as well as from a scrupulous technique and a great deal of study of earlier masters. His earliest researches into the simultaneous contrast of colours, based on a reading of Blanc and Chevreul and a study of Delacroix's use of colour, led to *Une baignade*, on which he worked for over a year and which he reworked in 1887. Seurat made thirteen preparatory oil sketches and numerous drawings for this work which, with its elemental composition, its monumental figures and banal industrial suburb for background, seems to be a secular reworking of Piero della Francesca's art. It certainly bears a relationship to the work of Seurat's Symbolist contemporary Puvis de Chavannes. Although the work is based on firmly moulded forms and a geometrical composition, the first traces of the pointillist technique can be discerned in the grass in the foreground. All the hues have a luminosity and intensity which derives from the use of pure and largely unmixed colours.

It was *La Grande Jatte*, showing Parisians relaxing on a Sunday afternoon, which was the first extreme example of pointillism and fully reveals the influence of scientific ideas on his work. All the colour is applied in small dots and strokes which, at a certain distance, are 'optically mixed' by the spectator's eye. Around the edge of this and future canvases is a thin border or 'false frame', which contrasts with adjacent colours. The figures are still and hieratic, as if seen in an atmospheric frieze, and the first traces of an elegant 'art nouveau' line can be traced in some of the forms. As with most of Seurat's major works,

La Grande Jatte was carefully composed over a long period from a large number of studies. After 1886, under the influence of the scientist and aesthetician Charles Henry, Seurat's work often deals with movement and he developed in his last years a complex linear style which was meant directly to affect the beholder's emotions by its formal arrangement. The emotional tones of pictures like *Le Chahut* (1889–90) and *Le Cirque* (1890–1) show the considerable impact of Henry's ideas concerning the relationships obtained between linear directions by measuring their angles with a *Rapporteur esthétique*, a sort of aesthete's protractor.

Seurat's own formulation of these theories was made in a letter to a friend, the writer Maurice Beaubourg, in August 1890, in which he stated, 'Art is Harmony. Harmony is the analogy of contrary and similar qualities in tone, colour and line, considered with reference to a Dominant and under the influence of a scheme of lighting in cheerful, calm or sad combinations.' These ideas had a major impact on later Symbolist and abstractionist theories of art and, in revising the tenets of Impressionism, led to the creation of more conceptual and schematic art forms than either Impressionism or traditional varieties of realism had offered. The Italian 'Divisionists', in particular Boccioni and Balla, were to develop these ideas into Futurism. Similar experiments in Germany by **Kandinsky** and **Klee** were to lay some of the foundations of a formally non-objective art. Like **Degas** and **Cézanne**, Seurat tried to reinvent the classical elements of structure and overall design in painting without sacrificing the mainly scientific advances that had been made since the advent of Impressionism. Seurat, in his scientific studies and researches, revived the image of the artist-philosopher in the tradition of Poussin and, before him, Leonardo.

Further reading

See: H. Dorra and J. Rewald, *Seurat* (Paris, 1960); *Seurat's Drawings*, ed. R.L. Herbert (1963);

W.I. Homer, *Seurat and the Science of Painting* (1964); J. Russell, *Seurat* (1965); J. Arguelles, *Charles Henry and the Formation of a Psychological Aesthetic* (1972); R. Thomson, *Seurat* (1985).

RICHARD HUMPHREYS

SHAW, George Bernard

1856–1950

Irish writer

'I am a typical Irishman,' Shaw told G.K. Chesterton, 'my family came from Yorkshire.' He was born in Dublin on 26 July 1856, the third and last child of George Carr Shaw, a redundant Civil Servant turned grain merchant, and his wife Lucinda Elizabeth, a lapsed Protestant who tampered with the occult. They were an unattractive couple and they achieved a miserable marriage that began in Synge Street – 'an awful little kennel', Shaw later described it. They did not physically ill-treat their son: they ignored him. If he had failed to come home from one of the genteel day schools to which he was sent, he did not think that either of them would have noticed.

Mrs Shaw despised her husband, who was a failed teetotaller, and she seems to have felt that their son was tainted by a similar ineffectualness. She looked down on all men: except one, 'a mesmeric conductor and daringly original teacher of Music' called George John Vandeleur Lee. The impact of this man on the Shaw household was revolutionary. Having discovered Mrs Shaw to be a fine mezzo-soprano, he trained her voice, made her the right-hand woman of his Amateur Musical Society and invited the Shaws to share both his smart house in Dublin and his seaside cottage at Dalkey. He banished family prayers, reduced Mr Shaw to nullity and filled the house with music. The ménage-à-trois was all the more remarkable in the strict caste society of Ireland since Lee was Catholic and the Shaws Protestant. But in 1873, in rather dubious circumstances, Lee suddenly left Dublin for London. A fortnight later, on her twenty-first wedding anniversary,

Mrs Shaw followed him. Though she was to bring both her daughters to live with her, she left 'Sonny' (as he had been called) in lodging with her husband. It was then, turning deprivation to advantage, that Shaw taught himself music from textbooks and the piano. After leaving school in 1871 he had become a junior clerk in 'a highly exclusive gentlemanly estate office', Uniacke Townshend & Co. Early in 1876 he resigned and, one of his sisters having died, went to take her room in his mother's home in London.

These first twenty years in Ireland had left Shaw bereft of all passions except two: the passion of laughter and a passion for reform. His early experiences were to control to an extraordinary degree the range and tone of his work. The art of paradox, which turned tragedy on its head and fulfilled a moral obligation to optimism, became his 'criticism of life'. Believing that he had inherited from his father the tendency to an obsession, he transferred it from drink to work, making himself, as he said, into a writing-machine. For professional purposes he dropped the name George (so uncomfortably shared by Lee and his father) and created a public being, G.B.S., a 'pantomime ostrich' which was modelled on the example of Lee whom he depicted as a phenomenon too impersonal to attract affection, but whose mercurial personality had won him the admiration, so much sought after by Sonny, of Mrs Shaw.

Shaw's progress in London at setting himself up as 'a professional man of genius' was dismayingly slow, and over the first nine years he calculated that he had earned less than ten pounds. 'I did not throw myself into the struggle for life: I threw my mother into it. I was not a staff to my father's old age: I hung on to his coat tails.' In this period he wrote five novels that were rejected by every publisher, though four of them eventually achieved publication in socialist magazines.

In 1884 Shaw joined the Fabian Society which, up to the First World War, often by means of permeating the Tories and Liberals with its socialist ideas, chiefly expressed the opinions of Shaw and Sidney Webb.

The Fabian Society became Shaw's new family and his socialist reforms a means of changing society so that no child should have to go through the sort of upbringing he had endured. Believing himself to be unlovable, he made out of Collectivism a weapon against individualist romantic propaganda. Shaw's socialism was composed of the abolition of private property plus the introduction of equality of income. To this, as a refinement to democracy, aimed at achieving efficiency and real adult suffrage, he proposed adding the Coupled Vote – every valid vote going to a man-and-woman. Shaw's socialism, which invades many of his plays and much of his journalism, found its outlet in numerous Fabian Tracts (of which he made a selection in *Essays in Fabian Socialism*), in *The Intelligent Woman's Guide to Socialism and Capitalism* (1928) and *Everybody's Political What's What* (1944). Shaw also spent a great deal of time speaking at street corners and working on committees, but eventually concluded that **William Morris** was right and that it had not been practical for socialists to enter the circus of party politics. Shaw believed that the Labour Party, so far from being a force for socialism against capitalism, was a trade union party dedicated to fighting the employer's federations in a new class war. A measure of his disenchantment with British politics may be seen from his enthusiasm for Soviet Russia, which he visited in 1931 and advertised on his return as an experimental Fabian colony.

Shaw was known as a journalist and critic long before he became famous as a playwright. His art reviews in *Our Corner and the World* (1885–9), though mainly anonymous, made him well known among his colleagues; while his celebrated musical criticism, first as 'Corno di Bassetto' in the *Star* (1888–90) and then as 'G.B.S.' in the *World* (1890–4), extended his fame. From 1895 to 1898 he contributed theatre criticism to the Saturday Review, making outrageous use of Shakespeare (whose politics, he claimed, 'would hardly impress the Thames Conservancy Board') to promote his campaign for a revolution on the late-Victorian stage. According to his successor

Max Beerbohm, he had become 'the most brilliant and remarkable journalist in London'.

But most critics agreed that he would have made a 'better Bishop than a playwright'. Almost all of them acknowledged that he could produce entertaining prose extravaganzas (*Arms and the Man, You Never Can Tell*), but they were based not on human emotions but piles of bluebooks, tracts, social statistics (*Widowers' Houses, Mrs. Warren's Profession*). Sometimes these compositions, amalgams of lecture and farce, the critics conceded, were almost as good as plays.

Success did not finally come until, during the Vedrenne-Barker management at the Court Theatre, the special furniture hired for a royal command performance of *John Bull's Other Island* on 11 March 1905 crashed beneath the king, who was laughing too hard, and flung Shaw's reputation high into the air. Despite his efforts to do so ('I am not in the popular entertainment business'), Shaw never fully recovered his unpopularity. *Fanny's First Play* ran for 622 performances in London (1912–13), and the number of revivals of *Pygmalion* (1913) and *Saint Joan* (1923) established him as a box-office success throughout the world.

But under the sparkle and to one side of the sermonizing lay an ingenious Shavian theme. He believed that he had inherited from his parents incompatible qualities that he must reconcile within himself. In *The Quintessence of Ibsenism* (1891) he had stressed the importance of efficiency over aspiration, but in later writings such as *Candida* (1894) and *The Perfect Wagnerite* (1898) he tried to expand this pragmatism so that it might serve not just a social but a religious purpose. From this process emerged his concept of the Life Force which is not a symbol of power but a unit of synthesis.

With this new religion came new drama in which, as a series of parables, Shaw rewrote past history and tried to navigate a course for the future. The synthesis of *Man and Superman* (1903) was a fantasy, and when in *John Bull's Other Island* (1904) and *Major Barbara* (1905) he tried to apply it to actual life he found that he could not reconcile all the separated elements. Like a conjuror with too many objects revolving in the air, he had to dispense with something and, in *Back to Methuselah* (1924), it was the body that he eliminated.

In later years Shaw lusted after a non-physical consummation – 'all life and no matter' – between earth and heaven. That man would have to change out of all recognition or be superseded by another species did not cause him to despair, for he had increasingly turned his attention away from the individual and the body as a vehicle of emotion. At times, like Ellie Dunn at the end of *Heartbreak House* (1919), he appears 'radiant at the prospect' of the human species being scrapped, and the Life Force taking another mate.

Shaw did not stop short at rewriting the past: he re-enacted it. Many of his affairs with women were three-cornered, often with the wife of some socialist friend. Shaw flirted, but never made love to anyone's wife. He acted his own version of Lee in other people's households – a sort of Sunday husband. In these relationships he was seeking a second childhood in which he received all the attention he had been denied. His liaisons became part of his theatrical life, the excitement producing an ejaculation of words from which plays were born. In 1898 he married Charlotte Payne Townshend, 'my green-eyed millionairess', who came from the same family as the Dublin estate agents. At Charlotte's request it was a *mariage blanc*. In their fashion they loved each other and when Charlotte died in 1943 Shaw was grief-stricken. Her death had been a great loss to him, he admitted; then at the last moment he turned it into a Shavian joke – 'a great financial loss'.

Further reading

See: the Standard Edition in thirty-six volumes published by Constable (1931–51); *Bernard Shaw and Mrs Patrick Campbell: Their Correspondence*, ed. Alan Dent (1952); *Ellen Terry and Bernard Shaw – A Correspondence*, ed. Christopher St John (1931); *Collected Plays* and their *Prefaces* in seven volumes

(1970–4) and *Collected Letters* ed. Dan H. Laurence (4 vols 1965–88). Among the many biographies, Michael Holroyd, *Bernard Shaw* (5 vols 1988–92) is perhaps definitive, while those by St John Ervine (1956) and Hesketh Pearson (1942, revised 1961) are also recommended. Critical and other studies include: Eric Bentley, *Shaw* (1946, revised 1957); Martin Meisel, *Shaw and the Nineteenth Century Theatre* (1963); J.M. Wisenthal, *The Marriage of Contraries* (1974); Alfred Turco Jr, *Shaw's Moral Vision* (1976); *The Genius of Shaw*, ed. Michael Holroyd (1979); and C. Innes (ed.), *The Cambridge Companion to George Bernard Shaw* (1998).

MICHAEL HOLROYD

SHOSTAKOVICH, Dmitri Dmitrievich

1906–75

Russian composer

Shostakovich was born in St Petersburg and took piano lessons from the age of nine. It soon became clear that he had exceptional talent and in 1919 he was enrolled at the Conservatoire in that city (by this time renamed Petrograd). He was obliged to support his family by playing for silent films but nevertheless completed his course with a First Symphony (1925) so well received that it immediately became part of the repertoire, first in Russia and then abroad, a position it has maintained to the present.

It revealed the composer as open to much of the exploratory music being written in the West at the time – Paul Hindemith's and **Berg's** in particular – as well as reflecting the conflicting Russian traditions: symphonic in the manner of **Tchaikovsky** and more Russophile after the example of the Five, the famous nineteenth-century group of composers, among whom **Rimsky-Korsakov** had been prominent. The latter's son-in-law, M. Steinberg, had been Shostakovich's composition teacher.

Shostakovich graduated as a pianist as well as composer and after leaving the Conservatoire won a prize at a recital contest in Warsaw and gave concerts throughout Russia. Composition remained of paramount importance to him, however, although he continued to give recitals, principally involving his own music, throughout his career.

In the late 1920s Shostakovich's musical modernism continued in the Second and Third Symphony, the ballets *The Golden Age* (1930) and *The Bolt* (1931), and the operas *The Nose* (1930) and *Lady Macbeth of Mtensk* (1934). Two current tendencies were present in Soviet music at the time – the 'proletarian' which insisted that music should be widely comprehensible and the 'modernistic' which asserted that revolution in art should accompany revolution in society. Both tendencies had their associations and both were wound up in the early 1930s as the ideas of Socialist Realism were formulated.

Shostakovich inclined towards the modernistic tendency but there are clear signs of stylistic crisis in his Fourth Symphony (withdrawn during rehearsal in 1936). An unwieldy and discursive structure supports a language that is not fully coherent and this problem, together with an article 'Chaos instead of Music', which appeared in *Pravda* in 1936 concerning his opera *Lady Macbeth of Mtensk*, forced on him a retrenchment as well as a reconsideration.

Starting with the Fifth Symphony (1937) his style becomes clearer and more traditional but equally more personal. Long-range tonal organization deriving from classical practice is allied with a detailed concentration on motif usually expressed in traditional forms. He turned to chamber music at this time, beginning his series of string quartets and producing two definitive works in piano chamber music – the Piano Quintet (1940) and the Piano Trio (1944). Both won **Stalin** Prizes as did the Seventh Symphony (1941), the *Leningrad*, composed and premiered under conditions of great privation during the German siege of that city. This work became the musical symbol of the Russian resistance when performed in concerts in the USA and unoccupied Europe.

At the end of the war Shostakovich failed to produce a victory symphony: instead his Ninth, perhaps from fear of comparison with Beethoven's, was a *jeu d'esprit* that revealed

nothing of the horrors of the previous years. This failure possibly contributed towards a government intervention in music in 1948 as the state's duty to have concern for all aspects of cultural life was reasserted. Between then and 1953 Shostakovich produced two types of work – the public, e.g. film scores, which won him Stalin Prizes and the title People's Artist, and the private, including the First Violin Concerto (1948) and the song cycle *From Jewish Folk Poetry*. Neither of the latter was released until 1953; at the same time the Tenth Symphony was performed.

Although still within a traditional idiom, these works reveal a widening of the language and a willingness to experiment a little with structure, and with the success of these pieces Shostakovich's final period was set. He turned increasingly towards the more personal medium of the string quartet and produced many fine works in this genre: Nos 7 and 8 (both from 1960), 12 (1968) and 13 (1970) and 15 (1974) are particularly remarkable pieces. Those dating from the late 1960s reveal an interest in twelve-note technique (cf. **Schoenberg**), always used within a diatonic context as a deepening of the expressive power of the music.

More public music from this period utilized the virtuosity of Russian performers, e.g. Oistrakh in the two Violin Concertos (the Second dating from 1967), and Rostropovitch in two Cello Concertos (1958 and 1967), or, alternatively, involved text in an exposition of the composer's increasing obsession with death.

In their various ways the Thirteenth and Fourteenth Symphonies (1962 and 1969) and *Suite to Poems by Michelangelo* (1974) make explicit a despair left implicit in the brooding chamber music of the time and, although honours continued to be showered on him both at home and abroad, the music of his last works is largely powerfully depressive, the more so for being contained within clearly defined structures.

In the context of European music Shostakovich was a conservative, like **Britten**, whose music he admired. But Schoenberg had said there was much good music still to be written in C major and Shostakovich undoubtedly contributed much to this quantity. In the field of Russian music he was the first internationally acclaimed musical talent to emerge from the Soviet Union and was its most prominent representative throughout his career. Because of the interventionist nature of its government his career may also function as a touchstone for relationships between music and society: a relationship that, in Shostakovich's case, was not always of the happiest.

Further reading

Other works include: two Piano Concertos (1933 and 1957); *24 Preludes and Fugues* for piano (1951); and the choral work *The Execution of Stepan Razin* (1964). See: D. Rabinovich, *Dmitri Shostakovich* (1959); N. Kay, *Shostakovich* (1971); R. Blokker with R. Dearling, *The Music of Shostakovich* (1979); *Testimony: The Memoirs of Shostakovich*, ed. S. Volkov (1979); Christopher Norris (ed.) *Shostakovich* (1982); Eric Roseberry, *Shostakovich: His Life and Times* (1982); and I. MacDonald, *The New Shostakovich* (1992). See also: Boris Schwarz, *Music and Musical Life in Soviet Russia 1917–70* (1972).

MALCOLM BARRY

SIBELIUS, Jean

1865–1957

Finnish composer

Jean Sibelius is Finland's greatest composer and a master of the symphony. His music bears witness to an all-consuming love of the nordic landscape and a preoccupation with its mythology, and more particularly, the repository of myth enshrined in the Finnish national epic, the *Kalevala*. Born in Hämeenlinna in Finland, he was christened Johan Julius Christian but subsequently Gallicized it, on discovering a set of visiting cards used by a sea-faring uncle who had adopted this form of the name. He showed an early talent for the violin and little interest in the law studies to which his family had set him. After some years in Helsinki as a pupil of Martin Wegelius, with whom he studied composition, he went abroad to Berlin in 1889 and the following year to Vienna, where he became a pupil of Goldmark. Up to this time his output comprised chamber music as opportunities to compose for the orchestra had been few. Helsinki did not possess a permanent symphony orchestra until 1888.

The *Kullervo Symphony*, an ambitious seventy-minute, five-movement work for soloists, male chorus and orchestra, put him on the map in 1892, and together with *En Saga* (1893), *Karelia* (1893) and the *Four Legends* (1895) established him as the leading figure in Finnish music. His popularity abroad began to grow a decade later with such works as *Finlandia* (1900) and *Valse triste* (1903). The 1890s show him developing as a nationalist composer, working within the Romantic musical tradition and responding positively to the influence of **Tchaikovsky**. His student works also show the influence of the Viennese classics and, of course, Grieg. After the Second Symphony (1902) and the Violin Concerto (1903, revised 1905), he moved away from the climate of post-Romanticism towards a more austere and classical language. His instinctive feeling for the Viennese classics strengthened, and works such as *Pohjola's Daughter* (1906) and the Third Symphony (1904–7) show a classicism at variance with the spirit of their time. In 1907 **Mahler** visited Helsinki and their oft-quoted exchange on the nature of the symphony reveals the difference of emphasis in their approach to the form. Sibelius said he admired 'its severity and style, and the profound logic that created an inner connection between all the motifs', to which Mahler replied, 'No, for me the symphony must be like the world: it must embrace everything.'

Championed by conductors, such as his countryman Robert Kajanus, Hans Richter, Sir Henry Wood and others, as well as such important critics as Rosa Newmarch and Ernest Newman, Sibelius's music gradually won acceptance both in England and America. In 1899 he had acquired the German publisher, Breitkopf and Härtel, and made numerous visits to both Germany and Italy. Busoni was among the figures who championed his music; he conducted both the Second Symphony and *Pohjola's Daughter* in Berlin. In 1909 Sibelius was operated on for a throat tumour, which may account for the greater austerity and depth of his Fourth Symphony (1911), as well as the greater seriousness and concentration of such scores as *The Bard* and *Luonnotar*.

With the outbreak of the First World War in 1914 he was cut off from his German royalties. He composed during this period a large number of light instrumental pieces in the hope of repeating the great success of *Valse triste*, the rights to which he had sold on derisory terms. From the war years comes the Fifth Symphony (1915), which he twice revised and which reached its definitive form only in 1919. The voyage from the climate of Slav romanticism that had fostered the First Symphony (1899) into the wholly isolated and profoundly original world of the Sixth (1923) and Seventh (1924), at a time when the mainstream of music was moving in other directions, was one of courageous spiritual discovery. Like all great artists, Sibelius's approach to the symphony is never the same. From the vantage point of the Fourth, it would be impossible to foretell the shape and character of the Fifth. Likewise, the Sixth is a wholly unpredictable phenomenon when viewed from the achievement of its predecessor, and in terms of the musical climate of the 1920s. There is no set of prescriptive rules for any Sibelius symphony: each differs from the other and from the genre as a whole. The Seventh's one movement is completely original in form, subtle in its handling of tempi, individual in its treatment of key and wholly organic in growth.

Tapiola (1926), in which his lifework culminated, united the symphonic process with his lifelong preoccupation with nature and myth. The sheer stature of the seven symphonies overshadowed Sibelius's achievement in the field of the tone-poem. This genre occupied him throughout his creative

life and his contribution to its literature is no less important than that of **Liszt** and **Richard Strauss**. Incidental music for the stage also constitutes an important part of his output and culminated in the ambitious and imaginative score he composed for the 1926 production of *The Tempest*. This saw the end of his creative career, though it is almost certain that an Eighth Symphony was composed and subsequently destroyed. After the 1920s, Sibelius gave up conducting and travelling and retired to the isolation of his home in Järvenpää, some miles outside Helsinki.

Further reading

See: Cecil Gray, *Sibelius: The Symphonies* (1931); Gerald Abraham (ed.), *Sibelius: A Symposium* (1947); Robert Layton, *Sibelius* (1965) and *Sibelius and His World* (1970); Erik Tawaststjerna, *Sibelius* (5 vols, 1968, abridged to 3 vols and translated by Robert Layton, 1976–97). See also F. Blum, *Jean Sibelius: An International Bibliography on the Occasion of the Centennial Celebration* (1965); G.D. Goss (ed.), *The Sibelius Symposium* (1996); T.L. Jackson and V. Murtomäki (eds), *Sibelius Studies* (2000).

ROBERT LAYTON

SINGER, Isaac Bashevis

1904–91

Polish/American novelist and short-story writer

Although Isaac Bashevis Singer has been called the last and greatest writer in Yiddish, most of his readers have been anglophone, and all his books were sooner or later translated into English. It was a process in which he actively took part, and he regarded these translations as 'second originals'.

Singer was born in Leoncyn, Poland; his sister Esther Singer (Kreitman) and brother Israel Yoshua Singer also became novelists. It was partly thanks to the Singer siblings that Yiddish fiction came of age. Much of Isaac's work is set in Poland among Jews before the Second World War. He said that he wanted to preserve the memory of a lifestyle which, because of secularization, assimilation and the Holocaust, had disappeared.

His father, a Hasidic rabbi, was a naïve, deeply religious man who didn't wish Isaac to study Polish, for the reason that the Messiah might appear any day and he would probably speak Hebrew. The mother was more intellectual, as was her own father, an orthodox rabbi. Isaac was reared on legends about Hasidic saints, but read the Kabbala and Spinoza as well. Among Isaac's favourite novelists were Balzac, Blixen, **Dickens**, **Dostoyevsky**, Gogol, **Thomas Mann** and **Tolstoy**. After two years at a rabbinical seminary in Warsaw, Singer worked in that city as a proofreader and translator. And he broke with Jewish orthodoxy, a decision that caused him considerable inner agony.

In all his work Singer would draw on his early years, but especially in the autobiographical novels *In My Father's Court* (1966), *A Little Boy in Search of God: Mysticism in a Personal Light* (1976), *A Young Man in Search of Love* (1978) and *Lost in America* (1981). Because of growing Polish antisemitism, Israel and Isaac emigrated to the USA (1934 and 1935, respectively). Isaac became a contributor to the *Jewish Daily Forward*, and married Alma Haimann; the couple had one son. Israel's premature death was a terrible shock to Isaac.

Fame didn't come to him until after the Second World War. It helped Singer that fiction about Jewish life had attained a certain dignity after the Holocaust. He had already promised himself never to write about people without passions, and never to create in cold blood.

In Singer's fiction there is a tension between belief in free will and a grim determinism. He asserted that God equals free will, while Satan stands for anything 'determined', unfree. Singer's characters tend to be the slaves of their own emotions, and unable to make free choices. There is a streak of mysticism in Singer as well, who defined a 'mystic' as 'a person who constantly feels surprised'.

His masterpiece is the trilogy *The Family Moskat* (1950), *The Manor* (1967) and *The Estate* (1969). These novels have reminded many of Mann, and their narrative mode is traditionally realistic. They are mostly set in Poland; the eponymous manor represents that country during the period of industrialization. Singer's enormous cast includes Gentiles as well as Jews. One of the themes is the struggle between orthodoxy and secularization. A claustrophobic feeling of predestined destruction characterizes *The Family Moskat*, which ends in 1939 when the Germans start bombing Warsaw.

Most critics have neglected Singer's prose style. One example of his carefully crafted imagery is *The Manor*, where it always seems to be winter. People skate or travel by sleigh. Snowflakes are dry as salt, and snow lies bunched up like cats on the branches of trees.

Other novels by Singer focus on individuals who are tempted or confronted by evil. *Satan in Goray* (1955) describes Messianism and mass hysteria in seventeenth-century Poland. Also *The Slave* (1962) presents Polish Jewry during that epoch. Jacob, the protagonist, may stand for the wandering, suffering Jew. *The Magician of Lublin* (1960) can be read as an allegory of the artist's life and development. There are allegorical elements also in *Shosha* (1978). The title figure, a girl who refuses to grow up, represents goodness and innocence. Singer sympathized with the plight of women in patriarchal societies. In 'Yentl the Yeshiva Boy' (*The Spinoza of Market Street and Other Stories*, 1961), a gifted Jewish girl disguises herself as a boy in order to become a scholar. The story was recast as a successful play (produced 1974, New York), and turned into a musical film, *Yentl* (1983), starring Barbra Streisand.

Singer's 'Zeitl and Rickel' (*The Séance and Other Stories*, 1968) is about a lesbian love affair in a small town.

His short stories, whether for adults or children, often use motifs from Jewish folklore, and have been compared to **Chagall's** paintings, with their naivism, supernatural details and stained-glass colours.

Singer received the Nobel Prize for Literature in 1978. In the USA he was the recipient of two National Endowment for the Arts grants and two National Book Awards.

Further reading

Other works include: *Enemies: A Love Story* (1972) and *Reaches of Heaven* (1980). See also: Grace Farrell (Lee), *From Exile to Redemption: The Fiction of Isaac Bashevis Singer* (1987); and Janet Hadda, *Isaac Bashevis Singer* (1997) – a biography.

SUSANNA ROXMAN

SIRK, Douglas

1900–87

Danish/German/US film director

It was only in the 1970s that the genius of Douglas Sirk was recognized. Even in his last years at Universal, when films like *All That Heaven Allows* (1955) and *Imitation of Life* (1959) were huge commercial successes, his mastery was ignored. His work, however, is important not only in itself as the richest body of melodrama to emerge from Hollywood, but also in terms of the complex aesthetic and stylistic questions it raises.

Sirk himself is the locus of many contradictions. Of all the German émigré population in Hollywood, Sirk was arguably the one most fascinated and stimulated by American culture. Yet he brought to Hollywood a breathtaking knowledge of European avant-garde theatre of the 1920s, painting, poetry and music.

Claus Detlef Sierck was born in Hamburg of Danish parents. After spending his early childhood in Skagen, he returned to Hamburg. His university education was wide-reaching: law in Munich, philosophy in Jena, and finally art history in Hamburg, where he studied under Erwin Panovsky. His mastery of lighting, composition and set-design undoubtedly owes much to this period. Another important formative experience was in Munich in 1919, when he witnessed the short-lived Bavarian Soviet, the only revolution to be masterminded and led by poets and intellectuals.

He entered the theatre in 1920, as a second-line *dramaturg* at the Deutsches Schauspielhaus, Hamburg. From 1923 to 1929, he was artistic director at the Schauspielhaus, Bremen, followed by seven years as *Direktor* at the Altes Theater, Leipzig. He proved an extremely gifted theatrical director, already demonstrating his ability to transform and to transcend awkward material. His knowledge of the structure of classical drama stemming from his productions of Molière, Shakespeare, Büchner and others, was to prove invaluable in enabling him to shape the intractable material with which he was confronted in Hollywood.

In 1934, his production of Shakespeare's *Twelfth Night* at the Berlin Volksbühne led to an invitation to join UFA, the leading German film studio. In spite of his left-wing reputation and the political controversy surrounding his period at Leipzig, Sierck was allowed considerable freedom at UFA. In his early films there (like *April, April*, 1935), he immediately displayed his extraordinary ability to transform recalcitrant material into something substantial and outstanding. His second feature, *Das Mädchen vom Moorhof* (1935), already filmed by Victor Sjöström, revealed many of what were to become Sirkian trademarks: the use of mirror shots, the dismantling of suspense and the theme of the exposure of hypocrisy.

His decision to make *Schlussakkord* (1936) was a landmark in his career, for in choosing an atrociously mawkish story on which he would make a full-blooded assault, he was breaking away from literary values to pursue the purely cinematic. He also made other major melodramas in Germany in 1937: *Zu Neuen Ufern*, which transformed Swedish actress Zarah Leander into a star, and *La Habanera*. In these tough, anti-colonialist films, he showed a mastery of the medium that was to be apparent in his later Hollywood masterpieces, *Written on the Wind* (1956) and *The Tarnished Angels* (1957).

In December 1937, Douglas Sirk (as he became known) left Germany for Hollywood, via Paris and Holland. After a difficult period at Columbia under the idiosyncratic Harry Cohn, and a happier period alfalfa farming, he signed with Universal in 1950. As 'house director', he had little control over the choice of projects, but could at least restructure material, shoot and edit as he wished. Only when maverick producer Albert Zugsmith spent a brief period at Universal was Sirk able to pursue two projects of his own choice: *The Tarnished Angels*, an adaptation of **William Faulkner's** novel of the Depression, *Pylon*, and *Written on the Wind*. To understand Sirk, it is instructive to compare these two masterpieces with the films he made with producer Ross Hunter, like *All That Heaven Allows* and *Imitation of Life*. All four are brilliant films, yet in those produced by Hunter, Sirk somehow triumphs over the material: in those produced by Zugsmith, he has the freedom to express his personal vision of America. Ross Hunter imposed on Sirk 'happy endings' which were at variance with Sirk's leanings towards themes of despair and disintegration, and which result in irony. In *The Tarnished Angels* and *Written on the Wind*, Sirk could follow through his vision of men and women driven to extremes in a society on the point of collapse. Both films deal with breakdown and with failure. In the latter, images of infirmity, of alcoholism, of sexual frustration and of fear of sterility abound. Throughout his work, images of illness recur, with individual illness representing social breakdown. Problems of vision also predominate, as characters suffer from blindness, or fail to see themselves, or others, clearly. Sirk's use of mirrors throughout his films also underlines this theme, suggestive too of the surfaces within which the characters are trapped.

Sirk believed that criticism and comment in art should be distanced, and that melodrama was the ideal genre at that particular historical conjecture to express his views on American society. He respected the rules of the genre, and used it to expose mercilessly the hypocrisy and deceit of Eisenhowerian America. His films shatter the complacency of American society in the 1950s, revealing the possibility of imminent collapse.

He was arguably the greatest stylist in Hollywood in the 1950s. In *Imitation of Life*, his last Hollywood film and one of Universal's most successful films commercially, he again succeeded in transcending a dreadful story through brilliant use of lighting, composition, camerawork and music. Sirk left Hollywood in 1958, leaving *Imitation of Life* as his farewell gesture. He returned to Europe, directing theatre in Germany, and teaching film at the Munich Film School. The influence of his work on a new generation of directors, ranging from **Rainer Werner Fassbinder** to Bernardo Bertolucci, became increasingly evident during the 1970s.

Further reading

See: Jon Halliday, *Sirk on Sirk* (1971); B. Klinger, *Melodrama and Meaning: History, Culture and the Films of Douglas Sirk* (1994); Jon Halliday (ed.), *Sirk on Sirk* (1997).

LINDA MILES

SKINNER, Burrhus Frederic
1904–90
US psychologist

The high priest of behaviourism – a now-outmoded but once vigorously challenging ideology in its application to human affairs – B.F. Skinner was born in Susquehanna, Pennsylvania, and educated at Hamilton College, New York, and at Harvard University. There he became a fellow in 1931, and Edgar Pierce Professor of Psychology from 1947 to 1975. His *Behaviour of Organisms* appeared in 1938, and *Science and Human Behaviour* in 1953. His most famous book, however, was, and remains, the utopian novel *Walden Two* (1948), while the definitive statement of his philosophical and scientific outlook is *Beyond Freedom and Dignity* (1971).

Most of Skinner's work as an experimental psychologist was concerned with behaviour modification in animals. The following is a typical example:

We study the height at which a pigeon's head is normally held, and select some line on the height scale which is reached only infrequently. Keeping our eye on the scale we begin to open the food tray very quickly whenever the head rises above the line. The result is invariable: we observe an immediate change in the frequency with which the head crosses the line.

(*Science and Human Behaviour*)

In this standard Skinnerian experiment, the food is termed the *reinforcer*; presenting the food whenever the desired response is produced is called *reinforcement*; the resulting change in the frequency with which the head is lifted is the process of *operant conditioning*.

Skinner's meticulous and painstaking research showed how such procedures can be extended to produce remarkably complex behavioural responses. But Skinner's importance lay not in his experimental results, impressive though they were, nor in the theory of conditioned response (which was first systematized by Sechenov and **Pavlov**), but in his insistence that it is proper, and indeed desirable, to apply the methods and procedures of behavioural psychology to the human domain. Skinner pioneered such ideas as the teaching machine and programmed learning; his inventions included mechanical baby-tenders, and the 'Skinner box' – a controlled environment for monitoring behavioural changes. Yet even this, for Skinner, was merely a beginning. While other behavioural psychologists adopted the techniques of conditioning to effect cures of specific mental disorders (cf. J.B. Watson), Skinner sought, via the same means, to recondition society itself. 'What would you do,' asks the hero of *Walden Two*, 'if you found yourself in possession of an effective science of behaviour? Suppose you found it possible to control the behaviour of men as you wished. What would you do?' Skinner's answer, made explicit in *Walden Two*, is that he would design a new society – a society in which stability, harmony and satisfaction would be, in the literal sense, behaviourally engineered.

The methods which Skinner advocated for this end were much simpler than the eugenics and hypnotherapy envisaged in **Aldous Huxley's** *Brave New World*. Skinner's 'technology of behaviour' relied largely on reinforcement, especially 'positive' rather than 'negative' reinforcement (in plain English, a system of rewards, rather than coercion or punishment).

We can achieve a sort of control under which the controlled, though they are following a code much more scrupulously than was ever the case under the old system, now *feel free*. That's the source of the tremendous power of positive reinforcement.

The vision of a controlled society was hardly unfamiliar. What was disturbing was Skinner's enthusiasm for it. It needs to be asked, in particular, what place remains, in Skinner's scheme of things, for individual freedom and responsibility. Skinner's answer was quite uncompromising. In *Beyond Freedom and Dignity* he proposed that we should abandon completely the notion of 'autonomous man' – the free, responsible agent who is the author of his actions.

As a science of behaviour adopts the strategy of physics and biology, the autonomous agent to which behaviour has traditionally been attributed is replaced by the environment – the environment in which the species evolved and in which the behaviour of the individual is shaped and maintained.

Autonomous man is simply 'a device used to explain what we cannot explain any other way. His abolition has been long overdue.'

To support his case, Skinner defended a radical form of philosophical behaviourism. Good science, claimed Skinner, has no place for appeal to internal mental states. To explain someone's conduct by reference to an inner feeling is as unhelpful as the ancient view that a falling body accelerates because it feels more jubilant as it finds itself nearer home. 'Young people refuse to get jobs not because they feel alienated, but because of defective social environments.'

Of the many criticisms that might be levelled against Skinner's approach, two are of particular relevance. First, the rejection of explanations appealing to inner mental states is too glib. Attributing jubilation to stones is unhelpful precisely because it is *anthropomorphic*: we are ascribing to stones person-like properties which they do not in fact possess. Yet this hardly shows that it is inappropriate to invoke such properties when we come to deal with an *anthropos*, a person; people, as we all know from direct personal experience, quite simply *do* possess feelings.

Second, and more generally, Skinner's version of a 'scientific' approach to society was flawed by a fundamental contradiction. Freedom and autonomy, he claimed, are a sham; all human behaviour is environmentally determined. Yet on the other hand, we are told that 'the intentional design of a culture and control of human behaviour is essential' (*Beyond Freedom and Dignity*). Intentional design and control *by whom?* Clearly, in Skinner's scheme of things there are, after all, autonomous agents – the behavioural technocrats and planners. These god-like creatures apparently stand outside the deterministic nexus that binds the rest of us: they take free and rational decisions about how our culture is to be designed. The upshot is that Skinner's insistence on a planned society presupposes the existence – at least for a minority – of the very autonomy that his deterministic behaviourism ruled out.

Despite its contradictions and lack of philosophical sophistication, Skinner's message exercised a firm hold over many of his contemporaries – though not **Noam Chomsky**, who in 1959 attacked his claims for the efficacy of 'reinforcement' in the context of linguistic behaviour. Perhaps just because it was so facile, the once celebrated slogan from *Walden Two* – 'When a science of behaviour has been achieved, there's no alternative to a planned society' – struck a chord with those who, in a post-war climate, sought simple solutions to enduring problems without thinking through the possible consequences.

In time Skinner's ideas were widely rejected, especially within liberal individualistic communities of the sort inspired by **Henry David Thoreau's** original *Walden*. It is admittedly true that all governments necessarily practice 'social engineering' to some degree, whatever name they care to give it, but Skinner's cardinal error may just have been that he overstated his case; for unless people are in some measure susceptible to inducements, it is difficult to conceive how any society can be managed, or manage itself.

Further reading

See: Tibor R. Machan, *The Pseudo-science of B.F. Skinner* (1974); John A. Weigel, *B.F. Skinner* (1977); A. Charles Catania and Stevan Hamad (eds), *The Selection of Behaviourism: The Operant Behaviourism of B.F. Skinner* (1988); James T. Todd and Edward K. Morris (eds), *Modern Perspectives on B.F. Skinner and Contemporary Behaviourism* (1995).

JOHN COTTINGHAM

SOLZHENITSYN, Aleksandr Isayevich
1918–2008
Russian writer

Solzhenitsyn was born in Kislovodsk. His father, a serving artillery officer, was accidentally killed six months beforehand. In 1924 his mother, a shorthand typist, moved to Rostov-on-Don where he received his first schooling. On leaving school in 1936 he hoped to be a writer but was obliged instead to take a degree course in mathematics and physics at Rostov University, although this was supplemented by a two-year correspondence course in literature. He married N.A. Reshetovskaya in 1940 and was appointed a physics teacher at Morozovka in the Rostov region. Called up in October 1940, he was commissioned as an artillery officer the following year, fought at Kursk in 1943 and participated in the advance towards Germany. In February 1945, during the battle for Koenigsberg, he was arrested for having made disrespectful references to **Stalin** in private correspondence and was returned to Moscow for investigation and sentencing to eight years' imprisonment followed by 'perpetual exile'. In July 1946 he was transferred from parquet-laying work in a block of flats on Lenin Prospekt to the 'Sharashka' at Marfino, north of Sheremet'yevo airport (Mavrino of *The First Circle, V kruge pervom,* 1968), where his scientific training was used to promote research into listening devices. He was later transferred to a Siberian labour camp, the setting of his first published work *One Day in the Life of Ivan Denisovich (Odin den' Ivana Denisovicha,* 1962), from which he was released in 1953. The first thing he learned on his release was news of Stalin's death. Serious recurrence of cancer obliged him to enter the Tashkent clinic that forms the setting for *Cancer Ward (Rakovy korpus,* 1969) where he eventually recovered. He was not released from 'perpetual exile' until 1956 and then chose to live in Torfoprodukt, near Vladimir, the scene of *Matryona's Place (Matryonin dvor,* 1963). Divorced by Reshetovskaya after his sentencing, it was at this time that they remarried and settled in Ryazan, where his literary fame and notoriety began.

The publication of *One Day in the Life of Ivan Denisovich* in Tvardovsky's journal *Novy Mir* in 1962 became a political event of the first magnitude. This masterpiece of twentieth-century prison literature was the first work published in the Soviet Union to give an explicit picture of life in Stalin's slave-labour camps. Although he became famous almost overnight and was publicly praised by Nikita Khrushchev, his increasingly outspoken criticism of Stalinism and the Soviet establishment soon proved too much for the authorities and by 1966 he had ceased to find official outlets for his work. His plays and novels were all refused publication, notwithstanding his frequent appeals to the Union of Soviet Writers, and had to be published abroad. When he was awarded the Nobel Prize for Literature in 1970 a campaign of vilification was launched against him, his *August 1914 (Avgust 14-ogo,* 1971) was banned and his role as spokesman of Soviet

dissidence began gradually to assume as great an importance as his role as a writer.

This reputation received endorsement with his decision to release for publication abroad in 1973 Parts I and II of *The Gulag Archipelago (Arkhipelag gulag),* his carefully documented exposure of the Soviet slave-labour system. The attacks on him and his associates increased in ferocity until, in February 1974, he was arrested, interrogated, stripped of his citizenship and summarily exiled to the West. He took up residence in Zurich, where he was joined by his second wife (formerly Natalya Svetlova) and their three sons. He later moved to an extensive estate in Vermont in the United States to live a reclusive life punctuated by occasional public appearances for interviews or speeches. Of the latter the most noteworthy was the speech delivered at Harvard on the award of an honorary Doctor of Letters in June 1978, when he denounced the West for its neglect of Christian responsibilities and its spiritual bankruptcy, or on the receipt of the Templeton Prize in London in 1983 when the religious emphasis in his thinking was especially marked.

His eighteen-year residence in the United States was spent mostly in the composition of 'knots' II, III and IV of *The Red Wheel (Krasnoe koleso)* and the third part of *The Gulag Archipelago* devoted to experiences of surviving the slave-labour system. Throughout the period of exile he remained convinced that he would eventually return to Russia, but to a Russia, in his view, modelled on neo-Slavophile principles and a socio-political form of subsidiarity reminiscent of the Swiss system. Hopefully, when the moment came for his return in 1994 after his citizenship had been restored in 1990, his message of a rebuilt Russia would have gone before him. Though his was a triumphant slow progress across Siberia from Magadan to Moscow by train, filmed for TV by the BBC, his welcome home was ultimately as characteristically lukewarm as that given to most prophets. He settled on an estate to the north of Moscow where, on the abandonment of his TV show and other public commitments, he lived until his death as reclusively as before, his most significant achievement at this time being the establishment of a generous literary prize.

Solzhenitsyn's literary reputation can be justifiably set within the tradition of Russian denunciatory literature that had its beginnings in the eighteenth century and the critical realism of much nineteenth-century writing. Denunciation and prophecy were never far apart in his work, with an increasing tendency for the publicistic element to overwhelm the literary. The harsh but memorable portrayal of the prisoners in *One Day* and *The First Circle*, the profound, often symbolic, analysis of the institutional forms and attitudes that gave rise to such gulag worlds, and the compressed power of his writing made his first works into outstanding examples of a literature combining denunciation of the Soviet system with universal literary values. His studies of the sickness pervading Soviet society in such brilliant pictures of enclosed, intimately observed worlds as those of *Cancer Ward* or his little masterpiece *Matryona's Place* demonstrated his remarkable authority as a writer whose range of critical assessment and philosophical awareness was matched by an equivalent understanding of the depths of emotion and commitment involved in human relationships. With the appearance of *August 1914* doubts about his imaginative power and ability to handle panoramic events on a scale matching **Leo Tolstoy's** were largely justified. The ensuing 'knots' of the tetralogy *The Red Wheel* comprising his longest work – *October 1916* (pub. 2 vols, 1984; trans. 1989), *Mart semnadtsatogo* (2 vols, 1986–8), *Aprel' semnadtsatogo* (1991) – were as much faction as fiction, designed to show a Russian readership the complex evolution of events, day by day and hour by hour, that led to the February Revolution of 1917 and **Lenin's** return from abroad. The crushing pressure exerted on the reader by *The Red Wheel's* ponderously detailed manner doubtless suggested realistically enough the slow, inevitable revolving of the wheel of history towards October.

Solzhenitsyn's birthright was the October Revolution and the Soviet Union that sprang from it. Even if he outlived it, his reputation must be largely confined to it. His commitment to Christianity derived from the bitterest personal experience, but his dislike of the Communist system, like his criticism of the West, transcended both the personal and the local in its insistence on sincere, if vaguely universal concepts of justice and responsibility that have their source in the human conscience. His most memorable pronouncements have concerned the writer's freedom of conscience, as, for example, his assertion that

> A writer's tasks ... concern the secrets of the human heart and conscience, of the conflict between life and death, the overcoming of spiritual sorrow and those laws extending throughout all humanity which were born in the immemorial depths of the millennia and will cease only when the sun is extinguished.

or a writer is both 'a humble apprentice beneath God's heaven' and 'a great writer is, so to speak, a second government. That is why no regime has ever loved its great writers, only its minor ones.' Solzhenitsyn, with his denunciatory exposure of the worst evils of the Soviet system, his readiness to denounce materialism, whether consumerist or ideological, his advocacy of spiritual values and his pleas for justice and freedom in his literary and publicistic work, was among the most significant moral authorities of the twentieth century.

Further reading

Other works include: *For the Good of the Cause* (1964); *Short Stories and Prose Poems* (1970); 'One Word of Truth Shall Outweigh the Whole World', The Nobel Speech (1972); *From under the Rubble, Lenin in Zurich*(1975); *The Oak and the Calf* (1980); *Invisible Allies* (1995). See: G. Lukacs, *Solzhenitsyn* (1970); L. Labedz, *Solzhenitsyn – A Documentary Record* (*1973*); M. Scammell,

Solzhenitsyn: A Biography (1984). J. Pearce, *Solzhenitsyn: A Soul in Exile* (1999); Harold Bloom (ed.), *Aleksandr Solzhenitsyn: Modern Critical Views* (2001).

RICHARD FREEBORN

SONDHEIM, Stephen

1930–

US musical theatre composer

Sondheim has spent his entire creative life living in Manhattan and writing musicals, or rather writing the music and lyrics for musicals, for the Broadway stage. This is a restrictive craft, one might think, essentially that of a songwriter, for unlike his teacher Oscar Hammerstein II, Sondheim leaves the 'book' – the spoken portion of a libretto – to others, which has not prevented the resulting musical plays being treated as though they were his, even when entire scenes play without music. His collaborators on the script have included Burt Shevelove (*A Funny Thing Happened on the Way to the Forum*, 1962; *The Frogs*, 1974, with Larry Gelbart); George Furth (*Company*, 1970; *Merrily We Roll Along*, 1981), James Goldman (*Evening Primrose*, for television, 1966; *Follies*, 1971), Hugh Wheeler (*A Little Night Music*, 1973; *Sweeney Todd*, 1979), John Weidman (*Pacific Overtures*, 1976; *Assassins*, 1991; *Bounce*, 2003) and James Lapine (*Sunday in the Park with George*, 1983; *Into the Woods*, 1987; *Passion*, 1994). As well as *Anyone Can Whistle* (1964), Arthur Laurents authored *West Side Story* (1957), *Gypsy* (1959) and *Do I Hear a Waltz?* (1965), the three shows for which Sondheim was asked to supply lyrics but not the music, which was by **Leonard Bernstein**, Jule Styne and Richard Rodgers respectively. An early show, *Saturday Night* (1954), was completed but not produced until 1997. The above titles furnish the Sondheim canon, augmented by occasional film songs (*Dick Tracy*, 1990) and one (non-musical) film score, *Stavisky* (1973). In show output Sondheim has outdistanced all the post-war Broadway masters including Rodgers and

Hammerstein (though Lloyd Webber, born on the same day seventeen years later, is fast creeping up on him). He has stuck to the game, often saying that the only way to overcome your critics is to outlive them.

At first Sondheim was seen as difficult and modernist. The episodic construction of *Company*, with its ambivalent ending, and the nervous breakdown in mid-song at the end of *Follies* (though this also happens in *Gypsy*), gave rise to much talk about 'concept musicals', their metaphoric packages deconstructing contemporary America in these two shows, as also its past in *Pacific Overtures* and *Assassins*; structural ideas are similarly part of the experience in *Merrily We Roll Along*, whose chronology runs backwards, *Sunday in the Park with George*, its second act set a hundred years after the first, and *Into the Woods*, which combines four fairy tales and places their 'happily ever after' only halfway through the narrative. But Bernstein's musical language in *West Side Story* was more aggressive and challenging than Sondheim's has ever been, and in the long run he is more likely to be viewed as the last classical master of the American musical in succession to Kern, **Gershwin**, **Porter**, Rodgers and their lesser contemporaries. Just as *Saturday Night* revealed his early melodiousness, *Bounce* (his last musical?) reinstates it, while his most musically affecting songs in between speak the common emotional language of tonality – 'What Can You Lose?' (*Dick Tracy*) a good example. Nevertheless, **Stravinsky** and musical minimalism had as far-reaching an effect on *Sweeney Todd* and *Sunday* as **Debussy** and **Rachmaninov** on 'Send in the Clowns' (*A Little Night Music*), Sondheim's best-known song. **Ravel** has been the most steadfast of his musical influences; those from pop music decidedly lacking (which separates Sondheim from Lloyd Webber), though jazzy pastiche occurs.

Sondheim the dramatist has accomplished the anatomy of twentieth-century manners, foibles and psychic *angst* with the devastating wit, logical cleverness and fundamental sympathy (though he was long judged cold) of an

Ayckbourn, a Neil Simon, perhaps an **Albee** when it comes to the downward trajectory. Lyrics accomplish this, and somehow so does the music; once again it hardly seems possible that he does not write the plays. **Stoppard** parallels the work he makes words do: 'Meanwhile' (its music too) structures a song and a philosophy in 'The Miller's Son' (*A Little Night Music*); 'Going, Going, Gone' cadences a melody, a metaphor, a relationship, an entire musical (*Merrily We Roll Along*); 'Today I Woke Too Weak to Walk' (*Forum*) takes algebra to explain its full network of melopoetic meanings. Sondheim's mind is extraordinary, its other outlets including published puzzles, two murder mysteries, and a town house full of artefacts that inspired Anthony Shaffer's *Sleuth*. Yet more important than this cleverness, his characters' monologues and their prickly or glowing harmonies have spoken to an era grasping at some epigrammatic beauty in the welter of urban postmodernity. Gays responded most; but the cultural resonances are far wider, with a Shakespearean richness in *Into the Woods* and *Sweeney Todd*.

Further reading

The complete piano/vocal scores of all the musicals, expensive but obtainable, are supplemented by a four-volume song anthology, *All Sondheim*. Most of the shows' playscripts are published with introductions. The essential book is Craig Zadan: *Sondheim & Co* (various editions); see also Stephen Banfield: *Sondheim's Broadway Musicals* (1993); Meryle Secrest: *Stephen Sondheim* (1998); and Mark Eden Horowitz: *Sondheim on Music* (2003).

STEPHEN BANFIELD

SPENCER, (Sir) Stanley

1881–1959

English artist

Stanley Spencer was one of the most eccentric artistic characters of the last century. Born in the small Berkshire town of Cookham, he studied at the Slade School of Art in London and was known to his roistering, Bohemian fellow students as 'Cookham' because of his habit of invariably going back there daily on the 5.08 train from Paddington.

Barely five feet tall, with a workhouse pudding basin haircut and a disastrous marital life, much recorded in his paintings and in an excellent play by Pam Gems called *Stanley*, he could, even when knighted, frequently be seen wheeling his painting gear around in a ramshackle perambulator.

He served, modestly and heroically, as a medical orderly in the Macedonian campaign in World War I; this gave rise to some notable war paintings which still dominate the permanent collection at the Imperial War Museum. In World War II he was an official war artist and painted remarkable large canvasses of the Port Glasgow Docks and factories. His other most notable war paintings are to be found in the frescoes he did for the Sandham Memorial Chapel at Burghclere in Hampshire, a private commission by the sister and brother-in-law of an army officer who also served in Macedonia but died there. When he secured the commission, being a great admirer of the Arena Chapel in Padua, he exclaimed, 'What ho, Giotto.'

Spencer, doubtless because of the complexity and failure of his marital life, devoted much energy to erotic drawings and paintings, and at one stage the awful anti-avant-garde President of the Royal Academy, Sir Alfred Munnings, tried unsuccessfully to get Spencer prosecuted by the Director of Public Prosecutions. His erotic masterpiece, known as the *Leg of Mutton* painting, is a bleak vision of sexual frustration.

Spencer once observed to his brother Gilbert, also a successful – although much more conventional – painter, that 'art is ninety per cent living'. This is doubtless why so much of his work is so personal in its imagery and why his student nickname of Cookham turned out to be so prophetic.

Apart from his war paintings and his highly charged pictures of wives and mistresses, his most notable pictures – and those for which he is most recognized – are his religious subjects, nearly all of which are set in an entirely recognizable Cookham high street and landscape. Spencer's daughter said that 'He was extremely sacramental', and religion was his second most cherished obsession after sex. Any broad description of his Cookham-fixated religious paintings could make him sound like a naïve artist, but this he was certainly was not. The almost architectonic skill of his vast compositions – *Resurrection, Cookham* of 1924–7 is 274 cm by 549 cm – is that of a highly sophisticated artist. As for the idea of placing Christ or various saints in a contemporary Berkshire countryside, he was simply following the practice of Renaissance artists who placed their holy men and women on the hillsides of Umbria or the campagna of Tuscany. (When Spencer went off to Macedonia and war he carried in his pockets little books of reproductions of paintings by Masaccio and Fra Angelico as well as Giotto.)

Not all his Cookham paintings are religious epics like *Resurrection* or *Christ's Entry into Jerusalem*. There are affectionate versions of the local regatta and even an immaculate and charming vision of a garage. Anything human interested him, although the religious and the erotic remained not only his most absorbing interests but also inspired his finest pictures. And while the *Leg of Mutton* painting is an agonized rendering of sexual dysfunction, the marvellous *On the Tiger Rug* is a joyous celebration of his affair with Daphne Charlton and presumably its title is meant to recall the doggerel: 'Would you like to sin/ With Elinor Glyn/On a tiger skin?'

Spencer was one of England's finest painters of the first half of the last century. He had no followers, had no influence because his style and his subject-matter were so personal, eccentric and idiosyncratic; but he is indispensable to the understanding of English art.

Further reading

See: Fiona MacCarthy, *Stanley Spencer: An English Vision* (1998); Maurice Collis, *Stanley Spencer (A Biography)* (1962); Keith Bell, *Stanley Spencer: A Complete Catalogue of the Paintings* (1993).

T.G. ROSENTHAL

SPIELBERG, Steven
1946–
American filmmaker

Born in Cincinnati, Ohio, raised in Scottsdale and Phoenix, Arizona, Steven Spielberg is now synonymous with Hollywood, the place and its metonymic associations, the film industry and film culture. At twelve years old he filmed an eight-minute Western; at fourteen he made a forty-minute war film; at sixteen he finished a feature-length science fiction movie. By the end of high school, he was working, as an office assistant, on the lot at Universal Studios. Though he was not accepted to film school, his short film *Amblin'* (1968) won a festival prize and got him another job at Universal, this time directing television dramas, including a *Columbo* mystery (1971) and a memorable episode of *Rod Serling's Night Gallery* (1970) starring Joan Crawford.

His first important film was the TV movie *Duel* (1971), which merited an international theatrical release. The story of a traveller harassed by an anonymous monolith, in this case a long-haul truck, would create a paradigm for the narrative structure of many of Spielberg's later films. In his first feature, *The Sugarland Express* (1974), an overwhelming force of police follow an escaped convict, his wife, and their hostage as the couple seek to reclaim their child. The monolith in *Jaws* (1975), of course, is the shark, the prototype for the dinosaurs of *Jurassic Park* (1993) and *The Lost World: Jurassic Park* (1997). With these films Spielberg also created an industrial model of turning best-selling adventure-thriller novels into blockbuster summer movies. *Raiders of the Lost Ark* (1981) and its second sequel, *Indiana Jones and the Last Crusade* (1989), exploit a monolithic evil of historical proportions, the Nazi party, its ideology and military power. War itself is the immeasurable, terrible adversary to be survived in *Empire of the Sun* (1987) and *Saving Private Ryan* (1998). And in *E.T. the Extra-Terrestrial* (1982) and *Minority Report* (2002) it is our own government and its unsympathetic, self-sustaining institutions that threaten the individual. A lone driver or adventurer, a small group of ordinary people, an abandoned child or alien – the protagonists of Spielberg's signature films are recognizable types (even the child-like E.T.) given mythic responsibilities, to find the intrepid soul within and prevail against unthinking, uncaring, seemingly unlimited enmity.

Several of Spielberg's most serious works complicate the paradigm. In *Amistad* (1997) government is challenged to repudiate the institution of slavery. His most complex work, *Schindler's List* (1993), analyses evil, investigating the psychology of Nazism and the vicissitudes and emotional toll of heroism. Commentators often note the recurring themes of family and fatherhood in most of Spielberg's work, from *The Sugarland Express* to *Catch Me If You Can* (2002). Steven Spielberg is the oldest of four children, has fathered four and adopted two, was distraught at his parents' divorce, and is divorced himself (and remarried to actress Kate Capshaw). In Spielberg films, fatherless families and failed, troubled husbands abound, like those in *Close Encounters of the Third Kind* (1977), *The Color Purple* (1985, from Alice Walker's Pulitzer-Prize novel) and *Artificial Intelligence: AI* (2001, taken over from **Stanley Kubrick**). Every kind of father figure and shade of fatherly behaviour, from the ideal (*Indiana Jones and the Temple of Doom*, 1984; *Saving Private Ryan*) to the demonic (*Jaws, Minority Report*) to the clash of both (*Hook*, 1991; *Jurassic Park, Schindler's List*), appear in Spielberg's filmography, and taken in total create an impressive exploration of the theme.

Spielberg's phenomenal popular success as a director – *E.T.* in the early 1980s and *Jurassic Park* in the early 1990s were both the largest grossing films ever – led to unrivalled power as a producer. In 1982 he formed Amblin Entertainment, a production company that created, among other projects, *Poltergeist* (1982), *Back to the Future* (1985), *Men in Black* (1997) and a number of his own most famous films. Amblin produced animated feature films and cartoon shorts and shows, and Spielberg was an executive producer on television series, such as *ER*, and mini-series, like *Band of Brothers* (2001). The Academy of Motion Picture Arts and Sciences awarded Spielberg the Irving G. Thalberg Memorial Award, an Oscar, in 1986 for producing a body of high-quality creative work in cinema. In 1994 he was one of the three founders of DreamWorks SKG, the first new fully functioning movie studio created in Hollywood in over seven decades. And after several nominations he won Academy Awards for Best Director for his work on *Schindler's List* and *Saving Private Ryan*. He has become a monolithic institution himself, a name above the title, but with such philanthropic projects as the Shoah Visual History Foundation, which records the testimony of Holocaust survivors and witnesses, he seeks to redress, to the extent that he can, the patterns of conflict and struggle throughout history and human psychology that his films record.

Further reading

See: Douglas Brode, *The Films of Steven Spielberg* (1995); Joseph McBride, *Steven Spielberg* (1997).

DENNIS PAOLI

STALIN, Joseph
1879–1953
Russian political leader

Joseph Vissarionovich Dzhugashvili – Stalin – was born at Gori in Tiflis province. A Georgian by nationality, he was the son of a shoemaker. In 1893 Stalin completed his studies at the ecclesiastical school in Gori. He entered the Tiflis Orthodox Seminary, which at that time was a hotbed of revolutionary ideas – populist, nationalist as well as Marxist. In 1897 Stalin became involved in Marxist circles there. In 1898 he officially joined the Tiflis Russian Social Democratic and Labour Party organization. Until his first arrest in March 1902 he was active in revolutionary politics. Over the next few years, but like thousands of the same generation, he was to be imprisoned and deported several times. Despite the mythology surrounding Stalin's early political years, it is clear that his overall role was only minor and his influence mainly provincial. He spoke no foreign languages. Unlike other Russian Marxists he had no experience of the European labour movement. As a Marxist theoretician he was irrelevant. He was above all an organization man whose roots were entirely Russian. It was for this reason alone that **Lenin** valued him. Stalin's one claim to early intellectual credibility, *Marxism and the National and Colonial Question* (1913, trans. 1936), was even written under Lenin's direction.

After the February Revolution in 1917, Stalin returned to Petrograd. For a short period and with Kamenev and Muranov, he led the Bolshevik Party. He declared himself in favour of lending critical support to the Provisional Government and of a Bolshevik–Menshevik unification. For fifteen days he opposed Lenin's 'April Theses' which called for a revolutionary transfer of power to the newly formed Soviets. His role during the October Revolution was marginal. The view, again fostered by Stalin in power, that he was Lenin's right-hand man and closest collaborator during the uprising is a complete distortion. Ironically, this description fits **Trotsky** far better.

During the Civil War Stalin, like many Bolsheviks, had military tasks thrust upon him. In this period his conflict with Trotsky, the main organizer of the Red Army, began to assume serious proportions. His ill will towards military 'specialists' of any kind and his refusal to obey orders during the Polish campaign were first shots in a long battle. In these conflicts Lenin consistently supported Trotsky.

Stalin's real role, however, was at the centre of the Party machine. With Sverdlov he kept the Party running during the repression of the Bolsheviks in July and August 1917; he was co-director of *Pravda*; one of the seven members of the Politburo, which was set up in October to prepare the

insurrection but never met; and he was Commissar for Nationalities. He was one of the four members of the 'small cabinet' of the Central Committee set up after October (Lenin, Trotsky, Sverdlov, Stalin). In 1919 Stalin was appointed Commissar for the Peasants' and Workers' Inspectorate (Rabkrin) and made one of the five established members of the first Politburo (Kamenev, Krestinsky, Lenin, Stalin, Trotsky); in April 1920 he became a member of the Orgburo. In April 1922 he was appointed as the Party's General Secretary. In the space of five years his organizational capacity and personal ambition at the centre of the merging party bureaucracy had led to an unbelievable accumulation of administrative posts.

In 1922 Lenin fell ill. In the course of the same year Stalin began to oppose Lenin on several fronts – on the foreign trade monopoly; on the Constitution of the USSR; on the Georgian nationality question; and on Lenin's increasing opposition to Stalin's power. In his Testament in 1922–3 Lenin finally called for Stalin's removal. Lenin's last heart attack in January 1923 probably saved Stalin.

With Lenin incapacitated (he died in January 1924), the oppositional tendencies divided and with his own control over the machine, Stalin's rise to power was assured. The receding prospects of world revolution, the political and social exhaustion inside Russia after the Civil War, and the general demoralization which pervaded the Party, all worked in Stalin's favour. The Left Opposition led by Trotsky, whatever the correctness of their views, were doomed to defeat. History was rapidly turning against a revolutionary programme.

Stalin's general strategy corresponded with the needs and aspirations of the growing Party bureaucracy. Socialism in one country, the campaign against egalitarianism, forced industrialization and collectivization and the whole conservative-nationalist retrenchment of the 1930s all related to their interests. The purges and destruction of the Old Bolshevik Party between 1936 and 1939 led to their final consolidation as a group.

Stalin's policy after 1929 was dictated by two considerations. One, was to ensure his own position and the second was rapid economic growth at any cost. The logic of this inevitably led to increasing repression, economic wastage and the extension of the forced labour camp system. Industrialization was thus purchased at enormous social and political cost.

The Second World War at first threw Stalin into disarray. It is clear that the Pact with **Hitler** (1939–41) had lulled the USSR into a false sense of security. Furthermore, the purges of the Red Army in 1937 had left the country dangerously exposed. All of these weaknesses were rapidly revealed in the early months of the war. However, Nazi racist savagery, the enormous sacrifice made by the Soviet people, and Allied military aid, finally helped turn the course of the war. Stalin, who had, in large part, prepared the ground for early Soviet setbacks, received much of the subsequent personal acclaim.

The post-war years saw no relief for the Soviet people. Sacrifice was still the order of the day. Repression in all spheres of life intensified – estimates of the total number of victims of Stalin's purges, policies and persecutions run as high as 17 million. The Cold War was functional for Stalin in so far as it provided the necessary justification for his harsh internal policies and his personal power. He died on 5 March 1953, revered, feared, but not loved; the USSR a world power, but clearly at variance with the socialist ideal.

Further reading

See: Boris Souvarine, *Stalin: A Critical Study of Bolshevism* (1939); Leon Trotsky, *Stalin: An Appraisal of the Man and His Influence* (2nd edn, 1946); Isaac Deutscher, *Stalin: A Political Biography* (2nd edn, 1966); Robert Conquest, *The Great Terror* (1968); Leonard Schapiro, *The Communist Party of the Soviet Union* (2nd edn, 1970); Robert Conquest, *Stalin: Breaker of Nations* (1991); Robert Service, *Stalin* (2004).

MICHAEL COX

STANISLAVSKY, Konstantin (Konstantin Sergeyevich ALEXEYEV)
1863–1938
Russian theatre director and actor

Stanislavsky was the stage-name of the son of a wealthy Moscow industrialist. He was, from an early age, fascinated by the theatre, and although, upon completion of his formal education, he joined the family business, Stanislavsky devoted much of his energy to amateur acting and directing. In 1888 he founded the Society of Art and Literature. In 1897 he met Vladimir Nemirovich-Danchenko, a successful playwright and teacher, and found they shared a profound disillusion with the state of contemporary Russian theatre. Out of their meeting came the establishment, in 1898, of the Moscow Art Theatre. The 'realism' of this new company made it an immediate success, with major productions of **Gorky**, Maeterlink, Shakespeare and, most important of all, **Chekhov**. From 1906 they frequently toured abroad. Although taking much of the directing upon himself, Stanislavsky also continued his own career as a performer, becoming one of Russia's leading actors, and the consummate interpreter of Chekhov. But Stanislavsky himself became increasingly dissatisfied with his own performances, and in 1906 attempted, for the first time, an analysis of acting techniques. From this he developed, over a period of years, a system of training actors which became known as the 'Stanislavskyan Method'.

Following the October Revolution, Stanislavsky continued to live and work in the USSR, making a major tour of Western Europe and the United States in 1922–4. During the 1920s he came in for considerable criticism at home, where he was accused of catering for bourgeois tastes. But, although producing several revolutionary dramas, he refused to give in to pressure, and was, during the 1930s, welcomed into the fold of official 'socialist realism'. In fact, the situation developed in which the methods of the bourgeois Stanislavsky were supported in opposition to those of the Marxist **Bertolt Brecht**. Stanislavsky spent his last years writing, and died in the city of his birth.

The essence of Stanislavsky's system is a rejection of the 'theatrical' in favour of the 'creative'. He recognized that much acting, including his own, was merely imitative, a series of stage-tricks slavishly repeated. In the work of a great actor, on the other hand, he saw an 'inner-truth', a sincerity which made a performance a 'reality' both for the actor and his audience. He wrote that, 'Nothing should take place … on the stage without having first gone through the filter of the artistic feeling for truth.' Acting, instead of being a conscious 'trick', should become a habit, a natural process. If someone 'acts' a role, rather than 'experiencing' it, his performance is a lie, and therefore, in Stanislavsky's terms, non-creative. He found that through total relaxation, attained by intensive physical and psychological exercises, it was possible to 'summon up' a performance at will, but always as a new experience, rather than a mechanical process. He called this the recreation of 'the life of the human spirit'.

It is a popular misconception that Stanislavsky's system demands that an actor be 'taken-over' by his part. On the contrary, it calls for a high degree of control, over voice, physical movement and the emotions. Stanislavsky often quoted the Italian actor Tommaso Salvini (1828–1916): 'An actor lives, weeps and laughs on the stage, and while weeping or laughing, he observes his laughter and tears.' It is impossible to overestimate the effect of Stanislavsky's ideas on the subsequent training of actors, especially in the United States, where Lee Strasberg, at the Actors Studio in New York, changed the whole face of American acting with his own idiosyncratic interpretation of 'the Method'.

Further reading

See: *My Life in Art* (1924, his only book to be published in the USSR during his lifetime); *An Actor Prepares* (1936); *Building a Character* (1949);

and *Creating a Role* (1961). See also: David Magarshack, *Stanislavsky: A Life* (1950) and *Stanislavsky on the Art of the Stage* (1950); R. Williams, *Drama in Performance* (1954); S. Moore, *The Stanislavski System* (1965); Jean Benedetti, *Stanislavski: A Biography* (1988); Sharon M. Carnicke, *Stanislavsky in Focus* (1998).

PAUL NICHOLLS

STEINBECK, John Ernst
1902–68
US novelist

John Steinbeck has always been popular with both European and American readers. As a serious novelist, however, he seems to have been more highly regarded outside his own country. Whereas the French included him in their honourable roll of '*les cinq grands*' modern American novelists, it is almost *de rigueur* for American critics to dismiss his achievement with some such adjective as 'sentimental' or 'primitive'. It is true that there is more than a streak of sentimentality in Steinbeck, and that his work, in general, showed a falling-off after *The Grapes of Wrath* (1939). He wrote some good things after that, however, and the sharpness of American critical comment makes one suspect an animus which has more to do with the sociology of his novels than with their literary merit.

There is a tendency, in other words, to criticize Steinbeck's treatment of social issues for being oversimplified and his characters for being grotesques. On both counts, the allegations are not without some justification. It is doubtful, however, whether it is valid criticism of a novel to say that *paisanos* never in real life lived like the characters of *Tortilla Flat* (1935), nor Oklahoma dirt-farmers like the Joads. The criterion is surely whether, given the terms within which he is working, the novelist's work as a whole has life and substance, and presents a convincing picture of human existence.

Steinbeck's best work – which is probably to be found in his short stories – does carry this kind of conviction. *The Red Pony* (1949) has that peculiar mixture of sympathy and savagery, an awareness of life's fundamentals, which all Steinbeck's best work has. When he attempts the larger canvas, however, his vision tends to become warped by the very sympathy which makes his shorter work so satisfying. This is true of *In Dubious Battle* (1936) and *The Grapes of Wrath* where fierce loyalties forced him nearer to propaganda than is healthy for a novelist. In quite another type of novel, *Of Mice and Men* (1937), not only the type of character chosen but also the manner in which the (simple-minded) protagonist is treated is more simple (and sentimental) than the highest standards require. Similarly, the near-whimsicality of *Tortilla Flat* turns into the gamey indulgence of *Cannery Row* (1945), without touching that norm of human conduct which, if Steinbeck only knew it, was his *forte*. Yet another attempt, *East of Eden* (1952) was too large, too rambling and too melodramatic for success, although, as one is always forced to recognize with Steinbeck's work, it is full of excellent things.

The quality of the *farouche* in Steinbeck spills over into his writings. Unlike **Hemingway**, he cannot seem to keep it in check for the sake of artistic perfection. Technically, there is some similarity between the two writers. Both, by selecting the minutiae of a given situation, render its inner emotion through a series of apparently objective notations. So far as their preoccupations are concerned, however, they seem to be working on different co-ordinates. Hemingway was always a conscious artist. Steinbeck comes near to achieving that kind of perfection only when, by a happy accident, his feeling for a simple human situation fuses with his talent for selecting significant detail. It is this quality which he so triumphantly achieves in *The Red Pony* and which could perhaps be called, after the French, 'poetic realism'. Here Steinbeck's 'primitivism' is subordinated to his humanity.

The so-called 'primitivism' of Steinbeck's view of life has been referred to his background. Born in 1902 in Salinas, California, he knew at first hand both the richness of nature and the poverty of man in 'The Long Valley'. From 1919 to 1925 he went to Stanford University, supporting himself by working as a labourer and 'sampling' courses that interested him. In 1925 he worked his way to New York on a cattle boat, as others had worked their way to Europe. Having written pieces for university magazines, his purpose was to make his living as a writer. After a short time as a reporter, however, he went back to California, and worked at whatever jobs he could get while writing his early novels.

The first to appear was *Cup of Gold*, an account, in fictional form, of the life of the buccaneer, Sir Henry Morgan. His early stories, all based on a Californian valley, were published in 1932 under the title of *The Pastures of Heaven*, a title taken from the Spanish and chosen with some ironical intention. *To a God Unknown*, in the following year, foreshadowed that feeling for the land, its nature and its rhythms, which was to be so strong a motif in Steinbeck's later work. During the twenty-seven years from *Tortilla Flat* to the award of the Nobel Prize in 1962, Steinbeck was a highly controversial figure, never lacking courage to attack the problems of the moment nor to present the joys and tribulations of people about whom only an act of self-abnegation would force the average novelist to write.

Steinbeck was always fascinated by biology. One remembers the land-turtle crawling across the Western highway at the beginning of *The Grapes of Wrath* and the comment that this implies on the 'Okies' who are to make their pilgrimage to California. Men may or may not have souls, he seems to be saying; this is something which cannot be measured or tested. What one *can* perceive, however, is that they are as subject to natural laws as the animals. This biological interest in human existence no doubt accounts for whatever simplification of human motive critics have found in Steinbeck's work. Yet despite this he never, as a narrower author might, gives the impression of being clinical, precisely because of the love and care he has for the simple people about whom he writes. He has an unembarrassed ability to speak out. He does not try to be clever or sophisticated. At his best he strikes a note of affirmation and this, coupled with his talent for selective detail, makes some of his characters and scenes stay in the mind long after the precise details of the novel or story have faded. Whether or not that makes him a great novelist is another matter. What is indisputable, however, is that he was a highly talented and serious one.

Further reading

See: E.W. Tedlock Jr and C.V. Wicker, *Steinbeck and His Critics: A Record of Twenty-Five Years* (1957); Peter Lisca, *The Wide World of John Steinbeck* (1958); Warren French, *John Steinbeck* (1961); F.W. Watt, *Steinbeck* (1962); P. McCarthy, *John Steinbeck* (1980); John H. Timmerman, *John Steinbeck's Fiction* (1986); Jay Parini, *John Steinbeck* (1994); John Steinbeck IV and Nancy Steinbeck, *The Other Side of Eden: Life with John Steinbeck* (2000).

GEOFFREY MOORE

STEVENS, Wallace

1879–1955

US poet

Now ranked with **Eliot**, **Pound** and **W.B. Yeats** as one of the outstanding English language poets of the twentieth century, it is only since his death that Wallace Stevens's technical mastery and seriousness have gradually assured him a reputation. There were perhaps two main reasons for this: first, his peculiar difficulty, arising from a conjunction of simple declarative grammar with extreme allusiveness of style; and, second, the unfashionableness of his poetic manner. In an age which demanded the bareness of later Yeats and the acerbity of early Eliot, Stevens's highly polished surfaces were impenetrable to all but the most persevering of readers. In particular some critics claimed that his poetry

lacked 'the urgency of human passion'. However, just as over the years most readers of poetry have grown familiar with Eliot's elliptical style, his personal references and highly subjective choice of literary allusions, so they have acclimatized themselves to Stevens. He is, in some respects, indeed easier for the 'unliterary' person – that ideal intelligent reader for whom even Eliot craved – since his difficulties are intrinsic and do not depend on reference to a body of literature which may or may not be known. Stevens's chief fault is a tendency towards whimsicality and aestheticism, but he is no more a mere player with words than Eliot is a mere paster-together of quotations. A meditative poet of the highest order, Stevens masked his seriousness with flippancy and bravura – mannerisms that were part of his literary *persona*.

Stevens was born in Reading, Pennsylvania, the son of Garret Barckalow Stevens and Mary Catherine Zeller Stevens. The Zeller family was Dutch and, according to Stevens's own account, went to America for religious reasons. After studying law at Harvard, where he was attracted to the teaching of Santayana, Stevens attended the New York University Law School. During the period between 1904, when he was admitted to the Bar, and 1916, when he became a member of the Hartford Accident and Indemnity Company, he practised both law and poetry in New York. He was associated with a Greenwich Village group of whom the leader was Alfred Kreymborg, and his poems were published in small magazines, among them Harriet Monroe's *Poetry*. It was not until he was forty-four that *Harmonium*, his first book, appeared. A second edition, revised and enlarged, was published in 1931, followed in 1935 by *Ideas of Order*. *Owl's Clover*, which he excluded from his *Collected Poems* (1954), came out in 1936, and was followed by *The Man with the Blue Guitar* (1937), *Parts of a World* and *Notes Toward a Supreme Fiction* (both 1942). *Esthétique du Mal* (1945), *Transport to Summer* (1947), *A Primitive Like an Orb* (1948), *Auroras of Autumn* (1950) complete the poetic canon, although since his death in

1955 Samuel French Morse has published plays and poems, either unprinted in book form or allowed to go out of print, in *Opus Posthumous* (1957). This book also contains Stevens's aphoristic 'Adagia' and other prose complementary to *The Necessary Angel: Essays on Reality and the Imagination* (1951).

A corporation lawyer in Hartford for nearly forty years of his life, Stevens negotiated the world of business with that mixture of diffidence and authority which is also part of the success of his poems. Behind what at first sight might seem like a charming example of Connecticut rococo, there stands the solidity of a Dutch barn, a toughness of mind scarcely equalled among poets of our time.

The surely savoured ambivalence of his situation reveals itself in the title of his first book. And the titles of the poems: 'Le Monocle de Mon Oncle', 'The Paltry Nude Starts on a Spring Voyage', 'The Worms at Heaven's Gate', 'Tea at the Palaz of Hoon' – what are we to make of them? Some have acute, if oblique, relevance; others are comments on the irony of the human situation as Stevens saw it. Stevens's poetic manner varies from the extravagant rhetoric of 'The Comedian as the Letter C' to the subtle sobriety of 'Esthétique du Mal'. Two main themes run through the bulk of his poetry: first, the matter of belief in the modern world, and second, the philosophical problem of appearance and reality. The 'belief poems' are central. From 'Sunday Morning' to 'Notes Toward a Supreme Fiction', Stevens was engaged by the problem of the religious man in a world whose religion he cannot accept. The woman in 'Sunday Morning' asks why she should 'give her bounty to the dead'. She feels that the things of this world are all that we know, in contrast to the myths of an afterlife which men in their hunger have fabricated for themselves. And yet, even despite her acceptance that 'divinity' must live within herself, she still feels the need for some 'imperishable bliss'. The answer that Stevens gives is a stoical one: that 'Death is the mother of beauty'. The awful fact of death, the knowledge that it is really the end

of existence, and that there is nothing beyond, enables us to savour the bitter-sweetness of the human situation. Stevens mocks the vision of paradise which we have created after our own image. There was a man called Jesus, but his tomb is no 'porch of spirits', only a grave. We are alone on this earth. No benign spirit watches over us. We have the world in our time, and that should be enough.

But it is not enough. If the reasoner is religious by nature, as Stevens was, age and maturity will yearly increase the necessity for belief in someone or something greater than man. Stevens found it in poetry, the 'supreme fiction'. As he said in a memorandum to Henry Church in 1940:

> The major poetic idea in the work is and always has been the idea of God. One of the visible movements of the modern imagination is the movement away from the idea of God. The poetry that created the idea of God will either adapt it to our different intelligence, or create a substitute for it, or make it unnecessary.

'Notes Toward a Supreme Fiction' deals with the basic philosophical and spiritual imperatives towards which Stevens had steadily been moving all his life. The imagination, in its attempt to abstract truth, brings up the idea of man, 'major man' – not the exceptional man, but the best in every man. Change, which we deplore as bringing death and destruction, is the source of vital freshness in life and its many forms. The flow of reality is that which brings us our moments of perfection, of happiness and love. The 'order' that Stevens seeks must be flexible, organic, partaking of the freshness of transformation. We must celebrate the world by a constant and amazed delight in the unexpectedness of each moment, a more difficult rigour than to follow ceremony in the form of traditional beliefs. This is the poet's way, and every man can be a poet, not necessarily by writing poems but by living with sensibility and wholeness.

'Notes Toward a Supreme Fiction' comprises an aggregate of ideas and feelings, expressed with such mutational amplitude, with such controlled jugglery of parenthetical impressions, that half a dozen lines of simultaneous commentary would be needed to do it justice. Yet, being supplied, they would, of course, do no justice at all, for it is the essence of Stevens's art that 'poetry is the subject of the poem' and that it 'must defeat the intelligence almost successfully'. Consistently, and with great courage, Stevens tackled what he saw to be the main problem of our time. Because he did it in poetry, and poetry which is very difficult, his art has not been sufficiently recognized. But by doing it this way, which was the only way he could – for he was a poet and not a philosopher – he could in a sense take his speculation further. His poetry begins where most other poetry leaves us, in a state of heightened awareness. Through the aesthetic experience he explored the possibility of a new epistemology, pushing the boundaries of poetic communication to a new limit. There is only one other modern American poet who is comparable with him in seriousness and range, and that is T.S. Eliot.

Further reading

See: Frank Kermode, *Wallace Stevens* 1960; Ashley Brown and Robert Haller, *The Achievement of Wallace Stevens* (1962); Marie Boroff, *Wallace Stevens, A Collection of Critical Essays* (1963); R.H. Pearce and J.H. Miller, *The Act of the Mind* (1965); Helen Vendler, *On Extended Wings* (1969); A. Walton Litz, *Introspective Voyager* (1972); Tony Sharpe, *Wallace Stevens: A Literary Life* (1999); Lee M. Jenkins, *Wallace Stevens: Rage for Order* (1999); Tim Morris, *Wallace Stevens: Poetry and Criticism* (2005).

GEOFFREY MOORE

STOCKHAUSEN, Karlheinz

1928–2007

German composer

It is not often that the trajectory of Western music, or any other art, has been decisively shaped by an orphaned farmhand. Yet that is exactly the situation in which the seventeen-year-old Karlheinz Stockhausen found himself at the end of the Second World War. Somehow, after a couple of years, he managed to enrol in a music education course at the conservatory (Musikhochschule) in Cologne. In August 1951 he went to the Summer Courses for New Music in Darmstadt, where he heard a recording of a radical, highly abstract new piano piece by **Olivier Messiaen**: *Mode de valeurs et d'intensités*. It was a classic epiphany: hearing this 'fantastic star-music' dispelled any residual post-war malaise: this was the path Stockhausen wanted to follow, and within a few months he was studying with Messiaen in Paris.

However, he didn't remain a 'follower' for long. Immediately after the Darmstadt experience, he had written *Kreuzspiel* ('Crossplay'), a piece whose rigorous numerical organization of every notated dimension – the pitches, length and loudness of notes, and even their timbre – made it, in retrospect, an early classic of so-called integral serialism. Such music constituted a conscious *tabula rasa*: it sought to sweep away everything that smacked of traditions (even the most recent ones) and start again from degree zero, but with a fanatical emphasis on the absolute conceptual unity of musical materials, and the need to recreate these materials 'uniquely' for each new work. When Stockhausen says that as a young composer he felt he had **Schoenberg** peering over one shoulder, and **Stravinsky** over the other, this had nothing to do with style, but everything to do with standards. His responsibility to the past was to surge beyond it: like **Rilke's** angels, he would 'obey by overstepping'.

Did Stockhausen's orphan status, coupled with his unquestionable genius, leave him ideally placed to head up this *tabula rasa*? Maybe so: at any rate, after returning to Cologne in 1953, for at least the next decade Stockhausen set the tone for the European avant-garde. Each new work opened up new perspectives, not only for himself, but for all the young composers around him. Within the newly evolving world of electronic music, it was he who set the standard – not just technically, but aesthetically: works like *Gesang der Jünglinge* ('Song of the Youths', 1956) and *Kontakte* ('Contacts', 1960) were unrivalled then, and in many respects remain so half a century later. But it wasn't just a matter of electronics: in his instrumental music there was an exploration of everything from the utmost control – as in *Gruppen* ('Groups') for three orchestras (1957), where each orchestral group plays highly complex music in a different tempo – to works in which the interpreter can significantly shape not only momentary detail, but even the overall form.

This was a time of stark polarities: of instrumental music versus electronic music, pitch versus noise, and European structuralism versus the seemingly anarchic freedom espoused by **John Cage** and his 'New York School'. Here, Stockhausen's genius lay not least in his capacity to posit seeming contradictions as opposite ends of a continuum, and to create aesthetically astounding works (such as *Kontakte*) that moved effortlessly through this continuum. But by the start of the 1960s, fuelled by what the composer and, subsequently somewhat regretfully, called 'utopian idealism', he was becoming increasingly fascinated by the idea of composition as a collaborative endeavour, to which he would contribute a structural framework and certain transformational processes, but leave their realization in 'real time' to his interpreters. A forerunner of this was *Plus Minus* (1963), a fascinating attempt – requiring careful realization – to formulate the creative act as a kind of genetic process where, in certain extreme situations, linear evolution leads to extinction or radical mutation.

In the short term this piece (which remains one of Stockhausen's most fascinating conceptions) was just too idealistic. In the following years there were three significant areas of exploration: one was live electronics, which brought sound transformations previously only available in the studio into the arena of live performance (the first examples are *Mixtur* and *Mikrophonie I*, both from

1964) and another was the expansion of new music's time scale to re-embrace works of epic proportions, such as *Hymnen* ('Anthems', 1967) and *Momente* (1965–72), both lasting a couple of hours. But perhaps the most striking and controversial strand in Stockhausen's work of the late 1960s is the series of 'process compositions' – for example *Prozession* (1967) and *Kurzwellen* ('Short-waves', 1968) – written for Stockhausen's own handpicked ensemble, where the scores were reduced to sequences of signs indicating how virtually any musical materials could be spontaneously transformed. The question of authorship implicit here became even more acute in the 'intuitive music' of *Aus den sieben Tagen* ('From the Seven Days', 1968), which comprises texts with instructions such as 'Play a vibration in the rhythm of the universe'. A priori, this may seem frankly absurd, but as the studio recordings from Darmstadt in 1969 show, it could give rise to a unique form of music-making, unthinkable without Stockhausen's involvement.

Yet if Stockhausen's open-form explorations of the late 1960s were controversial, the about-face signalled by *Mantra* (1970) for two electronically modified pianos proved even more so. It wasn't just a matter of returning to a very exactly structured music in which the central material had an almost 'retro' thematic content, but also of emphasizing a spiritual content that had always been implicit in his work but that most commentators had chosen to overlook. After the 1973 Parisian premiere of *Inori* ('Adorations'), a 70-minute work for praying mime and orchestra, Maurice Fleuret wrote, 'In drawing close to his God, Stockhausen is withdrawing from us.' And at least in a broad sense, it was true. Not only was he acutely aware of the spiritual gap that separated him from most of his more **Marxist**-orientated composer-contemporaries, but he had lost interest in being the avant-garde's figurehead. He had his own path to pursue: a music which sought to pave the way for a higher consciousness not necessarily defined by terrestrial models.

It is extraordinary to see how rapidly, especially in the early 1970s, former idolization turned to vilification, especially in Germany. It's as if, after the failures of 1960s idealism, people needed someone to hate and mock. The 'resentment against new music' that Theodor Adorno had invoked long before in relation to Schoenberg and his school now focused on Stockhausen, even – and in fact, especially – from within the ranks of the avant-garde. Former adherents, few of whom had achieved even a fraction of what Stockhausen had achieved, lost no opportunity to turn on him.

It was in this antagonistic context that Stockhausen embarked on a project that inevitably conjured up the name of **Wagner**. In 1977 he announced that the next twenty-five years of his life would be devoted to the composition of seven operas entitled *LICHT* – *the Seven Days of the Week*, and in fact this is (fairly) exactly what happened: the cycle was completed in 2003. The outcome – almost thirty hours of music, bound together by a 'Super-formula' that defines both macro- and micro-form – is perhaps the most extraordinary project in the history of Western music. Not least because of its overtly sacred orientation, it was initially the subject of trenchant criticism. Yet now, increasingly, its sheer musical substance is forcing a re-evaluation. Moreover, as the bland relativism implicit in postmodernist theorizing comes to seem ever more 'anti-aesthetic', Stockhausen's highly distinctive work provides an increasingly compelling counter-force.

Having completed *LICHT* ('LIGHT'), Stockhausen embarked on a new cycle of works entitled *KLANG* ('Sound', from 2004). Here, the 'Super-formula' concept of the previous twenty-five years was swept aside. Even in his seventies, Stockhausen constantly looked for new options.

Further reading

Other works include: *Zeitmaße* ('Time Measures', 1956) for wind quintet; *Carré* (1960) for four choirs and orchestra; *Trans* (1971) for orchestra; and *Sirius* (1975) for four soloists and electronic music. Stockhausen's own writings to 1991 are published in ten volumes of *Texte* ('Texts'). The main biography to date is Michael Kurtz, *Stockhausen: A Biography* (1992); the best English-language introduction to the music is Robin Maconie's somewhat idiosyncratic *The Works of Karlheinz Stockhausen* (2nd edn, 1990). Though over thirty years old, Jonathan Cott's book of interviews, *Stockhausen – Conversations with the Composer* (1973), can also be recommended. The Stockhausen entry in *The New Grove Dictionary of Music and Musicians* (2nd edn, 2001) includes a particularly comprehensive work list and bibliography.

RICHARD TOOP

STOPPARD, (Sir) Tom

1937–

British playwright

Tom Stoppard was a theatre critic before he was a dramatist, and it may have been this experience of watching things from out front that led him to declare, at a fairly early stage in his second career, that the audience owes the playwright absolutely *nothing*. He also said, equally sensibly, that the theatre ought to be in the hands of people who understand show business. This is also a playwright who has said that he would rather have written *The House at Pooh Corner* than the complete works of **Bertolt Brecht**, and who counts among his formative influences the memory of a line from *The Goon Show*: 'And then the monsoons came. And they couldn't have come at a worse time, right in the middle of the rainy season.' This is a playwright to love.

He has confessed to being driven by a consuming fear of being boring. To avoid this he has often filled his plays with contrasting elements: at one moment, metaphysical discussion, at another song-and-dance. Two of his major early plays, *Jumpers* (1972) and *Travesties* (1974), end with popular tunes ('Sentimental Journey' and 'My Blue Heaven' respectively) and their success may well have something to do with the fact that they sent their audiences home humming. Other playwrights have attempted to use music in the same way, but their efforts have usually come across as forced and programmatic. With Stoppard they seem spontaneous outgrowths of the exuberant dialogue and construction, which in turn are an expression of the writer's humanity. Other playwrights may treat of the human condition, social or metaphysical, with more obvious earnestness. He is almost alone in making the audience feel, through the actual texture of his work, that the condition is really worth bothering about – or, in plainer terms, that life might actually be worth living.

Stoppard used to divide his plays, in interviews, into 'nuts-and-bolts comedies' and seriously intended works. But this is misleading; the differences are more of scale than of kind. The obsessively neat patterning and verbal leap-frogging of *The Real Inspector Hound* (1968) parallel those in *Rosencrantz and Guildenstern are Dead* (1967 – the play that established him), *Jumpers* and *Travesties*. The long-running farce *Dirty Linen* (1976) may be slight but it deals with personal responsibility in public situations, as do the overtly political *Professional Foul* (television, 1976), *Every Good Boy Deserves Favour* (music by André Previn, 1977) and *Night and Day* (1978).

EGBDF deals with the persecution of dissidents in Soviet Russia, *Professional Foul* with state terror in Stoppard's native Czechoslovakia (which he left at the age of two). These plays prompted their first critics to welcome (or deplore) Stoppard's increasing 'seriousness'. But there is nothing in them that could not have been foreseen from *Jumpers,* the best comedy written in English since 1945. The play, which of all his work best achieves his stated aim of effecting a perfect marriage between play-of-ideas and madcap farce, is among other things a protest against intellectual bullying; and the introduction of a pugnacious (and electorally victorious) Radical-Liberal Party, represented on stage by a trendy and omnicompetent University Vice-Chancellor, is a clear indication of the ease with which this can extend to physical bullying. The nicest (though still dangerously self-absorbed) character on stage is the Professor of Ethics, trying to justify his belief in a moral force which he chooses, rather to his own embarrassment, to call God. In declaring that morality goes deeper than politics, and crucially influences it, Stoppard wrote a political play that made most others of the species look dangerously naive. *Travesties,* formally less satisfying, takes the argument a step further by examining the motives that make men into politicians, or for that matter artists: to each his own ego-trip. The play lines up **Joyce**, **Lenin**, the Dadaist **Tristan Tzara**; if the author's sympathies are obviously with the first, the artist, rather than with the two disparate (and highly plausible) philistines, this rarely upsets the comic balance.

Presiding over the whole, remembering it and usually getting it wrong, is the minor consular official Henry Carr, one of Stoppard's immortal onlooker figures (like Rosencrantz, Guildenstern, George of *Jumpers,* the theatre critics of *Inspector Hound* and the timid Moon of the 1966 novel *Lord Malquist and Mr Moon*). These culminate perhaps in the suaver academic philosopher of *Professional Foul* who is finally – perhaps marking a decisive breakthrough in Stoppard's work – nudged into action. He takes it by making exquisite and scrupulous use of the enemy's moral weapons, showing that Stoppard's symmetrical sense, of which an outward sign is his passion for puns, was as safe and as satisfying as ever.

The same critics who saluted Stoppard's new-found 'seriousness' also hailed the comparative naturalism of *Night and Day*, whose preoccupations included journalism and adultery. *The Real Thing* (1982) offered further comfort to those who wanted him to write the same kind of plays as everybody else, while dismaying those who would have preferred him to go on being himself. A fine revival in 1999, with far greater sexual presence, reassured both sides, revealing that he had in fact written a witty, painful and very personal play about love.

He seems to have dropped the distinction between serious plays and nuts-and-bolts assignments; his later works divide more into originals and adaptations. The latter category has been the likelier to release the funster in him, as in *On the Razzle* (1981, after Nestroy), in which virtually every line is a joke, and *Rough Crossing* (1984, after Molnar), which has a hilarious first act and a second which loses its audience by trying to make them follow a purposely incomprehensible plot. Curiously, he makes much the same mistake in the original and far more ambitious *Hapgood* (1988) which alienates its audience not with its discussion of quantum physics but with its hopelessly frustrating spy-story.

Among the adaptations must be included his many filmscripts including the excellent *The Russia House* (1990, from **John Le Carré**) and maybe the Oscar-winning *Shakespeare in Love* (1998) which seems to be a re-working of a script by Marc Norman (the two share credit) but which bears Stoppard's mark in almost every line. At any rate, it's an enchanting picture, crammed with characteristically telling anachronisms ('Their business is show,' cries a Puritan preacher, before being swept with the crowd into the first performance of *Romeo and Juliet*) and intoxicating as a love-letter to the theatre, whose 'natural condition' is definitively characterized as 'one of unsurmountable obstacles on the road to imminent disaster ... strangely enough it all turns out well'.

Back in the real theatre Stoppard reached mature twin peaks with *Arcadia* (1993) and *The Invention of Love* (1997). The former, juxtaposing nineteenth-century with modern action in the same country-house room, may be his most seamless structural achievement, both formally and intellectually; the latter may be his most moving, culminating in the cry of A.E. Housman – poet, scholar and unfulfilled homosexual – to his lifelong beloved: 'I would have died for you if I'd only had the luck.' It also has some of his sharpest jokes: 'I don't suppose I'll have time to meet everyone,' says Housman the classicist, on Charon's boat to the underworld: 'Oh

yes, you will,' says his conductor. His most recent play *The Coast of Utopia* (2002) has probably to be called his most ambitious; it's an uneven trilogy tracing the progress of the great generation of Russian idealists through the turbulent middle of the nineteenth century. The protagonist, Alexander Herzen, is told, 'You could be Minister of Paradox, with special responsibility for Irony,' which would be a fine office for Stoppard himself. He remains the wittiest and most humane of contemporary playwrights. Stoppard's literary and intellectual concerns have naturally made him a favourite subject for academic criticism, most of which reads like something that might be parodied in one of his plays. Few of the commentators (Jim Hunter is a notable exception) convey any sense of how his plays work in the theatre or of how blessedly funny they are.

Further reading

Other works include: *Enter a Free Man* (1968); *If You're Glad I'll be Frank* (radio, 1966); *Albert's Bridge* (radio, 1967); *After Magritte* (1970); *Dogg's Our Pet* (1971); *Artist Descending a Staircase* (radio, 1972); *New-Found-Land* (1976); *Dogg's Hamlet* and *Cahoot's Macbeth* (1979): *In the Native State* (radio, 1991); *Indian Ink* (1995) See: Tom Stoppard, *Conversations with Stoppard* (1995). See also: Ronald Hayman, *Tom Stoppard* (1977); Jim Hunter, *Tom Stoppard's Plays* (1982); Tim Brassell, *Stoppard: An Assessment* (1985); Michael Billington, *Stoppard the Playwright* (1987); Neil Sammells, *Tom Stoppard: The Artist as Critic* (1988); Anthony Jenkins, *The Theatre of Tom Stoppard* (1989); Jim Hunter, *Tom Stoppard* (2000); Katherine E. Kelly (ed.), *The Cambridge Companion to Tom Stoppard* (2001).

ROBERT CUSHMAN

STRAUSS, Johann
1825–99
Austrian composer

Johann Strauss was the most celebrated member of a distinguished Viennese family of musicians who made their names directing and composing for their own dance orchestras.

His father, the elder Johann Strauss (1804–49), had begun the family tradition, gaining acclaim during the second quarter of the nineteenth century not only in Vienna but also on extensive tours that included Britain in Queen Victoria's coronation season. Though nowadays remembered for his *Radetzky March* (1848), it was largely through the elder Strauss that the waltz became established not only as the principal attraction of elegant society balls but also as music worth playing and hearing for its own sake.

The father opposed his sons following in his footsteps, so that the younger Johann was at first intended for a banking career. However, with his mother's encouragement he had taken violin lessons from a member of his father's orchestra and subsequently studied theory with Joseph Drechsler (1782–1852). In October 1844 he made his début with his own small orchestra at a *soirée dansante* and soon began to establish himself as his father's most serious rival – a rivalry heightened when the two supported opposing factions in the Revolution of 1848.

After the father's death the younger Johann continued to extend the family reputation both in Vienna and further afield – eventually inheriting from his father the accolade of 'Waltz King'. In 1863 he was appointed to the official position of Music Director of the Court Balls. With the demand for his services increasing, he was fortunate to be able to enlist the services of his brothers Josef (1827–70) and Eduard (1835–1916). Now the orchestra could be split, to enable it to fulfil simultaneous engagements during Vienna's Carnival time (January/February) or to enable one portion to remain in Vienna while another went on tour. Johann himself conducted summer concerts at Pavlovsk in Russia annually from 1856 to 1865 and visited Paris and London in 1867 and Boston and New York in 1872.

By 1870, however, Strauss was increasingly recoiling from incessant public adulation. Simultaneously Viennese impresarios, alarmed at the dominance of the Viennese musical theatre by the imported works of Offenbach,

sought to enlist Strauss's services. He accepted, resigned his position as Music Director of the Court Balls and, with Josef now dead, left the direction of the family orchestra to Eduard. He continued to compose operettas for the rest of his life, while contriving to continue to provide new material for the ballroom by adapting themes from his operettas, as well as composing the occasional dance for special occasions. In the late 1880s his attention turned to the composition of a genuine opera, but the resulting *Ritter Pázmán* (Vienna Court Opera, 1 January 1892) enjoyed no more than a *succés d'estime*.

Besides his fifteen operettas, one opera and one ballet, Strauss's compositions number some 170 waltzes, 150 polkas, 30 polka-mazurkas, over 70 quadrilles and nearly 50 marches. His finest waltzes mostly date from the 1860s: *Accelerationen* ('Accelerations', 1860), *Morgenblätter* ('Morning Papers', 1864), *An der schönen blauen Donau* ('By the Beautiful Blue Danube', 1867), *Künsterleben* ('Artist's Life', 1867), *Geschichten aus dem Wienerwald* ('Tales from the Vienna Woods', 1868) and *Wein, Weib und Gesang* ('Wine, Woman and Song', 1869). Later examples include *Wiener Blut* ('Vienna Blood', 1873), *Rosen aus dem Süden* ('Roses from the South', 1880), the coloratura soprano showpiece *Frühlingsstimmen* ('Voices of Spring', 1883) and the *Kaiser-Walzer* ('Emperor Waltz', 1889). His most famous polkas include the *Annen-Polka* ('Anna Polka', 1852), the *Tritsch-Tratsch-Polka* ('Chit-Chat Polka', 1858), *Unter Donner und Blitz* ('In Thunder and Lightning', 1868) and the *Pizzicato Polka* (1869) composed jointly with Josef.

In assessing the stature of Johann Strauss's dance music one should not isolate his name from that of his brother Josef. Certainly Johann produced the more immediately striking and therefore more widely popular melodies. Josef, however, was perhaps the more cultivated musician, adding an extra sense of tenderness or emotional tension that leads many to consider his the greater talent. Between them, at any rate, they produced dance music unequalled by any of their many rivals, music which reflects the glamour and brilliance of the Habsburg monarchy at its height and which transcends the constraints of dance rhythms as never before or since. To the regular beat of the polka they added a unique range of picturesque invention, while always using with discretion the special effects that were often added to give a piece individuality. It was, however, in the rhythm of the waltz that they had the finest vehicle for their talents.

The standard pattern of the waltz had already been established in the works of the elder Strauss, with a sequence of simple waltz themes preceded by an introductory section and rounded off by a coda recapitulating the main themes. His sons developed the structure by building up the introductions into miniature tone poems, lengthening the span of the waltz melodies and extending their range of expression. None of their imitators ever approached their consistent freshness of invention, their ability to build upon a striking main theme and renew attention throughout, or the utterly natural way in which they integrated the various contrasted waltz sections. The refined shading of their orchestration has always been especially admired.

For the composition of operettas Strauss was far less well suited. He never became a good judge of a libretto and never acquired a taste for setting lyrics to music. Some of the best music came when, in possession of no more than an outline of the action, he built up an appropriately atmospheric sequence of melodies to which words were then fitted by his lyricist Richard Genée (1825–95). It was his prodigious melodic invention that enabled him to overcome his natural shortcomings and create the distinctive Viennese operetta based on the waltz – a form successfully developed in the twentieth century by such composers as Franz Lehár (1870–1948). Of Strauss's fifteen operettas three are acknowledged masterpieces, each with its own distinctive style – the sparkling *Die Fledermaus* ('The Bat', 1874), the graceful *Eine Nacht in Venedig* ('A Night in Venice', 1883) and the more solid *Der Zigeunerbaron* ('The Gipsy Baron', 1885).

In his time Strauss used the popularity of his orchestra to introduce new music to a wider public – introducing themes from **Wagner's** *Tristan und Isolde* to Vienna for the first time and giving the première of an early **Tchaikovsky** composition in Pavlovsk. In return he enjoyed the admiration of many of the greatest musicians, including **Brahms** who was a close personal friend. In our own time, too, his music continues to be performed around the world by the greatest orchestras, opera companies, conductors and singers to a degree enjoyed by no other composer of music for the ballroom and popular musical theatre.

Further reading

See: *Johann Strauss: Weltgeschichte im Walzertakt* (1975). Biographies in English include Joseph Wechsberg, *The Waltz Emperors* (1973), but the best assessment is the article (including list of works and bibliography) by Mosco Carner and Max Schönherr in *The New Grove Dictionary of Music and Musicians* (1980).

ANDREW LAMB

STRAUSS, Richard George
1864–1949
German composer and conductor

Strauss was born in Munich, a true Bavarian. His father was Germany's foremost horn-player and his mother was of the Pschorr Brewery family. Richard was brought up comfortably and first showed signs of unusual talent when he composed a Christmas song at the age of four. He entered the Munich Ludwigs-gymnasium in 1874, went to Munich University in 1882 and thence to the Academy of Music in 1894. By the time he was sixteen he had mastered every aspect of composition, and in 1885 was given his first musical post as assistant to Hans von Bülow in Meiningen. After only a month, Strauss was left in charge of the Ducal Orchestra, where he learned the repertoire by having to play it. Between 1886 and 1889 he was third conductor at the Munich Court Theatre where he suffered under two seniors, both jealous because of the demand for Strauss to conduct his own works elsewhere. In 1887 his *Aus Italien* branded him avant-garde in Munich itself. In 1889 he became a musical assistant at Bayreuth and conductor of the Weimar Court Theatre where his revolutionary tone-poem *Don Juan* was first heard. In 1894 his first opera *Guntram* was a failure (it was too Wagnerian in concept) but he married the prima donna, Pauline de Ahna, daughter of a general and his former pupil. From then on she ruled Strauss and his life with iron discipline.

Further tone-poems added lustre to his reputation for variety and instrumental skill, and in 1896 he returned to Munich as principal conductor. In 1897 his only child, Franz, was born and in the following year the family moved to Berlin where Strauss became principal conductor at the Court Opera, a post he retained until 1918. So far his output, apart from considerable conducting engagements, was in two forms: songs (*Lieder*) and the tone-poems.

In 1901 he redeemed the failure of *Guntram* with *Feuersnot* (Dresden), a light and indelicate opera produced as a tilt against the Munichers. In 1903 Strauss received his PhD degree from Heidelberg as token of their esteem, an honour which he always cherished and wrote into every signature. The first important opera *Salome* (Dresden 1905) was to his own libretto from a German translation of **Oscar Wilde's** play. This fascinatingly barbarous score scandalized the Kaiser and Kaiserin and was censored by the church in Vienna. But it soon brought Strauss sufficient royalties to enable him to build his ideal house in Garmisch at the foot of the Bavarian Alps. Next came *Elektra* (Dresden 1909), another morbid one-act opera, this time to a libretto by the brilliant Austrian poet Hugo von Hofmannsthal. At this point Strauss may be seen as leader of European music, verging on the emergent achievements of the Second Viennese School of composition (**Schoenberg**, **Berg** and **Webern**). Had he pushed his thoughts beyond *Elektra* into complete atonality, Strauss would have aligned himself with them. But instead he quickly succumbed to a charmingly romantic libretto by Hofmannsthal who did not want to lose such a collaborator. This was, in avant-garde terms, a retrograde step, for the opera was *Der Rosenkavalier* (Dresden 1911). It made a fortune for both Strauss and Hofmannsthal, and immediately Strauss made or authorized many popular arrangements of its melodies. Hofmannsthal's next libretto was more complex: a new translation of Molière *Le Bourgeois Gentilhomme* (as a play with incidental music) followed by the one-act opera *Ariadne auf Naxos* (Stuttgart 1912). In this cumbersome form the hybrid work was scarcely viable and only after much recrimination between its two creators was the opera prefaced by a sung prologue to make an evening's entertainment (Vienna 1916), and the play was abandoned. But in between the two versions of *Ariadne*, Strauss and Hofmannsthal embarked upon their most ambitious project, a huge fairy-tale moral, very complex in its story and making heavy demands upon producer and theatrical effects. This was *The Woman without a Shadow* (*Die Frau ohne Schatten*, Vienna 1919). Before it had been half finished, the First World War intervened.

Strauss lost his entire fortune, banked in London, and had to postpone his intention to give up conducting altogether in 1914, when he was fifty years old, so as to devote his full time to composing. In 1915 he completed a vast symphony that told a day's adventure in the Alps (*Eine Alpensinfonie*, 'Alpine Symphony', 1915) but this was – had to be – the last composition conceived in massive terms.

In 1919 Strauss became co-director of the Vienna Opera with Franz Schalk (they did not get on), and began to work on a bourgeois comedy as an opera to his own libretto. *Intermezzo* (Dresden 1924) was conceived in a series of almost filmic scenes, scored in a new and economic manner; but the two former collaborators again worked on *Die aegyptische Helena* (*The Egyptian Helen*, Dresden 1928), a less than satisfactory opera, and the partnership culminated with *Arabella* which attempted to be a later Viennese story in the *Rosenkavalier* vein. Hofmannsthal completed a difficult scene the day before his sudden death in 1929, leaving Strauss to finish composing, and to supervise the production (Dresden 1933) – a task which Hofmannsthal had always insisted upon undertaking.

In the same year Strauss returned to Bayreuth to conduct **Wagner's** *Parsifal* in the emergency of Arturo Toscanini's withdrawal on political grounds. This put him unintentionally into Nazi favour and helped to secure him the (unwanted) post of Head of the German Chamber of Music (Reichsmusikkammer) in 1934. Strauss was at a loss for an operatic partner until he found Stefan Zweig and his adaptation of Ben Jonson's *Epicoene*. Called *The Silent Woman* (*Die schweigsame Frau*, Dresden, 1935), the libretto suited Strauss admirably, and he quickly composed the complex, jovial score. But Zweig was Jewish and the Nazis were in full power in 1935. After four performances the opera was proscribed and, because of a politically tactless letter between Strauss and Zweig which the authorities intercepted, the composer was stripped of his office, reputation and all performances of his works in the Reich for a year.

Now unable to work any longer with Zweig, Strauss was recommended to a scholarly but extremely dull man called Joseph Gregor, whose three synopses (which all had their origins in previous ideas by Hofmannsthal or Zweig) were found to be acceptable. These operas, *Friedenstag*, *Daphne* and *Die Liebe der Danae*, were composed and were moderately successful between 1940 and 1946. By then the Second World War had begun and Strauss was again financially handicapped by lost royalties. He began to compose in an altogether fresh and economic manner as exemplified in the intellectual opera *Capriccio* (Munich 1942), and by several fragrant orchestral works of chamber proportions. He was mortified by the destruction of the principal German and Austrian opera houses in which his masterpieces had first

been presented, and his *Metamorphosen for 23 Solo Strings* expresses his grief in music.

Strauss's Jewish daughter-in-law and his two half-Jewish grandsons came under his protection in Garmisch, and in order to secure their immunity Strauss was forced to abide by detestable political actions in order to save them – which he did. At the end of the war he was a sick man, almost penniless, and disgusted at the vanquished regime. Sir Thomas Beecham organized a Strauss Festival in London in 1947, where he was fêted and made to feel most welcome. He died in 1949, with his final composition *The Four Last Songs* (*Vier letzte Lieder*, London 1950) a perfect epitaph.

Strauss's composing career bridged sixty years, from *Don Juan* in 1889 to the *Four Last Songs* in 1948. This included contemporary romanticism, through a period of almost atonality (and certainly abrasiveness) and back to lush romanticism at a time when the so-called leading composers were treading harsher paths. A fervent admirer of Mozart, Strauss had an unparalleled skill with orchestral sound, a 'lifelong love-affair with the soprano voice' and the instant ability to create a theme to highlight words, then to get as much out of that theme as he possibly could. As a first-rate conductor he came to minimize his gestures to a flicker, yet got enormous results thereby; and this practical ability not only earned him a great deal of money but put him constantly among working musicians, new works by others and the standard repertoire.

Further reading

Other works include: ballets: *The Legend of Joseph* (*Josephslegende*, Paris 1914); *Whipped Cream* (*Schlagobers*, Vienna 1924). Other tone-poems: *Death and Transfiguration* (*Tod und Verklärung*, 1890); *Thus Spake Zarathustra* (*Also sprach Zarathustra*, 1896); *Don Quixote* (1898); *A Hero's Life* (*Ein Heldenleben*, 1899). Concertos: Violin (1882); Horn No. 1 (1885); Horn No. 2 (1943); Piano (1890); Oboe (1946); *Duet Concertino* for Clarinet, Bassoon and Strings with Harp (1948). Chamber music: two Suites for thirteen winds (1882, 1884); two Sonatinas for sixteen winds

(1944, 1946). Songs: 197 songs for voice and piano; sixteen songs for voice and orchestra (1868–1950). About Strauss: *Strauss – Hofmannsthal Correspondence* (1952, trans. 1961); Norman Del Mar, *Richard Strauss: A Critical Commentary on His Life and Works* (1962, 1969, 1972); E. Krause, *Richard Strauss, Gestalt und Werk* (1956, *Richard Strauss: The Man and His Work*, 1964); *Richard Strauss. Correspondance. Fragments de Journal*, ed. R. Rolland (1951, *Strauss–Rolland Correspondence*, 1968); A. Jefferson, *Richard Strauss* (1973); Matthew Boyden, *Richard Strauss* (1999); Bryan Gilliam, *The Life of Richard Strauss* (1999); Michael Kennedy, *Richard Strauss* (2005).

ALAN JEFFERSON

STRAVINSKY, Igor Fedorovich

1882–1971

Russian composer

Born into a prosperous middle-class family, Stravinsky was a late starter as a composer. His father was a bass singer at the Maryinsky Theatre in St Petersburg, and Stravinsky had the Russian theatre, particularly ballet, in his blood. He attended St Petersburg University (1901–5), allegedly studying criminal law and legal philosophy, in fact developing his musicianship. It was not until 1902, with the death of his father, that he began to study composition, privately, with **Rimsky-Korsakov**. A close relationship thereafter developed between the young Stravinsky and this master, until the latter's death in 1908.

Stravinsky was twenty-eight when he was abruptly launched into international fame, which never left him, by *The Firebird* – the first of the glittering series of Russian ballets prompted and staged by his compatriot **Diaghilev**. But some of the works written prior to that date are of key importance, his *gradus ad Parnassum*. Starting with some derivative piano pieces, such as the *Scherzo* (1902) and the Sonata in F sharp minor (1903–4), his apprenticeship ends with the Symphony in E flat (1905–7). Three orchestral works follow which are of genuine artistic importance: the short fantasy *Fireworks* (1908), the *Scherzo Fantastique* (1907–8), and the lost *Chant Funèbre* (1908) in memory of Rimsky-Korsakov. The

Scherzo, for instance, even allowing for the sense of orchestral colour handed down from his teacher, the scherzando element of Mendelssohn, and a dash of **Wagner** and **Tchaikovsky**, still contains music which is recognizably Stravinsky's own. And it was after hearing a performance of this work, together with *Fireworks*, in early 1909, that Diaghilev invited Stravinsky to be associated with his new Ballets Russes.

Until 1913, when he moved to Switzerland, Stravinsky lived with his wife Catherine at Oustilug, a small village about a hundred miles south of Brest-Litovsk. His family included two sons, Theodore and Soulima, and two daughters, Ludmilla and Milena. The outbreak of war in 1914 cut him off from Russia, and he did not return there until 1962, when an official visit brought him back to the city renamed Leningrad. But in 1920, after spending the years of the First World War in Switzerland, he settled in France. It was there, as he said, particularly in Paris that 'the pulse of the world was throbbing most strongly'. In 1934 he became a French citizen; the following year he published his memoirs – in French. He remained in France until 1939, when he emigrated to America, following several visits to, and commissions from, that country. That was a year of triple bereavement for the composer, when his elder daughter Ludmilla, his wife Catherine and his mother all died. Soon after his arrival in America he was joined by Vera de Bosset, who became his second wife in March 1940. The couple settled in Los Angeles. Here they stayed until September 1969, when, largely for medical reasons, they moved to New York. There Stravinsky died in 1971, at the age of eighty-nine.

His output falls into three phases, Russian, neo-classical and serial. The first phase consists primarily of works written for the stage, of which there were nine: *The Firebird* (1910), *Petrushka* (1911), *The Rite of Spring* (1913), *The Nightingale* (1914), *Renard* (1916), *The Soldier's Tale* (1919), *Pulcinella* (1920), *Mavra* (1922), *The Wedding* (1923). The last of these was also the last to be written for Diaghilev, who produced all but one (*The Soldier's Tale*). Other works of this phase include some important songs, chiefly *Three Japanese Lyrics* (1913) – wrongly claimed by many as showing the influence of **Schoenberg**, whose *Pierrot Lunaire* had been heard by Stravinsky shortly before – *Pribaoutki* (short nonsense songs, 1914, for which no translation is possible), and the *Three Stories for Children* (1915–17); the cantata *The King of the Stars* (1912), which is a vision of the Last Judgement by the Symbolist poet Balmont; and the *chant funèbre* in memory of **Debussy**, called *Symphonies of Wind Instruments* (1920). It is assumed that this work contains similarities of scoring to the earlier piece written for Rimsky-Korsakov, unless and until that is discovered.

Stravinsky's second phase, which terminates with the opera *The Rake's Progress* (1948–51), is usually, and correctly, described as neo-classical. In the case of this composer, neo-classicism was not simply a retreat into the past, nor a form of academic pastiche, nor merely a series of quotations of other composers' ideas; rather, it was a re-thinking and a re-application of aesthetic principles of the classical period. Stravinsky's curiosity was insatiable, and it is interesting that as he moved forward and progressed, so his musical sources extended further into the past. Machaut and Gesualdo came to replace Bach and Beethoven. The majority of his neo-classical works are for the concert hall rather than the stage, and they culminate in the two great orchestral works, the Symphony in C (1940) and the *Symphony in Three Movements* (1945), first heard in Chicago and New York respectively. Indeed, after the Russian works of the first phase, the interest in Stravinsky's new compositions was stronger in America than it was in Europe – which was one factor in his deciding to emigrate to that country.

To this second phase belong some of Stravinsky's best-known and most performed works. Concert works include the *Symphony of Psalms* (1930), the Violin Concerto (1931), *Duo Concertant* (1932), and the *Mass* (1948); stage works include *Oedipus Rex* (1927), *Apollo* (1928), *Persephone* (1934), *Orpheus*

(1947). It will immediately be obvious that these titles show a marked predilection for classical Greek ideals. The exception is *The Card Party* (1936), though this is imbued, from first note to last, with the vocabulary of classic dancing and the classic tradition of the theatre. The same may be said for the ballet based on arrangements of Tchaikovsky's music, *The Fairy's Kiss* (1928).

In his third phase Stravinsky exploits the possibilities of serialism, following the example of **Webern**. Beginning hesitantly with the *Cantata* (1952) and the *Canticum Sacrum* (1956), which mark the transition, Stravinsky's characteristic style gradually reveals itself as being chiefly appropriate for vocal, religious music in this last stage of his life. Representative works are *Threni* (1958), *A Sermon, a Narrative and a Prayer* (1961), *Abraham and Isaac* (1963), and *Requiem Canticles* (1966), which was his last important work. It should be heard together with the *Introitus* in memory of **T.S. Eliot** (1965), which contains the opening words of the Requiem. Other works of this phase include, for the stage, *Agon* (1957) and *The Flood* (1962) and, for the concert hall, *Movements* for piano and orchestra (1959) and *Variations* (1964) in memory of **Aldous Huxley**. One of the chief fruits of his exploration into the possibilities of the serial method is his discovery of a new form of choral polyphony, based on canon. The creative impulse behind this was religious. He was a man of profound faith; as he says in *The Poetics of Music* (1947), quite explicitly, his creative work is the product of his conscience and his faith; indeed, the Russian Orthodox Church gave him just that spiritual *ordonnance* on which his life rested. Since choral, polyphonic music is traditionally the music of the church, it was through choral music that Stravinsky realized his religious nature. Moreover, serialism, as a principle of composition, is as remote as it could be from subjective emotion; and in this respect Stravinsky saw his new polyphony as most truly reflecting the spiritual aspiration of the universal church.

Stravinsky is the most representative of twentieth-century composers. His career began when, in the wake of Wagner, Western music had forsaken a single, common language. The period between the wars witnesses a polarization, between the Austro-German school on the one hand, whose representative was Schoenberg, and the Franco-Russian school on the other, of whom the most prominent was Stravinsky. The final period of his life witnessed his bringing together these two streams, so long divided. In this sense his work may be seen as reuniting and revitalizing twentieth-century music.

He has exercised a mesmeric hold over successive generations of European musicians, who no sooner would become acquainted with a particular aspect of his style, and maybe reproduce it themselves, than they would be disconcerted to see that its creator had moved off into some fresh territory. With each successive phase Stravinsky altered the face of Western music. He was incapable of repeating himself. Born outside the Austro-German tradition, he was not subject to the ardent yet limiting nationalism of the Second Viennese School, which claimed so many casualties in the first half of the twentieth century; at the same time he had the liveliest curiosity about everything that affected the *materia musica*, and about all aspects of music, from that of his contemporaries right back to the pre-classical period.

The Russian works of Stravinsky's first phase have a chief identifying characteristic – the development of rhythm, and metre, as an entity in itself. The nineteenth century, the age of Romanticism, had singled out harmony as the most important factor in musical composition; it was regarded as the parent of melody, the source of music's structures; rhythm was taken to be of subsidiary importance. *The Rite of Spring* abruptly changed that. Rhythm, as a separate structural element, was now emancipated – a fact which many later composers, notably **Messiaen** and **Elliott Carter**, have recognized as a turning-point in the evolution of Western music.

The neo-classicism of Stravinsky's second phase has frequently been criticized, even dismissed as irrelevant and reactionary, by the more radical avant-garde, particularly in Europe. **Pierre Boulez** may be taken as representative of this shade of opinion. But the criticism is usually based on a misunderstanding of Stravinsky's creative purpose, which was one of order, and the revitalizing of tradition. This feature is indeed a prominent one in works of all three phases, not least in his serial works. It was a view he shared with Webern. But whereas the latter interpreted the twelve-note laws of his teacher Schoenberg within the strict confines of the Viennese tradition, Stravinsky saw in Webern's technique the suggestion of something much broader; an entirely new concept of order, and fresh possibilities for the enrichment of the melodic/harmonic tradition of Western music as a whole. He discovered new areas of tonality beyond the limits of the major and minor keys. The range of the tonal spectrum appeared enormous, extending from, at the one end, primary chords and keys, to, at the other end, the most abstruse chromatic relationships. Serialism seemed to Stravinsky the means whereby this new resource, hitherto untapped, could be exploited. He said in 1958, which was the year of the *Threni* and *Movements*, 'My recent works are composed on the – my – tonal system' (in *Conversations*, see below). This fresh and latest discovery was to prove just as far-reaching and radical as his exploitation of rhythm in the works of his first phase.

Further reading

See: *Chroniques de ma vie* (1935, translated as *Chronicles of My Life*, 1936) and *An Autobiography* (1936). With Robert Craft: *Conversations with Igor Stravinsky* (1959); *Memories and Commentaries* (1960); *Expositions and Developments* (1962); *Dialogues and a Diary* (1963); *Themes and Episodes* (1966); *Retrospectives and Conclusions* (1969). By Robert Craft: *The Chronicle of a Friendship* (1972); *Prejudices in Disguise* (1074); *Stravinsky in Pictures and Documents* (1978). See also: N. Nabokov, *Igor*

Stravinsky (1964); Francis Routh, *Stravinsky* (1975); R. Vlad, *Stravinsky* (1958, trans. 1960, 3rd edn 1978); Stephen Walsh, *The Music of Stravinsky* (1993) and *Igor Stravinsky* (2000, first of a two-volume biography); Charles M. Joseph, *Stravinsky Inside Out* (2001); Stephen Walsh (ed.), *The New Grove Stravinsky* (2004). Stravinsky's music is published by Boosey and Hawkes, B. Schott's Sohne, and J. and W. Chester Ltd.

FRANCIS ROUTH

STRINDBERG, Johan August

1849–1912

Swedish playwright and author

Strindberg's father was a steamship agent who married his housekeeper in 1847, after she had already borne him three children. Her death when he was twelve left Strindberg feeling deprived. He was married three times to women who all put their own careers first, and did not want to mother him. He had a pietistic upbringing which marked him for life, and he was never at ease without God. Before he discovered his vocation as a writer Strindberg tried a number of occupations: student, doctor, actor and journalist. He wrote his first masterpiece *Master Olof (Mäster Olof)* in 1872, a play about the Lutheran reformer of the sixteenth century, Olaus Petri, but in spite of its deep psychological insight and brilliant dialogue it had to wait nine years for printing and performance. This was to be the pattern of Strindberg's career as a dramatist in Sweden. He never had more than brief periods of success, chiefly because he was always in advance of his times.

Fortunately for him he could write other things than plays. His seventy dramatic pieces are contained in only seventeen of the fifty-five volumes of his collected works. The rest contain poetry, novels, history, essays, pseudo-scientific and alchemistic writings. He made his breakthrough in Sweden with a novel, *The Red Room (Röda rummet,* 1879), a biting but light-hearted satire, written in sparkling Swedish, about his experiences in Stockholm. His first really successful play, *Lucky Peter's Travels (Lycko Pers resor,* 1882),

was also a satire about the folly of illusions, a favourite theme in his later plays. This was preceded and followed by works that made him so unpopular in Sweden that he went to live abroad. In Switzerland, hoping to reinstate himself, he wrote *Getting Married (Giftas,* I–II, 1884–5), two volumes of short stories about sex and married life. But the first volume precipitated a trial for blasphemy, engineered, as he thought, by the feminists whom, though he was acquitted, he attacked with great bitterness in the preface and in some of the stories of the second volume. 'The Breadwinner', the last story in the book, was seen as a slur on his first wife, the would-be actress Siri von Essen, and only served to increase his unpopularity. This was the first serious crisis in his life, mental and physical. Theatres were afraid to perform his plays, publishers to print his books. The second volume also established his reputation as a misogynist, later confirmed by the so-called 'naturalistic' plays, the only works by which he is widely known in this country. But though for a period Strindberg was fiercely anti-feminist, he was no misogynist. 'I love women and I adore children and, as a divorced man, I recommend marriage as the only commerce between the sexes,' he wrote in a letter of 1892. In many of his later dramas, including his historical plays, there is little trace of the woman-hater.

Strindberg was an omnivorous reader. Kierkegaard, Brandes, **Mill**, **Darwin** and Spencer were on his bookshelves before 1886; then, in order to understand the working of his own mind and the minds of others, he turned with enthusiasm to psychology and pathology, and studied among others the Frenchmen Jacoby, Ribot and Garnier, and the Englishman Maudsley, in whose book *The Pathology of Mind* he found a complete diagnosis of himself. It is difficult to say how far this reading coloured the self-portrait in his autobiographical work *The Son of a Servant (Tjänstekvinnans son,* 1886). He was an inveterate role-player, and what he says about himself must not be taken at its face value. He used his new knowledge to good effect when he wrote the three powerful plays which, in course of time, brought him international fame: *The Father* (*Fadren*, 1887), *Miss Julie* (*Fröken Julie*, 1888) and *Creditors* (*Fordringsägare*, 1889). These plays are called naturalistic, though they in no way resemble **Zola's** photographic naturalism. In his preface to *Miss Julie* Strindberg says: 'I believe I have observed that for modern people the psychological development is what most interests them, and that our inquiring minds are not satisfied with seeing something happen, we want to know why it happens.' *The Father* is a study of the effects of doubt and female oppression on a precariously balanced mind. The construction of the play is conventional but in its three acts every aspect of mental torture is portrayed, what Strindberg called 'psychic murder'. *Miss Julie* is another case history, a piece of brilliant analysis, acted in one continuous scene 'to maintain the author's magnetic hold over the audience'. This is not psychic murder. It is true that Jean and the absent father exercise a hypnotic influence at the end, but Julie commits suicide because she cannot face disgrace. In *Creditors*, another one-act play, Strindberg has introduced Max Nordau's idea that suggestion may be in dumb show: Gustav acts an epileptic fit, and Adolf has one and dies. Recognition of the greatness of these plays was slow to come everywhere except Paris and Berlin.

During this same period Strindberg wrote two of his most famous prose works: *A Madman's Defence* (*Le Plaidoyer d'un fou*, 1888) and *The People of Hemsö* (*Hemsöborna*, 1887). The first, written in French, and not meant for publication, is the vindictive story of his marriage to Siri, the second an amusing account of life in the Stockholm archipelago. In both the theme of sexual jealousy is prominent. Back in Stockholm he produced another important prose work, *By the Open Sea* (*I havsbandet*, 1890), a story about the disintegration of a human being when isolated from his intellectual equals, and persecuted by the masses. It was written during the period of his uneasy atheism, but is shot through with a longing for God. In 1892 he wrote seven plays, none of which were performed in Sweden though one, *Playing with Fire* (*Leka med elden*), has since gained international recognition. After this set-back and his divorce from Siri, which entailed the loss of his children, Strindberg again went into exile, first in Berlin, then in Paris. For the next six years he abandoned literature and turned to his own brand of science. His great plan was to write a work which would enable him to understand how the universe was governed. But he was no ordinary scientist. He was an artist, who believed in intuition, and though he did make some experiments he distrusted them. He was retreating into that inner world which became so real to him. This is the world of his novel *Inferno* (*Inferno*, 1897), the book that has always been taken as the clearest indication that he was mad. It is in fact a highly coloured account of what he called his 'occult' experiences in Paris from 1894 to 1896, the period known as his 'Inferno Crisis', though then, as always, Strindberg knew perfectly well what he was about. It is true that he experimented with madness, as he did with other things, but he never crossed the border line.

He emerged from this period a changed man. Swedenborg had revealed to him the meaning of his self-induced, but often terrifying, experiences: they were a punishment for sins committed in a previous existence. From being an atheist he became a believer. He knew this belief was a subjective matter. He needed God and so he believed, but in a very individual way. In this spirit he wrote one of his greatest dramas, *To Damascus* I–II–III (*Till Damaskus*, 1898–1901). These plays were quite unlike anything that had gone before. The technique was expressionistic, symbolism was freely used, and the dramatic unities were not observed. *To Damascus* is a journey, in the Kierkegaardian sense of *Stages on Life's Way*, in search of the self and of God. Both frequently elude the Unknown One, the protagonist of the play, but he persists, for, as he comes to realize, if you cannot know you must believe. Like most of what Strindberg wrote, *To Damascus* was before its time in Sweden, both in content and scenically. It was a precursor of the German expressionist movement of 1912.

The years from 1898 to 1903 were enormously productive. He wrote over twenty plays, some of them among his best. His cycle of historical dramas is the most effective dramatization of history since Shakespeare. The most popular of these is *Erik XIV* (1899), the Hamlet-like character, whom Strindberg himself called characterless. With *The Dance of Death* (*Dödsdansen*, 1901) Strindberg appears to be taking a step backwards to naturalism, but this is an illusion. The characters in this play are not men and women, they are types, elemental personifications of evil. As with many of Strindberg's dramas, episodes in his own life had fired his imagination, but it is the use he made of his source, not the source itself, that is important. As Ollén has pointed out: 'the details may correspond with uncanny precision ... but the whole is fantasy ... By magnifying, distorting, and freely associating ideas, he has created characters who live a fantasy life entirely independent of their origins.'

For Strindberg the climax of his work came with *A Dream Play* (*Ett Drömspel*, 1902). Like *To Damascus* it is a journey of the soul towards disillusionment and release. As illusions are burnt in the flames of the Growing Castle, the symbol of human life, the bud that crowns it bursts into bloom as the world did when Buddha ascended into nothingness. The action of the play takes place in an inconsequent dream world where anything may happen, but the dialogue is often very matter of fact:

The Daughter: People are pitiable
The Father: They are indeed. And it is a
    riddle to me what they live on. They
    marry on an income of four hundred
    pounds, when they need eight.

In 1907 Strindberg wrote some one-act chamber plays for his own Intimate Theatre,

among them *The Ghost Sonata* (*Spöksonaten*). It is often considered to be obscure; in fact it is a beautifully constructed play and demonstrates clearly that Strindberg knew exactly what he wanted to convey. The contending forces of good and evil are visually defined in the first scene, in the second the full extent of evil is revealed, both in the dialogue and in the setting, while in the third, in spite of the bright room in which it is set, darkness triumphs. The end is death, as it is in all but one of the chamber plays.

Strindberg was a great innovator; he had no more use for the well-made character than he had for the well-made play. 'Where is the self,' he wrote in 1886,

> which is supposed to be the character? It is neither in one place nor in the other, it is in both. The ego is not one unit; it is a multiplicity of reflexes, a complex of impulses, of demands, some suppressed at one moment, others let loose at another.

He showed that this complex self is more interesting than the straightforward character and, in his later plays, that the journey of the soul can be dramatically effective. He employed scenery in novel ways, and revolutionized dialogue by using everyday speech. His whole life was pilgrimage in search of himself. From the depths of his own experience he fashioned a new form of drama that gave expression to an inner world of trial and struggle, and his influence has been immense. Perhaps **Eugene O'Neill** springs most readily to mind, but there have been many others who could say with Strindberg: 'I find the joy of life in its fierce, cruel struggles, and my delight is in knowing something, in learning something.' People who can adopt this attitude will not find his plays depressing.

Further reading

See: *The Plays*, Vols I and II (trans. Michael Meyer, 1964–75); *The Vasa Trilogy* (trans. W. Johnson, 1950); *The Chamber Plays* (trans. E. Sprinchorn, 1962); *Twelve Plays* (trans. E. Sprigge, 1963); *The Red Room* (trans. E. Sprigge, 1967); *The Son of a*

Servant (trans. E. Sprinchorn, 1967); *A Madman's Defence* (trans. E. Sprinchorn, 1968); *Getting Married* (trans. M. Sandbach, 1972); *Inferno and From an Occult Diary* (trans. M. Sandbach, 1979). See: Mortensen and Downs, *Strindberg, His Life and Work* (1949); Gunnar Ollén, *August Strindberg* (1972); G. Brandell, *Strindberg in Inferno* (trans. 1974); W. Johnson, *Strindberg's Historical Dramas* (1962); M. Lamm, *August Strindberg* (trans. 1971). John Ward, *The Religious and Social Plays of August Strindberg* (1980), has an excellent bibliography. See also: Michael Robinson, *Strindberg and Autobiography: Writing and Reading a Life* (1986); Harry C. Carlson, *Out of Inferno: Strindberg's Reawakening as an Artist* (1996).

MARY SANDBACH

SULLIVAN, Louis Henry

1856–1924

US architect

Louis Sullivan's career rose with the evolution of the tall metal-framed commercial buildings, during the last decades of the nineteenth century. Through his talents, he showed that such structures could be artistically considered, and thus brought them within the realm of architecture. His efforts in bringing a new order and grace to this type of building were parallel with those of such as **Walt Whitman** and **Mark Twain**, who equally were searching for a true American voice, and to free their creative production from European influences. Born in Boston in 1856 of Irish and Swiss parents, both musical, Louis Sullivan's early architectural experience and training were restless and varied. He spent a short time at the École des Beaux Arts in Paris, and worked in many architects' offices, including the office of Frank Furness in Philadelphia. He arrived in Chicago in the 1870s, during the city's first great building boom. Shortly after arriving, Sullivan met and sufficiently impressed Dankmar Adler to be offered a partnership in the latter's established practice. Adler was to act as technician and trusted friend during the major part of Sullivan's career, from 1881 onwards.

Their early work was much influenced by the buildings of **H.H. Richardson**, particularly the exterior of their first major building, the Auditorium in Chicago of 1886. The interior, in its use of elemental geometry to organize the major spaces, was similarly influenced; the surfaces within, however, were extensively decorated, much of the decoration being remarkably inventive, derived from a combined use of geometry and natural form. Ornament in architecture was to be the most lasting theme in Sullivan's work. His use of it was organizational and metaphoric, to represent his deepest conviction in a natural law of form relating to function. Hating the Beaux Arts style, representing to him, as it did, Europe's tired decadence, he rejected the Beaux Arts principle of the dominance of the plan and its ancient role in carrying the meaning of the building, and consequently his work became increasingly elevational, to concentrate on the façade, the plans within seemingly wilfully indifferent. The finest examples of his ideas as applied to the new tall building form were the Wainwright Building of 1890–91 in St Louis and the Guaranty Building of 1894–5 in Buffalo. Sullivan's increasing facility with ornament can be traced developing through a series of tombs, the best of which, the Getty Tomb in Chicago of 1890 and the Wainwright Tomb in St Louis of 1892, are composed of sombre pure forms set alive by the application of running, vibrating decoration.

In his famous essay of 1896, 'The Tall Office Buildings Artistically Considered', he expounded his theories of the idea of the natural law as a basis of architecture. In doing this he was extending to buildings theories concerning fitness to purpose expounded earlier by Horatio Greenough, the American expatriate sculptor, and more generally, extending the essentially puritan New England natural Transcendentalism of **Thoreau** and Emerson. In so doing Sullivan was attempting to root this quintessential American spirit in the centres of the new booming cities. His conviction was that functionalism was a natural law, and that through a careful, ritualistic analysis of the needs that the building was to fulfil, by 'using nature's own machinery', the form would naturally emerge, like a plant from the earth. This belief allowed him to begin to form an architecture free from the wilful European formalism of the time. The poetry and potency of the idea is susceptible, however, to two major linked weaknesses. First, in its inability to recognize any conflict of interest, and in its dependence upon an intense spirituality for its fullness, the theory, through its workings as a conscious re-examination of the minutiae of requirement, could quickly decay into an unquestioning acceptance of the client's requirements, and a blindness to the larger social issues regarding, for instance, the relationship between the public and the private realms. It is, however, one of Sullivan's most lasting memorials that after him, the style of the American skyscraper remains to create public space within the building, adjacent to the street.

The second weakness revolves around the difficulty of defining any function clearly. One might confidently say of a bread knife what its purpose is, but such a straightforward implement might find itself being used purposefully, in, for instance, the hands of a murderer. Thus in the complexity of engagement with the living, where the rule of natural order should be most vivid, the idea of clarity of function becomes most endangered. With the less easily defined functions that the simplest building must accommodate, the idea tends to useless generalities, without some other, perhaps unspoken, controlling intention. One might feel some confidence in defining the functions of an office building, but what of a house? And yet Sullivan's edict that form follows function together with Le Corbusier's claim that the house was a machine for living in were to become the two major beliefs of the International Modern Movement in the early twentieth century, paradoxically because of the dependence of the central concept.

Clarity of function depends upon the larger idea of propriety of use, and its antithesis, abuse. In architecture, the idea becomes a concern with the correct use of space and this in turn depends upon a concern for the correctness of human behaviour. Thus a creed that would pretend to be essentially amoral is built upon and requires a necessarily determined morality. Thus functionalism is the unimpassioned mask of moral intentions and thus it was that the progressive European architects of the early twentieth century were able to engage with the idea of social programme, and in so doing created their plain white taut façades to contain the workings of an essentially nineteenth-century movement for social reform.

The hidden contradictions in Sullivan's thought concerning the programme for the tall commercial building has meant that the skyscraper remains enigmatic and challenging to American architects, unabsorbed as it is by either current theories, relating to the shingle style or the loosely termed postmodernist. The World Columbian Exposition, held in Chicago in 1893, represented a rejection by his adopted city of his thoughts and life's work. Apart from his own Transportation building, the predominant style was that of the Beaux Arts. Chicago had decided to appear, to represent its burgeoning wealth, as a *fin-de-siècle* mid-European city. Two years later, Adler withdrew from the partnership. This heavy double blow compounded his natural solitariness, resolved his path as that of the prophet alone, and ushered in the final phase of his life.

Sullivan's finest later works were a series of banks in small mid-west towns, notably in Owatoma, Minnesota, in Grinnell, Iowa, and in Sidney, Ohio, in which there is the finest realization of his style of ornament related to building. Despite the vagaries of available commissions, during a time of depression, which this was, it is difficult not to read in these late works a retreat from and disillusion with the city. During this period up to his death in 1924 he concentrated much effort on writing, exploring, notably in *Kindergarten Chats* (1901–2) and *Autobiography of an Idea* (1924), his deep concern for the relationship between democracy and the practice of his art.

In 1924 a series of large drawings under the title *A System of Architectural Ornament According with a Philosophy of Man's Powers* were published, which are the most beautiful accomplished exposition of his genius for marrying geometry and plant form. These undertakings, carried out in a period of apparent decline, represent his finest work, upon which, increasingly, his reputation will safely stand. It is a measure of his influence that his most brilliant assistant, Frank Lloyd Wright, would, in his mature work, carry further the major themes of Sullivan's life and work, the search for a democratic architecture, the relationship between ornament and building, and finally also, the retreat from the city.

Further reading

Other works include: *Kindergarten Chats and Other Writings* (reprinted 1918). See also: Hugh Morrison, *Louis Sullivan: Prophet of Modern Architecture* (1935); Willard Connely, *Louis Sullivan as He Lived* (1960); H. Frei, *Louis Henry Sullivan* (1992); Mario Manierielia, *Louis Henry Sullivan* (1997).

FREDERICK SCOTT

SULSTON, (Sir) John Edward

1942–

English scientist

John Sulston was born in Buckinghamshire, to a schoolteacher and an Anglican minister. As a child, he was fascinated with mechanisms, whether man-made or natural. In his 2002 Nobel Prize autobiography, he describes himself as always having been 'an artisan, a maker and doer'. Although from his early years Sulston differed with his father about religious belief and traditional social hierarchies, he attributes his relative indifference to material wealth and strong impulses to strive for the common good which have marked his career to his father's influence.

After a relatively unremarkable middle-class childhood, Sulston received a scholarship to attend Pembroke College, University of Cambridge, where he studied natural

sciences, specializing in organic chemistry. When an application to join the development charity Voluntary Service Overseas fell through at the last moment, he stayed on at Cambridge to do research and take his PhD, which focused on the synthesis of oligonucleotides (short segments of single-stranded DNA).

Sulston took a post-doctoral position at the Salk Institute in California with Leslie Orgel, a British theoretical chemist who was studying the origins of life, and there he 'discovered' the intersection of biology and chemistry. After two years at the Salk, Sulston met **Francis Crick** (co-discoverer of the structure of DNA), who interviewed him for a position at the Medical Research Council Laboratory of Molecular Biology (LMB) in Cambridge. Sulston was appointed staff scientist in 1969 in the laboratory group of Sydney Brenner. The LMB had been officially founded in the early 1960s, and hosted many important research projects to elucidate the basic mechanisms of molecular biology. By the late 1960s, Brenner had begun to study the small nematode worm *Caenorhabditis elegans* as a way to understand the basic mechanisms of genetics, development and neurobiology. Sulston was one of a few ongoing appointments to this research project, which was initially treated by many in the biological community with scepticism.

For nearly thirty years, Sulston worked on a range of phenomena in 'the worm,' as it is known, including neurotransmitters and mutations that interfere with normal development. In a task that many of his colleagues describe as monumental and which took nearly a decade, he used a light microscope with special interference optics to directly observe individual cells through an unfolding sequence of cell divisions in the transparent worm as it progressed from fertilized egg to adult, making an intricate series of hand-drawings to record the fate and position of each cell. Sulston and colleagues eventually mapped the entire cell lineage of the organism, making it the first such multi-organ organism to be so described. This research served as the basis for identifying the genetic controls that propel each cell towards its fate, including particular cells programmed to die as part of the normal processes of development. This process became recognized as a general and important biological phenomenon called 'apoptosis'. The last part of this project was the completion of the cell lineage of *C. elegans* embryo, for which Sulston was elected to the Royal Society in 1986.

Together with Robert Waterston of Washington University in St Louis (who had previously been a postdoctoral fellow at the LMB), Sulston and colleagues produced a physical map of the worm's six chromosomes, then sequenced its genes. The nematode's genomic sequence, the first of a multi-cellular organism to be completed, was published in 1998. This project served as a technological stepping stone to the major collaborative efforts associated with the international Human Genome Project (HGP). Sulston was appointed as the first head of the Wellcome Trust's Sanger Centre in Cambridgeshire, named after his long-time LMB mentor Fred Sanger and established in 1993 to house worm, human and other genome projects. He led a research group of several hundred scientists who sequenced nearly one-third of the three billion letters in the human genome as part of an international consortium.

As the project progressed, Sulston was drawn into a dispute with Celera Genomics, headed by the charismatic Craig Venter, which in 1998 made an aggressive bid to take over the HGP for profit. Venter promised to finish the sequence much more quickly than the public project would, using alternative technologies. This debate put Sulston into the political position of promoting the 'open science' ethos that had come to govern the HGP, codified in the group's 1996 Bermuda statement, namely that DNA sequence data should be publicly disclosed every day, and the human genome itself should not be owned or subject to commercial investment. This principle echoed those that formed the foundation of the worm community, which is well recognized for its mechanisms of communication which promote the sharing of data. Sulston believed that the HGP had progressed rapidly in large part because everyone shared data on the genetic and physical maps; mechanisms had been developed to facilitate this open access while still giving credit to individual accomplishments.

Sulston argued that the information gained through genomic research (but not the inventions that might be derived from it) should be freely released so that work could proceed efficiently and all could benefit, rather than limiting access through patenting or restrictive licensing. He contended that genes are merely discovered, not invented. The press eagerly picked up on this power struggle and what came to be known as the 'race' to sequence the genome, with Sulston portrayed as saintly or merely a naïve hippy, in juxtaposition to 'Darth' Venter who was viewed either as a savvy capitalist or an opportunistic scientist, whose drive originated from war experiences in Vietnam. Sulston's advocacy kept the human genome, as well as those of key model organisms such as the mouse, in the public domain. This public–private debate accelerated the sequencing of the human genome, perhaps at some cost to the initial accuracy of the data, and secured resources from both the private and public sectors, particularly when Sulston briefly threatened to leave the public project (ironically enough to start a private company). The nearly complete sequence was released to great fanfare in a ceremony hosted by US President Bill Clinton and UK Prime Minster Tony Blair in 2000, nearly five years ahead of the schedule for completing a human reference sequence.

In 2000, Sulston resigned as director of the Sanger Centre, though he continued some work on the HGP and the worm genome; he was knighted in 2001. Sulston views the data-sharing and ownership issues that arose with the human genome as fundamental to the practice of science, and argued for greater attention to free release of information and global equality in science and medicine in his book *The Common Thread: A Story of Science,*

Politics, Ethics and the Human Genome (2002), co-authored with UK science journalist Georgina Ferry. In 2002, he was awarded the Nobel Prize for Physiology or Medicine jointly with Brenner and Robert Horvitz for their work on understanding the development of the nematode and particularly the role of programmed cell death or apoptosis. A 2001 portrait of Sulston by the artist Marc Quinn hangs in the National Portrait Gallery, and it is composed of a sample of Sulston's DNA in agar jelly mounted in stainless steel, perhaps appropriate for a man known as 'a scientist's scientist'.

Further reading

See: Francis Harry Compton Crick.

RACHEL A. ANKENY

SUZUKI DAISETSU TEITARO

1870–1966

Japanese Buddhist philosopher

Since he was the son of Ryōjun Suzuki, a medical doctor and Confucian scholar whose family religion was Rinzai Zen, and Masu, who was an adherent of a mystic and unorthodox belief connected with the Shin sect (Jōdo Shinshū, or True Pure Land Sect), it is not a coincidence that Daisetsu Suzuki grew to become the greatest modern exponent of Zen and Shin, the two representative schools of Buddhist thought in Japan.

In his early twenties, while he was a student at Tokyo Imperial University, Suzuki dedicated himself to Zen meditation in Kamakura. At twenty-seven, he joined Paul Carus of La Salle, Illinois, to assist in translating Chinese Buddhist texts into English. While working on the editorial staff of the Open Court Publishing Company, he produced translations, including the *Discourse on the Awakening of Faith in the Mahayana* (1900). When he came to Europe in 1908, he was invited by the Swedenborg Society to translate *Heaven and Hell* into Japanese. After fourteen years abroad, he returned home to become a lecturer in English at Gakushū-in School, where he was later promoted to a professorship, and at Tokyo Imperial University. At forty-one he married an American, Beatrice Erskine Lane, and in 1921 moved to Kyoto to take the chair of Buddhist philosophy at Otani University. There he began publishing the *Eastern Buddhist*, one of the leading English-language Buddhist journals in the world. The rest of his life was dedicated to writing, translating and lecturing both at home and abroad. In 1936 Suzuki visited London to lecture on Zen at the First Convention of the World Congress of Faiths and also gave lectures on Zen at Oxford, Cambridge, Durham, Edinburgh and London Universities. At the age of ninety-five he resumed editorship of the new series of the *Eastern Buddhist* and died in July that year.

Suzuki's contributions to world spiritual culture are incalculable. The phenomenal popularity of Zen in the West after the Second World War is the direct result of his efforts. He was the first to write seriously about Zen in English, and he kept up his zeal and energy in introducing Zen to the West until his last days. It is also from his works that many Westerners have come to know about Shin teaching, which centres around Amida Buddha and emphasizes absolute trust in his power.

Suzuki's activity was not motivated by conventional religious fervour or mere evangelism. He really understood both Eastern and Western thought and endeavoured to make people of the East and West understand and appreciate each other's spiritual heritage. His Japanese translations of English works include Emanuel Swedenborg's *Heaven and Hell* (1910), *The Divine Love and the Divine Wisdom* (1914) and *The Divine Providence* (1915). *Mysticism, Christian and Buddhist* (1957) clearly shows his insight into world spiritual culture. His greatest contribution, however, lay in popularizing Buddhist concepts in the West. It is through his lucid explanation that one easily learns of the state called 'satori', where there is no subject–

object confrontation and where one attains 'absolute freedom, even from God' (*Essays in Zen Buddhism, First Series*, 1927).

Further reading

Suzuki's other works include: *Outlines of Mahayana Buddhism* (1907); *Essays in Zen Buddhism, Second Series* (1933), *Third Series* (1934); *Studies in the Lankavatara Sutra* (1930); *The Lankavatara Sutra* (a translation from the original Sanskrit, 1932); *An Index to the Lankavatara Sutra* (1933); *An Introduction to Zen Buddhism* (1934); *Manual of Zen Buddhism* (1935); *Zen Buddhism and its Influence on Japanese Culture* (1938); *The Essence of Buddhism* (1947); *The Zen Doctrine of No-Mind* (1949); *A Miscellany on the Shin Teaching of Buddhism* (1949); *Studies in Zen* (1955); and *Shin Buddhism* (1970). See: Rick Fields, *How the Swans Came to the Lake: A Narrative History of Buddhism in America* (1981); Masao Abe (ed.), *A Zen Life: D. T. Suzuki Remembered* (1986); William LaFleur's article on Suzuki in Mircea Eliade (ed.), *The Encyclopedia of Religion* (1993).

HISAO INAGAKI

T

TAGORE, Rabindranath

1861–1941

Bengali writer

A poet, novelist, dramatist, essayist, composer, painter and educationalist, Rabindranath Tagore was a modern-day Renaissance man, who dominated the cultural life of Bengal for the first half of the twentieth century. He was the seventh, and the youngest, son of Debendranath Tagore, a wealthy Brahmin landlord of Calcutta, who was a founder of the Brahmo Samaj, a reformist Hindu movement which emphasizes monotheism. He was tutored at home, and became proficient in Bengali, Sanskrit and English. At sixteen he was sent to England to study law, a subject that failed to interest him. After his marriage at twenty-three he left Calcutta to manage the family estate at Silaidaha. He did so for seventeen years, and then moved to Santiniketan (Abode of Peace), the family retreat near Bolpur, about a hundred miles north of Calcutta. Here he founded an experimental school for boys which blossomed into an international university, Visvabharati, twenty years later.

He began writing verses when he was in his teens, and published his first volume of poems at eighteen. Later, he was to find the running of the family estate artistically rewarding. The close contact with the enchanting Bengali landscape fired his poetic imagination, while the insight that he gained into peasant life served him well in his works of fiction. In the 1890s his considerable output of poetry was complemented by drama (*Chitrangada* and *Malini*) and fiction (*Chitra*). The sadness caused him by the deaths of his wife and two children, between 1902 and 1907, was to be reflected in the mellowed sharpness of his later work.

His poetic genius found its most accomplished achievement in *Gitanjali* ('Song Offerings'), which appeared in Bengali in 1910. The English translation published two years later, and praised by, among others, **Ezra Pound** and **W.B. Yeats**, won him the Nobel Prize for Literature in 1913. This, and the knighthood that came in 1915, made him an international celebrity. In his lecture tours of America, Europe, Japan and South-East Asia he stressed the need for blending the ancient heritage of the East with the material achievements of the West. His catholic humanism is well captured in *The Religion of Man* (1931), where he regards love as the key to human fulfilment and freedom, and the surplus energy that finds expression in creative art as the most outstanding characteristic of human nature.

Although he did not participate actively in the freedom struggle of his countrymen, he was not apolitical. He renounced his knighthood in protest against the Amritsar massacre, committed by imperial Britain, in 1919. India honoured him in 1947 by adopting 'Jan Gan Man' ('Mind of the People'), one of his songs, as the national anthem, as did Bangladesh, a quarter of a century later, with its adoption of his 'Sonar Bangla' ('Golden Bengal').

He left a deep mark on the arts of Bengal, and thus of India and Bangladesh. By releasing Bengali prose from the traditional form of classical Sanskrit he made literary Bengali accessible to the masses; and by introducing new types of metres he enriched Bengali poetry. His song-poems remain as popular with the Bengali elite as they do with the peasants. He also introduced the forms of short story and opera to Indian literature and theatre. By combining the classical Indian arts with the folk traditions, and encouraging a creative interchange between Eastern and Western artistic forms, at Visvabharati he blazed a new path in education.

Further reading

See: *The Collected Poems and Plays* (1936); *Hungry Stones and Other Stories* (1916); *Stories from Tagore* (1918); *My Reminiscences* (autobiography, 1917); *Sadhana: The Realization of Life* (essays, 1913); *Thought Relics* (essays, 1921); *The Religion of Man* (essays, 1931); and the novels *The Home and the World* (1919) and *Gora* (1924). *A Tagore Reader* (1961) is the best anthology. About Tagore: E. Rhys, *Rabindranath Tagore* (1915); E.J. Thompson, *Rabindranath Tagore: His Life and Work* (1921); S. Sen, *Political Philosophy of Tagore* (1929); H.R. Kripalani, *Rabindranath Tagore: A Biography* (1962); Edward John Thompson, *Rabindranath Tagore: His Life and Work* (1982); Kalyan Sen Gupta, *The Philosophy of Rabindranath Tagore* (2005).

DILIP HIRO

TÀPIES, Antoni

1923–

Spanish artist

Antoni Tàpies was born in Barcelona to Josep Tàpies i Mestre, a lawyer, and Maria Puig i Guerra, whose father was the mayor of the city and a Catalan nationalist. Brought up in a liberal and intellectual environment, the young Tàpies was introduced to the European avant-garde in 1934 through a special edition of the journal *D'Ací i D'Allá*. Although he pursued his interest in drawing and painting throughout his adolescence and early adulthood, at Barcelona University he studied law but never completed the programme.

In 1947, Tàpies befriended the poet Joan Brossa, through whom he met **Jóan Miró**. Along with a group of young artists and writers, Tàpies and Brossa founded the review *Dau al Set* in 1948, which published articles on many leading Surrealist artists, the occult, jazz and modern psychology. Steeped in the culture of Surrealism espoused by the *Dau al Set* group for whom Surrealism was an explicit critique of the repressive Franco régime, Tàpies began exploring Surrealist ideas of liberty and alternative modes of representation. His work of this period, such as *Dibuix* (1948) was heavily influenced by Miró, **Max Ernst** and **Paul Klee**, and experimented with unconventional materials such as thread, paper collage and thick pigment.

Around 1949, under the influence of João Cabral de Melo, the Communist consul from Brazil who advocated a more explicit connection between culture and politics, Tàpies began to reconsider the relevance of abstract art and began making more explicitly political work. Although Tàpies did not continue in this mode, his engagement with the political during this period contributed to his later attempts to articulate a language of painting that could at once embody the political goals of realism and the expressive ambitions of abstraction.

In 1950, Tàpies was awarded a scholarship through the French Institute of Barcelona, which enabled him to move to Paris. There, he developed his experiments with materials and calligraphic picture writing in the context of an international community of artists working to define a new mode of expression for the post-war period. Rejecting the traditional vocabulary of European painting as a moral and philosophical failure, these artists, among them **Jean Dubuffet**, Jean Fautrier and Antonin Artaud, defined Lyric Abstraction or Informel as a richer form of representation that incorporated the bodily and matter into painting. Tàpies' work from this period such as *Blanc et jaune* (1954) is fixated on the notion of the wall as silent witness, a material record of history, and through graffiti the place of clandestine expression. It was during the 1950s that Tàpies' artistic career took flight; he won the Carnegie Prize in 1950, showed at the Venice Biennale in 1952 and 1958 (where he won two prizes), won a purchase prize at the São Paolo Bienal in 1953, and participated in the Pittsburgh International in 1950, 1952, 1955 and 1958.

Tàpies has continued to produce strong, metaphysically charged work obsessed with matter, calligraphy and graffiti up to the present day. In the late 1960s and early 1970s, the artist became again more politically engaged, challenging the space of painting by making objects such as *Armari* (1973). In the 1980s, after the end of the fascist régime, Tàpies returned to the canvas. In 1993, he was chosen as the featured artist of the Spanish pavilion at the Venice Biennale, and had a one-person show at the Pace Wildenstein Gallery in New York in 2003.

Such European critics as Giulio Carlo Argan and Michel Tapié received Tàpies as an important voice in International Lyric Abstraction, and his work was seen as an existentialist project. In the USA, however, where the Cold War injected a politics of nationalism into International Lyric Abstraction, Tàpies was framed as a proponent of the 'Spanish school' in two important group exhibitions from 1960: *New Spanish Painting and Sculpture* at the Museum of Modern Art in New York and *Before Picasso After Miró* at the Solomon Guggenheim Museum. More recently, scholars such as Robert S. Lubar and Manuel S. Borja have attempted to rectify this perspective by situating his work in the international dialogue of Lyric Abstraction, of which it was such an integral part.

Further reading

See: Anna Agusti, *Tàpies, the Complete Works* (1989).

MING TIAMPO

TCHAIKOVSKY, Peter Ilich

1840–93

Russian composer

One of the most celebrated composers of the late Romantic musical period, Tchaikovsky was born at Votkinsk in central Russia where his father held a prominent position as a mining engineer. From an early age he showed great musical interest and was encouraged to learn the piano by his mother, to whom he had become neurotically attached. Her death when he was only eleven set the seal on an idealized view of women for the rest of his life. In 1855 the family moved to St Petersburg and the youth was sent to the prestigious School of Law, where he later graduated with honours. Accordingly he obtained a post in the Ministry of Justice where he remained for four years. However, the pull of music became so strong that he decided to enrol at the Conservatoire. Here he pursued full-time studies under Anton Rubinstein who had a high opinion of his composition exercises. Tchaikovsky's relinquishing of regular employment, just as he had become accustomed to a rather flamboyant lifestyle, meant a drastic drop in his living standards. He had to survive by giving lessons and acting as an accompanist for singers while writing his first compositions. Success in this field brought him a professorship of harmony at the new Moscow Conservatoire under Nikolai Rubinstein in 1866, and this enabled him greatly to increase his creative output. Compositions of this particularly fruitful period include the first three symphonies, the first piano concerto, three operas as well as *Romeo and Juliet* and the ballet *Swan Lake;* in addition, he was to produce articles for periodicals and become acquainted with many artistic contemporaries.

By his mid-thirties Tchaikovsky had met with sufficient acclaim both at home and abroad to fulfil short concert tours in Europe and purchase a house in the country for both rest and solitude. It is at this time that a curious correspondence was started with his new patroness Nadejda von Meck who over the thirteen years of their communications never made personal contact with the composer, though she did contribute greatly to his material needs. This, in contrast to his disastrous and short-lived marriage at the time, was to provide both platonic companionship and a secure income. In 1877, after recovering from a nervous breakdown and pathetic suicide attempt, he embarked on a travel programme which took him to Switzerland and Italy. Dissatisfied with his position at the Moscow Conservatoire he resigned in the following year and devoted more time to composition. New works soon included three orchestral suites, two symphonies, the second piano concerto, the violin concerto, *Sleeping Beauty*, the symphonic poems *Manfred*, *Hamlet* and *Voyevode,* together with four more operas.

Tchaikovsky spent his remaining five years touring Europe and promoting performances of his new scores. By the time von Meck had terminated their friendship he had directed concerts in Paris, Geneva, London, Leipzig, Berlin, Cologne, Hamburg and Prague. In 1891 he went to America and conducted concerts in New York, Baltimore and Philadelphia. A final move to a country house at Klin enabled him to complete the sixth symphony, subtitled 'Pathétique'. The award of an honorary doctorate by the University of Cambridge in 1893 was made immediately before the mysterious circumstances of his death which occurred in St Petersburg. His death from cholera has only very recently been disputed by the appearance of Russian sources which give the impression that he was directed to take his own life because of a homosexual affair with the relative of a high member of state.

Although Tchaikovsky's musical fame rests upon relatively few works, his output was of sizeable proportions and embraced most forms of the late nineteenth-century period. Compared with his colleagues in 'The Five' (Balakirev, Cui, **Borodin**, **Mussorgsky** and **Rimsky-Korsakov**), who chose to write strongly nationalistic works, Tchaikovsky's style was designed to appeal to international

audiences. Inevitably such influences do appear, as can be heard in his frequent use of long modal melodies and sequential repetitions reminiscent of folk song and Orthodox Chant. However, the fact that the infections of French and Italian cantilena figure strongly in his style and also that he adored the operatic works of Mozart, Rossini and **Verdi** contributes much to an understanding of his melodic characteristics. A great admirer of **Bizet's** *Carmen* and the ballets of Delibes, Tchaikovsky drew upon these models, injecting his own personal brand of hysteria, and evolved a style which placed much less emphasis on the constraints of traditional architectural form. Though his most famous compositions have a tendency to be theatrical, he had no interest in the romanticism of Beethoven or **Wagner** despite the fact that his contemporaries **Bruckner** and **Brahms** drew extensively from such influences for their symphonic writing.

Tchaikovsky's orchestral works can be divided into two groups: those with a definite programme and mostly cast as single movements, and the symphonies based on more traditional forms. In this first group can be placed the tone-poems *Romeo and Juliet* (1869), *The Tempest* (1875), *Francesca da Rimini* (1876) and *Hamlet* (1888). Taking *Romeo and Juliet* as reasonably representative of the composer's formal layout we can see that he invariably commences a work with a slow introduction and follows with a fast sonata section of two contrasted themes; these are treated freely both within the exposition and development sections. Again in this tone-poem, three stylistic elements are evident: the first theme is vigorous and frequently agitated while the second is mournful but eloquent. The whole is held together with extended running passages of a forceful nature. The second category includes the abstract works, namely the mature works for solo instrument with orchestra and the three late symphonies. Here the composer's first movements again employ much developmental material within the expositions, and frequently introductory themes recur in later movements also. In this procedure the over-emphasis of the same thematic materials tends to wear rather thin in long movements. However, the use of rhythmic devices such as syncopation or alternatively adept instrumental colouring frequently minimize any formal miscalculations on the part of the composer. Though the three early symphonies, No. 1 in G minor ('Winter Daydreams', Op. 13, 1866), No. 2 in C minor ('Little Russian', Op. 17, 1872) and No. 3 in D major ('Polish', Op. 29, 1875), show him grappling with just these problems, they are worthy predecessors to the more mature works. Much of their colourful orchestration is derived from Mendelssohn and Schumann who, like Tchaikovsky, were inspired by country scenes and local village dancing. Symphony No. 4 in F minor (Op. 36, 1877), which was written soon after his abortive marriage and dedicated to his new-found friend von Meck, represents a new depth of expression with its 'fate' motive on fanfare brass and melancholic waltz theme: the whole work could be termed auto-biographical, though the composer had no wish to be explicitly programmatic. The Symphony No. 5 in E minor (Op. 64, 1888) is more philosophical in its emotional attitude: the first three movements are Tchaikovsky at his best, while any formal weaknesses in the finale are mollified by the work's universal popularity. The same can be said for the sixth symphony in B minor (Op. 74, 1893), the 'Pathétique'. Written close to his death, this work shows him to have transcended the difficulties of form as well as present programmatic elements which bring the 'fate' theme to a convincing conclusion. Once again he draws from his palette feelings of utter despair as in the outer movements, and contrasts these with a balletic *valse à cinq temps* as the centrepiece.

Recently, much more acclaim has been given to the lengthy and programmatic *Manfred* symphony (Op. 58, 1885), based on the life of Lord Byron: the composer was ambivalent towards this symphony for it presented him with the problem of providing

themes capable of thematic transformation similar to those of Berlioz and **Liszt**.

Though there are several works for solo instrument with orchestra, only the first piano concerto in B flat minor (Op. 23, 1875) and the violin concerto in D major (Op. 35, 1878) have had any great following. Such works follow a narrower expressive range than the symphonies, though the latter is one of the finest written for the instrument since the death of Beethoven. Mention may also be made of the light-hearted *Variations on a Rococo Theme* (1876) for cello and orchestra which show an interest in pastiche later to be taken up in the opera *The Queen of Spades* (1890), and in *Mozartiana* (1887).

Tchaikovsky's three ballets – *Swan Lake* (1877), *The Sleeping Beauty* (1890) and *The Nutcracker* (1892) – provided the Russian ballet with a new kind of musical material with which to work. Prior to this audiences had to make do with French-style *divertissements* written by second-rate musicians who had been used to providing lightweight dance scores for operatic interludes or pageants for high society. Tchaikovsky built on this tradition by adding symphonic materials to the well-known folk forms of the polonaise, mazurka and minuet as well as drawing on such foreign dances as the tarantella and bolero. Within the first two ballets these, together with the concert waltz, are subjected to extensive development. His expertise in the portrayal of fairy tales via the use of scintillating orchestration can best be seen in the vignette-like miniatures of *The Nutcracker*, which owes a great deal to Delibes's *Sylvia* and *Coppélia* of twenty years earlier.

Of the dozen or so operas that Tchaikovsky wrote, only the Pushkin-inspired *Eugene Onegin* (1878) and the later *Queen of Spades* are regularly staged. The former is a masterpiece written at the time of crisis and owes more to the tragic lyricism of Bizet's *Carmen* than to the nationalist works of Glinka. The latter, with its biting satire and rococo style, can be traced to Mozart's treatment of the medium, though here the composer adds his own chromatic spice to the rather formal proceedings while ideally balancing lyricism and dramatic expressiveness.

For a long while the inflated popularity of a mere handful of orchestral compositions detracted from a wider appreciation of Tchaikovsky's complete oeuvres, particularly the beauty of the early quartets, many songs and piano pieces. These chamber works often achieve artistic greatness in their Slavonic individualism. It was this lighter side which was taken up by his successors Glazunov (1865–1936) and Miaskovsky (1881–1950): whether by way of *déjà-entendu* in **Rachmaninov's** symphonies or in the made-to-order 'socialist realism' of **Shostakovich's** ballets, the lilt of the Tchaikovsky concert waltz is instantly recognizable. Like many Romantic composers, his music contains many characteristic traits that have been copied. If the unstable side of his temperament frequently outweighs thematic and formal considerations, the humanity and sincerity of Tchaikovsky's artistry shines through.

Further reading

See: R. Newmarch, *Tchaikovsky* (1907); H. Weinstock, *Tchaikovsky* (1943); Gerald Abraham, *The Music of Tchaikovsky* (1945); E. Evans, *Tchaikovsky* (1966); John Warrack, *Tchaikovsky Symphonies and Concertos* (1974); Vladimir Volkoff, *Tchaikovsky* (1975); John Warrack, *Tchaikovsky Ballet Music* (1979); Alexander Poznansky, *Tchaikovsky's Last Days: A Documentary Study* (1996); Leslie Kearney (ed.) *Tchaikovsky and His World* (1998); Edward Garden, *Tchaikovsky* (2001).

MICHAEL ALEXANDER

TENNYSON, Alfred (Lord)

1809–92

English poet

Alfred Tennyson, first Baron Tennyson, was born in Somersby, Lincolnshire. His father was an emphatically gloomy country rector from whom the poet inherited a temperamental melancholy and from whom he received his early education, the rectory being well stocked with books. He began to write when he was eight years old. When he was eighteen, he and his brother issued *Poems by Two Brothers*. The next year Tennyson went to Trinity College, Cambridge, where he met Arthur Hallam. His discussions with the extremely clear-minded and sympathetic Hallam helped Tennyson to clarify his ideas about the nature of form in poetry and about poetic language. *Poems Chiefly Lyrical* (1830) and *Poems* (1833) established Tennyson in the eyes of Leigh Hunt, who had 'discovered' Keats, Shelley and Byron and set about promoting Tennyson. Hallam's death in 1833 marked Tennyson's life and affected his development as a poet. His most original and distinctive work was in a sense produced out of his dialogue with Hallam. He never had such another reader or friend. For nine years he published very little but was writing *In Memoriam* (published in 1850). *Poems* (1842) included earlier work but also 'Locksley Hall', 'Ulysses', 'Morte d'Arthur' (a prototype for the *Idylls of the King*) and other important work. *The Princess: A Medley* (1847) includes some of his best lyrics in a rather dull blank-verse flow from which they can fortunately be rescued to stand alone.

Fame was – for one of his temperament – a necessary burden. *Maud: A Monodrama* (1855) and the first four *Idylls* (1859) brought him much fame. *Enoch Arden* (1864) marked a decisive falling-off – not that Tennyson wrote badly after that date, only that he wrote dully, with a few vigorous exceptions. He became Poet Laureate in 1850 and held the post for forty-two years. His poetic 'working life' was among the longest in English literature – sixty-five years. His excursions into verse drama, as into narrative, were unconvincing, though he devoted his later years to them. His later collections were *Ballads and Other Poems* (1880), *Tiresias and Other Poems* (1885), *Demeter and Other Poems* (1889) and *The Death of Oenone* (1892). The 1885 collection took its title from an early poem he recovered and revised for publication.

His virtues as a lyric poet are essentially prosodic rather than conceptual. His narrative and dramatic limitations are clear from *Maud,* with its immediately memorable local passages and its eminently forgettable and sometimes absurd larger designs. Tennyson bases his dramatic procedure in the plays on what he takes to be Shakespeare's, but he is unable to give distinctive dictions to his speakers. His mimetic talents do not include the kind of self-effacement required of a dramatist nor the sense of thrift and pace which Shakespeare might have taught a brisker poet. Tennyson will talk through his characters: they reveal general states of feeling, not states of mind in specific context. The characters do not speak *in* character.

Even excluding the plays, Tennyson's output is huge. The good poems rise to the surface far more readily than they do in the work of a more integrated imagination – **Hardy's**, for instance – or of a more artificial one – for instance, **Browning's**. Tennyson had the desire and compulsion to write, but what he wrote did not always have the additional compulsion of emotional or psychological necessity. We distinguish the poems of feeling from the poems of conventional sentiment, but even they have prosodic merits. In some poems he thinks; in some he adopts, unimaginatively, other people's thoughts or the liberal sentiments of the age. As the 'Representative Voice', his politics and his religion are rooted in an idealizing memory of the past and a fear of the future.

Matthew Arnold discerned in 1860 that the Laureate, despite his vast accomplishments, 'is deficient in intellectual power'. This, of course, is one reason for the power of his lyric poems: they are not governed by ideas but by exquisitely held and apprehended feelings of a kind that 'intellectual power' might distrust, discard or ironize (as was the case with Browning, who – though one would hardly call him intellectually powerful – was no doubt clever, too clever to be seen to be sincere). Tennyson's poetic weakness is the narrowness of his register. He was technically omnicompetent; but he is truly accomplished only in a small area of his competence. His was a refining style which, when he tried to escape it, produced such disastrous work as 'Dora'.

Part of Tennyson's originality is in his mimetic conception of poetic language: sound and syntax could create, he believed, equivalents to motion and image, as 'The Palace of Art' and 'The Lotus Eaters' very differently demonstrate.

His idealization of the past provides him with epic and legendary figures, the best of them old men (whom he fleshed out in his youthful poems) – Tithonus and Ulysses especially. Those poems express – or seem to – through the vehicle of a *persona* Tennyson's deepest feelings and resolutions. The mask was for Browning a way of escaping the 'self'; for Tennyson it was a means of approach which suitably generalized the experience presented. No young poet has ever more effectively donned the mask of age.

His best long poem, *In Memoriam,* succeeds in part because it is an anthology of short poems arranged to follow the cycles of years and the gradual transformation of grief at the death of a friend into a kind of forced spiritual optimism. The lyrics – especially the melancholy ones – stand up well to reading out of context, as do the lyrics from *The Princess.* Organic units have been marshalled by Tennyson into mechanical structures. It is no wonder the structures do not hold; but the units retain unique force, the sum of the parts exceeding the whole. The language of *In Memoriam* is, for the most part, plain and direct with that refinement of sincerity which rejects the evasions of irony on the one hand and those of exaggeration in 'contextualizing' on the other.

The success of *In Memoriam* is its fragmentariness. Each section is an elegiac idyll. As one critic said, the faith is flimsy while the doubt is potent poetry. Tennyson was 'the voice of his age' in various ways – not least in a kind of nostalgic and intransitive eloquence, pure of designs on the reader beyond the design to pleasure and to move him – but not to impel him to action, rather to reflection. It is a poetry that – at its best – cannot be used, can only be valued.

One of the most rewarding contexts in which to set Tennyson's work is that of the first and second generation French Symbolists. The analogies are numerous and underline the freshness of his poetic intelligence and original imagination, his prosodic resourcefulness, whatever may have been the limitations of his more cognitive intellect.

Further reading

Other works include: *The Poems of Tennyson*, ed. Christopher Ricks (1969). See: Sir Charles Tennyson, *Alfred Tennyson* (1949); *Critical Essays on the Poetry of Tennyson*, ed. John Killham (1960); *Tennyson: The Critical Heritage*, ed. John D. Jump (1967); A. Sinfield, *Alfred Tennyson* (1986); D.S. Hair, *Tennyson's Language* (1991).

MICHAEL SCHMIDT

THOMAS, Dylan Marlais

1914–53

Welsh poet

Dylan Marlais Thomas was born on 27 October 1914 at 5 Cwmdonkin Drive in Swansea, where his father D.J. Thomas taught English at the grammar school and harboured unrealized ambitions to be a poet. D.J. gave his son the consciously literary names Dylan (the 'sea son' of the *Mabinogion*) and Marlais (a Welsh river adopted as bardic name by D.J.'s uncle) and encouraged him to read and recite poetry. Dylan stayed in his father's house until he was nineteen, referring to himself as 'the Rimbaud of Cwmdonkin Drive'.

If his home was excessively bookish, Dylan had no inclination for academic pursuits and liked to escape from 'splendidly ugly' Swansea. Near his house was Cwmdonkin Park, where he played and observed such unforgettable figures as 'The Hunchback in the Park'. Even more exciting were the summer holidays spent at Fern Hill dairy farm in north Carmarthenshire, the home of his aunt Ann Jones. Dylan drew on his adolescent experiences in poems like 'After the

Funeral' (in memory of Ann Jones who died in 1933) and the ecstatic 'Fern Hill' in which he recalled how he 'was young and easy under the apple boughs'.

Dylan left school in 1931 and spent his time acting with the Swansea Little Theatre, reporting for the *South Wales Daily Post* for fifteen months, and hanging about bars and cafés. He cultivated a romantic poetic persona but it was no sartorial pose; in the three years between leaving school in 1931 and leaving Swansea for London in 1934 he produced more than 200 poems including all the *18 Poems* (1934), most of the *Twenty-five Poems* (1936), early versions of many later poems and ideas that would subsequently be used in such works as *Under Milk Wood* (1954). It was the most creative period of his life and, by contrast, he wrote only eight poems in the last seven years of his life.

Thomas's poetry made an immediate and rather sensational impact on the public. His style was an individual mixture of the sensuous elements in poetry (as practised by Keats and **G.M. Hopkins**) and the linguistic experiments of **Joyce** and **Eliot**. When 'Light breaks where no sun shines' was published in the *Listener* of 14 March 1934 it provoked a storm of protest from readers who found the imagery obscene. However, Thomas's revitalization of the romantic tradition gained the admiration of Stephen Spender, Eliot, Edwin Muir and Edith Sitwell, who described the work *Twenty-five Poems* as 'nothing short of magnificent'. Thomas's early poetry was astonishingly dense in metaphor and treated sexual matters with surrealist manners. In a letter to Pamela Hansford Johnson – with whom he conducted an epistolary affair – he wrote in November 1933 that 'every idea, intuitive or intellectual, can be imaged and translated in terms of the body'.

Thomas had moved to London in 1934 and met Caitlin Macnamara, a twenty-two-year-old dancer who had been dismissed from the chorus line of the London Palladium. The couple spent a holiday together in the Welsh fishing village of Laugharne and returned there after getting married in July 1937 in Cornwall. Despite the great critical success of his poetry and the income derived from wartime film work and post-war broadcasting, Thomas was unable to control his domestic destiny. His drinking was reaching epic proportions and the marriage was punctuated by frequent periods of despair. In 1949 Margaret Taylor, wife of the historian A.J.P. Taylor, obtained for the Thomases the Boat House on the estuary of the River Taf in their beloved Laugharne and for the remaining four years of his life this was home for Dylan and Caitlin and their three children.

The cliffside house had a magnificent view of the bay, and in his garden shed, which he called 'the shack', Thomas composed poems like 'Over Sir John's hill', 'Author's Prologue' and 'Poem on his birthday'. Perhaps because he was suspicious of the apparently effortless precocity he had once enjoyed – or perhaps because he could no longer respond so readily to his insights – Thomas evolved an excruciatingly painstaking method of composition. He would retire to his shed in the afternoon after the pubs had closed and endlessly revise his poetry, sometimes making as many as 200 work-sheets for one poem. As a result Thomas's mature poetry became more and more formally intricate so that the finished product contained a complex of cross-association and a delicate embroidery of interweaving internal rhymes. Thomas was still an inspirational poet but the source of his poetry was no longer anatomical but natural; he was also anxious to live up to the Welsh tradition of technical expertise and to become a master of 'my craft or sullen art'.

In 1950 Thomas made, at the invitation of John Malcolm Brinnin, the first of four trips to America. His public performances of poetry delighted American audiences, for Thomas's incomparably rich delivery conformed to their expectations of a bard drunk on the music of words. His private performances as an obstreperous drunk scandalized his hosts who constructed, out of a few indiscreet incidents, a monument to Dylan as

an outrageous artistic clown. He was depressed by the malicious gossip that surrounded him in America, exhausted by the demands of extensive reading tours, and dismayed by the alcoholic pace his American admirers imposed on him. Yet he returned in triumph for his third trip in 1953. The previous year Thomas's Collected Poems (1952) had appeared to a crescendo of critical applause and he surpassed that with the New York reception of the stage version of his radio play Under Milk Wood (1954). The wit and brilliant linguistic invention of the play were enthusiastically appreciated and Thomas was well on the way to becoming an American institution; Boston University invited him to collaborate with **Stravinsky** on an opera on the re-creation of the world.

Thomas had earned substantial sums of money in America but had saved none of it so that life back in Laugharne, the setting of Under Milk Wood, became intolerable, and he embarked on his fourth and final visit to the USA to direct an expanded version of his play. His alcoholic decline was by this time complete and he suffered from delirium tremens and constant anxiety. When Thomas became uncontrollable his American doctor injected him with morphine; probably the effect of the drug, plus the intake of alcohol, proved fatal. On 4 November 1953 he was taken in a coma to St Vincent's Hospital, New York, and died five days later. The cause of death was diagnosed as 'Insult to the brain'. The poet's body was brought back to Wales to be buried in St Martin's Churchyard, Laugharne. Since then an academic industry has grown up around Thomas and his legend has been exhaustively examined; his poetry remains as the work of a virtuoso who created some of the finest lyrical works of the twentieth century.

Further reading

Other works include: The Poems (1971, revised 1974), ed. Daniel Jones; his broadcasts and stories can be sampled in Quite Early One Morning (1954) and A Prospect of the Sea (1955). See also: John Malcolm Brinnin, Dylan Thomas in America (1956);

Caitlin Thomas, *Leftover Life to Kill* (1957); Constantine FitzGibbon, *The Life of Dylan Thomas* (1965); and Paul Ferris, *Dylan Thomas* (1977); Caitlin Thomas with George Tremlett, *Caitlin: Life with Dylan Thomas* (1996); James A. Davies, *A Reference Companion to Dylan Thomas* (1998); Caitlin Thomas, *Double Drink Story* (1999); Paul Ferris, *Dylan Thomas: The Biography* (2000); Andrew Lycett, *Dylan Thomas: A New Life* (2003).

ALAN BOLD

THOMAS, Ronald Stuart

1913–2000

Welsh poet

As a young boy growing up on the farthest tip of the Welsh island of Anglesey, R.S. Thomas was captivated by the magisterial silhouette of distant Snowdonia. For him, deprived (in his view) of the Welsh language by his parents' snobbish choice, it represented the inaccessible, aboriginal, authentic Wales. Later, as a turbulent priest of the Church in Wales, he was to approach the Welsh geo-cultural heartland by cautious degrees, while attempting to gain full admission to it by becoming fluent in Welsh and substantially mastering the Welsh literary tradition. Yet, even when he finally settled on the Lleyn Peninsula, the psychic wound which, he was convinced, had been inflicted by the mother to whom he remained resentfully attached, failed to heal. Later in life, he was to concede that the powerful poetry he had written in what he regarded as the alien, and therefore self-alienating, English tongue had flowed from this wound. Echoing the words of **William B. Yeats**, who along with other 'Celtic' writers had been a considerably influence on his younger pan-Celtic self, he recognized that poetry proceeded from one's quarrel with oneself.

In Thomas's case, that quarrel took many different forms. It was encapsulated in the mesmerically contradictory figure of Iago Prytherch, the Welsh upland 'peasant' of his early poetry, and voiced as an obsessive, one-sided dialogue with a silent, deaf and implacably absent God throughout the last thirty years of his long life. Present in Thomas's railings against the 'Anglo-Welsh' it also erupted in fierce jeremiads against the modern world of technology and the 'Machine'. And it materialized in his aggressive support for direct political action on behalf of the Welsh language, his ambiguous attitude towards arson attacks on English holiday homes, and his championing of environmental causes.

The anguished concern at the plight of Wales that filled the poetry of Thomas's early decades found expression in poems some of which are classics of political engagement, but many of which are marred by shrillness, and disfigured by ugly hatreds. For Thomas himself, his defence of Wales (based on Saunders Lewis's nationalist vision) was only a local reaction to the threat of globalization, whose most powerful exponent was the US and which eroded the environment and unique cultural systems around the world.

In the latter years of his life, Thomas acted as the **Solzhenitsyn** of Wales – the uncomfortable, always extreme and at times bigoted voice of conscience of a Welsh people whom he despised as supinely acquiescing in the process of colonial assimilation by England. However, his dark charisma was based not only on his compelling public presence and sometimes scandalous utterance but also on his commanding stature as a poet. The equal but opposite of **Dylan Thomas**, the South Walian whose boyo personality and matching garrulity he affected to dismiss, Thomas produced a verbally austere poetry, apparently narrow in scope but correspondingly intense in focus. Repetitive in ways that seem claustrophobically restricting to many, his poems may also be seen as fruitfully obsessional, the frugal work of a profoundly meditative imagination. He was lastingly influenced by English Romantic poetry and continues to be viewed by some critics as an old-fashioned Georgian. But it can be argued that at his best he succeeded in refashioning traditional modes and discourses to produce a self-scrutinizing discourse capable of addressing the contemporary social, political and spiritual condition.

Although Thomas's first collection was published in 1946, it was only after the publication of *An Acre of Land* (1953) that the praise of John Betjeman, Kingsley Amis and others brought him to wide attention. The image of him that was fixed in the English imagination at that time – a Welsh country parson of attractively conservative style and subject – has unfortunately tended to recur in many circles. He has continued to serve as convenient example of one stubbornly persistent English stereotype of the Welsh – as rural, ruggedly remote, faintly exotic, and culturally reactionary. This is partly why token inclusion of Thomas's poems in anthologies of twentieth-century poetry almost always takes the form of Iago Prytherch. This remarkable psycho-mythic figure – 'just an ordinary man of the bald Welsh hills', his clothes 'sour with years of sweat', and by wholly unpredictable turns naturally wise and bestially ignorant – has been mistaken for social reality ever since Thomas first introduced him in *The Stones of the Field* (1946). In fact, Prytherch is a grotesque, born of Thomas's own deepest compulsions and pliant to his every obsession. He served his creator well for almost two decades as conduit for the vortex of his self-bewilderment.

So powerful did Prytherch ultimately become that he overshadowed the sensitive other poems that the earlier Thomas wrote about his wife, his mother and his son. During the last three decades of his life a like fate befell the fine painting poems and the powerfully original autobiographical sequence *The Echoes Return Slow* (1988), marginalized as they were by the poetry of repeated spiritual research. Most critics have condemned this poetry as rhythmically slack and imaginatively inert, lacking in the passion and linguistic impasto of the early writing. Alternatively they may be regarded as daringly innovative, seeking to pioneer a new discourse adequate to modern spiritual concerns, and uncannily attuned to the music of what mattered to the ageing and aged Thomas. Frequently turning on models and metaphors drawn from modern science, these spiritually sophisticated, self-cancelling poems constantly emphasize the provisional nature of their own conclusions and the incorrigible mortality of their would-be metaphysical language.

Despite its many palpable drawbacks, Thomas's *Collected Poems* made it evident that his lifetime's achievement had been as monumental as, to some, his poems seemed anorexically thin. While he was nominated for a Nobel Prize and admired in countries as distant as Japan, he remained a figure about whose literary stature there remained doubt and there raged dispute. It is, perhaps, the fitting legacy of a poet of unquiet spirit and unappeasable imagination. Echoing words uttered after **Matthew Arnold's** death, there were those who murmured at his passing: 'Poor old Thomas. He won't like God.'

Further reading

Collected Poems: 1945–1990 (1993) remains the standard text, but should be supplemented with Collected Later Poems: 1988–2000 (2004). Selected Poems (2004) was Thomas's final selection. For the prose, see Sandra Anstey (ed.), *R.S. Thomas, Selected Prose* (1995) and Jason Walford Davies, *Autobiographies* (1997). Justin Wintle, *Furious Interiors* (1996) is a fine first critical biography. Selected criticism includes M. Wynn Thomas (ed.), *The Page's Drift* (1993) and Damian Walford Davies (ed.), *Echoes to the Amen* (2003).

M. WYNN THOMAS

THOREAU, Henry David

1817–62

US author

Where Thoreau was known at all during his brief New England lifetime, it was essentially as an oddity, a figure of quirks and eccentric opinion. To many fellow New Englanders, in Boston and the surrounding townships of Cambridge and his birthplace, Concord, he seemed the very reverse of the gainful, purposive Yankee. He was a Harvard graduate but had settled to no recognizable occupation, as minister, lawyer or businessman.

Though perceived as a minor ripple in the larger Transcendentalist current, he was nonetheless literally closer than any to the master, Emerson's personal friend and protégé, and later a boarder and general handyman with the family. Then, despite the apparent outward severity of his character, a trait commented on not only by Emerson ('Henry is with difficulty sweet') but by Hawthorne, Thoreau's one-time neighbour in Concord, he was a committed family man, but as the lifelong bachelor who was a favourite uncle and loved brother. Though indubitably 'literary' in interests, he was also an alert and eloquent naturalist. No one knew better, or more first hand, the topographies of New England, its geology and Indian relics, the farms, ponds, flora and fauna. Above all, Thoreau confirmed his supposed oddness when he refused to pay his poll tax in protest at the unjust foreign war he believed his country was conducting in Mexico, having taken up residence in the summer of 1845 in the hut he built by Walden Pond, on land owned by Emerson, and stayed there for nearly two years, the action of a man who, apparently in earnest, talked of 'significant living'.

Given a reputation which, true to Thoreau's contrary style, now exceeds that of Emerson, his Transcendentalist mentor, perhaps the saddest paradox is that his age barely noticed him for the two full-length works published in his lifetime, *A Week on the Concord and Merrimack Rivers* (1849) and *Walden* (1854), or for the essays which have subsequently become classics in the literature of political dissent, 'On the Duty of Civil Disobedience' (1849) and 'A Plea for Captain John Brown' (1860). Yet these writings, *Walden* most especially, were no less than cornerstones in the American Renaissance, the mid-nineteenth-century efflorescence which includes **Melville**, **Whitman**, Hawthorne and a run of minor Transcendentalists, and which Emerson heralded in *Nature* (1836) and 'The American Scholar' (1837). Further, if Thoreau's published output looks scant, he was also the author of nearly forty journal

notebooks, extraordinary notations of a mind taking cognizance of its own inclinations and powers, and of a number of posthumous 'travel' books. As befits a writer who sought to hone down existence to 'essence', or as he puts it in *Walden* 'to drive life into a corner and reduce it to its lowest terms', Thoreau also evolved a literary idiom of rare distinction, aphoristic, wonderfully spare, layered with congenial Yankee wryness and wit.

Something of Thoreau's contrariness was recognized by **George Eliot** when she reviewed *Walden* for the *Westminster Review* in 1856. She saw his lakeside sojourn as 'a bit of pure American life', but retold 'through the medium of a deep poetic sensibility'. She testified to his 'unworldliness' yet also to his tempering 'sturdy sense'. Not unexpectedly, one of the most revealing estimates of Thoreau was offered by Emerson in the obituary essay he published in *Atlantic Monthly* in 1862. He emphasized, no doubt as much from personal knowledge of the daily routines of his so-called 'practical disciple' as of his writing, the obdurate, Spartan and as he termed it 'military' element in Thoreau, making reference to his 'inexorable demand on all for exact truth'. Emerson thought him 'a born protestant', who 'chose to be rich by making his wants few, and supplying them himself'. This radical self-sufficiency, which lies behind Thoreau's politics, and behind his wish to dissent from the prevailing orders of American capitalism and 'society', is everywhere reflected in his writing. Thoreau, according to *Walden,* wanted 'the flower and fruit of man', but only if seen and tested for himself. His bid for 'simplicity' thus was always highly complex, self-reliance not in the interests of conventionally defined rewards – material profit, possessions, social esteem – but as the path to higher 'essential' truths. Emerson was equally right to detect the 'Transcendental' ends to which Thoreau put his naturalism, the habit of seeing in nature's fine detail abiding spiritual meanings.

Born of English Channel Island and New England storekeeper stock which had gone bankrupt, Thoreau was educated at Concord Academy (1829–33), then Harvard (1833–7), where he read widely. After a brief interlude in Concord's public schools, he set up a school venture of his own with his brother John (1838–41), with whom also he travelled the Concord and Merrimack rivers in 1839. In 1840, he had his first essays and poems published in the Transcendentalist journal the *Dial*; moved in with the Emerson family (1841–3); did some tutoring on Staten Island (1843); and on 4 July 1845, an 'Independence Day' dramatically different in kind from that celebrated by the majority of his compatriots, moved to Walden Pond and his self-constructed hut. In the interim, like his brother John he had been turned down in marriage by Ellen Sewall; perfected a graphite process for his father's one-time lead pencil enterprise; acted as messenger and handyman for various of the townships; and begun his all-important notebooks. But by Walden Pond, where he had gone 'to transact some private business' and where, among other things, he wrote *A Week on the Concord and Merrimack Rivers,* he began the most significant act of his life, his two-year experiment as a 'community of one'. In 1846, he was arrested and kept in prison overnight for non-payment of the poll tax (the tax, to his annoyance, was paid by 'friends'). He travelled in 1846 to the Maine woods; lived again with the Emerson family in 1847–8; lectured on 'Civil Disobedience' (1848), a year before *A Week on the Concord and Merrimack Rivers* was published; made a sequence of trips to Cape Cod (in 1850 with his great friend and first biographer, the poet Ellery Channing); visited Walt Whitman in Brooklyn in 1856 (he called the second edition of *Leaves of Grass* 'an alarum or trumpet-note ringing through the American camp'); and in 1859 lectured on 'A Plea for Captain John Brown'. In 1860, during a camping trip, he caught cold, which exacerbated his hitherto dormant tuberculosis. Despite an excursion to Minnesota with Horace Mann Jr in hopes of recuperation, he died in Concord on 6 May 1862.

Ostensibly, *A Week on the Concord and Merrimack Rivers* re-creates the canoe journey Thoreau made with his brother into New Hampshire's White Mountains in 1839. Under his transforming design, however, it becomes also the transcript of another dimension of journeying, a diary of contemplation and thought and of Thoreau's testimony to nature as the repository of Emersonian-Transcendental spiritual 'laws'. He explains the metaphoric implications of his up-river, seven-day travel thus: 'True and sincere travelling is no pastime, but is as serious as the grave or any part of the human journey, and it requires a long probation to be broken into it.' This notion of figurative travel anticipates Thoreau's later, equally equivocal and teasing utterance, 'I have travelled much in Concord.' His 'week', in fact, is his version of the Genesis week, the Creation, as it were, retold in terms of a New England river expedition. The geography of the two rivers, and of the surrounding banks and ecology, not only yields a vivid, engaging portrait of nature itself, it acts for Thoreau as the means to his search for higher, ultimate meanings. *A Week* offers journey-narrative, thus, of a profoundly double kind, travel both outward and inward, into which Thoreau imports not only precise natural observations but a range of learning ancient and modern, different vignettes, maxims and aphorisms ('The traveller must be born again on the road, and earn a passport from the elements, the principal powers that be for him'), and various illustrative poems, including his own notable 'I am a Parcel of Vain Strivings'. Beginning from the Saturday and departure from river-source, each separate day is annotated in full, until the brothers re-arrive at the stiller waters of the port of Concord, home-coming as a time for retrospection and reflection. A line of comparable 'philosophic' nature writing might include John Aubrey's *Natural History,* or Gilbert White's *Natural History and Antiquities of Selborne,* or, closer to Thoreau's own time, Wordsworth's Lake poems.

As he used the emblematic span of the Genesis week for his first book, so in his masterpiece, *Walden*, Thoreau refashions the actual time he spent at Walden Pond into a cyclic representative year, another chronicle of 'awakening' which occurs to the rhythm of the seasons, summer, autumn, winter and the rebirth of spring. The heart of his endeavour is given in Chapter 2, 'Where I Lived, and What I Lived For':

> I went to the woods because I wished to live deliberately, to front only the essential facts of life, and see if I could not learn what it had to teach, and not, when I came to die, discover that I had not lived.

> I did not wish to live what was not life, living is so dear; nor did I wish to practise resignation, unless it was quite necessary I wanted to live deep and suck out all the marrow of life . . . to drive life into a corner, and reduce it to its lowest terms.

By this Thoreau intended no hermit-like avoidance of the world, but an exemplary act of self-realization, the individual life seeking to fulfil its best, most encompassing, possibilities. The attacks on the 'cost' of insignificant work, on mere money profit, and on the unneeded intrusions of state and society, Thoreau makes as the authentic anarch, a preserver and defender of self-acquired values. As the pond and its associated natural life turn, so Thoreau documents the turns of his own evolving consciousness, the self as a separate but complementary world. Most aspects of the pond – its changing seasonal colours, patterns and temperature, even its herbiage and fish – suggest to him analogies with basic human growth and change. And just as he develops, even more surely than in *A Week,* a magnificent account of nature, he insists on the need to be 'expert in home-cosmography', the scholar of the inner individual human landscape. The culminating point of his 'experiment', having taken his plumb-line to measure the pond and by clear implication his own being, lies in the arrival of the spring: 'As every season seems best to us in turn, so the coming in of the Spring is like the Creation of Cosmos out of Chaos and the realization of the Golden Age.' As

nature awakens in springtime, so each self, to Thoreau's perception, can awaken from past dormancy. Throughout *Walden,* and *A Week,* and in prose always subtly dual in angle, Thoreau adapts his observations of nature – and of 'economy' and 'profit' – to ends which are both moral and deeply existential. Typically, he writes at the conclusion of *Walden:* 'Let every one mind his own business, and endeavour to be what he was made.'

Thoreau's insistence upon the imperatives of unfettered selfhood equally marks out his essays. In 'Civil Disobedience', to which **Gandhi**, the pioneers of the British labour movement and a line of political 'resisters' have paid handsome acknowledgement, the ostensible object of attack is American slavery – but slavery not only as an actual historic and unconscionable indignity, but as the wider expression of how government always 'enslaves' its citizenry. Thoreau's spirited polemic seems to indict all statist systems, almost all imposed curbs on the claims of human liberty. Counter-arguments can, of course, be made. But the passion and controlling clarity of Thoreau's style make for one of the great, memorable formulations of dissent. Equally, Thoreau's espousal of John Brown in his famous 'Plea' is the argument of a philosophical radical to whom emancipation can, as at Harper's Ferry, justify murder. The other essays, and Thoreau's posthumous 'travel' pieces – *Excursions* (1863), *The Maine Woods* (1864), *Cape Cod* (1865) and *A Yankee in Canada* (1866) – have not had the currency of the earlier work, but they again underline his acute observational power and his principled insistence on individualism, the need for distinct, separate spheres of human consciousness.

Thoreau's 'eccentricity' is far less the expression of a man simply out of joint with his age, or with the American state and his inherited culture, but rather of a pragmatic, wholly undeferential, seeker after his own 'earned' truths. For him life was nothing if not lived in the particular, weighed and measured by individual inspection. The danger was always of solipsism, the self as all. But Thoreau's informed, radical respect for nature, and for the order of things as seen in his beloved New England forests and landscape, kept him mostly free of that impasse. Like Emerson he sought a 'transcendental' dimension, but only if gained through careful, meticulous personal experience. Here, as in almost every aspect of his life, he was the truest of Yankees, listening always, and never without irony, to his own drummer, the call of his own mind and conscience.

Further reading

See: Ellery Channing, *Thoreau: The Poet Naturalist* (1902); F.O. Mathiessen, *American Renaissance: Art and Expression in the Age of Emerson and Whitman* (1941); Joseph Wood Krutch, *Henry David Thoreau* (1948); *Thoreau: A Century of Criticism*, ed. Walter Harding (1954); R.W.B. Lewis, *The American Adam: Innocence, Tradition and Tragedy in the Nineteenth Century* (1955); J. Lyndon Shanley, *The Making of Walden, with the Text of the First Edition* (1957); Sherman Paul, *The Shores of America: Thoreau's Inward Exploration* (1958); *Thoreau: A Collection of Critical Essays*, ed. Sherman Paul (1962); *Twentieth Century Interpretations of Walden: A Collection of Critical Essays*, ed. Richard Ruland (1968); *The Recognition of Henry David Thoreau: Selected Criticism since 1848*, ed. Wendel Glick (1969); Raymond R. Borst, *Henry David Thoreau: A Descriptive Bibliography* (1982); Henry S. Salt, *The Life of Henry Thoreau* (1993); Edmund A. Schofield and Robert C. Baron, *Thoreau's World and Ours* (1993); Harmon D. Smith, *My Friend, My Friend: The Story of Thoreau's Relationship with Emerson* (1999); M. Sperber, *Henry David Thoreau: Cycles and Psyche* (2004).

A. ROBERT LEE

TIPPETT, (Sir) Michael

1905–98

English composer

Michael Tippett received an orthodox musical education, but developed late as a composer. It was only after two periods of study at the Royal College of Music in London (1923–8, 1930–2) that he began to assemble the elements of his personal, mature style.

The sinuous rhythms of Tudor polyphony, the exuberant syncopations and inflected harmonies of jazz, **Stravinsky's** avoidance of regular accentuation and traditional diatonic progressions, would all contribute to a distinctive energy and vitality. But it was the synthesis between fugue and sonata, between elaborately unified and intensely dramatic formal principles, so powerfully achieved in the music of Beethoven, which fired Tippett's imagination most decisively. His first completely characteristic and successful work, the *Concerto for Double String Orchestra* (1939), belongs to a series of symphonic compositions – four piano sonatas, five string quartets, four symphonies, a piano concerto, a concerto for string trio and orchestra and a concerto for orchestra – in which the energy of interacting contrapuntal lines often supports only occasional hints of traditional harmonic or modal thinking. And in the later works, for all their reliance on easily detectable thematic and textural recurrences, even that degree of tonal chordal practice may be dispensed with.

Tippett's early teaching and performing activities with amateurs, and his radical political sympathies, led to a permanent adherence to pacifism, for which he was briefly imprisoned in 1943. His oratorio, *A Child of Our Time* (1939–41), is his most politically explicit work, dealing with the murder of a German diplomat by a young Jew in 1938. But it was only when Tippett turned away from such documentary concerns to explore the symbols and themes of **Jungian** psychology in his first opera *The Midsummer Marriage* (1946–52) that he released a flow of inspired lyricism whose conviction and formal coherence triumphantly compensate for any obscurities or oddities in either plot or libretto. His later operas, *King Priam* (1958–61), *The Knot Garden* (1966–70), *The Ice Break* (1972–6) and *New Year* (1986–8), as well as the major choral works *The Vision of St Augustine* (1963–5) and *The Mask of Time* (1980–2), all explore human aspirations, stressing the need for individuals to comprehend the psychic as well as social forces within, around and beyond them. By writing his own texts (or choosing appropriate extracts, in the case of *The Vision of St Augustine* and *The Mask of Time*) Tippett revealed an idiosyncratic way with words, but an instinctive sense of the formulations needed to set his elaborate melodic lines in motion. In spite of the more naturalistic aspects of his later operas, and of the texts set as part of the Symphony No. 3 (1970–2), as well as in *The Mask of Time*, it is the exploration of myth and creative energy which remains most crucial. This is shown with particular clarity in his late setting of **Yeats's** *Byzantium* for soprano and orchestra (1989–90).

Tippett succeeds in communicating so forcefully because the importunate melodic eloquence and exhilarating superimpositions of his most characteristic textures are controlled by clear formal outlines, with easily perceptible repetitions and variations. Even in the absence of traditional tonal structures, there is a clear distinction between fundamental and ornamental aspects. Tippett's highly original style is always intensely coherent.

Further reading

Tippett's music is published by Schott. For his writings, see *Tippett on Music*, ed. M. Bowen (1995), and his autobiography *Those Twentieth-Century Blues* (1991). Important critical studies are Ian Kemp, *Tippett: The Composer and His Music* (1984) and David Clarke, *The Music and Thought of Michael Tippett* (2001).

ARNOLD WHITTALL

TOLKIEN, John Ronald Reuel

1892–1973

British writer and philologist

J.R.R. Tolkien was born in Bloemfontein, South Africa, but on his father's death in 1895 his family moved to Birmingham, at first to a cottage at Sarehole Mill outside the town, later into the city itself. He was educated at King Edward's School, Birmingham (with a short spell at St Philip's Grammar School), and went to Exeter College,

Oxford, as a scholar in 1911, reading Honour Moderations in classics and English language and literature, in which he was awarded a first class. His academic career was interrupted by military service between 1915 and 1918; after leaving the army he rapidly established himself as a distinguished philologist and successful academic, being appointed Reader in English Language at the University of Leeds in 1920 and Professor in 1924. In 1925 he was appointed Rawlinson and Bosworth Professor of Anglo-Saxon at Oxford, where he remained for the rest of his academic life. He became a friend of C.S. Lewis and was a member of the 'Inklings' circle.

The mythical fictions for which Tolkien became famous clearly grew from the same root as his professional and personal absorption in language (a talent he showed from an early age, not only becoming proficient in Anglo-Saxon and Gothic as a schoolboy, but also inventing languages at the same age). His imaginary world derived partly from a 'made-up' language, based on Finnish, begun in 1915, which needed a history to explain it (this language eventually became 'Elvish'). He began writing the poems and stories which eventually became *The Silmarillion* as early as 1916. His first published book of fantasy was, however, a children's book, *The Hobbit* (1936). The publishers, Allen & Unwin, expressed interest in a sequel, which finally emerged as a far more serious creation: *The Lord of the Rings*, written between 1939 and 1945, and published as a trilogy in 1954 (*The Fellowship of the Ring* and *The Two Towers*) and 1955 (*The Return of the King*). This, his most important work, achieved at first a respectable *succès d'estime* but went on to become a best-seller on both sides of the Atlantic and, on the face of it surprisingly, to become a campus cult particularly among the radical 'alternative culture' of the late 1960s. It was followed by the publication of slighter pieces, notably *Tree and Leaf* (1964) – a reprint of the well-known lecture 'On Fairy-Stories', and the short story 'Leaf by Niggle', both of which illuminate Tolkien's methods and intentions in *The Lord of the Rings*. *The Silmarillion*, a collection of legends and histories narrating the story of his imaginary world 'Middle-Earth' and 'Elvenhome' from its creation down to the end of its 'first Age', was published posthumously in 1977; it became a best-seller and was quickly followed by *Unfinished Tales of Numenor and Middle-Earth* (1980), both being edited by his son Christopher Tolkien. The popularity and continuing marketability of *The Lord of the Rings* and its largely fragmentary 'prequels', together with an accompanying 'Tolkien industry' of illustrated editions, guides to 'Middle-Earth', calendars, etc., were enormously increased by Peter Jackson's award-winning trio of films *The Lord of the Rings* in 2001–3 (the film titles following those of Tolkien's own trilogy). These were shot on location in New Zealand, with brilliant computer animations to represent the supernatural elements, the big battle-scenes and the monsters, including a finely grotesque and pitiful Gollum. The principal characters were played by leading actors, including Ian McKellen as a splendid Gandalf, Elijah Wood as Frodo, Ian Holm as Bilbo (a brilliant cameo role) and Orlando Bloom as a heroic Legolas. Although Jackson's films inevitably condense and to some extent simplify Tolkien's narrative, they remain remarkably faithful to their original, their dialogue even including some exchanges in Elvish (helpfully subtitled); they succeed particularly well in their portrayal of the set-piece battle-scenes and of the relation between Frodo and Gollum the corrupted hobbit. The enduring appeal of Tolkien's fantasy world is proved by Jackson's huge box-office success (not to mention the subsequent massive sales of role-playing computer games based on the film version of Tolkien's characters).

Tolkien believed in the making of fantasies as not only a legitimate and vital but a high form of art in which, as he wrote in the lecture 'On Fairy-Stories' (1939), man resembles God in the divinely granted faculty of 'sub-creation' of secondary worlds – as

opposed to the primary world created by God. Consistent with this was his habit of referring to his stories as 'discoveries', rather than inventions; and his imaginary Middle-Earth is, unsurprisingly, structured on firmly Christian lines.

Why what began as the spare-time hobby of a professor of Anglo-Saxon should have enjoyed such enduring and versatile popular success is an interesting question. In the first place, Tolkien's imagined world both feeds and stimulates a public appetite for myth, for heroism and for imaginary marvels, while presenting these with a novelist's attention to detail and privileged entry into the characters' consciousness. Tom Shippey has shown in his book *The Road to Middle-Earth* (by far the best critical study of Tolkien's writings) not only that *The Lord of the Rings* was profoundly influenced by its author's wide and deep knowledge of Dark Age and medieval Germanic literature, but also that although Tolkien's themes and imagery may be drawn from a wide variety of Old English, Old Norse and medieval sources, his narrative conventions are the familiar ones of realist fiction. Second, on a thematic level, *The Lord of the Rings* fits into a still-strong tradition of Romantic ruralist attacks on the evils of industrialism: Tolkien's insistence on the need for reverence towards non-human forms of life held a strong and continuing appeal to ecologically minded people alert to the threat posed to the biosphere by technological progress. Third, his world has the attraction of completeness; it has its own cosmology, mythology, history, variety of species, languages, literatures, scripts, maps, genealogies and even calendar. This world has also the ambiguous appeal of simplicity: there is hierarchy but no class, love-stories but no passionate sexuality, village life among the hobbits but no labour (unless you count Sauron's dimly glimpsed slaves) – in other words, a world without most of the problems which complicate human existence, dominated by a satisfactorily simple conflict between Good (the Elves and other 'Free Peoples') and Evil (Morgoth, Sauron and

Mordor). Finally, the elegiac mood of Tolkien's writing – *The Lord of the Rings* is set almost at the end of the imaginary era of Middle-Earth, and readers are constantly referred back to a vanished past still more remote and wonderful – increases the same nostalgic appetite for myth and remoteness on which it feeds.

Further reading

Other works: *Beowulf, the Monsters and the Critics* (1936); *Farmer Giles of Ham* (1949); *Adventures of Tom Bombadil* (1962); *Smith of Wootton Major* (1967); *Letters of J.R.R. Tolkien*, ed. Humphrey Carpenter (1981). See also the first of the authoritative twelve-volume *History of Middle-Earth*, ed. Christopher Tolkien (1983–96), beginning with *The Book of Lost Tales* (1983) and ending with *The Peoples of Middle-Earth* Vol. 12 (1996); this multiple edition contains all of Tolkien's fantasy writings, including early drafts of *The Lord of the Rings* and of *The Silmarillion*. See also the biographical studies by Humphrey Carpenter, *The Inklings* (1973) *J.R.R. Tolkien* (1977); *Letters of J.R.R. Tolkien* (1982). For a hostile view, see Edmund Wilson, 'Ooh, Those Awful Orcs!' in *The Bit Between My Teeth* (1956); for a strong defence, see Tom Shippey, *The Road to Middle-Earth* (1981), revised and reissued as *J.R.R. Tolkien: Author of the Century* (2000).

JANET MONTEFIORE

TOLSTOY, (Count) Lev Nikolaevich

1828–1910

Russian writer

Born in Yasnaya Polyana, near Tula, he was the fourth son of an aristocratic family of five children who were orphaned early by the death of their mother when Tolstoy was only two years of age. Given over to the guardianship of their Aunt Tatyana and their paternal grandmother, the children formed a close-knit group with their own nursery lore of an Ant Brotherhood and the legend of a little green stick on which the secret of happiness was written. The close intuitive understanding born of such relationships and the closed, protected world of Yasnaya Polyana itself, an estate supported by 800 or

so serfs, were to influence profoundly Tolstoy's view of the world by leading to his insistence on the importance of the family as the basis of the social contract and the moral superiority of the country to the city, of the rural peasantry to the urban masses. The death of his father when Tolstoy was only eight contributed to the family's desire to close ranks, but Tolstoy's own curiosity about life, brilliantly conveyed in his first semi-autobiographical work *Childhood* (*Detstvo,* 1852), was unorthodox in its directness and clarity. The conventional education by tutors offered him little, just as his years at the University of Kazan (1844–7) ended without his completing the course. His own rich inner life impelled him into making encyclopaedic plans for self-education, while his passionate masculine nature led to successive fruitless attempts at moral self-improvement, as his diaries testify. By the time he was twenty he was living the typically licentious life of a young Russian nobleman.

In 1849 he moved to St Petersburg with the intention of entering the university, but at the time of the arrests in connection with the Petrashevsky affair he appears to have returned hastily to Yasnaya Polyana. A superficially aimless lifestyle was soon interrupted when, in 1851, Tolstoy accompanied his brother Nikolay to the Caucasus and found himself involved in the Russian colonial wars against the hill tribesmen. The effect on him was of incalculable significance. It not only spurred him to write, but it also forced him to examine the nature of human motivation in war, the meaning of courage and the role of vanity in determining behaviour even at the limits of endurance. Such studies of Caucasian military life as *The Raid* (*Nabeg,* 1852) and *The Woodfelling* (*Rubka lesa,* 1855) supplied the groundwork for his masterly examination of war at its most brutal and senseless in his *Sevastopol Sketches* (*Sevastopol' v dekabre,* 1855; *Sevastopol v avguste,* 1856). Experience of the Crimean campaign in 1854–5 taught him that war was never glamorous, but that its only hero 'is he whom I love with all the strength of my spirit, whom

I have striven to depict in all his beauty and who always was, is and will be beautiful – truth'. Simultaneously he was completing the remaining parts of his autobiographical trilogy, *Boyhood* (*Otrochestvo*, 1854) and *Youth* (*Yunost'*, 1856).

By the end of the Crimean War he had become famous and he was lionized in the salons of St Petersburg during the winter of 1855–6, being cultivated particularly by Turgenev. It was with Turgenev as his companion for part of the time that he went to Europe in 1857. A public guillotining which he witnessed in Paris and the vulgar behaviour of English tourists in Lucerne (which gave rise to the first of his philosophical works, *Lucerne*, 1857) reinforced both his distaste for European standards and his sense of moral outrage. Upon his return to Russia, though he published *A Landowner's Morning* (*Utro pomeshchika*), *Three Deaths* (*Tri smerti*), *Albert* and the novella *Family Happiness* (*Semeynoye schast'ye*) during the following three years, he was gradually being drawn towards an interest in peasant education. The dilemma of conscience which faced so many members of the Russian nobility as the emancipation of the serfs approached (February 1861) took the form in Tolstoy's case of a desire to be of practical assistance to the peasants on his estate. This interest took him abroad again for the second and last time in his life between July 1860 and April 1861, when he studied educational practice in many European countries, visiting London, for example, where he attended a reading by **Dickens** and is supposed to have met **Matthew Arnold**. Back in Russia, he threw himself into the work of the peasant school which he established at Yasnaya Polyana and produced a dozen issues of an educational journal. Yet, at the age of thirty-four in 1862, he suddenly altered the pattern of his life by marrying Sonya Bers, sixteen years his junior, and settling down to raise a family.

In the following years the need for money obliged him to complete and publish *Polikushka*, his powerful study of peasant life, and his longest work to date, *The Cossacks*

(*Kazaki*), which had been ten years in the writing. Probably during the summer or autumn of the same year he began writing the monumental work about the Napoleonic invasion of Russia upon which his reputation still principally rests, though it was originally known simply as *1805* or *All's Well That Ends Well*. *War and Peace* was written over a period of seven years and was completed late in 1869. The immense effort involved may have brought him close to a nervous breakdown, for it is thought that he experienced a horrific vision of death while staying in a hotel in Arzamas at this time (described in *Notes of a Madman*, *Zapiski sumasshedshego*, 1897). In the ensuing decade his thinking, like his writing, showed a growing preoccupation with the purpose of life and ways to combat the apparent meaninglessness of death. Whether through his ABC book for schoolchildren or the writing of his great novel *Anna Karenina* (1873–7), he aimed to show the universal moral norms at work in society and the need for the educated and privileged to learn the true meaning of goodness from the peasantry.

The last pages of *Anna Karenina* point the way to the religious conversion which Tolstoy described in his *Confession* (*Ispoved'*, 1882). For the remaining three decades of his life he devoted himself chiefly to writing tracts which expounded the fundamental tenets of his religious philosophy. This philosophy, while outwardly concerned with non-resistance to evil by violence, the virtues of work, vegetarianism and abstinence from alcohol and sex, was basically a prolonged attempt by Tolstoy to reconcile through religious precept the gulf between rich and poor, especially the gulf between the intelligentsia and the peasantry, which divided Russian society. His outspoken attacks upon the church and the state undoubtedly brought him enormous moral authority, but also led to his excommunication by the Holy Synod in 1901. He also placed his immense powers as a writer at the service of his philosophy and, apart from writing a great many simple, edifying tales for the people, he turned such fine works as *The Death of Ivan Ilyich* (*Smert Ivan Il'yicha*, 1886), *The Kreutzer Sonata* (*Kreytserova sonata*, 1889) and *Resurrection* (*Voskreseniye*, 1899) into illustrative tracts. In the 1880s he also began writing for the theatre with his sombre study of peasant greed and murder, *The Power of Darkness* (*Vlast' t'my*, 1886), and his comedy about spiritualism and peasant guile, *The Fruits of Enlightenment* (*Plody prosveshcheniya*, 1889), though probably his most original work for the stage was *The Living Corpse* (*Zhivoy trup*, 1900). In his last years two works demand special mention: his treatise on art, *What is Art?* (*Chto takoye iskusstvo?*, 1897), in which a case is made for the idea that art is a kind of emotional infection, and his remarkable short novel drawn from his early experience of war in the Caucasus, *Hadji Murat* (completed 1904, published posthumously).

The contrast between his high-minded advocacy of a religious life and the fact that he remained in the relatively comfortable circumstances of Yasnaya Polyana naturally caused tension between himself and his family, especially his wife. She was concerned for the future security of his nine surviving children and less eager than her husband to renounce all earthly wealth. There was the added complication that she felt she had been replaced in his affections by the Tolstoyanists or cult followers surrounding him, with the result that their relations became clouded by suspicion, enmity and open feuding. In despair Tolstoy finally left home in November 1910 and was taken ill at the railway halt of Astapovo on the Ryazan–Ural railroad, where he died, aged eighty-two.

If Tolstoy's later renown as the founder of Tolstoyanism and an arbiter of morals for his time has faded to vanishing point since his death, his fame as a novelist has steadily increased. The reason for this is due largely to the fact that his religious and philosophical views were outdated even for the nineteenth century, deriving so clearly from an oversimplified, Enlightenment view of human capabilities and purposes, whereas his supreme gift as a writer was an outstanding clarity and freshness of viewpoint in depicting the world. His writer's vision had the straightforward, illustrative quality of photography, and he tended to represent life with all the kinetic vitality of the cinema. He deliberately avoided such artifices as plot-structure, narrated biographies of character or the domination of fiction by a single central portrayal, preferring to evoke the multiplicity of experience by offering successive and varied viewpoints through a multiplication of central figures with whom the reader can identify. Deliberately concealing his own authorial role in the fiction for the greater part, he dared to assume that fiction could represent life pictorially, always governed by a strict chronology, and that human nature changed with the passage of time and even discovered means to self-improvement. Probably the most daring of his achievements in this respect was his depiction of history and historical characters in *War and Peace* as relating to the same dimension as his fictional creations, so that the historical Kutuzov, the Russian commander, can be seen to know the fictional Pierre Bezukhov's wife, for example, and we as readers can appraise and appreciate Kutuzov through Pierre's eyes. Fiction and history here coalesce into a Tolstoyan truth which seems manifestly more real than the historian's.

For all the apparent breadth of vision and olympian skill with which Tolstoy moves us from a St Petersburg salon to the battlefields of Austerlitz or Borodino, from Pierre Bezukhov's world to the family world of the Rostovs, there are always certain limits of viewpoint and manner circumscribing the fiction and certain moralistic limitations or norms. In *War and Peace* the historical motivation imposes its own fatalism upon the lives of historical and fictional characters alike. Just as Napoleon is shown to be no more than a puppet of dynamic processes over which he can exert no real power, so Prince Andrey Bolkonsky can be seen to be predestined to act the role of doomed hero. There is perhaps a similar element of predestination about the evolution of the delightful Natasha Rostov into the matronly figure of the first epilogue. But the greatness of the fiction lies not in such fatalism, nor in the theory of history that turns its final pages (of the second epilogue) into a rather bullying tract; it lies in the assertion of the vital and positive ideas permeating the characters' lives. The role of the family, for instance, as exemplified by the Rostovs, is one that suggests stability, shared love and an instinctive hostility to all that threatens such an ethos, meaning chiefly the French invaders. Similarly, it is a search for a positive meaning in life that inspires Andrey Bolkonsky to replace his Napoleonic ideal by a faith in the boundlessness of love and equate such love with a divine force, or makes Pierre Bezukhov seek in freemasonry and numerology an answer to life's purpose that is finally revealed to him, in a simple equation of God with life, by the peasant Platon Karatayev. The epic size of *War and Peace* is therefore assessable both in terms of its enormous range of characters, its variety of locales and its timespan, and in terms of the profundity of the religious and philosophical ideas which concern the central characters.

Anna Karenina, though less ambitious in its scope, is no less daring as a novel in its portrayal of Anna herself – one of the most remarkable female characterizations ever achieved by a male author – and in its exploration of the manifold pressures in Russian society of the 1870s. A novel about marriage, female emancipation, the contrast between urban and rural life, between reason and faith, between suicide and religious purpose, *Anna Karenina* presupposes that there are certain norms, as rigid perhaps after their fashion as the railway lines which bring Anna into the fiction at the beginning and kill her at the end (of Part VII), and these norms point the way, so Tolstoy seems to be saying, either to personal fulfilment or to futility and suicide. Though a tragic mechanism may perhaps determine Anna's decision to leave her husband and son and give herself to Vronsky, the processes are so gradual and so subtle that her vitality seems always to

outpace them. The extinguishing of the vital candle of her life is an act of immolation that indicts all the pretensions, hypocrisies and falsehoods of the society to which she has fallen victim. In compensation for her tragedy, the parallel story of Konstantin Levin's marriage to Kitty and final discovery of an intuitive law of right and wrong known only to the peasantry is magnificent in its own right, but it scarcely prevails in its optimistic message against the darkness that finally engulfs Anna herself.

Tolstoy's realism is of a controlled richness in its detail, with emphasis always upon appearance and action, but at its heart is an awareness of both the physicality of experience – the sense, in short, that his characters inhabit bodies – and of the rational processes by which they may discover for themselves new truths and beliefs. However seriously he may have taken himself (and his work is not noteworthy for its humour), he was by nature the least pompous of men, and the gleam which shines from his eyes in so many of his portraits bespeaks a man who enjoyed life's peculiarities while recognizing its sinfulness and its grandeur.

Further reading

Other works include: *Twenty-Three Tales*; *What Then Must We Do?*; *On Life and Essays on Religion: Recollections and Essays*; *Tales of Army Life*; *The Kingdom of God and Peace Essays*; *The Snow Storm and Other Stories*; etc. A selection of his letters translated by R.F. Christian has recently been published in two volumes (1978). About Tolstoy: the two-volume biography by A. Maude, *The Life of Tolstoy* (1930), has been largely superseded by E.J. Simmons, *Leo Tolstoy* (1960), and H. Troyat, *Tolstoy* (1968). Recent critical works on Tolstoy (in alphabetical order) include an excellent work by J. Bayley, *Tolstoy and the Novel* (1966); the famous study of Tolstoy's theory of history by I. Berlin, *The Hedgehog and the Fox* (1953); T.G.S. Cain, *Tolstoy* (1977); R.F. Christian's 'critical introduction' to Tolstoy's work, *Tolstoy* (1969); a chapter devoted to *War and Peace* in R. Freeborn, *The Rise of the Russian Novel* (1973); E.B. Greenwood, *Tolstoy: The Comprehensive Vision* (1975); F.R. Leavis, *Anna Karenina and Other Essays* (1967); G.W. Spence's study of the dualism in Tolstoy's thought, *Tolstoy the Ascetic* (1967); E. Stenbock-Fermor's valuable, if eccentric, *The Architecture of 'Anna Karenina'* (1975); and E. Wasiolek's opinionated, but stimulating, *Tolstoy's Major Fiction* (1978). Two recent collections of critical essays on Tolstoy should also be mentioned: *Leo Tolstoy: A Critical Anthology*, ed. H. Gifford; and *New Essays on Tolstoy*, ed. M. Jones; John Bayley, *Leo Tolstoy* (1997).

RICHARD FREEBORN

TOULOUSE-LAUTREC, Henri de

1864–1901

French artist

Born near Albi in the south-west of France into one of the most aristocratic of families, Toulouse-Lautrec's full physical growth was retarded as a result of injuries to his legs. He remained permanently self-conscious with regard to his handicap until his death from alcoholism in 1901.

His artistic career started formally in Paris, first at the studio of Bonnat and then at that of Cormon where he met Émil Bernard, **Vincent Van Gogh** and Louis Anquetin, with whom he remained on friendly terms for many years, painting their portraits and corresponding when he or they left Paris.

Lautrec's work developed starting with influence from Bastien Lepage, then from the Impressionism of Pissarro, finally to his own personal style which took its main impetus from subtle and direct line drawing. This he at times adapted for the purposes of lithography. His subject-matter remained almost entirely that of people.

In 1884 Lautrec set up his studio in Montmartre where he spent hours in cafés and cabarets drawing the people who worked there and the patrons who gave them their living. At first he drew mostly those who came to Aristide Bruant's café cabaret, Le Mirliton, opened in 1885. Bruant wrote and sang many of the ballads performed at Le Mirliton himself. Before 1885 when he worked in a more expensive quarter of Paris his songs were light-hearted, at times amusing. Montmartre had the effect of providing

more tragic themes. It was these later ballads, based on the lives of the people in the locale of Le Mirliton – prostitutes, pimps, dancers, actresses, the homeless, forlorn or drunken – that provided Lautrec with subjects. Many of his paintings of the middle and late 1880s have titles taken from Bruant's ballads. *At Montrouge, Rosa la Rouge,* a single portrait of a girl of 1888, is a case in point.

It was at this time that Lautrec also adopted something of **Degas's** style and subject-matter, painting ballet girls with a light directional brush-stroke and achieving some acclaim for the work he exhibited. The brushwork then became less even and more open in handling and line began to separate itself from and dominate the colour areas. These portraits he carried out quickly but only after knowing and observing the person well. Generally he worked from memory and only rarely for commissions over which he was immensely conscientious, asking the sitter to pose dozens of times.

By the 1890s much of Lautrec's effort was directed towards lithography, in particular poster design. The most famous posters of this era must be those of La Goulu, can-can dancer at the Moulin Rouge.

In 1896 Lautrec painted and made lithographs entitled *Alone*. A prostitute is sympathetically portrayed resting on a bed. Other such pictures show moments of intimacy, of women combing their hair, tightening their corsets or waiting in a salon for customers.

Shortly before his death, while spending the summer as usual in Bordeaux, Lautrec became enchanted by opera as well as operettas and some of his last works are evocations of the mood of moments from *Messaline* or *La Belle Hélène.*

Lautrec's very early drawings as a child show a liking for caricature. Later in life this preference takes the form of feeling for character so that the essential elements not only of an individual's personal appearance, but also the objects that suggest his or her personal tastes and role or profession in life are included.

Often Lautrec's view is cynical, but frequently it is also compassionate as he surveys the difficulties with which the most vulnerable in Parisian society had to cope.

Many later artists, such as those of the German and Belgian Expressionist movement, owed as much to Lautrec as to Van Gogh. One can see La Goulu in Felicien Rops's skeletal women, fat clients of the brothel houses more sharply criticized by George Grosz in scenes of corruption in Berlin. The decadence of the 'Gay Nineties' then becomes the despair of the early 1920s and Lautrec's cynicism the paramount attitude

Further reading

See: Jean Adhémar, *Henri de Toulouse-Lautrec: Complete Lithographs and Drypoints* (1965); Eduouard Julien, *The Posters of Toulouse-Lautrec* (1966); M.G. Dortu and J.A. Méric, *Toulouse-Lautrec: The Complete Painting* (1981). See also: Henri Perruchot, *Toulouse-Lautrec: A Definitive Biography* (trans. 1969); André Fermigier, *Toulouse-Lautrec* (trans. 1969); Douglas Cooper, *Henri de Toulouse-Lautrec* (1981); Julia Frey, *Toulouse-Lautrec: A Life* (1994); David Sweetman, *Toulouse-Lautrec and the Fin-de-siècle* (1999).

PAT TURNER

TROLLOPE, Anthony

1815–82

English novelist

All authors may take courage from the extraordinary fortunes of Anthony Trollope, who enjoyed arguably even greater respect a century after his death than ever he did at the height of his Victorian success. His eminence is the more remarkable as resulting from a critical recovery after nearly half a century of contemptuous neglect, exacerbated at the outset by the publication, a year after his death, of his extremely blunt and straightforward *Autobiography* (1883), a plain statement of his aims and achievements as a man of letters and a professional employee of the Civil Service. Such frankness on the part of an artist was intolerable to an age which cherished artifice and performance; indeed, it was scarcely admissible that Trollope was an artist at all. His novels became swiftly relegated to the ranks of those relished rather guiltily by readers in search of a comfortable nostalgia. A work like *Framley Parsonage* (1861), fourth in the famous 'Barchester' series, was enjoyed almost solely for its superb characterization and neatly arranged plot, while its profounder and more abstract issues, dramatized to such ironic effect in the marital manoeuvres of Lucy Robarts, Griselda Grantly and Miss Dunstable, were totally ignored.

Writing was an inalienable part of the Trollope family heritage. Anthony's elder brother Tom produced a long and turgid set of works on Italian subjects and their father, a hopelessly unsuccessful barrister, made several attempts as a historian. The miserable childhood of the Trollope children, reared in an atmosphere of shabby gentility and feckless Micawberish optimism, was somewhat lightened by their indomitable mother, Frances, who gained considerable fame as a novelist dealing with social questions of the day and produced, after an unsuccessful attempt to carry culture to Cincinnati, the amusing and highly readable *Domestic Manners of the Americans* (1832).

Trollope was educated at Harrow and Winchester, and was eventually pushed into a Post Office clerkship at the age of nineteen. His careful cultivation of a bluff, even boorish exterior manner seems to have been designed to mask the acute sensitivity developed in him during his unhappy adolescence, and we can find traces of such characteristics in the awkward, gangling protagonists of certain of the novels. He appears to have put much of himself, for example, into Johnny Eames of *The Small House at Allington* (1864), and into Josiah Crawley, the gloomy curate hero of *The Last Chronicle of Barset* (1867).

The turn of his fortunes occurred in 1841 when he was transferred to Ireland to supervise postal operations in the central district. Here he was able to show a truly Victorian capacity for hard work and initiative, by which he soon won the respect of his superiors and sufficient funds to enable him to marry Rose Heseltine, the daughter of a Rotherham bank manager. He is almost exceptional among nineteenth-century novelists in having made a happy and successful marriage.

Ireland, its people and its problems offered him the material for his first and last novels, *The Macdermots of Ballycloran* (1847) and *The Landleaguers*, left unfinished at his death, and provided subject-matter elsewhere in his work. He returned to England to maintain the two careers in tandem throughout the 1850s and 1860s, fuelling each with the prodigious physical and mental energy which allowed him to indulge his other consuming enthusiasm, hunting. Thus his fiction is permeated throughout with an exactness of topographical detail acquired from journeyings across England on Post Office business, and several of his finest stretches of writing, notably in *Phineas Redux* (1874), *The Eustace Diamonds* (1873) and *The American Senator* (1877), are concerned with scenes in the hunting field.

His private and professional life was never marked by any especially dramatic events. As a thoroughly dependable official, despite a certain tendency to quarrelsomeness wherever he felt he was being overborne by bureaucracy, he was sent to Egypt, the Caribbean and the Pacific on postal assignments, and wrote an interesting account of post-Civil War America after visits to the principal eastern cities. It was on his last voyage to New York that he was seen by **Henry James**, whose account of the man and his work in *Partial Portraits* is one of the best of contemporary treatments. Trollope had a wide and loyal circle of friends, including **George Eliot**, **Browning** and the popular journalist George Augustus Sala, and died in the guise of a respected, if distinctly conservative, mainstay of the circulating library three-decker novel readership.

Few writers have been more honest in their assessments of personal achievement and few have done themselves a greater disservice

by being so. Only during the last thirty years has the literary public recovered sufficiently from being told by Trollope himself that he made £68,939 17s 5d from his novels and that it is not necessary to wait for inspiration before writing, and distanced itself enough from the Victorian era for us to have begun a wholesale and much-needed reappraisal of his work. Such a revaluation has brought him the attention of committed scholarship and placed him very high indeed among the English novelists of his age. Instead of viewing him as a mildly entertaining chronicler of clerical indiscretions in an English country town, we have been taught to see him as the quietly complex and admirably tolerant analyst of the strains imposed upon quintessentially normal people and societies by the conventions they accept. He is never, in any of his books, hysterical, dogmatic or pompous, and it is by virtue of what Henry James called his 'complete apprehension of the usual' that he so frequently triumphs.

His transcendent humanity prompts him to invoke our compassion for even the most transparently duplicit of his characters: the ironic solution which drives us to sympathize with Ferdinand Lopez in *The Prime Minister* (1876), with the impossible Lizzie Eustace in *The Eustace Diamonds*, with the unregenerate *fin-de-ligne* Sowerby of *Framley Parsonage*, or with gold-digging Arabella Trefoil as she prepares to marry Mounser Green in *The American Senator*, is always wholly acceptable. By the same method, other characters are made antipathetic by their unscrupulous cultivation of social orthodoxy: few are more chilling than the glacially correct and heartless Griselda Grantly of the Barchester novels or the monomaniacal Mr Kennedy in *Phineas Redux*, an offshoot of that profounder study of marital obsession, Louis Trevelyan in *He Knew He Was Right* (1869).

Pessimism, neurosis and the nightmare of social disgrace are always splendidly handled by the mature Trollope. His most perceptive treatment of these themes appears in *The Last Chronicle of Barset* and *The Way We Live Now* (1875). The first of these is, despite formal imperfections owing to an otiose sub-plot, an acknowledged masterpiece, in which the comic creations of the earlier Barchester novels are fleshed out with an impressively tragic dignity. The Lear-like figure of Josiah Crawley, learning survival through rejection and adversity, is cleverly opposed by the almost demonically self-destructive Mrs Proudie, the circumstances leading to whose death give the event a convincing pathos rarely equalled elsewhere in Victorian fiction. The second, the most ambitious work Trollope ever attempted, a mercilessly satirical indictment of debased values in the society of the 1870s, creates a comparable balance to the earlier book in counter-pointing the buccaneering financier Melmotte with the pillar of antique squirearchical virtue Roger Carbury.

Trollope does not wholly underwrite Carbury's standpoint and, as if in acknowledgment that his exalted moral standards are too lofty for most of us, makes the heroine Hetta reject him in favour of the far more doubtful but ultimately more full-blooded Paul Montague. There is no doubt, however, that Roger Carbury speaks for much of what Trollope admired, and a succession of the novels creates for us a consistent view of the English gentleman culminating in the fascinating figure of Plantagenet Palliser, whose appearances with his wife Glencora serve to link together a series of six books beginning with *Can You Forgive Her?* (1864) and concluding with *The Duke's Children* (1880) some sixteen years later.

Just as the Barchester series dealt in detail with the manners and trials of rural clergy and landowners, so the Palliser novels, with an equally sharp scrutiny, approach the world of politics and government. Though there is no evidence to suggest that Trollope planned either set through from start to finish, it is noteworthy that each is governed by the aura of a moral human presence – in the first case, that of Septimus Harding, hero of *The Warden* (1855), whose death in *The Last Chronicle of Barset* seems to ordain the sense of finality in the book rather than be ordained

by it; in the second, those of Plantagenet and Glencora. The latter, by a master-stroke, is made to die before *The Duke's Children* opens, and the power of her often anarchic influence is felt through the behaviour of her children.

As a stylist Trollope is among the plainest of Victorian writers. His handling of dialogue has been admired to the point of declaring it the best among nineteenth-century novelists and his comprehensive and refreshingly unsentimental treatment of female characters contrasts favourably with most of the other male fiction writers of the age. In his early work the influence of Thackeray can be felt too heavily, especially in the tiresome invocations to the reader in novels such as *Barchester Towers* (1857) and *The Three Clerks* (1858), and several of his later novels, such as *Kept in the Dark* (1882) and *The Fixed Period* (1882), show how fallacious was his reliance on a daily quota of written words. He is nearly always, however, a master of plotting, a talent displayed at its best in *The Eustace Diamonds* (though the structure has also been criticized for relying too heavily on sensationalism), the exuberantly comic *Ayala's Angel* (1881) and the nowadays critically lauded *Mr Scarborough's Family* (1883).

Unlike **Dickens**, **Hardy** and George Eliot, Trollope seldom attempts to write within a consciously historical perspective, though, like each of them, he attempted a historical romance and, as in each case, it is not considered the equal of his other books. Whereas works such as *Great Expectations*, *Middlemarch* and *The Mayor of Casterbridge* rely for their effect on our awareness of the tensions between a recently vanished world and our vivid memories of its existence, novels such as *Orley Farm* (1862), *Phineas Finn* (1869) and *John Caldigate* (1879) rely on our sense of them as taking place within the ordinary world of the mid-Victorian reader. It was Trollope's achievement to have dissected that world within its own frame of reference, in a manner often severe but invariably humane. Recognition of this achievement has been belated but wholly sincere. Yet perhaps the best tribute ever paid to him by another writer was in the form of a note written by **Tolstoy** during the composition of *Anna Karenina,* with its many Trollopian features: 'Trollope kills me, kills me with his excellence!'

Further reading

See: N.J. Hall (ed.), *The Letters of Anthony Trollope* (2 vols, 1983). See also: Michael Sadleir, *Trollope: A Commentary* (1928, rev. 1945); A.O.J. Cockshut, *Anthony Trollope: A Critical Study* (1955); P.D. Edwards, *Anthony Trollope* (1968); *Trollope: The Critical Heritage,* ed. Donald Smalley (1969); R.H. Super, *Trollope and the Post Office* (1981); V. Glendinning, *Trollope* (1992).

JONATHAN KEATES

TROTSKY, Leon
1879–1940
Russian revolutionary

Born Lev Davidovich Bronstein into a moderately prosperous Jewish farming family in the southern Ukraine, Trotsky early became active in the Russian workers' movement and embraced **Marxism**. He was arrested in 1898 for political activity in the town of Nikolayev, imprisoned, and deported to Siberia. Escaping in 1902, he travelled to London where he met **Lenin** for the first time and he began, with Lenin's encouragement, to write for the journal *Iskra* and to argue for its political standpoint – the building of a centralized Russian workers' party – in lectures and debates within Russian émigré circles in Europe. From the first he displayed a powerful literary and oratorical talent.

Present in 1903 at the Second Congress of the Russian Social-Democratic Party, at which the historic schism between Bolsheviks and Mensheviks occurred, Trotsky sided with the Mensheviks against Lenin. Though he would soon distance himself from them to stand outside both factions for more than a decade, on this issue he felt, and wrote, that Lenin's theory of organization was undemocratic, aiming to substitute the efforts of a

revolutionary elite for the initiative of the workers themselves.

Trotsky returned to Russia in 1905 to play a prominent part in the revolution of that year as a leader of the St Petersburg Soviet of Workers' Deputies. The lessons he drew from this experience included reflections on the nature of workers' democracy and the theory, identified with his name, of permanent revolution: he formulated this now in the argument that the Russian proletariat, contrary to any orthodox Marxist expectation held by Bolsheviks and Mensheviks alike, might embark upon socialist revolution before the workers of the more advanced capitalist countries.

For his part in the work of the Soviet, Trotsky was again imprisoned and condemned to exile in Siberia. In 1907, making another escape while under escort into exile, he returned to Europe to settle in Vienna until the First World War. During that conflict, which he spent in Paris and, briefly, New York, his was a leading voice in the revolutionary opposition to the war by the internationalist wing of European socialism.

After the February revolution in 1917, Trotsky again returned to Russia and at once made common cause with Lenin, eventually joining the Bolshevik Party. This had now, following a change of political position by Lenin, adopted a perspective essentially identical with Trotsky's own conception of permanent revolution. Trotsky became one of the Russian revolution's main leaders: brilliant orator, publicist, organizer, political strategist, President of the Petrograd Soviet. He prepared and led the October insurrection which delivered power into the Bolsheviks' hands. As Commissar of Foreign Affairs in the first Soviet government, he conducted the peace negotiations with Germany at Brest-Litovsk; as Commissar of War, supervised the construction of the Red Army through civil war and hostile foreign intervention; played a key role in the foundation and early congresses of the Communist International. Throughout these post-revolutionary years, he spoke and wrote on all important political issues, domestic and international, as also on literary, cultural and scientific topics.

From 1923 onwards, and especially after Lenin's death, Trotsky bent his efforts towards opposing the increasingly bureaucratic and authoritarian regime in the Communist Party, the rising power of **Stalin**, the latter's internal and foreign policies and the doctrine of 'socialism in one country' which he had begun to put forth. In this connection, Trotsky now developed and generalized the theory of permanent revolution. Defeated by Stalin, he was expelled from the Party in 1927, sent into remote exile near the Chinese border, and in 1929 deported from Russia altogether. During the next decade he would inhabit one brief and insecure refuge after another, in Turkey, then France, then Norway, finally Mexico. Isolated, beset by difficulties, bereft by family tragedies, he continued to write prodigiously: history, autobiography, diagnosis and warning concerning the danger of Nazism, analysis of the nature of Soviet society, defence of the authentic Leninist heritage, as he construed this, against its Stalinist despoliation, argument for the formation of a new revolutionary International. At work on a biography of Stalin, he was murdered in his home by one of Stalin's agents.

As political thinker and writer, Trotsky's importance is threefold. His work is one of the best examples of the creative application of Marxism in the area of political and historical analysis; between the time of Lenin's death and his own, Trotsky was in this respect without peer. His best writing, a clear, compelling and imaginative prose combining objectivity with the deepest commitment, achieved a standard of literary excellence first set by Marx himself and matched since by Marx's followers too rarely. Finally, he came to stand – against the currents dominant in the European workers' movement, gradualist and reformist on the one hand, Stalinist, authoritarian, on the other – for a socialism in which proletarian revolution and workers' democracy must sit side by side.

Trotsky's early analysis of the configuration of Russian society, and his prognosis about the character of the revolution that would emerge from it, provide one of the most striking instances of a Marxist theoretical projection confirmed in its broad outline by the immediately ensuing course of events. From 1905 onwards, he challenged the prevalent Russian Marxist belief that, in a backward country with a huge peasant majority, revolution could only mean bourgeois revolution, with its issue the extension of capitalist economy and the establishment of bourgeois–democratic political rule. In *Results and Prospects* (1906) and then *1905* (1910), Trotsky argued that, owing to the specific features of Russia's history in which capitalist development was fostered by the state and based largely on foreign capital, the indigenous forces of the Russian bourgeoisie were too weak, and Russian liberalism insufficiently bold, to lead a revolutionary assault against Tsarism. The Russian working class was small but highly concentrated. Like the compact, relatively advanced capitalist sector which had produced it, it was an expression of what Trotsky was later to call the 'law of combined and uneven development': as capitalism from its heartlands projected its consequences over the globe, heedless of traditional and national boundaries, so the features of modes of production that were, in the classical Marxist schema, distinct, would be found fused together within one social reality; so Russia now combined a modern industrial proletariat with pre-capitalist agrarian and political structures. A successful revolution here, Trotsky asserted, would have to be led by this small, militant proletariat, carrying behind it the land-hungry peasants, and because of this it could not remain a bourgeois revolution. The Russian workers once in power would not be able or willing to leave capitalist property relations intact. Establishing the first dictatorship of the proletariat, they would initiate the transition to socialism. But they could not complete this on their own without linking up with successful socialist revolutions in the West.

Confined to a backward country, the enterprise would be doomed to defeat.

The main tenets of this conception were part also of the outlook of Bolshevism by the time it led the Russian proletariat to power in 1917. Later, when revolutions to the west had failed, leaving the young Soviet state isolated, Stalin asserted first the possibility, then the reality, of a socialism constructed in Russia alone. In *The Permanent Revolution* (1930) and other writings, Trotsky reaffirmed and developed his original conception. He insisted that the fate of Russian socialism still depended on the outcome of the revolutionary process elsewhere. He extended to the analysis of this process in other backward societies the framework first applied in his treatment of Russia; arguing, in anticipation of much subsequent discussion of 'underdevelopment', that such societies could not reproduce the path followed by the first capitalist nations.

The geographical reach of Trotsky's writings on these and related themes was long, covering Britain and China, Germany, France and Spain, the Soviet Union itself. So extensive an output could not be wholly even in strength. Two of its notable achievements, however, were his analyses of fascism and of the character of the Soviet state, historically novel phenomena still to be assimilated within Marxist understanding. With growing urgency Trotsky warned against the Comintern's complacency towards the Nazi threat in Germany. Nazism triumphant, he predicted, would install not just one reactionary variant of capitalist rule among others, but a qualitatively distinct form catastrophic for the working class, predicated on the destruction of its organizations and its means of political self-defence through the mass mobilization against it of petty-bourgeois strata. The Soviet Union, he proposed in *The Revolution Betrayed* (1936), was neither socialist, as Stalin and his apologists claimed, nor some new type of class, or even capitalist, society, as some critics averred. It was a transitional formation in which the chief economic conquest of the October revolution, socialized property relations, was still extant despite the fact that a privileged bureaucracy had fashioned for itself a monopoly of political functions. To advance to socialism the workers would have to overturn this bureaucratic group by a political revolution. On both these issues Trotsky's contribution was original, level-headed and penetrating.

Trotsky was one of the great writers of his time. Keenly interested in literary and cultural subjects to which he devoted a significant part of his output and, in particular, the theoretical study *Literature and Revolution* (1923), his own literary achievement was considerable. It was built upon a lucid and incisive style and the ability to present ideas, persons, events in a complex and vivid way. It encompassed pages of cogent political argument, historical and literary interpretation finely integrating abstract theory with concrete perception, sketches of contemporaries acutely observed; an impressive account of the year *1905*, an autobiographical work, *My Life* (1930), unusual in the Marxist canon and remarkable by any standards, and an outstanding work of Marxist historiography, *The History of the Russian Revolution* (1931). This was his masterpiece, an epic, in which individuals and masses moved against the vast backdrop of Russia's history to transform the destiny of the whole world.

On questions of socialist democracy and organization, Trotsky's record over forty years was neither uniform nor unblemished. He opposed at first the Leninist party concept, representing it in *Our Political Tasks* (1904) as an attempt to hold the working class in tutelage. After 1917 he rejected out of hand all such interpretations of it, upheld it consistently against the charge of having begot the crimes of Stalin. His strictures of Lenin he came to see as unjust and mistaken. *Our Political Tasks* spoke in the name of a democratic socialism open to the struggle between different tendencies; *1905* depicted the soviet form, the workers' council, as the very embodiment of this democratic principle, born of direct proletarian action and expressing as directly as possible the diverse voices within the working class. Though he would share in the necessities, the expediencies and the errors of the Bolsheviks in power, Trotsky was later to return to and develop these themes in his struggle against Stalinism, arguing for the right of tendencies inside revolutionary organizations and, beyond, for a united front within which different currents in the workers' movement could openly compete. Taken all in all, across the inconsistencies, Trotsky's final record was clear: for a socialism both revolutionary and democratic in an atmosphere uncongenial to this synthesis, thus in lonely, but for this very reason vital, continuity with the best traditions of Marxism and of Leninism.

Further reading

Other works include: *The Permanent Revolution and Results and Prospects* (1962); *1905* (1972); *The Revolution Betrayed* (1965); *The Struggle Against Fascism in Germany* (1971); *Literature and Revolution* (1960); *My Life* (1960); *The History of the Russian Revolution* (1965); *Our Political Tasks* (1980). On Trotsky: Isaac Deutscher, *The Prophet Armed, The Prophet Unarmed* and *The Prophet Outcast* (1954, 1959 and 1963); Louis Sinclair, *Leon Trotsky: A Bibliography* (1972); Baruch Knei-Paz, *The Social and Political Thought of Leon Trotsky* (1978); Irving Howe, *Trotsky* (1978); Ernest Mandel, *Trotsky: A Study in the Dynamic of His Thought* (1979); Alex Callinicos, *Trotskyism* (1990); Antonovich Volkogorov, *Trotsky: The Eternal Revolutionary* (1996).

NORMAN GERAS

TURING, Alan

1912–54

English logician

Alan Turing was born in London and was educated at Sherborne and King's College, Cambridge. A fellowship at King's College (1935) led to two years (1936–8) working with Alonzo Church at Princeton. During the war Turing worked in the Communications Department at the Foreign Office, and in 1945 he joined the National Physical Laboratory to work on their early computer, known as ACE. In 1948 he took the post of Reader at Manchester University, again working on problems associated with computers. He died of poisoning, possibly accidental, in June 1954.

It is astonishing that Turing's famous paper on computable numbers was published in 1937. In it he performed an historic thought experiment: he postulated a computer which could take its instructions from a paper tape containing a sequence of 1s and 0s, could print new sequences of 1s and 0s, which would then, if necessary, join the sequence of instructions. In this way it would modify its own program. Turing showed that any machine which was capable of doing this much was, in a certain sense, the match of any other machine which could do this much. He called a machine of this kind a 'Universal Automaton'. (This is usually called a 'Turing Machine' today.) A small, slow Turing Machine will be capable of doing anything which can be done by a larger, faster Turing Machine, assuming that there are no physical limitations on the storage of the program. Essentially the smaller machine can always be programmed to plod on and to get there in the end.

The earliest steps in the development of computers were diverse, unco-ordinated, and mixed up with interests in tabulation, statistics, ballistics, telecommunications. Yet out of this somewhat confusing mêlée a wise strategic decision emerged: to build general-purpose machines capable of modifying their own programs. The hardware would be as flexible as possible: programs punched on paper tape would supply the specialist features required to meet any specific difficulty. The result was that most of the computers subsequently made embodied a potentially limitless computing facility: there was no knowing what they might be brought to do. This maintained the essentially 'magic' feeling of the machine, and acted as a sustained intellectual stimulus for programmers and analysts. Such machines were, in effect, the Universal Automatons Turing had foreseen in 1937.

It could easily have been otherwise. That it was not was largely due to the efforts of Alan Turing and John Von Neumann.

Further reading

Alan Turing's main papers were as follows: 'On Computable Numbers ... ' (1937); 'Systems of Logic Based on Ordinals' (1939); 'Computing Machinery and Intelligence' (1950); and 'The Chemical Basis of Morphogenesis' (1952). Unpublished in his lifetime, they can be found in *Collected Works of Alan Turing* (4 vols, 1992–2001). See also: S. Turing, *Alan M. Turing* (1959); Andrew Hodges, *Alan Turing: The Enigma* (1993); B.J. Copeland (ed.), *The Essential Turing* (2004); *Alan Turing's Automatic Computing Engine* (2005).

CHRISTOPHER ORMELL

TWAIN, Mark (Samuel Langhorne CLEMENS)

1835–1910

US novelist and essayist

When Twain was five the family moved within Missouri to Hannibal, the rich cultural location of his Tom Sawyer and Huckleberry Finn fictions. Brief schooling ended in apprenticeship on the Missouri *Courier*. In 1853 he worked his way east to New York and Philadelphia and back west to Iowa as journeyman printer. In 1857 he exchanged that life for apprentice and journeyman Mississippi riverboat pilot, vividly described in *Life on the Mississippi* (1883). Twain here has one of his very few cultural heroes without serious blemish, Horace Bixby, the dandy master pilot, the only acceptable heroic authority Twain acknowledged, and juxtaposes him with the bogus glories of 'the absolute South', with its aristocratic humbug and grotesque belief in itself as a civilization. But the Civil War closed the river. For about two weeks Clemens became second lieutenant in the Confederate army – his family were confirmed Unionists – and was then released for vague 'disabilities' (the affair is parodied in 'The Private History of a Campaign that Failed'). Discovering that being secretary

to his brother Orion, secretary to Nevada State, entailed no work and no pay, he unsuccessfully tried prospecting, turned to reporting, and in 1862 became city editor on the Virginia City (Nevada) *Enterprise*, using for the first time his pseudonym (a fathom call on the Mississippi boats but curiously indicative of the future schism in his character).

After an absurd duel (personal journalism proving a liability) he worked for newspapers in San Francisco, where he met Bret Harte and published 'The Celebrated Jumping Frog of Calaveras County', the just-about-funny story which made him famous and which he rightly did not value highly. The Sacramento *Union* assigned him travel reports in Hawaii, the Mediterranean and Palestine; the resulting *Innocents Abroad* (1869) combines the brash superiorities of the confident American tourist with a certain wariness of time and decay in monuments prior to America, largely brought on by the Sphinx gazing at Twain. The later tensions are already latent here: the overwhelming sense of time and eternity reducing men to transient data. With popular success and the editing of the Buffalo *Express,* he could marry Olivia, and their combined finances enabled him to buy a place in Hartford, Connecticut. His impulsive impracticality lost him a fortune in a typesetting machine already out of date, and in a publishing house which profited from General Grant's memoirs and then went bankrupt within ten years. Twain then wrote and lectured to pay debts and restore his finances. But inside national and international fame – between 1872 and 1900 he produced twenty-five books at least – private tragedy undermined him. A beloved daughter died, his only son died in infancy, his wife died in 1904 and another daughter in 1909. University honours were laid thickly upon him but, as he said, 'I take the same childish delight in a new degree that an Indian takes in a fresh scalp.' He finally left Hartford for Redding – still in Connecticut – and, having anticipated he would die with the return of Halley's comet, which had appeared at his birth, did so, of *angina pectoris.*

Twain's wit and humour constitute a balancing act, a controlled hysteria in the face of a contradictory and violent world, an edging towards the void of hopeless behaviourism and dehumanized determinism. Inside a witticism that the symbol of man ought to be an axe since 'every human being has one concealed about him somewhere, and is always seeking the opportunity to grind it', lies a sense of possible unbridled rapacity. The genteel fears of bourgeois society forced him to costume criticism and pain in ironic comedy, satire that excoriated cruelty, ignorance and hypocrisy, and farce resulting from the gap between established moral standards and the truth. *The Gilded Age* (1874), written in collaboration with Charles D. Warner, contains the exemplary figure of Colonel Beriah Sellers, epitome of the success ethic operating in the speculative corruptions of Washington, where his energies become a danger to youth by perpetuating a myth beyond practicality.

Shocks of recognition come through as nervous hilarity. His finest works retain an astonishing balance between buoyancy and despair. *The Adventures of Huckleberry Finn* (1884) is a pattern of duplicity and disguise, with a twelve-year-old boy, technically dead, discovering the adult hypocrisy of slavery, feuding Southern aristocrats in full stupidity, the confidence trickster who exemplifies capitalist fraud, the parent who exploits his child to extinction, and the training of another boy (Tom Sawyer) to believe in the competitive aggressions and romantic violence of the age. Huck's revolt against Christian society and the Fugitive Slave Law is one of the most moving and valuable moments in literature, a beacon of sense in a darkness of characteristic apologetics. But the brief days he and Nigger Jim spend on a piece of broken raft on the Mississippi cannot constitute a possible society, however idyllic and educative. Huck learns to respect a Negro and reject the shore societies, but can only then 'light out for the Territory', get clear of American lies by heading west. His inventive, explorative language – Twain created a rich

vehicle from his memories of Hannibal – carries him to articulate understanding which is useless in 'sivilized' America. In *A Connecticut Yankee at King Arthur's Court* (1889) the technology that Hank Morgan brings from the Colt factory to medieval feudalism, in order to transform serfdom, the chivalric order and a bigoted church into a reasonably humanitarian technocracy, turns to a violence which reflects American Civil War weaponry and the technological potentialities for aggression in the Philadelphia Exposition of 1876. A factory-colony is to turn 'groping and grubbing automata into men'. The revolution 'must *begin,* in blood, whatever may answer afterward. If history teaches anything, it teaches that.' Training is 'all there is *to* a person'. But the novel concludes with the nineteenth-century American mechanic roasting an army of knights on an electrified wire defence system. *Pudd'nhead Wilson* (1894) is one of the most savage and accurate exposures of racism and slavery ever written, but Twain also incorporates an analysis of American subservient snobbery before European aristocrats, the ruin of a young lawyer whose first mild joke is mistaken for stupidity by a stupid townspeople, and the lawyer's rehabilitation as a detective – a figure that will obsess American fiction in the following century and which Twain neatly mocked a few years later in *The Double Barrelled Detective Story* (1902). In 'The Man that Corrupted Hadleyburg' (1898) derision is the response to a town's untested reputation for honesty, or vanity disguised as self-righteous uprightness, the classic Christian social sin. Wealth attacks a society which believes that all things are ordered, including corruption; it is left praying: 'Lead us into temptation!'

These masterpieces manage, as works of art, to exhilarate the reader with wit, humour, skilled plots and critical vision, while impregnating him with recognitions of human cruelty and stupidity. But increasingly the famous novelist and much demanded after-dinner speaker began to lock manuscripts away from public scrutiny, in order to retain fame and fortune, to be honest with himself while entertaining the public who, as usual, demanded what it approved of. Mr Clemens divided from Mark Twain; the humorist's art could not fulfil the embittered conscience; the well-meaning censorship of his wife, W.D. Howells and others only exacerbated the schizoid life. The white-clothed public figure concealed the dark final phase of his genius. *What Is Man?* (1906) yields the creative impulse to mere train-ing, behaviourism and a cynical equation of Shakespeare and a machine or a rat. Human nature is always content with its condition 'no matter what its religion is, whether its master be tiger or house-cat'. 'Everything has been tried, without success', so do not waste feeling on the possibility of social change. In 1878, Twain wrote that 'To man all things are possible but one – he cannot have a hole in the seat of his breeches and keep his fingers out of it.' The later work explores the impulsive and irrational to the point where Twain can say, 'Fleas can be taught anything a Congressman can.' Man's boasted '*intellec-tual* superiority' to the contrary, 'the fact that he can *do* wrong proves his *moral* inferiority to any creature that cannot'. In *The Mysterious Stranger* (1916) the archangel Satan visits medieval Austria to reassure young Theodor that human history accurately reflects the vileness of mankind, especially in wars which religion and philosophy support. The rest is void:

> There is no God, no universe, no human race, no earthly life, no heaven, no hell. It is all a dream. Nothing exists but you. And you are but a thought, a useless thought, a homeless thought, wandering forlorn among the empty eternities!

Twain, like his contemporary Henry Adams, is a sceptical index of the twentieth century, prophetic of its state of continuous emer-gency and creedless hypocrisy. 'Two or three centuries from now it will be recognized that all the competent killers are Christians; then the pagan world will go to school to the Christian – not to acquire his religion, but his

guns': such is the chilling message to the modern world in *The Mysterious Stranger.* Angels, Satan adds, can only love each other; if they loved the human race, that love 'would consume its object like ashes. No, we cannot love men, but we can be harmlessly indifferent; we can also like them sometimes.' *Letters from the Earth* (1942) ridicules the inconsistencies and authoritarianism of Old Testament lore: 'The Biblical law says: "Thou shalt not kill". The law of God, planted in the heart of man at his birth, says: "Thou shalt kill".' Twain opened the way to American 'black' humour of the 1960s and the comedian of despair, Lenny Bruce.

Further reading

Other works include: *The Writings of Mark Twain,* ed. Albert Bigelow Paine (37 vols, 1922–5); *Letters from the Earth,* ed. Bernard de Voto (1942); *The Complete Humorous Sketches and Tales,* ed. Charles Neider (1961); *Notebooks and Journal of Mark Twain,* ed. Frederick Anderson, Michael B. Frank and Kenneth M. Sanderson (2 vols, 1976); *Mark Twain and the Damned Human Race,* ed. Janet Smith (1962). See: Walter Blair, *Mark Twain and Huck Finn* (1960); Henry Nash Smith, *Mark Twain: The Development of a Writer* (1962); Justin Kaplan, *Mr Clemens and Mark Twain* (1966); J.M. Cox, *Mark Twain: The Facts of Humour* (1967); Robert Keith Miller, *Mark Twain* (1983); Henry B. Wonham, *Mark Twain and the Art of the Tall Tale* (1993); Fred Kaplan, *The Singular Mark Twain: A Biography* (2003); Karen Lystra, *Dangerous Intimacy: The Untold Story of Mark Twain's Final Years* (2004); Louis Budd and Peter Messent (eds), *A Companion to Mark Twain* (2005).

ERIC MOTTRAM

TZARA, Tristan (Samuel ROSENSTOCK)
1896–1963
Romanian/French writer

A Romanian by birth, Tzara adopted the French language and in later life French nationality. His career as a cultural terrorist began in 1916 when, in neutral Zürich, he joined other refugees like Hugo Ball, Richard Huelsenbeck and **Jean Arp** to mount that brief but savage assault on Western cultural values known as Dada. Tzara was in his element as the ebullient impresario of this most anarchic of movements in the arts, contributing to the recitation of wild multilingual poems at the Cabaret Voltaire, setting up provocative exhibitions of Dada paintings, organizing stage performances at which the Dada group would, by their incoherent proclamations and insults, goad the audience into frenzied protest, and spreading the Dada message of subversion across Europe by way of publications and tireless correspondence with other avant-garde leaders like Apollinaire, **Marinetti**, Haussmann and **Breton**.

In 1920 Tzara settled in Paris, joining forces with André Breton and his Litérature group to launch a further series of outrageous spectacles. Eventually, though, bourgeois audiences began to enjoy being insulted and Dada scandal became a cultural commodity like any other. While Breton led the group into the new adventures of Surrealism, Tzara stuck to his individualist path, eventually to join up with the Surrealists again in the early 1930s, when he produced some of his best poetry. Later, Tzara's emergent **Marxist** concerns led him out of Surrealism: an active member of the Resistance during the Occupation, he entered the French Communist Party in 1947.

Tzara's most prized texts are his Dada manifestos, written to be performed in public and full of rumbustious tomfoolery and astringent wit. His is the language of a sophisticated savage, by turns silly, aggressive, and truculently paradoxical: 'I am writing a manifesto and there's nothing I want, and yet I'm saying certain things, and in principle I am against manifestos, as I am against principles ... I won't explain myself because I abhor common sense.'

The poems of the Dada period are characterized by extreme semantic and syntactic incoherence: improvised nonsense statements are interspersed with random slogans or headlines, with puns, invented words and printer's errors tossed into the mixture. The resultant texts exhibit a staccato singularity, a kind of sublime inarticulacy. 'Dada is an anti-nuance cream,' Tzara drily observed.

The remarkable thing is that Tzara persisted in this experiment in linguistic deviancy, maintaining a studied inconsequentiality until, by a mysterious reversal, his style modulated from unreadable gibberish into a seductive and fertile surrealist idiom. *L'Homme approximatif* (1931) is his best-known poem, an extended meditation on mental and elemental impulses in which the obscure play of words gives rise to felicitous lyrical passages with images of stunning beauty: 'sweet utterance at rest within my hand magic freshness/deep down in the cormorant at its breast flying spinning like an astral sign/light when expressed forfeits its petals.'

Essentially Tzara's poetry exemplifies the principle of new insights being generated through the exacerbation of singularity, as he indicated in an early aphorism:

> To concede to each element its identity, its autonomy, is the necessary condition for the creation of new constellations, since each has its place in the group. The thrust of the Word: upright, an image, a unique event, passionate, of dense colour, intensity, in communion with life.

Passing from Dada spontaneity through Surrealist automatic writing, Tzara arrived at a mature style of transparent simplicity in which disparate entities could be held together in a unifying vision.

In retrospect, harmony and contact had been Tzara's goals all along. The 'great destructive negative work' of Dada was a prelude to the renewal of mental perspectives, and the rampant nihilism of the *Dada Manifesto 1918* was counterbalanced by a desire to lay hold of the jostling realities of existence:

> Abolition of logic: DADA ... abolition of memory: DADA; abolition of archaeology: DADA; abolition of prophets: DADA; abolition of the future: DADA ... Liberty: *DADA DADA DADA*, the roaring of

contorted pains, the interweaving of contraries and of all contradictions, freaks and irrelevancies: LIFE.

Further reading

Other works include: *Vingt-cinq poèmes* ('Twenty-five Poems', 1918); *De nos oiseaux* ('Of Our Birds', 1929); *L'Antitête* ('The Anti-head', 1933); *A haute flamme* ('Flame Out Loud', 1955). In course of publication: *Oeuvres complètes* (Vol. I, 1975; Vol. II, 1977). In English: *Seven Dada Manifestos and Lampisteries* (trans. B. Wright, 1977). On Tzara: René Lacôte, *Tristan Tzara* (1952); Mary Ann Caws, *The Poetry of Dada and Surrealism* (1970); Sadie Plant, *The Most Radical Gesture: The Situationist International in a Postmodern Age* (1992).

ROGER CARDINAL

U

UPDIKE, John Hoyer

1932–

US novelist and poet

John Updike was born in Pennsylvania and educated at Harvard and the Ruskin School of Drawing and Fine Art at Oxford. Critical opinion has always been sharply divided over his literary status, many seeing him as the archetypal *New Yorker* short-story writer, producing mannered, vivid, yet vacuously descriptive prose concerned primarily with the banalities of fornication. However, beneath this exterior dwells a religious writer who has created a series of commonplace characters – especially 'Rabbit' Angstrom of *Rabbit Run* (1960), *Rabbit Redux* (1971), *Rabbit Is Rich* (1981) and *Rabbit At Rest* (1990) – muddled and incapable of controlling their lives or loves, yet whose very failure or incompetence has its roots in their perceptions of the inevitability of our solitude, frailty and death. This awareness cuts them off from identifying themselves with the roles they are asked to play, plunges their lives into chaos and cuckoldry, due to their paralysing sense of horror and compassion, and yet makes them the embodiment of value in their environments.

Many of these figures are conservatives, like George Caldwell in *The Centaur* (1963), an idealistic teacher fascinated by knowledge, Piet Hanema in *Couples* (1968), who is inwardly pious, and who tries to preserve old-fashioned skills and perfectionism in the building trade, or Thomas Marshfield in *A Month of Sundays* (1975), who is a Christian minister and eschews existentialist, ritualist and humanist revisions of his religion. However, this conservatism is not seen as a defence or protection against experience, nor an ethical straitjacket keeping their actions within the conventional, but rather a refusal to accept the easy solutions of American optimistic pragmatism, and instead to preserve a sense of the mystery out of which we seek to relate to others and our circumstances by words and actions which are always inadequate and misleading. Out of this, Updike creates both comedy and pathos, especially from the essential strangeness of the confrontation with another's body and the meanings it has for us.

Updike himself has summarized his literary quest as being 'to give the mundane its beautiful due'. A consummate craftsman, this most thoughtful of contemporary American novelists has also been the most consistent – hardly a year goes by without another Updike offering, quite apart from his collections of poetry, literary essays and art criticism. Only rarely, however, does he step outside the parameters he seems so carefully to have set himself. *The Witches of Eastwick* (1984), while still set in suburbia, is a vamp, in which a group of women are seduced by no less a figure than Satan, brilliantly played by Jack Nicholson in a film version of the same title. *Brazil* (1994) is a retelling of the Tristan and Iseult story. Only in *Gertrude and Claudius* (2000) – a sort of prequel to Shakespeare's *Hamlet* – does he stray into recognizably modernist territory. Little of his recent work has excited positive critical attention, but for Updike, whose essentially Christian faith is brought out into the open in his semi-confessional memoir *Self-Consciousness* (1989), sales and acclaim are clearly not everything that matter.

Further reading

Other works include: *The Carpentered Hen and Other Tame Creatures* (poems, 1958); *The Poorhouse Fair* (novel, 1959); *Pigeon Feathers and Other Stories* (1962); *Telephone Poles and Other Poems* (1963); *Of the Farm* (novel, 1965); *Mid Point and Other Poems* (1969); *Bech: A Book* (episodic novel, 1970); *Museums and Women and Other Stories* (1972); *Marry Me* (1974); *Buchanan* (play, 1976); *The Coup* (1978); *Roger's Version* (1988); *Memoirs of the Ford Administration* (1992); *Collected Poems* (1993); *Villages* (2004); and two volumes of art criticism, *Just Looking* (1989) and *Still Looking* (2005). Joyce B. Markle, *Fighters and Lovers: Theme in the Novels of John Updike* (1973); Edward P. Vargo, *Rainstorms and Fire: Ritual in the Novels of John Updike* (1973); George W. Hunt, *John Updike and the Three Great Things: Sex, Religion and Art* (1985); James Plath, *Conversations with John Updike* (1994).

DAVID CORKER
(REVISED AND UPDATED BY THE EDITOR)

V

VALÉRY, Paul

1871–1945

French poet and thinker

Of mixed Italian and Corsican blood, Valéry was born in Sète, a Mediterranean port which was to inform his whole imaginary world as a poet. Already by the age of nineteen he had written between two and three hundred poems, was engaged in painting and fascinated by music (in particular that of **Wagner**) and architecture. Then, as a law student at the University of Montpellier, he added mathematics and physics to his interests. Moving to Paris he continued to write poetry until 1892, assiduously frequenting the milieu of the Symbolists, who, with **Mallarmé** as their focal point, sought to make poetry as pure, abstract and evocative as music. In his late teens Valéry also came under the spell of the aesthetic theories of Edgar Allan Poe, according to which the poet must always be aiming at the effect that he is going to create on the reader. But neither Poe nor the Symbolists offered Valéry a satisfactory account of the world of the emotions, and it became his credo that the intellect should take control. Giving up poetry he decided to devote himself to a rigorous exploration of the way in which 'the closed system that is the mind' functions.

To this end he read widely not only in philosophy but also in the sciences. Believing that it was physicists and mathematicians who held the key to an understanding of consciousness, he endeavoured to discover algebraic formulae which would express the constants and the variables of human reactions. But the main source for his researches was his own self. Abandoning all received ideas, his enquiry focused on the question '*Que peut un homme?*' – 'Of what is a man capable?' *Une Soirée avec Monsieur Teste* (1894) presented a dialogue between Valéry and the strange character of Monsieur Teste, a fictional shadow employed to represent the intellect at its most abstract. Using a constant and constantly reflected self-awareness as his method, Teste attempts to transform even the inevitable weaknesses of the flesh and the knowledge of death into what he calls geometrical figures.

In his concern to establish a method of thinking Valéry next turned his attention to Leonardo da Vinci, whom he took as an exemplar of the universal mind. The *Introduction à la méthode de Leonardo da Vinci* (1895) establishes three stages of thought: a detailed observation of nature and man; the development of mental imagery, including the processes of induction and analogy; and, finally, construction. However, the core of his explorations into human possibilities was the famous *Cahiers* (2 vols, 1973–4), the notebooks to which, from 1894 until the end of his life, Valéry consigned the observations and ideas that he worked on in the early hours of each morning. Beside this formidable and perhaps unique enterprise, Montaigne's labyrinthine testings of himself, or **Gide's** fictional projections, seem digressive and self-indulgent. Valéry is not concerned with the contingent, surface individuality, but with what he calls *le moi pur*, later described in mathematical terms as the universal invariant, the pure functioning of the consciousness.

The author himself said that the *Cahiers* represented the best of him. Since they have been readily accessible to the public only since 1973, the full scale and portent of Valéry's activity is still being assessed. Before, it was widely accepted that between 1895 and 1912, when he again began to write poetry, there was a 'silence' broken only by one or two brilliant essays (including 'La Conquête allemande' of 1899, which prophesied the rise of German power). But the long poem which eventually emerged, and which immediately established Valéry as a leading poet, can now be seen in relation to a continuous intellectual activity. Working within the constraints of traditional form (which Valéry regarded as a necessary challenge), 'La Jeune Parque' (1917) – like the two collections that followed it, *Album de vers anciens* (1920) and *Charmes* (1922) – couples an intense cult of abstraction with an equally intense, palpitating sensuality. It is this, rather than any technical innovation, that marks Valéry's finest achievements as a poet.

With regard to 'La Jeune Parque', he claimed that the prolonged struggles with the combinatory qualities of language, the manipulation of the multiple possibilities of sound and sense inherent in words, were an important aspect of his understanding and mastery of himself. Although he insisted that his prime concern had been to exploit the musicality of verbal patterns, the poem is a profound examination of the working of consciousness in his symbolic human creation ('the young Fate'), its awakenings as she emerges from sleep, the gradual construction of her sense of identity, the physiological awareness of her sexuality and her simultaneous psychological reactions, and her recognition of recurrences and flux within her own being which reflect those of nature and interact with them.

Valéry's standing as a major poet was put beyond doubt with the publication of *Charmes*, which contained one of the most impressive pieces of the twentieth century, 'Le Cimetiére Marin'. Like 'La Jeune Parque', this poem springs initially from formal, musical preoccupations, but in this case it is the consciousness of a mature man at the height of his powers which is examined. Inserted into a diamantine Mediterranean setting, he experiences a fusion with nature which takes him to a peak of transcendence; but then, obeying the inevitable cyclical rhythms of nature, he drifts from the midday dazzle into a shadowed sense of mortality, until finally the lifting sea winds coincide with an invigorated acceptance of the limits of the human condition. The same coming-to-terms with the psyche through nature is sought elsewhere in the volume. 'Aurore' enacts the awakening of the poet in a garden at dawn; 'Le Rameur' brings together a rower's movement over water with his passage through time; and 'La Platane' and 'Palme' use trees as symbols of growth, of patience, and of the dual 'earth-rooted' heaven-seeking tendency of man.

Although there is evidence to suggest that Valéry continued to write poetry of a more experimental kind after 1922, he did not publish any. Instead he made his living as a critic and an essayist, the extraordinary breadth of his interests being attested in collected volumes such as *Variétés* (1924) and *Autres Rhumbs* (1927) and *Tel Quel* (1941). In 1925 he was elected to the French Academy, and in 1937 was appointed Professor of Poetics at the Collège de France. As a literary critic he was particularly forward-looking in his insistence on the impossibility of distinguishing between form and content, on taking a poem as an object – a view that has become a central tenet of much modern criticism. But if aesthetics were his profession, his relentless pursuit of his original question – '*Que peut un homme?*' – took him into widely different spheres. In this context three works, written in his favoured dialogue form, are of note. In the first, *Eupalinos*

(1922), the shades of Socrates and Phaedrus evoke the architect Eupalinos as a model of the thinker-constructor who is obliged to pit himself bodily against intractable matter, and then shape it according to the laws of his own mind. Thus, by constructing out of nature the creator learns how to construct himself. In the companion *L'Ame et la danse* (1922), Valéry discovers in the dancer's art a further aspect of creativity: the capacity of the human being to transcend apparent limitations, to go beyond the self. The third, *L'Idée fixe* (1932), reintroduces Monsieur Teste, and reflects Valéry's attempt to understand the new physics of Planck, **Einstein**, Schrödinger and **Heisenberg**. Numbering several of the leading French physicists of the day among his friends, including Paul Langevin and Louis de Broglie, he hoped that the theories which had so revolutionized man's way of looking at the world would be applied to the complex living organism itself. Thus, Monsieur Teste, using his familiar *tabula rasa* technique, interrogates a doctor on a number of crucial issues in psychotherapy: the function of the senses, of memory, of suggestibility, the differences between group and individual behaviour, how to account for the individual's appetites and repugnances, the nature of dreams, which he finds more interesting for their formal structure than for any apparent symbolism; and throughout sees man as a being turned always to the future with a potential which is always capable of development. Interestingly, at the end of the dialogue, it is Einstein who is introduced as a modern example of the universal thinker idealistically seeking the secrets of the unity of nature.

If, summing up Valéry's varied achievements, one had to pin-point his exemplary importance in the modern world, it would be his role as a *maître à penser*. 'I work for those who come after me,' he said. His method was to formulate those precise, unequivocal questions which are at least capable of precise, unequivocal answers. He teaches, by example, how to think, the what to think being constantly ahead.

Further reading

Other works include: *Oeuvres I & II* (1957 and 1960); and, in translation, *The Collected Works of Paul Valéry* (15 vols, 1956–75). See also: J. R. Lawler, *Lecture de Valéry* (1963); J. Robinson, *L'Analyse de l'esprit dans les Cahiers de Paul Valéry* (1963); Emilie Noulet, *Paul Valéry* (1950); W.N. Ince, *The Poetic Theory of Paul Valéry* (1970); Christine Crow, *Paul Valéry: Consciousness and Nature* (1972); C.G. Whiting, *Paul Valéry* (1979); Suzanne Guerlac, *Literary Polemics: Bataille, Satre, Valery, Breton* (1997); William Kluback, *Paul Valery: A Philosopher for Philosophers, the Sage* (1999).

MARGARET DAVIES

VAN GOGH, Vincent
1853–90
Dutch artist

Son of a pastor, the young Van Gogh was placed in 1869 in the Dutch branch of the art dealers' firm, Goupil and Co., in The Hague. During the next seven years he journeyed variously to Paris and London carrying out his duties until finally dismissed for rudeness to his employers.

If Van Gogh was a man of sorrows it was because the abnormalities of his behaviour rendered him by turn violently excitable and then melancholically withdrawn. Those people who befriended him had extreme difficulty in maintaining their relationship so that the painter constantly found himself to be a social outcast. It is thought that the cause of his unacceptably intense moods derived from a lesion in the brain occurring at his birth. As his life progressed the problems became more acute until at the age of thirty-five he suffered his first attack of insanity.

Highly intelligent, an avid reader with a good command of four languages including English, Van Gogh had decided prior to his dismissal by Goupil that he would follow a higher calling, similar to that of his father. In 1877 he entered a small Evangelical College in Brussels, completing his training the following year but, because of his peculiar personality, failing the course. Of his own initiative he settled in that bleak part of Belgium known as the Borinage. In this coal-mining area reminiscent of that in **Zola's** book *Germinal*, Van Gogh became a lay preacher. At the same time he began frequently to make drawings of the people in the area. He was much influenced in this activity by his collection of engravings cut from contemporary English magazines, such as the *Graphic*, which commented upon the social problems of the working poor in industrial areas of Britain. Soon after, in 1882, while at Nuenen, Van Gogh painted the famous *Potato Eaters* which portrays a poor family at the meal table. The dramatic contrasts of light and dark required only a low colour key and there is no hint of the colourist that the painter was to become.

By this time Van Gogh had realized his lack of aptitude for divine counselling and that he was better suited to the life of an artist. He left the church and settled for a time in Antwerp where he studied, among other works, those of Rubens. The appeal of these Baroque works probably lay in their warm colouring and lively movement. A further pleasure for the painter was his discovery of Japanese prints which he began to collect while at Antwerp. Their grace of line and simplicity of composition were as important to Van Gogh as they were to **Gauguin**.

It was not until the following year, 1886, when Van Gogh joined his brother Theo in Paris, that he finally met not only Gauguin but **Cézanne**, Bernard, Anguetin and Pissarro as well. While studying at Cormon's studio, Van Gogh, undergoing an immensely stimulating year, became interested in the flower paintings of Adolphe Monticelli, a Marseilles artist. Van Gogh experimented with flower pieces himself at this time, setting blues against complements of orange and playing with other such oppositions. These in conjunction with the use of an impasto technique strongly suggest a Monticelli influence. During the winter, however, Impressionism finally became apparent to the Dutchman who, in the spring of 1887,

lightened and unified his palette while working out of doors with Bernard on the banks of the Seine at Asnières.

Nonetheless, Van Gogh still had the idea of starting a society of painters with a lifestyle he imagined to be like that of the Japanese: simple, homogeneous, warm and gracious. He travelled south in February looking for a suitable place and decided upon Arles in Provence. Here he painted some glorious spring pictures of orchards while he prepared a small house for the arrival of Gauguin. He had hopes that the master of the school of artists in Brittany could be induced to set up a similar arrangement in the south. Throughout the summer he corresponded with Gauguin urging upon him all the good reasons for complying with his request. At the same time he painted some remarkable pictures, arriving at expressive solutions with non-naturalistic colour as an important poetic element. He wrote of his interior *The All-Night Café* (1888) that he had 'tried to express the idea that the café is a place where one can ruin oneself, go mad or commit a crime'. The use of powerful reds, assertive blue greens and hot orange yellows gives the work an almost painful intensity. It was also during the summer that Van Gogh painted a series of views of the public gardens at Arles. He said he felt there the presence, along with that of other famous figures of the past, of Petrarch, who had lived not far away at Avignon. These paintings called the *Poets' Garden* were to hang in Gauguin's own room to express the idea of the master of today meeting in Arles with the masters from history.

Short of money, induced by the funds provided by Theo Van Gogh and perhaps preferring to winter in a warmer climate, Gauguin consented to Vincent's proposal and arrived in Arles in October. However, the relationship between Vincent and Gauguin proved no happier than previous ones and in December Gauguin acknowledged that he would have to go north again. At this point the Dutchman's sanity finally gave way and he entered the asylum at St Rémy. Between bouts of manic violence he continued to paint with acute control of colour and tone but with an increasing wildness of shape and form. Rolling mountains, waving cypress and olive repeat the whirling of sun and stars. The whole of nature, seen through the ferment of Van Gogh's temperament, takes on a tumultuous aspect.

To be nearer the ever comforting Theo, his new wife and small baby, also named Vincent, the painter entered another hospital, near Paris, at Auvers. Here he painted and wrote as long as he could. His last important painting was of black crows flying against a strip of sky, so dark in its blueness that it is almost black. It lowers heavily over a corn-field the colour of bile. The work expresses not only a psychological state of being but also the physical sensations resulting from extreme anxiety. At the same time Van Gogh felt it to be a projection of the energy of nature. A short while later, after these terrifying hours, Van Gogh wrote a letter to Theo stating that 'painters themselves are fighting more and more with their backs to the wall'. He finally could no longer face the notion of continued insanity and, according to a letter found in his pocket after his suicide, had come to accept the inevitable end with comparative tranquillity of mind. He shot himself in the chest, dying later from the wound on 29 July 1890.

Further reading

Other works include: *Le Pont de Langlois* (1888); *Pink Peach Trees* (1888); *Café at Night Arles* (1888); *The Postman Roulin* (1888); *Van Gogh's Chair* (1888–89); *Sun Flowers* (1888); *Starry Night* (1889); *Yellow Cornfield* (1889). See: *The Complete Letters of Van Gogh*, trans. J. Van Gogh-Bonger and C. de Dood (1958); Meyer Schapiro, *Vincent Van Gogh* (1950); A.M. Hammacher, *Vincent Van Gogh* (1961); *Selected Letters of Van Gogh*, ed. Mark Roskill (1963); J. Meier Graefe, *Vincent Van Gogh: A Biographical Study* (trans. J. Reece, 2 vols, 1922), Nagera, *Vincent Van Gogh: A Psychological Study* (1967); J. Hulsker, *The New Complete Van Gogh: Paintings, Drawings, Sketches: Revised and Enlarged Edition of the Catalogue Raisonné of the Works of Vincent van Gogh* (1996).

PAT TURNER

VARGAS LLOSA, Mario

1936–

Peruvian novelist, playwright and critic

Mario Vargas Llosa was born in Arequipa, Peru, but was educated in Cochabamba, Bolivia, from 1937 to 1945 after his parents separated. He then moved to Piura in northern Peru. When his father returned to family life, Vargas Llosa was sent to the Leoncio Prado, a military academy outside Lima, to become a man, which would become the background to his scandalous first novel. Vargas Llosa always wanted to become a writer, but began as a journalist and broadcaster while studying at Lima's San Marcos University. In 1958 he won a scholarship to study for a doctorate at Madrid University, which he finally published in 1971, a meticulous study of his erstwhile friend **Gabriel García Márquez's** fiction (Vargas Llosa has refused to republish *García Márquez: historia de un deicidio*, and it hasn't been translated into English). He moved to Paris and then London, where he wrote and taught in different colleges at London University. He still lives part of the year in London, with his second wife, while their three grown-up children live around the world. Vargas Llosa has dual Spanish–Peruvian citizenship (with a flat in Madrid and a house in Barranco, Lima), and often teaches at prestigious universities. He is a brilliant lecturer, a wide-ranging columnist and continues to write immaculately crafted novels.

His first story appeared in 1956, collected in a book *Los jefes*, 1958 (*The Cubs and Other Stories*, 1980), but it was his first novel *La ciudad y los perros*, 1962 (*The Time of the Hero*, 1966) that catapulted Vargas Llosa to literary fame, winning the prestigious Bibliotecta Breve prize in Spain in 1962. A thousand copies were burnt in public by the military because he had defamed the military academy. The title refers to cheating and murder in the Leoncio Prado where the pupils are called *perros* (dogs). There are local characters from all Peruvian social classes, from a budding cowardly poet to a sensitive provincial officer to the slum-kid-turned-leader called El Jaguar. Most impressive is the unidentified monologue that traverses the novel. Combined with brilliant realism of place and dialogue, Vargas Llosa had written a formidable critique of *machismo* in Lima society. The first edition had a map of Peru, and a photo of the actual school. He had written this novel from abroad, and had sought the controversy it generated.

Vargas Llosa began writing with a Sartrian concern; fiction was serious and should explore what Peruvian society repressed. This earnest politicized writing, based on meticulous research and fine functional prose (Vargas Llosa has penned a study of **Flaubert**, *The Perpetual Orgy*, 1986), emerged in a critical realist vein that lasted until the late 1970s. This period mirrors his involvement and then rejection of Fidel Castro's revolution, and a general drift to the neo-liberal right. There's a discernible shift in tone, but not in teasing technique and realism, to more humorous novels. In the 1990s he reverted to his more serious phase, moving beyond Peruvian topics. Behind all his writing is a seamless crafting of the novel in terms of plot, character and suspense. He has combined readability, with serious concerns that few have matched in Latin American fiction.

The first earnest phase includes his second novel, *La casa verde*, 1965 (*The Green House*, 1968), a tour de force of technical innovation and realism about the setting up of a brothel, the Green House, in Piura, with long sections in Peru's Amazonian jungle region. An overlapping time-scheme throws characters back and forwards in unidentifiable ways where an Indian girl ends up as a whore and a Japanese trader a leper. It won the prestigious literary prize, the Rómulo Gallegos, in 1967. It was followed by a political analysis of the Odría dictatorship in Peru called *Conversación en La Catedral*, 1970 (*Conversation in the Cathedral,* 1975), which refers to bar conversations about political corruption. A later epic work about a rebellion in northern Brazil, *La guerra del fin del mundo*, 1981 (*The War of the End of the World*, 1984) debated Latin American utopianism and fanaticism.

Vargas Llosa's second but equally realistic mode began with a farce, *Pantaleón y las visitadoras*, 1973 (*Captain Pantoja and the Special Service*, 1978), set in the jungle near Iquitos, about furnishing whores to sex-starved soldiers. This lighter tone took off with his 1983 best-seller based on his own affair when eighteen years old with his thirty-two-year-old aunt, *La tía Julia y el escribidor*, 1977 (*Aunt Julia and the Scriptwriter*, 1982). It revolves around a soap-opera broadcaster, with many samples of his mad plots. Further novels in this vein involve his recurrent character Lituma, a policeman from *La casa verde* with common sense but not much culture, in *¿Quién mató a Palomino Molero?* (1986, *Who Killed Palomino Molero?*, 1987). Around a sadistic murder of a half-caste (*cholo*) bolero singer, Vargas Llosa brilliantly recreates Peruvian racism and coastal life in Piura. Lituma re-appears in *Lituma en los Andes*, 1993 (*Death in the Andes*, 1993), delving into Andean Peruvian identity during the bloody Sendero Luminoso revolt. *Historia de Mayta* (1984, *The Real Life of Alejandro Mayta*, 1986) explores a homosexual revolutionary who fails (Vargas Llosa often fictionalizes fanatics). Most amusing is his 1988 *Elogio de la madrastra* (*In Praise of the Stepmother*, 1990) where a boy seduces his stepmother, told with full accounts of their fantasy lives and coloured illustrations of paintings by Titian and **Bacon**. A follow-up in 1997 was *Los cuadernos de Don Rigoberto*, (*The Notebooks of Don Rigoberto*, 1998).

In 1990 Vargas Llosa stood as presidential candidate in Peru and was defeated by the fugitive Alberto Fujimori. Vargas Llosa's entry into politics as a neo-liberal failed, but led to his account of his life as a writer with political ambitions, *El pez en el agua: memorias* (1993, *A Fish in the Water: Memoirs*, 1994). He has always chronicled Peruvian and Latin American life from this independent angle, ruffling many feathers. He speaks his mind, and cares little about being ostracized by the left. His best essays can be read in *Making Waves* (1996).

He returned to his more serious mode in the late 1990s with a detailed exposure of the

Trujillo dictatorship in *La fiesta del Chivo* (2000, *The Feast of the Goat*, 2001). More recently, he has explored, in alternating chapters, **Gauguin's** last years and his grandmother, the revolutionary feminist Flora Tristan, in *El paraíso en la otra esquina* (2003, *The Way to Paradise*, 2003). He is also a playwright, and has written an untranslated study of Peru's great writer on indigenous matters, *La utopía arcaica: José María Arguedas y las ficciones del indigenismo*, 1996.

Further reading

See: Charles Rossman and Alan Warren Friedman (eds), *Mario Vargas Llosa: A Collection of Critical Essays* (1978); Dick Gerdes, *Mario Vargas Llosa* (1985); Efraín Kristal, *Temptation of the Word. The Novels of Mario Vargas Llosa* (1998).

JASON WILSON

VAUGHAN WILLIAMS, (Sir) Ralph

1872–1958

English composer

Vaughan Williams was slow to make an impression as a composer. His first published work, the very successful song 'Linden Lea', did not appear until 1902, and as late as 1908–10 he went to Paris to complete his studies under **Ravel**, having been previously the pupil of Parry and Stanford in London and of Max Bruch in Berlin. However, by the time he went to Paris the main features of his style were already formed. He had for some years been collecting English folk songs – his volume of *Folksongs from the Eastern Counties* was published in 1908 – and he had made use of this material in such utterly characteristic pastoral impressions as the orchestral *In the Fen Country* (1904). What he learned from Ravel was certainly not technique, for he could never boast anything like Ravel's precise craftsmanship, but confidence to continue along the path already mapped out. The Paris period saw not only his first important chamber work, the String Quartet in G minor (1908), but also his first

symphony, *A Sea Symphony* with soloists and chorus (1909), and three other important compositions: the song cycle *On Wenlock Edge* setting Housman for tenor and piano quintet (1909), the inventive overture to *The Wasps* (1909) and the *Fantasia on a Theme of Thomas Tallis* (1910).

This last work was remarkable for its rich interplay of different string groups – two orchestras and a quartet – and also for its use of Tudor music, which Vaughan Williams had come to appreciate as musical editor of the *English Hymnal* (1906). He made a more direct return to the world of Tallis and Byrd in his Mass in G minor for unaccompanied chorus (1920–1), but the pervasive influence of Tudor music is to be found in his very distinctive harmonic style, which had its origins also in the folk music he continued to collect, to arrange, and to use in such works as *A London Symphony* (1913) and *A Pastoral Symphony*, with soprano or tenor soloist (1921).

From this point his style was more or less fixed. He produced occasional surprises, notably in the aggressive and forceful manner of his Fourth Symphony (1931–4), but generally his music is marked by a flowing melodic ease, by his unusual handling of consonant harmony, and by moods of pastoral rambling or religious serenity. After **Elgar's** death in 1934 he was regarded as the outstanding British composer of his day and he produced a large quantity of the expected choral music, ranging from festival oratorios to psalms and anthems for the Anglican church. There were also five more symphonies, among which the *Sinfonia antartica* for wordless female voices and orchestra (1949–52) was derived from music he had written for the film *Scott of the Antarctic* (1948). In addition, he turned during this later period to the composition of opera, beginning with *The Shepherds of the Delectable Mountains* (1922), a one-act treatment of an episode from Bunyan which was eventually incorporated in his full-length 'morality' *The Pilgrim's Progress* (1906–51). This major testament was found undramatic when it at last reached the stage in 1951, and neither of

Vaughan Williams's other big operas, *Hugh the Drover* (1924) and *Sir John in Love* (1924–8, after *The Merry Wives of Windsor*), has proved successful. His setting of Synge's *Riders to the Sea* (1925–32), in which he found a subject better suited to the slow speed of his music's movement, is the most effective of his operas.

Vaughan Williams enjoyed a close friendship with Holst from 1895 until the latter's death in 1934, and each of them profited from criticism and understanding offered by the other. During his lifetime Vaughan Williams also had a great influence on younger English composers, but since his death he has been probably more realistically estimated as a curious offshoot from the tree of music and not a main branch.

Further reading

Other works include: *The Lark Ascending* for violin and orchestra (1914–20); *Job*, ballet (1930); *Fantasia on 'Greensleeves'* for orchestra (1934); *Five Tudor Portraits* for soloists, choir and orchestra (1935); *The Poisoned Kiss*, play with music (1936); *Dona nobis pacem* for soloists, choir and orchestra (1936); *Serenade to Music* for sixteen voices and orchestra (1938); Symphony No. 5 (1938–43); Symphony No. 6 (1944–7); Symphony No. 8 (1953–5); Symphony No. 9 (1956–7). Writings: *National Music* (1934); *Heirs and Rebels* (1959). See: Michael Kennedy, *The Works of Ralph Vaughan Williams* (1964); Ursula Vaughan Williams, *R.V.W.: A Biography of Ralph Vaughan Williams* (1964); Roy Douglas, *Working with R.V.W.* (1972); A. Frogley (ed.), *Vaughan Williams Studies* (1996); L. Foreman (ed.), *Ralph Vaughan Williams in Perspective* (1998); S. Heffer, *Vaughan Williams* (2000).

PAUL GRIFFITHS

VERDI, Giuseppe

1813–1901

Italian composer

The son of an innkeeper and a spinner, born in the tiny hamlet of Le Roncole, near Busseto in Parma, Verdi always stressed his humble origins, sometimes at the expense of the truth: the humbler his birth, the more dramatic would seem his ascent to spectacular success. He also insisted throughout his life that he had enjoyed no regular education. In actual fact he received a basic humanistic training at the Busseto *ginnasio*, formerly the local Jesuit school, which reopened in the year of Verdi's enrolment (1823); the teaching of the humanities was entrusted to Canon Pietro Seletti, who was also an amateur musician. Verdi was taught the rudiments of music, and organ playing, in his native village but regular music lessons began only in the autumn of 1822 with Ferdinando Provesi, a leading figure in Busseto's musical life. Soon Verdi was able to assist and deputize for his teacher in his various capacities as organist and head of the local Philharmonic Society (founded in 1816 jointly by Provesi and Antonio Barezzi, a rich Bussetan merchant). For this institution Verdi composed vocal pieces (arias, duets, trios), *sinfonie* (in the Italian sense of that term), virtuoso piano pieces and, on his own (perhaps somewhat mocking) later admission, 'marches for brass band by the hundred'. Also from this period came various pieces of church music, including a *Stabat Mater*.

By 1830 it was clear that the young musician's talent required further, less provincial teaching. An application to the Milan Conservatory was rejected, mainly on the grounds that Verdi was over-age and not a citizen of the Lombardo–Veneto kingdom, although the examiners' report bears witness to his talent for composition. But with financial support from Barezzi – who had in the meantime become Verdi's benefactor – private lessons were begun with Vincenzo Lavigna, former *maestro al cembalo* at La Scala, Milan. These, according to Verdi, consisted mostly of exercises in strict contrapuntal writing, although we learn from contemporary documents that *composizione ideale* (free composition) was also part of the training. At the same time Verdi established connections with a group of amateur musicians, mostly from the Milanese nobility, called the Philharmonic Society. Pietro Massini, who taught singing and was director of the society, soon detected talent in the young man, and under his guidance Verdi prepared performances of Haydn's *Creation* (April 1834) and Rossini's *Cenerentola* (April 1835). In July 1835 Verdi returned to Busseto to become, the following March, the town's music master, a job which was alien to his temperament and inclinations, now decidedly turned towards opera.

Between January and September 1836 Verdi wrote an operatic work, originally entitled *Rocester*, which after various revisions was eventually performed at La Scala in 1839 under the title *Oberto, conte di San Bonifacio*. This first opera reveals the various models (Donizetti, Mercadante, especially perhaps Bellini) to which the composer had been exposed during the – relatively long – period of composition and reworking. The moderate success of *Oberto* encouraged Bartolomeo Merelli, the impresario of La Scala, to offer Verdi a contract for two other operas, the first of which happened, of necessity, to be a comic one: *Un giorno di regno* (1840), based on the revision of an old libretto by Felice Romani, was one of Verdi's rare fiascos, and he returned to the comic vein only much later in his career.

But the next opera, based on a new libretto by Temistocle Solera, marked the beginning of Verdi's triumphant ascent. *Nabucco* (1842), realized through a few elementary contrasts and with an important role for the chorus, owes its success to a perfect match between the dramatic conception – a vast biblical fresco – and the musical language in which this is expressed. The next opera, *I Lombardi alla prima crociata* (1843), is based on the same pattern (though with a different plot articulation) and, not by chance, is also on a Solera libretto and first performed at La Scala. For the smaller, more intimate theatre of La Fenice, Venice, Verdi composed *Ernani* (1844), his first encounter with a Victor Hugo play. Here the drama centres on the conflicts between three male voices (tenor, baritone and bass) fighting for possession of a soprano; the 'abstract' quality of the characters and the action, developed almost exclusively through solo and ensemble set numbers, is emphasized by the absolute pre-eminence of the vocal writing.

With these operas Verdi established the basic patterns around which he worked in the following years. The immediate, enormous success of *Nabucco* and *Ernani* brought him to the forefront of the international operatic scene, and obliged him to fulfil demands for new scores from many of the most important theatres of Italy and abroad. In a period of about six years, from 1844 to 1850, he composed – or reworked – no fewer than twelve operas, gradually becoming aware of the necessity to realize a dramatic unity by musical means, of establishing relationships at the musical level between dramatically significant points in the action. He soon concluded that a motif announcing the appearance on stage of a major character (as in *I due Foscari*, 1845) was too simple and basically inarticulate; it was only on his encounter with Shakespeare, in the setting of *Macbeth* (1847), that we see the first successful attempt at solving the problem. From *Luisa Miller* (1849) until the end of his career, Verdi adopted a compositional procedure totally unknown in Italian tradition: he sketched the entire score on a small number of staves, notating only the vocal line(s), bass part and essential instrumental connective tissue. This 'continuity draft' helped him to establish musical connections between the various moments of the drama; in this way the set numbers, instead of being the basic dramatic unity (as they had been in previous Italian opera), became the means of establishing the duration of a section, a necessary tassel, outside of which, or even within which, the fundamental elements of the musical language were employed as powerful vehicles of dramatic conflicts.

Thus *Rigoletto* (1851) and *La traviata* (1853), based respectively on Hugo's *Le Roi s'amuse* and Dumas Fils's *La Dame aux camélias*, are directional music dramas in which the action evolves mainly through the characters' development, and particularly through their conflicts; set pieces (mostly duets) and freer musical structures (*arioso*, recitative and *scene*, variously articulated) alternate in equal proportions, forming a balanced, tensely poised whole. In *Il trovatore* (1853), on the other hand, Verdi for the last time builds his score almost exclusively through set pieces, a structure fully in accordance with the elusive nature of the plot and the characters' lack of development; structural symmetries and correspondences therefore dominate.

The central period of Verdi's output bears two distinct features: the relationships of his musical theatre to French *grand opéra* and the pre-eminence of political themes. (Concerning the latter, the development of political content in the operas parallels the composer's position in his country. The early works provided several choruses of a very 'singable' character which gained immense popularity and became vehicles of Italian patriotic feeling. As Verdi became an emblematic figure – as well as a member of the first Italian parliament, at Cavour's request – so political themes as such became central to his plots.) *Les Vêpres siciliennes* (1855) is a full-scale (though not altogether satisfactory) experiment with the French genre; *Simon Boccanegra* (1857; thoroughly reworked in 1881) is an opera where the amorous element has a decidedly secondary role, the plot being built on conflicts between classes and personalities struggling for power – hence the necessity to experiment with new kinds of musical language and, especially, new methods of structural articulation. *Un ballo in maschera* (1859), on a revised libretto by the famous French dramatist Eugène Scribe, combines and blends a basically Italian organization with certain essentially French characteristics and musical features; unity is achieved mainly through a masterful handling of the overall structure of the score, and through the composer's developing skill in fusing light and serious musical elements. *La forza del destino*, written for the Imperial Theatre of St Petersburg in 1862 and revised for La Scala in 1869, exploits a tendency – typical of *grand opéra* – for small, isolated episodes: the opera contains, among other things, the first entirely comic character in Verdi's mature theatre, the monk Fra Melitone. Yet again *La forza* invents new types of musical organization

for the set numbers, in particular employing articulation in the orchestral part rather than the voices. In *Don Carlos* (based on Schiller's play), written for the Paris Opéra in 1867 and much revised later, Verdi once again places the dramatic emphasis on conflicts of power and of political conception, the one influencing and eventually determining the other, thus creating the most complex of his dramatic structures. *Aida* (first performed at Cairo's newly opened opera house in 1871) is in fact an 'Italianization' of the *grand opéra* structure, a fusion of personal conflict and scenic display: the clash between individuals and power structures is again the unifying factor in the drama, and is matched at the musical level by an equally well-measured organization.

After *Aida* Verdi's increasing pessimism over the Italian musical scene, the influence of German music and consequent lack of national musical integrity, as well as his despair over the distortions which conventional performance practice caused to his precise view of music theatre, caused a halt in operatic composition.

In 1874, however, came the *Messa di requiem*, composed to celebrate the first anniversary of the death of Alessandro Manzoni. In this work Verdi's pessimistic vision of man in relation to his fellow beings is transferred to the problem of death and the hereafter. The *Requiem*'s remarkable blend of various influences (from Berlioz's *Grande Messe des morts* to 'classical' polyphonic forms such as the figue) creates a uniquely coherent conception which should not be underestimated: for many the *Requiem* contains some of Verdi's very greatest music.

A deepening contact with Arrigo Boito, encouraged by the publisher Giulio Ricordi, eventually gave rise to Verdi's final two Shakespearian masterpieces. In Boito, the composer at last found a collaborator with the perfect blend of musical awareness, theatrical understanding and ability to adapt (though not always passively) to his dramatic intuitions. After some intensive work together on the revision of *Simon Boccanegra*, the way was clear for *Otello* (first performed at La Scala in 1887). In comparison with the previous operas, *Otello* displays a simplified plot structure – although the decorative elements (basically the choral interventions) still perhaps lie rather uneasily in relation to the whole. But the force of the drama lies in the power with which the basic centres of attraction, the 'good' of Desdemona, the 'evil' of Iago, revolve around the protagonist as he inexorably plays out his tragedy. One of the many delights of *Falstaff* (also La Scala, 1893) is that the composer is summing up, consciously and ironically, the experiences of his operatic career. The opera, which begins with a pseudo sonata form and ends with a fugue sung by all the characters, is a constant, magnificent parody of the dramatic structures and problems of musical organization which Verdi had confronted during his long career. Verdi's final compositions were a series of religious choral pieces, the *Quattro pezzi sacri*, written between 1890 and 1896.

What mattered above all to Verdi was the creation of a musical object whose perfection of workmanship gave it a guarantee of contact, of direct relationship with the public; and in this he succeeded: the operas from *Nabucco* onwards have never left the repertoire of Italian theatres, and many of them are mainstays of the major opera houses of the world. Their extraordinary vitality comes primarily from their force as dramatic facts realized through the most suitable musical means, from the perfect functionality of the composer's musico-dramatic intuitions. It is this which explains the substantial unity of Verdi's oeuvre, from which many have learnt, but which none has attempted to intimate.

Further reading

Other works include: *Giovanna d'arco* (1845); *Alzira* (1845); *Attila* (1846); *I masnadieri* (1847); *Il corsaro* (1848); *La battaglia di Legnano* (1849); and *Stiffelio* (1850). See: Frank Walker, *The Man Verdi* (1962); Julian Budden, *The Operas of Verdi* (3 vols, 1973, 1978 and 1981); J. Rosselli, *Verdi* (2000);

A. Latham and R. Parker (eds), *Verdi in Performance* (2001).

PIERLUIGI PETROBELLI

VERLAINE, Paul
1844–96
French poet

Verlaine was inevitably an over-indulged child: his parents had been married for twelve years before his birth and his mother had suffered three miscarriages; there were no further children. In 1851, Verlaine's father, an army officer in the engineers, resigned his commission and the family moved to Paris. Verlaine's education here proceeded with a rapid loss of application, attrition of will, flirtation with illicit literature. Nascent alcoholism can be traced to 1862, the year he passed his *baccalauréat*. His father tried to draw him back to an ordered life and, in 1864, insisted that he take a job as a clerk, first in an insurance company and then in the Hôtel de Ville. Throughout this period, his literary interests and contacts had developed and 1866 saw the appearance of his first collection, *Poèmes saturniens*. The opening, in 1867, of the Salle Lacaze at the Louvre, with its collection of eighteenth-century canvases (Watteau, Fragonard, Boucher, Lancret) is one of the clues to Verlaine's second volume, *Fêtes galantes* (1869). It was in 1869, too, that he met the sixteen-year-old Mathilde Mauté whom he married the following year and to whom were addressed the poems of his third collection, *La Bonne Chanson* (1870).

His undiminished drinking habits intermittently led Verlaine to brutal treatment of both his mother and his wife. The early months of this marriage were further strained by the Franco-Prussian War, the Siege of Paris and the ensuing Commune; Verlaine's sympathies with the Communards lost him his job and made him something of a fugitive. His attempt to re-install himself in the world of bourgeois respectability was dealt a final blow by **Rimbaud's** arrival in Paris in September 1871, a month before the birth of

Verlaine's son, Georges. In July 1872, after more violence to his wife and son, Verlaine left with Rimbaud, first for Brussels and then for London. The months of wandering which followed and during which Verlaine sought both to reconcile himself with Mathilde and to keep Rimbaud came to an end on 10 July 1873, in Brussels, with Verlaine shooting Rimbaud in the wrist. Sentenced to two years' imprisonment, spent at Mons, Verlaine was converted to the faith in 1874, the year of the publication of *Romances sans paroles* and of Mathilde's legal separation from him.

Released from prison in January 1875, he returned to England to teach French and drawing at Stickney (Lincolnshire) and in 1876–7 was teaching French at Bournemouth. In October 1877, he returned to France and took up a teaching post at Rethel, where he struck up a relationship with one of his pupils, Lucien Létinois, a relationship which lasted through another visit to England, an abortive farming project at Juniville and until Lucien's death from typhoid in April 1883. In the meantime, *Sagesse*, containing the poems of his conversion, had appeared (December 1880). Having failed to be reinstated as a municipal employee, and after another short spell in prison for drunken attacks on his mother, Verlaine finally settled in Paris, in poverty and squalor. The last decade of his life, which, ironically, saw the steady growth of his poetic reputation, was a sequence of seedy lodgings, hospitals, bouts of drink, homosexual liaisons (principally with the artist Frédéric-Auguste Cazals) and affairs with prostitutes (particularly with Eugénie Krantz and Philomène Boudin). Lecture tours in Holland, Belgium and England, his election as Prince of Poets on the death of Leconte de Lisle (1894), the publication of more verse-collections of diminishing quality, preceded his death from bronchial pneumonia in January 1896.

Verlaine's finest poetry belongs to *Fêtes galantes*, poems using the *personae* of the *commedia dell'arte* and the pastoral tradition, in eighteenth-century park settings and inspired by the work of Watteau and others, and to *Romances sans paroles*, poems growing out of the Rimbaud adventure, caught between Rimbaud and Mathilde, backed by the cityscapes of Brussels and London. The *Poèmes saturniens* contain adumbrations of this flowering, but are given over largely to Parnassian and **Baudelairian** derivations. The early poems of *Sagesse* are also of the best vein; those of the conversion are more laboured and conventional.

Verlaine's is the poetry of a floating sensibility which operates in an ill-defined space between sensation and sentiment, self-surrender and anxious interrogation. His vocabulary is a vocabulary of etiolation (*blême, pâle, gris, vague, doux, incertain*), half-measure (*quasi, à peine, un peu*), of infantile diminutives, of locational uncertainty (*parmi, par, vers*), of oscillating or circular movement, pacifying and often mindless (*bercer, balancer, circuler, tourbillonner*). His is a world subject to reflexive or intransitive action, frequently evanescent (*s'évaporer, s'effacer, se noyer, se mêler*), a world of uncontrollable autonomies and apparently directionless motivations. All sense of causality is submerged, and the connections between things, between subject and object are scrambled by intervening barriers (mist, foliage, indeterminate noise). It is, then, a poetry of responses, of the almost imperceptible creations and transformations of temperamental conditions. It would be misleading to speak of feelings, in any Romantic sense of the word; the Romantics have confidence in the value of feeling and in their possession of feeling; they feel with purpose, because feeling is self-projection and self-assertion, born not of sensation but of ideology and moral imperative. With Verlaine, feelings are absorbed back into the more primitive state of sentience and a sentience peculiarly divorced from a sentient being. And repetition, so recurrent a habit in his work, situates the poem in a realm where obsession, hauntedness, ennui, self-hypnosis, formal self-consciousness cannot be put asunder. It is Verlaine's ability to capture the unfocused, almost undifferentiated ripplings of consciousness at its lower levels, the kinetics of the psyche, the flickering modulations of affective reaction, which gives his poetry its distinction. And the pleasure provided by his poetry is a pleasure in the act of reading rather than in subsequent reflection, a pleasure in the infinite resourcefulness and polymorphousness of his verse-art.

Verlaine's 'Art poétique', written in April 1874, appeared in *Jadis et naguère* (1884). Here he calls for music, an art that liberates response in a pure form and re-articulates the elements of semi-consciousness. This enterprise is aided by the use of the imparisyllabic line, which does not let verse-utterance settle, keeps it unstable, volatile, nervous, a safeguard against the portentous. He asks, too, that words be chosen with a certain carelessness, grammatical and semantic, so that precision and imprecision constantly shade into each other. The poet should prefer the nuance to the unambiguous colour, because nuance allows an unhindered trafficking between different kinds of dream, between different 'sonorities', the wistful and the resonant. He rejects satiric verse and the conceit, though the *Fêtes galantes* are given their peculiar alertness and textual crackle by a restless ironic undertone. Next, he attacks eloquence and rhyme. His own verse, with its familiar locutions, unfussy syntax, sudden changes of direction, never loses touch with common speech. What he faults in rhyme is its privilege, the way it monopolizes structural and semantic function, its exemplary conclusiveness. Verlaine seeks to reduce rhyme's prominence, to cast in doubt what it foregrounds, frequently by resorting to bold *enjambement*, by disregarding the traditional rules of rhyming (particularly the alternation of masculine and feminine rhyme-pairs, thus, paradoxically, liberating the expressive potentialities of rhyme gender), by reducing rhyme to assonance and by increasing line-internal music (alliteration, assonance, internal rhyme). Thus the way in which the reader locks into the verse is not rigorously coded; his attention is more uniformly and continuously engaged in a more uniform and

continuous diversity. Verlaine's *vers libéré* is not, however, *vers libre*; whatever liberties he took, he stoutly refused to do away with rhyme and syllabic regularity, and mocked the *verslibristes* for doing so. Traditional prosodic structure, however masked, was a necessary anchorage (moral? psychological? aesthetic?); it acted as a verse-consciousness which could be constantly sunk in, and salvaged from, a highly mobile, hesitant, somnambulistic verse-texture.

Jadis et naguère is the uncomfortable miscellany of poems previously laid aside and new poems that Verlaine's unimpressive late collections often are. It was his intention to follow through the two fundamental strains of his experience, the spiritual and the orgiastic, in parallel volumes. *Sagesse* was succeeded by *Amour* (1888), *Bonheur* (1891) and *Liturgies intimes* (1892). Simultaneously, the erotic thread was taken up by *Parallèlement* (1889), *Chansons pour elle* (1891), *Odes en son honneur* (1893), *Élégies* (1893), *Dans les limbes* (1894) and *Chair* (1896). But these collections are without momentum, falling back on the sentimental, the anecdotal, the rhetorical. Verlaine's poetry in these later years leaves his weaknesses untransformed: the infantile need for refuge, for the total passivity of naive belief or the oblivion of sensual self-immersion, and a mechanical reliance on poetic techniques now too conveniently a part of his growing reputation. There are also volumes of occasional verse: *Dédicaces* (1890), *Épigrammes* (1894), *Invectives* (1896).

If, in his earlier verse, Verlaine is a Symbolist, it is not because his poetry involves itself with metaphysical curiosity – though there is existential inquiry – or with essentialism, or with any excavation of idea from object. It is because his poems present, through sensory encounter, the shifting, polyvalent facets of a mood which is inhabitable but not definable; the poem unifies mood by harmonizing its multiplicity, not by resolving it into singleness. And if these earlier collections can be called Impressionist, it is because they cast anthropocentricity in doubt with their impersonal constructions, because they provide no dominant and stable perspective, because they relativize experience, because they totally subject concept to perception in a world of effects without causes, because they give peculiar substantiality to the half-realities of shadow and reflection, because they depict the mutual interpenetration of objects and surrounding space, because they pursue fugitivity in the free handling of their medium.

Verlaine's influence was marked but short-lived. In France, the Verlainian mode, that kind of poetry which veers between the most delicately musical tone and the prosy, which weds lyric indulgence in evanescent moods of disquiet and vague loss, moods often teased by erotic impulses, with a quizzical, often ironic, vigilance, leads through Laforgue to Apollinaire, but not beyond. Some critics have found a Verlainian transparency in Éluard's verse, but Éluard's verse is altogether firmer; where Verlaine's poems are so often self-consolatory chantings, *berceuses* by nature, Éluard's poems exude a confidence in their own public efficacy and his utterance is more lapidary. The Surrealists looked to Rimbaud, at Verlaine's expense: 'the over-valuation of Verlaine was the great mistake of the Symbolist school' (**Breton**).

In the Anglo-American world, Verlaine enjoyed a cult among the Nineties poets before slipping from sight with the Imagists. It was the neurasthenic strain in Verlaine which caught the fancy of the Nineties poets, the attractions of an experience governed by an atrophied will, by the subdued vyings of the sensual and the mystical, animated by the almost inaudible pulse of the subtlest and most transient sensations. Verlaine was translated (and copied) by Ernest Dowson, John Gray, Arthur Symons and others. In sending his poem 'Vanitas' to Victor Plarr (1891), for example, Dowson wrote: 'It's an attempt at mere sound verse, with scarcely the shadow of a sense in it: or hardly that so much as a vague, Verlainesque emotion.' **W.B. Yeats** had most of his familiarity with Verlaine's verse through Symons, and though he was unable to measure the extent of his debt, he indicated Verlaine's presence in *The Wind Among the Reeds* (1899); perhaps his pursuit of 'those wavering, meditative rhythms, which are the embodiment of the imagination, that neither desires nor hates' ('The Symbolism of Poetry', 1900) had something to do with Verlaine. But **Ezra Pound** found Verlaine to be of no pedagogic use, because he had not taken poetic art forward, as Gautier and Gourmont had done (letter to Harriet Monroe, 1913), an opinion hard to endorse.

Further reading

Other works include: criticism: *Les Poètes maudits* (1888), contributions to the series *Les Hommes d'aujourd'hui* (1885–93); fiction: *Louise Leclercq* (1886), *Les Mémoires d'un veuf* (1886); autobiography: *Mes Hôpitaux* (1891), *Mes Prisons* (1893), *Confessions* (1895); poetry: *Verlaine: Selected Poems*, ed. J. Richardson (1974). See: C. Chadwick, *Verlaine* (1973); C. Cuénot, *Le Style de Paul Verlaine* (1963); O. Nadal, *Verlaine* (1961); N. Osmond, 'Verlaine', in J. Cruickshank (ed.), *French Literature and Its Background*, Vol. 5 (1969); J.-P. Richard, 'Fadeur de Verlaine', in *Poésie et profondeur* (1955); E. Zimmermann, *Magies de Verlaine* (1967).

CLIVE SCOTT

VERNE, Jules
1828–1905
French novelist

The reputation of this prolific, popular writer of adventure stories, a pioneer of science fiction, has undergone some startling fluctuations. The 'New Criticism' in France inaugurated a stimulating rediscovery of works that had become scorned as mere edifying children's literature.

The son of a lawyer, Verne resisted pressure to follow the paternal example, preferring, in the 1850s, to write lightweight plays for the popular stage. In 1863, with the tale *Five Weeks in a Balloon (Cinq semaines en ballon)* he began publication of his *Extraordinary Journeys in Known and Unknown Worlds*, whose aim was described by the didactic publisher

Hetzel as 'to summarize all geographical, geological, physical, astronomical knowledge amassed by modern science'. The *Extraordinary Journeys* were to total a hundred volumes, constituting sixty-two novels, produced at the rate of two per annum. In a sense, they may be seen as imaginary compensation for Verne's own settled existence. The only science in which he had any expertise was geography: a member of the Société de Géographie, he worked on an *Illustrated Geography of France and Her Colonies* (1867–8). He also found time to act as municipal councillor in Amiens from 1884; despite the ambiguous suggestion of anarchist sympathies in novels such as *20,000 Leagues under the Sea* (*20,000 lieues sous les mers*, 1870), he followed a moderate, anti-radical line.

Verne's work may be said to belong to a tradition of imaginary journeys, for all the addition of nineteenth-century scientism. Indeed, the element of fantasy is supremely important. Verne criticism long took the form of 'prediction-spotting', but his science, we now know, was second-hand, culled from vulgarized sources; what we find in his work is not so much science as a mythology of science. 'Known worlds' shade disconcertingly into 'unknown worlds', science acts as threshold to myth. Overriding the paraphernalia of factual information are powerful recurrent images of mythic force, constituting what Michel Butor described as the essence of Verne's naive genius, 'the prodigious power to make us dream'.

A frequent theme is the quest for uncharted locations – the source of the Nile, the Pole (*Adventures of Captain Hatteras, Voyages et aventures du capitaine Hatteras*, 1866), the centre of the earth (*Journey to the Centre of the Earth, Voyage au centre de la terre*, 1864) – that take on quasi-mythical significance, suggesting to the modern reader something akin to the Surrealists' *point suprême* where all contradictions are resolved. In Verne's poetically powerful vision of the Pole ('that unknown point where all meridians cross'), snow and fire are united: Hatteras discovers a volcano

there, and goes mad in the attempt, Empedocles-like, to enter it. Repeatedly the volcano is associated (unscientifically!) with initiation: it is through an extinct volcano that the protagonists of the mythologically rich *Journey to the Centre of the Earth* begin their descent into the underworld, and it is through a live volcano that they are expelled out of the earth's innards in a fascinating transcription of the trauma of birth. Fire is a recurrent theme, often refined and purified in electricity, 'soul of the industrial world', as in *Clipper of the Clouds* (*Robur le conquérant*, 1886). Electricity is even curiously united with the trappings of Gothic horror in *Carpathian Castle* (*Le Château des Carpathes*, 1892). Verne's fascination with caverns, volcanoes, labyrinths and islands attains its finest synthesis in *The Mysterious Island* (*L'Île mystérieuse*, 1874–5). It is clear that much in his work can be read in terms of **Jungian** archetypes. Equally clear is the predominance of the initiation-pattern, together with a taste for cryptograms and word-play: the quest of *Journey to the Centre* begins from a coded message left by an Icelandic alchemist. Verne's imagination has much in common with the alchemical tradition, itself poised between science and mythology – gold and fire are suggestively united in *The Golden Volcano* (*Le Volcan d'or*, 1906).

Not surprisingly, characterization in these tales is rudimentary and largely reduced to standard types: eccentric scientists, young novices, initiates, mysterious holders of knowledge and power (Captain Nemo), humorous servants. The element of humour, to be found in most of his works, no doubt played a large part in the success of *Around the World in 80 Days* (*Le Tour du monde en 80 jours*, 1873). In a sense, humour acts as a check on the initiatory scope of these works, for Verne holds back from 'excessive' initiation. Transgressors, such as Hatteras, are punished, whereas in general the characters return to a settled bourgeois life after a hint, a vicarious thrill of revelation. **Roland Barthes** has commented (in *Mythologies*, 1957) on the bourgeois aspect of Verne's work: a cult of enclosedness, the desire to reconstruct, with the help of science, a comfortable universe in microcosm, whether submarine, island or lighthouse.

However, Verne is not simply a representative of the optimistic nineteenth-century ideology of science. His later novels show increasing doubts about progress – *Master of the World* (*Maître du monde*, 1904), *The Survivors of the 'Jonathan'* (*Les Naufragés du 'Jonathan'*, 1909). A final story, *The Eternal Adam* (*L'Eternel Adam*, 1910), completes the development into pessimism: human history now appears as absurdly cyclical. Having expressed the nineteenth century's dream of science, its mythology, Verne finally, on the threshold of a more sceptical age, passes judgement on that dream.

Further reading

Other works include: *From the Earth to the Moon* (*De la terre à la lune*, 1865); *The Children of Captain Grant* (*Les Enfants du capitaine Grant*, 1868); *Black Diamonds* (*Les Indes noires*, 1877); *The Begum's Fortune* (*Les Cinq Cents Millions de la Bégum*, 1879); *Mathias Sandorf* (1885). See: M. Butor, *Répertoire I* (1960); I.O. Evans, *Jules Verne and His Work* (1965); M. Moré, *Le Très Curieux Jules Verne* (1960); S. Vierne, *Jules Verne et le roman initiatique* (1973); Andrew Martin, *The Mask of the Prophet: Extraordinary Fictions of Jules Verne* (1990); Herbert R. Lottman, *Jules Verne: An Exploratory Biography* (1997).

DAVID MEAKIN

VIDAL, Gore

1925–

US novelist and essayist

Gore Vidal was born in 1925. He graduated from Phillips Exeter College in 1943, joined the maritime branch of the Army Transportation Corps and served in the Aleutian Islands (off the coast of Alaska). This experience provided the material for his first novel, *Williwaw* (1946), written at the age of nineteen. The next few years saw a rapid succession of novels, including the *succès de scandale*, *The City and the Pillar* (1948, revised

1965), a matter-of-fact account of homosexual pursuit and disillusion. In the 1950s and early 1960s Vidal also wrote a number of plays for Broadway and television as well as doing film work, including an uncredited share in the script for *Ben Hur* (1959). Linked with the **Kennedy** dynasty, descended from a political family (his maternal grandfather was an Oklahoman senator and a cousin is Al Gore, Bill Clinton's vice-president and a presidential candidate in his own right in 2000), Gore Vidal has always displayed an ambivalent attitude towards power and politics while contriving to remain on the margin of that world. But since Vidal seems to have known everyone – as shown by his highly entertaining and anecdotal memoir *Palimpsest* (1995) – it is a very glittering margin.

Impatient or dismissive of his national culture and its parochialism – America is 'the civilisation whose absence drove **Henry James** to Europe' is one of many agreeable asides in *Two Sisters: A Memoir in the Form of a Novel* (1970) – Vidal has for many years lived in European exile (in Ravello). Provokingly describing the great US authors as 'minor provincial writers', he has been influenced by European or classical models. Little indication of Vidal's development therefore was provided by *Williwaw*, a story he himself described as 'written in the national manner ... a bit simple-minded but useful'. The 'true voice and pitch' which the novelist has to discover are partially to be heard in *The Judgement of Paris* (1952), the account of a self-regarding odyssey made by a young American in Europe, and in the apocalyptic *Messiah* (1954), which describes the growth of a worldwide death-cult. Vidal's elegant, sombre and world-weary voice found its perfect pitch in *Julian* (1964), the story of the apostate Roman emperor who belatedly tried to substitute Hellenism for Christianity.

Vidal's status as an adroit, even outrageous satirist was confirmed by *Myra Breckinridge* (1968), the eponymous heroine of which is a film buff and sex-change who recovers his masculinity and a belief in Christian Science in the parodic happy ending. Other satires of this middle period include *Kalki* (1978), in which the author once again brings the world to an unlamented end, with a few survivors cavorting in an empty White House, the target of so much of his polemical writing and fiction. During the final third of the twentieth century, Vidal produced seven historical novels dealing with the American experience under the collective title 'Narratives of Empire'. These are serious and carefully researched fictions, whose tone veers between the iconoclastic and the elegiac. Chronologically, the sequence begins with *Burr* (1973) – an earlier work, *Washington D.C.* (1967) was later incorporated into the series – and concludes with *The Golden Age* (2000). In this final novel, Vidal himself emerges as a (marginal) character and, during a postmodern epilogue, dismisses his creations in gentle Shakespearian fashion. If the series can be said to have a single preoccupation it is, at least in its closing volumes, the inadvertent way in which America acquired an empire, subsequently justified through a messianic sense of destiny. *Empire* (1987) is the title of one of the finest books in the sequence. In their mingling of fictional characters with historical figures, and with their privileged-seeming insights into politics and power, these 'Narratives of Empire' look set to be Vidal's principal fictional legacy.

The George W. Bush presidency and the US response to the 9/11 attacks have amply confirmed Vidal's long-standing belief in governmental duplicity and conspiracy, and produced some of his most polemical work. There is no loss of cynical zest in his work. In his writing Vidal continues to circle like an urbane bird of prey round a society in decline; the refined mixture of regret, relief and anger is all his own.

Further reading

Other works include: *Homage to Daniel Shay: Collected Essays 1952–72* (1972); *Myron* (1975); *1876* (1976); *Creation* (1981); *Lincoln* (1984); *The Decline and Fall of the American Empire* (2002); *Imperial America: Reflections on the United States of Amnesia* (2004) See: Bernard F. Dick, *The Apostate Angel: A Critical Study of Gore Vidal* (1979); Fred Kaplan, *Gore Vidal: A Biography* (1999).

PHILIP GOODEN

VISCONTI, Luchino

1906–76

Italian filmmaker and theatre and opera director

Born into an aristocratic Milanese family, and brought up with a dilettantish interest in music and horses, Luchino Visconti was drawn to the cinema and to an involvement with left-wing politics when Coco Chanel introduced him to **Jean Renoir** in 1935. After a short period working with Renoir in the France of the Popular Front, he returned to Fascist Italy and made an extraordinary first film, *Ossessione* (1942), which was a direct challenge to the official culture of the period and was widely hailed, on its release after the war, as a precursor of neo-realism. In 1947 he made the mammoth *La terra trema,* an epic about a Sicilian fishing family, loosely inspired by Giovanni Verga's classic novel *I Malavoglia.* If *Ossessione* was a precocious forerunner of neo-realism, *La terra trema* equally precociously outran it. Shot on location, with non-professional actors speaking their own lines in incomprehensible dialect, *La terra trema* emerged, paradoxically, as closer in style to grand opera than to the documentary realism that it originally aspired to. With *Senso* (1954) Visconti attempted a historical spectacular which would be realist in the **Marxist** or at least Lukacsian sense of producing a narration that enabled the spectator to grasp the nature of historical reality. Set in the Risorgimento, *Senso* tells a complex story of betrayal and counterbetrayal, in which the personal and political are closely but ambiguously intertwined.

The historical process recounted in *Senso* is one of 'passive revolution' (in Gramsci's phrase) and of muted change achieved by accommodations and compromise. The same process also figures in *The Leopard* (1963), an adaptation of Giuseppe Tomasi di Lampedusa's novel. In both these Risorgimento films the mechanism of the plot works through betrayal, whether sexual or political, while the underlying thematic concern is with the survival or otherwise of class and family groupings in a context of historical change. In *Rocco and His Brothers* (1960) the same mechanisms are returned to a modern setting – the life of a family of southern immigrants in Milan during the 'economic miracle'. The peasant family is torn apart under the pressure of urban life and its destruction is seen as both tragic and necessary and as the price to be paid if the individuals composing it are to survive. In *Vaghe stelle dell'Orsa* (1965) (known in the US as *Sandra*) a family is also destroyed, but the forces motivating its destruction are more internal. The story of *Vaghe stelle* is that of the *Oresteia*, and in particular of Electra, the daughter dedicated to avenging her father's death at the hands of her mother and step-father. Again betrayal plays an important role. The daughter Sandra suspects her mother of having betrayed her father, a Jewish scientist, to the Nazis, resulting in his death in Auschwitz. Sandra in turn plays on her brother's (incestuous) love for her and betrays him, leading to his suicide. Sandra, however, survives and there is a sense at the end of the film that a future exists not only for her but for other survivors as well. History continues despite or even because of the family's destruction.

In his later films, however, Visconti shows himself more and more sceptical about history as a progressive development. In *The Damned* (*La caduta degli Dei,* 1969), the story of a German capitalist family destroyed by Nazism, there are no survivors. Nor are there in *Ludwig* (1972), where the mad king is incarcerated by his ministers leaving nothing behind him. Both these films are set in a recognizable history, whose development is cataclysmically blocked. In *Death in Venice* (1971) and *The Intruder* (*L'innocente,* 1976),

on the other hand, there is no history at all. The films are set in their own present, which is our past. They have neither a future of their own nor any connection forward, even implicit, to our present. This cutting off of the past from the present goes along with an increasing interest in deviant sexuality. The protagonists of these late films are the last of their line and can only live in the present, knowing it to be the end. Significantly, few children are procreated, and none survive. This contrasts sharply with the world of *Rocco* or *La terra trema,* where the break-up of the family leaves behind children who are free to grow and develop. How much this involution of Visconti's concerns connects with his own homosexuality and his approaching death (during the making of *Ludwig* he had a severe stroke from which he never fully recovered) and how much it has to do with political disappointments is hard to determine. Suffice it to say that the later films, for all their splendours, lack the urgent forward-looking drive that characterizes the early ones.

Visconti's film output was not very great – some fourteen features in thirty years – but each of his films is in some way remarkable. Throughout his filmmaking career he was also busy with theatre and opera productions, in London and Paris as well as in Italy. Among his finest opera productions were **Verdi's** *Traviata* and *Don Carlo* for Covent Garden. In the theatre he directed Shakespeare, Goldoni, Beaumarchais and **Chekhov** as well as contemporary plays and (as these names imply) his work in the theatre included a lot of comedy, generally treated in a realistic vein. Although he soon abandoned realism as an aesthetic, he retained a gift for incidental realistic touches, both in theatre and cinema, helping to give substance to productions which would otherwise occasionally seem to be merely spectacular.

Further reading

Other works include: *Bellissima* (1951); *White Nights* (1957); *Lo straniero* (1967; from Camus's *L'Etranger); Conversation Piece* (1975). See: Monica

Stirling, *A Screen of Time* (biography, 1979); Henry Bacon, *Visconti: Explorations of Beauty and Decay* (1998); Geoffrey Nowell-Smith, *Luchino Visconti* (2003).

GEOFFREY NOWELL-SMITH

VON STERNBERG, Josef

1894–1969

US film director

Josef Sternberg was born in Vienna in 1894. He moved to New York at the age of seven for three years, then returned to Vienna before settling permanently in the United States in 1908. Leaving school to work for a milliner and then a lace firm, he entered the film industry in 1911 as apprentice to a film-stock handler before moving to a job at the World Film Corporation in 1914. During the war he produced training films and was a Signal Corps photographer. Afterwards he worked as a cutter, writer, editor and assistant director in the United States and in Europe, ennobling his surname by the addition of 'von'.

His Hollywood career took off in the second half of the 1920s, following the prestige of his low-life (and low-budget) drama *The Salvation Hunters* (1925), which led to a contract with MGM, and, via *The Exquisite Sinner* (1925, now lost), to work for **Chaplin** on Edna Purviance's comeback picture, *The Sea Gull* (*A Woman of the Sea*, 1926), a film subsequently suppressed by Chaplin. The enormous success of Von Sternberg's *Underworld* (1927), one of the first gangster pictures, marked the beginning of his long relationship with Paramount and led to five films in the next three years, as well as re-editing work on Von Stroheim's *The Wedding March* (1927). The year 1928 saw *The Last Command*, the story of a Tsarist general reduced to the role of a Hollywood extra after the Revolution, *The Drag Net*, now lost, a follow-up to *Underworld*, and a further gangster picture, *The Docks of New York*. In 1929 Von Sternberg made *The Case of Lena Smith*, now lost, dealing with illegitimacy and class-relations in *fin-de-siècle* Vienna, and *Thunderbolt*, a 'gangster fantasy' (Weinberg) exploring the early possibilities of the sound cinema.

In 1930 Von Sternberg went to Europe to produce both English language and German versions of *The Blue Angel* (based on Heinrich Mann's novel *Professor Unrat*), the story of a schoolmaster who is bewitched and destroyed by a night-club singer. The film introduced Von Sternberg's new discovery, Marlene Dietrich, who then came to Hollywood to provide the cool and often mocking eroticism at the centre of Von Sternberg's love-dramas of the period, commencing with the North African romance *Morocco* (1930) and the spy story *Dishonoured* (1931). In 1931 Von Sternberg punctuated the Dietrich cycle with *An American Tragedy* – replacing the visiting Soviet director **Sergei Eisenstein** – before continuing with the 1932 Dietrich vehicles *Shanghai Express* and *Blonde Venus*. After *The Scarlet Empress* (1934), a sumptuous and grotesque account of the rise to power of Catherine the Great, came the last of the Von Sternberg/Dietrich collaborations, the Spanish caprice *The Devil is a Woman* (1935).

Von Sternberg's break with Dietrich and with Paramount led to a mixed bag of projects and associations. *Crime and Punishment* (1935) was followed by his version of an operetta on the life of Elizabeth of Austria, *The King Steps Out* (1936), and the unfinished *I, Claudius* (1937) for Alexander Korda. He moved on to the crime-drama *Sergeant Madden* (1939), followed by his return to oriental intrigue in *The Shanghai Gesture* (1941). After only one completed wartime project, the documentary short *The Town* (1943–4), Von Sternberg's career dwindled in the 1950s with the Cold War comic-strip *Jet Pilot* (1951) and the jewel-smuggling intrigue *Macao* (1952), both of which passed beyond his control. His last film, *The Saga of Anatahan* (1953), his most personal of the period, provides an oneiric account of a group of Japanese sailors who hide on an island for several years beyond the end of the Second World War, caught up in a cobweb of honour and desire with a man and woman from the island.

Von Sternberg is remembered for four main contributions to film history. First, for his totalizing attitude to film authorship, his ambitions in the direction of total creative control sometimes extending beyond mere perfectionism into the realms of sheer autocracy. Second, for his skills in intense pictorial stylization of frequently banal dramatic material through elaborate *mise-en-scène* and virtuoso cinematography. Third, for his contribution, in films like *Underworld*, *The Drag Net*, *The Docks of New York* and *Thunderbolt*, to the early evolution of the crime-film, a contribution later nuanced in such literary adaptations as *An American Tragedy* and *Crime and Punishment*. Finally, and above all, he is remembered for his representations of female eroticism through the figure of Marlene Dietrich in his middle-period Paramount films such as *The Blue Angel*, *Morocco*, *Dishonoured*, *Shanghai Express*, *Blonde Venus*, *The Scarlet Empress* and *The Devil is a Woman*.

Further reading

Other works include: *Fun in a Chinese Laundry* (1965); Andrew Sarris, *The Films of Josef von Sternberg* (1966); Herman G. Weinberg, *Josef von Sternberg* (1966); John Baxter, *The Cinema of Joseph von Sternberg* (1971); Carole Zucker, *The Idea of the Image: Josef von Sternberg's Dietrich Films* (1988); Gaylyn Studlar, *In the Realm of Pleasure: Von Sternberg, Dietrich and the Masochistic Aesthetic* (1993).

PHILIP DRUMMOND

VONNEGUT, Kurt, Jr

1922–2007

US novelist

Vonnegut's hip, breezy, atraditional style probably accounts for much of his enormous popularity, particularly among young adult readers. However, it is the tension between this light, humorous style and the seriousness of his themes and motifs that draws

widespread critical acclaim. In general, each Vonnegut novel asks this question: In a world where technology, power, and greed inevitably produce war, where wealth and prestige have replaced love and kindness, where society's goals have replaced the individual's, where free will has become an obsolete notion, is it possible for human beings to have purpose and to live according to meaningful values? The fourteen novels, three collections of stories, seven stage plays and other miscellaneous writings represent the search for an answer. Vonnegut has been variously labelled a science-fiction writer, a fantasist, an absurdist and a visionary. He is perhaps best understood as a black humorist, although Vonnegut preferred to see himself as an 'old fart with his Pall Malls'.

Vonnegut began writing for the *Daily Sun* while he was an undergraduate at Cornell. His formal education, mostly in the sciences and anthropology, was cut short by the Second World War; in 1943 he enlisted in the army. A year later, he was captured by the Germans and sent to a POW camp in Dresden. There he somehow survived the tragic Allied firebombing, and this experience obviously changed his view of modern man. Nevertheless, he returned to the United States and worked for the Chicago City News Bureau while attending the University of Chicago. In 1951, after working as a publicist for General Electric for four years, he quit to write full time. For many years he was able to support himself and his family only by publishing popular stories (many have been reprinted in *Canary in a Cat House*, 1961, and *Welcome to the Monkey House*, 1968), but from the mid-1960s his novels were financially successful, a fact that seemed to embarrass him.

It is no surprise that the first two novels, *Player Piano* (1952) and *Sirens of Titan* (1959), are stylistically more traditional than the later works. *Player Piano* is a reworking of *Brave New World* and *Sirens of Titan* is, at first glance, a somewhat ordinary science-fiction journey through space. However, these two books are seminal in the Vonnegut world.

The main characters, Dr Paul Proteus and Malachi Constant, struggle to find lives worth living. Proteus fights valiantly against a technological, machine-dominated society only to find, in the end, that most people are happy being automatons. Proteus's rebellion fails to save society, but he finds personal satisfaction and, perhaps, salvation in his effort. Constant, in *Sirens of Titan*, is transformed from debauched mogul into a loving, contented and sensitive man. It is no coincidence that he first finds this happiness on Titan; the implication is, of course, that love and peace are difficult in the chaos on Earth. During his journey, Constant discovers that all human evolution occurs in order to rescue a stranded Trafalmadore space traveller. So man has no universal purpose other than this mission and, therefore, humankind has absolutely no free will. Even with this discovery, Constant returns to Earth and asserts that human beings should live and love those around them. From these early novels, we learn that it is good, although futile, for the individual to struggle against inhumanity; at the same time, it is necessary for the individual to remain gentle and loving.

The next three novels, *Mother Night* (1962), *Cat's Cradle* (1963) and *God Bless You, Mr Rosewater* (1965), build on the discoveries made in the first two. For many critics, *Slaughterhouse Five* (1969) is Vonnegut's most significant work. Twenty-five years on, the author wrote about his Dresden experiences, and it is just this aesthetic distance that makes the novel so powerful. War and death are, of course, classic themes, but Vonnegut approaches these from a new perspective. Billy Pilgrim, survivor of Dresden, finds that he has no control over time, that he comes 'unstuck' and slips in and out from one moment to another. The Trafalmadores (space travellers) suggest cosmic detachment and advise Billy to cope with his chaotic world by enjoying the good moments and ignoring the bad. When catastrophe strikes, simply say, 'So it goes.' Then ignore it. Vonnegut clearly does not believe in this cosmic shrug; he illustrated, by the very act of writing this book, that the horrors of life are too important to ignore. However, one should not collapse into nihilism or withdraw into cosmic detachment under the weight of chaos; instead, one should face the bad (war, atrocities, greed, death, etc.) with grace, compassion and humour. *Slaughterhouse Five* is Vonnegut's testament to these values.

The same values inform much, if not all, of Vonnegut's subsequent work, which had a tendency to become self-absorbed, even eccentric – for example *Breakfast of Champions* (1973) and *Slapstick* (1976). The last novel to be published was *Timequake* (1997), though this was followed by *Bagombo Snuff Box* (1999), a collection of stories. In 2000 a serious fire broke out in the East Side Manhattan house where Vonnegut had lived with his photographer wife, Jill Krementz, since 1970. Narrowly surviving acute smoke inhalation, and losing his library and papers, Vonnegut abandoned New York for a safer haven in Northampton, Massachusetts. That asteroid number 25399 is named after him is a touch straight out of his own imagination.

Further reading

Other works include: *Happy Birthday, Wanda June* (1971) and *Between Time and Timbuktu* (1972) are both plays; *Wampeters, Foma, & Granfalloons: Opinions* (1974) and *God Bless You, Dr Kevorkian* (1999) are collections of essays. The later novels include *Jailbird* (1979); *Deadeye Dick* (1982); *Galápagos* (1982); *Bluebeard* (1987); *Hocus Pocus* (1990); and *A Man Without a Country* (2005). See: Richard Giannone, *Vonnegut: A Preface to His Novels* (1977); Jerome Klinkowitz and Donald Lawler, *Vonnegut in America* (1977); James Lundquist, *Kurt Vonnegut* (1977); William Rodney Allen, *Conversations with Kurt Vonnegut* (1988); Lawrence R. Broer, *Sanity Plea: Schizophrenia in the Novels of Kurt Vonnegut* (1994); Thomas F. Marvin, *Kurt Vonnegut: A Critical Companion* (2002); Donald E. Morse, *The Novels of Kurt Vonnegut: Imagining Being an American* (2003).

GARY THOMPSON
(REVISED AND UPDATED BY THE EDITOR)

W

WAGNER, Richard

1813–83

German music dramatist

Wagner's work has often been described in terms of its paradoxes. Yet the fact that these paradoxes reveal so much about the nineteenth century is due to Wagner's having been a dramatist as much as a composer. He championed a socialist Utopia free from financial cares where the pursuit of art could be held as the highest ideal: yet subtly he reinforced the Christian-bourgeois morality of his day. He was an idealist and, for the most part, an optimist, yet death cast the longest shadow over his work. He unleashed in his music a liberating new sensuality and energy, while arguing dramatically that redemption could be achieved only through sublimation, renunciation and self-sacrifice. He worked on a massive scale, but was celebrated for his unprecedented sensitivity to detail. As an artist, he was particular to the point of pedantry, but used his art to preach anti-intellectualism and a recognition of nature as the teacher of spontaneity. And while his operatic reforms and innovations were radical and international in their influence, they were, at the same time, rooted in a vast cultural and philosophical learning, and in mythic sources that were conspicuously German. Nowadays these opposites may readily be understood as interdependent. But earlier judgements of Wagner have, not surprisingly, been characterized by significant contradictions: he has been seen both as the high priest of love and as a dangerous, even malevolent, theatrical wizard.

Something of this critical perplexity owes to a further apparent dichotomy: between the high seriousness and tenacity of his work on the one hand, and the rash impetuosity of his personal and financial affairs on the other. This became evident even at an early stage of his life. Born in 1813, he matriculated from Leipzig University as a music student in 1831, at which time he studied composition privately with Theodore Weinlig (lessons recalled, perhaps, in *Die Meistersinger*). It was the epiphanies of this time, in drama (the plays of Shakespeare) and music (Beethoven's Ninth Symphony, Weber's *Der Freischütz* and (allegedly) Wilhelmine Schröder-Devrient singing Leonora in *Fidelio*), that were to lead in due course to the synthesis of the two arts into a 'higher' form. Also no less important for the development of his impeccable sense of theatre and stagecraft was the early and extensive first-hand knowledge he gained of the operatic repertoire as music director in Riga (1837) and Dresden (1843), and his experiences as a resident in Paris (1840), the operatic capital of Europe. As a consequence, his first three operas showed diverse influences: *Die Feen* (1833), *Das Liebesverbot* (1836) and the highly successful *Rienzi* (1840) owe as much to the examples of Bellini, Mehul, Auber, Meyerbeer and Spontini as they do to those of his German contemporaries. But these were also turbulent years privately. In 1836, he married Minna Planer whose early, but brief, elopement with a Königsberg merchant boded ill for the couple's future. In 1839, debts compelled him to flee Riga. After travels to Russia and England he settled in Paris, where his extravagance landed him for a short time in debtor's prison.

There was a similar pattern to the next decade. With *Der fliegende Holländer* (*The Flying Dutchman*, 1841), *Tannhäuser* (1847) and *Lohengrin* (1848), he found his own voice, took Romantic opera to its peak, uncovered most of his later dramatic concerns and provided a vital transition from sectionalized opera to operas where entire acts were unfolded as unbroken musical textures. He was also deeply absorbed in the socially iconoclastic Young Germany movement (which inspired his belief in free love), the Young Hegelians and the anti-Christian philosophy of Ludwig Feuerbach. Yet his participation in the Dresden uprisings of 1848–9 forced him to flee Saxony (Bakunin said he was too much of an idealist to be an effective revolutionary), and in the following financially unstable years he derived his income from concert-giving (he later wrote a monograph on conducting), which entailed further travels to Italy, England and France (his notorious pamphlet deploring the Jewish influence on music appears to have been triggered by Meyerbeer's refusal to promote his work).

In the 1850s, the affairs with Jessie Laussot and Mathilde Wesendonck that led eventually to Wagner's separation from Minna were evidently bound up with the great effort of gestation demanded by the music drama format that engaged him for the rest of his life. At this time his principal sources were Grimm's *German Mythology* and Greek drama in general (though Aeschylus especially), sources central to his attempt to restore to the theatre a lost communal consciousness (the argument was further developed in *The Birth of Tragedy* by Wagner's protégé, the philosopher **Friedrich Nietzsche**); and in *The Artwork of the Future* (*Das Kunstwerk der Zukunft*, 1849) and the comprehensive *Opera and Drama* (*Oper und Drama*, 1851) he

described how traditional technical features would in future have to be newly balanced and blended in order that music at all times could illumine the drama and not vice versa (this is what he meant by the *Gesamtkunstwerk*).

The main fruit of this undertaking was *Der Ring des Nibelungen*, a music drama in three evenings (*Die Walküre*, *Siegfried* and *Götterdämmerung*) preceded by an introductory evening, *Das Rheingold*. The libretto was begun in 1848, the music completed in 1874, and the whole performed in 1876. In the meantime, he composed two other works motivated to a greater or lesser extent by biographical concerns. Of *Tristan und Isolde* (1859) he had written to his lifelong friend Franz **Liszt**: 'As I have never in life felt the real bliss of love, I must erect a monument to the most beautiful of my dreams ... *Tristan and Isolde*.' And the extent to which he had absorbed the exotic nihilism of Schopenhauer's *The World as Will and Representation* emerges from his remark that 'freedom from all our dreams' – in other words, extinction – 'is our only salvation'. In the comedy *Die Meistersinger* (1867), however, he offered a defence of his own position as a German artist through the words of Hans Sachs and projected his aesthetic attitudes to the nature and function of high art.

But the end of the 1860s saw Wagner in changed circumstances. The publication of the poem of *Der Ring* had been prefaced by an appeal to an enlightened patron. In 1864, the young King of Bavaria, Ludwig II, declared himself ready and willing to respond. He eased Wagner's debts, promised him a regular income, and supported his projects – albeit intermittently – for the rest of his life. In 1861, Wagner had seen Minna for the last time (she died five years later); and two years after he had settled in Villa Tribschen near Lucerne, he was joined permanently by Cosima Liszt, at the time the wife of the conductor Hans von Bülow and daughter of the composer (according to whom she revered Wagner with a Senta-like devotion). Her diaries were to yield absorbing biographical information on Wagner's later years, following on from his autobiography (which had extended only as far as the mid-1860s). In 1871 Wagner moved to Bayreuth, and the last twelve years of his life were devoted to founding a specially designed festival theatre (which opened in 1876), to building his own house (Wahnfried, in 1874), to composing and producing his final music drama *Parsifal* (in part an idealization of Ludwig II), and to writing extensively on practical, musical and philosophical issues of the day. The organizational strain aggravated a heart condition (angina), and he died in Venice in 1883.

Although Wagner's art evolved extraordinarily during his lifetime, most of the main issues are essentially present in his first three mature works. In his transformation of Heine's account of *Der fliegende Holländer*, Wagner laid a special emphasis on the role of Senta. It is her self-sacrifice that redeems the Dutchman who had been destined to wander the seas eternally in punishment for his Promethean defiance of divinity. In the ballad that forms the kernel of the work, she reveals (with what **Thomas Mann** described as the 'lofty hysteria' of all Wagner's heroines) not merely love, but a deep, abnormal bonding with the more-than-human, timeless hero. On the other hand, his love for her is both a yearning for redemption and a longing for death (without her love, he is tragically doomed 'never to die'): her sacrifice is part of his self-fulfilment. But through it, they are both transfigured, and in a conclusion that reveals an essentially Christian morality, love emerges triumphant. Although the work is organized into discontinuous groups of scenes (Wagner soon came to prefer unbroken continuities in each act), it is powerfully homogeneous from a harmonic point of view – a feature of all Wagner's subsequent works.

If the Dutchman's quest for Senta represented part of the nineteenth century's (and Wagner's) quest for Goethe's *ewig Weibliche* (eternal womanhood), then the examination in *Tannhäuser* (a significant conflation of two sources from *Das Knaben Wunderhorn*) of

carnality (the court of Venus) and sublime purity (the Wartburg, the Minnesingers, Elizabeth and the pilgrims) established two poles important for Wagner's work generally. Their musical treatment through unstable harmony on the one hand, and pseudoarchaisms on the other, were to lead to the most characteristic sounds of *Tristan* and *Parsifal*. In the libretto, the two worlds are to a certain extent interdependent. Tannhäuser, a singer with whom Wagner identified closely, recognizes that through Venus 'every sweet wonder stems', but nevertheless proclaims that 'in the midst of joy, I crave pain'. On the other hand, the gravity of the saintly Elizabeth is at least partially sexually achieved: he has awoken in her 'emotions I had never experienced, longings I had never known'. Yet in its first version, the music (as with Senta's in *Der fliegende Holländer*) had not fully realized the feminine aspect of the text (Venus especially): and the post-Tristan revisions that developed the work's latent eroticism also unbalanced it stylistically. At the end of his life it remained the one work with which Wagner was still dissatisfied.

On the other hand, *Lohengrin* (derived from Wolfram von Eschenbach) is within its own terms consummately achieved. Here, humanity itself is put on trial, with only the divine and the superhuman exalted. Wagner saw in Lohengrin, a fearless emissary from the holy land of the Grail, a symbol of the artist, demanding unquestioning adherence to, and love for, his visions. Lohengrin agrees to defend and marry Elsa as long as she asks neither his name nor his origin. Inevitably, she is set upon by doubters, and after the wedding ceremony presses the forbidden question (why can't he trust her with his secret? she asks rather persuasively; how can love be ideal if she can't even address him?). Sadly, Lohengrin returns to the Grail, Elsa dies of shock and disappointment, and the moral is to be drawn – as **Gustav Mahler** put it – that 'the capacity for trust is masculine, suspicion is feminine'. More still, the audience is left to realize, as Kant had already done, that moral law is not achievable in this world but only in the transcendence of death. It was to become the dominant message of Wagner's oeuvre. But however two-edged Lohengrin's authoritarianism may be, there were three striking musical developments here: the impressive tableaux that portray an idealized medieval community are skilfully woven into a newly continuous texture; the music has a fresh synaesthetic splendour (**Baudelaire** revelled in the Lohengrin-Grail music); and the art of slow transition from one dramatic extreme (in Act III, festivity and private joy) to another (rupture, desolation and death) is effected by a large-scale control of harmony that adds a new dimension to the meaning of words.

Indeed, Wagner's theorizing in the early 1850s led to a new interdependence of word and music. Whereas previously, large-scale operatic continuity had been in part achieved by the use of 'reminiscence motives' – thematic entities that recurred with the effect of self-conscious quotations – Wagner now developed a constantly evolving orchestral web of thematic fragments, themselves significantly interrelated, which were symphonically developed in an 'unending' melodic flow according to dramatic circumstances. Over these 'leitmotives' (the term employed by Hans von Wolzogen) the voice sang in a heightened recitative (*Sprechgesang*), occasionally taking up the orchestral fragments to give them definitive meaning. This practice was also extended through new uses of harmony and versification. The orchestra thus assumed a narrative role similar to that of the chorus in Greek tragedy: the humans are the playthings of the gods, and the gods are subject to the force of destiny.

These new techniques are central to *Der Ring*, the quasi-Shakespearian complexity of which has attracted such a range of interpretation. The work opens with the depiction of original sin: the dwarf Alberich's seizure of power (symbolized by a ring) through the renunciation of love. He cruelly exploits his fellow dwarfs and places the curse of death on all the ring's future owners (the capitalist analogies here are what fascinated

G.B. Shaw). Conversely, it is dread of the loss of power that motivates Wotan, the all-too-human ageing head of the gods, to build Valhalla as a 'fortress against fear'. The cycle shows his fight against impending death, his acquiescence in it, and finally his combustion as flames consume Valhalla.

Importantly, however, there are two aspects to Wotan's personality, just as there were to Faust's. The male, mortal side schemes to perpetuate his power through the creation of a perfect hero, who, while being independent of himself, would represent a new and higher breed of being, capable of winning and guarding the ring. (Being fearless, Siegfried would be exempt from the curse: he is a cousin of Friedrich Schiller's fearless William Tell.) *Die Walküre* shows the failure of the hero's prototype, Siegmund; *Siegfried* shows the eponymous hero's schooling (from nature, not from received wisdom), and his winning of the highest prize, his bride Brünnhilde. *Götterdämmerung* reveals the truth of the comment made in *Das Rheingold* by Wotan's wife Fricka (the goddess of marriage and symbol of a legalistic, repressive society) that the god's eugenic plans are mere dreams: the 'tragic' destruction of Siegfried by Hagen (Alberich's son) is inevitable in a loveless world.

On the other hand, Wotan has a feminine, immortal side shown in two ways: first, in relation to Erda (the earth goddess), who represents the wisdom of the universe and his own deepest conscience. It is she who reminds him of the inexorability of destiny, and her decline matches his. Second, in relation to his daughter by Erda, the Valkyrie Brünnhilde. As his 'wish-child', she guards his deepest interests and intuitions. When the incensed Fricka insists that Wotan destroy his illegitimate child Siegmund (who is the lover of his own sister, herself the wife of another man), Brünnhilde refuses to execute the command as being contrary to Wotan's inner desires and a denial of the love Siegmund feels for Sieglinde. Wotan's strips her of her divinity, a punishment that gives her the independence to perform the Senta-like 'world-redeeming' act of self-sacrifice that atones for the sins committed against Siegfried: she casts herself on to the hero's funeral pyre. This act, together with the return of the ring to the Rhinemaidens, forms the basis for the underlying musical optimism with which the work ends (the conclusion, in fact, gave Wagner much trouble): the spirit of love remains if all else has perished.

What is so striking about this vast undertaking is the imaginative richness of its surface, especially in its use of the mythic, the elemental, the supernatural and the dynastic; in the complexity of its psychological situations (notably in *Die Walküre*); in the force of its dramatic parallelisms; in its energy (above all in the superlative third act of *Siegfried*); and not least in the invention and variety of the music at every level.

In *Tristan und Isolde*, an essentially private 'action', extinction is seen as the only true consummation of love: as Carl Dahlhaus observes, the love-potion which the maidservant substitutes for the intended poison, is, in a metaphysical sense, also a death-potion. But this nihilistic stance is not all that Wagner learnt from Schopenhauer. The life-enhancing eroticism of the music, so pre-eminent in Act II, derived its impetus from the key analogy drawn by the philosopher between the quality of music and the quality of the 'Will'. For he describes the 'Will' as the dynamic essence of things, the motivating energy of life before it has been refracted through, and tempered by, consciousness. The merging of the identities of the lovers in the duets is thus a shared return to the well-springs of nature, a rediscovery of what is usually found only in the night-time world of dreams. On the other hand, Wagner was too much of a moralist not to invest the day-time world of social contracts, embodied in the figure of King Marke, with its own dignity (Tristan appears to break honour in his love for Isolde); and the unification of the lovers in death – rather than in life – also offers a social answer to an illicit love (Marke's post-mortem absolution of Tristan and Isolde begs all kinds of

questions). Technically, the work is notable for two reasons: first, while Wagner adopted a more flexible treatment here than in the *Ring* of leitmotif and *Stabreim* (the creation of poetic continuity through the incantatory use of internal alliteration rather than end-rhyme); and second, the music derives new, complex and revolutionary means for obscuring its traditional tonal anchors without renouncing them, as a way of mirroring the language of the 'Will'.

Just as *Tristan* reinterprets human energy in erotic terms, so does *Die Meistersinger* see the justification of art in the need to sublimate aggression and promote itself as the highest activity of all. In this work – a comic appendage to *Tannhäuser* – the central figure is no longer the impetuous young knight (in this case Walther), but the cobbler Hans Sachs (alias Wagner). Sachs is now the older man who declines to play King Marke to Eva's Isolde. His advice is mellow and wise: art, he says, must be rooted in dreams and not rules (his teaching Walther how to compose *Stollen*, stanzas, has nothing to do with the impotent criticism of Beckmesser: he merely tames the socially disruptive aspects of Walther's earlier song); the older artist must learn to re-create the impulsive spontaneity of youth; and new art must build on the achievement of the old (here, the German masters, symbolizing the spirit of Germany itself). Accordingly, the musical language of not just the trial song but the entire opera does just this: its 'archaic' harmonies, its newly clarified tonality, its transparently articulated form, and the precision of its details have all benefited from Wagner's earlier innovations.

Wagner's final work, the 'sacred festival play' *Parsifal*, provoked a virulent attack from the estranged Nietzsche. The denial and sublimation of sexuality into Christian ritual (shown at its most theatrical), the covert misogyny, the obsession with the purity of blood (at this time Wagner cast doubt on Christ's Jewishness), the focused anti-intellectualism (Parsifal means 'so-pure-a-fool') and the invasion of pathology (the

Knights' protection of animals reflects the composer's vegetarianism), all contributed to what Nietzsche saw as a denial of the important elements in the earlier music dramas. Certainly, its winnowing, enervate sexuality is that of an older man, and its central premise – that redemption may be won through pity (for Wagner, the highest love; for Nietzsche, a form of contempt) – was indeed new. But for all that Nietzsche's Zarathustran ideals (as presented, for example, in the *Genealogy of Morals*) were, in part, founded on a self-conscious refutation of the *Parsifal* philosophy, the criticisms represented only a half-truth. For in this work, as in the *Ring*, the kinship relations touch extraordinary depths (especially the Oedipal temptation of Parsifal by Kundry), and the music (orchestrated with a wonderful diffused light) is no less resourceful than that of *Tristan*'s in pursuit of new extremes of expression. Moreover, Wagner was reviewing here the worlds of *Tannhäuser* and *Lohengrin*, albeit with a Sachsian mellowness.

While the refutation of *Parsifal* contributed to the emergence of existentialism and the exploration of the consequences of 'the Death of God', both Nietzsche and Wagner were seen by Thomas Mann as part of a chain of German thinking that extended back through Mann's own stories and the writings of **Freud** to Schopenhauer and Kant. It was this tradition that also provided a foundation for so much of the thought of **D.H. Lawrence**. In France, on the other hand, it was chiefly the musical and synaesthetic effects of the music dramas that exerted so powerful an effect upon composers (**Debussy**, and later **Messiaen**), painters (**Renoir** and **Cézanne**) and writers (Baudelaire, **Mallarmé** and **Proust**). **James Joyce** argued that the 'musical effects' of his Sirens chapter from the novel *Ulysses* were superior to those of *Die Walküre*, and in Molly's final monologue he created a literary equivalent for the perorations of Isolde and Brünnhilde, albeit cast in a demotic language. Indeed, female protagonists are central to the immediately post-Wagnerian German operas that take psycho-sexual

disorders to their extremes: **Schoenberg's** *Erwartung* (1909), **Richard Strauss's** *Salome* (1905) and *Elektra* (1909), and **Berg's** *Lulu* (1928–35). The technical innovations in harmony, melody and instrumentation introduced in these and other works derived their impetus directly from the most advanced, rootless aspects of the music in *Tristan* and *Parsifal*, and led in due course to the formulation by Schoenberg of the twelve-tone method. This method, and the line of development supporting it, did not pass unchallenged, though the challenges (as with Nietzsche) derived strength from their opposition: even **Stravinsky's** no less controversial 'neoclassicism' was rooted in a refutation of the Wagnerian aesthetic.

In the years since the Second World War, scholarship has had to address the dark side of Romanticism that undoubtedly underlies Wagner's work in general and his lifelong anti-Semitism in particular. Some scholars have left no stone unturned to reveal the scale of Wagner's hatreds; others have sought explanations; others still (including performers) have concentrated on the musical merits in their attempt to disassociate Wagner's name from the use to which it was put by Houston Stewart Chamberlain and the leaders of the Third Reich. Even Theodor Adorno, writing in 1963, advocated 'corrections' in modern productions. Thus today the paradox of Wagner is at its most acute: performances of Wagner's music in Israel arouse the strongest indignation, while opera houses and private companies around the world vie with each other to mount ever more outspoken interpretations. That is to say, Wagner's ability to transfigure the lives of his audiences remains entirely undiminished.

Further reading

See: *Wagner on Music and Drama* (1970). Still the best biography is Ernest Newman's *The Life of Richard Wagner* (4 vols, 1933–47), though Robert Gutman's *Richard Wagner, The Man, His Mind and His Music* (1968) is stimulating. G.B. Shaw's *The Perfect Wagnerite* (1922) is a classic study, and

Robert Donington's *Wagner's Ring and Its Symbols* (1960) is intriguing in its application of Jungian ideas. Carl Dahlhaus's *Richard Wagner's Music Dramas* (1971, trans. 1979), is a thoughtful recent introduction to the works. Barry Millington's *The Wagner Compendium* (1992) and U. Müller and P. Wapnewski's *Wagner Handbook* (1992) are both full of fascinating information, as is Michael Saffle's *Richard Wagner: A Guide to Research* (2002). The Jewish question is explored in Paul Lawrence Rose's *Wagner: Race and Revolution* (1992) and Michael Weiner's *Richard Wagner and the Anti-semitic Imagination* (1995). Other important writers on Wagner include Theodor Adorno, Dieter Borchmeyer, Warren Darcy, Martin Gregor-Dellin, Thomas Mann, Patrick McCreless, Jean-Jacques Nattiez, Friedrich Nietzsche and Curt von Westernhagen. The two volumes of *Cosima Wagner's Diaries* were published in English in 1978–80.

CHRISTOPHER WINTLE

WALCOTT, Derek

1930–

Caribbean poet, painter and dramatist

Derek Walcott was born in the town of Castries in St Lucia, one of the Windward Islands in the Lesser Antilles. The breath-taking beauty of the Caribbean landscape, with its immensity of sky and sea, has had a powerful shaping effect on his work, but so, too, has the painful colonial legacy of the place, with its disparate linguistic, cultural and religious traditions. Much of Walcott's poetry has been inspired by his profound sense of being 'divided to the vein' by his African and European ancestry. The English-speaking son of a Methodist family in a French-speaking Catholic community, Walcott quickly acquired an astute awareness of both the potential artistic fruitfulness and the personal and social conflicts that came with a complex multicultural inheritance. In his life and in his work, he has often been drawn by the compelling image of the cast-away, caught between different places, cultures and languages. Since the early 1980s, he has divided his time between the United States, working as Professor of Creative Writing at the University of Boston, and

Trinidad, his new home as a Caribbean poet and dramatist.

Although Walcott made an impressive early debut with *25 Poems* in 1948, it was *In a Green Night* (1962) that brought him recognition worldwide. The title, echoing Andrew Marvell's great poem of religious exile, 'Bermudas', is one of many rueful reminders that the Renaissance was a green age of learning, but also a time of colonial darkness and oppression. That troubling contradiction informs Walcott's 'Ruins of a Great House', a magnificent subversion of the English country house poem, in which 'men like Hawkins, Walter Raleigh, Drake' appear as 'Ancestral murderers and poets'. Ironically citing John Milton and William Blake, the poem laments the lost paradise and the green fields of the Caribbean, but it closes with a moving and forgiving reminder of John Donne's *Devotions* and his famous declaration that 'No man is an island'. 'A Far Cry from Africa' has a more urgent contemporary political relevance and stretches Walcott's allegiances to breaking point as he contemplates the Mau-Mau insurrection against British rule in Kenya in the 1950s: 'I who have cursed/The drunken officer of British rule, now choose/Between this Africa and the English tongue I love.'

Displacement and dislocation are abiding themes in Walcott's work, and are palpably evident in the titles of such volumes as *The Castaway* (1965) and *The Gulf* (1969). He attempts to come to terms with the psycho-logical effects of the African diaspora by finding parallels in the epic poetry of Homer, with its powerful images of voyage and exile. At the same time, Walcott is sensitively aware of what opponents might see as an elitist Eurocentrism. 'The classics can console,' he once wrote, 'but never enough.' Even so, the idea of the epic journey persists in his work, especially in *Omeros* (1990), with its punning emphasis on the Greek name for Homer and the circular quest for home. In several poems he imagines the Middle Passage, the sea journey that brought African slaves to the Caribbean, as a nightmarish odyssey. The epic journey also provides the structural underpinning for his long biographical poem, *Another Life* (1973), which both alludes to great autobiographical works in the English tradition (William Wordsworth's *Prelude* and **James Joyce's** *Portrait of the Artist as a Young Man*) and sets out to rediscover and repossess a distinctively Caribbean cultural inheritance. 'My generation,' he said, 'had looked at life with black skins and blue eyes.' In his next volume, *Sea Grapes* (1976), he returns to the sights and sounds of his native St Lucia, and in the rapturous 'Sainte Lucie' he closes a long passage of French creole with a passionate outburst in English: 'Come back to me my language.'

Although Walcott has tended to write in standard English, one of his most ambitious linguistic efforts was in the Trinidadian creole of 'The Schooner Flight', another sea-faring odyssey that appeared in *The Star Apple Kingdom* in 1979. The speaker is a Trinidadian sailor-poet, Shabine, who speaks eloquently for his creator: 'I'm just a red nigger who love the sea,/I had a sound colonial education,/I have Dutch, nigger and English in me,/and either I'm nobody, or I'm a nation.' There is a resolute refusal of identity politics here, at a time when 'hybridity' was just a glimpse in the eye of aspiring postcolonial theorists. Walcott refuses any simple categories of selfhood and nation, giving Shabine the last word on the matter: 'I had no nation now but the imagination.' In his 1974 essay, 'The Muse of History', he argues against a literature of either revenge or remorse, polemic or pathos, insisting that 'the truly tough aesthetic of the New World neither explains nor forgives history'.

That 'truly tough aesthetic' continues to be worked out in successive volumes, including *The Bounty* (1997), with its moving elegy for the poet's mother. *Tiepolo's Hound* (2000) is a painterly evocation of the life of Camille Pissarro, accompanied by Walcott's own watercolours, while *The Prodigal* (2004) is an exploration of European culture and the impact of the Old World on the New. Walcott's efforts to establish a distinctive New World aesthetic in poetry have been paralleled and complemented by his equal determination to construct a distinctive Caribbean theatrical tradition. His first major play, *Henri Christophe* (1950), reflects on the liberation of Haiti through a sustained psychological study of the enigmatic accomplice of Toussaint L'Ouverture. *The Sea at Dauphin* (1954) shows the influence of the Irish playwright, J.M. Synge, while *Ione* (1957) seeks to blend Caribbean folk elements with the legacy of classical drama. Walcott's determination to find a dramatic language that went beyond mimicry and to create a theatre where 'someone could do Shakespeare or sing calypso with equal conviction' was to be realized in Walcott's work with the Trinidad Theatre Workshop and in the production of powerfully engaging plays like *Ti-Jean and His Brothers* (1958) and *Dream on Monkey Mountain* (1967). Walcott has also collaborated on musicals such as *The Joker of Seville* (1974) and *O Babylon!* (1976), both with Galt MacDermot, and *The Capeman* (1998) with Paul Simon. He was awarded the Nobel Prize for Literature in 1992.

Further reading

Other works include: *Collected Poems 1948–1984* (1986). Bruce King's biography, *Derek Walcott: A Caribbean Life*, was in 2000. For stimulating critical commentary, see Paula Burnett, *Derek Walcott: Politics and Poetics* (2000), J. Edward Chamberlin, *Come Back to Me My Language: Poetry and the West Indies* (1993), and John Thieme, *Derek Walcott* (1999). *Agenda* magazine dedicated a special issue to Derek Walcott, edited by Maria Cristina Fumagalli (Vol. 39, Nos 1–3, Winter 2002–3).

STEPHEN REGAN

WARHOL, Andy (Andrew WARHOLA)

1928–87

US artist, filmmaker

Often categorized as a pioneer and leading exponent of Pop Art, Andy Warhol was born of Czech extraction in Philadelphia. He is best known for his paintings and films, but his activities, almost unrivalled in their diversity and volume, included producing the rock group The Velvet Underground (in the mid-1960s), designing record covers (notably for the **Rolling Stones'** album *Sticky Fingers*, with its openable zipper) and writing books (some of them taped conversations, some actually 'written'). From the late 1950s until 1968, when he was near-fatally shot by Valeria Solanis for motives that were never been clearly ascertained, most of his output flowed from the Factory, the idiosyncratic name given to his studio in Manhattan.

Warhol's fame was established by his silkscreen paintings of Campbell's soup cans and other everyday household objects in 1961–2. The popular, commercial images were transferred mechanically from the 'original' photographs to the silkscreen web, and then applied to paper or canvas. A reaction to Abstract Expressionism, they were in almost every respect, when they first appeared, a challenge to normal notions and practices of fine art. To begin with they were exhibited on the West Coast of the United States, not the East. Their subject-matter was drawn provocatively from an area that by definition was segregated from 'serious' artistic endeavour. But more revolutionary still was the idea of using *unchanged* and therefore *unlaboured* original material, and, further, reproducing this through assistants. This constituted, as Warhol intended it should, the almost total self-effacement of the artist's individuality, although purposely minor infringements (random marks, hand-pressure variations, drips) remained to belie the purity of the endeavour.

Paradoxically Warhol's denial of individuality made him a central personality in modern art. This predictable but illogical outcome naturally attracted suspicion, and Warhol's developments often raised the consideration: how much is expression and how much is ploy? Given the apparently successful de-individualization of his work, it is difficult to see what prompted its production in the first place. An incorrect summary might suggest that his admirers have mistaken the real target of his aesthetic, which was not the consumer product so much as consumer marketing. On the other hand there can be little doubt that Warhol significantly contributed to the refashioning of our sensibilities. A Campbell's soupcan is intrinsically neither funny nor sad, nor does it command any other emotional response when set apart from all other objects. The process of de-individualization has not stopped short at the artist, but extends to the viewer. But: are we being ironically rebuked for our willing self-immersion in the surface world of advertisement and brand promotion, or are we being offered a chance to empty out? Both of these, it could be claimed, are legitimate, if not conventional, functions for an artist to pursue.

While Warhol had worked as a commercial illustrator for *Harpers* early in his career, perhaps the more decisive experience was his involvement with a Brechtian theatre collective at the beginning of the 1950s. Interpreting **Brecht's** theoretical writings, he composed stage-sets in which drawings of interior objects were pasted or hung on the 'real' artefacts (thus the image of a chair might be attached to the chair which had been used as a model). This was done not as a scenic economy, but as a deliberate re-evaluation of space, of proximity and distanciation.

Not unlike Brecht, Warhol was concerned to undermine, wherever he could, illusionist representation, treating it as the ideology of truth and humanism which permeates, produces and is produced by Western cultural forms. In his paintings of Jacqueline Kennedy, **Elvis Presley**, Suicides and the Electric Chair, all major representational images during the 1960s, he offsets his highly charged subject-matter by a style that is wilfully mundane. These offer a critique of illusionist representation. For examples of non-illusionist representation we must turn back to the soupcans, or to Warhol's films, where he usually jettisons the identificatory processes of character, plot, drama, goal, fictive meaning and psychological truth.

Unavoidably, making a film requires 'labour'. Unless the camera is used nothing can be accomplished, and just how it is used involves strategy and decision-making. Warhol's solution to this problem was complex, and perhaps only partial. He evolved two techniques that, by not denying the procedure and process of filmmaking itself, allow for no 'effects' except for those which will be immediately recognizable as such. One is the use of a rigid, unmoving camera, sometimes sustained for hours at a time, so that the work seems to approach a zero point of stylelessness. The other is a camera which arbitrarily zooms, focuses, changes angle and depth of field and light intensity and 'sound focus', without apparent purpose. Both these serve, or seem to serve, as a forcing of the audience to the medium itself as a materialist practice. Other techniques, or ploys, include the sudden incorporation of unexposed footage which comes out as a brilliant white on the screen. These cinematographic habits, contrasted to normal 'editing', undermine the audience's status as a cohesive, uncontradictory consumer of an uncontradictory, pre-structured 'knowledge' of the real. This is Warhol's central project in all his work.

Warhol's aim was to discard the suspension of disbelief which is so necessary for dominant narrative cinema. The epitome of his filmwork is perhaps *Chelsea Girls* (1967), a three-and-a-half-hour double screen movie originally arranged so that its seven half-hour reels could be projected in any sequence. Many of the most well-known 'Andy Warhol' films, e.g. *Flesh*, *Trash*, etc., were produced and directed by his colleague Paul Morrissey, and Warhol himself ceased being personally involved in his films after 1969, with the important exception of the camerawork for *Women in Revolt* (1972), a study of conflictual sexual disorientations. Most of the 'real' Andy Warhol films have been hidden in a vault, possibly to make the Warhol/Morrissey films more attractive to their audiences, possibly as an annihilation ploy which, of course, produces precisely the opposite effect.

By the mid-1970s Warhol was undertaking commissioned portraits of politicians and wealthy socialites. His later paintings reincorporate much more abstract-expressionist hand-involvement, the mark, the scratch, the presence of the producer. But very often, as in the case of the ten *Mao* portraits (1972), each in editions of 250, they were produced in series, and this imposes a blandness that cancels out any suspected eruption of the artist's self. As in the earlier silkscreens, where only minor differences of tonality were noticeable, the emphasis remains on the mechanized and distanciated gesture, and it is for this quality, after a period in which other artists attempted to 'paint psychology', that Warhol is likely to be remembered.

Further reading

Other works include: *Screen Test*, stills from his films (1966); *The Index Book*, with fold-outs, pop-up soupcans, a record, a balloon, etc. (1967); *From A to B and Back Again* (1975). Among his films are: *Blowjob* (1963); *Empire, Couch, 13 Most Beautiful Women* (1964); *Vinyl, Kitchen, My Hustler, The Shopper* (1965); *Four Stars* (1966); *Lonesome Cowboys* (1978); and *Fuck* (*Blue Movie*, 1969). His silkscreens, paintings and lithographs are generally identified by their subjects, viz.: fruit tins, Coca-Cola labels, soupcans (1961); *Marilyn* (Monroe), *Liz* (Taylor), more soupcans (1962); car crashes, lynchings, suicides (1963); Brillo boxes, Kellogg's cornflakes cartons, flowers, *Jackie, Elvis* (from 1964); self-portraits, *Marlon Brando* (1965). Most of these and similar subjects were used in succeeding years. Others include: girls, boys, Indians, torsos, transvestites (1974); the Paul Anka T-shirt (1975); Hammer and Sickle (1976). About Andy Warhol: John Coplans, *Andy Warhol* (1971); Peter Gidal, *Andy Warhol: Films and Paintings* (1971); Stephen Koch, *Andy Warhol: Stargazer* (1973); Victor Bockris, *Warhol* (1990); Philippe Tretiack, *Warhol's America* (1997).

PETER GIDAL

WATSON, James Dewey

1928–

US biologist

In 1947 when J.D. Watson completed his bachelor's degree in biology at the University of Chicago, the science of genetics was well developed but little was known about the nature of the fundamental unit of that science – the gene. Watson's major contribution, in collaboration with the British-born scientist, **Francis H.C. Crick**, was to propose in 1953 a plausible structure for the chemical substance DNA, or deoxyribonucleic acid, and to show how it might account for many of the properties of the gene.

When Watson left Chicago to pursue graduate work at the University of Indiana he was only nineteen years of age. It was his acceptance by Indiana on condition that he study genetics or embryology which turned him from his intended career subject of ornithology.

Following upon his PhD research, Watson came to Europe and worked in Copenhagen and Cambridge, supported first by a Merck post-doctoral fellowship, and subsequently by the National Foundation for Infantile Paralysis. Returned to the United States in 1953 he continued as a research scientist in the California Institute of Technology, then he moved to Harvard where he became Full Professor in 1961. For eight years, beginning in 1968, he also directed the Cold Spring Harbor Laboratory on Long Island. He resigned from Harvard University in 1976 to devote all his energy to Cold Spring Harbor. The transformation that he made to this run-down, ailing institution has been perhaps his greatest achievement. As he expanded and modernized it he also preserved and enriched its history, opened up its educational potential and as opportunity permitted moved into fresh fields – first cancer research, then neuroscience. In 1988 he became Associate Director of the Human Genome Project, in 1989 until 1992 Director. On appointing a successor to the Directorship of the Cold Spring Harbor Laboratory he became its President in 1994, and in 2004 its Chancellor.

Watson's genetic research at Indiana concerned the effects of X-ray damage upon bacterial viruses. It was hoped that this approach might yield clues to viral multiplication, a process thought to be virtually identical with gene duplication. In the event, this indirect approach to the nature of the genetic material proved disappointing. By contrast the direct approach using the techniques of chemistry and physics upon the genetic material looked more promising for unravelling the secrets of the gene. Watson therefore studied the transfer of chemical constituents from infecting virus particles to progeny virus particles using radioactive tracers. Then, fired with enthusiasm after seeing X-ray diffraction pictures shown by the British biophysicist M.H.F. Wilkins, Watson altered his strategy yet again, turning to the study of molecular structure as deduced from X-ray diffraction pictures.

Using data obtained by Rosalind Franklin, Raymond Gosling and Maurice Wilkins at King's College, London, Watson collaborated in Cambridge with Crick. Having concluded that the genetic material was not a nucleoprotein but simply nucleic acid, they hoped that the structure of this substance would show how the gene works – how it duplicates, changes abruptly when it 'mutates', and expresses itself by giving rise to the heritable characteristics of organisms. Although their first attempt at a chemical structure was a failure, their second, just over a year later, was to be numbered among the most celebrated achievements of twentieth-century science. A preliminary description of their model was published in *Nature* in the spring of 1953, followed by a second paper on the implications for genetics suggested by the model. The third paper, almost entirely written by Watson, appeared in 1954. The rule book for the translation of the chemical sequence of the gene – the genetic code – had been discovered.

The idea, long discussed, that hereditary traits could be encoded in a specific chemical sequence was here identified with the sequence of 'bases'. Constancy of hereditary transmission, they suggested, was due to the faithful copying of the base sequence; changes or 'mutations' were due to errors in copying. The copying process itself was pictured as involving the opening of the two chains (the double helix) in such a way that new chains could be laid down on each of the originals.

The sequence of bases on a new chain was dictated by specific pairing with the bases of the original chain.

Despite modifications to the Watson–Crick model for DNA, its basic principles have been greatly strengthened over the succeeding two decades. Its authors' suggestions regarding its implications for genetics have been followed and confirmed. The chemical sequence of the gene – the genetic code – has been discovered. The mechanism by which this code is expressed, however, proved a far more complex process than Watson and Crick envisaged. Only a broad research programme of biochemistry and structural chemistry sufficed to unravel its mysteries. This triumph in analysis was catalysed by the many theoretical insights which Crick provided between 1956 and 1970. Watson, who was but twenty-five years of age in 1953, received with Crick and Wilkins the Nobel Prize for Medicine in 1962. Three years later, his textbook *The Molecular Biology of the Gene* (1965) appeared. He presented his subject boldly, because he believed the basic concepts provided by the molecular approach were now sound; in short, biology had by 1965 as sound a basis as chemistry had enjoyed since 1932 thanks to the Quantum Theory. It was time, he claimed, to reorient the teaching of biology and give 'the biologist of the future the rigor, the perspective, and the enthusiasm that will be needed to bridge the gap between the single cell and the complexities of higher organisms'.

After many revisions and some hard feeling within the scientific community, Watson published *The Double Helix*, an account of the period of his life spent in Europe which had led to the model for DNA. This very candid, at times corrosive, picture of an ambitious young American research scientist thirsting for the big discovery and winning a share in a Nobel Prize has undermined the public image of the unworldly scientist who solves problems by dedicated industry and accumulated expertise. The Watson of the *Double Helix* views much of the research going on in scientific institutions with a sceptical eye.

The Watson of Cold Spring Harbor Laboratory set high standards and made great demands in his reach for excellence. But more than a researcher he yearned to be a successful writer, and that he has achieved in two very different books: *The Double Helix* and *The Molecular Biology of the Gene*.

Further reading

Other works include *A Passion for DNA. Genes, Genomes, and Society* (2000). See: J. Cains, G. Stent and Watson (eds), *Phage and the Origin of Molecular Biology* (1968); R. Olby, *The Path of the Double Helix* (1974); J. Inglis, S. Sambrook and J. Wilkowski (eds), *Inspiring Science. Jim Watson and the Age of DNA* (2003); V.K. McElheny, *Watson and DNA. Making a Scientific Revolution* (2003).

ROBERT OLBY

WAUGH, Evelyn Arthur St John

1903–66

British novelist

The son of Arthur Waugh, publisher and literary critic, and younger brother of Alec Waugh, novelist, Evelyn Waugh was educated at Lancing and Hertford College, Oxford. After abortive attempts at schoolmastering and carpentry he turned to literature and in 1928 published a biographical study of **D.G. Rossetti**. His first novel, *Decline and Fall*, appeared later in the same year. Based loosely on his experiences as preparatory school teacher, it was a racy mixture of burlesque farce and social satire that brought him critical acclaim, a number of journalistic commissions, but little money. Popular success came with *Vile Bodies* (1930), which caught, with seemingly effortless precision, the frenetic social atmosphere of young upper-class London in the 1920s: the Bright Young People, their language, their parties and their aimlessness. Both in literature and in society Waugh became a fashionable figure, but his happiness was bitterly affected by the break-up, after a few months, of his first marriage. The behaviour of his wife left a scar that is visible in many of his subsequent writings. More immediately, it hastened his reception into the Roman Catholic Church in September 1930 – an event that Waugh regarded as the most important in his life.

Between then and the Second World War he travelled extensively in Europe, Africa, South America and Mexico. To this period belong: *Labels: A Mediterranean Journal* (1930); *Remote People* (1931); *Ninety-Two Days* (1934); *Waugh in Abyssinia* (1936). These travel books were later abridged into one volume, *When the Going was Good* (1946). The novels of this decade, which draw on the same experiences, are *Black Mischief* (1932), *A Handful of Dust* (1934), perhaps the climax of Waugh's early writings, and *Scoop* (1938).

In the course of the war, during which he served in the Royal Marines and later the Royal Horse Guards, he wrote *Put Out More Flags* (1942) and *Brideshead Revisited* (1945). The second of these, though attacked for its luxuriance and snobbery, was a best-seller in England and in America, bringing Waugh a measure of financial security and also heralding the deeper concern with religious themes that characterizes his later work. His main achievement during the last period of his life was the trilogy based on his wartime experiences: *Men at Arms* (1952), *Officers and Gentlemen* (1955) and *Unconditional Surrender* (1961). In 1965 these were published in one volume, with some revisions, as *Sword of Honour*. When he died, on Easter Day 1966, he had produced one volume of his autobiography, *A Little Learning* (1964), and was beginning work on the second.

Waugh is primarily a comic novelist, whose books display an anarchic imagination and cast an acute satirical eye on the manners of upper-class society. From the outset he was stimulated by the borderlands where civilization and savagery meet, where the sublime shades into the ridiculous, sanity into lunacy, sadness into hilarity. These oppositions fuelled his sense of the absurd, but also lent substance to his more serious preoccupations. If his work has a central theme, it is the triumph of barbarism in a civilization that has lost touch with the values on which

it was founded. Throughout his writings this nostalgia for the values of a happier age finds an image in the country house, beleaguered, encroached upon or destroyed by the agents of a graceless modern world. His growing disgust with 'the century of the common man' had a political and social complexion which many commentators have found repulsive. In later life Waugh developed an image of eccentric and extreme Toryism which is brilliantly portrayed by him in the opening chapter of his autobiographical novel, *The Ordeal of Gilbert Pinfold* (1957). But he was not a political figure; closer to the heart of both his life and his writings is a romanticism at odds with the conditions of his age and society.

The earlier novels use irony as their characteristic response. In a world of arbitrary cruelties and absurd injustices the novelist observes his creatures with a detachment that shields his own vulnerability. Later, the influence of religion begins to reveal the strain on his irony, making possible the achievement of the war trilogy, in which irony and despair are tempered by a kindling of religious charity that gives to the work an unaccustomed depth of humanity.

To Waugh the question of style was paramount: he looked on writing 'not as an exploration of character, but as an exercise in the use of language'. Hostile to the practices of most modernist writers, he developed a style that was elegant, lucid and precise, in which words were chosen with loving propriety and a strict regard for their etymology. Not surprisingly he was devoted to the works of **P.G. Wodehouse**, while another important influence on him was Ronald Firbank, about whom he wrote one of his best critical essays. Waugh remains, however, a writer who is difficult to identify with any particular school, and he has had no followers of note. He can be seen as an important cross-current to the dominant intellectual and artistic trends of post-war years. To be reactionary was in his view the necessary function of the artist in society. It is not a role that has endeared him to the arbiters of academic critical fashion, but he may yet be read for his humour and lucidity when writers of more importunate relevance and less embarrassing opinions have been forgotten.

Further reading

Other works include: *Edmund Campion* (1935) and *Ronald Knox* (1959), both biographies; *Helena* (1950) is a historical novel; *Scott-King's Modern Europe* (1947), *The Loved One* (1948), *Love Among Ruins* (1953) are short novels. *Work Suspended* (1942) is an unfinished fiction. The *Diaries*, ed. Michael Davie (1976) and *A Little Order*, a selection of his journalism, ed. Donat Gallagher (1977) appeared posthumously. About Waugh: M. Bradbury, *Evelyn Waugh* (1964); Alec Waugh, *My Brother Evelyn and Other Profiles* (1967); R.M. Davis (ed.), *Evelyn Waugh: A Checklist* (1972); D. Pryce-Jones (ed.), *Evelyn Waugh and His World* (1973); Christopher Sykes, *Evelyn Waugh: A Biography* (1975); Humphrey Carpenter, *The Brideshead Generation* (1989); Martin Stannard, *The Critical Heritage* (1984), *Evelyn Waugh: The Early Years: 1903–1939* (1986) and *Evelyn Waugh: No Abiding City: 1939–1966* (1992); Selina Hastings, *Evelyn Waugh: A Biography* (1995); Douglas Lane Patey, *The Life of Evelyn Waugh* (1998). His work is also discussed in Martin Green, *Children of the Sun* (1976).

IAN LITTLEWOOD

WEBER, Max

1864–1920

German sociologist

It is now generally recognized that sociology emerged as an important academic discipline not so much through the work of Auguste Comte, who first used the term 'sociology', but rather through the development of three traditions represented by the work of **Émile Durkheim** who wrote, it is true, in the tradition of Comte, of **Karl Marx**, whose work became one of the central intellectual and political facts in European history, and of Max Weber whose range of comparative and historical work approached from the intellectual standpoint of Neo-Kantianism was perhaps more comprehensive than either of the others.

Weber's father was prominent in the National Liberal Party during the Bismarck era. At Heidelberg his original studies were in law, but, by the time he came to write his doctoral and habilitation theses, his interest had shifted to economics and economic history. His first academic post was as a Professor of Economics in the University of Freiburg, but he moved to Heidelberg after three years in 1896. At Heidelberg he suffered a severe mental breakdown leading to total disablement for four years and to an inability to accept any academic appointment until 1917. His life during this period has been devotedly chronicled in one of the most dignified biographies ever written. The biography was by his wife, Marianne, with whom he is believed to have had an unusual marriage, which, though it may never have been sexually consummated, provided the basis for a remarkable intellectual and moral companionship.

Marianne Weber provided Weber with a home which served as the focus for the intellectual life of some of the greatest intellects of the time in the fields of history, philosophy, economics, politics and literature. He also worked within the *Verein für Sozialpolitik*, an organization concerned with the application of social science findings to politics, and for many years edited and wrote in its journal, the *Archiv für Sozialwissenschaft und Sozialpolitik*. He also participated very actively in German politics, even though the Kantian perspective which he shared with his intellectual companions led him to make a radical dissociation between what he conceived to be the tasks of science and those which he thought appropriate to the politician.

Weber's earliest writing was in economic history. One of his theses dealt with agrarian civilization in the ancient world and another with trading companies in the Middle Ages. His contribution in these writings were partly oriented to controversies in German historiography, but he also used these themes for the development of generally applicable sociological concepts and for the understanding of contemporary problems. His association with the *Verein für Sozialpolitik* led him to make investigations of such topics as the condition of agricultural labourers in East Germany and of the stock exchange. Informing these studies was a developing interest in studying the role of religious thought in shaping economic behaviour, and the nature of modern bureaucratic organization. Behind this lay a more far-reaching concern amounting to an implicit philosophy of history based upon a conception of the rationalization, secularization and disenchantment of the world. The best-known outcome of this concern was Weber's *The Protestant Ethic and the Spirit of Capitalism* (Vol. I of *Gesammelte Aufsätze zur Religionssoziologie*, 1920, trans. 1930), in which, stimulated by Ernst Troeltsch, he agreed that it was in Calvinism that the roots of capitalism were to be found, rather than in Judaism as had been suggested by Sombart. This work was supplemented by comparative studies of Chinese, Indian and Jewish civilization which set out to show the difference which religious thought made to economic behaviour, but which inevitably brought into focus many other structural variables which differentiated these civilizations one from another. Among many themes discussed were types of authority and administration, the relations between prophets, priests and administrators, the nature of urban settlements, guild and other occupational organizations, and class and status structures. These studies combined with Weber's early studies of ancient and medieval Europe and his study of contemporary issues to provide him with a range of comparative and historical knowledge which has probably had no equal in modern times.

In 1909 the publisher Paul Siebeck invited Weber to edit a new series of books which would replace the by then dated 'Handbook of Political Economy' edited by Gustav Schonberg. Although eventually contributions to this series were published, including those of distinguished authors such as Joseph Schumpeter, Werner Sombart, Robert

Michels, Karl Bucher and Alfred Weber, Max Weber grew impatient with the tardiness and the inadequacies of some of his proposed authors, and eventually decided to expand his own contribution on the social structures within which economic systems developed. The original title which Weber gave to his own contribution was 'The Economy and the Arena of De Facto and Normative Powers'. When this was eventually published, together with a new introduction, it was called simply *Economy and Society* (trans. 1967), but it is the original title which specifies Weber's exact intention. He attempts here to outline the basic types of economic action, their organization into alternative types of economic system, and the ways in which such systems operate within a context of legitimating idea systems and structures of power. There are thus book-length sections of the whole volume dealing with the comparative economic systems, the sociology of the world religions, the sociology of law, forms of legitimate authority and administration, and the city, as well as a number of minor themes such as domestic organization, village life and ethnic groups.

Economy and Society constitutes Weber's systematic sociology. No one who reads it could continue to give credence to the view widely held in the English-speaking world after the publication of *The Protestant Ethic and the Spirit of Capitalism* in translation that Weber was a bourgeois idealist anti-Marxist. Nor could it be maintained, as it sometimes is on the basis of Weber's methodological writings, that Weber held purely subjectivist views, believing that history had to be written only from limited value-laden perspectives. What is evident here is an almost brutal realism derived from a reading of history, which took violence and exploitation for granted. No volume in fact could more justifiably claim as its text Marx's assertion that 'All history is the history of class struggles' than Weber's volume on *The City*, which first appeared as a section of *Economy and Society*. Nonetheless there *are* also normative powers and these Weber treats both in terms of ideological content and in terms of their institutional embodiment in his sections on the Sociology of Religion and the Sociology of Law.

The perspective of *Economy and Society*, and still more the perspective of Weber's early writings, derives from a Kantian approach to history and the social sciences, which was shared ground between Weber and his colleagues who came to visit him. Weber never set out systematically to discuss this approach, nor did he have much to say about Kant. Nonetheless, in the sustained methodological polemics in which he engaged with contemporary authors in the pages of the *Archiv*, Weber's Kantianism is clear. The central Kantian notion which is taken for granted is that of the possibility of sustaining simultaneously a view of the world as consisting of phenomena organized in terms of the categories of space, time and causality, and an alternative view in which man lives in the realm of freedom, confronting the Moral Law, yet free to choose and to make value judgements for which he is responsible. It was from this perspective that Weber wrote about the notion of cause in history, about ideal types contrasted with empirical laws, about the relation between value perspectives and the discovery of causal sequences and about the tension between value freedom and value relevance in social science.

Probably the central idea which Weber has is that of 'relevance for value'. This idea, which he took over from Rickert and modified, suggested that there are a multitude of value starting points from which the manifold of social and cultural facts could be analysed, and it is necessary that every social science investigation should make its value starting points explicit, in order to distinguish these from the value-free investigation of the causal relations between social structures to which they subsequently lead. Unlike Rickert, Weber did not see any way in which an objective basis for value standpoints could be arrived at, and, in his determination to emphasize the responsibility of the individual for his own actions, he leaned towards almost

maintaining that the basis of value judgements themselves was arbitrary. Weber himself, however, would argue that to claim that discourse about values is distinct from scientific discourse is by no means to assert that it is irrational.

The second unifying theme in Weber's methodological writings is what might be called an attempt to give an account of the sociological *a priori*. Recognizing that the natural science categories of causation did not apply in the human studies, he sought to give an account of the way in which entities called social relations and groups might be thought of as being constructed, and the way in which they affected individual behaviour. As Weber saw it, social relations could be thought of as arising in meaningful action in which one actor took account of the behaviour of another. Thus the entities, which appear as compelling human behaviour from outside, are seen as human creations, potentially capable of being changed by human beings. This perspective is sometimes called methodological individualism and leads to Weber saying that explanations which are causally adequate should be supplemented by explanations which are adequate on the level of meaning. It is an approach which stands in sharp contrast to Durkheim's assertion that social facts should be treated as things. In these terms Weber went on to develop concepts of social structure which he called ideal types. At first these were types which were very specific and related to his own values. In *Economy and Society*, however, they were more abstract and less relativistic.

Weber has often been contrasted with Marx, and has been said to have 'carried on a lifelong dialogue with the ghost of Karl Marx', or to be the 'bourgeois Marx'. In fact, in most areas, his work is complementary to rather than opposed to Marx. He has the advantage over Marx in not having to come to terms with a Hegelian philosophical vocabulary, and some have argued that restating Marx in a language free of metaphysics would lead to accounts of the mode of production, social relations of production, social classes and the state which are very close to Weber's. It is not true that Weber offered some kind of spiritual determinism which was at an opposite extreme to Marx's materialist determinism. He explicitly denied this. What he did do was to give a structural and methodologically individualist account of the full range of social institutions in history, which included the institutions of production, but also all those other institutions which Marx was inclined to refer to, having the critique of Hegel in mind, as mere ideas, or institutions of the superstructure. Where perhaps Weber did differ from Marx was in his theory of class. He certainly distinguished class from status, as Marx would have done, but he saw class conflict as bargaining going on in any market situation, and going on indefinitely, because he had accepted marginalist economics, whereas Marx, basing himself on the labour theory of value, saw the concept of class as leading, not to bargaining, but to revolution.

At the end of his life Weber was much involved in politics and wrote some quite ephemeral documents, including an account of socialism designed to stop its spread in the army. He also offered himself unsuccessfully as a candidate in the elections in the new Weimar Republic. More interesting from a sociological point of view were his last lectures, which have been preserved from student notes and which are published under the title *General Economic History* (*Wirtschaftsgeschichte*, 1924, trans. 1961). On the political level he remained unconvinced that a transition of advanced industrial societies to socialism would mean anything else but the extension of rationalism and bureaucracy to its ultimate point, a prospect which he viewed with horror. To the end he remained a Kantian seeking to the point of despair to find a way in which individuals could remain free of an increasingly reified society.

Further reading

Other works include: *Economy and Society* (3 vols, 1968). The best introduction to Weber's methodological ideas can be found in *The Methodology of the Social Sciences* (1949), a selection and translation of his essays by E.A. Shils and H.A. Finch, to be taken with *Roscher and Knies* (1976), trans. Guy Oakes. Other translations include: *The Religion of China* (1953); *Ancient Judaism* (1952); *The Religion of India* (1958) – all from the *Gesammelte Aufsältze zur Religionssociologie; The Agrarian Sociology of Ancient Civilizations* (1974). See also *From Max Weber*, ed. H. Gerth and C. Wright Mills (1946). About Weber: Marianne Weber, *Max Weber* (*Max Weber, Ein Lebensbild*, 1926, trans. 1950); Reinhard Bendix, *Max Weber, An Intellectual Portrait* (1962); Julien Freund, *The Sociology of Max Weber* (*Sociologie de Max Weber*, 1966, trans. 1968); F. Ringer, *Max Weber: An Intellectual Biography* (2004).

JOHN REX

WEBERN, Anton von

1883–1945

Austrian composer

Born into the minor Austrian nobility, Webern studied music history with Guido Adler at the University of Vienna, and at the same time took private lessons in composition with **Arnold Schoenberg**, to whom he remained a lifelong 'friend and pupil', as did his fellow-student **Alban Berg**. In 1906 he was awarded a PhD for an edition of part of the *Choralis Constantinus* by Heinrich Isaac, a Flemish polyphonist of the late fifteenth century. Although he was to be busy for the rest of his life as a composer, he could never support himself financially by composing alone. Instead, he made up a living from conducting, private teaching (he never held an official teaching post) and work for his publishers. In the 1930s his music was vilified as 'cultural Bolshevism', and his later years were marked by an extreme withdrawal that nevertheless saw the development of an important friendship with the poetess Hildegard Jone. In September 1945 he was accidentally shot dead by an American soldier of the Occupation.

Webern's oeuvre is relatively small: apart from a sizeable quantity of early pieces, a few unpublished later works, and a number of arrangements, there are only thirty-one pieces that bear opus numbers. Over half of these are vocal, his talent being essentially lyrical rather than dramatic – indeed, Erwin Stein, another Schoenberg pupil, placed him in the line of Schubert and **Debussy**. His work divides into three periods: a tonal phase (until *c.* 1907), an experimental 'anti-tonal' and early twelve-tone phase (*c.* 1907–24), and a final phase in which he adopted Schoenberg's twelve-tone serialism. His development as a composer is inseparable from that of his teacher: in his early years especially he could seize upon and extend the radical elements in Schoenberg's music with an intensity that irked the older man. Unlike his teacher, however, he was a miniaturist by temperament, and few of his pieces last more than ten minutes. His individuality lay in the expressive concentration of his music, and his importance in the fastidiousness with which he refined and developed what he considered to be essentially traditional features of composition.

The works of the first, tonal period show an absorption of, on the one hand, the Classical formal principles of sonata and variation, and, on the other hand, the advanced melody, harmony, textures and instrumentation of composers such as **Richard Wagner**, **Richard Strauss**, **Hugo Wolf** and **Gustav Mahler**. Whereas the form of the *Passacaglia*, Op. 1, for example, may well have been suggested by the finale of **Brahms's** Fourth Symphony, the progressive transformation of its themes owes more, perhaps, to the practice of Strauss's tone-poems.

In the second phase, this principle of 'developing variation' gave way to that of 'constant variation'. Traditionally, music had proceeded through the statement, development and repetition of ideas. But now overt repetition was abandoned, leaving merely statement and continual development. This created a style analogous to written prose, and epitomized the predominantly negative virtues of this phase: nothing was to be too concrete. Directionally orientated harmony was replaced by 'wandering' harmony and a deliberate annulment of natural tonal hierarchies. The

avoidance of familiar formal prototypes led Webern, as it had Schoenberg, to an 'expressionist' reliance on texts to determine the formal outlines of his music, which at this time was predominantly vocal. Indeed, the imaginative world of Webern's music was inseparable from the work of the poets he set: George (Op. 3 and Op. 4), **Rilke** (Op. 8), Trakl (Op. 14), **Strindberg** (Op. 12) and Kraus (Op. 13). He also set Goethe (Op. 12), folk texts (Op. 15) and sacred works (Op. 16).

The rootless subjectivity of this music probably derived from the sensitivity of the word-setting in Wagner's music-dramas – indeed, Webern's lifelong fastidiousness in the observation of prosody would seem to owe to Wagner's *Sprechgesang* (speech-song, a heightened recitative). In Wagner the significance of the individual words could be enhanced through the inflexions of melody, harmony, rhythm and instrumental timbre. Similarly, a wide range of colour is the hallmark of Webern's second phase, particularly in his Mahler-like predilection for unusual combinations of solo instruments, and in the resourcefulness of his exploitation of individual instrumental effects. The increased intensity of Webern's music, however, lay in the use of frequently angular and wide-leaping lines, and in his dramatic juxtaposition of extreme contrasts in tempo, dynamics, texture and articulation. These features appear most notably in the instrumental works written between 1909 and 1914: *Five Pieces for String Quartet* (Op. 5); *Six Pieces for Large Orchestra* (Op. 6); *Four Pieces for Violin and Piano* (Op. 7); and the *Six Bagatelles for String Quartet* (Op. 9).

Of such brevity was this music that the publication of Op. 9 was accompanied by an apologia from Schoenberg: 'To express a novel in a gesture, joy in a single breath: such concentration can only be found where self-pity is lacking in equal measure.' In the years after the First World War, therefore, it was partly through an urge to create large structures, and partly through a wish to re-align himself with a musical tradition rooted in Bach, Beethoven and Brahms, that Webern chose to adopt his teacher's twelve-tone 'method'. By fixing the twelve notes of the chromatic scale into a series that was then unfolded in different versions and transpositions, a new formal classicism could be built out of the previous rootlessness. This neo-classicism extended into details of melodic structure and textural organization. After three exploratory vocal works (Opp. 17–19) we find that his new, predominantly instrumental music bears Classical titles: *Trio* (Op. 20), *Symphony* (Op. 21), *Quartet* (Opp. 22 and 28), *Concerto* (Op. 24), *Variations* (Opp. 27 and 30) and *Cantata* (Opp. 29 and 31; also *Das Augenlicht*, Op. 26, for chorus and orchestra).

Webern's understanding of the twelve-tone method was arguably more probing – and his use certainly more consistent – than Schoenberg's. Although Schoenberg combined series in a quasi-polyphonic manner, it was Webern who had a deeper grasp of what Milton Babbitt was to describe as 'combinatoriality'. His earlier procedure of developing small, motivic cells now led to the principle of 'derivation', the division of the chromatic scale into identically constituted cells. Webern also re-introduced – though at a remote level – pitch hierarchies based on the tritone, the diminished seventh or the augmented chord, to govern large-scale musical movement. His scholarly interest in Flemish polyphony had led in the second phase to an extensive exploration of canon, which assumed a greater significance in the twelve-tone works, especially through the exploitation of the harmonic properties of canon-by-inversion.

It was the radicalism of the aesthetic attitudes accompanying these works, however, that was to prove so influential, even though, or perhaps because, they were so deeply rooted in nineteenth- and early twentieth-century intellectual currents. Webern's account of music history was historicist and evolutionary: his own music was to be the latest, highest and most inevitable stage in the development of Western (German) music. It would render the need to study earlier theory

'obsolete'. He attempted a Bach-like integration of different ideas (polyphony, accompanied melody, etc.) with the newly conquered twelve-tone language. Above all he admired everything that led to the greatest possible structural unity, frequently citing Kraus's demands for a moral responsibility towards language, Goethe's work on colour theory and plant metamorphosis, and Bach's purely pedagogic work *The Art of Fugue*. The latter he described as the 'highest reality', on account of the 'abstract' complexities emanating from a single theme. In such works as the String Quartet Op. 28 he aimed at a comparable abstraction, convinced that 'composition with twelve-tone technique has achieved a degree of complete unity that was not even approximately there before'.

These attitudes, far from representing a *volte face* with respect to the preceding Expressionist works, merely redress the imbalance that these in turn had created with respect to his early music. Indeed, most of his later music retains something of the earlier spare, expressive urgency. In the post-1945 era, however, it was principally with abstraction, and less with expression, that Webern's name was associated. With the subsequent international movement towards the extension of the orderable domains of language, traditional concern with idea in Webern's music was deemed obsolete, and a complete schism with all but the most recent past was effected. While, since its inception, the adequacy of the twelve-tone system as a musical language has always been in dispute, the arguably deleterious effect of this schism on the composition, criticism, teaching and performance of modern music has only more recently been called into question.

Although it seems unlikely that Webern's reputation will ever again stand as high as it did in the 1950s, any revaluation can only emphasize the expressive qualities of some of his later music. Through setting the words of the nature-loving Hildegarde Jone (Opp. 23, 25, 26, 29 and 31), he developed a uniquely tender lyricism which finds its most perfect utterance in the second movement of the

Concerto Op. 24. It was with such pieces in mind that **Igor Stravinsky** remarked: 'Whether there are great, or only new and very individual feelings in his music is a question which I can only answer for myself, but for me Webern has a power to move.'

Further reading

Other works include: *The Path to the New Music* (trans. Leo Black, 1963), and *Letters to Hildegarde Jone and Josef Humplik* (trans. Cornelius Cardew, 1967). Important books on Webern include: W. Kolnedar, *Anton Webern* (trans. Humphrey Searle, 1961); H. Moldenhauer and D. Irvine (eds) *Anton von Webern: Perspectives* (1966); H. Moldenhauer, *Anton Webern: A Chronicle of His Life and Work* (1978); K. Bailey, *The Life of Webern* (1998); and *Die Reihe*, Vol. 2 (periodical). Other, mainly analytic, articles occur in *Perspectives of New Music, Music Quarterly, Score, Tempo, Music Review*. See also: R. Leibowitz, *Schoenberg and His School* (1949); G. Perle, *Serial Composition and Atonality* (1962).

CHRISTOPHER WINTLE

WELLES, George Orson

1915–85

US film director

Revered by Modernists such as **Jean–Luc Godard**, Welles's work centres on themes remote from Modernist concerns. From his appearance as Death in the early short *The Hearts of Age* (1934), the processes of mortality, corruption and the erosion of innocence haunt his films. Even if the perspectives are altered, the blueprint of classical tragedy, of hubris and nemesis, determines the structure of Welles's dramas, which are played out somewhere between life and legend. Two other traditions also meet in Welles: the ancient art of the storyteller, and the more recent association of the cinema, via Georges Méliès, with the **Barnum** skills of illusionism. Welles's delight in presenting himself as prestidigitateur is no peripheral eccentricity, but a reason for his exhilarated display of cinematic resources: 'This is the biggest electric train set any boy ever had,' he remarked of the set for *Citizen Kane* (1941).

The son of an inventor and a concert pianist, Orson Welles attended Todd School in Woodstock, Illinois, and there became active in theatre. After directing and acting in plays at the Gate Theatre, Dublin, he returned to America and founded the Mercury Theatre in 1937, and with its company presented a series of radio plays, including the notorious adaptation of **H.G. Wells's** *The War of the Worlds* which panicked many listeners into believing that a Martian invasion was actually taking place. This brought Welles a Hollywood contract that gave him an unusual degree of artistic and financial control, but also fuelled suspicion and dislike. His subsequent career casts light on the contradictions of an industry simultaneously demanding creativity and submission to standardized practices. Like Erich von Stroheim before him, Welles was frequently to discover that studios preferred him to be in front of rather than behind the camera.

His first still-born project was an adaptation of **Conrad's** *Heart of Darkness* (later the basis of **Coppola's** *Apocalypse Now*, 1979). *Citizen Kane* thus became Welles's astonishing début. Many of the stylistic devices of this deservedly famous film – deep-focus compositions, flashback structure, overlapping dialogue, chiaroscuro lighting effects, bizarre camera angles – had a clear lineage, and even the character of Kane himself can be seen as a hybrid of William Randolph Hearst, **Fitzgerald's** Gatsby, Howard Hughes and Welles himself; but Welles's massive achievement was to make all these elements entirely pristine as he found expressive use for what had frequently been mere decoration. Described by **Borges** as 'a centreless labyrinth', the film is built around a search for the key to the personality of the dead Kane. From a welter of recollections emerges a bleak tale of irremediable loss of innocence, betrayal of hope and love, and the misuse of great power. But because of Welles's exuberant visual style and the carefully woven web of symmetries and complexity, the impact of *Kane* is anything but bleak.

Following *Kane,* a critical success but relative financial failure, Welles directed *The Magnificent Ambersons* (1942), an elegiac evocation of the decline of a minor aristocratic family at the turn of the century, and his only completed picture in which he does not himself appear. New management at RKO led to its re-editing in Welles's absence and subsequent release in a version 45 minutes shorter than Welles's own. It was not the last time he was to experience such treatment. *Touch of Evil* (1958), a masterpiece of *film noir* which marked his return to Hollywood direction, was shrugged off by Universal without even a trade showing. Ostensibly a banal police story, *Touch of Evil* explores the contradictions between being 'a great detective but a lousy cop' in a meditation on the law that has the maturity to separate principles from their proponents. But, *Kane* apart, it was perhaps only in Shakespeare that Welles could find a physical space large enough for his characters. Three films based on Shakespearian drama (*Macbeth,* 1948; *Othello,* 1952; and *Falstaff,* or *Chimes at Midnight,* 1966), although uneven, project a personal vision without prejudice to the complexity of human nature. The increasing bitterness of his later works finds respite in *Chimes at Midnight,* hailed by some critics as a premature testament and product of a talent that had finally transcended the qualities that gave it birth.

Rejecting **Eisenstein's** practice of creating cinematic meaning through the juxtaposition of shots in montage and the isolation of images in close-up, Welles chose to organize his world through intricate camera movements, deep-focus compositions and long takes (the opening, three-minute tracking shot of *Touch of Evil* is a famous example). Such a style democratizes the image, allowing the audience to immerse itself in the dramatic reality of the scene, but the constant camera movement establishes a tension between involvement and distance, between compassion and irony – a tension that is central to Welles's work. Despite his troubled relationships with studio hierarchies, Welles has had

enormous influence on both Hollywood and European directors through his demonstration of the expressive powers of cinema, particularly those that derive from large-scale production, and through the magnanimity of his vision. Welles was a hard act to follow, but Francis Coppola, **Martin Scorsese** and **Stanley Kubrick** must all be considered at least partial inheritors.

Further reading

Other works include: *The Stranger* (1946); *The Lady from Shanghai* (1948); *The Trial* (1962); *The Immortal Story* (1968); and *F for Fake* (1973). Welles also directed a film version (1955, *Confidential Report* in the UK) of his own novel *Mr Arkadin* (1954). See: Andre Bazin, *Orson Welles* (rev. 1958, trans. 1978); Joseph McBride, *Orson Welles* (1972); Simon Callow, *The Road to Xanadu* (1995).

NIGEL ALGAR

WELLS, Herbert George

1866–1946

British writer

Journalist, novelist, popular historian and sociologist, H.G. Wells was a considerable influence in encouraging the modern mentality which brought scientific scepticism to bear on social, moral and religious questions during the early twentieth century. The logical outcome of the long curve which ran from the Renaissance through the Encyclopedists to **T.H. Huxley**, a curve sustained by the conviction that man was a rational being, Wells believed that once enlightened education had become universal and scientific techniques widely accepted, half the problems of humankind would be solved.

His beginnings were in complete contradiction to these lofty preoccupations. His father ran a shop in Bromley, Kent, which combined chinaware with cricket accessories, and Wells was born in a small bedroom over the shop. His mother, a simple woman of lower-middle-class origin, reached the height of her ambitions when she became housekeeper to Miss Featherstonhaugh who owned a mansion known as Uppark. It was at Uppark that Wells met some of the characters later to appear in his novel *Tono-Bungay* (1909), 'her leddyship' being drawn as a vivid caricature of his mother's employer.

A scant education led to his becoming a draper's assistant, but the life so appalled him that he quickly ran away. After several false starts he became a chemist's assistant, a post which revealed his lack of Latin. However, he astonished his tutor at Midhurst Grammar School by mastering the greater part of Smith's *Principia* in five hours, and after that nothing could stop his educational advance. At eighteen he won a scholarship to study biology at the Normal School of Science in London, then dominated by T.H. Huxley. The three years he spent there provided the scientific raw material from which he distilled the first wave of his scientific fiction.

Living in near-poverty as a teacher of science, he married his first cousin, Isabel Mary Wells, in 1891: an unfortunate choice which merely increased his financial problems. The *Pall Mall Gazette* printed his first article 'On the Art of Staying at the Seaside', in the same year, and thus began his lifelong habit of emptying his mind on the printed page in journalistic form whenever some urgent question demanded quick expression. Any conflict between his scientific training and his journalistic outpourings, however, was resolved when he wrote his first science-fiction story *The Time Machine* (1895), on the appearance of which W.T. Stead described Wells as 'a man of genius'. Constructing a brilliantly symbolized Time Machine, the Traveller flashes forward to the year 802701 and enters a society divided into two classes, the Morlocks, living and working in caves beneath the earth, and the Eloi, a class of graceful decadent sybarites. 'Man had not remained one species but had differentiated into two distinct animals', the result of the widening of differences between Capital and Labour. *The Time Machine* was a social allegory written with a poetic intensity its author never recaptured. Close on its heel came *The*

Wonderful Visit (1895), *The Island of Doctor Moreau* (1896), *The Invisible Man* (1897) and *The War of the Worlds* (1898). Wells knew just how to unlock the imaginative worlds, the latent excitements, buried beneath dull scientific data, but behind the virtuosity lay a deep concern for man and society. There were many comparisons with the work of **Jules Verne**, but the heroes of Verne's novels were idealized creatures turning invention to their own private account with little concern for the social problems that preoccupied Wells. He saw that he could harness scientific discovery to revolutionize our lives in ways as yet unforeseen. He also realized that science might run off in Frankenstein abandon, gathering more and more power over nature while the ordinary human being had less and less power over himself. He understood his scientific implications to be highly romantic, but each story carried a message, and it was the message that mattered when the drama had exhausted itself. Indeed, his concern for social problems soon drove him to abandon science fiction in favour of his lower-middle-class comedies: *Love and Mr Lewisham* (1900), *Kipps* (1905) and *The History of Mr Polly* (1910). Unlike with **Dickens**, what people did for a living became vital in his books, reflecting the organization of society, its greatest evil, the future always more important than the past or present. However, it was no accident that *Kipps* and *A Modern Utopia* were published in the same year. Wells was simply unable to express all his ideas in fiction. The scientist in him tried to shake off the novelist with *A Modern Utopia*, while the artist clamoured for comic simplicities untroubled by any vestige of science. In *Kipps* and *The History of Mr Polly* Wells drew heavily on his own attempts to climb from lower- to middle-class life, and he became the spokesman for millions of inarticulate people whose frustrations had never achieved such realistic expression in fiction before. Similarly, *Ann Veronica* (1909) crystallized the desire for greater freedom of thousands of young women in the period when the book was written. Here was a middle-class daughter who defied her father, ran off and threw herself into the arms of the man she loved. Wells once again brought to the surface the rational attitude to sexuality latent in the minds of many of his readers. Implicit in these novels, his belief in revolutionary progress found modified expression in *A Modern Utopia*, a vision of the future where society was divided into four entirely new classes: the Samurai, a voluntary nobility; the Poietic; the Kinetic; the Dull and the Base.

Attempting to translate theory into practice, Wells had joined the Fabian Society (a London-based group founded in 1883 and dedicated to transforming Great Britain into a socialist state) in 1903. Having created a following among many of the younger members, he quarrelled with the Executive, which included the Webbs, and challenged **G.B. Shaw**. Finally he resigned with a burst of that invective which came so readily from his pen. Always impatient, a man who overreacted to every situation, Wells now abandoned world-making to write what is perhaps his best novel, *Tono-Bungay*. This brought alive an ignorant little man, Uncle Ponderevo, a combination of Whitaker Wright (the financial fraud) and someone in the likeness of all ambitious shopkeepers, to foist on the world a patent medicine, following through its social and psychological consequences with a skill that impressed even **Henry James**. It was a devastating criticism of unfettered private enterprise in a capitalist society.

However, during the period of the First World War Wells's power as a novelist declined, and it was not until the 1920s that his reputation was restored when he took on the mantle of public educator with *The Outline of History* (1920), a massive survey of world history, and its altogether more successful 'introduction', *A Short History of the World* (1922). This was a vividly written account that traced the evolution of man from the biological beginnings to his technological incarnation. Already, in several of his novels, Wells had brought men together as a species, over-ruling national divisions and seeing them in the light of a common destiny. Now he set out to counteract the insidious distortions of national histories with the conception of One World, the outcome of one people and one history. Despite its journalistic shortcomings and lack of precision, it was a remarkable feat which reached an audience of millions. Wells followed it with a number of huge rambling books with all-embracing titles like *The Work, Wealth and Happiness of Mankind* (1932), compendiums of information intended to enlighten the average man.

His later work became repetitious, re-echoing his earlier messages and culminating finally in the despairing *Mind at the End of Its Tether* (1945), which pictured a jaded world 'devoid of recuperative power'. Written during the Second World War, its pessimism can also be attributed to the fact that Wells himself was under sentence of death: doctors told him he would not last another year, and on 13 August 1946 he duly died, aged eighty.

Born into a lower-class background, Wells might have remained a straightforward rebel against society, but it was in a voluntary nobility that he put his trust in the end. Devoted to the ways of science, his brave new worlds were more mystic than scientific. Since Wells was impatient when people were not driven to action by his plans, they were plans frequently incapable of practical interpretation. A devotee of collectivism, of the group, of the belief that the individual was only a biological device which would decline when it had outlived its use, he stood alone, himself against half the world, and spectacularly burst out of every group he joined. He was a prophet who expected to be honoured in his own land, a brilliant example of what the ordinary man could become with grave misgivings about the proletariat. As a science-fiction writer he alerted the world to the dangers and benefits of scientific technologies; as a novelist he brought enlightenment and entertainment to a very large audience; as a mass educator he opened areas of knowledge relatively unknown to his readers; as a prophet his predictions were sometimes true, sometimes false. If he never achieved academic respectability, that in his own eyes was a tribute to his powers.

Further reading

Other works include: science fiction: *When the Sleeper Wakes* (1899); *The First Men in the Moon* (1901); novels: *The New Machiavelli* (1911); *Mr Britling Sees It Through* (1916); non-fiction: *Anticipations* (1901); *New Worlds for Old* (1908); *The Open Conspiracy* (1928); *The Science of Life* (1931, with G.P. Wells); and the immensely readable *Experiment in Autobiography* (1934). About Wells: Geoffrey H. Wells, *H.G. Wells: A Sketch for a Portrait* (1930); Vincent Brome, *H.G. Wells* (1951); J. Kargalitski, *The Life and Thought of H.G. Wells* (trans. from the Russian, 1966); B. Murray, *H.G. Wells* (1990); P. Parrinder, *Shadows of the Future: H.G. Wells, Science Fiction and Prophecy* (1995).

VINCENT BROME

WHISTLER, James Abbot McNeill

1834–1903

US artist

James Abbot Whistler was born in 1834 in Lowell, Massachusetts, USA. In later life he replaced Abbot with his mother's maiden name, McNeill. Much of his childhood was spent in Russia, where his father was employed as an engineer. Having spent three years as a cadet at the prestigious West Point Military Academy, he left the United States for Paris in 1855, entering the studio of Charles Gleyre as a student of painting. He mixed widely in Paris with young British and French contemporaries, and was himself profoundly influenced by the work of Gustave Courbet, whose manifesto of Realism had been published in the year of Whistler's arrival in Europe. Having friends and relatives in London, he frequently visited England, where he gradually settled in the late 1850s. He met **D.G. Rossetti** and the members of his entourage in 1862, and for many years his name was associated with the declining Pre-Raphaelite movement. In England in the 1860s he moved away from his earlier Realist style in favour of an increasingly economic version of the prevailing climate of Symbolist painting, with its rejection of analytic Naturalism. He worked closely with Albert Moore in the late 1860s, and was also largely responsible for the revival of British etching.

Following a visit to South America in 1866 he commenced his series of *Nocturnes*, employing a musical as opposed to a literary metaphor in order to describe his pictures, a practice which was very much in keeping with the Aesthetic movement, of which he was a leading representative. In 1878 he sued the critic **John Ruskin** for libel, after the latter's momentously foolish remark that he had heard of cockney impudence, 'but never expected to hear a coxcomb ask two hundred guineas for flinging a pot of paint in the public's face'. Whistler was awarded only a farthing in damages and was in consequence bankrupted. Ruskin was discredited. Whistler's work in the 1880s became increasingly abstract. He was also active as an interior decorator, and published a number of highly polemical articles and essays which were eventually anthologized in 1890 under the title of *The Gentle Art of Making Enemies*. He continued to exhibit in England and France throughout the 1890s, his work being purchased by numerous state institutions. Whistler also sustained a high, and lucrative, reputation as a fashionable portrait painter. He was very badly affected by the premature death of his wife Beatrix in 1896, dying six years later, shortly after receiving *in absentia* an Honorary Degree of Law from Glasgow University, which possesses many of his finest paintings. He was buried at Chiswick cemetery.

The very ease with which Whistler moved between the avant-garde communities of London and Paris reveals the fundamental unity of concerns within the European Art For Art's Sake movement of the 1880s, and it is as a major international impresario and spokesman for Aestheticism that he will be best remembered. His reputation fell victim to Roger Fry's dogmatic Anglophobia, and his wildly over-simplified picture of the supposed relations between English and French art in the late nineteenth century, and has only been partially recuperated as the force and influence of that picture have gradually relaxed. For it was Whistler who stood between the historical figures of **Baudelaire** and **Oscar Wilde**, Whistler who reveals the shared cultural assumptions which lay beyond such ostensibly disparate tendencies as the influence of Japanese art and the Hellenism of the 1890s. A highly serious painter and art theorist, Whistler's entire career after his removal to England constituted an eloquent and provocative denial of the middle-class assumption that painting was a mere appendage to literature and morality, an attitude which was quite as prevalent in France as it was in England. As he argued in the Ten O'Clock Lecture of 1885, 'to say to the painter, that Nature is to be taken as She is, is to say to the player, that he may sit on the piano'. For such uncompromising attitudes he was not widely loved, and his subsequent reputation for maliciousness and personal animosity was perhaps the inevitable result of his uncomfortable historical position *vis-à-vis* the official art establishments of his day. Thus he was fated to be condemned as a 'Decadent' by many of his contemporaries, and those Post-Impressionists who, a few years later, were to repeat many of his arguments in defence of such painters as **Picasso** and **Matisse**. Whistler is undoubtedly a difficult figure to come to terms with in the late twentieth century. In his obsessive insistence on the quality of paint itself he clearly anticipated one major strand of Modernism, yet the very emphasis on close tonal values and his attendant vocabulary of 'daintiness' and the 'exquisite' sound as generally off-putting today as they did in 1914.

Whistler represents the *ne plus ultra* of what was a necessary response to the total epistemological confusion of late nineteenth-century aesthetics. His role in painting was strictly analogous to that of his friend **Mallarmé** in poetry, both men insisting on the specificity of the media in which they worked. He should also be regarded as a key figure in the genealogy of Romanticism

across the threshold of Victorianism and into the twentieth century, with his absolute denial of any social role for art, and his insistence on supposedly timeless and universal criteria for aesthetic evaluation and pleasure. In this respect his position was not unlike that of his near exact contemporary **Cézanne**, although the narrowness of concerns in his own painting, and the tendency to miniaturism in his later work, ensured that he exhausted the potential possibilities for developing his own style in his own lifetime. It was his lapidary wit more than his much vaunted *'valeurs gris'* which has sustained his influence. Yet just as he struck an exemplary dandy's pose between the courts of Baudelaire and Wilde, so, faced by Ruskin at the Old Bailey, he continues to represent the dignity and independence of the visual artist, albeit an independence which he himself embodied ambiguously, and not without irony, in his studied persona as 'The Butterfly', the matinée idol of Aestheticism.

Further reading

See: Elizabeth R. and Joseph Pennell's, *The Life of James McNeill Whistler* (2 vols, 1908). The best general introduction to his work and times is Robin Spencer, *The Aesthetic Movement* (1972). See: Hilary Taylor, *James McNeill Whistler* (1978); R. Spencer, *Whistler: A Retrospective* (1989); N. Thorp (ed.), *Whistler on Art: Selected Letters and Writings, 1849–1903* (1994); Stanley Weintraub, *Whistler: A Biography* (2001); Sarah Walden, *Whistler and His Mother* (2003).

SIMON WATNEY

WHITMAN, Walt

1819–92

US poet

Long Island – 'fish-shape Paumanock' – nourished Whitman's earliest childhood, and the old port of Brooklyn his young manhood: landscape and the sea, and the urban commerce of America, are the main spheres of his poetry. Following a short schooling he apprenticed at fourteen to a printer, beginning his career in printing, editing and newspapers, broken only by intermittent years of school-teaching – 'one of my best experiences and deepest lessons in human nature'. His journalism exposed the rough condition of New York society, the social unrest of the times, and the dirt of politics. His early poetry was as conventional and sentimental as his temperance novel *Franklin Evans* (1842); but he began to read philosophy and the literary classics, and practised as a well-known speaker for the Democrats. With these bases he moved into a seminal period for his maturity. New York newspaper jobs began to irritate him; reformism and the theatre preoccupied him; he knew nothing of the vast expanse of America. Discharged from the Brooklyn *Eagle*, partly for political reasons, in 1848 he obtained a job on the New Orleans *Crescent*, and the journey south, with his brother Jeff, opened up his American experience, taking him into the Mississippi heartlands. (Myths of Whitman's children – six in New Orleans, twins in Brooklyn, a silent-movie actor calling himself Walt Whitman and looking like him – develop from this period; but his deeper sensual interests were restricted to a few young men – in particular Peter Doyle, a streetcar conductor in Washington – and to himself.) He quarrelled with *Crescent*'s editor, and back in New York decided to cut a dandy figure – clothes, a cane, the theatre, Bohemian cafés – and edited the *Brooklyn Times*, helping to support his family and buying real estate. He practised his rhetorical abilities, wrote angry poems on liberty, and lectured on art theory. Important for his later poetry, he absorbed the *bel canto* lines of opera and the exhibition of the world's arts and crafts at the World's Fair of 1853. Then in 1855 he printed and published the first small edition of the eleven accumulative editions of *Leaves of Grass*. The title page carries no poet's name (it appears in the copyright) but a frontispiece shows the image of the new bard, self-named Walt, the persona of the twelve untitled poems within – a deliberately undignified pose in worker's dress, dark hat on cocked head, one hand in pocket and the other on his hip, open-necked shirt showing a dark vest (the engraver said it was red). The myth proclaimed itself: 'an American, one of the roughs, a kosmos,/Disorderly fleshy and sensual ... eating drinking and breeding', and not at all what he later called the tea-drinking British poet the American genteel copied. The persona enabled him to transcend his social and personal self into an ideal inquirer, on the road, looking for a sharing companion – 'I was the man, I suffered, I was there.' The book is his manifesto – 'who touches this touches a man' – and touch became a key word for his sensuous sociality. To the *Boston Post* the poems were 'foul and rank leaves of the poison-plant of egoism, irreverence and lust'; as Whitman said, 'I expected hell, and I got it.' But Emerson found the book 'fortifying & encouraging', although he, too, hedged at the sexuality of later editions. Undoubtedly, the long-breathed paragraphic lines, the personal punctuation, the *bel canto* freedom of the basically dactylic measures, the passionate rhetorical mode, the unveiled presence of love and death, the unashamed exhilaration and reverence in the self was an offensive pattern to those who wished simply to be confirmed in the narrowness and timidity. *Leaves of Grass* is a democratic book in its invitation to share openness to the mental and physical opportunity to expand and break with the sets of convention. It refuses the authoritarian impositions of fixed metrics and dominant heterosexuality.

Whitman's working man's dress became a necessity when the depression of 1857 made him poor. But he continued. The 1860–1 third edition contained 'Out of the Cradle Endlessly Rocking', a more personal poem than the persona celebrations of 'Song of Myself'. The Long Island boy experiences his first intuitions of love and death through the loves of two mocking birds; the adult poet recognizes the main instigation of his poetic life as a 'singer solitary, singing by yourself, projecting me ... Never more the cries of unsatisfied love be absent from me'. The tension with Walt increased: 'before all my arrogant poems the real Me stands yet untouch'd, untold, altogether unreach'd'. The third edition contained poems on sex ('Enfans d'Adam') which, when Emerson wanted to introduce Whitman to the famous Saturday Club, caused Longfellow, Oliver Wendell Holmes and others to refuse to meet him.

The frontispiece image of the great 1860 edition shows the poet now in bardic Byronic pose – large collar and large floppy cravat, curly hair, trimmed beard, jacket. But the double theme is still 'to make a song of These States' and to generate 'the evangel-poem of comrades and of love'. In Whitman's nationalist poems ('Chants Democratic') the poet accepts his respon-sibility for fusing the people into 'the com-pact organism of one nation'. In the love poems he speaks of 'my limbs, and the quiv-ering fire that ever plays through them, for reasons, most wondrous'. He pursued this double fecundity as a myth of resources necessary to make the nation positive and powerful – a new moral and social standard. In the 'Calamus' poems, focused on a phallic-shaped flag growing in the eastern states, the sense of lonely longing 'adhesiveness', his peculiar word for the total bonding of man to man, is therefore both personal and social in its vision. The Civil War shattered that American dream. Photographs of Whitman in his forties show him changing into a pre-maturely old man under the onslaught of his experiences as a wound-dresser in hospitals where more young men died than on the battlefields. His journals contain a remarkable account of these terrible years and of his exemplary ability to look after the men, some of whom never forgot his kindness. In his wartime poems, *Drum-Taps* (1865), he included the great elegy for **Lincoln**, 'When lilacs last in the dooryard bloom'd', one of his most formally accomplished poems.

His job as Department of the Interior clerk ended when the Secretary of the Interior discovered *Leaves of Grass*. The Attorney General's office took him on, but the sacking

was a sign of the public reception he could still expect. Whitman turned his attention to the healing of the split nation and a vision of universal peace under political and techno-logical progress: 'My spirit has pass'd in compassion and determination around the whole earth,/I have look'd for equals and lovers and found them ready for me in all lands,/I think some divine rapport has equalized me with them.' Living still in an unheated room, still managing to publish his work, he received surprising recognition from William Michael Rossetti in the 1867 London *Chronicle*, and, such was American genteel snobbery, this impressed local critics. And this year, the fourth edition of *Leaves of Grass* introduced him to Germany. He wrote arti-cles – primarily in response to Carlyle's pre-dictions that American democracy would destroy civilization – which became *Democratic Vistas* (1871), one of the few intelligent texts on the philosophy of democracy. Now magazines began to pay him for work. Swinburne praised the Lincoln elegy and compared him to Blake. A corre-spondence with Mrs Anne Gilchrist, widow of Blake's biographer, developed to the point where she proposed marriage in 1871. Whitman replied: 'I too send you my love ... My book is my best letter, my response, my truest explanation of all. In it I have put my body and spirit.' And later: 'Let me warn you about myself and yourself also.'

In 1871 the fifth *Leaves of Grass* appeared, reprinted in 1872 with 'Passage to India', a major visionary poem on the expansion of democracy westwards from America, across the Pacific into Asia, and so encircling the globe back to 'These States' (the poem is unaware of a possible imperialist interpreta-tion of such an action). Now, through ill-health, emotional strain and a certain quar-relsomeness retained from his youth, Whitman declined. In 1873 he suffered a paralytic stroke. He left Washington for Camden, New Jersey, to live with his brother George. Bored and lonely, he turned to Columbus as a stubborn visionary hero with whom in part to identify ('Let the old timbers part – I will not part!') and the figure of exploration ('anthems in new tongues I hear saluting me'). The subscription list for the Centennial Edition of *Leaves of Grass* included **Tennyson**, the **Rossettis**, George Saintsbury and many other famous names: the old man had made it. Mrs Gilchrist arrived in America; the romance did not develop. Whitman visited Colorado and St Louis (to see his brother Jeff), lectured in Boston, and had the seventh edition published by a prestigious Boston publisher (1881–2). **Oscar Wilde** visited him in 1887 ('like a great big, splendid boy', Whitman told a reporter). In 1884, he could afford a small house in Camden, where he held court and, on his deathbed, held the 1891 *Leaves of Grass*.

The preface to an early edition announced the essential image: the frontier poet – 'here are the roughs and beards and space and ruggedness and nonchalance that the soul loves', replacing 'old theories and forms' with fresh compositions opposed to European elitism: 'the attitude of great poets is to cheer up slaves and horrify despots'. The poetry therefore fuses the ideal body with an ideal society through the actualities of life in a huge space where the reader is invited to move freely as a rational and sexual creative being. 'Whatever satisfies the soul is truth' – 'One's self I sing, a simple separate person,/ yet utter the word Democratic, the word En-Masse' – 'The moth and the fish-eggs are in their place;/The suns I see, and the suns I cannot see, are in their place' – these are the bases of Whitman's poetic faith, his vision of 'the procreant urge of the world', a vision which encompasses a confrontation with death, in 'The Sleepers', as well as 'The Song of Sex and Amativeness, and even Animality' (1888). It includes an ability to let the body merge into nature which no other nineteenth-century poet possesses – 'Something I cannot see puts upward libidinous prongs;/Seas of bright juice suffuse heaven' – and a willingness to present national events, for example, 'Song of the Exposition', for the Philadelphia Centennial show. He invented and endlessly developed a major and still influential verse method which demonstrates the controlled freedom of measure which best suits the form-making body. Whitman remains an inspiration to American poets in his forms, his fresh sexuality and his buoyant futurity in the face of pressing catastrophe: 'Solitary, singing in the West, I strike up for a New World.'

Further reading

See: *The Complete Writings of Walt Whitman*, ed. R.M. Buckle and others (10 vols, 1902–68); *The Collected Writings of Walt Whitman*, ed. Gay Wilson Allen and E. Sculley Bradley (from 1961). See: Gay Wilson Allen, *The Solitary Singer* (1955, rev. 1967); Roger Asselineau, *The Evolution of Walt Whitman* (2 vols, trans. 1960 and 1962); Ezra Greenspan (ed.), *The Cambridge Companion to Walt Whitman* (1995); J.R. LeMaster and Donald D. Kummings (ed.), *Walt Whitman Encyclopedia* (1998).

ERIC MOTTRAM

WILDE, Oscar Fingal O'Flahertie Wills
1854–1900
Anglo-Irish writer, dramatist and wit

Oscar Wilde was born in Dublin, the son of Sir William Wilde, the eye surgeon, and Lady Wilde, who wrote Irish nationalist verses under the name 'Speranza'. A godson of the King of Sweden, he possessed immense curiosity and a remarkable memory and was from the outset the opposite of the 'ghetto' or 'partisan' type. He always tended to the wider world, to the universal, and so gravitated naturally towards a study of the classics. After the Portora Royal School and Trinity College, Dublin, where he won the Berkeley Gold Medal for Greek, he went on to Magdalen College, Oxford, in 1874, eventually taking a double first in Mods and Greats. In the long vacation of 1877 he travelled to Italy and Greece and subsequently wrote the poem *Ravenna* which won the Newdigate Prize in 1878. At Oxford, despite his gregarious manner and bulky physique, he gained notoriety as an aesthete, became the disciple of **Ruskin** and Pater, Swinburne, **D.G. Rossetti** and **Baudelaire**, and was excited by the glamour as well as the substance of art.

In 1879 Wilde moved to London and with a vigour that was characteristically Victorian achieved metropolitan celebrity by caricaturing – and so detaching himself from – his early influences. This capacity for detachment was one of his greatest strengths because Wilde sought to occupy in relation to the impulses of his personality the position of ringmaster and thereby acquire an individual gravitas sufficient, when married to his sense of purpose, to reconstitute his environment. This he increasingly managed to do but was finally dislodged from the creation of his own destiny by his love for Lord Alfred Douglas, which in Nietzschean style he interprets in *De Profundis* (the full text of this long letter to Douglas from prison was not published until 1962) as a failure of will. But Wilde himself set in motion the sequence of legal actions which led to his downfall, and when events were taken out of his hands he had established all the preconditions for the completion of his life as a perfect drama.

In 1881 Wilde published his first collection of poems, which are significant not so much as poetry as for the efficiency of Wilde's cannibalizing of his mentors. In 1882 he went on a year-long tour of the USA to lecture the Americans on beauty in connection with the performances there of Gilbert and Sullivan's *Patience*. This operetta, which had opened in London the previous year, was designed as a skit on Rossetti and Swinburne, but typically Wilde had turned it into an advertisement for himself. In 1883 he made the first of many visits to Paris, where he astonished and instructed its salons and leading literary figures. His pedagogic instinct, which repeatedly turned into parable, also operated in reverse. He parodied the teacher in himself and in this way he created a mask, as well as a vehicle, for his serious intentions.

In his espousal of a cause, from his preaching the doctrines of Aestheticism in the early 1880s onwards, high seriousness and high comedy always clash and flirt with each other. Wilde used ideas in motion, not at rest. That is to say, his relationship to his theories was always strategic, the very opposite of art for art's sake, and his method suggests the conceptual gymnastics of a Zen adept. Wilde's genius for contradiction permitted, for example, his hyperactive propagation of the cult of inaction; or the fervent individualism of a man who could function only in symbiosis (when, after his conviction for homosexual offences in 1895, he lost his audience, he lost also his motivation, writing nothing after his release from prison except *The Ballad of Reading Gaol*, 1898). This ambivalence disconcerted other artists, especially **Whistler**, and they resented the familiarity with which Wilde sometimes treated them. But society was fascinated by the brilliant talker who entertained with his epigrams and hypnotized with his stories.

In 1884 his travels and burlesque postures were curtailed by his marriage to Constance Lloyd. They moved into a house in Tite Street, Chelsea, and immediately had two sons (Cyril, 1885; Vyvyan, 1886). At the age of thirty he settled down to consolidate his position through journalism. This is Wilde at his most straightforward, the editor of *Woman's World* (1887–9), eliciting contributions from Marie Corelli, Sarah Bernhardt and the Queen of Roumania. At home he wrote for inspiration at a desk which had belonged to Carlyle, publishing short stories, essays, reviews and poems but only one book, *The Happy Prince* (1888). These fairy-tales catch something of Wilde's charm, mercuriality and freedom from malice, which Graham Robertson called an 'almost child-like love of fun' and Wilson Knight 'a boyish immaturity often difficult to distinguish from the integration of a seer'. In this he resembled Byron, as he did also in his androgynous nature and appearance.

Marriage organized Wilde but it also crystallized the deep conflict between social acceptance and self-betrayal, classical restraint and romantic passion, love of others and love of self. From this derive his most important works, beginning in 1891 with the publication of *Intentions* ('The Decay of Lying', 'Pen, Pencil and Poison', 'The Critic as Artist', 'The Truth of Masks', previously published essays much revised here), *Lord Arthur Savile's Crime and Other Stories*, *The Picture of Dorian Gray* (published the previous year in *Lippincott's Magazine* in a slightly less moral version) and a second volume of fairy-tales *A House of Pomegranates*. These books – indeed Wilde's entire oeuvre – are a complex and dangerous act of brinkmanship in which he attempts to subvert an entrenched world view without sacrificing his place in it. That is, he wished to affect humanity at large and not merely some convertible coterie. Hereafter, until his imprisonment and apart from a few poems and prose poems, he conducted his campaign exclusively in the theatre and in the real world.

Pater, in his essay on Coleridge, wrote 'Modern thought is distinguished from ancient by its cultivation of the "relative" spirit in place of the "absolute".' Wilde was the first man to enact this as well as think it, which exposed him to charges of shallowness but increased his range enormously. So on the one hand there is the voluptuous Byzantine Wilde of *Salomé* (written in French and first published in 1893), romantic in style but modern in content, in which all is flux and dispute and no one speaks with authority; on the other, the streamlined Mozartian Wilde of *The Importance of Being Ernest* (first performance 1895), classical in style, modern in content. The characters of this play well understand the provisional nature of a statement, the techniques of role playing and image games, governable only by a transcendental ego. *Salomé* is dark and tragic, steeped in superstition; *Ernest* is light and humorous in the realm of the sublime. Neither can provide an exhaustive truth. Both are facets of reality. For a nineteenth-century mind already made dizzy by **Darwinism**, Wilde made the vertiginous trauma of relativity tolerable by converting it into play: spectacle and symbol, insincerity and lying. This is

why he wished to detach his message from conventional morality. But he knew that a prerequisite of lying (except for the insane) is an apprehension of the truth. So in his system insincerity becomes the opposite of delusion.

By 1895 Wilde's success was very great and the world as it stood offered no challenge. The too-integrated personality can separate itself from life and float off like a balloon – this was **Nietzsche's** fate. Wilde rejected self-enclosure and plunged low to reconnect and stay sane (Alfred Douglas was both a poet and the most beautiful male aristocrat in the kingdom, and therefore worthy of symbolic behaviour). The spiritual effect of Wilde's downfall, which was to preserve and intensify his power, was the opposite of the social one. This was his final triumphant paradox: disaster rehumanizes him at the same time as it immortalizes him in myth.

He wrote:

> Understand that there are two worlds: the one that *is* without one's speaking about it; it is called the *real world* because there's no need to talk about it in order to see it. And the other is the world of art; that's the one which has to be talked about because it would not exist otherwise.

This is Wilde's challenge to entropy and takes us beyond Nietzsche into the regions of Gurdjieff, Aleister Crowley, Castaneda's Don Juan. Wilde belongs here too in that his ultimate concern is not with art but with power and transformation. But he scorned occultism and ridiculed it in the emblem of the green carnation.

Wilde was the last Romantic in his special claims for the artist in pursuit of ecstasy, and the first Modern in his knowledge of the relative manifestation of absolute being. In him these two opposed rotations are housed. As the first was overcome by the second, the capacity of Wilde's intellect and Wilde's sympathies enabled him – and only him – to hold them for a moment in dynamic balance, to accommodate both Salomé and

Ernest in a weightless reciprocity of opposites – then it is gone, and we are in the twentieth century.

Further reading

See: *The Collected Works of Oscar Wilde*, ed. G.F. Maine (1952), is convenient but untidy. See also *Letters*, ed. Rupert Hart-Davis (1962); Phillipe Jullian, *Oscar Wilde* (trans. 1969); Robert Hichens, *The Green Carnation* (1895); H. Montgomery Hyde, *The Trials of Oscar Wilde* (1948) and *Oscar Wilde: The Aftermath* (1963); Karl Beckson, *Oscar Wilde: The Critical Heritage* (1970); Richard Ellman, *Oscar Wilde* (1987); G. Woodcock, *Oscar Wilde* (1988).

DUNCAN FALLOWELL

WILLIAMS, Tennessee (Thomas Lanier)

1914–83

US playwright

Twice a Pulitzer Prize winner, with *A Streetcar Named Desire* (1947) and *Cat on a Hot Tin Roof* (1955), Tennessee Williams was a playwright of great popularity who utilized his own life and preoccupations to dramatic effect. He grew up, in Mississippi and Missouri, in an often poor household dominated by his mother, a former Southern belle making a difficult adjustment to the twentieth century, and coloured by the disturbing presence of a delicate and extremely neurotic sister. His father was almost always away. Masculinity and femininity, roles and relationships, the Old and New Souths, the individual and society, weak men and strong women, artists and outsiders, violence, maladjustment and alienation: these were the concerns of Williams's life and have become the themes of his plays. These can be read as documents and as analyses, but they also embody a perpetual quest for self-knowledge, on the part of Williams, his surrogates and the rest of his characters.

Williams's first important play, *The Glass Menagerie* (1945), deals movingly with that time of his life when his mother was struggling to keep the home together, his sister

was withdrawing from the world and he himself was faced with the necessity, as an artist, of leaving his womenfolk and of working out his own destiny. Nostalgia and hatred for a once halcyon, now debilitating past; reaction against and a desire for the conventional ties of home and family; mixed feelings of guilt and responsibility; a sense of yearning for ecstasy and self-expression – all were equally present in his next play, *A Streetcar Named Desire*, in which Marlon Brando so effectively created the role of Stanley Kowalski, the urban jungle brute, the 'Polack' who marries a genteel girl reared on a now bankrupt plantation and who is confronted, in a clash of cultures, by his wife's sister, Blanche Du Bois. Blanche is one of Williams's finest creations: a woman who feels she is virginal, sensitive and artistic, who in fact is promiscuous, selfish and superficially cultivated, yet who still represents, with pathos and power, whatever virtues may have accrued to civilization. In such later plays as *Summer and Smoke* (1948) and *Sweet Bird of Youth* (1959), Williams continued to represent the Old South as an aging belle and harsh contemporary reality as an aggressive young man. The two rarely come together, except with violence. Stanley rapes Blanche.

Williams admired **D.H. Lawrence** a great deal, and in 1951 he wrote a play dedicated to Lawrence, *I Rise in Flames, Cried the Phoenix*. But there is nothing as satisfying as the relationship between Lady Chatterley and her gamekeeper in Williams's plays. In fact, Williams consistently suggests not only that the times are out of joint but seems to subscribe, fatalistically, to a belief in the inevitably unsatisfactory nature of all relationships. Love is rarely returned. In *Cat on a Hot Tin Roof*, Big Mama loves Big Daddy, but the reverse is not true; similarly Maggie and Brick. Gooper and Mae are content with each other, but are unattractive to everybody else. Normality is unacceptable; but abnormality (Brick's homosexuality) offers no alternative.

Although obsessed with the isolation of the artist, with violence between individuals,

with heightened sexuality, especially homosexuality, Williams is able to distance himself
from his preoccupations. Few of his protagonists
are unsympathetic, whether nymphomaniacs
like Blanche or virgins like Hannah Jelkes in
The Night of the Iguana (1961) or shy bachelors
like Blanche's suitor Mitch. Only the cruel
and perverting Sebastian of *Suddenly Last
Summer* (1959) and the monstrous Boss Finley
in *Sweet Bird of Youth* are without redeeming
features. But only *Night of the Iguana*,
Williams's most philosophical play, suggests
that the playwright is, on occasion, reconciled to the human condition. Only in that
play is there a willingness on the part of all
the main characters to admit and accept the
limitations of themselves and their universe.
Most of Williams's characters are too large for
life. To act them requires strength, even
flamboyance; but when the casting is right –
Anna Magnani as the lusty, remorseful
Catholic widow, Serafina, in *The Rose Tattoo*
(1950), for instance – the effect is compelling.

Most often Williams worked to achieve
social realism, though he uses symbols (the
glass menagerie, the iguana, Blanche's lamp-
shade), a poeticized language and even neo-
expressionism to achieve his ends. *Camino Real*
(1953), for example, is a fascinating and
ambitious fable of love and death, and mixes
the myths of Old World and New – Casanova
and Don Quixote rub shoulders with Kilroy.
Williams experimented with forms other
than plays, publishing four collections of short
stories – *27 Wagons Full of Cotton* (1946), *One
Arm* (1948), *Hard Candy* (1956), *Eight Mortal
Ladies Possessed* (1975). One of his novels,
The Roman Spring of Mrs Stone (1950) is not
unimpressive. *In the Winter of Cities* (1956)
contains Williams's favourites among his
poems. His *Memoirs* (1970) are frank; so are
the prefaces to his plays and a book by his
mother Edwina Dakin Williams (as told to
Lucy Freeman), *Remember Me to Tom* (1963).

Further reading

See: Signi Falk, *Tennessee Williams* (1978); Jac
Tharpe (ed.), *Tennessee Williams* (1977); and
Richard Leavitt (ed.), *A Tribute to Tennessee
Williams* (1978); John S. McCann, *The Critical
Reputation of Tennessee Williams: A Reference Guide*
(1983); M.C. Roundane (ed.), *The Cambridge
Companion to Tennessee Williams* (1997).

ANN MASSA

WITTGENSTEIN, Ludwig Josef Johann
1889–1951
Austrian/British philosopher

Ludwig Wittgenstein was born in Vienna,
into a large and wealthy family; he was the
youngest of five brothers and three sisters,
and was educated at home until he was fourteen. He came to England at the age of
nineteen to study aeronautics at the
University of Manchester, but in 1912 he
met **Bertrand Russell** and spent five terms
studying logic under him at Cambridge. It
was during the Great War (he volunteered
for service in the Austrian artillery) that he
completed the notes for his *Logisch-Philosophische
Abhandlung*, a copy of which he sent to
Russell from a prison camp in Italy. It was
published first in 1921, and then in the following year, together with an English version, under the title *Tractatus Logico-
Philosophicus*. The introduction, by Russell,
described it as an achievement of 'extraordinary difficulty and importance'. Apart
from one short article, it was to be the only
work Wittgenstein published in his lifetime.

After completing the *Tractatus* Wittgenstein
gave up philosophy; he also gave away a large
inherited fortune. He qualified as an elementary schoolteacher and for several years taught
in various remote villages in southern Austria.
But in 1929 he returned to Cambridge, submitted the *Tractatus* (already an established
classic) as his PhD thesis, and was elected to a
research fellowship at Trinity College.
During the following decade he became a
legendary figure. His 'lectures', given to small
groups of devotees, were periods of intense
concentration during which Wittgenstein
'thought aloud'; impassioned questions to the
students would alternate with agonized

silences as the philosopher struggled to achieve a new insight. During this period he wrote the *Philosophische Bemerkungen* ('Remarks', 1964) and the lengthy *Philosophische Grammatik* (1969). He also began work on his most famous book, which was not to be completed until 1948 and was still not fully revised at his death. This was the *Philosophische Untersuchungen*, or *Philosophical Investigations*, which appeared posthumously in 1953.

Wittgenstein was appointed Professor of Philosophy at Cambridge in 1939, but he spent the war years working as a medical orderly in London and Newcastle. He returned to Cambridge in 1945 but found the life of a professor unendurable (he described it to a friend as a 'living death'), and he resigned his post two years later. He lived for a time in Ireland (in total isolation) and visited America; but on his return to England in 1949 it was discovered that he had cancer. He died in Cambridge.

There are three main reasons for the unique fascination of Wittgenstein. The austerity and deep seriousness of his life; his extraordinary writing style, which almost completely avoids 'philosophical argument' as it is traditionally understood; and the curious tension between his earlier work in the *Tractatus* and the later material of the *Investigations*. This last point needs some qualifying. The myth of a near-total split between the 'early' and the 'late' Wittgenstein has been sharply eroded: a study of some of the more recently published posthumous works has shown a more gentle transition and some elements of continuity. But it remains true that Wittgenstein's later views represent a marked retreat from the position taken in the *Tractatus* on the nature of language and its relation to the world.

The *Tractatus* is essentially a thesis about the limits of language and the limits of philosophy. 'The boundaries of my language mean the boundaries of my world' (Proposition 5.6). The book consists of seven brief propositions, each – save the last – followed by many further propositions (numbered in decimal system) which elucidate and develop what has gone before. An almost obsessive brevity marks the style; the compression does not always make for clarity, and several critics have complained that bald assertion often takes the place of reasoned argument.

The background presupposed by the author is the 'new logic' developed by Russell and the German philosopher Gottlob Frege, which replaced the old Aristotelian system of inference with a new symbolism based on analogies with mathematical functions. Part of Wittgenstein's purpose was to show how the 'truth value' (truth or falsity) of compound propositions depends on, or is a *function* of, the truth value of the elementary propositions out of which they are composed ('the proposition is a truth function of elementary propositions' – Proposition 5). To show this he employed the technique of *truth-tables* (now part of every introduction to logic); and he developed a symbolic notation to express the general form of any truth-function.

Alongside this technical apparatus for dealing with a proposition goes a theory about the relation of language to the world of which the key notion is that of a picture (*Bild*). The 'picture theory of meaning', as it has come to be known, is in one way very straightforward. The world, Wittgenstein asserts, is simply a collection of facts; the most basic kinds of fact are called 'states-of-affairs' or *Sachverhalten*. The proposition (*Sach*) now gets its meaning by being a kind of picture or model of a state-of-affairs. Wittgenstein admits that

> at first sight a proposition – one set out on the printed page for example – does not seem to be a picture of the reality with which it is concerned. But no more does musical notation at first sight seem to be a picture of music, nor our phonetic notation (the alphabet) to be a picture of our speech. Yet these sign languages prove to be pictures, even in the ordinary sense, of what they represent.
>
> (Proposition 4.011)

In a proposition, Wittgenstein goes on to say, 'one name stands for one thing, another for another thing, and they are combined with one another so that the whole group – like a *tableau vivant* – presents a state of affairs' (4.0311).

At first sight this theory looks innocent enough. Meaningful discourse consists of statements which can be broken down into elementary propositions which correspond (or fail to correspond) with the states-of-affairs they depict. But the austerity of Wittgenstein's conception can soon be seen from the fact that it allows no place for, for example, ethical or aesthetic judgements: these cannot be genuine propositions, since they are not pictures of facts in the world. They are beyond the limits of the sayable. Even logic can assert nothing significant beyond empty tautologies, which 'say nothing', their truth being guaranteed simply by their internal structure (6.1). Indeed, the whole of philosophy now becomes strictly unsayable: 'the correct method of philosophy would simply be this: to say nothing except what can be said, i.e. the propositions of natural science – i.e. something which has nothing to do with philosophy – and then, whenever someone wanted to say something metaphysical, to show him that he had failed to give a meaning to certain signs in his propositions' (6.53). The book ends with the famous warning '*Wovon man nicht sprechen kann, darüber muss man schweigen*' – 'What cannot be spoken must be passed over in silence.'

These conclusions anticipate in some important respects the Logical Positivist movement of the 1930s (which rejected as meaningless any proposition which could not be factually verified). A notorious difficulty with this type of philosophical position is that it seems to cut the ground from under its own feet: what is one to make of such philosophical claims as those in the *Tractatus* itself, since on the very theory which the book presents they must be meaningless? Wittgenstein himself admitted that 'anyone who understands me recognizes my propositions as nonsense'; but the nonsense was nonetheless supposed to be helpful

nonsense – like a ladder one climbs up and then throws away (6.54).

For all that, Wittgenstein was convinced that the *Tractatus* represented the final solution to the problems of philosophy. What compelled him to return to the subject, after a gap of some ten years, was not so much the type of difficulty just referred to, as some more technical problems about the logical independence of elementary propositions. More important, Wittgenstein gradually came to see that the way in which language is meaningful is very much more complex than the simple picturing model of the *Tractatus* had suggested. Words, he wrote in the *Philosophische Grammatik*, cannot be understood simply as the names of objects; they have as many different uses as money, which can buy an indefinite range of different kinds of item. Language, he wrote there and elsewhere, is like a toolbag, whose components are as diverse in function as hammer, saw and gluepot.

We have now arrived at one of the key slogans of Wittgenstein's later philosophy: 'The meaning of the word is its use in language' (*Philosophical Investigations* § 43). A detailed examination of the actual working of language in all its variety and complexity was to replace the insistence on a single model to which all meaningful propositions must conform.

The most famous concept Wittgenstein employs in presenting this new view of language is that of the *Sprachspiel* or *language-game*. We understand the meaning of a word by seeing the role it plays in any one of a vast number of language games. The important notions here are multiplicity and diversity. There is no one common essence that explains meaning, any more than there is one common feature shared by all games. In a famous passage Wittgenstein tells us to 'consider the proceedings that we call *games*. I mean board-games, card-games, ball-games, Olympic games … What is common to them all? Don't say *There must be something common or they would not be called games*, but *look and see*.' The conclusion is that there is no one essential feature or set of features, but instead 'a complicated network of similarities overlapping and criss-crossing' (§ 66).

'Overlapping and criss-crossing' is in fact characteristic of the style of the *Investigations*, which makes no pretence to be welded into a set of precisely stated philosophical conclusions. The author describes the book in the preface as 'a number of sketches of landscapes ... made in the course of ... long and involved journeyings'. The topic which begins to predominate as the sketches proceed is that of the philosophy of mind, the analysis of mental concepts, and in particular sensations.

Here Wittgenstein makes his most original contribution when he takes on the long-standing philosophical tradition which regards words like 'pain' as names for private sensations. In attacking this view, Wittgenstein manages to avoid the crude Behaviourist position which reduces sensations to their physical manifestations. Instead, his argument turns to the impossibility of what he calls a *private language*: words, to have meaning, must be subject to public rules for their application; so the picture of a man understanding the concept of pain by attending to an inner sensation and then christening it 'pain' is a fundamentally misleading one.

The controversy over the interpretation and validity of the 'private language argument' is still far from over. But as presented by Wittgenstein – as a struggle to free ourselves from a deceptive picture of how sensation words operate – it is characteristic of his later view of philosophy as a 'battle against the bewitchment of our intelligence by means of language' (§ 109). 'What is your aim in philosophy? To show the fly the way out of the fly-bottle' (§ 309).

Wittgenstein's influence has sometimes been destructive of good philosophy. Some philosophers of religion, for example, have taken the smug and cosy position that religious discourse can only be understood within its own 'language-game', which is apparently supposed to make it immune from scientific or other outside criticism. Other Wittgensteinians, trading on the idea that philosophy is purely the activity of linguistic clarification, have put forward the obscurantist doctrine that philosophical work on, for example, memory should confine itself to examining how we ordinarily use the word, and need take no account of physiological discoveries about how our brains work.

Wittgenstein himself would probably not have welcomed these developments. He had a horror of disciples, and once observed, 'The only seed I am likely to sow is a certain jargon.' In fact the harvest of Wittgenstein's thought is large, rich and still to be fully digested. Above all, there can be no doubt of his pioneering and lasting contribution to the two issues which have become definitive of so much contemporary philosophy – the nature of language and the function of philosophy itself.

Further reading

See: *Tractatus Logico-Philosophicus*, which presents an original German with an English translation by D.F. Pears and B.F. McGuinness (1961); the *Philosophical Investigations* is translated by G.E.M. Anscombe (1953). The *Blue and Brown Books* (1958) contain useful introductory material to the latter. Other posthumous texts include: *Protractatus* (1971); *Zettel* (1967); and *On Certainty* (1969). On Wittgenstein: G.E.M. Anscombe, *An Introduction to Wittgenstein's Tractatus* (1959); N. Malcolm, *Ludwig Wittgenstein: A Memoir* (1958); G. Pitcher (ed.), *Wittgenstein* (1971); P.M.S. Hacker, *Insight and Illusion – Wittgenstein on Philosophy and the Metaphysics of Experience* (1972); A. Kenny, *Wittgenstein* (1975); P.M.S. Hacker, *Insight and Illusion: Themes in the Philosophy of Wittgenstein* (revised edn., 1986); H. Sluga and D. Stern (eds), *The Cambridge Companion to Wittgenstein* (1996); M. McGinn, *Wittgenstein and the Philosophical Investigations* (1997).

JOHN COTTINGHAM

WODEHOUSE, (Sir) Pelham Grenville

1881–1974

English novelist

When Wodehouse left Dulwich College in 1900 he became a bank clerk. His career was not distinguished. He had an urge to write, and when he gained some success in journalism he left the bank. He had found his vocation. His first successes were his books for boys. For many years such works had been marked by pietism, mawkishness and an embarrassing sentimentality. Wodehouse, who never preached, wrote with humour, good sense and understanding of boys at school.

In 1909 he went to New York. For some time the publishers showed little interest in him. When he married Ethel Rowley, a young English widow, in 1914, they had just over a hundred dollars between them. But things changed. His collaboration in musical comedy with Guy Bolton produced plays which delighted audiences in America and England, and for fifty years Wodehouse wrote for the stage. His books, however, were more important, and he had a real triumph when his novel *Something Fresh* (1915) was accepted by the *Saturday Evening Post*. The paper had a vast circulation and an extremely high standard. He wrote twenty-one serials for it, and the English editions were snapped up as quickly as they could be printed.

In the following years he spent most of his time in England. His last visit was in 1939, when Oxford University conferred upon him the honorary degree of Doctor of Letters in recognition of his services to English literature. A little later, in France, the Germans interned him. In 1941 he delivered his broadcasts to neutral America. The reaction to this in England was hysterical and ill-informed. He was a traitor, a disciple of **Hitler**, and so on. In fact, the talks were a shrewd criticism of the incompetence of Germans in managing their prisons. In America they were looked on as models of anti-Nazi propaganda.

Before he returned to America in 1947 the animosity of his detractors in England had faded away. The sales of his books, far from falling, increased greatly, and there were many more to come.

He was always modest about his books. They might give readers an hour or so of amusement because of their absurdities and their remoteness from real life, but otherwise

they were valueless. He had no message for the world. Intelligent readers will not agree. His characters and their situations arouse laughter not because they are out of this world but because they are plainly within it. He was one of the great writers of the English comic tradition, and for all their lightness his books expose the shortcomings of society and all that is pretentious and unreal.

For many readers the genius of Wodehouse is best revealed in his series of stories about Bertie Wooster, his valet Jeeves and those about Lord Emsworth and Blandings Castle. They are brilliantly written with a continuous felicity of diction and metaphor, and it is in them that the peculiar flavour of the Wodehousian manner can be most fully savoured. It is odd that Bertie, who was in his middle twenties when he was created in 1919, is still of that age, and Emsworth, who in the first story about him was said to have been at Eton in the middle sixties of the last century, is not a day older now. But perhaps it is not so strange. They are of the immortals.

Further reading

See: Richard Usborne, *Wodehouse at Work* (1961), *Wodehouse at Work to the End* (1976), *Sunset at Blandings* (1977); R.B.D. French, *P.G. Wodehouse* (1966); Robert A. Hall, *The Comic Style of P.G. Wodehouse* (1976). *Performing Flea*, ed. W.T. Townend (1953), is a collection of letters sent to him by Wodehouse. See also: Robert McCrum: *Wodehouse: A Life* (2004); Brian Taves, *P.G. Wodehouse and Hollywood: Screenwriting, Satires and Adaptations* (2005).

R.B.D. FRENCH

WOLF, Hugo

1860–1903

Austrian composer

Wolf was born in Windischgraz, lower Styria (now part of Yugoslavia), the son of a tanner. He studied at the Vienna Conservatoire, where one of his fellow students was **Mahler**, with whom he later shared a room. His first important songs date from 1878; he had already composed piano and choral music. On leaving the conservatoire he supported himself mainly by teaching; a conducting post in Salzburg was abandoned after only three months. From 1884 to 1887 he was music critic of a fashionable Vienna weekly, the *Salonblatt*, where his outspoken criticisms made him notorious.

In 1888 he produced two of the great song-books on which his reputation rests; a third was begun in the same year. From now on he enjoyed increasing public success. His wish to write opera led to the composition of *Der Corregidor* (1895), his one completed work in that genre; a Hugo Wolf Society was established in 1897. But the same year saw a dramatic breakdown in his health, undermined by syphilis; insanity and paralysis followed; and he died in 1903.

Wolf is conventionally regarded, and rightly, as a major figure in the German *lieder* tradition, perhaps the last who is worthy of comparison with Schubert, Schumann and **Brahms**. Schubert and Schumann he venerated, so much so that he avoided setting poems already set to music by them. Brahms he detested with the passion of a true Wagnerian, though Brahms's influence can be heard in some of his very early songs. Wolf had come under the spell of **Wagner** in 1875, and had never escaped it; indeed, his greatest contribution to the *lied* may be the way he brings a Wagnerian intensity of emotion, and a Wagnerian harmonic language, to this miniature form. Other important influences were Berlioz, **Liszt** and Chopin.

Wolf's first great song-book was *Gedichte von Eduard Mörike* ('Poems of Eduard Mörike, for voice and piano, set to music by Hugo Wolf' – the emphasis on the poet is characteristic). The song entitled 'Lebewohl' is typical on several counts: its brevity (only twenty bars), its extreme dynamic range (from *pp* to *ff* and down again), its declamatory vocal writing (another Wagnerian trait), its chromatic texture (with a nod to Hans Sachs in bar 7), and its 'progressive tonality' (it ends in the dominant). The concept of the

song-book, or collection, devoted to the work of a single poet seems to have evolved partly from the great speed with which Wolf always composed; one song followed another as if by chain reaction. It led to an idealization of the poet on the composer's part: at times Mörike himself seems to be the subject of the song-book.

Wolf's *Eichendorff* song-book was conceived as a companion-piece to Schumann's Eichendorff *Liederkreis*, concentrating on the humorous figures which Schumann had ignored. This delight in musical characterization, much admired by Reger, is seen again in Wolf's *Goethe* song-book, especially in his settings of poems from *Wilhelm Meister*, where he tried to realize in music the characters of the novel. Wolf's fourth major song-book, the *Spanisches Liederbuch* (1889–90), sets translations of Spanish poems from the sixteenth and seventeenth centuries. It is in two sections, 'Sacred' and 'Profane', and the erotic/religious imagery inspires some of his most daring harmony; the piano writing, too, tends to be harsher than before, some of the sonorities anticipating **Bartók**. By contrast Wolf's final collection, the *Italienisches Liederbuch* (two volumes, 1890–1 and 1896: settings of Italian poems in translation), returns to a suaver, more lyrical style; here the vocal writing is perhaps his subtlest. Wolf himself said that many of the songs in the volume could be played equally well by a string quartet, and it is no coincidence that his most successful instrumental work, the Serenade in G (1887), is for this medium: it was later orchestrated as *Italienische Serenade*. Wolf's last songs are three to poems by Michelangelo (1897), in which the linear tendency combines with a bleak dissonance reminiscent of some of the Goethe songs.

Der Corregidor, based on Alarcón's *The Three-Cornered Hat*, is notable for its Spanish subject – a more substantial Mediterraneanizing of music than that found in *Carmen*. Its 'song-book' style has caused it to be criticized as undramatic, but this very lyricism, the containedness of the set numbers, gives it a Neoclassical quality far in advance of its time.

Wolf told a friend that in his next opera (*Manuel Venegas*, left unfinished at his death) he would orchestrate like Mozart; this remark may be a surer indication of his future development than the style of the Michelangelo songs.

Wolf's achievement lies in his mastery of a single medium, the *lied*, rather than in his versatility. His concern for truth of expression led to a style of declamation whose aims, at least, had something in common with those of **Mussorgsky** – and later with those of **Fauré**, **Debussy** and **Janáček**. At the same time the motivic concentration of his work – a predominantly German characteristic – links it with that of his detested Brahms. His influence has naturally been felt most strongly by other song-writers: by **Schoenberg**, **Webern** and Schoeck among the 'Austro-Germans', but also by the English composer Robin Holloway, while one of **Stravinsky's** last creative acts was to orchestrate two Wolf songs.

Further reading

Other works include: String Quartet in D minor (1878–84); *Penthesilea*, symphonic poem for orchestra (1883–5); *Christnacht* for soli, chorus and orchestra (1886–9). Wolf's works are published by the International Hugo Wolf Society under the editorship of Hans Jancik (Vienna). See: Frank Walker, *Hugo Wolf: A Biography* (2nd edn, 1968); Eric Sams, *The Songs of Hugo Wolf* (2nd edn, 1982), and 'Hugo Wolf', in *The New Grove Dictionary of Music and Musicians* (1981). See also: *The Music Criticism of Hugo Wolf*, trans. and ed. Henry Pleasants (1979); S. Youens, *Hugo Wolf: The Vocal Music* (2000) and *Hugo Wolf and the Mörike Songs* (2002).

DERRICK PUFFETT

WOLFE, Tom

1932–

US journalist and novelist

With the increasing tendency of post-**Joycean** fiction to move away from public reality into private exploration, and with the general lack of artistic ambition among journalists, there arose in the 1960s a middle ground in which some of the techniques, liberties and high purposes of creative writing were appropriated for the presentation of magazine non-fiction. It was **Matthew Arnold** who coined the phrase 'the new journalism' to describe the sharp, individualistic form of reviewing which arose in the 1880s and whose great exponent was to be **George Bernard Shaw**. Critics, of course, have always published in periodicals and many creative authors have also been gifted journalists – Coleridge, **Dostoevsky**, **Baudelaire** come to mind. But probably the first writers to use journalistic space as an experimental space were Vasily Rozanov in St Petersburg and Max Beerbohm in London, both at the end of the nineteenth century. In the 1920s and 1930s Cyril Connolly found himself unable to work easily in book form and produced an inventive series of jazz-rococo entertainments in journals and newspapers.

But Connolly was famously self-hating. He thought that the writer's purpose was to produce a masterpiece and not waste his talent in opportunistic journalism. Tom Wolfe, by contrast, stepped forward in an entirely unapologetic way. He was far from alone as a 'new journalist' – **Truman Capote** weighed in by claiming that his own book-long murder investigation *In Cold Blood* (1966) had started the whole thing – but Wolfe was the most audacious, systematic advocate of the cause, a position he later confirmed by editing and introducing with a passionate manifesto an anthology of articles by various authors under the title *The New Journalism* (1973) which claimed that this sort of work represented 'the most important literature being written in America today'. The emphasis in such journalism moved from the collation and analysis of fact towards the examination of personality, including the personality of the journalist. This chimed with the growing cult of celebrity and the proliferation of vanity columns, and it is no accident that some of the New Journalism's finest moments were in the interview, with its opportunities for dialogue and personal engagement.

Wolfe's approach to his material was generally mocking, as was that of his most outrageous protégé, Hunter S. Thompson, whose *Fear and Loathing in Las Vegas* (1971), developed from articles in *Rolling Stone* magazine, is the New Journalism's outstanding book (Thompson invented a substyle for it called 'gonzo journalism' in which the author becomes the Quixotic hero/ victim of the events going on around him). Wolfe's panache in debunking was made acceptable by the loving care with which he organized the foibles of social life into a subtle thesis. He was also able to adapt the prosodic adventures of modern fiction in a way which reached a large audience by harnessing them to popular idioms and concerns. In this fertile overlap of high and low culture, the arts, the media and the market place, he was as characteristic of the 1960s as were Warhol's Pop Art and the **Beatles'** records.

His language is colourful, overloaded, fast and slangy, with an obsession for microscopic detail which roots the subject in actuality. This linguistic flair was enormously influential. It was a style established in the title of his very first book, *The Kandy-Kolored Tangerine-Flake Streamline Baby* (1965). The demotic and sometimes philistine character (viz. *The Painted Word*, 1975, an attack on conceptual art) of his writing saw it published largely in leisure magazines such as *Esquire, Playboy* and *Rolling Stone*, which were generous with their fees, expenses and above all their space, allowing room to build a long, atmospheric, non-fiction story or thesis. Wolfe himself was a reporter for ten years after taking a PhD in American Studies at Yale 1957, and from 1968 a contributing editor to *New York Magazine*.

Wolfe is at his weakest when polemical (as is Hunter S. Thompson), the arguments being sentimental and glib. His true gift is for the comic mythologization of America's consumer society. However, he demonstrated a growing seriousness and a wish to eliminate his overt personality from the play of events (viz. *The Right Stuff*, 1979, about the world of the astronaut). At the same time the New Journalism was losing ground, eventually killed off by a later generation of mostly female magazine editors averse to risk-taking. It was not surprising, therefore, that Wolfe turned to the novel or that, when he did, he chose to reject the current fashion in literary fiction of writing *faux* confessionally in the first person, preferring the authorial overview. *The Bonfire of the Vanities* (1987), a celebration of Reaganite Manhattan, was compared to **Dickens's** work in capturing London. It was enormously successful, though working as it did within a long-established form, it did not make its author more interesting. The novels *A Man in Full* (1998) and *I am Charlotte Simmons* (2004) have sustained his reputation without adding to it.

Further reading

See: *The Pump House Gang* (1968); *The Electric Kool-Aid Acid Test* (1968); *Radical Chic and Mau-Mauing the Flak Catchers* (1970); *Mauve Gloves and Madmen, Clutter and Vine* (1976).

DUNCAN FALLOWELL

WOOLF, Adeline Virginia

1882–1941

English novelist

While Virginia Woolf's claim, in 'The Leaning Tower', that English writers tend to be firmly rooted in the middle class might not be altogether true or useful, it is certainly essential to an understanding of her own development. Daughter of Sir Leslie Stephen, critic, man of letters and editor of *The Dictionary of National Biography*, Virginia grew up in a London household in which distinguished writers and intellectuals were familiar figures, in which books and ideas were everywhere. Denied the formal education which Sir Leslie felt was appropriate for his sons but not his daughters, Virginia was at least given free access to his vast library, whose resources helped compensate for her exclusion from the educational opportunities offered to her two brothers. While she always resented the crippling patriarchal assumptions of life at 22 Hyde Park Gate, its rich intellectual ambience also nourished her and helped shape her early resolve to become a writer.

Liberated by Stephen's death in 1904, Virginia moved with her two brothers and sister Vanessa into Gordon Square, and into a new social life built around the Cambridge acquaintances of the Stephen boys. These new friendships, which fashioned the nucleus of the much deplored and admired 'Bloomsbury circle', also brought her a husband in the person of Leonard Woolf, Virginia's 'penniless Jew', who married her in 1911 after his return from Ceylon.

With the solidity of her marriage helping her to deal with the spells of incapacitating and, at times, suicidal depression which constantly assaulted her (until she finally took her life in 1941), Woolf began her novelistic career in 1915 with the publication of *The Voyage Out*. But neither this nor the book to follow, *Night and Day* (1919), is particularly successful or indicative of what was to come. Both are basically pedestrian works, written in the narrative, realist tradition she soon came to realize was an artistic dead-end for her. For Woolf, conventional techniques could produce only conventional fiction; and it was not until the publication of *Jacob's Room* in 1922 that she felt she had finally learned 'how to begin (at 40) to say something in my own voice'. Irrevocably breaking free with *Jacob's Room* from what she calls 'the appalling narrative business of the realist: getting on from lunch to dinner', Woolf devoted the next nineteen years to exploring the different possibilities of that newly discovered voice.

Woolf was not alone, of course, in rejecting traditional techniques. Such rejection accounts for the history of modern art in general and the modern novel in particular. But in many ways Woolf is a more radical

innovator than even **Conrad**, Ford Maddox Ford, **Lawrence**, **Joyce** and **Faulkner**. More totally than the others, she cuts herself off from any vestige of narrative energy. It is almost impossible to speak of 'the action' of a Woolf novel. As an artist Woolf was always absorbed with formal rather than substantive concerns, with trying to embody, as she says, 'the exact shapes my brain holds'. While she has frequently been associated with the 'stream of consciousness' novel her writing cannot, in fact, be understood by reference to any single label or technique. The astonishingly different forms of each novel – from the minutely detailed street life of *Mrs Dalloway* (1925) to the totally artificial, internalized depths of *The Waves* (1931), from the tripartite structure of *To the Lighthouse* (1927) to the day-long pageant of *Between the Acts* (1942) – suggest the single-minded purpose with which she sought to find fresh ways to express what the experience of living is like.

Woolf's own attempt to create shapes that can make sense out of the fluidity of life is paralleled by the same sort of quest going on inside the novels themselves. If it is possible to generalize about the meaning of the human activity in Woolf's fictional world, we can say that the characters all try, through widely different means, to fashion for themselves from the chaos surrounding them some coherent grasp of their world. Lily's painting in *To the Lighthouse*, Bernard's novel in *The Waves*, Miss LaTrobe's pageant in *Between the Acts*, and Clarissa's party in *Mrs Dalloway*, for example, are all efforts to effect what Woolf herself is seeking in her fiction. The workings of the creative imagination shaping different visions of order is the single great theme in Virginia Woolf's novels.

While Woolf's position as one of the important and original modern novelists seems now to be securely established, it is only recently that such canonization has taken place. During her lifetime and extending until the late 1960s, her critical reputation was extremely uneven, a result of both the inherent difficulties of the fiction itself and her involvement with the notorious

Bloomsbury circle of writers, artists and intellectuals. As the term 'Bloomsbury' was for years a highly pejorative designation, Woolf suffered from the same critical opprobrium generally lavished on all manifestations of the phenomenon. Snobbish, sexually effete, morally perverse, politically unaware – the charges brought against Bloomsbury by Sir John Rothenstein, Wyndham Lewis and the Leavises, among others, were also brought against Woolf, and she remained for years the most dismissible of the great modernists.

For reasons that are less literary than cultural, however, the metaphoric significance of 'Bloomsbury' and all its constituent parts – Lytton Strachey, Clive Bell, **E.M. Forster**, **Maynard Keynes** and the rest – has dramatically changed, so that what was once seen as trivial and pernicious is instead hailed as prophetic and socially redemptive. For a culture that is in the process of trying to divest itself of the rigidities of traditional sexual role-playing and masculine constraints, the value the Bloomsberries are seen to place on friendship and art, and their rejection of the use of power in personal relationships, bring them into the cultural mainstream from which they were so long excluded. And at the very centre of this rediscovery stands Woolf herself, the high priestess of Bloomsbury, embodying all the life-giving virtues attributed to it. In its denunciation of masculine oppression, her social criticism, most especially in *A Room of One's Own* (1929) and *Three Guineas* (1930), is revered by feminists and androgynists alike, and readers now find in her novels an anguished awareness of the plight of the creative woman trapped in a sexist society.

The cultic admiration surrounding Woolf is not altogether edifying. The arguments for her social relevance are grossly distorted, and her feminism is far more complicated than the polemicists of the women's movement make it out to be. Woolf's genuine achievement as a writer, however, should outlast the topical claims made for her. It is above all else in her ability to create the resonant forms of *Mrs Dalloway*, *To the Lighthouse*, *The Waves* and *Between the Acts* that her reputation will ultimately rest.

Further reading

Other works include: *Orlando* (1928); *Flush* (1933); *The Years* (1937); *Roger Fry: A Biography* (1940). The standard biography is Quentin Bell, *Virginia Woolf* (1972). See also: Avrom Fleishman, *Virginia Woolf: A Critical Reading* (1975); Phyllis Rose, *Woman of Letters* (1978); Michael Rosenthal, *Virginia Woolf* (1979); Hermione Lee, *Virginia Woolf* (1995); Regina Marler, *Bloomsbury Pie: The Story of the Bloomsbury Revival* (1997); Sue Roe and Susan Sellers (eds), *The Cambridge Companion to Virginia Woolf* (2000); Julia Briggs, *Virginia Woolf: An Inner Life* (2005).

MICHAEL ROSENTHAL

WRIGHT, Frank Lloyd

1869–1959

US architect

The great American architect died leaving behind the fruits of a working life that spanned some sixty years: years of prolific and original thinking that revolutionized architectural design by introducing a very sophisticated method of composition based on the subtle interplay of geometric forms which link all the elements of a building and its immediate environment into one essentially organic whole.

His initial training was in the School of Engineering at the University of Wisconsin but this formal education seems to have had little obvious lasting effect and was certainly less important to his work than the years of practical experience of long working days on his uncle's farm or the purposeful play induced by his mother's discovery of Froebel learning methods. His love for the land and the expressive possibilities of natural materials dates from this time.

Dissatisfied with the restrictive atmosphere at Wisconsin he moved to Chicago where he formed a close friendly relationship with the architect **Louis Sullivan** in whose office he eventually worked. Wright never lost his admiration for Sullivan and his faith in an architecture freed from convention based on the supposed great European tradition. As a Mid-West American Wright had no Beaux Arts training and much of the work he did with Sullivan during the six years he spent in Chicago, particularly the designs for private houses, clearly influenced the first buildings he developed as an independent architect – his Prairie houses, designed and built between 1900 and 1909.

Typified by the Willetts House of 1902, his 'house of the future' is composed of dramatic masses set around an articulate internal spatial arrangement, the geometric form of which is governed by purely functional needs. Embedded in its leafy surroundings it merges into the landscape, giving a sense of safe shelter and durability.

The designs for private houses grow in confidence and daring, culminating in the Robie House built in 1909 on a long narrow site in a wealthy area of Chicago. With its continuous flow of interesting planes and volumes, every component in the design including the fittings combines to give that total unity which Wright called an 'inner order'.

This concentration on housing for a rich minority has brought the obvious criticism that Wright avoided the real social issues of the day, and this is undoubtedly true, though it is equally true that it was their willingness to accept his ideas and to be able to pay for them to be put into practice that consequently influenced the evolution of modern architecture.

The public works are equally impressive. The Larkin Building, built in an industrial section of Buffalo in 1904 (and demolished in 1950), was far more than a new architectural form. It was a radical concept of what an office building should be and Wright concentrated on letting as much light as possible into the working area, which was open-plan with a series of galleries running around it and an open vertical court in which the employees could work in uninterrupted

space. The most internationally influential of the early works, double-glazing was first used in this building and, most interestingly, the first wall-hung latrines.

The year 1909 saw the end of the productive Prairie House phase, and dogged by personal pressures Wright left for Europe. In his immensely readable *An Autobiography* (1943) he gives an admittedly lurid account of the desperation he felt at the time and also of the tragic seemingly endless story of Taliesin and his attempts to start life afresh in Wisconsin where he had been so happy as a boy.

Taliesin 1 was built with a pioneer spirit of independence and a desire for self-sufficiency. Conceived as an integrated group of buildings and built into the hillside from which it took its form, the living accommodation meandered informally in marked contrast to the earlier Prairie houses. Random gardens and natural vegetation were allowed to flow freely, though hinting at ideas to be used later in the Kaufmann House known as Fallingwater.

Wright's concern for an ideal way of life for others was sadly doomed to failure. His Millard House, designed in 1923, is not unlike the box-like form associated with the European architect **Le Corbusier**, but there was an important difference in the social attitudes of the two men. Unlike Le Corbusier, Wright had no thoughts for mass-production and was still working for a wealthy elite.

Worldwide recognition came late to Wright and only in his last twenty years did large commissions come his way.

The Johnson Wax Factory is an office block with walls of brick and glass tubes and an interior with mushroom-like columns giving an air of pure fantasy. The laboratory block with its tree-like Research Tower added later is evidence of Wright's continuing inventiveness and versatility.

But it is his famous Fallingwater that is his masterpiece. Built in 1936 for yet another wealthy client, it is nothing if not dramatic, with its flat terraces poised precariously over the cascading waterfall, the cantilevering made possible by reinforced concrete. As Wright himself wrote:

> This structure might serve to indicate that the sense of shelter – the sense of space where used with sound structural sense – has no limitations as to form except the materials used and the methods by which they are employed for what purpose. The ideas involved here are in no wise changed from those of early work.
>
> (*Architectural Forum*, January 1938)

From the beginning, Wright's thinking had been concerned with the underlying structure of form and its subsequent meaning, and right until the end he stuck to his beliefs. Even the somewhat cumbersome and impractical Guggenheim Museum is not lacking in ingenious solutions.

His influence on others is complex, but in terms of the development of the Modern Movement the impact on J.J.P. Oud and the designers of the Dutch De Stijl group is probably the most significant. Wright's designs were published in Holland in 1910 and they were greeted with great enthusiasm for their strictly formal geometric rightness.

Frank Lloyd Wright was a complicated man with a simple approach to life, and with the ever-increasing awareness of the need for a unity between the new technology and a fundamental human self-sufficiency there is much still to be learnt from him and the utopian ideals of Taliesin.

Further reading

See: *Collected Writings of Frank Lloyd Wright*, ed. Bruce Brooks Pfeiffer (5 vols, 1992–5); Vincent Scully Jr, *Frank Lloyd Wright* (1960); H.A. Brooks, *The Prairie School* (1972); Patrick Joseph Meehan, *Frank Lloyd Wright: A Research Guide to Archival Sources* (1983); William Allin Storrer, *A Frank Lloyd Wright Companion* (1993); Joseph M. Siry, *Unity Temple: Frank Lloyd Wright and Architecture for Liberal Religion* (1996); Neil Levine, *The Architecture of Frank Lloyd Wright* (1996).

JOHN FURSE

WYETH, Andrew Newell
1917–
US artist

Andrew Wyeth is at once one of the most revered and most castigated painters at work in modern America. By seemingly turning his back on modernist procedures and obsessions, and by choosing instead to remain rooted in the definably provincial setting of his native rural Pennsylvania and nearby rural Maine, he has enraged the mainstream urban art establishment by consistently fetching the highest prices for his supposedly 'realist' and 'traditional' work. Yet such is the quality of his workmanship that his art if anything breaks down the divide between the provincial and the metropolitan; and that perhaps has been his real transgression. By sticking to his guns he has exposed the intolerance that nourishes the radical and the avant-garde in art, while always presenting his audience and his market with a vision of an alternative, now largely ignored America, that eschews the fashionable as much as it disdains the purely sentimental.

Wyeth was born, and grew up, in Chadd's Ford, Pennsylvania. His father, Newell Convers Wyeth (1882–1945), was a well-known illustrator, and it was from him that the young Andrew Wyeth learned his craft, in particular the craft of draughtsmanship. Because he was a sickly child he was schooled at home, though in his late teens he spent a season at art college in New York, and it was in New York that he enjoyed his first solo exhibition, as early as 1937, at the Macbeth Gallery. Within a day all his exhibits had been sold to an eager and responsive public. But Wyeth refused to be drawn in by the city, or by its values, and instead returned to Chadd's Ford. Later the family, which has included several other artists spread across three generations, acquired a property in Cushing, Maine, used as a summer residence. Throughout his professional life, Wyeth has oscillated between these two locations, deriving both his inspiration and his subject-matter from them, and has rarely stepped outside.

The term 'realist', applied to Wyeth, conceals more than it reveals. Although some of his work, in its even-handed attention to detail across a composition, is suggestive of realism's 'truth to life' imperatives, elsewhere his brushwork is more aggressive, hosting both impressionist and expressionist tendencies. While much of his best-known, and also best, work consists of either tempera or watercolour landscapes – characteristically broad, open and bare, touched but never dominated by the presence of humanity and its artefacts – he has also produced a volume of portraits, studies of flora and fauna, and rustic domestic still-lifes. His technical flair apart, his primary strength is compositional: Wyeth just knows how to re-invent a conventional rural aspect by reconfiguring both the point of view and, through the altered point of view, the weighting of its components. The root of a tree, or the corner of a boulder, thus becomes the true object, not an incidental, of the scene presented.

All of which is not to say that Wyeth never errs. In two of his most celebrated pictures – *Chill Wind* (1947) and *Christina's World* (1948) – human figures are pointedly exploited to encapsulate a raw romanticism: the reason, perhaps, for their popular appeal, as well as their critical rejection. Elsewhere Wyeth's romanticism is more carefully managed. The landscapes he depicts and the nature he pays homage to are seldom comfortable, either aesthetically or by narrative implication. Reared in the countryside, Wyeth knows the countryside's physical and social treachery, and comments on it in his art. There is, though, an insistence in his work that the bond between humankind and nature is something we abandon at our greater peril.

In this he can be seen as a perpetuator of American transcendentalism, as articulated by **Henry David Thoreau** and Ralph Waldo Emerson, and also as a kindred spirit of **Walt Whitman**. Or, in his own words: 'I dream a lot. I do more painting when I am not painting.'

To the surprise of many, in 1999 it emerged that Wyeth had, since 1930, been engaged on a series of personalized portraits of black Americans, drawn from a local 'Little Africa' community in Chadd's Ford, some of them nude female work. These were assembled for a touring exhibition that visited Mississippi and other southern cities, where they were welcomed and admired by black art critics. In the most startling of them – *Dryad* – his naked model, Senna Moore, is depicted stepping out of the trunk of a storm-ravaged oak tree, a naturally resplendent figure for whom the politics of race relations is neither here nor there, as, it may be presumed, must also be the case with the artist himself.

In 1963 **John F. Kennedy** presented Wyeth with the Presidential Medal of Freedom, the first time an artist had been so honoured. Twenty-seven years later, in 1990, Congress followed suit, with a Congressional Gold Medal.

Further reading

See: Andrew Wyeth, *Andrew Wyeth: Autobiography* (with Thomas Hoving, 1998); Andrew Wyeth and Betsy James Wyeth, *Andrew Wyeth: Close Friends* (2001). See also: Richard Meryman, *First Impressions: Andrew Wyeth* (1991) and *Andrew Wyeth: A Secret Life* (1998); Anne Knutson et al., *Andrew Wyeth: Memory and Magic* (2005).

SAMANTHA GOAT

Y

YEANG, Ken

1948–

Malaysian architect

Yeang pioneered a radically new climatically responsive architecture for the tropics which was to have a global influence on the debate about an ecologically responsible world architecture and which challenges the very notion of an 'international style'. *The Skyscraper Bioclimatically Considered* (1996) sets out his ideas for a climate-generated architecture and changed our preconceptions of appropriate high-rise building forms for the tropics.

There are two powerful pressures to introduce new building forms: the first is cultural, where an architecture related to the local climate engenders built forms more appropriate to the local way of life; and the second is climatic, where designing to optimize the ambient conditions also leads to low-energy structures.

Yeang revealed that imported Western high-rise building forms are fundamentally unsuited to a tropical climate. It can be argued that International Style Modernism is also ill suited to more temperate zones, but when transported to the tropics, design flaws become more obvious. Yeang's response was the development of the concept of the bioclimatic skyscraper as a more environmentally appropriate model which consumes less energy and also provides a better and more humane environment for its users and establishes a unique cultural identity related to the location. This led to his subsequent theoretical and technical work on ecological design.

Yeang studied architecture at the independent Architectural Association in London (1966–71) where there is a tradition of radical questioning and where international modernism had never been uncritically accepted. At that time there was a trend for departments of tropical studies in architecture to teach the climatic design of low-rise traditional structures rather than acknowledging the aspirations of countries in the tropical zones to also have a modern high-rise aesthetic. But Yeang appreciated the problem while still a student and started on his lifetime quest to develop alternatives and to consider wider environmental issues. Yeang's approach was influenced by **Buckminster Fuller's** ideas on synergy and his global approach to resources and energy, by **Cedric Price** for his ideas on choice and flexibility, by Archigram and especially Peter Cook for alternative ways of looking at architecture, and by Charles Jenks for his ideas on biomorphic architecture. Yeang's uniquely Asian perspective was encouraged by Kisho Kurokawa in addition to his ideas on biological analogies and on metabolism.

To develop a theoretical methodology Yeang enrolled for a doctorate at Cambridge University (1971–4) where sustainable architecture was a newly established area of research. Yeang's ideas rapidly expanded, influenced by Eugene Odum's work on ecosystems, by Alfred North Whitehead's work on the philosophy of the organism, by Ian McHarg's ideas of ecological land-use planning techniques, and by Ludwig von

Bertellanfy's systems theory. Yeang's newly formulated principles were first presented at the 1972 conference of the Royal Institute of British Architecture which took 'Designing for Survival' as its theme, echoing a growing public awareness of the major contribution of construction to environmental problems. The theoretical framework for an ecologically appropriate architecture which Yeang developed at this time underpinned his subsequent architectural practice and was the basis of several of his books, including *The Green Skyscraper* (1999).

He returned in 1974 to his native Malaysia, to form an architectural practice with Tengku Robert Hamzah. He researched the local vernacular and indigenous architecture and published books on the cultural aspirations of Asia: *The Tropical Verandah City* (1986), *Tropical Urban Regionalism* (1987) and *The Architecture of Malaysia (1992)*. He then developed a set of architectural bioclimatic design principles for the bioclimatic high-rise such as the location of the elevator core, the use of transitional spaces, solar orientation and shading, structural massing and vertical landscaping, publishing *Bioclimatic Skyscrapers* (1994) and *Designing with Nature* (1995), which established the initial theoretical bases for an ecologically sound architecture, later developed in *Ecodesign: A Manual for Ecological Design* (2005).

A number of dominant themes and concepts emerge: the integration of vegetation and vertical gardens, the use of sky courts and the influence of solar geometry to achieve self-shading structures. Yeang's practice maintains a strong research and development ethos, entirely funded out of real projects when the budget and enlightened clients allow.

Yeang's status as an innovator and international influence was clearly established by the mid 1990s, and is attested by many honours including the Aga Khan Award (1996) for his IBM Menara Mesiniaga project, the Prinz Claus Fonds Award (1999) for his work on bioclimatic high-rise design, professorships at leading world schools of architecture, and many other awards and international prizes.

Most important is Yeang's influence on others, not just in Asia and the tropics, but also in the West and more northern climes. **Richard Rogers'** Tomigaya Tower and **Norman Foster's** Commerzbank in Frankfurt are major projects cited by Ivor Richards as influenced by Yeang's thinking. And a new generations of students born into a world which is going to have to deal with the problems created by a previous generation of profligate energy design are increasingly learning of Yeang's pioneering work. His work is celebrated in *T.R. Hamzah and Yeang* in the *Master Architect* series (1999), where an introduction by Leon van Schaik demonstrates that in Yeang's vision ecological design need not be a retreating battle of sustainability, but can contribute positively to an ecologically responsible future through energy production.

Further reading

See: Robert Powell, *Ken Yeang: Rethinking the Environmental Filter* (1989) and *Rethinking the Skyscraper: The Complete Works of Ken Yeang* (1999); Ivor Richards, *The Ecology of the Sky* (2001).

JOHN HAMILTON FRAZER

YEATS, William Butler

1865–1939

Irish poet and dramatist

W.B. Yeats was born on 13 June 1865, the son of the eccentric but highly articulate John Butler Yeats, who in 1867 gave up a rather half-hearted career as a Dublin lawyer to become an art student in London. In 1863 he had married Susan Pollexfen, the eldest daughter of a Sligo mill-owning family of Cornish descent. Though the marriage itself turned out rather unsatisfactory, the union of the charming and gifted Yeats strain with the brooding introspective Pollexfens was, in J.B. Yeats's phrase, to 'give a tongue to the sea-cliffs' and to provide in W.B. Yeats and in his younger brother, Jack Yeats the painter, two artists of world repute. It was with the Pollexfens that W.B. Yeats spent a great deal of his youth, and the effect of the dramatic landscape around Sligo, with its visible reminders of the legendary past, combined with the influence of the Pollexfen family, and in particular his uncle George Pollexfen, to arouse his interest in astrology and Irish mythology, and turned the Sligo countryside into the symbolic landscape of his early poetry. Yet, despite the many shortcomings of J.B. Yeats as a father, he gave to his children an example of dedication to art which encouraged them in their own efforts. Like many fathers of men of genius his considerable talent foreshadowed, though it could not discipline itself to attain, the artistic flowering of the next generation.

Certainly Yeats seems to have learnt little in his formal education, first at the Godolphin School, Hammersmith, and later at the High School, Harcourt Street, Dublin, and the Dublin School of Art.

The Yeats family moved back to Ireland in 1880 and remained in and around Dublin until they returned to London in 1887, moving finally into a house in Bedford Park in 1887. It was in 1889 that Yeats's first substantial major poem, *The Wanderings of Oisin*, was published. This year, 1889, was a significant one for him in other ways: it was at this time that he began to frequent writers and artists who were to be his friends and associates in the Rhymers Club in the 1890s, and it was in this year too that he met and fell in love with Maud Gonne, whose total dedication to the cause of Irish independence and powerful, uncompromising nature were to torture and stimulate Yeats to some of his finest poetry. The year 1896 saw his meeting with another powerful feminine influence on his life, Lady (Augusta) Gregory, who collaborated with him in the collection and publication of Irish folk stories and in his work for the Irish theatre. Both she and J.M. Synge, whom he met in the same year, were inspired by him to write plays of Irish life and in 1904 the Abbey Theatre opened under his management. For the next six years he was engrossed in the job of producer and manager of the theatre. In 1917 he bought a ruined tower, Thoor Ballylee, near Coole Park, Lady Gregory's house in Galway, and the same year married Georgie Hyde-Lees. In 1922 he became a Senator of the Irish Free State and in 1923 was awarded the Nobel Prize for Literature. He died on 28 January 1939 at Cap Martin and was buried in Roquebrune. It was not until 1948 that his body was brought back to Ireland to be buried in the churchyard of Drumcliffe, near Sligo ('under bare Ben Bulben's head'), where his grandfather had been rector.

'I had,' wrote Yeats of himself as he was 'at twenty-three or twenty-four', 'three interests, interest in a form of literature, in a form of philosophy and a belief in nationality.' It was then that a 'sentence seemed to form in my mind ... "Hammer your thoughts into unity."' These preoccupations remained with him for the rest of his life.

At first sight Yeats is a man of seemingly irreconcilable contradictions. One expects of a major writer opinions and a consistent philosophy, a recognizable standpoint in relation to his subject. Yet Yeats is disconcertingly ambiguous in his attitudes: it is the clash between opinions, the tension engendered by ambiguities, that excites him ('Opinion is not worth a rush'). Where many modern writers, such as **T.S. Eliot**, have resolved their doubts to their own satisfaction by struggling through to a philosophical position which, however subtle and ambiguous, is still a position to which they can give emotional or philosophical assent, Yeats maintains a state of non-commitment. It is the conflict itself that he responds to, the forging of a mythology which can accommodate all opposites ('We make out of the quarrel with others, rhetoric, but of the quarrel with ourselves, poetry'). 'Opinions are accursed' because they harden and embitter the personality, and it is only through the free play of the mind, unfettered by dogma, that the greatness of man can be expressed. It is this ambiguous attitude that characterizes his dealings with, for example, Irish nationalism.

Have I not seen the loveliest woman born
Out of the mouth of Plenty's horn,
Because of her opinionated mind
Barter that horn and every good
By quiet natures understood
For an old bellows full of angry wind?

Perfection of the life and of the work can be attained only by discipline. Thoughts are hammered, not moulded, into unity; the bird on the golden bough can sing of what is past, or passing, or to come because it has itself passed through the purifying fire. The ideal is the dance, the total fusion of body, mind and soul, a Unity of Being symbolized by the whirling movement of the universe, the spinning-off of one spool of life on to the other, the eternal recurrence of the cycles of history.

It is often said that Yeats's 'philosophy' is nothing but elaborate rubbish; but the great purpose of *A Vision* (1937) is to create a myth that can be believed and disbelieved simultaneously. The truth of *A Vision* is an entirely symbolic truth: it is certainly not the truth of philosophy, and not even the truth of religion as it is commonly held by believers. When the so-called 'instructors' appeared 'on the afternoon of October 24th 1917' in response to Mrs Yeats's attempts at automatic writing, they produced such disjointed sentences that Yeats offered to dedicate his life to piecing together their jumbled message. 'No,' was the answer, 'we have come to give you metaphors for poetry.' Poetry for Yeats, as for **Mallarmé**, and others before him, held the key to existence itself. To give metaphors for poetry was to provide a 'supreme fiction' – supreme *because* fictional.

Some will ask whether I believe in the actual existence of my circuits of sun and moon ... To such a question I can but answer that if sometimes, overwhelmed by miracle as all men must be when in the midst of it, I have taken such periods literally, my reason has soon recovered ... They have helped me to hold in a single thought reality and justice.

As with **Baudelaire**, all Yeats touched he turned into symbol: Ireland, Byzantium, Maud Gonne, the Easter Rising, the Tower, religion, history, magic are all part of the great dance:

So the Platonic Year
Whirls out new right and wrong,
Whirls in the old instead;
All men are dancers and their tread
Goes to the barbarous clangour of a gong.

'The fascination of what's difficult', the unending search for a harder and more 'hammered' style, developed partly at the instigation of **Ezra Pound**, leads not only to the stark power of Yeats's last poems, but to the 'wild old wicked man' which was the mask which the sensitive youth of the 1890s had by the end of his life assumed, if only perhaps as another 'metaphor for poetry'. His life and his art became increasingly inseparable and both aimed at a powerful, unsentimental vision of things. As the vision of an Ireland that could in reality rival the imagined unity of being, represented to him by the image of Byzantium, receded from his mind, so the ideal country of the imagination became more significant.

Yeats thought of himself and his generation as the 'last Romantics', their theme tradition, their ideal community one in which craftsmanship and artistic creation could flourish, a state without politics; but 'Romantic Ireland' was for Yeats 'dead and gone'; modern society belongs to the politicians. Only in art can man move into a higher reality; only there is it possible that 'things can and cannot be'. Yet for all its rejection of the 'filthy modern tide', for all its prophecies of doom, Yeats's poetry is not ultimately pessimistic. By its firm grasp of the reality of the imagination it has achieved and teaches serenity and freedom.

Since the publication of the *Collected Poems* in 1950 Yeats has found an ever larger audience. Not only has his poetry been increasingly admired, but his prose and his plays – particularly his plays for dancers – have been much more commonly read and acted. Yeats's plays are notable for their very successful use of poetic language in the theatre and for their perhaps rather unexpected power when well performed, but it is in his lyric poetry that he writes with full conviction and mastery, and it is as the writer of some of the finest poems in the language that his work seems certain to survive changes of literary fashion.

Further reading

Other works include: *Collected Plays* (1952); *Autobiographies* (1956); *Mythologies* (1959); *Essays and Introductions* (1961); *Explorations* (1962); *Memoirs* (1972). See also: *Letters from W.B. Yeats to Dorothy Wellesley* (1940); *The Senate Speeches of W.B. Yeats*, ed. Donald Pearce (1961). The standard biographies are Joseph Hone, *W.B. Yeats 1865–1939* (1942) and R.F. Foster, *W.B. Yeats: A Life* (2 vols, 1997–2003). See: Louis MacNeice, *The Poetry of W.B. Yeats* (1941); Peter Ure, *Yeats the Playwright* (1963); Richard Ellmann, *Yeats: The Man and the Masks* (1949) and *The Identity of Yeats* (1954); Norman Jeffares, *W.B. Yeats, Man and Poet* (1949); John Unterecker, *A Reader's Guide to W.B. Yeats* (1959); A.G. Stock, *W.B. Yeats, His Poetry and Thought* (1961); Denis Donoghue, *Yeats* (1971); Frank Tuohy, *Yeats* (1976); Brenda Maddox, *George's Ghosts: A New Life of W.B. Yeats* (1999).

JOSEPH BAIN

Z

ZAMYATIN, Yevgeniy Ivanovich

1884–1937

Russian writer

Born into a middle-class background in Lebedyan', Tambov Province, Zamyatin attended the *gimnaziya* at Voronezh and then the Polytechnic Institute at St Petersburg, training as a naval architect. He graduated, despite imprisonment and exile for revolutionary activities on behalf of the Bolsheviks, travelled widely in connection with his work, and published his first short story in 1908. Best known of his early works was *A Provincial Tale* (*Uyezdnoye*, 1913). He continued his dual professions of naval engineering and literature up to 1931, with his mathematical training frequently influencing his literary work. In 1916–17 Zamyatin spent eighteen months in England, supervising the building of ice-breakers at Newcastle-upon-Tyne, and presenting a caustic picture of English life in his stories *The Islanders* (*Ostrovityane*, 1918, trans. 1978) and *A Fisher of Men* (*Lovets chelovekov*, 1922, trans. 1977). Returning to Russia just before the October Revolution, Zamyatin proceeded to question the direction of the revolution, and the future for literature under it, in a series of pungent stories and essays. His futuristic novel *We* (*My*, written 1920, published in English, New York 1924, and in Russian, New York 1952) was denounced as 'a malicious pamphlet on the Soviet government' and was never published in the Soviet Union. Under increasing attack as an 'inner émigré',

culminating in the 'Pil'nyak-Zamyatin affair' of 1929, Zamyatin requested of **Stalin**, and was surprisingly granted, permission to emigrate. He settled in Paris in 1931 and died in poverty in 1937, leaving an unfinished novel on the Roman Empire and Attila the Hun, the subject of an earlier play.

We, Zamyatin's only completed novel, depicts an apparently unsuccessful uprising against a totalitarian, glass-enclosed city-state of the distant future. Built on extreme mathematical and collectivist principles, 'The Singe State', having reduced its populace to 'numbers', determines to eradicate all remaining individuality by imposing an operation of 'fantasiectomy', to remove the imagination. *We* is notable for its linguistic and stylistic innovation, combining grotesque and primitivist elements with striking systems of imagery, as well as being a statement of Zamyatin's main philosophical preoccupations: the role of the heretic in the progression of human affairs, the necessity for an endless series of revolutions to combat the stagnation and philistinism of each successive status quo, and the cosmic struggle between energy and entropy. Influenced in its anti-utopianism and promotion of the irrational by **Dostoevsky** (*The Devils* and *The Notes from Underground*), and in its depiction of the future by **H.G. Wells**, *We* can be interpreted as a prophetic warning against tyranny, a work of science fiction in advance of its time, and a penetrating study of alienation and schizophrenia. Its plot and futuristic detail have been assumed, probably erroneously, to have influenced **Huxley's** *Brave New World* (1932), but had an acknowledged impact on **Orwell's** *1984* (1949). Parallels can also be drawn with near-contemporary works by Karel Čapek, and Georg Kaiser, and with **Fritz Lang's** film *Metropolis*.

An experimental prose writer and originator of the literary style of 'neo-realism', seen as a dialectical synthesis of Symbolism and Naturalism, Zamyatin was a leading figure of Russian modernism and an important influence on the prose of the 1920s, yet was far better known in the West than in the Soviet Union, where, unlike most of his disgraced contemporaries, he remained totally unpublished and rarely discussed.

Further reading

See: *A Soviet Heretic: Essays by Yevgeny Zamyatin* (1970); *The Dragon and Other Stories* (1975); *Mamay*, trans. Neil Cornwell, *Stand*, Vol. 17, No. 4 (1976). About Zamyatin: Alex M. Shane, *The Life and Works of Evgenij Zamjatin* (1968); Christopher Collins, *Evgenij Zamjatin, An Interpretative Study* (1973); E.J. Brown, *'Brave New World', '1984' and 'We': An Essay on Anti-Utopia* (1976); Gary Kern (ed.), *Zamyatin's 'We': A Collection of Critical Essays* (1998); Brett Cooke, *Human Nature in Utopia: Zamyatin's 'We'* (2002).

NEIL CORNWELL

ZOLA, Émile

1840–1902

French novelist

Zola was a naturalized French citizen, his family origins being Italian on the side of his father, who left his native Venice in 1821 eventually to set up practice as a civil engineer in Marseilles. The future novelist was born in Paris and spent his working career there, but his attachment to the sunlit landscapes of his childhood in Provence contributes to the sense in his writing of the power and beauty of nature behind the artifices and constraints of urban and industrialized society. Equally, the combination of being a first-generation immigrant, of reported persecution at school and of poverty brought on the family by the death, in 1847, of the energetic Francesco Zola, seems to have left the only child with feelings of insecurity and an intense desire to succeed which are translated into his whole approach to novel writing and into the values contained in his major novel series, *Les Rougon-Macquart* (1871–93).

Zola's early novels, of which the best known are *Claude's Confession* (*La Confession de Claude* 1865, trans. 1888), *Thérèse Raquin* (1867, trans. 1962) and *Madeleine Férat* (1868, trans. 1957), reveal a characteristic preoccupation with sexual guilt and a taste for melodrama, though here can also be discerned the radical conception of the individual as a complex of physiological forces which will find complete expression in the *Rougon-Macquart* volumes of the next two decades. In the 1868 preface to the second edition of *Thérèse Raquin*, Zola shows that he is aware of the dangers of oversimplification inherent in the confined scale of his first attempts at fiction and, in the broad canvases and massed characters of novels such as *Germinal* (1885, trans. 1954) and *Earth* (*La Terre*, 1887, trans. 1954), he will develop a literary form more appropriate to his dramatic social vision. Concerned to give a philosophical framework to his art, the novelist is drawn, during the 1860s, to contemporary work in physiology and biology, absorbing the general spirit of **Darwinian** evolutionary thought and the emphasis accorded by the positivist movement to the methods and achievements of science. After consulting, among other writings, Michelet's essays on women (*La Femme*, *L'Amour*), the study of Prosper Lucas on heredity (*Traité de l'hérédité naturelle*) and Taine's work on the influence of cultural and environmental factors on societies (*Introduction à l'histoire de la littérature anglaise*), Zola prepares, during the period 1868–9, a plan for his *Rougon-Macquart* series which is conceived as a natural and social history of a family under the Second Empire, subjected to the determinants of descent and the impact of the contemporary social and physical milieu.

Appreciation of Zola's novels was, for many years, clouded by legend and misunderstanding. What was seen as his gratuitous delight in the sordid and brutal side of life became a source of constant controversy, from brushes with the public prosecutor over his early books to the famous *Manifeste des cinq* ('The Manifesto of Five'), a public statement of protest made in 1887 by a group of young writers against the admittedly earthy *La Terre*. The novels of the series which deal with the problems of the working class, particularly *L'Assommoir* (1877, trans. 1970) and *Germinal*, were seized upon as political commentaries by those who chose to find in Zola's portrait of the proletariat a condemnation of the prevailing social order or who, alternatively, detected a patronizing and unfeeling demonstration to a middle-class reading public of the bestiality of the lower orders. A whole group of religiously inspired or disenchanted writers, among them Brunetière, Huysmans, Vogüé, would help to typecast Zola as the representative of a pessimistic and crudely materialist view of man as part of their call for a morally or spiritually uplifting literature as the century came to a close. A more enduring critical viewpoint, however, is that which challenges Zola's consistency in the theory and practice of literary Naturalism, particularly when the lyrical passages to be found in many of his novels and their barely concealed mythopoeic substructure are set against the claims made in such theoretical essays as *The Experimental Novel* (*Le Roman expérimental*, 1880) that his fiction is modelled on the procedures of experimental science. The case that Zola is at heart a romantic poet posing as a writer of sobriety and detachment appears easily substantiated when readers are confronted with descriptions such as those of 'Le Paradou', the exotic garden in *The Abbé Mouret's Sin* (*La Faute de l'abbé Mouret*, 1875, trans. 1957), or in *The Beast in Man* (*La Bête humaine*, 1890, trans. 1958) of the railway engine *Lison*, with a personality of its own. The strong impression of unity offered by the series, as well as by individual novels, nevertheless belies the presumption of an incoherent aesthetic or a novelist of incongruous objectives.

It is notably misleading to think of Zola's social vision as primarily political or economic; nor, despite the context given to the *Rougon-Macquart* series, should it be thought of as authentically historical. A superficial chronological framework locates the events of the series between the coup d'état of 1851 and the fall of the Second Empire in 1870, but an element of anachronism is apparent, lending to the early books in the series such as *The Kill* (*La Curée*, 1872, trans. 1895) the immediate atmosphere of a society in decay and to the later ones, including the war novel *The Debacle* (*La Débâcle*, 1892, trans. 1972), a mood of optimism and regenerative hope. It is sometimes held that this change of tone may be related to Zola's liaison, after eighteen years of childless marriage, with Jeanne Rozerot, a mistress some twenty-seven years his junior, and the birth (1889) of the first of two children by her. Beyond this, however, Zola's whole conception of time, in contrast with the linear historical perspective on the present to be found in Balzac's *Comédie humaine*, is both evolutionary and cyclical in that it is governed by the rhythms of all-powerful nature – for Zola the ultimate reality and force in the universe. While developing towards perfection, men and societies are conceived as subject to the seasonal flux of plant and animal life, so that the period of the Second Empire assumes the character of a phase of sickness or sterility, eventually emerging from the blood-letting of the 1870 war into new or potential fruitfulness. The constant ambivalence of a novel series which opens in an ancient graveyard (*La Fortune des Rougon*, 1871, translated as *The Fortune of the Rougons*, 1898) and ends in a celebration of the birth of a child (*Le Docteur Pascal*, 1893, translated as *Doctor Pascal*, 1957) is found in the idea that life and death are eternally interdependent. The intervening books of the series reinforce the correspondence between the ebb and flow of the natural cycle and that of human moral and social behaviour, a link which Zola, following Michelet, sees most clearly manifest in the biological cycle of woman, alternating between the destructively barren and the redemptively fertile. In Naturalism, instead of the environment of woman being man, the environment of man is woman, elevated through her association with the maternal deity, nature, to a representative of the space of man's world and a metaphor of human existence. For the individual, as for the microscopic seed, life is experienced as an arena of bewildering uncertainty, a vast uterine system, as suggested by the reiterated image of the labyrinth, whether formed by the vaults and avenues of the Paris market in *Savage Paris* (*Le Ventre de Paris*, 1873, trans. 1955), the 'terrible machine' of the department store in *Ladies' Delight* (*Au bonheur des dames*, 1883, trans. 1957) or, more obviously, the mine of *Germinal* with its endless passages and tunnels. Subject to nature's own experimental plan, humanity is faced with the uncompromising test of its capacity to fulfil a purpose which is unknown, apart from the characteristics revealed by nature herself. Energy, dynamism and fertility thus become the necessary qualities for evolutionary success by contrast with those which bring deceptive reward in an abortive society: sloth, self-indulgence, infertile lust. This stoical but fundamentally positive code of values is clearly very close to that adopted by the novelist in his personal cult of effort and self-discipline and one which, subordinating the struggles of politics and class to the spontaneous selection of the life force, is reflected in Étienne Lantier, still driving forward at the end of *Germinal*, as much as it is absent in his mother, the generous but passive and backward-looking Gervaise of *L'Assommoir*. Determinism vies with determination in Zola's thought. The thread of hereditary patterning connecting the members of his fictional family also represents for him the icy grip of the past, always threatening progress and natural fulfilment.

The philosophical vision behind Zola's Naturalism, embracing the individual, society and organic nature in a single whole, governs rather than is dictated by the mimetic considerations of his art. While Naturalism clearly derives many of its formal techniques from existing realism, Zola's literary theories and working notes tend to focus less on the problems of mimesis as an end in itself and to emphasize the importance of balance, logic and coherence as the instruments of a necessary verisimilitude. As his cycle of twenty books, each dealing with a separate social organ, may suggest, the novelist sets out to portray an integrated world, the validity of the picture being found in the whole rather than the individual constituents, in the combination of features which may appear in themselves distorted or exaggerated. Beginning with his boyhood friendship with **Cézanne**, who provided the inspiration for his novel *The Masterpiece* (*L'Oeuvre*, 1886, trans. 1950), Zola showed a keen interest in contemporary painting and particularly the work of the Impressionists. What Naturalism and Impressionism have most in common is that both represent a departure from academic realism in positing a phenomenological relationship between artist and subject, allowing eye or imagination to compose the perceived elements into a synthesis which is the sum of imprecise detail. 'We are all of us liars, more or less,' wrote Zola in an important letter of 1885 to his friend Céard, 'but what is the mechanism and the spirit of that falsehood? ... I consider my lies to be directed towards the truth.' It is here that the much questioned analogy with experimental procedures begins to have its meaning: even if, in *The Experimental Novel*, Zola can justly be accused of neglecting the specifically literary qualities of fiction in relation to science and its methods, the experimental is a definition of man's and the novelist's relationship to an enigmatic universe, forever seeking to advance, through trial and error, towards clarification and understanding.

It was perhaps as a natural conclusion to the inquiring stance of *Les Rougon-Macquart* that Zola should devote the last years of his life to writing novels concerned with advancing social solutions. Many of the values of these late works can be traced retrospectively to the twenty-volume series, but with a corresponding loss of literary and dramatic power as explicit statement and blatant moralizing replace the conflicts and suggestive imagery of the classic texts. The trilogy *Les Trois Villes* ('The Three Cities': *Lourdes*, 1894; *Rome*, 1896; *Paris*, 1898) represents Zola's affirmation of faith in scientific rationalism in the face of the mounting tide of contemporary religious reaction, the unfinished tetralogy *Les Quatre Évangiles* ('The Four Gospels': *Fécondité*, 1899; *Travail*, 1901; *Vérité*, 1903) the elaboration of his utopian vision of reform through prolific family life, the brotherhood of labour and enlightened education.

If such works have interest for the modern reader, it lies, as F.W.J. Hemmings suggests, in what they record of the prevailing social and intellectual climate at the turn of the century. It was this same climate which gave the novelist his final claim to public attention when in January 1898 under the title 'J'accuse', the editor of the newspaper *L'Aurore* published Zola's famous open letter to the president of the republic on the subject of the Dreyfus Affair. In an outburst of anger which was as uncharacteristic as the personal courage entailed was familiar, Zola denounced the conduct of the court-martial which, by acquitting Esterhazy of espionage in the face of all the evidence, served to confirm the trumped-up charge levelled four years before against the Jewish Captain Dreyfus. Zola himself was faced with a libel suit and forced to spend an uncomfortable year's exile in England to escape a prison sentence. He died in Paris in September 1902, poisoned by the fumes from a coal fire. The circumstances were judged accidental but, in view of his support for Dreyfus in a period of nationalist and anti-Semitic fervour, these have never been entirely free of suspicion.

Further reading

Other works include: *Oeuvres complètes*, ed. H. Mitterand (1966–9); *Les Rougon-Macquart*, ed. H. Mitterand (1960–7). Standard modern translations are referred to above. See also *Nana*, (trans. 1972) and *Zest for Life* (*La Joie de vivre*, trans. 1955). See: Angus Wilson, *Émile Zola: An Introductory Study of His Novels* (1952); E.M. Grant, *Émile Zola* (1966); F.W.J. Hemmings, *Émile Zola* (1966) and *The Life and Times of Émile Zola* (1977); P. Walker, *Émile Zola* (1968); G. King, *Garden of Zola* (1978); J.C. Lapp, *Zola before the 'Rougon-Macquart'* (1964); Joanna Richardson, *Zola* (1978); Frederick Brown, *Zola: A Life* (1995).

DAVID LEE

index

This is a subject and theme index only. See the two-volume set of this title for the full version.

Abbey Theatre 839

Aboriginal people 23

abortion laws 85

Abstract Expressionism 229, 383, 535, 542, 627, 801; De Kooning 171; Kitaj's reaction against 417; Oldenburg 571; Pollock 602; Rothko 660

abstraction: in Ben Nicholson's work 561; Hepworth's sculpture 338, 339–40; Kandinsky as pioneer of 395; in Klee's work 419–20; in Mondrian's painting 540; in Tàpies's painting 737; in Webern's music 811; *see also* Cubism; Futurism; Suprematism

Absurdism 119

academics: Arnold, Matthew 17–18; Ayer 30–31; Barthes 45; Bellow 59; Berlin, Isaiah 64–66; Galbraith, J.K. 268–70

Académie Française 452, 649

Action Painting 171, 602

activists *see* civil rights activists; political activists

actors: Armstrong, Louis ('Satchmo') 13–15; Chaplin, Charles S. 130–32; Fassbinder, Rainer Werner 231; Keaton, Buster 398–99; Lang, Fritz 434; Pinter, Harold 594–95; Polanski, Roman 600; Riefenstahl, Leni 640; Scorsese, Martin 684–85; Stanislavsky, Konstantin 710–11

advertising: Hirst's concern with 347; Koons's self-promotion 424; McLuhan's analyses 513, 514; Magritte's influence 476; television 686; Warhol's aesthetic 801

aestheticism: Baudelaire's idea of beauty 49; Cézanne 127; Nietzsche 564; Whistler 816, 817; Wilde 821

Afghanistan: American foreign policy 140; Jamal Uddeen Al Afghani 4; Osama bin Laden's activities 71–72, 72–73; Soviet retreat from 301

Africa: Riefenstahl's documentaries 641

African tribal art 539, 592

Afro-Americans *see* American Negroes/Afro-Americans

AG Gallery, New York 574

agrarian issues: Weber's writings 806–7

AIDS 251, 488–89

Al Urwat al Wuthqa (journal) 5

alcoholism: Dylan Thomas 744; Fitzgerald 239; Jack London 463; Kerouac 403; Pollock 602; Toulouse-Lautrec 757; Verlaine 782, 783

Algerian War 113, 183

Algiers: Camus 113, 113–14; Timothy Leary's visit 445

alienation: Marx's theory 510; in O'Neill's dramas 572

Amblin Entertainment 708

American Academy of Motion Picture Arts and Sciences 632, 708

American Civil War 209, 312, 459, 638, 765, 819

American Composers Alliance 149

American culture: in DeLillo's novels 177–78; DeMille's films 178

American Indians: Boas's studies 75–76; Lévi-Strauss's writings on myths of 452, 454

American Museum of Natural History 516

American Negroes/Afro-Americans: in Faulkner's novels 233; Gershwin's understanding of 287–88; importance of Duke Ellington 226; importance of Toni Morrison's work 550, 551

American South: in Faulkner's novels 233; in Tennessee Williams's plays 823

American Union 458–59

Analytical Engine 33–34

Analytical Society 32

anarchists 231, 425–26

anatomy: Huxley's lectures 363

ANC (African National Congress) 487–88, 488

Anglo-Saxon 751
animal behaviour *see* ethology
animation 382, 708; Disney 192–94
'anomie' 203
anthropologists: Boas, Franz 75–76; Lévi-Strauss, Claude 452–56; Malinowski, Bronislaw Kaspar 482–83; Mead, Margaret 515–16; *see also* ethnography; ethnology
anti-capitalism 140
anti-fascism: Camus 113; Eisenstein's *Alexander Nevsky* 216
anti-imperialism: Guevara's ideas 315; Jamal Uddeen Al Afghani 4–5; Mao Zedong 494; Said 672–73
anti-intellectualism: Wagner 793, 797–98; Waugh's reactionary role 805–6
anti-semitism: Eliot 224; Henry Ford 247; Hitler 349; impact on Herzl 340; perceived in *Oliver Twist* film 444; in Poland 698; Pound 610; Vichy regime 183; Wagner 794, 798; *see also* Dreyfus aair
Antwerp 775
Apple 67, 277, 285, 381, 381–82
Arabs: Camus's defence of 113; Israel–Arab wars 418, 672–73
archaeology, rejection of biblical chronology 164
archetypes 391–92
Archigram group 653, 837
architects: Aalto, Hugo 1–2; Foster, Norman 250–51; Fuller, Richard Buckminster 264–66; Gaudí, Antoni 278–81; Gehry, Frank O. 284–85; Gropius, Walter 313–15; Holabird, William 352–53; Le Corbusier 440–43; Mackintosh, Charles Rennie 474–75; Mies van der Rohe, Ludwig 524–27; Niemeyer, Oscar 561–62; Price, Cedric John 611–13; Richardson, Henry Hobson 637–40; Roche, Martin 352–53; Rogers, Richard George (Lord) 652–53; Sullivan, Louis Henry 730–32; Wright, Frank Lloyd 833–35; Yeang, Ken 837–38
Architectural Association, London 611, 613, 652, 837
architecture: Morris's interest in 548, 549; Ruskin's writings 666–67; *see also* International Modern Movement
Arctic, environment of *Nanook of the North* 240
Argentina: Borges and *ultraismo* 77
Arles 775
art and technology: Rauschenberg's work 627
art and text: Robbe-Grillet's collaborations 649
Art Brut movement 200
Art for Art's Sake 49, 127, 816
art market: Damien Hirst's tactics 346–47

Art Nouveau 36–37, 37, 52, 159, 422, 474, 481, 540, 551; *see also Jugendstil*
art theory/criticism: Baudelaire 48–49, 49; Beuys 70; Breton 94; Judd 38; Kandinsky 396; Lawrence 438; Ruskin 666–68; Seurat's influence 691; Shaw 693; Updike 770; Whistler 817
Art Workers Coalition 13
Artek 2
artists: Bacon, Francis 34–35; Chirico, Giorgio de 136–37; Dalí, Salvador 158–60; De Kooning, Willem 171–72; Dubuet, Jean-Philippe-Arthur 199–200; Ernst, Max 229–30; Gabo, Naum 267–68; Gauguin, Paul 281–84; Gilbert & George 292–93; Hirst, Damien 346–48; Hockney, David 351–52; Hopper, Edward 356–57; Judd, Donald 387–89; Klee, Paul 418–21; Klein, Yves 421–22; Klimt, Gustav 422–23; Koons, Je 423–24; Lawrence, David Herbert 436–39; Magritte, René-François-Ghislain 475–76; Malevich, Kazimir 480–82; Modigliani, Amedeo 538–40; Mondrian, Piet 540–41; Monet, Claude 541–43; Nicholson, Ben 560–61; Oldenburg, Claes 571–72; Ono, Yoko 574–75; Picasso, Pablo 592–94; Rauschenberg, Robert 626–27; Ray, Man 630–31; Rothko, Mark 660; Spencer, Stanley 706–7; Tàpies, Antoni 737–38; Toulouse-Lautrec, Henri de 757–58; Van Gogh, Vincent 774–76; Warhol, Andy 800–802; Whistler, James Abbot McNeill 816–17; Wyeth, Andrew 635–36; *see also* designers; illustrators; painters; photographers; sculptors
Arts Council of Great Britain 406
Arts and Crafts movement 313, 474, 548
Astronomical Society 32, 33
astrophysics: Hawking's *A Brief History of Time* 323–24; Oppenheimer's research 576
AT&T (American Telephone and Telegraph Company) 57
atheism: Buñuel 105; in Darwin's time 164; Dawkins 169–71
Atlantic magazine 42
Atlantic Monthly 372, 747
atom bomb 575, 576, 656
Atomic Energy Commission 576
atomic theory 212
L'Aurore 846
Auschwitz 418, 450, 451, 600, 687
Australia 23
Austria: Nazi occupation 89, 255
auteur cinema 685
auteur theory 248–49

authors: Barnum, Phineas Taylor 40–42; Carroll, Lewis 119–20; Heller, Joseph 331–33; Oates, Joyce Carol 568–69; Ōe Kenzaburō 569–71; Strindberg, Johan August 727–30; Thoreau, Henry David 746–50

autobiography: Alexander Calder 112; Anthony Burgess 107; in Fassbinder's films 232; in Fellini's films 237; Gide's works 291; Gorky's three volumes 302; Hughes's *Birthday Letters* 359–60; Joyce's *A Portrait* 385–86; J.S. Mill 528, 529, 530; Jung 390–91; Kate Millett 533; Lévi-Strauss's travel account 452; Mandela 489; in Mishima Yukio's novels 535; in Ōe Kenzaburō's work 50; in Pasternak's novels 586; Plath's *The Bell Jar* 599–600; Qutb's early novel 622; Sartre 676, 678; Strindberg 727; Tolstoy's works 753, 754; Trollope 758; Trotsky 763; Wagner 795; Waugh 805

automatism: in Surrealism 92, 158, 602, 660, 768; Yeats's experiments 840

automaton theory 377–78

Automobile Age 246

avant-garde: Brecht 91; Fauves 511; Godard's films 297–98; Henri Rousseau as hero of 663, 664; Hepworth's contact with 339; influence on Kawabata 397; Man Ray 631; Marinetti's influence 503; Penderecki's music 590, 591; Pirandello's links with 597; Russian art 481; Stockhausen's relationship with 715–16, 717; Tàpies 737

aviation, Bell's contributions to 57

Baader-Meinhof gang 286

ballet 39, 149, 173; Ballets Russes 37, 185–86, 268, 593, 614, 724; Bolshoi Ballet 624; Ravel's works 628; Tchaikovsky's music 740

bandleaders: Armstrong, Louis ('Satchmo') 13–14; Davis, Miles Dewey, Jr 168–69

Bangladesh 736

Barbizon school 281, 690

Barcelona: Gaudí 278–81; International Exhibition (1929) 525; Olympic Village 284; Picasso's time in 592

Bauhaus 313, 314, 396, 481

Bayreuth 722, 723

BBC (British Broadcasting Corporation) 15, 23–24, 36, 543, 578

Beacon Hill progressive school 671

Beat movement 107–8, 294, 402–3

behaviourism 588, 700–702, 766, 827

Belgium: Borinage 775

Bell Telephone Company 57

Bengal: famine 144, 689; Tagore 736, 737

Bengali stories 632

Benthamite ideas: Mill 528–29, 529–30

Berlin: Auden 25; Brecht 88; Capa 116–17; Einstein 212; Foster's Reichstag dome 250–51; Gabo 268; Grass 307; Gropius 313; Nabokov 555; National Art Gallery 526, 527; Schoenberg 681; Völkerkunde Museum 75

Berlin Wall 440

Berliner Ensemble 89, 91

Beyond the Fringe (revue) 543–44

BFI (British Film Institute) 685

Bhagavad Gita 273, 345, 575

The Bible: Marc's illustrations 500

Biblical epic films 179

biblical knowledge 170

biochemistry: Needham's work 557

biographers: Aldous Huxley 362; Anthony Burgess 107; Evelyn Waugh 804

biologists: Huxley, Thomas Henry 362–64; Lovelock, James Ephraim 467; Watson, James Dewey 802–4

biology: modern foundations 164–65

Birmingham, Alabama 412

Black civil rights: Kennedy's establishment of 400; Martin Luther King's leadership 411–13

black comedy: Dostoevsky's *The Possessed* 197; Pinter's plays 596; Polanski's films 601; Salinger's voice in *The Catcher in the Rye* 673; Vonnegut's novels 791

black consciousness: significance of Charlie Parker 583, 584; significance of Morrison's novels 550, 551

'black holes' 324

Black Mountain College, North Carolina 111, 156, 626

Black Panthers 286, 445

Der Blaue Reiter group 396, 419, 499, 500

Bloomsbury group 249, 406, 832, 833

blues music: Dylan's roots 206, 207; Gershwin 288

the body *see* mind-body

Boer War 143, 198

Bolivia 315, 316–17

Bolshevik Revolution *see* October Revolution

Bolsheviks 448, 470, 709, 764, 842

book design: Chagall 129; Grass 307

book illustration: Beardsley 51–52

Boston, Massachusetts 468, 675, 820

Boston University 744, 799

botanists: Mendel, Gregor 520–22

bourgeoisie: in Lenin's idea of revolution 448; Marx's view 506; Pasolini's critique 585; themes in Ibsen's plays 367

Brasilia 562
Brazil 561–62
Brechtian distancing devices 801
Bristol 102
British Association for the Advancement of Science 482
British Centre for Literary Translation 687
British Council 347
British Empire 219, 799; India 273–74
British Library 582
British Museum 251, 545
Brittany: Gauguin's art 282, 283
broadcasting 23–24; *see also* radio; television
Broadway shows 14, 63–64, 69, 153, 404, 606, 705, 787
Brownian motion 212
Die Brücke group 283, 499
Brussels 645
Buddhism 402, 452, 456, 685; *see also* Tibetan Buddhism; Zen Buddhism
Burma 577

Cahiers du Cinéma 296, 538
California: Hockney 351; Schoenberg's later life 682; Silicon Valley 381, 382; Steinbeck's background 712; Thomas Mann's home 491
California Institute of Technology (Caltech), Berkeley 575–76, 803
calligraphy: Tàpies 737, 738
Calvinism 468–9, 807
Cambodia 140
Cambridge University 406, 512, 543, 555, 557, 611, 764; Cavendish Institute 151–52, 575; Derrida controversy 182; Forster 249; Greer's experiences 310; honouring of Tchaikovsky 739; Lucasian Professor of Mathematics post 323; Russell's entry 668; Sen's experience 689; Sulston's studies 732; Wittgenstein's lectures 824–25; Yeang's experience 837
Camden, New Jersey 820
cancer research 803
Cannes Film Festival 296, 601
'capability approach' 609
capitalism: Galbraith's writings on 269; Havel's criticisms 322; H.G. Wells's critique 815; Keynes's criticisms 406; Lenin's writings on 447–48, 449; Marx's critique 507; Weber's theory 807
Caribbean: influence on Walcott's work 799, 800
cars 246–47
cartoons *see* animation
carvings: Hepworth 339

Catalonia: Gaudí and cultural movements 278–80; importance to Miró 534
Catholic Church *see* Roman Catholic Church
Caucasus: Tolstoy's experience 753, 755
celebrity: Hirst 346–48; Koons 423–24; Pasolini 585; Picasso 594; Tagore 736; Yoko Ono 574
censorship: attempts to ban Grass's work 307; Buñuel's films 105; by Nazis 60, 76, 434; Genet's novels 286; Ginsberg's activism against 293; Havel's plays 322; Joyce's work 385; Kubrick's films 426; Lawrence's *Lady Chatterley's Lover* 438
ceramicists: Gauguin, Paul 281–84; Miró, Jóan 534; Picasso, Pablo 594
CERN (European Council of Nuclear Research) 67, 68
chemical pollution 121
chemists: Lovelock, James Ephraim 466–68
Chicago: Art Institute 571; in Bellow's life and stories 58, 59; Frank Lloyd Wright's life and work 833; Holabird and Roche's skyscrapers 352–53; Louis Armstrong 13–14; Marshall Field building 640; Sullivan's architecture 730
Chicago school of economics 261, 261–62
children's authors: Carroll, Lewis 119–20; Hughes, Ted 358; Kipling, Joseph Rudyard 414; Tolkien, J.R.R. 751; Verne, Jules 785
children's music 166, 219, 628
Chile 261
China: annexation of Tibet 180, 317–18; Deng Xiaoping 179–82; Eve Arnold's photography 15; Mao Zedong 140, 494–99; Milton Friedman's visit 261
Chinati Foundation, Marfa, Texas 388
Chinese civilization: Needham's work 557–59; Weber's studies 807
Chinese Communist Party (CCP) 495, 496
Chinese poetry: Pound's versions 608
choreographers: Cunningham, Merce 156–57; Graham, Martha 305–6
Christianity: Arnold's writings 17; Auden's conversion 27; Dylan's 'born-again' phase 207; eect of natural selection on creation idea 170; George Eliot's Evangelism 220; Hopkins's faith 355; influences on Liszt 460; Lowell's battles with 468; Martin Luther King's faith 411; Nietzsche's war with 562; in Rimbaud's poetry 645; Solzhenitsyn's morality 703, 704; in Tolkien's world 752; T.S. Eliot's faith 225, 226; Updike's faith 771; Wagner's morality 795
Christmas 188
Chronicle (London) 891
CIA (Central Intelligence Agency) 71, 72

CIAM (Congrès Internationaux d'Architectes Modernes) 441, 562

cinema: Beatles films 53; British national cinema during 1940s 443–44; history of film 685; *The Lord of the Rings* trilogy 752; *mise-en-scène* technique 53, 791; montage 217, 271, 272, 444; *Monty Python* team's films 544; New Wave (*Nouvelle Vague*) 272, 296, 538; silent films 348, 398, 434, 633; *see also* film directors/makers; Hollywood

Circle (1937) 339, 561

circus 41–42

civil disobedience 487–88, 671, 748

civil rights activists: King, Martin Luther, Jr 411–13; Lowell, Robert 468; *see also* equal rights; human rights

Civil Service: Keynes 406, 408; Trollope's job 758; Turing's wartime post 764; *see also* public service

civil society 322, 323

class: in Chekhov's plays 135; in Fassbinder's films 231–32; in identification of Kipling 414, 415–16; issues addressed in Morrison's novels 550; Marx's theory 506–7; Waugh's Bright Young People 804; Weber's perspective 809; in Wells's novels 814; in Woolf's development 831

classical Greek thought: conception of culture 563; Nussbaum's account 567; *see also* Greek drama

Classicism: Dalí 159; Eisenstein's cinema 217; Picasso's period of 593; poetry 225; Pound's interest in 608

climate-sensitive architecture 837

CND (Campaign for Nuclear Disarmament) 671

Cold Spring Harbor Laboratory, Long Island 803, 804

Cold War 144, 245, 301, 439, 498, 575, 656, 657, 738

collage 293, 352, 512, 583, 593, 627

collective unconscious 390

collectivism: China 497; H.G. Wells's belief in 815; in Shaw's socialism 693; Western Progressivism towards 655–56

Cologne: Stockhausen 715–17

colonialism 113, 148, 799

colour: Bakst's ideas 37; in Kandinsky's work and thought 395, 396; in Klein's artwork 421; in Matisse's paintings 511; in Mondrian's painting 540; and optical laws 541, 691; in Rauschenberg's paintings 626; Rothko's use of 660; in Rouault's work 661, 662; Van Gogh's use of 776

Columbia University 532, 672

comedians: Allen, Woody 7–8

comedy: Keaton's films 398–99; *Monty Python* 543; in Proust's *Remembrance of Things Past* 617–18; Stoppard's farces 718; Tom Wolfe's writing 831; in Updike's fiction 770; in Waugh's novels 805; in Wells's novels 814; Wodehouse's writing 828; *see also* black comedy; humour; satire

comic books 456

commercial art 476

commercialism 549

commodification: in Koons's art 423

communication art 176, 177

communications: McLuhan's analysis 513–14; world wide web 67; *see also* telegraphy; telephone

Communism: Camus's view 114; China 180–82; DeMille's campaign against 179; Gide 292; Havel's critique of Czech regime 322; Mao Zedong's redefining of 494–95; Marx 505–6, 509, 509–10; Oppenheimer as victim of witch-hunt against 576; Orwell's polemics against 578; purge of Hollywood film industry 89, 131, 465; Russell's attack on Russian regime 671; and Surrealism 92–93; theory of socialist change 315

Communist Party of the Soviet Union (CPSU) 299–301, 509, 762

comparative studies: Weber's studies 807

composers: Adams, John Coolidge 2–4; Barber, Samuel 39–40; Bartók, Bela 46–48; Berg, Alban 59–61; Berlin, Irving 63–64; Bernstein, Leonard 68–70; Bizet, Georges 73–75; Boulez, Pierre 78–79; Brahms, Johannes 81–84; Britten, Benjamin 94–96; Bruckner, Anton 99–101; Cage, John 110–11; Carter, Elliott Cook 121–23; Copeland, Aaron 149; Davies, Peter Maxwell 165–68; Davis, Miles Dewey, Jr 168–69; Debussy, Claude 172–74; Dvořák, Antonin 204–5; Elgar, Sir Edward 218–19; Ellington, Duke 226–27; Fauré, Gabriel Urbain 234–36; Gershwin, George 287–88; Glass, Philip 294–96; Henze, Hans Werner 337–38; Ives, Charles Edward 368–70; Janáček, Leos Eugen 379–81; Liszt, Franz 459–62; Lutosławski, Witold 470–71; Mahler, Gustav 477–78; Messiaen, Olivier 522–24; Mussorgsky, Modest Petrovich 552–54; Penderecki, Krzysztof 590–92; Porter, Cole 605–6; Poulenc, Francis 606–7; Prokofiev, Sergei Sergeievich 613–15; Puccini, Giacomo 618–19; Rachmaninov, Sergei 624–26; Ravel, Maurice 627–29; Rimsky-Korsakov, Nikolay 646–47; Schoenberg, Arnold Franz Walter 681–84; Shostakovich, Dmitri Dmitrievich

694–96; Sibelius, Jean 696–97; Sondheim, Stephen 705–6; Stockhausen, Karlheinz 715–17; Strauss, Johann 719–21; Strauss, Richard George 721–24; Stravinsky, Igor 724–27; Tchaikovsky, Peter Ilich 738–41; Tippett, Sir Michael 750–51; Vaughan Williams, Sir Ralph 778–79; Verdi, Giuseppe 779–82; Webern, Anton 809–12; Wolf, Hugo 828–30

computer scientists: Berners-Lee, Timothy 67–68; Gates, Bill 276–78; Jobs, Steven 381–82; Turing, Alan 764–65

computers: Babbage's inventions 32–34; first commercial machine 67; technology of architecture 251; Turing's pioneering work 764–65; *see also* Apple; Microsoft Corporation

conceptual art: Klein 421–22

conditioned reflex (Pavlov's theory) 378, 588, 589–90, 620, 701

conductors: Adams, John Coolidge 2–4; Bernstein, Leonard 68–70; Britten, Benjamin 9; Bruckner, Anton 100; Mahler, Gustav 477; Strauss, Richard George 721–24

Confucianism 558

conscience collective 201, 203

conscientious objectors 457, 468, 594

consciousness: William James's theories 377–78

construction: Fuller's ecient principles 265

Constructivism 216, 267–68, 396, 481

consumerism 247, 583, 831

Cookham, Berkshire: Stanley Spencer 706, 706–7

co-operativism 425–26, 529

Cornhill Magazine 667

Cornwall 339–40, 561

corporations 269

correspondence theory 50

cosmology 214, 324

country music: Dylan 206, 207

countryside: in Hardy's novels 321; importance to Ted Hughes 357–58, 359; importance to Wyeth 836; spirituality of Palmer's paintings 581–82; Tolstoy's view 753; Yeats's symbolic landscape 839

Coventry Cathedral 95

Craiglockhart War Hospital, Edinburgh 579

creole 800

crime fiction *see* detective fiction

crime films 791

Crimean War 56, 753–54

Criterion (journal) 224

critical rationalism 604

criticism *see* art theory/criticism; cultural criticism/studies; literary criticism/studies; social criticism

critics: Arnold, Matthew 16–19; Barthes, Roland 43–46; Burgess, John Anthony 106–7; Collins, William Wilkie 146; Eliot, T.S. 223–26; Joyce, James 384; Machado de Assis, Joaquim Maria 472; Shaw 692; Stoppard's theatre reviews 717; Vargas Llosa, Mario 776–78; *see also* cultural criticism/studies; literary criticism/studies; social critics

Cuba: early telephone 56; Guevara's guerrilla activities and politics 315, 315–16; missile crisis 400

Cubism 87–88, 155, 283, 289, 441, 481, 540, 592–93, 663

cult/legendary figures: Dylan Thomas 744; Hemingway 333, 334; Herzog 343; Jack London 462; Kropotkin 426; Leary 444–47; Marley 503–5; Pollock 602; Tolkien 751; Wilde 822; Woolf 833

cultural anthropology 483, 515

cultural criticism/studies: Barthes 44; Dubuet 199; Lacan's influence 433

cultural identity: architecture 837

cultural memory: Scorsese's projects 685

Cultural Revolution 494, 498

cultural theory/studies: McLuhan's work 512–13; Nietzsche's importance 563–64

cyberneticians: Ashby, William Ross 20–21; ideas prefiguring world wide web 67

cybernetics 20–21

Czech music: Dvořák 204, 205

Czechoslovakia: Havel's views and activism 321–23; 'Prague Spring' 299, 301–2, 322; Stoppard's play about state terror 718

Dada/Dadaists 92, 191, 229, 583, 631, 768

Daily Telegraph 188

dance music: Strauss 720–21

dancers: Cunningham, Merce 156–57; Graham, Martha 305–6

Danzig 307, 308

Daoism 558

Dar as Salaam, Tanzania 72, 73

Darmstadt, Stockhausen's experience in 715, 716

Darwinian thought: influence on Zola 843; William James 375, 377, 378

Darwinism: Kropotkin's view 425; Thomas Huxley 362, 363, 364

Dasein (being-there) 329

Dau al Set (review) 737

De Stijl group 835

De Stijl magazine 540

Dean Gallery, Edinburgh 583

death: death drive 258, 433; in Hirst's art 347; in Mallarmé's poetics 484; in Munch's paintings 552; in Vonnegut's novels 792; in Whitman's poetry 818–19

deconstruction 182, 183–84

decorative art: Klimt's paintings and designs 422–23; Paolozzi's work 582–83

democracy: Gallup's polls 270–71; in idea of world wide web 67, 68; Ives's concern with 369; J.S. Mill's views 529, 530; Lincoln's commitment to 458; Whitman's writings 819

Depression 107, 116, 153, 193, 238, 407, 531, 537, 568, 818

design: Beardsley's drawings 52; Fuller's approach 264, 265, 265–66; Hirst's projects 347; Klimt's work 422; Le Corbusier's projects 441

designers: Aalto, Hugo 1–2; Mackintosh, Charles Rennie 474–75; Morris, William 547–50

Dessau: Bauhaus building 314

detective fiction 129, 130, 141, 147; Sherlock Holmes stories 198, 199

determinism 508, 766, 809

Deutscher Werkbund 313–14

Dewey lectures 690

Dial arts magazine 546

diarists: Dostoevsky 196; Gide 291; Whitman's account of Civil War years 819

Dierence Engine 33

Disney Concert Hall, Los Angeles 284, 285

Disneyland 193–94

DNA (deoxyribonucleic acid) 152, 164, 732, 803, 804

documentary films 240–41, 342–43, 637

documentary writing: Jack London 462

Dorset: Hardy's 'Wessex' 320

drama theory: Brecht 90–91

dramatists: Albee, Edward Franklin 6–7; Auden, Wystan Hugh 24–29; Chekhov, Anton P. 133–36; Collins, William Wilkie 146; Genet, Jean 285–87; Ibsen, Henrik 365–68; Lorca, Federico García 463–64; O'Neill, Eugene Gladstone 572–74; Pinter, Harold 594–96; Pirandello, Luigi 596–97; Sondheim, Stephen 705–6; Wilde, Oscar 820–23; Yeats, William Butler 838–41; *see also* playwrights

drawings: Cartier-Bresson 125; Giacometti 289; Hepworth 340; Hockney 351; Kitaj 417; Modigliani 539; Toulouse-Lautrec 757

DreamWorks SKG 708

Dresden: bombing of 144, 791; Vonnegut's wartime experience 791; Wagner's experiences 793, 794

Dreyfus aair 618, 846

drug culture/addiction: Burroughs 108, 109; D.G. Rossetti 658; Kerouac 403; Kesey 404; Leary's research and adventures with LSD 445, 446; Rolling Stones 654, 655

Düsseldorf Academy 70

Dutch masters 540

dynamite 566

East Anglia: in Sebald's life and work 687, 688

East Germany: Brecht's career 89, 91

Eastern Europe: fall of communist regimes 301

Eastern thought: The Beatles' involvement 53; Hesse's interest in 345

ecology: addressed in Yeang's architecture 837–38; *The Living Planet* 24

economic liberalization: China 181

economic policy: F.D. Roosevelt's reforms 655; Keynes's influence 405–6

economics: Cuba and Guevara's ideas 316; in Pound's *Cantos* 609–10; Weber's writings 806–7, 807–8

economists: Friedman, Milton 260–63; Galbraith, John Kenneth 268–70; Keynes, John Maynard 405–9; Marx, Karl Heinrich 505–11; Sen, Amartya 688–90

Edinburgh Review 528

editors: Boas, Franz 75; Breton, André 92; Dickens 187; Dostoevsky, Fyodor 196; Eliot, George 220; Eliot, T.S. 224; Galbraith, J.K. 268; Gandhi, Mahatma 274; Huxley, Aldous 362; Marinetti, Filippo Tommaso 502; Mill, John Stuart 528; Morris, William 548; Oates, Joyce Carol 568; Robbe-Grillet, Alain 648; Sen, Amartya 690; Twain, Mark 765; Weber, Max 806, 807; Wolfe, Tom 831

education: Lévi-Strauss's work 452; Matthew Arnold's work 16; Tolstoy's work for peasants 754; *see also* schools; scientific education

educators *see* teachers

Egypt: Afghani, Jamal Uddeen Al 4

Eiel Tower 210–11, 285

electric guitar music: Hendrix 335, 336

Electrician 502

electricity/electronics: Edison's work 210

electromagnetism 213–14

electronic music: Stockhausen 715–16

email 67

empiricism 388, 483, 587, 670

employment: Keynes's ideas 408

energy: Einstein's mechanics 214; Fuller's global approach 264–65, 265, 837

engineering and architecture: Millau viaduct 251

engineers: Brunel, Isambard Kingdom 101–4; Edison, Thomas Alva 209–10; Eiel, Gustave 210–11; Fuller, Richard Buckminster 264–66; Zamyatin, Yevgeniy Ivanovich 842

England: Frost's experiences 263; Gropius's work 314; identification of Kipling 414, 415–16; importance for Henry James 371, 372, 373; Losey's dicult time 465–66; Marconi's experiments 502; Sargent's experiences 674, 675; Verlaine's teaching posts 783; Zamyatin's job 842; Zola's exile 846

English folk songs 778

Englishness: aspect of D.G. Rossetti 658; Isaiah Berlin 66; Larkin 436

entertainment: Barnum's influence 40–42; Jobs's approach to computers 382; Price's architecture 612

entrepreneurs: Bell, Alexander Graham 56–57; Ford, Henry 247; Gates, Bill 276–78; Jobs, Steven 381–82

entropy 11, 21, 822

environmentalism: Carson's activism and influence 120–21; Galbraith's influence 269; Lovelock 466–68; Morris as pioneer of 549

epic: Pound's *Cantos* 608; Tolstoy's *War and Peace* 756; in Walcott's work 799–800

epistemology: eect of world wide web 68; Lévi-Strauss's framework 452–53; Russell's interest in 670; *see also* knowledge

equal rights 259–60, 458; *see also* Black civil rights; human rights

eroticism: in music 523, 797; in novels 243, 438, 555, 556; in Rimbaud's poetry 644; in visual art 52, 422, 423, 593, 706, 707; in Von Sternberg's films 790, 791

Esquire 445, 831

essayists: Arnold, Matthew 17, 17–18; Auden, Wystan Hugh 24–29; Borges, Jorge Luis 77–78; Collins, William Wilkie 146; Eliot, George 220; Mill, John Stuart 527–31; Orwell, George 577–78; Sartre, Jean-Paul 676–79

essays: Baudelaire 48–49; Havel 322; Heidegger 329; Huxley's output 362; Isaiah Berlin 65–66; John Barth 42; Joyce Carol Oates 569; Pirandello 597; Qutb 622; Ruskin 666; Thoreau 747; Valéry 773

etchings 354, 582

ethnography 75–76, 454, 482

ethnology 76, 164

ethnomusicology 47

ethology: Konrad Zacharias Lorenz 464–65

eugenics 57

Europe: importance to Henry James 371–72

European Court of Human Rights, Strasbourg 653

European science 558

European socialist movement 449, 450, 761

European Union 323

evolution: William James and Spencer's law 375–76

evolutionary theory: Darwin 160–65; and Gaia hypothsis 467

evolutionists: Darwin, Charles Robert 160–65; Dawkins, Richard 169–71; Gould, Stephen Jay 304–5

exile: Jean Renoir 633; Joyce 385; Lawrence 438; Lenin 447, 449; Losey 465–66; Nabokov 555; Neruda 560; Picasso 592; Solzhenitsyn 703; Thomas Mann 491; Trotsky 761, 762; Vidal 787; Zola 846

Existentialism 298, 328, 678, 679

Explorations (journal) 512–13, 514

explosives 566

Expressionism: French 511; German movement 283, 314, 499, 552; Modigliani 539–40; Schoenberg's music 681, 682, 683; Strindberg's dramatic technique 718–19; Toulouse-Lautrec's influence 758; Webern's works 811

Fabian Society 692–93, 815

The Factory 801

Fagus Shoe-Last Factory 313

fairy stories 752, 821

Fallingwater 834–35

family: Durkheim's sociology 202; Germaine Greer's criticism of 311; in Lawrence's novels 437; in Tennessee Williams's plays 823; themes in Ibsen's plays 365, 367; themes in Visconti's films 789; Tolstoy's view 753

fantasy: García Márquez's novels 275; Tolkien's theory 752; in Verne's work 786

Fascism: Hitler and National Socialism 349, 350; Marinetti's support of 503; Pound's attraction to 608–9; Spain 463; Trotsky's analysis 763; Visconti's challenge to 788

fashion: Bakst's designs 37; Barthes's cultural criticism 44; Man Ray's photography 631

Fauvism 86–87, 283, 396, 511, 540, 663

FBI (Federal Bureau of Investigation) 73

February Revolution, Russia 425, 709, 761

Fedayeen 286

feminists: Friedan 259–60; Greer 310–12; Millett 532–34; Oates 568; Woolf 833

Le Figaro 502

figurative art: Hopper 356–57; Kitaj 417

film directors/makers: Allen, Woody 7–8; Altman, Robert 8–10; Bergman, Ingmar 61–63; Buñuel, Luis 104–6; Chaplin, Charles S. 130–32; Coppola, Francis Ford 150–51; Cukor, George 153–54; DeMille, Cecil Blount 178–79; Disney, Walt 192–94; Eisenstein, Sergei Mikhailovich 215–18; Fassbinder, Rainer Werner 231–32; Fellini, Federico 236–38; Flaherty, Robert 240–41; Ford, John 247–49; Gance, Abel 271–73; Godard, Jean-Luc 296–98; Grith, D.W. 312–13; Hawks, Howard 325–26; Herzog, Werner 342–43; Hitchcock, Sir Alfred 348–49; Keaton, 'Buster' (Joseph Francis) 397–99; Kubrick, Stanley 426–27; Kurosawa, Akira 429–50; Lang, Fritz 433–35; Lean, Sir David 443–44; Losey, Joseph 465–66; Mizoguchi Kenji 537–38; Pasolini, Pier Paolo 584–85; Polanski, Roman 600–602; Ray, Satyajit 631–32; Renoir, Jean 632–33; Resnais, Alain 636–37; Riefenstahl, Leni 640–41; Robbe-Grillet, Alain 647–49; Scorsese, Martin 684–85; Scott, Ridley 686–87; Sirk, Douglas 699–700; Spielberg, Steven 707–8; Visconti, Luchino 788–90; Von Sternberg, Josef 790–91; Warhol, Andy 800–802; Welles, George Orson 812–13; see also cinema; Hollywood

film historians: Scorsese 684–85

film music 167; Glass 295; Penderecki 590; Prokofiev 615; Shostakovich 695; Vaughan Williams 778

film theory, Lacan's influence 433

Finland: Aalto, Hugo 1–2; Sibelius 696

First World War see World War I

Flower Power movement 53

Fluxus art group 70, 574

folk music: in Bartók's works 46–47; Dylan's re-synthesis of 206–7; elements in Janáček's work 380; influence on Lorca 463; Kubrick's films 426; see also Russian folk music

Ford Motor Company 246, 265

Fors Clavigera (periodical) 667–68

Foster Associates 250–51

Fourierism 50, 93

France: 1848 Revolution 243–44; Breton's influence 94; cultural life 113; Deng Xiaoping's time in 179–80; Faulkner's influence on fiction 234; German occupation/Vichy regime 114, 183, 272; Lévi-Strauss's influence 455; Rodin's government commissions 650; Stravinsky's time in 724; symbolism of Eiel Tower 211; Winslow Homer's time in 353

Frankfurt Theatre Festival (1969) 70–71

freedom of speech 140

Freiburg University 328, 806

French Communism: Jean Renoir's involvement 633; and Surrealism 92–93; Tzara's involvement 768

Freudian analysis 92

functionalism: Durkheim 202; Malinowski's anthrolopology 482–83, 483; Sullivan's architecture 730–31

furniture design: Mackintosh 474; Morris 548

Futurism: Italian precursors 691; Malevich's projects 481; Manifesto 502–3; Pasternak's association with 586; sculpture 228

Gaelic see Irish Gaelic

Gaia hypothesis 467, 467–68

Galapagos Islands 161–62

Gate Theatre, Dublin 812

gender: issues in Toni Morrison's novels 550; Millett's sexual politics 532, 533; Sen's concerns 688, 689

General Strike (1926) 143

genetics 732–33, 802–3, 803–4; Mendelian 258, 520–22

genre studies 512

geodesic domes 264, 265

geography: Verne's publication 786

geology: Darwin's interest and explorations 160, 161

Georg Büchner Prize 308

Georgian poets 263, 435

German Romanticism: and Beuys 70; in Ernst's art 230; influence on Herzog 343; Mahler's music 477–78

Germany: addressed in Sebald's novels 687; Churchill's recognition of threat 142, 143; Heisenberg's work under Nazis 331; Hitler's dictatorship 349–50; lieder tradition 829, 830; Nazi censorship 60, 76; refugees from 434, 682; represented in Fassbinder's films 231–32; represented in Grass's The Tin Drum 308; symbolism of Foster's Reichstag dome 250–51; unification (1990) 301

Glasgow School of Art 474–75

Gothic architecture 548

Göttingen University 575

GPO film unit 26

grati 738

Graphic (magazine) 775

graphics 351, 474, 552, 661, 662

gravitation theory 214–15

Great Exhibition (1851) 667

Great Western Railway 102–4

Great Western Steamship Company 104

Greek drama: in Wagner's works 794, 796; *see also* classical Greek thought

Greenwich: Millennial Dome 653

Group 47 306–7

Guatemala 315

guerrilla warfare 315, 316–17

Guggenheim Museum: Bilbao 284, 285; New York 534, 627

Guomindang 495, 496

Hamburg 699

'Happenings' 111

Harpers/Harper's Weekly 210, 353, 801

Harvard University: Gropius's experiences 314; J. D. Watson's achievements 803; notable architecture and designs 534, 639; sacking of Timothy Leary 444–45; Solzhenitsyn's speech 703

Hebrew *see* Modern Hebrew

Heidelberg 806

hermeticism: Mallarmé's poetics 484–86; Oldenburg's opposition to 571

Hertzian waves 501–2

Hinduism: Gandhi's social activism 273, 274

hippie culture 335, 344, 404, 467

Hiroshima 576

historians: Churchill, Winston Leonard Spencer 144; Kuhn, Thomas Samuel 427–29; Marx, Karl Heinrich 505–11; Needham, Joseph 557–59

historical determinism 508, 604

history: Foucault's view 253; H.G. Wells's survey 815; Lévi-Strauss's conception 453; philosophy of 807; in Tolstoy's *War and Peace* 755–56; in Verne's later novels 787; in Visconti's films 788–89, 789

history of ideas: Isaiah Berlin's views 64, 65

Hitler Youth 307

Holland 490, 540, 835

Hollywood: Arnold's photographs of stars 15; Brecht's period in 89; Chaplin's stardom 130; Cole Porter's involvement with 606; Coppola's status 150; DeMille's status 178, 179; Faulkner's scriptwriting 233; Ford's transcending of 248; Grith's historical importance 313; influence on Fassbinder 231; invitation to Buñuel 105; Spielberg's importance 707; Welles's status 813; *see also* film directors/makers

Holocaust *see* Jewish Holocaust

homosexuality 94, 252; in Fassbinder's films 232; Forster 249; in Genet's novels 286; Gide's championing of 291, 292; Hockney 351; Mishima 535; Pasolini 585; Proust 615; Verlaine 645, 783; Visconti 789; Whitman 818; Wilde 821; *see also* lesbianism

Hong Kong 181

horror films: Polanski 600, 601; soundtracks 591

House Un-American Activities Committee 89, 131, 576

housing: Frank Lloyd Wright's designs 834–35; Fuller's 'Dymaxion house' 264–65; Le Corbusier's projects 441, 442; Mies van der Rohe's projects 526–27

HRT (hormone replacement therapy) 311

human cultures: Lévi-Strauss's epistemological framework 452–53

Human Genome Project (HGP) 733, 803

human rights: Chomsky's polemics on 140; Havel's campaigns 322; Sen's contributions to 690; *see also* Black civil rights; civil rights activists; equal rights

humanism: in Bellow's novels 58, 59; Isaiah Berlin 66; in Kurisawa's films 430; Lutosławski 470; Tagore 736; Thomas Mann 493

humour: in Altman's films 10; in Elliott Carter's music 123; in García Márquez's novels 275; in Gide's works 291; in Gilbert & George's work 293; in Heller's stories 331; Lewis Carroll's inventiveness 119; in Miller's plays 532; in Pirandello's work 597; in Polanski's films 601; in Twain's work 766, 766–67; Wilde's wit 821, 823; Woody Allen 8; *see also* black comedy; comedy; satire

Hungary 46, 322

hybridization: Mendel's work towards genetics theory 520–22

hydrogen bomb 144

hypertext transfer protocols and commands (http and html) 67

IBM (International Business Machines) 277

Icelandic sagas 548

ideology: Marx's concept 508–9

Illinois Institute of Technology (IIT) 525, 526, 527

illusionism: Warhol's critique 801; in Welles's cinema 812

illustrators: Beardsley, Aubrey Vincent 51–52; Homer, Winslow 353; Hopper, Edward 356; *see also* artists; designers; painters; photographers; printmakers

imagination: Sartre's studies 676

Imagist movement 546, 785; Pound's links with 607, 608

Imperial War Museum 706

imperialism: Lenin's theory 449; *see also* anti-imperialism

impresarios: Diaghilev 185–86

Impressionism 86, 125, 126, 499; Degas's relationship with 175; Gauguin's work 281; influence on Sargent's painting 674–75; Manet's relationship with 489, 490; Monet's work 541–43; in music 173; Renoir's painting 633–34, 635; in Russian painting 395; Seurat's connection with 690, 691; Van Gogh's work 775; Zola's interest in 845

India: Afghani, Jamal Uddeen Al 4; background of Amartya Sen 688–89; Churchill's colonialist stance 143; in Forster's *Passage to India* 249; Gandhi's importance 273; importance of Tagore 736; influence on Hesse 343–44, 344; Jean Renoir's visit 633; in Kipling's writings 414; Ray's films 631–32; in Rushdie's work 664–65

Indian music 295

Indiana University 803

individuation 391–92

Indo-Chinese War 117

industrialists: Ford, Henry 246–47; Nobel, Alfred Bernhard 565–66

inequality: Sen's concerns 688, 689

Information Theory 21

instinct, concept of 377, 378

intellectuals: Berlin, Isaiah 64–66; Breton, André 94; Camus and colleagues 113; Eliot, T.S. 224; Gide, André 290–92; Said, Edward W. 672–73; Sartre, Jean-Paul 676, 678

intelligence services 439

interior design: Aalto 2; Mackintosh 474

International Modern Movement 1, 314, 441, 475, 524–25, 526, 561, 731, 835, 837

international organizations 690; *see also* United Nations (UN)

international relations: Rawls's view 630

internationalism: Gaudí 279; Paolozzi 582; Sen 688

internet 67

Inuit Eskimos 240

inventors: Babbage, Charles 32–34; Baird, John Logie 35–36; Bell, Alexander Graham 56–57; Edison, Thomas Alva 209–10; Fuller, Richard Buckminster 264–66

iPod 382

Ipswich *see* Willis Faber Dumas Building

Iran: Churchill's meddling in 144; Foucault's support for Islamic revolution 253; Jamal Uddeen al Afghani 4, 5; Khomeini's involvement with 409, 410, 411

Iraq 4, 5, 72, 140, 409

Ireland: environment in *Man of Aran* 240, 241; in Ford's films 248; in Joyce's writings 384–85, 386, 387; Shaw's early life 692; Trollope's life 758–59; Wittgenstein's time in 825; Yeats's vision and writings 839

Irish Gaelic 326, 327, 384

Irishness: importance to Heaney 326–27

irony: in art 293; in novels 242–43, 275–76, 291, 493–94, 618, 805

Islam: Dawkins's views 170; impact of *Satanic Verses* 665, 666

Islamic scholars: Khomeini, Ruhollah Musavi 409; Qutb, Sayyid Muhammad 622–23

Islamic teachers: Afghani, Jamal Uddeen Al 409; Khomeini, Ruhollah Musavi 409

Islamism: Bin Laden 71–73; Khomeini 409

Island Records 504

Israel 140, 212; Israel–Arab wars 418, 672–73

Istanbul 4

Italy: influence on Henze's music 337; influence on painters 159, 418; Palmer's sojourn 582; Pound's time in 607, 608–9; Racial Laws under Mussolini 451; Ruskin's visit 666; Visconti's challenge to Fascism 788; writers in 98, 249, 372

Jamaica 504

Japan: atomic bombs attacks on 576, 656; events aecting Mao Zedong 496; importance of Kurosawa's work 429–30; Mishima Yukio 535–36; Mizoguchi Kenji 537–38; Ōe Kenzaburō 569–71; Ono's break with traditions of 574; post-defeat period 429, 430, 537

Al Jazeera 73

jazz: elements in Tippett's music 750; Hendrix's involvement with 336; influence on Mondrian 541

Jazz Age 238, 313, 605

jazz musicians: Armstrong, Louis ('Satchmo') 13–15; Davis, Miles Dewey, Jr 168–69; Ellington, Duke 226–27; Parker, Charles Christopher, Jr (Bird) 583–84

Jesuits 355

Jewish folklore: in Chagall's pictures 127–28

Jewish Holocaust 140, 418, 451, 451–52, 575, 601, 698, 708

Jewish identity: in Arthur Miller's work 532; Kitaj's explorations 418; Roth's importance 658–60

Jews: discrimination against 255, 259; Hitler's persecution of 350; in Singer's work 697–98,

698; under Racial Laws in Fascist Italy 451; *see also* anti-semitism; Dreyfus aair; Zionism

jihad 72

journalism: Churchill's coverage of Boer War 143; Gallup's work 270; Hemingway 333; H. G. Wells 814; Joyce 385; Marx 505; natural talent of Mailer 480; Orwell's polemic 578; photojournalism of Cartier-Bresson 123–24; Shaw 692; Vonnegut 791; Whitman 818

journalists: Camus, Albert 113; Dickens, Charles 187; Greer, Germaine 310–12; Herzl, Theodor 340; Machado de Assis, Joaquim Maria 472; Twain, Mark 765; Wolfe, Tom 830–31

Jugendstil group 395, 422, 423, 500

Jungian psychology 38, 237, 389, 392, 599, 602, 750, 786

justice: Rawls's theory 629–30

Kansas City Evening Star 333, 335

Keynesian economics 261, 269

kitsch 423, 424

knowledge: Popper's 'problem-solving' 604–5; *see also* epistemology

Koran 5

Korean War 497, 559

Kraków 591, 600

Ku Klux Klan 312

language: Beckett's minimal style 55, 56; Boas's investigations 76; in Brecht's plays 91; Derrida's philosophy 183; Heaney's interest in politics of 327; Joyce's *Finnegans Wake* 387; Mallarmé's poetics 485–87; Pirandello's writing style 597; studies in McLuhan's *Explorations* 513; Tom Wolfe's style 831; Wittgenstein's ideas 825–27; *see also* linguistics; semiotics

Lapland 2

Larkin Building, Bualo 834

Lasky Feature Play Company 178

Latin America: Borges's influence on literature 77; in García Márquez's novels 275–76; Guevara's strategy 316; Neruda's consciousness and identity 560; Romanticism 472; Vargas Llosa's perspective 777

leaders: Deng Xiaoping 179–82; Gorbachev, Mikhail 299–302; *see also* political leaders; religious leaders; statesmen (and women)

League of Arab States 622

League of Nations 442, 656

lectures: Matthew Arnold 17; Thomas Huxley 363; Whistler 817; William Morris 548, 549

Leeds School of Art 339, 544–45

Leeds University 751

left-wing politics: and Existentialism 678; Fassbinder 231; Losey's plays 465; Visconti's involvement with 788

Leningrad 695

lesbianism 532–33

liberal humanism 249, 291

liberalism: F.D. Roosevelt's cause 656–57; Rawls's philosophy 629–30

liberty: negative and positive 66

libretti: Auden and Kallman 28, 337; for Poulenc's songs 607

linguistics: Boas's work 76; influences on Burgess's novels 106; performative utterances 29–30; *see also* language; semiotics

linguists: Chomsky, Avram Noam 137–41; Saussure, Mongin-Ferdinand de 679–81

Linnaean Society 162

Linz, Austria 100, 477

Listener (magazine) 743

literary criticism/studies: Arnold 18; Barthes 44; Beckett 54; Breton 94; McLuhan 512; Orwell 578; Qutb 622; Robbe-Grillet 648; Updike 770; Valéry 773

The Little Red Book 498

living sculptures 292, 293

Lodz Film School 600

Logical Positivism 30, 183, 603, 605, 826

logicians: Cantor, George F.L.P. 115–16; Russell's links with 669; Turing, Alan 764–65

London: Cartier-Bresson's time in 124; Chaplin's narrative settings 130; in Dickens's fiction 187; Epstein's sculpture 227–29; Henry James's experiences 372, 373; Jack London's account of East End 462; Marx's time in 505; Olympic Games of 2012 613; Pound's life in 607–8; Rimbaud's time in 644–45; Sargent's career as painter 675; Strauss Festival (1947) 723; 'underground' scene 310; Vargas Llosa's life 776; Whistler's time in 816; Yeats's time in 839; Yoko Ono's visit 574

London Eye 613

London School of Economics (LSE) 482, 483, 603

London Zoo 613

Long Island 817; *see also* Cold Spring Harbor Laboratory

Los Alamos, New Mexico 575, 576

Louvre 86, 664, 782

love: aspects addressed in Morrison's novels 551; Germaine Greer's writings on 311; Lawrence's veneration for 438; Neruda's poems 559; in Proust's *Remembrance of Things Past* 617; in Tennessee Williams's plays 823; in Tolstoy's

War and Peace 756; in Wagner's works 793, 795–96, 797; in Whitman's poetry 818–19, 819

LSD (lysergic acid diethylamide) 445, 446

Lyric Abstraction 737–38, 738

McCarthyism 531

magazines: Beardsley's ventures 52; Cartier-Bresson's photography 124; Dickens's editorship 187

Magical Realism 275–76, 551; Henri Rousseau's influence on 664; Rushdie's novels 655, 664–65

Magnum Photos 15, 117, 124

Maine 354

Malaya 106

Malaysia 838

Malvern, Worcestershire 218

Manchester: Ruskin's lectures 667; University 824

Manchuria 496

Manhattan Project 576

manufacturing: Edison's achievements 209–10

Marconi 209

Marine Biological Laboratory, Woods Hole, Massachusetts 120

market forces/values 269

market research: Gallup's polls 270–71

marriage: addressed in Tolstoy's *Anna Karenina* 756; eects on Wilde 821–22; Germaine Greer's criticism of 311; Lévi-Strauss's views 453–54; Strindberg's stories about 727

martial arts 536

Martinique 282

Marxism: Brecht 88, 90–91; Camus's views 114; Carl André's thinking 13; Deng Xiaoping's activism 179–80; influence on Mizoguchi Kenji 537; Kropotkin's views 425; Marx 505–8; Needham 557, 559; Neruda's sympathy with 559–60; Pasolini's war with 585; and Sartre's Existentialism 678, 679; Stalin 708–9; Trotsky 761, 762; Tzara 768

mass production 247

materialism: André's art and politics 12, 13

mathematicians: Babbage, Charles 32–34; Cantor, George F.L.P. 115–16; Hawking, Stephen 324; Russell, Bertrand 668

mathematics: in Valéry's thinking 772, 773

May 1968 events 93, 252, 297, 455

mechanics: Einstein's research 212–14

media: advertising 177; Germaine Greer's popularity 310; McLuhan's analyses 513, 514

Medical Research Council Laboratory of Molecular Biology (LMB) 732

medievalism: in Morris's work 548, 549, 550; in Tolkien's writings 752

melodrama: Grith's cinema 313; O'Neill's break with 572; Sirk's films 699; Wilkie Collins 146; in Zola's early novels 843

'memes' 170

memoirs/reminiscences: Heller 332; Hemingway 335; Kate Millett 533–34; Kerouac 401, 403; Proust's *Remembrance of Things Past* 617; Tennessee Williams 824

memory: Primo Levi's experiences at Auschwitz 450, 451; as source of Munch's paintings 552

Memphis, Tennessee 413

Menlo Park, New Jersey 209

Mensheviks 448, 761

Mercury Theatre 812

messianism: Bob Marley 504; Timothy Leary 445, 446

metaphysical painting 136

metaphysics: Principle of Verification 30

Mexico: Buñuel 105; Eisenstein's film about 216; Guevara 315; in Huxley's *Eyeless in Gaza* 362

Mickey Mouse 192, 193

Microsoft Corporation 276–78, 381, 382

Millau viaduct, France 251

mind-body theory 364

Minimalism 357; André's sculptures 12; Glass's music 295–96; Judd 388

Mir Iskusstva (World of Art), St Petersburg 36–37

misogyny: in Wagner's *Parsifal* 797–98

Mississippi: Whitman's American experience 818

MIT (Massachusetts Institute of Technology) 20, 68, 137, 138

'mobile' sculpture 111–12, 112

Modern Hebrew 137

Modern Movement *see* International Modern Movement

Modernism: architecture 284, 525, 526; Eisenstein 215–16; Faulkner 234; Flaubert 241, 244; Henri Rousseau's importance 664; Joyce's work 384; Larkin's rejection of 436; Lawrence's place in 438; Lutosławski's music 471; Marc's work 500–501; Moore's poetry 546–47; narration of *Moby Dick* 519; Penderecki's music 591; Rimbaud's place in 644; T.S. Eliot's poetry 226; Waugh's hostility towards 805; Welles's status 812; Whistler's connection with 817; in Wilde 822–23; Woolf's status 833; Zamyatin 843

modernity: in Manet's paintings 489, 490, 491; in Melville's writing 517

molecular biologists: Crick, Francis Harry
Compton 151–53, 164; Sulston, Sir John
Edward 732–34

monarchism: Eliot 224

monetarism: Friedman and Chicago School 261,
261–62

monumental sculture 652

moralists: Gide, André 290–92

morality: Buñuel's ideas 105; in Camus's activism
113; Dickens's approach to social problems
189; in Durkheim's sociology 202–3; eects of
world wide web 68; George Eliot's Realism
220; Gide's ideas 291; Hesse's rebellion against
344; in Isaiah Berlin's approach 65, 66; in
Nietzsche's psychology 563–65; in Nussbaum's
philosophy 567; outrage at Hardy's *Jude* 321; in
Stoppard's plays 718; in Tolstoy's philosophy
754–55, 755

Moscow: Deng Xiaoping's training 180; Trials
(1936) 93

Moscow Art Theatre 134, 216, 710

Moscow Conservatoire 624, 738–39

Moscow Jewish Theatre 128

Munich: Blaue Reiter group 396, 419, 681;
Fassbinder 231; Olympic Games 641; Richard
Strauss's early life 721–22; Rilke's experience
642; Sirk's time in 699

Munich Film School 700

murals: Le Corbusier 441; Matisse 512; Miró 534;
Sargent 675

Museum of Modern Art (MOMA), New York
124, 128, 228, 357, 662

music and technology 336

music and text 751

music hall 130

musical developments: Berg's work 61; Cage's
involvement 110; during Brahms's life 82, 83–
84; Mahler's style as pointer to 478;
Schoenberg 682; serialism 78, 725;
Stockhausen's genius 716; Webern 810, 811

musical drama/theatre: Verdi 780–82; Wagner
793–99; *see also* popular musicals

musical language: Messiaen 522–23, 524; Wagner
797; Webern 811

musicians: Bartók, Bela 46; The Beatles 53–54;
Bernstein, Leonard 69; Dylan, Bob 205–8;
Elgar, Sir Edward 218; Gershwin, George 287–
88; Hendrix, Jimi 335–37; Liszt, Franz 459–62;
Lorca, Federico García 463; Marley, Bob 503–
5; Rachmaninov, Sergei 624–26; The Rolling
Stones 653–55; *see also* composers; conductors;
jazz musicians; pop groups; singers

Muslim Brotherhood 622, 623

mysticism: in D.G. Rossetti's poetry 658; in
Singer's work 698

myths/mythologies: in Jung's idea of collective
unconscious 390; Lévi-Strauss's views 452, 454;
in Rothko's work 660; in Tolkien's world
752–53; Wagner's sources 793, 794; Yeats's
interest 839

Nagasaki 576

Nairobi, Kenya 72, 73

naïve art: Rousseau 663

National Gallery, London 664

National Organization for Women (NOW) 260

National Socialism *see* Nazism

nationalism: Whitman's poems 819

NATO (North Atlantic Treaty Organization) 656

Natural History (magazine) 305

natural sciences: Durkheim's model 201; Lévi-
Strauss's conception 453; Pavlov's ideas 587–88

natural selection 162–64, 169–70

Naturalism: Gauguin's struggle with 282; in
Strindberg's plays 727, 728; Zola 844–45

naturalists: Attenborough, Sir David Frederick
23–24; Carson, Rachel 120–21; Darwin,
Charles Robert 160–65; Thoreau, Henry David
747

nature: Neruda's imagery 559; in Rimbaud's
poetry 644; themes in Messiaen's music 523–
24; Van Gogh's vision 778

Nazis 349–50, 493, 682; book-burning (1933) 76;
commissions for Riefenstahl 640–41; Richard
Strauss's work under 723; suppression of
'degenerate art' 419, 499; suppression of music
60, 337

Nazism: Churchill's warning 143; Dalí's interest
in 159; depicted in Fassbinder's films 232;
Heidegger's vocabulary 328; and Nietzsche's
philosophy 565; refugees from 117, 212, 434,
682; Trotsky's warnings about 763

Negroes *see* American Negroes/Afro-Americans

neo-classicism: Lutosławski's music 470, 471;
Mies van der Rohe's architecture 525, 526;
Stravinsky's phase of 725; style of architecture
in America 638

neo-Impressionism 691

neo-liberalism: Vargas Llosa 777

neo-realism: Italian 633, 788; Zamyatin's style 843

nervism 588

neurobiology: Sulston's research 732–33

neurologists: Ashby, William Ross 20–21

neurology/neurophysiology: Freud's career
255–56

neuroscience: Crick's research 152

New Age culture 467

New Deal 655

New England: Thoreau 747, 748, 750

New German Cinema 342

New Gothic writing 568

New Guinea: anthropological studies 482, 515

New Journalism 830–31, 831

New Statesman 11, 612

New Worlds (journal) 38

New York: Abstract Expressionism 602; Bernstein's status 68; Burroughs's later years in 109; Charlie Parker 583–84; Eve Arnold's photography 15; Greenwich Village 335, 713; influences on Mondrian 541; Lévi-Strauss's educational work 452; Melville's home 517; Philip Glass Ensemble 295; reception of *Under Milk Wood* 744; Seagram Building, Park Avenue 527; Tin Pan Alley 63, 288; Wodehouse's time in 828; Wyeth's instant success 835; Yoko Ono 574, 575

New York Herald 19

New York Magazine 831

New York Philharmonic Orchestra (NYPO) 69, 477

New York Review of Books 140

New York School (poetry) 19

New York Times Book Review 446

New Yorker 118, 121, 770

New Zealand 603

Newcastle-upon-Tyne 842

Nietzschean ideas: connections with Wagner's work 798; 'superman' 253–54; vision of freedom 302–3

nihilism: elements in Rolling Stones' work 654; in Flaubert's novels 242, 244; Mishima Yukio 535; Wagner's leanings 794

Nitroglycerin Inc. 566

Nobel Prizes 566; Peace Prize 318, 411, 488; Prize for Economics 262, 688; Prize for Literature 55–56, 59, 113, 144, 233, 233–34, 291, 298, 299, 328, 344, 397, 491, 551, 560, 569, 586, 594, 671, 679, 698, 703, 712, 736, 800, 839; Prize for Physics 212, 331, 501; Prize for Physiology or Medicine 153, 464, 588, 734, 804

'non-fiction novel' 118

Norse literature 548

North Africa: Klee's travels 419

Northern Ireland 327

Norway: Ibsen's return 367

nouveau roman 616, 647–48

novelists: Ballard, James Graham 37–39; Barth, John 42–43; Beckett, Samuel 54–56; Bellow, Saul 58–59; Burgess, John Anthony 106–7; Burroughs, William Seward 107–9; Camus, Albert 113–14; Capote, Truman 117–18; Cheever, John 132–33; Coetzee, John Maxwell 144–46; Collins, William Wilkie 146–47; DeLillo, Don 176–78; Dickens, Charles 186–90; Doyle, Sir Arthur Conan 198–99; Eliot, George 219–23; Faulkner, William 232–34; Flaubert, Gustave 241–44; Forster, E.M. 249–50; García Márquez, Gabriel 274–76; Genet, Jean 285–87; Golding, Sir William 298–99; Greene, Graham 309–10; Hardy, Thomas 319–21; Hemingway, Ernest 333–35; Hesse, Hermann 343–46; Huxley, Aldous 360–62; James, Henry 371–75; Kafka, Franz 393–95; Kesey, Ken 403–5; Larkin, Philip Arthur 435; Le Carré, John 439–40; London, Jack 462–63; Mailer, Norman 479–80; Mann, Thomas 491–94; Morrison, Toni 550–51; Nabkov, Vladimir 555–56; Orwell, George 577–78; Pasternak, Boris Leonidovich 586–87; Pirandello, Luigi 596–97; Proust, Marcel 615–18; Pynchon, Thomas 619–21; Qutb, Sayyid Muhammad 622; Robbe-Grillet, Alain 647–49; Rushdie, Salman 664–66; Sartre, Jean-Paul 676–79; Singer, Isaac Bashevis 697–99; Steinbeck, John Ernst 711–13; Trollope, Anthony 758–61; Twain, Mark 765–67; Updike, John Hoyer 770–71; Vargas Llosa, Mario 776–78; Verne, Jules 785–87; Vonnegut, Kurt, Jr 791–92; Waugh, Evelyn Arthur St John 804–6; Wodehouse, P.G. 827–28; Wolfe, Tom 830–31; Woolf, Adeline Virginia 831–33; Zola, Émile 843–46

nuclear physics: Heisenberg's work 331; Oppenheimer's work 575–77

nuclear weapons: Cuba missile crisis 400; Ono-Lennon protest 575; Russell's activism against 671; testing of atom bomb 575, 576

Nürnberg 641

obscenity cases: Ginsberg's 'Howl' 294; Marinetti 503

October Revolution (1917) 216, 303, 396, 425, 449–50, 586, 709, 761, 842

old age: Friedan's study 260

Old English verse: Pound's versions 608

Ontario Review 568

ontology 329

Op Art movement 541

operas: Barber 39, 40; Bizet 73–74; Britten 95; Dvořák 205; Henze 337, 338; Johann Strauss's operettas 720, 721; Poulenc 607; Richard

Strauss's work 72–73, 722; Tippett 750–51; Visconti's productions 78

Orientalism 672

Orkney 167

the Other/otherness: Foucault's inquiry 252–53; in Lacan's theory of the unconscious 432

Oxford University 360, 439, 532, 543; honouring of Wodehouse 828; Hopkins's experiences 354; Larkin's generation 435; Professor of Poetry post 328; Rawls's experiences 629; Ruskin's reputation 666; Tolkien's achievement 751; Wilde's notoriety 820–21

pacifism 95, 212; anti-war message of *J'Accuse* 271; Gandhi 274; Hesse's writings 344–45; Russell 670–71; Tippett 750

Paimo Sanatorium, Finland 1

painters: Bacon, Francis 34–35; Bakst, Léon Samölivich 36–37, 52, 128; Braque, Georges 86–88; Cézanne, Paul 125–27; Chagall, Marc 127–29; Cummings, Edward Estlin 155; Dégas, Edgar 174–76; Freud, Lucian 254–55; Giacometti, Alberto 288–90; Homer, Winslow 353–54; Johns, Jasper 383–84; Kandinsky, Wassily 395–96; Kitaj, Ronald Brooks 416–18; Le Corbusier 440–43; Lichtenstein, Roy 456–57; Lorca, Federico García 463; Manet, Edouard 489–91; Marc, Franz 499–501; Matisse, Henri 511–12; Miró, Jóan 534–35; Munch, Edvard 551–52; Palmer, Samuel 581–82; Pollock, Jackson 602–3; Renoir, Pierre-Auguste 633–36; Rossetti, Dante Gabriel 657–58; Rouault, Georges 660–62; Rousseau, Henri 662–64; Sargent, John Singer 674–76; Seurat, Georges Pierre 690–92

Pakistan 71, 274, 664–65

paleontology: Stephen Jay Gould 304–5; Thomas Huxley's work 363

Palestine: Said's background and identity 672, 673; Zionism and Herzl's views 341

Palestinians 72, 140, 144

Pall Mall Gazette 814

Paramount 178, 216, 240, 313, 790

Paris: Brancusi's success 84; Capa's experiences 117; Diaghilev's theatrical career 186; Eiel 210–11; Gauguin's failure in 283; Giacometti's life in 289; Henri Rousseau's work 662–63; Hepworth and Nicholson 339; Joyce's experiences 386–87; Le Corbusier's activities 440–41; Manet's studio 489; Marx's time in 505; May 1968 events 93, 252, 297; Modigliani's life in 538–39; Mondrian's time in 540–41; Rimbaud and Verlaine 644, 782–83;

Sargent's training as painter 674; showing of Buñuel's first film 104; Strindberg's 'occult' experiences 718; Surrealists 136, 229, 768; Tolstoy's experience 754; Toulouse-Lautrec's Montmartre 757; UNICEF building 534; Van Gogh's activities 775; Whistler's time in 816; Wilde monument in Père Lachaise 228

Paris Commune 644, 782

Paris Conservatoire 522, 627

Paris Opera 129

pastoral traditions: Verlaine's poetry 783

pathology: in Wagner's *Parsifal* 797–98

patriarchy 533, 832

Penguin Books 438

Pennsylvania, University of 607

perestroika 300–301, 302

performance art: Gilbert & George 292–93; Klein 421–22; Yoko Ono 574, 575

performative utterances: Austin's notion 29–30

'permissiveness' 438

personality, in Pirandello's thinking 597

Peru: Vargas Llosa's background and perspective 776, 777

pesticides 120–21

phenomenology: in Heidegger's approach 329; Sartre's study 676

philanthropy: Alexander Graham Bell 57; Alfred Nobel 565–66; Bill Gates 278; Charles Dickens 187; Ruskin's ventures 667; Spielberg's projects 708

philologists: Nussbaum, Martha Craven 567; Tolkien, John Ronald Reuel 751–53

philosophers: Austin, John Langshaw 29–30; Ayer, Sir Alfred Jules 30–31; Berlin, Isaiah 64–65; Chomsky, Avram Noam 137–41; Derrida, Jacques 182–85; Foucault, Michel 251–54; Fuller, Richard Buckminster 264–66; Heidegger, Martin 328–29; James, William 375–79; Nietzsche, Friedrich 562–63; Nussbaum, Martha Craven 566–67; Popper, Sir Karl Raimund 603–5; Rawls, John Bordley 629–30; Russell, Bertrand Arthur William (Earl) 668–71; Sartre, Jean-Paul 676–79; Suzuki Daisetsu Teitaro 734–35; Wittgenstein, Ludwig Josef Johann 824–27

philosophy: background to Donald Judd's art 388; Camus's essays 113; Chinese 558; Hopkins's writings 355; influence of Mill's *A System of Logic* 529; Isaiah Berlin's views 64; Kantianism of Weber's thought 808; Sen's work 689–90; Tolstoy's moral authority 754–55; Yeats's *A Vision* 840; in Zola's writings 843, 845

philosophy of history: Weber 807

philosophy of science: Kuhn 427–29

phonograph 209

photographers: Arnold, Eve 15–16; Capa, Robert 116–17; Cartier-Bresson, Henri 123–25; Ray, Man 630–31; Riefenstahl, Leni 640–41

photography and text: Sebald's novels 688

photography in art: Gilbert & George 293; Hockney 352; Rauschenberg 627

physicists: Einstein, Albert 211–15; Hawking, Stephen 323–25; Heisenberg, Werner 329–31; Oppenheimer, J. Robert 575–77

physics: in Valéry's thinking 774

physiological studies: Pavlov 587–90

piano music: Liszt 460–62

picture theory of meaning 825–26

Pixar 382

planet Mars 467

Playboy magazine 80, 445, 514–15, 600–601, 831

playwrights: Beckett, Samuel 54–56; Brecht, Bertolt 88–92; Camus, Albert 113; Eliot, T.S. 223–26; Gorky, Maxim 303; Havel, Václav 321–22; Lawrence, David Herbert 436–39; Miller, Arthur 531–32; Stoppard, Sir Tom 717–19; Strindberg, Johan August 727–30; Vargas Llosa, Mario 776–78; Williams, Tennessee 823–24; *see also* dramatists

poetics: Auden's ideas 27; Baudelaire's ideas 49–51; Borges and *ultraismo* 77; Breton 92; Eliot's views 224–25; Ginsberg 293–94; Heaney's explorations 327–28; Hopkins's 'sprung rhythm' 355–56; Machado de Assis 473; Marinetti 503; Miró's paintings 534; musical settings 173; and Ray's photography 631; Stevens 714–15; Tennyson 741, 742; Verlaine 174, 783–84

poets: André, Carl 13; Arnold, Matthew 16–19; Ashbery, John Lawrence 19–20; Auden, Wystan Hugh 24–29; Baudelaire, Charles 48–51; Beckett, Samuel 54–56; Borges, Jorge Luis 77–78; Brecht, Bertolt 88–92; Breton, André 91, 93; Browning, Robert 96–99; Cummings, Edward Estlin 154–56; Dickinson, Emily 190–92; Dylan, Bob 206–8; Eliot, T.S. 223–26; Ernst, Max 230; Faulkner, William 232–33; Frost, Robert 263–64; Genet, Jean 285–87; Ginsberg, Allen 293–94; Hardy, Thomas 319–21; Heaney, Seamus 326–28; Hesse, Hermann 343–46; Hopkins, Gerard Manley 354–56; Hughes, Ted 357–60; Ibsen, Henrik 366; Kipling, Joseph Rudyard 414, 415; Larkin, Philip Arthur 435–36; Lawrence, David Herbert 436–39; Lorca, Federico García 463–64; Lowell, Robert 468–70; Mallarmé,

Stéphane 483–87; Moore, Marianne 546–47; Morris, William 549–50; Neruda, Pablo 559–60; Owen, Wilfred 579–80; Pasternak, Boris Leonidovich 586–87; Pirandello, Luigi 596–97; Plath, Sylia 598–600; Pound, Ezra Loomis 607–10; Proust, Marcel 616; Rilke, Rainer Maria 641–43; Rimbaud, Arthur 643–46; Rossetti, Dante Gabriel 657–58; Stevens, Wallace 713–15; Tennyson, Alfred (Lord) 741–43; Thomas, Dylan Marlais 743–45; Thomas, Ronald Stuart 745–46; Valéry, Paul 772–74; Verlaine, Paul 782–85; Walcott, Derek 799–800; Whitman, Walt 817–20; Yeats, William Butler 838–41

Poets Laureate 359, 741

Pointillisme 542, 691

Poland: Conrad 147; dissident acts of unions and intellectuals 322; Lutosławski 471; Penderecki's influence on music 590–91; Polanski's early life 600, 698; post-war boundaries 144; setting of Singer's work 697–98; *see also* Danzig

polemics: Chomsky 137–41; Orwell's writing 578; Thomas Huxley 363; Tom Wolfe 831; Vidal's opposition to American politics 788; Weber 808; Whistler 816

political activists: André, Carl 13; Beuys, Joseph 70; Camus, Albert 113; Capa's early activities 116; Carson, Rachel 121; Dylan, Bob 206; Gandhi, Mahatma 273–74; Ginsberg, Allen 293–94; Kropotkin, Petr Alekseyevich 425–26; Lowell, Robert 468; Morris, William 548; Neruda, Pablo 560; Qutb, Sayyid Muhammad 622–23; Said, Edward W. 673; Sartre, Jean-Paul 676–79; Weber, Max 806

political economy 269

political leaders: Guevara, Che 316; Gyatso Tenzin, 14th Dalai Lama 317–18; Havel, Václav 323; Herzl, Theodor 340–42; Hitler, Adolf 349–51; Khomeini, Ruhollah Musavi 409–11; Mandela, Nelson 487–89; Mao Zedong 494–99; Stalin, Joseph 708–10

political reformers: Gandhi, Mahatma 273–74; Kennedy, John F. 399–401

political theorists: Fuller, Richard Buckminster 265; Lenin, Vladimir Ilyich 447–50; Popper, Sir Karl Raimund 604; Rawls, John Bordley 629–30

political writers: André, Carl 13; Arnold, Matthew 17, 17–18; Brecht, Bertolt 88; Breton, André 9; Chomsky, Avram Noam 140–41; Dostoevsky 194–95, 195; Galbraith, J. K. 269; Genet, Jean 286, 287; Grass, Günter 306–8; Havel, Václav 322; Heaney, Seamus 327; Herzl, Theodor 341–42; Joyce, James 384,

385; Mailer, Norman 479–80; Mill, John Stuart 528–30; Millett, Kate 532, 533–34; Orwell, George 577–78; Pasolini, Pier Paolo 585; Pinter, Harold 596; Russell, Bertrand 670; Stoppard, Sir Tom 718; Vidal, Gore 787–88; Walcott, Derek 799–800; Weber, Max 809; Whitman, Walt 819; Zola, Émile 844

politicians: Churchill, Winston Leonard Spencer 142–44; Gandhi, Mahatma 273–74; Hitler, Adolf 349–51; Lincoln, Abraham 457–59; Roosevelt, Franklin Delano 655–57; Trotsky, Leon 761–62; *see also* leaders; statesmen (and women)

polyphonics 750, 781, 811

Pompidou Centre, Paris 125, 612, 613, 652, 653

Pop Art 351, 384, 476; Lichtenstein 456–57; Oldenburg 571–72; Paolozzi 582; Rauschenberg 627; Warhol 800–801

pop groups: The Beatles 53–54; Hendrix's career 335–36; The Rolling Stones 653–55

popular culture: McLuhan's views 513; Paolozzi's expression of 582–83; Tom Wolfe's use of 831

popular musicals: Bernstein 68, 69; Gershwin's music 287; Wodehouse's work with Bolton 828

popular science writers: Dawkins, Richard 169–71; Gould, Stephen Jay 304–5; Hawking, Stephen 323–24

pornography 68

positivism 331

post-colonial studies 144, 672

post-colonial writing 665

Post-Impressionism 36–37, 86, 395, 491, 499, 500, 540, 541, 817

postmodernism: Barth's novels 42–43; DeLillo's novels 177; Freud's influence 259; Lichtenstein as forerunner 457; Sebald's novels 688; Stockhausen's music as counterforce to 717

post-structuralism 183

post-totalitarianism 322

poverty: Sen's study 689

pragmatism 377

Prague: Rilke 642

Pre-Raphaelite Brotherhood 548, 657–58, 666, 667, 816

primitive art: influence on Henry Moore 545

primitivism: 'Blue Rider' artists 500; Gauguin's painting style 282, 283; in Modigliani's work 539; in Pasolini's later films 585; perceived in Steinbeck's work 711, 712; Picasso's art 592

Princeton University: Oates's work 568; Rawls's experience 629

printmakers: Kitaj, Ronald Brooks 416–18; Paolozzi, Sir Eduardo 582–83; Toulouse-Lautrec, Henri de 757; Warhol, Andy 801

privatization/deregularization 261

production relations 506–7

proletariat 506

propaganda: Kropotkin 425; McLuhan's analyses 513

protest: non-violent direct action 411–12, 413; Ono-Lennon performance 575; Zola's public activism 844, 846; *see also* May 1968 events

Prussian Academy of Arts 681

psychedelic research 445, 446

psychiatrists: Ashby, William Ross 20–21; Jung, Carl Gustav 389–92

psychoanalysis: in Hesse's fiction 344; Jung's work 390

psychoanalysts: Freud, Sigmund 255–59; Lacan, Jacques 431–33

psychologists: James, William 375–79; Skinner, Burrhus Frederic 700–702

psychology: Freud's work 256; in Hitchcock's films 348–49; Jung's theories 389, 390; Nietzsche's importance 563–64, 565; Pavlov's hostile views 590; Reichian thought 479; in Strindberg's plays 727, 728

public opinion: Gallup's polls 270–71

public service: Galbraith's work 268; Neruda's work as diplomat 559, 560; Tchaikovsky's post 738; Thomas Huxley's work 363; Verne's work 786; Whitman's job 819; *see also* Civil Service

publicity stunts: Phineas Taylor Barnum 40–42

publishing: Gollancz and Orwell 577; Kandinsky's ventures 396; Morris's Kelmscott Press 548; T. S. Eliot's contribution 224; world wide web 68

Pulitzer Prize 6, 7, 19, 133, 551, 620, 659, 823

pulp fiction 21, 38, 79, 129

punctutated equilibrium 304–5

Puritanism 191–92, 233, 368, 369

Al Qaida/al-Qaeda 72, 140

quantum mechanics 324, 329, 330

quantum theory 212–13, 330

racial issues: addressed in American novels 233, 550, 551, 568–69; Martin Luther King and Black civil rights 411–13

racism 80, 312, 411, 412, 465

radio: comedy series of 1950s and 1960s 543; Dylan Thomas's *Under Milk Wood* 744; Pound's broadcasts sponsored by Fascist Italy 609; Welles's involvement 812; Wodehouse's broadcasts 828 railways: Edison's achievements 211; *see also* Great Western Railway

Rank Organization 443–44

Rastafarian faith 504

Rationalism 139, 846

ready-mades 346, 583

real numbers 115

realism: in novels 220, 242, 302, 756, 777; in visual art 356, 542, 836

reality TV 311

reggae 504

Reith Lectures 653

relativity theory: general theory 212, 214–15, 324; special theory 213–14

religion: Arnold's writings 17, 18; Dawkins's views on 170; Durkheim's sociology 202, 203; Gide's experiences 291; impact of Darwinian theory 160, 164, 165; in Jung's conception of collective unconscious 390; Messiaen's sacred music 523, 524; Needham's leanings 557; Pasolini's leanings 585; and Penderecki's importance to Poland 591; Rodin's sensibilities 650; Scorsese's Catholic roots 684–85; Thomas Huxley's views 363; Tolstoy's philosophy and practice 754, 755; Van Gogh's studies and attempted vocation 774–75; Weber's comparative studies 807

religious artists 661–62, 706–7

religious leaders: Gyatso Tenzin, 14th Dalai Lama 317–18; Khomeini, Ruhollah Musavi 409–11

religious writers 191–92, 195, 354–56

Renaissance art 159, 675

Resistance 55, 113, 451, 768

revolutionaries: Guevara, Che 315–17; Lenin, Vladimir Ilyich 447–50; Mao Zedong 494–99; Marx, Karl Heinrich 505–11; Stalin, Joseph 708–9; Trotsky, Leon 761–64

rhythm and blues 653

RIBA (Royal Institute of British Architects) 251, 653, 838

right-wing nationalism, Mishima Yukio 535

Rio de Janeiro 561, 562

Robben Island 488

rock bands: The Rolling Stones 653–55; Warhol's projects with 801

rock festivals 336

rock 'n' roll musicians: Dylan, Bob 205–8; Presley, Elvis Aaron 610–11

Rolling Stone (magazine) 831

Roman Catholic Church 105, 287; J.F. Kennedy's faith 400; Joyce's opposition to 384; Lowell's period in 468; Pasolini's war with 585; Poulenc's sacred pieces 607; Scorsese's roots

684–85; vocation of Hopkins 354–55; Waugh's turn to 805

romances 463–64, 548, 550

Romanesque style 638–39

Romania: Brancusi 84, 85

Romanticism: art 52, 127; Cézanne 126, 127; D. G. Rossetti 657; Gorky 302; Hesse 344; influence on Liszt 460, 461; Morris 549–50; music 82, 236, 460, 726, 738, 741; Neruda's poetry 560; Palmer's landscape paintings 581; Plath's poetics 598; ruralism 752; Wagner's operas 794, 798; in Wilde 822–23; *see also* German Romanticism

Rome 236, 237, 366, 460

Rotherhithe Tunnel, London 102

Royal Academy of Arts 347, 353, 653, 675, 706

Royal Society 32, 33, 169, 323, 558, 733; Thomas Huxley 362–63, 363

Russia: after fall of Soviet Union 301; Cuba's relationship with 316; imperial domination of Poland 147; influence on Rilke 642; Kropotkin's political activism 425; Lenin's revolutionary activities 447–50; nuclear arms race 576; Pasternak's view in *Dr Zhivago* 58; revolution of 1905 449, 761; Russell's visit 670–71; scientists in late nineteenth century 588

Russian Constructivists 267

Russian folk culture: in Gorky's writings 303–4; Mussorgsky's interest in 553; in Rimsky-Korsakov's music 646–47; themes in Kandinsky's painting 395

Russian Orthodox Church 725

Russian theatre 134, 724

Sagrada Família, Barcelona 280–81, 284

St Lucia 799, 800

St Petersburg 588, 754; Conservatory 613–14, 646, 694, 738

Salk Institute for Biological Studies 152

Salonblatt (magazine) 829

San Francisc 404

Sandham Memorial Chapel, Burghclere 706

satire: in cinema 130, 237, 544, 601; in novels 11, 12, 233, 275, 361, 787, 805; in Pound's poetry 608; in Strindberg's plays 727

Saturday Club 819

Saudi Arabia 71, 72, 140

scepticism 564–65, 813

schizophrenia 390

schools: Thoreau's venture 748; Tolstoy's peasant school 754; *see also* education

science: antithesis with religion 160; Durkheim's sociology 200; H.G. Wells's ideas 814, 815;

Needham's work on history of 557–59; philosophy of 427–29; Popper views on scientific discovery 603–4

science fiction: Asimov's stories 21–23; Ballard's writing 38; Bradbury's stories 79–81; Lang's films 434; Verne's novels 785–87; Vonnegut's novels 791–92; Wells's stories 814, 815

Science Museum, South Kensington 34

scientific education 428

scientists see biologists; chemists; mathematicians; physicists; technologists

screenwriters: Coppola, Francis Ford 150–51; Fassbinder, Rainer Werner 231; Fellini, Federico 236–38; Greene, Graham 309; Kurosawa, Akira 429–50; Pasolini, Pier Paolo 585; Pinter, Harold 595; Robbe-Grillet, Alain 649; Stoppard, Sir Tom 719; Vidal, Gore 787

scriptwriting 89, 233, 434

sculptors: André, Carl 12–13; Beuys, Joseph 70–71; Brancusi, Constantin 84–86; Calder, Alexander 111–12; Dégas, Edgar 174–76; Epstein, Sir Jacob 227–29; Gabo, Naum 267–68; Giacometti, Alberto 288–90; Hepworth, Barbara 338–40; Millett, Kate 532; Miró, Jóan 534; Modigliani, Amedeo 539; Moore, Henry 544–45; Oldenburg, Claes 572; Paolozzi, Sir Eduardo 582–83; Renoir, Pierre-Auguste 636; Rodin, François-Auguste-René 649–52

Second World War see World War II

secularism 409

Selden Patent 246–47

semiology 45

semiotics: Barthes's theory and studies 44–45

September 11 attacks 73, 140, 788

set theory 115–16

sex/sexuality: in D.G. Rossetti's poetry 658; in Flaubert's novels 243, 244; Freud's ideas 257, 258; Germaine Greer's writings on 310–11; in Grass's novels 307; imagery in Dylan Thomas's poetry 743; issues in Mailer's writing 479–80; in James Bond novels 245; in Lacan's Imaginary 432; in Lawrence's novels 437, 438; in Munch's paintings 552; in Polanski's films 600–601; relationships in Hardy's novels 321; in Robbe-Grillet's novels 648; Russell's ideas on morality 671; scandal of Polanski 601; Strindberg's stories about 727; in Tennessee Williams's plays 824; themes in Visconti's films 789; in Wagner's works 795, 797–98; see also homosexuality

sexual politics 532–33

Sezession art 37, 423, 475

shell-shock 578

Shikoku 569, 570

Shoah Visual History Foundation 708

Shoreham, Kent: Palmer's landscapes 581–82

short fiction: Capote 118; Cheever 132–33; deLillo 176; Hemingway 333, 334; James 371, 372–73, 373–74; Joyce's Dubliners 385; Kafka 393–94; Kesey 405; Kipling 414, 414–15, 415; Lawrence 438; Machado de Assis 472–73, 473; Melville 519; Pirandello's writing 596–97; Proust 616; Salinger 673; Singer 697–99; Steinbeck 711–12; Tennessee Williams 824; Updike 770; Vonnegut 791, 792; Wilde 821, 822

showmanship: Barnum 40–42

Siberia: Dostoevsky's imprisonment 195; Lenin's imprisonment 447; Solzhenitsyn's imprisonment 703; Trotsky's exile 761

silkscreens: Warhol's paintings 801, 802

singers: Armstrong, Louis ('Satchmo') 13–15; The Beatles 53–54; Berlin, Irving 64; Dylan, Bob 206–8; Marley, Bob 503–5; Presley, Elvis Aaron 610–11

sinology: Needham's work 557–59

skyscrapers 352–53, 731

Slade School of Art 560, 706

slavery: abolition in America 459; legacy in Morrison's Beloved 551; as main issue during Lincoln's career 457, 458–59; Walcott's poems about Middle Passage 799–800

Sligo 839

social anthropology 455, 482

social choice 689

social criticism: in Bradbury's stories 79–80; in Eliot writings 225; in Woolf's writings 833; in Zola's work 844, 845–46

social critics: Arnold, Matthew 17, 17–18; Dickens, Charles 187; Gide, André 292; Havel, Václav 322–23; H.G. Wells 815; Ruskin, John 666–68; Van Gogh 775; in Wells's comedies 814

Social Darwinism 57, 164, 349

social policy 66

social realism 824

social reform: Gandhi 273–74

social theory: Marx's theory of social relations 506

socialism: demise of 656; Fabian Society 692–93; Guevara's ideas 315, 315–16, 316; Henze 337–38; in J.S. Mill's work 529; Keynes's circle 406; Kropotkin 425; Lenin and Social Democratic Party 448–49; Morris 548, 550; Orwell 577–78, 578; People's Republic of China 497; Trotsky's activities 763–64; in Wagner's idea of Utopia 793; Weber's account 809

Socialist League 548

Socialist Realism 217, 303, 695, 710–11

Société des Artistes Indépendants 690

society: Durkheim's conception 200–201

sociologists: Durkheim, Émile 200–204; Weber, Max 806–9

sociology 200, 604, 680, 806

Somalia 72

Somme, battle of 579

songwriters: Barber 40; The Beatles 53; Dylan, Bob 206–8

South Africa: apartheid 487; Coetzee 144–45; Gandhi's political activism 273; Mandela 487–89; see also Boer War

Southern Christian Leadership Conference (SCLC) 412

Soviet Union 88–89, 91; denunciation of Zamyatin's We 842; e.e. Cummings's journal 155; Eisenstein's work 215–16, 216; Gorbachev 299–301; Gorky's status 303–4; invasion of Czechoslovakia 322; Lenin and events leading to new state 449–50; Malevich's status 481–82; Pasternak's literary position 586; Prokofiev's return to 614–15; relations with US in Kennedy era 400; Shaw's enthusiasm for 692; Shostakovich's music 695–96; Stalin's policies 709–10; Stoppard's play about 718; Trotsky's analysis 763

Spain: censorship of Buñuel's films 105; motifs in Ravel's works 627–28; Neruda's time in 559

Spanish masters, influence on Manet 489, 490

Spanish Civil War 117, 140, 559, 577, 593–94

species: Darwin's evolutionary theory 160, 161–63; Mendel's hybridization experiments 520–22

'specific' art 387–88

spiritualism 198

spirituality: in Hughes's poetry 359; Jung's emphasis on 392; Kandinsky's search through painting 395, 396; in Marc's philosophy and paintings 499, 500; in Munch's paintings 552; Palmer's landscape paintings 581–82; in Stravinsky's music 725; Suzuki's contribution to 734

spy stories: Fleming's thrillers 244–46; Greene 309; Le Carré 439–40

Staordshire: Potteries Thinkbelt proposal 612

stained-glass windows: Chagall 129; Rouault's restoration work 661

Stalinism 93, 113, 300, 470; and Mao Zedong 180, 182; in Orwell's Animal Farm 578; Solzhenitsyn's criticism of 703; Trotsky's struggle against 762, 764

statesmen (and women): Churchill, Winston Leonard Spencer 142–44; Havel, Václav 321–23; Kennedy, John F. 399–401; Lenin, Vladimir Ilyich 447–50; Lincoln, Abraham 457–59; Mandela, Nelson 487–89; Roosevelt, Franklin Delano 655–57; see also leaders; politicians

statisticians: Gallup, George Horace 270–71

stream of consciousness 233, 378, 832

structural linguistics: Chomsky's break with tradition 137–40

Structuralism 44, 183, 253, 432, 455; Lévi-Strauss 452–53; Saussure 679–81

Sudan 72

suicide: Durkheim's sociology of 202; Mishima Yukio 535, 536; Primo Levi 450–51, 451; Rothko 660; Van Gogh 776; Woolf 832

Sunday Times 15

Suprematism 480, 481

Surrealism 38, 583; Breton 92–94; Buñuel 104–6; Dalí 158–59; De Chirico's relationship with 136, 137; Ernst 229–30; Giacometti's relationship with 289, 290; influence on Moore's sculpture 545; influence on Picasso 593; influence on Tàpies 737; Klee's relationship with 419; Lewis Carroll 119; in Lorca's works 463, 464; Messiaen's song cycles 523; Miró 534; in Neruda's poems 559; point suprême 786; Rimbaud's influence on 645; Rousseau's influence on 664; Tzara 768

sustainability 266; architecture 285, 837–38

Swinging Sixties 53

Switzerland: Einstein 211–12; Stravinsky's time in 724

Sydney Opera House 284

Symbolism 172–73, 291, 292, 484, 614, 690; painting 37, 282, 283, 422–23, 592, 816; poetry 51, 282, 743, 772, 784, 785

synaesthestics: Baudelaire's correspondence theory 50; in Wagner's music 796, 798

synergetics 265, 837

syntactic structures 138

Tahiti 283

Taiwan 494, 496

Taliban 72

Tate Gallery, London 35, 88, 228, 283, 542–43, 582

Tate Modern, London 12, 357

teachers: Barthes, Roland 43–46; Derrida, Jacques 183; Fauré, Gabriel Urbain 234; Foucault, Michel 251–52; Freud, Sigmund 255–56; Friedan, Betty 260; Gallup, George Horace

270; Hawking, Stephen 325; Heaney, Seamus
328; Heidegger, Martin 328–29; Huxley,
Aldous 362; Huxley, Thomas 364; Jung, Carl
Gustav 389, 392; Klee, Paul 419; Kuhn,
Thomas Samuel 427; Lacan, Jacques 431–32;
Leary, Timothy 444–45; Lévi-Strauss, Claude
452, 456; Malinowski, Bronislaw Kaspar 482,
483; Mallarmé, Stéphane 483; Mendel, Gregor
520; Morrison, Toni 551; Nietzsche, Friedrich
562; Oates, Joyce Carol 568; Owen, Wilfred
579; Paolozzi, Sir Eduardo 583; Pavlov, Ivan
Petrovich 588; Popper, Sir Karl Raimund 603;
Robbe-Grillet, Alain 649; Ruskin, John 667;
Said, Edward W. 672; Sartre, Jean-Paul 676;
Schoenberg, Arnold Franz Walter 681; Sebald,
Winfried Georg 687; Sirk, Douglas 700;
Skinner, Burrhus Frederic 700; Solzhenitsyn,
Aleksandr Isayevich 702; Suzuki Daisetsu
Teitaro 734; Tippett, Sir Michael 750; Vargas
Llosa, Mario 776–78; Verdi, Giuseppe 779;
Verlaine, Paul 783; Walcott, Derek 799–800;
Weber, Max 806; Wells, H.G. 814, 815;
Wittgenstein, Ludwig Josef Johann 824–27; see
also Islamic teachers
teaching: Alexander Graham Bell's career 57;
Anthony Burgess 106; Bruckner at Vienna
Conservatory 100; in Joseph Beuys's political
work 70
Technicolor 193
technologists: Marconi, Guglielmo 501–2
technology and architecture 251
technology and art see art and technology
teenage culture 53
Teignmouth, Devon 353, 354
telegraphy 56, 209, 501–2
telephone 56–57, 209
television 35–36, 238; commercials 686; David
Attenborough 23–24; dramas directed by
Bergman 62; Eve Arnold's *Beyond the Veil* 15;
Le Carré's *Tinker, Tailor, Soldier, Spy* 439;
Monty Python 543–45; *The Simpsons* 324, 620;
Vidal's plays 787; see also reality TV
Le Temps 5
Les Temps modernes 678
terrorism: Chomsky's polemics on 140; Genet's
controversial stance 286; Nazis 349–50; Al
Qaida and Bin Laden 72–73; see also September
11 attacks
textile designers: Bakst 37; William Morris 548,
549
theatre of the absurd 322, 596, 600
theatrical practitioners: Bakst, Léon Samölivich
36–37; Bergman, Ingmar 61–63; Beuys's set

designs 70–71; Brecht, Bertolt 88–92; Chagall's
designs 129; Cukor 153; DeMille's early career
178; designs for Ballets Russes 185, 186;
Eisenstein, Sergei Mikhailovich 215–16; Glass,
Philip 295; Hockney's set designs 352;
Marinetti's writings and plays 503; Miró's
designs 534; Picasso's ballet sets 593; Sirk,
Douglas 699; Sondheim, Stephen 705–6;
Stanislavsky, Konstantin 710–11; Visconti,
Luchino 788–90; Warhol, Andy 801; see also
actors; dancers; dramatists; playwrights
theology: Hopkins's studies 355; William James's
views 376, 379
Theosophical Society 396
Theosophy 540
thermodynamics 212–13
thinkers: Mill, John Stuart 527–31; Valéry, Paul
772–74; see also academics; Islamic scholars;
philosophers
Third Reich 350, 798
thriller genre: Chandler's writing 129–30;
Fleming's novels 244–46; Lang's films 434;
Ridley Scott's films 686
Tiananmen Square 181
Tibet 180, 317–18, 497
Tibetan Buddhism 317, 318
Time magazine 411
The Times 15, 52, 654, 666
Tokyo Imperial University 734
Toronto: Charlie Parker concert (1951) 584;
University 512
Toryism 805
totalitarianism 604
tower blocks 443, 527
town planning: Le Corbusier's projects 441,
442–43
trade unions 247, 322
tragedy: in O'Neill's dramas 572–73; in
Pirandello's fiction 597; in Welles's cinema 812
trans-sexualism: elements in Rolling Stones' act
654
Transcendentalism 369, 516, 621, 836; Thoreau
730, 747, 748, 750
translation: Arnold's lectures 17
translators: Baudelaire 49; Machado de Assis 472;
Marianne Moore's work 547; Pound's versions
of Confucius 609; Proust 616; Suzuki 734
trauma: emotional 256; war 258
travel books 362; Lawrence 438; Thoreau 747
travels: Ben Nicholson 560–61; Cartier-Bresson
124; Conrad 147; Darwin's voyage on HMS
Beagle 160–61; Gauguin 281, 282; Herzog 343;
James's experiences 372; Jung 389; Kerouac

401; Klee 418–19; Lawrence 438; Le Corbusier 440; Lévi-Strauss's account 452; Liszt 459, 460; Manet 489; Matisse 511; Melville's adventures 517–18, 519; Nietzsche 563; Rilke 642; Sargent's artistic visits 674; Tchaikovsky 739; Trollope 759; Verlaine 783; Wagner 794; Waugh 805; Wilde 820

Tribune 578

Trieste 385

Trinidad: Walcott 799, 800

Trinity College, Dublin 820

Trobiand Islands 482, 483

tuberculosis: Kafka 393; Modigliani 538; Orwell 578

Tunis 419

Turin 451

Turkey 4

Turun Samomat oces, Turku 1

UFA film studio 699

ultraismo 77

uncertainty principle 324, 329, 330–31

unconscious, concept of: Freud 259, 431; Lacan's updating of 431, 432–33; *see also* collective unconscious

unemployment 407

UNESCO (United Nations Educational, Scientific, and Cultural Organization) 557

Union of Soviet Writers 703

unions *see* trade unions

Unit One 339, 561

United Artists 312–13

United Nations (UN) 66, 260, 318, 656, 657; Human Development Index 690; Medal of Peace 504; Universal Declaration of Human Rights 630

United States: Bernstein's success 68–69; blacklisting of Needham 559; Chomsky's attack on foreign policy 140; Conrad's influence on novelists 148; context of Carl André's art 12; cult status of Timothy Leary 445–46; Declaration of Independence 458; Dvořák's time in 204; Dylan's American Nightmare 206; early television broadcasting 36; Edison legend 210; F.D. Roosevelt's government and reforms 655–57; feminism 259–60; Henry H. Richardson's vision 637–38; honours bestowed on Wyeth 836; impact of Kennedy's assassination 177, 401; importance of Winslow Homer 353, 354; intervention in World War II 143; investigation of film industry for Communism 89; Irving Berlin as parable of 63, 64; J.F. Kennedy's aims and political reforms

400–401; Kerouac's American myth 403; Khomeini's campaign against 410–11; Mahler's time in 477; Mailer's critique of American society 479–80; Marianne Moore's poetic status 546; Mies van der Rohe's work 526–27; Nabokov's career 555–56; nostalgia in Bradbury's stories 79–80; Oldenburg's Americanness 572; Pound's indictment for treason 609; psychoanalysis 259; Qutb's experience of 622; reception of Dylan Thomas 744; refugees from Nazism 212, 434, 682; Singer's emigration to 698; Sirk's use of film to criticize 700; Solzhenitsyn's life in 703–4; Stravinsky's emigration to 724; Thoreau and literary Renaissance 747; Vidal's polemics against 787, 788; Westerns 248; Wilde's lecture tour 821; *see also* American Civil War, etc.

Universal film studios 699, 700, 707, 813

University of East Anglia 687; Sainsbury Centre for the Visual Arts 250

UPA (United Productions of America) 193

urban living: images in Paolozzi's work 582, 583

urban regeneration: Price's projects 612

USSR *see* Soviet Union

utilitarianism: Rawls's alternative theory 629–30

Utopianism: in H.G. Wells's work 815; Morris's concerns 550; Wagner's idealism 793; Yves Klein's vision 421; Zola's vision 846

vaudeville 398

Velvet Revolution 323

Venice Biennale 112, 582, 738

Venice Film Festival 538, 640

Verein für Sozialpolitik 806, 807

Verification, Principle of 603–4

verse-art 784

Victorian era: Dickens's critique of society 187, 188–89; Hopkins's view of social conditions 355; Trollope's characteristics as typical of 758–59, 760; William Morris as rebel against 548, 549

video: Godard's explorations 297

Vienna: Brahms 81; Freud's work 255, 257; Klimt 422; Schoenberg's time in 681; Sibelius's time in 696; Strauss's acclaim 720; tradition of music 726; *see also* Sezession art

Vienna Circle 30, 603

Vienna Conservatory 100, 828

Vienna Opera 477, 722

Vienna University 520, 603, 809

Vietnam: Indo-Chinese War 117

Vietnam War 150, 309, 332, 403, 572; opposition to 140, 145, 413, 468, 480, 559, 575

Wafd Party 4

Wagnerian music 829

Wales, R.S. Thomas's relationship with 745, 746

wallpaper design: William Morris 548, 549

war: in Vonnegut's novels 792

War Artists Committee 675

web *see* world wide web

Weimar: Court Theatre 722; Liszt at court of 459

Weimar Republic 809

Weissenhof exhibition (1927) 526

Welsh language 355

Werkbund Exhibitions 313–14, 314

West Germany: context of Fassbinder's films 232

Westerns: DeMille 178; Ford 248

Westminster Review 220, 528, 747

Willis Faber Dumas Building, Ipswich 250, 251

Women's Art Colony Farm 533

women's emancipation: India 274; Mill's tract 530

women's movement: Plath's iconic status 598; *see also* feminism

wood engravings: Winslow Homer 354

Worcester 218

word association 389–90

world civilization: Needham's theory 557

The World Columbian Exposition, Chicago 731

World Islamic Front for Jihad against Crusaders and Jews 72

World War I 63, 88, 219, 238, 593, 603, 636; Churchill's policies 143; Cummings's experience 154–55; Gance's experiences 271; Golding's experience 298; Henry James's war eort 373; Hesse's pacifist writings 344–45; impact on Richard Strauss 722; impacts on Russia 449; Kipling's anti-German propaganda 415; Lang's experiences 433–34; Sibelius's compositions during 697; Stanley Spencer's service 706, 707; Trotsky's activities during 761; use of psychoanalysis for treating trauma 258; Von Sternberg's work during 790; Wilfred Owen's experiences and death 579; Wittgenstein's experiences 824

World War II 36, 38, 55, 63, 95, 225, 247; Americans' victory in Pacific 656; Arthur Miller's plays dealng with 531–32; Capa's assignments 117; Churchill's coalition government 142, 144; conscientious objectors 457; Gorbachev's experience 299; Heisenberg's work during 331; Henry Moore as War Artist 545; Ian Fleming's activities 245; impact on Mishima 535; impact on Richard Strauss 723; influence on Orwell 577–78; Isaiah Berlin's work 65; JFK's brave action 399; Joseph Beuys's experiences 70; Lutosławski's experience 470; Mead's work during 515–16; Messiaen's experience of internment 522; Mizoguchi Kenji's films during 537–38; Picasso's work during 594; Salinger's experience 673; Solzhenitsyn's activities and arrest 702–3; Stalin's achievements 710; Stanley Spencer as War Artist 706; Vidal's service 787; Vonnegut's experiences 791; Waugh's activities during 805

world wide web 67–68

World Zionist Organization 340, 341

World's Fair (1853) 818

Worpswede artists' colony 642

WPA (Works Progress Administration) project 171

writers: Afghani, Jamal Uddeen Al 4–5; Amis, Martin 10–12; Asimov, Isaac 21–23; Barthes, Roland 43–46; Beardsley, Aubrey Vincent 51–52; Borges, Jorge Luis 77–78; Bradbury, Ray 79–81; Breton, André 92–94; Camus, Albert 113–15; Chandler, Raymond Thornton 129–30; Cheever, John 132–33; Chekhov, Anton P. 133–36; Christie, Agatha 141–42; Conrad, Joseph 147–49; Dostoevsky, Fyodor 194–98; Fitzgerald, Francis Scott Key 238–40; Fleming, Ian 244–46; Gandhi, Mahatma 274; Gauguin, Paul 281–84; Gide, André 290–92; Gorky, Maxim 302–4; Grass, Günter 306–8; Greer, Germaine 310–12; Havel, Václav 321–23; Joyce, James 384–87; Kawabata Yasunari 396–97; Kerouac, Jack 401–3; Kipling, Joseph Rudyard 413–16; Leary, Timothy 446–47; Lenin, Vladimir Ilyich 447–48, 449, 450; Levi, Primo 450–52; Machado de Assis, Joaquim Maria 472–74; Marinetti, Filippo Tommaso 502–3; Melville, Hermann 516–20; Mishima Yukio 535–36; Morris, William 547–50; Pasolini, Pier Paolo 584–85; Roth, Philip Milton 658–60; Said, Edward W. 672–73; Salinger, Jerome David 673–74; Schoenberg's vast array of works 683; Sebald, Winfried Georg 687–88; Shaw, George Bernard 692–94; Solzhenitsyn, Aleksandr Isayevich 702–5; Tagore, Rabindranath 736–37; Tolkien, John Ronald Reuel 751–53; Tolstoy, Lev Nikolaevich 753–57; Tzara, Tristan 767–69; Wells, Herbert George 813–16; Wilde, Oscar 820–23; Zamyatin, Yevgeniy Ivanovich 842–43; *see also* authors; biographers; critics; dramatists; editors; essayists; journalists; novelists; playwrights; poets; political writers; satirists; screenwriters

X-ray dierentiation 152, 803

Yale University 482, 571–72, 652
Yiddish 697
Young British Artists 346, 347
Young Germany movement 794
youth culture: addressed in *The Catcher in the Rye* 673; Presley as inspirational figure 611; Rolling Stones' influence 654; Timothy Leary's influence 445

Zen Buddhism 109, 124, 673–74, 734–35
Zimbabwe 504
Zionism 66, 212, 340–42
Zürich 386, 387, 389, 767–68

Subculture
The Meaning of Style
Dick Hebdige

'Hebdige's *Subculture: The Meaning of Style* is so important: complex and remarkably lucid, it's the first book dealing with punk to offer intellectual content. Hebdige [. . .] is concerned with the UK's postwar, music-centred, white working-class subcultures, from teddy boys to mods and rockers to skinheads and punks.'

Rolling Stone

'With enviable precision and wit Hebdige has addressed himself to a complex topic – the meanings behind the fashionable exteriors of working-class youth subcultures – approaching them with a sophisticated theoretical apparatus that combines semiotics, the sociology of deviance and Marxism and come up with a very stimulating short book'

Time Out

'This book is an attempt to subject the various youth-protest movements of Britain in the last 15 years to the sort of Marxist, structuralist, semiotic analytical techniques propagated by, above all, Roland Barthes. The book is recommended whole-heartedly to anyone who would like fresh ideas about some of the most stimulating music of the rock era'

The New York Times

ISBN13: 978-0-415-03949-9